The Cambridge Handbook of Consciousness

The Cambridge Handbook of Consciousness is the first of its kind in the field, and its appearance marks a unique time in the history of intellectual inquiry on the topic. After decades during which consciousness was considered beyond the scope of legitimate scientific investigation, consciousness re-emerged as a popular focus of research toward the end of the last century, and it has remained so for nearly 20 years. There are now so many different lines of investigation on consciousness that the time has come when the field may finally benefit from a book that pulls them together and, by juxtaposing them, provides a comprehensive survey of this exciting field.

Philip David Zelazo is Professor of Psychology at the University of Toronto, where he holds a Canada Research Chair in Developmental Neuroscience. He is also Co-Director of the Sino-Canadian Centre for Research in Child Development, Southwest University, China. He was Founding Editor of the *Journal of Cognition and Development*. His research, which is funded by the Natural Sciences and Engineering Research Council (NSERC) of Canada, the Canadian Institutes of Health Research (CIHR), and the Canadian Foundation for Innovation

(CFI), focuses on the mechanisms underlying typical and atypical development of executive function – the conscious self-regulation of thought, action, and emotion. In September 2007, he will assume the Nancy M. and John L. Lindhal Professorship at the Institute of Child Development, University of Minnesota.

Morris Moscovitch is the Max and Gianna Glassman Chair in Neuropsychology and Aging in the Department of Psychology at the University of Toronto. He is also a Senior Scientist at the Rotman Research Institute of Baycrest Centre for Geriatric Care. His research focuses on the neuropsychology of memory in humans but also addresses attention, face recognition, and hemispheric specialization in young and older adults, and in people with brain damage.

Evan Thompson is Professor of Philosophy at the University of Toronto. He is the author of *Mind in Life: Biology, Phenomenoloy, and the Sciences of Mind* and *Colour Vision: A Study in Cognitive Science and the Philosophy of Perception*. He is also the co-author of *The Embodied Mind: Cognitive Science and Human Experience*. He is a former holder of a Canada Research Chair.

The Cambridge Handbook of Consciousness

Edited by

**Philip David Zelazo, Morris Moscovitch
and Evan Thompson**
University of Toronto

CAMBRIDGE UNIVERSITY PRESS
Cambridge, New York, Melbourne, Madrid, Cape Town, Singapore, São Paulo

Cambridge University Press
32 Avenue of the Americas, New York, NY 10013-2473, USA

www.cambridge.org
Information on this title: www.cambridge.org/9780521857437

First published 2007

Printed in the United States of America

A catalog record for this publication is available from the British Library.

Library of Congress Cataloging in Publication Data

The Cambridge handbook of consciousness / edited by Philip David Zelazo,
Morris Moscovitch, Evan Thompson.
    p.   cm.
Includes bibliographical references and index.
ISBN-13: 978-0-521-85743-7 (hardback)
ISBN-10: 0-521-85743-0 (hardback)
ISBN-13: 978-0-521-67412-6 (pbk.)
ISBN-10: 0-521-67412-3 (pbk.)
1. Consciousness.   I. Zelazo, Philip David.   II. Moscovitch, Morris, 1945–
III. Thompson, Evan.   IV. Title.
B808.9.C36   2007
153 – dc22   2006013843

ISBN   978-0-521-85743-7 hardback
ISBN   978-0-521-67412-6 paperback

To the memory of Francisco J. Varela (7 September 1946–28 May 2001)
– ET

To my growing family: Jill, Elana, David, Leora, and Ezra Meir
– MM

For Sam, and the next iteration
– PDZ

And a special dedication to Joseph E. Bogen (13 July 1926–22 April 2005)

Contents

List of Contributors

Ralph Adolphs, PhD
Department of Psychology
California Institute of Technology
HSS 228-77
Pasadena, CA 91125 USA
E-mail: radolphs@hss.caltech.edu

Bernard J. Baars, PhD
The Neurosciences Institute
10640 John Jay Hopkins Drive
San Diego, CA 92121 USA
E-mail: baars@nsi.edu

John A. Bargh, PhD
Department of Psychology
Yale University
2 Hillhouse Avenue
P.O. Box 208205
New Haven, CT 06520-8205 USA
E-mail: john.bargh@yale.edu

Jesse M. Bering, PhD
Institute of Cognition and Culture
Queen's University, Belfast
4 Fitzwilliam Street
Belfast, Northern Ireland BT7 1NN
E-mail: j.bering@qub.ac.uk

David F. Bjorklund, PhD
Department of Psychology
Florida Atlantic University
Boca Raton, FL 33431-0091 USA
E-mail: dbjorklund@fau.edu

Joseph E. Bogen, MD (Deceased)
Formerly of University of Southern California
    and the University of California, Los Angeles

Rebekah Bradley
Department of Psychiatry and Behavioral
    Sciences
Emory University
1462 Clifton Road
Atlanta, GA 30322 USA
E-mail: rbradl2@emory.edu

Wallace Chafe, PhD
Department of Linguistics
University of California, Santa Barbara
Santa Barbara, CA 93106 USA
E-mail: chafe@linguistics.ucsb.edu

Michael C. Corballis, PhD
Department of Psychology
University of Auckland
Private Bag 92019
Auckland 1020 NEW ZEALAND
E-mail: m.corballis@auckland.ac.nz

Diego Cosmelli, PhD
Centro de Estudios Neurobiológicos
Departomento de Psiquiatróa
P. Universidad Católica de Chile
Marcoleto 387, 2° piso
Santiago, Chile

(Also: Laboratoire de neurosciences Cognitives
    et Imagerie Cérébrale (LENA)
47 Bd de l'Hôpital, 75651 Paris FRANCE)
E-mail: diego.cosmelli@chups.jussieu.fr

JEAN-MARIE DANION, MD
INSERM Unité 405
Hôpital Civil de Strasbourg – Clinique
    Psychiatrique
1 place de l'Hôpital – BP n° 426
67091 STRASBOURG Cedex FRANCE
E-mail: jean-marie.danion@chru_strasbourg.fr

RICHARD J. DAVIDSON, PhD
W. M. Keck Laboratory for Functional Brain
    Imaging and Behavior
Waisman Center
University of Wisconsin-Madison
1500 Highland Avenue
Madison, WI 53703-2280 USA
E-mail: rjdavids@wisc.edu

STEVEN W. DAY, BSc
Department of Psychology
University of Illinois
603 East Daniel Street
Champaign, IL 61820 USA

GEORGES DREYFUS, PhD
Department of Religion
Williams College
E14 Stetson Hall
Williamstown, MA 01267 USA
E-mail: Georges.B.Dreyfus@williams.edu

JOHN D. DUNNE, PhD
Department of Religion
Emory University
Mailstop: 1535/002/1AA
537 Kilgo Circle
Atlanta, GA 30322 USA
E-mail: jdunne@emory.edu

STAN FRANKLIN, PhD
Institute for Intelligent Systems
The University of Memphis
Memphis, TN 38152 USA
E-mail: franklin@memphis.edu

HELENA HONG GAO, PhD
School of Humanities and Social Sciences
Nanyang Technological University
Singapore 639798
E-mail: helenagao@ntu.edu.sg

LISA GERACI, PhD
Department of Psychology
Washington University
One Brookings Drive

Campus Box 1125
St. Louis, MO 63130-4899 USA
E-mail: lgeraci@artsci.wustl.edu

DEBORAH E. HANNULA
Psychology Department
University of Illinois
603 E. Daniel Street, Room 807
Champaign, IL 61820 USA
E-mail: hannula@uiuc.edu

J. ALLAN HOBSON, MD
Massachusetts Mental Health Center
Psychiatry, S12
74 Fenwood Road
Boston, MA 02115 USA
E-mail: allan_hobson@hms.harvard.edu

CAROLINE HURON, MD, PhD
INSERM 0117
Service Hopitalo-Universitaire de Santé Mentale
    et Thérapeuthique
Hôpital Sainte-Anne
Université Paris V
Pavillon Broca
2 ter rue d'Alésia
75014 Paris FRANCE
E-mail: huron@broca.inserm.fr

JOHN F. KIHLSTROM, PhD
Department of Psychology, MC 1650
University of California, Berkeley
Tolman Hall 3210
Berkeley, CA 94720-1650 USA
E-mail: kihlstrm@socrates.berkeley.edu

ASHER KORIAT, PhD
Department of Psychology
University of Haifa
Haifa 31905 ISRAEL
E-mail: akoriat@research.haifa.ac.il

URIAH KRIEGEL, PhD
Department of Philosophy
Social Science Bldg. Rm 213
P.O. Box 210027
Tucson, AZ 85721-0027 USA
E-mail: kriegel@email.arizona.edu

JEAN-PHILIPPE LACHAUX
INSERM – Unité 280
Centre Hospitalier Le Vinatier
Bâtiment 452
95 Boulevard Pinel
69500 BRON, FRANCE
E-mail: lachaux@lyon.inserm.fr

CHARLES D. LAUGHLIN, PhD
Department of Sociology and Anthropology
Carleton University
125 Colonel By Drive
Ottawa, ON K1S 5B6 CANADA

ANTOINE LUTZ, PhD
W. M. Keck Laboratory for Functional Brain
    Imaging and Behavior
Waisman Center
University of Wisconsin-Madison
1500 Highland Avenue
Madison, WI 53703-2280 USA
E-mail: alutz@facstaff.wisc.edu

DREW MCDERMOTT, PhD
Department of Computer Science
Yale University
P.O. Box 208285
New Haven, CT 06520-8285 USA
E-mail: drew.mcdermott@yale.edu

KATHARINE MCGOVERN, PhD
California Institute of Integral Studies
1453 Mission Street
San Francisco, CA 94103 USA
E-mail: Mcgovernk@comcast.net

KEITH OATELY, PhD
Department of Human Development and
    Applied Psychology
Ontario Institute for Studies in
    Education/University of Toronto
252 Bloor Street West
Toronto, ON M5S 1V6 CANADA
E-mail: koatley@oise.utoronto.ca

SUPARNA RAJARAM, PhD
Department of Psychology
SUNY at Stony Brook
Stony Brook, NY 11794-2500 USA
E-mail: suparna.rajaram@sunysb.edu

HENRY L. ROEDIGER III, PhD
Department of Psychology, Box 1125
Washington University
One Brookings Drive
St. Louis, MO 63130-4899 USA
E-mail: roediger@artsci.wustl.edu

EDMUND T. ROLLS, PhD
University of Oxford
Department of Experimental Psychology
South Parks Road
Oxford OX1 3UD ENGLAND
E-mail: Edmund.Rolls@psy.ox.ac.uk

DANIEL L. SCHACHTER, PhD
Department of Psychology
Harvard University
Cambridge, MA 02138 USA
E-mail: dls@wjh.harvard.edu

WILLIAM SEAGER, PhD
Department of Philosophy
University of Toronto at Scarborough
265 Military Trail
Scarborough, ON M1C 1A4 CANADA
E-mail: seager@utsc.utoronto.ca

DANIEL J. SIMONS, PhD
Psychology Department
University of Illinois
603 E. Daniel Street, Room 807
Champaign, IL 61820 USA
E-mail: dsimons@uiuc.edu

SCOTT D. SLOTNICK
Department of Psychology
Boston College
McGuinn Hall
Chestnut Hill, MA 02467 USA
E-mail: sd.slotnick@bc.edu

HENRY STAPP, PhD
Lawrence Berkeley National Lab
Physics Division
1 Cyclotron Road Mail Stop 50A-5101
Berkeley, CA 94720-8153 USA
E-mail: hpstapp@lbl.gov

PETRA STOERIG, PhD
Institute of Physiological Psychology
Heinrich-Heine-University
Düsseldorf D-40225 GERMANY
E-mail: petra.stoerig@uni-duesseldorf.de

RON SUN, PhD
Cognitive Science Department
Rensselaer Polytechnic Institute
110 Eighth Street, Carnegie 302A
Troy, NY 12180 USA
E-mail: rsun@rpi.edu

EVAN THOMPSON, PhD
Department of Philosophy
University of Toronto
15 King's College Circle
Toronto, ON M5S 3H7 CANADA
E-mail: evan.thompson@utoronto.ca

C. JASON THROOP, PhD
Department of Anthropology
University of California, Los Angeles
341 Haines Hall
Los Angeles, CA 90095 USA
E-mail: jthroop@ucla.edu

REBECCA TODD, BA
Department of Human Development and
    Applied Psychology
Ontario Institute for Studies in
    Education/University of Toronto
252 Bloor Street West
Toronto, Ontario M5S 1V6 CANADA
E-mail: rtodd@oise.utoronto.ca

CARLO UMILTÀ, PhD
Dipartimeto di Psicologia Generale
Universita di Padova
via 8 Febbraio, 2-35122 Padova ITALY
E-mail: carlo.umilta@unipd.it

DAVID E. WARREN, BSc
Department of Psychology
University of Illinois
603 E. Daniel Street
Champaign, IL 61820 USA
E-mail:dewarrn1@uiuc.edu

JOEL WEINBERGER, PhD
Derner Institute
Adelphi University
Box 701
Garden City, NY 11530 USA
E-mail:Weinberg@panther.adelphi.edu

DREW WESTEN, PhD
Department of Psychology
Emory University
532 N. Kilgo Circle
Atlanta, GA 30322 USA
E-mail: dwesten@emory.edu

DAN ZAHAVI, PhD
Danish National Research Foundation
Center for Subjectivity Research
Kobmagergade 46
DK-1150 Copenhagen K DENMARK
E-mail: zahavi@cfs.ku.dk

PHILIP DAVID ZELAZO, PhD
Department of Psychology
University of Toronto
100 St. George Street
Toronto, ON M5S 3G3 CANADA
E-mail: zelazo@psych.utoronto.ca
(After September 2007:
Institute of Child Development
University of Minnesota
51 East River Road
Minneapolis, MN 55455 USA
E-mail: zelazo@umn.edu)

The Cambridge Handbook of Consciousness

CHAPTER 1

Consciousness: An Introduction

Philip David Zelazo, Morris Moscovitch, and Evan Thompson

The *Cambridge Handbook of Consciousness* brings together leading scholars from around the world who address the topic of consciousness from a wide variety of perspectives, ranging from philosophical to anthropological to neuroscientific. This handbook is the first of its kind in the field, and its appearance marks a unique time in the history of intellectual inquiry on the topic. After decades during which consciousness was considered beyond the scope of legitimate scientific investigation, consciousness re-emerged as a popular focus of research during the latter part of the last century and it has remained so for more than 20 years. Indeed, there are now so many different lines of investigation on consciousness that the time has come when the field may finally benefit from a book that pulls them together and, by juxtaposing them, provides a comprehensive survey of this exciting field.

By the mid-1990s, if not earlier, it was widely agreed that one could not get a full appreciation of psychological phenomena – for example, of perception or memory – without distinguishing between conscious and unconscious processes. The antecedents of this agreement are many, and it would be beyond the scope of this Introduction to do more than highlight a few (for further discussion, see Umiltà & Moscovitch, 1994). One of the most obvious is the so-called cognitive revolution in psychology and the subsequent emergence of cognitive science as an interdisciplinary enterprise. Whereas previously psychologists sought to describe lawful relations between environmental stimuli and behavioral responses, in the mid-1950s or so they began to trace the flow of information through a cognitive system, viewing the mind as a kind of computer program. It eventually became clear, however, that by focusing on the processing of information – the kind of thing a computer can do – psychology left out most of what really matters to us as human beings; as conscious subjects, it left us cold. The cognitive revolution opened the door to the study of such topics as attention and memory, and some time later, consciousness came on through.

The pre-1990s tendency to avoid discussions of consciousness, except in certain contexts (e.g., in phenomenological philosophy and psychoanalytic circles), may have been due, in part, to the belief that consciousness necessarily was a kind of ghost in the machine – one that inevitably courted the awful specter of dualism. Since then, however, our ontological suppositions have evolved, and this evolution may be a consequence of the growing trend toward interdisciplinary investigation – seen, for example, in the emergence of cognitive science and neuroscience as coherent fields. The transdisciplinary perspective afforded by new fields may have engendered an increased openness and willingness to explore problems that earlier were deemed too difficult to address. Certainly, it provided the means that made these problems seem soluble. Indeed, precisely because consciousness is such a difficult problem, progress in solving it probably depends on a convergence of ideas and methodologies: We are unlikely to arrive at an adequate understanding of consciousness in the absence of a transdisciplinary perspective.

Clinical sciences, and in particular neuropsychology, also played a prominent role in helping usher in a new willingness to tackle the problem of consciousness. Various unusual syndromes came to light in the latter half of the 20th century, and these syndromes seemed to demand an explanation in terms of consciousness. Blindsight is a good example: In this syndrome, patients with lesions to the occipital lobe of the brain are phenomenologically blind, but can nonetheless perform normally on a number of visual tasks. Another example is amnesia, in which people who are phenomenologically amnesic as a result of damage to medial temporal lobes or the diencephalon can acquire, retain, and recover information without awareness. Similar examples emerged in other domains, and it soon became clear that processes under conscious control complement, or compete with, unconscious processes in the control of cognition and behavior. These issues are also beginning to play a major role in the rigorous, scientific analysis of psychopathology, the one field in which concerns with the role of conscious and unconscious processes have played a steady role since Freud. More-

over, some of these same atypical phenomena (e.g., blindsight) have also been demonstrated in non-human animals, raising the possibility that consciousness is not associated exclusively with human beings.

A third prominent contribution to the current state of affairs is the development of new techniques that have made it possible to treat consciousness in a more rigorous and scientifically respectable fashion. Foremost among these is the development of neuroimaging techniques that allow us to correlate performance and subjective experience with brain function. These techniques include electrophysiological methods, such as magneto-encephalography (MEG), and various types of functional neuroimaging, including functional magnetic resonance imaging (fMRI). The analytic sophistication of these technologies is growing rapidly, as is the creation of new technologies that will expand our capabilities to look into the brain more closely and seek answers to questions that now seem impossible to address.

There is currently considerable interest in exploring the neural correlates of consciousness. There is also a growing realization, however, that it will not be possible to make serious headway in understanding consciousness without confronting the issue of how to acquire more precise descriptive first-person reports about subjective experience (Jack & Roepstorff, 2003, 2004). Psychologists, especially clinical psychologists and psychotherapists, have grappled with this issue for a long time, but it has gained new prominence thanks to the use of neuroimaging techniques. Here one guiding idea is that it may be possible to recover information about the highly variable neural processes associated with consciousness by collecting more precise, trial-by-trial first-person reports from experimental participants.

If ever it was possible to do so, certainly serious students of the mind can no longer ignore the topic of consciousness. This volume attempts to survey the major developments in a wide range of intellectual domains to give the reader an appreciation of the state of the field and where it is heading. Despite our efforts to provide a comprehensive overview of the field, however, there were several unavoidable omissions. Though we had hoped to include chapters on psychedelic drugs and on split-brain research, in the end we were unable to obtain these chapters in time. Readers interested in the latest scientific writing on drugs and consciousness may wish to see Benny Shanon's (2002) book on ayahuasca. Michael Gazzaniga's (1998) book, *The Mind's Past*, provides an accessible overview of work on split-brain research and its implications for subjective experience. We note, too, that although we were able to cover philosophical approaches to consciousness from a variety of cultural perspectives, including Continental phenomenology and Asian philosophy (particularly Buddhism), there were inevitably others that we omitted. We apologize for these unfortunate gaps.

The volume is organized mainly around a broad (sometimes untenable) distinction between cognitive scientific approaches and neuroscientific approaches. Although we are mindful of the truly transdisiplinary nature of contemporary work on consciousness, we believe this distinction may be useful for readers who wish to use this handbook as an advanced textbook. For example, readers who want a course in consciousness from a cognitive science perspective might concentrate on Chapters 2–24. Readers approaching the topic from the perspective of neuroscience might emphasize Chapters 25–31. A more sociocultural course could include Chapters 2–4, 13–15, 19–24, and 31. More focused topical treatments are also possible. For example, a course on memory might include Chapters 6–8, 10, 18, and 29.

The topic of consciousness is relevant to all intellectual inquiry – indeed, it is the foundation of this inquiry. As the chapters collected here show, individually and together, by ignoring consciousness, one places unnecessary constraints on our understanding of a wide range of phenomena – and risks grossly distorting them. Many mysteries remain (e.g., what are the neural substrates of consciousness? are there varieties or levels of consciousness within domains of functioning, across domains, across species, and/or across the lifespan?), but there has also been considerable progress. We hope this collection serves a useful function by helping readers see both how far we have come in understanding consciousness and how far we have to go.

Acknowledgments

The editors would like to thank Phil Laughlin, formerly of CUP, who encouraged us to prepare this volume, and Armi Macaballug and Mary Cadette, who helped us during the final production phases. Dana Liebermann provided valuable assistance as we planned the volume, and Helena Hong Gao helped us pull the many chapters together; we are very grateful to them both. We would also like to thank the contributors for their patience during the editorial process (the scope of this volume threatened, at times, to turn this process into an editorial nightmare . . .). Finally, we note with sadness the death of Joseph Bogen, one of the pioneers in research on consciousness. We regret that he was unable to see his chapter in print.

References

Gazzaniga, M. S. (1998). *The mind's past*. Berkeley, CA: University of California Press.

Jack, A. & Roepstorff, A. (Eds.) (2003). *Trusting the subject? The use of introspective evidence in cognitive science. Vol. 1*. Thorverton, UK: Imprint Academic.

Jack, A. & Roepstorff, A. (Eds.) (2004). *Trusting the subject? The use of introspective evidence in cognitive science. Vol. 2*. Thorverton, UK: Imprint Academic.

Shanon, B. (2002). *The antipodes of the mind: Charting the phenomenology of the ayahuasca experience*. New York: Oxford University Press.

Umiltà, C. & Moscovitch, M. (Eds.). (1994). *Conscious and nonconscious information processing: Attention and Performance XV: Conscious and nonconscious processes in cognition*. Cambridge, MA: MIT/Bradford Press.

Part I

THE COGNITIVE SCIENCE OF CONSCIOUSNESS

A. Philosophy

CHAPTER 2

A Brief History of the Philosophical Problem of Consciousness

William Seager

Abstract

The problem of consciousness, generally referred to as the mind-body problem although this characterization is unfortunately narrow, has been the subject of philosophical reflection for thousands of years. This chapter traces the development of this problem in Western philosophy from the time of the ancient Greeks to the middle of the 20th century. The birth of science in the 17th century and its subsequent astounding success made the problem of mind particularly acute, and produced a host of philosophical positions in response. These include the infamous interactionist dualism of Descartes and a host of dualist alternatives forced by the intractable problem of mind-matter interaction; a variety of idealist positions which regard mind as ontologically fundamental; emergentist theories which posit entirely novel entities, events, and laws which 'grow' out of the material substrate; panpsychist, double aspect, and 'neutral monist' views in which both mind and matter are somehow reflections of some underlying, barely knowable ur-material; and increasingly sophisticated forms of materialism which, despite failing to resolve the problem of consciousness, seemed to fit best with the scientific view of the world and eventually came to dominate thinking about the mind in the 20th century.

I. Forms of Consciousness

The term 'consciousness' possesses a huge and diverse set of meanings. It is not even obvious that there is any one 'thing' that all uses of the term have in common which could stand as its core referent (see Wilkes 1988). When we think about consciousness we may have in mind highly complex mental *activities*, such as reflective self-consciousness or introspective consciousness, of which perhaps only human beings are capable. Or we may be thinking about something more purely *phenomenal*, perhaps something as apparently simple and unitary as a momentary stab of pain. Paradigmatic examples of consciousness are the perceptual states of seeing and hearing, but the nature of the consciousness involved is actually complex and far from clear. Are the conscious elements of perception made up only of raw sensations from which we construct objects of perception in a quasi-intellectual operation? Or is perceptual consciousness always of 'completed' objects with their worldly properties?

The realm of consciousness is hardly exhausted by its reflective, introspective, or perceptual forms. There is distinctively *emotional* consciousness, which seems to necessarily involve both bodily feelings and some kind of cognitive assessment of them. Emotional states require a kind of evaluation of a situation. Does consciousness thus include distinctive evaluative states, so that, for example, consciousness of pain would involve both bodily sensations and a conscious sense of aversion? Linked closely with emotional states are familiar, but nonetheless rather peculiar, states of consciousness that are essentially other directed, notably empathy and sympathy. We visibly wince when others are hurt and almost seem to feel pain ourselves as we undergo this unique kind of experience.

Philosophers argue about whether all thinking is accompanied by or perhaps even constituted out of sensory materials (images have been the traditional favorite candidate material), and some champion the idea of a pure thought-consciousness independent of sensory components. In any event, there is no doubt that thought is something that often happens consciously and is in some way different from perception, sensation, or other forms of consciousness.

Another sort of conscious experience is closely associated with the idea of conscious thought but not identical to it: epistemological consciousness, or the sense of certainty or doubt we have when consciously entertaining a proposition (such as '2 + 3 = 5' or 'the word 'eat' consists of three letters'). Descartes famously appealed to such states of consciousness in the 'method of doubt' (see his *Meditations* 1641/1985).

Still another significant if subtle form of consciousness has sometimes been given the name 'fringe' consciousness (see Mangan 2001, following James 1890/1950, ch. 9), which refers to the background of awareness which sets the context for experience. An example is our sense of orientation or rightness in a familiar environment (consider the change in your state of consciousness when you recognize someone's face who at first appeared to be a stranger). Moods present another form of fringe consciousness, with clear links to the more overtly conscious emotional states but also clearly distinct from them.

But I think there is a fundamental commonality to all these different forms of consciousness. Consciousness is distinctive for its subjectivity or its first-person character. There is 'something it is like' to be in a conscious state, and only the conscious subject has direct access to this way of being (see Nagel 1974). In contrast, there is nothing it is like to be a rock, no subjective aspect to an ashtray. But conscious beings are essentially different in this respect. The huge variety in the forms of consciousness makes the problem very complex, but the core problem of consciousness focuses on the nature of subjectivity.

A further source of complexity arises from the range of possible explanatory targets associated with the study of consciousness. One might, for instance, primarily focus on the structure or contents of consciousness. These would provide a valid answer to one legitimate sense of the question, What is consciousness? But then again, one might be more interested in how consciousness comes into being, either in a developing individual or in the universe at large. Or one might wonder how consciousness, seemingly so different from the purely objective properties of the material world studied by physics or chemistry, fits in with the overall scientific view of the world. To address all these aspects of the problem of consciousness would require volumes upon volumes. The history presented in this chapter focuses on what has become perhaps the central issue in consciousness studies, which is the problem of integrating subjectivity into the scientific view of the world.

II. The Nature of the Problem

Despite the huge range of diverse opinion, I think it is fair to say that there is now something of a consensus view about the origin of consciousness, which I call here the *mainstream* view. It is something like the following. The world is a purely physical system created some 13 billion years ago in the prodigious event that Fred Hoyle labeled the big bang. Very shortly after the big bang the world was in a primitive, ultra-hot, and chaotic state in which normal matter could not exist, but as the system cooled the familiar elements of hydrogen and helium, as well as some traces of a few heavier elements, began to form. Then very interesting things started to happen, as stars and galaxies quickly evolved, burned through their hydrogen fuel, and went nova, in the process creating and spewing forth most of the elements of the periodic table into the increasingly rich galactic environments.

There was not a trace of life, mind, or consciousness throughout any of this process. That was to come later. The mainstream view continues with the creation of planetary systems. At first these systems were poor in heavier elements, but after just a few generations of star creation and destruction there were many Earth-like planets scattered through the vast – perhaps infinite – expanse of galaxies, and indeed some 7 or 8 billion years after the big bang, the Earth itself formed along with our solar system.

We do not yet understand it very well, but whether in a warm little pond, around a deeply submerged hydrothermal vent, amongst the complex interstices of some clay-like matrix, as a pre-packaged gift from another world, or in some other way of which we have no inkling, conditions on the early Earth somehow enabled the special – though entirely in accord with physical law – chemistry necessary for the beginnings of life.

But even with the presence of life or proto-life, consciousness still did not grace the Earth. The long, slow processes of evolu-tion by natural selection took hold and ultimately led at some time, somewhere to the first living beings that could *feel* – pain and pleasure, want and fear – and could experience sensations of light, sound, or odors. The mainstream view sees this radical development as being conditioned by the evolution of neurological behavior control systems in co-evolutionary development with more capable sensory systems. Consciousness thus *emerged* as a product of increasing biological complexity, from non-conscious precursors composed of non-conscious components.

Here we can raise many of the central questions within the problem of consciousness. Imagine we were alien exobiologists observing the Earth around the time of the emergence of consciousness. How would we know that certain organisms were conscious, while other organisms were not? What is it about the conscious organisms that explains why they are conscious? Furthermore, the appearance of conscious beings looks to be a development that sharply distinguishes them from their precursors, but the material processes of evolution are not marked by such radical discontinuities. To be sure, we do find striking differences among extant organisms. The unique human use of language is perhaps the best example of such a difference, but of course the apes exhibit a host of related, potentially precursor abilities, as do human beings who lack full language use. Thus we have possible models of at least some aspects of our prelinguistic ancestors which suggest the evolutionary path that led to language.

But the slightest, most fleeting spark of feeling is a full-fledged instance of consciousness which entirely differentiates its possessor from the realm of the non-conscious. Note here a dissimilarity to other biological features. Some creatures have wings and others do not, and we would expect that in the evolution from wingless to winged there would be a hazy region where it just would not be clear whether or not a certain creature's appendages would count as wings or not. Similarly, as we consider the evolutionary advance from non-conscious to conscious creatures, there would be a range of creatures about which we would be unclear whether they were conscious or not. But in this latter case, there is a fact whether or not the creatures in that range are feeling anything, however dimly or weakly, whereas we do not think there must be a fact about whether a certain appendage is or is not a wing (a dim or faint feeling is 100% a kind of consciousness, but a few feathers on a fore-limb is not a kind of wing). It is up to us whether to count a certain sort of appendage as a wing or not – it makes no difference, so to speak, to the organism what we call it. But it is not up to us to *decide* whether or not organism X does or does not enjoy some smidgen of consciousness – it either does or it does not.

Lurking behind these relatively empirical questions is a more basic theoretical, or metaphysical, issue. Given that creatures capable of fairly complex behavior were evolving without consciousness, why is consciousness necessary for the continued evolution of more complex behavior? Just as wings are an excellent solution to the problem of evolving flight, brains (or more generally nervous systems) are wonderful at implementing richly capable sensory systems and coordinated behavior control systems. But why should these brains be conscious? Although perhaps of doubtful coherence, it is useful to try to imagine our alien biologists as non-conscious beings. Perhaps they are advanced machines well programmed in deduction, induction, and abduction. Now, why would they ever posit consciousness in addition to, or as a feature of, complex sensory and behavioral control systems? As Thomas Huxley said, 'How it is that anything so remarkable as a state of consciousness comes about as a result of irritating nervous tissue, is just as unaccountable as the appearance of Djin when Aladdin rubbed his lamp' (1866, 8, 210). We might, rather fancifully, describe this core philosophical question about consciousness as how the genie of consciousness gets into the lamp of the brain, or why, to use Thomas Nagel's (1974) famous phrase, there is 'something it is like' to *be* a conscious entity?

III. Ancient Hints

Of course, the mainstream view has not long been mainstream, for the problem of consciousness cannot strike one at all until a fairly advanced scientific understanding of the world permits development of the materialism presupposed by the mainstream view. A second necessary condition is simply the self-recognition that we are conscious beings possessing a host of mental attributes. And that conception *has* been around for a long time. Our ancestors initiated a spectacular leap in conceptual technology by devising what is nowadays called folk psychology. The development of the concepts of behavior explaining states such as belief and desire, motivating states of pleasure and pain, and information-laden states of perceptual sensation, as well as the complex links amongst these concepts, is perhaps the greatest piece of theorizing ever produced by human beings. The power and age of folk psychology are attested by the universal animism of preliterate peoples and the seemingly innate tendencies of very young children to regard various natural or artificial processes as exemplifying agency (see, among many others, Bloom 2004; Gergeley et al. 1995; Perner 1991). The persistence of the core mentalistic notions of goal and purpose in Aristotle's proto-scientific but highly sophisticated theorizing also reveals the powerful hold these concepts had, and have, on human thought. But to the extent that mentalistic attributes are regarded as ubiquitous, no special problem of relating the mental to the non-mental realm can arise, for there simply is no such realm.

But interesting hints of this problem arise early on in philosophy, as the first glimmerings of a naturalistic world view occur. A fruitful way to present this history is in terms of a fundamental divergence in thought that arose early and has not yet died out in current debate. This is the contrast between emergence and panpsychism. The mainstream view accepts emergence: mind or consciousness appeared out of non-conscious precursors and non-conscious components (note there is both a synchronic and diachronic sense of emergence). Panpsychism is the alternative view that emergence is impossible and mind must be already and always present, in some sense, throughout the universe (a panpsychist might allow that mind emerges in the trivial sense that the universe may have been created out of nothing and hence out of 'non-consciousness'; the characteristically panpsychist position here would be that consciousness must have been created along with whatever other fundamental features of the world were put in place at the beginning). Of course, this divergence transcends the mind-body problem and reflects a fundamental difference in thinking about how the world is structured.

The Presocratic philosophers who flourished some 2,500 years ago in the Mediterranean basin were the first in the West to conceive of something like a scientific approach to nature, and it was their conception that eventually led to what we call science. Although their particular theories were understandably crude and often very fanciful, they were able to grasp the idea that the world could be viewed as composed out of elemental features, whose essential characterization might be hidden from human senses and which acted according to constant and universal principles or laws.

The Presocratics immediately recognized the basic dilemma: either mind (or, more generally, whatever apparently macroscopic, high-level, or non-fundamental property is at issue) is an elemental feature of the world, or it somehow emerges from, or is conditioned by, such features. If one opts for emergence, it is incumbent upon one to at least sketch the means by which new features emerge. If one opts for panpsychism (thus broadly construed), then one must account for the all too obviously apparent total lack of certain features at the fundamental level. For example, Anaxagoras (c. 500–425 BCE) flatly denied that emergence was possible

and instead advanced the view that 'everything is in everything'. Anaxagoras explained the obvious contrary appearance by a 'principle of dominance and latency' (see Mourelatos 1986), which asserted that some qualities were dominant in their contribution to the behaviour and appearance of things. However, Anaxagoras's views on mind are complex because he apparently regarded it as uniquely not containing any measure of other things and thus not fully in accord with his mixing principles. Perhaps this can be interpreted as the assertion that mind is ontologically fundamental in a special way; Anaxagoras did seem to believe that everything has some portion of mind in it while refraining from the assertion that everything has a mind (even this is controversial; see Barnes 1982, 405 ff.).

On the other hand, Empedocles, an almost exact contemporary of Anaxagoras, favoured an emergentist account based upon the famous doctrine of the four elements: earth, air, fire and water. All qualities were to be explicated in terms of ratios of these elements. The overall distribution of the elements, which were themselves eternal and unchangeable, was controlled by 'love and strife', whose operations are curiously reminiscent of some doctrines of modern thermodynamics, in a grand cyclically dynamic universe. It is true that Empedocles is sometimes regarded as a panpsychist because of the universal role of love and strife (see Edwards 1967, for example), but there seems little of the mental in Empedocles's conceptions, which are rather more like forces of aggregation and disaggregation, respectively (see Barnes 1982, 308 ff.).

The purest form of emergentism was propounded by the famed atomist Democritus (c. 460–370 BCE). His principle of emergence was based upon the possibility of multi-shaped, invisibly tiny atoms interlocking to form an infinity of more complex structures. But Democritus, in a way echoing Anaxagoras and perhaps hinting at the later distinction between primary and secondary properties, had to admit that the qualities of experience (what philosophers nowadays call qualia, the subjective features of conscious experience) could not be accounted for in this way and chose, ultimately unsatisfactorily, to relegate them to non-existence: 'sweet exists by convention, bitter by convention, in truth only atoms and the void'. Sorely missed is Democritus's account of how conventions themselves – the consciously agreed upon means of common reference to our subjective responses – emerge from the dancing atoms (thus, the ideas of Democritus anticipate the reflexive problem of modern eliminativist materialists [e.g., Churchland 1981] who would enjoin us to consciously accept a view which evidently entails that there is no such thing as conscious acceptance of views – see Chapter 3).

What is striking about these early struggles about the proper form of a scientific understanding of the world is that the mind and particularly consciousness keep rising as special problems. It is sometimes said that the mind-body problem is not an ancient philosophical issue on the basis that sensations were complacently regarded as bodily phenomena (see Matson 1966), but it does seem that the problem of consciousness was vexing philosophers 2,500 years ago, and in a form redolent of contemporary worries. Also critically important is the way that the problem of consciousness inescapably arises within the context of developing an integrated scientific view of the world.

The reductionist strain in the Presocratics was not favoured by the two giants of Greek philosophy, Plato and Aristotle, despite their own radical disagreements about how the world should be understood. Plato utterly lacked the naturalizing temperament of the Presocratic philosophers, although he was well aware of their efforts. He explicitly criticizes Anaxagoras's efforts to provide naturalistic, causal explanations of human behavior (see *Phaedo*, Plato 1961).

Of course, Plato nonetheless has a significant role in the debate because he advances positive arguments in favour of the thesis that mind and body are distinct. He also provides a basic, and perpetually influential, tri-component-based psychological theory (see *Republic*, Book 4, Plato 1961). These facets of his thought illustrate the two basic aspects of the problem of consciousness: the ontological question and the issue of how mind is structured. Plato's primary motivation for accepting a dualist account of mind and body presumably stems from the doctrine of the *forms*. These are entities which in some way express the intrinsic essence of things. The form of *circle* is that which our imperfect drawings of circles imitate and point to. The mind can grasp this form, even though we have never perceived a true circle, but only more or less imperfect approximations. The ability of the mind to commune with the radically non-physical forms suggests that mind itself cannot be physical. In the *Phaedo*, Plato (putting words in the mouth of Socrates) ridicules the reductionist account of Anaxogoras which sees human action as caused by local physical events. In its place, the mind is proposed as the final (i.e., teleological) cause of action, merely conditioned or constrained by the physical: 'if it were said that without such bones and sinews and all the rest of them I should not be able to do what I think is right, it would be true. But to say that is because of them that I do what I am doing, and not through choice of what is best – although my actions are controlled by mind – would be a very lax and inaccurate form of expression' (*Phaedo*, 98b ff.).

In general, Plato's arguments for dualism are not very convincing. Here's one. Life must come from death, because otherwise, as all living things eventually die, everything would eventually be dead. Life can come from death only if there is a distinct 'component', responsible for something being alive, that persists through the life-death-life cycle. That persistent component is soul or mind (*Phaedo* 72c-d). Another argument which Plato frequently invokes (or presupposes in other argumentation) is based on reincarnation. If we grant that reincarnation occurs, it is a reasonable inference that something persists which is what is reincarnated. This is a big 'if' to modern readers of a scientific bent, but the doctrine of reincarnation was widespread throughout ancient times and is still taken seriously by large numbers of people. The kernel of a more powerful argument for dualism lurks here as well, which was deployed by Descartes much later (see below).

Aristotle is famously more naturalistically inclined than Plato (Raphael's *School of Athens* shows Plato pointing upward to the heavens while Aristotle gestures downward to Earth as they stare determinedly at each other). But Aristotle's views on mind are complex and obscure; they are certainly not straightforwardly reductionist (the soul is *not*, for example, a particularly subtle kind of matter, such as fire). Aristotle's metaphysics deployed a fundamental distinction between matter and form, and any object necessarily instantiates both. A statue of a horse has its matter, bronze, and its form, horse. Aristotle is not using Plato's conception of form here. The form of something is not an other-world separate entity, but something more like the *way* in which the matter of something is organized or structured. Nor by matter does Aristotle mean the fundamental physical stuff we refer to by that word; matter is whatever relatively unstructured stuff is 'enformed' to make an object (English retains something of this notion in its use of matter to mean *topic*), so bronze is the matter of a statue, but soldiers would be the matter of an army. Objects can differ in matter, but agree in form (two identical pictures, one on paper and another on a computer screen) or vice versa. More abstractly, Aristotle regarded *life* as the form of plants and animals and named the form of living things *soul* ('the form of a natural body having life potentially within it' 1984, *De Anima*, bk. 2, ch. 1). Aristotle's views have some affinity both with modern biology's conception of life and the doctrine of psychophysical functionalism insofar as he stresses that soul is not a separate thing requiring another ontological realm, but also cannot be reduced to mere matter because its essential attribute is function and organization (for a close and skeptical look at the link between Aristotle's philosophy and modern functionalism

see Nelson 1990; see also Nussbaum and Putnam 1992).

Yet there are elements of Aristotle's account that are not very naturalistic. Early in the *De Anima* Aristotle raises the possibility that the relation between the body and the mind is analogous to that between sailor and ship, which would imply that mind is independent of body. Later Aristotle apparently endorses this possibility when he discusses, notoriously obscurely, the 'active intellect' – the 'part' of the soul capable of rational thought (*De Anima*, bk. 3, chs. 4–5). Aristotle clearly states that the active intellect is separable from body and can exist without it. For Aristotle, like Plato, the problematic feature of mind was its capacity for abstract thought and not consciousness per se, although of course these thinkers were implicitly discussing *conscious* thought and had no conception of mind apart from consciousness.

Discussion of one particular, and highly interesting if perennially controversial, feature of consciousness can perhaps be traced to Aristotle. This is the self-intimating or self-representing nature of all conscious states. Many thinkers have regarded it as axiomatic that one could not be in a conscious state without being aware of that state, and Aristotle makes some remarks that suggest he may belong to this school of thought. For example, in Book Three of *De Anima* Aristotle presents, rather swiftly, the following regress argument:

> *Since we perceive that we see and hear, it is necessarily either by means of the seeing that one perceives that one sees or by another [perception]. But the same [perception] will be both of the seeing and of the colour that underlies it, with the result that either two [perceptions] will be of the same thing, or it [the perception] will be of itself. Further, if the perception of seeing is a different [perception], either this will proceed to infinity or some [perception] will be of itself; so that we ought to posit this in the first instance.*

The passage is somewhat difficult to interpret, even in this translation from Victor Caston (2002) which forms part of an intricate (and controversial) mixed philosophical, exegetical, and linguistic argument in favor of the view that Aristotle accepted a self-representational account of conscious states which possessed unique phenomenal properties. Aristotle's argument appears to be that if it is essential to a conscious state that it be consciously apprehended then conscious states must be self-representing on pain of an infinite regress of states, each representing (and hence enabling conscious apprehension of) the previous state in the series. The crucial premise that *all* mental states must be conscious is formally necessary for the regress. Modern representational accounts of consciousness which accept that conscious states are self-intimating, such as the Higher Order Thought theory, can block the regress by positing non-conscious thoughts which make lower order thoughts conscious by being about them (see Seager 1999, Chapter 3, and see Chapters 3 and 4, this volume).

IV. The Scientific Revolution

Although the philosophy of the Middle Ages was vigorous and compendious, the problem of fitting consciousness into the natural world did not figure prominently (for an argument, following in the tradition of Matson 1966, that the medievals' views on the nature of sensation precluded the recognition of at least some versions of the mind-body problem, see King 2005). There were many acute studies of human psychology and innovative theoretical work on the content and structure of consciousness and cognition. Of special note is the 4th-century philosopher and Church Father, St. Augustine (354–430 CE). His writings exhibit important insights into the phenomenology of consciousness, especially with regard to the experience of time, will, and the self (see especially *Confessions* and *On Free Will*; 400/1998, 426/1998). He was one of the first philosophers to address the problem of other minds, arguing on the basis of introspection and analogy that because others behave as he behaves when he is aware of being in a

certain mental state, they too have mental states. In addition, he anticipated certain key features of Descartes' dualistic account of human beings, including Descartes' famous argument from his conscious self-awareness to the certainty of his own existence (*City of God*, Bk. 11, Ch. 21) and the idea that mind and body, although ontologically entirely distinct, somehow are united in the human person. Here Augustine also broaches one of the key puzzles of Cartesian dualism where he admits the 'mode of union' by which bodies and spirits are bound together to become animals is 'beyond the comprehension of man' (*City of God*, Bk. 21, Ch. 10). Although we see here that Augustine did not agree with Descartes in denying minds to animals, we can also note the complete lack of any idea that this mystery poses any special problem for our understanding of the natural world (see O'Daly 1987 for a detailed discussion of Augustine's philosophy of mind).

In fact, the tenets of Christian dogma, eventually wedded to a fundamentally Aristotelian outlook, conspired to suppress any idea that consciousness or mind could be, should be, or needed to be explained in naturalistic terms. It was the scientific revolution of the 16th and 17th centuries that forced the problem into prominence.

Galileo's distinction between primary and secondary properties, crucial for the development of science insofar as it freed science from a hopelessly premature attempt to explain complex sensible qualities in mechanical terms, explicitly set up an opposition between matter and consciousness: 'I think that tastes, odors, colors, and so on are no more than mere names so far as the object in which we place them is concerned, and that they reside only in the consciousness. Hence if the living creature were removed all these qualities would be wiped away and annihilated' (1623/1957, 274). The welcome consequence is that if there are therefore no colors in the world then science is free to ignore them. That was perhaps good tactics in Galileo's time, but it was a strategic time bomb waiting to go off when science could no longer delay investigating the mind itself.

The mind-body problem in its modern form is essentially the work of a single genius, René Descartes (1596–1650), who reformed the way we think about mind and consciousness, leaving us with a set of intuitions that persist to this day. To take just one topical example, the basic idea behind the fictional technology of the *Matrix* films is thoroughly Cartesian: what we experience is not directly related to the state of the environment, but is instead the result of a complex function – involving essential sensory and cognitive mediation based upon neural systems – from the environment to our current state of consciousness. Thus two brains that are in identical states ought to be in the same state of consciousness, no matter what differences there are in their respective environments. It now seems intuitively obvious that this is correct (so contemporary philosophers make exotic and subtle arguments against it) and that, to take another stock philosophical example, a brain in a vat, if kept alive in an appropriate chemical bath and if fed proper input signals into its severed nerve endings (cleverly coupled to the output of the brain's motor output nerves), would have experiences which could be indistinguishable from, say, those you are having at this very moment. This thought experiment reveals another of the reformations of philosophy instituted by Descartes: the invention of modern epistemology, for how could you *know* that you are not such a brain in a vat.

Descartes was of course also one of the creators of the scientific revolution, providing seminal efforts in mathematics and physics. But he also saw with remarkable prevision the outlines of neuropsychology. With no conception of how the nervous system actually works and instead deploying a kind of hydraulic metaphor, Descartes envisioned nerve-based sensory and cognitive systems and a kind of network structure in the brain, even – anticipating Hebb – suggesting that connections in the brain are strengthened through associated activation. His notorious discussion of animals as machines can be seen as the precursor of a materialist account of cognition.

But Descartes is most remembered and reviled for his insistence upon the strict separation of mind and body which, we are enjoined to believe, required sundering the world itself into radically distinct realms, thereby fundamentally splitting human beings from nature (including their own), denigrated emotion in favour of reason, and inspired a lack of respect for animals and nature in general. Why was Descartes a dualist? Some have suggested that Descartes lacked the courage to follow his science to its logical and materialist conclusion (the fate of Galileo is said to have had a strong effect on him, or it may be that Descartes really had no wish to harm the Catholic church). But Descartes did have *arguments* for his dualism, some of which still have supporters. These arguments also set out one of the basic strategies of anti-materialism.

To show that mind and body are distinct, it will suffice to show that mind has some property that matter lacks. The general principle here, which is that of the alibi, was codified by another 17th-century philosopher, Gottfried Leibniz (1646–1716) and is now known as Leibniz's Law: if x has a property which y lacks, then x and y are not identical. Descartes argued, for example, that although matter is extended in space, mind takes up no space at all. Thus, they could not be identical. It certainly does seem odd to ask how many cubic centimeters my *mind* takes up (does a broad mind take up more space than a narrow one?). But it is not obvious that this question is anything more than merely a feature of the conventional way we think about minds. An analogy would be an argument that machines cannot think because they are not *alive*; there is no particular reason to think that the heretofore constant and evident link between life and thought represents anything more than a kind of accident in the way minds happened to be created. In any event, this *strategy* is still at the core of the problem of consciousness. One current line of argument, for example, contends that consciousness has a kind of first-person subjectivity (the 'what it is like' to experience something), whereas matter is purely third-person objective – hence consciousness and matter must be fundamentally different phenomena.

Descartes, in the sixth of his *Meditations* (1641/1985), also invented an astonishingly novel kind of argument for dualism. The argument is couched in theological terms, but that was merely for purposes of clarity and forcefulness (in the 17th century, using God to explain one's argument was impeccable rhetoric). Descartes asked us to consider whether it was at least *possible* that God could destroy one's body while leaving one's mind intact. If it was possible then of course God could perform the feat if He wished. But nothing can be separated from itself! So if it is merely possible that God could sunder mind from body, then they must already be different things. So, anyone who thinks that, say, a consciousness persisting after bodily death is even so much as a bare possibility already thinks that consciousness is not a physical phenomenon. This argument is valid, but it has a little flaw: how do we know that what we think is possible is truly so? Many are the mathematicians labouring to prove theorems which will turn out to be unprovable (think of the centuries-long effort to square the circle) – what do they think they are doing? Nonetheless, it is a highly interesting revelation that the mere *possibility* of dualism (in the sense considered here) entails that dualism is true.

Cartesian dualism also included the doctrine of mind-body interaction. This seems like common sense: when someone kicks me, that causes me to feel pain and anger, and then it is my anger that makes me kick them back. Causation appears to run from body to mind and back again. But as soon as Descartes propounded his theory of mind, this interaction was seen to be deeply problematic. One of Descartes' aristocratic female correspondents, the Princess Elisabeth of Palatine, asked the crucial question: "How can the soul of man determine the spirits of the body, so as to produce voluntary actions (given that the soul is only a thinking substance)?" (from a letter of May 1643). It's a fair question and Descartes' only answer was that the mind-body union was instituted and maintained by God and was humanly incomprehensible. The Princess allowed herself less than *fully* satisfied with this reply.

It was also noticed that Descartes' dualism conflicted with the emerging understanding of the conservation of certain physical quantities. Descartes himself only accepted that the total amount, but not direction, of motion was conserved. Thus the mind's ability to wiggle the pineal gland (where Descartes posited the seat of the soul) would redirect motion without violating natural law. But it was soon discovered that it was momentum – or directed motion – that is conserved, and thus the mind-induced motion of the pineal gland would indeed contradict the laws of nature (one might try to regard this as a feature rather than a bug, because at least it makes Descartes' theory empirically testable in principle).

In addition to the ontological aspect of his views, Descartes had some interesting insights into the phenomenological side of consciousness. For Descartes, the elements of conscious experience are what he called 'ideas' (Descartes pioneered the modern use of this term to stand for mental items), and every idea possesses two kinds of reality: formal and objective. The formal reality of something is simply what it is in itself, whereas the objective reality is what, if anything, it represents (so, the formal reality of a picture of a horse is paper and paint; a horse is the objective reality). Though Descartes is often pilloried as one who believed that we are only ever conscious of our own ideas, it is far from clear that this is Descartes' position. It is possible to read him instead as a precursor of modern representational theories of consciousness [see Chapter 3], in which it is asserted that, although consciousness essentially involves mental representation, *what* we are conscious of is not the representations themselves but their content (rather in the way that although we must use words to talk about things, we are not thereby always talking *about* words). Descartes says that 'there cannot be any ideas which do not appear to represent some things . . .' (*Meditation* 3), and perhaps this suggests that even in cases of illusion

Descartes' view was that our experience is of the representational content of the ideas and that we do not, as it were, see our own ideas.

Finally, because Descartes is often misrepresented as denigrating bodily feelings and emotions in favour of pure reason, it is worth pointing out that he developed a sophisticated account of the emotions which stresses both their importance and the importance of the bodily feelings which accompany them (1649/1985). Descartes – perhaps contra Aristotle – strenuously denied that the mind was 'in' the body the way a pilot is in a ship, for the intimate connection to the body and the host of functionally significant feelings which the body arouses in the mind in the appropriate circumstances meant that the mind-body link was not a mere communication channel. Descartes declared instead that the mind and body formed a 'substantial union' and that emotional response was essential to cognition.

Despite the fact that *if* one is willing to endorse a dualism of mind and body then Descartes' interactive version seems to be the most intuitively reasonable, the difficulties of understanding how two such entirely distinct realms could causally interact created an avid market for alternative theories of the mind-body relation. Two broad streams of theory can be discerned, which I label, not altogether happily, *idealist* and *materialist*. Idealists regard mind or consciousness as the fundamental existent and deny the independent existence of the material world; its apparent reality is to be explained as a function of mentality. Materialists cannot follow such a direct route, for they have great difficulty in outright *denying* the existence of mind and generally content themselves with in some way identifying it with features of matter. The asymmetry in these positions is interesting. Idealists can easily assert that the material world is all illusory. Materialists fall into paradox if they attempt the same strategy – for the assertion that mind is illusory presupposes the existence of illusions, which are themselves mental entities. For a long time (centuries, I mean) the idealist

position seemed dominant, but the materialists, like the early mammals scrabbling under the mighty dinosaurs, were to have their day.

Early materialists had to face more than an intellectual struggle, because their doctrine stood in clear contradiction with fundamental beliefs endorsed by the Christian church, and many thinkers have been charged with softening their views to avoid ecclesiastical censure. One such is Pierre Gassendi (1592–1655), who espoused an updated version of ancient Epicurean atomism, but who added immortal and immaterial souls to the dance of the atoms. The souls were responsible, in a familiar refrain, for our higher *intellectual* abilities. On the materialist core of such a view, nature is ultimately composed of tiny, indivisible, and indestructible physical particles whose interactions account for all the complexity and behaviour of organized matter. Gassendi asserted that the 'sentient soul', as opposed to the immaterial 'sapient soul', was a material component of animals and humans, composed of an especially subtle, quick-moving type of matter which is capable of forming the system of images we call imagination and perception (Gassendi also endorsed the empiricist principle that all ideas are based on prior sensory experience). These are literally little images in the brain. Of course, there is a problem here: who is looking at these images? What good does it do to postulate them? For Descartes, the experience of sensory perception or imagination is similarly dependent upon corporeal imagery, but because the visual experience is a mental act, there really is someone to appreciate the brain's artwork. (Descartes in fact tried to use the imagistic quality of certain experiences as an argument for the existence of material objects, because real images need a material substrate in which they are realized – but Descartes concluded that this argument was far from conclusive.) A subtle distinction here may have directed philosophers' thinking away from this worry. This is the difference between what are nowadays called substance and property dualism. Descartes is a substance dualist (hence also a property dualist, but that is a rather trivial consequence of his view). Substance in general was understood as that which could exist independently (or perhaps requiring only the concurrence of God). Matter was thus a substance, but properties of matter were not themselves substantial, for properties require substance in which to be instantiated. According to Descartes, mind is a second kind of substance, with, naturally, its own set of characteristically mental properties. Thus one basic form of materialism involves merely the denial of mental substance, and the early materialists were keen to make this aspect of their views clear. But denial of substance dualism leaves open the question of the nature of mental properties or attributes (consciousness can be regarded as a feature of the brain, but is no less mysterious for being labeled a property of a physical object).

The problem is clearer in the work of another early materialist, Thomas Hobbes (1588–1679) who, entranced by the new science inaugurated by Galileo, declared that absolutely everything should be explicable in terms of the motions of matter and the efficient causal interaction of material contact. Eventually coming to consider the mind, Hobbes pursues motion into the brain to account for sensory phenomena: 'the cause of sense is the external body...which presses the organ proper to each sense...which pressure, by the mediation of the nerves...continues inwards to the brain...' (1651/1998, pt. 1, ch. 1). Hobbes goes out of his way to stress that there is nothing immaterial, occult, or supernatural here; there is just the various ways that physical events influence our material sense organs: 'neither in us that are pressed are they anything else but divers motions; for motion produceth nothing but motion' (1651/1998, pt. 1, ch. 1). But then Hobbes makes a curious remark: speaking of these 'divers motions' in the brain he says, 'but their appearance to us is fancy, the same waking that dreaming'. However, he elsewhere states that 'all fancies are motions within us' (1651/1998, pt. 1, ch. 3). Compounding the confusion he also describes our

appetites or motivations as motions, but says that pleasure and pain are the appearances of these motions (1651/1998, pt. 1, ch. 6). It would seem that 'appearance' is Hobbes's term for something like phenomenal consciousness, and he seems to be saying that such consciousness is *caused* by motions in the brain but is not identical to them, which of course flatly contradicts his claim that motion can only produce motion. Though obviously Hobbes is not clear about this problem, we might anachronistically characterize him as a substance materialist who is also a property dualist.

In any case, materialism was very far from the generally favoured opinion, and the perceived difficulties of Descartes' substance dualism led instead to a series of inventive alternatives to interactive substance dualism, the two most important being those of Baruch de Spinoza (1632–1677) and Leibniz. In an austerely beautiful if forbidding work, the *Ethics* (1677/1985), Spinoza laid out a theory which perhaps, logically, ought to have been that of Descartes. Spinoza notes that substance is that which exists independently of all other things, and thus there can be only one 'maximal' substance: God. If that is so, then matter and mind can only be features of the God-substance (Spinoza called them attributes and asserted there were an infinite number of them, although we are only aware of two). Spinoza's theory is an early form of what came to be called 'dual aspect theory', which asserts that mind and matter are mere aspects of some underlying kind of thing of which we have no clear apprehension. Particular material or mental individuals (as we would say) are mere modifications of their parent attributes (so your mind is a kind of short-lived ripple in the attribute of mind and your body a small disturbance in the material attribute). The attributes are a perfect reflection of their underlying substance, but only in terms of one aspect (very roughly like having both a climatographic and topographic map of the same territory). Thus Spinoza believed that the patterns within any attribute would be mirrored in all the others; in particular, mind and body would be synchronized automatically and necessarily. This explains the apparent linkage between mind and body – both are merely aspects of the same underlying substance – while at the same time preserving the causal completeness of each realm. In the illustrative scholium to proposition seven of book two of the *Ethics* (1677/1985) Spinoza writes, 'A circle existing in nature and the idea of the existing circle, which is also in God, are one and the same thing...therefore, whether we conceive nature under the attribute of Extension, or under the attribute of Thought...we shall find one and the same order, or one and the same connection of causes...'. On the downside, Spinoza does have to assume that every physical event has a corresponding mental event, and he is thus a kind of panpsychist. Even worse (from a 17th-century point of view) Spinoza's view is heretical, because it sees God as being literally in everything and thus as a material thing not separate from the world.

Leibniz never wrote down his metaphysical system in extensive detail (he was doubtless too busy with a multitude of other projects, such as inventing calculus, rediscovering binary arithmetic, building the first calculating machines, and writing endless correspondence and commentary, not to mention his day job of legal counsel and historian to the Hanoverian house of Brunswick), but his views can be reconstructed from the vast philosophical writings he left us. They can be caricatured, in part, as Spinoza's with an infinite number of substances replacing the unique God-substance. These substances Leibniz called monads (see Leibniz 1714/1989). Because they are true substances, and hence can exist independently of any other thing, and because they are absolutely simple, they cannot interact with each other in any way (nonetheless they are created by God, who is one of them – here Spinoza seems rather more consistent than Leibniz). Yet each monad carries within it complete information about the entire universe. What we call space and time are in reality sets of relations amongst these monads (or, better, the information which they contain), which are

in themselves radically non-spatial and perhaps even non-temporal (Leibniz's vision of space and time emerging from some more elementary systems of relations has always been tempting, if hard to fathom, and now fuels some of the most advanced physics on the planet).

However, Leibniz does not see the monadic substances as having both mental and material aspects. Leibniz's monads are fundamentally to be conceived mentalistically; they are in a way mentalistic automatons moving from one perceptual or apperceptual state to another, all exactly according to a God-imposed predefined rule. The physical world is a kind of logical construction out of these mental states, one which meets various divinely instituted constraints upon the relation between those aspects matching what we call 'material objects' with those we call 'states of consciousness' – Leibniz called this the pre-established harmony, and it is his explanation for the appearance of mind-body interaction. So Leibniz's view is one that favours the mental realm; that is, it is at bottom a kind of idealism as opposed to Spinoza's many aspect theory.

As we shall see, Leibniz's vision here had a much greater immediate impact on subsequent philosophy than Spinoza's. An important difference between the two theories is that, unlike Spinoza, Leibniz can maintain a distinction between things that have minds or mental attributes from those that do not, despite his panpsychism. This crucial distinction hinges on the difference between a 'mere aggregate' and what Leibniz sometimes calls an 'organic unity' or an organism. Each monad represents the world – in all its infinite detail – from a unique point of view. Consider a heap of sand. It corresponds to a set of monads, but there is no monad which represents anything like a point of view of the heap. By contrast, your body also corresponds to a set of monads, but one of these monads – the so-called dominant monad – represents the point of view of the system which is your living body. (There presumably are also sub-unities within you, corresponding to organized and functionally unified physiological, and hence also psychological, subsystems.) Organisms correspond to a hierarchically ordered set of monads; mere aggregates do not. This means that there is no mental aspect to heaps of sand as such, even though at the most fundamental level mind pervades the universe.

One last point: you might wonder why you, a monad that represents every detail of the entire universe, seem so relatively ignorant. The answer depends upon another important aspect of the conception of mentality. Leibniz allows that there are unconscious mental states. In fact, almost all mental states are unconscious, and low-level monads never aspire to consciousness (or what Leibniz calls apperception). You are aware, of course, only of your conscious mental states, and these represent a literally infinitesimal fraction of the life of your mind, most of which is composed of consciously imperceptible *petite perceptions* (it is galling to think that somewhere within each of our minds lies the invisible answers to such questions as whether there are advanced civilizations in the Andromeda galaxy, but there it is).

For Leibniz the material world is, fundamentally, a kind of illusion, but one of a very special kind. What Leibniz calls 'well grounded' phenomena are those that are in some way directly represented in every monad. Imagine aerial photographs of downtown Toronto taken from a variety of altitudes and angles. The same buildings appear in each photograph, though their appearance is more or less different. But, for example, sun flares caused by the camera lens will not appear in every picture. The buildings would be termed well grounded, the sun flare an illusion. So Leibniz can provide a viable appearance-reality distinction that holds in the world of matter (though it is tricky, because presumably the illusions of any one monad are actually reflected in all monads – hence the weasel word 'directly' above). Nonetheless, it is the domain of consciousness which is fundamental and, in the end, the totality of reality, with the physical world being merely a kind of construction out of the mental.

V. The Idealist Turn

In some way, Leibniz represents the culmination of the tradition of high metaphysics: the idea that reason could reveal the ultimate nature of things and that this nature is radically different from that suggested by common sense. But his model of the material world as mere appearance was taken to its logical next step by the, at least superficially, anti-metaphysical Immanuel Kant (1724–1804). In Kant (see especially 1781/1929) we see the beginning of the idealism which in one form or another dominated philosophy for more than a century afterward.

Once mind is established as the sole reality, the problem of consciousness and all the other traditional problems of relating matter to mind, virtually disappear. The problem that now looks big and important is in a way the inverse of the problem of consciousness: how exactly is the material world which we evidently experience to be constructed out of pure and seemingly evanescent consciousness. Two modes of response to this problem can be traced that roughly divide the thinkers of the British Isles (forgive me for including Ireland here) from those of continental Europe, although the geographic categorization becomes increasingly misleading as we enter the 20th century. Very crudely, these modes of idealism can be characterized respectively as phenomenalism (material objects are 'permanent possibilities of sensation') and transcendental idealism (a system of material objects represented in experience is a necessary condition for coherent experience and knowledge).

There were, of course, materialists lurking about in this period, though they were nowhere near the heart of philosophical progress; in fact they were frequently not philosophers at all, and quite a number came from the ranks of intellectually inclined medical doctors. One such was Julien de La Mettrie (1709–1751) who outraged Europe, or at least enough of France to require a retreat to Berlin, with his *L'Homme machine* (1748/1987) (see also the slightly earlier *L'Histoire naturelle de l'âme*; 1745). In this brisk polemical work, La Mettrie extends the Cartesian thesis that animals are 'mere' machines to include the human animal. But of note here is the same reluctance to shed all reference to the specialness of the mind that we observed in earlier materialists. La Mettrie is willing to deny that there are immaterial mental substances, but describes matter as having three essential attributes: extension, motion, and *consciousness*. In *L'Histoire naturelle de l'âme* (1745), La Mettrie makes the interesting points that the intrinsic nature of matter is utterly mysterious to us and that the attribution of mental properties to it should be no less strange than the attribution of extension and motion, in the sense that we understand what it is about matter itself that supports extension no better – that is not at all – than we understand how it can or cannot support mental properties. This idea has remained an important, if somewhat marginalized, part of the debate about the relation between mind and matter. Although not always very clear about their own positions, most materialists or quasi-materialists of the period, such as John Toland (1670–1722), Paul-Henri D'Holbach (1723–1789) (see Holbach 1970), Joseph Priestley (1733–1804) (see Priestley 1975), and Pierre-Jean-George Cabanis (1757–1808), agreed on the approach that denies substance dualism while allowing that matter may have properties that go beyond motion and extension, prominent among which are the various mental attributes.

The tide of philosophy was, however, running in favour of idealism. A central reason for this was independent of the problem of consciousness, but stemmed from the epistemological crisis brought about by Cartesian philosophy (itself but a partial reflection of the general cultural upheaval occasioned by the scientific revolution). Descartes had argued that the true nature of the world was quite unlike that apparently revealed by the senses, but that reality could be discovered by the 'light of reason'. Unfortunately, although everyone took to heart the skeptical challenge to conventional wisdom, Descartes' positive arguments convinced hardly anybody. The core problem was the disconnection between experience and the material world enshrined in Descartes' dualism. But what if the material world was somehow really a feature of the realm of consciousness for which we obviously seem to have infallible access? For example, suppose, as did George Berkeley (1685–1753), that material objects are nothing but ordered sequences of perceptions (1710/1998). We know by introspection that we have perceptions and that they obey certain apparent laws of succession. Under Berkeley's identification we thereby *know* that there are material objects and the epistemological crisis is resolved.

On the other side of the English Channel, Kant was investigating the deeper problem of how we could know that our perceptions really do follow law-governed patterns which guarantee that they can be interpreted in terms of a scientifically explicable material world. Kant accepted Leibniz's view that all we could possibly have knowledge of are constructions out of subjective experience and that any distinction between reality and appearance within the realm of perception and scientific investigation would have to be based upon some set of relations holding amongst our experiences. He added the remarkable idea that these relations were a reflection of the structure of the mind itself – concepts of space, time, and causation are necessary conditions for the existence of experience of an 'external world' and are 'discovered' in that world because they pre-exist in the mind. There is no reason at all to suppose that they reflect some deeper reality beyond appearances. But they are a necessary condition for having coherent experience at all and hence will and must be discovered in the world which is a construct out of such experience. Kant called this style of reasoning transcendental argumentation. In one sense, however, Kant was an impure idealist. He allowed for the existence of the 'thing-in-itself': the necessarily unknowable, mind-independent basis of experience. In this respect, Kant's philosophy is somewhat like Spinoza's, save of course that Spinoza was fully confident that reason could reveal something of the thing-in-itself. Idealists who followed Kant, such as A. Schopenhauer (1788–1869) and the absolute idealist G. Hegel (1770–1831) and many other continental philosophers, as well as the later followers of Hegel, such as the British philosopher F. Bradley (1846–1924), espoused purer forms of idealism (see Bradley 1987/1966; Hegel 1812/1969; Schopenhauer 1819/1966). Kant's hypothesis that it was a 'transcendental' condition for the very possibility of introspectible experience to be lawfully ordered led to a huge philosophical industry focused, to put it crudely, on the mind's contribution to the structures we find in the external world (an industry that eventually leads into the postmodern desconstructionist ghetto). But this industry, by its nature, did not face the problem of consciousness as defined here and so is not a main player in the drama of this chapter.

VI. Evolution and Emergence

Instead, as we now enter the heart of the 19th century, two crucial non-philosophical developments transformed the problem: the rise of Darwinism in biology and, drawn from the brow of philosophy itself, the beginning of scientific psychology. Above all else, the evolutionary theory of Charles Darwin (1809–1882) promised to unify the simple with the complex by suggesting some way that mere atoms could, guided only by the laws of physics, congregate into such complex forms as plants, animals, and even human beings. This led immediately to two deep questions: what is life and how does matter organized via natural selection acquire consciousness? These are both questions about *emergence*, for it certainly appears, if evolution be true, that life springs forth from the lifeless and consciousness appears in beings evolved from non-conscious ancestors composed of utterly non-conscious parts. The first question led to the vitalism controversy, which bears some analogy to the problem of consciousness. Vitalists contended that there was something more to life than mere material organization: a vital spark, or *élan vital*. This

view of life and its conflict with any materialist account can be traced back at least to the 17th century. Another of our philosophically inclined physicians, Nehemiah Grew (1641–1712), who helped found scientific botany and was secretary of the Royal Society in 1677, quaintly put the problem thus (see Garrett 2003), perhaps not atypically confusing the issues of life and consciousness:

> The Variety of the Mixture, will not suffice to produce Life... Nor will its being mechanically Artificial. Unless the Parts of a Watch, set, as they ought to be, together; may be said to be more Vital, than when they lye in a confused Heap. Nor its being Natural. There being no difference, between the Organs of Art and Nature; saving, that those of Nature are most of all Artificial. So that an Ear, can no more hear, by being an Organ; than an Artificial Ear would do... And although we add the Auditory nerves to the Ear, the Brain to the Nerves, and the Spirits to the Brain; yet is it still but adding Body to Body, Art to Subtility, and Engine or Art to Art: Which, howsoever Curious, and Many; can never bring Life out of themselves, nor make one another to be Vital. (Grew 1701, 33)

Vitalism flourished in the 19th century and persisted into the 20th, notably in the writings of Hans Driesch (1867–1941), who had discovered that fragments of sea urchin embryos would develop into normal sea urchins, contrary to then-current mechanist theory (indeed it is hard to understand how a few of the *parts* of a machine would go on to operate exactly as did the original whole machine). Vitalists thus assumed there must be some special added feature to living things which accounted for the ability to organize and reorganize even in the face of such assaults. It was the unfortunately delayed development of Mendelian 'information-based' genetics which suggested the answer to Driesch's paradox and led to the successful integration of evolution and heredity.

For our purposes, the decline of vitalism not only provides a cautionary tale but also highlights an important disanalogy between the problems of life and consciousness. Life was seen to be problematic from the materialist point of view because of what it could do, as in Driesch's sea urchins. It seemed hard to explain the behavioral capacities of living things in terms of non-organic science. Perhaps conscious beings, as living things, present the same problem. But this difficulty was ultimately swept away with the rise of genetics as an adjunct to evolutionary theory. However, in addition to and independent of the puzzle of behaviour, consciousness has an internal or subjective aspect, which life, as such, utterly lacks. What is especially problematic about consciousness is the question of why or how purely material systems could become such that there is 'something it is like' to be them.

Another aspect of Darwinism played directly into the mind-matter debate. Darwin himself, and for a long time all Darwinists, was a committed gradualist and assumed that evolution worked by the long and slow accumulation of tiny changes, with no infusions of radically new properties at any point in evolutionary history. Applying gradualism to the mind, Darwin went out of his way to emphasize the continuity in the mental attributes of animals and humans (see Darwin 1874).

Gradualism has its difficulties, which have long been noted and persist to this day in talk of punctuated equilibrium (see Eldredge & Gould 1972) and so-called irreducible complexity (Behe 1998, for example). The evolution of the eye was seen as very hard for evolution to explain even by Darwin himself: 'To suppose that the eye...could have been formed by natural selection, seems, I freely confess, absurd in the highest degree' (1859/1967, 167). Of course, the idea that a fully formed eye could appear as the result of one supremely lucky mutational accident is truly absurd and is not what is at issue here. But Darwin went on to give some basis for how the evolution of the eye was possible, and there are nowadays sophisticated accounts of how complex multi-part organs can evolve, as well as compelling theories of the evolution of particular organs, such as the eye (see e.g., Dawkins 1995).

But as noted above, in the most basic sense of the term, consciousness seems to be an all-or-nothing affair. No non-conscious precursor state seems to give the slightest hint that consciousness would be its evolutionary successor. The tiniest spark of feeling and the weakest and most obscure sensation are fully states of consciousness. Thus the emergence of consciousness at some point in evolutionary history appears to be an intrusion of true novelty at odds with the smoothly evolving complexity of organisms. William Clifford (1845–1879), a tragically short-lived philosophical and mathematical genius (he anticipated general relativity's unification of gravity with geometry and predicted gravitational waves), put the problem thus:

> ...we cannot suppose that so enormous a jump from one creature to another should have occurred at any point in the process of evolution as the introduction of a fact entirely different and absolutely separate from the physical fact. It is impossible for anybody to point out the particular place in the line of descent where that event can be supposed to have taken place (1874/1886, 266).

So, although Darwinism provided great support for and impetus to the materialist vision of the world, within it lurked the old, and still unresolved, problem of emergence.

Perhaps it was time to tackle the mind directly with the tools of science. During the 19th century, psychology broke away from philosophy to become a scientific discipline in its own right. Despite the metaphysical precariousness of the situation, no one had any doubt that there was a correspondence between certain physical states and mental states and that it ought to be possible to investigate that correspondence scientifically. The pseudo science of phrenology was founded on reasonably acceptable principles by Franz Gall (1758–1828) with the aim of correlating physical attributes of the brain with mental faculties, of which Gall, following a somewhat idiosyncratic system of categorization, counted some two dozen, including friendship, amativeness, and acquisitiveness. True, the categorization used is quaint and bizarrely 'high-level' and Gall's shortcut methodology of inferring brain structure from bumps on the skull dubious (to say the least), but the core idea retains vigorous life in today's brain imaging studies and the theory of mental/brain modules. As D. B. Klein said, 'Gall gave wrong answers to good questions' (Klein, 1970, 669).

Throughout the 19th century, one of the primary activities of psychological science and even the main impetus for its creation was discovering correlations between psychological states and physical conditions, either of the environment of the subject or brain anatomy discovered via postmortem investigation (but not of course brain *states*, which were entirely inaccessible to 19th-century science). Unlike in the quackery of phrenology, genuine and profound advances were made. Following foundational work on the physical basis of sensation by Hermann Helmholtz (1821–1894), also famed for introducing the hypothesis that unconscious inference accounts for many aspects of cognition and perception, important discoveries included the connection between certain brain regions and linguistic ability in the work of Paul Broca (1824–1880); seminal studies of stimulus strength and the introspected intensity of sensation by Gustav Fechner (1803–1887), who coined the phrase 'psycho-physical law' (1946), and the creation of the first psychological laboratory devoted to such studies by Wilhelm Wundt (1832–1920), who also developed the first distinctive research methodology of psychology – that of introspectionism (1892/1894).

From the point of view of the problem of consciousness these developments point to a bifurcation in the issue. Almost all the thinkers associated with the birth of psychology endorsed some form of idealism as the correct metaphysical account of mind and matter, and none of prominence were materialists. They were nonetheless keen on studying what we would call the neural bases of consciousness and never questioned the legitimacy of such studies. It is useful to distinguish the study of the structure of consciousness from the question of the ultimate nature of consciousness and its place in the natural world. The pioneers of psychology were, so to speak, officially interested in the structure of consciousness, both its introspectible experiential structure and its structural link to physical conditions (both internal and external to the body).

The growth of interest in these questions can also be seen in more purely philosophical work in the rise of the phenomenological movement, although of course the philosophers were not particularly interested in investigating correlations between mental and material conditions but rather focused on the internal structure of pure consciousness. Phenomenology was foreshadowed by Franz Brentano (1838–1917), who in a highly influential work, *Psychology from the Empirical Standpoint* (1874/1973, 121 ff.), advanced the view that mental states were self-intimating coupled with an updated version of Aristotle's regress argument (Brentano rather generously credits Aristotle for his whole line of thought here).

Brentano also reminded philosophers of a feature of mental states which had almost been forgotten since it had first been noted in the Middle Ages (though Descartes' notion of objective reality is closely related). Brentano labeled this feature *intentionality*, which is the 'directedness' or 'aboutness' of at least many mental states onto a content, which may or may not refer to an existing object. If I ask you to imagine a unicorn, you are easily able to do so, despite the fact that there are no unicorns. Now, what is your thought about? Evidently not any real unicorn, but neither is your thought about the image of a unicorn produced in your imagination or even just the idea of a unicorn. For if I asked you to think about your image or idea of a unicorn you could do that as well, but it would be a different thought, and a rather more complex one. One way to think about this is to say that any act of imagination has a certain representational content, and imagining a unicorn is simply the having of a particular unicorn-content (in the 'appropriate' way as well, for imagination must be distinguished from other content-bearing mental acts). The consciousness involved in such an act of imagination is the presentation of that content to your mind. This is not to say that you are aware of your mental state whenever you imagine, but rather it is through having such a state that you are conscious of what the state represents, although Brentano himself held that any conscious state presented *itself* as well as its content to the subject. The failure to notice the intentional aspect of consciousness had bedeviled philosophy, leading to a plethora of theories of thought and perception that left us in the awkward position of never being aware of anything but our own mental states.

Brentano went so far as to declare intentionality *the* mark of the mental, the unique property that distinguished the mental from the physical. Of course, many other things, such as pictures, words, images on television, electronic computation, and so on, have representational content, but arguably these all get their content derivatively, via a mental interpretation. Uniquely mental or not, intentionality poses an extremely difficult question: how is it that mental states (or anything else) can acquire representational content? Perhaps if one accepts, as so many of the thinkers of this period did, that mind is the bedrock reality, then one can accept that it is simply a brute fact, an essential property of mentality, that it carry representational content. No explanation of this basic fact can be given in terms of anything simpler or more fundamental.

However, if one aspires to a materialist account of mind, then one cannot avoid this issue. A frequent metaphor which materialists of the time appealed to was that of biological secretion, perhaps first explicitly articulated by Cabanis in his *Rapports du physique et du moral de l'homme* (1802/1981), who proclaimed that the brain secretes thought as the liver secretes bile. As it stands, this is little more than a declaration of loyalty to the materialist viewpoint, for we expect there should be an explication of the process and nature of such secretion just as there is such an account of the production

of bile. Just which part of the brain generates these 'secretions' and how do they manage to possess representational or phenomenal content? Nonetheless, the metaphor was effective. It was approved by Darwin himself (a closet materialist), who (privately) endorsed its repetition by John Elliotson (1791–1868) – physician, phrenologist, mesmerist, and the so-called strongest materialist of the day (see Desmond and Moore 1994, 250 ff.). In one of his private notebooks Darwin modified the metaphor in an interesting way, writing, 'Why is thought, being a secretion of brain, more wonderful than gravity as a property of matter'? This comment is striking because it clarifies how the metaphor implicitly suggests that it is a brute fact that brains produce thought, just as it is a brute fact that matter is associated with gravitation. Note also how the power to gravitate seems remote from matter's core properties of extension, exclusion, and mass and, at least in the Newtonian view, provides the almost miraculous ability to affect all things instantaneously at a distance. Nevertheless, the essential emptiness of the metaphor did not go unremarked. William James (1842–1910) wrote 'the lame analogy need hardly be pointed out ... we know of nothing connected with liver and kidney activity which can be in the remotest degree compared with the stream of thought that accompanies the brain's material secretions' (1890/1950, 102–3).

Leaving aside once again this metaphysical issue, workers focused on the structure and meaning of the contents of consciousness along with their empirically determinable relationship to a host of internal and external material conditions. I have referred to early scientific psychology above, but I would also put Sigmund Freud (1856–1939) in this group. Although an advocate of materialism, his theory of mind was focused on psychological structure, rather than explications of how matter gives rise to mind. In philosophy, this emphasis eventually led to the birth of a philosophical viewpoint explicitly dedicated to investigating the inner structure of consciousness: the phenomenology of Edmund Husserl

(1859–1938; see Chapter four). In the newly scientific psychology under the guidance of Wundt, introspection became the paradigmatic research methodology, raising such fundamental questions as whether all thought was necessarily accompanied by, or even constituted out of, mental imagery. Unfortunately, this methodology suffered from inherent difficulties of empirical verification and inter-observer objectivity, which eventually brought it into disrepute, probably overall to the detriment of scientific psychology.

Though James decried the gross metaphor of consciousness as a brain secretion, he introduced one of the most potent and durable metaphors, that of the *stream of consciousness*. In his remarkably compendious work, *The Principles of Psychology*, which remains to this day full of fresh insight, James devoted a chapter to the stream of thought in which he noted that ongoing consciousness is continuous, meaning 'without breach, crack or division' (1890/1950, 237) and that, by contrast, 'the breach from one mind to another is perhaps the greatest breach in nature'. James of course allowed that there were noticeable gaps in one's stream of consciousness, but these are peculiar gaps such that we sense that both sides of the gap belong together in some way; he also noted that the stream is a stream of *consciousness* and that *unnoticed* temporal gaps – which are perfectly conceivable – are simply not part of the stream. Throughout his writings James exhibits a keen and durable interest in the structure and contents of the stream of consciousness, even delving enthusiastically into mystical and religious experience.

Along with virtually all psychological researchers of the time, James was no materialist. His metaphysics of mind is complex and somewhat obscure, wavering between a neutral monism and a form of panpsychism (see Stubenberg 2005). James heaped scorn (and powerful counter-arguments) upon crude forms of 'molecular' panpsychism, what he called the 'mind dust' theory (see 1890/1950, ch. 5), but his monism leaned decidedly towards the mental pole.

In a notebook he wrote that 'the constitution of reality which I am making for is of the psychic type' (see Cooper 1990).

This lack of clarity may arise from the epistemological asymmetry between our apprehension of mind and matter. We seem to have some kind of direct access to the former – when we feel a pain there is an occurrence, at least some properties of which are made evident to us. We do not seem to have any similarly direct awareness of the nature of matter. Thus the avowed neutrality of neutral monism tends to slide towards some kind of panpsychism. From another point of view, the asymmetry encourages the association of some forms of phenomenalism with neutral monism.

For example, the highly influential British philosopher John Stuart Mill (1806–1873) endorsed a phenomenalism which regarded material objects as 'permanent possibilities of sensation'. This allows for the interposition of a *something we know not which* lurking behind our sensations (what might be called 'unsensed sensibilia' – see Mill 1865/1983 and Wilson 2003), but the seemingly unbridgeable gap between this ur-matter and our perceptual experiences creates a constant pressure to replace it with entirely mental sequences of sensations. To be sure, intuition suggests that material objects exist unperceived, but this 'existence' can, perhaps, be analysed in terms of dispositions to have certain sensations under certain *mentalistically* defined conditions. Furthermore, as our relation with the unknowable basis of matter is entirely mentalistic, why not accept that the primal material is itself mental (a view which can lead either back to idealism or to some form of panpsychism)? Bertrand Russell (1872–1970) devoted great effort to developing Mill's phenomenalism as a kind of neutral monism (see Russell 1927) in which what we call matter has intrinsic mental properties with which we are directly acquainted in experience – thus, Russell's seemingly bizarre remark that when a scientist examines a subject's brain he is really observing a part of his *own* brain (for an updated defense of a Russellian position see Lockwood 1991).

His one-time collaborator, Alfred North Whitehead (1861–1947), pursued the alternative panpsychist option in a series of works culminating in the dense and obscurely written *Process and Reality* (1929). Roughly speaking Whitehead proposed a radical reform of our conception of the fundamental nature of the world, placing *events* (or items that are more event-like than thing-like) and the ongoing *process* of their creation as the core feature of the world, rather than the traditional triad of matter, space, and time. His panpsychism arises from the idea that the elementary events that make up the world (which he called *occasions*) partake of mentality in some often extremely attenuated sense, metaphorically expressed in terms of the mentalistic notions of creativity, spontaneity, and perception. Whitehead's position nicely exposes the difficulty in maintaining a pure neutral monism. Matter must have some underlying intrinsic nature. The only intrinsic nature we seem to be acquainted with is consciousness. Thus it is tempting to simplify our metaphysics by assigning the only known intrinsic nature to matter. We thus arrive at panpsychism rather than neutral monism (for an introduction to Whitehead's philosophy of mind see Griffin 1998).

Such high metaphysical speculations, though evidently irresistible, seem far from the common-sense view of matter which was more or less enshrined in the world view of 19th-century science, which began then to fund the rapid and perpetual development of technology we are now so familiar with, and which greatly added to the social prestige of science. If we take the scientific picture seriously – and it came to seem irresponsible not to – then the central mystery of consciousness becomes that of the integration of mind with this scientific viewpoint. This is the modern problem of consciousness, which bypasses both idealist metaphysics and phenomenalistic constructionism.

But how could such integration be achieved? An important line of thought begins with some technical distinctions of Mill. In his *System of Logic* (1843/1963)

Mill attempted a compendious classification of scientific law, two forms of which he called 'homopathic' and 'heteropathic'. Homopathic laws are ones in which the resultant properties of a system are the mere additive results of the properties of the system's components. For example, the laws of motion are homopathic: the motion of an object is the result of all the forces acting on the object, and the resultant force is simply the vector addition of each separate force. Heteropathic laws are ones in which the resultant properties are *not* simply the sum of the properties of the components. It was George Lewes (1817–1878) – now best remembered as the consort of George Elliot – who coined the term 'emergent' to refer to heteropathic effects (he used 'resultant' to mean those features which Mill called homopathic effects). Here it is important to distinguish the more general notion of homopathic effects from what is sometimes called part-whole reductionism. The latter may well be false of the world: there are reasonable arguments that some physical properties are non-local and perhaps in some way holistic (both general relativity and quantum mechanics can be invoked to support these contentions). But the crucial question about homopathic versus heteropathic effects is whether the fundamental physical state of the world, along with the basic physical laws, determines all other, higher-level properties and laws. If not, we have true emergence.

The emergentists postulated that consciousness was a heteropathic effect, or emergent property, of certain complex material systems (e.g., brains). Emergentism may seem no more than extravagant metaphysical speculation, except that at the time it was widely conceded that there were excellent candidate emergent properties in areas other than consciousness. That is, it seemed there were independent grounds for endorsing the concept of emergence, which – thus legitimated – could then be fruitfully applied to the mind-body problem. The primary example of supposedly uncontentious emergent properties were those of chemistry. It was thought that, for example, the properties of water could not be accounted for in terms of the properties of oxygen and hydrogen *and* the laws of nature which governed atomic-level phenomena. Emergentists, of which two prominent ones were Conwy Lloyd Morgan (1852–1936) (see Morgan 1923) and C. D. Broad (1887–1971), recognized that the complexity of the interactions of the components of a system could present the appearance of emergence when there was none. Broad (1925) liked to imagine a 'mathematical archangel' who knew the laws of nature as they applied at the submergent level, knew the configuration of the components, and suffered from no cognitive limitations about deducing the consequences of this information. If the archangel could figure out that water would dissolve salt by considering only the properties of oxygen, hydrogen, sodium, and chlorine as well as the laws which governed their interaction at the atomic level, then this aspect of H_2O would fail to be an emergent property.

Thus the emergentists would have scoffed at current popular examples of emergence, such as John Conway's Game of Life and chaotic dynamical systems. Such examples represent nothing more than 'epistemological emergence'. Cognitive and physical limitations – albeit quite fundamental ones – on computational power and data acquisition prevent us (or our machines) from deducing the high-level properties of complex systems, but this is not a metaphysical barrier. The mathematical archangel could figure out the effect of the butterfly's flight on future weather.

But the emergentists believed that the world really did contain non-epistemological emergence; in fact, it was virtually everywhere. They regarded the world as an hierarchical cascade of emergent features built upon other, lower level emergent features. Unfortunately for them, their linchpin example, chemistry, was the masterpiece of the new quantum mechanics of the 1920s, which basically provided new laws of nature which opened the door – in principle – to the deduction of chemical properties from atomic states (nowadays we even have *de novo* calculation of some simple chemical features based on the quantum mechanical description of atomic components). Of course, this does not *demonstrate* that there is no real emergence in the world, but without any uncontentious example of it, and with the growing ability of physics to provide seemingly complete accounts of the basic structure of the world, the emergentist position was devastated (see McLaughlin 1992).

On the mainstream view articulated in Section II, emergentism seems no less metaphysically extravagant than the other positions we have considered. Emergentism espouses a form of property dualism and postulates that the novel emergent properties of a system would have distinctive causal powers, going beyond those determined solely by the basic physical features of the system (seemingly courting violation of a number of basic conservation laws).

Not that the science of psychology provided a more palatable alternative. Early in the 20th century, the introspectionist methodology as well as the sophisticated sensitivity to the issues raised by consciousness by such psychologists as James disappeared with the rise of a soulless behaviourism that at best ignored the mind and at worst denied its very existence. It took until halfway through the 20th century before philosophy and psychology grappled with the problem of the mind in new ways. In psychology, the so-called cognitive revolution made an appeal to inner mental processes and states legitimate once again (see Neisser 1967 for a classic introduction to cognitive psychology), although scientific psychology largely steered clear of the issue of consciousness until near the end of the 20th century.

In philosophy, the 1950s saw the beginning of a self-conscious effort to understand the mind and, eventually, consciousness as physical through and through in essentially scientific terms. This was part of a broader movement based upon the doctrine of scientific realism, which can be roughly defined as the view that it is science that reveals the ultimate nature of reality, rather than philosophy or any other non-empirical domain of thought. Applied to the philosophy of mind and consciousness, this led to the rise of the *identity theory* (see e.g., Smart 1959, or for a more penetrating and rather prescient account, Feigl 1958). This was a kind of turning point in philosophy, in which it was self-consciously assumed that because physical science should be the basis for our beliefs about the ultimate nature of the world, philosophy's job in this area would henceforth be to show how the mind, along with everything else, would smoothly fit into the scientific picture of the world. It embraced what I earlier called the mainstream view and began with high optimism that a scientific outlook would resolve not just the problem of consciousness but perhaps *all* philosophical problems. But subsequent work has revealed just how extraordinarily difficult it is to fully explicate the mainstream view, especially with regard to consciousness. In the face of unprecedented expansion in our technical abilities to investigate the workings of the brain and an active and explicit scientific, as well as philosophical, effort to understand how, within the mainstream view, consciousness emerges, we find that the ultimate problem remains intractable and infinitely fascinating.

References

Aristotle (1984). *The complete works of Aristotle* (J. Barnes, Ed.). Princeton: Princeton University Press.

Augustine (1998). *Confessions*. Oxford: Oxford University Press.

Augustine (1998). *City of God*. Cambridge: Cambridge University Press.

Barnes, J. (1982). *The Presocratic philosophers*. London: Routledge and Kegan Paul.

Behe, M. (1998). *Darwin's black box: The biochemical challenge to evolution*. New York: Free Press.

Berkeley, G. (1998). *A treatise concerning the principles of human knowledge*. Oxford: Oxford University Press. (Original work published 1710.)

Bloom, P. (2004). *Descartes's baby: How the science of child development explains what makes us human*. New York: Basic Books.

Bradley, F. (1966). *Appearance and reality* (2nd ed). Oxford: Clarendon Press. (Original work published 1897)

Brentano, Franz C. (1973). *Psychology from an empirical standpoint*. London: Routledge and Kegan Paul. (Original work published 1874.)

Broad, C. D. (1925). *The mind and its place in nature*. London: Routledge and Kegan Paul.

Cabanis, P. (1802/1981). *Rapports du physique et du moral de l'homme (On the relations between the physical and moral aspects of man*; G. Mora, Ed. & M. Saidi, Trans). Paris: Crapart, Caille et Ravier.

Caston, V. (2002). Aristotle on consciousness. *Mind*, 111(444), 751–815.

Clifford, William K. (1874). Body and mind. *Fortnightly Review*, December. (Reprinted in Leslie Stephen & Frederick Pollock (Eds.), *Lectures and essays*, 1876, London: Macmillan)

Churchland, Paul (1981). Eliminative materialism and propositional attitudes. *Journal of Philosophy*, 78, 67–90.

Cooper, W. E. (1990). William James's theory of mind. *Journal of the History of Philosophy*, 28(4), 571–93.

Darwin, C. (1967). *The origin of species by natural selection*. London: Dent (Everyman's Library). (Originally published 1859.)

Darwin, C. (1874). *The descent of man*. London: Crowell.

Dawkins, R. (1995). *River out of Eden*. New York: Basic Books.

Descartes, R. (1985). Meditations on first philosophy. In J. Cottingham, R. Stoothoff, & D. Murdoch (Eds.), *The philosophical writings of Descartes*. Cambridge: Cambridge University Press. (Originally published 1641.)

Descartes, R. (1985). The passions of the soul. In J. Cottingham, R. Stoothoff, & D. Murdoch (Eds.), *The philosophical writings of Descartes*. Cambridge: Cambridge University Press. (Originally published 1649.)

Desmond, A., & Moore, J. (1994). *Darwin: The life of a tormented evolutionist*. New York: Norton.

Edwards, P. (1967). Panpsychism. In P. Edwards (Ed.), *The encyclopedia of philosophy* (Vol. 5). New York: Macmillan.

Eldredge, N. & Gould, S. (1972). Punctuated equilibria: An alternative to phyletic gradualism. In T. Schopf (Ed.), *Models in paleobiology*. San Francisco: Freeman Cooper.

Fechner, G. (1946). *The religion of a scientist* (W. Lowrie, Ed. & Trans). New York: Pantheon.

Feigl, H. (1958). The mental and the physical. In H. Feigl, M. Scriven, & G. Maxwell (Eds.), *Minnesota studies in the philosophy of science: Vol. 2. Concepts, theories and the mind-body problem*. Minneapolis: University of Minnesota Press.

Galileo, G. (1957). *The assayer*. In D. Stillman (Ed.), *Discoveries and opinions of Galileo*. New York: Doubleday. (Originally published 1623.)

Garrett, B. (2003). Vitalism and teleology in the natural philosophy of Nehemiah Grew, *British Journal for the History of Science* 36(1), 63–81.

Gergeley, G, Z., Nádasdy, G. Csibra, & Biró, S. (1995). Taking the intentional stance at 12 months of age. *Cognition*, 56(2), 165–93.

Grew, N. (1701). *Cosmologia sacra: or a discourse of the universe as it is the creature and kingdom of God*. London: Rogers, Smith and Walford.

Griffin, D. (1998). *Unsnarling the world knot: Consciousness, freedom and the mind-body problem*. Berkeley: University of California Press.

Hegel, G. (1969). *The science of logic* (A. Miller, Trans.). London: Allen and Unwin. (Originally published 1812.)

Hobbes, T. (1998). *Leviathan* (J. Gaskin, Ed.). Oxford: Oxford University Press. (Originally published 1651.)

Holbach, Baron d' (1970). *Système de la nature; ou, Des lois du monde physique et du monde moral* (published under the pseudonym J. Mirabaud) (*The system of nature: or, laws of the moral and physical world*; H. Robinson, Trans.). (Originally published 1770.)

Huxley, T. (1866). *Lessons in elementary physiology*. London: Macmillan.

James, W. (1950). *The principles of psychology* (Vol. 1). New York: Dover. (Originally published 1890.)

Kant, I. (1929). *Critique of pure reason* (N. Kemp Smith, Ed. & Trans.). New York: St. Macmillan. (Originally published 1781.)

King, P. (2005). Why isn't the mind-body problem mediaeval? In H. Lagerlund & O. Pluta (Eds.), *Forming the mind – Conceptions of body and soul in late medieval and early modern philosophy*. Berlin and New York: Springer Verlag.

Klein, D. (1970). *A history of scientific psychology*. New York: Basic Books.

La Mettrie, J. (1745). *L'histoire naturelle de l'âme*. The Hague.

La Mettrie, J. (1987). *L'homme machine / Man a Machine*. La Salle, IL: Open Court. (Originally published 1748.)

Leibniz, G. (1989). *Monadology*. In R. Ariew & D. Garber (Eds. & Trans.), *G. W. Leibniz: Philosophical essays*. Indianapolis: Hackett. (Originally published 1714.)

Lockwood, M. (1991). *Mind, brain and the quantum*. Oxford: Blackwell.

Mangan, B. (2001). Sensation's ghost: The non-sensory 'fringe' of consciousness. *Psyche*, 7(18). http://psyche.cs.monash.edu.au/v7/psyche-7-18-mangan.html.

Matson, W. (1966). Why isn't the mind-body problem ancient? In P. Feyerabend & G. Maxwell (Eds.), *Mind, matter and method: Essays in philosophy and science in honor of Herbert Feigl*. Minneapolis: University of Minnesota Press.

McLaughlin, B. (1992). The rise and fall of British emergentism. In A. Beckermann, H. Flohr, & J. Kim (Eds.), *Emergence or reduction?* Berlin: De Gruyter.

Mill, J. (1963). *A system of logic*. In J. Robson (Ed.), *Collected works of John Stuart Mill* (Vols. 7 & 8). Toronto: University of Toronto Press. (Originally published 1843.)

Mill, J. (1963). *An examination of Sir William Hamilton's philosophy*, In J. Robson (Ed.), *Collected works of John Stuart Mill* (Vol. 9). Toronto: University of Toronto Press. (Originally published 1865.)

Morgan, C. (1923). *Emergent evolution*. London: Williams and Norgate.

Mourelatos, Alexander (1986). Quality, structure, and emergence in later Pre-Socratic philosophy. *Proceedings of the Boston Area Colloquium in Ancient Philosophy*, 2, 127–94.

Nagel, T. (1974). What is it like to be a bat? *Philosophical Review*, 83, 435–50.

Neisser, U. (1967). *Cognitive psychology*. New York: Appleton-Century-Crofts.

Nelson, J. (1990). Was Aristotle a functionalist? *Review of Metaphysics*, 43, 791–802.

Nussbaum, M. C., & Putnam, H. (1992). Changing Aristotle's mind. In M. Nussbaum & A. Rorty (Eds.), *Essays on Aristotle's De Anima* (pp. 27–56). Oxford: Clarendon Press.

O'Daly, G. (1987). *Augustine's philosophy of mind*. London: Duckworth.

Perner, J. (1991). *Understanding the representational mind*. Cambridge, MA: MIT Press.

Plato (1961). *Plato: Collected dialogues* (E. Hamilton & H. Cairns, Eds.). Princeton: Princeton University Press.

Priestley, J. (1975). *Disquisitions relating to matter and spirit*. New York: Arno Press. (Originally published 1777.)

Russell, B. (1927). *The analysis of matter*. London: Kegan Paul.

Schopenhauer, A. (1966). *The world as will and representation* (E. Payne, Trans.). New York: Dover Books. (Originally published 1819.)

Seager, W. (1999). *Theories of consciousness*, New York: Routledge.

Seager, W. (2005). Panpsychism. In E. Zalta (Ed.), *Stanford encyclopedia of philosophy*, http://plato.stanford.edu/archives/sum2005/entries/panpsychism.

Smart, J. (1959). Sensations and brain processes. *Philosophical Review*, 68, 141–56. Reprinted in slightly revised form in V. Chappell (ed.),

The philosophy of mind. Englewood Cliffs, NJ: Prentice-Hall.

Spinoza, B. (1677/1985). Ethics. In E. Curly (Ed. & Trans.), *The collected works of Spinoza* (Vol. 1). Princeton: Princeton University Press.

Stubenberg, L. (2005). 'Neutral Monism', *The Stanford Encyclopedia of Philosophy* (Spring 2005 Edition), Edward N. Zalta (ed.) http://plato.stanford.edu/.

Toland, J. (1704). *Letters to Serena*, London: Bernard Lintot.

Whitehead, A. (1929). *Process and reality: An essay in cosmology*. New York: Macmillan.

Wilkes, K. (1988). Yishi, duh, um, and consciousness. In A. Marcel & E. Bisiach (Eds.), *Consciousness in contemporary science*. Oxford: Oxford University Press.

Wilson, F. (2003). John Stuart Mill. In E. Zalta (Ed.), *Stanford encyclopedia of philosophy*. http://plato.stanford.edu/archives/fall2003/entries/mill

Wundt, W. (1894). *Vorlesungen über die Menschen- und Thierseele (Lectures on human and animal psychology*; J. Creighton & E. Titchener, Trans.). Hamburg: L. Voss. (Originally published 1892.)

CHAPTER 3

Philosophical Theories of Consciousness: Contemporary Western Perspectives

Uriah Kriegel

Abstract

This chapter surveys current approaches to consciousness in Anglo-American analytic philosophy. It focuses on five approaches, to which I will refer as mysterianism, dualism, representationalism, higher-order monitoring theory, and self-representationalism. With each approach, I will present in order (i) the leading account of consciousness along its line, (ii) the case for the approach, and (iii) the case against the approach. I will not issue a final verdict on any approach, though by the end of the chapter it should be evident where my own sympathies lie.

Introduction: The Concept of Consciousness

This chapter surveys current approaches to consciousness in Anglo-American analytic philosophy. It focuses on five approaches, to which I will refer as mysterianism, dualism, representationalism, higher-order monitoring theory, and self-representationalism.

With each approach, I will present in order (i) the leading account of consciousness along its line, (ii) the case for the approach, and (iii) the case against the approach.[1] I will not issue a final verdict on any approach, though by the end of the chapter it should be evident where my own sympathies lie.

Before starting, let us draw certain distinctions that may help fix our ideas for the discussion to follow. The term "consciousness" is applied in different senses to different sorts of things. It is applied, in one sense, to biological species, as when we say something like "Gorillas are conscious, but snails are not"; in a different sense, to individual organisms or creatures, as when we say "Jim is conscious, but Jill is comatose"; and in a third sense, to particular mental states, events, and processes, as when we say "My thought about Vienna is conscious, but Jim's belief that there are birds in China is not." To distinguish these different senses, we may call the first *species consciousness*, the second *creature consciousness*, and the third *state consciousness*.[2]

There appear to be certain conceptual connections among these three senses, such that they may be analyzable in terms of one another. Plausibly, species consciousness is analyzable in terms of creature consciousness: a species S is species-conscious just in case a prototypical specimen of S is creature-conscious. Creature consciousness may in turn be analyzable in terms of state consciousness: a creature C is creature-conscious just in case C has (or is capable of having) mental states that are state-conscious. If so, state consciousness is the most fundamental notion of the three.

State consciousness is itself ambiguous as between several senses. If Jim tacitly believes that there are birds in China, but never consciously entertained this belief, whereas Jill often contemplates consciously the fact that there are birds in China, but is not doing so right now, there is a sense of "conscious" in which we may want to say that Jim's belief is unconscious whereas Jill's is conscious. Let us call this *availability* consciousness.[3] By contrast, there is a sense of "conscious" in which a mental state is conscious when and only when there is *something it is like* for the subject – from the inside – to have it.[4] Thus, when I take in a spoonful of honey, there is a very specific – sweet, smooth, honey-ish, if you will – way it is like for me to have the resulting conscious experience. Let us call this *phenomenal consciousness*.

Some of the leading scientific theories of consciousness – such as Baars' (1988, 1997) Global Workspace Theory and Crick and Koch's (1990, 2003) synchrony-based "neurobiological theory" – shed much light on availability consciousness and neighboring notions. But there is a persistent feeling that they do not do much to explain phenomenal consciousness. Moreover, there is a widespread sense that there is something principled about the way in which they fail to do so. One way to bring out this feeling is through such philosophers' concepts as the *explanatory gap* (Levine, 1983) or the *hard problem* (Chalmers, 1995). According to Chalmers, for instance, the problems of explaining the various cognitive functions of conscious experiences are the "easy problems" of consciousness; the "hard problem" is that of understanding why there should be *something it is like* to execute these

functions.[5] The sense is that an insight of a completely different order would be needed to make scientific theories, and indeed science itself, at all relevant to our understanding of phenomenal consciousness. Some sort of conceptual breakthrough, which would enable us to conceive of the problem of consciousness in new ways, is required. This is where philosophical theories of consciousness come into the picture.[6,7]

Mysterianism

Some philosophers hold that science cannot and will not, in fact, help us understand consciousness. So-called mysterianists hold that the problem of consciousness – the problem of how there could be something like phenomenal consciousness in a purely natural world – is not a problem we are capable (even in principle) of solving. Thus consciousness is a genuine mystery, not merely a *prima facie* mystery that we may one day demystify.

We may introduce a conceptual distinction between two kinds of mysterianism – an ontological one and an epistemological one. According to ontological mysterianism, consciousness cannot be demystified because it is an inherently mysterious (perhaps supernatural) phenomenon.[8] According to epistemological mysterianism, consciousness is in no way inherently mysterious, and a greater mind could in principle demystify it – but it just so happens that we humans lack the cognitive capacities that would be required.

Epistemological mysterianism has actually been pursued by contemporary Western philosophers. The most comprehensive development of the view is offered in Colin McGinn's (1989, 1995, 1999, 2004) writings. We now turn to an examination of his account.

McGinn's Mysterianism

McGinn's theory of consciousness has two central tenets. First, the phenomenon of consciousness is in itself perfectly natural and in no way mysterious. Second, the human mind's conceptual capacities are too poor to demystify consciousness. That is, McGinn is an epistemological mysterianist: he does not claim that the world contains, in and of itself, insoluble mysteries, but he does contend that *we* will never understand consciousness.

At the center of McGinn's theory is the concept of *cognitive closure*. McGinn (1989, p. 529) defines cognitive closure as follows: "A type of mind M is cognitively closed with respect to a property P (or a theory T) if and only if the concept-forming procedures at M's disposal cannot extend to a grasp of P (or an understanding of T)."[9] To be cognitively closed to X is thus to lack the procedure for concept formation that would allow one to form the concept of X.

To illustrate the soundness and applicability of the notion of cognitive closure, McGinn adduces the case of animal minds and *their* constitutive limitations. As James Joyce writes in *A Portrait of the Artist as a Young Man*, rats' minds do not understand trigonometry. Likewise, snails do not understand quantum physics, and cats do not understand market economics. Why should humans be spared this predicament? As a natural, evolved mechanism, the human mind must have its own limitations. One such limitation, McGinn suggests, may be presented by the phenomenon of consciousness.

Interestingly, McGinn does *not* claim that we are cognitively closed to consciousness itself. Rather, his claim is that we are cognitively closed to that property of the brain responsible for the *production* of consciousness. As someone who does not wish to portray consciousness as inherently mysterious, McGinn is happy to admit that the brain has the capacity to somehow produce conscious awareness. But *how* the brain does so is something he claims we cannot understand. Our concept-forming procedures do extend to a grasp of consciousness, but they do not extend to a grasp of the *causal basis* of consciousness in the brain.

The Master Argument for Mysterianism

A natural reaction to McGinn's view is that it may be based upon an overly pessimistic induction. From the fact that all the theories of consciousness we have come up with to date are hopelessly unsatisfactory, it should not be concluded that our future theories will be the same. It may well be that a thousand years hence we will look back with amusement at the days of our ignorance and self-doubt.

However, McGinn's main argument for his position is not the inductive argument just sketched. Rather, it is a deductive argument based on consideration of our cognitive constitution. The argument revolves around the claim that we do not have a single mechanism, or faculty, that can access *both* consciousness and the brain. Our access to consciousness is through the faculty of introspection. Our access to the brain is through the use of our senses, mainly vision. But unfortunately, the senses do not give us access to consciousness proper, and introspection does not give us access to the brain proper. Thus, we cannot see with our eyes what it is like to taste chocolate. Nor can we taste with our buds what it is like to taste chocolate. We can, of course, taste chocolate. But we cannot taste the feeling of tasting chocolate. The feeling of tasting chocolate is something we encounter only through introspection. But alas, introspection fails to give us access to the brain. We cannot introspect neurons, and so could never introspect the neural correlates of consciousness.

Using the term "extrospective" to denote the access our senses give us to the world, McGinn's argument may be formulated as follows:

1) We can have introspective access to consciousness but not to the brain;
2) We can have extrospective access to the brain but not to consciousness;
3) We have no accessing method that is both introspective and extrospective; therefore,
4) We have no method that can give us access to both consciousness and the brain.

As we can see, the argument is based on considerations that are much more principled than a simple pessimistic induction from past theories. Dismayed as we may be by the prospects of mysterianism, we must not confuse McGinn's position for sheer despair. Instead, we must contend with the argument just formulated.

Some materialists would contest the first premise. Paul Churchland (1985) has repeatedly argued that we will one day be able to directly *introspect* the neurophysiological states of our brains. Perception and introspection are theory-laden, according to Churchland, and can therefore be fundamentally changed when the theory they are laden *with* is changed.[10] Currently, our introspective practice is laden with a broadly Cartesian theory of mind. But when we mature enough scientifically, and when the right neuroscientific theory of consciousness makes its way to our classroom and living room, this will change and we (or rather our distant offspring) will start thinking about ourselves in purely neurophysiological categories.

Other materialists may deny the second premise of the argument. As long as brain states are considered to be merely *correlates* of conscious states, the claim that the conscious states cannot be perceived extrospectively is plausible. But according to materialists, conscious states will turn out to be *identical with* the brain states in question, rather than merely *correlated* therewith. If so, perceiving those brain states would just *be* perceiving the conscious states.[11] To assume that we cannot perceive the conscious states is to beg the question against the materialist.

The Case Against Mysterianism

To repeat the last point, McGinn appears to assume that conscious states are *caused* by brain states. His argument does not go through if conscious states are simply *identical* to brain states. In other words, the argument does not go through unless any identity of conscious states with brain states is rejected.[12] But such rejection amounts to dualism. McGinn is thus committed to dualism.[13] On the view he presupposes, the conscious cannot be simply identified with the physical. Rather, there are two different

kinds of states a person or organism may be in: brain states on the one hand and conscious states on the other.

Recall that McGinn's mysterianism is of the epistemological variety. The epistemological claim now appears to be conditional upon an ontological claim, namely dualism. So at the end of the day, as far as the *ontology* of consciousness is concerned, McGinn is a straightforward dualist. The plausibility of his (epistemological) mysterianism depends, to that extent, on the plausibility of (ontological) dualism. In the next section, we consider the plausibility of dualism.

Before doing so, let us raise one more difficulty for mysterianism, and in particular the notion of cognitive closure. It is, of course, undeniable that rats do not understand trigonometry. But observe that trigonometric problems do not pose themselves to rats (Dennett, 1995, pp. 381–383). Indeed, it is precisely *because* rats do not understand trigonometry that trigonometric problems do not pose themselves to rats. For rats to grapple with trigonometric problems, they would have to understand quite a bit of trigonometry. Arguably, it is a mark of genuine cognitive closure that certain questions do not even pose themselves to the cognitively closed. The fact that certain questions about consciousness do pose themselves to humans may therefore indicate that humans are *not* cognitively closed to consciousness (or more accurately to the link between consciousness and the brain).[14]

Dualism

Traditionally, approaches to the ontology of mind and consciousness have been divided into two main groups: monism and dualism. The former holds that there is one kind of stuff in the world; the latter that there are two.[15] Within monism, there is a further distinction between views that construe the single existing stuff as material and views that construe it as immaterial; the former are *materialist* views, the latter *idealist*.[16]

Descartes framed his dualism in terms of two different kinds of *substance* (where a substance is something that can in principle exist all by itself). One is the extended substance, or matter; the other is the thinking substance, or mind. A person, on this view, is a combination of two different *objects*: a body and a soul. A body and its corresponding soul "go together" for some stretch of time, but being two separate objects, their existence is independent and can therefore come apart.[17]

Modern dualism is usually of a more subtle sort, framed not in terms of *substances* (or *stuffs*), but rather in terms of *properties*. The idea is that even though there is only one kind of stuff or substance, there are two kinds of properties, mental and physical, and neither can be reduced to the other.[18] This is known as *property dualism*. A particularly cautious version of property dualism claims that although most mental properties are reducible to physical ones, conscious or phenomenal properties are irreducible.

Chalmers' Naturalistic Dualism

For many decades, dualistic arguments were treated mainly as a *challenge* to a physicalist worldview, not so much as a basis for a non-physicalist alternative. Thus dualism was not so much an explanation or account of consciousness, but rather the avoidance of one. This state of affairs has been rectified in the past decade or so, mainly through the work of David Chalmers (1995, 1996, 2002a).

Chalmers' theory of consciousness, which he calls *naturalistic dualism*, is stronger than ordinary dualism, in that it claims not only that phenomenal properties are not *identical* to physical properties, but also that they fail to *supervene* – at least with metaphysical or logical necessity[19] – on physical properties.[20] We tend to think, for instance, that biological properties necessarily supervene on physical properties, in the sense that two systems cannot possibly differ in their biological properties if all their physical properties are exactly similar. But according to Chalmers, phenomenal properties are different: two systems *can* be exactly the same physically, but have different phenomenal properties.

At the same time, Chalmers does not take phenomenal properties to be accidental or random superpositions onto the physical world. On the contrary, he takes them to be causally grounded in physical laws. That is, instantiations of phenomenal properties are *caused* by instantiations of physical properties, and they are so caused in accordance with strict laws of nature.[21]

This means that phenomenal consciousness *can* be explained in physical terms. It is just that the explanation will not be a *reductive* explanation, but rather a *causal* explanation. To explain an event or phenomenon causally is to cite its cause, that is, to say what brought it about or gave rise to it.[22] According to Chalmers, one *could* in principle explain the instantiation of phenomenal properties by citing their physical causes.

A full theory of consciousness would uncover and list all the causal laws that govern the emergence of phenomenal properties from the physical realm. And a full description of nature and its behavior would have to include these causal laws on top of the causal laws obtained by "ultimate physics."[23]

Chalmers himself does not attempt to detail many of these laws. But he does propose a pair of principles to which we should expect such laws to conform. These are the "structural coherence" principle and the "organizational invariance" principle. The former concerns the sort of direct availability for global control that conscious states appear to exhibit, the latter the systematic correspondence between a system's functional organization and its phenomenal properties.[24]

The Case for Dualism

The best-known arguments in favor of property dualism about consciousness are socalled epistemic arguments. The two main ones are Frank Jackson's (1984) "Knowledge Argument" and Thomas Nagel's (1974) "what is it like" argument. Both follow a similar pattern. After describing a situation in which all physical facts about something are known, it is shown that some knowledge is still missing. It is then inferred that the missing knowledge must be knowledge of non-physical facts.

The Knowledge Argument proceeds as follows. Suppose a baby is kept in a black-and-white environment, so that she never has color experiences. But she grows to become an expert on color and color vision. Eventually, she knows all the physical facts about color and color vision. But when she sees red for the first time, she learns something new: she learns what it is like to see red. That is, she acquires a new piece of knowledge. Since she already knew all the physical facts, this new piece of knowledge cannot be knowledge of a physical fact. It is therefore knowledge of a non-physical fact. So, the fact thereby known (what it is like to see red) is a non-physical fact.

Nagel's argument, although more obscure in its original presentation, can be "formatted" along similar lines. We can know all the physical facts about bats without knowing what it is like to be a bat. It follows that the knowledge we are missing is not knowledge of a physical fact. Therefore, what it is like to be a bat is not a physical fact.

These arguments have struck many materialists as suspicious. After all, they infer an ontological conclusion from epistemological premises. This move is generally suspicious, but it is also vulnerable to a response that emphasizes what philosophers call the *intensionality* of epistemic contexts.[25] This has been the main response among materialists (Loar, 1990; Tye, 1986). The claim is that the Knowledge Argument's protagonist does not learn a new fact when she learns what it is like to see red, but rather learns an *old* fact in a new *way*; and similarly for the bat student.[26]

Consider knowledge that the evening star glows and knowledge that the morning star glows. These are clearly two different pieces of knowledge. But the fact thereby known is one and the same – the fact that Venus glows. Knowledge that *this* is what it is like to see red and knowledge that *this* is the neural assembly stimulated by the right wavelength may similarly constitute two separate pieces of knowledge that correspond to only one fact being known. So from the acquisi-

tion of a new piece of knowledge one cannot infer the existence of a new fact – and that is precisely the inference made in the above dualist arguments.[27,28]

A different argument for dualism that is widely discussed today is Chalmers' (1996) argument from the conceivability of zombies. Zombies are imaginary creatures that are physically indistinguishable from us but lack consciousness. We seem to be able to conceive of such creatures, and Chalmers wants to infer from this that materialism is false. The argument is often caricatured as follows:

1) Zombies are conceivable;
2) If As are conceivable, then As are (metaphysically) possible;[29] therefore,
3) Zombies are possible; but,
4) Materialism entails that zombies are not possible; therefore,
5) Materialism is false.

Or, more explicitly formulated:

1) For any physical property P, it is conceivable that P is instantiated but consciousness is not;
2) For any pair of properties F and G, if it is conceivable that F is instantiated when G is not, then it is (metaphysically) *possible* that F is instantiated when G is not; therefore,
3) For any physical property P, it is possible that P is instantiated and consciousness is not; but,
4) If a property F can be instantiated when property G is not, then F does not supervene on G;[30] therefore,
5) For any physical property P, consciousness does not supervene on P.

To this argument it is objected that the second premise is false, and the conceivability of something does not entail its possibility. Thus, we can conceive of water not being H_2O, but this is in fact impossible; Escher triangles are conceivable, but not possible.[31]

The zombie argument is more subtle than this, however. One way to get at the real argument is this.[32] Let us distinguish between the property of *being* water and the property of *appearing* to be water, or being *apparent* water.[33] For a certain quantity of stuff to *be* water, it must be H_2O. But for it to *appear* to be water, it need only be clear, drinkable, liquid, and so on – or perhaps only *strike normal subjects* as clear, drinkable, liquid, etc. Now, although the unrestricted principle that conceivability entails possibility is implausible, a version of the principle restricted to what we may call *appearance properties* is quite plausible. Thus, if we can conceive of apparent water not being H_2O, then it is indeed possible that apparent water should not be H_2O.

Once the restricted principle is accepted, there are two ways a dualist may proceed. The zombie argument seems to be captured more accurately as follows:[34]

1) For any physical property P, it is conceivable that P is instantiated but *apparent consciousness* is not;
2) For any pair of properties F and G, such that F is an *appearance* property, if it is conceivable that F is instantiated when G is not, then it is (metaphysically) possible that F is instantiated when G is not; therefore,
3) For any physical property P, it is possible that P is instantiated when apparent consciousness is not; but,
4) If a property F can be instantiated when property G is not, then F does not (metaphysically) supervene on G; therefore,
5) For any physical property P, apparent consciousness does not (metaphysically) supervene on P.

A materialist might want to reject this argument by denying Premise 2 (the restricted conceivability-possibility principle). Whether the restricted principle is true is something we cannot settle here. Note, however, that it is surely much more plausible than the corresponding unrestricted principle, and it is the only principle that the argument for dualism really needs.

Another way the argument could be rejected is by denying the *existence* of such properties as *apparent water* and *apparent consciousness*.[35] More generally, perhaps, while "natural" properties such as being

water or being conscious do exist, "unnatural" properties do not, and appearance properties are unnatural in the relevant sense.[36]

To avoid this latter objection, a dualist may proceed to develop the argument differently, claiming that in the case of consciousness, there is no distinction between appearance and reality (Kripke, 1980). This would amount to the claim that the property of being conscious is identical to the property of appearing to be conscious. The conceivability argument then goes like this:

1) For any physical property P, it is conceivable that P is instantiated but apparent consciousness is not;
2) For any pair of properties F and G, such that F is an *appearance* property, if it is conceivable that F is instantiated when G is not, then it is (metaphysically) possible that F is instantiated when G is not; therefore,
3) For any physical property P, it is *possible* that P is instantiated when apparent consciousness is not; but,
4) If property F can be instantiated when property G is not, then F does not supervene on G; therefore,
5) For any physical property P, apparent consciousness does not supervene on P; but,
6) Consciousness = apparent consciousness; therefore,
7) For any physical property P, consciousness does not supervene on P.

Materialists may reject this argument by denying that there is no distinction between appearance and reality when it comes to consciousness (the sixth premise).

The debate over the plausibility of the various versions of the zombie argument continues. A full critical examination is impossible here. Let us move on, then, to consideration of the independent case against dualism.

The Case against Dualism

The main motivation to avoid dualism continues to be the one succinctly worded by Smart (1959, p. 143) almost a half-century ago: "It seems to me that science is increasingly giving us a viewpoint whereby organisms are able to be seen as physico-chemical mechanisms: it seems that even the behavior of man himself will one day be explicable in mechanistic terms." It would be curious if consciousness stood out in nature as the only property that defied reductive explanation in microphysical terms. More principled arguments aside, this simple observation seems to be the chief motivating force behind naturalization projects that attempt to reductively explain consciousness and other recalcitrant phenomena.

As I noted above, against traditional dualists it was common to present the more methodological argument that they do not in fact propose any positive theory of consciousness, but instead rest content with arguing against existing materialist theories, and that this could not lead to real progress in the understanding of consciousness. Yet, this charge cannot be made against Chalmers, who does propose a positive theory of consciousness.

Chalmers' own theory is open to more substantial criticisms, however. In particular, it is arguably committed to epiphenomenalism about consciousness, the thesis that conscious states and events are *causally inert*. As Kim (1989a,b, 1992) has pointed out, it is difficult to find causal work for non-supervenient properties. Assuming that the physical realm is *causally closed* (i.e., that every instantiation of a physical property has as its cause the instantiation of another physical property), non-supervenient properties must either (i) have no causal effect on the physical realm or (ii) causally overdetermine the instantiation of certain physical properties.[37] But because pervasive overdetermination can be ruled out as implausible, non-supervenient properties must be causally inert vis-à-vis the physical world. However, the notion that consciousness is causally inert, or *epiphenomenal*, is extremely counter-intuitive: we seem to ourselves to act on our conscious decisions all the time and at will.

In response to the threat of epiphenomenalism, Chalmers pursues a two-pronged approach.[38] The first prong is to claim that epiphenomenalism is *merely* counter-intuitive, but does not face serious *argumentative* challenges. This is not particularly satisfying, however: all arguments must come to an end, and in most of philosophy, the end is bound to be a certain intuition or intuitively compelling claim. As intuitions go, the intuition that consciousness is not epiphenomenal is very strong.

The second prong is more interesting. Chalmers notes that physics characterizes the properties to which it adverts in purely relational terms – essentially, in terms of the laws of nature into which they enter. The resulting picture is a network of inter-related nodes, but the intrinsic character of the thus interrelated nodes remains opaque. It is a picture that gives us what Bertrand Russell once wittily called "the causal skeleton of the world." Chalmers' suggestion is that phenomenal properties may constitute the intrinsic properties of the entities whose relational properties are mapped out by physics. At least this is the case with intrinsic properties of obviously conscious entities. As for apparently inanimate entities, their intrinsic properties may be crucially *similar* to the phenomenal properties of conscious entities. They may be, as Chalmers puts it, "protophenomenal" properties.

Although intriguing, this suggestion has its problems. It is not clear that physics indeed gives us only the causal skeleton of the world. It is true that physics *characterizes* mass in terms of its causal relations to other properties. But it does not follow that the property thus characterized is nothing but a bundle of causal relations. More likely, the relational characterization of mass is what *fixes the reference* of the term "mass," but the referent itself is nonetheless an intrinsic property. The bundle of causal relations is the reference-fixer, not the referent. On this view of things, although physics characterizes mass in causal terms, it construes mass not as the *causing* of effects E, but rather as the *causer* (or just the *cause*) of E. It construes mass as the relatum, not the relation.

Furthermore, *if* physics did present us with the causal skeleton of the world, then *physical* properties would turn out to be epiphenomenal (or nearly so). As Block (1990b) argued, functional properties – properties of having certain causes and effects – are ultimately inert, because an effect is always caused by its cause, not by its causing. So if mass was the *causing* of E, rather than the *cause* of E, then E would not be caused by mass. It would be caused, rather, by the protophenomenal property that satisfies the relational characterization attached to mass in physics.[39] The upshot is that if mass *was* the causing of E, rather than the cause of E, mass would not have the causal powers we normally take it to have. More generally, if physical properties were nothing but bundles of causal relations, they would be themselves causally inert.[40]

Chalmers faces a dilemma, then: either he violates our strongly held intuitions regarding the causal efficacy of phenomenal properties, or he violates our strongly held intuitions regarding the causal efficacy of physical properties. Either way, half his world is epiphenomenal, as it were. In any event, as we saw above, the claim that physical properties are merely bundles of causal relations – which therefore call for the postulation of phenomenal and protophenomenal properties as the putative causal relata – is implausible.

Problems concerning the causal efficacy of phenomenal properties will attach to any account that portrays them as non-supervenient upon, or even as non-reducible to, physical properties. These problems are less likely to rear their heads for reductive accounts of consciousness. Let us turn, then, to an examination of the main reductive accounts discussed in the current literature.

Representationalism

According to the representational theory of consciousness – or for short, *representationalism* – the phenomenal properties of conscious experiences can be reductively explained in terms of the experiences' representational properties.[41] Thus, when I look up at the blue sky, what it is like for me to

have my conscious experience of the sky is just a matter of my experience's representation of the blue sky. The phenomenal character of my experience can be identified with (an aspect of) its representational content.[42]

This would be a theoretically happy result, since we have a fairly good notion as to how mental representation may be itself reductively explained in terms of informational and/or teleological relations between neurophysiological states of the brain and physical states of the environment.[43] The reductive strategy here is two-stepped, then: first reduce phenomenal properties to representational properties, then reduce representational properties to informational and/or other physical properties of the brain.

Tye's PANIC Theory

Not every mental representation is conscious. For this reason, a representational account of consciousness must pin down more specifically the kind of representation that would make a mental state conscious. The most worked-out story in this genre is probably Michael Tye's (1992, 1995, 2000, 2002) "PANIC Theory."[44]

The acronym "PANIC" stands for Poised, Abstract, Non-conceptual, Intentional Content. So for Tye, a mental representation qualifies as conscious when, and only when, its representational content is (a) intentional, (b) non-conceptual, (c) abstract, and (d) poised. What all these qualifiers mean is not particularly important, though the properties of non-conceptuality and poise are worth pausing to explicate.[45]

The content of a conscious experience is non-conceptual in that the experience can represent properties for which the subject lacks the concept. My conscious experience of the sky represents the sky not simply as being blue, but as being a very specific shade of blue, say blue$_{17}$. And yet if I am presented a day later with two samples of very similar shades of blue, blue$_{17}$ and blue$_{18}$, I will be unable to recognize which shade of blue was the sky's. This suggests that I lack the concept of blue$_{17}$. If so, my experience's representation of blue$_{17}$ is non-conceptual.[46]

The property of poise is basically a functional role property: a content is poised when it is ready and available to make a direct impact on the formation of beliefs and desires. Importantly, Tye takes this to distinguish conscious representation from, say, blindsighted representations. A square can be represented both consciously and blindsightedly. But only the conscious representation is poised to make a direct impact on the beliefs that the subject subsequently forms.

PANIC theory is supposed to cover not only conscious *perceptual* experiences but also all manners of phenomenal experience: somatic, emotional, and so on. Thus, a toothache experience represents tissue damage in the relevant tooth, and does so intentionally, non-conceptually, abstractly, and with poise.[47]

The Master Argument for Representationalism

The main motivation for representationalism may seem purely theoretical: it holds the promise of a reductive explanation of consciousness in well-understood informational and/or teleological terms. Perhaps because of this, however, the argument that has been most influential in making representationalism popular is a non-theoretical argument, one that basically rests on a phenomenological observation. This is the observation of the so-called *transparency of experience*. It has been articulated in a particularly influential manner by Harman (1990), but goes back at least to Moore (1903).

Suppose you have a conscious experience of the blue sky. Your attention is focused on the sky. You then decide to turn your attention *away* from the sky and onto your *experience* of the sky. Now your attention is no longer focused on the sky, but rather on the experience thereof. What are you aware of? It seems that you are still aware of the blueness of the sky. Certainly you are not aware of some *second* blueness, which attaches to your experience rather than to the sky. You are not aware of any *intermediary* blue quality interposed between yourself and the sky.

It appears, then, that when you pay attention to your experience, the only thing you become aware of is which features of the external sky your experience *represents*. In other words, the only introspectively accessible properties of conscious experience are its representational properties.

The transparency of experience provides a straightforward argument for representationalism. The argument may be laid out as follows:

1) The only introspectively accessible properties of conscious experience are its representational properties;
2) The phenomenal character of conscious experience is given by its introspectively accessible properties; therefore,
3) The phenomenal character of conscious experience is given by its representational properties.

The first premise is the thesis of transparency; the second one is intended as a conceptual truth (about what we mean by "phenomenal"). The conclusion is representationalism.

Another version of the argument from transparency, one that Tye employs, centers on the idea that rejecting representationalism in the face of transparency would require one to commit to an "error theory."[48] This version may be formulated as follows:

1) The phenomenal properties of conscious experience *seem* to be representational properties;
2) It is unlikely that the phenomenal properties of conscious experience are radically different from what they seem to be; therefore,
3) It is likely that the phenomenal properties of conscious experience *are* representational properties.

Here the transparency thesis is again the first premise. The second premise is the claim that convicting experience of massive error is to be avoided. And the conclusion is representationalism.

The Case against Representationalism

Most of the arguments that have been marshaled against representationalism are arguments by counter-example. Scenarios of varying degrees of fancifulness are adduced, in which allegedly (i) a conscious experience has no representational properties, or (ii) two possible experiences with different phenomenal properties have the same representational properties, or (iii) inversely, two possible experiences with the same phenomenal properties have different representational properties. For want of space, I present only one representative scenario from each category.

Block (1996) argues that phosphene experiences are non-representational. These can be obtained by rubbing one's eyes long enough so that when one opens them again, one "sees" various light bits floating about. Such experiences do not represent any external objects or features, according to Block.

In response, Tye (2000) claims that such experiences do represent – it is just that they *mis*represent. They misrepresent there to be small objects with phosphorescent surfaces floating around the subject's head.

A long-debated case in which phenomenal difference is accompanied by representational sameness is due to Peacocke (1983). Suppose you stand in the middle of a mostly empty road. All you can see in front of you are two trees. The two trees, A and B, have the same size and shape, but A is twice as far from you as B. Peacocke claims that, being aware that the two trees are the same size, you represent to yourself that they have the same properties. And yet B "takes up more of your visual field" than A, in a way that makes you experience the two trees differently. There is phenomenal difference without representational difference.

Various responses to this argument have been offered by representationalists. Perhaps the most popular is that although you represent the two trees to have the same size properties, you also represent them to have certain different properties – for example, B is represented to subtend a larger visual angle than A (DeBellis, 1991; Harman, 1990;

Tye, 2000). To be sure, you do not necessarily possess the concept of subtending a visual angle. But recall that the content of experience can be construed as non-conceptual. So your experience can represent the two trees to subtend different visual angles without employing the concept of subtending a visual angle. Thus a representational difference is matched to the phenomenal difference.

Perhaps the most prominent alleged counter-example is Block's (1990a) *Inverted Earth* case. Inverted Earth is an imaginary planet just like Earth, except that every object there has the color complementary to the one it has here. We are to imagine that a subject is clothed with color-inverting lenses and shipped to Inverted Earth unbeknownst to her. The color inversions due to the lenses and to the world cancel each other out, so that her phenomenal experiences remain the same. But externalism about representational contents ensures that the representational content of her experiences eventually change.[49] Her bluish experiences now represent a yellow sky. When her sky experiences on Inverted Earth are compared to her earthly sky experience, it appears that the two groups are phenomenally the same but representationally different.

This case is still being debated in the literature, but there are two representationalist strategies for accommodating it. One is to argue that the phenomenal character also changes over time on Inverted Earth (Harman, 1990); the other is to devise accounts of representational content that make the representational content of the subject's experiences remain the same on Inverted Earth, externalism notwithstanding (Tye, 2000).[50]

There may be, however, a more principled difficulty for representationalism than the myriad counter-examples it faces.[51] Representationalism seems to construe the phenomenal character of conscious experiences purely in terms of the *sensuous qualities* they involve. But arguably there is more to phenomenal character than sensuous quality. In particular, there seems to be a certain mineness, or for-me-ness, to them.

One way to put it is as follows (Kriegel, 2005a; Levine, 2001; Smith, 1986). When I have my conscious experience of the blue sky, there is a bluish way it is like for me to have my experience. A distinction can be drawn between two components of this "bluish way it is like for me": the bluish component, which we may call *qualitative character*, and the for-me component, which we may call *subjective character*. We may construe phenomenal character as the compresence of qualitative and subjective character. This subjective character, or for-me-ness, is certainly an elusive phenomenon, but it is present in every conscious experience. Indeed, its presence seems to be a condition of any phenomenality: it is hard to make sense of the idea of a conscious experience that does not have this for-me-ness to it. If it did not have this for-me-ness, it would be a mere subpersonal state, a state that takes place *in* me but is not *for* me in the relevant sense. Such a subpersonal state seems not to qualify as a conscious experience.

The centrality of subjective character (as construed here) to consciousness is something that has been belabored in the phenomenological tradition (see Chapter 4; Zahavi, 1999). The concept of *prereflective self-consciousness* – or a form of self-awareness that does not require focused and explicit awareness of oneself and one's current experience, but is rather built into that very experience – is one that figures centrally in almost all phenomenological accounts of consciousness.[52] But it has been somewhat neglected in analytic philosophy of mind.[53]

The relative popularity of representationalism attests to this neglect. While a representationalist account of sensuous qualities – what we have called qualitative character – may turn out to win the day (if the alleged counter-examples can be overcome), it would not provide us with any perspective on subjective character.[54] Therefore, even if representationalism turns out to be a satisfactory account of qualitative character, it is unlikely to be a satisfactory account of phenomenal consciousness proper.

Higher-Order Monitoring Theory

One theory of consciousness from analytic philosophy that *can* be interpreted as targeting subjective character is the higher-order monitoring theory (HOMT). According to HOMT, what makes a mental state conscious is the fact that the subject is *aware* of it in the right way. It is only when the subject is aware (in that way) of a mental state that the state becomes conscious.[55]

HOMT tends to anchor consciousness in the operation of a monitoring device. This device monitors and scans internal states and events and produces higher-order representations of some of them.[56] When a mental state is represented by such a higher-order representation, it is conscious. So a mental state M of a subject S is conscious when, and only when, S has another mental state, M*, such that M* is an appropriate representation of M. The fact that M* represents M guarantees that there is something it is like *for S* to have M.[57]

Observe that, on this view, what confers conscious status on M is something outside M, namely, M*. This is HOMT's reductive strategy. Neither M nor M* is conscious in and of itself, independently of the other state. It is their coming together in the right way that yields consciousness.[58]

Versions of the HOMT differ mainly in how they construe the monitoring device and/or the representations it produces. The most seriously worked out version is probably David Rosenthal's (1986, 1990, 2002a, b). Let us take a closer look at his "higher-order thought" theory.

Rosenthal's Higher-Order Thought Theory

According to Rosenthal, a mental state is conscious when its subject has a suitable higher-order thought about it.[59] The higher-order state's being a *thought* is supposed to rule out, primarily, its being a *quasi-perceptual* state.

There is a long tradition, hailing from Locke, of construing the monitoring device as analogous in essential respects to a sense organ (hence as being a sort of "inner sense") and accordingly as producing mental states that are crucially similar to perceptual representations and that may to that extent be called "quasi-perceptual." This sort of "higher-order perception theory" is championed today by Armstrong (1968, 1981) and Lycan (1987, 1996). Rosenthal believes that this is a mistake and that the higher-order states that confer consciousness are not analogous to perceptual representations.[60] Rather, they are intellectual, or cognitive, states – that is, thoughts.

Another characteristic of thoughts – in addition to being non-perceptual – is their being *assertoric*. An assertoric state is one that has a *thetic*, or mind-to-world, direction of fit.[61] This is to be contrasted with states (such as wanting, hoping, disapproving, etc.) that have primarily a *telic*, or world-to-mind, direction of fit.[62] A third characteristic of thoughts – at least the kind suitable for conferring consciousness – is that they are *occurrent* mental states.[63]

Crucially, a suitable higher-order thought would also have to be *non-inferential*, in that it could not be the result of a conscious inference from the lower-order state (or from any other state, for that matter).[64] To be sure, the thought is formed through some process of information processing, but that process must be automatic and unconscious. This is intended to reflect the *immediacy*, or at least *felt* immediacy, of our awareness of our conscious states.[65] The fact that my experience of the sky has for-me-ness entails that I am somehow aware of its occurrence; but not any sort of awareness would do – very mediated forms of awareness cannot confer conscious status on their objects.

One last characteristic Rosenthal ascribes to the "suitable" higher-order representation is that it represents the lower-order state as a state *of oneself*. Its content must be, as this is sometimes put, *de se* content.[66] So the content of the higher-order representation of my conscious experience of the sky is not simply something like "this bluish experience is occurring," but rather something like "I myself am having this bluish experience."[67]

It is worth noting that according to Rosenthal the second-order representation is normally an *unconscious* state. To be sure, it need not necessarily be: in the more introspective, or reflective, episodes of our conscious life, the second-order state becomes itself conscious. It is then accompanied by a *third*-order state, one that represents its occurrence in a suitable way. When I explicitly introspect and dwell on my conscious experience of the sky, there are three separate states I am in: the (first-order) experience, a (second-order) awareness of the experience, and a (third-order) representation of that awareness. When I stop introspecting and turn my attention back to the sky, however, the third-order state evaporates, and consequently the second-order state becomes unconscious again. In any event, at any one time the subject's highest-order state, the one that confers consciousness on the chain of lower-order states "below" it, is unconscious.[68]

In summary, Rosenthal's central thesis is that a mental state is conscious just in case the subject has a non-perceptual, non-inferential, assertoric, *de se*, occurrent representation of it. This account of consciousness is not intended as an account of introspective or reflective consciousness, but of regular, everyday consciousness.

The Master Argument for Higher-Order Monitoring Theory

The master argument for the higher-order monitoring approach to consciousness has been succinctly stated by Lycan (2001):

1) A mental state M of subject S is conscious when, and only when, S is aware of M in the appropriate way;
2) Awareness of X requires mental representation of X; therefore,
3) M is conscious when, and only when, S has a mental state M*, such that M* represents M in the appropriate way.

Although the second premise is by no means trivial, it is the first premise that has been the bone of contention in the philosophical literature (see, e.g., Dretske, 1993).

One can defend the claim that conscious states are states we are aware of having simply as a piece of conceptual analysis – as a platitude reflecting the very meaning of the word "conscious" (Lycan, 1996). To my ear, this sounds right: a mental state of which the subject is completely unaware is a sub-personal, and therefore unconscious, state.

To some, however, this seems plainly false. When I have an experience of the sky, I am attending to the sky, they stress, not to myself and my internal goings-on. By consequence, I am aware of the sky, not of my experience of the sky. I am aware *through* my experience, not *of* my experience.

This objection seems to rely, however, on an unwarranted assimilation of awareness and attention. There is a distinction to be made between attentive awareness and inattentive awareness. If S attends to X and not to Y, it follows that S is not attentively aware of Y, but it does not follow that S is completely unaware of Y. For S may still be inattentively aware of Y.

Consider straightforward visual awareness. The distinction between foveal vision and peripheral vision means that our visual awareness at any one time has a periphery as well as a focal center. Right now, I am (visually) focally aware of my laptop, but also (visually) peripherally aware of an ashtray at the far corner of my desk. A similar distinction applies to perceptual awareness in other modalities: I am now (auditorily) focally aware of Duke Ellington's voice and (auditorily) peripherally aware of the air conditioner's hum overhead.

There is no reason to think that a similar distinction would *not* apply to higher-order awareness. In reflective moods I may be focally aware of my concurrent experiences and feelings, but on other occasions I am just peripherally aware of them. The former is an attentive form of second-order awareness, the latter an inattentive one. Again, from the fact that it is inattentive it would be fallacious to infer that it is no awareness at all.

When it is claimed that conscious states are states we are aware of, the claim is not that we are focally aware of every conscious state we are in. That is manifestly false: the focus of our attention is mostly on the out-

side world. The claim is rather that we are at least peripherally aware of every conscious state we are in.[69] As long as M is conscious, S is aware, however dimly and inattentively, of M. Once S's awareness of M is extinguished altogether, M drops into the realm of the unconscious. This seems highly plausible on both conceptual and phenomenological grounds.[70]

The Case against Higher-Order Monitoring Theory

Several problems for the monitoring theory have been continuously debated in the philosophical literature. I focus here on what I take to be the main three.[71]

The first is the problem of animal and infant consciousness. It is intuitively plausible to suppose that cats, dogs, and human neonates are conscious, that is, they have conscious states; but it appears empirically implausible that they should have second-order representations (Lurz, 1999). The problem is particularly acute for Rosenthal's account, since it is unlikely that these creatures can have *thoughts*, and moreover of the complex form, "I myself am enjoying this milk."

There are two ways to respond to this objection. One is to deny that having such higher-order representations requires a level of sophistication of an order unlikely to be found in (say) cats. Thus, Rosenthal (2002b) claims that whereas *adult human* higher-order thoughts tend to be conceptually structured and employ a rich concept of self, these are not *necessary* features of such thoughts. There could be higher-order thoughts that are conceptually simple and employ a rudimentary concept of self, one that consists merely in the ability to distinguish oneself from anything that is not oneself. It may well turn out that worms, woodpeckers, or even day-old humans lack even this level of conceptual sophistication – in which case we would be required to deny them consciousness – but it is unlikely that cats, dogs, and *year*-old humans lack them.

The second possible line of response is to dismiss the intuition that animals, such as cats, dogs, and even monkeys, do in fact have conscious states. Thus, Carruthers (1998, 1999) claims that there is a significant amount of projection that takes place when we ascribe conscious states to, say, our pets. In reality there is very little evidence to suggest that they have not only perceptual and cognitive states but also conscious ones.

Both lines of response offer some hope to the defender of higher-order monitoring, but also implicate the theory in certain counter-intuitive and *prima facie* implausible claims. Whether these could somehow be neutralized, or accepted as outweighed by the theoretical benefits of HOMT, is something that is very much under debate.

Perhaps more disturbing is the problem of so-called targetless higher-order thoughts (or more generally, representations). When someone falsely believes that the almond tree in the backyard is blooming again, there are two ways he or she may get things wrong: (i) it may be that the backyard almond tree is *not* blooming, or (ii) it may be that there is no almond tree in the backyard (blooming or not). Let us call a false belief of type (ii) a *targetless* thought. HOMT gets into trouble when a subject has a targetless higher-order thought (Byrne, 1997).[72] Suppose at a time *t* subject S thinks (in the suitable way) that she has a throbbing toothache, when in reality she has no toothache at all (throbbing or not). According to HOMT, what it is like for S at *t* is the way it is like to have a throbbing toothache, even though S has no toothache at *t*. In other words, if S has an M* that represents M when in reality there is no M,[73] S will be under the impression that she is in a conscious state when in reality she is not. (She is not in a conscious state because M does not exist, and it is M that is supposed to bear the property of being conscious.) Moreover, on the assumption that a person is conscious at a time *t* only if she has at least one conscious state at *t*,[74] this would entail that when a subject harbors a targetless higher-order misrepresentation, she is not conscious, even though it feels to her as though she is. This is a highly counter-intuitive consequence: we want to say that a person cannot be under the impression that she is conscious when she is not.

There are several ways higher-order monitoring theorists may respond to this objection. Let us briefly consider three possible responses.

First, they may claim that when M* is targetless, the property of being conscious, although not instantiated by M, is instantiated by M*. But as we saw above, according to their view, M* is normally unconscious. So to say that M* instantiates the property of being conscious would be to say that it is, in the normal case, both conscious and not conscious – which is incoherent.[75]

Second, they may claim that the property of being conscious is, in reality, not a property of the discrete state M, but rather attaches itself to the compound of M and M*.[76] But this will not work either, because HOMT would then face the following dilemma. Either the compound state M + M* is a state we are aware of having, or it is not. If it is not, then HOMT is false, since it claims that conscious states are states we *are* aware of having. If it is, then according to the theory it must be represented by a third-order mental state, M**, in which case the same problem would recur when M** is targetless.

Third, they may claim that there are no targetless higher-order representations. But even if this can be shown to be the actual case (and it is hard to imagine how this would be done), we can surely conceive of counterfactual situations in which targetless higher-order representations do occur.[77]

A third problem for the HOMT is its treatment of the *epistemology* of consciousness (Goldman, 1993b; Kriegel, 2003b). Our knowledge that we are in a conscious state is first-person knowledge, knowledge that is not based on inference from experimental, or theoretical, or third-personal evidence. But if HOMT were correct, what would make our conscious states conscious is (normally) the occurrence of some unconscious state (i.e., the higher-order representation), so in order to know that we are in a conscious state we would need to know of the occurrence of that unconscious state. But knowledge of unconscious states is necessarily theoretical and third-personal, since we have no direct acquaintance with our unconscious states.

Another way to put the argument is this. How does the defender of HOMT know that conscious states are states of which we are aware? It does not seem to be something she knows on the basis of experimentation and theorization. Rather, it seems to be intuitively compelling, something that she knows on the basis of first-person acquaintance with her conscious states. But if HOMT were correct, it would seem that that knowledge would have to be purely theoretical and third-personal. So construed, this "epistemic argument" against HOMT may be formulated as follows:

1) If HOMT were correct, our awareness of our conscious states would normally be an unconscious state; that is,

2) We do not have non-theoretical, first-person knowledge of our unconscious states; therefore,

3) If HOMT were correct, we would not have non-theoretical, first-person knowledge of the fact that we are aware of our conscious states; but,

4) We do have non-theoretical, first-person knowledge of the fact that we are aware of our conscious states; therefore,

5) HOMT is incorrect.

The upshot of the argument is that the awareness of our conscious states must in the normal case be itself a conscious state. This is something that HOMT cannot allow, however, since within its framework it would lead to infinite regress. The problem is to reconcile the claim that conscious states are states we are aware of having with the notion that we have non-theoretical knowledge of this fact.

The Self-Representational Theory of Consciousness

One approach to consciousness that has a venerable tradition behind it, but has only very recently regained a modest degree of popularity, is what we may call the "self-representational theory." According to this view, mental states are conscious when, and only when, they represent their own occurrence (in the right way). Thus, my conscious experience of the blue sky represents both the sky and itself – and it is *in virtue* of representing itself that it *is* a conscious experience.

Historically, the most thorough development and elucidation of the self-representational theory is Brentano's (1874). Through his work, the view has had a significant influence in the phenomenological tradition. But apart from a couple of exceptions – Lehrer (1996, 1997) and Smith (1986, 1989) come to mind – the view had enjoyed virtually no traction in Anglo-American philosophy. Recently, however, versions of the view, and close variations on it, have been defended by a number of philosophers.[78]

Rather than focus on any one particular account of consciousness along these lines, I now survey the central contributions to the understanding of consciousness in terms of self-representation.

Varieties of Self-Representational Theory

Brentano held that every conscious state is intentionally directed at two things. It is *primarily* directed at whatever object it is about, and it is *secondarily* directed at itself. My bluish sky experience is directed primarily at the sky and secondarily at itself. In more modern terminology, a conscious state has two representational contents: an other-directed (primary) content and a self-directed (secondary) content. Thus, if S consciously fears that p, S's fear has two contents: the primary content is p, the secondary content is itself, the fear that p. The distinction between primary intentionality and secondary intentionality is presumably intended to capture the difference (discussed above) between attentive or focal awareness and inattentive or peripheral awareness.[79]

Caston (2002) offers an interesting gloss on this idea in terms of the type/token distinction. For Caston, S's conscious fear that p

is a single *token* state that falls under two separate state *types*: the fear-that-p type and the awareness-of-fear-that-p type. The state has two contents, arguably, precisely in virtue of falling under two types.

Brook and Raymont (2006) stress that the self-representational content of the conscious state is not simply that the state occurs, but rather that it occurs *within oneself* – that it is one's own state. Just as Rosenthal construed the content of higher-order states as "I myself am having that state," so Brook and Raymont suggest that the full self-representational content of conscious states is something like "I myself am herewith having this very state."[80]

For Brentano and his followers, the self-directed element in conscious states is an aspect of their intentionality, or content. In David Woodruff Smith's (1986, 2004) "modal account," by contrast, the self-directed element is construed not as an aspect of the representational content, but rather as an aspect of the representational attitude (or mode). When S consciously fears that p, it is not in virtue of figuring in its own secondary content that the fear is conscious. Indeed, S's fear does not *have* a secondary content. Its only content is p. The "reflexive character" of the fear, as Smith puts it, is rather part of the *attitude* S takes toward p. Just as the attitudes toward p can vary from fear, hope, expectation, and so on, so they can vary between self-directed or "reflexive" fear and un-self-directed or "irreflexive" fear. S's fear that p is conscious, on this view, because S takes the attitude of self-directed fear toward p.[81,82]

One way in which the self-representational thesis can be relaxed to make a subtler claim is the following. Instead of claiming that a mental state M of a subject S is conscious just in case M represents itself, the thesis could be that M is conscious just in case S has an M* that is a representation of M and there is a *constitutive, non-contingent* relation between M and M*.[83] One constitutive relation is of course identity. So one version of this view would be that M is conscious just in case M is identical with M* – this is how Hossack (2002) formulates his

thesis – and this seems to amount to the claim that M is conscious just in case it represents itself (constitutes a representation of itself). But the point is that there are other, weaker constitutive relations that fall short of full identity.

One such relation is the part-whole relation. Accordingly, one version of the view, the one defended by Gennaro (1996, 2006), holds that M* is a *part of* M; another version, apparently put forth by Kobes (1995), holds that M is part of M*; and yet another version, Van Gulick's (2001, 2006), holds that M is conscious when it has two parts, one of which represents the other.

In Van Gulick's "higher-order global states theory," S's fear that p becomes conscious when the fear and S's awareness of the fear are somehow integrated into a single, unified state. This new state supersedes its original components, though, in a way that makes it a genuine unity, rather than a sum of two parts, one of which happens to represent the other. The result is a state that, if it does not represent itself, does something very close to representing itself.[84]

The Master Argument for the Self-Representational Theory

The basic argument for the self-representational approach to consciousness is that it is the only way to accommodate the notion that conscious states are states we are aware of without falling into the pitfalls of HOMT.

The argument can be organized, then, as a disjunctive syllogism that starts from the master argument for HOMT, but then goes beyond it:

1) A mental state M of subject S is conscious when, and only when, S is aware of M;

2) Awareness of X requires mental representation of X; therefore,

3) M is conscious when, and only when, S has a mental state M*, such that M* represents M.

4) Either M* = M or M* ≠ M;

5) There are good reasons to think that it is not the case that M* ≠ M; therefore,

6) There are good reasons to think that it is the case that M* = M; therefore,

7) Plausibly, M is conscious when, and only when, M is self-representing.

The fourth premise could also be formulated as "either M* and M do not entertain a constitutive, non-contingent relation, or they do," with appropriate modifications in Premises 5 and 6 to suit. The conclusion of the relevantly modified argument would then be the thesis that M is conscious when, and only when, S has a mental state M*, such that (i) M* represents M and (ii) there is a constitutive, non-contingent relation between M and M*.

The fallacy in the master argument for HOMT is the supposition that if S is aware of M, then S must be so aware in virtue of being in a mental state that is *numerically different* from M. This supposition is brought to the fore and rejected in the argument just sketched.

The case for the fifth premise consists in all the reasons to be suspicious of HOMT, as elaborated in the previous section, although it must also be shown that the same problems do not bedevil the self-representational theory as well.

Consider first the epistemic argument. We noted that HOMT fails to account for the non-theoretical, first-person knowledge we have of the fact that we are aware of our conscious states. This is because it construes this awareness as (normally) an unconscious state. The self-representational theory, by contrast, construes this awareness as a conscious state, since it construes the awareness as the same state, or part of the state, of which one is thereby aware. So the self-representational theory, unlike HOMT, *can* provide for the right epistemology of consciousness.

Consider next the problem of targetless higher-order representations. Recall, the problem ensues from the fact that M* could in principle misrepresent not only that M is F when in reality M is not F, but also that M is F when in reality there is no M

at all. The same problem does not arise for self-representing states, however: although M could in principle misrepresent itself to be F when in reality it is not F, it could not possibly misrepresent itself to be F when in reality it does not exist at all. For if it did not exist it could not represent anything, itself included. Thus the problem of targetless higher-order representations has no bite against the self-representational theory.

These are already two major problems that affect gravely the plausibility of HOMT, but do not apply to the self-representational theory. They make a strong *prima facie* case for the fifth premise above. The fourth premise is a logical truism, and the first and second ones were defended above. So the argument appears to go through.

Problems for the Self-Representational Theory

One problem that does persist for the self-representational theory is the problem of animal consciousness. The ability to have self-representing states presumably requires all the conceptual sophistication that the ability to have higher-order monitoring states does (since the self-representational content of a conscious state is the same as the representational content that a higher-order state would have), and perhaps even greater sophistication.[85]

Another problem is the elucidation and viability of the notion of self-representation. What does it mean for a mental state to represent itself, and what sort of mechanism could subserve the production of self-representing states? There is something at least initially mysterious about the notion of a self-representing state that needs to be confronted.

In fact, one might worry that there are principled reasons why self-representation is incompatible with any known naturalist account of mental representation. These accounts construe mental representation as some sort of natural relation between brain states and world states. Natural relations, as opposed to conceptual or logical ones, are based on causality and causal processes. But causality is an anti-reflexive relation, that is, a relation that nothing can bear to itself. Thus no state can bring about its own occurrence or give rise to itself. The argument can be formulated as follows:

1) Mental representation involves a causal relation between the representation and the represented;

2) The causal relation is anti-reflexive; therefore,

3) No mental state can cause itself; and therefore,

4) No mental state can represent itself.

The basic idea is that there is no naturalist account of mental representation that could allow for self-representing mental representations.

Even more fundamentally, one may worry whether the appeal to self-representation really *explains* consciousness. Perhaps self-representation is a *necessary* condition for consciousness, but why think it is also a *sufficient* condition? A sentence such as "this very sentence contains six words" is self-representing, but surely there is nothing it is like to be that sentence.[86]

One may respond to this last point that what is required for consciousness is *intrinsic* or *original* self-representation, not *derivative* self-representation.[87] Sentences and linguistic expressions do not have any representational content in and of themselves, independently of being interpreted. But plausibly, mental states do.[88] The same goes for self-representational content: sentences and linguistic expressions may be derivatively self-representing, but only mental states can be non-derivatively self-representing. A more accurate statement of the self-representation theory is therefore this: A mental state M of a subject S is conscious when, and only when, M is non-derivatively self-representing.

Still, self-representing zombies are readily conceivable. It is quite easy to imagine unconscious mental states in our own cognitive system – say, states formed early on in visual processing – that represent themselves without thereby being conscious.[89] Furthermore, it is easy to imagine a crea-

ture with no conscious awareness whatsoever who harbors mental states that represent themselves. Thus Chalmers' zombie argument can be run in a particularized version directed specifically against the self-representational theory.[90]

Conclusion: Directions for Future Research

Much of the philosophical discourse on consciousness is focused on the issue of reducibility. As we just saw, the zombie argument and other dualist arguments can be tailored to target any particular reductive account of consciousness. This debate holds great intrinsic importance, but it is important to see that progress toward a scientific explanation of consciousness can be made without attending to it.

All three reductive approaches to consciousness we considered – the representational, higher-order monitoring, and self-representational theories – can readily be refashioned as accounts not of consciousness itself, but of the *emergence base* (or *causal basis*) of consciousness. Instead of claiming that consciousness *is* (or is *reducible to*) physical structure P, the claim would be that consciousness *emerges from* (or is *brought about by*) P. To make progress toward the scientific explanation of consciousness, we should focus mainly on what the right physical structure is – what P is. Whether P is consciousness itself or only the emergence base of consciousness is something we can set aside for the purposes of scientific explanation. If it turns out that P is consciousness itself (as the reductivist holds), then we will have obtained a *reductive* explanation of consciousness; if it turns out that P is only the emergence base of consciousness (as the dualist holds), then we will have obtained a *causal* explanation of consciousness. But both kinds of explanation are bona fide scientific explanations.

In other words, philosophers could usefully reorganize their work on consciousness around a distinction between two separate issues or tasks. The first task is to devise a positive account of the physical (or more broadly, natural) correlate of consciousness, without prejudging whether it will constitute a reduction base or merely an emergence base. Work along these lines will involve modifying and refining the representational, higher-order monitoring, and self-representational theories and/or devising altogether novel positive accounts. The second task is to examine the a priori and a posteriori cases for reducibility. Work here will probably focus on the issue of how much can be read off of conceivability claims, as well as periodic reconsideration of the intuitive plausibility of such claims in light of newer and subtler positive accounts of consciousness.[91]

Another front along which progress can certainly be made is tightening the connection between the theoretical and experimental perspectives on consciousness. Ultimately, one hopes that experiments could be designed that would test well-defined empirical consequences of philosophical (or more generally, purely theoretical) models of consciousness. This would require philosophers to be willing to put forth certain empirical speculations, as wild as these may seem, based on their theories of consciousness, and experimental scientists to take interest in the intricacies of philosophical theories in an attempt to think up possible ways to test them.

All in all, progress in our understanding of consciousness and the outstanding methodological and substantive challenges it presents has been quite impressive over the past two decades. The central philosophical issues are today framed with a clarity and precision that allow a corresponding level of clarity and precision in our thinking about consciousness. Even more happily, there is no reason to suppose that this progress will come to a halt or slow down in the near future.[92]

Notes

1. More accurately, I present *central aspects* of the main account, the case in favor, and the case against. Obviously, space and other limitations do not allow me to present the full story on each of these approaches.

2. The distinction between creature consciousness and state consciousness is due to Rosenthal (1986).

3. Availability consciousness as construed here is very similar to the notion of *access consciousness* as defined by Block (1995). There are certain differences, however. Block defines access consciousness as the property a mental state has when it is poised for free use by the subject in her reasoning and action control. It may well be that a mental state is availability-conscious if and only if it is access-conscious. For a detailed discussion of the relation between phenomenal consciousness and access consciousness, see Kriegel (2006b).

4. It is debatable whether thoughts, beliefs, desires, and other cognitive states can at all be conscious in this sense. I remain silent on this issue here. For arguments that they can be conscious, see Goldman (1993a), Horgan and Tienson (2002), and Siewert (1998).

5. The terms "easy problems" and "hard problem" are intended as mere labels, not as descriptive. Thus it is not suggested here that understanding any of the functions of consciousness is at all easy in any significant sense. Any scientist who has devoted time to the study of consciousness knows how outstanding the problems in this field are. These terms are just a terminological device designed to bring out the fact that the problem of why there is something it feels like to undergo a conscious experience appears to be of a different order than the problems of mapping out the cognitive functions of consciousness.

6. This is so even if phenomenal consciousness does not turn out to have much of a functional significance in the ordinary cognitive life of a normal subject – as some (Libet, 1985; Velmans, 1992; Wegner, 2002) have indeed argued.

7. In the course of the discussion I avail myself of philosophical terminology that may not be familiar to the non-philosophically trained reader. However, I have tried to recognize all the relevant instances and such and include an endnote that provides a standard explication of the terminology in question.

8. No major philosopher holds this view, to my knowledge.

9. Many of the key texts discussed in this chapter are conveniently collected in Block et al. (1997). Here, and in the rest of the chapter, I refer to the reprint in that volume.

10. This is what Churchland often discusses under the heading of the "plasticity of mind" (see especially Churchland, 1979).

11. It may not be perceiving those brain states *as* brain states. But it will nonetheless be a matter of perceiving the brain states.

12. The view – sometimes referred to as *emergentism* – that consciousness is caused by the brain, or causally emerges from brain activity, is often taken by scientists to be materialist enough. But philosophers, being interested in the *ontology* rather than *genealogy* of consciousness, commonly take it to be a form of dualism. If consciousness cannot be shown to be itself material, but only caused by matter, then consciousness is itself immaterial, as the dualist claims. At the same time, the position implicit in scientists' work is often that what is caused by physical causes in accordance with already known physical laws should be immediately considered physical. This position, which I have called elsewhere *inclusive materialism* (Kriegel, 2005b), is not unreasonable. But the present chapter is dedicated to *philosophers'* theories of consciousness, so I set it aside.

13. It should be noted that McGinn himself has repeatedly claimed that his position is not dualist. Nonetheless others have accused him of being committed to dualism (e.g., Brueckner and Berukhim, 2003). There is no doubt that McGinn does not *intend* to commit to dualism. In a way, his position is precisely that, because of our cognitive closure we cannot even know whether materialism or dualism is true. Yet it is a fair criticism to suggest that McGinn is committed to dualism despite himself because his argument for mysterianism would not go through unless dualism was true.

14. More generally, it is curious to hold, as McGinn does, that an organism's concept-forming procedures are powerful enough to *frame* a problem, without being powerful enough to *frame* the solution. To be sure, the wrong solution may be framed, but this would suggest not that the conceptual capabilities of the organism are at fault, but rather that the organism made the wrong turn somewhere in its reasoning. The natural thought is that if a conceptual scheme is powerful enough to frame a problem it should be powerful enough to frame the solution. Whether the correct solution will actually *be* framed is of course anyone's guess. But the problem cannot be a constitutive limitation on concept formation mechanisms. (For a more detailed development of this line of critique, see Kriegel, 2004a.) There is a counterexample of this sort of claim, however. Certain problems that can be framed within the theory of rational numbers cannot be solved within it; the conceptual machinery of irrational numbers must be brought in to solve these problems. It might be claimed, however, that this sort of exception is limited to formal systems and does not apply to theories of the natural world. Whether this claim is plausible is something I do not adjudicate here.

15. Monism divides into two subgroups: materialist monism, according to which the only kind of stuff there is is matter, and idealist monism, according to which the stuff in question is some sort of mindstuff.

16. Idealism is not really considered a live option in current philosophical discussions, although it *is* defended by Foster (1982). I do not discuss it here.

17. Such coming-apart happens, for Descartes, upon death of the physical body. We should note that Cartesian substance dualism drew much of its motivation from religious considerations, partly because it provided for the survival of the soul. The main difficulty historically associated with it is whether it can account for the causal interaction between the mind and the body.

18. So property dualism is compatible with substance monism. Unlike Descartes and other old-school dualists, modern dualists for the most part hold that there is only one kind of stuff, or substance, in the world – matter. But matter has two different kinds of *properties* – material and immaterial.

19. A kind of property F supervenes on a kind of property G with logical necessity – or for short logically supervenes on them – just in case two objects differing with respect to their F properties without differing with respect to their G properties would be in contravention of the laws of logic. A kind of property F supervenes on a kind of property G with metaphysical necessity – or for short

metaphysically supervenes on them – just in case it is impossible for two objects to differ with respect to their F properties without differing with respect to their G properties. Philosophers debate whether there is a difference between the two (logical and metaphysical supervenience). That debate does not concern us here.

20. This stronger claim will require a stronger argument. The claim that phenomenal properties are not identical to physical properties could be established through the now familiar argument from multiple realizability (Putnam, 1967). But multiple realizability does not entail failure of supervenience. To obtain the latter, Chalmers will have to appeal to a different argument, as we will see in the next subsection.

21. As a consequence, phenomenal properties do supervene on physical properties with *nomological* necessity, even though they do not supervene with metaphysical or logical necessity. A kind of property F supervenes on a kind of property G with nomological (or natural) necessity – or for short nomologically supervenes on them – just in case two objects differing with respect to their F properties without differing with respect to their G properties would be in contravention of laws of nature.

22. So causal explanation is the sort of explanation one obtains by citing the cause of the explanandum. For discussions of the nature of causal explanation, see (e.g., Lewis, 1993).

23. The latter will govern only the causal interaction *among* physical events. They will not cover causal interaction between physical and phenomenal, non-physical events. These will have to be covered by a special and new set of laws.

24. In Baars' (1988, 1997) Global Workspace Theory, consciousness is *reductively* explained in terms of global availability. In a functionalist theory such as Dennett's (1981, 1991), consciousness is *reductively* explained in terms of functional organization. Chalmers' position is that neither theory can explain consciousness *reductively*, though both may figure as part of the *causal* explanation of it. These theories are not discussed in the present chapter, because they are fundamentally psychological (rather than philosophical) theories of consciousness.

25. A linguistic context is intensional if it disallows certain inferences, in particular existential generalization (the inference from "a is F" to "there is an x, such that x is F") and substitution of co-referential terms *salva veritate* (the inference from "a is F" and "a = b" to "b is F"). Epistemic contexts – contexts involving the ascription of knowledge – are intensional in this sense.

26. Another popular materialist response to these arguments is that what is being gained is not new knowledge, but rather new abilities (Lewis, 1990; Nemirow, 1990). Upon being released from her room, the Knowledge Argument's protagonist does not acquire new knowledge, but rather a new set of abilities. And likewise what we lack with respect to what it is like to be a bat is not any particular knowledge, but a certain ability – the ability to imagine what it is like to be a bat. But from the acquisition of a new ability one can surely not infer the existence of a new fact.

27. Materialists reason that because what it is like to see red is identical to a neurophysiological fact about the brain, and *ex hypothesi* the Knowledge Argument's protagonist knows the latter fact, she already knows the former. So she knows the fact of what it is like to see red, but not *as* a fact about what it is like to see red. Instead, she knows the fact of what it is like to see red *as* a fact about the neurophysiology of the brain. What happens when she comes out of her room is that she comes to know the fact of what it is like to see red *as* a fact about what it is like to see red. That is, she learns in a new way a fact she already knew in another way. The same applies to knowledge of what it is like to be a bat: we may know all the facts about what it is like to see a bat, and still gain new knowledge about bats, but this new knowledge will present to us a fact we already know in a way we do not know it yet.

28. It could be responded by the dualist that some pieces of knowledge are so different that the fact known thereby could not possibly turn out to be the same. Knowledge that the evening star is glowing and knowledge that the morning star is glowing are not such. But consider knowledge that justice is good and knowledge that banana is good. The dualist could argue that these are such different pieces of knowledge that it is impossible that the facts thereby known should turn out to be one and the same. The concepts of evening star and morning star are not different enough to exclude the possibility that they pick out

the same thing, but the concepts of justice and banana are such that it cannot possibly be the case that justice should turn out to be the same thing as bananas.

29. The kind of possibility we are concerned with here, and in the following presentation of variations on this argument, is not practical possibility, or even a matter of consistency with the laws of nature. Rather it is possibility in the widest possible sense – that of consistency with the laws of logic and the very essence of things. This is what philosophers refer to as metaphysical possibility.

30. The modal force of this supervenience claim is concordant with that of the claim in Premise 2; that is, that of metaphysical necessity.

31. The reason it is impossible is that there is no such thing as *contingent identity*, according to the official doctrine hailing from Kripke. Since all identity is necessary, and necessity is cashed out as truth in all possible worlds, it follows that when a = b in the actual world, a = b in all possible worlds, that is, a is *necessarily* identical to b.

32. The interpretation I provide is based on certain key passages in Chalmers (1996, pp. 131–134), but I cast the argument in terms that are mine, not Chalmers'.

33. I mean the property of apparent water to be more or less the same as the property philosophers often refer to as "watery stuff" (i.e., the property of being superficially (or to the naked eye) the same as water – clear, drinkable, liquid, etc.).

34. Chalmers (1996, 132) writes, "…the primary intension [of "consciousness"] determines a *perfectly good property* of objects in possible worlds. The property of being watery stuff [or apparent water] is a perfectly reasonable property, even though it is not the same as the property of being H$_2$O. If we can show that there are possible worlds that are physically identical to ours but in which the properly introduced by the primary intension is lacking, then dualism will follow [italics added]."

35. Our discussion so far has presupposed a "latitudinous" approach to properties, according to which there is a property that corresponds to every predicate we can come up with. (Thus, if we can come up with the predicate, "is a six-headed space lizard or a flying cow," then there is the property of being a six-headed space lizard or a flying cow. This does

not mean, however, that the property is actually instantiated by any actual object.) But on a *sparse* conception of property – one that rejects the latitudinous assumption – there may not be appearance properties at all.

36. The notion of a natural property is hard to pin down and is the subject of philosophical debate. The most straightforward way of understanding natural properties is as properties that figure in the ultimate laws of nature (Armstrong, 1978; Fodor, 1974).

37. That is, they would have their causal efficacy restricted to bringing about physical events and property-instantiations that already have independent sufficient causes (and that would therefore take place anyway, regardless of the non-supervenient properties. (This is the second option of the dilemma.)

38. This is the strategy in Chalmers (1996). Later on, Chalmers (2002a) embraces a three-pronged approach, the third prong consisting in accepting causal overdetermination.

39. When a cause C causes an effect E, C's causing of E may have its own (mostly accidental) effects (e.g., it may surprise an observer who did not expect the causing to take place), but E is not one of them. This is because E is caused by C, not by C's causing of E. Dretske (1988) distinguished between *triggering* causes and *structuring* causes, the latter being causes of certain causal relations (such as C's causing of E), and offers an account of structuring causes. But this is an account of the *causes* of causal relations, not of their *effects*. To my knowledge, there is no account of the effects of causal relations, mainly because these seem to be chiefly accidental.

40. Or at least they would be nearly epiphenomenal, having no causal powers except perhaps to bring about some accidental effects of the sort pointed out in the previous endnote.

41. By "representational properties" it is meant properties that the experience has in virtue of what it represents – not, it is important to stress, properties the experience has in virtue of what does the representing. In terms of the distinction between vehicle and content, representational properties are to be understood as content properties rather than vehicular properties. We can also make a distinction between two kinds of vehicular properties: those that are essential to the vehicling of

the content and those that are not. (Block's (1996) distinction between mental paint and mental latex (later, "mental oil") is supposed to capture this distinction.) There is a sense in which a view according to which phenomenal properties are reductively accountable for in terms of vehicular properties essential to the vehicling is representational, but the way the term "representationalism" is used in current discussions of consciousness, it does not qualify as representationalism. A view of this sort is defended, for instance, by Maloney (1989), but otherwise lacks a vast following. I do not discuss it here.

42. By the "phenomenal character" of a mental state at a time t I mean the set of all phenomenal properties the state in question instantiates at t. By "representational content" I mean whatever the experience represents. (Experiences represent things, in that they have certain accuracy or veridicality conditions: conditions under which an experience would be said to get things right.)

43. See Dretske (1981, 1988) for the most thoroughly worked out reductive account of mental representation in informational and teleological terms. According to Dretske (1981), every event in the world generates a certain amount of information (in virtue of excluding the possibility that an incompatible event can take place). Some events also take place only when other events take place as well, and this is sometimes dictated by the laws of nature. Thus it may be a law of nature that dictates that an event type E_1 is betokened only when event type E_2 is betokened. When this is the case, E_1 is said to be *nomically dependent* upon E_2, and the tokening of E_1 carries the information that E_2 has been betokened. Or more accurately, the tokening of E_1 carries the information generated by the tokening of E_2. Some brain states bear this sort of relation to world states: the former come into being, as a matter of law, only when the latter do (i.e., the former are nomically dependent upon the latter). Thus, a certain type of brain state may be tokened only when it rains. This brain state type would thus carry the information that it rains. An informational account of mental representation is based on this idea: that a brain state can represent the fact that it rains by carrying information about it, which it does in virtue of nomically depending on it.

44. Other representational theories can be found in Byrne (2001), Dretske (1995), Lurz (2003),

Shoemaker (1994a, b, 1996, 2002) and Thau (2002). Some of these versions are importantly different from Tye's, not only in detail but also in spirit. This is particularly so with regard to Shoemaker's view (as well as Lurz's). For a limited defense and elaboration of Shoemaker's view, see Kriegel (2002a, b). In what way this defense is limited will become evident at the end of this section.

45. The properties of intentionality and abstractness are fairly straightforward. The former is a matter of intensionality; that is, the disallowing of existential generalizations and truth-preserving substitutions of co-referential terms. The second is a matter of the features represented by experience not being concrete entities (this is intended to make sense of misrepresentation of the same features, in which case no concrete entity is being represented).

46. This line of thought can be resisted on a number of scores. First, it could be argued that I do have a *short-lived* concept of blue$_{17}$, which I possess more or less for the duration of my experience. Second, it could be claimed that although I do not possess the *descriptive* concept "blue$_{17}$," I do possess the *indexical* concept "*this* shade of blue," and that it is the latter concept that is deployed in my experience's representational content. Be that as it may, the fact that conscious experiences can represent properties that the subject cannot recognize across relatively short stretches of time is significant enough. Even if we do not wish to treat them as non-conceptual, we must treat them at least as "sub-recognitional." Tye's modified claim would be that the representational content of experience is poised, abstract, sub-recognitional, intentional content.

47. To be sure, it does not represent the tissue damage *as* tissue damage, but it does represent the tissue damage. Since the representation is non-conceptual, it certainly cannot employ the concept of "tissue damage."

48. An error theory is a theory that ascribes a widespread error in commonsense beliefs. The term was coined by J. L. Mackie (1977). Mackie argued that values and value judgment are subjective. Oversimplifying the dialectic, a problem for this view is that such a judgment as "murder is wrong" appears to be, and is commonly taken to be, objectively true.

In response Mackie embraced what he termed an error theory: that the common view of moral and value judgments is simply one huge mistake.

49. Externalism about representational content, or "content externalism" for short, is the thesis that the representational content of experiences, thoughts, and even spoken statements is partially determined by objects outside the subject's head. Thus, if a person's interactions with watery stuff happen to be interactions with H_2O, and another person's interactions with watery stuff happen to be interactions with a superficially similar stuff that is not composed of H_2O, then even if the two persons cannot tell apart H_2O and the other stuff and are unaware of the differences in the molecular composition of the watery stuff in their environment, the representational contents of their respective water thoughts (as well as water pronouncements and water experiences) are different (Putnam, 1975). Or so externalists claim.

50. Another option is to go internalist with respect to the representational content that determines the phenomenal properties of conscious experiences. With the recent advent of credible account of narrow content (Chalmers, 2002b, Segal, 2000), it is now a real option to claim that the phenomenal properties of experience are determined by experience's narrow content (Kriegel, 2002a; Rey, 1998). However, it may turn out that this version of representationalism will not be as well supported by the transparency of experience.

51. For one such line of criticism, on which I do not elaborate here, see Kriegel (2002c).

52. Elsewhere, I construe this form of pre-reflective self-consciousness as what I call *intransitive self-consciousness*. Intransitive self-consciousness is to be contrasted with transitive self-consciousness. The latter is ascribed in reports of the form "I am self-conscious of my thinking that *p*," whereas the former is ascribed in reports of the form "I am self-consciously thinking that *p*." For details see Kriegel (2003b, 2004b).

53. Part of this neglect is justified by the thesis that the for-me-ness of conscious experiences is an illusory phenomenon. For an argument for the psychological reality of it, see Kriegel (2004b).

54. There are versions of representationalism that may be better equipped to deal with the subjective character of experience. Thus, according to Shoemaker's (2002) version, a mental state is conscious when it represents a subject-relative feature, such as the disposition to bring about certain internal states in the subject. It is possible that some kind of for-me-ness can be accounted for in this manner. It should be noted, however, that this is not one of the considerations that motivate Shoemaker to develop his theory the way he does.

55. Rosenthal prefers to put this idea as follows: conscious states are states we are conscious of. He then draws a distinction between consciousness and consciousness of – intransitive and transitive consciousness (Rosenthal, 1986, 1990). To avoid unnecessary confusion, I state the same idea in terms of awareness-of, rather than consciousness-of. But the idea is the same. It is what Rosenthal calls sometimes the "transitivity principle" (e.g., Rosenthal, 2000): a mental state is intransitively conscious only if we are transitively conscious of it.

56. The representation is "higher-order" in the sense that it is a representation of a representation. In this sense, a first-order representation is a representation of something that is not itself a representation. Any other representation is higher-order.

57. More than that, according to Rosenthal (1990), for instance, the particular *way* it is like for S to have M is determined by the particular *way* M* represents M. Suppose S tastes an identical wine in 1980 and in 1990. During the 1980s, however, S had become a wine connoisseur. Consequently, wines she could not distinguish at all in 1980 strike her in 1990 as worlds apart. That is, during the eighties she acquired a myriad of concepts for very specific and subtle wine tastes. It is plausible to claim that what it is like for S to taste the wine in 1990 is different from what it was like for her to taste it in 1980 – even though the wines' own flavors are identical. Arguably, the reason for the difference in what it is like to taste the wine is that the two wine-tasting experiences are accompanied by radically different higher-order representations *of* them. This suggests, then, that the higher-order representation not only determines *that* there is something it is like for S to have M, but also *what* it is like for S to have M.

58. I do not mean the term "yield" in a causal sense here. The higher-order monitoring theory does not claim that M*'s representing of M somehow *produces*, or *gives rise to*, M's being conscious. Rather, the claim is conceptual: M's being conscious *consists in*, or *is constituted by*, M*'s representing of M.

59. Other versions of the higher-order thought view can be found in Carruthers (1989, 1996), Dennett (1969, 1991), and Mellor (1978).

60. Rosenthal (1990, pp. 739–40) claims that it is essential to a perceptual state that it has a sensory quality, but the second-order representations do not have sensory qualities and are therefore non-perceptual. Van Gulick (2001) details a longer and more thorough list of features that are characteristic of perceptual states and considers which of them is likely to be shared by the higher-order representations. His conclusion is that some are and some are not.

61. The notion of direction of fit has its origins in the work of Anscombe (1957), but has been developed in some detail and put to extensive work mainly by Searle (1983). The idea is that mental states divide into two main groups, the cognitive ones (paradigmatically, belief) and the conative ones (paradigmatically, desire). The former are such that they are supposed to make the mind fit the way the world is (thus "getting the facts right"), whereas the latter are such that they are supposed to make the world fit the way the mind is (a change in the world is what would satisfy them).

62. Kobes (1995) suggests a version of higher-order monitoring theory in which the higher-order representation has essentially a telic direction of fit. But Rosenthal construes it as having only a thetic one.

63. Carruthers (1989, 1996, 2000), and probably also Dennett (1969, 1991), attempt to account for consciousness in terms of merely *tacit* or *dispositional* higher-order representations. But these would not do, according to Rosenthal. The reason for this is that a merely dispositional representation would not make the subject aware of her conscious state, but only *disposed* to being aware of it, whereas the central motivation behind the higher-order monitoring view is the fact that conscious states are states we are aware of having (Rosenthal 1990, p. 742).

64. Earlier on, Rosenthal (1990) required that the higher-order thought be not only non-inferential but also non-observational. This latter requirement was later dropped (Rosenthal, 1993).

65. A person may come to believe that she is ashamed about something on the strength of her therapist's evidence. And yet the shame state is not conscious. In terms of the terminology introduced in the introduction, the state may become availability-conscious, but not phenomenally conscious. This is why the immediacy of awareness is so crucial. Although the person's second-order belief constitutes an awareness of the shame state, it is not a non-inferential awareness, and therefore not immediate awareness.

66. *De se* content is content that is *of oneself*, or more precisely, of oneself *as oneself*. Castañeda (1966), who introduced this term, also claimed that *de se* content is irreducible to any other kind of content. This latter claim is debatable and is not part of the official higher-order thought theory.

67. Rosenthal's (1990, p. 742) argument for this requirement is the following. My awareness of my bluish experience is an awareness of *that particular* experience, not of the general type of experience it is. But it is impossible to represent a mental state as particular without representing in which subject it occurs. Therefore, the only way the higher-order thought could represent my experience in its particularity is if it represented it as occurring in me.

68. This is necessary to avert infinite regress. If the higher-order state was itself conscious, it would have to be itself represented by a yet higher-order state (according to the theory) and so the hierarchy of states would go to infinity. This is problematic on two scores. Firstly, it is empirically implausible, and perhaps impossible, that a subject should entertain an infinity of mental states whenever conscious. Secondly, if a mental state's being conscious is explained in terms of another conscious states, the explanation is "empty," inasmuch as it does not explain consciousness in terms of something other than consciousness.

69. This claim can be made on phenomenological grounds, instead of on the basis of conceptual analysis. For details, see Kriegel (2004b).

70. To repeat, the conceptual grounds are the fact that it seems to be a conceptual truth that

conscious states are states we are aware of having. This seems to be somehow inherent in the very concept of consciousness.

71. There are other arguments that have been leveled against the higher-order monitoring theory, or specific versions thereof, which I do not have the space to examine. For arguments not discussed here, see Block (1995), Caston (2002), Dretske (1995), Guzeldere (1995), Kriegel (2006a), Levine (2001), Natsoulas (1993), Rey (1988), Seager (1999), and Zahavi and Parnas (1998).

72. The argument has also been made by Caston (2002), Levine (2001), and Seager (1999). For a version of the argument directed at higher-order perception theory (and appealing to higher-order misperceptions), see Neander (1998).

73. Note that M* does not merely misrepresent M to be F when in reality M is not F, but misrepresents M to be F when in reality there is no M at all.

74. This would be a particular version of the supposition we made at the very beginning of this chapter, by way of analyzing creature consciousness in terms of state consciousness.

75. Furthermore, if M* were normally conscious, the same problem would arise with the third-order representation of it (and if the third-order representation were normally conscious, the problem would arise with the fourth-order state). To avert infinite regress, the higher-order monitoring theorist must somewhere posit an unconscious state, and when she does, she will be unable to claim that that state instantiates the property of being conscious when it misrepresents.

76. This appears to be Rosenthal's latest stance on the issue (in conversation).

77. There are surely other ways the higher-order monitoring theorist may try to handle the problem of targetless higher-order representations. But many of them are implausible, and all of them complicate the theory considerably. One of the initial attractions of the theory is its clarity and relative simplicity. Once it is modified along any of the lines sketched above, it becomes significantly less clear and simple. To that extent, it is considerably less attractive than it initially appears.

78. See Brook and Raymont (2006), Caston (2002), Hossack (2002), Kriegel (2003b), and Williford (2006). For the close variation, see Carruthers (2000, 2006), Gennaro (1996,

2002, 2006), Kobes (1995), Kriegel (2003a, 2005, 2006a), and Van Gulick (2001, 2004).

79. For fuller discussion of Brentano's account, see Caston (2002), Kriegel (2003a), Smith (1986, 1989) Thomasson (2000), and Zahavi (1998, 2004).

80. So the self-representational content of conscious states is *de se* content. There are places where Brentano seems to hold something like this as well. See also Kriegel (2003a).

81. For more on the distinction between content and attitude (or mode), see Searle (1983). For a critique of Smith's view, see Kriegel (2005a).

82. A similar account would be that conscious states are not conscious in virtue of standing in a certain relation to themselves, but this is because their secondary intentionality should be given an adverbial analysis. This is not to say that all intentionality must be treated adverbially. It may well be that the primary intentionality of conscious states is a matter of their standing in a certain informational or teleological relation to their primary objects. Thus, it need not be the case that S's conscious fear that *p* involves S's fearing *p*-ly rather than S's standing in a fear relation to the fact that *p*. But it *is* the case that S's *awareness* of her fear that *p* involves being aware fear-that-*p*-ly rather than standing in an awareness relation to the fear that *p*. To my knowledge, nobody holds this view.

83. A constitutive, non-contingent relation is a relation that two things do not just happen to entertain, but rather they would not be the things they are if they did not entertain those relations. Thus A's relation to B is constitutive if bearing it to B is part of what constitutes A's being what it is. Such a relation is necessary rather than contingent, since there is no possible world in which A does not bear it to B – for in such a world it would no longer be A.

84. Elsewhere, I have defended a view similar in key respects to Van Gulick's – see Kriegel (2003a, 2005, 2006a).

85. Indeed, the problem may be even more pressing for a view such as the higher-order global states theory. For the latter requires not only the ability to generate higher-order contents, but also the ability to *integrate* those with the right lower-order contents.

86. For a more elaborate argument that self-representation may not be a sufficient condition for consciousness, one that could provide

a reductive explanation of it, see Levine (2001, Ch. 6).

87. I am appealing here to a distinction defended, e.g., by Cummins (1979), Dretske (1988), and Searle (1992). Grice noted that some things that exhibit aboutness of meaningfulness, such as words, traffic signs, and arrows, do so only on the assumption that someone *interprets* them to have the sort of meaning they have. But these acts of interpretation are themselves contentful, or meaningful. So their own meaning must be either derived by further interpretative acts or be intrinsic to them and non-derivative. Grice's claim was that thoughts and other mental states have an aboutness all their own, independently of any interpretation.

88. This is denied by Dennett (1987), who claims that all intentionality is derivative.

89. One might claim that such states are less clearly conceivable when their self-representational content is fully specified. Thus, if the content is of the form, "I myself am herewith having this very bluish experience," it is less clearly the case that one can conceive of an unconscious state having this content.

90. The conceivability of unconscious self-representing states may not be *proof* of their possibility, but it is *evidence* of their possibility. It is therefore evidence against the self-representational theory.

91. The reductivist may claim that zombies with the same physical properties we have are conceivable only because we are not yet in a position to focus our mind on the right physical structure. As progress is made toward identification of the right physical structure, it will become harder and harder to conceive of a zombie exhibiting this structure but lacking all consciousness.

92. For comments on an earlier draft of this chapter, I would like to thank George Graham, David Jehle, Christopher Maloney, Amie Thomasson, and especially David Chalmers.

References

Armstrong, D. M. (1968). *A materialist theory of the mind*. New York: Humanities Press.

Armstrong, D. M. (1978). *A theory of universals*, Vol. 2. Cambridge: Cambridge University Press.

Armstrong, D. M. (1981). What is consciousness? In D. M. Armstrong (Ed.), *The nature of mind* (pp. 55–67). Ithaca, NY: Cornell University Press.

Anscombe, G. E. M. (1957). *Intention*. Oxford: Blackwell.

Baars, B. (1988). *A cognitive theory of consciousness*. New York: Cambridge University Press.

Baars, B. (1997). *In the theater of consciousness: The workspace of the mind*. Oxford: Oxford University Press.

Block, N. J. (1990a). Inverted earth. *Philosophical Perspective, 4,* 52–79.

Block, N. J. (1990b). Can the mind change the world? In G. Boolos (Ed.), *Meaning and method: Essays in honor of Hilary Putnam*. New York: Cambridge University Press.

Block, N. J. (1995). On a confusion about the function of consciousness. *Behavioral and Brain Sciences, 18,* 227–247.

Block, N. J. (1996). Mental paint and mental latex. *Philosophical Issues, 7,* 19–50.

Block, N. J., Flanagan, O., & Guzeldere, G. (Eds.). (1997). *The nature of consciousness: Philosophical debates*. Cambridge, MA: MIT Press.

Brentano, F. (1973). *Psychology from empirical standpoint* (O. Kraus, Ed. & A. C. Rancurello, D. B. Terrell, & L. L. McAlister, Trans.). London: Routledge and Kegan Paul. (Original work published 1874)

Brook, A., & Raymont, P. (2006). *A unified theory of consciousness*. Cambridge, MA: MIT Press.

Brueckner, A., & Berukhim, E. (2003). McGinn on consciousness and the mind-body problem." In Q. Smith & D. Jokic (Eds.), *Consciousness: New philosophical perspectives*. Oxford: Oxford University Press.

Byrne, D. (1997). Some like it HOT: Consciousness and higher order thoughts. *Philosophical Studies, 86,* 103–129.

Byrne, A. (2001). Intentionalism defended. *Philosophical Review, 110,* 199–240.

Carruthers, P. (1989). Brute experience. *Journal of Philosophy, 85,* 258–269.

Carruthers, P. (1996). *Language, thought, and consciousness*. Cambridge: Cambridge University Press.

Carruthers, P. (1998). Natural theories of consciousness. *European Journal of Philosophy*, 6, 203–222.

Carruthers, P. (1999). Sympathy and subjectivity. *Australasian Journal of Philosophy*, 77, 465–482.

Carruthers, P. (2000). *Phenomenal consciousness*. New York: Cambridge University Press.

Carruthers, P. (2006). Conscious experience versus conscious thought. In U. Kriegel & K. Williford (Eds.), *Consciousness and self-reference*. Cambridge, MA: MIT Press.

Castañeda, H.-N. (1966). 'He': A study in the logic of self-consciousness. *Ratio*, 8, 130–157.

Caston, V. (2002). Aristotle on consciousness. *Mind*, 111, 751–815.

Chalmers, D. J. (1995). Facing up to the problem of consciousness. *Journal of Consciousness Studies*, 2, 200–219.

Chalmers, D. J. (1996). *The conscious mind*. Oxford: Oxford University Press.

Chalmers, D. J. (2002a). Consciousness and its place in nature. In D. J. Chalmers (Ed.), *Philosophy of mind*. Oxford: Oxford University Press.

Chalmers, D. J. (2002b). The components of content. In D. J. Chalmers (Ed.), *Philosophy of mind*. Oxford: Oxford University Press.

Churchland, P. M. (1979). *Scientific realism and the plasticity of mind*. New York: Cambridge University Press.

Churchland, P. M. (1985). Reduction, qualia, and the direct introspection of brain states. *Journal of Philosophy*, 82, 8–28.

Crick, F., & Koch. C. (1990). Towards a neurobiological theory of consciousness. *Seminars in the Neurosciences*, 2, 263–275.

Crick, F., & Koch. C. (2003). A framework for consciousness. *Nature Neuroscience*, 6, 119–126.

Cummins, R. (1979). Intention, meaning, and truth conditions. *Philosophical Studies*, 35, 345–360.

DeBellis, M. (1991). The representational content of musical experience. *Philosophy and Phenomenological Research*, 51, 303–324.

Dennett, D. C. (1969). *Consciousness and content*. London: Routledge.

Dennett, D. C. (1981). Towards a cognitive theory of consciousness. In D. C. Dennett (Ed.), *Brainstorms*. Brighton: Harvester.

Dennett, D. C. (1987). *The intentional stance*. Cambridge, MA: MIT Press.

Dennett, D. C. (1991). *Consciousness explained*. Cambridge, MA: MIT Press.

Dennett, D. C. (1995). *Darwin's dangerous idea*. New York: Simon and Schuster.

Dretske, F. I. (1981). *Knowledge and the flow of information*. Oxford: Clarendon.

Dretske, F. I. (1988). *Explaining behavior*. Cambridge MA: MIT Press.

Dretske, F. I. (1993). Conscious experience. *Mind*, 102, 263–283.

Dretske, F. I. (1995). *Naturalizing the mind*. Cambridge MA: MIT Press.

Fodor, J. A. (1974). Special sciences. *Synthese*, 28, 97–115.

Foster, J. (1982). *The case for idealism*. London: Routledge.

Gennaro, R. J. (1996). *Consciousness and self-consciousness*. Philadelphia: John Benjamin.

Gennaro, R. J. (2002). Jean-Paul Sartre and the HOT theory of consciousness. *Canadian Journal of Philosophy*, 32, 293–330.

Gennaro, R. J. (2006). Between pure self-referentialism and (extrinsic) HOT theory. In U. Kriegel & K. Williford (Eds.), *Consciousness and self-reference*. Cambridge, MA: MIT Press.

Goldman, A. (1993a). The psychology of folk psychology. *Behavioral and Brain Sciences*, 16, 15–28.

Goldman, A. (1993b). Consciousness, folk psychology, and cognitive science. *Consciousness and Cognition*, 2, 364–383.

Grice, P. (1957). Meaning. *Philosophical Review*, 66, 377–388.

Guzeldere, G. (1995). Is consciousness the perception of what passes in one's own mind? In T. Metzinger (Ed.), *Conscious experience*. Padborn: Schoeningh-Verlag.

Harman, G. (1990). The intrinsic quality of experience. *Philosophical Perspectives*, 4, 31–52.

Horgan, T., & Tienson, J. (2002). The intentionality of phenomenology and the phenomenology of intentionality. In D. J. Chalmers (Ed.), *Philosophy of mind*. Oxford: Oxford University Press.

Hossack, K. (2002). Self-knowledge and consciousness. *Proceedings of the Aristotelian Society*, 163–181.

Jackson, F. (1984). Epiphenomenal qualia. *Philosophical Quarterly*, 34, 147–152.

Kim, J. (1989a). The myth of nonreductive materialism. *Proceedings and Addresses of the American Philosophical Association*, 63, 31–47.

Kim, J. (1989b). Mechanism, purpose, and explanatory exclusion. *Philosophical Perspectives*, 3, 77–108.

Kim, J. (1992). Multiple realization and the metaphysics of reduction. *Philosophy and Phenomenological Research*, 52, 1–26.

Kobes, B. W. (1995). Telic higher-order thoughts and Moore's paradox. *Philosophical Perspectives*, 9, 291–312.

Kriegel, U. (2002a). Phenomenal content. *Erkenntnis*, 57, 175–198.

Kriegel, U. (2002b). Emotional content. *Consciousness and Emotion*, 3, 213–230.

Kriegel, U. (2002c). PANIC theory and the prospects for a representational theory of phenomenal consciousness. *Philosophical Psychology*, 15, 55–64.

Kriegel U. (2003a). Consciousness, higher-order content, and the individuation of vehicles. *Synthese*, 134, 477–504.

Kriegel, U. (2003b). Consciousness as intransitive self-consciousness: Two views and an argument. *Canadian Journal of Philosophy*, 33, 103–132.

Kriegel, U. (2004a). The new mysterianism and the thesis of cognitive closure. *Acta Analytica*, 18, 177–191.

Kriegel, U. (2004b). Consciousness and self-consciousness. *The Monist* 87, 185–209.

Kriegel, U. (2005a). Naturalizing subjective character. *Philosophy and Phenomenological Research*, 71, 23–57.

Kriegel, U. (2005b). Review of Jeffrey Gray, *Consciousness: creeping up on the hard problem*. *Mind*, 114, 417–421.

Kriegel, U. (2006a). The same-order monitoring theory of consciousness In U. Kriegel & K. Williford (Eds.), *Consciousness and self-reference*. Cambridge, MA: MIT Press.

Kriegel, U. (2006b). The concept of consciousness in the cognitive sciences: Phenomenal consciousness, access consciousness, and scientific practice. In P. Thagard (Ed.), *Handbook of the philosophy of psychology and cognitive science*. Amsterdam: North-Holland.

Kriegel, U., & Williford, K. (eds.). (2006). *Self-representational approaches to consciousness*. Cambridge, MA: MIT Press.

Kripke, S. (1980). The identity thesis. Reprinted in N. J. Block, O. Flanagan, & G. Guzeldere (Eds.), (1997). *The nature of consciousness: Philosophical debates*. Cambridge, MA: MIT Press.

Lehrer, K. (1996). Skepticism, lucid content, and the metamental loop. In A. Clark, J. Ezquerro, & J. M. Larrazabal (Eds.), *Philosophy and cognitive science*. Dordrecht: Kluwer.

Lehrer, K. (1997). *Self-trust: A study of reason, knowledge, and autonomy*. Oxford: Oxford University Press.

Levine, J. (1983). Materialism and qualia: The explanatory gap. *Pacific Philosophical Quarterly*, 64, 354–361.

Levine, J. (2001). *Purple haze: The puzzle of consciousness*. Oxford: Oxford University Press.

Lewis, D. K. (1990). What experience teaches. In W. G. Lycan (Ed.), *Mind and cognition*. Oxford: Blackwell.

Lewis, D. K. (1993). Causal explanation. In D.-H. Ruben (Ed.), *Explanation*. Oxford: Oxford University Press.

Libet, B. (1985). Unconscious cerebral initiative and the role of conscious will in voluntary action. *Behavioral and Brain Sciences*, 8, 529–566.

Loar, B. (1990). Phenomenal states. *Philosophical Perspectives*, 4, 81–108.

Lurz, R. (1999). Animal consciousness. *Journal of Philosophical Research*, 24, 149–168.

Lurz, R. (2003). Neither HOT nor COLD: An alternative account of consciousness. *Psyche*, 9.

Lycan, W. G. (1987). *Consciousness*. Cambridge, MA: MIT Press.

Lycan, W. (1996). *Consciousness and experience*. Cambridge, MA: MIT Press.

Lycan, W. G. (2001). A simple argument for a higher-order representation theory of consciousness. *Analysis*, 61, 3–4.

McGinn, C. (1989). Can we solve the mind-body problem? *Mind*, 98, 349–366.

McGinn, C. (1995). Consciousness and space. *Journal of Consciousness Studies*, 2, 220–30.

McGinn, C. (1999). *The mysterious flame*. Cambridge, MA: MIT Press.

McGinn, C. (2004). *Consciousness and its objects*. Oxford: Oxford University Press.

Mackie, J. L. (1977). *Ethics: Inventing right and wrong*. New York: Penguin.

Maloney, J. C. (1989). *The mundane matter of the mental language*.New York: Cambridge University Press.

Mellor, D. H. (1978). Conscious belief. *Proceedings of the Aristotelian Society*, 78, 87–101.

Moore, G. E. (1903). The refutation of idealism. In G. E. Moore (Ed.), *Philosophical papers*. London: Routledge and Kegan Paul.

Nagel, T. (1974). What is it like to be a bat? *Philosophical Review*, 83, 435–450.

Natsoulas, T. (1993). What is wrong with appendage theory of consciousness? *Philosophical Psychology*, 6, 137–154.

Neander, K. (1998). The division of phenomenal labor: A problem for representational theories of consciousness. *Philosophical Perspectives*, 12, 411–434.

Nemirow, L. (1990). Physicalism and the cognitive role of acquaintance. In W. G. Lycan (Ed.), *Mind and cognition*. Oxford: Blackwell.

Peacocke, C. (1983). *Sense and content*. Oxford: Clarendon.

Putnam, H. (1967). The nature of mental states. In D. M. Rosenthal (Ed.), *The nature of mind*. Oxford: Oxford University Press.

Putnam, H. (1975). The meaning of 'meaning.' In H. Putnam (Ed.), *Mind, language, and reality*, New York: Cambridge University Press.

Rey, G. (1988). A question about consciousness. In H. Otto & J. Tueidio (Eds.), *Perspectives on mind*. Norwell: Kluwer Academic Publishers.

Rey, G. (1998). A narrow representationalist account of qualitative experience. *Philosophical Perspectives*, 12, 435–457.

Rosenthal, D. M. (1986). Two concepts of consciousness. *Philosophical Studies*, 94, 329–359.

Rosenthal, D. M. (1990). A theory of consciousness. ZiF Technical Report 40, Bielfield, Germany.

Rosenthal, D. M. (1993). Thinking that one thinks. In M. Davies & G. W. Humphreys (Eds.), *Consciousness: Psychological and philosophical essays*. Oxford: Blackwell.

Rosenthal, D. M. (2000). Consciousness and metacognition. In D. Sperber (Ed.), *Metarepresentation*. Oxford: Oxford University Press.

Rosenthal, D. M. (2002a). Explaining consciousness. In D. J. Chalmers (Ed.), *Philosophy of mind*. Oxford: Oxford University Press.

Rosenthal, D. M. (2002b). Consciousness and higher-order thoughts. In L. Nadel (Ed.),

Macmillan encyclopedia of cognitive science. New York: Macmillan.

Seager, W. (1999). *Theories of consciousness*. London: Routledge.

Searle, J. R. (1983). *Intentionality: An essay in the philosophy of mind*. New York: Cambridge University Press.

Searle, J. R. (1992). *The rediscovery of mind*. Cambridge, MA: MIT Press.

Segal, G. (2000). *A slim book on narrow content*. Cambridge, MA: MIT Press.

Shoemaker, S. (1994a). Phenomenal character. *Nous*, 28, 21–38.

Shoemaker, S. (1994b). Self-knowledge and 'inner sense.' Lecture III: The phenomenal character of experience. *Philosophy and Phenomenological Research*, 54, 291–314.

Shoemaker, S. (1996). Colors, subjective reactions, and qualia. *Philosophical Issues*, 7, 55–66.

Shoemaker, S. (2002). Introspection and phenomenal character. In D. J. Chalmers (Ed.), *Philosophy of mind*. Oxford: Oxford University Press.

Siewert, C. P. (1998). *The significance of consciousness*. Princeton, NJ: Princeton University Press.

Smart, J. J. C. (1959). Sensations and brain processes. *Philosophical Review*, 68, 141–156.

Smith, D. W. (1986). The structure of (self-) consciousness. *Topoi*, 5, 149–156.

Smith, D. W. (1989). *The circle of acquaintance*. Dordrecht: Kluwer Academic Publishers.

Smith, D. W. (2004). Return to consciousness. In D. W. Smith (Ed.), *Mind world*. New York: Cambridge University Press.

Thau, M. (2002). *Consciousness and cognition*. Oxford: Oxford University Press.

Thomasson, A. L. (2000). After Brentano: A one-level theory of consciousness. *European Journal of Philosophy*, 8, 190–209.

Tye, M. (1986). The subjective qualities of experience. *Mind*, 95, 1–17.

Tye, M. (1992). Visual qualia and visual content. In T. Crane (ed.), *The contents of experience*. New York: Cambridge University Press.

Tye, M. (1995). *Ten problems of consciousness*. Cambridge, MA: MIT Press.

Tye, M. (2000). *Consciousness, color, and content*. Cambridge, MA: MIT Press.

Tye, M. (2002). Visual qualia and visual content revisited. In D. J. Chalmers (Ed.), *Philosophy of mind*. Oxford: Oxford University Press.

Van Gulick, R. (1993). Understanding the phenomenal mind: Are we all just armadillos? Reprinted in N. J. Block, O. Flanagan, & G. Guzeldere (Eds.), (1997). *The nature of consciousness: Philosophical debates.* Cambridge, MA: MIT Press.

Van Gulick, R. (2001). Inward and upward – reflection, introspection needed and self-awareness. *Philosophical Topics*, 28, 275–305.

Van Gulick, R. (2006). Mirror mirror – is that all? In U. Kriegel & K. Williford (Eds.), *Consciousness and self-reference.* Cambridge, MA: MIT Press.

Velmans, M. (1992). Is human information processing conscious? *Behavioral and Brain Sciences*, 14, 651–669.

Wegner, D. M. (2002). *The illusion of conscious will.* Cambridge, MA: MIT Press.

Williford, K. W. (2006). The self-representational structure of consciousness. In U. Kriegel & K. Williford (Eds.), *Consciousness and self-reference.* Cambridge, MA: MIT Press.

Zahavi, D. (1998). Brentano and Husserl on self-awareness. *Études Phénomènologiques*, 27(8), 127–169.

Zahavi, D. (1999). *Self-awareness and alterity.* Evanston, IL: Northwestern University Press.

Zahavi, D. (2004). Back to Brentano? *Journal of Consciousness Studies*, 11, 66–87.

Zahavi, D., & Parnas, J. (1998). Phenomenal consciousness and self-awareness: A phenomenological critique of representational theory. *Journal of Consciousness Studies*, 5, 687–705.

CHAPTER 4

Philosophical Issues: Phenomenology

*Evan Thompson and Dan Zahavi**

Abstract

Current scientific research on consciousness aims to understand how consciousness arises from the workings of the brain and body, as well as the relations between conscious experience and cognitive processing. Clearly, to make progress in these areas, researchers cannot avoid a range of conceptual issues about the nature and structure of consciousness, such as the following: What is the relation between intentionality and consciousness? What is the relation between self-awareness and consciousness? What is the temporal structure of conscious experience? What is it like to imagine or visualize something, and how is this type of experience different from perception? How is bodily experience related to self-consciousness? Such issues have been addressed in detail in the philosophical tradition of phenomenology, inaugurated by Edmund Husserl (1859–1938)

and developed by numerous other philosophers throughout the 20th century. This chapter provides an introduction to this tradition and its way of approaching issues about consciousness. We first discuss some features of phenomenological methodology and then present some of the most important, influential, and enduring phenomenological proposals about various aspects of consciousness. These aspects include intentionality, self-awareness and the first-person perspective, time-consciousness, embodiment, and intersubjectivity. We also highlight a few ways of linking phenomenology and cognitive science in order to suggest some directions that consciousness research could take in the years ahead.

Introduction

Contemporary Continental perspectives on consciousness derive either whole or in part from phenomenology, the philosophical tradition inaugurated by Edmund Husserl (1859–1938). This tradition stands as one of the dominant philosophical movements

* Order of authors was set alphabetically, and each author did equal work.

of the last century and includes major 20th-century European philosophers, notably Martin Heidegger, Jean-Paul Sartre, and Maurice Merleau-Ponty, as well as important North American and Asian exponents (Moran, 2000). Considering that virtually all of the leading figures in 20th-century German and French philosophy, including Adorno, Gadamer, Habermas, Derrida, and Foucault, have been influenced by phenomenology, and that phenomenology is both a decisive precondition and a constant interlocutor for a whole range of subsequent theories and approaches, including existentialism, hermeneutics, structuralism, deconstruction, and post-structuralism, phenomenology can be regarded as the cornerstone of what is often (but somewhat misleadingly) called Continental philosophy.

The phenomenological tradition, like any other philosophical tradition, spans many different positions and perspectives. This point also holds true for its treatments and analyses of consciousness. Like analytic philosophy, phenomenology offers not one but many accounts of consciousness. The following discussion, therefore, is by necessity selective. Husserl's analyses are the main reference point, and the discussion focuses on what we believe to be some of the most important, influential, and enduring proposals about consciousness to have emerged from these analyses and their subsequent development in the phenomenological tradition.[1]

Furthermore, in recent years a new current of phenomenological philosophy has emerged in Europe and North America, one that goes back to the source of phenomenology in Husserl's thought, but addresses issues of concern to contemporary analytic philosophy of mind, philosophy of psychology, and cognitive science (see Petitot, Varela, Pachoud, & Roy, 1999, and the new journal *Phenomenology and the Cognitive Sciences*). This important current of phenomenological research also informs our discussion.[2] Accordingly, after introducing some features of the phenomenological method of investigation, we focus on the fol-

lowing topics relevant to cognitive science and the philosophy of mind: intentionality, self-awareness and the first-person perspective, time-consciousness, embodiment, and intersubjectivity.

Method

Phenomenology grows out of the recognition that we can adopt, in our own first-person case, different mental attitudes or stances toward the world, life, and experience. In everyday life we are usually straightforwardly immersed in various situations and projects, whether as specialists in one or another form of scientific, technical, or practical knowledge or as colleagues, friends, and members of families and communities. In addition to being directed toward more-or-less particular, 'thematic' matters, we are also overall directed toward the world as the unthematic horizon of all our activities (Husserl, 1970, p. 281). Husserl calls this attitude of being straightforwardly immersed in the world 'the natural attitude', and he thinks it is characterized by a kind of unreflective 'positing' of the world as something existing 'out there' more or less independently of us.

The 'phenomenological attitude', on the other hand, arises when we step back from the natural attitude, not to deny it, but to investigate the very experiences it comprises. If such an investigation is to be genuinely philosophical, then it must strive to be critical and not dogmatic, and therefore cannot take the naïve realism of the natural attitude for granted. Yet to deny this realistic attitude would be equally dogmatic. The realistic 'positing' of the natural attitude must rather be suspended, neutralized, or put to one side, so that it plays no role in the investigation. In this way, we can focus on the experiences that sustain and animate the natural attitude, but in an open and non-dogmatic manner. We can investigate experience in the natural attitude without being prejudiced by the natural attitude's own unexamined view of things. This investigation should be critical and not dogmatic, shunning metaphysical and scientific prejudices. It should be guided by what is actually given to experience, rather than by what we expect to find given our theoretical commitments.

Yet how exactly is such an investigation to proceed? What exactly are we supposed to investigate? Husserl's answer is deceptively simple: Our investigation should turn its attention toward the *givenness* or *appearance* of reality; that is, it should focus on the way in which reality is given to us in experience. We are to attend to the world strictly as it appears, the world as it is phenomenally manifest. Put another way, we should attend to the modes or ways in which things appear to us. We thereby attend to things strictly as correlates of our experience, and the focus of our investigation becomes the correlational structure of our subjectivity and the appearance or disclosure of the world.[3]

The philosophical procedure by which this correlational structure is investigated is known as the *phenomenological reduction*. 'Reduction' in this context does not mean replacing or eliminating one theory or model in favour of another taken to be more fundamental. It signifies rather a 'leading back' (*reducere*) or redirection of thought away from its unreflective and unexamined immersion in experience of the world to the way in which the world manifests itself to us. To redirect our interest in this way does not mean we doubt the things before us or somehow try to turn away from the world to look elsewhere. Things remain before us, but we envisage them in a new way; namely, strictly as they appear to us. Thus, everyday things available to our perception are not doubted or considered as illusions when they are 'phenomenologically reduced', but instead are envisaged and examined simply and precisely *as perceived* (and similarly for remembered things as remembered, imagined things as imagined, and so on). In other words, once we adopt the phenomenological attitude, we are interested not in *what* things are in themselves, in some naïve, mind-independent, or theory-independent sense, but rather in exactly *how* they appear,

and thus as strict relational correlates of our experience.

The phenomenological reduction, in its full sense, is a rich mode of analysis comprising many steps. Two main ones are crucial. The first leads back from the natural attitude to the phenomenological attitude by neutralizing the realistic positing of the natural attitude and then orienting attention toward the disclosure or appearance of reality to us. The second leads from this phenomenological attitude to a more radical kind of philosophical attitude. Put another way, this step leads from phenomenology as an empirical, psychological attitude (phenomenological psychology) to phenomenology as a 'transcendental' philosophical attitude (transcendental phenomenology).

'Transcendental' is used here in its Kantian sense to mean an investigation concerned with the *modes or ways in which objects are experienced and known*, as well as the a priori conditions for the possibility of such experience and knowledge. Husserl casts these two aspects of transcendental inquiry in a specific form, which is clearly related to but nonetheless different from Kant's (see Steinbock, 1995, pp. 12–15). Two points are important here. First, transcendental phenomenology focuses not on *what things are*, but on the *ways in which things are given*. For Husserl, this means focusing on phenomena (appearances) and the senses or meanings they have for us and asking how these meaningful phenomena are 'constituted'. 'Constitution' does not mean fabrication or creation; the mind does not fabricate the world. To constitute, in the technical phenomenological sense, means to bring to awareness, to present, or to disclose. The mind brings things to awareness; it discloses and presents the world. Stated in a classical phenomenological way, the idea is that objects are disclosed or made available to experience in the ways they are thanks to how consciousness is structured. Things show up, as it were, having the features they do, because of how they are disclosed and brought to awareness, given the structure of consciousness.

Such constitution is not apparent to us in everyday life, but requires systematic analysis to discern. Consider, for example, our experience of time. Our sense of the present moment as both simultaneously opening into the immediate future and slipping away into the immediate past depends on the formal structure of our consciousness of time. The present moment manifests as having temporal breadth, as a zone or span of actuality, instead of as an instantaneous flash, because of the way our consciousness is structured. Second, to address this constitutional problem of how meaningful phenomena are brought to awareness or disclosed, transcendental phenomenology tries to uncover the invariant formal principles by which experience necessarily operates in order to be constitutive. A fundamental example of this type of principle is the 'retentional-protentional' structure of time-consciousness, which we discuss in the later section, Temporality and Inner Time-Consciousness.

The purpose of the phenomenological reduction, therefore, contrary to many misunderstandings, is neither to exclude the world from consideration nor to commit one to some form of methodological solipsism. Rather, its purpose is to enable one to explore and describe the spatiotemporal world as it is given. For Husserl, the phenomenological reduction is meant as a way of maintaining this radical difference between philosophical reflection on phenomenality and other modes of thought.

Henceforth, we are no longer to consider the worldly object naïvely; rather, we are to focus on it precisely as a correlate of experience. If we restrict ourselves to that which shows itself (whether in straightforward perception or a scientific experiment), and if we focus specifically on that which tends to be ignored in daily life (because it is so familiar) – namely, on phenomenal manifestation as such, the sheer appearances of things – then we cannot avoid being led back (*re-ducere*) to subjectivity. Insofar as we are confronted with the appearance of an object – that is, with an object as presented,

perceived, judged, or evaluated – we are led back to the intentional structures to which these modes of appearance are correlated. We are led to the intentional acts of presentation, perception, judgement, and evaluation and thereby to the subject (or subjects), in relation to whom the object as appearing must necessarily be understood.

Through the phenomenological attitude we thus become aware of the givenness of the object. Yet the aim is not simply to focus on the object exactly as it is given, but also on the subjective side of consciousness. We thereby become aware of our subjective accomplishments, specifically the kinds of intentionality that must be in play for anything to appear as it does. When we investigate appearing objects in this way, we also disclose ourselves as 'datives of manifestation' (Sokolowski, 2000), as those to whom objects appear.

As a procedure of working back, as it were, from the objects of experience, as given to perception, memory, imagination, and so on, to the acts whereby one is aware of these objects – acts of perceiving, remembering, imagining, and so on – the phenomenological reduction has to be performed in the first person. As with any such procedure, it is one thing to describe its general theoretical character and another to describe it pragmatically, the concrete steps by which it is carried out. The main methodical step crucial for the phenomenological reduction Husserl calls the *epoché*. This term comes originally from Greek skepticism, where it means to refrain from judgement, but Husserl adopted it as a term for the 'suspension', 'neutralization', or 'bracketing' of both our natural 'positing' attitude (see above) and our theoretical beliefs or assertions (scientific or philosophical) about 'objective reality'. From a more concrete and situated first-person perspective, however, the epoché can be seen as a practiced mental gesture of shifting one's attention to how the object appears and thus to one's experiencing of the object: "Literally, the epoché corresponds to a gesture of suspension with regard to the habitual course of one's thoughts, brought about by an

interruption of their continuous flowing...
As soon as a mental activity, a thought
anchored to the perceived object alone,
turns me away from the observation of the
perceptual act to re-engage me in the perception of the object, I bracket it" (Depraz,
1999, pp. 97–98). The aim of this bracketing
is to return one's attention to the act of experiencing correlated to the object, thereby
sustaining the phenomenological reduction:
"in order that the reduction should always be
a living act whose freshness is a function of its
incessant renewal in me, and never a simple
and sedimented habitual state, the reflective
conversion [of attention] has to be operative
at every instant and at the same time permanently sustained by the radical and vig-
ilant gesture of the *epoché*" (Depraz, 1999,
p. 100).

One can discern a certain ambivalence
in the phenomenological tradition regarding the theoretical and practical or existential dimensions of the epoché. On the
one hand, Husserl's great concern was to
establish phenomenology as a new philosophical foundation for science, and so the
epoché in his hands served largely as a
critical tool of theoretical reason.[4] On the
other hand, because Husserl's theoretical
project was based on a radical reappraisal
of experience as the source of meaning
and knowledge, it necessitated a constant
return to the patient, analytic description of
lived experience through the phenomenological reduction. This impulse generated
a huge corpus of careful phenomenological analyses of numerous different dimensions and aspects of human experience –
the perceptual experience of space (Husserl,
1997), kinesthesis and the experience of
one's own body (Husserl, 1989, 1997),
time-consciousness (Husserl, 1991), affect
(Husserl, 2001), judgement (Husserl, 1975),
imagination and memory (Husserl, 2006),
and intersubjectivity (Husserl, 1973), to
name just a few. Nevertheless, the epoché
as a practical procedure – as a situated practice carried out in the first person by the
phenomenologist – has remained strangely
neglected in the phenomenological literature, even by so-called existential phenome-

nologists such as Heidegger and Merleau-
Ponty, who took up and then recast in
their own ways the method of the phenomenological reduction (see Heidegger,
1982; Merleau-Ponty, 1962).

For this reason, one new current in phenomenology aims to develop more explicitly the pragmatics of the epoché as a
'first-person method' for investigating consciousness (Depraz, 1999; Depraz, Varela,
& Vermersch, 2003; Varela & Shear 1999).
This pragmatic approach has also compared the epoché to first-person methods in other domains, such as contemplative practice (Depraz et al., 2003),
and has explored the relevance of first-
person methods for producing more refined
first-person reports in experimental psychology and cognitive neuroscience (Lutz &
Thompson, 2003; Varela, 1996). This latter endeavour is central to the research
programme known as 'neurophenomenology', introduced by Francisco Varela (1996,
1999) and developed by other researchers
(Lloyd, 2002, 2003; Lutz & Thompson,
2003; Rainville, 2005; Thompson, in press;
Thompson, Lutz, & Cosmelli, 2005; see also
Chapters 19 and 26).

Intentionality

Implicit in the foregoing treatment of phenomenological method is the phenomenological concept of *intentionality*. According
to Husserlian phenomenology, consciousness is intentional, in the sense that it 'aims
toward' or 'intends' something beyond itself.
This sense of intentional should not be confused with the more familiar sense of having a purpose in mind when one acts, which
is only one kind of intentionality in the
phenomenological sense. Rather, intentionality is a generic term for the pointing-
beyond-itself proper to consciousness (from
the Latin *intendere*, which once referred to
drawing a bow and aiming at a target).

Phenomenologists distinguish different
types of intentionality. In a narrow sense,
intentionality is defined as object-directedness. In a broader sense, which covers

what Husserl (2001, p. 206) and Merleau-Ponty (1962, p. xviii) called 'operative intentionality' (see below), intentionality is defined as openness toward otherness (or alterity). In both cases, the emphasis is on denying that consciousness is self-enclosed.

Object-directedness characterizes almost all of our experiences, in the sense that in having them we are exactly conscious *of* something. We do not merely love, fear, see, or judge; we love, fear, see, or judge *something*. Regardless of whether we consider a perception, a thought, a judgement, a fantasy, a doubt, an expectation, a recollection, and so on, these diverse forms of consciousness are all characterized by the intending of an object. In other words, they cannot be analyzed properly without a look at their objective correlates; that is, the perceived, the doubted, the expected, and so forth. The converse is also true: The intentional object cannot be analyzed properly without a look at its subjective correlate, the intentional act. Neither the intentional object nor the mental act that intends it can be understood apart from the other.

Phenomenologists call this act-object relation the 'correlational structure of intentionality'. 'Correlational' does not mean the constant conjunction of two terms that could be imagined to exist apart, but the necessary structural relation of mental act and intended object. Object-directed intentional experiences necessarily comprise these two inseparable poles. In Husserlian phenomenological language these two poles are known as the 'noema' (the object as experienced) and the 'noesis' (the mental act that intends the object).

There has been a huge amount of scholarly discussion about the proper way to interpret the Husserlian notion of the noema (see Drummond, 2003, for an overview). The discussion concerns the relation between the *object-as-intended* (the noema) and the *object-that-is-intended* (the object itself)– the wine bottle-as-perceived (as felt and seen) and the bottle itself. According to the representationalist interpretation, the noema is a type of representational entity, an ideal sense or meaning, that mediates the intentional relation between the mental act and the object. On this view, consciousness is directed toward the object by means of the noema and thus achieves its openness to the world only in virtue of the representational noema.

According to the rival non-representationalist interpretation, the noema is not any intermediate, representational entity; the noema is the object itself, but the object considered phenomenologically; that is, precisely as experienced. In other words, *the object-as-intended is the object-that-is-intended*, abstractly and phenomenologically considered; namely, in abstraction from the realistic positing of the natural attitude and strictly as experientially given. The noema is thus graspable only in a phenomenological or transcendental attitude. This view rejects the representationalism of the former view. Consciousness is intrinsically self-transcending and accordingly does not achieve reference to the world in virtue of intermediate ideal entities that bestow intentionality upon it. Experiences are intrinsically intentional (see Searle, 1983, for a comparable claim in the analytic tradition). Their being is constituted by being *of* something else. It would take us too far afield to review the twists and turns of this debate, so we simply state for the record that for a variety of reasons we think the representationalist interpretation of the noema is mistaken and the non-representationalist interpretation is correct (see Zahavi, 2003, 2004).

We have been considering object-directed intentionality, but many experiences are not object-directed – for example, feelings of pain and nausea, and moods, such as anxiety, depression, and boredom. Philosophers whose conception of intentionality is limited to object-directedness deny that such experiences are intentional (e.g., Searle, 1983). Phenomenologists, however, in distinguishing between intentionality as object-directedness and intentionality as openness, have a broader conception. It is true that pervasive moods, such as sadness, boredom, nostalgia, and anxiety, must be distinguished from intentional feelings, such as the desire for an apple or the admiration for a particular person. Nevertheless, moods are not without a reference to the world. They do not enclose us within ourselves, but are lived through as pervasive atmospheres that deeply influence the way the world is disclosed to us. Moods, such as curiosity, nervousness, or happiness, disclose our embeddedness in the world and articulate or modify our existential possibilities. As Heidegger argued, moods, rather than being merely attendant phenomena, are fundamental forms of disclosure: "Mood has always already disclosed being-in-the-world as a whole and first makes possible directing oneself toward something" (Heidegger, 1996, p. 129).

What about pain? Sartre's classic analysis in *Being and Nothingness* (1956) is illuminating in this case. Imagine that you are sitting late a night trying to finish reading a book. You have been reading most of the day and your eyes hurt. How does this pain originally manifest itself? According to Sartre, not initially as a thematic object of reflection, but by influencing the way in which you perceive the world. You might become restless and irritated and have difficulties in focusing and concentrating. The words on the page might tremble and quiver. The pain is not yet apprehended as an intentional object, but that does not mean that it is either cognitively absent or unconscious. It is not yet reflected-upon as a psychic object, but given rather as a vision-in-pain, as an affective atmosphere that influences your intentional interaction with the world.

Another important part of the phenomenological account of intentionality is the distinction among signitive (linguistic), pictorial, and perceptual intentionalities (Husserl, 2000). I can talk about a withering oak, I can see a detailed drawing of the oak, and I can perceive the oak myself. These different ways to intend an object are not unrelated. According to Husserl, there is a strict hierarchical relation among them, in the sense that they can be ranked according to their ability to give us the object as directly, originally, and optimally as possible.

The object can be given more or less directly; that is, it can be more or less present. One can also speak of different epistemic levels. The lowest and most empty way in which the object can appear is in the signitive acts. These (linguistic) acts certainly have a reference, but apart from that the object is not given in any fleshed-out manner. The pictorial acts have a certain intuitive content, but like the signitive acts, they intend the object indirectly. Whereas the signitive acts intend the object via a contingent representation (a linguistic sign), the pictorial acts intend the object via a representation (picture) that bears a certain similarity or projective relation to the object. It is only the perception that gives us the object directly. This is the only type of intention that presents the object in its bodily presence (*leibhaftig*).

Recollection and imagination are two other important forms of object-directed intentionality (empathy is a third: see the section, Intersubjectivity). These types are mediated; that is, they intend their objects by way of other, intermediate mental activities, rather than directly, as does perception. In recollection, I remember the withering oak (the object itself) by means of re-presenting (reproducing or re-enacting) a past perception of the oak. In imagination, I can either imagine the withering oak (the actual tree), or I can imagine a non-existent oak in the sense of freely fantasizing a different world. Either way, imagination involves re-presenting to myself a possible perceptual experience of the oak. Yet, in imagination, the assertoric or 'positing' character of this (re-presented) perceptual experience is said to be 'neutralized', for whereas an ordinary perceptual experience posits its object as actually there (regardless of whether the experience is veridical), imagination does not. In recollection, by contrast, this assertoric or positing feature of the experience is not neutralized, but remains in play, because the perception reproduced in the memory is represented as having actually occurred in the past. Husserl thus describes perception and recollection as positional (assertoric) acts, whereas imagination is non-positional (non-assertoric; see Husserl, 2006, and Bernet, Kern, & Marbach, 1993, for an overview).

We thus arrive at another crucial distinction, the distinction between intentional acts of *presentation* (*Gegenwärtigung*) and of *re-presentation* (*Vergegenwärtigung*). According to standard usage in the analytic philosophy of mind and cognitive science, the term 'representation' applies to any kind of mental state that has intentional content ('intentional content' and 'representational content' being used synonymously). In phenomenological parlance, on the other hand, 're-presentation' applies only to those types of mental acts that refer to their objects by way of intermediate mental activity, as in remembrance, imagination (imaging and fantasy), and pictorial consciousness (looking at a picture). Perception, by contrast, is not re-presentational, but presentational, because the object-as-experienced (the intentional object or objective correlate of the act) is 'bodily present' or there 'in flesh and blood' (regardless of whether the perceptual experience turns out to be veridical or not).

Perceptual intentionality can be further differentiated into, on the one hand, a thematic, explicit, or focal object-directed mode of consciousness and, on the other hand, a non-reflective tacit sensibility, which constitutes our primary openness to the world. This tacit sensibility, called 'operative [*fungierende*] intentionality', functions prereflectively, anonymously, and passively, without being engaged in any explicit cognitive acquisition. In this context it is important to distinguish between *activity* and *passivity*. One can be actively taking a position in acts of comparing, differentiating, judging, valuing, wishing, and so on. As Husserl (2001) points out, however, whenever one is active, one is also passive, because to be active is to react to something that has affected one. Every kind of active position-taking presupposes a prior and passive being affected.

Following Husserl one step further in his analysis, we can distinguish between *receptivity* and *affectivity*. Receptivity is taken to be the first, lowest, and most primitive type of intentional activity; it consists in responding to or paying attention to that which is affecting us passively. Even receptivity understood as a mere 'I notice' presupposes a prior 'affection' (meaning one's being *affectively influenced* or *perturbed*, not a feeling of fondness). Whatever becomes thematized (even as a mere noticing) must have been already affecting and stimulating one in an unheeded manner. Affectivity, however, is not a matter of being affected by an isolated, undifferentiated sense impression. If something is to affect us, impose itself on us, and arouse our attention, it must be sufficiently strong. It must be more conspicuous than its surroundings, and it must stand out in some way through contrast, heterogeneity, and difference. Thus, receptivity emerges from within a passively organized and structured field of affectivity.[5]

In summary, explicit, object-directed intentional experience arises against the background of a precognitive, operative intentionality, which involves a dynamic interplay of affectivity and receptivity and constitutes our most fundamental way of being open to the world.

Phenomenal Consciousness and Self-Awareness

In contemporary philosophy of mind the term 'phenomenal consciousness' refers to mental states that have a subjective and experiential character. In Nagel's words, for a mental state to be (phenomenally) conscious is for there to be something it is like for the subject to be in that state (Nagel, 1979). Various notions are employed to describe the properties characteristic of phenomenal consciousness – qualia, sensational properties, phenomenal properties, and the subjective character of experience – and there is considerable debate about the relation between these properties and other properties of mental states, such as their representational content or their being cognitively accessible to thought and verbal report ('access consciousness'). The examples used in these discussions are usually bodily sensations, such as pain, or perceptual experiences, such as the visual experience of colour. Much less frequently does one find discussion of the subjective character of emotion (feelings, affective valences, moods), to say nothing of memory, mental imagery, or thought.

According to Husserl, however, the phenomenal aspect of experience is not limited to sensory or even emotional states, but also characterizes conscious thought. In his *Logical Investigations*, Husserl (2000) argues that conscious thoughts have experiential qualities and that episodes of conscious thought are experiential episodes. Every intentional experience possesses two different, but inseparable 'moments' (i.e., dependent aspects or ingredients): (i) Every intentional experience is an experience of a specific type, be it an experience of judging, hoping, desiring, regretting, remembering, affirming, doubting, wondering, fearing, and so on. Husserl calls this aspect the *intentional quality* of the experience. (ii) Every intentional experience is also directed at or about something. He calls this aspect the *intentional matter* of the experience. Clearly, the same quality can be combined with different matters, and the same matter can be combined with different qualities. It is possible to doubt that 'the inflation will continue', doubt that 'the election was fair', or doubt that 'one's next book will be an international bestseller', precisely as it is possible to deny that 'the lily is white', to judge that 'the lily is white', or to question whether 'the lily is white'. Husserl's distinction between the intentional matter and the intentional quality thus bears a certain resemblance to the contemporary distinction between propositional content and propositional attitudes (though it is important to emphasize that Husserl by no means took all intentional experiences to be propositional in nature; see Husserl, 1975).

Nevertheless – and this is the central point – Husserl considered these cognitive differences to be also *experiential* differences. Each of the different intentional qualities has its own phenomenal character. There is an experiential difference between affirming and denying that Hegel was the greatest of the German idealists, as there is an experiential difference between expecting and doubting that Denmark will win the 2010 FIFA World Cup. What it is like to be in one type of intentional state is different from what it is like to be in another type of intentional state. Similarly, each of the different intentional matters has its own phenomenal character. To put it differently, a change in the intentional matter will entail a change in what it is like to undergo the experience in question. (This does not entail, however, that two experiences differing in what it is like to undergo them cannot intend the same object, nor that two experiences alike in this respect must necessarily intend the same object.) These experiential differences, Husserl argues, are not simply sensory differences.[6]

In summary, every phenomenally conscious state, be it a perception, an emotion, a recollection, an abstract belief, and so forth, has a certain subjective character, a certain phenomenal quality, corresponding to what it is like to live through or undergo that state. This is what makes the mental state in question phenomenally conscious.

This experiential quality of conscious mental states, however, calls for further elucidation. Let us take perceptual experience as our starting point. Whereas the *object* of my perceptual experience is intersubjectively (publicly) accessible, in the sense that it can in principle be given to others in the same way it is given to me, the case is different with *my perceptual experience itself*. Whereas you and I can both perceive one and the same cherry, each of us has his or her own distinct perception of it, and we cannot share these perceptions, precisely as we cannot share each other's pains. You might certainly realize that I am in pain and even empathize with me, but you cannot actually feel the pain the same way I do. This point can be formulated more precisely by saying that you have no access to the *first-personal givenness* of my experience. This first-personal quality of experience leads to the issue of self and self-awareness.

When one is directly and non-inferentially conscious of one's own occurrent thoughts, perceptions, feelings, or pains, they are characterized by a first-personal givenness that immediately reveals them as one's own. This first-personal givenness of experiential phenomena is not something incidental to their being, a mere varnish the experiences could lack without ceasing to be experiences. On the contrary, it is their first-personal givenness that makes the experiences *subjective*. To put it differently, their first-personal givenness entails a built-in self-reference, a primitive experiential self-referentiality. When I am aware of an occurrent pain, perception, or thought from the first-person perspective, the experience in question is given immediately and non-inferentially as *mine*. I do not *first* scrutinize a specific perception or feeling of pain and *then* identify it as mine.

Accordingly, self-awareness cannot be equated with reflective (explicit, thematic, introspective) self-awareness, as claimed by some philosophers and cognitive scientists. On the contrary, reflective self-awareness presupposes a prereflective (implicit, tacit) self-awareness. Self-awareness is not something that comes about only at the moment I realize that I am (say) perceiving the Empire State Building, or realize that I am the bearer of private mental states, or refer to myself using the first-person pronoun. Rather, it is legitimate to speak of a primitive but basic type of self-awareness whenever I am acquainted with an experience from a first-person perspective. If the experience in question, be it a feeling of joy, a burning thirst, or a perception of a sunset, is given in a first-personal mode of presentation to me, it is (at least tacitly) given as *my* experience and can therefore count as a case of self-awareness. To be aware of one*self* is consequently not to apprehend a pure self *apart* from the experience, but to be acquainted with an experience in its first-personal mode of presentation; that is, from 'within'. Thus, the subject or self referred to is not something standing opposed to, apart from, or beyond experience, but is rather *a feature or function of its givenness*. Or to phrase it differently, it is this first-personal givenness of the experience that constitutes the most basic form of selfhood (Zahavi, 1999, 2005).

In summary, any (object-directed) conscious experience, in addition to being of or about its intentional object is prereflectively manifest to itself. To use another formulation, transitive phenomenal consciousness (consciousness-of) is also intransitive self-consciousness (see Chapter 3). Intransitive self-consciousness is a primitive form of self-consciousness in the sense that (i) it does not require any subsequent act of reflection or introspection, but occurs simultaneously with awareness of the object; (ii) does not consist in forming a belief or making a judgement; and (iii) is passive in the sense of being spontaneous and involuntary. According to some phenomenologists (e.g., Merleau-Ponty, 1962), this tacit self-awareness involves a form of non-objective bodily self-awareness, an awareness of one's lived body (*Leib*) or embodied subjectivity, correlative to experience of the object (see the section, Embodiment and Perception). The roots of such prereflective bodily self-awareness sink to the passive and anonymous level of the interplay between receptivity and affectivity constitutive of 'operative intentionality' (see the section, Intentionality).

Phenomenology thus corroborates certain proposals about consciousness coming from neuroscience. Such theorists as Panksepp (1998a, b) and Damasio (1999) have argued that neuroscience needs to explain both how the brain enables us to experience the world outside us and how it "also creates a sense of self in the act of knowing ... how each of us has a sense of 'me'" (Parvizi & Damasio, 2001, pp. 136–137). In phenomenological terms, this second issue concerns the primitive sense of 'I-ness' belonging to consciousness, known as 'ipseity' (see also Chapter 19). As a number of cognitive scientists have emphasized, this core of self-awareness in consciousness is fundamentally linked to bodily processes of life-regulation, emotion, and affect, such that cognition and intentional action are emotive (Damasio, 1999; Freeman, 2000; Panksepp 1998a,b). A promising line of collaboration between phenomenology and affective-cognitive neuroscience could therefore centre on the lived body as a way of deepening our understanding of subjectivity and consciousness (Thompson, 2007).

Temporality and Inner Time-Consciousness

Why must an investigation of consciousness inevitably confront the issue of time? There are many reasons, of course, but in this section we focus on two main ones. First, experiences do not occur in isolation. The stream of consciousness comprises an ensemble of experiences that are unified both at any given time (synchronically) and over time (diachronically); therefore, we need to account for this temporal unity and continuity. In addition, we are able not only to recollect earlier experiences and recognize them as our own but also to perceive enduring (i.e., temporally extended) objects and events; hence, we need to account for how consciousness must be structured for there to be such experiences of coherence and identity over time. Second, our present cognitive activities are shaped and influenced conjointly by both our past experiences and our future plans and expectations. Thus, if we are to do justice to the dynamic character of cognition, we cannot ignore the role of time.

In a phenomenological context, the term 'temporality' does not refer to objective, cosmic time, measured by an atomic clock, or to a merely subjective sense of the passage of time, although it is intimately related to the latter. Temporality, or 'inner time-consciousness', refers to the most fundamental, formal structure of the stream of consciousness (Husserl, 1991).

To introduce this idea, we can consider what phenomenologists call 'syntheses of identity' in the flow of experience. If I move around a tree to gain a fuller appreciation of it, then the tree's different profiles – its front, sides, and back – do not appear as disjointed fragments, but as integrated features belonging to one and the same tree. The synthesis that is a precondition for this

integration is temporal in nature. Thus, time-consciousness must be regarded as a formal condition of possibility for the perception of any object. Yet, how must this experiential process be structured for identity or unity over time to be possible?

Phenomenological analyses point to the 'width' or 'depth' of the 'living present' of consciousness: Our experience of temporal enduring objects and events, as well as our experience of change and succession, would be impossible were we conscious only of that which is given in a punctual now and were our stream of consciousness composed of a series of isolated now-points, like a string of pearls. According to Husserl (1991), the basic unit of temporality is not a 'knife-edge' present, but a 'duration-block' (to borrow William James's words; see James, 1981, p. 574) i.e., a temporal field that comprises all three temporal modes of present, past, and future. Just as there is no spatial object without a background, there is no experience without a temporal horizon. We cannot experience anything except on the background of what it succeeds and what we anticipate will succeed it. We can no more conceive of an experience empty of future than one empty of past.

Three technical terms describe this temporal form of consciousness. There is (i) a 'primal impression' narrowly directed toward the now-phase of the object. The primal impression never appears in isolation and is an abstract component that by itself cannot provide us with a perception of a temporal object. The primal impression is accompanied by (ii) a 'retention', which provides us with a consciousness of the just-elapsed phase of the object, and by (iii) a 'protention', which in a more-or-less indefinite way intends the phase of the object about to occur. The role of the protention is evident in our implicit and unreflective anticipation of what is about to happen as experience progresses. That such anticipation belongs to experience is illustrated by the fact that we would be surprised if (say) the wax figure suddenly moved or if the door we opened hid a stone wall. It makes sense to speak of surprise only in light of anticipation, and because we can always be surprised, we always have a horizon of anticipation. The concrete and full structure of all lived experience is thus *primal impression-retention-protention*. Although the specific experiential contents of this structure from moment to moment progressively change, at any given moment this threefold structure is present (synchronically) as a unified whole. This analysis provides an account of the notion of the specious present that improves on that found in William James, C. D. Broad, and others (see Gallagher, 1998).

It is important to distinguish retention and protention, which are structural features of any conscious act, from recollection and expectation, understood as specific types of mental acts. There is a clear difference between, on the one hand, retaining notes that have just sounded and protending notes about to sound while listening to a melody, and, on the other hand, remembering a past holiday or looking forward to the next vacation. Whereas recollection and expectation presuppose the work of retention and protention, protention and retention are intrinsic components of any occurrent experience one might have. Unlike recollection and expectation, they are passive (involuntary) and automatic processes that take place without our active or deliberate contribution. Finally, they are invariant structural features that make possible the temporal flow of consciousness as we know and experience it. In other words, they are a priori conditions of possibility of there being 'syntheses of identity' in experience at all.

Husserl's analysis of the structure of inner time-consciousness serves a double purpose. It is meant to explain not only how we can be aware of objects with temporal extension but also how we can be aware of our own stream of experiences. To put it differently, Husserl's investigation is meant to explain not only how we can be aware of temporally extended units but also how consciousness unifies itself across time.

Like bodily self-awareness, temporality and time-consciousness are rich in potential for collaborative study by phenomenology and cognitive science. Work by Francisco Varela (1999) in particular has shown that phenomenological analyses of time-consciousness can be profitably linked to neurodynamical accounts of the brain processes associated with the temporal flow of conscious experience (see also Chapter 26 and Thompson, 2007). This linkage between phenomenology and neurodynamics is central to the research programme of neurophenomenology, mentioned above.

Embodiment and Perception

Conscious experience involves one's body. Yet what exactly is the relationship between the two? It is obvious that we can perceive our own body by (say) visually inspecting our hands. It is less obvious that our bodily being constitutes our subjectivity and the correlative modes or ways in which objects are given to us.

The phenomenological approach to the role of the body in its constitution of subjective life is closely linked to the analysis of perception. Two basic points about perception are important here: (i) the intentional objects of perceptual experience are public spatiotemporal objects (not private mental images or sense-data); and (ii) such objects are always given only partially to perception and can never present themselves in their totality. On the one hand, perception purports to give us experience of public things, not private mental images. On the other hand, whatever we perceive is always perceived in certain ways and from a certain perspective. We see things, for instance, as having various spatial forms and visible qualities (lightness, colour, etc.), and we are able to distinguish between constancy and variation in appearance (the grass looks uniformly green, but the shaded part looks dark, whereas the part in direct sunlight looks light). We see only one profile of a thing at any given moment, yet we do not see things as mere façades, for we are aware of the presence of the other sides we do not see directly. We do not perceive things in isolation; we see them in contexts or situations, in which they relate to and depend on each other and on dimensions of the environment in multifarious ways.

These invariant characteristics of perception presuppose what phenomenologists call the *lived body* (*Leib*). Things are perceptually situated in virtue of the orientation they have to our perceiving and moving bodies. To listen to a string quartet by Schubert is to enjoy it from a certain perspective and standpoint, be it from the street, in the gallery, or in the first row. If something appears perspectivally, then the subject to whom it appears must be spatially related to it. To be spatially related to something requires that one be embodied. To say that we perceive only one profile of something while being aware of other possible profiles means that any profile we perceive points beyond itself to further possible profiles. Yet this reference of a given profile beyond itself is equally a reference to our ability to exchange this profile for another through our own free movement (tilting our head, manipulating an object in our hands, walking around something, etc.). Co-given with any profile and through any sequence of profiles is one's lived body as the 'zero point' or absolute indexical 'here', in relation to which any appearing object is oriented. One's lived body is not co-given as an intentional object, however, but as an implicit and practical 'I can' of movement and perception. We thus rejoin the point made earlier (in the section, Phenomenality and Self-Awareness) that any object-directed (transitive) intentional experience involves a non-object-directed (intransitive) self-awareness, here an intransitive bodily self-awareness. In short, every object-experience carries with it a tacit form of self-experience.

The role of bodily self-experience in perception can be phenomenologically described in much greater detail. One important topic is the role it plays in the constitution (i.e., the bringing to awareness or disclosure) of both objects and space for perception. Perspectival appearances of the object bear a certain relation to kinaesthetic situations of the body. When I watch a bird in flight, the bird is given in conjunction with a sensing of my eye and head movements; when I touch the computer keys, the keys are given in conjunction with a sensing of my finger movements. Husserl's 1907 lectures on *Thing and Space* (Husserl, 1997) discuss how this relation between perception and kinaesthesis (including proprioception) is important for the constitution of objects and space. To perceive an object from a certain perspective is to be aware (tacitly or prereflectively) that there are other coexisting but absent profiles of the object. These absent profiles stand in certain sensorimotor relations to the present profile: They can be made present if one carries out certain movements. In other words, the profiles are correlated with kinaesthetic systems of possible bodily movements and positions. If one moves this way, then that aspect of the object becomes visible; if one moves that way, then this aspect becomes visible.

In Husserl's terminology, every perspectival appearance is kinaesthetically motivated. In the simple case of a motionless object, for instance, if the kinaesthetic experience (K_1) remains constant, then the perceptual appearance (A_1) remains constant. If the kinaesthetic experience changes (K_1 becomes K_2), then the perceptual appearance changes in correlation with it (A_1 becomes A_2). There is thus an interdependency between kinaesthetic experiences and perceptual appearances: A given appearance (A_1) is not always correlated with the same kinaesthetic experience (e.g., K_1), but it must be correlated with some kinaesthetic experience or other. Turning now to the case of perceptual space, Husserl argues that different kinaesthetic systems of the body imply different perceptual achievements with regard to the constitution of space. One needs to distinguish among the oculomotor systems of one eye alone and of two eyes together, the cephalomotor system of head movements, and the system of the whole body as it moves towards, away from, and around things. These kinaesthetic systems are hierarchically ordered in relation to the visual field: The cephalomotor visual field contains a continuous multiplicity of oculomotor fields; the egocentric field of the body as a whole contains a continuous multiplicity of cephalomotor fields. This hierarchy also reflects a progressive disclosure of visual space: The eyes alone give only a two-dimensional continuum; head movements expand the field into a spherical plane at a fixed distance (like a planetarium); and movement of the body as a whole introduces distance, depth, and three-dimensional structure. It is the linkage between the kinaesthetic system of whole-body movements (approaching, retreating, and circling) and the corresponding perceptual manifold of profiles or perspectival appearances that fully discloses the three-dimensional space of visual perception.

Insofar as the body functions as the zero-point for perception and action (i.e., considered in its function as a bodily first-person perspective), the body recedes from experience in favour of the world. My body supplies me with my perspective on the world, and thus is first and foremost not an object on which I have a perspective. In other words, bodily awareness in perception is not in the first instance a type of object-consciousness, but a type of non-transitive self-awareness (see the section on Phenomenal and Self-awareness and Chapter 3). Although one can certainly experience one's body as an object (e.g., in a mirror), bodily self-awareness is more fundamentally an experience of one's body as a unified subjective field of perception and action. A full account of bodily experience thus reveals the body's double or ambiguous character as both a subjectively lived body (*Leib*) and a physical (spatiotemporal) objective body (*Körper*).

The phenomenological analyses of embodiment and perception summarized in this section are relevant to current trends in cognitive science. In recent years cognitive scientists have increasingly challenged the classical view that perception and action are separate systems. Although phenomenologists have long emphasized the constitutive role of motor action in perceptual experience, cognitive scientists often seem unaware of this important body of research (but see Rizzolatti

et al., 1997, for an exception). For example, neuropsychologists Milner and Goodale write in their influential book, *The Visual Brain in Action*: "For most investigators, the study of vision is seen as an enterprise that can be conducted without any reference whatsoever to the relationship between visual inputs and motor outputs. This research tradition stems directly from phenomenological intuitions that regard vision purely as a perceptual phenomenon" (Milner & Goodale 1995, p. 13). It can be seen from our discussion in this section, however, that it is important to distinguish between uncritical common-sensical intuitions and the critical examination of perceptual experience found in the phenomenological tradition. The intuitions Milner and Goodale target do not belong to phenomenology. On the contrary, Husserl's and Merleau-Ponty's analyses of the relation between perception and kinaesthesis clearly indicate that perception is also a motor phenomenon. Indeed, these analyses anticipate the so-called dynamic sensorimotor approach to perception (Hurley, 1998; Hurley & Noë, 2003; Noë, 2004; O'Regan & Noë, 2001). Rather than looking to the intrinsic properties of neural activity to understand perceptual experience, this approach looks to the dynamic sensorimotor relations among neural activity, the body, and the world. This approach has so far focused mainly on the phenomenal qualities of perceptual experience, but has yet to tackle the perceptual constitution of space, intransitive bodily self-awareness, or the relationship between perception and affectively motivated attention, all long-standing topics in phenomenology. Further development of the dynamic sensorimotor approach might therefore benefit from the integration of phenomenological analyses of embodiment and perception (see Thompson, 2007).

Intersubjectivity

For many philosophers, the issue of intersubjectivity is equated with the 'problem of other minds': How can one know the mental states of others, or even that there are any other minds at all (see Dancy, 1985, pp. 67–68)? One classical attempt to deal with this problem takes the form of trying to justify our belief in other minds on the basis of the following argument from analogy: The only mind I have direct access to is my own. My access to the mind of another is always mediated by my perception of the other's bodily movements, which I interpret as intentional behaviour (i.e., as behaviour resulting from internal mental states). But what justifies me in this interpretation? How can the perception of another person's bodily movements provide me with information about his mind, such that I am justified in viewing his movements as intentional behaviour? In my own case, I can observe that I have experiences when my body is causally influenced and that these experiences frequently bring about certain actions. I observe that other bodies are influenced and act in similar manners, and I therefore infer by analogy that the behaviour of foreign bodies is associated with experiences similar to those I have myself. Although this inference does not provide me with indubitable knowledge about others, it gives me reason to believe in their existence and to interpret their bodily movements as meaningful behaviour.

This way of conceptualizing self and other can also be discerned, to varying degrees, in certain approaches to social cognition in cognitive science. Thus, both certain versions of the 'theory-theory' (e.g., Gopnik, 1993) and the 'simulation-theory' (e.g., Goldman, 2000) have crucial features in common with the traditional argument from analogy. According to the theory-theory, normal human adults possess a common-sense or folk-psychological 'theory of mind' that they employ to explain and predict human behaviour. Advocates of the theory-theory consider this folk-psychological body of knowledge to be basically equivalent to a scientific theory: Mental states are unobservable entities (like quarks), and our attribution of them to each other involves causal-explanatory generalizations (comparable in form to those of empirical science)

that relate mental states to each other and to observable behaviour. According to the simulation-theory, on the other hand, 'mind-reading' depends not on the possession of a tacit psychological theory, but on the ability to mentally 'simulate' another person – to use the resources of one's own mind to create a model of another person and thereby identify with that person, projecting oneself imaginatively into his or her situation (Goldman, 2000). In either case, intersubjectivity is conceptualized as a cognitively mediated relation between two otherwise isolated subjects. Both theories take intersubjective understanding to be a matter of how one represents unobservable, inner mental states on the basis of outward behaviour (what they disagree about is the nature of the representations involved). Thus, both theories foster a conception of the mental as an inner realm essentially different from outward behaviour.

Phenomenologists do not frame the issue of intersubjectivity in this way, for they reject the presuppositions built into the problem of other minds (see Zahavi, 2001a, 2001b). Two presuppositions in particular are called into question. The first is that one's own mind is given to one as a solitary and internal consciousness. The problem with this assumption is that our initial self-acquaintance is not with a purely internal, mental self, for we are embodied and experience our own exteriority, including our bodily presence to the other. The second assumption is that, in perceiving the other, all we ever have direct access to is the other's bodily movements. The problem with this assumption is that what we directly perceive is intentional or meaningful behaviour – expression, gesture, and action – not mere physical movement that gets interpreted as intentional action as a result of inference. Thus, on the one hand, one's own subjectivity is not disclosed to oneself as a purely internal phenomenon, and on the other hand, the other's body is not disclosed as a purely external phenomenon. Put another way, both the traditional problem of other minds and certain cognitive-scientific conceptions of 'mind-reading' rest on a deeply problematic conception of the mind as essentially inner, the body as essentially outer, and intentional behaviour as arising from a purely contingent and causal connection between these two spheres.

Phenomenological treatments of intersubjectivity start from the recognition that, in the encounter with the other, one is faced neither with a mere body nor a hidden psyche, but with a unified whole. This unified whole is constituted by the *expressive relation* between mental states and behaviour, a relation that is stronger than that of a mere contingent, causal connection, but weaker than that of identity (for clearly not every mental state need be overtly expressed). In other words, expression must be more than simply a bridge supposed to close the gap between inner mental states and external bodily behaviour; it must be a direct manifestation of the subjective life of the mind (see Merleau-Ponty, 1962, Part One, Chapter 6). Thus, one aspect of the phenomenological problem of intersubjectivity is to understand how such manifestation is possible.

Phenomenologists insist that we need to begin from the recognition that the body of the other presents itself as radically different from any other physical entity, and accordingly that our perception of the other's bodily presence is unlike our perception of physical things. The other is given in its bodily presence as a *lived body* according to a distinctive mode of consciousness called *empathy* (see Husserl, 1989; Stein, 1989). Empathy is a unique form of intentionality, in which one is directed towards the other's lived experiences. Thus, any intentional act that discloses or presents the other's subjectivity from the second-person perspective counts as empathy. Although empathy, so understood, is based on perception (of the other's bodily presence) and can involve inference in difficult or problematic situations (where one has to work out how another person feels about something), it is not reducible to some additive combination of perception and inference.

The phenomenological conception of empathy thus stands opposed to any theory according to which our primary mode of understanding others is by perceiving their bodily behaviour and then inferring or hypothesizing that their behaviour is caused by experiences or inner mental states similar to those that apparently cause similar behaviour in us. Rather, in empathy, we experience the other directly as a person, as an intentional being whose bodily gestures and actions are expressive of his or her experiences or states of mind (for further discussion, see Thompson, 2001, 2005, 2007).

Phenomenological investigations of intersubjectivity go beyond intentional analyses of empathy, however, in a variety of ways (see Zahavi, 2001b). Another approach acknowledges the existence of empathy, but insists that our ability to encounter others cannot simply be taken as a brute fact. Rather, it is conditioned by a form of alterity (otherness) internal to the embodied self. When my left hand touches my right, or when I perceive another part of my body, I experience myself in a manner that anticipates both the way in which an other would experience me and the way in which I would experience an other. My bodily self-exploration thus permits me to confront my own exteriority. According to Husserl (1989), this experience is a crucial precondition for empathy: It is precisely the unique subject-object status of the body, the remarkable interplay between ipseity (I-ness) and alterity characterizing body-awareness, that provides me with the means of recognizing other embodied subjects.

Still another line of analysis goes one step further by denying that intersubjectivity can be reduced to any factual encounter between two individuals, such as the face-to-face encounter (see Zahavi, 2001a, b). Rather, such concrete encounters presuppose the existence of another, more fundamental form of intersubjectivity that is rooted a priori in the very relation between subjectivity and world. Heidegger's (1996) way of making this point is to describe how one always lives in a world permeated by references to others and already furnished with meaning by others. Husserl (1973) and Merleau-Ponty (1962) focus on the public nature of perceptual objects. The subject is intentionally directed towards objects whose perspectival appearances bear witness to other possible subjects. My perceptual objects are not exhausted in their appearance for me; each object always possesses a horizon of coexisting profiles, which although momentarily inaccessible to me, could be perceived by other subjects. The perceptual object as such, through its perspectival givenness, refers, as it were, to other possible subjects, and is for that very reason already intersubjective. Consequently, prior to any concrete perceptual encounter with another subject, intersubjectivity is already present as co-subjectivity in the very structure of perception.

Finally, there is a deep relation between intersubjectivity so understood and objectivity. My experience of the world as objective is mediated by my experience of and interaction with other world-engaged subjects. Only insofar as I experience that others experience the same objects as myself do I really experience these objects as objective and real. To put this point in phenomenological language, the objectivity of the world is intersubjectively constituted (i.e., brought to awareness or disclosed). This is an idea not foreign to Anglo-American philosophy, as the following remark by Donald Davidson indicates: "A community of minds is the basis of knowledge; it provides the measure of all things. It makes no sense to question the adequacy of this measure, or to seek a more ultimate standard" (Davidson 2001, p. 218).

Conclusion

Phenomenology and analytic philosophy are the two most influential philosophical movements of the twentieth century. Unfortunately, their relationship in the past was not one of fruitful cooperation and exchange, but ranged from disregard to outright hostility. To the extent that cognitive science (especially in North America) has been informed by analytic philosophy of mind, this attitude was at times perpetuated between phenomenology and cognitive science.

In recent years, however, this state of affairs has begun to change and is rapidly coming to seem outdated, as this volume itself indicates. Conferences on consciousness (such as the biannual 'Towards a Science of Consciousness' conference held in Tucson, Arizona, and the annual meetings of the Association for the Scientific Study of Consciousness) now routinely include colloquia informed by phenomenology alongside cognitive science and analytic philosophy. In 2001 there appeared a new journal, *Phenomenology and the Cognitive Sciences*. Other journals, such as *Consciousness and Cognition* and the *Journal of Consciousness Studies*, include articles integrating phenomenological, cognitive-scientific, and analytic approaches to consciousness. Given these developments, the prospects for cooperation and exchange among these traditions in the study of consciousness now look very promising. To this end, in this chapter we have called attention to a number of related areas in which there is significant potential for collaborative research – intentionality, self-awareness, temporality, embodiment and perception, and intersubjectivity. We have also sketched a few ways of linking phenomenology and cognitive science in these areas in order to suggest some directions such research could take in the years ahead.

Notes

1. For a recent discussion of the unity of the phenomenological tradition, see Zahavi (2006).

2. An important forerunner of the current interest in the relation between phenomenology and cognitive science is the work of Hubert Dreyfus (1982). Dreyfus has been a pioneer in bringing the phenomenological tradition into the heartland of cognitive science through his important critique of artificial intelligence (Dreyfus, 1991) and his groundbreaking studies on skillful knowledge and action (Dreyfus, 2002; Dreyfus & Dreyfus, 1982). Yet this work is also marked by a peculiar (mis)interpretation and use of Husserl. Dreyfus presents Husserl's phenomenology as a form of representationalism that anticipates cognitivist and computational theories of mind. He then rehearses Heidegger's criticisms of Husserl thus understood and deploys them against cognitivism and

artificial intelligence. Dreyfus reads Husserl largely through a combination of Heidegger's interpretation and a particular analytic philosophical (Fregean) reconstruction of one aspect of Husserl's thought (the representationalist interpretation of the noema). Thus, Husserlian phenomenology as Dreyfus presents it to the cognitive science and analytic philosophy of mind community is a problematic interpretive construct and should not be taken at face value. For a while Dreyfus's interpretation functioned as a received view in this community of Husserl's thought and its relation to cognitive science. This interpretation has since been seriously challenged by a number of Husserl scholars and philosophers (see Zahavi, 2003, 2004, for further discussion; see also Thompson, 2007). These studies have argued that (i) Husserl does not subscribe to a representational theory of mind; (ii) Husserl is not a methodological solipsist (see the section on methodology; (iii) Husserl does not assimilate all intentionality to object-directed intentionality (see the section on intentionality); (iv) Husserl does not treat the 'background' of object-directed intentional experiences as simply a set of beliefs understood as mental representations (see the section on intentionality); and (v) Husserl does not try to analyze the 'lifeworld' into a set of sedimented background assumptions or hypotheses (equivalent to a system of frames in artificial intelligence). In summary, although Dreyfus is to be credited for bringing Husserl into the purview of cognitive science, it is important to go beyond his interpretation and to re-evaluate Husserl's relationship to cognitive science on the basis of a thorough assessment of his life's work. This re-evaluation is already underway (see Petitot, Varela, Pachoud & Roy, 1999) and can be seen as part of a broader reappropriation of phenomenology in contemporary thought.

3. Does Husserl thereby succumb to the so-called philosophical myth of the given? This is a difficult and complicated question, and space prevents us from addressing it here. There is not one but several different notions of the 'given' in philosophy, and Husserl's thought developed considerably over the course of his life, such that he held different views at different times regarding what might be meant by it. Suffice it to say that it is a mistake to label Husserl as a philosopher of the given in the sense originally targeted by Wilfrid Sellars,

for two main reasons: First, the given in the phenomenological sense is not non-intentional sense-data, but the phenomenal world as disclosed by consciousness. Second, the phenomenality of the world is not understandable apart from the constitutive relation that consciousness bears to it. For recent discussions of some of these issues see Botero (1999) and Roy (2003).

4. This sense of the epoché is well put by the noted North American and Indian phenomenologist, J. N. Mohanty (1989, pp. 12–13): "I need not emphasize how relevant and, in fact, necessary is the method of phenomenological epoché for the very possibility of genuine description in philosophy. It was Husserl's genius that he both revitalized the descriptive method for philosophy and brought to the forefront the method of epoché, without which one cannot really get down to the job. The preconceptions have to be placed within brackets, beliefs suspended, before philosophy can begin to confront phenomena as phenomena. This again is not an instantaneous act of suspending belief in the world or of directing one's glance towards the phenomena as phenomena, but involves a strenuous effort at recognizing preconceptions as preconceptions, at unraveling sedimented interpretations, at getting at presuppositions which may pretend to be self-evident truths, and through such processes aiming asymptotically at the prereflective experience."

5. We can discern here another reason for not interpreting Husserl as a philosopher who relies on any simple or straightforward notion of an uninterrupted given in experience: Passive affection is not the reception of simple and unanalyzable sense impressions, but has a field structure.

6. When we think a certain thought, the thinking will often be accompanied by a non-vocalized utterance or aural imagery of the very string of words used to express the thought. At the same time, the thought will also frequently evoke certain mental images. It could be argued that the phenomenal qualities encountered in abstract thought are constituted by such imagery. Husserl makes clear in his *Logical Investigations*, however, that this attempt to deny that thought has any distinct phenomenality beyond such sensorial and imagistic phenomenality is problematic. There is a marked difference between what it is like to imagine aurally a certain string of meaningless

noise, and what it is like to imagine aurally the very same string while understanding and meaning something by it (Husserl, 2000, I., pp. 193–194, II., p. 105). Because the phenomenality of the sensory content is the same in both cases, the phenomenal difference must be located elsewhere, namely, in the thinking itself. The case of homonyms and synonyms also demonstrates that the phenomenality of thinking and the phenomenality of aural imagery can vary independently of each other. As for the attempt to identify the phenomenal quality of thought with the phenomenal quality of visualization, a similar argument can be employed. Two different thoughts, say, 'Paris is the capital of France', and 'Parisians regularly consume baguettes', might be accompanied by the same visualization of baguettes, but what it is like to think the two thoughts remains different. Having demonstrated this much, Husserl then proceeds to criticize the view according to which the imagery actually constitutes the very meaning of the thought – that to understand what is being thought is to have the appropriate 'mental image' before one's inner eye (Husserl, 2000, I., pp. 206–209). The arguments he employs bear striking resemblance to some of the ideas that were subsequently used by Wittgenstein (1999) in his *Philosophical Investigations*: (i) From time to time, the thoughts we are thinking, for instance 'every algebraic equation of uneven grade has at least one real root', will in fact not be accompanied by any imagery whatsoever. If the meaning were actually located in the 'mental images', the thoughts in question would be meaningless, but this is not the case. (ii) Frequently, our thoughts, for instance 'the horrors of World War I had a decisive impact on post-war painting', will in fact evoke certain visualizations, but visualizations of quite unrelated matters. To suggest that the meanings of the thoughts are to be located in such images is absurd. (iii) Furthermore, the fact that the meaning of a thought can remain the same although the accompanying imagery varies also precludes any straightforward identification. (iv) An absurd thought, like the thought of a square circle, is not meaningless, but cannot be accompanied by a matching image (a visualization of a square circle being impossible in principle). (v) Finally, referring to Descartes' famous example in the *Meditations*, Husserl points out that we can easily distinguish thoughts like 'a chiliagon is a many

sided polygon', and 'a myriagon is a many sided polygon', although the imagery that accompanies both thoughts might be indistinguishable. Thus, as Husserl concludes, although imagery might function as an aid to the understanding, it is not what is understood; it does not constitute the meaning of the thought (Husserl, 2000, I., p. 208).

References

Bernet, R., Kern, I., & Marbach, E. (1993). *An introduction to Husserlian phenomenology.* Evanston, IL: Northwestern University Press.

Botero, J.-J. (1999). The immediately given as ground and background. In J. Petitot, F. J. Varela, B. Pachoud, & J.-M. Roy (Eds.), *Naturalizing phenomenology: Issues in contemporary phenomenology and cognitive science* (pp. 440–463). Stanford, CA: Stanford University Press.

Damasio, A. R. (1999). *The feeling of what happens: Body and emotion in the making of consciousness.* New York: Harcourt Brace.

Dancy, J. (1985). *An introduction to contemporary epistemology.* Oxford: Basil Blackwell.

Davidson, D. (2001). *Subjective, intersubjective, objective.* Oxford: Oxford University Press.

Depraz, N. (1999). The phenomenological reduction as praxis. *Journal of Consciousness Studies,* 6, 95–110.

Depraz, N., Varela, F. J., & Vermersch, P. (2003). *On becoming aware: A pragmatics of experiencing.* Amsterdam and Philadelphia: John Benjamins Press.

Dreyfus, H. (1982). Introduction. In H. Dreyfus & H. Harrison (Eds.), *Husserl, intentionality and cognitive science.* Cambridge, MA: MIT Press.

Dreyfus, H. (1991). *What computers still can't do.* Cambridge, MA: MIT Press.

Dreyfus, H. (2002). Intelligence without representation – Merleau-Ponty's critique of mental representation. *Phenomenology and the Cognitive Sciences,* 1, 367–383.

Dreyfus, H., & Dreyfus, S. (1982). *Mind over machine.* New York: Free Press.

Drummond, J. J. (2003). The structure of intentionality. In D. Welton (Ed.), *The new Husserl: A critical reader* (pp. 65–92). Bloomington: Indiana University Press.

Freeman, W. J. (2000). Emotion is essential to all intentional behaviors. In M. D. Lewis

& I. Granic (Eds.), *Emotion, development, and self-organization. Dynamic systems approaches to emotional development* (pp. 209–235). Cambridge: Cambridge University Press.

Gallagher, S. (1998). *The inordinance of time.* Evanston, IL: Northwestern University Press.

Goldman, A. I. (2000). Folk psychology and mental concepts. *Protosociology, 14,* 4–25.

Gopnik, A. (1993). How we know our minds: The illusion of first-person knowledge of intentionality. *Behavioral and Brain Sciences, 16,* 1–14.

Heidegger, M. (1982). *The basic problems of phenomenology* (A. Hofstadter, Trans.). Bloomington, IN: Indiana University Press.

Heidegger, M. (1996). *Being and time* (J. Stambaugh, Trans). Albany, NY: State University of New York Press.

Hurley, S. L. (1998). *Consciousness in action.* Cambridge, MA: Harvard University Press.

Hurley, S. L., & Noë, A. (2003). Neural plasticity and consciousness. *Biology and Philosophy, 18,* 131–168.

Husserl, E. (1970). *The crisis of European sciences and transcendental phenomenology* (D. Carr, Trans.). Evanston, IL: Northwestern University Press.

Husserl, E. 1973. *Zur Phänomenologie der Intersubjektivität, Dreiter Teil: 1929–1935. Husserliana* (Vol. 15). The Hague: Martinus Nijhoff.

Husserl, E. (1975). *Experience and judgment* (J. S. Churchill, Trans.) Evanston, IL: Northwestern University Press.

Husserl, E. (1987). *Aufsätze und Vorträge (1911–1921).* Husserliana XXV. Dordrecht: Martinus Nijhoff.

Husserl, E. (1989). *Ideas pertaining to a pure phenomenology and to a phenomenological philosophy, second book* (R. Rojcewicz & A. Schuwer, Trans). Dordrecht: Kluwer Academic Publishers.

Husserl, E. (1991). *On the phenomenology of the consciousness of internal time (1893–1917)* (J. B. Brough, Trans.) Dordrecht: Kluwer Academic Publishers.

Husserl, E. (1997). *Thing and space: Lectures of 1907* (R. Rojcewicz, Trans.) Dordrecht: Kluwer Academic Publishers.

Husserl, E. (2000). *Logical investigations I–II* (J. N. Findley, Trans.). London: Routledge Press.

Husserl, E. (2001). *Analyses concerning passive and active synthesis. Lectures on transcendental logic* (A. J. Steinbock, Trans.) Dordrecht: Kluwer Academic Publishers.

Husserl, E. (2006). *Phantasy, image consciousness, and memory (1898–1925)* (J. B. Brough, Trans.). Dordrecht, The Netherlands: Springer.

James, W. (1981). *The principles of psychology.* Cambridge, MA: Harvard University Press.

Lloyd, D. (2002). Functional MRI and the study of human consciousness. *Journal of Cognitive Neuroscience, 14,* 818–831.

Lloyd, D. (2003). *Radiant cool. A novel theory of consciousness.* Cambridge, MA: MIT Press.

Lutz, A., & Thompson, E. (2003). Neurophenomenology: Integrating subjective experience and brain dynamics in the neuroscience of consciousness. *Journal of Consciousness Studies, 10,* 31–52.

Merleau-Ponty, M. (1962). *Phenomenology of perception* (C. Smith, Trans.) London: Routledge Press.

Milner, A. D., & Goodale, M. A. (1995). *The visual brain in action.* New York: Oxford University Press.

Mohanty, J. N. (1989). *Transcendental phenomenology.* Oxford: Basil Blackwell.

Moran, D. (2000). *Introduction to phenomenology.* London: Routledge Press.

Nagel, T. (1979). What is it like to be a bat? In T. Nagel (Ed.), *Mortal questions* (pp. 165–180). New York: Cambridge University Press.

Noë, A. (2004). *Action in perception.* Cambridge, MA: MIT Press.

O'Regan, J. K., & Noë, A. (2001). A sensorimotor account of vision and visual consciousness. *Behavioral and Brain Sciences, 24,* 939–1031.

Panskepp, J. (1998a). *Affective neuroscience: The foundations of human and animal emotions.* Oxford: Oxford University Press.

Panskepp, J. (1998b). The periconscious substrates of consciousness: Affective states and the evolutionary origins of self. *Journal of Consciousness Studies, 5,* 566–582.

Parvizi, J., & Damasio, A. (2001). Consciousness and the brainstem. *Cognition, 79,* 135–159.

Petitot, J., Varela, F. J., Pachoud, B., & Roy, J.-M. (Eds.). (1999). *Naturalizing phenomenology: Issues in contemporary phenomenology and cognitive science.* Stanford, CA: Stanford University Press.

Rainville, P. (2005). Neurophénoménologie des états et des contenus de conscience dans l'hypnose et l'analgésie hypnotique. *Théologique*, 12, 15–38.

Rizzolatti, G. L., Fadiga, L., Fogassi, L., & Gallese, V. (1997). The space around us. *Science*, 277, 190–191.

Roy, J.-M.(2003). Phenomenological claims and the myth of the given. In E. Thompson (Ed.), *The problem of consciousness: New essays in phenomenological philosophy of mind. Canadian Journal of Philosophy*, Suppl. Vol. 29 (pp. 1–32). Calgary, AL: University of Alberta Press.

Sartre, J.-P. (1956). *Being and nothingness* (H. Barnes, Trans). New York: Philosophical Library.

Searle, J. R. (1983). *Intentionality: An essay in the philosophy of mind*. Cambridge: Cambridge University Press.

Stein, E. (1989). *On the problem of empathy* (W. Stein, Trans.) Washington, DC: ICS Publications.

Steinbock, A. (1995). *Home and beyond: Generative phenomenology after Husserl*. Evanston, IL: Northwestern University Press.

Sokolowski, R. (2000). *An introduction to phenomenology*. Cambridge: Cambridge University Press.

Thompson, E. (2001). Empathy and consciousness. In E. Thompson (Ed.), *Between ourselves: Second-person issues in the study of consciousness* (pp. 1–32). Thorverton, UK: Imprint Academic.

Thompson, E. (2005). Empathy and human experience. In J. D. Proctor (Ed.), *Science, religion, and the human experience* (pp. 261–285). New York: Oxford University Press.

Thompson, E. (2007). *Mind in life: Biology, phenomenology, and the sciences of mind*. Cambridge, MA: Harvard University Press.

Thompson, E., Lutz, A., & Cosmelli, D. (2005). Neurophenomenology: An introduction for neurophilosophers. In A. Brook & K. Akins (Eds.), *Cognition and the brain: The philosophy and neuroscience movement* (pp. 40–97). New York: Cambridge University Press.

Varela, F. J. (1996). Neurophenomenology: A methodological remedy for the hard problem. *Journal of Consciousness Studies*, 3, 330–350.

Varela, F. J. (1999). The specious present: A neurophenomenology of time consciousness. In J. Petitot, F. J. Varela, B. Pachoud, & J.-M. Roy (Eds.), *Naturalizing phenomenology: Issues in contemporary phenomenology and cognitive science* (pp. 266–314). Stanford, CA: Stanford University Press.

Varela, F. J., & Shear, J. (1999). *The view from within. First-person approaches to the study of consciousness*. Thorverton, UK: Imprint Academic.

Wittgenstein, L. (1999). *Philosophical investigations* (3d ed.; G. E. M. Anscombe, Trans.) Englewood Cliffs, NJ: Prentice Hall.

Zahavi, D. (1999). *Self-awareness and alterity. A phenomenological investigation*. Evanston, IL: Northwestern University Press.

Zahavi, D. (2001a). *Husserl and transcendental intersubjectivity*. Athens, OH: Ohio University Press.

Zahavi, D. (2001b). Beyond empathy: Phenomenological approaches to intersubjectivity. *Journal of Consciousness Studies*, 8, 151–167.

Zahavi, D. (2003). *Husserl's phenomenology*. Stanford, CA: Stanford University Press.

Zahavi, D. (2004). Husserl's noema and the internalism-externalism debate. *Inquiry*, 47, 42–66.

Zahavi, D. (2005). *Subjectivity and selfhood: Investigating the first-person perspective*. Cambridge, MA: MIT Press.

Zahavi, D. (2006). The phenomenological tradition. In D. Moran (Ed.), *Routledge companion to twentieth-century philosophy*. London: Routledge.

CHAPTER 5

Asian Perspectives: Indian Theories of Mind

Georges Dreyfus and Evan Thompson

Abstract

This chapter examines Indian views of the mind and consciousness, with particular focus on the Indian Buddhist tradition. To contextualize Buddhist views of the mind, we first provide a brief presentation of some of the most important Hindu views, particularly those of the Sāṃkhya school. Whereas this school assumes the existence of a real transcendent self, the Buddhist view is that mental activity and consciousness function on their own without such a self. We focus on the phenomenological and epistemological aspects of this no-self view of the mind. We first discuss the Buddhist Abhidharma and its analysis of the mind in terms of awareness and mental factors. The Abhidharma is mainly phenomenological; it does not present an epistemological analysis of the structure of mental states and the way they relate to their objects. To cover this topic we turn to Dharmakīrti, one of the main Buddhist epistemologists, who offers a comprehensive view of the types of cognition and their relation to their objects.

Introduction

In discussing Asian views of mind and consciousness, we must start from the realization that this topic presents insurmountable challenges. The diversity of Asian cultures from China to India to Iran is so great that it is impossible to find coherent ways to discuss the mental concepts of these cultures over and above listing these conceptions and noting their differences. Hence, rather than chart a territory that hopelessly extends our capacities, we have chosen to examine Indian views of the mind, with a special focus on the Indian Buddhist tradition, which can be traced back to the first centuries after the life of Siddhartha Gautama, the Buddha (566–483 BCE), and which continued to develop in India through the 7th and 8th centuries CE. This approach allows us to present a more grounded and coherent view of the mind as conceived in the Indian philosophical tradition and to indicate some areas of interest that this tradition offers to cognitive scientists and philosophers of mind.

In talking about the mind, it is important to define the term, for it is far from unambiguous. In most Indian traditions, the mind is neither a brain structure nor a mechanism for treating information. Rather, mind is conceived as a complex cognitive process consisting of a succession of related mental states. These states are at least in principle phenomenologically available; that is, they can be observed by attending to the way in which we experience feeling, perceiving, thinking, remembering, and so on. Indian thinkers describe these mental states as cognizing (*jñā*) or being aware (*buddh*) of their object. Thus, the mind is broadly conceived by traditional Indian thinkers as constituted by a series of mental states that cognize their objects.

This general agreement breaks down quickly, however, when we turn to a more detailed analysis of the nature and structure of the mind, a topic on which various schools entertain vastly different views. Some of these disagreements relate to the ontological status of mental states and the way they relate to other phenomena, particularly physical ones. Such disagreements are related to well-known ideas in the Western tradition, particularly the mind-body dualism that has concerned Western philosophy since Descartes. But many of the views entertained by Indian thinkers are not easily mapped in Western terms, as we see in this chapter.

Most Indian thinkers do not consider the ontological status of mental states to be a particularly difficult question, for most of them accept that there is an extra-physical reality. Among all the schools, only the Materialist, the Cārvāka, reduces the mental to physical events. For its proponents, mental states do not have any autonomous ontological status and can be completely reduced to physical processes. They are just properties of the body, much like the inebriating property of beer is a property of beer. Most other thinkers reject this view forcefully and argue that the mind can neither be eliminated nor reduced to the material. Their endorsement of an extra-physical reality does not, however, necessar-

ily amount to a classical mind-body dualism (of the sort found in Descartes' *Meditations* or Plato's *Phaedo*). Moreover, although they agree in rejecting the materialist view, they strongly disagree in their presentations of the mind.

In this chapter, we focus mostly on the Buddhist tradition, exploring some of its views of the mind. One of the most salient features of this tradition is that its accounts of the mind and consciousness do not posit the existence of a self. According to this tradition, there is no self, and mental activity cannot be understood properly as long as one believes in a self. The Hindu tradition, by contrast, maintains that mental life does involve a permanent self. Thus, to contextualize Buddhist views of the mind, we begin with a brief presentation of some of the most important Hindu views. We then present the Buddhist Abhidharma and its analysis of the mind in terms of awareness and mental factors. Traditionally, the Abhidharma makes up one of the 'three baskets' into which Buddhists divide their scriptures – *Sutra* or sayings of the Buddha, *Vinaya* or monastic discipline, and *Abhidharma*, which systematizes Buddhist teachings in the form of detailed analyses of experience. In examining the Abhidharma, we examine the ways in which this tradition analyzes the different functions of the mind without positing the existence of a self. These analyses are in certain ways reminiscent of those in cognitive science that aim to account for cognitive processing without invoking a homunculus or 'little man' inside the head who oversees the workings of the mind (or merely passively witnesses the results; see Varela, Thompson, & Rosch, 1991, for further discussion of this parallel). The Abhidharma, however, is phenomenological; its concern is to discern how the mind works as evidenced by experience (but especially by mentally disciplined and refined contemplative experience). Although thus it is also epistemological, the Abhidharma does not present any developed epistemological analysis of the structure of mental states and the way they relate to their objects so as to produce knowledge. To cover this topic we turn to

Dharmakīrti (c. 600 CE), one of the main Buddhist epistemologists, who offers a comprehensive view of the types of cognition and their relation to their objects.

The phenomenological analyses contained in the Abhidharma and the epistemological analyses of Dharmakīrti offer significant resources for cognitive scientists and philosophers of mind in their efforts to gain a better understanding of consciousness. These analyses also constitute the theoretical framework for the ways in which the Buddhist tradition conceives of meditation and mental training, both with regard to the phenomenology of contemplative mental states and the epistemology of the types of knowledge that these states are said to provide. Given the increasing scientific interest in the physiological correlates and effects of meditation and their relation to consciousness (see Chapter 19), it is important for the scientific community to appreciate the phenomenological and philosophical precision with which these states are conceptualized in the Buddhist tradition.

Self and Mental States: A Sāṃkhya View

One of the most important views of the mind in the Hindu tradition is found in the Sāṃkhya school. Traditionally this school is said to have been founded by the philosopher Kapila, a legendary figure who may have lived as early as the 7th century BCE, but the earliest Sāṃkhya text we possess dates from the 3rd century CE. The Sāṃkhya tradition is one of the six classical schools of Hindu philosophy (Nyaya, Vaisesika, Sāṃkhya, Yoga, Purva Mimamsa, and Vedānta). Its influence extends to the other schools, particularly the Vedānta school, which later became especially important in the development of Hindu thought. The Sāṃkhya was in fact less a school proper than a way of thinking based on the categorization of reality. It was crucial in the formation of Indian philosophical thinking before and after the start of the Common Era, and hence it is unsurprising that its view of the

mind has been largely adopted in the Hindu tradition and beyond.[1]

The Sāṃkhya approach rests on a dualistic metaphysics built on the opposition between material primordial nature (*pradhāna*) or materiality (*prakṛti*) and a spiritual self (*ātman*) or person (*puruṣa*).[2] Nature is the universal material substratum out of which all phenomena other than the self emerge and evolve. These phenomena, which make up the world of diversity, are physical transformations of the three qualities (*guṇa*) that compose primordial nature. These three qualities are *sattva* (transparency, buoyancy), *rajas* (energy, activity), and *tamas* (inertia, obstruction). They are principles or forces, rather than building blocks. All material phenomena, including the intellect and organs of perception, are understood to be made up of a combination of these three principles. The one principle not included in this constant process of transformation is the self, which is permanent, non-material, and conscious or aware. The self is also described as the conscious presence that witnesses the transformations of nature, but does not participate in them. As such it is passive, though it witnesses the experiences deriving from the transformations of the world of diversity.[3]

Although the Sāṃkhya analysis of mind is dualistic, it does not fit within classical mind-body dualism. For the Sāṃkhya, the mind involves a non-material spiritual element, namely the self. The self, however, is not the same as the mind. Rather, the self is the mere presence to or pure witnessing of the mental activities involved in the ordinary awareness of objects. This pure witnessing, untainted by the diversity of the material world, is not sufficient for mental activities, for mental activities are representational or semantic and require more than passive mirroring. Mental activity is the apprehension of an object, and this activity requires active engagement with objects and the formation of ideas and concepts necessary for purposeful action in the world. The self cannot account for such activity, however, because it is changeless and hence passive. To account for our cognitive activities, we therefore need other elements that participate in the world of diversity. Because any element that participates in the world of change must emerge out of primordial materiality and hence be material, it follows that the analysis of mental states cannot be limited to their spiritual dimension (the self), but must also involve material elements. Hence, for the Sāṃkhya, mental activity requires the cooperation of the two fundamental types of substance that make up the universe, passive consciousness and material nature.

Having described the Sāṃkhya metaphysics, we can now sketch its influential analysis of mental activity.[4] This analysis starts with *buddhi*, which is usually translated as 'the intellect' and is the ability to distinguish and experience objects. This ability provides the prereflective and presubjective ground out of which determined mental states and their objects arise; it is also the locus of all the fundamental predispositions that lead to these experiences. The intellect emerges out of primordial matter and therefore is active, unlike the non-material and passive self. The self is described metaphorically as a light, for it passively illuminates objects, making it possible for the intellect to distinguish them. The intellect operates in a representational way by taking on the form of what is known. This representational ability works in two directions – toward the conscious and uninvolved self and toward the objects. The intellect, thanks to its quality of clarity and transluscence (*sattva*), takes on the form of the self by reflecting it. As a result, it seems as if the self experiences the diversity of objects, when it is actually the intellect that undergoes these experiences, the self being the mere witness of them. This ability of the intellect to usurp the function of consciousness helps the intellect in its apprehension of objects, for by itself the intellect is active but unconsious. Awareness of objects arises only when the intellect takes on the light of the self and reflects it on objects, much like pictures are created when light is projected onto a film. In this way, the intellect becomes able to take on the form of the object and thus to discern it.

The intellect's reflecting the self and taking on the form of an object are not, however, sufficient to fully determine experience. To become fully cognitive, experience requires the formation of subjective and objective poles. Experience needs to be the experience of a particular individual apprehending a particular object. The formation of the subjective pole is the function of the 'ego-sense' (*ahaṃkāra*), the sense of individual subjectivity or selfhood tied to embodiment. This sense colors most of our experiences, which involve a sense of being a subject opposed to an object. The determination of the objective pole, on the other hand, is the function of 'mentation' (*manas*), which oversees the senses and whose special function is discrimination. This function allows mentation to serve as an intermediary between the intellect and the senses. Mentation organizes sensory impressions and objects and integrates them into a temporal framework created by memories and expectations. In this way, our experience of objects in the world is created.

Although the dualistic metaphysics associated with this view was rejected in the history of Indian philosophy, the Sāṃkhya model of the mind was taken over by other Hindu schools. It serves as a foundation of the philosopher Patañjali's (c. 2nd century BCE) Yoga view of mind, which is similar to the Sāṃkhya.[5] The Yoga view also rests on the opposition between passive self and active mental activities (*citta*), a rubric under which intellect, ego-sense, and mentation are grouped. Similarly, Śamkara (788–820 CE), who savaged the dualism of the Sāṃkhya, took over its model of the mind in his Advaita Vedānta, emphasizing the contrast between the transcendence of the self and the mental activities of the 'inner sense' (*antaḥkarava*) belonging to the person.[6] Hence, the Sāṃkhya view can be taken as representative of the Hindu view of the mind, especially in its emphasis on the difference between a passive witnessing consciousness and mental activity.

According to this view, as we have seen, mental events come about through the conjunction of two heterogeneous factors – a transcendent self and a diversity of mental activities. It is a basic presupposition of the Hindu tradition that mental life involves a permanent self. Yet because mental life also undeniably involves change, it cannot be reduced to this single, motionless factor of the self; hence the need for the complicated analysis briefly summarized here. This tension in accounts of the mind and consciousness between identity and change, unity and diversity, is of course also prevalent throughout Western philosophy and persists in cognitive science. We turn now to the Buddhist tradition, which presents a different perspective on this issue.

The Abhidharma Tradition and its View of the Mind

The Buddhist tradition is based on the opposite view of no-self (*anātman*). For the Buddhists, there is no self, and hence mental activity is not in the service of such an entity, but rather functions on its own. In short, for the Buddhists there is no self that is aware of the experiences one undergoes or the thoughts one has. Rather the thoughts themselves are the thinker, and the experiences the experiencer.

How, then, do Buddhists explain the complexities of the mind? How do they explain mental regularities if there is no central controller to oversee the whole process?

For an answer, we turn to the Abhidharma, one of the oldest Buddhist traditions, which can be traced back to the first centuries after the Buddha (566–483 BCE). First elaborated as lists,[7] the Abhidharma contains the earlier texts in which Buddhist concepts were developed and hence is the source of most philosophical developments in Indian Buddhism. But the Abhidharma is not limited to this role as a source of Buddhist philosophical development. It remained a vital focus of Buddhist thought and kept evolving, at least until the 7th or 8th century CE. In this chapter, we focus on two Indian thinkers from the 4th or 5th century CE, Asaṅga and Vasubandhu, and ignore

the diversity of opinions and debates that has animated this tradition.

The object of the Abhidharma is to analyze both the realm of sentient experience and the world given in such experience into its components in language that avoids the postulation of a unified subject. This analysis concerns the whole range of phenomena, from material phenomena to nirvana (the state of enlightenment, understood as the direct realization of the nature of reality, including especially the lack of any essential self and the consequent liberation from suffering). For example, there are elaborate discussions of the four primary and four secondary elements that make up matter (see de la Vallée Poussin, 1971, I: 22). There are also lengthy treatments of the nature, scope, and types of soteriological practices prescribed by the Buddhist tradition, a central focus of the Abhidharma. But a large part of the Abhidharmic discourse focuses on the analysis of mental phenomena and their various components. It is this part of the Abhidharma that we examine in this chapter.

In considering experience, the Abhidharma proceeds in a rather characteristic way that may be disconcerting for newcomers, but reflects its historical origin as mnemonic lists of elements abstracted from the Buddha's discourses. For each type of phenomenon considered, the Abhidharma analyzes it into its basic elements (*dharma*), lists these elements, and groups them into the appropriate categories (examples are given below). The study of the Abhidharma thus often revolves around the consideration of series of extended lists.

In elaborating such lists of components of experience and the world given in experience, the Abhidharma follows the central tenets of Buddhist philosophy, in particular the twin ideas of non-substantiality and dependent origination. According to this philosophy, the phenomena given in experience are not unitary and stable substances, but complex and fleeting formations of basic elements that arise in dependence on complex causal nexuses. Such non-substantiality is particularly true of the person, who is not a substantial self, but a changing construct dependent on complex configurations of mental and material components. This analysis, which is diametrically opposed to the Sāṃkhya view, is not just limited to the person, but is applied to other objects.

All composite things are thus analyzed as being constituted of more basic elements. Moreover, and this point is crucial, these basic elements should not be thought of as reified or stable entities, but as dynamically related momentary events instantaneously coming into and going out of existence. Thus, when the Abhidharma analyzes matter as being made up of basic components, it thinks of those components not as stable particles or little grains of matter, but rather as fleeting material events, coming into and going out of existence depending on causes and conditions. Similarly, the mind is analyzed into its basic components; namely, the basic types of events that make up the complex phenomenon we call 'mind'.

This Abhidharmic analysis is not just philosophical but it also has practical import. Its aim is to support the soteriological practices that the Buddhist tradition recommends. The lists of material and mental events are used by practitioners to inform and enhance their practices. For example, the list of mental factors we examine shortly is a precious aid to various types of meditation, providing a clear idea of which factors need to be developed and which are to be eliminated. In this way, the Abhidharma functions not just as the source of Buddhist philosophy but also informs and supports the practices central to this tradition.

In the Abhidharma the mind is conceived as a complex cognitive process consisting of a succession of related momentary mental states. These states are phenomenologically available, at least in principle: They can be observed by turning inwardly and attending to the way we feel, perceive, think, remember, and so on. When we do so, we notice a variety of states of awareness, and we also notice that these states change rapidly. It is these mental states arising in quick succession that the Abhidharma identifies as being the basic elements of the mind.

It should be clear from this preliminary characterization that in elaborating a theory of the mind the Abhidharma relies primarily on what we would call a first-person approach. It is by looking directly at experience that we gain an understanding of mind, not by studying it as an object and attending to its external manifestations. This approach of the Ahbidharma is not unlike that of such Western thinkers as James, Brentano, and Husserl, who all agree that the study of the mind must be based on attention to experience (see Chapter 4). This approach is well captured by James's famous claim that in the study of the mind, "Introspective Observation is what we have to rely on first and foremost and always" (James, 1981, p. 185).

As James himself recognizes, however, first-person observation of the mind, although it might seem a straightforward enterprise, is not a simple affair and raises numerous questions. What does it mean to observe the mind? Who observes? What is being observed? Is the observation direct or mediated? In addition to these difficult epistemological issues (some of which we take up in the next section), there are also questions about the reliability of observation. We are all able to certain degrees to observe our own minds, but it is clear that our capacities to do so differ. Whose observations are to be considered reliable? This question is significant for the Abhidharmists, who may include in their data not only ordinary observations but also the observations of trained meditators. This inclusion of observation based on contemplative mental training and meditative experience marks an important difference between the Abhidharma and James, as well as other Western phenomenologists. Nevertheless, the degree to which meditative experience is relevant to Buddhist theories of the mind is not a straightforward matter, as we see shortly.

The comparison between the Abhidharma and James goes further, however, than their reliance on an introspective method. They also share some substantive similarities, the most important of which is perhaps the idea of the *stream of consciousness*.

For the Abhidharma, mental states do not arise in isolation from each other. Rather, each state arises in dependence on preceding moments and gives rise to further moments, thus forming a mental stream or continuum (*santāna, rgyud*), much like James's 'stream of thought'. This metaphor is also found in the Buddhist tradition in which the Buddha is portrayed as saying, "The river never stops: there is no moment, no minute, no hour when the river stops: in the same way, the flux of thought" (de la Vallée Poussin, 1991, p. 69, translation from the French by Dreyfus).

Unsurprisingly, there are also significant differences between James and the Abhidharma. One difference of interest to contemporary research is the issue of whether mental states arise in continuity or not (see Varela, Thompson, & Rosch, 1991, pp. 72–79). James's view is well known: "Consciousness does not appear to itself chopped up in bits" (James, 1981, p. 233). Although the content of consciousness changes, we experience these changes as smooth and continuous, without any apparent break. The Abhidharma disagrees, arguing that although the mind is rapidly changing, its transformation is discontinuous. It is only to the untrained observer that the mind appears to flow continuously. According to the Abhidharma, a deeper observation reveals that the stream of consciousness is made up of moments of awareness, moments that can be introspectively individuated and described.

Several Abhidharma texts even offer measurements of this moment, measurements one would expect to be based on empirical observation. Yet such claims are problematic, for different Abhidharma traditions make claims that at times are strikingly at odds with one another. For example, the *Mahavibhāṣā*, an important text from the first centuries of the Common Era, states that there are 120 basic moments in an instant. The text further illustrates the duration of an instant by equating it to the time needed by an average spinner to grab a thread. Not at all, argues another text: This measurement is too coarse. A moment

is the 64th part of the time necessary to click one's fingers or blink an eye (see de la Vallée Poussin, 1991, pp. 70–71). Although these measurements differ, one could argue that given the imprecision of premodern measurement, there is a rough agreement between these accounts, which present a moment of awareness as lasting for about 1/100th of a second. This is already significantly faster than pyschophysical and electrophysiological estimates of the duration of a moment of awareness as being on the order of 250 milliseconds or a quarter of a second (see Pöppel, 1988; Varela, Thompson, & Rosch, 1991, pp. 72–79). But consider the claim made by a Theravada Abhidharma text that "in the time it takes for lightning to flash or the eyes to blink, billions of mind-moments can elapse" (Bodhi, 1993, p. 156). The time scale in this account, which is standard in the Theravada tradition, is faster by many orders of magnitude.

This dramatic discrepancy alerts us to some of the difficulties of accounts based on observation. For whom are we to believe? On which tradition should we rely? Moreover, we cannot but wonder about the sources of these differences. Do they derive from the observations of meditators, or are they the results of theoretical elaborations? It is hard to come to a definitive conclusion, but it seems reasonable to believe that these accounts are not simply empirical observations, but largely theoretical discussions, perhaps supplemented by observation reports. Hence one must be cautious and not assume that these texts reflect empirical findings. Although some may, they are mostly theoretical elaborations, which cannot be taken at face value, but require critical interpretation. Finally, another Abhidharma text seems to muddy the waters further by claiming that the measure of a moment is beyond the understanding of ordinary beings. Only enlightened beings can measure the duration of a moment (de la Vallée Poussin, 1991, p. 73). Thus it is not surprising that we are left wondering!

According to the Abhidharma, the mental episodes that compose a stream of consciousness take as their objects either real or fictional entities. This object-directed character of mind has been called 'intentionality' by Western philosophers, such as Brentano and Husserl. Brentano claimed that intentionality is an essential feature of consciousness and proposed it as a criterion of the mental. All acts of awareness are directed toward or refer to an object, regardless of whether this object is existent or not. We cannot think, wish, or dread unless our mind is directed toward something thought about, wished for, or dreaded, which thus appears to the mind. Therefore, to be aware is for something to appear to the mind. The Abhidharma seems to share this view, holding that every moment of cognition relates to particular objects, and hence it assumes that intentionality and consciousness are inseparable.[8]

The Abhidharma also holds that this stream of consciousness is not material. It is associated with the body during this lifetime, but will come to exist in dependence on other bodies after the death of this body. It is crucial to recognize, however, that the immaterial stream of consciousness is not a soul in the Platonic or Cartesian sense, but an impersonal series of mental events. Buddhist philosophers do not believe in an ontology of substances – that reality comprises the existence of independent entities that are the subjects of attributes or properties. Rather, they argue that reality is made up of events consisting of a succession of moments. Thus, mind and matter are not substances, but evanescent events, and mental and material events interact in a constantly ongoing and fluctuating process. Moreover, Buddhist philosophers partake of the general Indian reluctance to separate the mental and the material. Hence they do not hold that the divide between the material and mental spheres is absolute. Nevertheless, for the Buddhists, in contrast to the *Sāṃkhya*, there is a sharp divide between the mental, which is intentional and conscious, and other elements. In this respect, Buddhists are perhaps the closest among Indian philosophers to a classical mind-body dualism.

The Abhidharma, however, does not stop at a view of the mind as a succession of mental states, but goes much further in its analysis, breaking down each mental state into its components. According to the Abhidharma schema, which is to our knowledge unique, each mental state is analyzed as having two aspects: (i) the *primary factor of awareness* (citta), whose function is to be aware of the object, and (ii) *mental factors* (caitesika), whose function is to qualify this awareness by determining its qualitative nature as pleasant or unpleasant, focused or unfocused, calm or agitated, positive or negative, and so on. The philosopher Vasubandhu (c. 4th or 5th century CE), one of the great Abhidharmists, explains this distinction between awareness and mental factors as follows:

> Cognition or awareness apprehends the thing itself, and just that; mental factors or dharmas *associated with cognition such as sensation, etc., apprehend special characteristics, special conditions (de la Vallée Poussin, 1971, I: 30).*[9]

The basic insight is that mental states have two types of cognitive functions – (1) awareness and (2) cognitive and affective engagement and characterization. The mental state is aware of an object. For example, the sense of smell is aware of a sweet object. But mental states are not just states of awareness. They are not passive mirrors in which objects are reflected. Rather, they actively engage their objects, apprehending them as pleasant or unpleasant, approaching them with particular intentions, and so forth. For example, a gustatory cognition of a sweet object is not just aware of the sweet taste but also apprehends the object as pleasant, distinguishes certain qualities such as its texture, and so on. It also categorizes the object as being (say) one's favorite Swiss chocolate. Such characterization of the object is the function of the mental factors. We now describe this distinction between the *primary factor of awareness* and *mental factors* in more detail.

The Primary Factor of Awareness

The primary factor of awareness (citta) is also described as *vijñāna*, a term often translated as *consciousness* or *cognitive aware-ness*. It is the aspect of the mental state that is aware of the object. It is the very activity of cognizing the object, not an instrument in the service of an agent or self (which, as we have seen, the Buddhist philosophers argue is nonexistent). This awareness merely discerns the object, as in the above example where one apprehends the taste of what turns out to be one's favorite Swiss choco-late. Thus Vasubandhu speaks of awareness as the "bare apprehension of each object" (de la Vallée Poussin, 1971, I: 30).

In most Abhidharma systems, there are six types of awareness: five born from the five physical senses (sight, hearing, smell, taste, and touch) and mental cognition. Each type of sensory cognition is produced in depen-dence on a sensory basis (one of the five physical senses) and an object. This aware-ness arises momentarily and ceases imme-diately, to be replaced by another moment of awareness, and so on. The sixth type of awareness is mental. It is considered a sense by the Abhidharma, like the five phys-ical senses, though there are disagreements about its basis (see Guenther, 1976, pp. 20–30).

Some Abhidharma texts, such as Asaṅga's (Rahula, 1980), argue that these six types of consciousness do not exhaust all the possi-ble forms of awareness. To this list Asaṅga adds two types of awareness: the *store-consciousness* (*ālaya-vijñāna, kun gzhi rnam shes*) and *afflictive mentation* (*kliṣṭa-manas, nyon yid*; Rahula, 1980, p. 17).[10] The idea of a store-consciousness is based on a dis-tinction between the six types of awareness, which are all described as manifest cognitive awareness (*pravṛtti-vijñāna, 'jug shes*), and a more continuous and less manifest form of awareness, which is the store-consciousness. This awareness is invoked to answer the fol-lowing objection: If there is no self and the mind is just a succession of mental states, then how can there be any continuity in our mental life? Asaṅga's answer is that there is a more continuous form of consciousness, which is still momentary, but exists at all times. Because it is subliminal, we usually do not notice it. It is only in special circum-stances, such as fainting, that its presence can be noticed or at least inferred. This con-sciousness contains all the basic habits, ten-dencies, and propensities (including those that persist from one life to the next) accu-mulated by the individual. It thus provides a greater degree of continuity than manifest cognitive awareness on its own.

The store-consciousness is mistaken by the afflictive mentation as being a self. In this way one's core inborn sense of self is formed. From a Buddhist point of view, however, this sense of self is fundamentally mistaken. It is a mental imposition of unity where there is in fact only the arising of a multiplicity of interrelated physical and mental events. The sense of control belonging to one's sense of self is thus largely illusory. There is really nobody in charge of the physical and men-tal processes, which arise according to their own causes and conditions, not our whims. The mind is not ruled by a central unit, but by competing factors whose strength varies according to circumstances.

Thus Asaṅga, allegedly Vasubandhu's half-brother, posits as many as eight types of consciousness, a doctrine usually asso-ciated with a particular Buddhist school, the Yogācāra. This school contains many interesting insights, without which there is no complete understanding of the depth of Buddhist views of the mind, but there is not space to discuss these insights here. Let us simply point out that there are some interesting similarities between the Yogācāra and the Sāṃkhya views. The store-consciousness, in acting as the holder of all the potentialities accumulated by an individual, is not unlike the intellect (*buddhi*), whereas the afflictive mentation seems similar to the ego-sense (*ahaṃkāra*). Furthermore, mental cognition does not seem too different from mentation (*manas*). These similarities indicate the reach of the Sāṃkhya model, even in a tradition whose basic outlook is radically different.

Mental Factors

Mental states are not just states of awareness; they also actively engage their objects, qualifying them as pleasant or unpleasant, approaching them with a particular attitude, and so on. Mental factors, which are aspects of the mental state that characterize the object of awareness, account for this engagement. In other words, whereas consciousness makes known the mere presence of the object, mental factors make known the particulars of the content of awareness, defining the characteristics and special conditions of its object. They qualify the apprehension of the object as being pleasant or unpleasant, attentive or distracted, peaceful or agitated, and so forth.

The translation of these elements of the mind (*caitesika*) as *factors* is meant to capture the range of meanings that the Abhidharma associates with this term. The relation between cognitive awareness and mental factors is complex. At times the Abhidharma construes this relation diachronically as being causal and functional. Factors cause the mind to apprehend objects in particular ways. At other times, the Abhidharma seems to emphasize a synchronic perspective in which cognitive awareness and mental factors coexist and cooperate in the same cognitive task.[11]

In accordance with its procedure, the Abhidharma studies mental factors by listing them, establishing the ways in which they arise and cease, and grouping them in the appropriate categories. Each Abhidharma tradition has a slightly different list. Here we follow a list of 51 mental factors distributed in 6 groups.[12] The mental typology presented in this list has a number of interesting features in relation to more familiar Western philosophical and scientific typologies:

- Five omnipresent factors: feeling, discernment, intention, attention, and contact
- Five determining factors: aspiration, appreciation, mindfulness, concentration, and intelligence
- Four variable factors: sleep, regret, investigation, and analysis
- Eleven virtuous factors: confidence/faith, self-regarding shame, other-regarding shame, joyful effort, pliability, conscientiousness, detachment, non-hatred

(lovingkindness), wisdom, equanimity, and non-harmfulness (compassion).
- Six root-afflictions: attachment, anger, ignorance, pride, negative doubt, and mistaken view.
- Twenty branch-afflictions: belligerence, vengefulness, concealment, spite, jealousy, avarice, pretense, dissimulation, self-satisfaction, cruelty, self-regarding shamelessness, other-regarding shamelessness, inconsideration, mental dullness, distraction, excitement, lack of confidence/faith, laziness, lack of conscientiousness, and forgetfulness.

The nature of this complex typology becomes clearer when one realizes that these six groups can be further reduced to three. The first three groups contain all the neutral factors. They are the factors that can be present in any mental state, whether positive or negative. Hence these factors are neither positive nor negative in and of themselves. The next three groups are different. These factors are ethically determined. The eleven virtuous factors are positive in that they do not compel us toward attitudes that lead to suffering. They leave us undisturbed, open to encounter reality with a more relaxed and freer outlook. The twenty-six afflictive factors, on the other hand, disturb the mind, creating frustration and restlessness. They are the main obstacles to the life of the good as understood by the Buddhist tradition. The very presence of these factors marks the mental state as virtuous or afflictive. Thus it is clear that the Abhidharma typology is explicitly ethical.

This presentation also offers interesting insights concerning the cognitive functions of the mind. In particular, the analysis of the five omnipresent factors – feeling, discernment, intention, attention, and contact – shows some of the complexities of Abhidharmic thinking. These five are described as omnipresent because they are present in every mental state. Even in a subliminal state such as the store-consciousness these five factors are present. The other factors are not necessary for the performance of the most minimal cognitive task (the apprehension of an object, however dimly and indistinctly). Hence they are not present in all mental states, but only in some.

One striking feature of this list is the pre-eminent place of feeling (*vedanā, tshor ba*) as the first of the factors. This emphasis reflects the fundamental outlook of the tradition, which views humans as being first and foremost sentient. But it also reflects a distinctive view of the cognitive realm that emphasizes the role of spontaneous value attribution. For the Abhidharma, a mental state is not only aware of an object but at the same time it also evaluates this object. This evaluation is the function of the feeling tone that accompanies the awareness and experiences of the object as either pleasant, unpleasant, or neutral. This factor is central in determining our reactions to the events we encounter, because, for the most part, we do not perceive an object and then feel good or bad about it out of considerate judgments. Rather, evaluation is already built into our experiences. We may use reflection to come to more objective judgments, but those mostly operate as correctives to our spontaneous evaluations.

Feeling is not the only important factor, however. A mental state involves not only awareness and feeling but also discernment (*saṃjñā, 'du shes* also often translated as perception or recognition). This factor involves the mind's ability to identify the object by distinguishing it from other objects. This concept of discernment presents some difficulties, however. In its most elaborate form, discernment is based on our semiotic ability to make distinctions, mostly through linguistic signs. But for the Abhidharma, the mind's ability to identify objects is not limited to linguistic distinctions, however important they may be. Infants and non-human animals are understood to have the ability to make distinctions, although they do not use symbolic thinking. Are these prelinguistic cognitions nevertheless semiotic? Do they involve non-linguistic signs, or do they make distinctions without the use of signs? It seems plausible to argue that some of these states involve non-linguistic signs, as in the case of visual cognitions that distinguish objects

on the basis of visual clues. For the Abhidharma, however, this question strikes deeper, because several meditative states in the Buddhist tradition are described as signless (*animitta, mthan med*).[13] Can the mind in these states identify its object without making distinctions? Or is it the case that even in the case of signless states the mind still makes distinctions, although they are not linguistic or even conceptual? In a short chapter such as this one, we cannot delve into this issue, despite its relevance to the dialogue between Buddhism and the sciences of mind.

Other factors are also significant. Intention (*cetanā, sems pa*) is a central and omnipresent factor, which determines the moral (not ethical) character of the mental state. Every mental state approaches its object with an intention, a motivation that may be evident to the person or not. This intention determines the moral nature of the mental state, whether it is virtuous, non-virtuous, or neutral. This factor is associated with the accomplishment of a goal and hence is also thought of as a focus of organization for the other factors.

Also important is the role of attention (*manasikāra, yid la byed pa*), another one of the five omnipresent factors. It is the ability of the mind to be directed to an object. A contemporary commentator explains attention this way: "Attention is the mental factor responsible for the mind's advertence to the object, by virtue of which the object is made present to consciousness. Its characteristic is the conducting of the associated mental states [i.e., factors] to the object. Its function is to yoke the associated mental states [i.e., factors] to the object" (Bodhi, 1993, p. 81). Every mental state has at least a minimal amount of focus on its object; hence attention is an omnipresent factor.

Attention needs to be distinguished from two other related factors. The first is concentration (*samādhi, ting nge 'dzin*), the ability of the mind to dwell on its object single-pointedly. The second is mindfulness (*smṛti, dran pa*, also translated as recollection), which is the mind's ability to keep the object in focus without forgetting, being distracted, wobbling, or floating away from the object.

Both abilities are not present in every mental state. Concentration differs from attention in that it involves the ability of the mind not just to attend to an object but also to sustain this attention over a period of time. Similarly, mindfulness is more than the simple attending to the object. It involves the capacity of the mind to hold the object in its focus, preventing it from slipping away in forgetfulness. Hence both factors, which are vital to the practice of Buddhist meditation (see Chapter 19), are included among the determining factors. They are present only when the object is apprehended with some degree of clarity and sustained focus.

The factors discussed so far are mainly cognitive, but the Abhidharma list also includes mental factors we would describe as emotions. Consider the ethically determined factors, starting with the eleven virtuous ones: confidence/faith, self-regarding shame, other-regarding shame, joyful effort, pliability, conscientiousness, detachment, non-hatred (lovingkindness), wisdom, equanimity, and non-harmfulness (compassion).

We would describe several of these factors, such as lovingkindness and compassion, as emotions. These two factors belong to what we would characterize as the affective domain, although here they are understood not with regard to their affectivity, but rather in relation to their ethical character.[14] Hence they are grouped with other factors, such as wisdom and conscientiousness, that are more cognitive than affective. For the Abhidharma all these factors are grouped together. They are all positive in that they promote well-being and freedom from the inner compulsions that lead to suffering.

The afflictive factors, on the other hand, are precisely those that lead to suffering. They are by far the most numerous group and are clearly a major focus of this typology:

• Six root-afflictions: attachment, anger, ignorance, pride, negative doubt, and mistaken view.

• Twenty branch-afflictions: belligerence, vengefulness, concealment, spite, jealousy, avarice, pretense, dissimulation, self-satisfaction, cruelty, self-regarding shamelessness, other-regarding shamelessness, inconsideration, mental dullness, distraction, excitement, lack of confidence/faith, laziness, lack of conscientiousness, and forgetfulness.

Here again we notice that this list contains factors that look quite different. Some factors such as ignorance are clearly cognitive, whereas others such as anger and jealousy are more affective. They are grouped together because they are afflictive: They trouble the mind, making it restless and agitated. They also compel and bind the mind, preventing one from developing more positive attitudes. This afflictive character may be obvious in the case of attachment and jealousy, which directly lead to dissatisfaction, frustration, and restlessness. Ignorance – that is, our innate and mistaken sense of self – is less obviously afflictive, but its role is nonetheless central here, because it brings about the other more obviously afflictive factors.

Although there are many elements in the typology of mental factors that we can identify as emotions (anger, pride, jealously, lovingkindness, and compassion), there is no category that maps onto our notion of emotion. Most of the positive factors are not what we would call emotions, and although most of the negative factors are affective, not all are. Hence it is clear that the Abhidharma does not recognize the notion of emotion as a distinct category of a mental typology. There is no Abhidharma category that can be used to translate our concept of emotion, and similarly our concept of emotion is difficult to use to translate the Abhidharma terminology. Rather than opposing rational and irrational elements of the psyche, or cognitive and emotive systems of the mind (or brain), the Abhidharma emphasizes the distinction between virtuous and afflictive mental factors. Thus, our familiar Western distinction between cognition and emotion simply does not map onto the Abhidharma typology. Although the cognition/emotion distinction has recently been called into question by some scientists (see Chapter 29 and Damasio, 1995), it remains central to most of contemporary cognitive science and philosophy of mind. The Abhidharma typology offers a different approach, one in which mental factors are categorized according to their ethical character. This typology could prove fruitful for psychologists and social and affective neuroscientists interested in studying the biobehavioral components of human well-being (see Goleman, 2003).

The analyses of mental factors we have reviewed indicate the complexity, sophistication, and uniqueness of the Abhidharma mental typology. For this reason, the Abhidharma is often called, somewhat misleadingly, 'Buddhist psychology'.[15] Yet the Abhidharma analysis does not answer all the questions raised by the Buddhist view of the mind as lacking a real self. In particular, it leaves out the issue of the cognitive or epistemic structure of the mental states that make up the stream of consciousness. To examine this issue, we turn to another Indian Buddhist tradition, the logico-epistemological tradition of Dignāga and Dharmakīrti (see Dreyfus, 1997; Dunne, 2004).

Buddhist Epistemology

This tradition was started by Dignāga around 500 CE and was expanded significantly more than a century later by Dharmakīrti, the focus of our analysis. Its contribution was the explicit formulation of a complete Buddhist logical and epistemological system. The importance of this system in India can be seen in the continuous references to it by later Buddhist thinkers and the numerous attacks it received from orthodox Hindu thinkers. It gradually came to dominate the Indian Buddhist tradition, even eclipsing the Abhidharma as the prime focus of intellectual creativity.

The concern of this tradition is the nature of knowledge. In the Indian context, this issue is formulated as this question: What

is the nature of valid cognition (pramāṇa) and what are its types? Hindu thinkers tend to present a realist theory, which liberally allows a diversity of instruments of valid cognition. For example, the Sāṃkhya asserts that there are three types of valid sources of knowledge: perception (pratyakṣa), inference (anumāna), and verbal testimony (śabda). The Nyāya, perhaps the most important Hindu logico-epistemological tradition, added a fourth type of valid cognition, analogy (upamāna). This fourfold typology provided the most authoritative epistemological typology in India. Buddhist epistemology, however, rejects these typologies and offers a more restrictive view, limiting knowledge to inference and perception. It is in its examination of inference as a source of knowledge that the Buddhist tradition analyzes reasoning, in particular the conditions necessary for the formation of sound reasons and all their possible types. Hence this tradition is often described, also somewhat misleadingly, as 'Buddhist logic'.[16]

The interpretation of the word pramāṇa is itself a topic of debate among Buddhist and Hindu thinkers. For the latter, this word, in accordance with its grammatical form, refers to 'means of valid cognition'. This understanding also accords with the basic view of this school that knowledge is owned by a subject, the self, to whom knowledge is ultimately conveyed. For example, the Nyāya asserts that knowledge is a quality of the self. It is only when I become conscious of something that I can be said to know it. This view is energetically rejected by Dharmakīrti, who follows the classical Buddhist line that there is no knowing self, only knowledge. Hence, pramāṇa should not be taken in an instrumental sense, but as referring to the knowledge-event, the word itself being then interpreted as meaning valid cognition. This type of cognition is in turn defined as that cognition that is non-deceptive (avisaṃvādi-jñāna):

> Valid cognition is that cognition [that is] non-deceptive (avisaṃvādi). Non-deceptiveness [consists] in the readiness

[for the object] to perform a function (Dharmakīrti, Commentary on Valid Cognition II: 1, *translated by Dreyfus, in Miyasaka,* 1971–2).

This statement emphasizes that *pramāṇa* is not the instrument that a knowing self uses to know things. There is no separate knowing subject, but just knowledge, which is *pramāṇa.* According to this account, a cognition is valid if, and only if, it is non-deceptive. Dharmakīrti in turn interprets non-deceptiveness as consisting of an object's readiness to perform a function that relates to the way it is cognized. For example, the non-deceptiveness of a fire is its disposition to burn, and the non-deceptiveness of its perception is its apprehension as burning. This perception is non-deceptive because it practically corresponds to the object's own causal dispositions, contrary to the apprehension of the fire as cold.

The scope of the discussion of *pramāṇa,* however, is not limited to the analysis of knowledge, but constitutes a veritable philosophical method used in investigating other philosophical and even metaphysical topics. All pronouncements about the world and our ways of knowing it must rest on some attested forms of knowledge, such as perception and inference, if they are to be taken seriously. No one can simply claim truth, but must be able to establish statements by pinning down their epistemic supports. The advantage of this method is that it provides intertraditional standards of validation and the development of a relatively neutral framework within which philosophical and metaphysical claims can be assessed, without regard to religious or ideological backgrounds. This procedure is different from the Abhidharmic approach, which presupposes Buddhist ideas and vocabulary.

In analyzing the mind, Dharmakīrti starts from the same view of mind as the Abhidharma. Mind is made up of momentary mental states that arise in quick succession. Each moment of consciousness comes to be and disappears instantaneously, making a place for other moments of awareness. Moreover, each moment apprehends the object that

appears to it and in the process reveals the object that is apprehended. In this way, each mental state cognizes its object. But as an epistemologist, Dharmakīrti investigates issues left out by the Abhidharma, tackling questions that are central to any philosophical exploration of the mind. In this chapter, we examine some of these questions. First, we consider Dharmakīrti's analysis of the nature of cognitive events. We examine his view of the mind as apprehending representations of external objects, rather than the objects themselves, and the consequences that this view has for the issue of whether the mind is inherently reflexive (self-revealing and self-aware). We also examine Dharmakīrti's theory of perception, as well as some of his views on the nature of conceptuality and its relation to language. Finally, we revisit the issue of intentionality, showing the complexity of this notion and attempting to disentangle its several possible meanings within the context of a Buddhist account of the mental.

The Reflexive Nature of Mental Events

We commonly assume that we have unproblematic access to our environment through our senses. Even casual first-person investigation shows, however, that such access may well not be the case. There are cases of perceptual illusions, and even when we are not deceived, the perceptions of individuals vary greatly. Hence philosophy cannot take for granted the common-sense view of perceptual knowledge. Many Western philosophers have argued that our perceptual knowledge goes well beyond the sensible experiences that give rise to it. Although this claim is debatable, we cannot assume without examination that we understand the way in which cognition apprehends its objects.

In thinking about the nature of cognition, Dharmakīrti relies crucially on the concept of *aspect* (*ākāra*), a notion that goes back to the Sāṃkhya, but has been accepted by several other schools. The idea behind this position, which is called in Indian philosophy *sākāravāda* ('assertion of aspect'), is that cognition does not apprehend its object nakedly, but rather through an aspect, which is the reflection or imprint left by the object on the mind. For example, a visual sense consciousness does not directly perceive a blue color, but captures the likeness of blue as imprinted on cognition. Thus, to be aware of an object does not mean apprehending this object directly, but having a mental state that has the form of this object and being cognizant of this form. The aspect is the cognitive form or epistemic factor that allows us to distinguish mental episodes and differentiate among our experiences. Without aspects, we could not distinguish, for instance, a perception of blue from a perception of yellow, for we do not perceive yellow directly. The role of the aspect is thus crucial in Dharmakīrti's system, for it explains a key feature of consciousness: Consciousness is not the bare seeing that direct realism and common sense suppose, but rather the apprehension of an aspect that represents this object in the field of consciousness. The aspect is not external to consciousness. It is not only the form under which an external object presents itself to consciousness but also the form that consciousness assumes when it perceives its object. Thus an aspect is a representation of objects in consciousness, as well as the consciousness that sees this representation.

The implication of this analysis is that perception is inherently reflexive. Awareness takes on the form of an object and reveals that form by assuming it. Thus, in the process of revealing external things, cognition reveals itself. This view of cognition as 'self-luminous' (*svayam prakāśa*) and self-presencing is not unique to Dignāga, its first Buddhist propounder, or to Dharmakīrti, his follower. It is also accepted by other thinkers, particularly the Hindu Vedāntins, who identify consciousness as the self and describe it as being 'only known to itself' (*svayaṃvedya*) and 'self-effulgent' (*svayamprabha*; see Gupta 1998, 2003; Mayeda, 1979/1992, pp. 22, 44). For Dignāga and Dharmakīrti, however, the inherently reflexive character of consciousness is not a consequence of its transcendent and pure nature, but of its consisting of the beholding of an internal representation. From one side, consciousness has an externally oriented feature, called the objective aspect (*grāhyākāra*). This feature is the form that a mental state assumes under the influence of an external object. The second side is the internal knowledge of our own mental states. It is called the subjective aspect (*grāhakākāra*), the feature that ensures that we are aware of the objective aspect, the representation of the object. These two parts do not exist separately. Rather, each mental state consists of both and hence is necessarily reflexive (aware of itself in being aware of its object).

The necessary reflexivity of consciousness is understood by Dharmakīrti and his followers as a particular type of perception called *self-cognition* (*svasaṃvedana*). Self-cognition can be compared to what Western philosophers call *apperception*; namely, the knowledge that we have of our own mental states. It is important to keep in mind, however, that apperception does not imply a second and separate cognition directed toward a given mental state of which one is thereby aware. For Dharmakīrti, apperception is not introspective or reflective, for it does not take inner mental states as its objects. It is instead the self-cognizing factor inherent in every mental episode, which provides us with a non-thematic awareness of our mental states. For Dharmakīrti, reflexivity is a necessary consequence of his analysis of perception, according to which a subjective aspect beholds an objective aspect that represents the external object within the field of consciousness. Self-cognition is nothing over and above this beholding.

Self-cognition is the intuitive presence that we feel we have toward our own mental episodes. We may not be fully aware of all the aspects and implications of our experiences, but we do seem to keep track of them. Tibetan scholars express this idea by saying that there is no person whose mental states are completely hidden to him- or herself. This limited self-presence is not due to a metaphysical self, but to self-cognition. Because apperception does not rely on reasoning, it is taken to be a form of perception.

Apperception does not constitute, however, a separate reflective or introspective cognition. Otherwise, the charge that the notion of apperception opens an infinite regress would be hard to avoid.

Dharmakīrti's ideas are not unlike those Western philosophers who have argued that consciousness implies self-consciousness (see Chapters 3 and 4). Such philosophers include (despite their otherwise vast differences) Aristotle, Descartes, Locke, Kant, Husserl, and Sartre (see Wider, 1997, pp. 7–39). According to Locke, a person is conscious of his or her own mental states. He defines consciousness as "the perception of what passes in a man's mind" (*Essay Concerning Human Understanding* II: ii, 19). Leibniz, in his *New Essays Concerning Human Understanding* (II: i, 19), criticizes Locke, pointing out that this view leads to an infinite regress, for if every cognitive act implies self-awareness, self-knowledge must also be accompanied by another awareness, and so on ad infinitum. This regress arises, however, only if knowledge of one's mental states is assumed to be distinct from knowledge of external objects. This assumption is precisely what Dharmakīrti denies. A consciousness is aware of itself in a non-dual way that does not involve the presence of a separate awareness of consciousness. The cognizing person simply knows that he or she cognizes without the intervention of a separate perception of the cognition. This knowledge is the function of apperception, which thus provides an element of certainty with respect to our mental states. Apperception does not necessarily validate these states, however. For example, one can take oneself to be seeing water without knowing whether that seeing is veridical. In this case, one knows that one has an experience, but one does not know that one knows. The determination of the validity of a cognition is not internal or intrinsic to that cognition, but is to be established by practical investigation.

Several arguments are presented by Dharmakīrti to establish the reflexive nature of consciousness.[17] One of his main arguments concerns the nature of suffering and happiness as it reveals the deeper nature of mental states. For Dharmakīrti, as for the Abhidharma, suffering and happiness are not external to consciousness, but integral to our awareness of external objects. Our perceptions arise with a certain feeling-tone, be it pleasant, unpleasant, or neutral; this feeling-tone is a function of the presence of the mental factor of feeling as described by the Abhidharma. This feeling needs to be noticed, however; otherwise we would not be aware of how the apprehension of the object feels. Because this noticing cannot be the function of another mental state without incurring the problem of an infinite regress, it must be the mental state apprehending the external object that becomes aware at the same time of the feeling. This conclusion indicates, for Dharmakīrti, the dual nature of mental states. In a single mental state, two aspects can be distinguished: (1) the objective aspect, the representation of the external object in consciousness, and (2) the subjective aspect, the apprehension of this appearance or self-cognition.

For Dharmakīrti, a mental state thus has two functions. It apprehends an external object (*ālambana*) and beholds itself. The apprehension of an external object is not direct, but results from the causal influence of the object, which induces cognition to experience (*anubhava*) the object's representation. Hence, mind does not experience an external object, but beholds an internal representation that stands for an external object. Cognition cannot be reduced to a process of direct observation, but involves a holding of an inner representation. This beholding is not, however, an apprehension in the usual sense of the word, for the two aspects of a single mental episode are not separate. It is an 'intimate' contact, a direct experiencing of the mental state by itself through which we become aware of our mental states at the same time as we perceive things.

Theory of Perception

This view of cognition as bearing only indirectly on external objects has obvious consequences for the theory of perception. The theory of perception is an important element of Dharmakīrti's epistemology, for we have access to external reality first and foremost through perception, the primary valid cognition. But this access is not as unproblematic as one might think. Although it might seem commonsensical that perception results from our encounter with the world, in reality consciousness does not directly cognize the object, but only indirectly cognizes it. For Dharmakīrti, as we have seen, the mind has direct access only to the representational *aspect* caused by the object; the object itself remains inaccessible to consciousness. The similarity between object and aspect – and hence between object and consciousnesss, the aspect being the cognitive form of the object that stands for the object in the field of consciousness – is the crucial element in this causal theory of perception. This similarity ensures that perception is not locked up in its own appearances, as conceptions are. Consciousness is not in direct contact with the external world, but only with an internal impression caused by the external object. Hence the external object remains hidden, though not completely.

When pressed by these problems, Dharmakīrti sometimes shifts between the views of two different Buddhist philosophical schools, using one perspective to bypass problems that arise in the other. These two views are the Sautrāntika theory of perception, which is representationalist in the ways just described, and the Yogācāra theory, which is idealist and denies that there is anything outside of consciousness. Following Dignāga's example and his strategy of ascending scales of philosophical analysis, Dharmakīrti holds that the Yogācāra theory is truer and hence higher on the scale of analysis. This theory denies that there are any external objects over and above the direct objects of perception. Thus its view of perception is phenomenalist: It reduces external objects to interpreted mental data, but such data are no longer taken to stand for external objects (because it is now held that nothing exists outside of consciousness). This theory, however, is counter-intuitive, and so Dharmakīrti refers to it only occasionally, prefer-

ring to argue on the basis of the commonsensical assumption that external objects exist. His theory of perception thus has a peculiar two-tiered structure, in which he presupposes the existence of external objects, which he then ultimately rejects to propound a form of idealism.

Among these two tiers, the one Dharmakīrti most often refers to is the Sautrāntika representationalist theory of perception. According to this view, consciousness does not have direct access to external objects, but grasps objects via the intermediary of an aspect caused by and similar to an external object. He sometimes replaces this view by a Yogācāra view, which holds that internal impressions are not produced by external objects, but by internal tendencies. This shift into full-blown idealism allows Dharmakīrti to bypass the difficulties involved in explaining the relation between internal perceptions and external objects. Because there are no external objects, the problem of the relation between internal impressions and external objects does not arise. At this level, his philosophy of perception can be described as phenomenalist, for it holds that there is no external object outside of aspects.

Another major feature of Dharmakīrti's account is his sharp separation between perception and conception, a separation enshrined in his definition of perception as the cognition that is unmistaken (*abhrānta*) and free from conceptions (*kalpanāpoḍha*) (*Commentary on Valid Cognition*, III: 300 cd). Because perception is unmistaken and conception is mistaken, perception must be free from conception. This analysis of perception differs sharply from the dominant account in India, the epistemological realism of the Nyāya school and its assertion of the existence of a determinate (*savikalpaka*) form of perception. For the Nyāya, perception does not stop with the simple taking in of sensory stimuli, but also involves the ability to categorize this input. Although we may start with a first moment of indeterminate perception, in which we merely take in external reality, we do not stop there but go on to formulate perceptual judgments. Moreover, and this is the crux of the question, these judgments are for the Nyāya fully perceptual. They are not mistaken conceptual overlays, but true reflections of reality.

This commonsensical view of perception is not acceptable to Dharmakīrti, for it leads to an unenviable choice: either accept the reality of the abstract entities necessary for the articulation of the content of perception or reject the possibility of an unmistaken cognition. Because neither possibility is acceptable for Dharmakīrti, he holds that perception can only be non-conceptual. There is no determinate perception, for the judgments induced by perception are not perceptual, but are just conceptual superimpositions. They do not reflect the individual reality of phenomena, but instead address their general characteristics. Because those are only constructs, the cognitions that conceive them cannot be true reflections of reality. Hence for perception to be undistorted in a universe of particulars, it must be totally free from conceptual elaborations. This position implies a radical separation between perception, which merely holds the object as it is in the perceptual ken, and interpretation of this object, which introduces conceptual constructs into the cognitive process.

This requirement that perception be non-conceptual is the cornerstone of the Buddhist theory of perception. But it creates problems for Dharmakīrti. It would seem that given his privileging of perception he should hold an empiricist view, according to which perception boils down to a bare encounter with reality and knowledge is given to the senses. Dharmakīrti should hold the view that the aspects through which we come to perceive reality are fully representational like Locke's ideas, that they stand for external objects, and that their apprehension is in and of itself cognitive. Dharmakīrti's view of perception, however, is more complex, for he shares with Sellars (1956) the recognition that knowledge, even at the perceptual level, does not boil down to an encounter with reality, but requires active categorization. We do not know things by sensing them, for perception does not deliver articulated objects, but only impressions, which by themselves are not forms of knowledge but become so only when they are integrated within our categorical schemes. For example, when we are hit on the head, we first have an impression. We just have a sensation of pain, which is not by itself cognitive. This sensation becomes cognitive when it becomes integrated into a conceptual scheme, in which it is explained as being an impact on a certain part of our body due to certain causes. It is only then that the impression of being hit becomes fully intentional. Prior to this cognitive integration, the impression, or to speak Dharmakīrti's language, the aspect, does not yet represent anything in the full sense of the word. It only becomes so when interpreted conceptually.

This view of perception agrees with Dharmakīrti's analysis of the validity of cognitions, which consists in their being 'non-deceptive', a term interpreted in practical terms. Cognitions are valid if, and only if, they have the ability to lead us toward successful practical actions. In the case of perception, however, practical validity is not as straightforward as one might think. Achieving practical purposes depends on correctly describing the objects we encounter. It is not enough to see an object that is blue; we must also see it *as* being blue. To be non-deceptive, a cognition depends on the appropriate identification of the object as being this or that. Perceptions, however, do not identify their objects, for they are not conceptual. They cannot categorize their objects, but only hold them without any determination. Categorization requires conceptual thought under the form of a judgment. Such a judgment subsumes its object under an appropriate universal, thereby making it part of the practical world where we deal with long-lasting entities that we conceive of as parts of a determined order of things. For example, we sense a blue object that we categorize as blue. The perceptual aspect (the blue aspect) is not yet a representation in the full sense of the word, because its apprehension, the perception of blue, is not yet cognitive. It is only when it is interpreted by a conception that the aspect becomes a full-fledged intentional object standing for an external object. Hence, Dharmakīrti's account of perception leads us to realize the importance of categorical interpretation in the formation of perceptual knowledge, a position that is not without problems for his system, given his emphasis on the primacy and non-conceptuality of perception. Nevertheless, the merit of this analysis is that it disentangles the processes through which we come to know the world, explaining the role of perception as a way to contact the world while emphasizing the role of conceptual categorization in the formation of practical knowledge.

Thought and Language

In examining thought (*kalpanā*), Dharmakīrti postulates a close association with language. In fact, the two can be considered equivalent from an epistemological point of view. Language signifies through conceptual mediation in the same way that thought conceives of things. The relation between the two also goes the other way: We do not first understand things independently of linguistic signs and then communicate this understanding to others. Dharmakīrti recognizes a cognitive import to language; through language we identify the particular things we encounter, and in this way we integrate the object into the meaningful world we have constructed. The cognitive import of language is particularly obvious in the acquisition of more complex concepts. In these cases, it is clear that there is nothing in experience that could possibly give rise to these concepts without language. Without linguistic signs thought cannot keep track of things to any degree of complexity. Dharmakīrti also notes that we usually remember things by recollecting the words associated with those things. Thus concepts and words mutually depend on each other.

This close connection between thought and language, inherited from Dignāga, differentiates Dharmakīrti from classical empiricists, such as Locke and modern sense-data theorists, who believe in what Sellars (1956) describes as the 'myth of the given'. Locke, for example, holds that concepts and words are linked through association. The word 'tree' acquires its meaning by becoming connected with the idea *tree*, which is the mental image of a tree. Hence for Locke the representation of the tree is not formed through language, but is given to sensation (Dharmakīrti's perception). We understand a tree as a tree through mere acquaintance with its representation without recourse to concepts. Dharmakīrti's philosophy is quite different, for it emphasizes the constitutive and constructive nature of language. This conception of language is well captured by one of Dharmakīrti's definitions of thought:

> *Conceptual cognition is that consciousness in which representation (literally, appearance) is fit to be associated which words* (Ascertainment of Valid Cognition 40: 6–7, in Vetter, 1966).

Thought identifies its object by associating the representation of the object with a word. When we conceive of an object we do not apprehend it directly, but through the mediation of its aspect. Mediation through an aspect also occurs with perception, but here the process of mediation is different. In the case of perception there is a direct causal connection between the object and its representation, but no such link exists for thought. There is no direct causal link between the object and thought, but rather an extended process of mediation in which linguistic signs figure prominently.

For Dharmakīrti, the starting point of this process is our encounter with a variety of objects that we experience as being similar or different. We construct concepts in association with linguistic signs to capture this sense of experienced similarity and difference. This linguistic association creates a more precise concept in which the representations are made to stand for a commonality that the objects are assumed to possess. For example, we see a variety of trees and apprehend a similarity between these objects. At this level, our mental representations have yet to yield a concept of tree. The concept of tree is formed when we connect our representations with a socially formed and communicated sign and assume that they stand for a treeness that we take individual trees to share. In this way experiences give rise to mental representations, which are transformed into concepts by association with a linguistic sign. The formation of a concept consists of the assumption that mental representations stand for an agreed-upon imagined commonality. Thus concepts come to be through the conjunction of the experience of real objects and the social process of language acquisition. Concept formation is connected to reality, albeit in a mediated and highly indirect way.

But concept formation is also mistaken, according to this view. A concept is based on the association of a mental representation with a term that enables the representation to stand for a property assumed to be shared by various individuals. In Dharmakīrti's nominalist world of individuals, however, things do not share a common property; rather, the property is projected onto them. The property is manufactured when a representation is made to stand for an assumed commonality, which a variety of individuals are mistakenly taken to instantiate. Hence this property is not real; it is merely a pseudo-entity superimposed (adhyāropa) on individual realities. This property is also not reducible to a general term. In other words, the commonality that we project onto things does not reside in using the same term to designate discrete individuals. Upon analyzing the notion of sameness of terms, we realize that identifying individual terms as being the same presupposes the concept of sameness of meaning, in relation to which the individual terms can be identified. Thus commonality is not due simply to a term, but requires the formation of concepts on the basis of the mistaken imputation of commonality onto discrete individuals.

What does it mean, however, for a concept to be based on an assumed commonality? Here Dharmakīrti's theory must be placed within its proper context, the apoha or exclusion theory of language, which was created by Dignāga. This complex topic is beyond the scope of this chapter. Suffice it to say that the apoha theory is a way to explain how language signifies in a world of individuals. Linguistic meaning poses a particularly acute problem for Dignāga and Dharmakīrti, for they are committed to a connotationist view of language, in which sense has primacy over reference. Such a view, however, is difficult to hold in a nominalist ontology that disallows abstract entities, such as meaning.[18]

The apoha theory tries to solve this conundrum by arguing that language does not describe reality positively through universals, but negatively by exclusion. Language is primarily meaningful, but this does not mean that there are real senses. Rather, we posit agreed-upon fictions that we construct for the sake of categorizing the world according to our purposes. Thus 'cow' does not describe Bessie through the mediation of a real universal (cowness), but by excluding a particular (Bessie) from the class of non-cow. Matilal describes Dignāga's view this way:

> Each name, as Dignāga understands, dichotomizes the universe into two: those to which the name can be applied and those to which it cannot be applied. The function of a name is to exclude the object from the class of those objects to which it cannot be applied. One might say that the function of a name is to locate the object outside of the class of those to which it cannot be applied (Matilal, 1971, p. 45).

Although linguistic form suggests that we subsume an individual under a property, analysis reveals that words merely exclude objects from being included in a class to which they do not belong. The function of a name is to locate negatively an object within a conceptual sphere. The impression that words positively capture the nature of objects is misleading.

This theory was immediately attacked by Hindu thinkers, such as Kumārila and Uddyotakara, who raised strong objections. One of them was that this theory is counterintuitive, because we do not perceive ourselves to eliminate non-cows when we conceive of cows. Dharmakīrti's theory of concept formation is in many ways an attempt to answer these attacks. It argues that the *apoha* theory is not psychological, but epistemological. In conceiving of objects we do not directly eliminate other objects, but instead rely on a representation that is made to stand in for an assumed commonality shared by several particulars. It is this fictional commonality that is the result of an exclusion. There is nothing over and above particulars, which are categorized on the basis of their being excluded from what they are not. The concept that has been formed in an essentially negative way is projected onto real things. In the process of making judgments such as 'this is a tree', the real differences that exist between the different trees come to be ignored and the similarities are reified into a common universal property, which is nothing but a socially agreed-upon fiction.

The eliminative nature of thought and language is psychologically revealed when we examine the learning process. The word 'cow', for instance, is not learned only through a definition, but by a process of elimination. We can give a definition of 'cow', but the definition works only if its elements are known already. For example, we can define cows as animals having dewlaps, horns, and so on (the traditional definition of 'cow' in Indian philosophy). But how do we know what counts as a dewlap? Not just by pointing to the neck of a cow, but by eliminating the cases that do not fit. In this way, we establish a dichotomy between those animals that fit, and other animals or things that do not, and on the basis of this negative dichotomy we construct a fictive property, cowness. This construction is not groundless, however, but proceeds through an indirect causal connection with reality. Concepts are not formed a priori, but elaborated as a result of experiences. Dharmakīrti's solution to the problem of thought and meaning is thus to argue that in a world bereft of real abstract entities (properties), there are only constructed intensional (linguistic) pseudo-entities, but that this construction is based on experience; that is, perception.

This grounding in perception ensures that, although conception is mistaken in the way reviewed above, it is neither baseless nor random and hence can lead to the formation of concepts that will be attuned to the causal capacities of particulars.

Dharmakīrti and Abhidharma: Intentionality Revisited

Dharmakīrti's analysis has in certain respects a great deal of continuity with the Abhidharma. Both view the mind as constituted by a succession of mental states in accordance with their ontological commitments, which privilege the particular over the general. Reality is made up of a plurality of elements (here moments of awareness), and generality, when it is not a figment of our imagination, is at best the result of aggregation. This emphasis on the particular derives from the central tenets of the Buddhist tradition; namely, non-substantiality and dependent origination. In Dharmakīrti's epistemological approach, this emphasis expresses itself in valuing perception over conception, and in the problematic but necessary cooperation between the two forms of cognition. We do not come to know things by merely coming across them, but by integrating them into our conceptual schemes on the basis of our experiences.

One question raised by this analysis concerns intentionality. The Abhidharma tradition had assumed all along that cognitions were intentional, but did not provide a systematic analysis of intentionality. Dharmakīrti fills this gap, analyzing the way in which various types of cognition bear on their objects. But because he makes a sharp distinction between perception and conception, his analysis does not yield a single concept of intentionality, but on the contrary leads us to realize that this central notion may have to be understood in multiple ways. The cognitive process starts with our encounter with the world through perceptions, but this encounter is not enough to bring about knowledge. Only when we are able to integrate the objects delivered through the senses into our categorical schemes can we be said to know them in the full sense of the word. Hence, if we understand intentionality as cognitive – that is, as pertaining to knowledge – we may well have to agree with Dharmakīrti that perception is not in and of itself fully intentional. Only when perception is coordinated with conception does it become intentional; hence it can be said to be intentional only in a derived sense of the word. Perception is not in and of itself cognitive, but only inasmuch as it has the ability to induce conceptual interpretations of its objects. This does not mean, however, that perception is completely blank or purely passive. It has an intentional function, that of delivering impressions that we take in and organize through our conceptual schemes. Hence, perception can be said to have a phenomenal intentionality, which may be revealed in certain forms of meditative experiences.

Dharmakīrti alludes to such experiences when he describes a form of meditation, in which we empty our mind without closing it completely to the external world (*Commentary on Valid Cognition* III: 123–5, in Miyasaka 1971–2). In this state of liminal awareness, things appear to us but we do not identify them. We merely let them be. When we come out of this stage, the usual conceptual flow returns, and with it the conceptualization that allows us to identify things as being this or that. This experience shows, Dharmakīrti argues, that identification is not perceptual, but is due to conceptualization. In such a state, perception takes place but not conceptualization. Hence, perception is a non-conceptual sensing onto which interpretations are added.

Due to the speed of the mental process, the untrained person cannot differentiate conceptual from non-conceptual cognitions. It is only on special occasions, such as in some form of meditation, that a clear differentiation can be made. There, the flow of thought gradually subsides, and we reach a state in which there is a bare sensing of things. In this state, what we call shapes and colors are seen barely (i.e., as they are delivered to our senses without the adjunctions of conceptual interpretations). When one gradually emerges from such a non-conceptual state, the flow of thoughts gradually reappears, and we are able to make judgments about what we saw during our meditation. One is then also able to make a clear differentiation between the products of thoughts and the bare delivery of the senses and to distinguish cognitive from phenomenal intentionality.

The analysis of intentionality, however, may have to go even further to account for all the forms of cognition known to Buddhist traditions. We alluded above to the Abhidharmic idea of a store-consciousness, a subliminal form of cognition that supports all the propensities, habits, and tendencies of a person. Although such a store-consciousness is usually asserted by the Yogācāra to support their idealist view, it is known to other traditions under other names and hence has to be taken seriously within a Buddhist account of the mind, regardless of the particular views that are associated with it. But given the particularities of this form of consciousness, its integration within a Buddhist view of the mind is not without problems. The difficulties come from the fact that the store-consciousness does not seem to have cognitive or even phenomenal intentionality. Because it does not capture any feature, it cannot be said to know its object, like conceptions. Because it is subliminal, it is difficult to attribute to it a phenomenal content able to induce categorization, like perceptions. How then can it be intentional?

To respond to this question would necessitate an analysis that goes well beyond the purview of this chapter. Several avenues are open to us. We could argue that the store-consciousness is not intentional and hence that intentionality is not the defining characteristic of the mental, but only of certain forms of cognitions. We would then be faced with the task of explaining the nature of the mental in a way that does not presuppose intentionality. Or we could extend the concept of intentionality, arguing that the store-consciousness is not intentional in the usual cognitive or phenomenal senses of the word, but rather that its intentionality consists in its having a dispositional ability to generate more explicit cognitive states. Some Western phenomenologists, notably Husserl and

Merleau-Ponty, distinguish 'object directed intentionality' from 'operative intentionality' (see Chapter 4). Whereas the former is what we usually mean by intentionality, the latter is a non-reflective tacit sensibility, a spontaneous and involuntary level that makes us ready to respond cognitively and affectively to the world, though it is not by itself explicitly cognitive. This most basic form of intentionality is important in explaining our openness to the world. It also seems an interesting avenue for exploring the cognitive nature of the store-consciousness.

Conclusion

We can now see the richness and the complexities of the Indian Buddhist analyses of the nature of the mind and consciousness. The Abhidharma provides the basis of these analyses, with its view of the mind as a stream of moments of consciousness and its distinction between the primary factor of awareness and mental factors. This tradition also emphasizes the intentional nature of consciousness, the ability of consciousness to be about something else. As we have seen, however, this concept is far from self-evident and needs further philosophical clarification. This clarification is one of the important tasks of Dharmakīrti's philosophy. In accomplishing this task, Dharmakīrti critically explores the variety of human cognitions, distinguishing the conceptual from the perceptual modes of cognition and emphasizing the constructed nature of the former and its close connection with language. Yet, as we have also seen, this philosophy is not always able to account for all the insights of the Abhidharma, particularly those concerning the deeper layers of consciousness.

When we look at the Indian Buddhist tradition, we should not look for a unified and seamless view of the mind. Like any other significant tradition, Indian Buddhist philosophy of mind is plural and animated by debates, questions, and tensions. This rich tradition has a great deal to offer contemporary mind science and philosophy, includ-ing rich phenomenological investigations of various aspects of human cognition and exploration of various levels and types of meditative consciousness. This tradition also shows, however, that it would be naïve to take these investigations of consciousness as being objectively given or established. Rather, they are accounts of experience that are often intertwined with doctrinal formulations and hence are open to critique, revision, and challenge, like any other human interpretation. Indeed, these formulations need to be taken seriously and examined with the kind of critical spirit and rigorous philosophical thinking exhibited by Dharmakīrti. Only then, can we do justice to the insights of this tradition.

Glossary

Sāṃkhya

Pradhāna: primordial nature or prakṛti, materiality. The primordial substance out of which the diversity of phenomena arise. It is composed of three qualities (guṇa): sattva (transparency, buoyancy), rajas (energy, activity), and tamas (inertia, obstruction). They are the principles or forces whose combination produces mental and material phenomena.

Atman: spiritual self or puruṣa, person. The non-material spiritual element that merely witnesses the mental activities involved in the ordinary awareness of objects.

Buddhi: usually translated as 'the intellect'. It has the ability to distinguish and experience objects. This ability provides the prereflective and presubjective ground out of which determined mental states and their objects arise. It is also the locus of all the fundamental predispositions that lead to these experiences.

Ahaṃkāra: egoity or ego-sense. This is the sense of individual subjectivity or selfhood tied to embodiment, which gives rise to the subjective pole of cognition.

Manas: mentation. It oversees the senses and discriminates between objects. By serving as an intermediary between the intellect and the senses, mentation organizes sensory impressions and objects and integrates them into a temporal framework created by memories and expectations.

Citta: mental activities or *antahkarana,* internal organ. This is the grouping of *buddhi, ahamkāra,* and *manas.*

Pramāṇa: instrument of valid cognition of the self. The Sāṃkhya recognizes three such instruments: perception, inference, and testimony. The Nyāya adds a fourth one, analogy.

Buddhist

Citta: primary factor of awareness or *vijñāna,* consciousness. It is the aspect of the mental state that is aware of the object, or the bare apprehension of the object. It is the awareness that merely discerns the object, the activity of cognizing the object.

Caitesika: mental factor. Mental factors are aspects of the mental state that characterize the object of awareness and account for its engagement. In other words, whereas consciousness makes known the mere presence of the object, mental factors make known the particulars of the content of awareness, defining the characteristics and special conditions of its object.

Alaya-vijñāna: store-consciousness. This continuously present subliminal consciousness is posited by some of the Yogācāra thinkers to provide a sense of continuity in the person over time. It is the repository of all the basic habits, tendencies, and propensities (including those that persist from one life to the next) accumulated by the individual.

Bhavaṅga citta: life-constituent consciousness. Although this consciousness is not said to be always present and arises only during the moments where there is no manifest mental activity, it also provides a sense of continuity for the Theravada school, which asserts its existence.

Kliṣṭa-manas: afflictive mentation. This is the inborn sense of self that arises from the apprehension of the store-consciousness as being a self. From a Buddhist point of view, however, this sense of self is fundamentally mistaken. It is a mental imposition of unity where there is in fact only the arising of a multiplicity of interrelated physical and mental events.

pramāṇa: valid cognition. Not the instrument of a self but the knowledge-event itself. There are only two types of valid cognition admissible in Buddhist epistemology, *pratyakṣa,* perception, and *anumāna,* inference.

Svasaṃvedana: self-cognition. This is the limited but intuitive presence that we feel we have toward our own mental episodes, which is due not to the presence of a metaphysical self but to the non-thematic reflexive knowledge that we have of our own mental states. Because self-cognition does not rely on reasoning, it is taken to be a form of perception. It does not constitute, however, a separate reflective or introspective cognition. Otherwise, the charge that the notion of apperception opens an infinite regress would be hard to avoid.

Notes

1. Presenting the Sāṃkhya view in a few lines is problematic given its evolution over a long period of time, an evolution shaped by the addition of numerous refinements and new analyses in response to the critiques of Buddhists and Vedāntins. For a quick summary, see Mahalingam (1977). For a more detailed examination, see Larson and Bhattacharya (1987).

2. Contrary to Vedānta, the Sāṃkhya holds that there are many individual selves rather than a universal ground of being such as *Brahman.*

3. The notion of a pure and passive 'witness consciousness' is a central element of many Hindu views about consciousness (see Gupta, 1998, 2003).

4. For a thoughtful discussion of this view of the mind, see Schweizer (1993).

5. Numerous translations of Patañjali's *Yoga Sutras* are available in English.

6. For discussion of the Advaita Vedānta view of consciousness, see Gupta (2003, Chapter 5). For a philosophical overview of Advaita Vedānta, see Deutsch (1969).

7. For a glimpse of the origins of the Abhidharma, see Gethin (1992).

8. For Husserl, by contrast, not all consciousness is intentional in the sense of being object-directed. See Chapter 4 and the final section of this chapter.

9. All quotations from this work are translated from the French by G. Dreyfus.

10. See Rahula (1980, p. 17). Although the Theravada Abhidharma does not recognize a distinct store-consciousness, its concept of *bhavaçga citta*, the life-constituent consciousness, is similar. For a view of the complexities of the *bhavaçga*, see Waldron (2003, pp. 81–87).

11. They are then said to be conjoined (*sampayutta, mtshungs ldan*), in that they are simultaneous and have the same sensory basis, the same object, the same aspect or way of apprehending this object, and the same substance (the fact that there can be only one representative of a type of consciousness and mental factor at the same time). See Waldron (2003, p. 205).

12. This list, which is standard in the Tibetan tradition, is a compilation based on Asaçga's *Abhidharma–samuccaya*. It is not, however, Asaçga's own list, which contains 52 items (Rahula 1980, p. 7). For further discussion, see Napper (1980) and Rabten (1978/1992). For the lists of some of the other traditions, see Bodhi (1993, pp. 76–79) and de la Vallée Poussin (1971, II: 150–178).

13. Although some of these states may be soteriologically significant and involve the ability to transcend duality, not all need be. The practice of concentration can involve signless meditative states, and so too does the practice of some of the so-called formless meditative states.

14. For a discussion of whether compassion and lovingkindness, seen from a Buddhist point of view, are emotions, see Dreyfus (2002).

15. For a brief but thoughtful discussion of the idea of Buddhism as a psychology, see Gomez (2004).

16. For discussion of the characteristics of Indian logic, see Matilal (1985) and Barlingay (1975). On Buddhist logic, see Kajiyama (1966). For an analysis of Dharmakīrti's philosophy, see Dreyfus (1997) and Dunne (2004).

17. For a detailed treatment of Dharmakīrti's arguments and their further elaboration in the Tibetan tradition, see Dreyfus (1997, pp. 338–341, 400–415).

18. For more on this difficult topic, see Dreyfus (1997) and Dunne (2004).

References

Barlingay, S. S. (1975). *A modern introduction to Indian logic*. Delhi: National.

Bodhi, B. (Ed.). (1993). *A comprehensive manual of Abhidharma*. Seattle, WA: Buddhist Publication Society.

Damasio, A. (1995). *Descartes' error: Emotion, reason and the human brain*. New York: Harper Perennial.

de la Vallée Poussin, L. (1971). *L'Abhidharmakośa de Vasubandhu*. Bruxelles: Institut Belge des Hautes Etudes Chinoises.

de la Vallée Poussin, L. (1991). Notes sur le moment ou ksana des bouddhistes. In H. S. Prasad (Ed.), *Essays on time*. Delhi: Sri Satguru.

Deutsch, E. (1969). *Advaita Vedanta: A philosophical reconstruction*. Honolulu: University Press of Hawaii.

Dreyfus, G. (1997). *Recognizing reality: Dharmakīrti's philosophy and its Tibetan interpretations*. Albany, NY: State University of New York Press.

Dreyfus, G. (2002). Is compassion an emotion? A cross-cultural exploration of mental typologies. In R. Davidson & A. Harrington (Eds.), *Visions of compassion: Western scientists and Tibetan Buddhists examine human nature* (pp. 31–45). Oxford: Oxford University Press.

Dunne, J. D. (2004). *Foundations of Dharmakīrti's philosophy*. Boston: Wisdom.

Gethin, R. (1992). The Mātrikās: Memorization, mindfulness and the list. In J. Gyatso (Ed.), *In *the mirror of memory* (pp. 149–172). Albany, NY: State University of New York Press.

Goleman, D. (2003). *Destructive emotions. A scientific dialogue with the Dalai Lama*. New York: Bantam.

Gomez, L. (2004). Psychology. In R. Buswell (Ed.), *Encyclopedia of Buddhism* (pp. 678–692). New York: MacMillan.

Guenther, H. (1976). *Philosophy and psychology in the Abhidharma*. Berkeley, CA: Shambala Press, 1976.

Gupta, B. (1998). *The disinterested witness. A fragment of Advaita Vedanta phenomenology*. Evanston, IL: Northwestern University Press.

Gupta, B. (2003). *Cit. consciousness*. New Delhi: Oxford University Press.

James, W. (1981). *Principles of psychology*. Cambridge, MA: Harvard University Press.

Kajiyama, Y. (1966). *Introduction to Buddhist logic*. Kyoto: Kyoto University.

Larson, J., & Bhattacharya, R. S. (1987). *Encyclopedia of Indian philosophies: Sāṃkhya, A dualist tradition in Indian philosophy*. Delhi: Motilal.

Mahalingam, I. (1977). Sāṃkhya-Yoga. In B. Carr & I. Mahalingam (Eds.), *Companion encyclopedia of Asian philosophy*. London: Routledge Press.

Matlilal, B. K. (1971). *Epistemology, logic, and grammar in Indian philosophical analysis*. The Hague: Mouton.

Matilal, B. K. (1985). *Logic, language, and reality*. Delhi: Matilal Banarsidas.

Mayeda, S. (1992). *A thousand teaching: The Upadeśashasrī*. Albany, NY: State University of New York Press. Original work published 1979.

Miyasaka, Y. (Ed.) (1971–2). Pramanavarttika-karika. *Acta Indologica* 2.

Napper, E. (1980). *Mind in Tibetan Buddhism*. Ithaca, NY: Snow Lion.

Pöppel, E. (1988). *Mindworks: Time and conscious experience*. Boston: Harcourt Brace Jovanovich.

Rabten, G. (1992). *The mind and its functions*. Mt. Pélerin: Rabten Choeling. Original work published 1978.

Rahula, W. (1980). *Le Compendium de la Super-Doctrine de Asaçga*. Paris: Ecole Française d'Extrême-Orient.

Schweizer, P. (1993). Mind/consciousness Dualism in Samkhya-Yoga philosophy. *Philosophy and Phenomenological Research*, 53, 845–859.

Sellars, W. (1956). Empiricism and the philosophy of mind. In H. Feigl & M. Scriven (Eds.), *Minnesota studies in the philosophy of science. Vol. 1: The foundations of science and the concepts of psychology and psychoanalysis* (pp. 253–329). Minneapolis, MN: University of Minnesota Press.

Varela, F. J., Thompson, E., & Rosch, E. (1991). *The embodied mind: Cognitive science and human experience*. Cambridge, MA: MIT Press.

Vetter, T. (1966). *Dharmakīrti's Pramanaviniscayah 1. Kapitel: Pratyaksam*. Vienna: Österreichische Akademie der Wissenschaften.

Waldron, W. (2003). *The Buddhist unconscious*. London: Routledge Press.

Wider, K. (1997). *The bodily nature of consciousness: Sartre and contemporary philosophy of mind*. Ithaca, NY: Cornell University Press.

B. Computational Approaches to Consciousness

CHAPTER 6

Artificial Intelligence and Consciousness

Drew McDermott

Abstract

Consciousness is only marginally relevant to artificial intelligence (AI), because to most researchers in the field other problems seem more pressing. However, there have been proposals for how consciousness would be accounted for in a complete computational theory of the mind from such theorists as Dennett, Hofstadter, McCarthy, McDermott, Minsky, Perlis, Sloman, and Smith. One can extract from these speculations a sketch of a theoretical synthesis, according to which consciousness is the property a system has by virtue of modeling itself as having sensations and making free decisions. Critics such as Harnad and Searle have not succeeded in demolishing a priori this or any other computational theory, but no such theory can be verified or refuted until and unless AI is successful in finding computational solutions to difficult problems, such as vision, language, and locomotion.

Introduction

Computationalism is the theory that the human brain is essentially a computer, although presumably not a stored-program, digital computer like the kind Intel makes. *Artificial intelligence* (AI) is a field of computer science that explores computational models of problem solving, where the problems to be solved are of the complexity of those solved by human beings. An AI researcher need not be a computationalist because he or she might believe that computers can do things that brains do non-computationally. However, most AI researchers are computationalists to some extent, even if they think digital computers and brains-as-computers compute things in different ways. When it comes to the problem of phenomenal consciousness, however, the AI researchers who care about the problem and believe that AI can solve it are a tiny minority, as shown in this chapter. Nonetheless, because I count myself in that minority,

I do my best here to survey the work of its members and defend a version of the theory that I think represents that work fairly well.

Perhaps calling computationalism a theory is not exactly right here. One might prefer calling it a working hypothesis, assumption, or dogma. The evidence for computationalism is not overwhelming, and some even believe it has been refuted by a priori arguments or empirical evidence. But, in some form or other, the computationalist hypothesis underlies modern research in cognitive psychology, linguistics, and some kinds of neuroscience. That is, there would not be much point in considering formal or computational models of mind if it turned out that most of what the brain does is not computation at all, but, say, some quantum-mechanical manipulation (Penrose, 1989). Computationalism has proven to be a fertile working hypothesis, although those who reject it typically think of the fertility as similar to that of fungi or of pod people from outer space.

Some computationalist researchers believe that the brain is nothing more than a computer. Many others are more cautious and distinguish between modules that are quite likely to be purely computational (e.g., the vision system) and others that are less likely to be so, such as the modules, or principles of brain organization, that are responsible for creativity or for romantic love. There is no need, in their view, to require that absolutely everything be explained in terms of computation. The brain could do some things computationally and other things by different means, but if the parts or aspects of the brain that are responsible for these various tasks are more or less decoupled, we could gain significant insight into the pieces that computational models are good for and could then leave the other pieces to some other disciplines, such as philosophy and theology.[1]

Perhaps the aspect of the brain that is most likely to be exempt from the computationalist hypothesis is its ability to produce consciousness; that is, to experience things. There are many different meanings of the word "conscious," but I am talking here about the "Hard Problem" (Chalmers, 1996), the problem of explaining how it is that a physical system can have vivid experiences with seemingly intrinsic "qualities," such as the redness of a tomato or the spiciness of a taco. These qualities usually go by their Latin name, *qualia*. We all know what we are talking about when we talk about sensations, but they are notoriously undefinable. We all learn to attach a label such as "spicy" to certain tastes, but we really have no idea whether the sensation of spiciness to me is the same as the sensation of spiciness to you.

Perhaps tacos produce my "sourness" in you, and lemons produce my "spiciness" in you.[2] We would never know, because you have learned to associate the label "sour" with the quale of the experience you have when you eat lemons, which just happens to be very similar to the quale of the experience I have when I eat tacos. We can't just tell each other what these qualia are like; the best we can do is talk about comparisons. But we agree on such questions as, Do tacos taste more like Szechuan chicken or more like lemons? I focus on this problem because other aspects of consciousness raise no special problem for computationalism, as opposed to cognitive science generally.

The purpose of consciousness, from an evolutionary perspective, is often held to have something to do with the allocation and organization of scarce cognitive resources. For a mental entity to be conscious is for it to be held in some globally accessible area (Baars, 1988, 1997). AI has made contributions to this idea, in the form of specific ideas about how this global access works, going under names such as the "blackboard model" (Hayes-Roth, 1985), or "agenda-based control" (Currie & Tate, 1991). One can evaluate these proposals by measuring how well they work or how well they match human behavior. But there does not seem to be any *philosophical* problem associated with them.

For phenomenal consciousness, the situation is very different. Computationalism seems to have nothing to say about it, simply because computers do not have experiences.

I can build an elaborate digital climate-control system for my house, which keeps its occupants at a comfortable temperature, but the climate-control system never feels overheated or chilly. Various physical mechanisms implement its temperature sensors in various rooms. These sensors produce signals that go to units that compute whether to turn on the furnace or the air conditioner. The result of these computations causes switches to close so that the furnace or air conditioner does actually change state. We can see the whole path from temperature sensing to turning off the furnace. Every step can be seen to be one of a series of straightforward physical events. Nowhere are you tempted to invoke conscious sensation as an effect or element of the causal chain.

This is the *prima facie* case against computationalism, and a solid one it seems to be. The rest of this chapter is an attempt to dismantle it.

An Informal Survey

Although one might expect AI researchers to adopt a computationalist position on most issues, they tend to shy away from questions about consciousness. AI has often been accused of being over-hyped, and the only way to avoid the accusation, apparently, is to be so boring that journalists stay away from you. As the field has matured and as a flock of technical problems have become its focus, it has become easier to bore journalists. The last thing most serious researchers want is to be quoted on the subject of computation and consciousness.

To get some kind of indication of what positions researchers take on this issue, I conducted an informal survey of Fellows of the American Association for Artificial Intelligence (AAAI) in the summer of 2003. I sent the following e-mail to all of them:

> Most of the time AI researchers don't concern themselves with philosophical questions, as a matter of methodology and perhaps also opinion about what is ultimately at stake. However, I would like to find out

> how the leaders of our field view the following problem: Create a computer or program that has "phenomenal consciousness," that is, the ability to experience things. By "experience" here I mean "qualitative experience," the kind in which the things one senses seem to have a definite but indescribable quality, the canonical example being "looking red" as opposed to "looking green." Anyway, please choose from the following possible resolutions of this problem:

> 1. The problem is just too uninteresting compared to other challenges
> 2. The problem is too ill defined to be interesting; or, the problem is only apparent, and requires no solution
> 3. It's an interesting problem, but AI has nothing to say about it
> 4. AI researchers may eventually solve it, but will require new ideas
> 5. AI researchers will probably solve it, using existing ideas
> 6. AI's current ideas provide at least the outline of a solution
> 7. My answer is not in the list above. Here it is: ...

> Of course, I don't mean to exclude other branches of cognitive science; when I say "AI" I mean "AI, in conjunction with other relevant disciplines." However, if you think neuroscientists will figure out phenomenal consciousness, and that their solution will entail that anything not made out of neurons cannot possibly be conscious, then choose option 3. Because this topic is of passionate interest to a minority, and quickly becomes annoying to many others, please direct all follow up discussion to fellows-discuss@aaai.org. Directions for subscribing to this mailing list are as follows: ...

> Thanks for your time and attention.

Of the approximately 207 living Fellows, I received responses from 34. The results are as indicated in Table 6.1.

Of those who chose category 7 (None of the above) as answer, here are some of the reasons why:

- "Developing an understanding of the basis for conscious experience is a central, long-term challenge for AI and related

Table 6.1. Results of survey of AAAI fellows

1 Problem uninteresting	3%	
2a Ill-defined	11%	19%
2b Only apparent	8%	
3 AI silent	7%	
4 Requires new ideas	32%	
5 AI will solve it as is	3%	
6 Solution in sight	15%	
7 None of the above	21%	

Percentages indicate fraction of the 34 who responded.

disciplines. It's unclear at the present time whether new ideas will be needed. . . . "

- "If two brains have isomorphic computation then the 'qualia' must be the same. Qualia must be just another aspect of computation – whatever we say of qualia must be a property of the computation viewed as computation."

- "There are two possible ways (at least) of solving the problem of phenomenal consciousness, 'explaining what consciousness is' and 'explaining consciousness away.' It sounds like you are looking for a solution of the first type, but I believe the ultimate solution will be of the second type."

- "The problem is ill-defined, and always will be, but this does not make it uninteresting. AI will play a major role in solving it."

If Table 6.1 seems to indicate no particular pattern, just remember that what the data show is that the overwhelming majority (173 of 207) refused to answer the question at all. Obviously, this was not a scientific survey, and the fact that its target group contained a disproportionate number of Americans perhaps biased it in some way. Furthermore, the detailed responses to my questions indicated that respondents understood the terms used in many different ways. But if 84% of AAAI Fellows don't want to answer, we can infer that the questions are pretty far from those that normally interest them. Even the 34 who answered include very few optimists (if we lump categories 5 and 6 together), although about the same number (categories 1 and 2) thought the problem didn't really need to be solved. Still, the outright

pessimists (category 3) were definitely in the minority.

Research on Computational Models of Consciousness

In view of the shyness about consciousness shown by serious AI researchers, it is not surprising that detailed proposals about phenomenal consciousness from this group should be few and far between.

Moore/Turing Inevitability

One class of proposals can be dealt with fairly quickly. Hans Moravec, in a series of books (1988, 1999), and Raymond Kurzweil (1999) have more or less assumed that continuing progress in the development of faster, more capable computers will cause computers to equal and then surpass humans in intelligence and that computer consciousness will be an inevitable consequence. The only argument offered is that the computers will talk as though they are conscious; what more could we ask?

I believe a careful statement of the argument might go like this:

1. Computers are getting more and more powerful.

2. This growing power allows computers to do tasks that would have been considered infeasible just a few years ago. It is reasonable to suppose, therefore, that many things we think of as infeasible will eventually be done by computers.

3. Pick a set of abilities such that if a system had them we would deal with it as we would a person. The ability to carry on a conversation must be in the set, but we can imagine lots of other abilities as well: skill in chess, agility in motion, visual perspicacity, and so forth. If we had a talking robot that could play poker well, we would treat it the same way we treated any real human seated at the same table.

4. We would feel an overwhelming impulse to attribute consciousness to such a robot. If it acted sad when losing money or made

whimpering sounds when it was damaged, we would respond as we would to a human who was sad or in pain.

5. This kind of overwhelming impulse is our only evidence that a creature is conscious. In particular, it is the only real way we can tell that *people* are conscious. Therefore, our evidence that the robot was conscious would be as good as one could have. Therefore the robot would *be* conscious, or be conscious for all intents and purposes.

I call this the "Moore/Turing inevitability" argument because it relies both on Moore's Law (Moore, 1965), which predicts exponential progress in the power of computers, and on a prediction about how well future programs will do on the "Turing Test," proposed by Alan Turing (1950) as a tool for rating the intelligence of a computer.[3] Turing thought all questions about the *actual* intelligence (and presumably degree of consciousness) of a computer were too vague or mysterious to answer. He suggested a behaviorist alternative. Let the computer carry on a conversation over a teletype line (or via an instant-messaging system, we would say today). If a savvy human judge could not distinguish the computer's conversational abilities from those of a real person at a rate better than chance, then we would have some measure of the computer's intelligence. We could use this measure *instead of* insisting on measuring the computer's *real* intelligence, or *actual* consciousness. This argument has a certain appeal. It certainly seems that *if* technology brings us robots that we cannot help treating as conscious, then in the argument about whether they really are conscious the burden of proof will shift, in the public mind, to the party-poopers who deny that they are. But so what? You can't win an argument by imagining a world in which you've won it and declaring it inevitable.

The anti-computationalists can make several plausible objections to the behavioral-inevitability argument:

• Just because computers have made impressive strides does not mean that

they will eventually be able to carry out *any* task we set them. In particular, progress in carrying on conversations has been dismal.[4]

• Even if a computer could carry on a conversation, that would not tell us *anything* about whether it really was conscious.

• Overwhelming impulses are not good indicators for whether something is true. The majority of people have an overwhelming impulse to believe that there is such a thing as luck, so that a lucky person has a greater chance of winning at roulette than an unlucky person. The whole gambling industry is based on exploiting the fact that this absurd theory is so widely believed.

I come back to the second of these objections in the section on Turing's test. The others I am inclined to agree with.

Hofstadter, Minsky, and McCarthy

Richard Hofstadter touches on the problem of consciousness in many of his writings, especially the material he contributed to Hofstadter and Dennett (1981). Most of he what he writes seems to be intended to stimulate or tantalize one's thinking about the problem. For example, in Hofstadter (1979) there is a chapter (reprinted in Hofstadter & Dennett, 1981) in which characters talk to an anthill. The anthill is able to carry on a conversation because the ants that compose it play roughly the role neurons play in a brain. Putting the discussion in the form of a vignette allows for playful digressions on various subjects. For example, the anthill offers the anteater (one of the discussants) some of its ants, which makes vivid the possibility that "neurons" could implement a negotiation that ends in their own demise.

It seems clear from reading this story that Hofstadter believes that the anthill is conscious, and therefore one could use integrated circuits rather than ants to achieve the same end. But most of the details are left out. In this as in other works, it's as if he wants to invent a new, playful style of argumentation, in which concepts are broken up and tossed together into so many configurations that the original questions one might have asked get shunted aside. If you're already convinced by the computational story, then this conceptual play is delightful. If you're a skeptic, I expect it can get a bit irritating.

I put Marvin Minsky in this category as well, which perhaps should be called "Those who don't take consciousness very seriously as a problem." He wrote a paper in 1968 (Minsky, 1968b) that introduced the concept of *self-model*, which I argue is central to the computational theory of consciousness.

> To an observer B, an object A* is a model of an object A to the extent that B can use A* to answer questions that interest him about A. . . . If A is the world, questions for A are experiments. A* is a good model of A, in B's view, to the extent that A*'s answers agree with those of A, on the whole, with respect to the questions important to B. When a man M answers questions about the world, then (taking on ourselves the role of B) we attribute this ability to some internal mechanism W* inside M.

This part is presumably uncontroversial. But what is interesting is that W*, however it appears, will include a model of M himself, M*. In principle, M* will contain a model of W*, which we can call W**. M can use W** to answer questions about the way he (M) models the world. One would think that M** (the model of M* in W**) would be used to answer questions about the way M models himself, but Minsky has a somewhat different take: M** is used to answer general questions about himself. Ordinary questions about himself (e.g., how tall he is) are answered by M*, but very broad questions about his nature (e.g., what kind of a thing he is, etc.) are answered, if at all, by descriptive statements made by M** about M*.

Now, the key point is that the accuracy of M* and M** need not be perfect.

> A man's model of the world has a distinctly bipartite structure: One part is concerned with matters of mechanical, geometrical, physical character, while the other is associated with things like goals, meanings, social matters, and the like. This division of W*

> carries through the representations of many things in W*, especially to M itself. Hence, a man's model of himself is bipartite, one part concerning his body as a physical object and the other accounting for his social and psychological experience.

This is why dualism is so compelling. In particular, Minsky accounts for free will by supposing that it develops from a "strong primitive defense mechanism" to resist or deny compulsion.

> If one asks how one's mind works, he notices areas where it is (perhaps incorrectly) understood, that is, where one recognizes rules. One sees other areas where he lacks rules. One could fill this in by postulating chance or random activity. But this too, by another route, exposes the self to the . . . indignity of remote control. We resolve this unpleasant form of M** by postulating a third part, embodying a will or spirit or conscious agent. But there is no structure in this part; one can say nothing meaningful about it, because whenever a regularity is observed, its representation is transferred to the deterministic rule region. The will model is thus not formed from a legitimate need for a place to store definite information about one's self; it has the singular character of being forced into the model, willy-nilly, by formal but essentially content-free ideas of what the model must contain.

One can quibble with the details, but the conceptual framework offers a whole new way of thinking about consciousness by showing that introspection is mediated by models. There is no way for us to penetrate through them or shake them off, so we must simply live with any "distortion" they introduce. I put "distortion" in quotes because it is too strong a word. The concepts we use to describe our mental lives were developed over centuries by people who all shared the same kind of mental model. The distortions are built in. For instance, there is no independent notion of "free will" beyond what we observe by means of our self-models. We cannot even say that free will is a dispensable illusion, because we have no way of getting rid of it and living to tell the tale.

Minsky's insight is that to answer many questions about consciousness we should focus more on the models we use to answer the questions than on the questions themselves.

Unfortunately, in that short paper, and in his later book *The Society of Mind* (Minsky, 1986), Minsky throws off many interesting ideas, but refuses to go into the depth that many of them deserve. He has a lot to say about consciousness in passing, such as how Freudian phenomena might arise out of the "society" of subpersonal modules that he takes the human mind to be. But there is no solid proposal to argue for or against.

John McCarthy has written a lot on what he usually calls "self-awareness" (McCarthy, 1995b). However, his papers are mostly focused on robots' problem-solving capacities and how they would be enhanced by the ability to introspect. An important example is the ability of a robot to infer that it doesn't know something (such as whether the Pope is currently sitting or lying down). This may be self-awareness, but the word "awareness" here is used in a sense that is quite separate from the notion of phenomenal consciousness that is our concern here.

McCarthy (1995a) specifically addresses the issue of "zombies," philosophers' term for hypothetical beings who behave exactly as we do but do not experience anything. This paper is a reply to an article by Todd Moody (1994) on zombies. He lists some introspective capacities it would be good to give to a robot ("... Observing its goal structure and forming sentences about it. ... Observing how it arrived at its current beliefs. ..."). Then he concludes abruptly:

> Moody isn't consistent in his description of zombies. On page 1 they behave like humans. On page 3 they express puzzlement about human consciousness. Wouldn't a real Moody zombie behave as though it understood as much about consciousness as Moody does?

I tend to agree with McCarthy that the idea of a zombie is worthless, in spite of its initial plausibility. Quoting Moody:

> Given any *functional* [=, more or less, computational] *description of cognition, as detailed and complete as one can imagine, it will still make sense to suppose that there could be insentient beings that exemplify that description. That is, it is possible that there could be a behaviourally indiscernible but insentient simulacrum of a human cognizer: a zombie.*

The plausibility of this picture is that it does indeed seem that an intricate diagram of the hardware and software of a robot would leave consciousness out, just as with the computer-controlled heating system described in the introduction to this chapter. One could print the system description on rose-colored paper to indicate that the system was conscious, but the color of the paper would play no role in what it actually did. The problem is that in imagining a zombie one tends at first to forget that the zombie would say exactly the same things non-zombies say about their experiences. It would be very hard to convince a zombie that it lacked experience, which means, as far as I can see, that we might be zombies, at which point the whole idea collapses.

Almost everyone who thinks the idea is coherent sooner or later slips up the way Moody does: They let the zombie *figure out* that it is a zombie by noticing that it has no experience. By hypothesis, this is something zombies cannot do. Moody's paper is remarkable only in how obvious the slip-up in it is.

> Consider, for example, the phenomenon of dreaming. Could there be a cognate concept in zombie-English? How might we explain dreaming to them? We could say that dreams are things that we experience while asleep, but the zombies would not be able to make sense[z] of this.[5]

Of course, zombies would talk about their dreams (or dreams[z]?) exactly as we do; consult the intricate system diagram to verify this.

McCarthy's three-sentence reply is just about what Moody's paper deserves. But meanwhile philosophers such as Chalmers (1996) have written weighty tomes based on the assumption that zombies make sense. McCarthy is not interested in refuting them.

Similarly, McCarthy (1990b) discusses when it is legitimate to ascribe mental properties to robots. In some ways his treatment is more formal than that of Dennett, which I discuss below. But he never builds on this theory to ask the key question: Is there more to your having a mental state than having that state ascribed to you?

Daniel Dennett

Daniel Dennett is not a researcher in artificial intelligence, but a philosopher of mind and essayist in cognitive science. Nonetheless, he is sympathetic to the AI project and bases his philosophy on computational premises to a great degree. The models of mind that he has proposed can be considered to be sketches of a computational model and therefore constitute one of the most ambitious and detailed proposals for how AI might account for consciousness.

Dennett's (1969) Ph.D. dissertation proposed a model for a conscious system. It contains the sort of block diagram that has since become a standard feature of the theories of such psychologists as Bernard Baars (1988, 1997), although the central working arena is designed to account for introspection more than for problem-solving ability.

In later work, Dennett has not built upon this model, but, in a sense, has been rebuilding it from the ground up. The result has been a long series of papers and books, rich with insights about consciousness, free will, and intentionality. Their very richness makes it hard to extract a brisk theoretical statement, but that is my aim.

Dennett has one overriding methodological principle, to be distrustful of introspection. This position immediately puts him at odds with such philosophers as Nagel, Searle, and McGinn, for whom the first-person point of view is the alpha and omega of consciousness. On his side Dennett has many anecdotes and experimental data that show how wildly inaccurate introspection can be, but his view does leave him open to the charge that he is ruling out all the competitors to his theory from the start. From a computationalist's vantage point, this is all

to the good. It's clear that any computationalist theory must eventually explain the mechanism of the first-person view in terms of third-person components. The third person is that which you and I discuss and therefore must be observable by you and me, and by other interested parties, in the same way. In other words, the term "third-person data" is just another way of saying "scientific data." If there is to be a scientific explanation of the first person, it will surely seem more like an "explaining away" than a true explanation. An account of how yonder piece of meat or machinery is conscious will almost certainly invoke the idea of the machinery playing a trick on itself, the result of which is for it to have a strong belief that it has a special first-person viewpoint.

One of Dennett's special skills is using vivid images to buttress his case. He invented the phrase "Cartesian Theater" to describe the hypothetical place in the brain where the self becomes aware of things. He observes that belief in the Cartesian Theater is deep-seated and keeps popping up in philosophical and psychological writings, as well as in common-sense musings. We all know that there is a lot going on the brain that is preconscious or subconscious. What happens when a train of events becomes conscious? According to the view Dennett is ridiculing, to bring it to consciousness is to show it on the screen in the Cartesian Theater. When presented this way, the idea does seem silly, if for no other reason than that there is no plausible homunculus to put in the audience. What's interesting is how hard it is to shake this image. Just about all theorists of phenomenal consciousness at some point distinguish between "ordinary" and "conscious" events by making the latter be accessible to . . . what, exactly? The system as a whole? Its self-monitoring modules? One must tread very carefully to keep from describing the agent with special access as the good old transcendental self, sitting alone in the Cartesian Theater.

To demolish the Cartesian Theater, Dennett uses the tool of discovering or inventing situations in which belief in it leads to absurd conclusions. Many of these situations are experiments set up by psychology researchers. Most famous are the experiments by Libet (1985), whose object was to determine exactly when a decision to make a motion was made. What emerged from the experiments was that at the point where subjects *think* they have made the decision, the neural activity preparatory to the motion has already been in progress for hundreds of milliseconds. Trying to make sense of these results using the homuncular models leads to absurdities. (Perhaps the choice causes effects in the person's past?) But it is easy to explain them if you make a more inclusive picture of what's going on in a subject's brain. Libet and others tended to assume that giving a subject a button to push when the decision had been made provided a direct route to . . . that pause again . . . the subject's self, perhaps? Or perhaps the guy in the theater? Dennett points out that the neural apparatus required to push the button is part of the overall brain system. Up to a certain resolution, it makes sense to ask someone, "When did you decide to do *X*?" But it makes no sense to try to tease off a subsystem of the brain and ask it the same question, primarily because there is no subsystem that embodies the "will" of the whole system.

Having demolished most of the traditional model of consciousness, Dennett's next goal is to construct a new one, and here he becomes more controversial, and in places more obscure. A key component is human language. It is difficult to think about human consciousness without pondering the ability of a normal human adult to *say* what they are thinking. There are two possible views about why it should be the case that we can introspect so easily. One is that we evolved from animals that can introspect, so naturally when language evolved one of the topics it was used on was the contents of our introspections. The other is that language plays a more central role than that; without language, we would not be conscious at all, at least full-bloodedly. Dennett's view is the second. He has little to say about animal consciousness, and what he does say is disparaging.

Language, for Dennett, is very important, but not because it is spoken by the homunculus in the Cartesian Theater. If you leave it out, who is speaking? Dennett's answer is certainly bold: In a sense, the language speaks itself. We take it for granted that speaking feels like it emanates from our "transcendental self" or, less politely, from the one-person audience in the Theater. Whether or not that view is correct now, it almost certainly was not correct when language began. In its original form, language was an information-transmission device used by apes whose consciousness, if similar to ours in any real respect, would be about the same as a chimpanzee's today. Messages expresssed linguistically would be heard by one person and, for one reason or another, be passed to others. The messages' chance of being passed would depend, very roughly, on how useful their recipients found them.

The same mechanism has been in operation ever since. Ideas (or simple patterns unworthy of the name "idea" – advertising jingles, for instance) tend to proliferate in proportion to how much they help those who adopt them or in proportion to how well they tend to stifle competing ideas – not unlike what genes do. Dennett adopts Dawkins' (1976) term *meme* to denote a linguistic pattern conceived of in this way. One key meme is the idea of talking to oneself; when it first popped up, it meant literally talking out loud and listening to what was said. Although nowadays we tend to view talking to oneself as a possible symptom of insanity, we have forgotten that it gives our brains a whole new channel for its parts to communicate with each other. If an idea – a pattern of activity in the brain – can reach the linguistic apparatus, it gets translated into a new form, and, as it is heard, gets translated back into a somewhat different pattern than the one that started the chain of events. Creatures that start to behave this way start to think of themselves in a new light, as someone to talk to or listen to. Self-modeling, according to Dennett (and Jaynes, 1976) starts as modeling this person to whom we are talking. There is nothing special about this kind of model; it is as crude as most of the models we make. But memes for self-modeling have been some of the most successful in the history (and prehistory) of humankind. To a great degree, they make us what we are by giving us a model of who we are that we then live up to. Every child must recapitulate the story Dennett tells, as he or she absorbs from parents and peers all the ways to think of oneself, as a being with free will, sensations, and a still small voice inside.

The theory has one striking feature: It assumes that consciousness is based on language and not vice versa. For that matter, it tends to assume that for consciousness to come to be, there must be in place a substantial infrastructure of perceptual, motor, and intellectual skills. There may be some linguistic abilities that depend on consciousness, but the basic ability must exist *before* and *independent of* consciousness.

This conclusion may be fairly easy to accept for the more syntactic aspects of language, but it is contrary to the intuitions of many when it comes to semantics. Knowing what a sentence means requires knowing how the sentence relates to the world. If I am told, "There is a lion on the other side of that bush," I have to understand that "that bush" refers to a particular object in view, I have to know how phrases like "other side of" work, and I have to understand what "a lion" means so that I have a grasp of just what I'm expecting to confront. Furthermore, it's hard to see how I could know what these words and phrases meant without knowing that I know what they mean.

Meditating in this way on how meaning works, the late 19th-century philosopher Franz Brentano developed the notion of *intentionality*, the power that mental representations seem to have of pointing to – "being about" – things outside of, and arbitrarily far from, the mind or brain containing those representations. The ability of someone to warn me about that lion depends on that person's sure-footed ability to reason about that animal over there, as well as on our shared knowledge about the species *Panthera leo*. Brentano and many philosophers since have argued that intentionality

is at bottom a property *only* of mental representations. There seem to be many kinds of "aboutness" in the world; for instance, there are books about lions, but items such as books can be about a topic only if they are created by humans using language and writing systems to capture thoughts about that topic. Books are said to have *derived* intentionality, whereas people have *original* or *intrinsic* intentionality.

Computers seem to be textbook cases of physical items whose intentionality, if any, is derived. If one sees a curve plotted on a computer's screen, the surest way to find out what it's about is to ask the person who used some program to create it. In fact, that's the *only* way. Digital computers are syntactic engines par excellence. Even if there is an interpretation to be placed on every step of a computation, this interpretation plays no role in what the computer does. Each step is produced purely by operations dependent on the formal structure of its inputs and prior state at that step. If you use TurboTax to compute your income taxes, then the numbers being manipulated represent real-world quantities, and the number you get at the end represents what you actually do owe to the tax authorities. Nonetheless, TurboTax is just applying formulas to the numbers. It "has no idea" what they mean.

This intuition is what Dennett wants to defeat, as should every other researcher who expects a theory of consciousness based on AI. There is really no alternative. If you believe that people are capable of original intentionality and computers are not, then you must believe that something will be missing from any computer program that tries to simulate humans. That means that human consciousness is fundamentally different from machine consciousness, which means that a theory of consciousness based on AI is radically incomplete.

Dennett's approach to the required demolition job on intrinsic intentionality is to focus on the prelinguistic, non-introspective case. In a way, this is changing the subject fairly radically. In the introspective set-up, we are talking about elements or aspects of the mind that we are routinely acquainted with, such as words and images. In the non-introspective case, it's not clear that those elements or aspects are present at all. What's left to talk about if we're not talking about words, "images," or "thoughts"? We will have to shift to talking about neurons, chips, firing rates, bits, pointers, and other "subpersonal" entities and events. It's not clear at all whether these things are even capable of exhibiting intentionality. Nonetheless, showing that they are is a key tactic in Dennett's attack on the problem of consciousness (see especially Appendix A of Dennett, 1991b). If we can define what it is for subpersonal entities to be intentional, we can then build on that notion and recover ·the phenomenal entities we (thought we) started with. "Original" intentionality will turn out to be a secondary consequence of what I call *impersonal intentionality*.

Dennett's approach to the problem is to call attention to what he calls the *intentional stance*, a way of looking at systems in which we impute beliefs and goals to them simply because there's no better way to explain what they're doing. For example, if you're observing a good computer chess program in action, and its opponent has left himself vulnerable to an obvious attack, then one feels confident that the program will embark on that attack. This confidence is not based on any detailed knowledge of the program's actual code. Even someone who knows the program well won't bother trying to do a tedious simulation to make a prediction that the attack will occur, but will base their prediction on the fact that the program almost never misses an opportunity of that kind. If you refuse to treat the program as though it had goals, you will be able to say very little about how it works. The intentional stance applies to the innards of the program as well. If a data structure is used by the program to make decisions about some situation or object S, and the decisions it makes are well explained by assuming that one state of the data structure means that P is true of S, and that another means P', then those states *do* mean P and P'.

It is perhaps unfortunate that Dennett has chosen to express his theory this way,

because it is easy to take him as saying that all intentionality is observer-relative. This would be almost as bad as maintaining a distinction between original and derived intentionality, because it would make it hard to see how the process of intentionality attribution could ever get started. Presumably my intuition that I am an intentional system is indubitable, but on what could it be based? It seems absurd to think that this opinion is based on what others tell me, but it seems equally absurd that I could be my own observer. Presumably to be an observer you have to be an intentional system (at least, if your observations are to be *about* anything). Can I bootstrap my way into intentionality somehow? If so, how do I tell the successful bootstrappers from the unsuccessful ones? A computer program with an infinite loop, endlessly printing, "I am an intentional system because I predict, by taking the intentional stance, that I will continue to print this sentence out," would not actually be claiming anything, let alone something true.

Of course, Dennett does not mean for intentionality to be observer-relative, even though many readers think he does. (To take an example at random from the Internet, the online *Philosopher's Magazine*, in its "Philosopher of the Month" column in April, 2003 (Douglas & Saunders, 2003), writes, "Dennett suggests that intentionality is not so much an intrinsic feature of agents, rather, it is more a way of looking at agents.") Dennett has defended himself from this misinterpretation more than once (Dennett, 1991a). I come back to this issue in my attempt at a synthesis in the section, "A Synthetic Summary."

Perlis and Sloman

The researchers in this section, although they work on hard-headed problems in artificial intelligence, do take philosophical problems seriously and have contributed substantial ideas to the development of the computational model of consciousness.

Donald Perlis's papers build a case that consciousness is ultimately based on self-consciousness, but I believe he is using the term "self-consciousness" in a misleading and unnecessary way. Let's start with his paper (Perlis, 1994), which I think lays out a very important idea. He asks, Why do we need a dichotomy between appearance and reality? The answer is, Because they could disagree (i.e., because I could be wrong about what I think I perceive). For an organism to be able to reason explicitly about this difference, it must be able to represent both X (an object in the world) and quote-X, the representation of X in the organism itself. The latter is the "symbol," the former the "symboled." To my mind the most important consequence of this observation is that it must be possible for an information-processing system to get two kinds of information out of its X-recognizer: signals meaning "there's an X" and signals meaning "there's a signal meaning 'there's an X.'"

Perlis takes a somewhat different tack. He believes there can be no notion of appearance without the notion of appearance *to* someone. So the self-model cannot get started without some prior notion of self to model.

> When we are conscious of X, we are also conscious of X in relation to ourselves: It is here, or there, or seen from a certain angle, or thought about this way and then that. Indeed, without a self model, it is not clear to me intuitively what it means to see or feel something: it seems to me that a point of view is needed, a place from which the scene is viewed or felt, defining the place occupied by the viewer. Without something along these lines, I think that a "neuronal box" would indeed "confuse" symbol and symboled: to it there is no external reality, and it has no way to "think" (consider alternatives) at all. Thus I disagree [with Crick] that self-consciousness is a special case of consciousness: I suspect that it is the most basic form of all.

Perlis continues to elaborate this idea in later publications. For example, "*Consciousness is the function or process that allows a system to distinguish itself from the rest of the world.*... To feel pain or have a vivid experience requires a self" (Perlis, 1997) (italics in original). I have trouble following his

arguments, which often depend on thought experiments, such as imagining cases where one is conscious but not *of* anything, or of as little as possible. The problem is that introspective thought experiments are just not a very accurate tool. One may perhaps conclude that Perlis, although housed in a Computer Science department, is not a thoroughgoing computationalist at all. As he says, "I conjecture that we may find in the brain special amazing structures that facilitate true self-referential processes, and constitute a primitive, bare or ur-awareness, an 'I.' I will call this the *amazing-structures-and-processes paradigm*" (Perlis, 1997) (italics in original). It is not clear how amazing the "amazing" structures will be, but perhaps they will not be computational.

Aaron Sloman has written prolifically about philosophy and computation, although his interests range far beyond our topic here. In fact, although he has been interested in conscious control, both philosophically and as a strategy for organizing complex software, he has tended to shy away from the topic of phenomenal consciousness. His book *The Computer Revolution in Philosophy* (Sloman, 1978) has almost nothing to say about the subject, and in many other writings the main point he has to make is that the concept of consciousness covers a lot of different processes, which should be sorted out before hard questions can be answered. However, in a few of his papers he has confronted the issue of qualia, notably (Sloman & Chrisley, 2003). I think the following is exactly right:

> Now suppose that an agent A ... uses a self-organising process to develop concepts for categorising its own internal virtual machine states as sensed by internal monitors. ... If such a concept C is applied by A to one of its internal states, then the only way C can have meaning for A is in relation to the set of concepts of which it is a member, which in turn derives only from the history of the self-organising process in A. These concepts have what (Campbell, 1994) refers to as 'causal indexicality'. This can be contrasted with what happens when

A interacts with other agents in such a way as to develop a common language for referring to features of external objects. Thus A could use 'red' either as expressing a private, causally indexical, concept referring to features of A's own virtual-machine states, or as expressing a shared concept referring to a visible property of the surfaces of objects. This means that if two agents A and B have each developed concepts in this way, then if A uses its causally indexical concept Ca, to think the thought 'I am having experience Ca', and B uses its causally indexical concept Cb, to think the thought 'I am having experience Cb' the two thoughts are intrinsically private and incommunicable, even if A and B actually have exactly the same architecture and have had identical histories leading to the formation of structurally identical sets of concepts. A can wonder: 'Does B have an experience described by a concept related to B as my concept Ca is related to me?' But A cannot wonder 'Does B have experiences of type Ca', for it makes no sense for the concept Ca to be applied outside the context for which it was developed, namely one in which A's internal sensors classify internal states. They cannot classify states of B.

This idea suggests that the point I casually assumed at the beginning of this chapter, that two people might wonder if they experienced the same thing when they ate tacos, is actually incoherent. Our feeling that the meaning is clear is due to the twist our self-models give to introspections of the kind Sloman and Chrisley are talking about. The internal representation of the quale of redness is purely local to A's brain, but the self-model says quite the opposite – that objects with the color are recognizable by A because they have that quale. The quale is made into an objective entity that might attach itself to other experiences, such as my encounters with blue things or B's experiences of red things.

Brian Cantwell Smith

The last body of research to be examined in this survey is that of Brian Cantwell Smith. It is hard to dispute that he is a computational-ist, but he is also an antireductionist, which places him in a unique category. Although it is clear in reading his work that he considers consciousness to be a crucial topic, he has been working up to it very carefully. His early work (Smith, 1984) was on "reflection" in programming languages; that is, how and why a program written in a language could have access to information about its own subroutines and data structures. One might conjecture that reflection might play a key role in a system's maintaining a self-model and thereby being conscious. But since that early work Smith has moved steadily away from straightforward computational topics and toward foundational philosophical ones. Each of his papers seems to take tinier steps from first principles than the ones that have gone before, so as to presuppose as little as humanly possible. Nonetheless, they often express remarkable insight. His paper (Smith, 2002) on the "Foundations of Computing" is a gem. (I also recommend Sloman (2002) from the same collection [Scheutz, 2002].)

One thing both Smith and Sloman argue is that Turing machines are misleading as ideal vehicles for computationalism, which is a point often missed by philosophers. For example, Wilkes (1990) says that "... computers (as distinct from robots) produce at best only linguistic and exclusively 'cognitive' – programmable – 'behaviour': the emphasis is on internal psychological processes, the cognitive 'inner' rather than on action, emotion, motivation, and sensory experience." Perhaps I've misunderstood him, but it's very hard to see how this can be true, given that all interesting robots are controlled by digital computers. Furthermore, when computers and software are studied isolated from their physical environments, it's often for purely tactical reasons (from budget or personnel limitations, or to avoid endangering bystanders). If we go all the way back to Winograd's (1972) SHRDLU system, we find a simulated robot playing the role of conversationalist, not because Winograd thought real robots were irrelevant, but precisely because he was thinking of a long-term project in which an actual robot would be used. As Smith (2002) says,

> In one way or another, no matter what construal [of formality] they pledge allegiance to, just about everyone thinks that computers are formal. . . . But since the outset, I have not believed that this is necessarily so. . . . Rather, what computers are . . . is neither more nor less than the full-fledged social construction and development of intentional artifacts. *(Emphasis in original.)*

The point he is trying to make (and it can be hard to find a succinct quote in Smith's papers) is that computers are *always* connected to the world, whether they are robots or not, and therefore the meaning their symbols possess is more determined by those connections than by what a formal theory might say they mean. One might want to rule that the transducers that connect them to the world are non-computational (cf. Harnad, 1990), but there is no principled way to draw a boundary between the two parts, because ultimately a computer is physical parts banging against other physical parts. As Sloman puts it,

> . . . The view of computers as somehow essentially a form of Turing machine . . . is simply mistaken. . . . [The] mathematical notion of computation . . . is not the primary motivation for the construction or use of computers, nor is it particularly helpful in understanding how computers work or how to use them (Sloman, 2002).

The point Smith makes in the paper cited above is elaborated into an entire book, *On the Origin of Objects* (Smith, 1995). The problem the book addresses is the basic ontology of physical objects. The problem is urgent, according to Smith, because the basic concept of intentionality is that a symbol S stands for an object X, but we have no prior concept of what objects or symbols are. A geologist might see a glacier on a mountain, but is there some objective reason why the glacier is an object (and the group of stones suspended in it is not)? Smith believes that all object categories are to some extent carved out by subjects (i.e., by information-processing systems like us and maybe someday by robots as well).

The problem with this point of view is that it is hard to bootstrap oneself out of what Smith calls the Criterion of Ultimate Concreteness: "No naturalistically palatable theory of intentionality – of mind, computation, semantics, ontology, objectivity – can presume the identify or existence of any individual object whatsoever" (1995. p. 184). He tries valiantly to derive subjects and objects from prior . . . umm . . . "entities" called s-regions and o-regions, but it is hard to see how he succeeds. In spite of its length of 420 pages, the book claims to arrive at no more than a starting point for a complete rethinking of physics, metaphysics, and everything else.

Most people will have a hard time following Smith's inquiry, not least because few people agree on his opening premise, that everyday ontology is broken and needs to be fixed. I actually do agree with that, but I think the problem is much worse than Smith does. Unlike him, I am reductionist enough to believe that physics is the science of "all there is"; so how do objects emerge from a primordial superposition of wave functions? Fortunately, I think this is a problem for everyone and has nothing to do with the problem of intentionality.[6] If computationalists are willing to grant that there's a glacier over there, anyone should be willing to consider the computational theory of how systems refer to glaciers.

A Synthetic Summary

In spite of the diffidence of most AI researchers on this topic, I believe that there is a dominant position on phenomenal consciousness among computationalists; it is dominant in the sense that among the small population of those who are willing to take a clear position, this is more or less the position they take. In this section I try to sketch that postion, pointing out the similarities and differences from the positions sketched in the preceding section.

The idea in a nutshell is that phenomenal consciousness is the property a computational system X has if X models itself as experiencing things. To understand it, I need to explain the following three things:

1. what a computational system is;
2. how such a system can exhibit intentionality; and
3. that to be conscious is to model oneself as having experiences.

The Notion of Computational System

Before we computationalists can really get started, we run into the objection that the word "computer" doesn't denote the right kind of thing to play an explanatory role in a theory of any natural phenomenon. A computer, so the objection goes, is an object that people[7] *use to compute things*. Without people to assign meanings to its inputs and outputs, a computer is just an overly complex electronic kaleidoscope, generating a lot of pseudo-random patterns. We may interpret the output of a computer as a prediction about tomorrow's weather, but there's no other sense in which the computer is predicting anything. A chess computer outputs a syntactically legal expression that we can take to be its next move, but the computer doesn't actually intend to make that move. It doesn't intend *anything*. It doesn't care whether the move is actually made. Even if it's displaying the move on a screen or using a robot arm to pick up a piece and move it, these outputs are just meaningless pixel values or drive-motor torques until *people* supply the meaning.

In my opinion, the apparent difficulty of supplying an objective definition of syntax and especially semantics is the most serious objection to the computational theory of psychology, and in particular to a computational explanation of phenomenal consciousness. To overcome it, we need to come up with a theory of computation (and eventually semantics) that is observer-independent.

There are two prongs to this attack, one syntactic and the other semantic. The syntactic prong is the claim that even the symbols we attribute to computers are observer-relative. We point to a register in the computer's memory and claim that it contains a number. The critic then says that the mapping of states that causes this state to encode "55,000" is entirely arbitrary; there are an infinite number of ways of interpreting the state of the register, none of which is the "real" one in any sense. Therefore, all we can talk about is the *intended* one. A notorious example given by John Searle (1992) exemplifies this kind of attack; he claims that the wall of his office could be considered to be a computer under the right encoding of its states.

The semantic prong is the observation, discussed in the sections on Daniel Dennett and on Brian Cantwell Smith, that even after we've agreed that the register state encodes "55,000," there is no objective sense in which this figure stands for "Jeanne D'Eau's 2003 income in euros." If Jeanne D'Eau is using the EuroTax software package to compute her income tax, then such semantic statements are nothing but a convention adopted by her and the people who wrote EuroTax. In other words, the only intentionality exhibited by the program is derived intentionality.

To avoid these objections, we have to be careful about how we state our claims. I have space for only a cursory overview here; see McDermott (2001) for a more detailed treatment. First, the idea of computer is prior to the idea of symbol. A *basic computer* is any physical system whose subsequent states are predictable given its prior states. By "state" I mean "partial state," so that the system can be in more than one state at a time. An *encoding* is a mapping from partial physical states to some syntactic domain (e.g., numerals). To view a system as a computer, we need two encodings, one for inputs and one for outputs. It computes $f(x)$ with respect to a pair $\langle I, O \rangle$ of encodings if and only if putting it into the partial state encoding x under I causes it to go into a partial state encoding $f(x)$ under O.

A *memory element* under an encoding E is a physical system that, when placed into a state s such that $E(s) = x$, tends to remain in the set of states $\{s: E(s) = x\}$ for a while.

A *computer* is then a group of basic computers and memory elements viewed under a consistent encoding scheme, meaning merely that if changes of component 1's state cause component 2's state to change, then the encoding of 1's outputs is the same as the encoding of 2's inputs. *Symbol sites* then appear as alternative possible stable regions of state space, and symbol *tokens* as chains of symbol sites such that the occupier of a site is caused by the presence of the occupier of its predecessor site. Space does not allow me to discuss all the details here, but the point is clear: The notions of *computer* and *symbol* are not observer-relative. Of course, they are encoding-relative, but then velocity is "reference-frame-relative." The encoding is purely syntactic, or even presyntactic, because we have said nothing about what syntax an encoded value has, if any. We could go on to say more about syntax, but one has the feeling that the whole problem is a practical joke played by philosophers on naive AI researchers. ("Let's see how much time we can get them to waste defining 'computer' for us, until they catch on.") I direct you to McDermott (2001) for more of my theory of syntax. The important issue is semantics, to which we now turn.

One last remark: The definitions above are not intended to distinguish digital from analog computers, or serial from parallel ones. They are broad enough to include anything anyone might ever construe as a computational system. In particular, they allow neural nets (Rumelhart et al., 1986), both natural and artificial, to count as computers. Many observers of AI (Churchland, 1986, 1988; Wilkes, 1990) believe that there is an unbridgeable chasm between some classical, digital, traditional AI and a revolutionary, analog, connectionist alternative. The former is the realm of von Neumann machines, the latter the realm of artificial neural networks – "massively parallel" networks of simple processors (meant to mimic neurons), which can be trained to learn different categories of sensory data (Rumelhart et al., 1986). The "chasm" between the two is less observable in practice than you might infer from the literature. AI researchers are omnivorous consumers of algorithmic techniques and think of neural nets as one of them – entirely properly, in my opinion. I return to this subject in the section, "Symbol Grounding."

Intentionality of Computational Systems

I have described Dennett's idea of the "intentional stance," in which an observer explains a system's behavior by invoking such intentional categories as beliefs and goals. Dennett is completely correct that there is such a stance. The problem is that we sometimes adopt it inappropriately. People used to think thunderstorms were out to get them, and a sign on my wife's printer says, "Warning! This machine is subject to breakdown during periods of critical need." What could it possibly mean to say that a machine demonstrates *real* intentionality when it is so easy to indulge in a mistaken or merely metaphorical "intentional stance"?

Let's consider an example. Suppose someone has a cat that shows up in the kitchen at the time it is usually fed, meowing and behaving in other ways that tend to attract the attention of the people who usually feed it. Contrast that with the case of a robot that, whenever its battery is low, moves along a black trail painted on the floor that leads to the place where it gets recharged, and, when it is over a large black cross that has been painted at the end of the trail, emits a series of beeps that tend to attract the attention of the people who usually recharge it. Some people might refuse to attribute intentionality to either the cat or the robot and treat as purely metaphorical such comments as, "It's trying to get to the kitchen [or recharging area]," or "It wants someone to feed [or recharge] it." They might take this position, or argue that it's tenable, on the grounds that we have no reason to suppose that either the cat or the robot has mental states, and hence nothing with the kind of "intrinsic aboutness" that people exhibit. High catologists[8] are sure cats do have mental states, but the skeptic will view this as just another example of someone falling into the metaphorical pit of "as-if" intentionality.

I believe, though, that even hard-headed low catologists think the cat is truly intentional, albeit in the impersonal way discussed in the section on Daniel Dennett. They would argue that if you could open up its brain you would find neural structures that "referred to" the kitchen or the path to it, in the sense that those structures became active in ways appropriate to the cat's needs: They were involved in steering the cat to the kitchen and stopping it when it got there. A similar account would tie the meowing behavior to the event of getting food, mediated by some neural states. We would then feel justified in saying that some of the neural states and structures *denoted* the kitchen, or the event of being fed.

The question is, are the ascriptions of impersonal intentionality so derived arbitrary, or are they objectively true? It's difficult to make either choice. It feels silly saying that something is arbitrary if it takes considerable effort to figure it out, and if one is confident that if others independently undertook the same project they would reach essentially the same result. But it also feels odd to say that something is objectively true if it is *inherently* invisible. Nowhere in the cat will you find labels that say "This means X," nor little threads that tie neural structures to objects in the world. One might want to say that the cat is an intentional system because there was evolutionary pressure in favor of creatures whose innards were tied via "virtual threads" to their surroundings. I don't like dragging evolution in because it's more of a question stopper than a question answerer. I prefer the conclusion that the reluctance to classify intentionality as objectively real simply reveals an overly narrow conception of objective reality.

A couple of analogies should help.

CODE BREAKING

A code breaker is sure he or she has cracked a code when the message turns into meaningful natural-language text. That's because there are an enormous number of possible messages and an enormous number of possible ciphers, out of which there is (almost certainly) only one combination of natural-language text and simple cipher that produces the encrypted message.

Unfortunately for this example, it involves interpreting the actions of people. So even if there is no observer-relativity from the cryptanalyst's point of view, the intentionality in a message is "derived" according to skeptics about the possible authentic intentionality of physical systems.

GEOLOGY

A geologist strives to find the best explanation for how various columns and strata of rock managed to place themselves in the positions in which they are found. A good explanation is a series of not-improbable events that would have transformed a plausible initial configuration of rocks into what we see today.

In this case, there is no observer-relativity, because there was an actual sequence of events that led to the current rock configuration. If two geologists have a profound disagreement about the history of a rock formation, they cannot both be right (as they might be if disagreeing about the beauty of a mountain range). Our normal expectation is that any two geologists will tend to agree on at least the broad outline of an explanation of a rock formation and that as more data are gathered the areas of agreement will grow.

These examples are cases where, even though internal harmoniousness is how we judge explanations, what we get in the end is an explanation that is true, *independent of the harmoniousness*. All we need to do is allow for this to be true even though, in the case of intentionality, even a time machine or mind reader would not give us an independent source of evidence. To help us accept this possibility, consider the fact that geologists can never actually get the entire story right. What they are looking at is a huge structure of rock with a detailed microhistory that ultimately accounts for the position of every pebble. What they produce in the end is a coarse-grained history that talks only about large intrusions, sedimentary layers, and such. Nonetheless we say that it is objectively true, even though the objects it speaks of don't even exist unless the account is true. It explains how a particular "intrusion" got to be there, but if geological theory isn't more or less correct, there might not be such a thing as an intrusion; the objects might be parsed in a totally different way.

If processes and structures inside a cat's brain exhibit objectively real impersonal intentionality, then it's hard not to accept the same conclusion about the robot trying to get recharged. It might not navigate the way the cat does – for instance, it might have no notion of a place it's going to, as opposed to the path that gets it there – but we see the same fit with its environment among the symbol structures in its hardware or data. In the case of the robot the hardware and software were designed, and so we have the extra option of asking the designers what the entities inside the robot were *supposed* to denote. But it will often happen that there is conflict between what the designers intended and what actually occurs, and *what actually occurs wins*. The designers don't get to say, "This boolean variable means that the robot is going through a door," unless the variable's being true tends to occur if and only if the robot is between two door jambs. If the variable is correlated with something else instead, then *that's* what it actually means. It's appropriate to describe what the roboticists are doing as debugging the robot so that its actual intentionality matches their intent. The alternative would be to describe the robot as "deranged" in the sense that it continuously acts in ways that are bizarre given what its data structures mean.

Two other remarks are in order. What the symbols in a system mean is dependent on the system's environment. If a cat is moved to a house that is so similar to the one it's familiar with that the cat is fooled, then the structures inside it that used to refer to the kitchen of house 1 now refer to the kitchen of house 2. And so forth; and there will of course be cases in which the denotation of a symbol breaks down, leaving no coherent story about what it denotes, just as in the geological case an event of a type unknown to geology, but large enough to cause large-scale effects, will go unhypothesized, and some parts of geologists' attempts to make sense of what they see will be too incoherent to be true or false or even to refer to anything.

The other remark is that it might be the case that the sheer size of the symbolic systems inside people's heads might make the impersonal intentionality story irrelevant. We don't, of course, know much about the symbol systems used by human brains, whether there is a "language of thought" (Fodor, 1975) or some sort of connectionist soup but clearly we can have beliefs that are orders of magnitude more complex than those of a cat or a robot (year-2006 model). If you walk to work, but at the end of the day absentmindedly head for the parking lot to retrieve your car, what you will believe once you get there has the content, "My car is not here." Does this belief correspond to a symbol structure in the brain whose pieces include symbol tokens for "my car," "here," and "not"? We don't know. But if anything like that picture is accurate, then assigning a meaning to symbols such as "not" is considerably more difficult than assigning a meaning to the symbols a cat or robot might use to denote "the kitchen." Nonetheless, the same basic story can still be told: that the symbols mean what the most harmonious interpretation says they mean. This story allows us to assign arbitrarily abstract meanings to symbols like "not"; the price we pay is that for now all we have is an IOU for a holistic theory of the meanings inside our heads.

Modeling Oneself as Conscious

I have spent a lot of time discussing intentionality because once we can establish the concept of an impersonal level of meaning in brains and computers, we can introduce the idea of *a self-model*, a device that a robot or a person can use to answer questions about how it interacts with the world. This idea was introduced by Minsky almost forty years ago (Minsky, 1968a) and has since been explored by many others, including Sloman (Sloman & Chrisley, 2003), McDermott (2001), and Dennett (1991b). As I have mentioned, Dennett mixes this idea with the concept of meme, but self-models don't need to be made out of memes.

We start with Minsky's observation that complex organisms use models of their environments to predict what will happen and decide how to act. In the case of humans, model making is taken for granted by psychologists (Johnson-Laird, 1983); no one really knows what other animals' capacities for using mental models are. A *mental model* is some sort of internal representation of part of the organism's surroundings that can be inspected, or even "run" in some way, so that features of the model can then be transformed back into inferred or predicted features of the world. For example, suppose you're planning to go grocery shopping, the skies are threatening rain, and you're trying to decide whether to take an umbrella. You enumerate the situations where the umbrella might be useful and think about whether on balance it will be useful enough to justify having to keep track of it. One such situation is the time when you emerge from the store with a cartload of groceries to put in the car. Will the umbrella keep you or your groceries dry?[9]

This definition is general (and vague) enough to cover non-computational models, but the computationalist framework provides an obvious and attractive approach to theorizing about mental models. In this framework, a model is an internal computer set up to simulate something. The organism initializes it, lets it run for a while, reads off its state, and interprets the state as a set of inferences that then guide behavior. In the umbrella example, one might imagine a physical simulation, at some level of resolution, of a person pushing a cart and holding an umbrella while rain falls.

A mental model used by an agent A to decide what to do must include A itself, simply because any situation A finds itself in will have A as one of its participants. If I am on a sinking ship, and trying to pick a lifeboat to jump into, predicting the number of people on the lifeboat must not omit the "+ 1" required to include me. This seemingly minor principle has far-reaching conse-quences because many of A's beliefs about itself will stem from the way its internal surrogates participate in mental models. We call the beliefs about a particular surrogate a *self-model*, but usually for simplicity I refer to *the* self-model, as if all those beliefs are pulled together into a single "database." Let me state up front that the way things really work is likely to be much more complex and messy. Let me also declare that the self-model is *not* a Cartesian point of transcendence where the self can gaze at itself. It is a resource accessible to the brain at various points for several different purposes.

We can distinguish between *exterior* and *interior* self-models. The former refers to the agent considered as a physical object, something with mass that might sink a lifeboat. The latter refers to the agent considered as an information-processing system. To be concrete, let's look at a self-model that arises in connection with the use of *any-time algorithms* to solve *time-dependent planning problems* (Boddy & Dean, 1989). An any-time algorithm is one that can be thought of as an asynchronous process that starts with a rough approximation to the desired answer and gradually improves it; it can be stopped at any time, and the quality of the result it returns depends on how much run time it was given. We can apply this idea to planning robot behavior, in situations where the objective is to minimize the total time required to solve the problem, which is equal to time (t_P) to find a plan P + time $(t_E(P))$ to execute P.

If the planner is an any-time algorithm, then the quality of the plan it returns improves with t_P. We write $P(t_P)$ to indicate that the plan found is a function of the time allotted to finding it. Because quality is execution time, we can refine that statement and say that $t_E(P(t_P))$ decreases as t_P increases. Therefore, to optimize

$$t_P + t_E(P(t_P))$$

we must find the smallest t_P such that the time gained by planning Δt longer than that would probably improve t_E by less than Δt. The only way to find that optimal t_P is to have an approximate model of how fast $t_E(P(t_P))$ changes as a function of t_P. Such a model would no doubt reflect the law of diminishing returns, so that finding the optimal t_P is an easy one-dimensional optimization problem. The important point for us is that this model is a model of the planning component of the robot, and so counts as an interior self-model.

Let me make sure my point is clear: Interior self-models are no big deal. Any algorithm that outputs an estimate of something plus an error range incorporates one. The mere presence of a self-model does not provide us some kind of mystical reflection zone where we can make consciousness pop out as an "emergent" phenomenon. This point is often misunderstood by critics of AI (Block, 1997; Rey, 1997) who attribute to computationalists the idea that consciousness is nothing but the ability to model oneself. In so doing, they tend to muddy the water further by saying that computationalists confuse consciousness with self-consciousness. I hope in what follows I can make these waters a bit clearer.

Today's information-processing systems are not very smart. They tend to work in narrow domains and outperform humans only in certain areas, such as chess and numerical computation, in which clear formal ground rules are laid out in advance. A robot that can walk into a room, spy a chessboard, and ask if anyone wants to play is still far in the future. This state of affairs raises a huge obstacle for those who believe that consciousness is built on top of intelligence, rather than vice versa, that obstacle being that everything we say is hypothetical. It's easy to counter the computationalist argument. Just say, "I think you're wrong about intelligence preceding consciousness, but even if you're right I doubt that computers will ever reach the level of intelligence required."

To which I reply, Okay. But let's suppose they do reach that level. We avoid begging any questions by using my hypothetical chess-playing robot as a concrete example. We can imagine it being able to locomote, see chessboards, and engage in simple conversations: "Want to play?" "Later." "I'll

be back." We start by assuming that it is not conscious and then think about what it would gain by having interior self-models of a certain class. The starting assumption, that it isn't conscious, should be uncontroversial.

One thing such a robot might need is a way to handle perceptual errors. Suppose that it has a subroutine for recognizing chessboards and chess pieces.[10] For serious play only Staunton chess pieces are allowed, but you can buy a chessboard with pieces of almost any shape; I have no doubt that Disney sells a set with Mickey and Minnie Mouse as king and queen. Our robot, we suppose, can correct for scale, lighting, and other variations of the appearance of Staunton pieces, but just can't "parse" other kinds of pieces. It could also be fooled by objects that only appeared to be Staunton chess pieces.

Now suppose that the robot contained some modules for improving its performance. It might be difficult to calibrate the perceptual systems of our chess-playing robots at the factory, especially because different owners will use them in different situations. So we suppose that after a perceptual failure a module we will call the *perception tuner* will try to diagnose the problem and change the parameters of the perceptual system to avoid it in the future.

The perception tuner must have access to the inputs and outputs of the chess recognition system and, of course, access to parameters that it can change to improve the system's performance. It must have a self-model that tells it how to change the parameters to reduce the likelihood of errors. (The "backpropagation" algorithm used in neural nets (Rumelhart et al., 1986) is an example.) What I want to call attention to is that the perception tuner interprets the outputs of the perceptual system in a rather different way from the decision-making system. The decision-making system interprets them (to oversimplify) as being about the environment; the tuning system interprets them as being about the perceptual system. For the decision maker, the output "Pawn at x, y, z" means that there is a pawn at a certain place. For the tuner, it means that the perceptual system *says* there is a pawn; in other words, that there *appears to be* a pawn.

Here is where the computationalist analysis of intentionality steps in. We don't need to believe that either the decision maker or the tuner literally "thinks" that a symbol structure at a certain point means a particular thing. The symbol structure S means X if there is a harmonious overall interpretation of the states of the robot in which S means X. The perceptual-tuner scenario suggests that we can distinguish two sorts of access to a subsystem: normal access and introspective access. The former refers to the flow of information that the subsystem extracts from the world (Dretske, 1981). The latter refers to the flow of information it produces *about* the normal flow.[11] For our robot, normal access gives it information about chess pieces; introspective access gives it information about ... what, exactly? A datum produced by the tuner would consist of a designator of some part of the perceptual field that was misinterpreted, plus information about how it was interpreted and how it should have been. We can think of this as being information about "appearance" vs. "reality."

The next step in our story is to suppose that our robot has "episodic" memories; that is, memories of particular events that occurred to it. (Psychologists draw distinctions between these memories and other kinds, such as learned skills [e.g., the memory of how to ride a bicycle] and abstract knowledge [e.g., the memory that France is next to Germany], sometimes called *semantic memory*.) We take episodic memory for granted, but presumably flatworms do without it; there must be a reason why it evolved in some primates. One possibility is that it's a means to keep track of events whose significance is initially unknown. If something bad or good happens to an organism, it might want to retrieve past occasions when something similar happened and try to see a pattern. It's hard to say why the expense of maintaining a complex "database" would be paid back in terms of reproductive success, especially given

how wrong-headed people can be about explaining patterns of events. But perhaps all that is required is enough paranoia to avoid too many false negatives in predicting catastrophes.

The final step is to suppose that the robot can ask fairly general questions about the operation of its perceptual and decision-making systems. Actually, this ability is closely tied to the ability to store episodic memories. To remember something one must have a notation to express it. Remembering a motor skill might require storing a few dozen numerical parameters (e.g., weights in neural networks, plus some sequencing information). If this is correct, then, as argued above, learning a skill means nudging these parameters toward optimal values. Because this notation is so lean, it won't support recording the episodes during which skill was enhanced. You may remember your golf lessons, but those memories are independent of the "memories," encoded as numerical parameters, that manifest themselves as an improved putt. Trying to think of a notation in which to record an arbitrary episode is like trying to think of a formal notation to capture the content of a Tolstoy novel. It's not even clear what it would mean to record an episode. How much detail would there be? Would it always have to be from the point of view of the creature that recorded it? Such questions get us quickly into the realm of Knowledge Representation, and the Language of Thought (Fodor, 1975). For that matter, we are quickly led to the topic of ordinary human language, because the ability to recall an episode seems closely related to the abilities to tell about it and to ask about it. We are far from understanding how language, knowledge representation, and episodic memory work, but it seems clear that the mechanisms are tightly connected, and all have to do with what sorts of questions the self-model can answer. This clump of mysteries accounts for why Dennett's (1991b) meme-based theory is so attractive. He makes a fairly concrete proposal that language came first and that the evolution of the self-model was driven by the evolution of language.

Having waved our hands a bit, we can get back to discussing the ability of humans, and presumably other intelligent creatures, to ask questions about how they work. We will just assume that these questions are asked using an internal notation reminiscent of human language, and then answered using a Minskyesque self-model. The key observation is that the self-model need not be completely accurate or, rather, that there is a certain flexibility in what counts as an accurate answer, because what it says can't be contradicted by other sources of information. If all people's self-models say they have free will, then free will can't be anything but whatever it is all people think they have. It becomes difficult to deny that we have free will, because there's no content to the claim that we have it over and above what the chorus of self-models declare.[12]

Phenomenal experience now emerges as the self-model's answer to the question, What happens when I perceive something? The answer, in terms of appearance, reality, and error, is accurate up to a point. It's when we get to qualia that the model ends the explanation with a just-so story. It gives more useful answers on such questions as whether it's easier to confuse green and yellow than green and red, or what to do when senses conflict, or what conditions make errors more or less likely. But to questions such as, How do I know this is red in the first place?, it gives an answer designed to stop inquiry. The answer is that red has this quality (please focus attention on the red object), which is intrinsically different from the analogous quality for green objects (now focus over here, if you don't mind). Because red is "intrinsically like . . . *this*," there is no further question to ask. Nor should there be. I can take steps to improve my classification of objects by color, but there's nothing I can do to improve my ability to tell red from green (or, more plausibly, to tell two shades of red apart) once I've obtained optimal lighting and viewing conditions.[13]

The computationalist theory of phenomenal consciousness thus ends up looking like a spoil-sport's explanation of a magic trick.

It comes down to this: "Don't look over there! The key move is over here, where you weren't looking!"[14] *Phenomenal consciousness is not part of the mechanism of perception, but part of the mechanism of introspection about perception.*

It is easy to think that this theory is similar to Perlis's model of self-consciousness as ultimately fundamental, and many philosophers have misread it that way. That's why the term "self-consciousness" is so misleading. Ordinarily what we mean by it is consciousness of self. But the self-model theory of consciousness aims to explain *all* phenomenal consciousness in terms of *subpersonal* modeling by an organism R of R's own perceptual system. Consciousness of self is just a particular sort of phenomenal consciousness, so the theory aims to explain it in terms of modeling by R of R's own perceptual system in the act of perceiving R. In these last two sentences the word "self" does not appear except as part of the *definiendum*, not as part of the *definiens*. Whatever the self is, it is not lying around waiting to be perceived; the act of modeling it defines what it is to a great extent. There is nothing mystical going on here. When R's only view of R is R^*, in Minsky's terminology, then it is no surprise if terms occur in R^* whose meaning depends at least partly on how R^* fits into everything else R is doing, and in particular on how (the natural-language equivalents of those) terms are used by a community of organisms to which R belongs.

I think the hardest part of this theory to accept is that perception is normally not mediated, or even accompanied, by qualia. In the introduction to this chapter, I invited readers to cast their eyes over a complex climate-control system and observe the absence of sensation. We can do the same exercise with the brain, with the same result. It just doesn't need sensations to do its job. But if you *ask* it, it will claim it does. A quale exists only when you look for it.

Throughout this section, I have tried to stay close to what I think is a consensus position on a computational theory of phenomenal consciousness. But I have to admit that the endpoint to which I think we are driven is one that many otherwise fervent computationalists are reluctant to accept. There is no alternative conclusion on the horizon, just a wish for one, as in this quote from (Perlis, 1997):

> ... Perhaps bare consciousness is in and of itself a self-distinguishing process, a process that takes note of itself. If so, it could still be considered a quale, the ur-quale, what it's like to be a bare subject.... What might this be? That is unclear....

Perlis believes that a conscious system needs to be "strongly self-referring," in that its modeling of self is modeled in the very modeling, or something like that. "Why do we need a self-contained self, where referring stops? Negotiating one's way in a complex world is a tough business...." He sketches a scenario in which Ralph, a robot, needs a new arm:

> Suppose the new arm is needed within 24 hours. He cannot allow his decision-making about the best and quickest way to order the arm get in his way, i.e., he must not allow it to run on and on. He can use meta-reasoning to watch his reasoning so it does not use too much time, but then what is to watch his meta-reasoning?... He must budget his time. Yet the budgeting is another time-drain, so he must pay attention to that too, and so on in an infinite regress... Somehow he must regard [all these modules] as himself, one (complex) system reasoning about itself, including that very observation. He must strongly self-refer: he must refer to that very referring so that its own time-passage can be taken into account. (Emphasis in original.)

It appears to me that two contrary intuitions are colliding here. One is the hardheaded computationalist belief that self-modeling is all you need for consciousness; the other is the nagging feeling that self-modeling alone can't quite get us all the way. Yet when he tries to find an example, he winds up with a mystical version of the work by Boddy and Dean (1989) that I cited above as a prosaic example of self-modeling. It seems clear to me that the only reason Perlis needs the virtus dormi-

tiva of "strong self-reference" is because the problem-solving system he's imagining is not an ordinary computer program, but a transcendental self-contemplating mind – something not really divided into modules at all, but actively dividing itself into time-shared virtual modules as it shifts its attention from one aspect of its problem to another, then to a meta-layer, a meta-meta-layer, and so forth. If you bite the bullet and accept that all this meta-stuff, if it exists at all, exists only in the system's self-model, then the need for strong self-reference, and the "ur-quale," goes away, much like the ether in the theory of electromagnetism. So I believe, but I admit that most AI researchers who take a position probably share Perlis's reluctance to let that ether go.

The Critics

AI has always generated a lot of controversy. The typical pattern is that some piece of research captures the public's imagination, as amplified by journalists, then the actual results don't fit those public expectations, and finally someone comes along to chalk up one more failure of AI research. Meanwhile, often enough the research does succeed, not on the goals hallucinated by the popular press, but on those the researchers actually had in mind, so that the AI community continues to gain confidence that it is on the right track. Criticism of AI models of consciousness doesn't fit this pattern. As I observed at the outset, almost no one in the field is "working on" consciousness, and certainly there's no one trying to write a conscious program. It is seldom that a journalist can make a breathless report about a *robot that will actually have experiences*!!¹⁵

Nonetheless, there has been an outpouring of papers and books arguing that mechanical consciousness is impossible and that suggestions to the contrary are wasteful of research dollars and possibly even dangerously dehumanizing. The field of "artificial consciousness" (AC) is practically *defined* by writers who deny that such a thing is possible. Much more has been written by

AC skeptics than by those who think it is possible. In this section I discuss some of those criticisms and refute them as best I can.

Due to space limitations, I try to focus on critiques that are specifically directed at computational models of consciousness, as opposed to general critiques of materialist explanation. For example, I pass over Jackson's (1982) story about "Mary, the color scientist" who learns what red looks like. There are interesting things to say about it, which I say in McDermott (2001), but Jackson's critique is not directed at, and doesn't mention, computationalism in particular. I also pass over the vast literature on "inverted spectrum" problems, which is a somewhat more complex version of the sour/spicy taco problem.

Another class of critiques that I omit are those whose aim is to show that computers can never achieve human-level intelligence. As discussed in the section on research on computational models of consciousness, I concede that if computers can't be intelligent then they can't be conscious either. But our focus here is on consciousness, so the critics I try to counter are those who specifically argue that computers will never be conscious, even if they might exhibit intelligent behavior. One important group of arguments this leaves out are those based on Gödel's proof that Peano arithmetic is incomplete (Nagel & Newman, 1958; Penrose, 1989, 1994). These arguments are intended to show a limitation in the abilities of computers to reason, not specifically a limitation on their ability to experience things; in fact, the connection between the two is too tenuous to justify talking about the topic in detail.

Turing's Test

Let's start where the field started: with Turing's Test (Turing, 1950). As described earlier, it consists of a judge trying to distinguish a computer from a person by carrying on typed conversations with both. If the judge gets it wrong about 50% of the time, then the computer passes the test.

Turing's Test is not necessarily relevant to the computational theory of consciousness. Few of the theorists discussed in this chapter have invoked it as a methodological tool. Where it comes in is when reliance on it is *attributed* to computationalists. A critic will take the computationalist's focus on the third-person point of view as an endorsement of behaviorism and then jump to Turing's Test as the canonical behaviorist tool for deciding whether an entity is conscious. That first step, from "third-person" to "behaviorist," is illegitimate. It is, in fact, somewhat ludicrous to accuse someone of being a behaviorist who is so eager to open an animal up (metaphorically, that is) and stuff its head with intricate block diagrams. All the "third-personist" is trying to do is stick to scientifically, that is, publicly, available facts. This attempt is biased against the first-person view, and that bias pays off by eventually giving us an *explanation* of the first person.

So there is no particular reason for a computationalist to defend the Turing Test. It doesn't particularly help develop theoretical proposals, and it gets in the way of thinking about intelligent systems that obviously can't pass the test. Nonetheless, an objection to computationalism raised in the section, "Moore/Turing Inevitability," does require an answer. That was the objection that even if a computer could pass the Turing Test, this achievement wouldn't provide any evidence that it actually was conscious. I disagree with this objection on grounds that should be clear at this point: To be conscious is to model one's mental life in terms of things like sensations and free decisions. It would be hard to have an intelligent robot that wasn't conscious in this sense, because everywhere the robot went it would have to deal with its own presence and its own decision making, and so it would have to have models of its behavior and its thought processes. Conversing with it would be a good way of finding out how it thought about itself; that is, what its self-models were like.

Keep in mind, however, that the Turing Test is not likely to be the standard method to check for the presence of consciousness in a computer system, if we ever need a standard method. A robot's self-model, and hence its consciousness, could be quite different from ours in respects that are impossible to predict given how far we are from having intelligent robots. It is also just barely possible that a computer not connected to a robot could be intelligent with only a very simple self-model. Suppose the computer's job was to control the traffic, waste management, and electric grid of a city. It might be quite intelligent, but hardly conscious in a way we could recognize, simply because it wouldn't be present in the situations it modeled the way we are. It probably couldn't pass the Turing Test either.

Somewhere in this thicket of possibilities there might be an artificial intelligence with an alien form of consciousness that could *pretend* to be conscious on our terms while knowing full well that it wasn't. It could then pass the Turing Test, wine tasting division, by faking it. All this shows is that there is a slight possibility that the Turing Test could be good at detecting intelligence and not so good at detecting consciousness. This shouldn't give much comfort to those who think that the Turing Test systematically distracts us from the first-person viewpoint. If someone ever builds a machine that passes it, it will certainly exhibit intentionality and intelligence and almost certainly be conscious. There's a remote chance that human-style consciousness can be faked, but no chance that intelligence can be.[16]

The Chinese Room

One of the most notorious arguments in the debate about computational consciousness is Searle's (1980) "Chinese Room" argument. It's very simple. Suppose we hire Searle (who speaks no Chinese) to implement a computer program for reading stories in Chinese and then answering questions about those stories. Searle reads each line of the program and does what it says. He executes the program about a million times slower than an actual CPU would, but if we don't

mind the slow motion we could carry on a perfectly coherent conversation with him.

Searle goes on:

Now the claims made by strong AI are that the programmed computer understands the stories and that the program in some sense explains human understanding. But we are now in a position to examine these claims in light of our thought experiment.

1. *As regards the first claim, it seems to me quite obvious in the example that I do not understand a word of the Chinese stories. I have inputs and outputs that are indistinguishable from those of the native Chinese speaker, and I can have any formal program you like, but I still understand nothing. . . .*

2. *As regards the second claim, that the program explains human understanding, we can see that the computer and its program do not provide sufficient conditions of understanding since the computer and the program are functioning, and there is no understanding.*

It's hard to see what this argument has to do with consciousness. The connection is somewhat indirect. Recall that in the section, "Intentionality of Computational Systems," I made sure to discuss "impersonal" intentionality, the kind a system has by virtue of being a computer whose symbol structures are causally connected to the environment so as to denote objects and states of affairs in that environment. Searle absolutely refuses to grant that there is any such thing as impersonal or subpersonal intentionality (Searle, 1992). The paradigm case of any mental state is always the conscious mental state, and he is willing to stretch mental concepts only far enough to cover unconscious mental states that could have been conscious (repressed desires, for instance). Hence there is no understanding of Chinese unless it is accompanied by a conscious awareness or feeling of understanding.

If Searle's stricture were agreed upon, then all research in cognitive science would cease immediately, because it routinely assumes the existence of non-conscious symbol processing to explain the results of experiments.[17]

Searle seems to have left an escape clause, the notion of "weak AI":

I find it useful to distinguish what I will call 'strong' AI from 'weak' or 'cautious' AI. . . . According to weak AI, the principal value of the computer in the study of the mind is that it gives us a very powerful tool. For example, it enables us to formulate and test hypotheses in a more rigorous and precise fashion. But according to strong AI, the computer is not merely a tool in the study of the mind; rather, the appropriately programmed computer really is a mind, in the sense that computers given the right programs can be literally said to understand and have other cognitive states (Searle, 1980).

Many people have adopted this terminology, viewing the supposed weak version of AI as a safe harbor in which to hide from criticism. In my opinion, the concept of weak AI is incoherent. Suppose someone writes a program to simulate a hurricane, to use a common image. The numbers in the simulation denote actual or hypothetical air pressures, wind velocities, and the like. The simulation embodies differential equations that are held to be more or less true statements about how wind velocities affect air pressures and vice versa, and similarly for all the other variables involved. Now think about "computer simulations of human cognitive capacities" (Searle's phrase). What are the analogues of the wind velocities and air pressures in this case? When we use the simulations to "formulate and test hypotheses," what are the hypotheses *about?* They might be about membrane voltages and currents in neurons, but of course they aren't, because neurons are "too small." We would have to simulate an awful lot of them, and we don't really know how they're connected, and the simulation would just give us a huge chunk of predicted membrane currents anyway. So no one does that. Instead, they run simulations at a much higher level, at which symbols and data structures emerge. This is true even for neural-net researchers, whose models are much, much smaller than the real thing, so that each connection weight represents an abstract summary of a huge collection of real weights. What, then, is the ontological status of these symbols and data structures? If we believe that these symbols and the computational processes over them are really present in the brain, and really explain what the brain does, then we are back to strong AI. But if we don't believe that, then why the hell are we simulating them? By analogy, let us compare strong vs. weak computational meteorology. The former is based on the belief that wind velocities and air pressures really have something to do with how hurricanes behave. The latter allows us to build "powerful tools" that perform "computer simulations of [hurricanes' physical] capacities," and "formulate and test hypotheses" about . . . something *other* than wind velocities and air pressures?

Please note that I am not saying that all cognitive scientists are committed to a computationalist account of consciousness. I'm just saying that they're committed to a computationalist account of whatever it is they're studying. If someone believes that the EPAM model (Feigenbaum & Simon, 1984) accounts for human errors in memorizing lists of nonsense syllables, they have to believe that structures isomorphic to the discrimination trees in EPAM are actually to be found in human brains. If someone believes that there is *no* computationalist account of intelligence, then they must also believe that a useful computer simulation of intelligence must simulate something *other* than symbol manipulation, perhaps ectoplasm secretions. In other words, given our lack of *any* non-computational account of the workings of the mind, they must believe it to be pointless to engage in simulating intelligence *at all* at this stage of the development of the subject.

There remains one opportunity for confusion. No one believes that a simulation of a hurricane could blow your house off the beach. Why should we expect a simulation of a conscious mind to be conscious (or expect a simulation of a mind to be a mind)? Well, we need not expect that, exactly. If a simulation of a mind is disconnected from an environment, then it would remain a mere simulation.

However, once the connection is made properly, we confront the fact that a sufficiently detailed simulation of computation C *is* computation C. This is a property of formal systems generally. As Haugeland (1985) observes, the difference between a game like tennis and a game like chess is that the former involves moving a physical object, the ball, through space, whereas the latter involves jumping from one legal board position to the next, and legal board positions are not physical entities. In tennis, one must hit a ball with certain prescribed physical properties using a tennis racket, which must also satisfy certain physical requirements. Chess requires only that the state of the game be represented with enough detail to capture the positions of all the pieces.[18] One can use any 8×8 array as a board, and any collection of objects as pieces, provided they are isomorphic to the standard board and pieces. One can even use computer data structures. So a detailed simulation of a good chess player *is* a good chess player, provided it is connected by some channel, encoded however you like, between its computations and an actual opponent with whom it is alternating moves. Whereas for a simulation of a tennis player to be a tennis player, it would have to be connected to a robot capable of tracking and hitting tennis balls.

This property carries over to the simulation of any other process that is essentially computational. So, if it happens that consciousness is a computational phenomenon, then a sufficiently faithful simulation of a conscious system would be a conscious system, provided it was connected to the environment in the appropriate way. This point is especially clear if the computations in question are somewhat modularizable, as might be the case for a system's self-model. The difference between a non-conscious tennis player and a conscious one might involve connections among its internal computational modules, and not the connections from there to its cameras and motors. There would then be no difference between the "consciousness module" and a detailed simulation of that "module"; they would be interchangeable, provided that they didn't differ

too much in speed, size, and energy consumption. I use scare quotes here because I doubt that things will turn out to be that tidy. Nonetheless, no matter how the wires work out, the point is that nothing *other than* computation need be involved in consciousness, which is what Strong AI boils down to. Weak AI boils down to a sort of "cargo cult" whose rituals involve simulations of things someone only guesses might be important in some way.

Now that I've clarified the stakes, let's look at Searle's argument. It is ridiculously easy to refute. When he says that "the claims made by strong AI are that the programmed computer understands the stories and that the program in some sense explains human understanding," he may be right about the second claim (depending on how literally you interpret "explains"), but he is completely wrong about the first claim, that the programmed computer understands something. As McCarthy says, "The Chinese Room Argument can be refuted in one sentence: Searle confuses the mental qualities of one computational process, himself for example, with those of another process that the first process might be interpreting, a process that understands Chinese, for example" (McCarthy, 2000). Searle's slightly awkward phrase "the programmed computer" gives the game away. Computers and software continually break our historically founded understanding of the identity of objects across time. Any computer user has (too often) had the experience of not knowing "whom" they're talking to when talking to their program. Listen to a layperson try to sort out the contributions to their current state of frustration made by the e-mail delivery program, the e-mail reading program, and the e-mail server. When you run a program you usually then talk to it. If you run two programs at once you switch back and forth between talking to one and talking to the other.[19] The phrase "programmed computer" makes it sound as if programming it changes *it* into something you can talk to. The only reason to use such an odd phrase is because in the story Searle himself plays the role of the programmed computer, the entity that doesn't understand. By pointing at the "human CPU" and shouting loudly, he hopes to distract us from the abstract entity that is brought into existence by executing the story-understanding program.

We can state McCarthy's argument vividly by supposing that *two* CPUs are involved, as they might well be. The story-understanding program might be run on one for a while, then on the other, and so forth, as dictated by the internal economics of the operating system. Do AI researchers imagine that the ability to "understand" jumps back and forth between the two CPUs? If we replace the two CPUs by two people, does Strong AI predict that the ability to understand Chinese will jump back and forth between the two people (McDermott, 2001)? Of course not.

Symbol Grounding

In both of the preceding sections, it sometimes seems as if intentionality is the real issue, or what Harnad (1990, 2001) calls the *symbol-grounding problem*. The problem arises from the idea of a disembodied computer living in a realm of pure syntax, which we discussed in the section on Brian Cantwell Smith. Suppose that such a computer ran a simulation of the battle of Waterloo. That is, we intend it to simulate that battle, but for all we know there might be another encoding of its states that would make it be a simulation of coffee prices in Ecuador.[20] What connects the symbols to the things they denote? In other words, what *grounds* the symbols?

This problem underlies some people's concerns about the Turing Test and the Chinese Room because the words in the Turing Test conversation might be considered to be ungrounded and therefore meaningless (Davidson, 1990) and the program and data structures being manipulated by the human CPU John Searle seem also to be disconnected from anything that could give them meaning.

As should be clear from the discussion in the section, "Intentionality of Computa-

tional Systems," symbols get their meanings by being causally connected to the world. Harnad doesn't disagree with this, but he thinks that the connection must take the special form of neural networks, natural or artificial.[21] The inputs to the networks must be sensory transducers. The outputs are neurons that settle into different stable patterns of activation depending on how the transducers are stimulated. The possible stable patterns and the way they classify inputs are learned over time as the network is trained by its owner's encounters with its surroundings.

How does the hybrid system find the invariant features of the sensory projection that make it possible to categorize and identify objects correctly? Connectionism, with its general pattern-learning capability, seems to be one natural candidate (though there may well be others): Icons, paired with feedback indicating their names, could be processed by a connectionist network that learns to identify icons correctly from the sample of confusable alternatives it has encountered, by dynamically adjusting the weights of the features and feature combinations that are reliably associated with the names in a way that (provisionally) resolves the confusion. It thereby reduces the icons to the invariant (confusion-resolving) features of the category to which they are assigned. The net result is that the grounding of the name to the objects that give rise to their sensory projections and their icons would be provided by neural networks (Harnad, 1990).

The symbol-grounding problem, if it is a problem, requires no urgent solution, as far as I can see. I think it stems from a basic misunderstanding about what computationalism is and what the alternatives are. According to Harnad, "The predominant approach to cognitive modeling is still what has come to be called 'computationalism' . . . , the hypothesis that cognition is computation. The more recent rival approach is 'connectionism' . . . , the hypothesis that cognition is a dynamic pattern of connections and activations in a 'neural net'" (Harnad, 2001). Put this way, it seems clear that neural nets would be welcome under computationalism's "big tent," but Harnad spurns the invitation by imposing a series of fresh requirements. By "computation" he means "symbolic computation," which consists of syntactic operations on "symbol tokens." Analog computation is ruled out. Symbolic computation doesn't depend on the medium in which it is implemented, just so long as it is implemented somehow (because the syntactic categories of the symbol tokens will be unchanged). And last, but certainly not least, "the symbols and symbol manipulations in a symbol system [must be] systematically interpretable (Fodor & Pylyshyn, 1988): They can be assigned a semantics, and they mean something (e.g., numbers, words, sentences, chess moves, planetary motions, etc.)." The alternative is "trivial" computation, which produces "uninterpretable formal gibberish."

As I argue in McDermott (2001), these requirements have seldom been met by what most people call "computational" systems. The average computer programmer knows nothing about formal semantics or systematic interpretability. Indeed, in my experience it is quite difficult to teach a programmer about formal systems and semantics. One must scrape away layers of prior conditioning about how to "talk" to computers. Furthermore, as I write in the section, "The Notion of a Computational System," few AI practitioners refuse to mix and match connectionist and symbolic programs. One must be careful about how one interprets what they *say* about their practice. Clancey (1999), in arguing for a connectionist architecture, calls the previous tradition modeling the brain as a "wet" computer similar in important respects to the "dry" computers we use as models. He argues that we should replace it with a particular connectionist architecture. As an example of the change this would bring, he says (p. 30), "Cognitive models have traditionally treated procedural memory, including inference rules ('if X then Y'), as if human memory is just computer random-access memory...." He proposes to "explore the hypothesis that a sequential association, such as an inference-rule..., is a temporal relation of activation,

such that if X implies Y," what is recorded is a "relation...of temporal activation, such that when X is presently active, Y is a categorization that is potentially active next" (p. 31). But he remains a committed computationalist through this seemingly discontinuous change. For instance, in discussing how the new paradigm would actually work, he writes, "The discussion of [insert detailed proposal here] illustrates how the discipline of implementing a process in a computer representation forces distinctions to be rediscovered and brings into question consistency of the theory" (p. 44).

The moral is that we must be careful to distinguish between two ways in which computers are used in psychological modeling: as implementation platform and as metaphor. The digital-computer metaphor might shed light on why we have a single stream of consciousness ($\sim$ von Neumann instruction stream?), why we can only remember 7 ± 2 things ($\sim$ size of our register set?), and why we have trouble with deep center-embedded sentences like "The boy the man the dog bit spanked laughed" ($\sim$ stack overflow?). The metaphor may have had some potential in the 1950s, when cognitive science was just getting underway, but it's pretty much run out of steam at this point. Clancey is correct to point out how the metaphor may have affected cognitive science in ways that seemed too harmless to notice, but that in retrospect are hard to justify. For instance, the program counter in a computer makes pursuing a rigid list of tasks easy. If we help ourselves to a program counter in implementing a cognitive model, we may have begged an important question about how sequentiality is achieved in a parallel system like the brain.

What I argue is that the essence of computationalism is to believe that (a) brains are essentially computers and (b) digital computers can simulate them in all important respects, even if they aren't digital at all. Because a simulation of a computation *is a* computation, the "digitality" of the digital computer cancels out. If symbol grounding is explained by some very special properties of a massively parallel neural network of a *particular sort*, then if that net can be simulated in real time on a cluster of parallel workstations, the cluster becomes a virtual neural net, which grounds symbols as well as a "real" one would.

Perhaps this is the place to mention the paper by O'Brien and Opie (1999) that presents a "connectionist theory of phenomenal experience." The theory makes a basic assumption, that a digital simulation of a conscious connectionist system would not be conscious. It is very hard to see how this could be true. It's the zombie hypothesis, raised from the dead one more time. The "real" neural net is conscious, but the simulated one, in spite of operating in exactly the same way (plus or minus a little noise), would be experience-less – another zombie lives.

Conclusions

The contribution of artificial intelligence to consciousness studies has been slender so far, because almost everyone in the field would rather work on better defined, less controversial problems. Nonetheless, there do seem to be common themes running through the work of AI researchers that touches on phenomenal consciousness. Consciousness stems from the structure of the *self-models* that intelligent systems use to reason about themselves. A creature's models of itself are like models of other systems, except for some characteristic indeterminacy about what counts as accuracy. To explain how an information-processing system can *have* a model of something, there must be a prior notion of intentionality that explains why and how symbols inside the system can refer to things. This theory of *impersonal intentionality* is based on the existence of harmonious match-ups between the states of the system and states of the world. The meanings of symbol structures are what the match-ups say they are.

Having established that a system's model of that very system is a non-vacuous idea, the next step is to show that the model almost certainly will contain ways of thinking about

how the system's senses work. The difference between appearance and reality arises at this point, and allows the system to reason about its errors in order to reduce the chance of making them. But the self-model also serves to set boundaries to the questions that it can answer. The idea of a sensory quale arises as a useful way of cutting off useless introspection about how things are ultimately perceived and categorized.

Beyond this point it is hard to find consensus between those who believe that the just-so story the self-model tells its owner is all you need to explain phenomenal consciousness, and those who think that something more is needed. Frustratingly, we won't be able to create systems and test hypotheses against them in the foreseeable future, because real progress on creating conscious programs awaits further developments in enhancing the intelligence of robots. There is no guarantee that AI will *ever* achieve the requisite level of intelligence, in which case this chapter has been pretty much wasted effort.

There are plenty of critics who don't want to wait to see how well AI succeeds, because they think they have arguments that can shoot down the concept of machine consciousness or rule out certain forms of it, right now. We examined three such arguments: the accusation that AI is behaviorist on the subject of consciousness, the "Chinese Room" argument, and the symbol-grounding problem. In each case the basic computationalist working hypothesis survived intact: that the embodied brain is an "embedded" computer and that a reasonably accurate simulation of it would have whatever mental properties it has, including phenomenal consciousness.

Notes

1. I would be tempted to say there is a spectrum from "weak" to "strong" computationalism to reflect the different stances on these issues, but the terms "weak" and "strong" have been used by John Searle (1980) in a quite different way. See the section on the "Chinese room."

2. I am taking this possibility seriously for now because everyone will recognize the issue and its relationship to the nature of qualia. But I follow Sloman & Chrisley (2003) in believing that cross-personal comparison of qualia makes no sense. See section on Perlis and Sloman and McDermott (2001).

3. Turing actually proposed a somewhat different test. See Davidson (1990) for discussion. Nowadays this version is the one everyone works with.

4. The Loebner Prize is awarded every year to the writer of a program that appears "most human" to a panel of judges. You can see how close the programs are getting to fooling anyone by going to its Web site, http://www.loebner.net/Prizef/loebner-prize.html.

5. The "[z]" is used to flag zombie words whose meanings must not be confused with normal human concepts.

6. Even more fortunate, perhaps, is the fact that few will grant that foundational ontology is a problem in the first place. Those who think elementary particles invented us, rather than vice versa, are in the minority.

7. Or intelligent aliens, but this is an irrelevant variation on the theme.

8. By analogy with Christology in Christian theology, which ranges from high to low depending on how superhuman one believes Jesus to be.

9. For some readers this example will elicit fairly detailed visual images of shopping carts and umbrellas, and for those readers it's plausible that the images are part of the mental-model machinery. But even people without much visual imagery can still have mental models and might still use them to reason about grocery shopping.

10. I have two reasons for positing a chessboard-recognition subroutine instead of a general-purpose vision system that recognizes chessboards and chess pieces in terms of more "primitive" elements: (1) Many roboticists prefer to work with specialized perceptual systems, and (2) the qualia-like entities we will predict will be different in content from human qualia, which reduces the chances of jumping to conclusions about them.

11. Of course, what we'd like to be able to say here is that normal access is the access it was designed to support, and for most purposes that's what we will say, even when evolution

is the "designer." But such basic concepts can't depend on historical events arbitrarily that are far in the past.

12. For the complete story on free will, see McDermott (2001, Chapter 3). I referred to Minsky's rather different theory above; McCarthy champions his own version in McCarthy & Hayes (1969).

13. One may view it as a bug that a concept, qualia, whose function is to end introspective questioning, has stimulated so much conversation! Perhaps if human evolution goes on long enough natural selection will eliminate those of us who persist in talking about such things, especially while crossing busy streets.

14. Cf. Wittgenstein (1953): "The decisive movement in the conjuring trick has been made, and it was the very one we thought quite innocent."

15. One occasionally hears news reports about attempts to build an artificial nose. When I hear such a report, I picture a device that measures concentrations of substances in the air. But perhaps the average person imagines a device that "smells things," so that, for example, the smell of a rotten egg would be unpleasant for it. In any case, these news reports seem not to have engendered much controversy so far.

16. I realize that many people, for instance Robert Kirk (1994), believe that in principle something as simple as a lookup table could simulate intelligence. I don't have space here to refute this point of view, except to note that in addition to the fact that the table would be larger than the known universe and take a trillion years to build, a computer carrying on a conversation by consulting it would not be able to answer a question about what time it is.

17. There is a popular belief that there is such a thing as "nonsymbolic" or "subsymbolic" cognitive science, as practiced by those who study artificial neural nets. As I mentioned in the section, "The Notion of Computational System," this distinction is usually unimportant, and the present context is an example. The goal of neural-net researchers is to explain conscious thought in terms of unconscious computational events in neurons, and as far as Searle is concerned, this is just the same fallacy all over again (Searle, 1990).

18. And a couple of other bits of information, such as whether each player still has castling as an option.

19. Technically I mean "process" here, not "program." McCarthy's terminology is more accurate, but I'm trying to be intelligible by technical innocents.

20. I believe these particular examples (Waterloo and Ecuador) were invented by someone other than me, but I have been unable to find the reference.

21. The fact that these are called "connectionist" is a mere pun in this context – I hope.

References

Baars, B. J. (1988). *A cognitive theory of consciousness*. New York: Guilford Press.

Baars, B. J. (1997). *In the theater of consciousness: The work space of the mind*. New York: Oxford University Press.

Block, N. (1997). On a confusion about a function of consciousness. In N. Block, O. Flanagan, & G. Güzeldere (Eds.), *The nature of consciousness: Philosophical debates* (pp. 375–415). Cambridge, MA: MIT Press.

Block, N., Flanagan, O., & Güzeldere, G. (Eds.) (1997). *The nature of consciousness: Philosophical debates*. Cambridge, MA: MIT Press.

Boddy, M., & Dean, T. (1989). Solving time-dependent planning problems. *Proceedings of the 11th International Joint Conference on Artificial Intelligence*, 979–984.

Campbell, J. (1994). *Past, space and self*. Cambridge, MA: MIT Press.

Chalmers, D. (1996). *The conscious mind: In search of a fundamental theory*. New York: Oxford University Press.

Churchland, P. (1986). *Neurophilosophy: Toward a unified science of the mind-brain*. Cambridge, MA: MIT Press.

Churchland, P. (1988). *Matter and consciousness: A contemporary introduction to the philosophy of mind*. Cambridge, MA: MIT Press.

Clancey, W. J. (1999). *Conceptual coordination: How the mind orders experience in time*. Mahwah, NJ: Erlbaum.

Currie, K., & Tate, A. (1991). O-plan: The open planning architecture. *Artificial Intelligence*, 52(1), 49–86.

Davidson, D. (1990). Turing's test. In K. M. Said, W. Newton-Smith, R. Viale, & K. Wilkes (Eds.), *Modelling the mind* (pp. 1–11). Oxford: Clarendon Press.

Dawkins, R. (1976). *The selfish gene*. Oxford: Oxford University Press.

Dennett, D. C. (1969). *Content and consciousness*. London: Routledge & Kegan Paul.

Dennett, D. C. (1991a). Real patterns. *Journal of Philosophy*, 88, 27–51.

Dennett, D. C. (1991b). *Consciousness explained*. Boston: Little, Brown.

Douglas, G., & Saunders, S. (2003). Dan Dennett: Philosopher of the month. *TPM Online: The Philosophers' Magazine on the internet*. Retrieved August 2, 2005, from http://www.philosophers.co.uk/cafe/phil apr2003.htm.

Dretske, F. I. (1981). *Knowledge and the flow of information*. Cambridge, MA: MIT Press.

Feigenbaum, E. A., & Simon, H. A. (1984). Epam-like models of recognition and learning. *Cognitive Science*, 8(4), 305–336.

Fodor, J. (1975). *The language of thought*. New York: Thomas Y. Crowell.

Fodor, J., & Pylyshyn, Z. (1988). Connectionism and cognitive architecture: A critical analysis. In S. Pinker, & J. Mehler (Eds.), *Connections and symbols* (pp. 3–72). Cambridge, MA: MIT Press.

Harnad, S. (1990). The symbol grounding problem. *Physica D*, 42, 335–346.

Harnad, S. (2001). Grounding symbols in the analog world with neural nets – a hybrid model. *Psycoloquy*. Retrieved August 2, 2005, from http://psycprints.ecs.soton.ac.uk/archive/00000163/.

Haugeland, J. (1985). *Artificial intelligence: The very idea*. Cambridge, MA: MIT Press.

Hayes-Roth, B. (1985). A blackboard architecture for control. *Artificial Intelligence*, 26(3), 251–321.

Hofstadter, D. R. (1979). *Gödel, Escher, Bach: An eternal golden braid*. New York: Basic Books.

Hofstadter, D. R., & Dennett, D. C. (1981). *The mind's I: Fantasies and reflections on self and soul*. New York: Basic Books.

Jackson, F. (1982). Epiphenomenal qualia. *Philosophical Quarterly*, 32, 127–136.

Jaynes, J. (1976). *The origins of consciousness in the breakdown of the bicameral mind*. Boston: Houghton Mifflin.

Johnson-Laird, P. N. (1983). *Mental models*. Cambridge, MA: Harvard University Press.

Kirk, R. (1994). *Raw feeling: A philosophical account of the essence of consciousness*. Oxford: Oxford University Press.

Kurzweil, R. (1999). *The age of spiritual machines: When computers exceed human intelligence*. New York: Penguin Books.

Libet, B. (1985). Unconscious cerebral initiative and the role of conscious will in voluntary action. *Behavioral and Brain Sciences*, 8, 529–566.

McCarthy, J. (1990b). Ascribing mental qualities to machines. In J. McCarthy (Ed.), *Formalizing commonsense*. Norwood, NJ: Ablex.

McCarthy, J. (1995a). Todd Moody's zombies. *Journal of Consciousness Studies*. Retrieved June 26, 2006, from http://www-formal.stanford.edu/jmc/zombie/zombie.html.

McCarthy, J. (1995b). Making robots conscious of their mental states. *Proceedings of the Machine Intelligence Workshop*. Retrieved August 2, 2005, from http://www-formal.stanford.edu/jmc/consciousness.html.

McCarthy, J. (2000). John Searle's Chinese room argument. Retrieved August 2, 2005, from http://www-formal.stanford.edu/jmc/chinese.html.

McCarthy, J. & Hayes, P. (1969). Some philosophical problems from the standpoint of artificial intelligence. In B. Meltzer, & D. Michie (Eds.), *Machine intelligence 4* (pp. 463–502). Edinburgh: Edinburgh University Press.

McDermott, D. (2001). *Mind and mechanism*. Cambridge, MA: MIT Press.

Meltzer, B., & Michie, D. (Eds.). (1969). *Machine intelligence 4*. Edinburgh: Edinburgh University Press.

Minsky, M. (Ed.). (1968a). *Semantic information processing*. Cambridge, MA: MIT Press.

Minsky, M. (1968b). Matter, mind, and models. In M. Minsky (Ed.), *Semantic information processing* (pp. 425–432). Cambridge, MA: MIT Press.

Minsky, M. (1986). *The society of mind*. New York: Simon and Schuster.

Moody, T. C. (1994). Conversations with zombies. *Journal of Consciousness Studies*, 1(2), 196–200.

Moore, G. E. (1965). Cramming more components onto integrated circuits. *Electronics*, 38(8), pp. 114–117.

Moravec, H. P. (1988, Summer). Sensor fusion in certainty grids for mobile robots. *AI Magazine*, 9, 61–74.

Moravec, H. (1999). *Robot: Mere machine to transcendent mind*. New York: Oxford University Press.

Nagel, E., & Newman, J. R. (1958). *Goedel's proof*. New York: New York University Press.

O'Brien, G., & Opie, J. (1999). A connectionist theory of phenomenal experience. *Behavioral and Brain Sciences*, 22, 127–148.

Penrose, R. (1989). *The emperor's new mind: Concerning computers, minds, and the laws of physics*. New York: Oxford University Press.

Penrose, R. (1994). *Shadows of the mind: A search for the missing science of consciousness*. New York: Oxford University Press.

Perlis, D. (1994). An error-theory of consciousness. Unpublished material, *University of Maryland Computer Science*, CS-TR-3324, College Park, MD.

Perlis, D. (1997). Consciousness as self-function. *Journal of Consciousness Studies*, 4(5/6), 509–525.

Pinker, S., & Mehler, J. (1988). *Connections and symbols*. Cambridge, MA: MIT Press.

Rey, G. (1997). A question about consciousness. In N. Block, O. Flanagan, & G. Güzeldere (Eds.), *The nature of consciousness: Philosophical debates* (pp. 461–482). Cambridge, MA: MIT Press.

Rumelhart, D. E., McClelland, J. L., & the PDP Research Group (1986). *Parallel distributed processing: Explorations in the microstructure of cognition*. Cambridge, MA: MIT Press.

Said, K. M., Newton-Smith, W., Viale, R., & Wilkes, K. (1990). *Modelling the mind*. Oxford: Clarendon Press.

Scheutz, M. (Ed.) (2002). *Computationalism: New directions*. Cambridge, MA: The MIT Press.

Searle, J. R. (1980). Minds, brains, and program. *The Behavioral and Brain Sciences*, 3, 417–424.

Searle, J. R. (1990). Is the brain's mind a computer program? *Scientific American*, 262, 26–31.

Searle, J. R. (1992). *The rediscovery of the mind*. Cambridge, MA: MIT Press.

Sloman, A. (1978). *The computer revolution in philosophy*. Hassocks, Sussex: Harvester Press.

Sloman, A. (2002). The irrelevance of Turing machines to artificial intelligence. In M. Scheutz, M, (Ed.), *Computationalism: New directions* (pp. 87–127). Cambridge, MA: The MIT Press.

Sloman, A., & Chrisley, R. (2003). Virtual machines and consciousness. *Journal of Consciousness Studies, 10*(4–5), 6–45.

Smith, B. C. (1984). Reflection and semantics in Lisp. *Proceedings of the Conference on Principles of Programming Languages, 11*, 23–35.

Smith, B. C. (1995). *On the origins of objects.* Cambridge, MA: MIT Press.

Smith, B. C. (2002). The foundations of computing. In M. Scheutz, M, (Ed.), *Computationa-*

lism: New directions (pp. 23–58). Cambridge, MA: The MIT Press.

Turing, A. (1950). Computing machinery and intelligence. *Mind, 49*, 433–460.

Wilkes, K. (1990). Modelling the mind. In K. M. Said, W. Newton-Smith, R. Viale, & K. Wilkes (Eds.), *Modelling the mind* (pp. 63–82). Oxford: Clarendon Press.

Winograd, T. (1972). *Understanding natural language.* New York: Academic Press.

Wittgenstein, L. (1953). *Philosophical investigations.* New York: MacMillan.

CHAPTER 7

Computational Models of Consciousness: A Taxonomy and Some Examples

Ron Sun and Stan Franklin

Abstract

This chapter aims to provide an overview of existing computational (mechanistic) models of cognition in relation to the study of consciousness, on the basis of psychological and philosophical theories and data. It examines various mechanistic explanations of consciousness in existing computational cognitive models. Serving as an example for the discussions, a computational model of the conscious/unconscious interaction, utilizing the representational difference explanation of consciousness, is described briefly. As a further example, a software agent model that captures another explanation of consciousness (the access explanation of consciousness) is also described. The discussions serve to highlight various possibilities in developing computational models of consciousness and in providing computational explanations of conscious and unconscious cognitive processes.

Introduction

In this chapter, we aim to present a short survey and a brief evaluation of existing computational (mechanistic) models of cognition in relation to the study of consciousness. The survey focuses on their explanations of the difference between conscious and unconscious cognitive processes on the basis of psychological and philosophical theories and data, as well as potential practical applications.

Given the plethora of models, theories, and data, we try to provide in this chapter an overall (and thus necessarily sketchy) examination of computational models of consciousness in relation to the available psychological data and theories, as well as the existing philosophical accounts. We come to some tentative conclusions as to what a plausible computational account should be like, synthesizing various operationalized psychological notions related to consciousness.

We begin by examining some foundational issues concerning computational approaches toward consciousness. Then, various existing models and their explanations of the conscious/unconscious distinction are presented. After examining a particular model embodying a two-system approach, we look at one embodying a unified (one-system) approach and then at a few additional models.

Computational Explanations of Consciousness

Work in the area of computational modeling of consciousness generally assumes the sufficiency and the necessity of mechanistic explanations. By mechanistic explanation, we mean any concrete computational processes, in the broadest sense of the term "computation." In general, computation is a broad term that can be used to denote any process that can be realized on generic computing devices, such as Turing machines (or even beyond if there is such a possibility). Thus, mechanistic explanations may utilize, in addition to standard computational notions, a variety of other conceptual constructs ranging, for example, from chaotic dynamics (Freeman, 1995), to "Darwinian" competition (Edelman, 1989), and to quantum mechanics (Penrose, 1994). (We leave out the issue of complexity for now.)

In terms of the *sufficiency* of mechanistic explanations, a general working hypothesis is succinctly expressed by the following statement (Jackendoff, 1987):

> *Hypothesis of computational sufficiency: every phenomenological distinction is caused by/supported by/projected from a corresponding computational distinction.*

For the lack of a clearly better alternative, this hypothesis remains a viable working hypothesis in the area of computational models of consciousness, despite various criticisms (e.g., Damasio, 1994; Edelman, 1989; Freeman, 1995; Penrose, 1994; Searle, 1980).

On the other hand, the necessity of mechanistic explanations, according to the foregoing definition of mechanistic processes, should be intuitively obvious to anyone who is not a dualist. If one accepts the universality of computation, then computation, in its broadest sense, can be expected to include the necessary conditions for consciousness.

On the basis of such intuition, we need to provide an explanation of the computational/mechanistic basis of consciousness that answers the following questions. What kind of mechanism leads to conscious processes, and what kind of mechanism leads to unconscious processes? What is the functional role of conscious processes (Baars, 1988, 2002; Sun, 1999a, b)? What is the functional role of unconscious processes? There have been many such explanations in computational or mechanistic terms. These computational or mechanistic explanations are highly relevant to the science of consciousness as they provide useful theoretical frameworks for further empirical work.

Another issue we need to address before we move on to details of computational work is the relation between biological/physiological models and computational models in general. The problem with biologically centered studies of consciousness in general is that the gap between phenomenology and physiology/biology is so great that something else may be needed to bridge it. Otherwise, if we rush directly into complex neurophysiological thickets (Edelman, 1989; Crick & Koch, 1990; Damasio et al., 1990; LeDoux, 1992,), we may lose sight of the forests. Computation, in its broadest sense, can serve to bridge the gap. It provides an intermediate level of explanation in terms of processes, mechanisms, and functions and helps determine how various aspects of conscious and unconscious processes should figure into the architecture of the mind (Anderson & Lebiere, 1998; Sun, 2002). It is possible that an intermediate level between phenomenology and physiology/neurobiology might be more apt to capture fundamental characteristics of consciousness (Coward & Sun, 2004). This notion of an intermediate level of explanation has been variously expounded recently; for example, in terms of virtual machines by Sloman and Chrisley (2003).

Different Computational Accounts of Consciousness

Existing computational explanations of the conscious/unconscious distinction may be categorized based on the following different emphases: (1) differences in knowledge organization (e.g., the SN+PS view, to be detailed later), (2) differences in knowledge-processing mechanisms (e.g., the PS+SN view), (3) differences in knowledge content (e.g., the episode+activation view), (4) differences in knowledge representation (e.g., the localist+distributed view), or (5) different processing modes of the same system (e.g., the attractor view or the threshold view).

Contrary to some critics, the debate among these differing views is not analogous to a debate between algebraists and geometers in physics (which would be irrelevant). It is more analogous to the wave vs. particle debate in physics concerning the nature of light, which was truly substantive. Let us discuss some of the better known views concerning computational accounts of the conscious/unconscious distinction one by one.

First of all, some explanations are based on recognizing that there are two separate systems in the mind. The difference between the two systems can be explained in terms of differences in either knowledge organization, knowledge-processing mechanisms, knowledge content, or knowledge representation:

- *The SN+PS view*: an instance of the explanations based on differences in knowledge organization. As originally proposed by Anderson (1983) in his ACT* model, there are two types of knowledge: Declarative knowledge is represented by semantic networks (SN), and it is consciously accessible, whereas procedural knowledge is represented by rules in a production system (PS), and it is inaccessible.

The difference lies in the two different ways of organizing knowledge – whether in an action-centered way (procedural knowledge) or in an action-independent way (declarative knowledge). Computationally, both types of knowledge are represented symbolically (using either symbolic semantic networks or symbolic production rules).[1] The semantic networks use parallel spreading activation (Collins & Loftus, 1975) to activate relevant nodes, and the production rules compete for control through parallel matching and firing. The models embodying this view have been used for modeling a variety of psychological tasks, especially skill learning tasks (Anderson, 1983, Anderson & Lebiere, 1998).

- *The PS+SN view*: an instance of the explanations based on differences in knowledge-processing mechanisms. As proposed by Hunt and Lansman (1986), the "deliberate" computational process of production matching and firing in a production system (PS), which is serial in this case, is assumed to be a conscious process, whereas the spreading activation computation (Collins & Loftus, 1975) in semantic networks (SN), which is massively parallel, is assumed to be an unconscious process. The model based on this view has been used to model controlled and automatic processing data in the attention-performance literature (Hunt & Lansman, 1986). Note that this view is the exact opposite of the view advocated by Anderson (1983), in terms of the roles of the two computational mechanisms involved. Note also that the emphasis in this view is on the processing difference of the two mechanisms, serial vs. parallel, and not on knowledge organization.

- *The algorithm+instance view*: another instance of the explanations based on differences in knowledge-processing mechanisms. As proposed by Logan (1988) and also by Stanley et al. (1989), the computation involved in retrieval and use of instances of past experience is considered to be unconscious (Stanley et al., 1989) or automatic (Logan 1988), whereas the use of "algorithms" involves conscious awareness. Here the term "algorithm" is not clearly defined and apparently refers to computation more complex than instance retrieval/use. Computationally, it was suggested that the use of an algorithm is under tight control and carried out in a serial, step-by-step way, whereas instances can be retrieved in parallel and effortlessly (Logan, 1988). The emphasis here is again on the differences in processing mechanisms. This view is also similar to the view advocated by Neal and Hesketh (1997), which emphasizes the unconscious influence of what they called episodic memory. Note that the views by Logan (1988), Stanley et al. (1989), and Neal and Hesketh (1997) are the exact opposite of the view advocated by Anderson (1983) and Bower (1996), in which instances/episodes are consciously accessed rather than unconsciously accessed.

- *The episode+activation view*: an instance of the explanations based on differences in knowledge content. As proposed by Bower (1996), unconscious processes are based on activation propagation through strengths or weights (e.g., in a connectionist fashion) between different nodes representing perceptual or conceptual primitives, whereas conscious processes are based on explicit episodic memory of past episodes. What is emphasized in this view is the rich spatial-temporal context in episodic memory (i.e., the ad hoc associations with contextual information, acquired on a one-shot basis), which is termed type-2 associations as opposed to regular type-1 associations (which are based on semantic relatedness). This emphasis somewhat distinguishes this view from other views concerning instances/episodes (Logan, 1988; Neal & Hesketh, 1997; Stanley et al. 1989).[2] The reliance on memory of specific events in this view bears some resemblance to some neurobiologically moti-

vated views that rely on the interplay of various memory systems, such as that advocated by Taylor (1997) and McClelland et al. (1995).

- *The localist+distributed representation view*: an instance of the explanations based on differences in knowledge representation. As proposed by Sun (1994, 2002), different representational forms used in different components may be used to explain the qualitative difference between conscious and unconscious processes. One type of representation is symbolic or localist, in which one distinct entity (e.g., a node in a connectionist model) represents a concept. The other type of representation is distributed, in which a non-exclusive set of entities (e.g., a set of nodes in a connectionist model) are used for representing one concept, and the representations of different concepts overlap each other; in other words, a concept is represented as a pattern of activations over a set of entities (e.g., a set of nodes). Conceptual structures (e.g., rules) can be implemented in the localist/symbolic system in a straightforward way by connections between relevant entities. In distributed representations, such structures (including rules) are diffusely duplicated in a way consistent with the meanings of the structures (Sun, 1994), which captures unconscious performance. There may be various connections between corresponding representations across the two systems. (A system embodying this view, CLARION, is described later.)

In contrast to these two-systems views, there exist some theoretical views that insist on the unitary nature of the conscious and the unconscious. That is, they hold that conscious and unconscious processes are different manifestations of the same underlying system. The difference between conscious and unconscious processes lies in the different processing modes for conscious versus unconscious information within the same system. There are several possibilities in this regard:

- *The threshold view*: As proposed by various researchers, including Bowers et al. (1990), the difference between conscious and unconscious processes can be explained by the difference between activations of mental representations above a certain threshold and activations of such representations below that threshold. When activations reach the threshold level, an individual becomes aware of the content of the activated representations; otherwise, although the activated representations may influence behavior, they will not be accessible consciously.

- *The chunking view*: As in the models described by Servan-Schreiber and Anderson (1987) and by Rosenbloom et al. (1993), a chunk is considered a unitary representation and its internal working is opaque (although its input/output are accessible). A chunk can be a production rule (as in Rosenbloom et al., 1993) or a short sequence of perceptual-motor elements (as in Servan-Schreiber & Anderson, 1987). Because of the lack of transparency of the internal working of a chunk, it is equated with implicit learning (Servan-Schreiber & Anderson, 1987) or automaticity (Rosenbloom et al., 1993). According to this view, the difference between conscious and unconscious processes is the difference between using multiple (simple) chunks (involving some consciousness) and using one (complex) chunk (involving no consciousness).

- *The attractor view*: As suggested by the model of Mathis and Mozer (1996), being in a stable attractor of a dynamic system (a neural network in particular) leads to consciousness. The distinction between conscious and unconscious processes is reduced to the distinction of being in a stable attractor and being in a transient state. O'Brien and Opie (1998) proposed an essentially similar view. This view may be generalized to a general coherence view – the emphasis may be placed on the role of internal consistency in producing consciousness. There has been support for this possibility from neuroscience, for example, in terms of a coherent "thalamo-cortical core" (Edelman & Tononi, 2000).

- *The access view*: As suggested by Baars (1988), consciousness is believed to help mobilize and integrate mental functions that are otherwise disparate and independent. Thus, consciousness is aimed at solving the relevance problem – finding the exact internal resources needed to deal with the current situation. Some evidence has been accumulated for this view (Baars, 2002). A computational implementation of Baars' theory in the form of IDA (a running software agent system; Franklin et al., 1998) is described in detail later. See also Coward and Sun (2004).

The coexistence of these various views of consciousness seems quite analogous to the parable of the Blind Men and the Elephant. Each of them captures some aspect of the truth about consciousness, but the portion of the truth captured is limited by the view itself. None seems to capture the whole picture.

In the next two sections, we look into some details of two representative computational models, exemplifying either two-system or one-system views. The models illustrate what a plausible computational model of consciousness should be like, synthesizing various psychological notions and relating to various available psychological theories.

A Model Adopting the Representational Difference View

Let us look into the representational difference view as embodied in the cognitive architecture CLARION (which stands for Connectionist Learning with Rule Induction ON-line; Sun 1997, 2002, 2003), as an example of the two-system views for explaining consciousness.

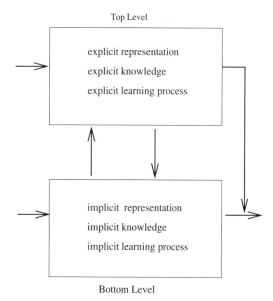

Figure 7.1. The CLARION model.

The important premises of subsequent discussions are the *direct accessibility* of conscious processes and the *direct inaccessibility* of unconscious processes. Conscious processes should be *directly* accessible – that is, directly verbally expressible – without involving intermediate interpretive or transformational steps, which is a requirement prescribed and/or accepted by many theoreticians (see, e.g., Clark, 1992; Hadley, 1995).[3] Unconscious processes should be, in contrast, inaccessible directly (but they might be accessed indirectly through some

interpretive processes), thus exhibiting different psychological properties (see, e.g., Berry & Broadbent, 1988; Reber, 1989; more discussions later).

An example model in this regard is CLARION, which is a two-level model that uses the localist and distributed representations in the two levels, respectively, and learns using two different methods in the two levels, respectively. In developing the model, four criteria were hypothesized (see Sun, 1994), on the basis of the aforementioned considerations: (1) direct accessibility of conscious processes; (2) direct inaccessibility of unconscious processes; and furthermore, (3) linkages from localist concepts to distributed features: once a localist concept is activated, its corresponding distributed representations (features) are also activated, as assumed in most cognitive models, ranging from Tversky (1977) to Sun (1995);[4] and (4) linkages from distributed features to localist concepts: under appropriate circumstances, once some or most of the distributed features of a concept are activated, the localist concept itself can be activated to "cover" these features (roughly corresponding to categorization; Smith & Medin, 1981).

The direct inaccessibility of unconscious knowledge can be best captured by a "subsymbolic" distributed representation such as that provided by a backpropagation network (Rumelhart et al., 1986), because representational units in a distributed representation

Dimensions	bottom	top
Cognitive phenomena	implicit learning	explicit learning
	implicit memory	explicit memory
	automatic processing	controlled processing
	intuition	explicit reasoning
Source of knowledge	trial-and-error	external sources
	assimilation of explicit knowledge	extraction from the bottom level
Representation	distributed (micro) features	localist conceptual units
Operation	similarity-based	explicit symbol manipulation
Characteristics	more context sensitive, fuzzy	more crisp, precise
	less selective	more selective
	more complex	simpler

Figure 7.2. Comparisons of the two levels of the CLARION architecture.

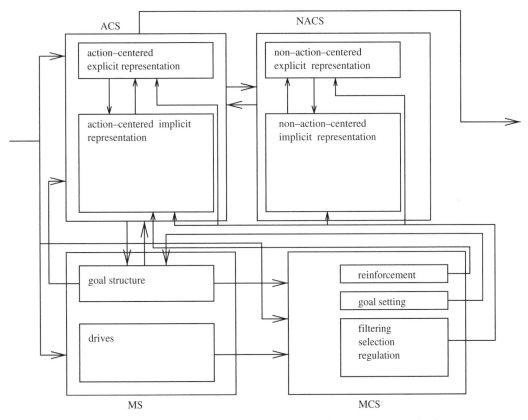

Figure 7.3. The implementation of CLARION. ACS denotes the action-centered subsystem, NACS the non-action-centered subsystem, MS the motivational subsystem, and MCS the metacognitive subsystem. The top level contains localist encoding of concepts and rules. The bottom level contains multiple (modular) connectionist networks for capturing unconscious processes. The interaction of the two levels and the information flows are indicated with arrows.

are capable of accomplishing tasks but are generally uninterpretable directly (see Rumelhart et al., 1986; Sun, 1994). In contrast, conscious knowledge can be captured in computational modeling by a symbolic or localist representation (Clark & Karmiloff-Smith, 1993; Sun & Bookman 1994), in which each unit has a clear conceptual meaning/interpretation (i.e., a semantic label). This captures the property of conscious processes being directly accessible and manipulable (Smolensky, 1988; Sun, 1994). This difference in representation leads to a two-level structure whereby each level uses one type of representation (Sun, 1994, 1995, 1997; Sun et al., 1996, 1998, 2001). The bottom level is based on distributed representation, whereas the top level is based on localist/symbolic representation. For learn-

ing, the bottom level uses gradual weight tuning, whereas the top level uses explicit, one-shot hypothesis testing learning, in correspondence with the representational characteristics of the two levels. There are various connections across the two levels for exerting mutual influences. See Figure 7.1 for an abstract sketch of the model. The different characteristics of the two levels are summarized in Figure 7.2.

Let us look into some implementational details of CLARION. Note that the details of the model have been described extensively in a series of previous papers, including Sun (1997, 2002, 2003), Sun and Peterson (1998), and Sun et al. (1998, 2001). It has a dual representational structure – implicit and explicit representations being in two separate "levels" (Hadley, 1995; Seger,

1994). Essentially it is a dual-process theory of mind (Chaiken & Trope, 1999). It also consists of a number of functional subsystems, including the action-centered subsystem, the non-action-centered subsystem, the metacognitive subsystem, and the motivational subsystem (see Figure 7.3).

Let us first focus on the action-centered subsystem of CLARION. In this subsystem, the two levels interact by cooperating in actions, through a combination of the action recommendations from the two levels, respectively, as well as cooperating in learning through a bottom-up and a top-down process (to be discussed below). Actions and learning of the action-centered subsystem may be described as follows:

1. Observe the current state x.

2. Compute in the bottom level the "values" of x associated with each of all the possible actions a_i's: $Q(x, a_1)$, $Q(x, a_2)$, ..., $Q(x, a_n)$ (to be explained below).

3. Find out all the possible actions $(b_1, b_2, ..., b_m)$ at the top level, based on the input x (sent up from the bottom level) and the rules in place.

4. Compare or combine the values of the a_is with those of b_js (sent down from the top level), and choose an appropriate action b.

5. Perform the action b, and observe the next state y and (possibly) the reinforcement r.

6. Update Q-values at the bottom level in accordance with the *Q-Learning-Backpropagation* algorithm (to be explained later).

7. Update the rule network at the top level using the *Rule-Extraction-Refinement* algorithm (to be explained later).

8. Go back to Step 1.

In the bottom level of the action-centered subsystem, implicit reactive routines are learned: A Q-value is an evaluation of the "quality" of an action in a given state: $Q(x, a)$ indicates how desirable action a is in state x (which consists of some sensory input). The agent may choose an action in any state based on Q-values (for example, by choosing the action with the highest Q-value). To acquire the Q-values, one may use the *Q-learning* algorithm (Watkins 1989), a reinforcement learning algorithm. It basically compares the values of successive actions and adjusts an evaluation function on that basis. It thereby develops reactive sequential behaviors.

The bottom level of the action-centered subsystem is modular; that is, a number of small neural networks coexist, each of which is adapted to specific modalities, tasks, or groups of input stimuli. This coincides with the modularity claim (Baars, 1988; Cosmides & Tooby, 1994; Edelman, 1987; Fodor, 1983; Hirschfield & Gelman, 1994; Karmiloff-Smith, 1986) that much processing in the human mind is done by limited, encapsulated (to some extent), specialized processors that are highly effcient. Some of these modules are formed evolutionarily; that is, given a priori to agents, reflecting their hard-wired instincts and propensities (Hirschfield & Gelman, 1994). Some of them can be learned through interacting with the world (computationally through various decomposition methods; e.g., Sun & Peterson, 1999).

In the top level of the action-centered subsystem, explicit conceptual knowledge is captured in the form of rules. Symbolic/localist representations are used. See Sun (2003) for further details of encoding (they are not directly relevant here).

Humans are clearly able to learn implicit knowledge through trial and error, without necessarily utilizing a priori explicit knowledge (Seger, 1994). On top of that, explicit knowledge can be acquired, also from ongoing experience in the world, and possibly through the mediation of implicit knowledge (i.e., bottom-up learning; see Karmilof-Smith, 1986; Stanley et al., 1989; Sun, 1997, 2002; Willingham et al., 1989). The basic process of bottom-up learning is as follows (Sun, 2002). If an action decided by the bottom level is successful, then the agent extracts a rule that corresponds to the action selected by the bottom level and adds the rule to the top level. Then, in subsequent interaction with the world, the agent verifies the extracted rule by considering the outcome of applying the rule: If the outcome is not successful, then the rule should be made more specific and exclusive of the current case, and if the outcome is successful, the agent may try to generalize the rule to make it more universal (e.g., Michalski, 1983). The details of the bottom-up learning algorithm (the Rule-Extraction-Refinement algorithm) can be found in Sun and Peterson (1998). After rules have been learned, a variety of explicit reasoning methods may be used. Learning explicit conceptual representation at the top level can also be useful in enhancing learning of implicit reactive routines (reinforcement learning) at the bottom level.

Although CLARION can learn even when no a priori or externally provided knowledge is available, it can make use of it when such knowledge is available (cf. Anderson, 1983; Schneider & Oliver, 1991). To deal with instructed learning, externally provided knowledge (in the forms of explicit conceptual structures, such as rules, plans, routines, categories, and so on) should (1) be combined with autonomously generated conceptual structures at the top level (i.e., internalization) and (2) be assimilated into implicit reactive routines at the bottom level (i.e., assimilation). This process is known as top-down learning. See Sun (2003) for further details.

The non-action-centered subsystem represents general knowledge about the world, which is equivalent to the notion of semantic memory (as in, e.g., Quillian, 1968). It may be used for performing various kinds of retrievals and inferences. It is under the control of the action-centered subsystem (through the actions of the action-centered subsystem). At the bottom level, associative memory networks encode non-action-centered implicit knowledge. Associations are formed by mapping an input to an output. The regular backpropagation learning algorithm can be used to establish such associations between pairs of input and output (Rumelhart et al., 1986).

On the other hand, at the top level of the non-action-centered subsystem, a general knowledge store encodes explicit non-action-centered knowledge (Sun, 1994). In this network, chunks are specified through dimensional values. A node is set up at the top level to represent a chunk. The chunk node (a symbolic representation) connects to its corresponding features (dimension-value pairs) represented as nodes in the bottom level (which form a distributed representation). Additionally, links between chunks at the top level encode explicit associations between pairs of chunks, known as associative rules. Explicit associative rules may be formed (i.e., learned) in a variety of ways (Sun, 2003).

On top of associative rules, similarity-based reasoning may be employed in the non-action-centered subsystem. During reasoning, a known (given or inferred) chunk may be automatically compared with another chunk. If the similarity between them is sufficiently high, then the latter chunk is inferred (see Sun, 2003, for details). Similarity-based and rule-based reasoning can be intermixed. As a result of mixing similarity-based and rule-based reasoning, complex patterns of reasoning emerge. As shown by Sun (1994), different sequences of mixed similarity-based and rule-based reasoning capture essential patterns of human everyday (mundane, common-sense) reasoning.

As in the action-centered subsystem, top-down or bottom-up learning may take place in the non-action-centered subsystem, either to extract explicit knowledge in the top level from the implicit knowledge in the bottom level or to assimilate explicit knowledge of the top level into implicit knowledge in the bottom level.

The motivational subsystem is concerned with drives and their interactions (Toates, 1986). It is concerned with why an agent does what it does. Simply saying that an agent chooses actions to maximizes gains, rewards, or payoffs leaves open the question of what determines these things. The relevance of the motivational subsystem to the action-centered subsystem lies primarily in the fact that it provides the context in which the goal and the payoff of the action-centered subsystem are set. It thereby influences the working of the action-centered subsystem and, by extension, the working of the non-action-centered subsystem.

A bipartite system of motivational representation is again in place in CLARION. The explicit goals (such as "finding food") of an agent (which is tied to the working of the action-centered subsystem) may be generated based on internal drive states (for example, "being hungry"). See Sun (2003) for details.

Beyond low-level drives concerning physiological needs, there are also higher-level drives. Some of them are primary, in the sense of being "hardwired." For example, Maslow (1987) developed a set of these drives in the form of a "need hierarchy." Whereas primary drives are built-in and relatively unalterable, there are also "derived" drives, which are secondary, changeable, and acquired mostly in the process of satisfying primary drives.

The metacognitive subsystem is closely tied to the motivational subsystem. The metacognitive subsystem monitors, controls, and regulates cognitive processes for the sake of improving cognitive performance (Nelson, 1993; Sloman & Chrisley, 2003; Smith et al., 2003). Control and regulation may be in the forms of setting goals for the action-centered subsystem, setting essential parameters of the action-centered and the non-action-centered subsystem, interrupting and changing ongoing processes in the action-centered and the non-action-centered subsystem, and so on. Control and regulation may also be carried out through setting reinforcement functions for the action-centered subsystem on the basis of drive states. The metacognitive subsystem is also made up of two levels: the top level (explicit) and the bottom level (implicit).

Note that in CLARION, there are thus a variety of memories: procedural memory (in the action-centered subsystem) in both implicit and explicit forms, general "semantic" memory (in the non-action-centered subsystem) in both implicit and explicit forms, episodic memory (in the non-action-centered subsystem), working memory (in the action-centered subsystem), goal structures (in the action-centered subsystem), and so on. See Sun (2003) for further details of these memories. As touched upon before, these memories are important for accounting for various forms of conscious and unconscious processes (also see, e.g., McClelland et al., 1995; Schacter, 1990; Taylor, 1997).

CLARION has been successful in accounting for a variety of psychological data. A number of well-known skill learning tasks have been simulated using CLARION; these span the spectrum ranging from simple reactive skills to complex cognitive skills. The tasks include serial reaction time (SRT) tasks, artificial grammar learning (AGL) tasks, process control (PC) tasks, the categorical inference (CI) task, the alphabetical arithmetic (AA) task, and the Tower of Hanoi (TOH) task (see Sun, 2002). Among them, SRT, AGL, and PC are typical implicit learning tasks, very much relevant to the issue of consciousness as they operationalize the notion of consciousness in the context of psychological experiments (Coward & Sun, 2004; Reber, 1989; Seger, 1994; Sun et al., 2005), whereas TOH and AA are typical high-level cognitive skill acquisition tasks. In addition, extensive work have been done on a complex minefield navigation task (see Sun & Peterson, 1998; Sun et al., 2001). Metacognitive and motivational simulations have also been undertaken, as have social simulation tasks (e.g., Sun & Naveh, 2004).

In evaluating the contribution of CLARION to our understanding of consciousness, we note that the simulations using CLARION provide detailed, process-based interpretations of experimental data related to consciousness, in the context of a broadly scoped cognitive architecture and a unified theory of cognition. Such interpretations are important for a precise, process-based understanding of consciousness and other aspects of cognition, leading to better appreciations of the role of consciousness in human cognition (Sun, 1999a). CLARION also makes quantitative and qualitative predictions regarding cognition in the areas of memory, learning, motivation, metacognition, and so on. These predictions either have been experimentally tested already or are in the process of being tested (see, e.g., Sun, 2002; Sun et al., 2001, 2005). Because of the complex structures and their complex interactions specified within the framework of CLARION, it has a lot to say about the roles that different types of processes, conscious or unconscious, play in human cognition, as well as their synergy (Sun et al., 2005).

Comparing CLARION with Bower (1996), the latter may be viewed as a special case of CLARION for dealing specifically with implicit memory phenomena. The type-1 and type-2 connections, hypothesized by Bower (1996) as the main explanatory constructs, can be equated roughly to top-level representations and bottom-level representations, respectively. In addition to making the distinction between type-1 and type-2 connections, Bower (1996) also endeavored to specify the details of multiple pathways of spreading activation in the bottom level. These pathways were phonological, orthographical, semantic, and other connections that store long-term implicit knowledge. In the top level, associated with type-2 connections, it was claimed on the other hand that rich contextual information was stored. These details nicely complement the specification of CLARION and can thus be incorporated into the model.

The proposal by McClelland et al. (1995) that there are complementary learning systems in the hippocampus and neocortex is also relevant here. According to their account, cortical systems learn slowly, and the learning of new information destroys the old, unless the learning of new information is interleaved with ongoing exposure to the old information. To resolve these two problems, new information is initially stored in the hippocampus, an explicit memory system, in which crisp, explicit representations are used to minimize interference of information (so that catastrophic interference is avoided there). It allows rapid learning of new material. Then, the new information stored in the hippocampus is assimilated into cortical systems. The assimilation is interleaved with the assimilation

of all other information in the hippocampus and with the ongoing events. Weights are adjusted by a small amount after each experience, so that the overall direction of weight change is governed by the structure present in the ensemble of events and experiences, using distributed representations (with weights). Therefore, catastrophic interference is avoided in cortical systems. This model is very similar to the two-level idea of CLARION, in that it not only adopts a two-system view but also utilizes representational differences between the two systems. However, in contrast to this model, which captures only what may be termed top-down learning (that is, learning that proceeds from the conscious to the unconscious), CLARION can capture both top-down learning (from the top level to the bottom level) and bottom-up learning (from the bottom level to the top level). See Sun et al. (2001) and Sun (2002) for details of bottom-up learning.

Turning to the declarative/procedural knowledge models, ACT* (Anderson, 1983) is made up of a semantic network (for declarative knowledge) and a production system (for procedural knowledge). ACT-R is a descendant of ACT*, in which procedural learning is limited to production formation through mimicking, and production firing is based on log odds of success. CLARION succeeds in explaining two issues that ACT did not address. First, whereas ACT takes a mostly top-down approach toward learning (i.e, from given declarative knowledge to procedural knowledge), CLARION can proceed bottom-up. Thus, Clarion can account for implicit learning better than ACT (see Sun, 2002, for details). Second, in ACT both types of knowledge are represented in explicit, symbolic forms (i.e., semantic networks and productions), and thus it does not explain, from a representational viewpoint, the differences in conscious accessibility (Sun, 1999b). CLARION accounts for this difference based on the use of two different forms of representation. Top-level knowledge is represented explicitly and thus consciously accessible, whereas bottom-level knowledge is represented implicitly and thus inaccessible. Thus, this distinction in CLARION is intrinsic, instead of assumed as in ACT (Sun, 1999b).

Comparing CLARION with Hunt and Lansman's (1986) model, there are similarities. The production system in Hunt and Lansman's model clearly resembles the top level in CLARION, in that both use explicit manipulations in much the same way. Likewise, the spreading activation in the semantic network in Hunt and Lansman's model resembles the connectionist network in the bottom level of CLARION, because the same kind of spreading activation was used in both models, although the representation in Hunt and Lansman's model was symbolic, not distributed. Because of the uniformly symbolic representations used in Hunt and Lansman's model, it does not explain convincingly the qualitative difference between conscious and unconscious processes (see Sun, 1999b).

An Application of the Access View

Let us now examine an application of the access view on consciousness in building a practically useful system. The access view is a rather popular approach in computational accounts of consciousness (Baars, 2002), and therefore it deserves some attention. It is also presented here as an example of various one-system views.

Most computational models of cognitive processes are designed to predict experimental data. IDA (Intelligent Distribution Agent), in contrast, models consciousness in the form of an autonomous software agent (Franklin & Graesser, 1997). Specifically, IDA was developed for Navy applications (Franklin et al., 1998). At the end of each sailor's tour of duty, he or she is assigned to a new billet in a process called distribution. The Navy employs almost 300 people (called detailers) to effect these new assignments. IDA's task is to play the role of a detailer.

Designing IDA presents both communication problems and action selection problems involving constraint satisfaction. It must communicate with sailors via e-mail and in English, understanding the content and producing human-like responses. It must access a number of existing Navy databases, again understanding the content. It must see that the Navy's needs are satisfied while adhering to Navy policies. For example, a particular ship may require a certain number of sonar technicians with the requisite types of training. It must hold down moving costs. And it must cater to the needs and desires of the sailor as well as possible. This includes negotiating with the sailor via an e-mail correspondence in natural language. Finally, it must authorize the finally selected new billet and start the writing of the sailor's orders.

Although the IDA model was not initially developed to reproduce experimental data, it is nonetheless based on psychological and neurobiological theories of consciousness and does generate hypotheses and qualitative predictions (Baars & Franklin, 2003; Franklin et al., 2005). IDA successfully implements much of the global workspace theory (Baars, 1988), and there is a growing body of empirical evidence supporting that theory (Baars, 2002). IDA's flexible cognitive cycle has also been used to analyze the relation of consciousness to working memory at a fine level of detail, offering explanations of such classical working memory tasks as visual imagery to gain information and the rehearsal of a telephone number (Baars & Franklin, 2003; Franklin et al., 2005).

In his global workspace theory (see Figure 7.4 and Chapter 8), Baars (1988) postulates that human cognition is implemented by a multitude of relatively small, special-purpose processors, which are almost always unconscious (i.e., the modularity hypothesis as discussed earlier). Communication between them is rare and over a narrow bandwidth. Coalitions of such processes find their way into a global workspace (and thereby into consciousness). This limited capacity workspace serves to broadcast the message of the coalition to all the unconscious processors in order to recruit other processors to join in handling the current novel situation or in solving the current

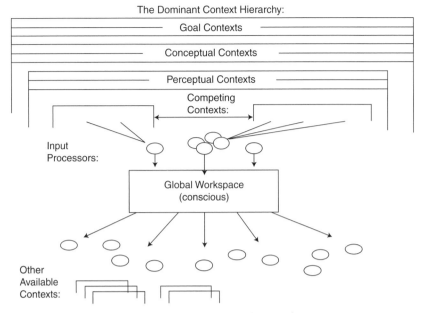

Figure 7.4. Baars' global workspace theory.

problem. Thus consciousness, in this theory, allows us to deal with novel or problematic situations that cannot be dealt with efficiently, or at all, by habituated unconscious processes. In particular, it provides access to appropriately useful resources. Global workspace theory offers an explanation for the limited capacity of consciousness. Large messages would be overwhelming to tiny processors. In addition, all activities of these processors take place under the auspices of contexts: goal contexts, perceptual contexts, conceptual contexts, and/or cultural contexts. Though contexts are typically unconscious, they strongly influence conscious processes.

Let us look into some details of the IDA architecture and its main mechanisms. At the higher level, the IDA architecture is modular with module names borrowed from psychology (see Figure 7.5). There are modules for Perception, Working Memory, Autobiographical Memory, Transient Episodic Memory, Consciousness, Action Selection, Constraint Satisfaction, Language Generation, and Deliberation.

In the lower level of IDA, the processors postulated by the global workspace theory are implemented by "codelets." Codelets are small pieces of code running as indepen-

dent threads, each of which is specialized for some relatively simple task. They often play the role of "demons,"[5] waiting for a particular situation to occur in response to which they should act. Codelets also correspond more or less to Edelman's neuronal groups (Edelman, 1987) or Minsky's agents (Minsky, 1985). Codelets come in a number of varieties, each with different functions to perform. Most of these codelets subserve some high-level entity, such as a behavior. However, some codelets work on their own, performing such tasks as watching for incoming e-mail and instantiating goal structures. An important type of codelet that works on its own is the attention codelets that serve to bring information to "consciousness."

IDA senses only strings of characters, which are not imbued with meaning but which correspond to primitive sensations, like, for example, the patterns of activity on the rods and cones of the retina. These strings may come from e-mail messages, an operating system message, or from a database record.

The perception module employs analysis of surface features for natural-language understanding. It partially implements perceptual symbol system theory (Barsalou, 1999); perceptual symbols serve as a uniform

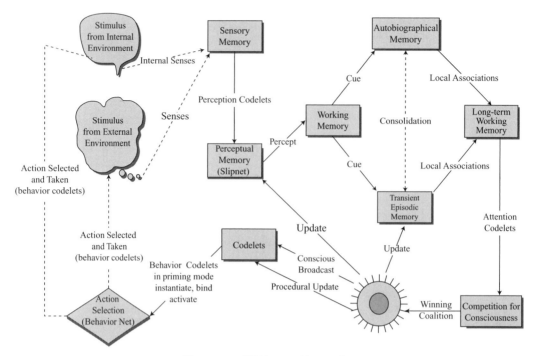

Figure 7.5. IDA's cognitive cycle.

system of representations throughout the system. Its underlying mechanism constitutes a portion of the Copycat architecture (Hofstadter & Mitchell, 1994). IDA's perceptual memory takes the form of a semantic net with activation passing, called the slipnet (see Figure 7.6). The slipnet embodies the perceptual contexts and some conceptual contexts from the global workspace theory. Nodes of the slipnet constitute the agent's perceptual symbols. Perceptual codelets recognize various features of the incoming stimulus; that is, various concepts. Perceptual codelets descend on an incoming message, looking for words or phrases they recognize. When such are found, appropriate nodes in the slipnet are activated. This activation passes around the net until it settles. A node (or several) is selected by its high activation, and the appropriate template(s) is filled by codelets with selected items from the message. The information thus created from the incoming message is then written to the workspace (working memory, to be described below), making it available to the rest of the system.

The results of this process, information created by the agent for its own use, are written to the workspace (working memory, not to be confused with Baars' global workspace). (Almost all of IDA's modules either write to the workspace, read from it, or both.)

IDA employs sparse distributed memory (SDM) as its major associative memory (Anwar & Franklin, 2003; Kanerva, 1988). SDM is a content-addressable memory. Being content addressable means that items in memory can be retrieved by using part of their contents as a cue, rather than having to know the item's address in memory.

Reads and writes, to and from associative memory, are accomplished through a gateway within the workspace called the focus. When any item is written to the workspace, another copy is written to the read registers of the focus. The contents of these read registers of the focus are then used as an address to query associative memory. The results of this query – that is, whatever IDA associates with this incoming information – are written into their own registers in the focus.

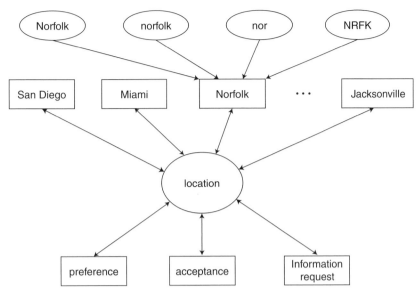

Figure 7.6. A portion of the slipnet in IDA.

This may include some emotion and some action previously taken. Thus associations with any incoming information, either from the outside world or from some part of IDA itself, are immediately available. (Writes to associative memory are made later and are described below.)

In addition to long-term memory, IDA includes a transient episodic memory (Ramamurthy, D'Mello, & Franklin, 2004). Long-term, content-addressable, associative memories are not typically capable of retrieving details of the latest of a long sequence of quite similar events (e.g., where I parked in the parking garage this morning or what I had for lunch yesterday). The distinguishing details of such events tend to blur due to interference from similar events. In IDA, this problem is solved by the addition of a transient episodic memory implemented with a sparse distributed memory. This SDM decays so that past sequences of similar events no longer interfere with the latest such events.

The apparatus for producing "consciousness" consists of a coalition manager, a spotlight controller, a broadcast manager, and a collection of attention codelets that recognize novel or problematic situations. Atten-

tion codelets have the task of bringing information to "consciousness." Each attention codelet keeps a watchful eye out for some particular situation to occur that might call for "conscious" intervention. Upon encountering such a situation, the appropriate attention codelet will be associated with the small number of information codelets that carry the information describing the situation. This association should lead to the collection of this small number of codelets, together with the attention codelet that collected them, becoming a coalition. Codelets also have activations. The attention codelet increases its activation in proportion to how well the current situation fits its particular interest, so that the coalition might compete for "consciousness," if one is formed.

In IDA, the coalition manager is responsible for forming and tracking coalitions of codelets. Such coalitions are initiated on the basis of the mutual associations between the member codelets. At any given time, one of these coalitions finds it way to "consciousness," chosen by the spotlight controller, which picks the coalition with the highest average activation among its member codelets. Baars' global workspace theory calls for the contents of "consciousness" to be broadcast to each of the codelets in the system, and in particular, to the behavior codelets. The broadcast manager accomplishes this task.

IDA depends on the idea of a behavior net (Maes, 1989; Negatu & Franklin, 2002) for high-level action selection in the service of built-in drives. It has several distinct drives operating in parallel, and these drives vary in urgency as time passes and the environment changes. A behavior net is composed of behaviors and their various links. A behavior has preconditions as well as additions and deletions. A behavior also has an activation, a number intended to measure the behavior's relevance to both the current environment (external and internal) and its ability to help satisfy the various drives it serves.

The activation comes from activation stored in the behaviors themselves, from the external environment, from drives, and from internal states. The environment awards activation to a behavior for each of its true preconditions. The more relevant it is to the current situation, the more activation it receives from the environment. (This source of activation tends to make the system opportunistic.) Each drive awards activation to every behavior that, by being active, will help satisfy that drive. This source of activation tends to make the system goal directed. Certain internal states of the agent can also send activation to the behavior net. This activation, for example, might come from a coalition of codelets responding to a "conscious" broadcast. Finally, activation spreads from behavior to behavior along links.

IDA's behavior net acts in consort with its "consciousness" mechanism to select actions (Negatu & Franklin, 2002). Suppose some piece of information is written to the workspace by perception or some other module. Attention codelets watch both it and the resulting associations. One of these attention codelets may decide that this information should be acted upon. This codelet would then attempt to take the information to "consciousness," perhaps along with any discrepancies it may find with the help of associations. If the attempt is successful, the coalition manager makes a coalition

of them, the spotlight controller eventually selects that coalition, and the contents of the coalition are broadcast to all the codelets. In response to the broadcast, appropriate behavior-priming codelets perform three tasks: an appropriate goal structure is instantiated in the behavior net, the codelets bind variables in the behaviors of that structure, and the codelets send activation to the currently appropriate behavior of the structure. Eventually that behavior is chosen to be acted upon. At this point, information about the current emotion and the currently executing behavior is written to the focus by the behavior codelets associated with the chosen behavior. The current contents of the write registers in the focus are then written to associative memory. The rest of the behavior codelets associated with the chosen behavior then perform their tasks. Thus, an action has been selected and carried out by means of collaboration between "consciousness" and the behavior net.

This background information on the IDA architecture and mechanisms should enable the reader to understand IDA's cognitive cycle (Baars & Franklin, 2003: Franklin et al., 2005). The cognitive cycle specifies the functional roles of memory, emotions, consciousness, and decision making in cognition, according to the global workspace theory. Below, we sketch the steps of the cognitive cycle; see Figure 7.5 for an overview.

1. *Perception.* Sensory stimuli, external or internal, are received and interpreted by perception. This stage is unconscious.

2. *Percept to Preconscious Buffer.* The percept is stored in preconscious buffers of IDA's working memory.

3. *Local Associations.* Using the incoming percept and the residual contents of the preconscious buffers as cues, local associations are automatically retrieved from transient episodic memory and from long-term autobiographical memory.

4. *Competition for Consciousness.* Attention codelets, whose job is to bring relevant, urgent, or insistent events to consciousness, gather information, form coalitions, and actively compete against each other.

(The competition may also include attention codelets from a recent previous cycle.)

5. *Conscious Broadcast.* A coalition of codelets, typically an attention codelet and its covey of related information codelets carrying content, gains access to the global workspace and has its contents broadcast. The contents of perceptual memory are updated in light of the current contents of consciousness. Transient episodic memory is updated with the current contents of consciousness as events. (The contents of transient episodic memory are separately consolidated into long-term memory.) Procedural memory (recent actions) is also updated.

6. *Recruitment of Resources.* Relevant behavior codelets respond to the conscious broadcast. These are typically codelets whose variables can be bound from information in the conscious broadcast. If the successful attention codelet was an expectation codelet calling attention to an unexpected result from a previous action, the responding codelets may be those that can help rectify the unexpected situation. (Thus consciousness solves the relevancy problem in recruiting resources.)

7. *Setting Goal Context Hierarchy.* The recruited processors use the contents of consciousness to instantiate new goal context hierarchies, bind their variables, and increase their activation. Emotions directly affect motivation and determine which terminal goal contexts receive activation and how much. Other (environmental) conditions determine which of the earlier goal contexts receive additional activation.

8. *Action Chosen.* The behavior net chooses a single behavior (goal context). This selection is heavily influenced by activation passed to various behaviors influenced by the various emotions. The choice is also affected by the current situation, external and internal conditions, by the relation between the behaviors, and by the residual activation values of various behaviors.

9. *Action Taken.* The execution of a behavior (goal context) results in the behavior codelets performing their specialized tasks, which may have external or internal consequences. The acting codelets also include an expectation codelet (see Step 6) whose task is to monitor the action and to try and bring to consciousness any failure in the expected results.

IDA's elementary cognitive activities occur within a single cognitive cycle. More complex cognitive functions are implemented over multiple cycles. These include deliberation, metacognition, and voluntary action (Franklin, 2000).

The IDA model employs a methodology that is different from that which is currently typical of computational cognitive models. Although the model is based on experimental findings in cognitive psychology and brain science, there is only qualitative consistency with experiments. Rather, there are a number of hypotheses derived from IDA as a unified theory of cognition. The IDA model generates hypotheses about human cognition and the role of consciousness through its design, the mechanisms of its modules, their interaction, and its performance.

Every agent must sample and act on its world through a sense-select-act cycle. The frequent sampling allows for a fine-grained analysis of common cognitive phenomena, such as process dissociation, recognition vs. recall, and the availability heuristic. At a high level of abstraction, the analyses support the commonly held explanations of what occurs in these situations and why. At a finer-grained level, the analyses flesh out common explanations, adding details and functional mechanisms. Therein lies the value of these analyses.

Unfortunately, currently available techniques for studying some phenomena at a fine-grained level, such as PET, fMRI, EEG, implanted electrodes, etc., are lacking either in scope, in spatial resolution, or in temporal resolution. As a result, some of the hypotheses from the IDA model, although testable in principle, seem not to be testable at the

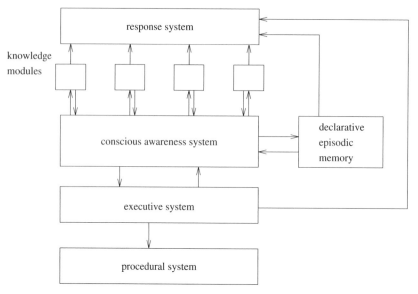

Figure 7.7. Schacter's model of consciousness.

present time for lack of technologies with suitable scope and resolution.

There is also the issue of the breadth of the IDA model, which encompasses perception, working memory, declarative memory, attention, decision making, procedural learning, and more. How can such a broad model produce anything useful? The IDA model suggests that these various aspects of human cognition are highly integrated. A more global view can be expected to add additional understanding to that produced by more specific models. This assertion seems to be borne out by the analyses of various cognitive phenomena (Baars & Franklin, 2003; Franklin et al., 2005).

Sketches of Some Other Views

As we have seen, there are many attempts to explain the difference in conscious accessibility. Various explanations have been advanced in terms of the content of knowledge (e.g., instances vs. rules), the organization of knowledge (e.g., declarative vs. procedural), processing mechanisms (e.g., spreading activation vs. rule matching and firing), the representation of knowledge (e.g., localist/symbolic vs. distributed), and

so on. In addition to the two views elaborated on earlier, let us look into some more details of a few other views. Although some of the models that are discussed below are not strictly speaking computational (because they may not have been fully computationally implemented), they are nevertheless important because they point to possible ways of constructing computational explanations of consciousness.

We can examine Schacter's (1990) model as an example. The model is based on neuropsychological findings of the dissociation of different types of knowledge (especially in brain-damaged patients). It includes a number of "knowledge modules" that perform specialized and unconscious processing and may send their outcomes to a "conscious awareness system," which gives rise to conscious awareness (see Figure 7.7). Schacter's explanation of some neuropsychological disorders (e.g., hemisphere neglect, blindsight, aphasia, agnosia, and prosopagnosia) is that brain damages result in the disconnection of some of the modules from the conscious awareness system, which causes their inaccessibility to consciousness. However, as has been pointed out by others, this explanation cannot account for many findings in implicit memory research (e.g., Roediger,

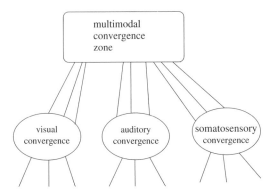

Figure 7.8. Damasio's model of consciousness.

1990). Revonsuo (1993) advocated a similar view, albeit from a philosophical viewpoint, largely on the basis of using Schacter's (1990) data as evidence. Johnson-Laird's (1983) model was somewhat similar to Schacter's model in its overall structure in that there was a hierarchy of processors and consciousness resided in the processes at the top of the hierarchy. Shallice (1972) put forward a model in which a number of "action systems" could be activated by "selector input" and the activated action systems correspond to consciousness. It is not clear, however, what the computational (mechanistic) difference between conscious and unconscious processes is in those models, which did not offer a mechanistic explanation.

We can compare Schacter's (1990) model with CLARION. It is similar to CLARION in that it includes a number of "knowledge modules" that perform specialized and unconscious processing (analogous to bottom-level modules in CLARION) and send their outcomes to a "conscious awareness system" (analogous to the top level in CLARION), which gives rise to conscious awareness. Unlike CLARION's explanation of the conscious/unconscious distinction through the difference between localist/symbolic versus distributed representations, however, Schacter's model does not elucidate in computational/mechanistic terms the qualitative distinction between conscious and unconscious processes, in that the "conscious awareness system" lacks any apparent qualitative difference from the unconscious systems.

We can also examine Damasio's neuroanatomically motivated model (Damasio et al., 1990). The model hypothesizes the existence of many "sensory convergence zones" that integrate information from individual sensory modalities through forward and backward synaptic connections and the resulting reverberations of activations, without a central location for information storage and comparisons; it also hypothesizes the global "multimodal convergence zone," which integrates information across modalities also through reverberation (via recurrent connections; see Figure 7.8). Correlated with consistency is global information availability; that is, once "broadcast" or "reverberation" is achieved, all the information about an entity stored in difference places of the brain becomes available. This was believed to have explained the accessibility of consciousness.[6] In terms of CLARION, different sensory convergence zones may be roughly captured by bottom-level modules, each of which takes care of sensory inputs of one modality (at a properly fine level), and the role of the global multi-modal convergence zone (similar to the global workspace in a way) may be played by the top level of CLARION, which has the ultimate responsibility for integrating information (and also serves as the "conscious awareness system"). The widely recognized role of reverberation (Damasio, 1994; Taylor, 1994) may be captured in CLARION through using recurrent connections within modules at the bottom level and through multiple top-down and bottom-up information flows across the two levels, which leads to the unity of consciousness that is the synthesis of all the information present (Baars, 1988; Marcel, 1983).

Similarly, Crick and Koch (1990) hypothesize that synchronous firing at 35–75 Hz in the cerebral cortex is the basis for consciousness – with such synchronous firing, pieces of information regarding different aspects of an entity are brought together, and thus consciousness emerges. Although consciousness has been experimentally observed to be somewhat correlated with synchronous firing at 35–75 Hz, there is no explanation of *why* this is the case and there is no computational/mechanistic explanation of any *qualitative* difference between 35–75 Hz synchronous firing and other firing patterns.

Cotterill (1997) offers a "master-module" model of consciousness, which asserts that consciousness arises from movement or the planning of movement. The master-module refers to the brain region that is responsible for motor planning. This model sees the conscious system as being profligate with its resources: Perforce it must plan and organize movements, even though it does not always execute them. The model stresses the vital role that movement plays and is quite compatible with the IDA model. This centrality of movement was illustrated by the observation that blind people were able to read braille when allowed to move their fingers, but were unable to do so when the dots were moved against their still fingers (Cotterill, 1997).

Finally, readers interested in the possibility of computational models of consciousness actually producing "conscious" artifacts may consult Holland (2003) and other work along that line.

Concluding Remarks

This chapter has examined general frameworks of computational accounts of consciousness. Various related issues, such as the utility of computational models, explanations of psychological data, and potential applications of machine consciousness, have been touched on in the process. Based on existing psychological and philosophical evidence, existing models were compared and contrasted to some extent. It appears inevitable at this stage that there is the coexistence of various computational accounts of consciousness. Each of them seems to capture some aspect of consciousness, but each also has severe limitations. To capture the whole picture in a unified computational framework, much more work is needed. In this regard, CLARION and IDA provide some hope.

Much more work can be conducted on various issues of consciousness along this computational line. Such work may include further specifications of details of computational models. It may also include reconciliations of existing computational models of consciousness. More importantly, it may, and should, include the validation of computational models through empirical and theoretical means. The last point in particular should be emphasized in future work (see the earlier discussions concerning CLARION and IDA). In addition, we may also attempt to account for consciousness computationally at multiple levels, from phenomenology, via various intermediate levels, all the way down to physiology, which will likely lead to a much more complete computational account and a much better picture of consciousness (Coward & Sun, 2004).

Acknowledgments

Ron Sun acknowledges support in part from Office of Naval Research grant N00014-95-1-0440 and Army Research Institute grants DASW01-00-K-0012 and W74V8H-04-K-0002. Stan Franklin acknowledges support from the Office of Naval Research and other U.S. Navy sources under grants N00014-01-1-0917, N00014-98-1-0332, N00014-00-1-0769, and DAAH04-96-C-0086.

Notes

1. There are also various numerical measures involved, which are not important for the present discussion.
2. Cleeremans and McClelland's (1991) model of artificial grammar learning can be viewed as instantiating half of the system (the unconscious half), in which implicit learning takes place based on gradual weight changes in response to practice on a task and the resulting changes in activation of various representations when performing the task.
3. Note that the accessibility is defined in terms of the surface syntactic structures of the

objects being accessed (at the level of outcomes or processes), not their semantic meanings. Thus, for example, a LISP expression is directly accessible, even though one may not fully understand its meaning. The internal working of a neural network may be inaccessible even though one may know what the network essentially does (through an interpretive process). Note also that objects and processes that are directly accessible at a certain level may not be accessible at a finer level of details.

4. This activation of features is important in subsequent uses of the information associated with the concept and in directing behaviors.

5. This is a term borrowed from computer operating systems that describes a small piece of code that waits and watches for a particular event or condition to occur before it acts.

6. However, consciousness does not necessarily mean accessibility/availability of all the information about an entity; for otherwise, conscious inference, deliberate recollection, and other related processes would be unnecessary.

References

Anderson, J. R. (1983). *The architecture of cognition*. Cambridge, MA: Harvard University Press.

Anderson, J., & Lebiere, C. (1998). *The atomic components of thought*. Mahwah, NJ: Erlbaum.

Anwar, A., & Franklin, S. (2003). Sparse distributed memory for "conscious" software agents. *Cognitive Systems Research, 4*, 339–354.

Baars, B. (1988). *A cognitive theory of consciousness*. New York: Cambridge University Press.

Baars, B. (2002). The conscious access hypothesis: Origins and recent evidence. *Trends in Cognitive Science, 6*, 47–52.

Baars, B., & Franklin, S. (2003). How conscious experience and working memory interact. *Trends in Cognitive Science, 7*, 166–172.

Barsalou, L. (1999). Perceptual symbol systems. *Behavioral and Brain Sciences, 22*, 577–609.

Berry, D., & Broadbent, D. (1988). Interactive tasks and the implicit-explicit distinction. *British Journal of Psychology, 79*, 251–272.

Bower, G. (1996). Reactivating a reactivation theory of implicit memory. *Consciousness and Cognition, 5*(1/2), 27–72.

Bowers, K., Regehr, G., Balthazard, C., & Parker, K. (1990). Intuition in the context of discovery. *Cognitive Psychology, 22*, 72–110.

Chaiken, S., & Trope, Y. (Eds.). (1999). *Dual process theories in social psychology*. New York: Guilford Press.

Clark, A. (1992). The presence of a symbol. *Connection Science. 4*, 193–205.

Clark, A., & Karmiloff-Smith, A. (1993). The cognizer's innards: A psychological and philosophical perspective on the development of thought. *Mind and Language, 8*(4), 487–519.

Cleeremans, A., & McClelland, J. (1991). Learning the structure of event sequences. *Journal of Experimental Psychology: General, 120*, 235–253.

Collins, A., & Loftus, J. (1975). Spreading activation theory of semantic processing. *Psychological Review, 82*, 407–428.

Cosmides, L., & Tooby, J. (1994). Beyond intuition and instinct blindness: Toward an evolutionarily rigorous cognitive science. *Cognition, 50*, 41–77.

Cotterill, R. (1997). On the mechanism of consciousness. *Journal of Consciousness Studies, 4*, 231–247.

Coward, L. A., & Sun, R. (2004). Criteria for an effective theory of consciousness and some preliminary attempts. *Consciousness and Cognition, 13*, 268–301.

Crick, F., & Koch, C. (1990). Toward a neurobiological theory of consciousness. *Seminars in the Neuroscience, 2*, 263–275.

Damasio. A., et al. (1990). Neural regionalization of knowledge access. *Cold Spring Harbor Symposium on Quantitative Biology, LV*.

Damasio, A. (1994). *Descartes' error*. New York: Grosset/Putnam.

Dennett, D. (1991), *Consciousness explained*. Boston: Little Brown.

Edelman, G. (1987). *Neural Darwinism*. New York: Basic Books.

Edelman, G. (1989). *The remembered present: A biological theory of consciousness*. New York: Basic Books.

Edelman, G., & Tononi, G. (2000). *A universe of consciousness*. New York: Basic Books.

Freeman, W. (1995). *Societies of brains*. Hillsdale, NJ: Erlbaum.

Fodor, J. (1983). *The modularity of mind*. Cambridge, MA: MIT Press.

Franklin, S. (2000). Deliberation and voluntary action in 'conscious' software agents. *Neural Network World*, 10, 505–521.

Franklin, S., Baars, B. J., Ramamurthy, U., & Ventura, M. 2005. The Role of consciousness in memory. *Brains, Minds and Media*, 1, 1–38.

Franklin, S., & Graesser, A. C. (1997). Is it an agent, or just a program?: A taxonomy for autonomous agents. *Intelligent agents III*, 21–35.

Franklin, S., Kelemen, A., & McCauley, L. (1998). IDA: A cognitive agent architecture. *IEEE Conference on Systems, Man and Cybernetics*.

Hadley, R. (1995). The explicit-implicit distinction. *Minds and Machines*, 5, 219–242.

Hirschfeld, L., & Gelman, S. (1994). *Mapping the Mind: Domain Specificity in Cognition and Culture*. New York: Cambridge University Press.

Hofstadter, D., & Mitchell, M. (1994). The copycat project: A model of mental fluidity and analogy-making. In K. J. Holyoak, & J. A. Barnden (Eds.), *Advances in connectionist and neural computation theory, Vol. 2: Logical connections*. Norwood, NJ: Ablex.

Holland, O. (2003). *Machine consciousness*. Exeter, UK: Imprint Academic.

Hunt, E., & Lansman, M. (1986). Unified model of attention and problem solving. *Psychological Review*, 93(4), 446–461.

Jackendoff, R. (1987). *Consciousness and the computational mind*. Cambridge, MA: MIT Press.

Johnson-Laird, P. (1983). A computational analysis of consciousness. *Cognition and Brain Theory*, 6, 499–508.

Kanerva, P. (1988). *Sparse distributed memory*. Cambridge MA: MIT Press.

Karmiloff-Smith, A. (1986). From meta-processes to conscious access: Evidence from children's metalinguistic and repair data. *Cognition*, 23, 95–147.

LeDoux, J. (1992). Brain mechanisms of emotion and emotional learning. *Current Opinion in Neurobiology*, 2(2), 191–197.

Logan, G. (1988). Toward a theory of automatization. *Psychological Review*, 95(4), 492–527.

Maes, P. (1989). How to do the right thing. *Connection Science*, 1, 291–323.

Marcel, A. (1983). Conscious and unconscious perception: An approach to the relations between phenomenal experience and perceptual processes. *Cognitive Psychology*, 15, 238–300.

Maslow, A. (1987). *Motivation and personality* (3d ed.). New York: Harper and Row.

Mathis, D., & Mozer, M., (1996). Conscious and unconscious perception: A computational theory. *Proceedings of the 18th Annual Conference of the Cognitive Science Society*, 324–328.

McClelland, J., McNaughton, B., & O'Reilly, R. (1995). Why there are complementary learning systems in the hippocampus and neocortex: Insights from the successes and failures of connectionist models of learning and memory. *Psychological Review*, 102(3), 419–457.

Michalski, R. (1983). A theory and methodology of inductive learning. *Artificial Intelligence*, 20, 111–161.

Minsky, M. (1985). *The society of mind*. New York: Simon and Schuster.

Moscovitch, M., & Umilta, C. (1991). Conscious and unconscious aspects of memory. In *Perspectives on cognitive neuroscience*. New York: Oxford University Press.

Neal, A., & Hesketh, B. (1997). Episodic knowledge and implicit learning. *Psychonomic Bulletin and Review*, 4(1), 24–37.

Negatu, A., & Franklin, S. (2002). An action selection mechanism for 'conscious' software agents. *Cognitive Science Quarterly*, 2, 363–386.

Nelson, T. (Ed.) (1993). *Metacognition: Core Readings*. Boston, MA: Allyn and Bacon.

O'Brien. G., & Opie, J. (1998). A connectionist theory of phenomenal experience. *Behavioral and Brain Sciences*, 22, 127–148.

Penrose, R. (1994). *Shadows of the mind*. Oxford: Oxford University Press.

Quillian, M. R. (1968). Semantic memory. In M. Minsky (Ed.), *Semantic information processing* (pp. 227–270). Cambridge, MA: MIT Press.

Ramamurthy, U., D'Mello, S., & Franklin, S. (2004). Modified sparse distributed memory as transient episodic memory for cognitive software agents. In *Proceedings of the International Conference on Systems, Man and Cybernetics*. Piscataway, NJ: IEEE.

Reber, A. (1989). Implicit learning and tacit knowledge. *Journal of Experimental Psychology: General*, 118(3), 219–235.

Revonsuo, A. (1993). Cognitive models of consciousness. In M. Kamppinen (Ed.), *Consciousness, cognitive schemata and relativism* (pp. 27–130). Dordrecht, Netherlands: Kluwer.

Roediger, H. (1990). Implicit memory: Retention without remembering. *American Psychologist*, 45(9), 1043–1056.

Rosenbloom, P., Laird, J., & Newell, A. (1993). *The SOAR papers: Research on integrated intelligence*. Cambridge, MA: MIT Press.

Rosenthal, D. (Ed.). (1991). *The nature of mind*. Oxford: Oxford University Press.

Rumelhart, D., McClelland, J., & the PDP Research Group, (1986). *Parallel distributed processing: Explorations in the microstructures of cognition*. Cambridge, MA: MIT Press.

Schacter, D. (1990). Toward a cognitive neuropsychology of awareness: Implicit knowledge and anosagnosia. *Journal of Clinical and Experimental Neuropsychology*, 12(1), 155–178.

Schneider, W., & Oliver, W. (1991). An instructable connectionist/control architecture. In K. VanLehn (Ed.), *Architectures for intelligence*. Hillsdale, NJ: Erlbaum.

Searle, J. (1980). Minds, brains, and programs. *Brain and Behavioral Sciences*, 3, 417–457.

Seger, C. (1994). Implicit learning. *Psychological Bulletin*, 115(2), 163–196.

Servan-Schreiber, E., & Anderson, J. (1987). Learning artificial grammars with competitive chunking. *Journal of Experimental Psychology: Learning, Memory, and Cognition*, 16, 592–608.

Shallice, T. (1972). Dual functions of consciousness. *Psychological Review*, 79(5), 383–393.

Sloman, A., & Chrisley, R. (2003). Virtual machines and consciousness. *Journal of Consciousness Studies*, 10, 133–172.

Smith, E., & Medin, D. (1981). *Categories and concepts*. Cambridge, MA: Harvard University Press.

Smith, J. D., Shields, W. E., & Washburn, D. A. (2003). The comparative psychology of uncertainty monitoring and metacognition. *Behavioral and Brain Sciences*. 26, 317–339.

Smolensky, P. (1988). On the proper treatment of connectionism. *Behavioral and Brain Sciences*, 11(1), 1–74.

Stanley, W., Mathews, R., Buss, R., & Kotler-Cope, S. (1989). Insight without awareness: On the interaction of verbalization, instruction and practice in a simulated process control task.

Quarterly Journal of Experimental Psychology, 41A(3), 553–577.

Sun, R. (1994). *Integrating rules and connectionism for robust commonsense reasoning*. New York: John Wiley and Sons.

Sun, R. (1995). Robust reasoning: Integrating rule-based and similarity-based reasoning. *Artificial Intelligence*, 75(2), 241–296.

Sun, R. (1997). Learning, action, and consciousness: A hybrid approach towards modeling consciousness. *Neural Networks*, 10(7), 1317–1331.

Sun, R. (1999a). Accounting for the computational basis of consciousness: A connectionist approach. *Consciousness and Cognition*, 8, 529–565.

Sun, R. (1999b). Computational models of consciousness: An evaluation. *Journal of Intelligent Systems [Special Issue on Consciousness]*, 9(5–6), 507–562.

Sun, R. (2002). *Duality of the mind*. Mahwah, NJ: Erlbaum.

Sun, R. (2003). *A tutorial on CLARION*. Retrieved from http://www.cogsci.rpi.edu/~rsun/sun.tutorial.pdf.

Sun, R., & Bookman, L. (Eds.). (1994). *Computational architectures integrating neural and symbolic processes*. Norwell, MA: Kluwer.

Sun, R., Merrill, E., & Peterson, T. (2001). From implicit skills to explicit knowledge: A bottom-up model of skill learning. *Cognitive Science*, 25(2), 203–244.

Sun, R., & Naveh, I. (2004, June). Simulating organizational decision making with a cognitive architecture CLARION. *Journal of Artificial Society and Social Simulation*, 7(3). Retrieved from http://jasss.soc.surrey.ac.uk/7/3/5.html.

Sun, R., & Peterson, T. (1998). Autonomous learning of sequential tasks: Experiments and analyses. *IEEE Transactions on Neural Networks*, 9(6), 1217–1234.

Sun, R., & Peterson, T. (1999). Multi-agent reinforcement learning: Weighting and partitioning. *Neural Networks*, 12(4–5). 127–153.

Sun, R., Peterson, T., & Merrill, E. (1996). Bottom-up skill learning in reactive sequential decision tasks. *Proceedings of 18th Cognitive Science Society Conference*. Hillsdale, NJ: Lawrence Erlbaum Associates.

Sun, R., Merrill, E.. & Peterson, T. (1998). A bottom-up model of skill learning. *Proceedings of the 20th Cognitive Science Society Conference* (pp. 1037–1042). Mahwah, NJ: Lawrence Erlbaum Associates

Sun , R., Slusarz, P., & Terry, C. (2005). The interaction of the explicit and the implicit in skill learning: A dual-process approach. *Psychological Review*, 112, 159–192.

Taylor, J. (1994). Goal, drives and consciousness. *Neural Networks*, 7 (6/7), 1181–1190.

Taylor, J. (1997). The relational mind. In A. Browne (Ed.), *Neural network perspectives on cognition and adaptive robotics*. Bristol, UK: Institute of Physics.

Toates, F. (1986). *Motivational systems*. Cambridge: Cambridge University Press.

Tversky, A. (1977). Features of similarity. *Psychological Review*, 84(4), 327–352.

Watkins, C. (1989). *Learning with delayed rewards*. PhD Thesis, Cambridge University, Cambridge, UK.

Willingham, D., Nissen, M., & Bullemer, P. (1989). On the development of procedural knowledge. *Journal of Experimental Psychology: Learning, Memory, and Cognition*, 15, 1047–1060.

C. Cognitive Psychology

CHAPTER 8

Cognitive Theories of Consciousness

Katharine McGovern and Bernard J. Baars

Abstract

Current cognitive theories of consciousness focus on a few common themes, such as the limited capacity of conscious contents under input competition; the wide access enabled by conscious events to sensation, memory, problem-solving capacities, and action control; the relation between conscious contents and working memory; and the differences between implicit and explicit cognition in learning, retrieval, and other cognitive functions. The evidentiary base is large. A unifying principle in the midst of these diverse empirical findings is to treat consciousness as an experimental variable and, then, to look for general capacities that distinguish conscious and unconscious mental functioning. In this chapter, we discuss three classes of theories: information-processing theories that build on modular elements, network theories that focus on the distributed access of conscious processing, and globalist theories that combine aspects of these two. An emerging consensus suggests that conscious cognition is a global aspect of human brain functioning. A specific conscious content, like the sight of a coffee cup, is crucially dependent on local regions of visual cortex. But, by itself, local cortical activity is not conscious. Rather, the conscious experience of a coffee cup requires both local and widespread cortical activity.

Introduction

When consciousness became a scientifically respectable topic again in the 1980s, it was tackled in a number of different scholarly disciplines – psychology, philosophy, neuroscience, linguistics, medicine, and others. By the late 1990s, considerable interdisciplinary cooperation evolved in consciousness studies, spurred by the biennial Tucson Conferences and the birth of two new scholarly journals, *Consciousness and Cognition* and the *Journal of Consciousness Studies*. The domain of consciousness studies originated in separate disciplines, but has since become cross-disciplinary. Thus, a number of early theories of consciousness can justifiably be called purely cognitive theories of consciousness, whereas most recent theories are neurocognitive hybrids – depending on evidence from the brain as well as behavior. In this chapter, we have, for the most part, restricted discussion to cognitive or functional models of consciousness with less reference to the burgeoning neuroscientific evidence that increasingly supports the globalist position that we develop here.

Operationally Defining Consciousness

Cognitive Methods That Treat Consciousness as a Variable

There is a curious asymmetry between the assessment of conscious and unconscious processes. Obtaining verifiable experiential reports works very nicely for specifying conscious representations, but unconscious ones are much more slippery. In many cases of apparently unconscious processes, such as all the things the reader is *not* paying attention to at this moment, it could be that the "unconscious" representations may be momentarily conscious, but so quickly or vaguely that we cannot recall them even a fraction of a second later. Or suppose people cannot report a word shown for a few milliseconds: Does this mean that they are truly unconscious of it? Such questions continue to lead to controversy today. William James understood this problem very well and suggested, in fact, that there were no unconscious psychological processes at all (1890, p. 162ff.). This has been called the "zero point" problem (Baars, 1988). It should be emphasized, however, that problems with defining a zero point do not prevent scientists from studying phenomena as variables. Even today, the precise nature of zero temperature points, such as the freezing point of water, continues to lead to debate. But physicists have done extremely productive work on thermodynamics for centuries. Zero points are not the sole criterion for useful empirical variables.

The discovery that something we take for granted as a constant can be treated as a variable has led to scientific advances before. In the late 1600s, contemporaries of Isaac Newton were frustrated in their attempts to understand gravity. One key to Newton's great achievement was to imagine the presence *and the absence* of gravity, thus permitting gravity to be treated as a variable. In the same way, a breakthrough in the scientific study of consciousness occurred when psychologists began to understand that consciousness can be treated as a variable. That is, behavioral outcomes can be observed when conscious cognitions are present and when they are absent. The process of generalizing across these observations has been called *contrastive analysis* (explained below).

Beginning in the 1980s, a number of experimental methods gained currency as means of studying comparable conscious and non-conscious processes. In much of cognitive science and neuroscience today, the existence of unconscious cognitive processes, often comparable to conscious ones, is taken for granted. Table 8.1 highlights methods that have produced behavioral data relevant to the study of consciousness.

Working Definitions of "Conscious" and "Unconscious"

In the history of science, formal definitions for concepts like "heat" and "gene" tend to come quite late, often centuries after adequate operational definitions are developed. The same point may apply to conscious cognition. Although there is ongoing debate about what consciousness "really" is, there has long been a scientific consensus on its observable index of verbal report. This index can be generalized to any other kind of voluntary response, such as pressing a button or even voluntary eye movements in "locked-in" neurological patients. Experiential reports can be analyzed with sophisticated methods, such as process dissociation and signal detection. Thus, empirically, it is not difficult to assess conscious events in humans with intact brains, given good experimental conditions. We propose the

Table 8.1. Empirical methods used in the study of conscious and unconscious processes

Class of Methods	Experimental Paradigm	Outcome
Divided attention	Dichotic listening	Two dense streams of speech are offered to the two ears, and only one stream at a time can receive conscious word-level processing. Evidence suggests that the unconscious stream continues to receive some processing.
	Selective ("double exposure") viewing	When two overlaid movies are viewed, only one is perceived consciously.
	Inattentional blindness	Aspects of visual scenes to which attention is not directed are not consciously perceived; attended aspects of the same scenes are perceived.
	Binocular rivalry/dichoptic viewing (including flash suppression)	Presenting separate visual scenes to each eye; only one scene reaches consciousness, but the unconscious scene receives low-level processing.
Dual task paradigms	Driving and talking on a cell phone	To the extent that tasks require conscious initiation and direction, they compete and degrade the performance of each other; once automatized, multiple tasks interfere less.
	Rehearsing words and doing word verification	
Priming	Supraliminal and subliminal priming	When a "prime" stimulus is presented prior to a "target" stimulus, response to the "target" is influenced by the currently unconscious nature and meaning of the "prime." Supraliminal priming generally results in a more robust effect.
	Priming of one interpretation of ambiguous words or pictures	
Visual backward masking		When supra-threshold visual stimuli are followed immediately by visual masking stimuli (visual noise), the original stimuli are not consciously perceived, though they are locally registered in early visual cortex.
Implicit learning	Miniature grammar learning	Consciously perceived stimuli give rise to knowledge structures that are not available to consciousness.
Process dissociation and ironic effects		Participants are told to exclude certain memorized items from memory reports; if those items nevertheless appear, they are assumed to be products of non-conscious processing.
Fixedness, decontextualization, and being blind to the obvious (related to availability)	Problem-solving tasks, functional fixedness tasks (Duncker), chess playing, garden path sentences, highly automatized actions under novel conditions	Set effects in problem solving can exclude otherwise obvious conclusions from consciousness. "Breaking set" can lead to recovery of those conclusions in consciousness.

Table 8.2. Contrastive analysis in perception and imagery

Conscious Events	Comparable Unconscious Events
1. Perceived stimuli	1. Processing of stimuli lacking in intensity or duration, or centrally masked stimuli
	2. Preperceptual processing of stimuli
	3. Habituated or automatic stimulus processing
	4. Unaccessed versions of ambiguous stimuli/words
	5. Contexts of interpretation for percepts and concepts
	6. Unattended streams of perceptual input (all modalities)
	7. Implicit expectations about stimuli
	8. Parafoveal guidance of eye movements in reading
	9. Stimulus processing under general anesthesia
10. Images in all sense modalities	10. Unretrieved images in memory
11. a. Newly generated visual images	11. Automatized visual images
b. Automatic images that encounter some difficulty	
12. Inner speech: words currently rehearsed in working memory	12. Inner speech, not currently rehearsed in working memory
13. Fleetingly conscious phrases and belief statements	13. Automatized inner speech; the "jingle channel"
14. Visual search based on conjoined features	14. Visual search based on single features
15. Retrieval by recall	15. Retrieval by recognition
16. Explicit knowledge	16. Implicit knowledge

following as de facto operational definitions of conscious and unconscious that are already in very wide experimental use in perception, psychophysics, memory, imagery, and the like.

We can say that mental processes are *conscious* if they

(a) are claimed by people to be conscious; and

(b) can be reported and acted upon,

(c) with verifiable accuracy,

(d) under optimal reporting conditions (e.g., with minimum delay between the event and the report, freedom from distraction, and the like).

Conversely, mental events can be defined as *unconscious* for practical purposes if

(a) their presence can be verified (through facilitation of other observable tasks, for example); although

(b) they are not claimed to be conscious;

(c) and they cannot be *voluntarily* reported, operated upon, or avoided,

(d) even under optimal reporting conditions.

The Method of Contrastive Analysis

Using the logic of experimental research, consciousness can be treated as a controlled variable; then, measures of cognitive functioning and neural activity can be compared under two levels of the independent variable – consciousness-present and consciousness-absent. If there is no clearly unconscious comparison condition, a low-level conscious condition may be used, as in drowsiness or stimuli in background noise. The point, of course, is to have at least two quantitatively different levels for comparison.

DATA FROM CONTRASTIVE ANALYSIS
Examples of conscious versus non-conscious contrasts from studies of perception, imagery, memory, and attention appear in Table 8.2. In the left column, conscious mental events are listed; on the right are

Table 8.3. Capability contrasts between comparable conscious and non-conscious processes

Conscious Processes	Unconscious Processes
1. Are computationally inefficient with • Many errors • Relatively low speed • Mutual interference between conscious processes.	1. Are very efficient in routine tasks with • Few errors • High speed • Little mutual interference.
2. Have a great range of contents • Great ability to relate different conscious contents to each other • Great ability to relate conscious events to unconscious contexts • *Flexible*	2. Taken individually, unconscious processes have a *limited range* of contents • Each routine process is relatively isolated and autonomous • Each routine process is relatively context-free, operates in a range of contexts • *Fixed pattern*
3. • have high *internal consistency* at any single moment • have *seriality* over time • have *limited processing capacity*	3. The set of routine, unconscious processes, taken together, is: • *diverse,* • can operate *concurrently* • have great *processing capacity*
4. The *clearest* conscious contents are *perceptual or quasi-perceptual* (e.g., imagery, inner speech, and internally generated bodily feelings)	4. Unconscious processes are involved in *all* mental tasks, not limited to perception and imagery, but including memory, knowledge representation and access, skill learning, problem-solving, action control, etc.
5. Are associated with *voluntary* actions	5. Are associated with *non-voluntary* actions

corresponding non-conscious processes. Theoretically, we are interested in finding out what is common in conscious processing across all these cases.

Capability Contrasts

The difference in mental and neural functioning between consciousness-present and consciousness-absent processing – taken across many experimental contexts – reveals stable characteristics attributable to consciousness. *Conscious processes* are phenomenally serial, internally consistent, unitary at any moment, and limited in capacity. *Nonconscious mental processes* are functionally concurrent, often highly differentiated from each other, and relatively unlimited in capacity, when taken together. Table 8.3 summaries these general conclusions.

These empirical contrasts in the capabilities of conscious and unconscious mental processes can become the criteria against which models of consciousness can be evaluated. Any adequate theory of consciousness

would need to account for these observed differences in functioning. Thus, we have a way of judging the explanatory adequacy of proposals concerning the nature and functioning of consciousness. We can keep these capability contrasts in mind as we review contemporary cognitive models of consciousness.

Given the tight constraints that appear repeatedly in studies of conscious processing – that is, limited capacity, seriality, and internal consistency requirements – we might ask, Why? Would it not be adaptive to do *several* conscious things at the same time? Certainly human ancestors might have benefited from being able to gather food, be alert for predators, and keep an eye on their offspring simultaneously; modern humans could benefit from being able to drive their cars, talk on cell phones, and put on lipstick without mutual interference. Yet these tasks compete when they require consciousness, so that only one can be done well at any given moment. The question then is, Why are conscious functions so limited in a neuropsychological architecture that is so large and complex?

Functions of Consciousness in the Architecture of Cognition

A Note about Architectures

The metaphor of "cognitive architectures" dates to the 1970s when cognitive psychologists created information-processing models of mental processes. In many of these models, different mental functions, such as memory, language, attention, and sensory processes, were represented as modules, or sets of modules, within a larger information-processing system. The functional layout and the interactions of the parts of the system came to be called the cognitive architecture. We have adopted this terminology here to capture the idea that consciousness operates within a larger neuropsychological system that has many constituents interacting in complex ways.

Consciousness Serves Many Functions

William James believed that "[t]he study . . . of the distribution of consciousness shows it to be exactly such as we might expect in an organ added for the sake of steering a nervous system grown too complex to regulate itself (1890, p. 141)." More recently, Baars (1988) identified eight psychological functions of consciousness, which are defined in Table 8.4.

Note that each proposed function of consciousness is served through an interplay of conscious and unconscious processes. It has been argued that consciousness fulfills all eight functions by providing *access* or priority entrance into various subparts of the cognitive system (Baars, 2002). For example, the error-detection function can be accomplished only when information about an impending or actual error, which cannot be handled by "canned" automatisms, can gain access to consciousness. Subsequently, editing occurs when this conscious information is "broadcast" or distributed to other parts

of the system that are capable of acting to recognize and correct it. Consciousness functions as the central distributor of information, which is used by subparts of the cognitive system or architecture.

Consciousness Creates Access

A strong case can be made that we can create access to any part of the brain by way of conscious input. For example, to gain voluntary control over alpha waves in the occipital cortex we merely sound a tone or turn on a light when alpha is detected in the EEG, and shortly the subject will be able to increase the power of alpha at will. To control a single spinal motor unit we merely pick up its electrical activity and play it back over headphones; in a half-hour, subjects have been able to play drum rolls on single motor units. Biofeedback control over single neurons and whole populations of neurons anywhere in the brain is well established (Basmajian, 1979). Consciousness of the feedback signal seems to be a necessary condition to establish control, though the motor neural activities themselves remain entirely unconscious. It is as if mere consciousness of results creates access to unconscious neuronal systems that are normally quite autonomous.

Psychological evidence leads to similar conclusions. The recognition vocabulary of educated English speakers contains about 100,000 words. Although we do not use all of them in everyday speech, we can understand each word as soon as it is presented in a sentence that makes sense. Yet each individual word is already quite complex. The *Oxford English Dictionary* devotes 75,000 words to the many different meanings of the word "set." Yet all we do as humans to access these complex unconscious bodies of knowledge is to become conscious of a target word. It seems that understanding language demands the gateway of consciousness. This is another case of the general principle that consciousness of stimuli creates widespread access to unconscious sources of knowledge, such as the mental lexicon, meaning, and grammar.

Table 8.4. Explaining the psychological functions of consciousness

Function of Consciousness	Function Explained
1. Definition and context-setting	By relating input to its contextual conditions, consciousness defines a stimulus and removes ambiguities in its perception and understanding.
2. Adaptation and learning	The more novelty and unpredictability to which the psychological system must adapt, the greater the conscious involvement required for successful problem solving and learning.
3. Prioritizing and access control	Attentional mechanisms exercise selective control over what will become conscious by relating input to unconscious goal contexts. By consciously relating an event or circumstance to higher-level goals, we can raise its access priority, making it conscious more often and therefore increasing the chances of successful adaptation to it.
4. Recruitment and control of thought and action	Conscious goals can recruit subgoals and behavior systems to organize and carry out flexible, voluntary action.
5. Decision-making and executive function	Consciousness creates access to multiple knowledge sources within the psychological system. When automatic systems cannot resolve some choice point in the flow of action, making it conscious helps recruit knowledge sources that are able to help make the decision; in case of indecision, making the goal conscious allows widespread recruitment of conscious and unconscious sources acting for and against the goal.
6. Error detection and editing	Conscious goals and plans are monitored by unconscious rule systems that will act to interrupt execution if errors are detected. Though we often become aware of making an error in a general way, the detailed description of what makes an error an error is almost always unconscious.
7. Reflection and self-monitoring	Through conscious inner speech and imagery we can reflect upon and to some extent control and plan our conscious and unconscious functioning.
8. Optimizing the tradeoff between organization and flexibility	Automatized, "canned" responses are highly adaptive in predictable circumstances. However, in unpredictable environments, the capacity of consciousness to recruit and reconfigure specialized knowledge sources is indispensable in allowing flexible responding.

Or consider autobiographical memory. The size of long-term episodic memory is unknown, but we do know that simply by paying attention to as many as 10,000 distinct pictures over several days without attempting to memorize them, we can spontaneously recognize more than 90% a week later (Standing, 1973). Remarkable results like this are common when we use recognition probes, merely asking people to choose between known and new pictures. Recognition probes apparently work so well because they re-present the original conscious experience of each picture in its entirety. Here the brain does a marvelous job of memory search, with little effort. It seems that humans create memories of the stream of input merely by paying attention, but because we are always paying attention to something, in every waking moment, this suggests that autobiographical memory may be very large indeed. Once again we have a vast unconscious domain, and we gain access to it using consciousness. Mere consciousness of some event helps store a recognizable memory of it, and when we experience it again, we can distinguish it accurately from millions of other experiences.

The ability to access unconscious processes via consciousness applies also to the vast number of unconscious automatisms that can be triggered by conscious events, including eye movements evoked by conscious visual motion, the spontaneous inner speech that often accompanies reading, the hundreds of muscle groups that control the vocal tract, and those that coordinate and control other skeletal muscles. None of these automatic neuronal mechanisms are conscious in any detail under normal circumstances. Yet they are triggered by conscious events. This triggering function is hampered when the conscious input is degraded by distraction, fatigue, somnolence, sedation, or low signal fidelity.

Consciousness seems to be needed to access at least four great bodies of unconscious knowledge: the lexicon of natural language, autobiographical memory, the automatic routines that control actions, and even the detailed firing of neurons and neuronal populations, as shown in biofeedback training. Consciousness seems to create access to vast unconscious domains of expert knowledge and skill.

Survey of Cognitive Theories of Consciousness

Overview

In the survey that follows, cognitive theories of consciousness are organized into three broad categories based on the architectural characteristics of the models. The first group consists of examples of *information-processing theories that emphasize modular processes*: Johnson-Laird's Operating System Model of Consciousness, Schacter's Model of Dissociable Interactions and Conscious Experience (DICE), Shallice's Supervisory System, Baddeley's Early and Later Models of Working Memory, and Schneider and Pimm-Smith's Message-Aware Control Mechanism. The second group includes *network theories that explain consciousness as*

patterns of system-wide activity: Pribram's Holonomic Theory, Tononi and Edelman's Dynamic Core Hypothesis, and Walter Freeman's Dynamical Systems Approach. The third group includes globalist models that combine aspects of information-processing theories and network theories: Baars' Global Workspace Theory, Franklin's IDA as an implementation of GW theory, and Dehaene's Global Neuronal Network Theory. Theories have been selected that represent the recent history of cognitive modeling of consciousness from the 1970s forward and that account in some way for the evidence described above concerning the capability contrasts of conscious and unconscious processes.

Information-Processing Theories That Emphasize Modular Processes: Consciousness Depends on a Kind of Processing

Theories in this group emphasize the information-processing and action control aspects of the cognitive architecture. They tend to explain consciousness in terms of "flow of control" or flow of information among specialist modules.

JOHNSON-LAIRD'S OPERATING SYSTEM MODEL OF CONSCIOUSNESS

Johnson-Laird's (1988) operating system model of consciousness emphasizes its role in controlling mental events, such as directing attention, planning and triggering action and thought, and engaging in purposeful self-reflection. Johnson-Laird proposes that the cognitive architecture performs parallel processing in a system dominated by a control hierarchy. His system involves a collection of largely independent processors (finite state automata) that cannot modify each other but that can receive messages from each other; each initiates computation when it receives appropriate input from any source. Each passes messages up through the hierarchy to the operating system that sets goals for the subsystems. The operating system does not have access to the detailed operations of the subsystems – it receives

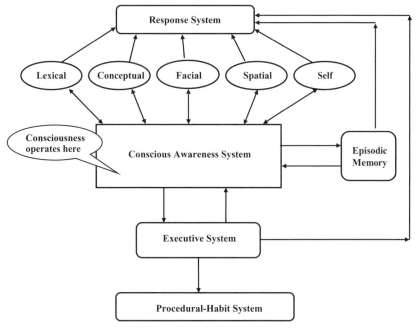

Figure 8.1. Schacter's Dissociable Interactions and Conscious Experience
(DICE) Model. (Redrawn from Schacter, 1990). Phenomenal awareness depends
on intact connections between the conscious awareness system and the
individual knowledge modules or episodic memory. The conscious awareness
system is the gateway to the executive system, which initiates voluntary action.

only their output. Likewise, the operating
system does not need to specify the details
of the actions it transmits to the processors –
they take in the overall goal, abstractly specified, and elaborate it in terms of their own
capabilities.

In this model, conscious contents reside
in the operating system or its working memory. Johnson-Laird believes his model can
account for aspects of action control, self-
reflection, intentional decision making, and
other metacognitive abilities.

SCHACTER'S MODEL OF DISSOCIABLE
INTERACTIONS AND CONSCIOUS
EXPERIENCE (DICE)

Accumulating evidence regarding the neuropsychological disconnections of processing from consciousness, particularly implicit
memory and anosagnosia, led Schacter
(1990) to propose his Dissociable Interactions and Conscious Experience (DICE)
model (see Figure 8.1): "The basic idea motivating the DICE model . . . is that the pro-

cesses that mediate conscious identification
and recognition – that is, phenomenal awareness in different domains – should be sharply
distinguished from modular systems that
operate on linguistic, perceptual, and other
kinds of information" (pp. 160–161, 1990).

Like Johnson-Laird's model, Schacter's
DICE model assumes independent memory
modules and a lack of conscious access to
details of skilled/procedural knowledge. It
is primarily designed to account for memory dissociations in normally functioning and
damaged brains. There are two main observations of interest. First, with the exception of coma and stupor patients, failures
of awareness in neuropsychological cases
are usually restricted to the domain of the
impairment; these patients do not have difficulty generally in gaining conscious access to
other knowledge sources. Amnesic patients,
for example, do not necessarily have trouble reading words, whereas alexic individuals do not necessarily have memory
problems.

Second, implicit (non-conscious) memory of unavailable knowledge has been demonstrated in many conditions. For example, name recognition is facilitated in prosopagnosic patients when the name of the to-be-identified face is accompanied by a matching face – even though the patient does not consciously recognize the face. Numerous examples of implicit knowledge in neuropsychological patients who do not have deliberate, conscious access to the information are known (see Milner & Rugg, 1992). These findings suggest an architecture in which various sources of knowledge function somewhat separately, because they can be selectively lost; these knowledge sources are not accessible to consciousness, even though they continue to shape voluntary action.

In offering DICE, Schacter has given additional support to the idea of a conscious capacity in a system of separable knowledge sources, specifically to explain spared implicit knowledge in patients with brain damage. DICE does not aim to explain the limited capacity of consciousness or the problem of selecting among potential inputs. In agreement with Shallice (see below) the DICE model suggests that the primary role of consciousness is to mediate voluntary action under the control of an executive. However, the details of these abilities are not spelled out, and other plausible functions are not addressed.

SHALLICE'S SUPERVISORY SYSTEM

Shallice shares an interest in the relation of volition and consciousness with James (1890), Baars (1988), and Mandler (1975). In 1972, Shallice argued that psychologists needed to have a rationale for using the data of introspection. To do so, he said, the nature of consciousness would need to be considered. He thought at that time that the selector of input to the dominant action system had properties that corresponded to those of consciousness. Shallice's early theory (1978) focused on conscious selection for a dominant action system, the set of current goals that work together to control thought and action. Subsequently, Shallice (1988; Norman & Shallice, 1980) modified and refined the theory to accommodate a broader range of conscious functions (depicted in Figure 8.2).

Shallice describes an information-processing system as having five characteristics. First, it consists of a very large set of specialized processors, with several qualifications on their "modularity":

- There is considerable variety in the way the subsystems can interact.
- The overall functional architecture is seen as partly innate and partly acquired, as with the ability to read.
- The "modules" in the system include not only input processors but also specialized information stores, information management specialists, and other processing modules.

Second, a large set of action and thought schemata can "run" on the modules. These schemata are conceptualized as well-learned, highly specific programs for routine activities, such as eating with a spoon, driving to work, etc. Competition and interference between currently activated schemata are resolved by another specialist system, CONTENTION SCHEDULING, which selects among the schemata based on activation and lateral inhibition. Contention scheduling acts during routine operations.

Third, a SUPERVISORY SYSTEM functions to modulate the operation of contention scheduling. It has access to representations of operations, of the individual's goals, and of the environment. It comes into play when operation of routinely selected schemata does not meet the system's goals; that is, when a novel or unpredicted situation is encountered or when an error has occurred.

Fourth, a LANGUAGE SYSTEM is involved that can function either to activate schemata or to represent the operations of the supervisory system or specialist systems.

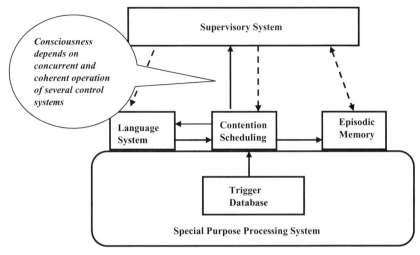

Figure 8.2. Shallice's Supervisory System Model of Conscious Processing. Solid arrows represent obligatory communications; dashed arrows represent optional communications. (Drawn from Shallice, 1988.)

Fifth, more recently an EPISODIC MEMORY component containing event-specific traces has been added to the set of control processes.

Thus, the supervisory system, contention scheduling, the language system, and episodic memory all serve higher-level or control functions in the system. As a first approximation, one of these controllers or several together might be taken as the "conscious part" of the system. However, as Shallice points out, consciousness cannot reside in any of these control systems taken individually. No single system is either necessary or sufficient to account for conscious events. Consciousness remains even when one of these control systems is damaged or disabled, and the individual control systems can all operate autonomously and unconsciously. Instead, Shallice suggests that consciousness may arise on those occasions where there is concurrent and coherent operation of several control systems on representations of a single activity. In this event, the contents of consciousness would correspond to the flow of information between the control systems and the flow of information and control from the control systems to the rest of the cognitive system.

Shallice's (1988) model aims primarily to "reflect the phenomenological distinc-tions between willed and ideomotor action" (p. 319). Shallice identifies consciousness with the control of coherent action subsystems and the emphasis on the flow of information among the subsystems.

BADDELEY'S EARLY AND LATER MODELS OF WORKING MEMORY: 1974 TO 2000
Working memory is a functional account of the workings of temporary memory (as distinct from long-term memory). Baddeley and Hitch (1974) first proposed their multi-component model of working memory (WM) as an advance over single-store models, such as Short-Term Memory (STM; Atkinson & Shiffrin, 1968). The original WM model was simple, composed of a central executive with two subsystems, the phonological loop and the visuospatial sketchpad. WM was designed to account for short duration, modality-specific, capacity-limited processing of mnemonic information. It combined the storage capacity of the older STM model with an executive process that could "juggle" information between two slave systems and to and from long-term memory. The evolving model of WM has been successful in accounting for behavioral and neurological findings in normal participants and in neuropsychological patients. From the beginning, working memory,

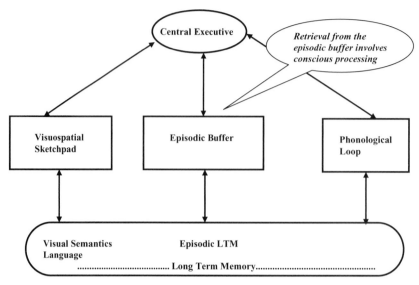

Figure 8.3. Baddeley's Model of Working Memory. This model incorporates the episodic buffer. (Adapted from Baddeley, 2000.)

particularly transactions between the central executive and the subsystems, has been associated with conscious and effortful information processing. However, these were rarely stated in terms of the question of consciousness as such.

Recently, Baddeley (2000, 2001) has proposed an additional WM component called the episodic buffer (see Figure 8.3 for a depiction of the most recent model). This addition to the WM architecture means that the central executive now becomes a purely attentional, controlled process while multimodal information storage devolves onto the episodic buffer. The episodic buffer "comprises a limited capacity system that provides temporary storage of information held in a multimodal code, which is capable of binding information from the subsidiary systems, and from long-term memory, into a unitary episodic representation. Conscious awareness is assumed to be the principal mode of retrieval from the buffer" (Baddeley, 2000, p. 417). Baddeley (2001) believes that the binding function served by the episodic buffer is "the principal biological advantage of consciousness" (p. 858).

Conscious processing in WM appears to reside in the *transactions* of the central executive with the episodic buffer (and perhaps

with the visuospatial sketchpad and phonological loop), in which the central executive controls and switches attention while the episodic buffer creates and makes available multimodal information.

Baddeley's episodic buffer resembles other models of consciousness in its ability to briefly hold multimodal information and to combine many information sources into a unitary representation. A major difference between WM and other models is that WM was not proposed as a model of consciousness in general. It is restricted to an accounting of mnemonic processes – both conscious and unconscious. In addition, the WM model does not assume that contents of the episodic buffer are "broadcast" systemwide as a means of organizing and recruiting other non-mnemonic processes. No account is given of the further distribution of information from the episodic buffer, once it is accessed by the central executive.

SCHNEIDER AND PIMM-SMITH'S
MESSAGE-AWARE CONTROL MECHANISM
Schneider and Pimm-Smith have proposed a model of cognition that incorporates a conscious processing component and allows widespread distribution of information from specialist modules (Schneider &

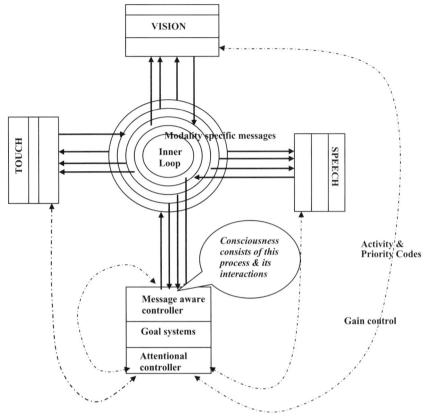

Figure 8.4. A simplified view of Schneider and Pimm-Smith's Message-Aware Control Mechanism.

Pimm-Smith, 1997). The model is an attempt to capture the adaptive advantage that consciousness adds to cognitive processing. According to Schneider and Pimm-Smith, "consciousness may be an evolutionary extension of the attentional system to modulate cortical information flow, provide awareness, and facilitate learning particularly across modalities. . . . According to [the] model, consciousness functions to monitor and transmit global messages that are generally received by the whole system serially to avoid the cross-talk problem (pp. 65, 76)." The conscious component of this model, the conscious controller, stands between the serially arriving high-level messages forwarded by the specialist modules and the attentional controller, which sends scalar messages back to the specialist modules according to their value in ongoing activities. The conscious controller is not privy

to all information flowing within the system, examining data only after lower-level modules have produced invariant codes and selecting those messages that relate to currently active goals. Figure 8.4 illustrates the functional relations among components in Schneider and Pimm-Smith's model.

The message-aware control mechanism model of consciousness depends on localized specialist processors – auditory, haptic, visual, speech, motor, semantic, and spatial modules – which each have their own internal levels of processing. These modules feed their output codes serially and separately to other modules and to the consciousness controller via an inner loop. According to Schneider and Pimm-Smith, "Consciousness is a module on the inner loop that receives messages that evoke symbolic codes that are utilized to control attention to specific goals (p. 72)." Furthermore, "consciousness is the message awareness of the controller. . . . This message awareness allows control decisions based on the specific messages transmitted in the network rather than labeled line activity or priority codes from the various modules in the network (pp. 72–73)." There is also information sharing through non-conscious channels. The attentional controller receives activity and priority signals from specialist modules marking the availability of input through non-conscious outer loop channels, and it sends gain control information back to the specialists.

Schneider and Pimm-Smith's model has several notable characteristics: (1) information is widely distributed; (2) particular content is created by localized specialist modules, which themselves have levels of processing; (3) consciousness is identified as a separable and separate function that modulates the flow of information throughout the system: and (4) access to consciousness is through reference to goal systems. This elegant model accounts for the modulation of attention by reference both to current goals and to the recruitment of specialist modules in the service of goals through the global distribution of conscious messages.

Network Theories That Explain Consciousness as Patterns of System-Wide Activity

Although the information-processing theories in the previous section attempted to model consciousness in terms of the selection and interactions of specialized, semiautonomous processing modules, the theories described in the present section build on networks and connectionist webs. It may be helpful to view the information-processing models as macroscopic and the network theories as microscopic. It is possible that the activities attributed to modules in the information-processing models could, in fact, be seen to be carried out by connectionist networks when viewed microscopically. As we examine network theories, it should be kept in mind that, although network theorists often make comparisons with and assumptions about networks composed

of neurons, most network theories, including those described here, are in fact functional descriptions of activities that are presumed to occur in the brain. Brain networks themselves are not directly assessed.

PRIBRAM'S HOLONOMIC THEORY

Karl Pribram has developed a holographic theory (more recently, holonomic theory) of brain function and conscious processing (Pribram, 1971). He has built on the mathematical formulations of Gabor (1946), combining holography and communication theory. To state things in simple form, the holonomic model postulates that the brain is holograph machine. That is, the brain handles, represents, stores, and reactivates information through the medium of "wetware" holograms. Holograms, though complex mathematically, are familiar to us as the three-dimensional images found on credit cards and driver's licenses. Such a hologram is a photograph of an optical interference pattern, which contains information about intensity and phase of light reflected by an object. When illuminated with a coherent source of light, it will yield a diffracted wave that is identical in amplitude and phase distribution with the light reflected from the original object. The resulting three-dimensional image is what we see on our credit cards.

In a holonomic model, Pribram says, information is encoded by wave interference patterns rather than by the binary units (BITs) of computer science. Rather than encoding sensory experience as a set of features that are then stored or used in information processing, sensory input in the holonomic view is encoded as the interference pattern resulting from interacting waves of neuronal population activity. Stated in the language of visual perception, the retinal image is understood to be coded by a spatial frequency distribution over visual cortex, rather than by individual features of the visual scene. Because the surface layer of the cortex consists of an entangled "feltwork" of dendrites, Pribram suggests that cortex represents a pattern of spatial correlations in a continuous dendritic medium, rather than by discrete, localized features expressed by the firing of single neurons. The dendritic web of the surface layers of cortex is the medium in which representations are held. Functionally, it is composed of oscillating graded potentials. In Pribram's view, nerve impulses have little or no role to play in the brain web. However, dendritic potentials obviously trigger axonal firing when they rise above a neuronal threshold, so that long-distance axons would also be triggered by the dendro-dendritic feltwork.

The holonomic model finds support in the neuropsychological finding that focal brain damage does not eliminate memory content. Further, it is consistent with the fact that each sensory neuron tends to prefer one type of sensory input, but often fires to different inputs as well. Neurons do not operate individually but rather participate in different cell assemblies or active populations at different times; the cell assemblies are themselves "kaleidoscopic."

In a hologram, the information necessary to construct an image is inherently distributed. Pribram explains how the notion of distributed information can be illustrated with a slide projector (Pribram & Meade, 1999). If one inserts a slide into the projector and shows a "figure," then removes the lens from the front of the projector, there is only a fuzzy bright area. There is nothing, "no-*thing*," visible on the screen. But that does not mean there is no information in the light. The information can be re-visualized by placing a pair of reading glasses into the light beam. On the screen, one now again sees the "figure" in the slide. Putting two lenses of the eyeglasses in the beam, one sees two "figures" that can be made to appear in any part of the bright area. Thus any part of the beam of light carries all the information needed to reconstruct the picture on the slide. Only resolution is lost.

According to the holonomic theory, no "receiver" is necessary to "view" the result of the transformation (from spectral holographic to "image"), thus avoiding the homunculus problem (the problem of infinite regress, of a little man looking at the visual scene, which in turn needs a little

man in its brain, and so on ad infinitum). It is the activity of the dendro-dendritic web that gives rise to the experience. Correspondingly, remembering is a form of re-experiencing or re-constructing the initial sensory input, perhaps by cuing a portion of the interference pattern. Finally, Pribram believes that we *"become aware of* our conscious experience due to a delay between an incoming pattern of signals before it matches a previously established outgoing pattern" (Pribram & Meade, 1999, p. 207).

Pribram's holonomic model is attractive in that it can account for the distributed properties of memory and sensory processing. The model makes use of the dendritic feltwork that is known to exist in the surface layer of cortex. However, the model fails to help us understand the difference between conscious and unconscious processing or the unique functions of consciousness *qua* consciousness. Pribram has not treated consciousness as a variable and cannot tell us what it is that consciousness adds to the cognitive system.

EDELMAN AND TONONI'S DYNAMIC CORE HYPOTHESIS

Edelman and Tononi's theory of consciousness (2000; see also Tononi & Edelman, 1998) combines evidence from large-scale connectivities in the thalamus and cortex, behavioral observation, and mathematical properties of large-scale brain-like networks. Based on neuropsychological and lesion evidence that consciousness is not abolished by losses of large volumes of brain tissue (Penfield, 1958), Edelman and Tononi reject the idea that consciousness depends on participation of the whole brain in an undifferentiated fashion. At the same time, they, along with many others, reject the view that consciousness depends only on local properties of neurons. Tononi and Edelman cite, for example, PET evidence suggesting that moment-to-moment awareness is highly correlated with increasing functional connectivity between diverse cortical regions (see, for example, McIntosh, Rajah, & Lobaugh, 1999). In other words, the same cortical areas seem to participate in conscious experience or not at different times, depending on their current dynamic connectivity. This idea is resonant with Pribram's description of neural assemblies being "kaleidoscopic."

The fundamental idea in Edelman and Tononi's theory is the *dynamic core hypothesis*, which states that conscious experience arises from the activity of an ever-changing functional cluster of neurons in the thalamocortical complex of the brain, characterized by high levels of differentiation as well as strong reciprocal, re-entrant interaction over periods of hundreds of milliseconds. The particular neurons participating in the dynamic core are ever changing while internal integration in the dynamic core is maintained through re-entrant connections. The hypothesis highlights the functional connections of distributed groups of neurons, rather than their local properties; thus, the same group of neurons may at times be part of the dynamic core and underlie conscious experience, whereas at other times, this same neuronal group will not be part of the dynamic core and will thus be part of unconscious processing. Consciousness in this view is not a thing or a brain location but rather, as William James argued, a process, occurring largely within the re-entrant meshwork of the thalamocortical system.

Edelman and Tononi (2000) take issue with Baars' (1988) concept of global broadcasting (see below) as a way to explain capacity limits and wide access in conscious processing. In Baars' view, the information content of any conscious state is apparently contained in the single message that is being broadcast to specialist systems throughout the brain at any one moment; information content is thus limited but widely distributed. Edelman and Tononi (2000) argue for an alternative view: that the information is not in the message, but rather in the number of system states that can be brought about by global interactions within the system itself. In place of Baars' broadcasting or theater metaphor, they offer an alternative:

[A] better metaphor would be . . . a riotous parliament trying to make a decision, signaled by its members raising their hands.

Before counting occurs, each member of parliament is interacting with as many other members as possible not by persuasive rhetoric . . . but by simply pushing and pulling. Within 300 msec., a new vote is taken. How informed the decision turns out to be will depend on the number of diverse interactions within the parliament. In a totalitarian country, every member will vote the same; the information content of constant unanimity is zero. If there are two monolithic groups, left and right, such that the vote of each half is always the same, the information content is only slightly higher. If nobody interacts with anyone, the voting will be purely random, and no information will be integrated within the system. Finally, if there are diverse interactions within the parliament, the final vote will be highly informed (Edelman & Tononi, 2000, pp. 245–246).

A constantly changing array of ever-reorganized mid-sized neuronal groups in a large system of possible groups has high levels of complexity and integration – characteristics of conscious states. Within this model, unconscious specialist systems are local, non-integrated neuronal groups. How the unconscious specialists are recruited into the dynamic core is not made entirely clear in the theory. Edelman and Tononi say that consciousness in its simplest form emerges in the re-entrant linkage between current perceptual categorization and value-category memory (short-term and long-term memory). Conscious experience is actually a succession of 100-ms snapshots of the current linkages that constitute the "remembered present."

Perhaps Baars and Tononi and Edelman are not so different on closer examination. Baars' (1988, 1998) model supposes that there is reciprocal exchange between the global workspace (GW) and specialist systems in the architecture of consciousness; it is difficult to see why this is different from the re-entrant linkages between neuronal groups in Edelman and Tononi's theory. Furthermore, within any one "snapshot" of the system, the pattern of dynamically linked elements in Baars' model – GW and specialists that are able to receive the particular

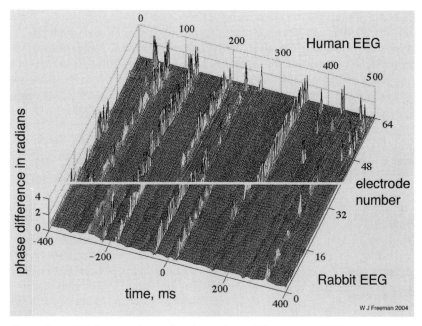

Figure 8.5. A Hilbert analysis of analytic phase differences in EEG across cortical surface measured over 400 ms in rabbit and human conscious processing. Phase differences are calculated in the beta band (12–30 Hz) for human EEG and in the gamma band (20–50 Hz) for the rabbit EEG. (With permission of the author.) (See color plates.)

message that has been disseminated – looks very much like the pattern of momentarily linked neuronal groups in Tononi and Edelman's model that are recruited in the moment depending on environmental input and value memories. Two strengths of the Tononi and Edelman model are its acknowledgment of long-distance connectivity among specialist brain regions as a characteristic of conscious processes, as well as the dynamic nature of these connections.

WALTER FREEMAN'S DYNAMICAL SYSTEMS
APPROACH: FRAMES IN THE CINEMA
Like Pribram, Walter Freeman has worked to obtain empirical support for a cortex-wide dynamic neural system that can account for behavioral data observed in conscious activities. Freeman's Dynamical Systems approach to consciousness is built on evidence for repetitive global phase transitions occurring simultaneously over multiple areas of cortex during normal behavior (see Figure 8.5 Freeman, 2004;

Freeman & Rogers, 2003). Freeman and his colleagues have analyzed EEGs, recorded from multiple high-density electrode arrays (64 electrodes) fixed on the cortex of rabbits and on the scalp of human volunteers. An index of synchronization was obtained for pairs of signals located at different cortical sites to detect and display epochs of mutual engagement between pairs. The measure was adapted to derive an index of global synchronization among all four cortices (frontal, parietal, temporal, and occipital) – global epochs of phase stabilization ("locking") involving all cortices under observation during conscious perceptual activity. These epochs of phase locking can be seen in the "plateaus" of global coherence in Figure 8.5. The peaks in the figure indicate momentary, global decoherence.

To understand Freeman's findings, we have to understand the basics of Hilbert analysis as it is shown in Figure 8.5. Hilbert analysis of the EEGs recorded from electrode arrays produces a three-dimensional graphical representation. In it, the phase difference between pairs of cortical electrodes within a particular EEG band is plotted against time (in milliseconds) and spatial location (represented by electrode number). The resulting plot is called a Hilbert space. The Hilbert space can be read like a topographical map. In the plot in Figure 8.5, we can see many flat plateau areas lying between peaked ridges. The plateaus represent time periods (on the order of 50 ms) in which many pairs of EEG signals from different cortical locations are found to be in phase with each other. The ridges represent very short intervals when all of these pairs are simultaneously out of phase, before returning to phase locking. These out-of-phase or decoherent epochs appear to be non-conscious transitions between moments of consciousness.

According to Freeman (2004),

The EEG shows that neocortex processes information in frames like a cinema. The perceptual content is found in the phase plateaus from rabbit EEG; similar content is predicted to be found in the plateaus of human scalp EEG. The phase jumps show the shutter. The resemblance across a 33-fold difference in width of the zones of coordinated activity reveals the self-similarity of the global dynamics that may form Gestalts (multisensory percepts). (Caption to cover illustration, p. i)

Freeman's data are exciting in their ability to map the microscopic temporal dynamic changes in widespread cortical activity during conscious perception – something not found in other theories. As a theory of consciousness, the dynamical systems approach focuses primarily on describing conscious perceptual processing at the cortical level. It does not attempt to explain the conscious/non-conscious difference or the function of consciousness in the neuropsychological system. With many neurocognitive theorists, we share Freeman's question about how the long-range global state changes come about virtually simultaneously. Freeman's hypothesis of Self-organized Criticality suggests that the neural system is held in a state of dynamic ten-

sion that can change in an all-or-none fashion with small environmental perturbations. He says "a large system can hold itself in a near-unstable state, so that by a multitude of adjustments it can adapt to environments that change continually and unpredictably" (Freeman & Rogers, 2003, p. 2882).

Globalist Models That Combine Aspects of Information-Processing Theories and Network Theories

BAARS' GLOBAL WORKSPACE THEORY

A theater metaphor is the best way to approach Baars' Global Workspace (GW) theory (Baars, 1988, 1998, 2001). Consciousness is associated with a global "broadcasting system" that disseminates information widely throughout the brain. The metaphor of broadcasting explicitly leaves open the precise nature of such a wide influence of conscious contents in the brain. It could vary in signal fidelity or degree of distribution, or it might not involve "labeled line" transmission at all, but rather activation passing, as in a neural network. Metaphors are only a first step toward explicit theory, and some theoretical decision points are explicitly left open.

If consciousness is involved with widespread distribution or activation, then conscious capacity limits may be the price paid for the ability to make single momentary messages act upon the entire system for purposes of coordination and control. Because at any moment there is only one "whole system," a global dissemination capacity must be limited to one momentary content. (There is evidence that the duration of each conscious "moment" may be on the order of 100 ms, one-tenth of a second – see Blumenthal, 1977).

Baars develops these ideas through seven increasingly detailed models of a global workspace architecture, in which many parallel unconscious experts interact via a serial, conscious, and internally consistent global workspace (1983, 1988). Global workspace architectures or their functional equivalents have been developed by cognitive scientists since the 1970s; the notion of a "blackboard" where messages from specialized subsystems can be "posted" is common to the work of Baars (1988), Reddy and Newell (1974), and Hayes-Roth (1984). The global workspace framework has a family resemblance to the well-known integrative theories of Herbert A. Simon (General Problem Solver or EPAM), Allan Newell (SOAR, 1992), and John R. Anderson (ACT*, 1983). Architectures much like this have also seen some practical applications. GW theory is currently a thoroughly developed framework, aiming to explain an large set of evidence. It appears to have fruitful implications for a number of related topics, such as spontaneous problem solving, voluntary control, and even the Jamesian "self" as agent and observer (Baars, 1988; Baars, Ramsoy, & Laureys, 2003).

GW theory relies on three theoretical constructs: unconscious specialized processors, a conscious Global Workspace, and unconscious contexts.

The first construct is the *unconscious specialized processor*, the "expert" of the psychological system. We know of hundreds of types of "experts" in the brain. They may be single cells, such as cortical feature detectors for color, line orientation, or faces, or entire networks and systems of neurons, such as cortical columns, functional areas like Broca's or Wernicke's areas, and basal ganglia. Like human experts, unconscious specialized processors may sometimes be quite "narrow-minded." They are highly efficient in limited task domains and able to act independently or in coalition with each other. Working as a coalition, they do not have the narrow capacity limitations of consciousness, but can receive global messages. By "posting" messages in the global workspace (consciousness), they can send messages to other experts and thus recruit a coalition of other experts. For routine missions they may work autonomously, without conscious involvement, or they may display their output in the global workspace, thus making their work conscious and available throughout the system. Answering a question like "What is your mother's maiden name?" requires a mission-specific coalition

of unconscious experts, which report their answer to consciousness. Figure 8.6 shows the major constructs in GW theory and the functional relations among them.

The second construct is, of course, the *global workspace (GW)* itself. A global workspace is an architectural capability for system-wide integration and dissemination of information. It is much like the podium at a scientific meeting. Groups of experts at such a meeting may interact locally around conference tables, but to influence the meeting as a whole any expert must compete with others, perhaps supported by a coalition of like-minded experts, to reach the podium, whence global messages can be broadcast. New links among experts are made possible by global interaction via the podium and can then spin off to become new local processors. The podium allows novel expert coalitions to form that can work on new or difficult problems, which cannot be solved by established experts and committees. Tentative solutions to problems can then be globally disseminated, scrutinized, and modified.

The evidence presented in Tables 8.2 and 8.3 falls into place by assuming that information in the global workspace corresponds to conscious contents. Because conscious experience seems to be oriented primarily toward perception, it is convenient to imagine that preperceptual processors – visual, auditory, or multimodal – can compete for access to a brain version of a global workspace. For example, when someone speaks to us, the speech stream receives preperceptual processing through the speech specialist systems before the message in the speech stream is posted in consciousness. This message is then globally broadcast to the diverse specialist systems and can become the basis for action, for composing a verbal reply, or for cuing related memories. In turn, the outcome of actions carried out by expert systems can also be monitored and returned to consciousness as action feedback.

Obviously the abstract GW architecture can be realized in a number of different ways in the brain, and we do not know at this point which brain structures provide

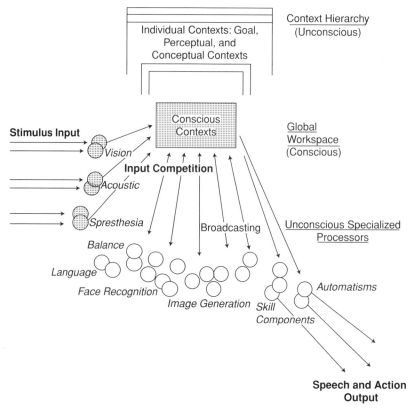

Figure 8.6. Global Workspace Architecture: Basic constructs and their relations.

the best candidates. Although its brain correlates are not entirely clear at this time, there are possible neural analogs, including the reticular and intralaminar nuclei of the thalamus, one or more layers of cortex, long-range cortico-cortico connections, and/or active loops between sensory projection areas of cortex and the corresponding thalamic relay nuclei. Like other aspects of GW theory, such neural candidates provide testable hypotheses (Newman & Baars, 1993). All of the neurobiological proposals described in this chapter provide candidates (Freeman, 2004; Dehaene & Naccache, 2001; Edelman & Tononi, 2000; Tononi & Edelman, 1998), and some have been influenced by GW theory.

Context, the third construct in GW theory, refers to the powers behind the scenes of the theater of mind. Contexts are coalitions of expert processors that provide the director, playwright, and stagehands behind the scenes of the theater of mind. They can

be defined functionally as knowledge structures that constrain conscious contents without being conscious themselves, just as the playwright determines the words and actions of the actors on stage without being visible. Conceptually, contexts are defined as pre-established expert coalitions that can evoke, shape, and guide global messages without themselves entering the global workspace.

Contexts may be momentary, as in the way the meaning of the first word in a sentence shapes an interpretation of a later word like "set," or they may be long lasting, as with life-long expectations about love, beauty, relationship, social assumptions, professional expectations, worldviews, and all the other things people care about. Although contextual influences shape conscious experience without being conscious, contexts can also be set up by conscious events. The word "tennis" before "set" shapes the interpretation of "set," even when "tennis" is already gone from consciousness. But "tennis" was

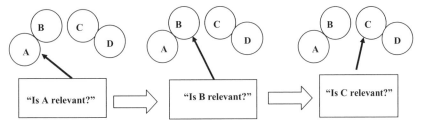

Figure 8.7. A naive processor approach to environmental novelty.

initially conscious and needed to be conscious to create the unconscious context that
made sense of the word "set."

Thus conscious events can set up unconscious contexts. The reader's ideas about
consciousness from years ago may influence
his or her current experience of this chapter,
even if the memories of the earlier thoughts
do not become conscious again. Earlier experiences typically influence current experiences as contexts, rather than being brought
to mind. It is believed for example that
a shocking or traumatic event earlier in
life can set up largely unconscious expectations that may shape subsequent conscious
experiences.

SHANAHAN: AN ANSWER TO THE
MODULARITY AND FRAME PROBLEMS
Shanahan and Baars (2005) suggest that
the global workspace approach may provide a principled answer to the widely discussed "modularity" and "frame" problems.
Fodor (1983) developed the view that cognitive functions like syntax are performed
by "informationally encapsulated" modules,
an idea that has some empirical plausibility. However, as stated by Fodor and
others, modules are so thoroughly isolated
from each other that it becomes difficult to
explain how they can be accessed, changed,
and mobilized on behalf of general goals.
A closely related difficulty, called the frame
problem, asks how an autonomous agent can
deal with novel situations without following
out all conceivable implications of the novel
event. For example, a mobile robot on a cart
may roll from one room to another. How
does it know what is new in the next room
and what is not, without explicitly testing

out all features of the new environment?
This task quickly becomes computationally prohibitive. Shanahan and Baars (2005)
point out that the following:

*What the global workspace architecture
has to offer . . . is a model of information
flow that explains how an informationally unencapsulated process can draw on
just the information that is relevant to the
ongoing situation without being swamped
by irrelevant rubbish. This is achieved
by distributing the responsibility for deciding relevance to the parallel specialists
themselves. The resulting massive paral-
lelism confers great computational advantage without compromising the serial flow
of conscious thought, which corresponds to
the sequential contents of the limited capacity global workspace. . . .*

Compare the naive processor's inefficient
approach (depicted in Figure 8.7) with a
massively parallel and distributed global
workspace approach (depicted in Figure 8.8)
to dealing with environmental novelty.

The key point here is that the GW
architecture permits widely distributed local
responsibility for processing global signals.
As was pointed out above, conscious and
non-conscious process differ in their capabilities – they are two different modes of processing that, when combined, offer powerful
adaptive possibilities.

FRANKLIN'S IDA AS AN IMPLEMENTATION
OF GW THEORY
Stan Franklin and colleagues (Franklin, 2001;
Franklin & Graesser, 1999) have developed
a practical implementation of GW theory
in large-scale computational agents to test
its functionality in complex practical tasks.

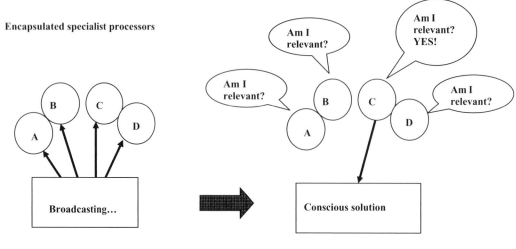

Figure 8.8. A GW approach to environmental novelty.

IDA, or Intentional Distribution Agent, the current implementation of the extended GW architecture directed by Franklin, is designed to handle a very complex artificial intelligence task normally handled by trained human beings (see Chapter 7). The particular domain in this case is interaction among U.S. Navy personnel experts and sailors who move from job to job. IDA interacts with sailors via e-mail and is able to combine numerous regulations, sailors' preferences, and time, location, and travel considerations into human-level performance. Although it has components roughly corresponding to human perception, memory, and action control, the heart of the system is a GW architecture that allows input messages to be widely distributed, so that specialized programs called "codelets" can respond with solutions to centrally posed problems (see Figure 8.9).

Franklin writes, "The fleshed out global workspace theory is yielding hopefully testable hypotheses about human cognition. The architectures and mechanisms that underlie consciousness and intelligence in humans can be expected to yield information agents that learn continuously, adapt readily to dynamic environments, and behave flexibly and intelligently when faced with novel and unexpected situations"

(see http://csrg.cs.memphis.edu). Although agent simulations do not prove that GW architectures exist in the brain, they demonstrate their functionality. Few if any large-scale cognitive models can be shown to actually perform complex human tasks, but somehow the real cognitive architecture of the brain does so. In that respect, the test of human-level functionality is as important in its way as any other source of evidence.

DEHAENE'S GLOBAL NEURONAL
NETWORK THEORY

Stanislas Dehaene and his colleagues (Dehaene & Naccache, 2001; Dehaene, Kerszberg, & Changeux, 1998) have recently proposed a *global neuronal workspace theory* of consciousness based on psychological and neuroscientific evidence quite similar to that cited by Baars and others. Dehaene and colleagues identify three empirical observations that any theory of consciousness must be able to account for: "namely (1) a considerable amount of processing is possible without consciousness, (2) attention is a prerequisite of consciousness, and (3) consciousness is required for some specific cognitive tasks, including those that require durable information maintenance, novel combinations of operations, or

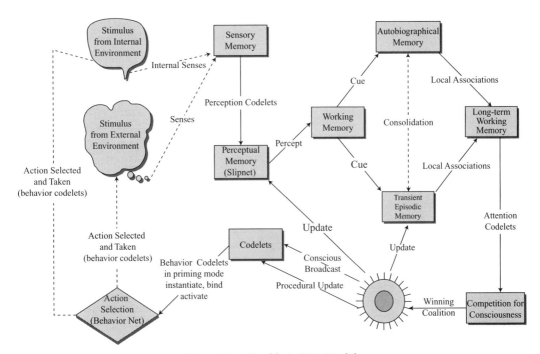

Figure 8.9. Franklin's IDA Model.

the spontaneous generation of intentional behavior" (p. 1). The Dehaene and Naccache model depends on several well-founded assumptions about conscious functioning.

The first assumption is that non-conscious mental functioning is modular. That is, many dedicated non-conscious modules can operate in parallel. Although arguments remain as to whether psychological modules have immediate correlates in the brain, Dehaene and Naccache (2001) say that the "automaticity and information encapsulation acknowledged in cognitive theories are partially reflected in modular brain circuits." They tentatively propose that "a given process, involving several mental operations, can proceed unconsciously only if a set of adequately interconnected modular systems is available to perform each of the required operations" (p. 12; see Figure 8.10).

The second assumption, one shared by other cognitive theories, is that controlled processing requires an architecture in addition to modularity that can establish links among the encapsulated processors. Dehaene et al. (1998) argue that a distributed neural system or "workspace" with

long-distance connectivity is needed that can "potentially interconnect multiple specialized brain areas in a coordinated, though variable manner" (p. 13).

The third assumption concerns the role of attention in gating access to consciousness. Dehaene and Naccache (2001) review evidence in support of the conclusion that considerable processing can occur without attention, but that attention is required for information to enter consciousness (Mack & Rock, 1998). They acknowledge a similarity between Michael Posner's hypothesis of an attentional amplification (Posner, 1994) and their own proposal. Attentional amplification explains the phenomena of consciousness as due to the orienting of attention, which causes increased cerebral activation in attended areas and a transient increase in their efficiency. According to Dehaene & Nacache (2001),

[I]nformation becomes conscious . . . if the neural population that represents it is mobilized by top-down attentional amplification into a brain-scale state of coherent activity that involves many neurons distributed throughout the brain. The long-distance

connectivity of these 'workspace neurons' can, when they are active for a minimal duration, make the information available to a variety of processes including perceptual categorization, long-term memorization, evaluation, and intentional action. (p. 1)

An implication of the Dehaene and Naccache model is that consciousness has a granularity, a minimum duration of long-distance integration, below which broadcast information will fail to be conscious.

It is worth noting a small difference between Baars' version of global workspace and that of Dehaene and colleagues. (Dehaene & Naccache, 2001; Dehaene et al., 1998). They believe that a separate attentional system intervenes with specialized processors to allow their content to enter the global workspace and become conscious. Baars (1998), on the other hand, sees attention not as a separate system but rather as the name for the process of gaining access to global workspace by reference to long-term or current goals. Clearly, further refinement is needed here in thinking through what we mean by attention or an attentional system as separate from the architecture of consciousness, in this case, varieties of GW architecture.

Dehaene, Sargent, and Changeux (2003) have used an implementation of the global neuronal workspace model to successfully simulate attentional blink. Attentional blink is a manifestation of the all-or-none characteristic of conscious processing observed when participants are asked to process two successive targets, T_1 and T_2. When T_2 is presented between 100 and 500 ms after T_1, the ability to report it drops, as if the participants' attention had "blinked." During this blink, T_2 fails to evoke a P300 potential but still elicits event-related potentials associated with visual and semantic processing (P1, N1, and N400). Dehaene et al. (2003) explain,

Our simulations aim at clarifying why some patterns of brain activity are selectively associated with subjective experience. In short, during the blink, bottom-up activ-

ity, presumably generating the P1, N1, and N400 waveforms, would propagate without necessarily creating a global reverberant state. However, a characteristic neural signature of long-lasting distributed activity and g-band emission, presumably generating the P300 waveform, would be associated with global access. (p. 8520)

In the simulation, a network modeled the cell assemblies evoked by T_1 and T_2 through four hierarchical stages of processing, two separate perceptual levels and two higher association areas. The network was initially assigned parameters that created spontaneous thalamocortical oscillations, simulating a state of wakefulness. Then, the network was exposed to T_1 and T_2 stimulation at various interstimulus intervals (ISI). T_1 excitation was propagated bottom-up through all levels of the processing hierarchy, followed by top-down amplification signals that resulted in sustained firing of T_1 neurons. Dehaene et al. (2003) hypothesized that this sustained firing and global broadcasting may be the neural correlate of conscious reportability. In contrast, the activation evoked by T_2 depended closely on its timing relative to T_1. For simultaneous and long ISIs, T_2 excitation evoked sustained firing. Importantly, when T_2 was presented during T_1-elicited global firing, it evoked activation only in the low-level perceptual assemblies and resulted in no global propagation. Dehaene and colleagues conclude that this detailed simulation has provided tentative links between subjective reports and "objective physiological correlates of consciousness on the basis of a neurally plausible architecture" (2003, p. 8524).

The Globalist Argument: An Emerging Consensus

In the last two decades, a degree of consensus has developed concerning the role of consciousness in the neuropsychological architecture. The general position is that consciousness operates as a distributed and flexible system offering nonconscious expert systems global accessibility

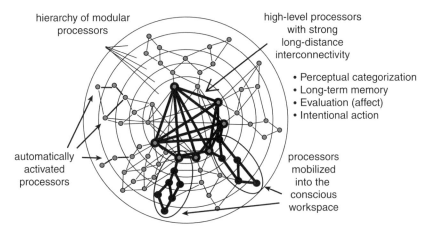

hierarchy of modular processors

high-level processors with strong long-distance interconnectivity

• Perceptual categorization
• Long-term memory
• Evaluation (affect)
• Intentional action

automatically activated processors

processors mobilized into the conscious workspace

Figure 8.10. A global neuronal network account of conscious processes (Dehaene & Naccache, 2001, p. 27).

to information that has a high concurrent value to the organism. Although consciousness is not itself an executive system, a global distribution capacity has obvious utility for executive control, in much the way that governments can control nations by influencing nation-wide publicity.

Excerpted below are the views of prominent researchers on consciousness revealing considerable agreement.

• **Baars (1983)**: "Conscious contents provide the nervous system with *coherent, global information.*"

• **Damasio (1989)**: "Meaning is reached by time-locked multiregional retroactivation of widespread fragment records. Only the latter records can become contents of consciousness."

• **Freeman (1991)**: "The activity patterns that are formed by the (sensory) dynamics *are spread out over large areas of cortex*, not concentrated at points. Motor outflow is likewise *globally distributed....* In other words, the pattern categorization does not correspond to the selection of a key on a computer keyboard but to an induction of a global activity pattern." [Italics added]

• **Tononi and Edelman (1998)**: "The dynamic core hypothesis avoids the category error of assuming that certain local, intrinsic properties of neurons have,

in some mysterious way, a privileged correlation with consciousness. Instead, this hypothesis accounts for fundamental properties of conscious experience by linking them to global properties of particular neural processes" (p. 1850).

• **Llinas et al. (1998)**: "... *the thalamus represents a hub from which any site in the cortex can communicate with any other such site or sites....* temporal coincidence of specific and non-specific thalamic activity generates the functional states that characterize human cognition" (p. 1841).

• **Edelman and Tononi (2000)**: "When we become aware of something...it is as if, suddenly, many different parts of our brain were privy to information that was previously confined to some specialized subsystem.... the wide distribution of information is guaranteed mechanistically by *thalamocortical and corticocortical reentry*, which facilitates the interactions among distant regions of the brain" (pp. 148–149).

• **Dennett (2001)**: "Theorists are converging from quite different quarters on a version of the global neuronal workspace model of consciousness" (p. 42).

• **Kanwisher (2001)**: "... it seems reasonable to hypothesize that awareness of a particular element of perceptual information must entail not just a strong enough neural representation of information, but also access to that information by most of the rest of the mind/brain."

- **Dehaene and Naccache (2001):** "We propose a theoretical framework...the hypothesis of a global neuronal workspace....We postulate that this global availability of information through the workspace is what we subjectively experience as the conscious state."

- **Rees (2001):** "One possibility is that activity in such a distributed network might reflect stimulus representations gaining access to a 'global workspace' that constitutes consciousness" (p. 679).

- **John et al. (2001):** "Evidence has been steadily accumulating that information about a stimulus complex is distributed to many neuronal populations dispersed throughout the brain."

- **Varela et al. (2001):** "...the brain ...transiently settling into a globally consistent state...[is] the basis for the unity of mind familiar from everyday experience."

- **Cooney and Gazzaniga (2003):** "Integrated awareness emerges from modular interactions within a neuronal workspace....The presence of a large-scale network, whose long-range connectivity provides a neural workspace through which the outputs of numerous, specialized, brain regions can be interconnected and integrated, provides a promising solution...In the workspace model, outputs from an array of parallel processors continually compete for influence within the network" (p. 162).

- **Block (2005):** "Phenomenally conscious content is what differs between experiences as of red and green, whereas access conscious content is information which is 'broadcast' in the global workspace."

Although debate continues about the functional character of consciousness, the globalist position can be summarized in the following propositions:

1. The architecture of consciousness comprises numerous, semi-autonomous specialist systems, which interact in a dynamic way via a global workspace.

2. The function of the workspace is global distribution of information in order to recruit resources in the service of current goals.

3. Specialist systems compete for access to the global workspace; information that achieves access to the workspace obtains system-wide dissemination.

4. Access to the global workspace is "gated" by a set of active contexts and goals.

DISSENTING VIEWS

The globalist position argues that consciousness provides a momentary unifying influence for a complex system through global distribution and global access. In this sense, consciousness may be said to have unity. Alternative views chiefly depart from the globalist position on this point. They argue, in one way or another, that consciousness is not fundamentally unified.

One alternative view is that of Marcel (1993) who argued for "slippage" in the unity of consciousness. In part, he made his case based on his observation that different reporting modalities (blink vs. finger tap) could produce conflicting reports about conscious experience. Marcel took this to indicate that consciousness itself is not unified in any real sense.

Marcel's argument bears some similarity to Dennett's "multiple drafts" argument (Dennett, 1991). Dennett pointed to the puzzle posed by the phi phenomenon. In the phi phenomenon, we observe a green light and a red light separated by a few degrees in the field of vision as they are flashed in succession. If the time between flashes is about one second or less, the first light flashed appears to move to the position of the second light. Further, the color of the light appears to change midway between the two lights. The puzzle is explaining how we could see the color change before we see the position of the second light. Dennett hypothesizes that the mind creates different analyses or narratives (multiple drafts) of the scene at different moments from different sensory inputs. All of the accounts are available to influence behavior and report. A given scene can give rise to more than one interpretation. In contrast, with global broadcasting models, Dennett says there is no single version of the scene available anywhere in the psychological system.

Simiarly, Zeki (2001, 2003) has argued on neurological grounds that there is "disunity" in the neural correlates of consciousness. With many others, Zeki notes that the visual brain consists of many separate, functionally specialized processing systems that are autonomous with respect to one another. He then supposes that activity at each node reaches a perceptual endpoint at a different time, resulting in a perceptual asynchrony in vision. From there, Zeki makes the inference that activity at each node generates a microconsciousness. He concludes that visual consciousness is therefore distributed in space and time, with an organizing principle of abstraction applied separately within each processing system. It remains to be seen whether Zeki's microconsciousnesses can be examined empirically via contrastive analysis and whether the microconsciousnesses are necessarily conscious or simply potentially conscious. The globalist position would argue that all neural processing is potentially conscious, depending on the needs and goals of the system. Clearly, this is a point for future discussion.

Conclusion

This chapter suggests that current cognitive theories have much in common. Almost all suggest an architectural function for consciousness. Although the reader's experience of *these words* is no doubt shaped by feature cells in visual cortex, including word recognition regions, such local activity is not sufficient for consciousness of the words. In addition, some widespread functional brain capacity is widely postulated. Direct functional imaging evidence for that hypothesis is now abundant. In that sense, most current models are globalist in spirit, which is not to deny, of course, that they involve multiple

local specializations as well. It is the *integration* of local and global capacities that marks these theoretical approaches. Given the fact that scientists have only "returned to consciousness" quite recently, this kind of convergence of opinion is both surprising and gratifying.

Future work should focus on obtaining neuroscientific evidence and corresponding behavioral observations that can address global access as the distinguishing feature of consciousness. Additional work could contribute simulations of the kind offered by Dehaene, Sargent, and Changeux (2003), supporting the plausibility of all-or-none global propagation of signals as models of the neurocognitive architecture of consciousness, and of Franklin, documenting the real-world potential of global workspace architectures as intentional agents. Further work is also needed to resolve the issue of whether consciousness is all-or-none, as Baars, Freeman, and Dehaene and his colleagues argue, or whether there are multiple drafts (Dennett, 1991) or microconsciousnesses (Zeki, 2001, 2003) playing a role in the architecture of consciousness (see also Chapter 15).

References

Atkinson, R., & Shiffrin, R. (1968). Human memory: A proposed system and its control processes. In K. W. Spence & J. Spence (Eds.), *Advances in the psychology of learning and motivation: Research and theory* (Vol. 2, pp. 89–195). New York: Academic Press.

Baars, B. J. (1983). Conscious contents provide the nervous system with coherent, global information. In R. J. Davidson, G. Schwartz, & D. Shapiro (Eds.), *Consciousness and self-regulation* (Vol. 3, pp. 41–79). New York: Plenum Press.

Baars, B. J. (1988). *A cognitive theory of consciousness.* New York: Cambridge University Press.

Baars, B. J. (1998). *In the theater of consciousness: The workspace of the mind.* New York: Oxford University Press.

Baars, B. J. (2002). The conscious access hypothesis: Origins and recent evidence. *Trends in Cognitive Sciences*, 6(1), 47–52.

Baars, B. J., Ramsoy, T., & Laureys, S. (2003). Brain, conscious experience, and the observing self. *Trends in Neurosciences, 26*(12), 671–675.

Baddeley, A. D. (2000). The episodic buffer: A new component of working memory? *Trends in Cognitive Sciences, 4*, 417–423.

Baddeley, A. D. (2001). Is working memory still working? *American Psychologist, 56*(11), 851–864.

Baddeley, A. D., & Hitch, G. J. (1974). Working memory. In G. A. Bower (Ed.), *Recent advances in learning and motivation* (Vol. 8, pp. 47–90). New York: Academic Press.

Basmajian, J. (1979). *Biofeedback: Principles and practice for the clinician.* Baltimore: Williams & Wilkins.

Block, N. (2005). Two neural correlates of consciousness, *Trends in Cognitive Sciences, 9*, 46–52.

Blumenthal, A. L. (1977). *The process of cognition.* Englewood Cliffs, NJ: Prentice-Hall.

Cooney, J. W., & Gazzaniga, M. S. (2003). Neurological disorders and the structure of human consciousness. *Trends in Cognitive Sciences, 7*(4), 161–165.

Damasio, A. (1989). Time-locked multiregional retroactivation: A systems-level proposal for the neural substrates of recall and recognition. *Cognition, 33*, 25–62.

Dehaene, S., & Naccache, L. (2001). Towards a cognitive neuroscience of consciousness: Basic evidence and a workspace framework. *Cognition, 79*, 1–37.

Dehaene, S., Kerszberg, M., & Changeux, J. P. (1998). A neuronal model of a global workspace in effortful cognitive tasks. *Proceedings of the National Academy of Sciences USA, 95*, 14529–14534.

Dehaene, S., Sargent, C., & Changeux, J. (2003). A neuronal network model linking subjective reports and objective physiological data during conscious perception. *Proceedings of the National Academy of Science USA, 100*(14), 8520–8525.

Dennett, D. (1991). *Consciousness explained.* Boston: Back Bay Books.

Dennett, D. E. (2001). Are we explaining consciousness yet? *Cognition, 79*, 221–237.

Edelman, G. M., & Tononi, G. (2000). *A universe of consciousness.* New York: Basic Books.

Fodor, J. (1983). *The modularity of mind: An essay on faculty psychology.* Cambridge, MA: MIT Press.

Franklin, S. (2001). Conscious software: A computational view of mind. In V. Loia & S. Sessa (Eds.), *Soft computing agents: New trends for designing autonomous systems* (pp. 1–46). Berlin: Springer (Physica-Verlag).

Franklin, S., & Graesser, A. (1999). A software agent model of consciousness. *Consciousness and Cognition, 8*, 285–301.

Freeman, W. J. (2004). Origin, structure, and role of background EEG activity. Part 1. Analytic amplitude. *Clinical Neurophysiology, 115*, 2077–2088 (Including issue cover).

Freeman, W. J. (1991). The physiology of perception. *Scientific American, 264*, 78–85.

Freeman, W. J., & Rogers, L. (2003). A neurobiological theory of meaning in perception. Part V. Multicortical patterns of phase modulation in gamma EEG. *International Journal of Bifurcation and Chaos in Applied Sciences and Engineering, 13*(10), 2867–2887.

Gabor, D. (1946, November). Theory of communication. *Journal of the IEE (London), 93*(26), 429–457.

Hayes-Roth, B. (1984). A blackboard model of control. *Artificial Intelligence, 16*, 1–84.

James, W. (1890). *The principles of psychology.* New York: Holt.

John, E. R., Prichep L. S., Kox, W., Valdes-Sosa, P., Bosch-Bayard, J., Aubert, E., Tom, M., di Michele, F., & Gugino, L. D. (2001). Invariant reversible qeeg effects of anesthetics. *Consciousness and Cognition, 10*, 165–183.

Johnson-Laird, P. N. (1988). A computational analysis of consciousness. In A. Marcel & E. Bisiach (Eds.), *Consciousness in contemporary science* (pp. 357–368). Oxford: Clarendon.

Kanwisher, N. (2001). Neural events and perceptual awareness. *Cognition, 79*, 89–113.

Llinas, R., Ribary, U., Contreras, D., & Pedroarena, C. (1998). The neuronal basis of consciousness. *Philosophical Transaction of the Royal Society, London, 353*, 1841–1849.

Mack, A., & Rock, I. (1998). *Inattentional blindness.* Cambridge, MA: MIT Press.

Marcel, A. (1993). Slippage in the unity of consciousness. *CIBA Foundation Symposium. 174*, 168–80; discussion, pp. 180–186.

Mandler, G. A. (1975). Consciousness: Respectable, useful and probably necessary. In R. Solso (Ed.), *Information processing and cognition: The Loyola Symposium*. Hillsdale, NJ: Erlbaum.

McIntosh, A. R., Rajah, M. N., & Lobaugh, N. J. (1999). Interactions of prefrontal cortex in relation to awareness in sensory learning. *Science*, 284, 1531–1533.

Milner, B., & Rugg, M. D. (Eds.), (1992). *The neuropsychology of consciousness*. London: Academic Press.

Newell, A. (1992). SOAR as a unified theory of cognition: Issues and explanations. *Behavioral and Brain Sciences*, 15(3), 464–492.

Newman, J., & Baars, B. J. (1993). A neural attentional model for access to consciousness: A global workspace perspective. *Concepts in Neuroscience*, 4(2), 255–290.

Norman, D. A., & Shallice, T. (1980). *Attention to action: Willed and automatic control of behaviour* (CHIP Report No. 99). San Diego: University of California.

Penfield, W. (1958). *The excitable cortex in conscious man*. Springfield, IL: Thomas.

Posner, M. (1994). Attention: The mechanisms of consciousness. *Proceedings of the National Academy of Sciences USA*, 91, 7398–7403.

Pribram, K. H. (1971). *Languages of the brain: Experimental paradoxes and principles in neuropsychology*. Englewood Cliffs, NJ: Prentice-Hall.

Pribram, K., & Meade, S. D. (1999). Conscious awareness: Processing in the synaptodendritic web. *New Ideas in Psychology*, 17(205), 214.

Reddy, R., & Newell, A. (1974). Knowledge and its representations in a speech understanding system. In L. W. Gregg (Ed.), *Knowledge and cognition* (pp. 256–282). Potomac, MD: Erlbaum.

Rees, G. (2001). Seeing is not perceiving. *Nature Neuroscience*, 4, 678–680.

Schacter, D. L. (1990). Toward a cognitive neuropsychology of awareness: Implicit knowledge and anosognosia. *Journal of Clinical and Experimental Neuropsychology*, 12(1), 155–178.

Schneider, W., & Pimm-Smith, M. (1997). Consciousness as a message-aware control mechanism to modulate cognitive processing. In J. D. Cohen & J. W. Schooler (Eds.), *Scientific approaches to consciousness* (pp. 65–80). Mahwah, NJ: Erlbaum.

Shallice, T. (1972). The dual functions of consciousness. *Psychological Review*, 79(5), 383–393.

Shallice, T. (1978). The dominant action system: An information processing approach to consciousness. In K. S. Pope & J. L. Singer (Eds.), *The stream of consciousness: Scientific investigations into the flow of experience* (pp. 117–157). New York: Plenum.

Shallice, T. (1988). Information-processing models of consciousness: Possibilities and problems. In A. J. Marcel & E. Bisiach (Eds.), *Consciousness in contemporary science* (pp. 305–333). Oxford: Clarendon Press.

Shanahan, M., & Baars, B. J. (2005), Applying global workspace theory to the frame problem. *Cognition*, 98, 157–176.

Standing, L. (1973). Learning 10,000 pictures. *Quarterly Journal of Experimental Psychology*, 525, 207–222.

Tononi, G., & Edelman, G. (1998). Consciousness and complexity. *Science*, 282, 1846–1851.

Varela, F., Lachaux, J., Rodriguez, E., & Martinerie, J. (2001). The brainweb: Phase synchronization and large-scale integration. *Nature Neuroscience*, 2, 229–239.

Zeki, S. (2001). Localization and globalization in conscious vision. *Annual Review of Neuroscience*, 24, 57–86.

Zeki, S. (2003). The disunity of consciousness. *Trends in Cognitive Science*, 7(5), 214–218.

CHAPTER 9

Behavioral, Neuroimaging, and Neuropsychological Approaches to Implicit Perception

Daniel J. Simons, Deborah E. Hannula, David E. Warren, and Steven W. Day

Abstract

For well over a century, the idea that rich, complex perceptual processes can occur outside the realm of awareness has either intrigued or exasperated researchers. Although popular notions of implicit processing largely focus on the practical consequences of implicit perception, the empirical literature has addressed more focused, basic questions: (a) Does perception occur in the absence of awareness? (b) what types of information are perceived in the absence of awareness? and (c) what forms of processing occur outside of awareness? This chapter discusses recent advances in the study of implicit perception, considering the ways in which they do and do not improve on earlier approaches. We contrast the conclusions a skeptic and a believer might draw from this literature. Our review considers three distinct but related classes of evidence: behavioral studies, neuroimaging, and brain-damaged patient case studies. We conclude by arguing that qualitative differences between perceptual mechanisms are interesting regardless of whether or not they demonstrate the existence of perception without awareness.

Introduction

... [T]here is now fairly widespread agreement that perception can occur even when we are unaware that we are perceiving. (Merikle & Joordens, 1997a, p. 219)

Unconscious cognition is now solidly established in empirical research (Greenwald, 1992, p. 766).

My contention is that most, if not all, claims for SA/CI [semantic activation without conscious identification] in dichotic listening, parafoveal vision, and visual masking are in reality based on the failure of these experimental methods to reveal whether or not the meaning of the critical stimulus was available to consciousness at the time of presentation (Holender, 1986, p. 3; brackets added)

For well over a century, the idea that rich, complex perceptual processes can occur outside the realm of awareness has either intrigued or exasperated researchers. The notion that many of the cognitive processes that occur with awareness might also occur without awareness is both exciting and frightening; it would not only reveal untapped or unnoticed powers of mind but would also raise the specter of undesirable mechanisms of mind. If implicit cognitive processes are rich and powerful, then given the right tools, we might be able to exploit these resources – we might be capable of using far more information than reaches awareness. Alternatively, implicit processes might counteract our explicitly held attitudes, thereby changing our behavior without our knowledge (Greenwald & Banaji, 1995).

This fear has its roots in psychodynamic views of unconscious processing that attribute many psychological problems to unconscious conflicts and motivations (Freud, 1966). It manifests itself in the fear that subliminal advertising can affect our beliefs against our will (Pratkanas, 1992). These desires and fears drive a large market in subliminal self-help tapes as well as public outcry about apparent attempts at implicit influence. Yet, evidence for subliminal persuasion of this sort is scant at best (Greenwald, Spangenberg, Pratkanis, & Eskenazi, 1991; Pratkanis, Eskenazi, & Greenwald, 1994).

Although popular notions of implicit processing focus largely on the practical consequences of implicit perception, the empirical literature has addressed more focused, basic questions: (a) Does perception occur in the absence of awareness? (b) What types of information are perceived in the absence of awareness? and (c) What forms of processing occur outside of awareness? Few researchers question the idea that some perceptual processing occurs outside of awareness. For example, we are not usually aware of the luminance changes that lead to the perception of motion. Rather, we just perceive the motion itself. Some processing of the luminance boundaries occurs outside of awareness even if we are aware of the stimulus itself.

The more subtle, more interesting question is whether the meaning of a stimulus is processed without awareness. This problem is of fundamental theoretical importance because any evidence of semantic processing in the absence of awareness strongly supports late-selection models of attention and awareness (Deutsch & Deutsch, 1963). Presumably, implicit processes occur independent of explicit attentional selection, so if the meaning of a stimulus can be perceived implicitly, selective attention is not necessary for semantic processing. Each of these questions, at its core, asks how implicit perception is like explicit perception.

For more than a century, strong claims for the existence of complex perceptual processes in the absence of awareness have been dismissed on methodological grounds. In one early study, for example, observers viewed a card with a letter or digit on it, but their viewing distance was such that the character was hard to see – it was reported to be blurry, dim, or not visible at all. Although subjects could not consciously report the nature of the stimulus, they accurately guessed whether it was a letter or digit, and they could even guess its identity better than chance (Sidis, 1898). This lack of a clear conscious percept combined with better performance on an indirect, guessing task might provide evidence for implicit perception. However, alternative interpretations that require no implicit perception are equally plausible. For example, observers might simply be more conservative when asked to produce the name of a digit or letter than they would be when making a forced-choice decision (see Azzopardi & Cowey, 1998, for a similar argument about blindsight). This bias alone could account for better performance on a forced-choice task even if there were no difference in conscious perception. Moreover, the forced-choice task might just be a more sensitive measure of conscious awareness, raising the possibility that the dissociation between the two tasks is a dissociation within conscious perception rather than between conscious and non-conscious perception. Finally, the measure of awareness – the ability to recognize the character from a distance – might be inadequate as an assessment of awareness, leaving open the possibility that some conscious perception had occurred.

This example illustrates some of the weaknesses inherent in many studies of implicit perception. Although the behavioral and methodological tools for studying implicit perception became far more sophisticated toward the end of the 20th century, and despite some claims to the contrary (e.g., Greenwald, 1992; Merikle, Smilek, & Eastwood, 2001), the controversy over the mere existence of implicit perception persists (Dulany, 2004). Often, the same data are taken by some as convincing support for the existence of implicit perception and by others as unpersuasive (see the critique and responses in Holender, 1986).

In fact, theoretical reviews of the existing literature often arrive at strikingly different conclusions. Whereas Holender (1986) concludes that most demonstrations of implicit semantic processing are unconvincing, others consider the converging support for implicit effects to be overwhelming (e.g., Greenwald, 1992). In part, these divergent conclusions simply reflect different default assumptions. "Skeptics" assume the absence of implicit perception unless definitive evidence supports its presence. "Believers" assume the presence of implicit perception given converging evidence, even if none of the evidence is strictly definitive. At its core, the debate often devolves into little more than arguments over parsimony or over the criteria used to infer implicit processing.

The goal of this chapter is not to resolve this controversy. Nor is it to provide a thorough review of this century-old debate. Rather, we discuss recent advances in the study of implicit perception, considering the ways in which they do and do not improve on earlier approaches. We also contrast the conclusions a skeptic and a believer might draw from this literature. Since the mid-1980s, claims about implicit perception have become more nuanced, focusing less on the mere existence of the phenomenon and more on the nature of the information that might be implicitly perceived and on the mechanisms underlying implicit perception. Our review considers three distinct but related classes of evidence: behavioral studies, neuroimaging, and brain-damaged patient case studies.

Limits on the Scope of our Chapter

Given the availability of many excellent and comprehensive reviews/critiques of the early literature on implicit perception (e.g., Greenwald, 1992; Holender, 1986; Merikle, 1992), our chapter focuses primarily on the theoretical and methodological innovations introduced in recent years. Many disciplines include claims about implicit processing, and incorporating all of them in a single overview would be impractical. Instead, we highlight claims for implicit perceptual or semantic processing of discrete stimuli, largely overlooking implicit skill learning, artificial grammar learning, or other forms of procedural knowledge that might well be acquired without awareness. Our neglect of these areas does not imply any denigration of the evidence for implicit perception they have produced. Although we limit our review to the possibility of semantic processing without awareness and closely related questions, we also consider recent arguments about how best to study implicit perception. Finally, we discuss how qualitative differences in the nature of perceptual processing may be of theoretical significance even without a clear demonstration that processing occurs entirely outside of awareness.

Early Evidence for and against Implicit Perception

Claims for and against implicit perception received extensive empirical attention starting in the late 1950s, with sentiment in the field vacillating between acceptance and skepticism. Many early studies used a dichotic listening method in which observers attend to a stream of auditory information in one ear and verbally shadow that content while simultaneously ignoring another stream in their other ear (Cherry, 1953; Moray, 1959; Treisman, 1960, 1964). If the ignored channel is actually unattended and information from the ignored channel intrudes into awareness, then the ignored information must have been processed implicitly. With this technique, observers occasionally hear their own name in an ignored channel (Moray, 1959), and they sometimes momentarily shift their shadowing to the ignored channel when the auditory information presented to each ear is swapped (Treisman, 1960). If ignored information is truly unattended, then these findings support a strong form of late selection in which unattended information is processed to a semantic level and sometimes intrudes on awareness. Other studies using this dichotic listening technique found evidence for skin conductance changes to words in the ignored stream that were semantically related to shock-associated words (Corteen & Dunn, 1974; Corteen & Wood, 1972).

Of course, the central assumption underlying these conclusions is that an ignored auditory stream is entirely unattended. If participants periodically shift attention to the "ignored" channel, then the influence of semantic information in the ignored channel might occur only with attention. To conclude that perception of the semantic content of the ignored stream was caused by implicit processing, the experimenter must show that it did not result from explicit shifts of attention at the time of presentation. The difficulty of verifying that attention was never directed to the ignored channel gave meat to skeptics (Holender, 1986). In fact, this critique can be applied far more generally. The vast majority of studies of implicit perception, including those in the past 20 years, rely on what is commonly known as the dissociation paradigm (Merikle, 1992). To demonstrate the existence of implicit perception, experimenters must eliminate explicit perception and show that something remains. Applied to dichotic listening, the task for experimenters is to rule out attention to the ignored stream and then show that something remains. The failure of the premise, that ignored means unattended in the case of dichotic listening, weakens evidence for implicit perception. Given the fairly convincing critiques of evidence based on dichotic listening (Holen-der, 1986), few current studies use dichotic listening to study implicit perception. The dissociation paradigm, however, remains the dominant approach to studying implicit perception.

The modern use of the dissociation paradigm in the study of implicit perception was triggered by a series of experiments in the 1980s in which masked primes were shown to influence subsequent processing of a target stimulus even though observers did not notice the primes themselves (Marcel, 1983a, b). This approach is a classic application of the dissociation paradigm: Rule out explicit awareness of the prime stimulus and show that it still influences performance in some other way. Importantly, these studies provided evidence not just that something was perceived but also that its meaning was processed as well; the semantic content of a masked word served as a prime for a subsequent response to a semantically related target word (Marcel, 1983b). Many of the recent behavioral studies of implicit perception use variants of this masked prime approach.

The Merits and Assumptions of the Dissociation Paradigm

The dissociation paradigm is particularly appealing because it requires no assumptions about the nature of or mechanisms underlying implicit perception. In its purest form, the dissociation paradigm has a single constraint: Implicit perception can only be demonstrated in the absence of explicit perception. Superficially, this constraint seems straightforward. Yet, it amounts to confirming the null hypothesis – demonstrating no effect of explicit perception – leading some to decry its usefulness for the study of implicit perception (Merikle, 1994). Given that most claims for implicit perception are based on the dissociation paradigm, most critiques of these claims focus on violations of this assumption, often producing evidence that some contribution from explicit perception can explain the residual effects previously attributed to implicit perception (see Mitroff, Simons, & Franconeri, 2002 for a similar approach to critiquing evidence for implicit change detection). For example, critiques of dichotic listening studies typically focus on the possibility that subjects devoted some attention to the ignored stream (Holender, 1986). Given that the dichotic listening paradigm does not allow a direct measure of the absence of attention to the ignored channel, it cannot rule out the possibility that explicit factors contributed to perception of ignored material. More subtle critiques raise the possibility that observers were momentarily aware of ignored or unattended material, but rapidly forgot that they had been aware. If so, then explicit awareness could have contributed to any effects of the "unattended" information. This "amnesia" critique has been applied more recently to such phenomena as inattentional blindness (Wolfe, 1999).

To meet the assumptions of the dissociation paradigm, the measure of explicit perception must be optimally sensitive – it must exhaustively test for explicit influences on performance (Merikle, 1992). If a maximally sensitive measure reveals no evidence of explicit perception, we can be fairly confident that explicit factors did not contribute to performance, and any residual effects can be attributed to implicit perception. This criterion was adopted by some of the more ardent critics of the early literature on implicit perception (Holender, 1986). The explicit measure most typically adopted as a sensitive measure of explicit awareness is the simple detection of the presence of a stimulus. If subjects cannot detect the presence of a stimulus, but the stimulus still has an effect on performance, then that effect presumably resulted from implicit perception. In essence, this approach served as the basis for early work on priming by masked stimuli (Marcel, 1983b). If a masked prime cannot be detected but still influences performance, it must have been implicitly perceived. Note, however, that even a simple detection task may not exhaustively measure all explicit influences on performance and residual effects of a stimulus that cannot be detected might still reflect some explicit processing (Merikle, 1992). Later

in this chapter, we review new behavioral studies that attempt to meet these assumptions, but we also note that few of them systematically demonstrate null explicit sensitivity to the presence of a stimulus.

Objective vs. Subjective Thresholds – What Is the Appropriate Measure of Awareness?

One recurring controversy in the study of implicit perception concerns whether the threshold for explicit perception should be based on an *objective* or *subjective* criterion. Although the notion of thresholds has fallen into disfavor with the advent and increased use of signal detection theory in perception (e.g., Green & Swets, 1966; Macmillan, 1986), it still has intuitive appeal in the study of implicit perception. Later in this chapter, we discuss the importance of using signal detection to measure awareness in the dissociation paradigm. In the interim, the distinction between *objective* and *subjective* thresholds may still provide a useful rubric for explaining some of the continuing controversy in the literature.

Most studies of implicit perception rely on a subjective threshold to determine whether or not a stimulus was explicitly noticed; this approach assumes that observers will report a stimulus if they are aware of it and will not if they are unaware. For example, blindsight patients typically will report no awareness of a static stimulus presented to their blind field – the stimulus falls below their subjective threshold. Use of the subjective threshold to rule out explicit perception essentially treats the observers' reports of their experiences as the best indicator of whether or not they were aware. More often than not, studies using subjective thresholds are interested in performance on each individual trial, and claims about implicit perception are derived from the consequences of a specific stimulus that was not reported. This approach is appealing because it treats observers' reports of their own mental states as more legitimate than the experimenter's ability to infer the observers' state of awareness.

Objective thresholds are based on the idea that observers might fail to report a stimulus even if they did have some explicit awareness of its presence. They might adopt a conservative response bias, responding only when certain. Or, they might lack the means to express verbally what they saw. Typically, objective thresholds are measured across a large set of trials. The threshold is that level at which a stimulus is *not perceivable* rather than simply not perceived. In using this approach, experimenters often adopt the standard of null explicit sensitivity required by the dissociation paradigm, assuming that if a series of trials show that a stimulus is not explicitly perceivable, then it could not have been perceived on any individual trial. Consequently, any influence of that stimulus must be implicit. Unlike the subjective threshold approach, objective thresholds are based on the idea that observers might fail to report a stimulus not because they failed to see it, but because they adopted too conservative a criterion. This approach does not trust an observer's subjective experience on a given trial to be a true indicator of his or her actual awareness of the stimulus.

In a sense, the terms "objective" and "subjective" are misnomers. Both approaches rely on explicitly reported experiences, so both are subjective. Subjective thresholds are based on experiences on each trial, whereas objective thresholds are based on cumulative experiences across a larger number of trials. Thus, when measuring an objective threshold, responses on individual trials do not necessarily indicate the observer's awareness. Observers might respond that they saw a stimulus, but that response might simply be a guess. Similarly, they might report having no conscious experience, even if they had some vague inkling that failed to surpass their criterion for responding. Finding an objective threshold requires manipulating the stimulus presentation such that judgments of stimulus presence are no better than chance over a reasonably large number of trials. If responding to this sort of explicit task is at chance over a set of trials, then presumably any individual trial is based on a guess. The challenge is in demonstrat-

ing that explicit performance was truly random and not somewhat better than would be expected by chance alone.

The use of an objective threshold can lead to a seeming paradox wherein subjects report no conscious awareness of a stimulus (i.e., they report guessing) but still show better than chance performance; their performance exceeds the objective threshold even though their subjective impression is of guessing. Those adopting a subjective threshold approach would conclude that such a finding reflects implicit processing. The appeal of relying on the subjective threshold is that it accepts what the observer reports at face value. If observers report no awareness, then they had no awareness. However, it also relies on the observer's ability to judge probabilities over a series of trials. Does the subjective report of no awareness really mean that they were guessing, or does it mean that they *thought* that they were guessing? If observers lack precise access to their probability of a successful response, they might report guessing when in actuality, they were slightly, but significantly performing better than chance.

The primary difference between the objective threshold approach and the subjective threshold approach is that objective thresholds take the responsibility of estimating the extent of correct responding out of the observer's hands. Rather than relying on the observer to estimate when they felt they were guessing, the objective threshold technique objectively measures when their actual performance across a series of trials reflected guessing. In both cases, though, the subjects' subjective experience on a given trial contributes to the assessment of whether or not they were aware of the critical stimulus.

Differential reliance on objective and subjective thresholds underlies much of the controversy in the field. Most critiques of implicit perception simply show that performance actually exceeded an objective threshold for awareness. For example, evidence for implicit priming from masked stimuli was premised on the idea that subjects were no better than chance at determining whether or not the prime was present – explicit performance did not exceed the objective threshold (Marcel, 1983b). Yet critiques of those studies suggest that the thresholds were not adequately measured and that explicit performance might well have exceeded threshold (Holender, 1986). Even studies that do attempt to demonstrate that explicit detection was no better than chance rarely meet the statistical requirements necessary to infer null explicit sensitivity (Macmillan, 1986). Many studies, especially those of patients, make no attempt to measure an objective threshold, but instead rely entirely on the observer's self-assessment of awareness, much as early behavioral studies did (e.g., Sidis, 1898). Such studies are open to the criticism that explicit perception might well affect performance even when subjects do not consciously report the presence of a stimulus.

As we discuss later in this chapter, this issue is only of importance when questioning whether or not an example of perception is entirely implicit. Finding a dissociation in the types of processing that occur above and below a subjective threshold would still be of theoretical (and practical) import even if explicit perception contributed to both types of processing. For example, in studies of inattentional blindness, observers view a single critical trial and quite often fail to notice the presence of salient but unexpected objects and events (Mack & Rock, 1998; Most et al., 2001; Simons, 2000; Simons & Chabris, 1999). When counting the total number of times one team of basketball players passes a ball and simultaneously ignoring another team of players passing a ball, approximately 50% of observers fail to notice a person in a gorilla suit who walks through the display (Simons & Chabris, 1999). The interesting aspect of these studies is that observers can fail to notice or consciously detect surprisingly salient unexpected events. Most people expect that they would notice such events, and the fact that they do not report objects as unusual as a gorilla is startling (see Levin,

Momen, Drivdahl, & Simons, 2000 for similar examples from the change blindness literature).

Unfortunately, the studies are not ideal for demonstrating implicit perception. Imagine, for instance, that observers in this study reported not noticing the gorilla, but then showed priming for the word "monkey." Would that provide evidence for implicit perception of the gorilla? The study uses the dissociation paradigm, and subjects subjectively report no awareness of a gorilla. This finding suggests that any priming effects might be implicit. However, observers might have had some awareness of the gorilla, or they might have had momentary awareness of some furry object, even if they failed to report noticing anything unusual. Given that the method only allows one critical trial and the "gorilla" is demonstrably perceivable (i.e., it is above the objective threshold), the possibility of some residual explicit awareness cannot be eliminated.

Arguments for implicit perception on the basis of such one-trial studies rest on the plausibility of the alternative explanations for the priming effects. As the measure of explicit awareness becomes less "objective" and more reliant on the observer's self-assessment, it is more likely to miss some aspect of explicit processing. The sufficiency of the measure of explicit awareness, regardless of whether it is considered objective or subjective, rests on the plausibility of the possibility that some explicit awareness was not tapped by the measure. Of course, even if the gorilla exceeded an objective threshold for awareness, this hypothetical finding would still be interesting because it would reveal a discrepancy between what people see and what they can explicitly report. Moreover, their surprise at having missed the gorilla suggests that their awareness of it likely was limited. Consequently, evidence for inattentional blindness may have important practical consequences even if some residual awareness of the unexpected event exists.

Rather than viewing the objective-subjective difference as a dichotomy, we prefer to characterize it as a continuum that varies along the dimension of the *experimenter's* confidence in the accuracy of the subjective judgments. With a subjective judgment on a single trial, the experimenter should lack confidence in the veracity of the observer's claim of no explicit awareness. One-trial approaches do not systematically eliminate the possibility that the stimulus was perceived and then forgotten, that some less-easily-reportable aspect of the stimulus was consciously perceived, or that the stimulus was explicitly detected and partially but not completely identified.

Critiques of the Dissociation Paradigm

Although the dissociation paradigm has intuitive appeal, some critics argue that the exhaustiveness requirement is a fatal shortcoming – that no task can fully satisfy the exhaustiveness assumption (Merikle, 1992). Even if a task were optimally sensitive to explicit perception and even if it showed null sensitivity, some other unmeasured aspect of explicit perception could still influence performance. Logically, this view is unassailable. Even if a task showed null sensitivity for all known explicit influences, it might neglect some as yet unknown and unmeasured explicit influence. Practically, however, if a task eliminates all known, plausible explicit influences, then claims of implicit perception might be more parsimonious than defaulting to some unknown explicit factor.

A second critique of the dissociation paradigm rests on the idea that no task measures just explicit or just implicit perception (Reingold & Merikle, 1988). Performance on any task involves a mixture of implicit and explicit influences. Consequently, finding null sensitivity on an "explicit" task might also eliminate implicit perception because the task likely measures aspects of both. By analogy, a sledgehammer to the head would eliminate all explicit awareness, but it also would eliminate most implicit effects on performance. Any manipulation that leads to null explicit sensitivity might simply be so draconian that no measure would be suffi-

ciently sensitive to detect any implicit processes.

This *exclusivity* critique is based on the premise that tasks do not provide a pure measure of either implicit or explicit perception. Whether or not this premise is valid, the exclusiveness critique carries less force than the exhaustiveness critique. The failure to use an exclusive measure of explicit awareness is one reason why studies using the dissociation paradigm might *fail* to find evidence for implicit perception. The lack of exclusivity can only *decrease* the probability of finding implicit perception, and it should not spuriously produce evidence for implicit perception. Thus, positive evidence for implicit perception derived from the dissociation paradigm cannot be attributed to the lack of pure measures of implicit and explicit processing. If evidence for implicit perception using the dissociation paradigm is not forthcoming, failed exclusivity would provide a plausible explanation for how implicit perception might occur but be undetectable via the dissociation paradigm.

Recent Behavioral Approaches to Studying Implicit Perception

Despite concerns about the need for exhaustive measures of awareness, most recent studies of implicit perception have relied heavily on the dissociation logic. The approaches to studying implicit perception have become somewhat more refined in their treatment of the problem. In this section, we review several relatively new behavioral approaches to studying implicit perception. In some cases, these approaches follow the dissociation logic, but with improved attempts to exhaustively measure explicit influences. Others dismiss the dissociation paradigm as flawed and propose new approaches to measuring implicit perception. For each topic, we consider possible criticisms of the evidence for implicit perception, and at the end of the section, we provide contrasting conclusions that might be drawn by a believer and by a skeptic.

Modern Applications of the Dissociation Paradigm

Since the mid-1980s, the tools and techniques used to measure implicit perception have developed substantially, largely at the goading of skeptics (Holender, 1986). However, straightforward applications of the dissociation logic still dominate studies of implicit perception, and many (if not most) of them neglect to address the standard critiques of the dissociation paradigm. This shortcoming is particularly true of neuroimaging work and of studies using patient populations, where failures to provide an adequate exhaustive measure of awareness are commonplace (see Hannula, Simons, & Cohen, 2005 for a detailed discussion of neuroimaging evidence for implicit perception). In part, the methods in these studies are constrained by the need to include imaging measures or by the nature of the patient's deficit. However, behavioral studies of implicit perception are not limited in these ways, and a number of new techniques have emerged to provide sensitive and relatively rigorous tests of the existence of implicit perception.

Some of the simplest approaches are based closely on early studies of masked priming, focusing on the ability to perceive a target as a function of an unseen prime (e.g., Bar & Biederman, 1998; Watanabe, Nanez, & Sasaki, 2001). For example, one study examined naming accuracy for briefly presented line drawings (Bar & Biederman, 1998). For the first time a stimulus was presented, subjects were only able to name it correctly approximately 15% of the time. However, when the same stimulus was presented a second time, subjects were far more successful, suggesting that having seen the stimulus before, even without being able to name it, facilitated subsequent processing. This priming benefit only occurred when the same object was presented (a different exemplar of the same category received no priming) and was maximal when the object was presented in the same location. These results suggest that implicit processing of the prime stimulus led to facilitated naming of the target

stimulus even when subjects typically were unsuccessful at naming the prime. Although this study is consistent with implicit perception, critics might well raise the objection that the explicit measure (naming) was not an exhaustive test of explicit awareness. Given that the logic of this task follows from that of the dissociation paradigm, unless explicit awareness of the prime is eliminated, naming improvements could result from residual explicit awareness.

Other studies adopted the repetition approach with a more rigorous measure of awareness of the initial stimulus (Watanabe et al., 2001), although these studies focused on perceptual learning rather than priming per se. While subjects performed a primary task involving the perception of letters in the center of a display, a set of dots behind were organized into somewhat coherent motion; most of the dots moved randomly, but a subset moved in a coherent direction. Critically, a small enough subset of the dots (5%) was coherent that subjects could not reliably discriminate the coherent motion displays from displays in which all dots moved randomly. The dots were entirely irrelevant to the primary task during the first phase of the experiment. Then, in a later phase, subjects attempted to judge the direction of coherent motion of another set of dot arrays, this time with somewhat more coherence (10%). Subjects were reliably better at determining the direction of these dot displays if they moved in the same direction as the previously viewed displays. Thus, even though subjects were unable to determine that the dots were moving coherently at all in the first phase of the experiment, the frequent repetition of a particular motion direction led to better performance with a somewhat easier judgment task. This indirect test provides evidence for implicit perception of the coherent motion of dots in the first phase, even though subjects had no conscious awareness of their motion. This approach is an elegant instance of the dissociation paradigm; subjects could not reliably detect the presence of coherent motion in the prime stimulus, but the motion coherence still affected subsequent judgments. Perceptual learning approaches like this one have distinct advantages over typical priming experiments in that awareness of the prime stimulus can be psychophysically eliminated. Other more recent priming studies have attempted to adopt more rigorous measures of awareness as well.

Many of these recent studies exploit response compatibility as an indirect, but sensitive measure of perceptual processing. For example, an experiment might measure response latency to a supraliminal target preceded by a supposedly subliminal prime. If the target would require a different response than the prime, subjects might be slowed by the presence of the prime. If subjects do not consciously detect the prime, then response compatibility effects likely resulted from implicit processing of the prime. One large advantage of this approach over traditional semantic priming studies in the dissociation paradigm is that response compatibility effects can be positive, negative, or absent, allowing additional ways to measure the effects of an unseen stimulus.

Given that this approach adopts the dissociation logic, experiments must provide direct evidence for the invisibility of the prime. As for studies of masked semantic priming, most decrease detectability by limiting presentation times and by adding masking stimuli before and/or after the prime (e.g., Eimer & Schlaghecken, 2002; Naccache & Dehaene, 2001b). Others have used small differences in contrast to camouflage primes against a background of a similar color (e.g., Jaskowski, van der Lubbe, Schlotterbeck, & Verleger, 2002). Even within the masked presentation approach, however, studies vary in terms of how systematically they manipulate the visibility of the prime. Some studies use a single stimulus duration, contrast level, or type of masking for all subjects (e.g., Naccache & Dehaene, 2001b), whereas others adjust the stimulus presentation to account for individual differences in perceptibility (Greenwald, Draine, & Abrams, 1996). Both approaches can work provided that neither shows any evidence of explicit detection of the prime stimulus. Unfortunately, many of the studies using a constant prime and mask across subjects do

not entirely eliminate explicit perceptibility for all subjects, raising some concerns about the exhaustiveness assumption.

Although early studies of priming by masked stimuli focused on semantic priming by words, more recent studies using response compatibility have adopted a host of different stimuli and judgment tasks, including left/right discrimination of arrows (Eimer, 1999; Eimer & Schlaghecken, 2002; Klapp & Hinkley, 2002); concrete/abstract word discrimination (Damian, 2001); lexical decision (Brown & Besner, 2002); words and pictures in animacy judgments (Dell'Acqua & Grainger, 1999; Klinger, Burton, & Pitts, 2000); words and nonword stimuli in Stroop interference tasks (Cheesman & Merikle, 1984; Daza, Ortells, & Fox, 2002); words in positive/negative valence judgments (Abrams & Greenwald, 2000; Abrams, Klinger, & Greenwald, 2002); numerals and number words in relative magnitude judgments (Greenwald, Abrams, Naccache, & Dehaene, 2003; Naccache & Dehaene, 2001b; Naccache, Blandin, & Dehaene, 2002;); names in male/female judgment (Greenwald et al., 1996); and diamonds and rectangles in shape categorization (Jaskowski et al., 2002). Despite the varied stimuli and judgment tasks, the results of these studies are remarkably consistent.

Moreover, all of these approaches to compatibility effects fall into roughly four types: (1) centrally presented masked primes followed by a target, (2) centrally presented masked primes followed by a target with a limited interval for an allowed response (i.e., a "response window"), (3) masked flanker tasks, and (4) Stroop tasks. Findings from the first two approaches are reviewed below. A few of these studies were accompanied by neuroimaging results, some of which are discussed in this section and some of which are considered in the section on neuroimaging evidence for implicit perception.

Masked Priming without a Response Window

The influence of masked primes on response time and accuracy to subsequently presented target items varies as a function of the compatibility of the responses mapped to those items (Dehaene et al., 1998; Eimer, 1999; Eimer & Schlaghecken, 1998; Koechlin, Naccache, Block, & Dehaene, 1999; Naccache & Dehaene, 2001b; Neumann & Klotz, 1994). In many cases, target items elicit faster, more accurate responses when the target and prime require the same, compatible response than when they require different or incompatible responses (Dehaene et al., 1998; Koechlin et al., 1999; Naccache & Dehaene, 2001b; Neumann & Klotz, 1994). In one task, subjects judged whether an Arabic numeral or number word target was greater than or less than 5 (Dehaene et al., 1998; Koechlin et al., 1999; Naccache & Dehaene, 2001a; Naccache & Dehaene, 2001b). Target numbers were preceded by a compatible or incompatible number prime (e.g., if 6 were the target, a prime of 7 would be compatible and a prime of 4 would be incompatible). In this case, compatible primes benefited performance regardless of whether or not the prime was masked (Koechlin et al., 1999). Moreover, the compatibility effects persisted even when the notation of the target and prime were different (i.e., Arabic numerals primed both Arabic numerals and number words), suggesting that the priming effect must be more abstract than feature-based visual matching.

Not all studies show a positive effect of compatibility, however. In fact, some studies show a negative compatibility effect (NCE) in which responses are slower and more error prone for compatible primes (Eimer & Schlaghecken, 1998)! For example, when a post-masked priming arrow pointed in the same direction as a subsequent target arrow, subjects were slower and less accurate than when the prime arrow pointed in the opposite direction (Eimer & Schlaghecken, 1998). One explanation for these contradictory results appeals to the effects of delays between the prime and the response on compatibility effects. In one experiment that systematically manipulated the delay, positive compatibility effects were found for short delays between the prime and the response, but negative effects of compatibil-

ity resulted from delays longer than 350–400 ms (Eimer, 1999; Eimer & Schlaghecken, 1998).

The transition from positive to negative effects has been characterized more completely using recordings of ERPs. The lateralized readiness potential (LRP), detected via ERP recording, measures the activation from motor cortex of the hemisphere opposite the response hand (Coles, Gratton, & Donchin, 1988) and provides a direct way to determine whether a stimulus leads to activation of motor cortex. On incompatible trials, the prime should elicit transient activation of motor cortex ipsilateral to the responding hand followed by contralateral motor cortex activation in response to the target. With a compatible prime and target, this ipsilateral activation should be absent. In fact, the behavioral compatibility studies often incorporated ERP recording and consistently found LRPs in response to masked primes (Dehaene et al., 1998; Eimer, 1999; Eimer & Schlaghecken, 1998). Ipsilateral activation was evident shortly after the prime, both for arrow primes and numerical stimuli. Assuming that the masked primes were not consciously perceived, these LRPs provide evidence of processing in the absence of awareness.

The time course of neural activation corresponding to a masked prime might also help explain the paradoxical negative compatibility effect sometimes observed with longer lags between the prime and response (Eimer, 1999; Eimer & Schlaghecken, 1998). The burgeoning neural activity associated with a subliminal prime diminishes rapidly when observers do not make an overt response. If inhibitory mechanisms, not yet fully characterized, are responsible for preventing an overt motor response to the masked prime (Eimer, 1999), then they might also induce a refractory period during which activation consistent with the prime is suppressed. Thus, activation in response to the consistent target would overlap temporally with this refractory period, leading to the paradoxical result of slowed responses with compatible primes. Regardless of whether the prime produces a positive or negative compatibility effect, these studies confirm that masked primes activate corresponding motor cortices.

Together, the behavioral and ERP evidence for compatibility effects suggests that unseen primes influence both performance and neural activity. However, these studies still follow the logic of the dissociation paradigm, and any claims for implicit perception must satisfy the exhaustiveness assumption. Otherwise, differences between visible and "subliminal" primes might just reflect different levels of explicit activation rather than a dissociation between explicit and implicit perception. In most response compatibility studies, the perceptibility of the prime is measured not during the primary task, but in a separate set of trials or separate control experiments (e.g., Naccache & Dehaene, 2001b). Although few subjects report having seen the primes after the primary task, performance in these separate prime perceptibility trials implies some awareness of the "subliminal" primes. For example, sensitivity using signal detection measure (d′) ranged from o for some subjects to as high as 1.3 for other subjects (Naccache & Dehaene, 2001b). Given that d′ levels of as low as .3 can reflect some reliable sensitivity to the presence of a prime and a d′ level of 1 represents fairly good sensitivity, these studies do not adequately eliminate explicit awareness of the prime stimuli. Consequently, claims of compatibility effects that are devoid of any explicit awareness are not entirely supported; the masked primes might well have been explicitly detected by some of the subjects on some trials.

Masked Priming with a Response Window

One recent refinement of the masked priming approach involves the use of a speeded response to maximize the effects of implicit processing (Draine & Greenwald, 1998; Greenwald et al., 1996; Greenwald, Schuh, & Klinger, 1995). In this approach, subjects must make their judgment within a fixed temporal window after the presentation of the target (e.g., between 383 and 517 ms instead of a more typical response latency of about 600 ms). The goal in forcing speeded

responses is to maximize any implicit compatibility effects based on the premise that such implicit compatibility effects might be short-lived. As is typical of implicit response compatibility studies, prime visibility was measured by asking subjects to detect the masked prime stimulus either in a simple detection task or in a discrimination task (e.g., distinguish between a word prime and a random string of digits). Not surprisingly given the fixed prime presentation durations, a number of subjects had d′ levels above o. However, these studies did not simply look at performance on the compatibility task and then presume that explicit awareness was nil. Rather, a new analytical approach was adopted: Regression was used to predict the level of the compatibility effect when explicit awareness was absent (d′ = o). If the intercept of the regression of the compatibility effect on explicit sensitivity is greater than o, then the study provides evidence for implicit perception. That is, implicit processing is revealed when the indirect measure reveals some consequence of the perception of the prime even when explicit sensitivity is extrapolated to d′ = o. This approach revealed significant response compatibility effects for prime durations ranging from 17–50 ms when explicit sensitivity was extrapolated to d′ = o.

This approach was premised on the assumption that the response window was necessary to detect implicit compatibility effects. Another experiment tested the validity of this assumption by varying the stimulus onset asynchrony (SOA) between the prime and the target (Greenwald et al., 1996). If more than 67 ms elapsed between the prime and target onsets, masking the prime eliminated the compatibility effect. In contrast, unmasked primes produced compatibility effects at a wide range of SOAs. This finding represents an important qualitative difference between visible and subliminal primes. Moreover, the regression technique and the response-window methodology are valuable contributions to the study of implicit perception.

More importantly, the findings raise some important limitations on implicit processing. Findings from this response-window technique suggest that implicit effects are extremely short-lived and are disrupted by even slight increases to the delay between the prime and the target. If this form of perception proves to be the only reliable way to find evidence for implicit perception, it would undermine more radical claims about the pervasiveness of implicit processes, especially implicit persuasion. Most hypothesized processes of implicit persuasion would require a much longer delay between the priming stimulus and the changed belief or action. These findings also provide an explanation for why studies of implicit perception often fail to replicate – the effects are ephemeral.

Although the response compatibility effects seem to provide evidence for implicit semantic processing, many of the findings could be attributed to motor interference rather than to semantic priming. Subjects learn responses to a stimulus, and it is the responses that conflict, not the abstract or semantic representations of those stimuli. In the response-window approach, semantic priming effects are difficult to produce, and most results can be attributed to response compatibility rather than any more abstract priming (Klinger et al., 2000). In fact, the effects, at least in some cases of word primes, seem not due to the semantic content of the word, but rather to response associations formed earlier in the experiment. In one striking example, subjects were asked to make positive/negative valence judgments about words. In the critical trials, words that previously had been used as targets were recombined in a way that changed the valence and then were used as a prime word. For example, the targets "smut" and "bile" would become the prime word "smile." Although the semantic representation of "smile" should lead to a compatibility benefit for a positive target, it instead facilitated processing of negative words (Abrams & Greenwald, 2000; Greenwald et al., 2003)! Moreover, unless a word or part of a word had been consciously perceived as a target during an earlier phase of the experiment, it produced no priming at all. In fact, other evidence not using a response-window technique suggests that not only must a word

be consciously perceived to later serve as an effective prime but it must also have been used as a target such that the word would be associated with a motor response (Damian, 2001). In the example above, the word "smile" without prior exposure to "smut" and "bile" did not prime positive or negative words (Abrams & Greenwald, 2000; Greenwald et al., 2003). This claim directly contradicts other evidence of implicit semantic processing (Dehaene et al., 1998; Koechlin et al., 1999; Naccache & Dehaene, 2001b) by suggesting that only fragments of words are processed implicitly and that the associations they prime are developed through conscious experience as part of the experiment. Yet, evidence for priming of Arabic numerals by number words implies priming of more abstract representations, and such studies also showed priming from stimuli that had not previously been the target of a judgment (Naccache & Dehaene, 2001b). Moreover, switching the required response did not eliminate priming, so the effect cannot be entirely due to some automated form of response priming (Abrams et al., 2002).

In a recent intriguing paper, the primary adversaries in the argument over the nature of priming in the response-window paradigm combined their efforts to determine whether the effects were due to more than response compatibility (Greenwald et al., 2003). These experiments adopted numerical stimuli (Naccache & Dehaene, 2001b) in a response-window task. The stimuli were all two-digit Arabic numerals, and the judgment task required subjects to determine whether the target was greater or less than 55. Unfortunately, the use of two-digit numbers precluded the assessment of cross-notation priming, which was one of the strongest arguments for semantic processing in earlier experiments (Naccache & Dehaene, 2001b). The experiment replicated the finding of response compatibility effects with stimuli that had not previously been used as targets, refuting the argument that subjects must have formed a response association to a stimulus for it to produce priming (Abrams & Greenwald, 2000; Damian, 2001). However, the study also replicated the counter-intuitive finding that prior judgments affect the directionality of priming (Abrams & Greenwald, 2000). If 73 had served as a target, then subsequently using 37 as a prime enhanced response times to numbers greater than 55! Taken together, these findings imply that previously unclassified primes can produce compatibility effects and that they do so based on long-term semantic representations. However, such representations are overridden once a prime has been consciously classified, and then its features lead to priming based on the response association formed during the experiment.

Interim Conclusions

The response-window and regression approach lend new credibility to the traditional dissociation technique, and they show exceptional promise as a way to produce consistent evidence for priming by masked stimuli. Although some of the findings using this method are counter-intuitive and others are contradictory, the basic approach represents one of the best existing attempts to meet the challenges of critics of implicit perception (e.g., Holender, 1986). The approach is firmly couched in the dissociation logic, and most experiments make a laudable attempt to eliminate explicit sensitivity. The regression approach, in particular, is a clever way to examine performance in the absence of awareness. However, the existing literature does leave plenty of wiggle room for skeptics unwilling to accept the existence of implicit perception. First, because the approach adopts the dissociation paradigm, the measures of explicit sensitivity might fail to measure explicit sensitivity exhaustively (Merikle & Reingold, 1998).

Perhaps of greater concern to those who are otherwise willing to adopt the dissociation logic is the nature of the regression approach itself. The approach has been criticized for making assumptions about the nature of the relationship between the direct and indirect tasks and measures (Dosher, 1998). For example, the conclusions from the regression approach often depend on extrapolation, with relatively few subjects (e.g., 25%) performing at chance on the explicit detection task and a sizable minority of subjects (25%) showing substantial explicit sensitivity with d' levels greater than 1 (Greenwald et al., 1996). If most subjects show greater than chance explicit sensitivity, the extrapolation to zero sensitivity might not be appropriate. A skeptic could easily imagine a non-linearity in the relationship between implicit and explicit measures when explicit performance is just barely above $d' = 0$. Perhaps there is a qualitative difference between minimal sensitivity and fairly good sensitivity. If so, then extrapolating to no sensitivity from fairly good sensitivity would not allow a clear conclusion in favor of implicit effects. Of course, this concern could be remedied with a more systematic manipulation of prime visibility within rather than across subjects, thereby obviating the need for any extrapolation. Given the trend toward progressively more sophisticated analyses and methodologies in this literature, this new approach shows great promise as an effective use of the dissociation paradigm.

Alternatives to Dissociation

The concerns about exhaustiveness and the possible role of failed exclusivity in minimizing evidence for implicit perception have spurred a new approach to studying implicit perception: Concentrate on qualitative or quantitative differences between tasks that purportedly measure implicit perception to different degrees. Examining differences in performance on these tasks as a function of an experimental manipulation can reveal the operation of distinct implicit and explicit processes. Two types of "relative differences" methodologies have used this logic: (1) the *relative sensitivity procedure*, which looks for greater sensitivity to stimulus presence with indirect measures than with direct measures of awareness, and (2) the *process dissociation procedure*, which looks for qualitatively different performance for implicit and explicit perception. Neither methodology requires process-pure measures of implicit or explicit perception. Rather, both assume that all tasks have implicit and explicit components. Carefully designed experiments can pull apart the underlying processes, revealing differences between the implicit and explicit processing in a given task. Both approaches also assume that implicit and explicit processes underlie functionally different types of behavior; explicit processes underlie intentional actions, whereas implicit processes govern automatic (non-intentional) behaviors. A behavior may result from a conscious, deliberate decision or from an automatic predisposition, or a combination of the two. The relative differences methodologies attempt to show that such automatic and deliberate processes can lead to qualitatively different performance.

Relative Sensitivity: An Alternative to Dissociation

The goal of the relative sensitivity procedure is to reveal implicit processes by showing instances in which indirect measures are more sensitive than comparable direct measures in making a given discrimination. This approach assumes that performance of any task involves both implicit and explicit contributions, neither of which can be measured exclusively by any task. Direct tasks measure performance when subjects are instructed to use their percept of a critical stimulus to make a judgment or discrimination. Indirect tasks involve an ostensibly unrelated behavior or judgment that nevertheless can be influenced by perception of a critical stimulus. Although the direct task might not exclusively measure explicit contributions, on its face it is demonstrably more explicit than the indirect task. Any decision-making process that relies on conscious awareness of the critical stimulus should lead to better performance on a direct measure than on an indirect measure because subjects should optimally rely on their conscious percept. In contrast, indirect measures do not require conscious perception of the critical stimulus, so subjects are unlikely to rely on conscious processing of that stimulus in making their

judgment. Therefore, if indirect measures reveal better performance than direct measures, implicit processes must have influenced performance.

One critical component of this paradigm is that the two tasks must be equated in most respects. Unless the visual displays are equivalent and the task requirements comparable, any performance differences could be caused by the differences between the displays or the task demands and requirements. Proponents of this approach rightly take pains to make sure that the only difference between the direct and indirect tasks are in the instructions (a similar approach has been adopted in the study of implicit memory; see Schacter, 1987).

Note that this criterion – equivalency across direct and indirect measures – is not often met in studies of implicit perception. Many experiments use entirely distinct indirect and direct measures, making comparability more difficult. When observers report no awareness of a stimulus on a direct measure, indirect measures such as eye movements, patterns of neural activation, skin-conductance changes, or ERPs might reveal sensitivity to the presence of a stimulus. Although these sorts of indirect measurements certainly provide important insight into the nature of the processing of the stimulus, they do not provide conclusive evidence for processing in the absence of awareness. They might only reveal greater sensitivity of the measure itself; using such measures to provide corroborating evidence for qualitative differences in implicit and explicit processing may prove more fruitful (see the neuroimaging evidence section below). For the inference of implicit processing to follow from the relative sensitivity of direct and indirect measures, however, the measures must be comparable.

In one of the first experiments to adopt the relative sensitivity approach for the study of implicit perception (Kunst-Wilson & Zajonc, 1980), subjects viewed a series of briefly presented pictures of geometric shapes. Then, they either performed an old/new recognition task (the direct task) or they picked which of two shapes they preferred (the indirect task). When performing the direct task, subjects performed no better than chance at discriminating previously viewed from novel shapes. In contrast, when performing the indirect preference judgment task, they preferred the previously studied shape over a novel shape at rates significantly above chance levels. In other words, a direct measure of conscious recognition showed less sensitivity to the presence of a representation than an indirect measure of preference. This experiment meets the standards necessary for inferring implicit processing in the relative sensitivity approach: (a) the experimental environment was constant across tasks, with only the task instructions changing across conditions, and (b) performance on the indirect task exceeded that on the direct task. By the logic of the relative sensitivity approach, the direct task represents a putatively better measure of conscious awareness, so the relatively increased sensitivity of the indirect task must have resulted from implicit processes.

One possible concern about this conclusion derives from the use of separate study and test phases rather than testing performance at the time of presentation; subjects may have perceived and forgotten the consciously experienced shape even if a vague, explicitly generated preference persisted longer and affected performance on the indirect task. Furthermore, subjects might have been less motivated to make the more difficult intentional recognition judgments than the simpler preference judgment, so they were more likely to select responses randomly. If so, then responding in both cases might reflect access to an explicit representation, with the relative increase in sensitivity for the indirect task resulting not from implicit processing but from a differential effect of motivation (cf. Visser & Merikle, 1999).

One representative experiment pitted a recognition task (direct) against a perceptual contrast judgment (indirect) in which subjects judged the contrast of a word against the background (Merikle & Reingold, 1991). In a study phase, subjects viewed pairs of words and were asked to read the cued one. Then, in the test phase, they viewed individual words against a noise background and either judged whether it was old or new (a direct recognition task) or judged whether it was presented in high or low contrast (an indirect measure). Performance on the contrast judgment task revealed greater sensitivity to the presence of a word in the study phase than did the direct recognition task (at least for the first block of trials). Presumably, the prior presentation reduced the processing demands, leading to a subjective impression that the words were easier to see against a noisy background even if the words were not recognized. Once again, the study used comparable stimuli in the direct and indirect tasks and found greater performance for the indirect task, suggesting implicit processing.

Problems with Relative Sensitivity as an Approach

Although this approach is touted as an alternative to the classic dissociation paradigm, any positive evidence for implicit perception is subject to many of the same assumptions. Positive evidence for implicit perception requires some task to have a greater implicit contribution than explicit contribution. Otherwise, performance on the indirect task could not exceed that on any task with a greater explicit component. If some task has a greater implicit than explicit component, then it should also be possible to make the task sufficiently difficult that the explicit component would be eliminated, leaving only the residual implicit component. That is, the "indirect > direct" approach is a superset of the standard dissociation paradigm that does not require the elimination of an explicit component. Yet, any case in which the indirect > direct approach reveals implicit perception would also support the possibility that the dissociation paradigm could reveal implicit perception. In essence, this approach amounts to a more liberal variant of the dissociation paradigm in which explicit processing need not be eliminated. However, as critics of early work on implicit perception have noted, whenever a stimulus is consciously perceptible, explicit factors may contaminate estimates of implicit processing.

A more general concern about this paradigm is that it assumes a unitary explicit contribution and a unitary implicit contribution. In arguing that a direct measure involves a greater explicit contribution than an indirect measure, the assumption is that the explicit contributions to each task are of the same sort. If more than one sort of explicit contribution exists, then a "direct" task might exceed an "indirect" task on some forms of explicit contribution but not others. Unless the direct task exceeds the indirect task on all explicit contributions, the logic underlying the paradigm fails. Just as the dissociation paradigm suffers from the problem of exhaustively eliminating all possible explicit contributions, the indirect > direct approach requires that the two tasks measure the same explicit component and only that explicit component. Consequently, for the logic of the paradigm to hold, the experimenter must exhaustively eliminate any extraneous explicit contributions to the indirect task that might explain superior performance on the indirect task. Given that this exhaustiveness assumption applies to the relative sensitivity approach, its advantage over the standard dissociation paradigm is somewhat unclear.

Qualitative Differences

One criterion often used to infer the existence of implicit perception relies on differences in the patterns of performance derived from implicit and explicit processes. When the pattern of performance diverges from what would be expected with explicit perception, then the processes leading to this qualitative difference might well be implicit. Qualitative differences in performance for implicit and explicit tasks or measures often provide an intuitive way to infer the existence of implicit perception. The negative compatibility effects described earlier provide one illustration of the importance of such differences for inferring implicit processing (Eimer, 1999). However, the inter-

pretation of qualitative differences is often muddied by the challenge of determining whether differences in performance are qualitative rather than quantitative. An effect that initially appears to reflect a qualitative difference might simply be a difference along a non-linear dimension.

More importantly, though, qualitative differences in performance can occur even when subjects are aware of the stimulus (Holender, 1986). That is, qualitative differences are possible within explicit perception, so the existence of a qualitative difference in performance alone does not unequivocally demonstrate implicit perception. Rather, the qualitative difference must be accompanied by an exhaustive measure of explicit awareness. Consequently, qualitative differences can provide converging evidence for the existence of implicit perception, but they are not definitive in and of themselves (Holender, 1986). Perhaps the best example of the use of qualitative differences in studies of implicit perception comes from the use of the process dissociation paradigm (otherwise known as the "exclusion" paradigm).

Process Dissociation

In the process dissociation technique, implicit and explicit performance are put in opposition (Jacoby, 1991). As in the relative sensitivity approach, direct and indirect measures are thought to rely differentially on explicit and implicit processing. In this approach, intentional actions are assumed to be under explicit control, whereas automatic responses are thought to reflect implicit processing. Presumably, people will use consciously available information to guide their intentional actions. In contrast, information available only to implicit processes will be less subject to intentional control. Consequently, when subjects produce responses that differ from those associated with intentional actions, they may have been influenced by non-conscious processes. The critical difference between the process dissociation procedure and the relative sensitivity procedure is that the task instructions and goals are constant. Subjects always perform the same task. Rather than manipulating the task across conditions, the perceptibility of the critical stimulus itself is varied so that some responses are consistent with awareness of the stimulus and others are not.

Subjects are instructed to respond one way if they are aware of a stimulus, but implicit or indirect influences lead them to respond the opposite way by default. For example, in the original instantiation of this approach in the memory literature, subjects studied a list of words and then were asked to complete word fragments with words that had *not* been on the studied list (Jacoby, 1991). Presumably, if they remembered the studied word, they would successfully avoid it in the fragment task. If they did not explicitly remember the word, they might automatically or implicitly be more likely to complete a fragment with a studied word than a non-studied word. Implicit influences should increase the likelihood of completing fragments with studied words, whereas explicit influences should decrease the likelihood of completing fragments with studied words. The same logic can be applied to implicit and explicit perception: If subjects explicitly detect the presence of a word, they should avoid using it to complete a word fragment. However, if they do not detect it and it still influences performance implicitly, they should be more likely to complete a fragment with a studied word than a non-studied word.

Studies using this procedure have been taken to support the existence of implicit perception. For example, one study varied the presentation time for words. Immediately after viewing each word, subjects were given a word stem completion task in which they were asked to complete the stem with a word other than the one that had been presented (Debner & Jacoby, 1994). With long presentation durations, subjects were aware of the words and successfully avoided completing stems with the "studied" words relative to the baseline performance of subjects who had never been shown the word. In contrast, with shorter presenta-

tions, subjects completed the stems with the "studied" word more often than the baseline condition. Even when they were unable to use their memory for the word to guide their intentional actions (i.e., choose another word), the briefly presented word still received enough processing to increase its availability in the stem completion task.

A similar pattern emerges when attentional focus rather than presentation duration is manipulated (see Merikle et al., 2001 for an overview). In one study, subjects viewed a briefly presented cross and judged which of its two lines was longer. During a subset of trials, a word was presented briefly along with the cross (see Mack & Rock, 1998 for the origins of this method). Depending on the condition, subjects were asked to focus attention either on the cross judgment or on the words. In both conditions, subjects subsequently attempted to complete a word stem with a word that had not been presented (this study was described by Merikle et al., 2001). Those subjects who focused on the words performed well, rarely using the presented words to complete the stem. In contrast, those who focused attention on the cross judgment completed the stem with presented words more often than would be expected based on a previously determined baseline (see also Mack & Rock, 1998). When the words were the focus of attention, they presumably were available to awareness, and subjects could use that information to exclude them in the stem completion task. However, when subjects focused attention on the cross judgment, they were less aware of the words, but automatic processing of the words biased them to use the presented words in the stem completion task.

A variety of exclusion tasks have been used to study implicit perception. For example, subjects show differential effects of interference in a variant of the Stroop task when aware and unaware of a stimulus. Typically, when color patches are incongruent with a preceding word (e.g., a green patch preceded by the word "red"), subjects are slower to identify the color of the patch than if the two matched. However, if mismatches occur on a large proportion of trials (80%), subjects use this information to perform faster when the word and patch *mismatch* than when they match (see Merikle & Joordens, 1997b for a discussion of these studies). When words were presented long enough to be consciously detected, subjects used their explicit knowledge to override Stroop interference. In contrast, briefly presented words were not consciously detected, and subjects were significantly slowed when a word-color patch mismatch occurred (Merikle & Joordens, 1997a,b). Stroop interference can be counteracted if subjects are aware of the word and of the predictiveness of the word, but if the word is not consciously perceived, subjects cannot override these automatic interference effects.

Other exclusion studies have used similar manipulations of target predictability in response compatibility paradigms (e.g., McCormick, 1997). Subjects were asked to decide whether an X or O was in the display, and this target item was presented either on the right or left side of the fixation cross. Before the presentation, a cue appeared on the left or right side of the display. On approximately 80% of trials, the cue was on the side opposite where the target would appear. Thus, the cue predicted that the target would be on the opposite side of the display. When the cue was presented for long enough to be consciously detected, subjects responded more rapidly to targets on the side opposite the cue. In contrast, when the cue was presented too briefly to be consciously detected, subjects were faster to respond when the cue and target were on the same side of the display (McCormick, 1997). Presumably, the cue automatically attracts attention, and only with awareness can subjects override this automatic shift of attention. Without awareness, the cue automatically draws attention, leading to better performance when the target appears at the cued location. Although this finding does not involve semantic processing without awareness, it does suggest that attention shifts can be induced without awareness of the inducing stimulus.

Problems with Process Dissociation as a Measure of Implicit Perception

This approach has promise as a means of studying implicit perception. One concern about this approach, however, is that it might be subject to biases and motivational factors that affect the criterion that subjects adopt. If so, estimates of implicit processing might be inflated (Visser & Merikle, 1999). Any case in which the subject's criterion is differentially affected by exclusion and inclusion instructions can produce a change in the criterion that could then influence estimates of unconscious processing. For example, increasing incentives to exclude studied items led to improved performance, thereby decreasing estimates of unconscious processing (Visser & Merikle, 1999). More broadly, variations in the degree of confidence or certainty in a representation or a percept can lead to different degrees of success on the exclusion task. Given that the exclusion task provides the basis for inferring implicit representations, such variations are problematic. A word that is explicitly detected, but with low confidence, might lead to a failure to exclude that item on a stem completion task even though there was an explicit contribution to perception. In terms of signal detection, if subjects were conservatively biased when reporting explicit detection, estimates of implicit perception would be inflated. Thus, as in the dissociation paradigm, the explicit task must demonstrably eliminate all explicit detection and must not be subject to conservative response biases for this paradigm to provide a clear estimate of implicit perception.

A Believer's Interpretation

The past 15 years have seen tremendous improvements in the behavioral methods used to study implicit perception. More importantly, many of the early critiques of the implicit perception literature have been addressed. Most studies using the dissociation paradigm now use signal detection theory to determine the explicit perceptibility of the prime stimulus, thereby providing a more convincing demonstration that priming results from implicit processing rather than from explicit contamination. The recently introduced technique of regressing performance on an indirect measure (e.g., a response compatibility effect) on performance on an explicit detection task provides a more nuanced approach to the dissociation technique. Even when performance on the explicit task is extrapolated to null sensitivity, performance on some indirect measures is still better than chance. The use of response compatibility allows an indirect measure that can, under the right circumstances, reveal implicit semantic processing. For example, priming persists even when the format of a number (text vs. Arabic numeral) changes from prime to test. The combination of the regression technique and response compatibility paradigms provides a powerful new tool to study implicit perception, one that has produced consistent and replicable evidence for implicit perception. Finally, work using process dissociation and relative sensitivity approaches reveals evidence for qualitative differences between implicit and explicit processing. These qualitative differences suggest that different mechanisms underlie implicit and explicit perception, thereby providing further evidence for the existence of implicit perception. In sum, evidence from a wide variety of tasks and measures provides support for implicit perception and even for semantic processing in the absence of awareness. Given the wide variety of tools used in the study of implicit perception, the converging evidence for the existence of implicit perception is overwhelming.

A Skeptic's Interpretation

The tools and techniques used to study implicit perception have improved immensely over the past 20 years. Many studies have adopted signal detection theory as a way to verify the absence of explicit perception, thereby making evidence from the dissociation paradigm less subject to the standard criticisms. Moreover, seeking evidence of qualitative differences using the process dissociation paradigm or other relative sensitivity approaches is a promising avenue for the exploration of implicit perception. However, none of these approaches or studies provides airtight evidence for implicit perception, and all are subject to fairly plausible alternative explanations that rely solely on explicit mechanisms. For example, in studies using the regression approach, the direct measure often reveals sensitivity to the presence of the prime stimulus at levels far above $d' = 0$ (Naccache & Dehaene, 2001b); the prime is readily visible to some subjects. Consequently, the inference for implicit perception relies on extrapolation of performance to $d' = 0$ from a number of subjects who show positive sensitivity to the stimulus. This extrapolation is potentially hazardous, particularly if the distribution of subjects is not centered on d' of 0. If the relationship between explicit perception and the indirect measure is non-linear, the extrapolation may be invalid (Dosher, 1998). Moreover, the presence of a positive indirect effect might require only a minimal amount of explicit sensitivity. No published studies have examined the effect of varying explicit sensitivity systematically (within subjects) on the magnitude of the indirect response compatibility effect. Any application of the dissociation paradigm, including the regression approach, depends critically on demonstrating null sensitivity to the presence of the critical stimulus. None of the studies to date have done so adequately.

Evidence from the process dissociation paradigm suggests a qualitative difference between implicit and explicit perception, something that would be more difficult to explain via explicit contamination. Most studies of implicit perception simply reveal "implicit" effects that are weaker versions of what would be expected with explicit processing. The process dissociation procedure, in contrast, suggests that implicit and explicit mechanisms differ. However, as accurately noted in critiques of the implicit perception literature, qualitative differences alone are insufficient to claim evidence for implicit perception. The qualitative difference could simply be a dissociation between two forms of explicit perception rather than between implicit and explicit perception. Moreover, inferences of implicit perception depend on the extent to which the explicit, intentional response fully measures all of the explicit processing. The only studies to address this question suggest that performance on the explicit task can be enhanced via motivation manipulations, thereby decreasing the evidence for implicit perception (Visser & Merikle, 1999).

In sum, the new tools introduced to study implicit perception may be promising, but the evidence for implicit perception is not yet convincing. Moreover, the implicit effects that have been reported are small and tend to vary with the extent of demonstrated explicit awareness, hinting that the "implicit" effects might well be driven by residual explicit processing. For a study using the dissociation paradigm to make a strong claim for implicit perception, no subject should show explicit sensitivity to the visibility of the critical stimulus; no study to date has met this strict criterion. Converging solid evidence from a variety of techniques can provide powerful support for a claim of implicit perception, but the convergence of weak and controvertible evidence for implicit perception does not merit strong support for the claim. If all of the evidence can be explained by plausible explicit confounds, then there is no need to infer the existence of a separate mechanism or set of mechanisms.

Evidence for Implicit Perception – Neuroimaging Data

Neuroimaging approaches provide several distinct advantages over behavioral approaches in the study of implicit perception. First, the effects of a subliminal stimulus can be assessed without an overt response; neuroimaging techniques provide an additional dependent measure of the consequences of perception, one that may allow dissociations that would be impossible with strictly behavioral measures. Moreover, dif-

ferences in the pattern of activation for explicit and implicit perception might reveal additional qualitative differences between these forms of processing even if behavioral responses show no difference; neuroimaging might simply provide a more sensitive measure. Finally, the known functions of various brain regions can be mapped onto the pattern of activation produced in response to seen and unseen stimuli, allowing yet another way to determine the richness of implicit percepts.

Although such approaches have great promise as a new tool for the study of implicit perception, in many respects the existing research on the neural bases of implicit perception falls prey to the same critiques leveled at the behavioral research. Perhaps more importantly, as our review suggests, the neural activity elicited by implicit perception often is similar to that corresponding to overt perception, just diminished in amplitude. In the absence of qualitative differences in the pattern of activation, such diminished effects might well result from low-level overt perception. In such cases, the same standards and criteria applied to the use of the dissociation paradigm in behavioral research must be applied to the neuroimaging methods (see Hannula et al., 2005 for a detailed treatment of these issues).

A wide array of neuroimaging tools, most notably functional magnetic resonance imaging (fMRI) and event-related potentials (ERPs), have been adapted to the study of implicit perception. Most often, these investigations draw on existing knowledge of the functional brain regions likely to be involved in overt perception of a class of stimuli (e.g., emotional faces, words, etc.), and then try to determine whether those same regions are active even when observers report no awareness of the stimuli. Neuroimaging studies of implicit perception typically rely on several different types of processing and stimulus classes, and for the sake of organizing this rapidly expanding field, we consider three types of evidence for implicit perception: implicit perception of faces, implicit perception of words and numbers, and ERPs in priming studies. Within the neuroimaging literature, most inferences about implicit perception depend critically on the pattern of neural localization or the magnitude of activation resulting from explicitly detected and implicitly perceived stimuli.

Implicit Perception of Faces

Face processing represents one of the more promising avenues for the study of implicit perception because the neural regions activated in response to faces are fairly well described in the neuroimaging literature. A slew of recent neuroimaging studies of face perception reveal an area in the fusiform gyrus that responds relatively more to faces than to other stimuli (the Fusiform Face Area, or FFA; Kanwisher, McDermott, & Chun, 1997; McCarthy, Puce, Gore, & Allison, 1997). Is this area active even when observers are unaware of the presence of a face stimulus? Also, fearful faces are associated with activation of the amygdala (Breiter et al., 1996; Morris et al., 1996). Do fearful faces lead to amygdala activation even when they are not consciously perceived? Finally, recent neuroimaging studies using the phenomenon of binocular rivalry have explored the areas that are activated by stimuli when they are consciously perceived and when rivalry removes them from awareness.

Recent neuroimaging studies of visual extinction patients have explored whether an extinguished face leads to activation in the FFA (Rees et al., 2000; Vuilleumier et al., 2001). Unilateral brain lesions, particularly those located in the right posterior inferior parietal lobe, are associated with spatial neglect of the contralesional visual field. Many neglect patients exhibit visual extinction, accurately detecting isolated stimuli presented in either visual field, but failing to identify a contralesional stimulus when items are presented simultaneously in both visual fields. Behavioral research (discussed in later sections of this chapter) provides evidence for residual processing of extinguished stimuli, perhaps due to intact striate and extrastriate cortex along with ventral inferotemporal areas that process object identity.

One study required a patient to respond differently to a stimulus presented solely on the left, solely on the right, or simultaneously on the left and right (Rees et al., 2000). Given that the patient had right inferior parietal lobe damage, extinction would be revealed by incorrect "right-side" responses when a stimulus was presented on both the left and the right simultaneously. By comparing fMRI data corresponding to correct "right-side" responses and incorrect "right-side" responses on extinction trials, residual neural activity associated with extinction could be revealed. Extinguished stimuli activated striate and early extrastriate cortex in the damaged right hemisphere – a pattern of activation no different from that elicited by left-side stimuli that were consciously perceived. This activation of early visual cortex occurred regardless of whether the patient was aware of the stimulus, suggesting that these areas are not sufficient for conscious awareness. More importantly, a region of interest analysis revealed low-threshold, category-specific activation in the right FFA in association with extinguished face stimuli, suggesting that the extinguished face was processed by the same regions as for consciously perceived faces (for reviews of evidence for preserved activation in response to unreported stimuli, see Driver & Vuilleumier, 2001; Driver, Vuilleumier, Eimer, & Rees, 2001).

This basic pattern was replicated in a similar experiment using both fMRI and ERPs (Vuilleumier et al., 2001). An extinction patient with right-lateralized posterior inferior parietal damage indicated on each trial whether or not a face was presented. Stimuli (i.e., schematic faces and shapes) were presented unilaterally in the right or left hemifield or bilaterally. Again, extinguished faces activated right striate cortex as well as an area of inferior temporal cortex just lateral to the FFA, although the level of activation was much reduced relative to that for visible face stimuli. Furthermore, ERPs revealed a right-lateralized negativity over posterior temporal regions approximately 170–180 ms after a face was presented in the left hemifield. This N170, a component known to be face-selective, was evident regardless of whether the face was perceptible or not. Interestingly, this experiment varied the duration of the bilateral presentations in order to vary whether or not extinction occurred. Awareness of the left visual field stimulus evoked activation of striate cortex and fusiform gyrus coupled with increased activation of a network of frontal and parietal brain regions, reflecting the sorts of long-range associations or widespread activation thought to accompany consciousness (Baars, 1988). Thus, differences in activation strength and functional connectivity distinguish conscious from unconscious perception.

Evidence from patients with bilateral amygdala damage (e.g., Adolphs, Tranel, Damasio, & Damasio, 1995) and neuroimaging of intact individuals (Breiter et al., 1996; Morris et al., 1996) support a role for the amygdala in processing fear-related stimuli, such as fearful faces. At least one theory suggests that a direct short-latency pathway between the thalamus and the amygdala might underlie the processing of emotional stimuli even in the absence of awareness (Le Doux, 1996). In one fMRI study (Whalen et al., 1998), fearful and happy faces were presented for 33 ms followed immediately by a neutral-face mask. Based on previous behavioral studies, the 33-ms masked presentation was assumed to be below the threshold for awareness. Post-study questioning found that eight of ten subjects denied having seen emotional faces and did not select these faces as having been in the stimulus set. Under these conditions, the unnoticed fearful faces did elicit a relatively circumscribed increase in amygdala activation relative to masked happy faces and a fixation baseline. This amygdala activation was attenuated with repeated exposure to masked fearful faces, a finding consistently observed with visible faces as well. Further, increased activation in response to both masked fearful and happy faces extended into the adjacent sublenticular substantia innominata of the basal forebrain, a region thought to be involved in more general processing of emotional stimuli and arousal

(although activation was more pronounced for fearful faces). This pattern of results is consistent with the notion that the amygdala is selectively recruited when subliminal fear stimuli are presented (for additional evidence of early affective word processing in the absence of awareness see Bernat, Bunce, & Shevrin, 2001a), but as for similar behavioral results, such dissociations must be interpreted with caution because of methodological shortcomings in the assessment of awareness. For example, awareness was not measured directly on each trial – doing so might change the subject's strategy from one of passive viewing to active search (Whalen et al., 1998).

In another study, relative to neutral faces, fearful faces were associated with significant activation of the left amygdala, left fusiform, lateral orbitofrontal, and right intraparietal cortex (Vuilleumier et al., 2002). Activation of fusiform gyrus in response to extinguished faces was much reduced relative to activation for visible faces though, and the activation evident in association with extinguished stimuli may be a consequence of feedback from the amygdala. Together, these findings suggest that emotional stimuli can receive substantial processing even if they fail to reach awareness. Emotional stimuli are among the most promising approaches to the study of implicit processing, precisely because of the hypothesized existence of a direct, perhaps more primitive neural pathway that bypasses higher cognitive areas.

These studies provide interesting, suggestive support for the hypothesized short-latency pathway originating in the thalamus (LeDoux, 1996). Such a pathway might reasonably allow for processing even in the absence of more complex cognitive processes, and by inference without awareness. More importantly, amygdala activation was not significantly modulated by awareness (Vuilleumier et al., 2002), suggesting that processing of extinguished stimuli extends beyond early visual processing areas and that activation need not be less robust in the absence of conscious detection. Similar approaches have been taken in the study of implicit processing of unnoticed, emotionally arousing stimuli (see Lane & Nadel, 2000 for an overview of work on the cognitive neuroscience of emotion).

Another neuroimaging-based approach to studying processing in the absence of awareness relies on the phenomenon of binocular rivalry. When two patterns are presented simultaneously, one to each eye, the contents of conscious awareness spontaneously alternate between one monocular percept and the other over time. The visual percepts compete for awareness such that only one image is consciously perceived, and the other is suppressed (Levelt, 1965; Wheatstone, 1838). The oscillation of perceptual awareness between two simultaneously presented stimuli provides a useful tool to identify the neural correlates of conscious awareness (for reviews, see Rees, Kreiman, & Koch, 2002; Tong, 2001, 2003).

A growing number of investigations have been conducted using fMRI to address, in particular, the contributions of specific brain regions to perceptual awareness of rivalrous stimuli. One recent study using fMRI (Tong, Nakayama, Vaughan, & Kanwisher, 1998) presented face and house images separately to each eye and measured the neural activity in two predefined regions of interest: the FFA, which responds preferentially to faces (Kanwisher et al., 1997; McCarthy et al., 1997), and a parahippocampal region that responds most strongly to places and less so to faces (the Parahippocampal Place Area, or PPA; Epstein & Kanwisher, 1998). During imaging, participants continuously reported whether they saw a face or a house, and the pattern of neural activity extracted from a region of interest analysis was time-locked to these conscious perceptual experiences. Interestingly, neural activation corresponded to the conscious perceptual experience, even though the stimulus pair was invariant within a trial; FFA activation increased when participants reported perception of a face stimulus, and PPA activation increased when they reported a house. Critically, the pattern of activation when subjects consciously per-

ceived a face or a house when both were present (in the rivalrous stimulus) was no different than when the face or house was presented alone, suggesting that the competitive neural interactions responsible for rivalry are largely resolved before conscious perception occurs.

This finding might suggest that activation in the FFA or the PPA produces visual awareness of the presence of a face or a house. However, the FFA also is active when faces are not consciously reported (Rees et al., 2000), suggesting that reliable FFA activation is not sufficient for conscious perception of a face. This discrepancy might result from different degrees of activation, though. If neural activity is graded with respect to the level of perceptual awareness (i.e., low-level activity reflects low-level awareness) or if activity must surpass some threshold before conscious awareness occurs, then it is entirely possible that sufficient activation of the FFA or PPA does correspond to conscious awareness of a face or house, respectively. Stricter criteria for measuring conscious awareness are needed to determine whether activation in these specialized processing regions is sufficient for conscious perception.

Implicit Processing of Words and Numbers

Just as consciously perceived emotional stimuli activate the amygdala, read words tend to activate a prescribed set of brain regions more than do other stimuli (e.g., left-lateralized extrastriate cortex, fusiform gyrus, and precentral sulcus). Therefore, studies of implicit word perception can use neuroimaging evidence to determine whether words activate a similar set of regions without awareness. Such studies first assess the visibility of the critical words using behavioral measures. In one study (Dehaene et al., 2001), masked words were presented such that they were detected only 0.7% of the time (a rate slightly higher than the false alarm rate of 0.2% for trials in which no word was presented) and almost never named successfully (see also Rees, 2001). Moreover, recognition tests after the imaging portion of the study revealed no memory for the masked words. Of course, subjects might adopt a conservative criterion for indicating whether or not a word was present if they knew they would then be asked to name it. If so, then the task might not exhaustively measure conscious awareness, raising the possibility that the masked words were at least temporarily available to consciousness.

Assuming that low detection rates and failed recognition performance imply the absence of conscious awareness of the presence of the masked words, and if neural activity is consistent with reading, then perception presumably occurred implicitly. Interestingly, when compared to control conditions that mimicked the masking conditions of the critical trials but without any masked words, the unseen stimuli activated the previously mentioned set of brain regions known to be associated with reading (Dehaene et al., 2001). This pattern is consistent with the idea that the unseen stimuli were processed similarly to visible words. However, the pattern of neural activity evoked by the masked words in the ventral visual pathway was less widely distributed and of smaller magnitude than that obtained with consciously perceived words. The discrepancy was increasingly evident from posterior to anterior brain regions, suggesting that visual masking begins to suppress neural activity early in the visual processing stream, rendering later stages of visual processing less likely. Furthermore, visible words elicited neural activity in parietal, prefrontal, and cingulate cortices, but corresponding activation was not evident when the words were not available to conscious awareness. Finally, increased correlated activity among the ventral visual stream, parietal, and prefrontal areas was evident only when the words were visible. Some of these differences might well result from the naming task used in the study rather than from the perceptibility of the stimuli. Visible words could be named, but the masked words were not. However, it cannot be determined on the basis of these results whether some of the activity associated with visible words is a consequence of the naming task. In sum, masking resulted in less robust neural activation, but also in reduced correlated neural activity that might contribute to conscious awareness.

Similar patterns have emerged in neuroimaging studies of the perception of numerical stimuli (Naccache & Dehaene, 2001a). Neuroimaging and lesion data suggest a role for the parietal lobe (and particularly the intraparietal sulcus) in the mental representation and understanding of the quantity meaning of numbers (for a review, see Dehaene, Piazza, Pinel, & Cohen, 2003). Can implicit stimuli lead to similar patterns of activation? A recent paper (Naccache & Dehaene, 2001a) reanalyzed earlier neuroimaging data (Dehaene et al., 1998) and addressed this issue by using the phenomenon of repetition suppression. A number of imaging studies have shown that when a stimulus is repeated, localized neural activity associated with processing of that stimulus or its attributes typically decreases (Schacter, Alpert, Savage, Rauch, & Albert, 1996; Schacter & Buckner, 1998; Squire et al., 1992). Whole brain analysis of fMRI data revealed two isolated brain regions with reduced activity when the target repeated the prime relative to an otherwise categorically congruent prime: the left and right intraparietal sulci (Naccache & Dehaene, 2001a). The priming effect was not influenced by the use of different notations for the prime and target (1 vs. one), suggesting that the intraparietal sulcus encodes numbers in a more abstract format. Assuming that the prime stimuli were not consciously perceived, these effects indicate that repetition suppression can occur even when observers are unaware of the repetition. Presumably, this effect reflects the fairly extensive processing of an implicitly perceived stimulus.

Additionally, ERP studies of the response compatibility effect reveal covert activation from an incongruent prime – a lateralized readiness potential (LRP) on the incorrect side of response – presumably because the incongruent prime activates the incorrect motor response (Dehaene et al., 1998). fMRI data revealed greater overall activation in right motor cortex when both the prime and target were consistent with a left hand response (and vice versa), providing additional evidence for processing of the prime stimulus without awareness (Dehaene et al., 1998). In all of these studies, perception of the prime in the absence of awareness was not limited to sensory mechanisms alone, but also influenced higher-level processing.

ERPs in Priming Experiments

The influence of an unseen prime stimulus has been explored by examining general changes in ERPs to a target as a result of the presence of a prime. These studies measure the influence of an implicit prime indirectly, looking for changed neural processing of the target rather than activation directly in response to the prime stimulus. Studies of priming by masked stimuli represent the paradigmatic application of the dissociation paradigm, and the use of ERPs in conjunction with this approach may well contribute to a more complete assessment of the processing of an unseen stimulus. To the extent that semantic processing of a prime takes place, it should lead to modulation of the N400 (i.e., a negative-going ERP component sensitive to manipulations of semantic relatedness). Experiments with supraliminal words and sentences consistently find larger deflections in N400 amplitude for incongruent than for congruent targets (Kutas & Hillyard, 1980). For example, the N400 generated in response to the word "lemon" would likely be more negative when preceded by the unrelated prime "chair" than when preceded by the related prime "citrus."

Unfortunately, studies of N400 modulation by semantically related, unseen primes have produced mixed results (for a review, see Deacon & Shelley-Tremblay, 2000). For instance, in one experiment, masked primes led to faster responses to semantically related targets, but modulation of N400 was evident only when primes were completely visible (Brown & Hagoort, 1993). This finding implied that the N400 might constitute an electrophysiological marker of conscious semantic processes. Yet, other experiments that account for potential methodological shortcomings of this experiment induce modulation of the N400 even when the primes were consciously inaccessible (e.g., Deacon, Hewitt, Yang, & Nagata, 2000; Kiefer, 2002). Moreover, the effects of a prime on the N400 are qualitatively different for visible and masked primes. Masked primes modulate the N400 with a short SOA between the prime and target, but not with a longer SOA. In contrast, for visible primes, the modulation of the N400 increases as the SOA increases (Kiefer & Spitzer, 2000). This qualitative difference suggests that implicit and explicit perception of prime stimuli might rely on different processing mechanisms.

Taken together, these studies provide support for N400 activation in response to an unseen prime. However, they are subject to many of the critiques leveled at the dissociation paradigm (Holender, 1986). For example, visibility of the prime on some trials might well contribute to the observed effects – the measure of awareness might not have been exclusive. One recent ERP study made a valiant effort to address many of the requirements of the dissociation paradigm (Stenberg, Lindgren, Johansson, Olsson, & Rosen, 2000). Most dissociation paradigm studies attempt to render the prime invisible using a masking procedure, assuming that the prime is invisible to all subjects on all trials. An alternative approach is to vary the visibility of the target itself and to measure the ERP response to an unseen target stimulus (Stenberg et al., 2000). This approach has the advantage of allowing the trial-by-trial assessment of target visibility.

In these experiments (Stenberg et al., 2000), a visible category name (the prime) was followed by a word that either was from the primed category or from a different category. Target perceptibility was varied across blocks so that individual subjects could successfully name the target on 50% of trials. Because this subjective naming task leaves criterion setting in the hands of the subject and does not sample conscious awareness exhaustively, several measures of conscious awareness were also administered at the end of each trial: (a) subjects indicated whether or not the word had been a member of the prime category, (b) they named the word (guessing if necessary), and (c) they attempted to select the target word from either a 2- or 6-alternative forced-choice test. The 6-alternative test was considered the most sensitive, hence the most exhaustive measure of awareness. Interestingly, the semantic priming effect (i.e., N400) distinguished between categorically consistent and categorically inconsistent words, irrespective of visibility. Although modulation of the N400 was less pronounced when the words could not be explicitly identified, the topographical pattern of activation did not differ across conditions. Qualitative differences in hemispheric lateralization were evident in an extended positive-going complex that typically accompanies cognitive tasks like the one employed in these experiments. This ERP component remained consistent irrespective of categorical classification, but had a different topography depending upon whether or not targets were explicitly identified. Consciously reported targets were associated with left- lateralized activity, whereas implicitly perceived targets elicited more distributed or right-lateralized activity, suggesting that different neural populations were recruited under these circumstances (Stenberg et al., 2000).

Together, the consistency of the N400 irrespective of visibility and differences in lateralization of raw amplitudes for visible and implicit targets strengthen claims for semantic processing of words that are not readily identified. When the criterion for conscious awareness was based on the more conservative 6-alternative forced-choice test, 30% of the words that could not be named were correctly identified and dropped from subsequent analyses. The binary categorization responses collected on the remaining trials were used to calculate d', which was not different from 0 – providing even stronger evidence that the remaining target words were not available to conscious awareness. Despite using a more stringent objective criterion, modulation of the N400 remained intact (Stenberg et al., 2000). In fact, when a regression analysis was conducted to determine whether the N400 was more sensitive to categorical deviations than the binary-choice discrimination task, the intercept was reliably greater than 0. This experiment adopts most of the controls needed to make clear inferences from behavioral studies using the dissociation paradigm, but also adds a more sensitive neuroimaging measure to provide additional evidence for both quantitative and qualitative differences in the processing of consciously perceived and implicitly perceived stimuli.

Additional evidence for a change in the ERP pattern in response to an unseen stimulus comes from studies of the P300, a component typically occurring 260–500 ms after exposure to a relatively rare stimulus. In this case, the "rarity" of the target stimulus depends on its relation to other stimuli presented in the study. Would the target stimulus reveal this rarity response if the other stimuli were not consciously perceived? A number of studies have explored this question (e.g., Brazdil, Rektor, Dufek, Jurak, & Daniel, 1998; Devrim, Demiralp, & Kurt, 1997), but most are subject to the critique that subjects were aware of the regular or frequent stimuli and that they had a strong response bias when awareness was assessed in a separate block of trials (Bernat, Shevrin, & Snodgrass, 2001b).

One more recent experiment (Bernat et al., 2001b) showed modulation of the P300 to a rare target word even when more rigorous criteria for measuring conscious awareness were applied to make sure that the frequent words were not consciously detected (for a review, see Shevrin, 2001). The words LEFT and RIGHT were presented tachistoscopically in an oddball design with an 80:20 frequent-to-rare ratio. Frequent stimuli were made subliminal by presenting them for only 1 ms, and subjects were given a forced-choice detection block after the experiment. Collapsed across subjects, d' did not differ from 0, but not all subjects showed a d' of 0. Consequently, the effect could be driven by a few subjects who showed awareness on some trials. However, the correlation between the d′ score for a given subject and their P300 was negative, suggesting that more awareness of the frequent stimuli actually diminished the P300 amplitude. Moreover, a regression of P300 magnitude against d′ revealed a significant P300 effect even when d′ was extrapolated to 0.

Summary

One recurrent theme in this overview of the neuroimaging of implicit perception is that, when stimuli are not consciously perceptible, activation is often reduced relative to when they are consciously perceived. Importantly, activation in response to an unseen stimulus is not limited to early sensory processing and often activates brain regions associated with processing that particular type of stimulus. These findings suggest that implicit perception might be a weaker version of the same processes occurring for explicit perception. As for most studies of implicit perception, neuroimaging studies rely almost exclusively on the dissociation paradigm, attempting to eliminate explicit awareness and then attributing the residual effects to implicit perception. To the extent that these studies fail to meet the exhaustiveness assumption of the dissociation paradigm, they are subject to the same critiques often leveled at behavioral studies (Hannula et al., 2005). The strength of the evidence for implicit perception based on neuroimaging approaches depends on the extent to which the studies successfully demonstrate that processing has really occurred in the absence of awareness.

A Believer's Interpretation

Although some of the experiments fail to address the exhaustiveness assumption sufficiently, others provide more convincing tests of explicit awareness. Few individual studies provide unequivocal evidence for the effects of an unseen stimulus on brain activity; however, when considered holistically, the literature provides strong converging evidence. Some experiments provide evidence that

processing was implicit and simultaneously demonstrate neural consequences of implicit perception. The strongest evidence comes from studies of differences in N400 amplitude in response to an implicitly perceived stimulus (Stenberg et al., 2000). Reliable differences in N400 amplitude were evident even when a fairly conservative 6-alternative forced-choice task was used to rule out explicit awareness on a trial-by-trial basis. By probing for awareness of the critical stimulus immediately after presentation, this study reduced concerns about fleeting conscious perception of the stimuli (i.e., memory failure following conscious perception). Further, the study adopted the regression technique (Greenwald et al., 1995) to show that N400 patterns persisted even when the d′ measure was extrapolated to null sensitivity. Finally, and perhaps most importantly, the patterns of neural activity elicited by implicitly and explicitly visible stimuli were qualitatively different, suggesting different neural mechanisms for the processing of implicit and explicit stimuli. Each piece of evidence can be criticized if considered in isolation, but taken together they provide one of the most complete and convincing demonstrations of implicit perception.

Further valuable evidence for implicit perception comes from fMRI studies of emotionally valenced faces (Whalen et al., 1998). Implicitly perceived fearful faces produce amygdala activation, and a subtraction analysis revealed no additional activation of visual cortex relative to happy faces, suggesting the possibility that fearful faces are processed automatically via a non-cortical route. Of course, this subtraction does not eliminate the possibility of cortical activation; both happy and fearful faces could produce visual cortex activation, and the subtraction just reveals the lack of additional cortical processing of fearful faces. Even so, the fact that amygdala activation was greater for fearful faces in the absence of greater activation of visual cortex is suggestive of an alternative, non-cortical source of the activation. Together, for these results provide converging support for implicit perception.

A Skeptic's Interpretation

Although these investigations provide some of the strongest evidence for implicit perception, and despite the advantages of using sensitive neuroimaging measures, all of them adopt the dissociation paradigm without fully meeting the exhaustiveness assumption for each subject (Hannula et al., 2005). Most of these studies find diminished responses to less visible stimuli, raising the possibility that the effect results from residual explicit processing rather than from a different mechanism altogether. That is, these findings are consistent with a failure to meet the exhaustiveness assumption. Moreover, neural activation might not be as sensitive a measure as we assume. Perhaps a sizable amount of conscious processing is necessary to produce robust neural activation and to produce the distributed processing that is typically attributed to consciousness. If so, then "implicit" stimuli may have been fleetingly or weakly perceived, and the amount of conscious information available might not be enough to drive robust neural activation. This distinction might account for qualitative differences in the pattern of activation for identified and unidentified words (Stenberg et al., 2000). The unidentified words might have received an insufficient amount of conscious processing to produce the pattern typically associated with full awareness; however, that qualitative difference does not imply the absence of explicit processing. Implicitly and explicitly perceived stimuli may produce qualitatively different patterns of activation only because the implicit stimuli received less conscious processing (not no conscious processing).

The strongest evidence reviewed here is the N400 effect for unseen stimuli. This series of studies represents the most careful and systematic exploration of implicit perception that we are aware of in any of the studies discussed in this chapter. The studies carefully segregated aware and unaware trials on the basis of both subjective (word identification) and objective (6-alternative forced-choice [6AFC] decisions)

measures and then examined the N400 for both correct and incorrect/absent responses. Although explicit sensitivity (measured using d' for a binary category decision task) was effectively nil for mistaken responses in the 6AFC task, it was reliably above chance for the word identification task (in Experiments 2 and 3). Thus, the identification task clearly was not exhaustive. The 6AFC task comes closer, but a skeptic could quibble with several of the procedures in this study. First, the mean d' was often greater than 0, and some subjects had d' values greater than 0.5 on the binary choice. Although the regression method revealed an intercept significantly greater than 0, suggesting implicit processing even when d' was extrapolated to 0, the fact that many observers had greater than nil sensitivity raises concerns that a few of the subjects might partially drive the results. A better approach would be to set the stimulus characteristics separately for each subject such that d' is as close as possible to 0 on the explicit task. Another concern is that the task used to measure d' was a binary category judgment (in the category vs. not in the category). This task might not be as sensitive as a presence/absence judgment, raising the possibility that a more sensitive measure might reveal some explicit processing even when observers show no sensitivity in the category judgment. These critiques aside, this study represents one of the greatest challenges to a skeptic because it uses multiple explicit measures and a sensitive imaging measure to examine implicit processing.

Evidence for Implicit Perception – Patient Data

Studies of brain-damaged patients provide some of the most compelling evidence for implicit perception. In fact, some have noted the surprising acceptance of evidence for implicit perception in brain-damaged subjects even by researchers who reject similar methods in the study of unimpaired subjects (Merikle & Reingold, 1992). In part, this acceptance of evidence from patient populations derives from the belief that brain damage can entirely disrupt some aspects of conscious perception or memory. If so, then the brain damage may provide the most effective elimination of explicit perception, much more so than simply reducing the visibility of a stimulus via masking. In unimpaired populations, the mechanisms for conscious perception are potentially available, leaving the persistent concern that any evidence for implicit perception might derive from explicit contamination. However, if the mechanisms themselves are eliminated by brain damage, then any residual processing must be attributed to implicit processes.

The challenge for researchers wishing to provide evidence for implicit perception is different for patient studies. Rather than trying to show that a particular task rules out the use of explicit perception, researchers must demonstrate that the patient entirely lacks the capacity for explicit processing in any task. Given that most such "natural experiments" are inherently messy, with some spared abilities intermixed with impairments, conclusions from patient studies depend on a systematic exploration of the nature and extent of the deficit in processing. In many cases, such studies require the same level of empirical precision necessary in behavioral studies, but they are further hampered by the limited subject population.

In this section, we consider three different sorts of evidence for a distinction between implicit and explicit processing. In two of these cases, conclusions rely heavily on the data of a relatively small number of patients. First, we consider the implications of studies of DF who is a visual form agnosic. We then consider two different classes of brain-damage phenomena, each of which has led to striking findings of preserved processing in the absence of awareness: blindsight and visual neglect.

DF and the Two Pathways Argument

The visual form agnosic patient DF (Goodale & Milner, 1992; Milner & Goodale, 1995) acquired her deficit from bilateral damage to portions of extrastriate visual cortex in the ventral visual processing stream. Although she can perceive and discriminate surface features such as color and texture, she shows a strikingly impaired ability to visually discriminate figural properties of objects, such as form, size, and orientation. Her preserved haptic and auditory discrimination of objects reveals preserved general knowledge and object recognition abilities; her deficit is one of visual object perception. Despite her inability to recognize objects visually, she can use the visual structure of objects to guide her motor responses. For example, she shows normal performance when trying to insert a slate into a slot, using the proper orientation and directed movement even though she cannot report the orientation of the slate in the absence of a motor interaction (Goodale, Milner, Jakobson, & Carey, 1991). Furthermore, she cannot report the orientations of blocks placed on tables, but can still reach out and pick up the blocks with appropriate grip aperture and limb movements (Jakobson & Goodale, 1991).

These results countermand the intuition that perception produces a unitary representation of the world, that interactions with the visual world should rely on the same representations and mechanisms as visual interpretation of the world. The dissociation in DF's ability to interpret and act on the world provides evidence for two distinct mechanisms to process visual information. One system involves the phenomenal recognition of parts of the visual world, and the other, operating without our awareness of the identities of objects, allows us to act on the world. In other words, this system seems to allow guided motor responses to objects even if we are unaware of what those objects might be.

The case of DF does not provide evidence for implicit perception in the same sense discussed throughout the rest of this chapter; at some level, DF is aware of the existence of the object even if she cannot name it. However, the case has some interesting parallels, and it reveals the importance of looking for qualitative differences in performance. One obvious parallel is that a visual stimulus can elicit an appropriate action or response even if some aspects of it are unavailable to consciousness. Visual analysis of an object does not guarantee conscious perception of its properties. More importantly, some aspects of visual processing occur outside of what can be consciously reported. The case of DF differs from other studies of implicit perception in that her spared abilities do not involve the processing of symbolic representations outside of awareness. Rather, she can engage in actions toward objects without needing to use a symbolic representation or any recognition-based processes. Most studies of implicit perception focus on whether or not implicit symbol manipulation or representation is possible (Dulany, 2004).

Blindsight

Neurologists had long speculated that some visual functioning might persist even in patients blinded by cortical damage (see Teuber, Battersby, & Bender, 1960 for a review), but the phenomenology of "blindsight" was not convincingly demonstrated until the 1970s (Pöppel, Held, & Frost, 1973; Weiskrantz, Warrington, Sanders, & Marshal, 1974). Patients suffering damage to primary visual cortex (V1) experience a visual scotoma; they fail to consciously perceive objects that fall into the affected portion of their visual field. They do not perceive a black hole or an empty space. Rather, the missing region of the visual field simply does not reach awareness, much as neurologically intact individuals do not normally notice their blind spot when one eye is closed. Blindsight refers to the finding that some cortically blind patients show evidence of perception in their damaged field in the absence of awareness. In essence, such patient evidence constitutes an application of the dissociation logic; the patient reports no awareness of the stimulus but still shows some effect of it. In a classic study of blindsight (Weiskrantz et al., 1974), lights were flashed in the damaged visual field of patient DB. Although DB reported no awareness of the lights, he could point out the loca-

tion of the light more accurately than would be expected by chance. This finding suggests that V1 contributes to visual awareness, because in its absence, patients do not consciously experience visual stimuli. Perhaps the most established explanation for blindsight posits two routes to visual perception: (a) a pathway via V1 that leads to conscious awareness and (b) a more primitive pathway bypassing V1, perhaps via the superior colliculus. The latter route presumably allows perception in the absence of awareness. Indeed, in animals, cells in MT specialized for the detection of motion continue to respond normally to moving stimuli in the scotoma (Rosa, Tweedale, & Elston, 2000).

The two-routes hypothesis provides a strong claim about the nature of implicit perception, with one route operating outside awareness and the other generating awareness. Over the past 20 years, this hypothesis has faced a number of challenges designed to undermine the claim that conscious perception is entirely absent in blindsight. In other words, these alternative explanations question the exhaustiveness of the measure of conscious awareness, which in this case is the subjective report of the subject. For example, damage to V1 might be incomplete, with islands of spared cortex that function normally, thereby allowing degraded visual experience in small portions of the scotoma region (Fendrich, Wessinger, & Gazzaniga, 1992, 1993; Gazzaniga, Fendrich, & Wessinger, 1994; Wessinger, Fendrich, & Gazzaniga, 1997). Brain imaging of blindsight patients has returned mixed results: at least one patient (CLT) showed a small region of metabolically active visual cortex (Fendrich et al., 1993), whereas other researchers found no evidence for intact visual cortex in structural scans of other blindsight patients (e.g., Trevethan & Sahraie, 2003; Weiskrantz, 2002). Moreover, lesions of V1 in animals produce blindsight-like behavior even though these controlled lesions likely are complete (e.g., Cowey & Stoerig, 1995). Another alternative is that neurologically spared regions surrounding the scotoma receive differential sensory input as a result of the presence of an item in the blind region, thereby allowing better-than-chance guessing (Campion, Latto, & Smith, 1983). For example, a light source in the blind field might also generate some visual input for regions outside the blind field via scattering of light, thereby indicating the presence of something unseen (see the commentary in Campion et al., 1983 for a discussion). A final challenge comes from the argument that blindsight itself might indicate a change in response criterion rather than a change in awareness or sensitivity per se (Azzopardi & Cowey, 1998). This challenge is based on the idea that subjective reports on single trials do not fully measure awareness and that a signal detection approach is needed to verify that the response criterion cannot entirely account for the results. We address this final alternative in more detail here because it is the most theoretically relevant to the topic of this chapter.

Most evidence for blindsight comes from a comparison of performance on two tasks: a presence/absence judgment (direct measure of awareness) and a forced-choice task (indirect measure of perception), and most data are reported in terms of percentage correct (Azzopardi & Cowey, 1998). Yet, the use of percent correct to compare performance in these two tasks could well lead to spurious dissociations between implicit and explicit perception because percent correct measures are affected by response biases (Campion et al., 1983). For example, subjects tend to adopt a fairly conservative response criterion (responding only when certain) when asked to make a presence/absence judgment about a near-threshold stimulus. Furthermore, subjects may well vary their criterion from trial to trial. In contrast, when subjects are forced to choose between two alternative stimuli or to pick which temporal interval contained a stimulus, response bias is less of a concern; subjects have to choose one of the two stimuli. Direct comparisons of presence/absence and forced choice performance are therefore pitting.

To examine the possibility of bias, a frequently tested blindsight patient's (GY) sensitivity to the presence of stimuli was mea-sured with d' (or d_a where appropriate) along with his response criterion for a variety of tasks often used to study blindsight (Azzopardi & Cowey, 1998). As expected, responding was unbiased in a forced-choice task. In contrast, response criterion in a presence/absence judgment was fairly conservative ($c = 1.867$), and interestingly, it was substantially reduced by instructing GY to guess when unsure ($c = .228$). These findings reveal the danger of relying on percent correct as a primary measure of blindsight; with sensitivity set to $d' = 1.5$, these levels of bias elicit 75% correct responding for a forced-choice task, but 55% performance for a presence/absence judgment. In fact, any $d' > 1$ would lead to an apparent dissociation in percentage correct, but the result could entirely be attributed to response criterion rather than differential sensitivity. Using this signal detection approach, GY showed greater sensitivity for static displays in forced-choice responses than in presence/absence responses, but the same did not hold for moving displays. Thus, evidence for "blindsight" to motion stimuli in which patients report no awareness (presence/absence) but still show accurate forced-choice performance might result entirely from shifts in response criterion. These results underscore the danger of relying on percent correct scores in investigations employing blindsight patients and highlight the benefits of using bias-free tasks. To date, relatively few investigations of blindsight have adopted these important methodological changes, despite an active literature that possesses surprising scope given the apparent rarity of blindsight patients.

Inferences from one recent study are less subject to the criterion problem (Marcel, 1998). Two patients (TP and GY) completed a series of tasks that required forced-choice judgments, and only some showed evidence of implicit perception. For example, neither showed much priming from single letters presented to their blind field when the task was to pick the matching letter. Also, neither was more likely to select a synonym of a word presented to the blind field. However, when defining a polysemous word, both showed priming in their choice of a definition when a word presented to the blind field disambiguated the meaning. Given that these tasks all involve forced-choice decisions, differences between them are unlikely to result from response biases. Interestingly, the finding that the least direct measure shows an effect implies that semantic concepts are activated without activating the representation of the word itself.

One intriguing finding is that some blindsight patients apparently consciously experience afterimages of stimuli presented to their blind field (Marcel, 1998; Weiskrantz, 2002). Such afterimages, if frequently experienced by blindsight patients, might explain some residual perception in the damaged field. Interestingly, the afterimages can arise after information from the blind and sighted fields have been combined. When different colored filters were used for the blind and sighted field, patient DB experienced an afterimage that was specific to the combination of those two colors, suggesting that information from the blind field was processed beyond the point required to resolve binocular differences (Weiskrantz, 2002).

The phenomenon of blindsight represents one of the most striking demonstrations of non-conscious perception. It provides potentially important insights into the need for V1 in order to consciously perceive our environment. However, the approaches typically used to study blindsight are subject to methodological critiques because they often do not account for response biases in the measurement of awareness. Perhaps more importantly, most such studies are couched in the dissociation framework, inferring implicit perception based on the absence of direct evidence for conscious perception. Consequently, blindsight findings are subject to many of the same objections raised for behavioral work on implicit perception.

Parietal Neglect

Visual neglect involves deficient awareness of objects in the contralesional visual field, typically resulting from damage to the posterior inferior parietal lobe in the right hemisphere, secondary to middle cerebral artery infarction. Although both blindsight and neglect are associated with spared processing in the absence of awareness, neglect is characterized as an attentional (rather than sensory) deficit, and commonly occurs in the absence of a visual scotoma (or blind spot). The damage in neglect occurs later in the perceptual processing stream than it does in cases of blindsight, raising the possibility that neglected stimuli might be processed semantically to a greater extent as well (see Driver & Mattingley, 1998 for a review). In many patients, the failure to notice or attend to contralesional stimuli is exacerbated when stimuli are presented simultaneously to both left and right visual fields, presumably because these stimuli compete for attention (visual extinction, as described earlier). For example, neglect patients might fail to eat food on the left side of their plate. Some patients fail to dress the left side of their body or to brush the left side of their hair. Although neglect can affect other processing modalities (e.g., haptic and auditory processing), we limit our discussion to visual neglect.

Evidence for preserved processing of neglected visual stimuli takes several forms: (a) successful same/different discrimination of bilaterally presented stimuli despite a failure to report the contralesional stimulus, (b) intact lexical and semantic processing of extinguished stimuli, and (c) activation of responses consistent with an extinguished prime. Here we review evidence from each of these areas, and we also describe experiments designed to test the claim that extinguished stimuli are not consciously perceived.

Many studies demonstrate the preserved ability to discriminate identical pairs of items from those that are physically or categorically dissimilar (Berti et al., 1992; Verfaellie, Milberg, McGlinchey-Berroth, & Grande, 1995; Volpe, Ledoux, & Gazzaniga, 1979). Typically, two pictures or words are briefly presented to the right and left of fixation, and patients judge whether they are the same (have the same name) or are different. Both patients and intact control subjects perform this task better than chance even when the object orientations differ or when they are two different exemplars of the same category (e.g., two different cameras). Further, patients can reliably indicate that physically similar (and semantically related) items are in fact different from one another. In all cases, patients report little or no awareness of the stimulus in the contralesional visual field.

These findings suggest that neglect patients can process extinguished stimuli semantically and that their representation of these unseen stimuli is fairly complex and complete. The dissociation between the naming and matching indicates that visual processing of extinguished stimuli proceeds relatively normally despite the absence of awareness (but see Farah, Monheit, & Wallace, 1991). However, more concrete evidence for the absence of explicit awareness of extinguished stimuli is required for a clear conclusion in favor of implicit perception. This approach is logically equivalent to the dissociation paradigm; demonstrate that subjects cannot perceive a stimulus and then look for residual effects on performance. Subjects claim no conscious experience of extinguished stimuli but still are able to perform a fairly complex discrimination on the basis of the stimulus presentation. In fact, when patients were required to name both stimuli, they frequently named only the ipsilesional item. However, some of them felt that something had appeared on the contralesional side. None of these studies demonstrate that sensitivity to the presence of the extinguished stimulus is objectively no better than chance.

An alternative to examining preserved judgments about extinguished stimuli is to explore whether such stimuli produce lexical or semantic priming. To the extent that neglect is only a partial disruption of the ability to form representations, the inability to name extinguished stimuli might result from a failure to access existing representations rather than a failure to form a representation (McGlinchey-Berroth, Milberg, Verfaellie, Alexander, & Kilduff, 1993). Repetition priming tasks have been used to examine lexical, orthographic, or

phonological priming by neglected stimuli (Schweinberger & Stief, 2001), and semantic priming studies have explored whether neglected primes receive more extensive cognitive processing (e.g., Ladavas, Paladini, & Cubelli, 1993; McGlinchey-Berroth et al., 1993). Primes are presented briefly in either the contralesional or ipsilesional visual field followed by a visible target stimulus, and priming is reflected in faster processing of the target stimulus. Lexical priming apparently survives visual neglect: Priming was evident for both patients and normal controls only when word stimuli were repeated and not when non-word stimuli were repeated, suggesting that the neglected word activated an existing representation (Schweinberger & Stief, 2001). Furthermore, the magnitude of priming was comparable in the contralesional and ipsilesional visual fields. In fact, left visual field priming was actually greater than that of normal controls for patients who neglected their left visual field. This counter-intuitive finding may result from a center-surround mechanism that increases activation for weakly accessible or subconscious visual stimulus while simultaneously inhibiting activation of other related items (see Carr & Dagenbach, 1990).

Similar claims have been made with respect to higher-level semantic processing of neglected visual stimuli. In one of these experiments (McGlinchey-Berroth et al., 1993), pictures, used as prime stimuli, were presented peripherally in the left or the right visual field, and filler items (a meaningless visual stimulus made up of components of the target items) were presented on the side opposite. After 200 ms, the pictures were replaced by a central target letter string, and subjects indicated whether or not the string was a word. Semantic priming should lead to faster lexical decisions if the prime pictures were related to the word. Although patients responded more slowly than controls, they showed semantic priming even though they could not identify the prime pictures in a 2-alternative forced-choice task (McGlinchey-Berroth et al., 1993). Other semantic priming tasks have found faster processing of a right-lateralized word following a left-lateralized prime word (Ladavas et al., 1993). Given that the patient in this study was unable to read a single word presented in the left visual field, and performed no better than chance with lexical decision, semantic discrimination, and stimulus detection tasks even without a bilateral presentation, the prime presumably was not consciously perceived.

However, none of the studies discussed thus far provided an exhaustive test for conscious awareness of left-lateralized stimuli, leaving open the possibility that residual awareness of the "neglected" stimulus might account for preserved priming effects. More generally, the use of different paradigms or stimuli in tests of awareness and measures of priming does not allow a full assessment of awareness during the priming task; measures of awareness may not generalize to the experiment itself. Many of the priming studies also introduce a delay interval between the prime and target, leaving open the possibility that patients shift their attention to the extinguished stimulus in advance of target presentation (see Cohen, Ivry, Rafal, & Kohn, 1995).

Other studies of implicit perception in visual neglect have adopted a response compatibility approach in which a central target item is flanked by an irrelevant item on either the left or right side of fixation (Cohen et al., 1995). These flanker items were either compatible, incompatible, or neutral with respect to the response required for the target. Interestingly, responses to the target were slower when the flanker was incompatible, even when it was presented to the contralesional visual field. In a control experiment using the same materials, the patients were asked to respond to the flankers and were given unlimited time to respond. Responses were reliably slower and more error prone for stimuli presented to the contralesional visual field. This finding confirms the impairment of processing of stimuli in the contralesional visual field, but it also undermines the response compatibility results as a demonstration of implicit perception. That subjects could,

when instructed, direct their attention to the "neglected" contralesional stimulus implies that they might have had some residual awareness of flankers presented to the contralesional visual field. The patients in this experiment also had more diffuse damage than is typical in neglect experiments, and one had left-lateralized damage. The diffuse damage might affect performance on the flanker task for reasons other than hemispatial neglect.

Most studies of implicit perception by neglect patients have focused on determining the richness of processing of neglected stimuli, but relatively few studies have focused on producing convincing demonstrations that neglected stimuli truly escape conscious awareness. One recent study adopted the process dissociation procedure in an attempt to provide a more thorough demonstration that processing of neglected stimuli is truly implicit (Esterman et al., 2002). A critical picture appeared in one visual field and a meaningless filler picture appeared in the other. After a 400-ms delay, a two-letter word stem appeared in the center of the screen, and subjects were either instructed to complete the stem with the name of the critical picture (inclusion) or to complete it with any word other than the picture name (exclusion). Relative to normal control subjects, patients were less likely to complete word stems with picture names in the inclusion task, particularly when the picture was presented in the neglected visual field. In contrast, patients were more likely than controls to complete the stems with picture names in the exclusion task when the picture was presented in the neglected field. Moreover, they completed such stems with the picture name more frequently than in a baseline condition with no pictures. If patients had explicitly perceived the stimulus, they would not have used it to complete the word stem. However, they still processed it enough that it influenced their stem completion. Although this study provides clearer evidence for implicit perception of neglected stimuli, the methods are subject to the same critiques discussed in our review of behavioral evidence using the exclusion paradigm. Clearly, more systematic assessments of explicit perception of neglected words are needed before unequivocal claims about implicit perception in neglect are possible.

A Believer's Interpretation

Perhaps more interesting than the evidence itself is the face validity of evidence for implicit perception in patient populations. Neglect and blindsight illustrate the serious behavioral ramifications of the absence of awareness, and their normal behaviors are in essence a constant, real-world version of the process dissociation paradigm. Such patients' daily actions reflect their lack of awareness of some aspects of their visual world, and if they had awareness of those aspects, they would perform differently. Evidence for perception despite the absence of awareness in these patients is particularly convincing because the absence of explicit awareness is their primary deficit. In combination with behavioral and neuroimaging evidence, these data confirm that implicit perception is possible in the absence of awareness.

A Skeptic's Interpretation

Studies of patient populations rely extensively on the logic of the dissociation paradigm; patients lack awareness of parts of their visual world, so any residual processing of information in those areas must reflect implicit perception. Unfortunately, few studies exhaustively eliminate the possibility of partial explicit processing of visual information in the face of these deficits. Nobody doubts that explicit awareness is affected in both blindsight and neglect. These deficits of awareness have clear behavioral consequences. However, impaired awareness does not mean absent awareness. One of the few studies of blindsight to measure awareness using signal detection theory found that many of the most robust findings supporting implicit perception could be attributed to bias rather than residual sensitivity (Azzopardi & Cowey, 1998). This study reveals the dan-

ger in relying solely on subjective reports of awareness rather than on systematic measurement of performance. Most patient studies use subjects' ability to report their visual experience as the primary measure of explicit awareness, with implicit perception inferred from any spared processing in the "blind" field. Such subjective reports in the context of the dissociation paradigm do not provide an adequately exhaustive measure of explicit perception. Consequently, performance on indirect measures might reflect residual explicit perception rather than implicit perception.

What do Dissociations in Perception Mean?

Despite protestations to the contrary, the century-old debate over the mere existence of implicit perception continues to this day. The techniques and tools have improved, but the theoretical arguments are surprisingly consistent. In essence, believers argue that the converging evidence provides overwhelming support for the existence of implicit perception, whereas skeptics argue that almost all findings of implicit perception fail to provide adequate controls for explicit contamination. As with most such debates, different conclusions can be drawn from the same data. Believers can point to improved methodologies that provide more sensitive measures of implicit processing or that more effectively control for explicit processing. Skeptics can point to the fact that none of these controls are airtight and that the effects, when present, tend to be small. Believers point to converging evidence from patients and from imaging studies with neurologically intact individuals, and skeptics point to the even greater inadequacies of the controls for explicit processing in those domains. The conclusions drawn from these data are colored by assumptions about the parsimony of each conclusion. Believers find the conclusion in favor of implicit processing more parsimonious because a variety of critiques, some fairly convoluted, are needed to account for all of the converging support for implicit processing. Skeptics find conclusions in favor of implicit processing unappetizing because they often posit the existence of additional mechanisms when all of the data can potentially be explained using solely explicit processing.

More recent behavioral techniques have made progress toward eliminating the more obvious objections of skeptics. Qualitative differences, signal detection measures of sensitivity, and regression techniques are appropriate first steps toward overcoming the critiques of the dissociation paradigm, although a staunch critic might never be satisfied. From this possibly irresolvable debate, perhaps some additional insights can be gleaned. Regardless of whether or not implicit perception exists, what can we learn about perceptual processing from attempts to reveal implicit perception? What do dissociations in perception, whether between implicit and explicit or entirely within explicit processing, tell us about the nature of awareness and about the nature of perception? What do these dissociations mean for our understanding of perception?

For the moment, let's assume that implicit perception exists. If it does exist, what does it do? Does it play a functional role in the survival of the perceiver? Our perceptual systems exist to extract information from the world to allow effective behavior. The world, then, presents a challenge to a perceptual system: The information available far exceeds our ability to consciously encode and retain it. Our perceptual systems evolved to extract order and systematicity from the available data, to encode those aspects of the world that are relevant for the behavioral demands of our ecological niche (Gibson, 1966). Our perceptual systems adapted to extract signal from the noise, allowing us to survive regardless of whether we are aware of the variables that influence our behavior.

We are only aware of a subset of our world at any time, and we are, of course, unaware of those aspects that fail to reach awareness. Just as a refrigerator light is always on whenever we look inside, any time we examine the outputs of perceptual processing, we are aware of those outputs. Someone unfamiliar with the workings of a refrigerator might assume that the light is on when the door is closed. Similarly, given that the only information available to consciousness is that information that has reached awareness, an intuitive inference would be to assume that all processing involves awareness – we never "see" evidence of processing without awareness. Claims that mental processes happen outside of consciously mediated operations run counter to this intuitive belief. That same belief might also underlie the willingness to accept subjective reports as adequate measures of conscious processing (see the subjective vs. objective threshold discussion above). The goal of the implicit perception literature is to determine whether or not perceptual processing occurs with the metaphorical refrigerator light out.

A fundamental issue in the implicit perception literature concerns the similarities of the types of processing attributed to implicit and explicit mechanisms. Is there a commonality to those operations that apply with and without awareness? If implicit perception exists, do the implicit mechanisms apply to everything outside of awareness equally, or is there some selectivity? Does the spotlight of consciousness perpetually move about, randomly illuminating implicitly processed information, thereby bringing it to awareness? Or are there fundamental differences between implicit and explicit processes? This question is, in many respects, more interesting and important than the question of whether or not implicit perception exists at all. Implicit perception would lack its popular appeal and broad implications if it produced nothing more than a weak version of the same processing that would occur with awareness. The broad popular appeal (or fear) of the notion of implicit processing is that it could, under the right circumstances, lead to behaviors different from those we would choose with awareness.

One way to conceptualize the implicit/explicit distinction is to map it onto the intentional/automatic dichotomy. Consciousness presumably underlies intentional actions (Searle, 1992), those in which perceivers can perform new operations, computations, or symbol manipulations on the information in the world. Automatic behaviors, in contrast, reproduce old operations, computations, or symbol manipulations, repeating processes that were effective in the past in the absence of intentional control. Automatic computations occur in a data-driven, possibly encapsulated fashion (Fodor, 1986). Much of the evidence for perception without awareness is based on this sort of data-driven processing that could potentially affect explicit processing, but that occurs entirely without conscious control. Previous exposure to a stimulus might lead to more automatic processing of it the next time. Or, if the implicit and explicit processing mechanisms overlap substantially, a prior exposure might provide metaphorical grease for the gears, increasing the likelihood that bottom-up processing will lead to explicit awareness.

The vast majority of evidence for implicit perception takes this form, producing behavioral responses or neural activation patterns that mirror those we might expect from explicit processing. Behavioral response compatibility findings are a nice example of this form of implicit perception: The interference shown in response to an implicitly perceived prime is comparable to that we might expect from a consciously perceived prime (except for NCE effects). Similarly, much of the fMRI evidence for implicit perception shows that activation from unseen stimuli mirrors the pattern of activation that would occur with awareness.

These findings are not as theoretically interesting as cases in which the outcome of implicit perception differs from what we would expect with conscious perception – cases in which implicit and explicit processes lead to qualitatively different outcomes. When the results are the same for implicit and explicit processing, the standard skeptical critiques weigh heavily. The failure to meet the assumptions of the dissociation paradigm adequately leaves open the possibility that "implicit" behaviors result from explicit processing. In contrast, qual-

itative differences are theoretically significant regardless of whether or not they reflect a difference between implicit and explicit processing. Take, for example, the case of DF (Goodale & Milner, 1992). She can accurately put an oriented card through a slot, but lacks conscious access to the orientation of the card. Although she cannot subjectively perceive the orientation, other mechanisms allow her to access that information and to use it in behavior. In other words, the dissociation implies the operation of two different processes. Moreover, the finding is significant even if her accurate behavior involves some degree of explicit awareness. The dissociation reveals the operation of two different processes and different uses of the same visual information. If the behavior happened to result entirely from implicit perception, that would be interesting as well, but it is not as important as the finding that two different processes are involved. Similarly, evidence for amygdala activation from unreported fearful faces is interesting not because the faces cannot be reported but because it suggests a possible alternative route from visual information to neural activation (LeDoux, 1996). Subsequent control experiments might show that the unreported faces were explicitly perceivable. However, the more interesting question is whether a subcortical route exists, not whether that subcortical route operates entirely without awareness. Of course, to the extent that inferences about alternative processing mechanisms depend on the complete absence of awareness, these findings will always be open to critique. Although evidence from the process dissociation paradigm is subject to shifts in bias and motivation (Visser & Merikle, 1999), the underlying goal of that paradigm has at its base the demonstration of a qualitative difference in performance. Whether or not this difference reflects the distinction between implicit and explicit processing or between two forms of explicit processing is of secondary importance.

In sum, the evidence for implicit perception continues to be mixed and likely will remain that way in spite of improved tools and methods. A diehard skeptic likely will be able to generate some alternative, however implausible, in which explicit processing alone can explain a dissociation between implicit and explicit perception. Similarly, believers are unlikely to accept the skeptic's discomfort with individual results, relying instead on the convergence of a large body of evidence. Methodological improvements might well force the skeptic to adopt more convoluted explanations for the effects, but are unlikely to eliminate those explanations altogether.

Here we propose a somewhat different focus for efforts to explore perception with and without awareness. Rather than trying to eliminate all aspects of explicit perception, research should focus instead on demonstrating differences in the perceptual mechanisms that vary as a function of manipulating awareness. Qualitative differences in perception are interesting regardless of whether they reflect purely implicit perception. Differences between performance when most explicit processes are eliminated and performance when all explicit processes can be brought to bear are interesting in their own right and worthy of further study.

References

Abrams, R. L., & Greenwald, A. G. (2000). Parts outweigh the whole (word) in unconscious analysis of meaning. *Psychological Science, 11*(2), 118–124.

Abrams, R. L., Klinger, M. R., & Greenwald, A. G. (2002). Subliminal words activate semantic categories (not automated motor responses). *Psychonomic Bulletin & Review, 9*(1), 100–106.

Adolphs, R., Tranel, D., Damasio, H., & Damasio, A. R. (1995). Fear and the human amygdala. *Journal of Neuroscience, 15*, 5879–5891.

Azzopardi, P., & Cowey, A. (1998). Blindsight and visual awareness. *Consciousness & Cognition, 7*(3), 292–311.

Baars, B. J. (1988). *A cognitive theory of consciousness*. New York: Cambridge University Press.

Bar, M., & Biederman, I. (1998). Subliminal visual priming. *Psychological Science, 9*(6), 464–469.

Bernat, E., Bunce, S., & Shevrin, H. (2001). Event-related brain potentials differentiate positive and negative mood adjectives during both supraliminal and subliminal visual processing. *International Journal of Psychophysiology, 42*, 11–34.

Bernat, E., Shevrin, H., & Snodgrass, M. (2001). Subliminal visual oddball stimuli evoke a P300 component. *Clinical Neurophysiology, 112*(1), 159–171.

Berti, A., Allport, A., Driver, J., Dienes, Z., Oxbury, J., & Oxbury, S. (1992). Levels of processing for visual stimuli in an "extinguished" field. *Neuropsychologia, 30*, 403–415.

Brazdil, M., Rektor, I., Dufek, M., Jurak, P., & Daniel, P. (1998). Effect of subthreshold target stimuli on event-related potentials. *Electroencephalography & Clinical Neurophysiology, 107*, 64–68.

Breiter, H. C., Etcoff, N. L., Whalen, P. J., Kennedy, W. A., Rauch, S. L., Buckner, R. L., et al. (1996). Response and habituation of the human amygdala during visual processing of facial expression. *Neuron, 17*, 875–887.

Brown, C., & Hagoort, P. (1993). The processing nature of the N400: Evidence from masked priming. *Journal of Cognitive Neuroscience, 5*, 34–44.

Brown, M., & Besner, D. (2002). Semantic priming: On the role of awareness in visual word recognition in the absence of an expectancy. *Consciousness and Cognition, 11*(3), 402–422.

Campion, J., Latto, R., & Smith, Y. M. (1983). Is blindsight an effect of scattered light, spared cortex, and near-threshold vision? *Behavioral & Brain Sciences, 6*(3), 423–486.

Carr, T. H., & Dagenbach, D. (1990). Semantic priming and repetition priming from masked words: Evidence for a center-surround attentional mechanism in perceptual recognition. *Journal of Experimental Psychology: Learning, Memory and Cognition, 16*, 341–350.

Cheesman, J., & Merikle, P. M. (1984). Priming with and without awareness. *Perception & Psychophysics, 36*(4), 387–395.

Cherry, E. C. (1953). Some experiments upon the recognition of speech, with one and with two ears. *Journal of the Acoustical Society of America, 25*, 975–979.

Cohen, A., Ivry, R. B., Rafal, R. D., & Kohn, C. (1995). Activating response codes by stimuli in the neglected visual field. *Neuropsychology, 9,* 165–173.

Coles, M. G., Gratton, G., & Donchin, E. (1988). Detecting early communication: Using measures of movement-related potentials to illuminate human information processing. *Biological Psychology, 26,* 69–89.

Corteen, R. S., & Dunn, D. (1974). Shock-associated words in a nonattended message: A test for momentary awareness. *Journal of Experimental Psychology, 102* (6), 1143–1144.

Corteen, R. S., & Wood, B. (1972). Autonomic responses to shock-associated words in an unattended channel. *Journal of Experimental Psychology, 94* (3), 308–313.

Cowey, A., & Stoerig, P. (1995). Blindsight in monkeys. *Nature, 373,* 247–249.

Damian, M. (2001). Congruity effects evoked by subliminally presented primes: Automaticity rather than semantic processing. *Journal of Experimental Psychology: Human Perception and Performance, 27* (1), 154–165.

Daza, M. T., Ortells, J. J., & Fox, E. (2002). Perception without awareness: Further evidence from a Stroop priming task. *Perception & Psychophysics, 64* (8), 1316–1324.

Deacon, D., Hewitt, S., Yang, C., & Nagata, M. (2000). Event-related potential indices of semantic priming using masked and unmasked words: Evidence that N400 does not reflect a post-lexical process. *Cognitive Brain Research, 9,* 137–146.

Deacon, D., & Shelley-Tremblay, J. (2000). How automatically is meaning accessed: A review of the effects of attention on semantic processing. *Frontiers in Bioscience, 5,* E82–94.

Debner, J., & Jacoby, L. (1994). Unconscious perception: Attention, awareness and control. *Journal of Experimental Psychology: Learning, Memory, and Cognition, 20* (2), 304–317.

Dehaene, S., Naccache, L., Cohen, L., Le, B., D., Mangin, J., Poline, J., et al. (2001). Cerebral mechanisms of word masking and unconscious repetition priming. *Nature Neuroscience, 4* (7), 752–758.

Dehaene, S., Naccache, L., Le Clech, G., Koechlin, E., Mueller, M., Dehaene-Lambertz, G., et al. (1998). Imaging unconscious semantic priming. *Nature, 395* (6702), 597–600.

Dehaene, S., Piazza, M., Pinel, P., & Cohen, L. (2003). Three parietal circuits for number processing. *Cognitive Neuropsychology, 20* (3–6), 487–506.

Dell'Acqua, R., & Grainger, J. (1999). Unconscious semantic priming from pictures. *Cognition, 73* (1), B1–B15.

Deutsch, J. A., & Deutsch, D. (1963). Attention: Some theoretical considerations. *Psychological Review, 70* (1), 80–90.

Devrim, M., Demiralp, T., & Kurt, A. (1997). The effects of subthreshold visual stimulation on P300 response. *Neuroreport, 8,* 3113–3117.

Dosher, B. A. (1998). The response-window regression method – some problematic assumptions – comment on Draine and Greenwald (1998). *Journal of Experimental Psychology: General, 127* (3), 311–317.

Draine, S. C., & Greenwald, A. G. (1998). Replicable unconscious semantic priming. *Journal of Experimental Psychology: General, 127* (3), 286–303.

Driver, J., & Mattingley, J. B. (1998). Parietal neglect and visual awareness. *Nature Neuroscience, 1,* 17–22.

Driver, J., & Vuilleumier, P. (2001). Perceptual awareness and its loss in unilateral neglect and extinction. *Cognition, 79* (1–2), 39–88.

Driver, J., Vuilleumier, P., Eimer, M., & Rees, G. (2001). Functional magnetic resonance imaging and evoked potential correlates of conscious and unconscious vision in parietal extinction patients. *Neuroimage, 14,* S68–75.

Dulany, D. E. (2004). Higher order representation in a mentalistic metatheory. In R. J. Gennaro (Ed.), *Higher-order theories of consciousness.* Amsterdam: John Benjamins.

Eimer, M. (1999). Facilitatory and inhibitory effects of masked prime stimuli on motor activation and behavioural performance. *Acta Psychologica, 101* (2–3), 293–313.

Eimer, M., & Schlaghecken, F. (1998). Effects of masked stimuli on motor activation: Behavioral and electrophysiological evidence. *Journal of Experimental Psychology: Human Perception and Performance, 24,* 1737–1747.

Eimer, M., & Schlaghecken, F. (2002). Links between conscious awareness and response inhibition: Evidence from masked priming. *Psychonomic Bulletin & Review, 9* (3), 514–520.

Epstein, R., & Kanwisher, N. (1998). A cortical representation of the local visual environment. *Nature, 392,* 598–601.

Esterman, M., McGlinchey-Berroth, R., Verfaellie, M., Grande, L., Kilduff, P., & Milberg, W.

(2002). Aware and unaware perception in hemispatial neglect: Evidence from a stem completion priming task. *Cortex, 38*(2), 233–246.

Farah, M. J., Monheit, M. A., & Wallace, M. A. (1991). Unconscious perception of "extinguished" visual stimuli: Reassessing the evidence. *Neuropsychologia, 29,* 949–958.

Fendrich, R., Wessinger, C. M., & Gazzaniga, M. S. (1992). Residual vision in a scotoma: Implications for blindsight. *Science, 258,* 1489–1491.

Fendrich, R., Wessinger, C. M., & Gazzaniga, M. S. (1993). Sources of blindsight – Reply to Stoerig and Weiskrantz. *Science, 261,* 493–495.

Fodor, J. (1986). Modularity of mind. In Z. W. Pylyshyn & W. Demopoulos (Ed.), *Meaning and cognitive structure: Issues in the computational theory of mind* (pp. 129–167). Norwood, NJ: Ablex.

Freud, S. (1966). *Introductory lectures on psychoanalysis* (J. Strachey, Trans.). New York: W. W. Norton.

Gazzaniga, M. S., Fendrich, R., & Wessinger, C. M. (1994). Blindsight reconsidered. *Current Directions in Psychological Science, 3*(3), 93–96.

Gibson, J. J. (1966). *The senses considered as perceptual systems.* Boston: Houghton Mifflin.

Goodale, M. A., & Milner, A. D. (1992). Separate visual pathways for perception and action. *Trends in Neurosciences, 15*(1), 20–25.

Goodale, M. A., Milner, A. D., Jakobson, L. S., & Carey, D. P. (1991). A neurological dissociation between perceiving objects and grasping them. *Nature, 349,* 154–156.

Green, D. M., & Swets, J. A. (1966). *Signal detection theory and psychophysics.* New York: Wiley.

Greenwald, A. G. (1992). New Look 3: Unconscious cognition reclaimed. *American Psychologist, 47,* 766–779.

Greenwald, A., Abrams, R., Naccache, L., & Dehaene, S. (2003). Long-term semantic memory versus contextual memory in unconscious number processing. *Journal of Experimental Psychology: Learning, Memory, and Cognition, 29*(2), 235–247.

Greenwald, A. G., & Banaji, M. R. (1995). Implicit social cognition: Attitudes, self-esteem, and stereotypes. *Psychological Review, 102*(4–27).

Greenwald, A. G., Draine, S. C., & Abrams, R. L. (1996). Three cognitive markers of unconscious semantic activation. *Science, 273*(5282), 1699–1702.

Greenwald, A. G., Schuh, E. S., & Klinger, M. R. (1995). Activation by marginally perceptible (subliminal) stimuli: Dissociation of unconscious from conscious cognition. *Journal of Experimental Psychology: General, 124*(1), 22–42.

Greenwald, A. G., Spangenberg, E. R., Pratkanis, A. R., & Eskenazi, J. (1991). Double-blind tests of subliminal self-help audiotapes. *Psychological Science, 2*(119–122).

Hannula, D. E., Simons, D. J., & Cohen, N. J. (2005). Imaging implicit perception: Promise and pitfalls. *Nature Reviews Neuroscience, 6,* 247–255.

Holender, D. (1986). Semantic activation without conscious identification in dichotic listening, parafoveal vision, and visual masking: A survey and appraisal. *Behavioral and Brain Sciences, 9,* 1–66.

Jacoby, L. L. (1991). A process dissociation framework: Separating automatic and intentional uses of memory. *Journal of Memory & Language, 30,* 513–541.

Jakobson, L. S., & Goodale, M. A. (1991). Factors affecting higher-order movement planning: A kinematic analysis of human prehension. *Experimental Brain Research, 8,* 199–208.

Jaskowski, P., van der Lubbe, R. H. J., Schlotterbeck, E., & Verleger, R. (2002). Traces left on visual selective attention by stimuli that are not consciously identified. *Psychological Science, 13*(1), 48–54.

Kanwisher, N., McDermott, J., & Chun, M. M. (1997). The fusiform face area: A module in human extrastriate cortex specialized for face perception. *Journal of Neuroscience, 17,* 4302–4311.

Kiefer, M. (2002). The N400 is modulated by unconsciously perceived masked words: Further evidence for an automatic spreading activation account of N400 priming effects. *Cognitive Brain Research, 13*(1), 27–39.

Kiefer, M., & Spitzer, M. (2000). Time course of conscious and unconscious semantic brain activation. *Neuroreport, 11*(11), 2401–2407.

Klapp, S., & Hinkley, L. (2002). The negative compatibility effect: Unconscious inhibition influences reaction time and response selection. *Journal of Experimental Psychology: General, 131*(2), 255–269.

Klinger, M., Burton, P., & Pitts, G. (2000). Mechanisms of unconscious priming: I. Response competition, not spreading activation. *Journal* of Experimental Psychology: Learning, Memory, and Cognition, 26(2), 441–455.

Koechlin, E., Naccache, L., Block, E., & Dehaene, S. (1999). Primed numbers: Exploring the modularity of numerical representations with masked and unmasked semantic priming. Journal of Experimental Psychology: Human Perception & Performance, 25(6), 1882–1905.

Kunst-Wilson, W. R., & Zajonc, R. B. (1980). Affective discrimination of stimuli that cannot be recognized. Science, 207, 557–558.

Kutas, M., & Hillyard, S. A. (1980). Reading senseless sentences: Brain potentials reflect semantic incongruity. Science, 207, 203–205.

Ladavas, E., Paladini, R., & Cubelli, R. (1993). Implicit associative priming in a patient with left visual neglect. Neuropsychologia, 31, 1307–1320.

Lane, R. D., & Nadel, L. (2000). Cognitive neuroscience of emotion. New York: Oxford University Press.

Le Doux, J. E. (1996). The emotional brain. New York: Simon & Shuster.

Levelt, W. J. M. (1965). On binocular rivalry. Assen, The Netherlands: Royal VanGorcum.

Levin, D. T., Momen, N., Drivdahl, S. B., & Simons, D. J. (2000). Change blindness blindness: The metacognitive error of overestimating change-detection ability. Visual Cognition, 7, 397–412.

Mack, A., & Rock, I. (1998). Inattentional blindness. Cambridge, MA: MIT Press.

Macmillan, N. A. (1986). The psychophysics of subliminal perception. Behavioral and Brain Sciences, 9, 38–39.

Marcel, A. J. (1983a). Conscious and unconscious perception: An approach to the relations between phenomenal experience and perceptual processes. Cognitive Psychology, 15, 238–300.

Marcel, A. J. (1983b). Conscious and unconscious perception: Experiments on visual masking and word recognition. Cognitive Psychology, 15, 197–237.

Marcel, A. J. (1998). Blindsight and shape perception: Deficit of visual consciousness or of visual function? Brain, 121(8), 1565–1588.

McCarthy, J. C., Puce, A., Gore, J. C., & Allison, T. (1997). Face-specific processing in the human fusiform gyrus. Journal of Cognitive Neuroscience, 9, 604–609.

McCormick, P. (1997). Orienting attention without awareness. Journal of Experimental Psychology: Human Perception & Performance, 23(1), 168–180.

McGlinchey-Berroth, R., Milberg, W. P., Verfaellie, M., Alexander, M., & Kilduff, P. T. (1993). Semantic processing in the neglected visual field: Evidence from a lexical decision task. Cognitive Neuropsychology, 10, 79–108.

Merikle, P. (1992). Perception without awareness. Critical issues. American Psychologist, 47(6), 766–779.

Merikle, P. M. (1994). On the futility of attempting to demonstrate null awareness. Behavioral & Brain Sciences, 17(3), 412.

Merikle, P., & Joordens, S. (1997a). Parallels between perception without attention and perception without awareness. Consciousness & Cognition, 6(2–3), 219–236.

Merikle, P. M., & Joordens, S. (1997b). Measuring unconscious influences. In J. W. Schooler (Ed.), Scientific approaches to consciousness (pp. 109–123). Mahwah, NJ: Erlbaum.

Merikle, P. M., & Reingold, E. M. (1991). Comparing direct (explicit) and indirect (implicit) measures to study unconscious memory. Journal of Experimental Psychology: Learning, Memory, and Cognition, 17(2), 224–233.

Merikle, P. M., & Reingold, E. M. (1992). Measuring unconscious perceptual processes. In T. S. Pittman (Ed.), Perception without awareness: Cognitive, clinical, and social perspectives (pp. 55–80). New York: Guilford Press.

Merikle, P., & Reingold, E. (1998). On demonstrating unconscious perception – Comment on Draine and Greenwald (1998). Journal of Experimental Psychology: General, 127(3), 304–310.

Merikle, P., Smilek, D., & Eastwood, J. (2001). Perception without awareness: Perspectives from cognitive psychology. Cognition, 79(1–2), 115–134.

Milner, A. D., & Goodale, M. A. (1995). The visual brain in action. New York: Oxford University Press.

Mitroff, S. R., Simons, D. J., & Franconeri, S. L. (2002). The siren song of implicit change detection. Journal of Experimental Psychology: Human Perception & Performance, 28(4), 798–815.

Moray, N. (1959). Attention in dichotic listening: Affective cues and the influence of instructions. Quarterly Journal of Experimental Psychology, 11, 56–60.

Morris, J. S., Frith, C. D., Perrett, D. I., Rowland, D., Young, A. W., Calder, A. J., et al. (1996). A differential neural response in the human amygdala to fearful and happy facial expressions. *Nature, 383*, 812–815.

Most, S. B., Simons, D. J., Scholl, B. J., Jimenez, R., Clifford, E., & Chabris, C. F. (2001). How not to be seen: The contribution of similarity and selective ignoring to sustained inattentional blindness. *Psychological Science, 12* (1), 9–17.

Naccache, L., Blandin, E., & Dehaene, S. (2002). Unconscious masked priming depends on temporal attention. *Psychological Science, 13* (5), 416–424.

Naccache, L., & Dehaene, S. (2001a). The priming method: Imaging unconscious repetition priming reveals an abstract representation of number in the parietal lobes. *Cerebral Cortex, 11* (10), 966–974.

Naccache, L., & Dehaene, S. (2001b). Unconscious semantic priming extends to novel unseen stimuli. *Cognition, 80*, 223–237.

Neumann, O., & Klotz, W. (1994). Motor responses to nonreportable, masked stimuli: Where is the limit of direct paramater specification? In M. Moscovitch (Ed.), *Attention and performance* (Vol. XV, pp. 123–150). Cambridge, MA: MIT Press.

Pöppel, E., Held, R., & Frost, D. (1973). Residual visual function after brain wounds involving the central visual pathways in man. *Nature, 243*, 295–296.

Pratkanis, A. R. (1992). The cargo-cult science of subliminal persuasion. *Skeptical Inquirer, 16*, 260–272.

Pratkanis, A., Eskenazi, J., & Greenwald, A. (1994). What you expect is what you believe (but not necessarily what you get) – A test of the effectiveness of subliminal self-help audiotapes. *Basic & Applied Social Psychology, 15* (3), 251–276.

Rees, G. (2001). Seeing is not perceiving. *Nature Neuroscience, 4* (7), 678–680.

Rees, G., Kreiman, G., & Koch, C. (2002). Neural correlates of consciousness in humans. *Nature Reviews Neuroscience, 3*, 261–270.

Rees, G., Wojciulik, E., Clarke, K., Husain, M., Frith, C., & Driver, J. (2000). Unconscious activation of visual cortex in the damaged right hemisphere of a parietal patient with extinction. *Brain, 123* (8), 1624–1633.

Reingold, E., & Merikle, P. (1988). Using direct and indirect measures to study perception without awareness. *Perception & Psychophysics, 44* (6), 563–757.

Rosa, M. G. P., Tweedale, R., & Elston, G. N. (2000). Visual responses of neurons in the middle temporal area of new world monkeys after lesions of striate cortex. *Journal of Neuroscience, 20* (14), 5552–5563.

Schacter, D. L. (1987). Implicit memory: History and current status. *Journal of Experimental Psychology: Learning, Memory, and Cognition, 13*, 501–518.

Schacter, D. L., Alpert, N. M., Savage, C. R., Rauch, S. L., & Albert, M. S. (1996). Conscious recollection and the human hippocampal formation: Evidence from positron emission tomography. *Proceedings of the National Academy of Sciences, 93* (1), 321–325.

Schacter, D. L., & Buckner, R. L. (1998). On the relations among priming, conscious recollection, and intentional retrieval: Evidence from neuroimaging research. *Neurobiology of Learning & Memory, 70* (1–2), 284–303.

Schweinberger, S., & Stief, V. (2001). Implicit perception in patients with visual neglect: Lexical specificity in repetition priming. *Neuropsychologia, 39* (4), 420–429.

Searle, J. R. (1992). *The rediscovery of the mind.* Cambridge, MA: MIT Press.

Shevrin, H. (2001). Event-related markers of unconscious processes. *International Journal of Psychophysiology, 42*, 209–218.

Sidis, B. (1898). *The psychology of suggestion.* New York: D. Appleton.

Simons, D. J. (2000). Attentional capture and inattentional blindness. *Trends in Cognitive Sciences, 4* (4), 147–155.

Simons, D. J., & Chabris, C. F. (1999). Gorillas in our midst: Sustained inattentional blindness for dynamic events. *Perception, 28*, 1059–1074.

Squire, L. R., Ojemann, J. G., Miezin, F. M., Petersen, S. E., Videen, T. O., & Raichle, M. E. (1992). Activation of the hippocampus in normal humans: A functional anatomical study of memory. *Proceedings of the National Academy of Sciences, 89* (5), 1837–1841.

Stenberg, G., Lindgren, M., Johansson, M., Olsson, A., & Rosen, I. (2000). Semantic processing without conscious identification: Evidence from event-related potentials. *Journal of Experimental Psychology: Learning, Memory, & Cognition, 26* (4), 973–1004.

Teuber, H. L., Battersby, W. S., & Bender, M. B. (1960). *Visual field defects after penetrating missile wounds of the brain*. Cambridge, MA: Harvard University Press.

Tong, F. (2001). Competing theories of binocular rivalry: A possible resolution. *Brain and Mind*, 2, 55–83.

Tong, F. (2003). Primary visual cortex and visual awareness. *Nature Reviews Neuroscience*, 4, 219–229.

Tong, F., Nakayama, K., Vaughan, J. T., & Kanwisher, N. (1998). Binocular rivalry and visual awareness in human extrastriate cortex. *Neuron*, 21, 753–759.

Treisman, A. M. (1960). Contextual cues in selective listening. *Quarterly Journal of Experimental Psychology*, 12, 242–248.

Treisman, A. (1964). Monitoring and storage of irrelevant messages in selective attention. *Journal of Verbal Learning and Verbal Behavior*, 3, 449–459.

Trevethan, C. T., & Sahraie, A. (2003). Spatial and temporal processing in a subject with cortical blindness following occipital surgery. *Neuropsychologia*, 41(10), 1296–1306.

Verfaellie, M., Milberg, W. P., McGlinchey-Berroth, R., & Grande, L. (1995). Comparison of cross-field matching and forced-choice identification in hemispatial neglect. *Neuropsychology*, 9, 427–434.

Visser, T., & Merikle, P. (1999). Conscious and unconscious processes: The effects of motivation. *Consciousness & Cognition*, 8(1), 94–113.

Volpe, B. T., Ledoux, J. E., & Gazzaniga, M. S. (1979). Information processing of visual stimuli in an "extinguished" field. *Nature*, 282, 722–724.

Vuilleumier, P., Armony, J., Clarke, K., Husain, M., Driver, J., & Dolan, R. (2002). Neural response to emotional faces with and without awareness: Event-related fMRI in a parietal patient with visual extinction and spatial neglect. *Neuropsychologia*, 40(12), 2156–2166.

Vuilleumier, P., Sagiv, N., Hazeltine, E., Poldrack, R. A., Swick, D., Rafal, R. D., et al. (2001). Neural fate of seen and unseen faces in visuospatial neglect: A combined event-related functional MRI and event-related potential study. *Proceedings of the National Academy of Sciences*, 98(6), 3495–3500.

Watanabe, T., Nanez, J., & Sasaki, Y. (2001). Perceptual learning without perception. *Nature*, 413(6858), 844–848.

Weiskrantz, L. (2002). Prime-sight and blindsight. *Consciousness & Cognition*, 11(4), 568–581.

Weiskrantz, L., Warrington, E. K., Sanders, M. D., & Marshal, J. (1974). Visual capacity in the hemianopic field following a restricted occipital ablation. *Brain*, 97, 709–728.

Wessinger, C. M., Fendrich, R., & Gazzaniga, M. S. (1997). Islands of residual vision in hemianopic patients. *Journal of Cognitive Neuroscience*, 9(2), 203–221.

Whalen, P. J., Rauch, S. L., Etcoff, N. L., McInerney, S. C., Lee, M. B., & Jenike, M. A. (1998). Masked presentations of emotional facial expressions modulate amygdala activity without explicit awareness. *Journal of Neuroscience*, 18, 411–418.

Wheatstone, C. (1838). Contributions to the physiology of vision – Part the first. On some remarkable and hitherto unobserved phenomena of binocular vision. *Philosophical Transactions of the Royal Society of London*, 128, 371–394.

Wolfe, J. M. (1999). Inattentional amnesia. In V. Coltheart (Ed.), *Fleeting memories: Cognition of brief visual stimuli* (pp. 71–94). Cambridge, MA: MIT Press.

CHAPTER 10

Three Forms of Consciousness
in Retrieving Memories

Henry L. Roediger III, Suparna Rajaram,
and Lisa Geraci

Abstract

The study of conscious processes during
memory retrieval is a relatively recent
endeavor. We consider the issue and review
the literature using Tulving's distinctions
among autonoetic (self-knowing), noetic
(knowing), and anoetic (non-knowing) types
of conscious experience during retrieval.
One index of autonoetic consciousness is the
experience of remembering (mental time
travel to recover past events and the sense of
re-experiencing them). We review the literature on judgments of remembering (expressing autonoetic consciousness) and those of
knowing (being confident something happened without remembering it, an expression of noetic consciousness). These introspective judgments during retrieval have
produced a sizable body of coherent literature, even though the field remains filled
with interesting puzzles (such as how to
account for the experience of remembering
events that never actually occurred). Priming on implicit memory tests can be considered an index of anoetic consciousness, when
past events influence current behavior without intention or awareness. In addition to
reviewing the Remember/Know judgment
literature and the topic of priming, we consider such related topics as objective measures of conscious control in Jacoby's process
dissociation procedure and the thorny issue
of involuntary conscious memory.

Accessing Memories: Three Forms
of Consciousness

During most of the first hundred years
that researchers worked on issues in human
memory, considerations of conscious experience were rare. Scholars interested in conscious experience did not consider states of
consciousness during retrieval from memory,
and memory researchers rarely considered
conscious states of awareness of their subjects performing memory tasks. Consciousness and memory were considered separate
areas of inquiry, with few or no points of
contact. Researchers working on the vexing problem of consciousness were interested in such topics as sleeping and waking,

hypnosis, states of alertness and awareness, and how skilled tasks become automatic and appear to drop out of conscious control, among other issues. Researchers working in traditions of human memory considered the products of memory – what people recalled or recognized when put through their paces in experimental paradigms – but they generally did not concern themselves with the state of conscious awareness accompanying the memory reports.

In fact, in the first empirical studies of memory, Ebbinghaus (1885/1964) championed his savings method of measuring retention because it avoided reliance on "introspective" methods of assessing memory (recall and recognition). Nonetheless, Ebbinghaus did clearly state his opinion of the relation of consciousness and memory, and the relevant passage is still worth quoting today:

> Mental states of every kind – sensations, feelings, ideas, – which were at one time present in consciousness and then have disappeared from it, have not with their disappearance ceased to exist . . . they continue to exist, stored up, so to speak, in the memory. We cannot, of course, directly observe their present existence, but it is revealed by the effects which come to our knowledge with a certainty like that with which we infer the existence of stars below the horizon. These effects are of different kinds.
>
> In a first group of cases we can call back into consciousness by an exertion of the will directed to this purpose the seemingly lost states . . . that is, we can produce them voluntarily . . .
>
> In a second group of cases this survival is even more striking. Often, even after years, mental states once present in consciousness return to it with apparent spontaneity and without any act of the will; that is, they are produced involuntarily . . . in the majority of the cases we recognize the returned mental state as one that has already been experienced; that is, we remember it.
>
> Finally, there is a third and large group to be reckoned with here. The vanished mental states give indubitable proof of their continuing existence even if they themselves do not return to consciousness at all . . . The boundless domain of the effect of accumu-

lated experiences belongs here . . . Most of these experiences remain concealed from consciousness and yet produce an effect which is significant and which authenticates their previous existence (Ebbinghaus, 1885/1964, pp. 1–2).

In today's terminology, we might say that Ebbinghaus was outlining different means of retrieval or accessing information from memory. The first case, voluntary recollection, resembles retrieval from episodic memory (Tulving, 1983) or conscious, controlled recollection (Jacoby, 1991). The second case, involuntary recollection, has several modern counterparts, but perhaps the most direct is the concept of involuntary conscious memory discussed by Richardson-Klavehn, Gardiner, and Java (1996), among others. Finally, the idea that aftereffects of experience may be expressed in behavior and the person may never be conscious of the fact that current behavior is so guided is similar to the contemporary idea of priming on implicit or indirect tests of memory (Schacter, 1987).

Although Ebbinghaus raised the issue of the relation of consciousness to memory on the first two pages of his great book that began the empirical investigation of memory, later generations of researchers generally did not take up the puzzles he posed, at least until recently. Today, research on consciousness and memory is proceeding apace, although the field is still fumbling toward a lucid and encompassing theory. One origin of the current interest in consciousness among memory researchers can be traced, quite after the fact, to the 1980s, with the rise of the study of priming in what are now called implicit or indirect memory experiments.

Warrington and Weiskrantz (1968, 1970) first showed that amnesic patients could perform as well as normal control subjects on indirect tests of memory, such as completing fragmented pictures or words. When the corresponding pictures or words had been studied recently, patients could complete the fragments as well as control subjects (see too Graf, Squire, & Mandler, 1984).

However, these same patients did much more poorly than controls on free recall and recognition tests. The critical difference between these types of test was the instructions given to subjects. In standard memory tests like recall and recognition, subjects are explicitly told to think back to the recent experiences to be retrieved. These are called explicit or direct tests of memory. In what are now called implicit (or indirect tests), subjects are presented with material in one guise or another in an experiment and are later told to perform the criterial task (naming fragmented words or pictures, answering general knowledge questions, among many others) as well and quickly as possible. Usually no mention is made about the test having anything to do with the prior study episode, and often researchers go to some effort to disguise the relation between the two. The finding, as in the work of Warrington and Weiskrantz (1968, 1970), is that prior experience with a picture or word facilitates, or primes, naming of the fragmented items. The phenomenon is called priming and has been much studied in the past 25 years. Because retention is measured indirectly and the study of memory is implicit in the procedure, these tasks are called implicit or indirect memory tasks. Graf and Schacter (1985) first used the terms "explicit" and "implicit memory" to refer to these different types of measures. Schacter (1987) provided a fine historical review of the concept of implicit memory, and a huge amount of research has been conducted on this topic. Here we make only a few points about this research to set the stage for the chapter.

First, hundreds of experiments have shown dissociations between measures of explicit memory and implicit memory with both neuropsychological variables (different types of patients relative to control subjects; see Moscovitch, Vriezen, & Goshen-Gottstein, 1993) and variables under experimental control (e.g., type of study condition, type of material, and many others; see Roediger & McDermott, 1993). Sometimes a variable can have a powerful effect on an explicit task and no effect on priming (Jacoby & Dallas, 1981), whereas in other cases the situation is reversed (Church & Schacter, 1994). And a variable can even have opposite effects on an explicit and implicit task (e.g., Blaxton, 1989; Jacoby, 1983b; Weldon & Roediger, 1987), even under conditions when all variables except instructions to the subjects are held constant (Java, 1994). There is no doubt that explicit and implicit measures are tapping different qualities of memory.

Second, one straightforward and appealing way to think of the contrast between explicit and implicit forms of memory is to align them with states of consciousness. Explicit memory tests are thought to be reflections of memory with awareness, or conscious forms of memory, whereas implicit memory tests are thought to reflect an unaware, unconscious, or even automatic form of memory. This appealing argument, which was put forward in one form or another by many authors in the 1980s (e.g., Graf & Schacter, 1985; Jacoby & Witherspoon, 1982, among others) seems valid up to a point, but that point is quickly reached, and in 2006, no researcher would agree with this assessment. States of consciousness (e.g., aware and unaware) cannot be directly equated with performance on explicit and implicit tests. Jacoby (1991) refers to this as a process purity assumption (that a task and state of consciousness in performing the task can be equated). He argued that it is difficult to provide convincing evidence that an implicit test does not involve some component of conscious awareness and even harder to show that an explicit test does not involve unconscious components. His process dissociation procedure was developed in the same paper as a promising way to cut this Gordian knot and measure conscious and unconscious components underlying task performance. Another method of measuring these components that makes different assumptions is the Remember/Know paradigm originally created by Tulving (1985) and developed by others (Gardiner, 1988; Rajaram, 1993). Still, no method is generally agreed upon in the field to perfectly measure consciousness or its role (or lack thereof) in various memory tasks.

In this chapter we adopt Tulving's (1985) tripartite distinction among three states of consciousness to provide coherence to our review of the literature. Tulving distinguished among autonoetic, noetic, and anoetic forms of consciousness, which refer, respectively, to self-knowing, knowing, and non-knowing states of consciousness. (We define each concept more fully below.) Even though Tulving's distinctions are not necessarily used by all psychologists, we see his theory as a fruitful and useful way of organizing our chapter, and we consider it the leading theory on the relations of conscious states of awareness to memory performance. The Remember/Know paradigm just mentioned was intended to measure autonoetic consciousness (remembering) and noetic consciousness (knowing). We turn to the first of these concepts in the next section.

Autonoetic Consciousness

Tulving (1985) defined autonoetic consciousness of memory as one's awareness that she has personally experienced an event in her past. This ability to retrieve and, in a sense, relive events from the past has been characterized as a kind of mental time travel that allows one to "become aware of [their] protracted existence across subjective time" (Wheeler, Stuss, & Tulving, 1997, p. 334). By this definition, autonoetic consciousness constitutes what most people think of as memory: thinking back to a particular episode in life and mentally reliving that event. In addition to imagining oneself in the past, autonoetic consciousness allows one to imagine the future and make long-term plans. In this section, we focus on the autonoetic consciousness that is associated with mental time travel into the past, or remembering.

Autonoetic consciousness includes not only the ability to travel mentally through time but also the complementary ability to recognize that a particular mental experience is from one's past (as opposed to being perceived for the first time). This recognition of one's past gives rise to a feeling that

is uniquely associated with remembering, and it is this recognition of oneself in the past that characterizes the kind of memory that people with amnesia lack. When Tulving described K. C., "a man without autonoetic consciousness" (1985), he illustrated the distinction between the rich reliving of one's past, an ability of which most people are capable, and the cold fact-like knowledge of one's life that most memory-impaired patients retain. K. C. does not seem to have the concept of personal time. Tulving noted that K. C. can understand the concept of yesterday, but cannot remember himself yesterday. Similarly, he can understand the concept of tomorrow, but cannot imagine what he might do tomorrow. When asked what he thinks when he hears a question about tomorrow, K. C. describes his mind as "blank" (p. 4).

Measurement Issues and Theoretical Accounts

Tulving (1985) introduced the concepts of autonoetic and noetic consciousness and the Remember/Know paradigm for measuring these states of consciousness. The basic paradigm for studying these two different forms of subjective experience involves giving subjects explicit memory instructions (to think back to some specific point in time) and asking them either to recall or recognize events from this time. For a recognition test, subjects are told that if they recognize the item from the study episode (if they judge it "old" or "studied"), then they should try to characterize their experience of recognition as involving the experience of either remembering or knowing. They are told that they should assign a Remember response to items when they can vividly remember having encountered the item; that is, they can remember some specific contextual detail (e.g., what they were thinking or the item's position in the study list) that would provide supporting evidence that they are indeed remembering the item's occurrence (see Rajaram, 1993, for published instructions given to subjects). Subjects are told that they should assign a Know response to a recognized item when they are sure that the item occurred in the study list, but they cannot recollect its actual occurrence; they cannot remember any specific details associated with the item's presentation at study. In short, subjects know it was presented in the past, but they cannot remember its occurrence.

In the example just given, subjects are asked first to make a yes/no recognition decision and then to assign either a Remember or Know response to the recognized item. This variety of the task is the most widely used version of the Remember/Know procedure. A small number of studies have used a different procedure where the recognition and Remember/Know judgments are made simultaneously rather than sequentially; that is, subjects are asked to say for each test item whether they remember or know that the item was on the study list or whether the item is new.

Research shows that the results using the Remember/Know procedure can change critically depending on whether the sequential or simultaneous method is used (Hicks & R. Marsh, 1999). The standard sequential method of measurement implicitly assumes that the Remember/Know judgments are post-recognition judgments, whereas the other method assumes that remembering and knowing drive recognition. As we discuss later, this difference in assumption parallels the debate as to whether these judgments should be considered as subjective states that a person assesses after recognition or as subjective states that uniquely map onto two processes that drive recognition judgments. Regardless, Hicks and R. Marsh argue that the simultaneous decision is more difficult than the sequential method, because the judgment for each test item has to be weighed against two other possibilities (e.g., "Do I remember or know that the item was on the study list, or is it a new item?"). In contrast, in the sequential method, subjects only have to weigh the judgment against one other possibility (e.g., "Was the item presented earlier or not?" and "Do I remember it or do I know it?"). In support of this hypothesis, Hicks and R. Marsh found

that, as compared to the sequential method, the simultaneous method leads subjects to respond more liberally and increases the recognition hit rate as well as the false alarm rate.

In addition to these differences in procedure, several important measurement issues have arisen that reflect fundamental points of disagreement regarding what processes Remember and Know responses measure. Most of the measurement controversies surround the theoretical question of what states of awareness or processes are reflected by remembering and by knowing. As we describe in the next section, there are several accounts of remembering and knowing (see Yonelinas, 2002, for a recent review).

Remembering, Knowing, and Confidence

One proposal is that remembering and knowing reflect different levels of confidence that can be explained by appealing to a signal detection model (Donaldson, 1996; Hirshman & Masters, 1997; Inoue & Bellezza, 1998; Wixted & Stretch, 2004). The idea is that subjects place two thresholds on a continuum of strength; the more stringent threshold is used for making Remember judgments, and the more lenient threshold is used for making Know judgments. In other words, when people are very confident that they recognize an item, they assign it a Remember response, and when they are less confident, they assign it a Know response. By this view, certain independent variables influence these judgments by affecting the amount of memory information available at retrieval. The availability of this information, in turn, determines where people place their criteria (if they do not have much information, they may be very conservative and set a high threshold for responding). Thus, these models conceptualize Remember/Know judgments as quantitatively different judgments that vary along a single continuum of degree of confidence. It follows from this view that Know judgments are isomorphic with low-confidence judgments and do not capture any other experiential state. This criterion shift model can fit several different patterns of Remember and Know data (see Dunn, 2004, for a recent review from this perspective).

Although single-process models do a good job of accounting for various associations and dissociations, they seem to lack explanatory power. It is difficult to know what determines the placement of criteria at particular points on the continuum in these models and how this placement might vary with different experimental conditions. More problematic for this view are the reports that both meta-analyses of a large set of studies (Gardiner & Conway, 1999; Gardiner, Ramponi, & Richardson-Klavehn, 2002) and analyses of sets of individual data (Gardiner & Gregg, 1997) have not supported a key prediction of single-process models. These models predict that the bias-free estimates for Remember judgments should be comparable to that obtained for overall recognition (that includes both Remember and Know judgments). In other words, Know judgments are assumed to contribute little to the bias-free estimate, but contrary to this prediction, overall recognition shows a larger bias-free estimate than do Remember judgments by themselves (but see Wixted & Stretch, 2004, for an alternative view).

Other empirical evidence is also inconsistent with the view that Remember and Know judgments simply reflect high- and low-confidence judgments. Gardiner and Java (1990) had shown in an earlier study that memory-intact subjects give significantly more Remember judgments to words than non-words and significantly more Know judgments to non-words than words. In contrast, words and non-words simply produce a main effect on high- and low-confidence judgments. Single-process models can account for the double dissociation observed for Remember/Know judgments and the main effect observed for confidence judgments by assuming certain shifts of criteria, but it is not clear why the criteria would shift in different ways for the two sets of judgments (Remember/Know and high/low confidence) if the types of judgment are isomorphic.

To test for the presumed equivalence between Remember/Know and high/low confidence judgments, Rajaram, Hamilton and Bolton (2002) adapted Gardiner and Java's design and conducted the study with amnesic subjects. Impaired conscious experience is a hallmark of amnesia, and both Remember judgments (to a greater extent) and Know judgments (to a lesser extent) are impaired in amnesia. Consistent with these findings, Rajaram et al. (2002) showed that amnesic subjects were severely impaired at making Remember/Know judgments, and they did not produce even a hint of the double dissociation observed with matched-control subjects. In contrast, the performance of matched-control and amnesic subjects did not differ for high- and low-confidence judgments. Such findings are quite difficult to reconcile with the notion that Remember and Know judgments are redundant with confidence judgments.

The findings described here show that confidence judgments and experiential judgments can be differentiated. Clearly though, one is highly confident when reporting that one remembers an event, and so it is likely that recollective experience is closely tied to confidence. Roediger (1999) suggested that "...theorists may have the relation backwards. Rather than differing levels of confidence explaining Remember/Know responses, it may well be that the study of retrieval experience through the Remember/Know technique may help explain why subjects feel more or less confident" (p. 231). According to this view, confidence and recollective experience can be correlated, but confidence does not explain remembering. Remembering explains confidence.

Remember/Know Responses and Dual-Process Models of Recognition

Dual-process models in general suggest that remembering and knowing reflect two independent processes in memory, termed "recollection" and "familiarity," respectively (Jacoby, 1991; Jacoby, Yonelinas, & Jennings, 1997). Applied to the Remember/Know paradigm, Remember judgments reflect primarily recollection-based memory, whereas Know judgments reflect primarily familiarity-based memory performance. According to this model, recollection and familiarity represent independent processes: They can work together or separately to affect memory performance. This means that Remember judgments can arise from a recollective process alone or from occasions when recollection and familiarity co-occur. Know responses, on the other hand, arise from a familiarity process that occurs in the absence of recollection. By this view, Know responses alone can underestimate the true contribution of familiarity-driven processes to recognition performance. If one assumes that Remember and Know responses reflect the contribution of recollection and familiarity processes, then it is important to measure Remember and Know responses in a slightly different manner than is usually reported in the literature. The Independence Remember Know (IRK) procedure (Jacoby et al., 1997; Lindsay & Kelley, 1996; Yonelinas & Jacoby, 1995) addresses this issue by measuring familiarity as a proportion of Know judgments divided by the opportunity to make a Know response (or K/1-Remember).

Implicit in this view of remembering and knowing is the assumption that the processes driving Remember responses overlap with those that drive Know responses. That is, events that are remembered can also be known. However, there are other ways to conceive of the relation between remembering and knowing (see Jacoby et al., 1997). For example, one could assume that everything that is remembered is also known, but events that are known are not always remembered (e.g., Joordens & Merikle, 1993). Or, one could assume that the two responses are exclusive: things are either remembered or known (Gardiner & Parkin, 1990). How one conceives of the relation between these two states of awareness and the processes underlying these states will have implications for how they should be measured (Rotello, Macmillan, & Reeder, 2004).

Another dual-process model proposes that remembering and knowing are graded

differently (e.g., Yonelinas, 1994). According to this view, only responding based on familiarity or fluency (as measured by Know responses) can be modeled by a signal detection theory that assumes a shifting criterion. In contrast, responding that is driven by recollection, as measured by Remember responses, does not fit this model. Instead, these responses reflect a retrieval process that can be characterized as an all-or-none threshold process. The idea is that participants can recall various types of information about an event (e.g., its appearance, sound, or associated thoughts) that either exceed or do not exceed some set retrieval threshold. If any one of these qualities exceeds some threshold, then participants determine that they remember the item. If these qualities do not exceed this threshold, then participants might rely on various levels of familiarity when endorsing the item as recognized. Therefore, unlike a signal detection model of Remember and Know responses, this model can be considered a dual-process model (see Jacoby, 1991). Recognition can be characterized by two distinct processes that behave differently and give rise to distinct subjective states of awareness: Remember responses are associated with a threshold retrieval process that is driven by the qualitative features of an event, whereas Know responses are associated with a familiarity retrieval process that is driven by sheer memory strength. In this model, remembering is an all-or-none process, whereas knowing is based purely on familiarity.

The varying assumptions of these models are tied to different conceptualizations about the ways in which Remember and Know judgments denote states of consciousness. The assumption that a single process underlies both states of retrieval puts the emphasis on overall memory performance, but at the cost of shifting focus from capturing (through experimentation) the conscious states that accompany performance. The dual-process assumption recognizes the role of conscious states more overtly, although some versions of dual-process models place greater emphasis on the relation of performance to distinct underlying processes, whereas other dual-process models focus directly on the functional states of consciousness that accompany retrieval.

Measurement Issues and the Role of Instructions

Another measurement issue has to do with the instructions that one gives to subjects. This topic has not been the focus of many discussions on the Remember/Know procedure (but see Geraci & McCabe, 2006). Like the other topics discussed so far, how subjects interpret the Remember/Know distinction based on the instructions given to them may determine what these responses reflect. As such, the issue of interpretation of instructions also has theoretical implications. We note that for Remember judgments, the issue of instructions may be less of a problem. People tend to be in agreement over what remembering means. For knowing, the psychological experience that elicits this response may depend on the instructions. Some published instructions (Rajaram, 1993) tell subjects to give a Know judgment when they are certain that the event has occurred, but their recognition lacks the recollective detail that was described to them. By this definition, Know responses should, and probably do, reflect high confidence, similar to Remember responses. With these instructions, the distinction between the two judgments is likely to be based on distinct conscious experiences. However, because Know instructions differ across experimenters and across labs, the definition of knowing may also differ from lab to lab. If the instructions say something along these lines of "Give a Remember judgment if you vividly remember the item from the study list. Otherwise, give it a Know judgment," then knowing could reflect high- or low-confident memory, some sort of feeling or familiarity, or simple guessing (see Java, Gregg, & Gardiner, 1997, for examples of the variety of ways in which subjects interpret this instruction). Kelley and Jacoby (1998) capture these various interpretations when they suggest, "A

Know response is defined as the inability to recollect any details of the study presentation in combination with a feeling of familiarity or certainty that the word was studied" (p. 134). As we see in the next section on noetic consciousness, these possibilities map onto the theoretical debate in the literature regarding the definition of knowing.

The nature of the instructions given to subjects also has been used to argue for exclusivity of the responses. Gardiner and Java (1993) have suggested that the instructions implicitly suggest that remembering and knowing are two states of conscious experience that cannot coexist. They argue, "A person cannot at one and the same time experience conscious recollection and feelings of familiarity in the absence of conscious recollection" (p. 179). They note that one state can lead to the other across time and repeated retrievals, but that retrieval on any one occasion will be associated with either one state of awareness or the other. Although this idea is consistent with the instructions researchers give to subjects, it is at odds with Jacoby's conception that events that are remembered are also familiar (Jacoby et al., 1997). Recall that this independence view assumes that the two underlying processes (recollection and familiarity) are separate and can therefore act together or in opposition. That is, recognition can be driven by both recollection and familiarity, by just recollection, or by just familiarity. Researchers disagree on which conception is the right one, but it may be that both are correct but in different situations. This matter awaits future research.

Factors That Increase Autonoetic Consciousness

Another way to understand the distinction between remembering and knowing has been to examine the various factors that give rise to each state of recollective experience. Several factors increase reports of remembering and include conceptual or elaborative processing, generation, imagery, and distinctive processing. Alongside this collection of empirical findings, several complementary theories have arisen. In this section, we discuss these findings and theories together. Lastly, we discuss other factors that selectively influence remembering by decreasing it. These factors include various forms of brain damage associated with amnesia and the cognitive decline associated with aging.

Several studies have provided empirical evidence for the experiential distinction between remembering and knowing by showing that these two states are selectively affected by different independent variables. Because the body of evidence is now large, we classify the effects of various independent variables into general categories of conceptual processing, imagery and generation, distinctiveness, and emotion.

CONCEPTUAL INFLUENCES
ON REMEMBERING

Several accounts of remembering suggest that this recollective state is driven largely by prior conceptual processing. This idea follows from dual-process theories of recognition (Atkinson & Juola, 1973; 1974; Jacoby, 1983a, b; Jacoby & Dallas, 1981; Mandler, 1980) that propose that the recollective component of recognition memory is affected by conceptual or elaborative processing, whereas the familiarity component is driven by perceptual processes. Based on this processing distinction, Gardiner (1988) proposed that Remember responses are affected by conceptual processing that arises from the episodic memory system, and Know responses are affected by perceptual processing that arises from the semantic or procedural memory system. In support of this idea, Gardiner showed that reports of remembering increased when subjects performed some meaningful processing at study. Using a level of processing manipulation (Craik & Lockhart, 1972), this study found that people's reports of remembering increased after studying words for their meaning (as opposed to their lexical or physical properties). Also, using a generation manipulation (Jacoby, 1978; Slamecka & Graf, 1978), this same study showed that people's reports of remembering increased

after generating study targets to semantic cues, rather than simply reading them.

A similar hypothesis emphasized the role of processing rather than different memory systems and proposed that remembering is affected by conceptual processing (Rajaram, 1993). This work showed that ostensibly conceptually driven memory effects, including the levels of processing effect and the picture superiority effect, were obtained and selectively associated with remembering. That is, subjects' reports of remembering (but not their reports of knowing) increased when they studied words for meaning and when they saw pictures at study. This work not only showed that remembering is influenced by conceptual processing but it also demonstrated that knowing was differently influenced by perceptual processing (we discuss factors that affect knowing in the next section on noetic consciousness).

Subsequently, a number of studies have been conducted that support the proposal that remembering is associated with prior conceptual processing and knowing is associated with prior perceptual processing (see Gardiner & Richardson-Klavehn, 2000; Rajaram, 1999; Rajaram & Roediger, 1997; Richardson-Klavehn, Gardiner, & Java, 1996; Roediger, Wheeler, & Rajaram, 1993, for reviews). For example, reports of remembering increase after elaborative rehearsal (as compared to rote rehearsal) at study (Gardiner, Gawlick, & Richardson-Klavehn, 1994). Reports of remembering are also affected by attention at study: Remember responses increase after study under full attention as compared to divided attention (Gardiner & Parkin, 1990; Mangels, Picton, & Craik, 2001; Parkin, Gardiner, & Rosser, 1995; Yonelinas, 2001). Because dividing attention at study has been interpreted as a manipulation that decreases elaborative, conceptual processing but not perceptual processing, the findings showing selective effects of dividing attention on Remember responses can be taken as support for the idea that remembering is associated with prior conceptual processing.

Although the evidence just reviewed supports the idea that conceptual processes underlie remembering and perceptual processes underpin knowing, more recent data have undercut these claims. These data are inconsistent with both sides of the argument: They show that remembering can be influenced by perceptual processes and that knowing can be influenced by conceptual process (Conway, Gardiner, Perfect, Anderson, & Cohen, 1997; Mantyla, 1997; Rajaram, 1996, 1998; Rajaram & Geraci, 2000). For now, we focus on research that is inconsistent with the remembering side of the account. Two perceptual manipulations have been found to affect remembering. Changes in both size and orientation of objects across study and test influence Remember responses, but have little effect on Know responses (Rajaram, 1996; see also Yonelinas & Jacoby, 1995). This work shows that reports of remembering increase when objects are presented in the same size and orientation at study and at test and decrease when the size and orientation are different at test. In retrospect, the possibility that both meaning and perceptual features influence remembering is not altogether surprising because much of autonoetic consciousness is associated with retrieval of vivid perceptual details. The challenge then is to ascertain a priori the nature of variables – conceptual or perceptual – that would influence remembering (or autonoetic consciousness) and thereby develop a framework that can generate useful predictions.

To this end, Rajaram (1996, 1998; Rajaram & Roediger, 1997) developed an alternative theory that involved distinctiveness of processing. This alternate hypothesis proposes that autonoetic consciousness or remembering reflects distinctiveness of the processing at study (Rajaram, 1996, 1998), whereas knowing, or noetic consciousness, is influenced by the fluency of processing at study (Rajaram, 1993; Rajaram & Geraci, 2000). This interpretation that autonoetic consciousness especially reflects distinctive processing during encoding can accommodate many of the studies mentioned so far, as well as more recent findings, which are discussed next.

DISTINCTIVENESS EFFECTS ON REMEMBERING

Recent work shows that the distinctiveness of the study episode influences reports of remembering; importantly, this work shows that both perceptual and conceptual sources of distinctiveness cause increases in remembering. First, take for example a manipulation of distinctiveness that arises from perceptual oddities of the word form, such as orthographic distinctiveness. Words with unusual letter combinations, such as "subpoena," are remembered better than words with more common letter combinations, such as "sailboat" (Hunt & Elliott, 1980; Hunt & Mitchell, 1978; 1982; Hunt & Toth, 1990; Zechmeister, 1972). The effects of such orthographic distinctiveness on Remember and Know judgments were examined in one study by asking subjects to study a list of orthographically common and distinct words. Replicating the standard finding in the literature, results showed that people had superior recognition for the orthographically distinct words. Critically, this manipulation selectively affected Remember responses, and not Know responses (Rajaram, 1998). In other words, remembering increased with the perceptual distinctiveness of the items at study.

Similarly, noting the distinctive features of a face affects remembering and not knowing (Mantyla, 1997). In this study, subjects studied faces and either examined the differences among them by noting the facial distinctiveness of various features or categorized faces together based on general stereotypes, such as "intellectual" or "party-goer." Distinctive processing of individual features increased Remember responses, whereas categorizing faces increased Know responses. These results all converge on the conclusion that distinctive processing leads to conscious recollection as reflected in Remember responses.

EFFECTS OF EMOTION ON REMEMBERING

Defining what constitutes a distinctive event in memory is difficult (see Schmidt, 1991), although the issue has received a resurgence of investigation and theorizing (Geraci & Rajaram, 2006; Hunt, 1995, 2006; McDaniel & Geraci, 2006). Does distinctiveness refer to information that is simply unusual against a background context (e.g., von Restorff, 1933)? Is something considered distinctive if it is surprising or unexpected within a certain context? Is particularly salient information distinctive? Or, does distinctiveness refer to a type of processing, as Hunt and McDaniel (1993) proposed in distinguishing between distinctive and relational processing?

Emotionally laden events are often considered distinctive and are well remembered (but see Schmidt, 2006, for conditions under which emotionally arousing events affect memory differently from other distinctive events). Evidence that emotional information is remembered well and in vivid detail comes both from studies investigating emotional experimental stimuli, such as arousing words or pictures, and from studies investigating powerful emotional occurrences outside the lab in what are called flashbulb memories (Brown & Kulik, 1977). Flashbulb memories are so named because dramatic life events seem to be remembered in striking detail, just as is a picture caught in a photographic flash (although later research shows that the term may be something of a misnomer). Many studies of flashbulb memory have examined subjects' memory for large-scale naturally occurring events, such as JFK's assassination, the Challenger explosion of 1996, or more recently, the terrorist attacks of September 11, 2001. Although there are doubtless important differences between laboratory and naturally occurring emotional memories, in general findings from these studies demonstrate that emotional events produce more vivid memories for the events in question. We review evidence from the two types of study in turn.

Several laboratory experiments demonstrate that retention is superior for emotionally laden items presented as pictures, words, or sentences relative to neutral items (see Buchanan & Adolphs, 2002 and Hamann, 2001, for reviews). This work attempts to provide a laboratory analog to emotional events that people experience outside the lab. Because the hallmark of a flashbulb memory is that people report being able to remember many contextual details from having first encoded the emotional event (e.g., people often report that they can remember where they were and what they were wearing when they first heard the news that JFK had been shot; Neisser & Harsch, 1992; Rubin & Kozin, 1984), recent investigation is aimed at examining the quality of these emotional memories.

To examine whether emotional memories are qualitatively different from nonemotional or neutral memories, some studies have begun examining metamemory judgments for these events, including Remember/Know responses and source judgments (Kensinger & Corkin, 2003; Ochsner, 2000). In the Ochsner study, subjects studied positive pictures (e.g., a flower), negative pictures (e.g., a burned body), and neutral pictures (e.g., a house) that systematically varied in the amount of arousal they produced. Results showed that participants had best retention of the negative pictures, followed by the positive pictures, with the worst memory for the neutral pictures. Importantly for our purposes, people were much more likely to indicate that they had a rich and vivid memory for emotional pictures that were at least mildly arousing relative to the neutral pictures. Subjects assigned a higher proportion of Remember responses to emotional than to neutral pictures, whereas Know responses were associated mostly with neutral and positive items. Kensinger and Corkin further demonstrated that not only were people more likely to remember the emotional events but they were also more likely to remember accurate source details from the emotional events.

Similar to the studies just described, people often report that their flashbulb memories of real-life events are also extremely vivid and full (e.g., Christianson & Loftus, 1990). Of course, the term *flashbulb memory* was developed to suggest this very fact. Although, flashbulb memories may feel vivid, much debate has ensued regarding the accuracy of these events and the relation between accuracy and vivid memory reports (see Conway, 1995, for a review).

A recent study examined the relation between accuracy and subjective experience using the Remember/Know paradigm to examine flashbulb memories for the events of September 11th (Talarico & Rubin, 2003). Participants were asked questions about their flashbulb memories of September 11th (e.g., when they first heard what happened, who told them, etc.), and they were asked questions about everyday sorts of events from before the attack. People were more likely to assign Remember responses to their flashbulb memories as compared to control (common) events. This pattern held when participants were tested on September 12, 2001 and became more pronounced at longer delays. Talarico and Rubin found that people claimed to remember the emotional events more vividly than the everyday events despite the fact that they were no more accurate at recalling the flashbulb memories as compared to the everyday memories. Thus, flashbulb memories may be quite susceptible to error despite the great confidence with which they are held, especially after long delays (see also Neisser & Harsch, 1992; Schmolck, Buffalo, & Squire, 2000).

Recollective Experience and Memory for Source

As the preponderance of the evidence reviewed so far indicates, autonoetic consciousness is characterized by vivid, detailed feelings associated with one's personal past, at least for distinctive events. Using the Remember/Know paradigm, "vividness" is characterized by using a single Remember response, whereas the lack of this vivid detail constitutes a Know response. However, this memory for details has also been examined by requiring subjects to assess the quality of their memories by assigning the correct source of these memories (see Johnson, Hashtroudi, & Lindsay, 1993). In this line of research, source is defined broadly and can include, for example, one list of items versus another, items presented in one voice versus another, in one location or another, on a computer monitor, and so on. A particularly interesting case (called reality monitoring) asks subjects to determine whether an event actually occurred or was imagined. In some sense, all recognition judgments require source-specifying information of some sort.

According to the source-monitoring framework (e.g., Johnson, 1988), people often rely on the qualities of their memories to determine their source by comparing the characteristics of the retrieved memory to memories generally associated with that source. For example, with a reality monitoring decision, people may rely on the knowledge that memories of perceived or experienced events tend to be more vivid and have more associated details than memories of imagined events. Conversely, they may rely on the knowledge that memories from imagined sources tend to be characterized by more information about cognitive processes associated with cognitive effort and elaboration relative to those that are perceived (e.g., Johnson, Foley, Suengas, & Raye, 1988; Johnson, Hashtroudi, & Lindsay, 1993; Johnson, Raye, Foley, & Foley, 1981). As with the Remember/Know studies, much research on source (or reality) monitoring focuses on defining the information that characterizes memories from various sources and shows that sources can be discriminated flexibly among many dimensions. The dimensions include perceptual features of the target (e.g., Ferguson, Hashtroudi, & Johnson, 1992; Henkel, Franklin, & Johnson, 2000; Johnson, DeLeonardis, Hashtroudi, & Ferguson, 1995; Johnson, Foley, & Leach, 1988), cognitive processes (e.g., Finke, Johnson, & Shyi, 1988), the plausibility of remembered details (e.g., Sherman & Bessenoff, 1999), as well as related experiences (Geraci & Franklin, 2004; Henkel & Franklin, 1998). Thus, source decisions rely on multiple aspects of experience that give rise to autonoetic consciousness.

Some studies have compared Remember/Know responses and source judgments. Conway and Dewhurst (1995) had subjects watch, perform, or imagine doing a series of tasks. Later, they were presented with the task and asked about its source: Was it watched, performed, or imagined? Accurate source memory for tasks that the subjects performed was primarily associated with Remember responses, whereas accurate source memory for tasks that they only imagined performing was associated mostly with Know responses. Accurate source memory for the observed tasks was associated more equally with both Remember and Know responses. These results corroborate the idea that Remember responses can reflect detailed perceptual memories associated with personally experienced events.

In conjunction with asking source questions, subjects are often asked to rate the qualities of their memories using the Memory Characteristics Questionnaire (MCQ; Johnson, Foley, Suengas, & Raye, 1988). The MCQ asks people to assess the qualities of their remembrances; in this context, we may think of the MCQ as a further attempt to gain introspective knowledge of autonoetic states of consciousness. Remember/Know responses have also been compared to MCQ ratings (Mather, Henkel, & Johnson, 1997). The Mather et al. study was designed to determine why people falsely remember words that they never saw using the Deese-Roediger-McDermott (DRM) false memory paradigm (Deese, 1959; Roediger & McDermott, 1995) in which subjects study lists of related words (bed, rest, awake, tired, dream...) and often remember a word that was not presented on the list (sleep, in this example). To examine the basis of these false Remember responses, this study examined their qualities using MCQ ratings. (We include more discussion on the topic of illusory remembering toward the end of this chapter.) Results from the MCQ ratings showed that people did report less auditory perceptual detail for false Remembered items than for correct Remembered items (see also Norman & Schacter, 1997), whereas both types of items were associated with details of semantic associations. These findings show that autonoetic consciousness is influenced by a number of variables,

including perceptual and emotional qualities of the information. Interestingly, autonoetic consciousness as reflected in memory for details is not always associated with accurate memory, as we also observed in discussing emotional memories. However, the qualitatively distinct nature of memory – accurate or inaccurate – that is accompanied by autonoetic consciousness provides greater consistency and confidence in subjects' judgments. Finally, these studies also show that remembering is the central process in conscious recollections of our past, and that Tulving's (1985) Remember/Know procedure and Johnson's Memory Characteristics Questionnaire are useful methodological tools for investigating the nature of autonoetic consciousness.

Noetic Consciousness

In Tulving's (1983, 1985) theory, noetic consciousness is associated with the experience of knowing and with the semantic memory system (Tulving, 1985). In this sense, Know judgments should be associated with semantic knowledge. However, in experimental practice, Know judgments seem to capture various types of awareness. In particular, subjects generally give Know judgments for two types of cognitive experiences – knowledge and familiarity. In fact, in some theoretical treatments (e.g., Jacoby, Jones & Dolan, 1998), Know judgments are aligned with the process of familiarity.

At the experiential level, noetic consciousness lacks the intensity and immediacy that are associated with autonoetic consciousness. This is true by definition because noetic consciousness represents the less personal and the more generic sense in which we retrieve factual events and information. This lack of personal involvement in the retrieved information applies not only to general knowledge about the world (the usual definition of semantic memory) but also can apply to knowledge about ourselves and our own experiences. We may know we had a fifth birthday party without it being remembered. In this case the memory takes on an impersonal quality. Another example of the operation of noetic consciousness can be seen in one's memory of a trip by airplane taken ten years ago. Although a person may know that he or she traveled from New York to Calcutta, any remembrance of the events of the trip may have vanished. The argument is that noetic consciousness differs from autonoetic consciousness not only in terms of the content of retrieval but also in the very nature of the retrieval process. We know about the airplane ride in the same way that we know that Thomas Jefferson was president of the United States.

The Influence of Instructions on the Interpretations of Know Judgments

The interpretation of Know judgments can be traced back to the specific instructions provided to subjects. An abbreviated version of these instructions (taken from Rajaram, 1996) is provided here to illustrate this point. We include here the instructions for Remember judgments as well, because Know judgments are typically operationalized in experimental studies in the context of Remember judgments:

> Remember judgments: If your recognition of the item is accompanied by a conscious recollection of its prior occurrence in the study list, then write R. "Remember" is the ability to become consciously aware again of some aspect or aspects of what happened or what was experienced at the time the word was presented (e.g., aspects of the physical appearance of the word, or of something that happened in the room, or of what you were thinking and doing at the time). In other words, the "remembered" word should bring back to mind a particular association, image, or something more personal from the time of study or something about its appearance or position (i.e., what came before or after that word).
>
> Know judgments: "Know" responses should be made when you recognize that the word was in the study list, but you cannot consciously recollect anything about its actual occurrence, or what happened, or what was experienced at the time of its occurrence. In other words, write K (for

know) when you are certain of recognizing the words but these words fail to evoke any specific conscious recollection from the study list.

> To further clarify the difference between these two judgments (i.e., R versus K), here are a few examples. If someone asks for your name, you would typically respond in the "know" sense without becoming consciously aware of anything about a particular event or experience; however, when asked the last movie you saw, you would typically respond in the "Remember" sense, that is, becoming consciously aware again of some aspects of the experience.

It is clear from these instructions that Know judgments may be used in the sense of knowledge (as in the semantic sense of knowing one's own name or knowing Thomas Jefferson was president) or as a sense of familiarity where no specific details can be evoked from the study phase (e.g., recognizing a face as familiar but not being able to recover who the person is or where you met her). In other words, Know judgments are defined in terms of what they are not (they are confident memories that lack detail), rather than what they are. However, the examples and description provided in the instructions do lead to the two interpretations – knowledge and familiarity – that are most commonly associated with Know judgments.

Knowing and Retrieval from Semantic Memory

It is common for people to know that Mt. Everest is in the Himalayas, that mango is a tropical fruit, and that Chicago in November is colder than Houston. However, people almost certainly do not know when and where they learned these bits of knowledge. The conception of semantic memory is not without its critics, and the very definition of semantic memory is sometimes a source of debate. Nevertheless, according to Tulving's theory within which the Remember/Know distinction is embedded, semantic memory is defined as a repository of organized information about concepts, words, people, events, and their interrelations in the world. Information from semantic memory is retrieved as facts and without memory for the details of the learning experience or the time and place where learning took place.

An understanding of the process by which the sense of knowing may be associated with semantic memory requires a systematic investigation of the learning and testing conditions. This approach has the potential to lead us to an understanding of the ways in which specific experimental conditions give rise to noetic consciousness associated with memory.

The original sense of knowing as awareness associated with semantic knowledge is perhaps best illustrated in a study by Martin Conway and his colleagues (Conway, Gardiner, Perfect, Anderson, & Cohen, 1997). In this study, subjects gave Remember and Know judgments to different types of course material learned over an extended period of time. Conway and colleagues asked subjects to make an important distinction in their study between two different interpretations of noetic consciousness by asking them to judge between Just Knowing and Familiarity. This distinction was made for the precise reason of separating knowledge from a sense of familiarity. The authors also studied two types of courses. One type consisted of lecture materials (Introduction to Psychology, Physiological Psychology, Cognitive Psychology, and Social and Developmental Psychology), and another type consisted of learning scientific methodology (research methods courses). The nature of learning differs in these two types of courses: Lecture courses entail learning massive amounts of content material, whereas methodology courses usually require active learning and application in smaller class settings. The nature of awareness systematically varied with this distinction; subjects gave more Remember judgments to information learned in lecture courses and more Just Know judgments to material from the methodology courses. Furthermore, there was a shift from Remember to Just Know judgments over time, further supporting the idea that once episodic details were lost, information became schematized and conceptually organized.

This sense of knowing (or just knowing) has not been used frequently in the literature, even though the distinction led to interesting results in the Conway et al. (1997) study. Several reasons may exist for the scant use of Know judgments as a measure of semantic knowledge. For example, the Conway et al. study clearly found numerous repetitions of material to be necessary for schematization to occur and to lead to just knowing the response. Spacing between repetitions may also be important for conceptual organization to occur. The variety of content and learning experience accumulated over time may also interact with repetition and spacing and create memories that can shift from remembering to just knowing, instead of being simply forgotten over time. These are but three notable variables, and there are probably more. Classroom education in the Conway et al. (1997) study brought together these conditions of repetition, spacing, and varied encoding quite nicely, but it is usually difficult to create such conditions in the laboratory.

In a recent study, Rajaram and Hamilton (2005) created the following laboratory conditions as a first step toward testing the effects of varied and deep encoding on Remember and Know states of awareness. Subjects studied unrelated word pairs either once or twice where the repeated presentation varied the context and was spaced apart (e.g., a single presentation might be *penny-cousin*, whereas a repeated presentation would have been *fence-bread*, then *guard-bread*). At test, subjects gave recognition and Remember/Know judgments to the target words (cousin, bread). Among several conditions in this study, the most relevant for our present purposes are those that involved a deep level of processing at encoding. The results showed that even after 48 hours of delay (relative to 30 minutes), subjects gave significantly more Remember responses to words repeated under different contexts than to once-presented target words. Importantly for the present discussion, subjects also gave significantly more Know responses after 48 hours than after 30 minutes. Thus, Know judgments were responsive to both conceptual encoding and varied repetition even after considerable delay.

A recent study by E. Marsh, Meade, and Roediger (2003) reported a paradigm that could be very useful for investigating knowing as a measure of semantic memory. In this study, E. Marsh et al. investigated whether reading a story before being tested on general knowledge questions can influence subjects' ability to identify correctly the story or prior knowledge as the source of their answers. Both immediate source judgments and retrospective source judgments on the general knowledge answers showed that subjects attributed many details from the story to being part of their prior knowledge. This finding nicely illustrates that episodic information was converted to facts or semantic memory. Other experiments using this paradigm and ones like it might answer the question about how information that once held great recollective detail may be transformed into impersonal knowledge over time, or how remembering becomes knowing.

Knowing as Fluency and Familiarity

In contrast to the limited experimental work on knowing as a measure of semantic memory, there has been a flurry of research aimed at characterizing Know judgments as a measure of fluency or familiarity. This effort may be attributed, in large part, to the ways in which Know judgments are defined through instructions. As described earlier, subjects are asked to give Know judgments when they have a feeling that something has been encountered recently but no details come to mind about that encounter. In an interesting project on the actual reports by subjects, Gardiner, Ramponi, and Richardson-Klavehn (1998) examined subjects' transcripts of reasons they gave Know judgments and found they did so typically based on a feeling of familiarity as expressed in some of the statements made by subjects ("It was one of those words that

rang a bell," "There was no association, I just had a feeling that I saw it, I was sure" [p. 7].)

The fluency-familiarity interpretation of Know judgments has featured prominently in our own conceptualization (see Rajaram, 1993, 1996, 1999; Rajaram & Geraci, 2000; Rajaram & Roediger, 1997). This approach proposes that Remember judgments are influenced by the processing of distinctive attributes of the stimuli, whereas Know judgments are sensitive to the fluency or ease with which stimuli are processed. Considerable evidence supports this interpretation of Know judgments. For example, subjects give more Know responses to words that are preceded by a masked repetition of the same word (hence increasing fluency) compared to words that are preceded by a masked presentation of an unrelated word (Rajaram, 1993). Similarly, words that are preceded by a very brief (250 ms) presentation of semantically related words elicit more Know judgments than words that are preceded by unrelated words (Rajaram & Geraci, 2000; see also Mantyla, 1997; Mantyla & Raudsepp, 1996). Along these lines, having modality match across study and test occasions (e.g., items presented visually in both cases) increases perceptual fluency and selectively increases Know judgments relative to when the modalities mismatch between study and test (Gregg & Gardiner, 1994).

The idea that fluency or familiarity increases Know judgments and the supporting evidence are also consistent with Gardiner and colleagues' original proposal about the nature of Know judgments (Gardiner, 1988; Gardiner & Java, 1990; Gardiner & Parkin, 1990). According to this view, Know judgments are mediated by processes of the procedural memory system. This view ties Know judgments not only to the familiarity process but also to perceptual priming. In more recent works, Gardiner and his associates have reconsidered Tulving's original classification system of associating Know judgments with semantic memory that we described in an earlier section (see for example, Gardiner & Gregg, 1997; Gardiner, Java, & Richardson-Klavehn,

1996; Gardiner, Kaminska, Dixon, & Java, 1996).

Other recent theories that distinguish between a recollective basis and a familiarity basis of recognition memory have also contributed to the interpretation of Know judgments as reflecting the fluency or familiarity process (Jacoby, et al., 1997; Yonelinas, 2001). These dual-process models are based on the process dissociation procedure (Jacoby, 1991) that was developed to measure the independent and opposing influences of recollective (consciously controlled) and familiarity (more automatic) processes. According to this view, Know judgments in Tulving's (1985) Remember/Know procedure provide an underestimation of the extent to which the familiarity process contributes to memory performance. As noted in an earlier section, Jacoby and colleagues have assumed independence between these processes and have proposed a mathematical correction (Know/(1-Remember)) to compute the influence of familiarity. On this point these dual-process models diverge from the frameworks and models described earlier, but these models are nevertheless in agreement with the main point under consideration here – Know judgments measure the effects of fluency or familiarity.

Know Judgments and Perceptual Priming

Some of the theoretical interpretations reviewed in the previous section suggest the strong possibility that the same processes should mediate Know judgments and perceptual priming. Issues surrounding this proposal are tricky, however, and the evidence is mixed. We review the issues and evidence here, albeit briefly.

Perceptual priming is measured with implicit memory tasks, such as word stem completion, word fragment completion, and perceptual identification (see Roediger, 1990 and Roediger & McDermott, 1993, for reviews.) For example, on a task such as word fragment completion, subjects first study a list of words (e.g., elephant) and are later asked to complete the first word that comes

to mind in response to fragmented word cues that could be solved with studied words (e.g., _ l _ p h _ n _ for elephant) or nonstudied words (e.g., _ a _ l b _ a _ for sailboat). The advantage in completing fragments of studied words compared to nonstudied words is that it gives a measure of priming, and priming can be dissociated from explicit measures of memory by many variables. Extensive experimental efforts are made in these studies to discourage subjects from using explicit retrieval strategies and to exclude subjects who nevertheless use explicit or deliberate retrieval to complete these tasks. Thus, such tasks are assumed to measure a relatively automatic process that contributes to memory performance. Furthermore, a subset of this class of tasks is also particularly, though not exclusively, sensitive to match or mismatch in the perceptual attributes of study and test stimuli. For example, changes in the presentation modality (from auditory to visual) reduce the magnitude of priming compared to matched modality across study and test (visual to visual; Rajaram & Roediger, 1993; Roediger & Blaxton, 1987; see also Weldon & Roediger, 1987, for similar conclusions based on changes in surface format across pictures and words.) Thus, perceptual priming is a measure of performance on implicit memory tasks where perceptual features exert a strong influence on the magnitude of priming.

In contrast to perceptual priming, Know judgments reflect retention while subjects are engaged in the explicit retrieval of studied information. Therefore, the possibility that these two measures, one derived from implicit memory tasks and the other from explicit memory tasks, have the same underlying basis is intriguing. The earlier proposal of Gardiner and colleagues that Know judgments are influenced by processes of the procedural memory system suggests such equivalence because perceptual priming is assumed to be mediated by the procedural memory system (Tulving & Schacter, 1990).

Furthermore, dual-process models proposed by Jacoby, Yonelinas, and colleagues also suggest such equivalence. In these approaches, automatic processes and familiarity processes appear to be interchangeable concepts; the former is typically associated with priming on implicit tests, and the latter is associated with the Know component of explicit memory performance. Whether or not these measures are isomorphic, and the evidence reviewed below is mixed on this issue, it seems intuitive to assume that Know judgments share some of the properties both of perceptual priming and of explicit memory. If priming is placed at one end of the continuum of conscious awareness and Remember judgments at the other end, Know judgments by definition fall in between, albeit on the conscious side of this continuum. By virtue of being at the brink of conscious awareness, some processing component of Know judgments might share its basis with priming.

As just mentioned, the evidence seems mixed on this issue, although only a handful of studies have addressed it. For instance, dividing attention during study with an auditory tone or digit monitoring task (when the subjects' main task is to read the words) adversely affects explicit memory tasks, but leaves perceptual priming intact (Jacoby, Woloshyn, & Kelley, 1989; Parkin & Russo, 1990). Parallel effects of tone monitoring during study are observed on Remember and Know judgments, respectively (Gardiner & Parkin, 1990). Similarly, a study of pictures and words dissociates performance on explicit memory tasks and implicit memory tasks such that the picture superiority effect (better memory for pictures than words – Madigan, 1983) is reliably observed on the explicit memory task, but this effect reverses on the perceptual priming task of word fragment completion (Weldon & Roediger, 1987). This dissociative pattern has been reported for Remember and Know judgments as well, where the picture superiority effect was observed for Remember judgments and its reversal was observed on Know judgments (Rajaram, 1993, Experiment 2).

In contrast to these findings where independent variables affected Know judgments in ways similar to their effects on priming tasks, other studies have not shown such parallels. For example, the generation effect (when words generated from semantic cues are better recalled and recognized than words that are simply read) that is reliably observed in explicit memory tasks (e.g., Jacoby, 1978; Slamecka & Graf, 1978) is usually reversed in perceptual priming (Blaxton, 1989; Srinivas & Roediger, 1990), but such a reversal is not observed for Know judgments (Gardiner & Java, 1990) even under optimally designed conditions (Java, 1994). This result clearly undermines any straightforward notion that Know judgments solely reflect perceptual priming.

Word frequency effects across a repetition priming task and a recognition memory task also challenge the notion that Know judgments and priming performance are similarly responsive to independent variables. For example, Kinoshita (1995) reported that on a priming task of making lexical decisions (where subjects decide whether a letter string is a word or a non-word), low-frequency words yielded greater priming than high-frequency words even following unattended study conditions. This finding suggests that low-frequency words should lead to greater Know judgments than high-frequency words. However, Gardiner and Java (1990) had previously reported an unambiguous advantage for low-frequency words over high-frequency words in *Remember* judgments, and this variable had little effect on Know judgments. Other recent evidence also suggests a distinction between types of familiarity processes that mediate recognition relative to priming. For example, Wagner, Gabrieli, and Verfaellie (1997) have reported that the familiarity process associated with recognition is more conceptually based than processes that underlie perceptual priming. Wagner and Gabrieli (1998) have further argued that processes supporting perceptual priming and the familiarity component of recognition are both functionally and anatomically distinct.

The evidence on this issue is also mixed in studies of individuals with anterograde amnesia. Whereas explicit memory performance is severely impaired in amnesia, perceptual priming for single words or picture is found to be intact (see Moscovitch, Vriezen, & Goshen-Gottstein, 1993; Schacter, Chiu, & Ochsner, 1993; Verfaellie & Keane, 2002, for reviews). Preserved perceptual priming in amnesia suggests that Know judgments (or the familiarity component of recognition) should also be preserved if perceptual priming and knowing have the same bases. Recent evidence has started to delineate conditions in the Remember/Know paradigm that show that amnesic subjects can indeed utilize the familiarity component to boost their Know judgments (Verfaellie, Giovanello, & Keane, 2001). However, converging evidence from different paradigms (see Knowlton & Squire, 1995; Schacter, Verfaellie, & Pradere, 1996; Verfaellie, 1994) has also shown a deficit in Know judgments in amnesic patients, although this deficit is far lower in magnitude than the deficit in Remember judgments (see Yonelinas, Kroll, Dobbins, Lazzara, & Knight, 1998). Evidence from studies with amnesic patients has further identified neuroanatomical regions that are differentially associated with remembering and knowing. Specifically, evidence from studies of amnesic patients (Moscovitch & McAndrews, 2002, Yonelinas et al., 2002) suggests that Remember judgments are mediated by the hippocampus, whereas familiarity is mediated by parahippocampal structures in the medial temporal lobe region. Neuroimaging evidence also supports this distinction (but see Squire, Stark, & Clark, 2004, for a different view on the proposed structural dichotomies).

Together, a comparison between perceptual priming and Know judgments has revealed at best mixed evidence. As some have noted, the key to the differences between processes that affect perceptual priming and Know judgments (or familiarity) may lie in the greater involvement of conceptual processes in explicit recognition (Verfaellie & Keane, 2002, Wagner et al., 1997.) It is clear that both for theoretical

reasons outlined earlier and mixed empirical evidence reviewed here, this area is ripe for extensive investigation.

Knowing and Confidence

Earlier we considered the contention that judgments of knowing may simply reflect low-confidence judgments. That is, perhaps people give Remember judgments when they are highly confident that an event occurred previously and Know judgments when they believe it occurred but are less confident. Proponents of this view (e.g., Donaldson, 1996) argue that the Remember/Know distinction is merely a quantitative one (how much "memory strength" does the tested event have?), rather than a qualitative difference (reflecting, say, recollection and fluency). To review a few points made previously, the signal detection models with several criteria can often account for data after the fact, but lack true explanatory power in predicting dissociations and associations between Remember and Know judgments. It is difficult to know what determines the placement of criteria at particular points on the continuum in these models and how this placement might vary with different experimental conditions. Further, experimental evidence cited in the earlier part of the chapter (e.g., Rajaram et al., 2002) revealing different effects of independent and subject variables on Remember/Know judgments and confidence judgments is inconsistent with the idea the Know judgments merely reflect confidence. Although confidence and Remember/Know judgments are related, remembering may explain confidence judgments rather than the other way around.

Knowing and Guessing

A potential problem in interpreting the nature of Know judgments is the extent to which subjects include guesses when making Know judgments. In this situation, Know judgments would reflect not only memory processes but also pure guesses, thereby complicating the inferences we might draw about the nature of knowing. An even more serious concern might be that Know judgments simply reflect guesses and nothing more. However, neither of these concerns seems to compromise the data typically obtained for Know judgments. The first concern is circumvented in most studies by the careful use of instructions that strongly discourage guessing. In fact, the generally low false alarm rates that are typical in these studies suggest that this approach is largely successful. The second concern about Know judgments simply being equivalent to guesses is addressed by Gardiner and colleagues in studies where they required subjects to make Remember, Know, and Guess judgments to items presented in recognition memory tests (see Gardiner & Conway, 1999; Gardiner, Java, & Richardson-Klavehn, 1996; Gardiner, Kaminska, Dixon, & Java, 1996; Gardiner, Ramponi, & Richardson-Klavehn, 1998; Gardiner, Richardson-Klavehn, & Ramponi, 1997). By and large, Know and Guess responses turn out to be functionally distinct such that Know judgments reflect memory for prior information and Guess judgments do not. As Gardiner and Conway (1999) note, the relevance of taking guesses into account in the Remember/ Know paradigm seems to be to minimize noise for Know judgments. We note that this could be achieved either by including a separate response category or by instructing subjects to refrain from guessing. As discussed in a previous section, the potential variations across laboratories in communicating Remember/Know instructions may account for some differences in the literature. For these reasons, we have emphasized elsewhere the care and effort that are needed to administer the Remember/Know task properly (Rajaram & Roediger, 1997). Despite these concerns, the experimental effort of nearly 20 years has yielded fairly systematic, informative, and interesting findings about the nature of Know judgments. This effort has also answered as many questions as it has raised critical issues for future investigation. Finally, this empirical effort in the literature has begun to identify the nature

of memory that is associated with noetic consciousness.

Knowing and Other Metamemory Judgments

Remember/Know judgments are by definition metamemory judgments – subjects indicate their assessment of retrieval experience for items that they have recalled or recognized. People are able to make other judgments that may seem similar to Know judgments, but are in fact quite distinct. For example, people can reliably report feelings-of-knowing indicating that they can recognize an item on a multiple-choice test even though they are unable to recall it (see Koriat, 1995), and people can also reliably differentiate whether or not they are in a tip-of-the-tongue state (where they feel that the answer or the word they are looking for is on the tip of their tongue and could be retrieved; see Brown, 1991, for a review). Both of these types of experiences differ from Know judgments in that the latter experience is associated with information that is already retrieved (as in recall) or has been presented (as in recognition). That is, Know judgments characterize a particular experiential state that accompanies retrieved information. There has been little experimental effort as yet directed toward the possible relation between Know judgments and these other states of awareness.

Concluding Remarks about Interpreting Know Judgments

The preceding sections bring into focus both the difficulties in characterizing Know judgments and the successes that have been accomplished so far in doing so. Know judgments have been defined both in terms of what they are (semantic memory, fluency, familiarity), what they are not (low-confidence responses, guesses, and other metamemorial judgments), and what they might or might not partly reflect (perceptual priming.) These efforts show the challenges associated with distinguishing different states of consciousness – autonoetic and noetic – experimentally and the role research can play in successfully delineating these mental states. As such, these findings have refined the questions and sharpened the direction for future studies aimed at understanding the relationship between noetic consciousness and memory.

Anoetic Consciousness

So far our discussion has focused on two types of conscious experience: autonoetic consciousness where one feels as though one is mentally reliving a past experience in the present and noetic consciousness where one simply knows that one has experienced the event before, but cannot vividly relive it. These two states of conscious awareness have in common that they both indicate knowledge of past events. However, there is a third class of memory phenomena that is characterized by the lack of awareness that an event occurred in the past even though the event changes behavior. Ebbinghaus (1885/1964) described this class of event and Tulving (1985) referred to this occurrence as exemplifying anoetic, or non-knowing, consciousness. One could quibble that the characteristic of "non-knowing" means that subjects are not conscious, and so this state should not be included in the list. However, in other realms of inquiry, being asleep or in a coma is referred to as a state of consciousness even though both indicate the absence of awake consciousness.

In anoetic consciousness, a person is fully awake and alert, but is unaware that some past event is influencing current behavior. Unlike the first two states that accompany performance on explicit memory tests like free recall and recognition, anoetic consciousness is associated with memory performance on a separate class of memory tests, called implicit memory tests. Of course, many phenomena in other areas of psychology (particularly social psychology) might also be said to refer to anoetic consciousness because all sorts of factors affect behavior without the person becoming aware of the critical variables controlling behavior (e.g., Wegner, 2002; Wilson, 2002). Here we confine our remarks to responding on implicit memory tests.

Measurement Issues: Responding on Implicit Tests

Implicit memory tests differ from explicit ones because they are designed to measure retention when people are not aware of the influence of prior events on their behavior. As discussed previously, implicit tests measure memory indirectly (and therefore are also called indirect tests) by having subjects perform tasks that, unbeknownst to them, can be accomplished using previously studied items. These tasks may include filling in fragmented words or naming fragmented pictures, generating items that belong to a category, or simply answering general knowledge questions. Subjects can perform the task at some level whether or not they have studied relevant material. However, they are more likely to fill in a fragmented word, for example, if they had been exposed to it previously than if the fragment is filled by a word that was not studied. The study experience is said to prime the correct completion, so the phenomenon is called priming. Paul Rozin (1976) was among the first to call attention to this notion. Importantly, priming, by definition, occurs without autonoetic or noetic awareness of the study episode. In this way, implicit tests measure memory that is associated with anoetic consciousness. However, once a person has produced an item on the test, he or she may become aware, after the fact, that it was from a recently experienced episode. In this case, retrieval of the item seems to occur automatically, but the experience of recognition occurs later; this type of experience has been referred to as involuntary conscious memory by Richardson-Klavehn and Gardiner (2000) and is discussed in a later section.

Perceptual and Conceptual Tests

All implicit tests are designed to measure anoetic consciousness, but they differ in the nature of the processes they require. Roediger and Blaxton (1987) first proposed that there were (at least) two types of implicit and explicit tests, perceptual and conceptual tests. It is probably best to think of perceptual and conceptual dimensions as separate continua, so that tests could rely mostly on perceptual processes or conceptual processes or some combination of the two (see Roediger, Weldon & Challis, 1989, for a discussion of converging operations that can be applied to define tests). Most explicit tests are primarily conceptual in nature. Similarly, implicit tests have been broadly classified into those that require primarily perceptual analysis of the target items and those that require primarily meaningful analysis. According to the transfer appropriate processing view (Blaxton, 1989; Kolers & Roediger, 1984; Roediger, 1990; Roediger, Weldon, & Challis, 1989), retention on both explicit and implicit tests benefits to the extent that the tests require similar stimulus analysis (i.e., similar conceptual or perceptual processing between study and test), regardless of whether one is consciously aware of the study episode. A large body of work is consistent with this prediction (although there are clear exceptions, too). Here, we describe just a few examples of these classes of tests that have emerged from this line of thinking (see Toth, 2000, for a comprehensive list of implicit memory tests).

Perceptual implicit memory tests generally require participants to identify a physically degraded or rapid presentation of a stimulus. Priming on these tests is influenced by the perceptual format used at encoding, such as modality (auditory or visual) or form (e.g., picture or word) of presentation. Conversely, these tests are relatively unaffected by meaningful analysis, such as the semantic analysis required by levels-of-processing manipulations (e.g., Jacoby & Dallas, 1981). There are several popular perceptual implicit memory tests, and here we describe only a few.

The word stem completion test is one of the most popular perceptual implicit tests. In verbal versions of this task, subjects are exposed to a list of words in one phase of the experiment (e.g., elephant) and then, in a later phase, presented with the first three letters of words (e.g., "ele___") and are asked

to complete them with the first words that come to mind (Warrington & Weiskrantz, 1968). There are usually ten or more possible solutions in this kind of test (element, elegant, etc.) so priming is measured by the bias to produce elephant after study of that word relative to the case in which it has not been studied. Similarly, the word fragment completion test requires subjects to complete words with missing letters, such as e_e_h_n_, with the first word that comes to mind (e.g., Tulving, Schacter & Stark, 1982). Priming in both tests is measured by the proportion of fragments completed with studied solutions minus the proportion completed with non-studied solutions. The picture fragment completion test provides fragmented pictures (following study of intact pictures) with instructions for subjects to name the pictures (Weldon & Roediger, 1987).

Other perceptual tests require naming of degraded words or pictures. These are called word identification and picture identification because people are required to identify words or pictures presented very briefly (and sometimes followed by a backward mask). A variant on this task requires participants to identify increasingly complete fragments of stimuli. Here, the item is revealed slowly, and what is measured is the level of clarity needed to identify the item, either a picture (e.g., Snodgrass & Corwin, 1988; Snodgrass, Smith, Feenan, & Corwin, 1987) or a word (e.g., Hashtroudi, Ferguson, Rappold, & Cronsniak, 1988; Johnston, Hawley & Elliot, 1991). Again, priming on these tasks is measured by the percentage of clarity required for identification when the item was studied relative to when it was not studied.

Conceptual tests represent the other class of implicit memory tests (Roediger & Blaxton, 1987). These tests are largely unaffected by perceptual manipulations at encoding (e.g., the modality of presentation does not affect priming). Instead, priming on these tests is affected by meaningful factors manipulated during study, such that more priming occurs with more meaningful analyses. One commonly used conceptual implicit test is the word association test (see Shimamura & Squire, 1984). In this test, participants see words (some of which are associated with the studied words; e.g., elephant) during study and are asked to quickly produce all the associated words that come to mind in response to the cue word presented during the test (e.g., lion). In a similar test, the category exemplar production test, participants see category names at test (animals) and are asked to quickly produce as many examples from the category that come to mind (e.g. Srinivas & Roediger, 1990). As always, priming in both tests is obtained by comparing performance when a relevant item was studied to when it was not studied. The category verification test (e.g., Tenpenny & Shoben, 1992) is similar to the category production test, except that participants do not have to produce the category exemplar. Instead, they are given the category name and a possible exemplar and must indicate whether or not the item is a member of the category (animals: elephant). Priming on this task is measured by examining the decrease in reaction time to studied exemplars as compared to non-studied exemplars. Finally, general knowledge tests can function as a conceptual implicit memory test (e.g. Blaxton, 1989). In this test, participants attempt to answer general knowledge questions (e.g., "What animal did the Carthagenian general Hannibal use in his attack on Rome?"). Priming is obtained when participants are more likely to answer the questions correctly when they have studied the answer than when they have not.

The Problem of Contamination

Implicit memory tests are designed to measure anoetic consciousness, but these tests can become contaminated by consciously controlled uses of memory. That is, despite the test instructions to complete the fragment or answer the question with the first word that comes to mind, subjects may recognize the items they produce as being from the earlier phase in the experiment, and they may change their retrieval strategy to attempt explicit recollection. Whether contamination should be considered a great problem for implicit memory research is up for debate (see Roediger & McDermott, 1993), but certainly it is possible that neurologically intact participants may treat implicit tests like explicit ones (see Geraci & Rajaram, 2002). Given this possibility, several researchers have provided recommendations to help limit participants' awareness of the study-test relation and to devise procedures for determining when the implicit test is compromised by this conscious recollection. Many of these strategies have been described at length elsewhere (Roediger & Geraci, 2004; Roediger & McDermott, 1993) so we discuss them here only briefly.

EXPERIMENTAL METHODS TO MINIMIZE CONTAMINATION

One suggestion has been to give incidental learning instructions at encoding to try to disguise the fact that participants have entered a memory experiment. It may also help to use several filler tasks between the study and test phases of the experiment so that the criterial test seems, to the subjects, to be just one more task in a long series. If intentional learning instructions are required at encoding, then the implicit test itself can be disguised as a filler test before an expected explicit memory test (e.g., Weldon & Roediger, 1987). In fact, one can even give an example of the expected explicit test (e.g., a recognition test or a cued recall test) before encoding, so that participants will be less likely to recognize the implicit test as a memory test and think of it as only another filler task before the explicit test they expect. In addition to including a good cover story, the test list can be constructed such that studied items make up a smaller proportion of test items than non-studied or filler items, and appear later in the list. With this test construction, participants may be less likely to notice the studied items (but see Challis & Roediger, 1993, for evidence on whether this factor matters). Finally, there is some evidence that rapid presentation of the test fragments or stems (for example) helps promote performance associated with anoetic consciousness (Weldon, 1993).

METHODS FOR DETECTING AUTONOETIC (OR NOETIC) CONSCIOUSNESS IN IMPLICIT TESTS

Despite using the recommendations outlined above, it is still possible that subjects will become aware that they encountered the test items recently. There are several procedures for measuring whether implicit tests have been compromised by this level of awareness. Perhaps the simplest measure is to use a post-test questionnaire to assess autonoetic and noetic consciousness (e.g., Bowers & Schacter, 1990). Many studies of implicit memory have used this technique, and data from these questionnaires have permitted the partitioning of subjects into those who are aware and unaware of the relations between the study and test phases; critical dissociations between aware and unaware participants are sometimes obtained as a function of independent variables (e.g., Geraci & Rajaram, 2002). As an aside, we note that the data from these questionnaires may overestimate the level of participants' awareness because (1) participants may only become aware at the time of the questioning, especially if the questions are leading ones, and (2) participants may not have had time or motivation to engage in conscious recollection when performing the task, even if they did become aware during the test. This latter possibility can be thought of as illustrating autonoetic consciousness occurring after automatic retrieval; as noted above, this phenomenon is called involuntary conscious recollection (or memory) and is discussed in depth below (Richardson-Klavehn, Gardiner, & Java, 1994).

A second procedure that has been developed to assess whether implicit memory tests are compromised by autonoetic consciousness is the retrieval intentionality criterion (Schacter, Bowers, & Booker, 1989). This procedure is based on the fact that explicit tests of memory reliably show certain encoding effects, such as the levels of processing effect (superior memory for words processed for meaning as opposed to surface detail). If the criterial test is a perceptual implicit memory test, one can manipulate the nature of the encoding task (physical or semantic processing) to determine if the perceptual implicit test is compromised by explicit processes. If the implicit test shows a level of processing effect, then one can conclude that the test is contaminated by explicit recollection; if there is little or no effect of this powerful variable on the perceptual implicit test, then it is probably a relatively pure measure of priming in an anoetic state (see Roediger, Weldon, Stadler, & Riegler, 1992). Note, however, that this specific procedure only works for perceptual implicit tests, because conceptual implicit tests, by definition, are sensitive to meaningful processing. Other techniques must be used for conceptual tests (e.g., Hashtroudi, Ferguson, Rappold, & Crosniak, 1988).

A third procedure for separating consciously controlled from automatic processes is the process dissociation procedure (Jacoby, 1991). Jacoby argued that attempts to isolate pure types of processing (incidental or automatic processing on the one hand, and intentional or consciously controlled processing, on the other) are unlikely to be completely successful even when using questionnaires or the retrieval intentionality criterion. So, although implicit tests are designed and often assumed to rely on unconscious automatic processes, they are not immune to more consciously controlled processes. Similarly, and just as seriously, explicit memory tests may be affected by incidental or automatic retrieval. To address these issues Jacoby and his colleagues developed the process dissociation procedure (PDP) that incorporates a technique called the opposition method (see Jacoby, 1991, 1998; Jacoby, Toth, & Yonelinas, 1993). Here we sketch in the logic of the procedure, but the method can be a bit tricky to use; perhaps the best general "user's guide" to the PDP is Jacoby (1998).

In the PDP technique as applied to implicit memory tests, participants study a set of material, such as words in a list (often under several encoding conditions), and then take one of two types of tests using different retrieval instructions called inclusion and exclusion instructions. The test cues are held constant (e.g., the same word stems might be presented on both the inclusion and exclusion test). Consider again a word-stem completion test (see Jacoby et al., 1993, for an experiment that used this procedure). After studying a long list of words such as *mercy* under various encoding conditions, participants are given the stems of words, such as "mer__", that could either be completed with a studied word on the previous list (e.g., *mercy*) or a non-studied (e.g., *merit*). On a typical cued recall test, people would be given a cue and asked to use it to remember the studied word. Here, as in all explicit memory tests, correct recall of the item could be achieved through either intentional recollection of the study episode or by a more automatic process in which the item pops to mind and is then recognized. The inclusion test instructions are similar to those in a typical explicit memory task in that participants are asked to respond to the cue with an item from the study list; however, if they cannot remember the item, they are instructed to guess, so the test includes both the product of intentional recollection and, failing that, incidental or automatic priming due to familiarity.

On an exclusion test, participants are told to respond to the word stem *without* using a word from the studied list. So, if *mercy* comes to mind and they recognize it from the list, they should not respond with *mercy*, but they must respond with *merit* or *merchant* or some other word beginning with *mer*. Now participants' use of conscious recollection opposes their responding with a list word; if they respond with the list word (above the non-studied base rate of producing the list word when it has not been recently studied) then this effect is due to incidental retrieval that is unopposed by recollection.

The logic of the PDP is that inclusion performance is driven both by intentional and incidental (or automatic) retrieval, whereas exclusion performance is produced only by incidental (automatic) retrieval. If we assume that these processes are independent, then an estimate of intentional recollection in a particular condition or a particular participant can be derived by sub-

tracting performance under the exclusion instruction from performance under inclusion instruction. That is, if Inclusion performance = Probability of retrieval using intentional recollection + Probability of recollection using automatic retrieval, whereas Exclusion performance = Probability of recollection using automatic retrieval, then the difference between the two reflects the influence of intentional recollection.

Probability of recall in the exclusion condition represents a measure of performance that is driven by incidental or automatic processes. This automatic use of memory is analogous to implicit memory in that it is the information that leaks into memory and affects behavior without intention or awareness. However, several researchers (Richardson-Klavehn & Gardiner, 1996; Richardson-Klavehn, Gardiner, & Java, 1994) have suggested that the automatic form of memory measured by the PDP may not be completely analogous to priming on implicit memory tests because of involuntary recollection. We turn to that issue next.

Involuntary Conscious Recollection

Some researchers have suggested that automatic forms of memory measured by the process dissociation procedure may not be completely analogous to priming on implicit memory tests due to the bugaboo of involuntary conscious recollection (Richardson-Klavehn, et al. (1994); Richardson-Klavehn, et al. 1996). The criticism arises from the fact that controlled processes and automatic processes are often, but not always, accompanied by autonoetic consciousness and anoetic consciousness, respectively. The process dissociation procedure assumes that forms of memory that are automatic are also unconscious. However, it is logically possible that people may vividly remember events after they come to mind spontaneously (see the Ebbinghaus quote at the beginning of the chapter). A procedure used to capture this kind of memory experience instructs subjects to try *not* to produce studied items to fit a cue (e.g., a word stem), but instead to complete the stems with only non-studied words; this is Jacoby's exclusion test and embodies the logic of opposition. If the subject produces any studied words under these instructions, the assumption can be made that the words came to mind automatically. However, Richardson-Klavehn and his colleagues altered the test to determine whether this spontaneous retrieval is associated with later awareness. To do this, after the exclusion test they gave subjects an opportunity to write the word again next to the fragment if they recognize it as having been in the list earlier. Words that were studied and "accidentally" used to complete the fragments but are then later recognized as having been studied provide a measure of involuntary conscious (aware) memory. To the extent that such recognition occurs during exclusion tests, the automatic component from the PDP may be underestimated.

Interestingly, this form of memory appears to be useful in reconciling some contradictory results in the literature regarding whether cross-modality priming (e.g., the effect of auditory presentation on a visual test, Rajaram & Roediger, 1993) results from explicit memory contamination. Using the retrieval intentionality criterion, Craik, Moscovitch, and McDowd (1994) argued that valid cross-modal priming occurs on perceptual implicit memory tests and that it is not the result of explicit memory processes being used on the implicit test. On the other hand, another set of results using the process dissociation procedure indicated that the effect is not associated with automatic processes (Jacoby et al., 1997). The two methods therefore lead to different conclusions. These paradoxical results can be reconciled if it is assumed that the process dissociation procedure conflates awareness with volition. Using the procedure to study involuntary conscious recollection outlined above, Richardson-Klavehn and Gardiner (1996) showed that cross-modality priming was associated both with awareness and with automatic retrieval. Cross-modality priming does occur due to an automatic (priming) component, and the apparent lack of an automatic influence using the PDP occurs

because the PDP overestimates the amount of conscious recollection (by mixing in involuntary conscious recollection).

Recently, Kinoshita (2001) has attempted to provide a theoretical account of involuntary aware memory. Following Moscovitch's component process model of memory (1992, 1994), Kinoshita distinguishes between the memory systems involved in intentional retrieval and those involved in awareness of the past. According to Moscovitch, the frontal lobes are responsible for our ability to intentionally retrieve the past, whereas the medial-temporal lobes are responsible for binding the features of an event together, including time and place information that helps define the episode in memory. The idea is that cues at retrieval (either ones provided experimentally or those produced internally) automatically reactivate memories, bringing events to mind. (Tulving [1983, 1985] referred to this kind of process as *ecphory*). If the subject is in an explicit memory experiment at the time of this ecphoric process and is by definition required to use the cue to retrieve the past, then volition and awareness work together: The subject both intends to retrieve the past and is also aware of the past. If, on the other hand, the subject is in an implicit memory experiment and is not required to intentionally retrieve the past, then volition and awareness can either occur together or separately. Because the medial-temporal lobes bind episodic information associated with the study context together, this information can become automatically available at retrieval, despite the lack of intention to recall these events.

Our interpretation of this argument is that if all aspects of the event including the episodic features of that event (the time and place) are activated, then one may become aware of the past even in the absence of an intention to retrieve (hence involuntary conscious recollection). That is, this process associated with the medial-temporal lobes allows for involuntary aware memory. As Kinoshita suggests, "... this retrieval of a trace imbued with consciousness accounts for the felt experience of remembering, the feeling of reexperiencing the event" (2001, p. 61).

Although it is possible for awareness to accompany automatic retrieval, the converse is possible as well. Even on a free recall test a person may simply know that the retrieved item was presented earlier, indicating retrieval accompanied by noetic consciousness (e.g., Hamilton & Rajaram, 2003; Tulving, 1985). Similarly, the phenomenon of recognition failure of recallable words (Tulving & Thomson, 1973) indicates that a person can fail to recognize retrieved items as from the past (an example of anoetic consciousness). The point is that volition, or intention to retrieve, is a separate and orthogonal construct from conscious awareness. The thorny thicket of issues surrounding these complex issues of intention, awareness, and memory performance are just beginning to be investigated and understood.

Illusions of Remembering and Knowing

So far we have discussed conscious experiences associated with accurate memories – instances when people vividly remember a past event, when they know that the event has occurred, or when the event (unbeknownst to them) influences their behavior. In all three cases, we are concerned with the various levels of conscious experience associated with memory for events that actually occurred. However, one of the most compelling findings from recent studies is that subjects sometimes report vivid conscious experiences (Remember responses) for events that never occurred (e.g., Roediger & McDermott, 1995). This phenomenon has been termed false remembering (Roediger & McDermott, 1995), illusory recollection (Gallo & Roediger, 2003), or phantom recollection (Brainerd, Payne, Wright, & Reyna, 2003).

The paradigm that has been used most frequently to study this phenomenon involves having subjects study lists of 15 associatively related words (bed, rest, awake tired, dream, slumber....) and is called the Deese-Roediger-McDermott paradigm or DRM (after its originators; Deese, 1959; Roediger & McDermott, 1995). The lists are all associates of one word that is not presented, *sleep* in this case, as determined by word association norms. The finding is that, even on immediate recall tests with warnings against guessing, subjects recall the critical non-presented words at levels comparable to those of words that were presented (Roediger & McDermott, 1995). The effect also occurs on cued recall tests (e.g., E. Marsh, Roediger, & McDermott, 2004). When given a recognition test, the subjects falsely recognize the critical item at the same level as the list words. Even more importantly for present purposes, when asked to provide Remember/Know judgments on recognized items, subjects judge the critical words like *sleep* to be remembered just as often as they do for the list words that were actually studied. The fact that subjects vividly remember these falsely recognized items produces an interesting paradox, because in most recognition studies (often with unrelated words) false alarms are assigned Know rather than Remember responses. (After all, if the item was never presented, shouldn't it just be known because it was familiar? How could subjects remember features associated with the moment of occurrence of a word that was never presented?)

The finding of false recall, false recognition, and false remembering using the DRM paradigm has been confirmed and studied by many other researchers (e.g., Gallo & Roediger, 2003; Gallo, McDermott, Percer, & Roediger, 2001; Neuschatz, Payne, Lampinen, & Toglia, 2001). In addition, illusory recollection is obtained using other paradigms that produce high levels of false alarms in recognition (Lampinen, Copeland, & Neuschatz, 2001; Miller & Gazzaniga, 1998) and also in cases of false recall in the Loftus misinformation paradigm (Roediger, Jacoby, & McDermott, 1996).

Remember judgments are sometimes viewed as a purified form of episodic recollection, so the finding of false Remember responses raises the issue of veracity of Remember judgments. The outcome is perplexing for theories of remembering and knowing (see Rajaram, 1999; Rajaram & Roediger, 1997, for further discussion). One idea is that people misattribute (Gallo & Roediger, 2003) or incorrectly bind (Hicks & Hancock, 2002) features from studied items to the related non-studied item (the critical lure, in this case). When subjects study lists of words that are associated to the critical item, many of the studied words may spark associative arousal (at either a conscious or unconscious level, or both). Therefore, features from studied events become bound to the critical item even though it is never explicitly presented. Norman and Schacter (1997) required subjects to justify their Remember responses in a DRM experiment by providing details they remembered. Subjects had no trouble doing so for items such as *sleep*, and in fact the levels of false remembering were just as high in an instructional condition in which subjects had to justify responses as in other conditions in which no justification was required (as is customary in Remember/Know experiments).

A related idea is that reports of illusory recollection are driven in part by accurate episodic memory for the surrounding list context (Geraci & McCabe, 2006). In support of this hypothesis, Geraci and McCabe showed that reports of false Remember responses decreased when subjects were given modified Remember instructions that did not contain the instruction to use recollection of surrounding items. When subjects were not instructed to rely on recollection for the surrounding words as a basis for remembering, the magnitude of the illusion decreased (although it did not vanish). These results suggest that Remember responses to falsely recognized items are driven partly by retrieval of studied items. These findings further highlight the critical role of instructions in affecting reports of conscious experience, which has been a theme of this chapter.

A critic might complain that the fact that subjects can have full-blown recollective experiences of events that never occurred might cast doubt on the utility of studying

Remember/Know judgments. Don't these results from the DRM paradigm show they are invalid? We believe that such skepticism is misplaced. The fact that autonoetic consciousness is subject to illusions is quite interesting, but in our opinion does not cast doubt on this type of conscious experience. Consider the case of visual perception and our conscious experience of seeing the world. Complex cognitive processes can give rise to powerful visual illusions in which our percepts differ dramatically from the objects in the world that give rise to them. Still, no one doubts the conscious experience of seeing just because what we see sometimes differs from what we ought to see. Just as errors of perception do not invalidate the notion of seeing, so we do not think that errors of recollection invalidate the concept of remembering.

Conclusion

As noted at the outset of this chapter, the issue of states of consciousness in the study of memory has only recently become an active topic of study. The discussion of mental states associated with various forms of retrieval was avoided through much of the history of cognitive psychology, probably because investigators worried about the legacy of introspection. Introspective studies of attention and perception conducted early in the 20th century are today largely considered blind alleys into which the field was led. Yet even Ebbinghaus (1885/1964), the great pioneer who eschewed introspective methods in his own work, began his famous book with a lucid discussion of mental states during retrieval.

In this chapter, we have described two empirical movements, with their attendant theoretical frameworks, that have shaped the recent study of consciousness in relation to memory. The first breakthrough can be traced to the reports of implicit memory in severely amnesic individuals. The dissociative phenomena of conscious or explicit memory and indirect or implicit memory provided, in retrospect, one important way to characterize two distinct states of consciousness associated with retrieval. The second impetus – this a deliberate effort to map the relation between consciousness and memory – came from the distinction Endel Tulving introduced in 1985 between remembering and knowing. Unlike the explicit/implicit distinction, where the former signified conscious memory and the latter non-conscious memory, the experiences of remembering and knowing both denote conscious memory but of two different forms. The two states can be distinguished by subjects given careful instructions and seem to map onto experiences people have every day. Remembering represents the ability to mentally travel across the temporal continuum of the personal past with attendant feelings of immediacy and warmth, whereas knowing represents memory for the past in terms of facts, knowledge, or familiarity but without any re-experiencing of the events.

We have used Tulving's tripartite distinction among autonoetic, noetic, and anoetic states of consciousness to organize some of the key research findings in memory. This approach helps us understand the properties of these three states of consciousness in relation to different forms of memory – remembering, knowing, and priming, respectively. An interesting observation to emerge from this approach is that the experience of remembering can be documented with considerable clarity. Even though remembering – the mental time travel associated with this form of memory – seems introspective and highly personal, it represents a state of consciousness and a form of memory that neurologically intact subjects can use. The experimental work that has been produced using the Remember/Know procedure (and related techniques) has resulted in a sizable body of research with consistent and replicable effects across laboratories. The unreliability of introspective reports, which undermined certain research programs promulgated by Wundt and Titchener, does not seem to afflict this modern work, which is robust and replicable. Research on remembering, knowing, and priming reveals the systematic responsiveness of these measures to the influence of specific independent and subject variables.

The study of remembering is in some ways more advanced that the study of knowing, which presents unique challenges. Knowing is relatively more difficult to communicate in experiments, and the usual tactic of instructions is to define knowing in relation to remembering, rather than as an experience in its own right. Noetic consciousness can, in the abstract, be defined on its own (the conscious state of knowing, just as we know the meaning of *platypus* without remembering when and where we first learned about this creature), but in experimental practice has been defined in relation to remembering. This methodological challenge of definition through instructions is manifested in our attempts at theoretical interpretations as well. We have identified these challenges in the section on noetic consciousness, and we consider these issues to be important topics for future investigation (see also Rajaram, 1999). Better characterization of the nature of knowing remains an important piece of the puzzle to solve in our pursuit of relating consciousness to memory.

The third state of consciousness under consideration here – anoetic consciousness – is best described in memory research in terms of priming on implicit memory tests under conditions when conscious awareness of the study/test relation can be eliminated or minimized. Priming has been documented most dramatically in individuals with severe anterograde amnesia who show intact priming with little or no capacity for conscious recollection. This non-knowing or non-aware state of consciousness and its expression in priming on implicit memory tests have also been extensively studied in individuals with intact memory. In these latter cases, much effort has been expended to control, minimize, or eliminate the issue of consciously controlled processes affecting performance that is supposed to be, in Tulving's terms, anoetic. The great challenge in the work reported in this chapter is to separate and study the three states of awareness, attempts that have been partially successful. Of course, in many situations the subject's mind may slip among the various states of consciousness in performing tasks, and the challenge would be to chart the ebb and flow of different states of consciousness during memory tasks.

In 1885 Ebbinghaus provided examples of states of conscious awareness during memory retrieval. One hundred years later, Tulving named and delineated a theory of three states of conscious awareness and, most importantly, provided a method by which they might be studied. We may hope that by 2085 great progress will have been made in studying consciousness and memory. Our chapter is a progress report (written in 2006) that marks the steps taken along the first fifth of the path. Although we as a field have made good progress in the past 20 years, it is clear to us that great breakthroughs must lay ahead because we are far from our goal of understanding the complex relations of memory and consciousness.

References

Atkinson, R. C., & Joula, J. F. (1973). Factors influencing speed and accuracy of word recognition In S. Kornblum (Ed.), *Attention and performance* (Vol. 4, pp. 583–612). San Diego: Academic Press.

Atkinson, R. C., & Joula, J. F. (1974). Search and decision processes in recognition memory. In D. H. Krantz & R. C. Atkinson (Eds.), *Contemporary developments in mathematical psychology: I. Learning, memory, and thinking* (p. 299). Oxford: W. H. Freeman.

Blaxton, T. A. (1989). Investing dissociations among memory measures: Support for a transfer-appropriate processing framework. *Journal of Experimental Psychology: Learning, Memory, and Cognition, 15*, 657–668.

Bowers, J. S., & Schacter, D. L. (1990). Implicit memory and test awareness. *Journal of Experimental Psychology: Learning, Memory, and Cognition, 16*, 404–416.

Brainerd, C. J., Payne, D. G., Wright, R., & Reyna, V. F. (2003). Phantom recall. *Journal of Memory & Language, 48*, 445–467.

Brown, R. (1991). A review of the tip-of-the-tongue experience. *Psychological Bulletin, 109*, 204–223.

Brown, R., & Kulik, J. (1977). Flashbulb memories. *Cognition, 5*, 73–99.

Buchanan, T. W., & Adolphs, R. A. (2002). The role of the human amygdala in emotional modulation of long-term declarative memory. In S. Moore & M. Oaksford (Eds.), *Emotional cognition: From brain to behavior*. London: John Benjamins.

Challis, B. H., & Roediger, H. L. (1993). The effect of proportion overlap and repeated testing on primed word fragment completion. *Canadian Journal of Experimental Psychology, 47*, 113–123.

Christianson, S., & Loftus, E. F. (1990). Some characteristics of people's traumatic memories. *Bulletin of the Psychonomic Society, 28*, 195–198.

Church, B. A., & Schacter, D. L. (1994) Perceptual specificity of auditory priming: Implicit memory for voice intonation and fundamental frequency. *Journal of Experimental Psychology: Learning, Memory, and Cognition, 20*, 521–533.

Conway, M. A. (1995). *Flashbulb memories*. Hillsdale, NJ: Erlbaum.

Conway, M. A., & Dewhurst, S. A. (1995). Remembering, familiarity, and source monitoring. *Quarterly Journal of Experimental Psychology: Human Experimental Psychology, 48A*, 125–140.

Conway, M. A., Gardiner, J. M., Perfect, T. J., Anderson, S. J., & Cohen, G. M. (1997). Changes in memory awareness during learning: The acquisition of knowledge by psychology undergraduates. *Journal of Experimental Psychology: General, 126*, 393–413.

Craik, F. I. M., & Lockhart, R. S. (1972). Levels of processing: A framework for memory research. *Journal of Verbal Learning and Verbal Behavior, 11*, 671–684.

Craik, F. I. M., Moscovitch, M., & McDowd, J. M. (1994). Contributions of surface and conceptual information to performance on implicit and explicit memory tasks. *Journal of Experimental Psychology: Learning, Memory, and Cognition, 20*, 864–875.

Deese, J. (1959). On the prediction of occurrence of particular verbal intrusions in immediate recall. *Journal of Experimental Psychology, 58*, 17–22.

Donaldson, W. (1996). The role of decision processes in remembering and knowing. *Memory & Cognition, 24,* 523–533.

Dunn, J. C. (2004). Remember-know: A matter of confidence. *Psychological Review, 111,* 524–542.

Ebbinghaus, H. (1964). *Memory: A contribution to experimental psychology* (H. A. Ruger & C. E. Bussenius, Trans.). New York: Dover Publications. (Original work published 1885).

Ferguson, S. A., Hashtroudi, S., & Johnson, M. K. (1992). Age differences in using source-relevant cues. *Psychology and Aging, 7,* 443–452.

Finke, R. A., Johnson, M. K., & Shyi, G. C. (1988). Memory confusions for real and imagined completions of symmetrical visual patterns. *Memory & Cognition, 16,* 133–137.

Gallo, D. A., McDermott, K. B., Percer, J. M., & Roediger, H. L., III. (2001). Modality effects in false recall and false recognition. *Journal of Experimental Psychology: Learning, Memory, & Cognition, 27,* 339–353.

Gallo, D. A., & Roediger, H. L., III. (2003). The effects of associations and aging on illusory recollection. *Memory & Cognition, 31,* 1036–1044.

Gardiner, J. M. (1988). Functional-aspects of recollective experience. *Memory & Cognition, 16,* 309–313.

Gardiner, J. M., & Conway, M. A. (1999). Levels of awareness and varieties of experience. In B. H. Challis & B. M. Velichkovsky (Eds.), *Stratification in cognition and consciousness* (pp. 237–254). Amsterdam: John Benjamins.

Gardiner, J. M., Gawlick, B., & Richardson-Klavehn, A. (1994). Maintenance rehearsal affects knowing, not remembering; elaborative rehearsal affects remembering, not knowing. *Psychonomic Bulletin and Review, 1,* 107–110.

Gardiner, J. M., & Gregg, V. H. (1997). Recognition memory with little or no remembering: Implications for a detection model. *Psychonomic Bulletin and Review, 4,* 474–479.

Gardiner, J. M., & Java, R. I. (1990). Recollective experience in word and nonword recognition. *Memory & Cognition, 18,* 23–30.

Gardiner, J. M., & Java, R. I. (1993). Recognizing and remembering. In A. F. Collins, S. E. Gathercole, M. A. Conway, & P. E. Morris (Eds.), *Theories of memory* (pp. 163–188). Hillsdale, NJ: Erlbaum.

Gardiner, J. M., Java, R. I., & Richardson-Klavehn, A. (1996). How level of processing really influences awareness in recognition memory. *Canadian Journal of Experimental Psychology, 50,* 114–122.

Gardiner, J. M., Kaminska, Z., Dixon, M., & Java, R. I. (1996). Repetition of previously novel melodies sometimes increases both remember and know responses in recognition memory. *Psychonomic Bulletin and Review, 3,* 366–371.

Gardiner, J. M., & Parkin, A. J. (1990). Attention and recollective experience in recognition memory. *Memory & Cognition, 18,* 579–583.

Gardiner, J. M., Ramponi, C., & Richardson-Klavehn, A. (1998). Experiences of remembering, knowing, and guessing. *Consciousness and Cognition: An International Journal, 7,* 1–26.

Gardiner, J. M., Ramponi, C., & Richardson-Klavehn, A. (2002). Recognition memory and decision processes: A meta-analysis of remember, know, and guess responses. *Memory, 10,* 83–98.

Gardiner, J. M., & Richardson-Klavehn, A. (2000). Remembering and knowing. In E. Tulving & F. I. M. Craik (Eds.), *Handbook of memory*. Oxford: Oxford University Press.

Gardiner, J. M., Richardson-Klavehn, A., & Ramponi, C., (1997). On reporting recollective experiences and "direct access to memory systems." *Psychological Science, 8,* 391–394,

Geraci, L., & Franklin, N. (2004). The influence of linguistic labels on source monitoring decisions. *Memory, 12,* 571–585.

Geraci, L., & McCabe, D. P. (2006). Examining the basis for illusory recollection: The role of Remember/Know Instructions. *Psychonomic Bulletin & Review, 13,* 466–473.

Geraci, L., & Rajaram, S. (2002). The orthographic distinctiveness effect on direct and indirect tests of memory: Delineating the awareness and processing requirements. *Journal of Memory and Language, 47,* 273–291.

Geraci, L., & Rajaram, S. (2006). The distinctiveness effect in explicit and implicit memory. In R. R. Hunt & J. Worthen, (Eds.), *Distinctiveness and memory* (pp. 211–234). New York: Oxford University Press.

Graf, P., & Schacter, D. L. (1985). Implicit and explicit memory for new associations in normal and amnesic subjects. *Journal of Experimental Psychology: Learning, Memory, and Cognition, 11,* 501–518.

Graf, P., Squire, L. R., & Mandler, G. (1984). The information that amnesic patients do not forget. *Journal of Experimental Psychology: Learning, Memory, and Cognition, 10,* 164–178.

Gregg, V. H., & Gardiner, J. M. (1994). Recognition memory and awareness: A large effect of the study-test modalities on "know" responses following a highly perceptual orienting task. *European Journal of Cognitive Psychology*, 6, 131–147.

Hamilton, M., & Rajaram, S. (2003). States of awareness across multiple memory tasks: Obtaining a "pure" measure of conscious recollection. *Acta Psychologica*, 112, 43–69.

Hamann, S. (2001). Cognitive and neural mechanisms of emotional memory. *Trends in Cognitive Sciences*, 5, 394–400.

Hashtroudi, S., Ferguson, S. A., Rappold, V. A., & Cronsniak, L. D. (1988). Data-driven and conceptually driven processes in partial-word identification and recognition. *Journal of Experimental Psychology: Learning, Memory, and Cognition*, 14, 749–757.

Henkel, L. A., & Franklin, N. (1998). Reality monitoring of physically similar and conceptually related objects. *Memory & Cognition*, 26, 659–673.

Henkel, L. A., Franklin, N., & Johnson, M. K. (2000). Cross-modal source monitoring confusions between perceived and imagined events. *Journal of Experimental Psychology: Learning, Memory, and Cognition*, 26, 321–335.

Hicks, J. L., & Hancock, T. (2002). The association between associative strength and source attributions in false memory. *Psychonomic Bulletin & Review*, 9, 807–815.

Hicks, J. L., & Marsh, R. L. (1999). Remember-know judgments can depend on how memory is tested. *Psychonomic Bulletin & Review*, 6, 117–122.

Hirshman, E., & Masters, S. (1997). Modeling the conscious correlates of recognition memory: Reflections on the remember-know paradigm. *Memory & Cognition*, 25, 345–351.

Hunt, R. R. (1995). The subtlety of distinctiveness: What von Restorff really did. *Psychonomic Bulletin & Review*, 2, 105–112.

Hunt, R. R. (2006). What is the meaning of distinctiveness for memory research? In R. R. Hunt & J. Worthen, (Eds.), *Distinctiveness and memory*. Oxford: Oxford University Press.

Hunt, R. R., & Elliot, J. M. (1980). The role of nonsemantic information in memory: Orthographic distinctiveness effects on retention. *Journal of Experimental Psychology: General*, 109, 49–74.

Hunt, R. R. & McDaniel, M. A. (1993). The enigma of organization and distinctiveness. *Journal of Memory and Language*, 32, 421–445.

Hunt, R. R., & Mitchell, D. B. (1978). Specificity in nonsemantic orienting tasks and distinctive memory traces. *Journal of Experimental Psychology: Human Learning and Memory*, 4, 121–135.

Hunt, R. R., & Mitchell, D. B. (1982). Independent effects of semantic and nonsemantic distinctiveness. *Journal of Experimental Psychology: Learning, Memory, and Cognition*, 8, 81–87.

Hunt, R. R., & Toth, J. P. (1990). Perceptual identification, fragment completion, and free recall: Concepts and data. *Journal of Experimental Psychology: Learning, Memory, and Cognition*, 16, 282–290.

Inoue, C., & Bellezza, F. S. (1998). The detection model of recognition using know and remember judgments. *Memory & Cognition*, 26, 299–308.

Jacoby, L. L. (1978). On interpreting the effects of repetition: Solving a problem versus remembering a solution. *Journal of Verbal Learning and Verbal Behavior*, 17, 649–667.

Jacoby, L. L. (1983a). Perceptual enhancement: Persistent effects of an experience. *Journal of Experimental Psychology: Learning, Memory, and Cognition*, 9, 21–38.

Jacoby, L. L. (1983b). Remembering the data: Analyzing interactive processes in reading. *Journal of Verbal Learning and Verbal Behavior*, 22, 485–508.

Jacoby, L. L. (1991). A process dissociation framework: Separating automatic from intentional uses of memory. *Journal of Memory and Language*, 30, 513–541.

Jacoby, L. L. (1998). Invariance in automatic influences of memory: Toward a user's guide for the process-dissociation procedure. *Journal of Experimental Psychology: Learning, Memory, & Cognition*, 24, 3–26.

Jacoby, L. L., & Dallas, M. (1981). On the relationship between autobiographical memory and perceptual learning. *Journal of Experimental Psychology: General*, 110, 306–340.

Jacoby, L. L., Jones, T. C. & Dolan, P. O. (1998). Two effects of repetition: Support for a dual-process model of knowledge judgments and exclusion errors. *Psychonomic Bulletin & Review*, 5, 705–709.

Jacoby, L. L., Toth, J. P., & Yonelinas, A. P. (1993). Separating conscious and unconscious influences of memory: Measuring recollection. *Journal of Experimental Psychology: General, 122*, 139–154.

Jacoby, L. L., & Witherspoon, D. (1982). Remembering without awareness. *Canadian Journal of Psychology, 36*, 300–324.

Jacoby, L. L., Woloshyn, V., & Kelley, C. (1989). Becoming famous without being recognized: Unconscious influences of memory produced by dividing attention. *Journal of Experimental Psychology: General, 118*, 115–125.

Jacoby L. L., Yonelinas, A. P., & Jennings, J. M. (1997). The relation between conscious and unconscious (automatic) influences: A declaration of independence. In J. D. Cohen & J. W. Schooler (Eds.), *Scientific approaches to consciousness* (pp. 13–47). Hillsdale, NJ: Erlbaum.

Java, R. I. (1994). States of awareness following word stem completion. *European Journal of Cognitive Psychology, 6*, 77–92.

Java, R. I., Gregg, V. H., & Gardiner, J. M. (1997). What do people actually remember (and know) in "remember/know" experiments? *European Journal of Cognitive Psychology, 9*, 187–197.

Johnson, M. K. (1988). Discriminating the origin of information. In T. F. Oltmanns & B. A. Maher (Eds.), *Delusional beliefs* (pp. 34–65). Oxford: John Wiley and Sons.

Johnson, M. K., DeLeonardis, D. M., Hashtroudi, S., & Ferguson, S. A. (1995). Aging and single versus multiple cues in source monitoring. *Psychology and Aging, 10*, 507–517.

Johnson, M. K., Foley, M. A., & Leach, K. (1988). The consequences for memory of imagining in another person's voice. *Memory & Cognition, 16*, 337–342.

Johnson, M. K., Foley, M. A., Suengas, A. G., & Raye, C. L. (1988). Phenomenal characteristics of memories for perceived and imagined autobiographical events. *Journal of Experimental Psychology: General, 117*, 371–376.

Johnson, M. K., Hashtroudi, S., & Lindsay, D. S. (1993). Source monitoring. *Psychological Bulletin, 144*, 3–28.

Johnson, M. K., Raye, C. L., Foley, H. J., & Foley, M. A. (1981). Cognitive operations and decision bias in reality monitoring. *American Journal of Psychology, 94*, 37–64.

Johnston, W. A., Hawley, K. J., & Elliott, J. M. (1991). Contribution of perceptual fluency to recognition judgments. *Journal of Experimental Psychology, Learning, Memory, and Cognition, 17*, 210–223.

Joordens, S., & Merikle, P. M. (1993). Independence or redundancy: 2 models of conscious and unconscious influences. *Journal of Experimental Psychology: General, 122*, 462–467.

Kelley, C. M., & Jacoby, L. L. (1998). Subjective reports and process dissociation: Fluency, knowing, and feeling. *Acta Psychologica, 98*, 127–140.

Kensinger, E. A., & Corkin, S. (2003). Memory enhancement for emotional words: Are emotional words more vividly remembered than neutral words? *Memory & Cognition, 31*, 1169–1180.

Kinoshita, S. (1995). The word frequency effect in repetition memory versus repetition priming. *Memory & Cognition, 23*, 569–580.

Kinoshita, S. (2001). The role of involuntary aware memory in the implicit stem and fragment completion tasks: A selective review. *Psychonomic Bulletin & Review, 8*, 58–69.

Knowlton, B. J., & Squire, L. R. (1995). Remembering and knowing: Two different expressions of declarative memory. *Journal of Experimental Psychology: Learning, Memory, and Cognition, 21*, 699–710.

Kolers, P. A., & Roediger, H. L., III. (1984). Procedures of mind. *Journal of Verbal Learning and Verbal Behavior, 23*, 425–449.

Koriat, A. (1995). Dissociating knowing and the feeling of knowing: Further evidence for the accessibility model. *Journal of Experimental Psychology: General, 124*, 311–333.

Lampinen, J. M., Copeland, S. M., & Neuschatz, J. S. (2001). Recollections of things schematic: Room schemas revisited. *Journal of Experimental Psychology: Learning, Memory, and Cognition, 27*, 1211–1222.

Lindsay, D. S., & Kelley, C. M. (1996). Creating illusions of familiarity in a cued recall remember/know paradigm. *Journal of Memory and Language, 35*, 197–211.

Madigan, S. (1983). Picture memory. In J. C. Yuille (Ed.), *Imagery, memory, and cognition: Essays in honor of Allan Paivio* (pp. 65–89). Hillsdale, NJ: Erlbaum.

Mandler, G. (1980). Recognizing: The judgment of previous occurrence. *Psychological Review, 87*, 252–271.

Mangels, J. A., Picton, T. W., & Craik, F. I. M. (2001). Attention and successful episodic encoding: An event-related potential study. *Cognitive Brain Research, 11*, 77–95.

Mantyla, T. (1997). Recollections of faces: Remembering differences and knowing similarities. *Journal of Experimental Psychology: Learning, Memory, and Cognition, 23*, 1–14.

Mantyla, T., & Raudsepp, J. (1996). Recollective experience following suppression of focal attention. *European Journal of Cognitive Psychology, 8*, 195–203.

Marsh, E. J., Meade, M. L., & Roediger, H. L. (2003). Learning facts from fiction. *Journal of Memory and Language, 49*, 519–536.

Marsh, E. J., Roediger, H. L., & McDermott, K. B. (2004). Does test-induced priming play a role in the creation of false memories? *Memory, 12*, 44–55.

Mather, M., Henkel, L. A., & Johnson, M. K. (1997). Evaluating characteristics of false memories: Remember/know judgments and memory characteristics questionnaire compared. *Memory & Cognition, 25*, 826–837.

McDaniel, M. A., & Geraci, L. (2006). Encoding and retrieval processes in distinctiveness effects: Toward an integrative framework. In R. R. Hunt & J. Worthen (Eds.), *Distinctiveness and memory* (pp. 65–88). Oxford: Oxford University Press.

Miller, M. B., & Gazzaniga, M. S. (1998). Creating false memories for visual scenes. *Neuropsychologia, 36*, 513–520.

Moscovitch, M. (1992). Memory and working-with-memory: A component process model based on modules and central systems. *Journal of Cognitive Neuroscience, 4*, 257–267.

Moscovitch, M. (1994). Memory and working with memory: Evaluation of a component process model and comparisons with other models. In D. L. Schacter & E. Tulving (Eds.), *Memory systems 1994* (pp. 269–310). Cambridge, MA: MIT Press.

Moscovitch, D. A., & McAndrews, M. P. (2002). Material-specific deficits in "remembering" in patients with unilateral temporal lobe epilepsy and excisions. *Neuropsychology, 40*, 1335–1342.

Moscovitch, M., Vriezen, E., & Goshen-Gottstein, Y. (1993). Implicit tests of memory in patients with focal lesions or degenerative brain disorders. In H. Spinnler & F. Boller (Eds.), *Handbook of neuropsychology* (Vol. 8, pp. 133–173). Amsterdam: Elsevier.

Neisser, U. & Harsch, N. (1992). Phantom flashbulbs: False recollections of hearing the news about the Challenger. In E. Winograd & U. Neisser (Eds.), *Affect and accuracy in recall: Studies of "flashbulb" memories* (pp. 9–31). New York: Cambridge University Press.

Neuschatz, J. S., Payne, D. G., Lampinen, J. M., & Toglia, M. P. (2001). Assessing the effectiveness of warnings and the phenomenological characteristics of false memories. *Memory, 9*, 53–71.

Norman, K. A., & Schacter, D. L. (1997). False recognition in older and younger adults: Exploring the characteristics of illusory memories. *Memory & Cognition, 25*, 838–848.

Ochsner, K. (2000). Are affective events richly recollected or simply familiar? The experience and process of recognizing feelings past. *Journal of Experimental Psychology: General, 129*, 242–261.

Parkin, A. J., Gardiner, J. M., & Rosser, R. (1995). Functional aspects of recollective experience in face recognition. *Consciousness and Cognition: An International Journal, 4*, 387–398.

Parkin, A. J., & Russo, R. (1990). Implicit and explicit memory and the automatic/effortful distinction. *European Journal of Cognitive Psychology, 2*, 71–80.

Rajaram, S. (1993). Remembering and knowing: Two means of access to the personal past. *Memory & Cognition, 21*, 89–102.

Rajaram, S. (1996). Perceptual effects on remembering: Recollective processes in picture recognition memory. *Journal of Experimental Psychology: Learning, Memory, and Cognition, 22*, 365–77.

Rajaram, S. (1998). The effects on conceptual salience and conceptual distinctiveness on conscious recollection. *Psychonomic Bulletin & Review, 5*, 71–78.

Rajaram, S. (1999). Assessing the nature of retrieval experience: Advances and challenges. In B. H. Challis & B. M. Velichkovsky (Eds.), *Stratification in cognition and consciousness* (pp. 255–275). Amsterdam: John Benjamins.

Rajaram, S., & Geraci, L. (2000). Conceptual fluency selectively influences knowing. *Journal of Experimental Psychology: Learning, Memory, and Cognition, 26*, 1070–1074.

Rajaram, S., & Hamilton, M. (2005). Conceptual processes can enhance both Remembering and Knowing even after delay: Effects of contextually-varied repetition, meaningful encoding, and test delay. Unpublished manuscript, Stony Brook University, Stony Brook, N.Y.

Rajaram, S., Hamilton, M., & Bolton, A. (2002). Distinguishing states of awareness from confidence during retrieval: Evidence from amnesia. *Cognitive, Affective, and Behavioral Neuroscience, 2*, 227–235.

Rajaram, S. & Roediger, H. L. (1993). Direct comparison of four implicit memory tests. *Journal of Experimental Psychology: Learning, Memory, and Cognition, 19*, 765–776.

Rajaram, S. & Roediger, H. L. (1997) Remembering and knowing as states of consciousness during retrieval. In J. D. Cohen & J. W. Schooler (Eds.), *Scientific approaches to consciousness.* (pp. 213–240). Hillsdale, NJ: Erlbaum.

Richardson-Klavehn, A. & Gardiner, J. M. (2000). Remembering and knowing. In E. Tulving & F. I. M. Craik (Eds.), *The Oxford handbook of memory* (pp. 229–244). New York, N.Y., U.S.: Oxford University Press.

Richardson-Klavehn, A., Gardiner, J. M., & Java, R. I. (1994). Involuntary conscious memory and the method of opposition. *Memory, 2*, 1–29.

Richardson-Klavehn, A., Gardiner, J. M, & Java, R. I. (1996). Memory: Task dissociations, process dissociations and dissociations of consciousness. In G. D. M. Underwood (Ed.), *Implicit cognition* (pp. 85–158). New York, N.Y., U.S.: Oxford University Press.

Roediger, H. L. (1990). Implicit memory: Retention without remembering. *American Psychologist, 45*, 1043–1056.

Roediger, H. L. (1999). Retrieval experience: A new arena of psychological study. In B. H. Challis & B. M. Velichkovsky (Eds.), *Stratification of cognition and consciousness* (pp. 229–235). Amsterdam: John Benjamins.

Roediger, H. L., & Blaxton, T. A. (1987). Effects of varying modality, surface features, and retention interval on priming in word-fragment completion. *Memory & Cognition, 15*, 379–388.

Roediger, H. L., & Geraci, L. (2004). Conducting implicit memory research: A practical guide. In A. Wenzel & D. Rubin (Eds.), *A guide to implementing cognitive methods with clinical populations.* Washington, DC: APA Books.

Roediger, H. L., Jacoby, J. D., & McDermott, K. B. (1996). Misinformation effects in recall: Creating false memories through repeated retrieval. *Journal of Memory & Language, 35*, 300–318.

Roediger, H. L., & McDermott, K. B. (1993). Implicit memory in normal human subjects. In F. Boller & J. Grafman (Eds.), *Handbook of neuropsychology* (Vol. 8, pp. 63–131). Amsterdam: Elsevier.

Roediger, H. L., & McDermott, K. B. (1995). Creating false memories: Remembering words not presented in lists. *Journal of Experimental Psychology: Learning, Memory, & Cognition, 21*, 803–814.

Roediger, H. L., Weldon, M. S., & Challis, B. H. (1989). Explaining dissociations between implicit and explicit measures of retention: A processing account. In H. L. Roediger & F. I. M. Craik (Eds.), *Varieties of memory and consciousness: Essays in honour of Endel Tulving* (pp. 3–41). Hillsdale, NJ: Erlbaum.

Roediger, H. L., Weldon, M. S., Stadler, M. L., & Riegler, G. L. (1992). Direct comparison of two implicit memory tests: Word fragment and word stem completion. *Journal of Experimental Psychology: Learning, Memory, & Cognition, 18*, 1251–1269.

Roediger, H. L. III, Wheeler, M. A., & Rajaram, S. (1993). Remembering, knowing, and reconstructing the past. *Psychology of Learning and Motivation: Advances in Research and Theory, 30*, 97–134.

Rotello, C. M., Macmillan, N. A., & Reeder, J. A. (2004). Sum-difference theory of remembering and knowing: a two-dimensional signal-detection model. *Psychological Review, 111*, 588–616.

Rozin, P. (1976). The psychobiological approach to human memory. In M. R. Rosenzweig & E. L. Bennett (Eds.), *Neural Mechanisms of Learning and Memory* (pp. 3–48). Cambridge, MA: MIT Press.

Rubin, D. C., & Kozin, M. (1984). Vivid memories. *Cognition, 16*, 81–95.

Schacter, D. L. (1987). Implicit memory: History and current status. *Journal of Experimental Psychology: Learning, Memory, and Cognition, 13*, 501–518.

Schacter, D. L., Bowers, J., & Booker, J. (1989). Intention awareness, and implicit memory: The retrieval intentionality criterion. In S. Lewandowsky, J. C. Dunn, et al. (Eds.), *Implicit memory: Theoretical issues* (pp. 47–65). Hillsdale, NJ: Erlbaum.

Schacter, D. L., Chiu, C. Y. P., & Ochsner, K. N. (1993). Implicit memory: A selective review. *Annual Review of Neuroscience, 16*, 159–182.

Schacter, D. L., Verfaellie, M., & Pradere, D. (1996). The neuropsychology of memory illusions: False recall and recognition in amnesic patients. *Journal of Memory and Language*, 35, 319–334.

Schmidt, S. R. (1991). Can we have a distinctive theory of memory? *Memory & Cognition*, 19, 523–542.

Schmidt, S. (2006). Emotion, significance, distinctiveness, and memory. In R. R. Hunt & J. Worthen (Eds.), *Distinctiveness and memory*. Oxford: Oxford University Press.

Schmolck, H., Buffalo, E. A., & Squire, L. R. (2000). Memory distortions develop over time: Recollections of the O. J. Simpson trial verdict after 15 and 32 months. *Psychological Science*, 11, 39–45.

Sherman, J. W., & Bessenoff, G. R. (1999). Stereotypes as source-monitoring cues: On the interaction between episodic and semantic memory. *Psychological Science*, 10, 106–110.

Shimamura, A. P., & Squire, L. R. (1984). Paired-associated learning and priming affects in amnesia: A neuropsychological study. *Journal of Experimental Psychology: General*, 113, 556–570.

Slamecka, N. J., & Graf, P. (1978). The generation effect: Delineation of a phenomenon. *Journal of Experimental Psychology: Human Learning and Memory*, 4, 592–604.

Snodgrass, J. G., & Corwin, J. (1988). Perceptual identification thresholds for 150 fragmented pictures from the Snodgrass and Vanderwart picture set. *Perceptual and Motor Skills*, 67, 3–36.

Snodgrass, J. G., Smith, B., Feenan, K., & Corwin, J. (1987). Fragmenting pictures on the Apple Macintosh computer for experimental and clinical applications. *Behavior Research Methods, Instruments and Computers*, 19, 270–274.

Squire, L. R., Stark, C. E. L., & Clark, R. E. (2004). The medial temporal lobe. *Annual Review of Neuroscience*, 27, 279–306.

Srinivas, K., & Roediger, H. L. (1990). Classifying implicit memory tests: Category association and anagram solution. *Journal of Memory and Language*, 29, 389–412.

Talarico, J. M., & Rubin, D. C. (2003). Confidence, not consistency, characterizes flashbulb memories. *Psychological Science*, 14, 455–461.

Tenpenny, P. L., & Shoben, E. J. (1992). Component processes and the utility of the conceptually-driven/data-driven distinc-

tion. *Journal of Experimental Psychology: Learning, Memory, and Cognition*, 18, 25–42.

Toth, J. P. (2000). Nonconscious forms of human memory. In E. Tulving & F. I. M. Craik (Eds.), *The Oxford handbook of memory* (pp. 245–261). New York: Oxford University Press.

Tulving, E. (1983). *Elements of episodic memory*. Oxford: Oxford University Press.

Tulving, E. (1985). Memory and consciousness. *Canadian Psychology*, 26, 1–12.

Tulving, E.. & Schacter, D. L. (1990). Priming and human memory systems. *Science*, 247, 301–306.

Tulving, E., Schacter, D. L., & Stark, H. A. (1982). Priming effects in word-fragment completion are independent of recognition memory. *Journal of Experimental Psychology: Learning, Memory, and Cognition*, 8, 336–342.

Tulving, E., & Thompson, D. M. (1973). Encoding specificity and retrieval processes in episodic memory. *Psychological Review*, 80, 352–373.

Verfaellie, M. (1994). A re-examination of recognition memory in amnesia: Reply to Roediger and McDermott. *Neuropsychology*, 8, 289–292.

Verfaellie, M., Giovanello, K. S., & Keane, M. M. (2001). Recognition memory in amnesia: Effects of relaxing response criteria. *Cognitive, Affective, and Behavioral Neuroscience*, 1, 3–9.

Verfaellie, M., & Keane, M. M. (2002). Impaired and preserved memory processes in amnesia. In L. R. Squire & D. L. Schacter (Eds.), *Neuropsychology of memory* (3d ed., pp. 36–45). New York: Guilford Press.

von Restorff, H. (1933). Uber die wirkung von Bereichsblidungen im spurenfeld. *Psychologishe Forschung*, 18, 299–342.

Wagner, A. D., & Gabrieli, J. D. E. (1998). On the relationship between recognition familiarity and perceptual fluency: Evidence for distinct mnemonic processes. *Acta Psychologia*, 98, 211–230.

Wagner, A. D., Gabrieli, J. D. E., & Verfaellie, M. (1997). Dissociations between familiarity processes in explicit recognition and implicit perceptual memory. *Journal of Experimental Psychology: Learning, Memory, and Cognition*, 23, 305–323.

Warrington, E. K., & Weiskrantz, L. (1968). A study of learning and retention in amnesic patients. *Neuropsychologia*, 6, 283–291.

Warrington, E. K., & Weiskrantz, L. (1970). Amnesic syndrome: Consolidation or retrieval? *Nature*, 228, 628–630.

Wegner, D. M. (2002). *The illusion of conscious will*. Cambridge, MA: MIT Press.

Weldon, M. S. (1993). The time course of perceptual and conceptual contributions to word fragment completion priming. *Journal of Experimental Psychology: Learning, Memory, and Cognition*, 19, 1010–1023.

Weldon, M. S., & Roediger, H. L. (1987). Altering retrieval demands reverses the picture superiority effect. *Memory & Cognition*, 15, 269–280.

Wheeler, M. A., Stuss, D. T., & Tulving, E. (1997). Toward a theory of episodic memory: The frontal lobes and autonoetic consciousness. *Psychological Bulletin*, 121, 331–354.

Wilson, T. D. (2002). *Strangers to ourselves: Discovering the adaptive unconscious*. Cambridge, MA: Harvard University Press.

Wixted, J., & Stretch, V. (2004). In defense of the signal detection interpretation of remember/know judgments. *Psychonomic Bulletin & Review*, 11, 616–641.

Yonelinas, A. P. (1994). Receiver-operating characteristics in recognition memory: evidence for a dual-process model. *Journal of Experimental Psychology: Learning, Memory, and Cognition*, 20, 1341–1354.

Yonelinas, A. P. (2001). Consciousness, control, and confidence: The 3 Cs of recognition memory. *Journal of Experimental Psychology: General*, 130, 361–379.

Yonelinas, A. P. (2002). The nature of recollection and familiarity: A review of 30 years of research. *Journal of Memory and Language*, 46, 441–517.

Yonelinas, A. P., & Jacoby, L. L. (1995). The relation between remembering and knowing as bases for recognition-effects of size congruency. *Journal of Memory and Language*, 34, 622–643.

Yonelinas, A. P., Kroll, N. E. A., Dobbins, I., Lazzara, M., & Knight, R. T. (1998). Recollection and familiarity deficits in amnesia: Convergence of remember-know, process dissociation, and receiver operating characteristic data. *Neuropsychology*, 12, 323–339.

Yonelinas, A. P., Kroll, N. E. A., Quamme, J. R., Lazzara, M. M., Sauve, M., Widaman, K. F., & Knight, R. T. (2002). Effects of extensive temporal lobe damage or mild hypoxia on recollection and familiarity. *Nature Neuroscience*, 5, 1236–1241.

Zechmeister, E. B. (1972). Orthographic distinctiveness as a variable in word recognition. *American Journal of Psychology*, 85, 425–430.

CHAPTER 11

Metacognition and Consciousness

Asher Koriat

Abstract

The study of metacognition can shed light on some fundamental issues about consciousness and its role in behavior. Metacognition research concerns the processes by which people self-reflect on their own cognitive and memory processes (monitoring) and how they put their metaknowledge to use in regulating their information processing and behavior (control). Experimental research on metacognition has addressed the following questions. First, what are the bases of metacognitive judgments that people make in monitoring their learning, remembering, and performance? Second, how valid are such judgments and what are the factors that affect the correspondence between subjective and objective indexes of knowing? Third, what are the processes that underlie the accuracy and inaccuracy of metacognitive judgments? Fourth, how does the output of metacognitive monitoring contribute to the strategic regulation of learning and remembering? Finally, how do the metacognitive processes of monitoring and control affect actual performance? This chapter reviews research addressing these questions, emphasizing its implications for issues concerning consciousness; in particular, the genesis of subjective experience, the function of self-reflective consciousness, and the cause-and-effect relation between subjective experience and behavior.

Introduction

There has been a surge of interest in metacognitive processes in recent years, with the topic of metacognition pulling under one roof researchers from traditionally disparate areas of investigation. These areas include memory research (Kelley & Jacoby, 1998; Metcalfe & Shimamura, 1994; Nelson & Narens, 1990; Reder, 1996), developmental psychology (Schneider & Pressley, 1997), social psychology (Bless & Forgas, 2000; Jost, Kruglanski, & Nelson, 1998; Schwarz, 2004), judgment and decision making (Gilovich, Griffin, & Kahneman, 2002; Winman & Juslin, 2005), neuropsychology (Shimamura, 2000), forensic psychology (e.g., Pansky, Koriat,

& Goldsmith, 2005; Perfect, 2002), educational psychology (Hacker, Dunlosky, & Graesser, 1998), and problem solving and creativity (Davidson & Sternberg, 1998; Metcalfe, 1998a). The establishment of metacognition as a topic of interest in its own right is already producing synergy among different areas of investigation concerned with monitoring and self-regulation (e.g. Fernandez-Duque, Baird, & Posner, 2000). Furthermore, because some of the questions discussed touch upon traditionally ostracized issues in psychology, such as the issues of consciousness and free will (see Nelson, 1996), a lively debate has been going on between metacognitive researchers and philosophers (see Nelson & Rey, 2000). In fact, it appears that the increased interest in metacognition research derives in part from the feeling that perhaps this research can bring us closer to dealing with (certainly not resolving) some of the metatheoretical issues that have been the province of philosophers of the mind.

Definition

Metacognition concerns the study of what people know about cognition in general, and about their own cognitive and memory processes, in particular, and how they put that knowledge to use in regulating their information processing and behavior. Flavell (1971) introduced the term "metamemory," which concerns specifically the monitoring and control of one's learning and remembering. Metamemory is the most researched area in metacognition and is the focus of this chapter.

Nelson and Narens (1990) proposed a conceptual framework that has been adopted by most researchers. According to them, cognitive processes may be divided into those that occur at the object level and those that occur at the meta level: The object level includes the basic operations traditionally subsumed under the rubric of information processing – encoding, rehearsing, retrieving, and so on. The meta level is assumed to oversee object-level operations (monitoring) and return signals to regulate them actively in a top-down fashion (con-

trol). The object level, in contrast, has no control over the meta level and no access to it. For example, the study of new material involves a variety of basic, object-level operations, such as text processing, comprehending, rehearsing, and so on. At the same time, metacognitive processes are engaged in planning how to study, in devising and implementing learning strategies, in monitoring the course and success of object-level processes, in modifying them when necessary, and in orchestrating their operation. In the course of studying new material, learners are assumed to monitor their degree of comprehension online and then decide whether to go over the studied material once again, how to allocate time and effort to different segments, and when to end studying.

We should note, however, that the distinction between cognitive and metacognitive processes is not sharp because the same type of cognitive operation may occur at the object level or at the meta level, and in some cases it is unclear to which level a particular operation belongs (Brown, 1987).

Research Traditions

Historically, there have been two main lines of research on metacognition that proceeded almost independently of each other, one within developmental psychology and the other within experimental memory research. The work within developmental psychology was spurred by Flavell (see Flavell, 1979; Flavell & Wellman, 1977), who argued for the critical role that metacognitive processes play in the development of memory functioning (see Flavell, 1999). Within memory research, the study of metacognition was pioneered by Hart's (1965) studies on the feeling-of-knowing (FOK), and Brown and McNeill's (1966) work on the tip-of-the-tongue (TOT).

There is a difference in goals and methodological styles between these two research traditions. The basic assumption among developmental students of metacognition is that learning and memory performance depend heavily on monitoring and regulatory proficiency. This assumption has resulted in attempts to specify the components of metacognitive abilities, to trace their development with age, and to examine their contribution to memory functioning. Hence a great deal of the work is descriptive and correlational (Schneider, 1985). The focus on age differences and individual differences in metacognitive skills has also engendered interest in specifying "deficiencies" that are characteristic of children at different ages and in devising ways to remedy them. This work has expanded into the educational domain: Because of the increasing awareness of the critical contribution of metacognition to successful learning (Paris & Winograd, 1990), educational programs have been developed (see Scheid, 1993) designed to make the learning process more "metacognitive." Several authors have stressed specifically the importance of metacognition to transfer of learning (see De Corte, 2003).

The conception of metacognition by developmental psychologists is more comprehensive than that underlying much of the experimental work on metacognition. It includes a focus on what children know about the functioning of memory and particularly about one's own memory capacities and limitations. Developmental work has also placed heavy emphasis on strategies of learning and remembering (Bjorklund & Douglas, 1997; Brown, 1987; Pressley, Borkowski, & Schneider, 1987). In addition, many of the issues addressed in the area of theory of mind (Perner & Lang, 1999) concern metacognitive processes. These issues are, perhaps, particularly important for the understanding of children's cognition.

In contrast, the experimental-cognitive study of metacognition has been driven more by an attempt to clarify basic questions about the mechanisms underlying monitoring and control processes in adult memory (for reviews, see Koriat & Levy-Sadot, 1999; Nelson & Narens, 1990; Schwartz, 1994). This attempt has led to the emergence of several theoretical ideas as well as specific experimental paradigms for examining the monitoring and control processes that occur during learning, during the attempt to retrieve information from memory, and following the retrieval of candidate answers (e.g., Metcalfe, 2000; Schwartz, 2002).

In addition to the developmental and the experimental-memory lines of research, there has been considerable work on metacognition in the areas of social psychology and judgment and decision making. Social psychologists have long been concerned with questions about metacognition, although their work has not been explicitly defined as metacognitive (see Jost et al., 1998). In particular, social psychologists share the basic tenets of metacognitive research (see below) regarding the importance of subjective feelings and beliefs, as well as the role of top-down regulation of behavior. In recent years social psychologists have been addressing questions that are at the heart of current research in metacognition (e.g., Winkielman, Schwarz, Fazendeiro, & Reber, 2003; Yzerbyt, Lories, & Dardenne, 1998; see Metcalfe, 1998b). Within the area of judgment and decision making, a great deal of the work concerning the calibration of probability judgments (Fischhoff, 1975; Lichtenstein, Fischhoff, & Phillips, 1982; Winman & Juslin, 2005) is directly relevant to the issues raised in metacognition.

Research Questions

This chapter emphasizes the work on metacognition within the area of adult memory research. It is organized primarily around the five main questions that have been addressed in experimental research on metamemory. First, what are the bases of metacognitive judgments; that is, how do we know that we know (e.g., Koriat & Levy-Sadot, 1999)? Second, how valid are subjective intuitions about one's own knowledge; that is, how accurate are metacognitive judgments, and what are the factors that affect their accuracy (e.g., Schwartz & Metcalfe, 1994)? Third, what are the processes underlying the accuracy and inaccuracy of metacognitive judgments? In particular, what are the processes that lead to illusions of knowing and to dissociations between knowing and the feeling of knowing (e.g., Benjamin & Bjork, 1996; Koriat, 1995)? Fourth, what are the processes underlying the strategic regulation of learning and remembering? In particular, how does the output of monitoring affect control processes (e.g., Barnes, Nelson, Dunlosky, Mazzoni, & Narens, 1999; Son & Metcalfe, 2000)? Finally, how do the metacognitive processes of monitoring and control affect actual memory performance (e.g., Koriat & Goldsmith, 1996a; Metcalfe & Kornell, 2003)?

Although these questions focus on relatively circumscribed processes of memory and metamemory, they touch upon some of the issues that are at the heart of the notions of consciousness and self-consciousness. Thus, the study of the subjective monitoring of knowledge addresses a defining property of consciousness, because consciousness implies not only that we know something but also that we know that we know it. Thus, consciousness binds together knowledge and metaknowledge (Koriat, 2000b). This idea is implied, for example, in Rosenthal's (2000) "higher-order thought" (HOT) philosophical theory of consciousness: A "lower-order" mental state is conscious by virtue of there being another, higher-order mental state that makes one conscious that one is in the lower-order state (see Chapter 3). Clearly, the subjective feelings that accompany cognitive processes constitute an essential ingredient of conscious awareness. Rather than taking these feelings (and their validity) at their face value, the study of metacognition attempts to uncover the processes that shape subjective feelings and contribute to their validity or to their illusory character. Furthermore, the study of monitoring-based control has implications for the question of the function of conscious awareness, and for the benefits and perils in using one's own intuitive feelings and subjective experience as a guide to judgments and behavior.

Basic Assumptions about Agency and Consciousness

The increased interest in metacognition seems to reflect a general shift from the stimulus-driven, behavioristic view of the person to a view that acknowledges the importance of subjective processes and top-down executive functions (see Koriat, 2000b). The study of metacognition is generally predicated on a view of the person as an active organism that has at its disposal an arsenal of cognitive operations that can be applied at will toward the achievement of various goals. The strategic choice and regulation of these operations are assumed to be guided in part by the person's subjective beliefs and subjective feelings.

Embodied in this view are two metatheoretical assumptions (see Koriat, 2002). The first concerns agency – the assumption that self-controlled processes have measurable effects on behavior. Although most researchers would acknowledge that many cognitive processes, including some that are subsumed under the rubric of executive function, occur outside of consciousness, there is also a recognition that the person is not a mere medium through which information flows. Rather, people have some freedom and flexibility in regulating actively their cognitive processes during learning and remembering. Furthermore, it is assumed that such self-regulation processes deserve to be studied not only because they can have considerable effects on performance but also because they are of interest in their own right.

This assumption presents a dilemma for experimental researchers because self-controlled processes have been traditionally assumed to conflict with the desire of experimenters to exercise strict experimental control. Of course, there are many studies in which learning and remembering strategies have been manipulated (through instructions) and their effects investigated (e.g., Craik & Lockhart, 1972). Unlike such experimenter-induced strategies, however, self-initiated strategies generally have been seen as a nuisance factor that should be avoided or neutralized. For example, laboratory studies typically use a fixed-rate presentation of items rather than a self-paced presentation (see Nelson & Leonesio, 1988). Also, in measuring memory performance, sometimes forced-choice tests are preferred over free-report tests to avoid having to deal with differences in "guessing," or else some correction for guessing procedure is used to achieve a pure measure of "true" memory (see Koriat & Goldsmith, 1996a; Nelson & Narens, 1994). Needless to say, people in everyday life have great freedom in regulating their memory processes, and the challenge is to find ways to bring these self-controlled metacognitive processes into the laboratory (Koriat, 2000a; Koriat & Goldsmith, 1996a).

The second assumption concerns the role of self-reflective, subjective experience in guiding controlled processes. This is, of course, a debatable issue. It is one thing to equate controlled processes with conscious processes (e.g., Posner & Snyder, 1975); it is another to assume that subjective experience plays a causal role in behavior. Students of metacognition not only place a heavy emphasis on subjective experience but also assume that subjective feelings, such as the feeling of knowing, are not mere epiphenomena, but actually exert a causal role on information processing and behavior (Koriat, 2000b; Nelson, 1996).

A similar growing emphasis on the role of subjective feelings in guiding judgments and behavior can be seen in social-psychological research (Schwarz & Clore, 2003) and in decision making (Slovic, Finucane, Peters, & MacGregor, 2002). Also, the work on memory distortions and false memories brings to the fore the contribution of phenomenological aspects of remembering to source monitoring and reality monitoring (see Kelley & Jacoby, 1998; Koriat, Goldsmith, & Pansky, 2000; Mitchell & Johnson, 2000).

It should be stressed, however, that not all students of metacognition subscribe to the assumptions discussed above. In particular, Reder (1987) has argued that a great deal of strategy selection occurs without conscious deliberation or awareness of the factors that influence one's choice. Of course, there is little doubt that many monitoring and control processes occur without consciousness (Kentridge & Heywood, 2000), so the question becomes one of terminology, like the question whether feelings must be conscious or can also be unconscious (Clore, 1994;

Winkielman & Berridge, 2004). However, by and large, much of the experimental research in metacognition is predicated on the tacit assumption that the metacognitive processes studied entail conscious control. Nonetheless, although the term "metacognition" is generally understood as involving conscious awareness, it should be acknowledged that monitoring and control processes can also occur unconsciously (Spehn & Reder, 2000).

I now review some of the experimental work on metamemory, focusing on research that may have some bearing on general questions about phenomenal experience and conscious control.

Experimental Paradigms in the Study of Online Metamemory

A variety of metacognitive judgments have been studied in recent years that ought to be included under the umbrella of metacognition (Metcalfe, 2000). Among these are ease-of-learning judgments (Leonesio & Nelson, 1990), judgments of comprehension (Maki & McGuire, 2002), remember/know judgments (Gardiner, & Richardson-Klavehn, 2000), output monitoring (Koriat, Ben-Zur, & Sheffer, 1988), olfactory metacognition (Jönsson & Olsson, 2003), and source monitoring (Johnson, 1997). However, the bulk of the experimental work has concerned three types of judgments.

First are judgments of learning (JOLs) elicited following the study of each item. For example, after studying each paired-associate in a list, participants are asked to assess the likelihood that they will be able to recall the target word in response to the cue in a future test. These item-by-item judgments are then compared to the actual recall performance.

Second are FOK judgments elicited following blocked recall. In the Recall-Judgment-Recognition (RJR) paradigm introduced by Hart (1965), participants are required to recall items from memory (typically, the answers to general knowledge questions). When they fail to retrieve the answer, they are asked to make FOK judgments regarding the likelihood that they would be able to select the correct answer from among several distractors in a forced-choice test to be administered later. The validity of FOK judgments is then evaluated by the correspondence between these judgments and performance on the recognition test. Finally, after retrieving an answer from memory or after selecting an answer, the subjective confidence in the correctness of that answer is elicited, typically in the form of a probability judgment reflecting the assessed likelihood that the answer is correct. Whereas JOLs and FOK judgments are prospective, involving predictions of future memory performance, confidence judgments are retrospective, involving assessments about a memory that has been produced.

Many different variations of these general paradigms have been explored, including variations in the type of memory studied (semantic, episodic, autobiographical, eyewitness-type events, etc.), the format of the memory test (free recall, cued recall, forced-choice recognition, etc.), and the particular judgments elicited (item-by-item judgments or global judgments, using a probability or a rating scale, etc.).

How Do We Know That We Know? The Bases of Metacognitive Judgments

As we see later, metacognitive judgments are accurate by and large. JOLs made for different items during study are generally predictive of the accuracy of recalling these items at test. FOK judgments elicited following blocked recall predict the likelihood of recalling or recognizing the elusive target at some later time, and subjective confidence in the correctness of an answer is typically diagnostic of the accuracy of that answer. Thus, the first question that emerges is, How do we know that we know?

This question emerges most sharply with regard to the tip-of-the-tongue (TOT) state, in which we fail to recall a word or a name, and yet we are convinced that we know it

and can even sense its imminent emergence into consciousness. What is peculiar about this experience is the discrepancy between subjective and objective knowing. So how can people monitor the presence of information in memory despite their failure to retrieve it? In reviewing the verbal learning literature more than 30 years ago, Tulving and Madigan (1970), in fact, argued that one of the truly unique characteristics of human memory is its knowledge of its own knowledge. They proposed that genuine progress in memory research depends on understanding how the memory system not only can produce a learned response or retrieve an image but also can estimate rather accurately the likelihood of its success in doing it. A great deal of research conducted since 1970 has addressed this question.

The Direct-Access View

A simple answer to the question about the basis of feelings of knowing is provided by the direct-access view according to which people have direct access to memory traces both during learning and during remembering and can base their metacognitive judgments on detecting the presence and/or the strength of these traces. For example, in the case of JOLs elicited during study, it may be proposed that learners can detect directly the memory trace that is formed following learning and can also monitor online the increase in trace strength that occurs in the course of study as more time is spent studying an item (e.g., Cohen, Sandler, & Keglevich, 1991). Of course, to the extent that learners can do so, they can also decide to stop studying (under self-paced conditions) when trace strength has reached a desirable value (Dunlosky & Hertzog, 1998).

A direct-access account has also been advanced by Hart (1965) with regard to FOK. Hart proposed that FOK judgments represent the output of an internal monitor that can survey the contents of memory and can determine whether the trace of a solicited memory target exists in store. Thus, the feeling associated with the TOT state may be assumed to stem from direct, privileged access to the memory trace of the elusive target (see also Burke, MacKay, Worthley, & Wade, 1991; Yaniv & Meyer, 1987). Hart stressed the functional value of having such a monitor, given the general fallibility of the memory system: If the monitor "signals that an item is not in storage, then the system will not continue to expend useless effort and time at retrieval; instead, input can be sought that will put the item into storage" (Hart, 1965; p. 214).

Direct-access (or trace-access) accounts, which assume that monitoring involves a direct readout of information that appears in a ready-made format, have two merits. The first is that they can explain not only the basis of JOLs and FOK judgments but also their accuracy. Clearly, if JOLs are based on accessing the strength of the memory trace that is formed following learning, then they ought to be predictive of future recall, which is also assumed to depend on memory strength. Similarly, if FOK judgments monitor the presence of the memory trace of the unrecalled item, they should be expected to predict the future recognition or recall of that item.

The second merit is that they would seem to capture the phenomenal quality of metacognitive feelings: the subjective feeling, such as that which accompanies the tip-of-the-tongue state, that one monitors directly the presence of the elusive target in memory and its emergence into consciousness (James, 1890). In fact, metacognitive feelings are associated with a sense of self-evidence, which gives the impression that people are in direct contact with the contents of their memories and that their introspections are inherently accurate.

The Cue-Utilization View of Metacognitive Judgments

Although the direct-access view has not been entirely abandoned (see Burke et al., 1991; Metcalfe, 2000), an alternative view has been gaining impetus in recent years. According to this view, metacognitive judgments are inferential in origin, based on a variety of cues and heuristics that have some

degree of validity in predicting objective memory performance (Benjamin & Bjork, 1996). To the extent that such indeed is the case, then the accuracy of metacognitive judgments is not guaranteed, but should depend on the validity of the cues on which it rests.

Inferential, cue-utilization accounts generally distinguish between information-based (or theory-based) and experience-based metacognitive judgments (see Kelley & Jacoby, 1996a; Koriat & Levy-Sadot, 1999; Matvey, Dunlosky, & Guttentag, 2001; Strack, 1992). This distinction parallels a distinction between two modes of thought that has been proposed in other domains (see Kahneman, 2003, and see further below). Thus, it is assumed that metacognitive judgments may be based either on a deliberate use of beliefs and memories to reach an educated guess about one's competence and cognitions, or on the application of heuristics that result in a sheer subjective feeling.

Theory-Based Monitoring

Consider first theory-based metacognitive judgments. Developmental students of cognition placed a great deal of emphasis on what Flavell called "metacognitive knowledge;" that is, on children's beliefs and intuitions about their own memory capacities and limitations and about the factors that contribute to memory performance (Brown, 1987). Such beliefs have been found to affect the choice of learning strategies, as well as people's predictions of their own memory performance (see Flavell, 1999; Schneider & Pressley, 1997).

In contrast, the experimental research on adult metacognition contains only scattered references to the possible contribution of theories and beliefs to metacognitive judgments. For example, in discussing the bases of JOLs, Koriat (1997) proposed to distinguish between two classes of cues for theory-based online JOLs, intrinsic and extrinsic. The former includes cues pertaining to the perceived a priori difficulty of the studied items (e.g., Rabinowitz, Ackerman, Craik, & Hinchley, 1982). Such cues seem to affect

JOLs, particularly during the first study trial, as suggested by the observation that normative ratings of ease of learning are predictive both of JOLs and of recall of different items (e.g., Koriat, 1997; Leonesio & Nelson, 1990; Underwood, 1966). The second class includes extrinsic factors that pertain either to the conditions of learning (e.g., number of times an item has been presented, presentation time, etc., Mazzoni, Cornoldi, & Marchitelli, 1990; Zechmeister & Shaughnessy, 1980) or to the encoding operations applied by the learner (e.g., level of processing, interactive imagery, etc.; Begg, Vinski, Frankovich, & Holgate, 1991; Matvey et al., 2001; Rabinowitz et al., 1982; Shaw & Craik, 1989). For example, participants' JOLs seem to draw on the belief that generating a word is better for memory than reading it (Begg et al., 1991; Matvey et al., 2001). Koriat (1997) proposed that JOLs are comparative in nature. Hence, they should be more sensitive to intrinsic cues pertaining to the relative recallability of different items within a list than to factors that affect overall performance (see Begg, Duft, Lalonde, Melnick, & Sanvito, 1989; Carroll, Nelson, & Kirwan, 1997; Shaw & Craik, 1989). Indeed, he obtained evidence indicating that, in making JOLs, the effects of extrinsic factors are discounted relative to those of intrinsic factors that differentiate between different items within a list.

Another major determinant of people's metacognitive judgments is their perceived self-efficacy (Bandura, 1977). In fact, people's preconceived notions about their skills in specific domains predict their assessment of how well they did on a particular task. For example, when students are asked to tell how well they have done on an exam, they tend to overestimate greatly their performance on the test, and this bias derives in part from the tendency of people to base their retrospective assessments on their preconceived, inflated beliefs about their skills in the domain tested, rather than on their specific experience with taking the test (Dunning, Johnson, Ehrlinger, & Kruger, 2003). In a study by Ehrlinger and Dunning (2003), two groups of participants took the same test; those who believed that the test measured abstract reasoning ability (on which they had rated themselves highly) estimated that they had achieved higher scores than did those who thought that they had taken a computer programming test. This was so despite the fact that the two groups did not differ in their actual performance.

Another finding that points to the effects of one's a priori beliefs comes from studies of the relationship between confidence and accuracy. People's confidence in their responses is generally predictive of the accuracy of these responses in the case of general knowledge questions but not in the case of eyewitness memory (Perfect, 2002). Perfect (2004) provided evidence that this occurs because people's confidence is based in part on their preconceptions about their abilities. Such preconceptions are generally valid in the case of general knowledge questions, for which people have had considerable feedback and hence know their relative standing. Such is not the case with eyewitness memory, for which they lack knowledge about how good they are and, by implication, how confident they ought to be. Thus, people's confidence in their performance seems to be based in part on their preconceived beliefs about their own competence in the domain of knowledge tested.

Evidence for the effects of beliefs and theories also comes from studies of correction processes in judgment. People often base their judgments directly on their subjective feelings (see Schwarz & Clore, 1996; Slovic et al., 2002). However, when they realize that their subjective experience has been contaminated by irrelevant factors, they may try to correct their judgments according to their beliefs about how these judgments had been affected by the irrelevant factors (Strack, 1992). For example, in the study of Schwarz, Bless, Strack, Klumpp, Rittenauer-Schatka, and Simons (1991), participants who were asked to recall many past episodes demonstrating self-assertiveness reported lower self-ratings of assertiveness than those who were asked to recall a few such episodes, presumably because of the greater difficulty experienced in recalling many episodes. However, when led to believe that the experienced difficulty had been caused by background music, participants relied more heavily on the retrieved content, reporting higher ratings under the many-episodes condition than under the few-episodes condition. These and other findings suggest that the correction process is guided by the person's beliefs about the factors that make subjective experience an unrepresentative basis for judgment. Although most researchers assume that the correction process requires some degree of awareness (see Gilbert, 2002), others suggest that it may also occur unconsciously (Oppenheimer, 2004).

More recent work in social cognition (see Schwarz, 2004) suggests that the conclusions that people draw from their metacognitive experience, such as the experience of fluent processing, depend on the naïve theory that they bring to bear. Furthermore, people can be induced to adopt opposite theories about the implications of processing fluency, and these theories modulate experience-based judgments. These suggestions deserve exploration with regard to judgments of one's own knowledge.

Another line of evidence comes from studies that examined how people determine that a certain event did not happen. Strack and Bless (1994) proposed that decisions of nonoccurrence may be based on a metacognitive strategy that is used when rememberers fail to retrieve any feature of a target event that they have judged to be highly memorable. In contrast, in the absence of a clear recollection of a non-memorable event, people may infer that the event had actually occurred (but had been forgotten). Indeed, non-occurrence decisions are made with strong confidence for events that would be expected to be remembered (e.g., one's name, a salient item, etc.; Brown, Lewis, & Monk, 1977; Ghetti, 2003). On the other hand, studying material under conditions unfavorable for learning (or expecting fast forgetting, Ghetti, 2003) results in a relatively high rate of false alarms for non-memorable distrac-

tors. Brainerd, Reyna, Wright, and Mojardin (2003) also discussed a process termed "recollection rejection" in which a distractor that is consistent with the gist of a presented item may be rejected when the verbatim trace of that item is accessed. However, they argued that this process can occur automatically, outside conscious awareness.

The evidence reviewed thus far supports the idea that metacognitive judgments may be based on one's beliefs and theories. For example, the subjective confidence in the correctness of one's memory product (e.g., a selected answer in a quiz) can be based on a logical, analytic process in which one evaluates and weighs the pros and cons (Gigerenzer, Hoffrage & Kleinbölting, 1991; Koriat, Lichtenstein, & Fischhoff, 1980). FOK judgments, too, may draw on theories or beliefs resulting in an educated guess about the likelihood of retrieving or recognizing an elusive word in the future (Costermans, Lories, & Ansay, 1992). Such judgments may not be qualitatively different from many predictions that people make in everyday life.

Experience-Based Monitoring

Experience-based metacognitive judgments, in contrast, are assumed to entail a qualitatively different process from that underlying theory-based judgments. Consider, for example, the TOT experience. The strong conviction that one knows the elusive target is based on a sheer subjective feeling. That feeling, however, appears to be the product of an inferential process that involves the application of nonanalytic heuristics (see Jacoby & Brooks, 1984; Kelley & Jacoby, 1996a; Koriat & Levy-Sadot, 1999) that operate below full consciousness and give rise to a sheer subjective experience. Indeed, the idea that subjective experience can be influenced and shaped by unconscious inferential processes has received support in the work of Jacoby, Kelley, Whittlesea, and their associates (see Kelley & Jacoby, 1998; Whittlesea, 2004). Koriat (1993) argued that the nonanalytic, unconscious basis of metacognitive judgments is responsible for the phenomenal quality of the feeling of knowing as representing an immediate, unexplained intuition, similar to that which is associated with the experience of perceiving (see Kahneman, 2003). According to this view, sheer subjective experience, which lies at the core of conscious awareness, is in fact the end product of processes that lie below awareness.

Several cues have been proposed as determinants of JOL, FOK, and subjective confidence. These cues have been referred to collectively as "mnemonic" cues (Koriat, 1997). With regard to JOLs and FOK, these cues include the ease or fluency of processing of a presented item (Begg et al., 1989), the familiarity of the cue that serves to probe memory (Metcalfe, Schwartz, & Joaquim, 1993; Reder & Ritter, 1992; Reder & Schunn, 1996), the accessibility of pertinent partial information about a solicited memory target (Dunlosky & Nelson, 1992; Koriat, 1993; Morris, 1990), and the ease with which information comes to mind (Kelley & Lindsay, 1993; Koriat, 1993; Mazzoni & Nelson, 1995). Subjective confidence in the correctness of retrieved information has also been claimed to rest on the ease with which information is accessed and on the effort experienced in reaching a decision (Kelley & Lindsay, 1993; Nelson & Narens, 1990; Robinson & Johnson, 1998; Zakay & Tuvia, 1998).

These cues differ in quality from those underlying theory-based judgments. Whereas the latter judgments draw upon the *content* of domain-specific beliefs and knowledge that are retrieved from memory, the former rely on contentless mnemonic cues that pertain to the quality of processing, in particular, the fluency with which information is encoded and retrieved. As Koriat and Levy-Sadot (1999) argued, "The cues for feelings of knowing, judgments of learning or subjective confidence lie in structural aspects of the information processing system. This system, so to speak, engages in a self-reflective inspection of its own operation and uses the ensuing information as a basis for metacognitive judgments" (p. 496).

Consider experience-based JOLs. These have been claimed to rely on the ease with which the items are encoded during learning or on the ease with which they are retrieved. Both of these types of cues become available in the course of learning and disclose the memorability of the studied material. Such cues have been assumed to give rise to a sheer feeling of knowing. Indeed, there is evidence suggesting that JOLs monitor the ease with which studied items are processed during encoding (Begg, et al., 1989; Koriat, 1997; Matvey et al., 2001). For example, Begg et al. (1989) reported results suggesting that JOLs are sensitive to several attributes of words (e.g., concreteness-abstractness) that affect ease of processing. Other findings suggest that JOLs are affected by the ease and probability with which the to-be-remembered items are retrieved during learning (Benjamin & Bjork, 1996; Benjamin, Bjork, & Schwartz, 1998; Koriat & Ma'ayan, 2005). For example, Hertzog, Dunlosky, Robinson, and Kidder (2003) reported that JOLs increased with the speed with which an interactive image was formed between the cue and the target in a paired-associates task. Similarly, Matvey et al. (2001) found that JOLs increased with increasing speed of generating the targets to the cues at study. These results are consistent with the view that JOLs are based on mnemonic cues pertaining to the fluency of encoding or retrieving to-be-remembered items during study.

With regard to FOK judgments, several heuristic-based accounts have been proposed. According to the *cue familiarity* account, first advanced by Reder (1987; see also Metcalfe et al., 1993), FOK is based on the familiarity of the pointer (e.g., the question, the cue term in a paired-associate, etc., see Koriat & Lieblich, 1977) that serves to probe memory (Reder, 1987). Reder argued that a fast, preretrieval FOK is routinely and automatically made in response to the familiarity of the terms of a memory question to determine whether the solicited answer exists in memory. This preliminary FOK can guide the question answering strategy. Indeed, the latency of speeded FOK judgments was found to be shorter than that of providing an answer. Furthermore, in several studies, the advance priming of the terms of a question was found to enhance speeded, preliminary FOK judgments without correspondingly increasing the probability of recall or recognition of the answer (Reder, 1987, 1988). Schwartz and Metcalfe (1992) extended Reder's paradigm to show that cue priming also enhances (unspeeded) FOK judgments elicited following recall failure. Additional evidence for the cue-familiarity account comes from studies using a proactive-interference paradigm (Metcalfe et al., 1993). Remarkable support was also obtained using arithmetic problems: When participants made fast judgments whether they knew the answer to an arithmetic problem and could retrieve it, or whether they had to compute it, Know judgments were found to increase with increasing frequency of previous exposures to the same parts of the problem, not with the availability of the answer in memory (Reder & Ritter, 1992). This was true even when participants did not have enough time to retrieve an answer (Schunn, Reder, Nhouyvanisvong, Richards, & Stroffolino, 1997; see Nhouyvanisvong & Reder, 1998, for a review).

Consistent with the cue-familiarity account are also the results of studies of the feeling-of-not-knowing. Glucksberg and McCloskey (1981) and Klin, Guzman, and Levine (1997) reported results suggesting that lack of familiarity can serve as a basis for determining that something is not known. Increasing the familiarity of questions for which participants did not know the answer increased the latency of Don't Know responses as well as the tendency to make a Know response erroneously.

According to the *accessibility* account of FOK, in contrast, FOK is based on the overall accessibility of pertinent information regarding the solicited target (Koriat, 1993). This account assumes that monitoring does not precede retrieval but follows it: It is by trying to retrieve a target from memory that a person can appreciate whether the target is "there" and worth continuing to search for. This occurs because, even when retrieval fails, people may still access a variety of partial clues and activations, such as fragments of the target, semantic and episodic

attributes, and so on (see Koriat, Levy-Sadot, Edry, & de Marcas, 2003; Miozzo & Caramazza, 1997). These partial clues may give rise to a sheer feeling that one knows the answer. An important assumption of the accessibility account is that participants have no direct access to the accuracy of the partial clues that come to mind, and therefore both correct and wrong partial clues contribute to the FOK.

Support for the accessibility account comes from a study on the TOT state (Koriat & Lieblich, 1977). An analysis of the questions that tend to induce an overly high FOK suggested that the critical factor is the amount of information they tend to elicit. For example, questions that contain redundancies and repetitions tend to produce inflated feelings of knowing, and so are questions that activate many "neighboring" answers. Thus, accessibility would seem to be a global, unrefined heuristic that responds to the mere amount of information irrespective of its correctness. Because people can rarely specify the source of partial information, they can hardly escape the contaminating effects of irrelevant clues by attributing them to their source. Such irrelevant clues sometimes precipitate a strong illusion of knowing (Koriat, 1995, 1998a) or even an illusory TOT state – reporting a TOT state even in response to questions that have no real answers (Schwartz, 1998), possibly because of the activations that they evoke.

Indeed, Schwartz and Smith (1997) observed that the probability of reporting a TOT state about the name of a fictitious animal increased with the amount of information provided about that animal, even when the amount of information did not contribute to the probability of recalling the name of the animal. In addition, FOK judgments following a commission error (producing a wrong answer) are higher than following an omission error (Koriat, 1995; Krinsky & Nelson, 1985; Nelson & Narens, 1990), suggesting that FOK judgments are sensitive to the mere accessibility of information.

In Koriat's (1993) study, after participants studied a nonsense string, they attempted to recall as many of the letters as they could and then provided FOK judgments regarding the probability of recognizing the correct string among lures. The more letters that participants could access, the stronger was their FOK regardless of the accuracy of their recall. When the number of letters accessed was held constant, FOK judgments also increased with the ease with which information came to mind, as indexed by recall latency.

If both correct and incorrect partial information contribute equally to the feeling that one knows the elusive memory target, how is it that people can nevertheless monitor their knowledge accurately? According to Koriat (1993) this happens because much of the information that comes spontaneously to mind (around 90%; see Koriat & Goldsmith, 1996a) is correct. Therefore, the total amount of partial information accessible is a good cue for recalling or recognizing the *correct* target. Thus, the accuracy of metamemory is a byproduct of the accuracy of memory: Memory is by and large accurate in the sense that what comes to mind is much more likely to be correct than wrong.

A third account still assumes a combined operation of the familiarity and accessibility heuristics. According to this account both heuristics contribute to FOK, but whereas the effects of familiarity occur early in the microgenesis of FOK judgments, those of accessibility occur later, and only when cue familiarity is sufficiently high to drive the interrogation of memory for potential answers (Koriat, & Levy-Sadot, 2001; Vernon & Usher, 2003). This account assumes that familiarity, in addition to affecting FOK judgments directly, also serves as a gating mechanism: When familiarity is high, participants probe their memory for the answer, and then the amount of information accessible affects memory performance. When familiarity is low, the effects of potential accessibility on FOK are more limited.

It should be noted, however, that results obtained by Schreiber and Nelson (1998) question the idea that FOK judgments are sensitive to the mere accessibility of partial clues about the target. These results indicate that FOK decreases with the number of pre-experimental, neighboring concepts that are linked to a cue, suggesting that these judgments are sensitive to the competition between the activated elements.

Subjective confidence in the correctness of one's answers has also been assumed to rest sometimes on mnemonic cues deriving from the process of recalling or selecting an answer. Thus, people express stronger confidence in the answers that they retrieve more quickly, whether those answers are correct or incorrect (Nelson & Narens, 1990). Similarly, in a study by Kelley and Lindsay (1993), retrieval fluency was manipulated through priming. Participants were asked to answer general information questions and to indicate their confidence in the correctness of their answers. Prior to this task, participants were asked to read a series of words, some of which were correct answers and some were plausible but incorrect answers to the questions. This prior exposure was found to increase the speed and probability with which those answers were provided in the recall test and, in parallel, to enhance the confidence in the correctness of those answers. Importantly, these effects were observed for both correct and incorrect answers. These results support the view that retrospective confidence is based in part on a simple heuristic: Answers that come to mind easily are more likely to be correct than those that take longer to retrieve.

The imagination inflation effect also illustrates the heuristic basis of confidence judgments. Asking participants to imagine some childhood events increased confidence that these events did indeed happen in the past (Garry, Manning, Loftus, & Sherman, 1996). Merely asking about the event twice also increased subjective confidence. Possibly imagination of an event and attempting to recall it increase its retrieval fluency, which in turn contributes to the confidence that the event has occurred (see also Hastie, Landsman & Loftus, 1978).

In sum, although metacognitive judgments may be based on explicit inferences that draw upon a priori beliefs and knowledge, much of the recent evidence points to the heuristic basis of such judgments, suggesting that feelings of knowing are based on the application of nonanalytic heuristics that operate below conscious awareness. These heuristics rely on mnemonic cues pertaining to the quality of processing and result in a sheer noetic experience. Thus, it would seem that sheer subjective feelings, such as the feeling of knowing, which are at the core of subjective awareness, are the product of unconscious processes (Koriat, 2000b).

The distinction between information-based and experience-based processes has important implications that extend beyond metacognition. It shares some features with the old distinction between reason and emotion (see Damasio, 1994), but differs from it. It implies a separation between two components or states of consciousness – on the one hand, sheer subjective feelings and intuitions that have a perceptual-like quality and, on the other hand, reasoned cognitions that are grounded in a network of beliefs and explicit memories. It is a distinction between what one "feels" and "senses" and what one "knows" or "thinks." The extensive research in both cognitive psychology and social psychology (e.g., Jacoby & Whitehouse, 1989; Strack, 1992) indicates that these two components of conscious awareness are not only dissociable, but may actually conflict with each other, pulling judgments and behavior in opposite directions (Denes-Raj & Epstein, 1994). The conflict between these components is best illustrated in correction phenomena (e.g., Jacoby & Whitehouse, 1989; Strack, 1992), which suggest that when people realize that their subjective experience has been contaminated, they tend to change their judgments so as to correct for the assumed effects of that contamination (Strack, 1992).

Dissociations between Knowing and the Feeling of Knowing

The clearest evidence in support of the idea that metacognitive judgments are based on inference from cues rather than on direct access to memory traces comes from observations documenting a dissociation between subjective and objective indexes of knowing. Several such dissociations have been reported. These dissociations also bring to the fore the effects of specific mnemonic cues on metacognitive judgments.

With regard to JOLs, Begg et al. (1989) found that high-frequency words, presumably fluently processed, yielded higher JOLs but poorer recognition memory than low-frequency words (see also Benjamin, 2003). Narens, Jameson and Lee (1994) reported that subthreshold target priming enhanced JOLs, perhaps because it facilitated the processing of the target, although it did not affect eventual recall.

Bjork (1999) described several conditions of learning that enhance performance during learning but impair long-term retention and/or transfer. According to Bjork and Bjork (1992), these manipulations facilitate "retrieval strength" but not "storage strength." As a result, the learners, fooled by their own performance during learning, may experience an illusion of competence, resulting in inflated predictions about their future performance. For example, massed practice typically yields better performance than spaced practice in the short term, whereas spaced practice yields considerably better performance than massed practice in the long term. Massed practice, then, has the potential of leading learners to overestimate their future performance. Indeed, Zechmeister and Shaughnessy (1980) found that words presented twice produced higher JOLs when their presentation was massed than when it was distributed, although the reverse pattern was observed for recall. A similar pattern was reported by Simon and Bjork (2001) using a motor-learning task: Participants asked to learn each of several movement patterns under blocked conditions predicted better performance than when those patterns were learned under random (interleaved) conditions, whereas actual performance exhibited the opposite pattern.

Benjamin et al. (1998) reported several experiments documenting a negative relation between recall predictions and actual recall performance, presumably deriving from reliance on retrieval fluency when retrieval fluency was a misleading cue for future recall. For example, they had participants answer general information questions and assess the likelihood that they would be able to free recall each answer in a later test. The more rapidly participants retrieved an answer to a question, the higher was their estimate that they would be able to free recall that answer at a later time. In reality, however, the opposite was the case.

Another type of dissociation was reported by Koriat, Bjork, Sheffer, and Bar (2004). They speculated that, to the extent that JOLs are based on processing fluency at the time of study, they should be insensitive to the expected time of testing. This should be the case because the processing fluency of an item at the time of encoding should not be affected by when testing is expected. Indeed, when participants made JOLs for tests that were expected either immediately after study, a day after study, or a week after study, JOLs were entirely indifferent to the expected retention interval, although actual recall exhibited a typical forgetting function. This pattern resulted in a dissociation such that predicted recall matched actual recall very closely for immediate testing. For a week's delay, however, participants predicted over 50% recall, whereas actual recall was less than 20%.

That study also demonstrated the importance of distinguishing between experience-based and theory-based JOLs: When a new group of participants were presented with all three retention intervals and asked to estimate how many words they would recall at each interval, their estimates closely mimicked the forgetting function exhibited by the first group's actual recall. Thus, the effects of forgetting on recall performance seem to emerge under conditions that activate participants' beliefs about memory.

Dissociations have also been reported between FOK judgments and actual memory performance. First are the findings in support of the cue-familiarity account reviewed above. These findings indicate that manipulations that enhance the familiarity of the terms of a question enhance FOK judgments associated with that question without correspondingly affecting actual recall performance. A similar dissociation, inspired by the accessibility account, has been demonstrated by Koriat (1995): The results of that study suggest that FOK judgments for general information questions tend to be accurate as long as these questions bring to mind more correct than incorrect partial information. However, deceptive questions (Fischhoff, Slovic, & Lichtenstein, 1977), which bring to mind more incorrect than correct information, produce unduly high FOK judgments following recall failure and, in fact, yield a dissociation to the extent that FOK judgments are *negatively* correlated with subsequent recognition memory performance.

With regard to confidence judgments, Chandler (1994) presented participants with a series of target and non-target stimuli, each consisting of a scenic nature picture. In a subsequent recognition memory test, a dissociation was observed such that targets for which there existed a similar stimulus in the non-target series were recognized less often, but were endorsed with stronger confidence than targets for which no similar non-target counterpart was included. Thus, seeing a related target seems to impair memory while enhancing confidence.

Busey, Tunnicliff, Loftus, and Loftus (2000) had participants study a series of faces appearing at different luminance conditions. For faces that had been studied in a dim condition, testing in a bright condition reduced recognition accuracy, but increased confidence, possibly because it enhanced their fluent processing during testing.

In sum, several researchers, motivated by the cue-utilization view of metacognitive judgments, have deliberately searched for conditions that produce a dissociation between memory and metamemory. Interestingly, all of the manipulations explored act in one direction: inflating metacognitive judgments relative to actual memory performance. Some of the experimental conditions found to engender illusions of knowing are ecologically unrepresentative, even contrived. However, the demonstrated dissociations clearly speak against the notion that metacognitive judgments rest on privileged access to the contents of one's own memory.

The Validity of Metacognitive Judgments

How valid are subjective feelings of knowing in monitoring actual knowledge? How accurate are people's introspections about their memory? Earlier research has sought to establish a correspondence between knowing and the feeling of knowing as an attempt to support the trace-access view of metacognitive judgments. Later studies, in contrast, inspired by the inferential view, have concentrated on producing evidence for miscorrespondence and dissociation, as just reviewed. Although the conditions used in these studies may not be ecologically representative, the results nevertheless suggest that the accuracy of metacognitive judgments is limited. Furthermore, these results point to the need to clarify the reasons for accuracy and inaccuracy and to specify the conditions that affect the degree of correspondence between subjective and objective measures of knowing.

Two aspects of metacognitive accuracy must be distinguished. The first is calibration (Lichtenstein et al., 1982) or "bias" or "absolute accuracy" (see Nelson & Dunlosky, 1991), which refers to the correspondence between mean metacognitive judgments and mean actual memory performance and reflects the extent to which metacognitive judgments are realistic. For example, if confidence judgments are elicited in terms of probabilities, then the mean probability assigned to all the answers in a list is compared to the proportion of correct answers. This comparison can indicate whether probability judgments are well calibrated or whether they disclose an overconfidence bias (inflated confidence relative to performance) or an underconfidence bias. Calibra-

tion or bias can also be assessed by eliciting global or aggregate predictions (Hertzog, Kidder, Powell-Moman, & Dunlosky 2002; Koriat, Sheffer, & Ma'ayan, 2002; Liberman, 2004), for example, by asking participants to estimate how many answers they got right and comparing that estimate to the actual number of correct answers.

It should be stressed that calibration can be evaluated only when judgments and performance are measured on equivalent scales. Thus, for example, if confidence judgments are made on a rating scale, calibration cannot be evaluated unless some assumptions are made (e.g., Mazzoni & Nelson, 1995).

Such is not the case for the second aspect of metacognitive accuracy, resolution (or relative accuracy). Resolution refers to the extent to which metacognitive judgments are correlated with memory performance across items. This aspect is commonly indexed by a within-subject gamma correlation between judgments and performance (Nelson, 1984). For example, in the case of JOLs and FOK judgments, resolution reflects the extent to which a participant can discriminate between items that she will recall and those that she will not. In the case of confidence, it reflects the ability to discriminate between correct and incorrect answers.

The distinction between calibration and resolution is important. For example, in monitoring one's own competence during the preparation for an exam, calibration is pertinent to the decision when to stop studying: Overconfidence may lead to spending less time and effort than are actually needed. Resolution, in turn, is relevant to the decision how to allocate the time between different parts of the material. Importantly, resolution can be high, even perfect, when calibration is very poor. Also, calibration and resolution may be affected differentially. For example, Koriat et al. (2002) observed that practice studying the same list of items improves resolution but impairs calibration, instilling underconfidence.

We should note that much of the experimental work on the accuracy of JOLs and

FOK judgments has focused on resolution. In contrast, research on confidence judgments, primarily the work carried out within the judgment and decision tradition, has concentrated on calibration.

With regard to JOLs elicited during study, the results of several investigations indicate that by and large item-by-item JOLs are well calibrated on the first study-test trial (e.g., Dunlosky & Nelson, 1994; Mazzoni & Nelson, 1995). Judgments of comprehension, in contrast, tend to be very inflated. One reason for this is that in monitoring comprehension people assess familiarity with the general domain of the text instead of assessing knowledge gained from that text (Glenberg, Sanocki, Epstein, & Morris, 1987).

Two interesting trends have been reported with regard to the calibration of JOLs. First is the aggregate effect. When learners are asked to provide an aggregate judgment (i.e., predict how many items they will recall), their estimates, when transformed into percentages, are substantially lower than item-by-item judgments. Whereas the latter judgments tend to be relatively well calibrated or even slightly inflated, aggregate judgments tend to yield underconfidence (Koriat et al., 2002, 2004; Mazzoni & Nelson, 1995). A similar effect has been observed for confidence judgments (Griffin & Tversky, 1992).

Second is the underconfidence-with-practice (UWP) effect (Koriat et al., 2002): When learners are presented with the same list of items for several study-test cycles, their JOLs exhibit relatively good calibration on the first cycle, with a tendency toward overconfidence. However, a shift toward marked underconfidence occurs from the second cycle on. The UWP effect was found to be very robust across several experimental manipulations and was obtained even for a task involving the monitoring of memory for self-performed tasks.

Turning next to resolution, the within-person correlation between JOLs and subsequent memory performance tends to be relatively low, particularly when the studied material is homogeneous. For example,

the JOL-recall gamma correlation averaged .54 across several studies that used lists of paired-associates that included related and unrelated pairs (Koriat et al., 2002). In contrast, in Dunlosky and Nelson's (1994) study, in which all pairs were unrelated, the gamma correlation averaged .20.

Monitoring seems to be particularly poor when it concerns one's own actions. When participants are asked to perform a series of minitasks (so called self-performed tasks) and to judge the likelihood of recalling these tasks in the future, the accuracy of their predictions is poor, and much lower than that for the study of a list of words (Cohen et al., 1991). It has been argued that people sometimes have special difficulties in monitoring their own actions (e.g., Koriat, Ben-Zur, & Druch, 1991).

However, two types of procedures have been found to improve JOL resolution. The first procedure is repeated practice studying the same list of items. As noted earlier, although repeated practice impairs calibration, it does improve resolution (King, Zechmeister, & Shaughnessy, 1980; Koriat, 2002; Mazzoni et al., 1990). Thus, in Koriat et al.'s (2002) analysis, in which the JOL-recall gamma correlation averaged .54 for the first study-test cycle, that correlation reached .82 on the third study-test cycle. Koriat (1997) produced evidence suggesting that the improved resolution with practice occurs because (a) with increased practice studying a list of items, the basis of JOLs changes from reliance on pre-experimental intrinsic attributes of the items (e.g., perceived difficulty) toward a greater reliance on mnemonic cues (e.g., processing fluency) associated with the study of these items, and (b) mnemonic cues tend to have greater validity than intrinsic cues, being sensitive to the immediate processing of the items during study. Rawson, Dunlosky, and Thiede (2000) also observed an improvement in judgments of comprehension with repeated reading trials.

A second procedure that proved effective in improving JOL accuracy is that of soliciting JOLs not immediately after studying each item, but a few trials later.

In paired-associate learning, delaying JOLs has been found to enhance JOL accuracy markedly (Dunlosky & Nelson, 1994; Nelson & Dunlosky, 1991). However, the delayed-JOL effect occurs only when JOLs are cued by the stimulus term of a paired-associate, not when cued by an intact stimulus-response pair (Dunlosky & Nelson, 1992). It would seem that the condition in which JOLs are delayed and cued by the stimulus alone approximates the eventual criterion test, which requires access to information in long-term memory in response to a cue. Indeed, Nelson, Narens, and Dunlosky (2004) reported evidence suggesting that, in making delayed JOLs, learners rely heavily on the accessibility of the target, which is an effective predictor of subsequent recall. When JOLs are solicited immediately after study, the target is practically always retrievable, and hence its accessibility has little diagnostic value. There is still controversy, however, whether the delayed-JOL effect indeed reflects improved metamemory (Dunlosky & Nelson, 1992) or improved memory (Kimball & Metcalfe, 2003; Spellman & Bjork, 1992).

Koriat and Ma'ayan (2005) reported evidence suggesting that the basis of JOLs changes with delay: As the solicitation of JOLs is increasingly delayed, a shift occurs in the basis of JOLs from reliance on encoding fluency (the ease with which an item is committed to memory) toward greater reliance on retrieval fluency (the ease with which the target comes to mind in response to the cue). In parallel, the validity of retrieval fluency in predicting recall increases with delay and becomes much better than that of encoding fluency. These results suggest that metacognitive judgments may be based on the flexible and adaptive utilization of different mnemonic cues according to their relative validity in predicting memory performance.

The results of Koriat and Ma'ayan suggest that repeated practice and delay may contribute to JOL accuracy by helping learners overcome biases that are inherent in encoding fluency. Koriat and Bjork (2005) described an illusion of competence – *foresight bias* – that arises from an inherent discrepancy between the standard conditions of learning and the standard conditions of testing. On a typical memory test, people are presented with a question and are asked to produce the answer. In contrast, in the corresponding learning condition, both the question and the answer generally appear in conjunction, meaning that the assessment of one's future memory performance occurs in the presence of the answer. This difference has the potential of creating unduly high feelings of competence that derive from the failure to discount what one now knows. This situation is similar to what has been referred to as the "curse of knowledge" – the difficulty in discounting one's privileged knowledge in judging what a more ignorant other knows (Birch & Bloom, 2003). Koriat and Bjork produced evidence suggesting that learners are particularly prone to a foresight bias in paired-associate cue-target learning when the target (present during study) brings to the fore aspects of the cue that are less apparent when the cue is later presented alone (at test). Subsequent experiments (Koriat & Bjork, 2006) indicated that foresight bias, and associated overconfidence, can be alleviated by conditions that enhance learners' sensitivity to mnemonic cues that pertain to the testing situation, including study-test experience, particularly test experience, and delaying JOLs.

Another way in which JOLs can be made more sensitive to the processes that affect performance during testing was explored by Guttentag and Carroll (1998) and Benjamin (2003). They obtained the typical result in which learners predict superior recognition memory performance for common than for uncommon words (although in reality the opposite is the case). However, when during the recognition test learners made postdictions about the words that they could not remember (i.e., judged the likelihood that they would have recognized the word if they had studied it), they actually postdicted superior recognition of the uncommon words. Furthermore, the act of making postdictions for one list of items was found to rectify predictions made for a second list of items studied later.

As far as the accuracy of FOK judgments is concerned, these judgments are relatively well calibrated (Koriat, 1993) and are moderately predictive of future recall and recognition. Thus, participants unable to retrieve a solicited item from memory can estimate with above-chance success whether they will be able to recall it in the future, produce it in response to clues, or identify it among distractors (e.g., Gruneberg & Monks, 1974; Hart, 1967). In a meta-analysis, Schwartz and Metcalfe (1994) found that the accuracy of FOK judgments in predicting subsequent recognition performance increases with the number of test alternatives. The highest correlations were found when the criterion test was recall.

Assuming that metacognitive judgments are based on internal, mnemonic cues, then their accuracy should depend on the validity of the cues on which they rest. However, only a few studies examined the validity of the mnemonic cues that are assumed to underlie FOK judgments. Koriat (1993) showed that the correlation between the amount of partial information retrieved about a memory target (regardless of its accuracy) is a good predictor of eventual memory performance, and its validity is equal to that of FOK judgments. Whereas the overall accessibility of information about a target (inferred from the responses of one group of participants) predicted the magnitude of FOK judgments following recall failure, the output-bound accuracy of that information was predictive of the accuracy (resolution) of these FOK judgments (Koriat, 1995). In a similar manner, cue familiarity may contribute to the accuracy of FOK judgments because in the real world cues and targets (or questions and answers) typically occur in tight conjunction; therefore familiarity with the clue should predict familiarity with the target (Metcalfe, 2000).

Turning finally to retrospective confidence judgments, these have received a great deal of research in the area of judgment and decision making. When participants are presented with general knowledge questions and are asked to assess the probability that the chosen answer is correct, an overconfidence bias is typically observed, with mean probability judgments markedly exceeding the proportion of correct answers (Lichtenstein et al., 1982). This overconfidence has been claimed to derive from a confirmation bias (see Koriat et al., 1980; Nickerson, 1998; Trope & Liberman, 1996) – the tendency to build toward a conclusion that has already been reached by selectively gathering or utilizing evidence that supports that conclusion. However, it has also been argued that part of the observed overconfidence may be due to the biased sampling of items by researchers – the tendency to include too many deceptive items. Indeed, when items are drawn randomly, the overconfidence bias decreases or disappears (Gigerenzer et al., 1991).

More recently, attempts have been made to show that confidence in a decision is based on the sampling of events from memory, with overconfidence resulting from a biased sampling (Winman & Juslin, 2005). Indeed, Fiedler and his associates (Fiedler, Brinkmann, Betsch, & Wild, 2000; Freytag & Fiedler, 2006) used a sampling approach to explain several biases in judgment and decision making in terms of the notion of *metacognitive myopia*. According to this approach, many environmental entities have to be inferred from the information given in a sample of stimulus input. Because samples are rarely representative, an important metacognitive requirement would be to monitor sampling biases and control for them. People's responses, however, are finely tuned to the information given in the sample, and biased judgments, including overconfidence, derive from the failure to consider the constraints imposed on the generation of the information sample.

It is important to note that overconfidence is not ubiquitous: When it comes to sensory discriminations, participants exhibit underconfidence, thinking that they did worse than they actually did (Björkman, Juslin, & Winman, 1993). Also, whereas item-by-item confidence judgments yield overconfidence, aggregate (or global) judgments (estimating the number of correct answers), as noted earlier, typically yield underconfidence (Gigerenzer et al., 1991; Griffin & Tversky, 1992). The underconfidence for aggregate judgments may derive in part from a failure to make an allowance for correct answers likely to result from mere guessing (Liberman, 2004).

A great deal of research has been carried out also on the confidence-accuracy (C-A) relation, with variable results. The general pattern that emerges from this research is that the C-A relation is quite strong when calculated within each participant (which is what was referred to as resolution), but very weak when calculated between participants (see Perfect, 2004). Consider the latter situation first. Research conducted in the domain of eyewitness testimony, focusing on the ability of participants to recall a particular detail from a crime or to identify the perpetrator in a lineup, has yielded low C-A correlations (Wells & Murray, 1984). That research has typically focused on a between-individual analysis, which is, perhaps, particularly relevant in a forensic context: It is important to know whether eyewitnesses can be trusted better when they are confident in the testimony than when they express low confidence. Similarly, if there are several witnesses, it is important to know whether the more confident among them is likely to be the more accurate. Thus, in this context the general finding is that a person's confidence in his or her memory is a poor predictor of the accuracy of that memory.

On the other hand, research focusing on within-person variation has typically yielded moderate-to-high C-A correlations. Thus, when participants answer a number of questions and for each question report their confidence in the correctness of the answer, the cross-item correlation between confidence and accuracy tends to be relatively high (e.g. Koriat & Goldsmith, 1996a). The same is true when the questions concern the episodic memory for a previously experienced event (Koriat, Goldsmith, Schneider, & Nakash-Dura, 2001). Thus, people can generally discriminate between answers (or memory reports) that are likely to be correct and those that are likely to be false.

Why are the between-participant correlations very low? Several studies suggest that these low correlations stem from the low level of variability among witnesses in experimental laboratory studies. Such studies typically maintain the same conditions across participants. In contrast, under naturalistic conditions the correlation is generally much higher, and it is that type of correlation that would seem to be of relevance in a forensic context (Lindsay, Read & Sharma, 1998). A second reason, mentioned earlier, is that retrospective confidence judgments tend to be based in part on participants' preconceptions about their ability in the domain tested, and these preconceptions tend to be of low validity when they concern eyewitness memory (e.g., lineup identification).

Several studies explored the subjective mnemonic cues that may mediate the within-person C-A correlation. These cues include retrieval latency and the perception of effortless retrieval. The correlation was higher for recall than for recognition presumably because recall provides more cues pertaining to ease of retrieval than recognition (Koriat & Goldsmith, 1996a; Robinson, Johnson, & Herndon, 1997). Robinson, Johnson, & Robertson (2000) found that ratings of vividness and detail for a videotaped event contributed more strongly to confidence judgments than processing fluency and were also more diagnostic of memory accuracy. Attempts to enhance the C-A relation in eyewitness identification by inducing greater awareness of the thoughts and reasoning process involved in the decision process have been largely ineffective or even counterproductive (Robinson & Johnson, 1998).

In sum, the accuracy of metacognitive judgments has attracted a great deal of interest because of its theoretical and practical implications. The results are quite variable, although by and large JOLs, FOK judgments, and confidence ratings are moderately predictive of item differences in actual memory performance.

The Control Function of Metacognition

As noted earlier, much of the work in metacognition is predicated on the assumption that consciousness is not a mere epiphenomenon. Rather, subjective feelings and subjective judgments exert a causal role on behavior. In metacognition research this idea has been expressed in terms of the hypothesis that monitoring affects control (Nelson, 1996). Indeed, several observations suggest a causal link between monitoring and control so that the output of monitoring serves to guide the regulation of control processes.

With regard to the online regulation of learning, it has been proposed that JOLs affect the choice of which items to relearn and how much time to allocate to each item. Indeed, it has been observed that under self-paced conditions, when learners are given the freedom to regulate the amount of time spent on each item, they tend to allocate more time to items that are judged to be difficult to learn than to those that are judged to be easier (for a review see Son & Metcalfe, 2000). It was proposed that the effects of item difficulty on study time allocation are mediated by a monitoring process in which learners judge the difficulty of each item and then invest more effort in studying the judged-difficult items to compensate for their difficulty (Nelson & Leonesio, 1988).

Dunlosky and Hertzog (1998; see also Thiede & Dunlosky, 1999) proposed a discrepancy-reduction model to describe the relation between JOLs and study time allocation. Learners are assumed to monitor online the increase in encoding strength that occurs as more time is spent studying an item and to cease study when a desired level of strength has been reached. This level, which is referred to as "norm of study" (Le Ny, Denhiere, & Le Taillanter, 1972), is preset on the basis of various motivational factors, such as the stress on accurate learning versus fast learning (Nelson & Leonesio, 1988). Thus, in self-paced learning, study continues until the perceived degree of learning meets or exceeds the norm of study.

In their review of the literature, Son and Metcalfe (2000) found that indeed, in 35 of 46 published experimental conditions, learners exhibited a clear preference for studying the more difficult materials. There are two exceptions to this rule, however.

First, Thiede and Dunlosky (1999) showed that when learners are presented with an easy goal (e.g., to learn a list of 30 items with the aim of recalling at least 10 of them), they tended to choose the easier rather than the more difficult items for restudy. Thiede and Dunlosky took these results to imply a hierarchy of control levels: At a superordinate level, learners may plan to invest more effort studying either the easier or the more difficult items. This strategy is then implemented at the subordinate level to control the amount of time allocated to each item and to select items for restudy.

Second, Son and Metcalfe (2000) had participants learn relatively difficult materials with the option to go back to materials that had previously been studied. Under high time pressure, participants allocated more study time to materials that were judged as easy and interesting. When the time pressure was not so great, however, they tended to focus on the more difficult items.

These results indicate that study time allocation is also affected by factors other than the output of online monitoring. Indeed, other studies indicated, for example, that learners invest more study time when they expect a recall test than when they expect a recognition test (Mazzoni & Cornoldi, 1993) and when the instructions stress memory accuracy than when they stress speed of learning (Nelson & Leonesio, 1988). Also, the allocation of study time to a given item varies according to the incentive for subsequently recalling that item and according to the expected likelihood that the item would be later tested (Dunlosky & Thiede, 1998).

Altogether, these results suggest that study time allocation is guided by an adaptive strategy designed to minimize effort and improve learning.

With regard to FOK judgments, several studies indicated that they predict how long people continue searching for a memory target before giving up: When people feel that they know the answer or that the answer is on the tip-of-the-tongue, they search longer than when they feel that they do not know the answer (Barnes et al., 1999; Costermans et al., 1992; Gruneberg, Monks, & Sykes, 1977; Schwartz, 2001). FOK judgments are also predictive of the speed of retrieving an answer, so that in the case of commission responses the correlation between FOK judgments and retrieval latency is positive, whereas for omission responses the correlation between FOK and the latency of the decision to end search is negative (see Nelson & Narens, 1990).

Search time is also affected by other factors in addition to FOK judgments: When participants are penalized for slow responding, they tend to retrieve answers faster but produce more incorrect answers (Barnes et al., 1999).

As noted earlier, Reder (1987) proposed that preliminary FOK judgments also guide the selection of strategies for solving problems and answering questions. In her studies, the decision whether to retrieve a solution to an arithmetic problem (Know) or to compute it was affected by manipulations assumed to influence cue familiarity. These studies suggest that FOK judgments that are misled by cue familiarity can misguide the decision to retrieve or compute the answer.

Retrospective monitoring can also affect behavior. When people make an error in performing a task they can detect that without an external feedback and can often immediately correct their response. Following the detection of an error, people tend to adjust their speed of responding to achieve a desirable level of accuracy (Rabbit, 1966).

Confidence judgments have also been shown to affect choice and behavior and do so irrespective of their accuracy. As noted earlier, people are often overconfident in their knowledge. Fischhoff et al. (1977) showed that people had sufficient faith in their confidence judgments that they were willing to stake money on their validity.

Consider the finding, mentioned earlier, that when judging how well they have done on a test, people tend to base their judgments on their preconceptions about their abilities in the domain tested. Ehrlinger and Dunning (2003) reasoned that because women tend to perceive themselves as less scientifically talented than men, they should

be expected to rate their performance on a quiz of scientific reasoning lower than men rate themselves. Such was indeed the case, although in reality there was no gender difference in actual performance. When asked later if they would like to participate in a science competition, women were more likely to decline, and their reluctance correlated significantly with their self-rated performance on the quiz. Thus, their choices were affected by their confidence even when confidence was unrelated to actual performance.

A systematic examination of the control function of confidence judgments was conducted by Koriat and Goldsmith (1994, 1996a,b) in their investigation of the strategic regulation of memory accuracy. Consider the situation of a person on the witness stand who is sworn to "tell the whole truth and nothing but the truth." To meet this requirement, that person should monitor the accuracy of every piece of information that comes to mind before deciding whether to report it or not. Koriat and Goldsmith proposed a model that describes the monitoring and control processes involved. The rememberer is assumed to monitor the subjective likelihood that each candidate memory response is correct and then compare that likelihood to a preset threshold on the monitoring output to determine whether to volunteer that response or not. The setting of the control threshold depends on the relative utility of providing as complete a report as possible versus as accurate a report as possible. Several results provided consistent support for this model. First, the tendency to report an answer was very strongly correlated with subjective confidence in the correctness of the answer (the intra-subject gamma correlations averaged more than .95; Koriat & Goldsmith, 1996b, Experiment 1; see also Kelley & Sahakyan, 2003). This result suggests that people rely completely on their subjective confidence in deciding whether to volunteer an answer or withhold it. In fact, participants were found to rely heavily on their subjective confidence even when answering a set of "deceptive" general knowledge questions, for which subjective confidence was quite undiagnostic of accuracy (Koriat & Goldsmith, 1996b, Experiment 2). Second, participants given a high accuracy incentive (e.g., "you win one point for each correct answer but lose all of your winnings if even a single answer is incorrect") adopted a stricter criterion than participants given a more moderate incentive (a 1:1 penalty-to-bonus ratio), suggesting that the strategic regulation of memory reporting is flexibly adapted to the emphasis on memory accuracy. Third, the option to volunteer or withhold responses (which is often denied in traditional memory experiments) allowed participants to boost the accuracy of what they reported, in comparison with a forced-report test. This increase occurred by sacrificing some of the correct answers; that is, at the expense of memory quantity performance. This implies that eyewitnesses generally cannot "tell the whole truth" and also "tell nothing but the truth," but must find a compromise between the two requirements. Importantly, however, the extent of the quantity-accuracy tradeoff was shown to depend critically on monitoring effectiveness: In fact, when monitoring resolution is very high (that is, when a person can accurately discriminate between correct and wrong answers), the accuracy of what is reported may be improved significantly under free report conditions at little or no cost in quantity performance. Thus, in the extreme case when monitoring is perfect, a person should be able to exercise a perfect screening process, volunteering all correct items of information that come to mind and withholding all incorrect items.

Koriat and Goldsmith's model was applied to study the strategic regulation of memory accuracy by school-aged children (Koriat et al., 2001). Even second-to-third-grade children were effective in enhancing the accuracy of their testimony when given the freedom to volunteer or withhold an answer under a 1:1 penalty-to-bonus ratio, and they were able to enhance the accuracy of their reports even further when given stronger incentives for accurate reporting. However, both the children in this study (see also Roebers, Moga, & Schneider, 2001) and elderly adults in other studies (Kelley &

Sahakyan, 2003; Pansky, Koriat, Goldsmith, & Pearlman-Avnion, 2002) were found to be less effective than young adults (college students) in utilizing the option to withhold answers to enhance their accuracy. These results have implications for the dependability of children's testimony in legal settings.

Interestingly, results suggest that the relationship between monitoring and control, what Koriat and Goldsmith (1996b) termed "control sensitivity," may be impaired to some extent in aging (Pansky et al., 2002) and in certain psychotic disorders, such as schizophrenia (Danion, Gokalsing, Robert, Massin-Krauss, & Bacon, 2001; Koren et al., 2004). In the Koren et al. study, for instance, the correlation between confidence judgments in the correctness of a response and the decision to volunteer or withhold that response was highly diagnostic of the degree of insight and awareness that schizophrenic patients showed concerning their mental condition – more so than traditional measures of executive control, such as the Wisconsin Card Sorting Task. Patients exhibiting low control sensitivity were also less able to improve the accuracy of their responses when given the option to choose which answers to volunteer and which to withhold.

The research reviewed above has direct bearing on the question of how people can avoid false memories and overcome the contaminating effects of undesirable influences. Using fuzzy-trace theory as a framework, Brainerd et al. (2003) proposed a mechanism for false-memory editing that allows children and adults to reject false but gist-consistent events. The model also predicts the occurrence of erroneous recollection rejection, in which true events are inappropriately edited out of memory reports.

Payne, Jacoby, and Lambert (2004) investigated the ability of participants to overcome stereotype-based memory distortions when allowed the option of free report. Reliance on subjective confidence allowed participants to enhance their overall memory accuracy, but not to reduce stereotype bias. The results suggested that whereas subjective confidence monitors the accuracy of one's report, stereotypes distort memory through an unconscious-accessibility bias to which subjective confidence is insensitive. Hence the effects of stereotypes are difficult to control.

The work of Johnson and her associates on source monitoring (see Johnson, 1997; Johnson, Hashtroudi, & Lindsay, 1993) also has important implications for the editing of memory reports. According to the source-monitoring framework, there are several phenomenal cues that can be used by a rememberer to specify the source of a mental record, including such mnemonic cues as vividness, perceptual detail, and spatial and temporal information. Because mental experiences from different sources (e.g., perception versus imagination) differ on average in their phenomenal qualities (e.g., visual clarity), these diagnostic qualities can support source monitoring by using either a heuristically based process or a more strategic, systematic process. Both types of processes require setting criteria for making a judgment, as well as procedures for comparing activated phenomenal information to the criteria.

The broader implication of the work on the strategic regulation of memory accuracy (Koriat & Goldsmith, 1996b) is that, to investigate the complex dynamics between (a) memory (the quality of the information that is available to the rememberer), (b) monitoring, (c) control, and (d) overt accuracy and quantity performance, one must include a situation in which participants are free to decide what to report and what not to report. In fact, in everyday life people have great freedom in reporting an event from memory: They can choose what perspective to adopt, what to emphasize and what to skip, how much detail to provide, and so forth. Such strategic regulation entails complex monitoring and control processes that go beyond the decision to volunteer or withhold specific items of information, and these, too, deserve systematic investigation.

In fact, the conceptual framework of Koriat and Goldsmith was extended to incorporate another means by which people normally regulate the accuracy of what they report: control over the *grain size* (pre-

cision or coarseness) of the information that is reported (Goldsmith & Koriat, 1999; Goldsmith, Koriat, & Pansky, 2005; Goldsmith, Koriat, & Weinberg-Eliezer, 2002). For example, when not completely certain about the time of an event, a person may simply report that it occurred "late in the afternoon" rather than "at four-thirty." Neisser (1988) observed that when answering open-ended questions, participants tend to provide answers at a level of generality at which they are not likely to be mistaken. Of course, more coarsely grained answers, although more likely to be correct, are also less informative. Thus, Goldsmith et al. (2002) found that when participants are allowed to control the grain size of their report, they do so in a strategic manner, sacrificing informativeness (degree of precision) for the sake of accuracy when their subjective confidence in the more precise informative answer is low, and taking into account the relative payoffs for accuracy and informativeness in choosing the grain size of their answers. Moreover, the monitoring and control processes involved in the regulation of memory grain size appear to be similar to those underlying the decision to volunteer or withhold specific items of information, implying perhaps the use of common metacognitive mechanisms. A more recent study by Goldsmith et al. (2005), which examined changes in the regulation of grain size over different retention intervals, also yielded results consistent with this model: Starting with the well-known finding that people often remember the gist of an event though they have forgotten its details, Goldsmith et al. (2005) asked whether rememberers might exploit the differential forgetting rates of coarse and precise information to strategically regulate the accuracy of the information that they report over time. The results suggested that when given control over the grain size of their answers, people tend to provide coarser answers at longer retention intervals, in the attempt to maintain a stable level of report accuracy.

In sum, the few studies concerning the control function of metacognition suggest that people rely heavily on their subjective, metacognitive feelings and judgments in choosing their course of action. In addition to the monitoring output, however, they also take into account a variety of other considerations, such as the goals of learning and remembering, time pressure, emphasis on accuracy versus quantity, and the emphasis on accuracy versus informativeness.

The Effects of Metacognitive Regulation on Memory Performance

Given the dynamics of monitoring and control processes discussed so far, it is of interest to ask, To what extent does the self-regulation of one's processing affect actual memory performance? There are only a few studies that have examined this issue systematically. As noted earlier, under self-paced learning conditions, when participants are free to allocate study time to different items, they tend to divide their time unevenly among the items. Does the self-allocation of study time affect actual memory performance? Nelson and Leonesio (1988) coined the phrase "labor-in-vain effect" to describe the phenomenon that large increases in self-paced study time yielded little or no gain in recall. Specifically, they observed that the amount of self-paced study time increased substantially under conditions that emphasized accuracy in comparison with a condition that emphasized speed. However, the increase in study time resulted in little or no gain in recall.

Metcalfe and her associates (Metcalfe, 2002; Metcalfe & Kornell, 2003) examined systematically the effectiveness of the policy of study time allocation for enhancing memory performance. They found, for example, that learners allocated most time to medium-difficulty items and studied the easiest items first (in contrast to what would be expected from the discrepancy-reduction model, Dunlosky & Hertzog, 1998). When study time was experimentally manipulated, the best performance resulted when most time was given to the medium-difficulty items, suggesting that the strategy that peo-

ple use under self-paced conditions is largely appropriate. These and other results were seen to accord with the region of proximal learning framework according to which learning proceeds best by attending to concepts and events that are nearest to one's current understanding and only later going on to integrate items that are more difficult.

Thiede, Anderson, and Therriault (2003) used a manipulation that affected the learner's monitoring accuracy in studying text. They found that improved accuracy resulted in a more effective regulation of study and, in turn, in overall better test performance. Thus, learners seem to rely on their metacognitive feelings in regulating their behavior, and to the extent that these feelings are accurate, such self-regulation helps improve memory performance.

With regard to confidence judgments, as noted earlier, the work of Koriat and Goldsmith (1994, 1996b) indicates that when given the option of free report, people enhance their memory accuracy considerably in comparison to forced-report testing and do so by relying on the subjective confidence associated with each item that comes to mind. Because confidence is generally predictive of accuracy, reliance on confidence judgments is effective in enhancing accuracy when accuracy is at stake. However, the effective regulation of memory accuracy comes at the cost of reduced memory quantity, and both the increase in memory accuracy achieved under the free-report option and the reduction in memory quantity depend heavily on monitoring effectiveness.

Koriat and Goldsmith (1996b) evaluated the effectiveness of the participants' control policies given their actual levels of monitoring effectiveness. The participants were found to be quite effective in choosing a control policy that would maximize their joint levels of free-report accuracy and quantity performance, compared to an "optimal" control policy that could be applied directly, based on the confidence judgments assigned to the individual answers under forced report. The effectiveness of the participants' control of grain size in the

Goldsmith et al. (2002) study was much less impressive, however, perhaps because of the greater complexity of the incentive structure (differential payoffs for correct answers at different grain sizes, a fixed penalty for incorrect answers, regardless of grain size). In fact, one of the interesting findings of that study was that participants seemed to adopt a simple "satisficing" heuristic based on the payoff (whether explicit or implicit) and confidence for the more precise-informative answer alone, rather than to compare the expected subjective utility (confidence multiplied by subjective payoff) of potential answers at different grain sizes. Monitoring effectiveness for the correctness of the answers at different grain sizes was, however, also relatively poor (see also Yaniv & Foster, 1997). Thus, it may be that there are limits on the complexity and efficiency of both monitoring and control processes that in turn place limits on the performance benefits that can be achieved through such control.

In sum, only a few studies explored the effectiveness of metacognitive monitoring and control processes in enhancing actual memory performance. More work in this vein is needed.

Metacognition and Consciousness: Some General Issues

In concluding this chapter I would like to comment on how the research on metacognition relates to some of the fundamental issues regarding consciousness and its role in behavior. I discuss three issues: the determinants of subjective experience, the control function of subjective experience, and the cause-and-effect relation between consciousness and behavior.

The Genesis of Subjective Experience

The study of the bases of metacognitive judgments and their accuracy brings to the fore an important process that seems to underlie the shaping of subjective experience. The unique qualities of that process are best highlighted by contrasting experience-based judgment and theory-based judgments. Similar contrasts have been proposed by researchers in both cognitive psychology and social psychology who drew a distinction between two general modes of cognition (see Chaiken & Trope, 1999), and each of these contrasts highlights a particular dimension. Thus, different researchers have conceptualized the distinction in terms of such polarities as Nonanalytic versus Analytic cognition (Jacoby & Brooks, 1984), Associative versus Rule-Based Systems (Sloman, 1996), Experiential versus Rational Systems (Epstein & Pacini, 1999), Impulsive versus Reflective processes (Strack & Deutsch, 2004), Experience-Based versus Information-Based processes (Kelley & Jacoby, 1996a; Koriat & Levy-Sadot, 1999), Heuristic versus Deliberate modes of thought (Kahneman, 2003), and Experiential versus Declarative information (Schwarz, 2004). Stanovich and West (2000) used the somewhat more neutral terms System 1 versus System 2, which have been adopted by Kahneman (2003) in describing his work on judgmental biases.

In this chapter I focused on the contrast between theory-based and experience-based judgments, which seems to capture best the findings in metacognition. As far as metacognitive judgments are concerned, the important assumption is that both experience-based and theory-based judgments are inferential in nature. They differ, however, in two respects. First, theory-based judgments draw upon the content of declarative (semantic and/or episodic) information that is typically stored in long-term memory. Experience-based judgments, in contrast, are assumed to rely on mnemonic cues stemming from the current processing of the task at hand. Such cues as fluency of processing or ease of access pertain to the quality and efficacy of object-level processes as revealed online. Hence, as Koriat (1993) argued, experience-based FOK judgments, for example, monitor the information accessible in short-term memory rather than the information available in long-term memory. It follows that the accuracy of theory-based judgments depends on the validity of the theories and knowledge on which they are based, whereas the accuracy of experience-based judgments should depend on the diagnosticity of the effective mnemonic cues.

Second, they differ in the nature of the underlying process. Theory-based judgments are assumed to rely on an explicitly inferential process: The process is assumed to be deliberate, analytic, slow, effortful, and largely conscious. In contrast, experience-based judgments involve a two-step process: A fast, unconscious, automatic inference results in a sheer subjective experience, and that subjective experience can then serve as the basis for noetic judgments. Therefore, as Koriat and Levy-Sadot argued (1999), the processes that take off from subjective experience generally have no access to the processes that have produced that experience in the first place.

It is experience-based metacognitive judgments that have attracted the attention of memory researchers who asked the question, How do we know that we know? (e.g., Hart, 1965; Tulving & Madigan, 1970). Experience-based judgments have the quality of immediate, direct impressions, similar to what would follow from the trace-access view of metacognitive judgments. However, as argued earlier, this phenomenal quality could be explained in terms of the idea that experience-based judgments are based on an inferential process that is not available to consciousness, and hence the outcome of that process has the phenomenal quality of a direct, self-evident intuition (see Epstein & Pacini, 1999).

Thus, the work on metacognition nicely converges on the proposals advanced by Jacoby and Kelley (see Kelley & Jacoby, 1993) and by Whittlesea (2002, 2004) on the shaping of subjective experience. These proposals also parallel ideas in the area of social psychology on the genesis of various subjective feelings (see Bless & Forgas, 2000; Strack, 1992). However, although it is theoretically comforting that the distinction between experience-based and theory-based metacognitive processes converges on similar distinctions that have emerged in other domains, a great deal can be gained

by attempting to place the metacognitive distinction within a broader framework that encompasses other similar distinctions. For example, research in social psychology suggests that the interplay between declarative and experiential information is greater than has been realized so far (see Schwarz, 2004). However, little is known about the possibility that a similar interplay between the effects of theories and knowledge and those of mnemonic cues occurs also with regard to metacognitive judgments. Also, little research has been carried out that examines the possible effects of attribution and misattribution on metacognitive judgments. Furthermore, processing fluency has been shown to affect a variety of phenomenal experiences, such as liking, truth judgments, recognition decisions, and so on. Again, it is important to examine noetic feelings in the context of these other phenomenal experiences.

The Control Function of Subjective Experience

The issue of metacognitive control emerges most sharply when we ask, What is the status of metacognitive monitoring and control processes within the current distinction between implicit and explicit cognition? In light of the extensive research on both of these areas of research, one would expect the answer to be quite straightforward. However, such is not the case. In an edited volume on *Implicit Memory and Metacognition* (Reder, 1996), the discussions of the participants revealed a basic ambivalence: Kelley and Jacoby (1996b) claimed that "metacognition and implicit memory are so similar as to not be separate topics" (p. 287). Funnell, Metcalfe, and Tsapkini (1996), on the other hand, concluded that "the judgment of what and how much you know about what you know or will know is a classic, almost definitional, explicit task" (p. 172). Finally, Reder and Schunn (1996) stated, "Given that feeling of knowing, like strategy selection, tends to be thought of as the essence of a metacognitive strategy, it is important to defend our claim that this rapid feeling of knowing is actually an *implicit process* rather than an *explicit process*" (p. 50).

Koriat (1998b, 2000b) argued that this ambivalence actually discloses the two faces of metacognition. He proposed a *crossover model* that assigns metacognition a pivotal role in mediating between unconscious and conscious determinants of information processing. Thus, metacognitive judgments were assumed to lie at the interface between implicit and explicit processes. Generally speaking, a rough distinction can be drawn between two modes of operation: In the explicit-controlled mode, which underlies much of our daily activities, behavior is based on a deliberate and conscious evaluation of the available options and on a deliberate and controlled choice of the most appropriate course of action. In the implicit-automatic mode, in contrast, various factors registered below full consciousness may influence behavior directly and automatically, without the mediation of conscious control (see Bargh, 1997; Wegner, 2002).

Metacognitive experiences are assumed to occupy a unique position in this scheme: They are implicit as far as their antecedents are concerned, but explicit as far as their consequences are concerned. Although a strong feeling of knowing or an unmediated subjective conviction is certainly part and parcel of conscious awareness, they may themselves be the product of an unconscious inference, as reviewed earlier. Once formed, however, such subjective experiences can serve as the basis for the conscious control of information processing and action.

The crossover model may apply to other types of unmediated feelings (Koriat & Levy-Sadot, 1999). Thus, according to this view, sheer subjective feelings, which lie at the heart of consciousness, may themselves be the product of unconscious processes. Such feelings represent an encapsulated summary of a variety of unconscious influences, and it is in this sense that they are informative (see Schwarz & Clore, 1996): They contain information that is relevant to conscious control, unlike the implicit, unconscious processes that have given rise to these feelings. Koriat (2000b) speculated that the function

of immediate feelings, such as experience-based metacognitive feelings, is to augment self-control; that is, to allow some degree of personal control over processes that would otherwise influence behavior directly and automatically, outside the person's consciousness and control.

The Cause-and-Effect-Relation between Monitoring and Control

A final metatheoretical issue concerns the assumption underlying much of the work in metacognition (and adopted in the foregoing discussion) – that metacognitive feelings play a causal role in affecting judgments and behavior. However, the work of Jacoby and his associates (see Kelley & Jacoby, 1998) and of Whittlesea (2004) suggests a process that is more consistent with the spirit of the James-Lange view of emotion (see James, 1890): Subjective experience is based on an interpretation and attribution of one's own behavior, so that it *follows* rather than precedes controlled processes. In fact, the assumption that metacognitive feelings monitor the dynamics of information processing implies that such feelings are sometimes based on the feedback from self-initiated object-level processes. For example, the accessibility model of FOK (Koriat, 1993) assumes that FOK judgments are based on the feedback from one's attempt to retrieve a target from memory. Hence they follow, rather than precede, controlled processes. Thus, whereas discussions of the *function* of metacognitive feelings assume that the subjective experience of knowing drives controlled action, discussions of the *bases* of metacognitive feelings imply that such feelings are themselves based on the feedback from controlled action, and thus follow rather than precede behavior.

Recent work that addressed the cause-and-effect relation between metacognitive monitoring and metacognitive control (Koriat, in press; Koriat, Ma'ayan, & Nussinson, 2006; see Koriat, 2000b) suggests that the interplay between them is bidirectional: Although metacognitive monitoring can drive and guide metacognitive control, it may itself be based on the feedback from controlled operations. Thus, when control effort is *goal driven*, greater effort enhances metacognitive feelings, consistent with the "feelings-affect-behavior" hypothesis. For example, when different incentives are assigned to different items in a study list, learners invest more study time on the high-incentive items and, in parallel, make higher JOLs for these items than for the low-incentive items. This is similar to the idea that we run away because we are frightened, and therefore the faster we run away the safer we feel. In contrast, when control effort is *data driven*, increased effort is correlated with lower metacognitive feelings, consistent with the hypothesis that such feelings are based on the feedback from behavior. For example, under self-paced learning the more effort learners spend studying an item the *lower* is their JOL, and also the lower is their subsequent recall of that item. This is similar to the idea that we are frightened because we are running away, and therefore the faster we run the more fear we should experience. Thus, the study of metacognition can also shed light on the long-standing issue of the cause-and-effect relation between consciousness and behavior.

In sum, some of the current research in metacognition scratches the surface of metatheoretical issues concerning consciousness and its role in behavior and is beginning to attract the attention of philosophers of mind (see Nelson & Rey, 2000).

Acknowledgments

The preparation of this chapter was supported by a grant from the German Federal Ministry of Education and Research (BMBF) within the framework of German-Israeli Project Cooperation (DIP). The chapter was prepared when the author was a fellow at the Centre for Advanced Study, Norwegian Academy of Science, Oslo. I am grateful to Morris Goldsmith, Sarah Bar, and Rinat Gil for their help on this chapter.

References

Bandura, A. (1977). Self-efficacy: Toward a unifying theory of behavioral change. *Psychological Review, 84*, 191–215.

Bargh, J. A. (1997). The automaticity of everyday life. In R. S. Wyer, Jr. (Ed.), *Advances in social cognition* (Vol. 10, pp. 1–61). Mahwah, NJ: Erlbaum.

Barnes, A. E., Nelson, T. O., Dunlosky, J., Mazzoni, G., & Narens, L. (1999). An integrative system of metamemory components involved in retrieval. In D. Gopher & A. Koriat (Eds.), *Attention and performance XVII: Cognitive regulation of performance: Interaction of theory and application* (pp. 287–313). Cambridge, MA: MIT Press.

Begg, I., Duft, S., Lalonde, P., Melnick, R., & Sanvito, J. (1989). Memory predictions are based on ease of processing. *Journal of Memory and Language, 28*, 610–632.

Begg, I., Vinski, E., Frankovich, L., & Holgate, B. (1991). Generating makes words memorable, but so does effective reading. *Memory and Cognition, 19*, 487–497.

Benjamin, A. S. (2003). Predicting and postdicting the effects of word frequency on memory. *Memory and Cognition, 31*, 297–305.

Benjamin, A. S., & Bjork, R. A. (1996). Retrieval fluency as a metacognitive index. In L. Reder (Ed.), *Implicit memory and metacognition* (pp. 309–338). Hillsdale, NJ: Erlbaum.

Benjamin, A. S., Bjork, R. A., & Schwartz, B. L. (1998). The mismeasure of memory: When retrieval fluency is misleading as a metamnemonic index. *Journal of Experimental Psychology: General, 127*, 55–68.

Birch, S. A. J., & Bloom, P. (2003). Children are cursed: An asymmetric bias in mental-state attribution. *Psychological Science, 14*, 283–286.

Bjork, R. A. (1999). Assessing our own competence: Heuristics and illusions. In D. Gopher & A. Koriat (Eds.), *Attention and performance XVII: Cognitive regulation of performance: Interaction of theory and application* (pp. 435–459). Cambridge, MA: MIT Press.

Bjork, R. A., & Bjork, E. L. (1992). A new theory of disuse and an old theory of stimulus fluctuation. In A. F. Healy, S. M. Kosslyn, & R. M. Shiffrin (Eds.), *Essays in honor of William K. Estes, Vol. 1: From learning theory to connectionist theory, Vol. 2 : From learning processes to cognitive processes* (pp. 35–67). Hillsdale, NJ: Erlbaum.

Bjorklund, D. F., & Douglas, R. N. (1997). The development of memory strategies. In N. Cowan (Ed.), *The development of memory in childhood* (pp. 201–246). Hove, England: Taylor & Francis.

Björkman, M., Juslin, P., & Winman, A. (1993). Realism of confidence in sensory discrimination: The underconfidence phenomenon. *Perception and Psychophysics, 54,* 75–81.

Bless, H., & Forgas, J. P. (Eds.). (2000). *The message within: The role of subjective experience in social cognition and behavior.* Philadelphia: Psychology Press.

Brainerd, C. J., & Reyna, V. F., Wright, R., & Mojardin, A. H. (2003). Recollection rejection: False-memory editing in children and adults. *Psychological Review, 110,* 762–784.

Brown, A. L. (1987). Metacognition, executive control, self-regulation, and other more mysterious mechanisms. In F. E. Weinert & R. H. Kluwe (Eds.), *Metacognition, motivation, and understanding* (pp. 95–116). Hillsdale, NJ: Erlbaum.

Brown, J., Lewis, V. J., & Monk, A. F. (1977). Memorability, word frequency and negative recognition. *Quarterly Journal of Experimental Psychology, 29,* 461–473.

Brown, R., & McNeill, D. (1966). The "tip of the tongue" phenomenon. *Journal of Verbal Learning and Verbal Behavior, 5,* 325–337.

Burke, D. M., MacKay, D. G., Worthley, J. S., & Wade, E. (1991). On the tip of the tongue: What causes word finding failures in young and older adults? *Journal of Memory and Language, 30,* 542–579.

Busey, T. A., Tunnicliff, J., Loftus, G. R., & Loftus, E. (2000). Accounts of the confidence accuracy relation in recognition memory. *Psychonomic Bulletin & Review, 7,* 26–48.

Carroll, M., Nelson, T. O., & Kirwan, A. (1997). Tradeoff of semantic relatedness and degree of overlearning: Differential effects on metamemory and on long-term retention. *Acta Psychologica, 95,* 239–253.

Chaiken, S., & Trope, Y. (Eds.). (1999). *Dual process theories in social psychology.* New York: Guilford Press.

Chandler, C. C. (1994). Studying related pictures can reduce accuracy, but increase confidence, in a modified recognition test. *Memory & Cognition, 22,* 273–280.

Clore, G. L. (1994). Can emotions be nonconscious. In P. Ekman & R. J. Davidson (Eds.), *The nature of emotion: Fundamental questions. Series in affective science* (pp. 283–299). London: Oxford University Press.

Cohen, R. L., Sandler, S. P., & Keglevich, L. (1991). The failure of memory monitoring in a free recall task. *Canadian Journal of Psychology, 45,* 523–538.

Costermans, J., Lories, G., & Ansay, C. (1992). Confidence level and feeling of knowing in question answering: The weight of inferential processes. *Journal of Experimental Psychology: Learning, Memory, and Cognition, 18,* 142–150.

Craik, F. I. M., & Lockhart, R. S. (1972). Levels of processing: A framework for memory research. *Journal of Verbal Learning and Verbal Behavior, 11,* 671–684.

Damasio, A. R. (1994). *Descartes' error: Emotion, reason, and the human brain.* New York: Putnam.

Danion, J. M., Gokalsing, E., Robert, P., Massin-Krauss, M., & Bacon, E. (2001). Defective relationship between subjective experience and behavior in schizophrenia. *American Journal of Psychiatry, 158,* 2064–2066.

Davidson, J. E., & Sternberg, R. J. (1998). Smart problem solving: How metacognition helps. In D. J. Hacker, J. Dunlosky, & A. C. Graesser (Eds.), *Metacognition in educational theory and practice* (pp. 47–68). Mahwah, NJ: Erlbaum.

De Corte, E. (2003). Transfer as the productive use of acquired knowledge, skills, and motivations. *Current Directions in Psychological Science, 12,* 142–146.

Denes-Raj, V., & Epstein, S. (1994). Conflict between intuitive and rational processing: When people behave against their better judgment. *Journal of Personality and Social Psychology, 66,* 819–829.

Dunlosky, J., & Hertzog, C. (1998). Training programs to improve learning in later adulthood: Helping older adults educate themselves. In D. J. Hacker (Ed.), *Metacognition in educational theory and practice* (pp. 249–275). Mahwah, NJ: Erlbaum.

Dunlosky, J., & Nelson, T. O. (1992). Importance of the kind of cue for judgments of learning (JOL) and the delayed-JOL effect. *Memory & Cognition, 20,* 374–380.

Dunlosky, J., & Nelson, T. O. (1994). Does the sensitivity of judgments of learning (JOLs) to the effects of various study activities depend on when the JOLs occur? *Journal of Memory and Language, 33*, 545–565.

Dunlosky, J., & Thiede, K. W. (1998). What makes people study more? An evaluation of factors that affect self-paced study. *Acta Psychologica, 98*, 37–56.

Dunning, D., Johnson, K., Ehrlinger, J., & Kruger, J. (2003). Why people fail to recognize their own incompetence. *Current Directions in Psychological Science, 12*, 83–87.

Ehrlinger, J., & Dunning, D. (2003). How chronic self-views influence (and potentially mislead) estimates of performance. *Journal of Personality and Social Psychology, 84*, 5–17.

Epstein, S., & Pacini, R. (1999). Some basic issues regarding dual-process theories from the perspective of cognitive-experiential self-theory. In S. Chaiken & Y. Trope (Eds.), *Dual process theories in social psychology* (pp. 462–482). New York: Guilford Press.

Fernandez-Duque, D., Baird, J., & Posner, M. (2000). Awareness and metacognition. *Consciousness and Cognition, 9*, 324–326.

Fiedler, K., Brinkmann, B., Betsch, T., & Wild, B. (2000). A sampling approach to biases in conditional probability judgments: Beyond base rate neglect and statistical format. *Journal of Experimental Psychology: General, 129*, 399–418.

Fischhoff, B. (1975). Hindsight is not equal to foresight: The effect of outcome knowledge on judgment under uncertainty. *Journal of Experimental Psychology: Human Perception and Performance, 1*, 288–299.

Fischhoff, B., Slovic, P., & Lichtenstein, S. (1977). Knowing with certainty: The appropriateness of extreme confidence. *Journal of Experimental Psychology: Human Perception and Performance, 3*, 552–564.

Flavell, J. H. (1971). First discussant's comments: What is memory development the development of? *Human Development, 14*, 272–278.

Flavell, J. H. (1979). Metacognition and cognitive monitoring: A new area of cognitive-developmental inquiry. *American Psychologist, 34*, 906–911.

Flavell, J. H. (1999). Cognitive development: Children's knowledge about the mind. *Annual Review of Psychology, 50*, 21–45.

Flavell, J. H., & Wellman, H. M. (1977). Metamemory. In R. V. Kail & J. W. Hagen (Eds.), *Perspectives on the development of memory and cognition* (pp. 3–33). Hillsdale, NJ: Erlbaum.

Freytag, P. & Fiedler, K. (2006). Subjective validity judgements as an index of sensitivity to sampling bias. In K. Fiedler & P. Juslin (Eds.), *Information sampling and adaptive cognition* (pp. 127–146). New York: Cambridge University Press.

Funnell, M., Metcalfe, J., & Tsapkini, K. (1996). In the mind but not on the tongue: Feeling of knowing in an anomic patient. In L. M. Reder, (Ed.) *Implicit memory and metacognition* (pp. 171–194). Hillsdale, NJ: Erlbaum.

Gardiner, J. M., & Richardson-Klavehn, A. (2000). Remembering and knowing. In E. Tulving & F. I. M. Craik (Eds.), *The Oxford handbook of memory* (pp. 229–244). London: Oxford University Press.

Garry, M., Manning, C. G., Loftus, E. F., & Sherman, S. J. (1996). Imagination inflation: Imagining a childhood event inflates confidence that it occurred. *Psychonomic Bulletin and Review, 3*, 208–214.

Ghetti, S. (2003). Memory for nonoccurrences: The role of metacognition. *Journal of Memory and Language, 48*, 722–739.

Gigerenzer, G., Hoffrage, U., & Kleinbölting, H. (1991). Probabilistic mental models: A Brunswikian theory of confidence. *Psychological Review, 98*, 506–528.

Gilbert, D. T. (2002). Inferential correction. In T. Gilovich, D. Griffin, & D. Kahneman (Eds.), *Heuristics and biases: The psychology of intuitive judgment* (pp. 167–184). New York: Cambridge University Press.

Gilovich, T., Griffin, D. & Kahneman, D. (Eds.). (2002). *Heuristics and biases: The psychology of intuitive judgment*. New York: Cambridge University Press.

Glenberg, A. M., Sanocki, T., Epstein, W., & Morris, C. (1987). Enhancing calibration of comprehension. *Journal of Experimental Psychology: General, 116*, 119–136.

Glucksberg, S., & McCloskey, M. (1981). Decisions about ignorance: Knowing that you don't know. *Journal of Experimental Psychology: Human Learning and Memory, 7*, 311–325.

Goldsmith, M., & Koriat, A. (1999). The strategic regulation of memory reporting: Mechanisms and performance consequences. In D. Gopher & A. Koriat (Eds.), *Attention and performance*

XVII: Cognitive regulation of performance: Inter-action of theory and application (pp. 373–400). Cambridge, MA: MIT Press.

Goldsmith, M., Koriat, A., & Pansky, A. (2005) Strategic regulation of grain size in memory reporting over time. Journal of Memory and Language, 52, 505–525.

Goldsmith, M., Koriat, A., & Weinberg-Eliezer, A. (2002). Strategic regulation of grain size memory reporting. Journal of Experimental Psychology: General, 131, 73–95.

Griffin, D., & Tversky, A. (1992). The weighing of evidence and the determinants of confidence. Cognitive Psychology, 24, 411–435.

Gruneberg, M. M., & Monks, J. (1974). "Feeling of knowing" and cued recall. Acta Psychologica, 38, 257–265.

Gruneberg, M. M., Monks, J., & Sykes, R. N. (1977). Some methodological problems with feelings of knowing studies. Acta Psychologica, 41, 365–371.

Guttentag, R., & Carroll, D. (1998). Memorability judgments for high- and low-frequency words. Memory and Cognition, 26, 951–958.

Hacker, D. J., Dunlosky, J., & Graesser, A. C. (Eds.). (1998). Metacognition in educational theory and practice. Mahwah, NJ: Erlbaum.

Hart, J. T. (1965). Memory and the feeling-of-knowing experience. Journal of Educational Psychology, 56, 208–216.

Hart, J. T. (1967). Second-try recall, recognition, and the memory-monitoring process. Journal of Educational Psychology, 58, 193–197.

Hastie, R., Landsman, R., & Loftus, E. F. (1978). The effects of initial questioning on subsequent eyewitness testimony. Jurimetrics Journal, 19, 1–8.

Hertzog, C., Dunlosky, J., Robinson, A. E., & Kidder, D. P. (2003). Encoding fluency is a cue used for judgments about learning. Journal of Experimental Psychology: Learning, Memory, and Cognition, 29, 22–34.

Hertzog, C., Kidder, D. P., Powell-Moman, A., & Dunlosky, J. (2002). Aging and monitoring associative learning: Is monitoring accuracy spared or impaired? Psychology and Aging, 17, 209–225.

Jacoby, L. L., & Brooks, L. R. (1984). Nonanalytic cognition: Memory, perception, and concept learning. In G. H. Bower (Ed.), The psychology of learning and motivation: Advances in research and theory (pp. 1–47). New York: Academic Press.

Jacoby, L. L., & Whitehouse, K. (1989). An illusion of memory: False recognition influenced by unconscious perception. Journal of Experimental Psychology: General, 118, 126–135.

James, W. (1890). The principles of psychology. New York: Holt.

Johnson, M. K. (1997). Identifying the origin of mental experience. In M. S. Myslobodsky (Ed.), The mythomanias: The nature of deception and self-deception (pp. 133–180). Hillsdale, NJ: Erlbaum.

Johnson, M. K., Hashtroudi, S., & Lindsay, D. S. (1993). Source monitoring. Psychological Bulletin, 114, 3–28.

Jönsson, F. U., & Olsson, M. J. (2003). Olfactory metacognition. Chemical Senses, 28, 651–658.

Jost, J. T., Kruglanski, A. W., & Nelson, T. O. (1998). Social metacognition: An expansionist review. Personality and Social Psychology Review, 2, 137–154.

Kahneman, D. (2003). A perspective on judgment and choice: Mapping bounded rationality. American Psychologist, 58, 697–720.

Kelley, C. M., & Jacoby, L. L. (1993). The construction of subjective experience: Memory attributions. In M. Davies & G. W. Humphreys (Eds.), Consciousness: Psychological and philosophical essays. Readings in mind and language (Vol. 2, pp. 74–89). Malden, MA: Blackwell.

Kelley, C. M., & Jacoby, L. L. (1996a). Adult egocentrism: Subjective experience versus analytic bases for judgment. Journal of Memory and Language, 35, 157–175.

Kelley, C. M., & Jacoby, L. L. (1996b). Memory attributions: Remembering, knowing, and feeling of knowing. In L. M. Reder (Ed.), Implicit memory and metacognition (pp. 287–308). Hillsdale, NJ: Erlbaum.

Kelley, C. M., & Jacoby, L. L. (1998). Subjective reports and process dissociation: Fluency, knowing, and feeling. Acta Psychologica, 98, 127–140.

Kelley, C. M., & Lindsay, D. S. (1993). Remembering mistaken for knowing: Ease of retrieval as a basis for confidence in answers to general knowledge questions. Journal of Memory and Language, 32, 1–24.

Kelley, C. M., & Sahakyan, L. (2003). Memory, monitoring, and control in the attainment of memory accuracy. Journal of Memory and Language, 48, 704–721.

Kentridge, R. W., & Heywood, C. A. (2000). Metacognition and awareness. *Consciousness and Cognition, 9,* 308–312.

Kimball, D. R., & Metcalfe, J. (2003). Delaying judgments of learning affects memory, not metamemory. *Memory and Cognition, 31,* 918–929.

King, J. F., Zechmeister, E. B., & Shaughnessy, J. J. (1980). Judgments of knowing: The influence of retrieval practice. *American Journal of Psychology, 93,* 329–343.

Klin, C. M., Guzman, A. E., & Levine, W. H. (1997). Knowing that you don't know: Metamemory and discourse processing. *Journal of Experimental Psychology: Learning, Memory, and Cognition, 23,* 1378–1393.

Koren, D., Seidman, L. J., Poyurovsky, M., Goldsmith, M., Viksman, P., Zichel, S., & Klein, E. (2004). The neuropsychological basis of insight in first-episode schizophrenia: A pilot metacognitive study. *Schizophrenia Research, 70,* 195–202.

Koriat, A. (1993). How do we know that we know? The accessibility model of the feeling of knowing. *Psychological Review, 100,* 609–639.

Koriat, A. (1995). Dissociating knowing and the feeling of knowing: Further evidence for the accessibility model. *Journal of Experimental Psychology: General, 124,* 311–333.

Koriat, A. (1997). Monitoring one's own knowledge during study: A cue-utilization approach to judgments of learning. *Journal of Experimental Psychology: General, 126,* 349–370.

Koriat, A. (1998a). Illusions of knowing: The link between knowledge and metaknowledge. In V. Y. Yzerbyt, G. Lories, & B. Dardenne (Eds.), *Metacognition: Cognitive and social dimensions* (pp. 16–34). London: Sage.

Koriat, A. (1998b). Metamemory: The feeling of knowing and its vagaries. In M. Sabourin, F. I. M. Craik, & M. Robert (Eds.), *Advances in psychological science* (Vol. 2, pp. 461–469). Hove, UK: Psychology Press.

Koriat, A. (2000a). Control processes in remembering. In E. Tulving & F. I. M. Craik (Eds.), *The Oxford handbook of memory* (pp. 333–346). London: Oxford University Press.

Koriat, A. (2000b). The feeling of knowing: Some metatheoretical implications for consciousness and control. *Consciousness and Cognition, 9,* 149–171.

Koriat, A. (2002). Metacognition research: An interim report. In T. J. Perfect & B. L. Schwartz (Eds.), *Applied metacognition* (pp. 261–286). Cambridge: Cambridge University Press.

Koriat, A. (in press). Are we frightened because we run away? Some evidence from metacognitive feelings. In B. Uttl, N. Ohta, & A. L. Siegenthaler (Eds.), *Memory and emotions: Interdisciplinary perspectives.* Malden, MA: Blackwell.

Koriat, A., Ben-Zur, H., & Druch, A. (1991). The contextualization of memory for input and output events. *Psychological Research, 53,* 260–270.

Koriat, A., Ben-Zur, H., & Sheffer, D. (1988). Telling the same story twice: Output monitoring and age. *Journal of Memory and Language, 27,* 23–39.

Koriat, A., & Bjork, R. A. (2005). Illusions of competence in monitoring one's knowledge during study. *Journal of Experimental Psychology: Learning, Memory and Cognition, 31,* 187–194.

Koriat, A., & Bjork, R. A. (2006). Illusions of competence during study can be remedied by manipulations that enhance learners' sensitivity to retrieval conditions at test. *Memory & Cognition, 34,* 959–972.

Koriat, A., & Bjork, R. A., Sheffer, L., & Bar, S. K. (2004). Predicting one's own forgetting: The role of experience-based and theory-based processes. *Journal of Experimental Psychology: General, 133,* 643–656.

Koriat, A., & Goldsmith, M. (1994). Memory in naturalistic and laboratory contexts: Distinguishing the accuracy-oriented and quantity-oriented approaches to memory assessment. *Journal of Experimental Psychology: General, 123,* 297–315.

Koriat, A., & Goldsmith, M. (1996a). Memory metaphors and the real-life/laboratory controversy: Correspondence versus storehouse conceptions of memory. *Behavioral and Brain Sciences, 19,* 167–228.

Koriat, A., & Goldsmith, M. (1996b). Monitoring and control processes in the strategic regulation of memory accuracy. *Psychological Review, 103,* 490–517.

Koriat, A., Goldsmith, M., & Pansky, A. (2000). Toward a psychology of memory accuracy. *Annual Review of Psychology, 51,* 481–537.

Koriat, A., Goldsmith, M., Schneider, W., & Nakash-Dura, M. (2001). The credibility of children's testimony: Can children control the accuracy of their memory reports? *Journal of Experimental Child Psychology, 79,* 405–437.

Koriat, A., & Levy-Sadot, R. (1999). Processes underlying metacognitive judgments: Information-based and experience-based monitoring of one's own knowledge. In S. Chaiken & Y. Trope (Eds.), *Dual process theories in social psychology* (pp. 483–502). New York: Guilford Press.

Koriat, A., & Levy-Sadot, R. (2001). The combined contributions of the cue-familiarity and accessibility heuristics to feelings of knowing. *Journal of Experimental Psychology: Learning, Memory, and Cognition, 27*, 34–53.

Koriat, A., Levy-Sadot, R., Edry, E., & de Marcas, S. (2003). What do we know about what we cannot remember? Accessing the semantic attributes of words that cannot be recalled. *Journal of Experimental Psychology: Learning, Memory, and Cognition, 29*, 1095–1105.

Koriat, A., Lichtenstein, S., & Fischhoff, B. (1980). Reasons for confidence. *Journal of Experimental Psychology: Human Learning and Memory, 6*, 107–118.

Koriat, A., & Lieblich, I. (1977). A study of memory pointers. *Acta Psychologica, 41*, 151–164.

Koriat, A., & Ma'ayan, H. (2005). The effects of encoding fluency and retrieval fluency on judgments of learning. *Journal of Memory and Language, 52*, 478–492.

Koriat, A., Ma'ayan, H., & Nussinson, R. (2006). The intricate relationships between monitoring and control in metacognition: Lessons for the cause -and-effect relation between subjective experience and behavior. *Journal of Experimental Psychology: General, 135*, 36–69.

Koriat, A., Sheffer, L., & Ma'ayan, H. (2002). Comparing objective and subjective learning curves: Judgments of learning exhibit increased underconfidence with practice. *Journal of Experimental Psychology: General, 131*, 147–162.

Krinsky, R., & Nelson, T. O. (1985). The feeling of knowing for different types of retrieval failure. *Acta Psychologica, 58*, 141–158.

Le Ny, J. F., Denhiere, G., & Le Taillanter, D. (1972). Regulation of study-time and interstimulus similarity in self-paced learning conditions. *Acta Psychologica, 36*, 280–289.

Leonesio, R. J., & Nelson, T. O. (1990). Do different metamemory judgments tap the same underlying aspects of memory? *Journal of Experimental Psychology: Learning, Memory, and Cognition, 16*, 464–470.

Liberman, V. (2004). Local and global judgments of confidence. *Journal of Experimental Psychology: Learning, Memory, and Cognition, 30*, 729–732.

Lichtenstein, S., Fischhoff, B., & Phillips, L. D. (1982). Calibration of probabilities: The state of the art to 1980. In D. Kahneman, P. Slovic, & A. Tversky (Eds.), *Judgment under uncertainty: Heuristics and biases* (pp. 306–334). New York: Cambridge University Press.

Lindsay, D. S., Read, D. J., & Sharma, K. (1998). Accuracy and confidence in person identification: The relationship is strong when witnessing conditions vary widely. *Psychological Science, 9*, 215–218.

Maki, R. H., & McGuire, M. J. (2002). Metacognition for text: Findings and implications for education. In T. Perfect & B. Schwartz (Eds.), *Applied metacognition* (pp. 39–67). Cambridge: Cambridge University Press.

Matvey, G., Dunlosky, J., & Guttentag, R. (2001). Fluency of retrieval at study affects judgments of learning (JOLs): An analytic or nonanalytical basis for JOLs? *Memory and Cognition, 29*, 222–233.

Mazzoni, G., & Cornoldi, C. (1993). Strategies in study time allocation: Why is study time sometimes not effective? *Journal of Experimental Psychology: General, 122*, 47–60.

Mazzoni, G., Cornoldi, C., & Marchitelli, G. (1990). Do memorability ratings affect study-time allocation? *Memory and Cognition, 18*, 196–204.

Mazzoni, G., & Nelson, T. O. (1995). Judgments of learning are affected by the kind of encoding in ways that cannot be attributed to the level of recall. *Journal of Experimental Psychology: Learning, Memory, and Cognition, 21*, 1263–1274.

Metcalfe, J. (1998a). Cognitive optimism: Self-deception or memory-based processing heuristics? *Personality and Social Psychology Review, 2*, 100–110.

Metcalfe, J. (Ed.). (1998b). Metacognition. [Special issue]. *Personality and Social Psychological Review, 2*.

Metcalfe, J. (2000). Metamemory: Theory and data. In E. Tulving & F. I. M. Craik (Eds.), *The Oxford handbook of memory* (pp. 197–211). London: Oxford University Press.

Metcalfe, J. (2002). Is study time allocated selectively to a region of proximal learning? *Journal *of Experimental Psychology: General, 131,* 349–363.

Metcalfe, J., & Kornell, N. (2003). The dynamics of learning and allocation of study time to a region of proximal learning. *Journal of Experimental Psychology: General, 132,* 530–542.

Metcalfe, J., Schwartz, B. L., & Joaquim, S. G. (1993). The cue-familiarity heuristic in metacognition. *Journal of Experimental Psychology: Learning, Memory, and Cognition, 19,* 851–864.

Metcalfe, J., & Shimamura, A. P. (Eds.). (1994). *Metacognition: Knowing about knowing.* Cambridge, MA: MIT Press.

Miozzo, M., & Caramazza, A. (1997). Retrieval of lexical-syntactic features in tip-of-the tongue states. *Journal of Experimental Psychology: Learning, Memory, and Cognition, 23,* 1410–1423.

Mitchell, K. J., & Johnson, M. K. (2000). Source monitoring: Attributing mental experiences. In E. Tulving & F. I. M. Craik (Eds.), *The Oxford handbook of memory* (pp. 179–195). London: Oxford University Press.

Morris, C. C. (1990). Retrieval processes underlying confidence in comprehension judgments. *Journal of Experimental Psychology: Learning, Memory, and Cognition, 16,* 223–232.

Narens, L., Jameson, K. A., & Lee, V. A. (1994). Subthreshold priming and memory monitoring. In J. Metcalfe & A. P. Shimamura (Eds.), *Metacognition: Knowing about knowing* (pp. 71–92). Cambridge, MA: MIT Press.

Neisser, U. (1988). Time present and time past. In M. M. Gruneberg, P. Morris, & R. Sykes (Eds.), *Practical aspects of memory: Current research and issues* (Vol. 2, pp. 545–560). Chichester, England: Wiley.

Nelson, T. O. (1984). A comparison of current measures of the accuracy of feeling-of-knowing predictions. *Psychological Bulletin, 95,* 109–133.

Nelson, T. O. (1996). Consciousness and metacognition. *American Psychologist, 5,* 102–116.

Nelson, T. O., & Dunlosky, J. (1991). When people's judgments of learning (JOLs) are extremely accurate at predicting subsequent recall: The "delayed-JOL effect." *Psychological Science, 2,* 267–270.

Nelson, T. O., & Leonesio, R. J. (1988). Allocation of self-paced study time and the "labor-in-vain effect." *Journal of Experimental Psychology: Learning, Memory, and Cognition, 14,* 676–686.

Nelson, T. O., & Narens, L. (1990). Metamemory: A theoretical framework and new findings. In G. Bower (Ed.), *The psychology of learning and motivation: Advances in research and theory* (pp. 125–173). New York: Academic Press.

Nelson, T. O., & Narens, L. (1994). Why investigate metacognition. In J. Metcalfe & A. P. Shimamura (Eds.), *Metacognition: Knowing about knowing* (pp. 1–25). Cambridge, MA: MIT Press.

Nelson, T. O., Narens, L., & Dunlosky, J. (2004). A revised methodology for research on metamemory: Pre-judgment Recall and Monitoring (PRAM). *Psychological Methods, 9,* 53–69.

Nelson, T. O., & Rey, G. (Eds.). (2000). Metacognition and consciousness: A convergence of psychology and philosophy [Special issue]. *Consciousness and Cognition, 9(2).*

Nickerson, R. S. (1998). Confirmation bias: A ubiquitous phenomenon in many guises. *Review of General Psychology, 2,* 175–220.

Nhouyvanisvong, A., & Reder, L. M. (1998). Rapid feeling-of-knowing: A strategy selection mechanism. In V. Y. Yzerbyt, G. Lories, & B. Dardenne (Eds.), *Metacognition: Cognitive and social dimensions* (pp. 35–52). London: Sage.

Oppenheimer, D. M. (2004). Spontaneous discounting of availability in frequency judgment tasks. *Psychological Science, 15,* 100–105.

Pansky, A., Koriat, A., & Goldsmith, M. (2005). Eyewitness recall and testimony. In N. Brewer & K. D. Williams (Eds.), *Psychology and law: An empirical perspective* (pp. 93–150). New York: Guilford.

Pansky, A., Koriat, A., Goldsmith, M., & Pearlman-Avnion, S. (March, 2002). *Memory accuracy and distortion in old age: Cognitive, metacognitive, and neurocognitive determinants.* Poster presented at the 30th Anniversary Conference of the National Institute for Psychobiology, Jerusalem, Israel.

Paris, S. G., & Winograd, P. (1990). How metacognition can promote academic learning and instruction. In B. F. Jones & L. Idol (Eds.), *Dimensions of thinking and cognitive instruction* (pp. 15–51). Hillsdale, NJ: Erlbaum.

Payne, B. K., Jacoby, L. L., & Lambert, A. J., (2004). Memory monitoring and the control of stereotype distortion. *Journal of Experimental Social Psychology, 40,* 52–64.

Perfect, T. J. (2002). When does eyewitness confidence predict performance? In T. J. Perfect

& B. L. Schwartz (Eds.), *Applied metacognition* (pp. 95–120). Cambridge: Cambridge University Press.

Perfect, T. J. (2004). The role of self-rated ability in the accuracy of confidence judgments in eyewitness memory and general knowledge. *Applied Cognitive Psychology, 18*, 157–168.

Perner, J., & Lang, B. (1999). Development of theory of mind and executive control. *Trends in Cognitive Sciences, 3*, 337–344.

Posner, M. I., & Snyder, C. R. R. (1975). Attention and cognitive control. In R. L. Solso (Ed.), *Information processing and cognition: The Loyola Symposium* (pp. 55–85). Hillsdale, NJ: Erlbaum.

Pressley, M., Borkowski, J. G., & Schneider, W. (1987). Cognitive strategies: Good strategy users coordinate metacognition and knowledge. *Annals of Child Development, 4*, 89–129.

Rabinowitz, J. C., Ackerman, B. P., Craik, F. I. M., & Hinchley, J. L. (1982). Aging and metamemory: The roles of relatedness and imaginary. *Journal of Gerontology, 37*, 688–695.

Rabbitt, P. M. A. (1966). Errors and error correction in choice reaction tasks. *Journal of Experimental Psychology, 71*, 264–272.

Rawson, K. A., Dunlosky, J., & Theide, K. W. (2000). The rereading effect: Metacomprehension accuracy improves across reading trials. *Memory and Cognition, 28*, 1004–1010.

Reder, L. M. (1987). Strategy selection in question answering. *Cognitive Psychology, 19*, 90–138.

Reder, L. M. (1988). Strategic control of retrieval strategies. In G. H. Bower (Ed.), *The psychology of learning and motivation: Advances in research and theory* (Vol. 22, pp. 227–259). San Diego: Academic Press.

Reder, L. M. (Ed.). (1996). *Implicit memory and metacognition.* Mahwah, NJ: Erlbaum.

Reder, L. M., & Ritter, F. E. (1992). What determines initial feeling of knowing? Familiarity with question terms, not with the answer. *Journal of Experimental Psychology: Learning, Memory, and Cognition, 18*, 435–451.

Reder, L. M. & Schunn, C. D. (1996). Metacognition does not imply awareness: Strategy choice is governed by implicit learning and memory. In L. M. Reder (Ed.), *Implicit memory and metacognition* (pp. 45–77). Mahwah, NJ: Erlbaum.

Robinson, M. D., & Johnson, J. T. (1998). How not to enhance the confidence-accuracy relation: The detrimental effects of attention to the identification process. *Law and Human Behavior, 22*, 409–428.

Robinson, M. D., Johnson, J. T., & Herndon, F. (1997). Reaction time and assessments of cognitive effort as predictors of eyewitness memory accuracy and confidence. *Journal of Applied Psychology, 82*, 416–425.

Robinson, M. D., Johnson, J. T., & Robertson, D. A. (2000). Process versus content in eyewitness metamemory monitoring. *Journal of Experimental Psychology: Applied, 6*, 207–221.

Roebers, C. M., Moga, N., & Schneider, W. (2001). The role of accuracy motivation on children's and adults' event recall. *Journal of Experimental Child Psychology, 78*, 313–329.

Rosenthal, D. M. (2000). Consciousness, content, and metacognitive judgments. *Consciousness and Cognition, 9*, 203–214.

Scheid, K. (1993). *Helping students become strategic learners: Guidelines for teaching.* Cambridge, MA: Brookline Books.

Schneider, W. (1985). Developmental trends in the metamemory-memory behavior relationship: An integrative review. In D. L. Forest-Pressley, G. E. MacKinnon, & T. G. Waller (Eds.), *Metacognition, cognition, and human performance* (Vol. 1, pp. 57–109). Orlando, FL: Academic Press.

Schneider, W., & Pressley, M. (1997). *Memory development between two and twenty* (2d ed.). Mahwah, NJ: Erlbaum.

Schreiber, T. A., & Nelson, D. L. (1998). The relation between feelings of knowing and the number of neighboring concepts linked to the test cue. *Memory and Cognition, 26*, 869–883.

Schunn, C. D., Reder, L. M., Nhouyvanisvong, A., Richards, D. R., & Stroffolino, P. J. (1997). To calculate or not to calculate: A source activation confusion model of problem familiarity's role in strategy selection. *Journal of Experimental Psychology: Learning, Memory, and Cognition, 23*, 3–29.

Schwartz, B. L. (1994). Sources of information in metamemory: Judgments of learning and feeling of knowing. *Psychonomic Bulletin & Review, 1*, 357–375.

Schwartz, B. L. (1998). Illusory tip-of-the-tongue states. *Memory, 6*, 623–642.

Schwartz, B. L. (2001). The relation of tip-of-the-tongue states and retrieval time. *Memory and Cognition, 29*, 117–126.

Schwartz, B. L. (2002). *Tip-of-the-tongue states: Phenomenology, mechanism, and lexical retrieval*. Mahwah, NJ: Erlbaum.

Schwartz, B. L., & Metcalfe, J. (1992). Cue familiarity but not target retrievability enhances feeling-of-knowing judgments. *Journal of Experimental Psychology: Learning, Memory, and Cognition, 18*, 1074–1083.

Schwartz, B. L., & Metcalfe, J. (1994). Methodological problems and pitfalls in the study of human metacognition. In J. Metcalfe & A. P. Shimamura (Eds.), *Metacognition: Knowing about knowing* (pp. 93–113). Cambridge, MA: MIT Press.

Schwartz, B. L., & Smith, S. M. (1997). The retrieval of related information influences tip-of-the-tongue states. *Journal of Memory and Language, 36*, 68–86.

Schwarz, N. (2004). Meta-cognitive experiences in consumer judgment and decision making. *Journal of Consumer Psychology, 14*, 332–348.

Schwarz, N., Bless, H., Strack, F., Klumpp, G., Rittenauer-Schatka, H., & Simons, A. (1991). Ease of retrieval as information: Another look at the availability heuristic. *Journal of Personality and Social Psychology, 61*, 195–202.

Schwarz, N., & Clore, G. L. (1996). Feelings and phenomenal experiences. In E. T. Higgins & A. W. Kruglanski (Eds.), *Social psychology: Handbook of basic principles* (pp. 433–465). New York: Guilford Press.

Schwarz, N., & Clore, G. L. (2003). Mood as information: 20 years later. *Psychological Inquiry, 14*, 296–303.

Shaw, R. J., & Craik, F. I. M. (1989). Age differences in predictions and performance on a cued recall task. *Psychology and Aging, 4*, 131–135.

Shimamura, A. P. (2000). Toward a cognitive neuroscience of metacognition. *Consciousness and Cognition, 9*, 313–323.

Simon, D. A., & Bjork, R. A. (2001). Metacognition in motor learning. *Journal of Experimental Psychology: Learning, Memory, and Cognition, 27*, 907–912.

Sloman, S. A. (1996). The empirical case for two systems of reasoning. *Psychological Bulletin, 119*, 3–22

Slovic, P., Finucane, M., Peters, E., & MacGregor, D. G. (2002). The affect heuristic. In T. Gilovich, D. Griffin, & Kahneman, D. (Eds.), *Heuristics and biases: The psychology of intu-*itive judgment (pp. 397–420). New York: Cambridge University Press.

Son, L. K., & Metcalfe, J. (2000). Metacognitive and control strategies in study-time allocation. *Journal of Experimental Psychology: Learning, Memory, and Cognition, 26*, 204–221.

Spehn, M. K., & Reder, L. M. (2000). The unconscious feeling of knowing: A commentary on Koriat's paper. *Consciousness and Cognition, 9*, 187–192.

Spellman, B. A., & Bjork, R. A. (1992). When predictions create reality: Judgments of learning may alter what they are intended to assess. *Psychological Science, 3*, 315–316.

Stanovich, K. E., & West, R. F. (2000). Individual differences in reasoning: Implications for the rationality debate. *Behavioral and Brain Sciences, 23*, 645–665.

Strack, F. (1992). The different routes to social judgments: Experiential versus informational strategies. In L. L. Martin & A. Tesser (Eds.), *The construction of social judgments* (pp. 249–275). Hillsdale, NJ: Erlbaum.

Strack, F., & Bless, H. (1994). Memory for nonoccurrences: Metacognitive and presuppositional strategies. *Journal of Memory and Language, 33*, 203–217.

Strack, F., & Deutsch R. (2004). Reflective and impulsive determinants of social behavior. *Personality and Social Psychology Review, 8*, 220–247.

Thiede, K. W., Anderson, M. C. M., & Therriault, D. (2003). Accuracy of metacognitive monitoring affects learning of texts. *Journal of Educational Psychology, 95*, 66–73.

Thiede, K. W., & Dunlosky, J. (1999). Toward a general model of self-regulated study: An analysis of selection of items for study and self-paced study time. *Journal of Experimental Psychology: Learning, Memory, and Cognition, 25*, 1024–1037.

Trope, Y., & Liberman, A. (1996). Social hypothesis testing: Cognitive and motivational mechanisms. In E. T. Higgins & A. W. Kruglanski (Eds.), *Social psychology: Handbook of basic principles* (pp. 239–270). New York: Guilford Press.

Tulving, E., & Madigan, S. A. (1970). Memory and verbal learning. *Annual Review of Psychology, 21*, 437–484.

Underwood, B. J. (1966). Individual and group predictions of item difficulty for free learning.

Journal of Experimental Psychology, 71, 673–679.

Vernon, D., & Usher, M. (2003). Dynamics of metacognitive judgments: Pre- and postretrieval mechanisms. *Journal of Experimental Psychology: Learning, Memory, and Cognition, 29,* 339–346.

Wegner, D. M. (2002). *The illusion of conscious will.* Cambridge, MA: MIT Press.

Wells, G. L., & Murray, D. M. (1984). Eyewitness confidence. In G. L. Wells & E. F. Loftus, (Eds.), *Eyewitness testimony: Psychological perspectives* (pp. 155–170). New York: Cambridge University Press.

Whittlesea, B. W. A. (2002). Two routes to remembering (and another to remembering not). *Journal of Experimental Psychology: General, 131,* 325–348.

Whittlesea, B. W. A. (2004). The perception of integrality: Remembering through the validation of expectation. *Journal of Experimental Psychology: Learning, Memory, and Cognition, 30,* 891–908.

Winkielman, P., & Berridge, K. C. (2004). Unconscious emotion. *Current Directions in Psychological Science, 13,* 120–123.

Winkielman, P., Schwarz, N., Fazendeiro, T. A., & Reber, R. (2003). The hedonic marking of processing fluency: Implications for evaluative judgment. In J. Musch & K. C. Klauer (Eds.), *The psychology of evaluation: Affective processes in cognition and emotion* (pp. 189–217). Mahwah, NJ: Erlbaum.

Winman, A., & Juslin, P. (2005). "I'm *m/n* confident that I'm correct": Confidence in foresight and hindsight as a sampling probability. In K. Fiedler & P. Juslin (Eds.), *Information sampling and adaptive cognition.* Cambridge, UK: Cambridge University Press.

Yaniv, I., & Foster, D. P. (1997). Precision and accuracy of judgmental estimation. *Journal of Behavioral Decision Making, 10,* 21–32.

Yaniv, I., & Meyer, D. E. (1987). Activation and metacognition of inaccessible stored information: Potential bases for incubation effects in problem solving. *Journal of Experimental Psychology: Learning, Memory, and Cognition, 13,* 187–205.

Yzerbyt, V. Y., Lories, G., & Dardenne, B. (Eds.). (1998). *Metacognition: Cognitive and social dimensions.* Thousand Oaks, CA: Sage.

Zakay, D., & Tuvia, R. (1998). Choice latency times as determinants of post-decisional confidence. *Acta Psychologica, 98,* 103–115.

Zechmeister, E. B., & Shaughnessy, J. J. (1980). When you know that you know and when you think that you know but you don't. *Bulletin of the Psychonomic Society, 15,* 41–44.

CHAPTER 12
Consciousness and Control of Action

Carlo Umiltà

Abstract

Any voluntary action involves at least three stages: intention to perform an action, performance of the intended action, and perception of the effects of the performed action. In principle, consciousness may manifest itself at all three stages. Concerning the first stage, research suggests that intentions for carrying out voluntary actions may be generated unconsciously and retrospectively referred consciously to the action when it has been executed. There is a mechanism that binds together in consciousness the intention to act and the consequences of the intended action, thus producing the experience of free will.

Human beings consistently show visual illusions when they are tested with perceptual measures, whereas the illusions do not manifest themselves when they are tested with motor measures. These dissociations concern the stage of performing the intended action and recall blindsight and visual agnosia, in which patients can perform visually guided tasks without conscious visual experience. The explanation is that action execution depends on a sensorimotor or "how" system, which controls visually guided behavior without access to consciousness. The other is a cognitive or "what" system, which gives rise to perception, is used consciously in pattern recognition, and produces normal visual experience. The processes of this second stage do not have access to consciousness either.

In contrast, we are aware of some aspects of the current state of the motor system at the third stage in the sequence that leads to the execution of an action. When performing an action, we are aware of the prediction of its effects, which depend on the motor commands that were planned in the premotor and motor cortical areas.

Introduction: The Notion of Intentionality

In the present chapter, I am concerned exclusively with motor (i.e., bodily) actions.

Although actions usually manifest themselves as bodily movements, in accord with Marcel (2004) an action can be distinguished from a mere movement because the former has a goal and an effect, belongs to a semantic category (i.e., it has a content), and has some degree of voluntariness.

With the term "intentional action" we normally mean an action that one is conscious of; that is, an action that is performed consciously (Marcel, 2004). Other terms that can be used in place of "intentional" action are "deliberate" action or "volitional" action or "willed" action. As Zhu (2004, pp. 2–3) has maintained,

> *A central task for theories of action is to specify the conditions that distinguish voluntary and involuntary bodily movements. . . . A general way to understand the nature of action is to view actions as bodily movements preceded by certain forms of thought, such as appropriate combinations of beliefs, desires, intentions, and reasons. It is these particular forms of thought that characterize the voluntariness of human action.*

The critical question in Zhu's view is, "[H]ow can a certain piece of thought bring about physical bodily movement?"

It is important to point out, however, that the terms "conscious" and "intentional" should not be used interchangeably when referring to action. In fact, consciously performed actions are not necessarily actions that are performed intentionally. One can be conscious of performing an action that is non-intentional, or automatic, in nature. This distinction between conscious and intentional applies to all cognitive processes. Research has found that the vast majority of human thinking, feeling, and behavior operates in automatic fashion with little or no need for intentional control (see, e.g., Dehaene & Naccache, 2001; and chapters in Umiltà & Moscovitch, 1994; also, see Prochazka, Clarac, Loeb, Rothwell, & Wolpaw, 2000, for a discussion of voluntary vs. reflexive behavior). Once certain triggering conditions occur, cognitive processes can proceed automatically and autonomously until their completion, independent of intentional initiation and online intentional control. That does not mean, however, that the observer is not conscious of the fact that those cognitive processes are in progress or, to be more precise, of their intermediate and final outputs (i.e., representations; in fact, we are never conscious of the inner workings of our cognitive processes, but only of their outputs). Very likely, therefore, the observer becomes conscious of the representations that are produced by the cognitive processes that operate automatically. Thus, the question concerning what aspects of action we are conscious of is relevant for both intentional and automatic actions.

In our daily life we quite often experience conscious intentions to perform specific actions and have the firm belief that those conscious intentions drive our bodily movements, thus producing the desired changes in the external world. In this view, which no doubt is shared by the vast majority of people, the key components of an intentional action constitute a causal chain that can be described as follows, though in an admittedly oversimplified way. At the beginning of the chain that leads to an intentional action there is a goal-directed conscious intention. As a direct consequence of the conscious intention, a series of movements occurs. Then, effects – that is changes in the external world – manifest themselves and are consciously linked to the intention to act and to the series of performed movements.

However, an apparently goal-directed behavior does not necessarily signal intentionality. There can be little doubt that an organism may manifest goal-directed behavior without satisfying the criteria for performing an intentional action. Most lower-order organisms do exactly that. The characterization of an intentional action that I have adopted implies that, to define an action as intentional, one has to consciously experience a link, through the movements performed to achieve the goal, between the mental state of intention and the effects of the performed movements. That is, one can claim that a given goal-directed behavior satisfies the criteria for an intentional action only if the organism produces that behavior along with a conscious mental representation of its own internal state and of the state of the external world.

It is generally agreed that intentional actions engage processes different from those engaged by automatic actions (e.g., Prochazka et al., 2000). Here the fundamental principle is that *consciousness is necessary for intentional action*. In some cases, this principle is explicitly stated in one of a variety of different forms, whereas in some other cases it is simply implied. At any rate, the (explicit or implicit) accepted view is that conscious awareness of intentions, and of the motor and environmental consequences (effects) they cause, is required to construct the subjective experience of intentional action.

In summary, it seems that consciousness can manifest itself at three stages: intention to perform an action, performance of the intended action, and perception of the effects of the performed action. It is possible that the closeness in time of these three stages allows one to unify the conscious experiences that accompany them. This unification in turn is how we construct the strong subjective association among intentions, actions, and action effects (Haggard, Aschersleben, Gehrke, & Prinz, 2002a).

Note that the second stage, consciousness of performing the intended action, may be subdivided into two aspects (Marcel, 2004). One aspect is consciousness of the action we are actually performing; that is, the extent to which we are aware of what we are doing. The other aspect is consciousness of some events that take place during the action we are performing; that is, awareness of the nature of the specific components and of the precise details of our current action. In what follows, I am concerned almost exclusively with the first aspect because very little experimental evidence is available concerning the second aspect.

Also, it is worth noting that this traditional view of how we perform intentional actions may acquire a dangerously dualist connotation and becomes thus difficult to reconcile with the reductionism of neuroscience and cognitive science. At first sight, the toughest problem would be to provide an answer to the question Zhu (2004), among many others, asked above; that is, how a mental state (i.e., the observer's conscious intention) interacts with the neural events in the motor and premotor brain areas that produce body movements. That would no longer be a problem, however, if we accepted that the so-called mental state is in fact a specific neural state: It is a neural state representing or mediating intentionality that acts on another neural state mediating or representing movements and their consequences. Therefore, it is only phrasing the problem the way Zhu does that creates a dualistic separation where there may be none (also, see Wegner, 2005, and commentaries therein). The question I address in the first part of this chapter is quite different and is in fact concerned with the relative timing of two sets of neural events, those that represent (accompany?) the subjective experience of intentional action and those that represent (accompany?) the execution of the intended action.

Intention to Perform an Action (Unawareness of Intention)

Regardless of the difficulties of the traditional view and the danger of dualism it creates, there can be little doubt that very often we introspectively feel we can generate our actions; that is, we are conscious of our actions and of why they are initiated. Our experience of willing our own actions is so profound that it tempts us to believe that our actions are caused by consciousness. We first experience the conscious intention to perform a specific action; then, after a variable number of intermediate states, the desired action takes place. In spite of its apparent plausibility, this causal chain is likely incorrect.

It is important to keep in mind that there are two issues here, which should not be confounded. The first is whether the observer's conscious intention (i.e., a mental state) causes the neural events in the motor and premotor brain areas, which in turn produce body movements. This is a dualistic viewpoint that is at odds with current cognitive neuroscience. The other is whether the neural state representing conscious intentionality precedes or follows the neural states that produce movements. I am concerned almost exclusively with this latter issue, even if for simplicity I sometimes make recourse to mentalistic terms.

Concerning the dualistic issue, suffice it to say that, contrary to what introspection seems to suggest, conscious intention that leads to actions in fact arises as a result of brain activity, and not vice versa (Haggard & Eimer, 1999; Haggard & Libet, 2001; Haggard & Magno, 1999; Haggard et al., 2002a; Haggard, Clark, & Kalogeras, 2002b; Libet, 1985, 1999; Libet, Gleason, Wright, & Pearl, 1983). Or, as Wegner (2003, page 65) puts it, "You think of doing X and then do X – not because conscious thinking causes doing, but because other mental processes (that are not consciously perceived) cause both the thinking and the doing." This sentence is phrased in mentalistic terms, but it is easy to rephrase by substituting "conscious thinking" with "neural events that represent conscious thinking" and "other mental processes" with "neural events that represent other mental processes."

The celebrated experiments by Libet and his collaborators (Libet 1985, 1999; Libet et al., 1983) challenged the classical notion of conscious intention as action initiator and provided evidence that the conscious intention that is experienced does not correspond to causation. In a non-dualistic view, these experiments suggest that the neural events that represent conscious intentions, and that we think determine voluntary action, actually occur after the brain events that underlie action execution. Precisely, although the experience of conscious intention precedes the movement (flexing a finger, for example), it occurs well after the relevant brain events. This fact is taken to show that the experience of consciously willing an action begins after brain events that set the action into motion. Thus, the brain creates both the intention and the action, leaving the person to infer that the intention is causing the action.

Libet et al. (1983; also see McCloskey, Colebatch, Potter, & Burke, 1983) asked their participants to watch a clock face with a revolving hand and to report either the time at which they "felt the urge" to make a freely willed endogenous movement (W judgment) or the time the movement actually commenced (M judgment). The voluntary movement consisted in flexing the wrist at a time the participants themselves chose. Also, they were asked to note and to report the position of the hand when they first became conscious of wanting to move; that is, the moment at which they first consciously experienced the will to move. The W judgment was considered to be the first moment of conscious intention. The exact moment at which the action began was estimated by measuring the electrical activity in the muscles involved. The preparatory activity in the motor areas of the brain (the readiness potential, RP) was measured through the electrical activity recorded by a scalp electrode placed over the motor cortex. The RP is a gradual increase in electrical activity in the motor cortical regions, which typically precedes willed actions by 1 s or longer, and is known to be related closely to the cognitive processes required to generate the action.

Assuming that the cause precedes the effect, the temporal order of the W judgment and PR onset allows one to investigate which event is the cause and which event is the effect. If the moment of the W judgment (i.e., the moment of conscious intention or, to be more precise, of the neural event representing conscious intention) precedes the onset of RP, then the idea that conscious intention can initiate the subsequent preparation of movement is tenable. In contrast, if the moment of the W judgment follows the onset of RP, then conscious intention (i.e., the neural state representing conscious intention) would be a consequence of activity in the motor areas, rather than the cause of it. It should be noted, however, that Dennett (1998) has made the interesting point that conscious experience does not occur instantaneously, but rather develops over time. That means that the conscious experience of the onset of the neural event that produces a movement may evolve along with the movement itself. Therefore, it is likely wrong to expect a precise point in time when one becomes conscious of the initiation of a movement.

The sequence of events observed by Libet et al. (1983) is as follows: RP began between 1,000 and 500 ms before onset of the actual body movement, participants only experienced a conscious intention (i.e., W judgments) about 200 ms before movement onset, and conscious intention was experienced between 500 and 350 ms after RP onset. That indicated that a brain process in the motor areas initiated the intentional process well before participants were aware of the intention to act. The conclusion is that the brain is preparing the action that is apparently caused by a conscious intention before the participant is aware that he or she intends to act. All this goes directly against the traditional view that the conscious intention to perform an action initiates the neural events in the motor areas of the brain, which in turn produce the desired action. Also, it challenges the folk notion of free will, implying that the feeling of having made a decision is merely an illusion (e.g., Eagleman & Holcombe, 2002).

The notion that free will is a mere construct of our own minds, and we are only aware in retrospect of what our brain had already started some time ago, was not accepted lightly. Several critiques of Libet et al.'s (1983) study were advanced in response to a target article by Libet (1985). The more damaging one was that participants are often poor at judging the synchrony of two events, and especially so if the two events occur in different perceptual streams. Even more importantly, the so-called prior entry phenomenon may occur, according to which events in an attended stream appear to occur earlier than simultaneous events in an unattended stream. Because participants in the Libet et al. study very likely attempted to divide their

attention between the external clock and their own internal states in order to make the W judgment, the value of 200 ms as the interval by which the W judgment preceded movement onset is uncertain. However, even the largest estimates of the prior entry effect are much smaller than the gap between RP and W judgment that Libet et al. found (e.g., Haggard & Libet, 2001; Haggard et al., 2002b).

In conclusion, it seems that Libet et al.'s results, as well as those of Haggard and his colleagues (Haggard & Eimer, 1999; Haggard & Magno, 1999; Haggard et al., 2002a,b), are fully consistent with the view that consciousness of intention to perform an action (i.e., the brain events that represent the conscious intention to perform an action) is the consequence, rather than the cause, of activity in the cortical motor areas. That does not mean to deny that there must be an identifiable link between having an intention and the action that is subsequently performed to achieve the goal indicated by the intention. It simply means that the timing between the brain events involved is not necessarily the one corresponding to the subjective experience of the observer.

Note, however, that the studies by Haggard and his colleagues (Haggard & Eimer, 1999; Haggard & Magno, 1999; Haggard et al., 2002a,b) suggest that the processes underlying the so-called lateralized readiness potential (LRP) are more likely than those underlying the RP to cause awareness of movement initiation. The LRP measures the additional negativity contralateral to the actual movement that is being performed, over and above that in the ipsilateral motor cortex, and it can be considered to be an indicator of action selection. This is based on the reasoning that, once the LRP has begun, the selection of which action to make must have been completed. In the studies by Haggard and his colleagues the onset of the RP and W judgment did not covary, whereas the onset of the LRP and W judgment did. That is, the LRP for early W awareness trials occurred earlier than the LRP for late W awareness trials. This finding would seem to rule out the RP as the unconscious cause of the conscious state upon which W judgment depends, but it is consistent with LRP having that role. Therefore, there is a clear indication that (a) the initial awareness of a motor action is premotor, in the sense of deriving from the specifications for movement rather than the movement itself (i.e., a stage later than intention but earlier than movement itself; Marcel, 2004), and (b) awareness of initiating action relates to preparing a specific action, rather than a general abstract state of intending to perform an action of some kind.

In this connection, a study of Fried, Katz, McCarthy, Sass, Williamson, Spencer, and Spencer (1991) is of interest. They stimulated, through surface electrodes that were implanted for therapeutic reasons, the premotor areas (Broadmann's area 6, BA6, in particular) of epileptic patients. Weak stimulation of some of the more anterior electrode sites caused the patients to report a conscious intention to move or a feeling that they were about to move specific body parts. Stronger stimulation evoked actual movements of the same body parts. Fried et al.'s results too are clearly consistent with a causation chain that goes from motor areas to intention and not vice versa.

The results of the studies that Haggard and his colleagues (Haggard & Eimer, 1999; Haggard & Magno, 1999; Haggard et al., 2002a,b) conducted by following Libet's seminal work (also see Marcel, 2004) point to the stage of motor specifications as the stage at which that initial awareness of action arises. By the term "motor specifications" they refer to the operations of preparing, planning, and organizing forthcoming movements (including selection of the effectors), which Haggard and Magno (1999) attributed to a specific premotor area, the Supplementary Motor Area (SMA), and which Haggard and Eimer (1999) associated with LRPs. The stage of motor specifications is downstream of the stage of intention formation, but prior to the stage of activation of the primary motor cortex, which controls execution of the movements themselves.

It is worth pointing out that, having disproved the traditional concept of mind-brain causation, Libet (1985, 1999) salvaged an important consequence of conscious intention. He claimed that, although actions seem not to be initiated consciously, they may be inhibited or stopped consciously. This is because there is sufficient time between W judgment (i.e., W awareness) and movement onset for a conscious veto to operate. Thus, although conscious intention to act does not seem to initiate the intended action, consciousness might still allow the unconsciously initiated action to go to completion, or veto it and prevent the actual action from occurring. The view of consciously vetoing an unconsciously initiated action may be altered to one according to which the action is only consciously modified (Haggard & Libet, 2001). That clearly is not a critical alteration. The critical point is that the neural onset of a voluntary movement precedes the conscious experience of having had the intention to act, and the causal role of conscious intention is confined to the possibility of suppressing the movement.

It must be conceded that one does not easily accept the notion that intention of action follows its initiation. That is, the activation of the neural mechanisms that give rise to the intention to act follows the activation of the neural mechanisms that cause initiation of the action. What seems to have been asked in all studies that to date have addressed this issue is whether perception of the time of intentionality precedes or follows action. Suppose, however, we have a poor awareness of the time when we believe our intentionalty occurs: Then, all the evidence collected so far becomes suspect.

Even if one accepts the notion that the neural state of intention follows the neural state of action, it is still necessary to indicate what distinguishes voluntary from involuntary actions. It seems we have not yet uncovered the neural correlate of intention formation, which should always be a prerequisite for voluntary actions, regardless of whether such a correlate follows or precedes the neural events that lead to an action. As we see in one of the following sections, a signal that is available to consciousness before a voluntary action is initiated is the prediction of the sensory consequences of the action; that is, the anticipatory representations of their intended and expected effects. Perhaps, this is the direction in which to look for differences between voluntary and involuntary actions.

Performing the Intended Action (Unawareness of Action)

Studies on Neurologically Intact Participants

In what follows I summarize evidence that an unconscious visual system can accurately control visually guided behavior even when the unconscious visual representation on which it depends conflicts with the conscious visual representation on which perception depends.

In the human brain, visual information follows many distinct pathways that give rise to many distinct representations of the visual world (e.g., Milner & Goodale, 1995; Rossetti & Pisella, 2002). Of these, two are more important than the others. One produces conscious perceptual representations (i.e., perception) and governs object recognition, whereas the other produces non-conscious representations and controls visually guided behavior. Because of this organization, human beings can simultaneously hold two representations of the same visual display without becoming aware of the conflict when they are incongruent. One representation is perceptual and is perceived consciously and directly. The other representation is not consciously perceived, is unconscious, and manifests itself only through its behavioral effects. In spite of that, a healthy observer experiences one coherent visual world and performs fully appropriate motor actions to interact with that world, a conscious representation of which he or she is at the same time perceiving. This occurs because the outputs of the two visual pathways normally do not conflict, but rather lead to perceptual experiences and to actions that are consistent with one another. Therefore, demonstrating their dissociability requires studies that disrupt this

congruence as a result either of experimental intervention in healthy participants or of certain types of brain injury in neurological patients. In recent years, many studies (for reviews, see Glover, 2002, 2004; Rossetti & Pisella, 2002) have shown that introspection, on the basis of which we are convinced of perceiving a coherent visual world that is identical to the visual world that is the object of our actions, is in error: At least two visual representations operate simultaneously and in parallel when we interact with the visual world. Several of those studies have exploited perceptual illusions to explore double dissociations between perceptual and sensorimotor visual systems in non-brain-damaged participants.

One of these illusions is a variation of the Roelofs effect (Roelofs, 1935), which has been studied extensively by Bridgeman and his colleagues (e.g., Bridgeman, 2002; Bridgeman, Peery, & Anand, 1997). The location of a rectangular frame shown off-center in the visual field is misperceived so that a frame presented on the left side of the visual field, for example, will appear less eccentric than it is, and the right edge will appear somewhat to the right of the observer's center. In a typical experiment, the target is presented within the asymmetrically located frame, and its location is misperceived in the direction opposite the offset of the frame. That is, misperception of frame position induces misperception of target position (i.e., an induced Roelofs effect). In their studies, Bridgeman and his colleagues asked participants to perform two tasks when faced with a display that induced the Roelofs effect. One task was to describe the target's position verbally, and based on the verbal response, the Roelofs effect was reliably observed. In contrast, a jab at the target, performed just after it had disappeared from view, was not affected by the frame's position: The direction of the jab proved accurate despite the consciously perceived (and consciously reported) perceptual mislocation. The result is different, however, if a delay is imposed between disappearance of the target and execution of the motor response. After a delay of just 4 s, participants have the tendency to jab in the direction of the perceptual mislocation.

Aglioti, DeSouza, and Goodale (1995) made use, for a similar purpose, of the Ebbinghaus illusion (also called the Titchener circle illusion). In it, a circle is presented in the center of a circular array, composed of circles of either smaller or larger than the central one. The circle in the center appears to be larger if it is surrounded by smaller than by larger circles. One can build displays with central circles of physically different sizes that appear perceptually equivalent in size. In a 3-D version of this illusion, Aglioti et al. required participants to grasp the central circle between thumb and index finger and measured the maximal grip aperture during the reaching phase of the movement. They found that grip size was largely determined by the true, physical size of the circle to be grasped and not by its illusory size. In a subsequent study, Haffenden and Goodale (1998) measured the circle illusion either by asking participants to indicate the apparent size of a circle or to pick it up, without vision of hand and target. In both tasks the dependent variable was the distance between thumb and forefinger, so that the output mode was controlled, and only the source of information varied. The illusion appeared in both tasks, but was much smaller for the grasp response.

Similarly, Daprati and Gentilucci (1997; also see Gentilucci, Chieffi, Daprati, Saetti, & Toni, 1996) used the Mueller-Lyer illusion for contrasting grasp and perception. This illusion induces the perception of longer or shorter length of a line ended by outward- or inward-pointing arrows. In the study by Daprati and Gentilucci, participants were required to reach and grasp a wooden bar that was superimposed over the line. Results showed that the illusion was smaller when measured with grasp than with perception, even though there was some illusion under both conditions. That is, hand shaping while grasping the bar with thumb and index finger was influenced by the illusion configurations on which it was superimposed. This effect, however, was smaller than that

observed in two tasks in which participants were required to reproduce the length of the line with the same two fingers. As is the case for the Roelofs effect (see above), the difference between grasp and perception disappeared when participants were asked to delay their response. With the delay, the illusion in the motor condition became as large as in the perceptual condition.

Additional evidence of a dissociation between perception and action derives from other studies that made use of paradigms different from those based on visual illusions. The perturbation paradigm is one of these (see review in Desmurget, Pelisson, Rossetti, & Prablanc, 1998). It involves a task in which the participant is asked to reach and grasp a target. Then, often coincident with the onset of the movement by the participant, a characteristic of the target, typically its location and/or size, is changed suddenly. Many studies have demonstrated the ability of the sensorimotor system to adjust to change in the characteristics of the target well before the perceptual system can even detect the change. For example, Paulignan, MacKenzie, Marteniuk, and Jeannerod (1991) placed three dowels on a table and, by manipulating the lighting of the dowels, were able to create the impression that the target had changed location on some trials. They found that the acceleration profile of the grasping movement changed only 100 ms after the perturbation. Castiello, Bennett, and Stelmach (1993) studied the effect of size perturbation on hand shaping in a thumb and finger grasp of a target object and found that hand shaping could respond to a size perturbation in as little as 170 ms.

In a series of experiments (Castiello & Jeannerod, 1991; Castiello, Paulignan, & Jeannerod, 1991; also, see Jeannerod, 1999), participants made a simple vocal utterance to signal their awareness of the object perturbation in a version of the perturbation paradigm. Comparison of the hand motor reaction time and the vocal reaction time showed that the vocal response consistently took place after the motor correction had started. As in the Paulignan et al. (1991) study, the change in the hand trajectory occurred as early as 100 ms following the object's perturbation, whereas the vocal response by which they reported awareness of the perturbation was not observed until more than 300 ms later. The conclusion was that awareness of the perturbation lagged behind the motor action performed in response to this perturbation.

Because our perceptual system is able to disregard motion of images on the retina during eye movements, it is very difficult to detect small displacements (perturbations) that occur in the visual field during a saccade; that is, a rapid eye movement from one point to another. Often objects can be moved several degrees of visual angle during a saccade without the displacement being perceived. This phenomenon is known as saccadic suppression (see, e.g., Bridgeman, Hendry, & Stark, 1975, and Chekaluk & Llewelynn, 1992, for a review). A seminal study on this subject is the one by Bridgeman, Lewis, Heit, and Nagle (1979). It was instrumental in starting the whole line of research on the distinction between processing for action, which produces non-conscious representations, and processing for perception, which produces conscious representations. Participants were asked to point at a target that had been displaced during the saccade and then extinguished. It was found that the displacement often went undetected (saccadic suppression), but was not accompanied by corresponding visuomotor errors. That is, the pointing movement after a target jump remained accurate, irrespective of whether the displacement could be verbally reported or not. Not only did participants fail to detect the target displacement but they also failed to detect their own movement corrections.

The paradigm just described is also called the double-step paradigm, in which the first step is target presentation and the second step is target displacement. It was further exploited by Goodale, Pélisson, and Prablanc (1986) and Pélisson, Prablanc, Goodale, and Jeannerod (1986). They confirmed that participants altered the amplitude of their movements to compensate for (most) of the target displacement, even though they were not able to detect either the target jump or their own movement correc-

tions. Not even forced-choice guesses about the direction of the jump could discriminate between forward and backward target perturbations.

Visual masking too has been used to study the dissociation between motor control and conscious perception (e.g., Kunde, Kiesel, & Hoffman, 2003; Neumann & Klotz, 1994; Taylor & McCloskey, 1990; Vorberg, Mattler, Heinecke, Schmidt, & Schwarzbach, 2003; see Bar, 2000, and Price, 2001, for reviews). It seems that masking (and metacontrast) eliminates conscious perception of the stimulus, whereas the ability of the (non-perceived) stimulus to trigger an action (a motor response) remains largely intact. In the study of Neumann and Klotz, for example, the observer was unable to discriminate reliably the presence from the absence of the masked stimulus, but the masked (and undetected) stimulus affected the speed of voluntary responses, even in a two-choice situation that required integrating form information with position information. Thus, this study clearly confirmed that motor action in response to a visual stimulus can be dissociated from the verbal report about detection of that same stimulus. Similarly, Vorberg et al. (2003) showed that experimental manipulations that modify the subjective visual experience of invisible masked stimuli do not affect the speed of motor responses to those same stimuli. In addition, they found that, over a wide range of time courses, perception and unconscious behavioral effects of masked visual stimuli obey different temporal laws.

The studies I have summarized above used different procedures, but the results converge toward supporting a rather counter-intuitive conclusion: An unconscious visual system controls visually guided actions and operates more or less simultaneously with the conscious visual system. When the representations produced by the unconscious visual system conflict with the representations produced by the conscious visual system, the former prevail and guide action. Here, as well as in the studies that are summarized in the following section, two dissociations emerge. One is between (conscious) perceptual and (unconscious) sensorimotor visual systems. The other, more interesting dissociation is between awareness of the representations, produced by the perceptual system, which one believes guide action, and the lack of awareness of the representations, produced by the sensorimotor system, which actually guide action.

Studies on Brain-Damaged Patients

The deficits observed in some neuropsychological patients lend further (and perhaps more convincing) support to the notion of dissociability between perceptual and sensorimotor visual systems. In particular, optic ataxia and visual agnosia patients not only strongly support the case for a double dissociation between perceptual recognition of objects and reaching and grasping of the same objects but also suggest that the neurological substrates for these two systems are located selectively in the ventral (object perception) and dorsal (object-directed action) streams of the visual pathways (e.g., Milner & Goodale, 1995).

A patient, DF, first reported by Goodale, Milner, Jakobson, and Carey (1991; also see Milner & Goodale, 1995), perhaps provides the clearest evidence to date for dissociation between perception and action, showing a reciprocal pattern to optic ataxia (see below). DF developed a profound visual-form agnosia following a bilateral lesion of the occipito-temporal cortex. She was unable to recognize object size, shape, and orientation. She failed even when she was asked purposively to match her forefinger-thumb grip aperture to the size of visually presented target objects. In sharp contrast, when instructed to pick up objects by performing prehension movements, the patient was quite accurate, and the maximum size of her grip correlated normally with the size of the target object. Apparently, DF possessed the ability to reach out and grasp objects with remarkable accuracy and thus could process visual information about object features that she could not perceive accurately, if at all. However, although her ability to grasp target objects was truly remarkable, it had certain limitations. In normal participants, grip size still correlates well with object width even when a temporal delay of up to 30 s is interposed between disappearance of the target object and execution of the motor response. In DF, instead, evidence of grip scaling was no longer present after a delay of just 2 s.

If DF's performance is compared with the performance of patients with posterior parietal lesions, impairments in perceptual recognition of objects and in object-directed action seem to be clearly dissociated. Jeannerod (1986) and Perenin and Vighetto (1988) reported patients with lesions to the posterior parietal lobe, who showed a deficit that is termed optic ataxia. Patients with optic ataxia have difficulties in directing actions to objects presented in their peripheral visual field. Their visually directed reaching movements are inaccurate, often systematically in one direction. In addition, these movements are altered kinematically, especially concerning duration, peak velocity, and deceleration phase. However, patients with optic ataxia, in contrast to visual agnosic patients, are not impaired in the recognition of the same objects that they are unable to reach correctly.

In addition to optic ataxia and visual agnosia, blindsight is another neurological deficit that provides support to the dissociation between conscious perception and non-conscious motor control. Patients with extensive damage to the primary visual area in the occipital lobe (area V_1 or BA_{17}) are regarded as cortically blind because they do not acknowledge seeing stimuli in the affected parts of their visual fields. It is possible, however, to demonstrate that their behavior can still be controlled by visual information (e.g., Farah, 1994; Milner & Goodale, 1995; Weiskrantz, 1986). The paradoxical term "blindsight" was initially coined by Sanders, Warrington, Marshall, and Weiskrantz (1974) to refer to all such non-conscious visual capacities that are spared in cortically blind parts of the visual field. The first of the many reports that patients with cortical blindness can use visuospatial information to guide their actions within the blind field showed this by asking patients to move their eyes toward a light that they insisted they could not see. Their movements were statistically correlated with the location of the light (Poeppel, Held, & Frost, 1973). Further, Zihl (1980; Zihl & von Cramon, 1985) found that accuracy of their saccadic responses can be improved markedly as a consequence of training. Even more striking evidence was provided by Perenin and Jeannerod (1978), who showed accurate pointing within the blind fields in several patients. It is clear that considerable visual control of the direction and amplitude of both eye and arm movements is present in cortically blind patients.

In addition, it turns out that some patients with blindsight seem to have a residual ability to use shape and size information. Perenin and Rossetti (1996) asked a completely hemianoptic patient to "post" a card into a slot placed at different angles within his blind field. His performance was statistically well above chance. Yet, when asked to make perceptual judgments of the slot's orientation, either verbally or by manual matching, the patient was at chance level in his affected field. Perenin and Rossetti also demonstrated that the patient, when tested with the same tasks as those used to test agnosic patient DF, and the task of "posting" the card was one of them, could reach out and grasp rectangular objects with a certain accuracy in his affected field: As in normal participants, the wider the object, the greater the anticipatory hand-grip size during reaching. Yet again the patient failed when asked to make perceptual judgments: With either verbal or manual response his attempts were uncorrelated with object size. As was the case with agnosic patient DF, orientation and size can be processed in cortically blind visual fields, but only when used to guide a motor action and not for perceptual tasks. Remember, however, that patients with optic ataxia show the converse dissociation. They are unable to use visual information to guide motor acts, such as reaching and grasping, but they still retain the ability to perceive consciously the objects on which they are unable to act.

The evidence summarized above strongly supports the notion that the human brain produces at least two functionally distinct representations of a given visual display, which, under some conditions, can be different. One originates from a conscious system that performs visual object (pattern) recognition. The other is a motor-oriented representation that is unconscious, can be in conflict with the conscious perceptual representation, and can accurately control visually guided behavior in spite of the potential conflict with the conscious representation. The distinction between these two pathways originated nearly 40 years ago (Schneider, 1967; Trevarthen, 1968). Trevarthen named the two systems "focal" and "ambient": The focal system was postulated to be based on the geniculostriate pathway and to be devoted to pattern recognition; the ambient system was thought to be based on the superior colliculus and related brainstem structures and to be devoted to visually guided behavior. This anatomical and functional distinction became known as the now classical distinction between a system specialized for answering the question "what is it" and a system specialized for answering the question "where is it" (Schneider, 1969). Later on, both systems were shown also to have a cortical representation: The successor to the focal system (i.e., the "what" system) comprises an occipito-temporal pathway, whereas the ambient system (i.e., the "where" system) includes an occipito-parietal pathway as well as the superior colliculus (Ungerleider & Mishkin, 1982).

More precisely, the cortical pathway for the "what" system is the ventral occipito-temporal route that links striate cortex (V1 or BA17) to prestriate areas and from there reaches the inferotemporal cortex on both sides via callosal connections. Lesions to this pathway abolish object discrimination without damaging perception of spatial relations among objects (visual-form agnosia). The other, dorsal pathway diverges from the ventral one after the striate cortex and links the prestriate areas to the posterior part of the parietal lobe. Lesions to this pathway produce visuospatial deficits characterized by errors in establishing the relative positions of spatial landmarks and by localization deficits during object-directed actions (optic ataxia).

As described above, cases of optic ataxia, visual-form agnosia, and blindsight, as well as a number of studies on healthy participants, have shown that the anatomical dorsal-ventral distinction relates more precisely to a distinction between the processing of what an object is and of how to direct action, rather than of where an object is located (Milner & Goodale, 1995).

The phenomenon of blindsight merits a few additional words (Milner & Goodale, 1995; Stoerig & Cowey, 1997). The dorsal stream also has substantial inputs from several subcortical visual structures in addition to input from V1. In contrast, the ventral stream depends on V1 almost entirely for its visual input. As a consequence, damage to V1, even though it affects either stream, deprives the ventral stream of all its input, leaving instead the dorsal stream with much of its input from its associated subcortical structures (the superior colliculus, in particular). It is possible, thus, to demonstrate that their behavior can be controlled by visual information provided by intact subcortical visual structures via the dorsal stream. What these patients are unable to do is to process visual information through the ventral stream, which depends primarily on V1 for its visual input. In addition, it is impossible for these patients to give any but the most rudimentary kind of perceptual report about their visual experiences (regions of brightness, motion, or change).

As already noted, differences between immediate and delayed actions have been reported in neurologically intact observers, as well as in neurological patients (see Rossetti & Pisella, 2002, for an extensive discussion of this issue). In general, what emerges is that the insertion of a temporal gap between target presentation and response execution renders the features of the representation on which the motor action depends more similar to the perceptual representation on which the verbal report depends. In partic-

ular, the delay seems to bring about a shift from reliance on a (non-conscious) representation formed online, and used for immediate action control, to a (conscious) representation retrieved from memory and used for verbal report. The former would be short-lived and would compute stimulus location in egocentric coordinates, whereas the latter would last much longer and would compute stimulus location in allocentric coordinates. Egocentric coordinates have their origin in the observer, often in its body midline. Allocentric coordinates have their origin outside the observer, often in an external object. While an action is being performed, the location of its target seems to be computed in terms of egocentric coordinates. In contrast, if a delay is introduced between target presentation and verbal report, target location seems to be computed in terms of allocentric coordinates.

Evidence is available that supports this distinction. In a study reported by Rossetti and Pisella (2002), for example, immediate and delayed pointing toward proprioceptive targets was tested in blindfolded participants. On each trial a target was presented on one out of six possible locations lying on a circle centered in the starting point. In a preliminary session participants had been trained to point to these positions and to associate a number (from 1 to 6) with each target. When the task was to point to the target immediately, the participants' pointing distribution was unaffected by the target array and was elongated in the movement direction. That showed the use of an egocentric reference frame. In contrast, when pointing was delayed and/or was accompanied by a simultaneous verbal response of the target number, the participants' pointing distribution tended to align with the target array, perpendicular to movement direction. That showed the use of an allocentric frame of reference. In the words of Rossetti and Pisella (2002, p. 86), "when action is delayed and the object has disappeared, the parameters of object position and characteristics that are used by the action system can only be accessed from a cognitive sustained representation. This type of representation . . . relies on different reference frames with respect to the immediate action system."

In conclusion, it is clear that the sensorimotor representations that support immediate action are not conscious and are short-lived. If a delay is introduced, long-term and conscious perceptual representations take over. The frames of reference on which immediate and delayed actions depend also differ, consistent with the needs of an action system and a perceptual representational system.

Perception of the Effects of the Performed Action

So far I have reviewed evidence that suggests that many aspects of action, from initiation to appreciation of the percepts that guide them, occur without awareness (i.e., unconsciously). Now I argue that one aspect of an action that is normally available to awareness is the sensory consequence(s) of that action, or, more precisely, the prediction of the sensory consequences of that action (Blakemore & Frith, 2003; also see Frith, Blakemore, & Wolpert, 2000; Jeannerod, Farrer, Franck, Fourneret, Posada, Daprati, & Georgieff, 2003). However, although there is only limited awareness of the actual sensory consequences of an action (i.e., of action effects) when they are successfully predicted in advance, we are very often aware of the actual action effects when they deviate from what we expect.

As was pointed out by Blakemore and Frith (2003), here the important point is to distinguish between the predicted action effects and the actual action effects. Normally, we are aware of the former but not of the latter, unless the latter do not conform to our expectations, in which case they too become conscious. In some circumstances, however, not even quite large deviations from the expected action effects reach consciousness (see, e.g., Fourneret & Jeannerod, 1998). When a task is overlearned and becomes automatic with practice, and thus can be carried out without the intervention of executive functions (see below), we are not aware of the predicted consequences of our actions, as well as of the intended actions and of the motor programs that are executed to achieve the actions' goals.

Representations of action effects have at least two functions in performing an action (a special issue of *Psychological Research/Psychologische Forschung*, edited by Nattkemper and Ziessler, 2004, was devoted to the role of action effects in the cognitive control of action). First, after having executed a particular action, one needs to compare the obtained effects with the effects that the action intended to accomplish. Hence, anticipatory effect representations are involved in the evaluation of action results. Second, one plans and executes actions with the aim of producing some desired effects. Hence, anticipations of action goals are involved in action control. Both functions require representations of an action goal and of action effects.

The notion that intentional actions are controlled by anticipatory representations of their intended and expected effects goes back at least to James (1890). It is termed the "ideomotor theory," which basically proposes that actions are represented in memory by their effects and in turn these effects are used to control actions. In the last 15 years or so, the ideomotor approach has been reformulated within the framework of cognitive psychology by Prinz and his colleagues (e.g., Prinz, 1997; Hommel, Muesseler, Aschersleben, & Prinz, 2001), who used the term "common coding theory of perception and action."

The simplest idea would, of course, be that our awareness of initiating an action originated from sensory signals arising in the moving limbs. This seems unlikely, though, because such signals are not available until after the limbs have started to move. Instead, our awareness seems to depend on a signal that precedes the action. A signal that is available before an action is initiated is the prediction of the sensory consequences of the action; that is, the anticipatory representations of their intended and expected effects.

Haggard and Magno (1999), by using Libet's paradigm (see above), found a dissociation between perceived onset and action initiation. They showed that the perceived time of action onset is slightly delayed (by about 75 ms) if the motor cortex is stimulated with transcranial magnetic stimulation (TMS), whereas this stimulation causes a greater delay (of about 200 ms) in the initiation of the actual movement. This finding is compatible with the notion that it is the prediction of the effects of the action that corresponds to the onset of the action. However, it is not evidence of such a relation. In a subsequent study, which too exploited Libet's paradigm, Haggard et al. (2002b; also, see Eagleman & Holcombe, 2002; Frith, 2002) explored the time course of the binding of actions and their effects in consciousness by investigating the sensory consequences of an event being causally linked to an observer's action. Their aim was to clarify what happens to our subjective judgment of timing of events when an event is causally linked to an observer's intentional action. They showed that the perceived time of intentional actions and the perceived time of their sensory consequences were attracted together in consciousness, so that participants perceived intentional movements as occurring later and their sensory consequences as occurring earlier than they actually did. In the voluntary condition, participants noted, by watching a revolving hand on a clock face, the time of onset of their intention to perform an action (i.e., a key-press). In the TMS condition, they noted the time of a muscle twitch produced by magnetic stimulation of the motor cortex. In the sham TMS condition, they noted the time of an audible click made by TMS in the absence of motor stimulation. In the auditory condition, they just noted the time of a tone.

When the first three conditions were followed, after 250 ms, by a tone, large perceptual shifts occurred in the time of awareness of conscious intention, the TMS-induced twitch, and click produced by the sham TMS. Only awareness of the voluntary key-press and awareness of the tone were perceived as being closer in time than they actu-

ally were. Awareness of the voluntary key-press was shifted later in time, toward the consequent tone, whereas awareness of the tone was shifted earlier in time, toward the action. The involuntary, TMS-induced movement produced perceptual shifts in the opposite direction. The sham TMS showed minimal perceptual shifts. Based on these findings Haggard et al. (2002b) suggested the existence of a mechanism that associates (or binds) together awareness of a voluntary action and awareness of its sensory consequences, bringing them closer in perceived time. In other words, "the brain would possess a specific mechanism that binds intentional actions to their effects to construct a coherent conscious experience of our own agency" (p. 385). Note that several other behavioral studies confirmed that representations of actions and their effects tend to be integrated (see chapters by Hazeltine, by Stoet & Hommel, and by Ziesser & Nattkemper in Prinz & Hommel, 2002) and the observation of the existence of attraction effects between percepts of stimuli and percepts of movements that might have caused the occurrence of those same actions.

Even if ample empirical evidence suggests that motor actions are cognitively coded based on their sensory effects, it does not imply that they are initiated by consciously accessing their sensory effects. It is entirely possible that binding between actions and their consequences and/or action retrieval via action consequences occur unconsciously (Haggard et al., 2002a). For example, Kunde (2004) reasoned that, based on the ideomotor theory, initiating a certain action is mediated by retrieving its perceptual effects, which then in turn activate the particular motor pattern that normally brings about these anticipated perceptual effects. Also, the ideomotor theory implies that actions (as motor patterns) should become activated by presenting the effect codes that represent their consequences. In other words, actions should be induced by perceiving their effects. Kunde found that responding to a visual target was faster and more accurate when the target was briefly preceded by the visual effect of the required response. Interestingly, this response priming that was induced by the action effects was independent of prime perceptibility and occurred when the prime was not consciously perceived. That indicates that consciousness is not a necessary condition for action effects to evoke their associated actions (motor patterns).

Regardless of whether binding among intention, action, and consequence occurs consciously or unconsciously, or, more likely, in part consciously and in part unconsciously, it has both unconscious and conscious elements (Haggard et al., 2002a); inference based on timing plays a critical role in producing the illusion of consciously willed actions. The conscious experiences of intention, action, and action effects are compressed in time. This unification is instrumental in producing the experience of voluntary action. Even though he overlooked the role of action effects, Wegner (2003, p. 67) has clearly expressed this notion, by saying, "When a thought appears in consciousness just before an action (priority), is consistent with the action (consistency), and is not accompanied by conspicuous alternative causes of the action (exclusivity), we experience conscious will and ascribe authorship to ourselves for the action."

Before leaving this section it is perhaps useful briefly to touch on the work on mirror neurons. Mirror neurons (see Rizzolatti & Craighero, 2004, for a recent and extensive review) are found in the premotor and parietal cortex of the monkey. They selectively discharge both when the monkey performs a given action and when the monkey observers another living being perform a similar action. Thus, mirror neurons code specific actions performed by the agent or by others. Evidence exists that a mirror-neuron system, similar to that of the monkey, is present in humans. The notion that mirror neurons are involved in action understanding is corroborated by the observation that they discharge also in conditions in which the monkey does not see the action but nonetheless is provided sufficient clues to create a mental representation of what action is being performed (Kohler, Keysers,

Umiltà, Fogassi, Gallese, & Rizzolatti, 2002; Umiltà, Kohler, Gallese, Fogassi, Fadiga, & Rizzolatti, 2001). Visual clues of the action can be critical to trigger mirror neurons only if they allow the observer to understand the action. Auditory clues originating from an action performed behind a screen can replace visual clues if auditory clues convey the crucial information about the meaning of the action. However, an fMRI study (Buccino, Lui, Canessa, Patteri, Lagravinese, & Rizzolatti, 2004) showed that only actions belonging to the motor repertoire of the observer excite the human mirror system, whereas actions that do not belong to the motor repertoire of the observer do not. They are recognized through a different, purely visual mechanism.

Especially interesting in the present context are studies (e.g., Schubotz & von Cramon, 2002) that showed that the human frontal mirror region is important not only for the understanding of goal-directed actions but also for recognizing predictable patterns of visual change. In conclusion, it seems clear that mirror neurons play a role in coding intended actions and their consequences.

Executive Functions

Another popular view is that investigation of the processes underlying intentional actions are related closely to executive functions (also termed "control processes"), such as those involved in planning, problem solving, inhibition of prepotent response, and response to novelty. If the notion is to be preserved that consciousness is necessary for intentional actions, and intentional actions belong to the realm of executive functions, then drawing on the Supervisory Attentional System model (SAS; Norman & Shallice, 1986; Shallice, 1988, 1994) can be useful in this context.

It is widely accepted that the vast majority of our cognitive processes operate in automatic fashion, with little or no need for conscious, intentional control: When specific conditions occur, automatic mental processes are triggered and run autonomously to completion, independent of intentional initiation and conscious guidance (e.g., Dehane & Naccache, 2001, and chapters in Umiltà & Moscovitch, 1994). In the information-processing accounts of consciousness developed in the 1970s, the unitary nature and control functions of consciousness were explained in terms of the involvement of a limited capacity higher-level processing system (Mandler, 1975; Posner & Klein, 1973; Umiltà, 1988). However, because of the diversification of processing systems that originated from the research in cognitive psychology, cognitive neuropsychology, and cognitive neuroscience, and because of the realization that processing systems are often informationally encapsulated (Fodor, 1983; Moscovitch & Umiltà, 1990), it became less plausible to associate the unitary characteristics of consciousness with the operations of any single processing system. Shallice (Norman & Shallice, 1986; Shallice, 1988, 1994) put forward an alternative approach by proposing that a number of high-level systems have a set of special characteristics that distinguish them from the cognitive systems devoted to routine informationally encapsulated processes. He maintained that the contrast between the operations of these special systems and those realizing informationally encapsulated processes corresponded in phenomenological terms to that between conscious and nonconscious processes.

His model is clearly concerned with action selection and thus is very relevant to the present discussion. It has three main processing levels. The lowest is that of special-purpose processing subsystems, each specialized for particular types of operations. There are a large number of actions and thought schemas, one for each well-learned routine task or subtask. Schemas are selected for operation through a process involving mutually inhibitory competition (contention scheduling). To cope with non-routine situations, an additional system – SAS – provides modulating activating input to schemas in contention scheduling. In later versions of the SAS, the SAS is held to

contain a variety of special-purpose subsystems localized in different parts of the prefrontal cortex and in the anterior cingulate.

This model relates to consciousness of action if one assumes that conscious processes require the mediation of the SAS and lead directly to the selection in contention scheduling of a schema for thought or action. On this view, consciousness of a particular content causes the selection of a schema. Once a schema is selected, and provided that it does not conflict with a strongly established schema for a different action (as in cases requiring inhibition of prepotent response), then action may proceed without any transfer of information from the SAS. Therefore, the principle that consciousness is necessary for intentional action can be stated more precisely as the hypothesis that tasks involving intentional action recruit conscious processes, whereas automatic actions do not. Keep in mind, however, that, as Block (1995) argued, such attempts to account for the functional role of conscious information ("access-consciousness") do not address the phenomenological properties of conscious experience ("phenomenological-consciousness").

Some results are especially important for a precise specification of the relation between consciousness and intentional action. Studies on blindsight (see above) show that awareness of the location of the stimulus is not necessary for accurate performance on a simple pointing task when participants are asked to guess. As was maintained by Marcel (1988; also, see Natsoulas, 1992), blindsight patients can learn to initiate goal-directed actions (e.g., reaching), which means that their actions can be visually guided in the absence of conscious visual representations on which the actions are based. Very strikingly, patients protest that they are not performing the visually guided behavior that they are in fact performing. However, awareness of the presence of the visual stimulus has to be provided by an auditory cue for the initiation of the pointing action to occur (Weiskrantz, 1997). That seems to indicate that the blindsight patient requires input via the SAS to initiate a pre-existing schema for pointing. Once that schema is initiated, non-conscious information held in special-purpose processing systems can serve to guide action.

Lesion studies in monkeys and humans indicate that prefrontal lesions (i.e., SAS lesions) have little effect on performance in automatic tasks, but instead have a strong effect on tasks that seem to be crucially dependent on conscious processes, among which is the spontaneous generation of intentional actions. A striking consequence of a deficit of the SAS is the so-called utilization behavior sign. It manifests itself as a component of a very grave dysexecutive syndrome and is typically observed in patients with a bilateral focal frontal lesion. If there is some object that can be used or manipulated within the patient's field of view and within reach, the patient will use it to perform actions appropriate to the object, even though they have been explicitly and insistently asked not to do so. It is clear that in utilization behavior the non-intended actions are environment-driven with the mediation of contention scheduling. The SAS plays very little role or no role at all in them. In effect, most current explanations of this bizarre behavior suggest a weakening of whatever mechanism is responsible for ensuring the implementation of intended actions, such that it overrides, under normal circumstances, automatic or environmentally driven actions. Apparently, utilization behavior is attributable to the failure to inhibit inappropriate actions, rather than a failure to select appropriate actions.

Environmentally driven actions are quite common in normal people under circumstances that suggest a diminished influence of the SAS, such as when we are in a distracted state or when we are engaged in another task; this is especially so when the level of arousal is low. In these cases, an apparently intentional action is initiated in the absence of full awareness. Examples include reaching for and drinking from a glass while talking, slips of highly routine actions that involve action lapses of the "capture" error type, and changing gears or braking while driving (Norman, 1981; Norman & Shallice, 1986; Reason, 1984; Shallice, 1988). It is not clear whether it would be correct to speak of these actions as completely unconscious. Probably not. These anomalous cases are explained by distinguishing between the influence of the stimulus on contention scheduling, and the influence on the SAS. The selection of well-learned and relatively undemanding schemas need not require the SAS involvement. As already mentioned in the context of action effects, overlearned tasks are common examples of actions (schemas) that can be carried out with very limited awareness. With sufficient practice many tasks can become automatic and can be carried out without the intervention of the SAS; that is, without any need to consciously control the actions required by the task.

Deficits in the Control of Action That Co-Occur with Abnormalities in Consciousness

At first sight one of the most striking abnormalities in the control of action would not seem to be accompanied by abnormality of consciousness, but rather by disownership of action. This abnormality is termed the "anarchic hand" sign, which was first described by Della Sala, Marchetti, and Spinnler (1991, 1994; also see Frith, Blakemore, & Wolpert, 2000; Marcel, 2004, for extensive discussions). It is often confused with the "alien hand" sign (Marchetti & Della Sala, 1998; Prochazka et al., 2000) or with the utilization behavior sign (e.g., Lhermitte, 1983; also, see above), which too are abnormalities in the control of action. The anarchic hand sign is unimanual, and patients describe the anarchic hand as having a "will of its own," which, of course, terrifies them. The affected hand performs unintended (even socially unacceptable) but complex, well-executed, goal-directed actions that compete with those performed by the non-affected hand. Sometimes the patient talks to his or her anarchic hand, asking it to desist, and often the patient succeeds in stopping it only by holding it down with the other hand. The patient seems to lack any sense of intention for what concerns the anarchic action performed by the affected hand.

It is important to keep in mind that the patient is aware that the anarchic hand belongs to him or her. What is alien, what the patient disowns, is the action the hand performs, not the hand itself. In contrast, in the case of the alien hand sign, the affected hand does not feel to be one's own. This seems to be a sensory phenomenon and has little to do with motor action. As I have already noted when I discussed the dysexecutive syndrome, patients with damage to the frontal lobe may show utilization behavior that is characterized by the fact that the sight of an object elicits a stereotyped action that is inappropriate in the current context. The abnormal aspect of consciousness that accompanies utilization behavior is not so much lack of awareness of the action or lack of awareness of the intention to act, but rather the erroneous experience that those inappropriate and unwanted actions are experienced as intended (also, see Frith et al., 2000).

The anarchic hand sign is often associated with unilateral damage to the SMA contralateral to the hand affected by the pathological sign. Considering that the function of the anterior part of the SMA is likely to be essentially inhibitory, and a movement can only be initiated by the primary motor cortex (M1 or BA4) when activity in the anterior part of the SMA declines, Frith et al. (2000) have suggested that the anarchic hand sign manifests itself when the anterior part of the SMA is damaged. In the absence of the inhibitory influence by the SMA on one side, appropriate stimuli would trigger the automatic action of the corresponding hand. In support of the inhibitory role of the SMA is the observation of its preferential activation when movements are imagined but their execution must be inhibited. It is clear that this hypothesis renders the anarchic hand sign very similar, if not identical, to the utilization behavior sign. Actually, the former would be a special case of the latter. Marcel (2004), however, has con-

vincingly argued that that is not the case. His main point is that the patient who shows utilization behavior does not disown the hand that performs it. If the SMA is the source of the LRP (see above) and the LRP is correlated with voluntary action, it makes sense that damage to the SMA would be associated with lack of awareness, or distortions in awareness, associated with movement initiation and execution.

A possibility, with which Marcel (2004) would not agree, though, is that disownership of action in the anarchic hand sign is attributable to lack of awareness of the intention that guides the affected hand's behavior. In other words, the patient would disown the action (not the hand that performs it, as happens in the alien hand sign) because the intention that has initiated that action is not available to consciousness. If that is so, then the anarchic hand sign would after all be a deficit in the control of action that co-occurs with an abnormality of consciousness. Perhaps, it is caused by an abnormality of consciousness of the predicted action effects.

By following Frith et al. (2000), I have maintained (see above) that what normally reaches consciousness is the prediction of the action effects, rather than the actual action effects. Frith et al. suggest that the same is true of the state of the limbs after a movement; that is, the conscious experience of a limb would normally be based on its predicted state, rather than on its actual state. In effect, the predicted state would play a greater role than sensory feedback. That, after all, is not surprising, considering that one of the effects of an action is to bring about a new state of the limbs that were involved in performing the action.

As argued by Frith et al. (2000), the notion that the conscious experience of a limb originates from its predicted state is supported by the phenomenon of the "phantom limb." After amputation of all or part of a limb, patients may report that, in spite of the fact they know very well that there is no longer a limb, they still feel the presence of it. Although the limb is missing because of the amputation, the premotor and the motor cortex can still program a movement of it, which causes computation of the predicted state. Because the predicted state becomes available, the phantom limb will be experienced as moving. It is interesting to note that Ramachandran and Hirstein (1998) have proposed that the experience of the phantom limb depends on mechanisms located in the parietal lobes, and Frith et al. (2000) have independently suggested that parietal lobes are involved in the representation of predicted limb positions.

The phantom limb may also manifest itself after deafferentation of a limb that in fact is still present. Patients may or may not be aware of the existing but deafferented limb. If they are, then the phantom limb is experienced as a supernumerary limb. One or more supernumerary limbs can be experienced even if the real limbs are not deafferented. Frith et al. (2000) have proposed that these phenomena are all attributable to the failure to integrate two independent sources of information concerning the position of the limbs. One derives from the motor commands, which are issued from the cortical premotor and motor areas independent of whether the limb is still present. The other source derives from sensory feedback and of course is available only if the limb is still present.

After right-hemisphere damage, leading to paralysis of the left side (usually associated with anesthesia of that same side), patients may show anosognosia for hemiplegia. By that term it is meant that they are unaware of the impairment that concerns the motor control of their left limb(s) (see, e.g., Pia, Neppi-Modona, Ricci, & Berti, 2004, for a review). Anosognosia for hemiplegia is often associated with unilateral neglect for the left side of space and the location of the lesion is in the right parietal lobe. The interesting question here is why patients with this condition develop the false belief that there is nothing wrong with the paralyzed limb, even to the point of claiming to have moved it to command when in fact no movement has occurred. The explanation provided by Frith et al. (2000) once more makes recourse to the hypothesis that awareness of initiating a movement is based on a representation of the predicted action effects, rather than of the actual action effects. A representation of the predicted action effects can be formed as long as the motor commands can be issued. Thus, a patient with a paralyzed limb would have the normal experience of initiating a movement with that limb as long as the motor commands can be issued. The belief that the movement was performed is not contradicted by the discrepancy between the predicted action effects and the actual action effects because, as I have already noted, even healthy individuals may have a remarkably limited awareness of this discrepancy (Fourneret & Jeannerod, 1998). In addition, when patients have suffered a parietal lesion, damage to the parietal cortex is likely to impair awareness of the state of the motor system and cause a failure to detect the discrepancies between the actual and the predicted action effects.

Finally, according to Frith et al. (2000; also, see Kircher & Leube, 2003) the same explanation is applicable to those patients with schizophrenia who describe experiences of alien control, in which actions (as well as thoughts or emotions) are performed by external agent, rather than by their own will. In healthy individuals, self-monitoring systems enable one to distinguish the products of self-generated actions (or thoughts) from those of other-generated actions (or thoughts). It has been postulated that self-monitoring is normally based on a comparison between the intention underlying an action and its observed effects (Jeannerod, 1999; Jeannerod et al., 2003). The proposal of Frith et al. is that the experience of alien control arises from a lack of awareness of the predicted limb position (action effect). In particular, they suggest "that, in the presence of delusions of control, the patient is not aware of the predicted consequences of a movement and is therefore not aware of initiating a movement" (2000, p.1784).

In conclusion, it would seem that the proposal according to which it is the prediction of the action effects, rather than the actual action effects, that reaches consciousness can explain some odd and apparently unrelated phenomena. In the case of the phantom limb, for example, the limb is of course missing because of the amputation. However, the premotor and motor cortical areas are intact and can still program a movement of the missing limb. The action effects are computed and reach consciousness, thus producing the conscious experience of a limb. Similarly, anosagnosic patients may be unaware of their paralyzed limb because they can still compute the predicted action effects of that limb. Conversely, in the case of the anarchic hand and of schizophrenic patients, the action effects would not be computed in advance, causing the feeling of lack of intention, which in turn would induce the patient to disown the action and attribute it to an external agent.

Conclusion

Although being aware of initiating and controlling actions is a major component of conscious experience, empirical evidence shows that much of the functioning of our motor system occurs without awareness. That is to say, it appears that, in spite of the contents of our subjective experience, we have only limited conscious access to the system by which we control our actions. This limited access is certainly not concerned with the detailed mechanisms of the motor system. Even higher-order processes seem to be denied access to consciousness. Awareness of initiating an action occurs after the movement has begun in the brain area devoted to motor processes. Similarly, awareness of choosing one action rather than another occurs after brain correlates indicate that the choice already has been made. Therefore, it is important to provide an answer to the question of what are the (few) levels, in the process of action generation, and execution, that can be accessed consciously while many more levels occur without awareness.

With much simplification, it can be said that voluntary actions, from the simplest to the most complex ones, involve the following three stages: intention to perform an action, performance of the intended action, and perception of the effects of the performed action. In principle, therefore, consciousness may manifest itself at all three stages. At the first stage, conscious intention to perform an action may arise. At the second stage, the intended action may be consciously performed. At the third stage, the effects of the performed action may be consciously perceived.

For the first stage, research suggests that intentions for carrying out voluntary actions are generated unconsciously and retrospectively referred consciously to the action when it has been executed. That is, the evidence is that consciousness of intention to perform an action is the consequence, rather than the cause, of activity in the brain. There is a mechanism that binds together in consciousness the intention to act and the consequences of the intended action, thus producing the illusion of free will. That represents a paradox: An individual may accurately attribute the origin of an action to him- or herself and yet lack online consciousness of the events that have led to that action.

The interpretation outlined above is the most obvious one of the available evidence. However, there is still the possibility that there is something wrong with it. In particular, what seems to be missing in that interpretation is a clear indication of what differentiates willed (voluntary) actions from involuntary actions. Perhaps what is needed is an intention whose brain correlates begin to initiate an action before we can signal exactly when that intention began. The advanced representations of the effects of an action might prove instrumental in contrasting a voluntary action with one that is truly automatic.

Human beings consistently show visual illusions when they are tested with perceptual measures, whereas the illusions do not manifest themselves when they are tested with motor measures. They can point accurately to targets that have been illusorily displaced by induced motion. A target can be moved substantially during a saccadic eye movement, and the observer will deny perceiving the displacement even while pointing correctly to the new, displaced position. These dissociations recall the situation in blindsight and visual agnosia, where patients can perform visually guided tasks without visual experience and without awareness of the accuracy of their behavior. The explanation is that action execution depends on one of two visual systems. There is a sensorimotor or "how" system, which controls visually guided behavior without access to consciousness. Its memory is very brief, only long enough to execute an act, but it possesses an egocentrically calibrated metric visual space that the other system lacks. The other is a cognitive or "what" system, which gives rise to perception and is used consciously in pattern recognition and normal visual experience. The processes that compose the second stage do not have access to consciousness either.

In contrast, we certainly are aware of some aspects of the current state of the motor system at the third stage in the sequence that leads to execution of an action. These, however, do not seem to be concerned with the perception of the action effects. Normally, we are not aware of the action effects if they match our prediction of the expected effects; that is, of the effect we predict the action should produce. Rather, we are aware of the stream of motor commands that have been issued to the system. Or, to be more precise, when performing an action, we are aware of the prediction of its effects, which, of course, depend on the motor commands that were planned in the premotor and motor cortical areas.

The conclusion that we are not aware of most of our own behavior is disturbing, but the evidence to date clearly indicates that very few aspects of action generation and execution are accessible to consciousness.

Acknowledgments

Preparation of this chapter was supported by grants from MIUR and the University of Padua. The author thanks Morris Moscovitch for very helpful suggestions on a previous version of the chapter.

References

Agliotti, S., DeSouza, J. F. X., & Goodale, M. A. (1995). Size-contrast illusions deceive the eye but not the hand. *Current Biology*, 5, 679–685.

Bar, M. (2000). Conscious and nonconscious processing of visual identity. In Y. Rossetti & A. Revonsuo (Eds.), *Beyond dissociation: Interaction between dissociated implicit and explicit processing* (pp. 153–174). Amsterdam: John Benjamins.

Blakemore, S. J.-, & Frith, C. D. (2003). Self-awareness and action. *Current Opinions in Neurobiology*, 13, 219–224.

Block, N. (1995). On a confusion about a function of consciousness. *Behavioral Brain Sciences*, 18, 227–287.

Bridgeman, B. (2002). Attention and visually guided behavior in distinct systems. In W. Prinz & B. Hommel (Eds.), *Attention and performance XIX: Common mechanisms in perception and action* (pp. 120–135). Oxford: Oxford University Press.

Bridgeman, B., Hendry, D., & Stark, L. (1975). Failure to detect displacement of the visual world during saccadic eye movements. *Vision Research*, 15, 719–722.

Bridgeman, B., Lewis, S., Heit, F., & Nagle, M. (1979). Relation between cognitive and motor-oriented systems of visual perception. *Journal of Experimental Psychology: Human Performance and Attention*, 5, 692–700.

Bridgeman, B., Peery, S., & Anand, S. (1997). Interaction of cognitive and sensorimotor maps of visual space. *Perception and Psychophysics*, 59, 456–469.

Buccino, G., Lui, F., Canessa, N., Patteri, I., Lagravinese, G., & Rizzolatti, G. (2004). Neural circuits involved in the recognition of actions performed by non-conspecifics: An fMRI study. *Journal of Cognitive Neuroscience*, 16, 1–14.

Castiello, U., Bennett, K., & Stelmach, G. (1993). Reach to grasp: The natural response to perturbation of object size. *Experimental Brain Research*, 94, 163–178.

Castiello, U., & Jeannerod, M. (1991). Measuring time of awareness. *Neuroreport*, 2, 797–800.

Castiello, U., Paulignan, Y., & Jeannerod, M. (1991). Temporal dissociation of motor responses and subjective awareness. *Brain*, 114, 2639–2655.

Chekaluk, E., & Llewelynn, K. (1992). Saccadic suppression: A functional viewpoint. In E. Chekaluk & K. Llewelynn (Eds.), *Advances in psychology, 88: The role of eye movements in perceptual processes* (pp. 3–36). Amsterdam: Elsevier.

Daprati, E., & Gentilucci, M. (1997). Grasping an illusion. *Neuropsychologia, 35*, 1577–1582.

Dehaene, S., & Naccache, L. (2001). Towards a cognitive neuroscience of consciousness: Basic evidence and a workspace framework. *Cognition, 79*, 1–37.

Della Sala, S., Marchetti, C., & Spinnler, H. (1991). Right-sided anarchic (alien) hand: A longitudinal study. *Neuropsychologia, 29*, 1113–1127.

Della Sala, S., Marchetti, C., & Spinnler, H. (1994). The anarchic hand: A fronto-mesial sign. In F. Boller & J. Grafman (Eds.), *Handbook of neuropsychology* (Vol. 9, pp. 204–248). Amsterdam: Elsevier.

Dennett, D.C. (1998). The myth of double transduction. In S. R. Hameroff, A. W. Kaszniak, & A. C. Scott (Eds), *Towards a science of consciousness. II. The second Tucson discussions and debates* (pp. 97–107). Cambridge, MA: MIT Press.

Desmurget, M., Pelisson, D., Rossetti, Y., & Prablanc, C. (1998). From eye to hand: Planning goal-directed movements. *Neuroscience and Biobehavioral Review, 22*, 761–788.

Eagleman, D. M., & Holcombe, A. O. (2002). Causality and perception of time. *Trends in Cognitive Sciences, 6*, 323–325.

Farah, M. J. (1994). Visual perception and visual awareness after brain damage: A tutorial review. In C. Umiltà & M. Moscovitch (Eds.), *Attention and performance XV: Conscious and nonconscious information processing* (pp. 37–76). Cambridge, MA: MIT Press.

Fodor, J. (1983). *The modularity of mind.* Cambridge, MA: MIT Press.

Fourneret, P., & Jeannerod, M. (1998). Limited conscious monitoring of motor performance in normal subjects. *Neuropsychologia, 36*.

Fried, I., Katz, A., McCarthy, G., Sass, K. J., Williamson, P., Spencer, S. S., & Spencer, D. D. (1991). Functional organization of human supplementary motor cortex studied by electrical stimulation. *Journal of Neuroscience, 11*, 3656–3666.

Frith, C. D. (2002). Attention to action and awareness of other minds. *Consciousness and Cognition, 11*, 481–487.

Frith, C. D., Blakemore, S.-J., & Wolpert, D. M. (2000). Abnormalities in the awareness and control of action. *Philosophical Transactions of the Royal Society, London B, 355*, 1771–1788.

Gentilucci, M., Chieffi, S., Daprati, E., Saetti, M. C., & Tonil. (1996). Visual illusions and action. *Neuropsychologia, 34*, 369–376.

Glover, S. (2002). Visual illusions affect planning but not control. *Trends in Cognitive Sciences, 6*, 288–292.

Glover, S. (2004). Separate visual representations in the planning and control of action. *Behavioral and Brain Sciences, 27*, 3–78.

Goodale, M. A., Milner, D. A., Jakobson, L. S., & Carey, D. P. (1991). A neurological dissociation between perceiving objects and grasping them. *Nature, 349*, 154–156.

Goodale, M. A., Pélisson, D., & Prablanc, C. (1986). Large adjustments in visually guided reaching do not depend on vision of the hand or perception of target displacement. *Nature, 320*, 748–750.

Haffenden, A., & Goodale, M. A. (1998). The effect of pictorial illusion on prehension and perception. *Journal of Cognitive Neurosciences, 10*, 122–136.

Haggard, P., Aschersleben, G., Gehrke, J., & Prinz, W. (2002a). Action, binding, and awareness. In W. Prinz & B. Hommel (Eds.), *Attention and performance XIX: Common mechanisms in perception and action* (pp. 266–285). Oxford: Oxford University Press.

Haggard, P., Clark, S., & Kalogeras, J. (2002b). Voluntary actions and conscious awareness. *Nature Neuroscience, 5*, 382–385.

Haggard, P., & Eimer M. (1999). On the relation between brain potentials and awareness of voluntary movements. *Experimental Brain Research, 126*, 128–133.

Haggard, P., & Libet, B. (2001). Conscious intention and brain activity. *Journal of Consciousness Studies, 11*, 47–63.

Haggard, P., & Magno, E. (1999). Localising awareness of action with transcranial magnetic stimulation. *Experimental Brain Research, 17*, 102–107.

Hazeltine, E. (2002). The representational nature of sequence learning: evidence for goal-based codes. In W. Prinz & B. Hommel (Eds.),

Attention and performance XIX: Common mechanisms in perception and action (pp. 673–689). Oxford: Oxford University Press.

Hommel, B., Muesseler, J., Aschersleben, G., & Prinz, W. (2001). The theory of event coding (TEC): A framework for perception and action planning. *Behavioral and Brain Sciences*, 24, 849–937.

James, W. (1890). *Principles of psychology*. New York: Holt.

Jeannerod, M. (1986). The formation of finger grip during prehension: A cortically mediated visuomotor pattern. *Behavioral Brain Research*, 19, 99–116.

Jeannerod, M. (1999). To act or not to act: Perspectives on the representation of actions. *Quarterly Journal of Experimental Psychology*, 52 A, 1–29.

Jeannerod, M., Farrer, M., Franck, N., Fourneret, P., Posada, A., Daprati, E., & Georgieff, N. (2003). Action recognition in normal and schizophrenic subjects. In T. Kircher & A. David (Eds.), *The self in neuroscience and psychiatry* (pp. 119–151). Cambridge: Cambridge University Press.

Kircher, T. T. J., & Leube, D. T. (2003). Self-consciousness, self-agency, and schizophrenia. *Consciousness and Cognition*, 12, 656–669.

Kohler, E., Keysers, C., Umiltà, M. A., Fogassi, L., Gallese, V., & Rizzolatti, G. (2002). Hearing sounds, understanding actions: Action representation in mirror neurons. *Science*, 297, 846–848.

Kunde, W. (2004). Response priming by supraliminar and subliminar action effects. *Psychological Research / Psychologische Forschung*, 68, 91–96.

Kunde, W., Kiesel, A., & Hoffman, J. (2003). Conscious control over the content of unconscious cognition. *Cognition*, 88, 223–242.

Lhermitte, F. (1983). 'Utilization behavior' and its relation to lesions of the frontal lobes. *Brain*, 106, 237–255.

Libet, B. (1985). Unconscious cerebral initiative and the role of conscious will in voluntary action. *Behavioral and Brain Sciences*, 8, 529–566.

Libet, B. (1999). Do we have free will? *Journal of Consciousness Studies*, 6, 47–57.

Libet, B., Gleason, C. A., Wright, E. W., & Pearl, D. K. (1983). Time of conscious intention to act in relation to onset of cerebral activity (readiness-potential): The unconscious initiation of freely voluntary act. *Brain*, 106, 623–642.

Mandler, G. (1975). *Mind and emotion*. New York: Wiley.

Marcel, A. J. (1988). Phenomenal experience and functionalism. In A. J. Marcel & E. Bisiach (Eds.), *Consciousness in contemporary science* (pp. 121–158). Oxford: Oxford University Press.

Marcel, A. J. (2004). The sense of agency: Awareness and ownership of action. In J. Roessler & N. Eilan (Eds.), *Agency and self-awareness* (pp. 48–93). Oxford: Clarendon.

Marchetti, C., & Della Sala, S. (1998). Disentangling the alien and anarchic hand. *Cognitive Neuropsychiatry*, 3, 191–207.

McCloskey, D. I., Colebatch, J. G., Potter, E. K., & Burke, D. (1983). Judgements about onset of rapid voluntary movements in man. *Journal of Neurophysiology*, 49, 851–863.

Milner, D. A., & Goodale, M. A. (1995). *The visual brain in action* (Oxford Psychology Series 27). Oxford: Oxford University Press.

Moscovitch, M., & Umiltà, C. (1990). Modularity and neuropsychology: Implications for the organization of attention and memory in normal and brain-damaged people. In M. F. Schwartz (Ed.), *Modular deficits in Alzheimer-type dementia* (pp. 1–59). Cambridge, MA: MIT Press.

Natsoulas, T. (1992). Is consciousness what psychologists actually examine? *American Journal of Psychology*, 105, 363–384.

Nattkemper, D., & Ziessler, M. (Eds.). (2004). Cognitive control of action: The role of action effects. *Psychological Research / Psychologische Forschung*, 68(2/3).

Neumann, O., & Klotz, W. (1994). Motor responses to nonreportable, masked stimuli: Where is the limit of direct parameter specification? In C. Umiltà & M. Moscovitch (Eds.), *Attention and performance XV: Conscious and nonconscious information processing* (pp. 123–150). Cambridge, MA: MIT Press.

Norman, D. A. (1981). Categorisation of action slips. *Psychological Review*, 88, 1–15.

Norman, D. A., & Shallice, T. (1986). Attention to action: Willed and automatic control of behaviour. In R. J. Davidson, G. E. Schwartz, & D. Shapiro (Eds.), *Consciousness and self regulation* (Vol. 4, pp. 189–234). New York: Plenum.

Paulignan, Y., MacKenzie, C. L., Marteniuk, R. G., & JeannerodM. (1991). Selective perturbation of visual input during prehension movements. I. The effect of changing object position. *Experimental Brain Research*, 83, 502–512.

Pélisson, D., Prablanc, C., Goodale, M. A., & Jeannerod, M. (1986). Visual control of reaching movements without vision of the limb. II. Evidence of fast unconscious processes correcting the trajectory of the hand to the final position of double-step stimulus. *Experimental Brain Research*, 62, 303–311.

Perenin, M.-T., & Jeannerod, M. (1978). Visual function within the hemianoptic field following early cerebral hemidecortication in man. 1. Spatial localization. *Neuropsychologia*, 16, 1–13.

Perenin, M.-T., & Rossetti, Y. (1996). Grasping without form discrimination in a hemianopic field. *Neuroreport*, 7, 793–797.

Perenin, M.-T., & Vighetto, A. (1988). Optic ataxia. *Brain*, 111, 643–674.

Pia, L., Neppi-Modona, M., Ricci, R., & Berti, A. (2004). The anatomy of anosognosia for hemiplegia: A meta-analysis. *Cortex*, 40, 367–377.

Poeppel, E., Held, R., & Frost, D. (1973). Residual visual function after brain wounds involving the central visual pathways in man. *Nature*, 243, 295–296.

Posner, M. I., & Klein, R. M. (1973). On the function of consciousness. In S. Kornblum (Ed.), *Attention and Performance IV* (pp. 21–35). New York: Academic Press.

Price, M.C. (2001). Now you see it, now you don't. Preventing consciousness with visual masking. In P.G. Grossenbacher (Ed.), *Finding consciousness in the brain: A neurocognitive approach (Advances in consciousness research* (Vol. 8, pp. 25–60). Amsterdam: John Benjamins.

Prinz, W. (1997). Perception and action planning. *European Journal of Cognitive Psychology*, 9, 129–154.

Prinz, W., & Hommel, B. (Eds.). (2002) *Attention and Performance XIX: Common mechanisms in perception and action*. Oxford: Oxford University Press.

Prochazka, A., Clarac, F., Loeb, G. E., Rothwell, J. C., & Wolpaw, J. R. (2000). What do *reflex* and *voluntary* mean? Modern views on an ancient debate. *Experimental Brain Research*, 130, 417–432.

Ramachandran, V. S., & Hirstein, W. (1998). The perception of phantom limbs. *Brain*, 121, 1603–1630.

Reason, J. T. (1984). Lapses of attention. In R. Parasuraman, R. Davies, & J. Beatty (Eds.), *Varieties of attention* (pp. 151–183). Orlando, FL: Academic Press.

Rizzolatti, G. & Craighero, L. (2004). The mirror-neuron system. *Annual review of neuroscience* 27, 169–192.

Roelofs, C. (1935). Optische Localisation. *Archiv fuer Augenheilkunde*, 109, 395–415.

Rossetti, Y., & Pisella, L. (2002). Several 'vision for action' systems: A guide to dissociating and integrating dorsal and ventral functions (Tutorial). Attention and visually guided behavior in distinct systems. In W. Prinz & B. Hommel (Eds.), *Attention and performance XIX: Common mechanisms in perception and action* (pp. 62–119). Oxford: Oxford University Press.

Sanders, M. D., Warrington, E. K., Marshall, J., & Weiskrantz, L. (1974). 'Blindsight': Vision in a field defect. *Lancet*, 20, 707–708.

Schneider, G. E. (1967). Contrasting visuomotor functions of tectum and cortex in the golden hamster. *Psychologische Forschung*, 31, 52–62.

Schneider, G. E. (1969). Two visual systems. *Science*, 163, 895–902.

Schubotz, R. I., & von Cramon, D. Y. (2002). Predicting perceptual events activates corresponding motor schemes in lateral premotor cortex: An fMRI study. *Neuroimage*, 15, 787–796.

Shallice, T. (1988). *From neuropsychology to mental structure*. Cambridge: Cambridge University Press.

Shallice, T. (1994). Multiple levels of control processes. In C. Umiltà & M. Moscovitch (Eds.), *Attention and performance XV: Conscious and nonconscious information processing* (pp. 395–420). Cambridge, MA: MIT Press.

Stoerig, P., & Cowey, A. (1997). Blindsight in man and monkey. *Brain*, 120, 535–559.

Stoet, G., & Hommel, B. (2002). Interaction between feature binding in perception and action. In W. Prinz & B. Hommel (Eds.), *Attention and performance XIX: Common mechanisms in perception and action* (pp. 538–552). Oxford: Oxford University Press.

Taylor, T. L., & McCloskey, D. (1990). Triggering of preprogrammed movements as reactions to masked stimuli. *Journal of Neurophysiology*, 63, 439–446.

Trevarthen, C. B. (1968). Two mechanisms of vision in primates. *Psychologische Forschung*, 31, 299–337.

Umiltà, C. (1988). The control operations of consciousness. In A. J. Marcel & E. Bisiach (Eds.), *Consciousness in contemporary science* (pp. 334–356). Oxford: Oxford University Press.

Umiltà, C., & Moscovitch, M. (1994) (Eds.). *Attention and performance XV: Conscious and nonconscious information processing.* Cambridge, MA: MIT Press.

Umiltà, M. A., Kohler, E., Gallese, V., Fogassi, L., Fadiga, L., & Rizzolatti, G. (2001). "I know what you are doing": A neurophysiological study. *Neuron*, 32, 91–101.

Ungerleider, L. G., & Mishkin, M. (1982). Two cortical visual systems. In D. Ingle, M. A. Goodale, & R. J. W. Mansfield (Eds.), *Analysis of visual behavior* (pp. 549–586). Cambridge, MA: MIT Press.

Vorberg, D., Mattler, U., Heinecke, A., Schmidt, T., & Schwarzbach, J. (2003). Different time courses for visual perception and action priming. *Proceedings of the National Academy of Science USA*, 100, 6275–6280.

Wegner, D. M. (2003). The mind's best trick: How we experience conscious will. *Trends in Cognitive Sciences*, 7, 65–69.

Wegner, D. M. (2005). Précis of the illusion of conscious will. *Behavioral and Brain Sciences*, 27, 649–659.

Weiskrantz, L. (1986). *Blindsight. A case study and implications.* Oxford: Oxford University Press.

Weiskrantz, L. (1997). *Consciousness lost and found. A neuropsychological exploration.* Oxford: Oxford University Press.

Zhu, J. (2004). Locating volition. *Consciousness and Cognition*, 13, 1–21.

Ziesser, M., & Nattkemper, D. (2002). Effect anticipation in action planning. In W. Prinz & B. Hommel (Eds.), *Attention and performance XIX: Common mechanisms in perception and action* (pp. 645–672). Oxford: Oxford University Press.

Zihl, J. (1980). Blindsight: Improvement of visually guided eye movements by systematic practice in patients with cerebral blindness. *Neuropsychologia*, 18, 71–77.

Zihl, J., & von Cramon D. (1985). Visual field recovery from scotoma in patients with postgeniculate damage: A review of 55 cases. *Brain*, 108, 335–365.

D. Linguistic Considerations

CHAPTER 13

Language and Consciousness

Wallace Chafe

Abstract

This chapter focuses on two distinct, linguistically oriented approaches to language and consciousness taken by Ray Jackendoff and Wallace Chafe. Jackendoff limits consciousness to uninterpreted imagery, and he presents evidence that such imagery is external to thought because it is too particular, does not allow the identification of individuals, and fails to support reasoning. If all we are conscious of is imagery and imagery does not belong to thought, it follows that we are not conscious of thought. Chafe distinguishes between immediate consciousness, involved in direct perception, and displaced consciousness, involved in experiences that are recalled or imagined. He sees the former as including not only the sensory experiences discussed by Jackendoff but also their interpretation in terms of ideas. Displaced consciousness includes sensory imagery that is qualitatively different from immediate sensory experience, but it too is accompanied by ideational interpretations that resemble those of immediate experience. Both the imagistic and the ideational components of consciousness are held to be central to thought as thought is usually understood. Both approaches are supported with linguistic data, but data that are different in kind.

Introduction

How are language and consciousness related? Can the study of language shed light on the nature of consciousness? Can an improved understanding of consciousness contribute to an understanding of language? Some scholars in the past have gone so far as to equate conscious experience with linguistic expression. Within philosophy, as one example, we find Bertrand Russell (1921, p. 31) writing, "A desire is 'conscious' when we have told ourselves that we have it." In psychology we have Jean Piaget's statement (1964/1967, p. 19) that "thought becomes conscious to the degree to which the child is able to communicate it." Given our current knowledge, however, we might want to go beyond simply equating consciousness with language. This chapter focuses on some possible insights originating in linguistics, the discipline for which language is the primary focus, including the relation of language to broader aspects of humanness. It may be that a language-centered approach can provide some answers that have eluded those in other disciplines who have approached these questions from their own perspectives.

Consciousness-related questions were rarely asked within linguistics in the 20th century, a period during which most scholars in that field would have found them irrelevant or pointless. Stamenov (1997, p. 6) mentions correctly that "there is at present little research in linguistics, psycholinguistics, neurolinguistics and the adjacent disciplines which explicitly addresses the problem of the relationships between language and consciousness." This neglect can be traced historically to the association of consciousness with "mentalism," a supposedly unscientific approach to language that was forcefully rejected by Leonard Bloomfield and his followers, who dominated linguistics during the second quarter of the 20th century. Bloomfield often repeated statements such as the following, taken from his obituary of Albert Paul Weiss, a behaviorist psychologist who strongly influenced him: "Our animistic terms (mind, consciousness, sensation, perception, emotion, volition, and so on) were produced, among the folk or by philosophers, in pre-scientific times, when language was taken for granted" (Bloomfield, 1931, p. 219). Bloomfield's enormous influence led his followers to regard such notions as pointless appeals to something akin to magic. Noam Chomsky, whose influence eclipsed that of Bloomfield in the latter half of the 20th century, departed from Bloomfield by expressing an interest in the mind, but his interests were restricted to an abstract variety of syntax that in basic respects remained loyal to Bloomfield's constraints and that, by its very nature, precluded a significant role for consciousness.

Language Structure, Discourse and the Access to Consciousness, a book characterized by its editor, M. I. Stamenov, as "the first one dedicated to a discussion of some of the aspects of this topic" (1997, p. 6),

includes various authors who show that at least some aspects of language structure lie *outside* of consciousness. Langacker (1997, p. 73), for example, concludes his chapter by saying that "it should be evident that grammar is shaped as much by what we are not consciously aware of as by what we are." Although that may be true, the discussion to follow explores the question of whether and to what extent consciousness and the structure of language are mutually interactive.

This exploration can hardly proceed without taking into account ways in which both language and consciousness are related to other mental phenomena, and especially to those captured by such words as *thought* and *imagery*. These are, of course, words in the English language, and they can mean different things to different people. Natsoulas (1987) discusses six different ways of understanding *consciousness*, and exactly what is meant by *thought* and *imagery* is hardly uncontroversial. The underlying problem, of course, is that consciousness, thought, and imagery all refer to private phenomena that are inaccessible to direct public observation. Although their referents may seem obvious to introspection and may be pervasive ingredients of people's mental lives, it can be frustratingly difficult to achieve agreement on what they include or where their boundaries lie.

It may seem presumptuous to suggest new solutions to problems that have occupied scholars for millennia, but continuing advances in both scholarship and supporting technology have encouraged new approaches to old puzzles in many areas, including the study of language and its relation to the mind. This chapter focuses on two partially different answers to the questions raised at the beginning of this introduction. One has been proposed by Ray Jackendoff, the other by Wallace Chafe. Both agree that people are conscious of imagery and affect. Beyond that, however, their conclusions differ. Jackendoff limits consciousness to imagery and excludes imagery from thought, above all because it is unable to account for inferences and other logical processes. It follows that people are not conscious of thought. Chafe suggests that imagery is inseparable from its interpretation in terms of ideas and orientations of ideas and that thought exhibits both imagistic and ideational components that are simultaneously available to consciousness. Both scholars support their suggestions with evidence from language, but the evidence is of different kinds.

Is Thought Unconscious?

We can consider first the view that people are conscious only of imagery and that imagery is not an element of thought, a view that was forcefully presented by Jackendoff in his book, *Consciousness and the Computational Mind* (1987) and subsequently refined in Chapter 8 of *The Architecture of the Language Faculty* (1997), which was in turn a somewhat modified version of Jackendoff (1996). He identifies three basic levels of information processing. At the outermost level, closest to "the outside world," are brain processes of which we are totally unconscious; among these processes are such visual phenomena as fusing the retinal images from the two eyes into a perception of depth or stabilizing the visual field when the eyes are moving. We are conscious of the results of these processes – depth perception and a stabilized visual field – but not of how they happen. When it comes to auditory phenomena, we may be conscious of speech sounds, such as vowels, consonants, syllables, and pitch contours, but not of how raw sound comes to be interpreted in those ways. Mechanisms at the outer layer of perception do their work outside of consciousness.

What we *are* conscious of are the visual forms, speech sounds, and so on that belong to what Jackendoff calls the intermediate level of information processing. It is intermediate between unconscious perceptual processes and a deeper level inhabited by thought, of which we are also not conscious. In short, we are conscious of imagery associated with the various sense modalities, and we are also conscious of affect, but that is all. We certainly *have* thoughts, but it is only through their manifestations in imagery, nonverbal or verbal, that we can be

conscious of what they are. We may hear the sounds of language overtly or in our heads, but the thoughts expressed by those sounds lie outside of consciousness. "We become aware of thought taking place – we catch ourselves in the act of thinking – only when it manifests itself in linguistic form, in fact phonetic form" (1997, p. 188). Nonverbal imagery provides other conscious manifestations of thought, but it too is distinct from thought itself.

Jackendoff discusses several kinds of evidence that thought is unconscious. For one thing, our minds sometimes seem to solve problems without our being conscious of them doing it: "We have to assume that the brain is going about its business of solving problems, but not making a lot of conscious noise about it; reasoning is taking place without being expressed as language" (1997, p. 188). He emphasizes the role of reasoning as a fundamental aspect of thought, suggesting that if he were to say to you *Bill killed Harry*, you would know from that statement that Harry died. You might at first think you knew it because you had an image of Bill stabbing Harry and Harry falling dead, but this image is too specific because "the thoughts expressed by the words *kill* and *die*, not to mention the connections between them, are too general, too abstract to be conveyed by a visual image." Thus, the knowledge that killing entails dying must belong to unconscious thought. He also mentions the problem of identification. "How do you know that those people in your visual image are Bill and Harry respectively?" Beyond that, there are many concepts like *virtue* or *social justice* or *seven hundred thirty-two* for which no useful images may be available. Such words express elements of thought of which there is no way to be directly conscious.

Jackendoff takes pains to separate thought from language. A major ingredient of consciousness is inner speech, and we may for that reason be tempted to equate inner speech with thought. But, for one thing, "thinking is largely independent of what language one happens to think in" (1997, p. 183). Whether one is speaking English or French or Turkish, one can, he says, be having essentially the same thoughts. The form of a particular language is irrelevant to the thoughts it conveys, as shown by the fact that an English speaker can be having the same thoughts as a Japanese speaker, even though the English speaker puts the direct object after the verb and the Japanese speaker before it. Furthermore, one can be conscious of linguistic form that is dissociated from any thought at all, as with the rote learning of a ritual in an unfamiliar language. Conversely, in the tip-of-the-tongue phenomenon "one feels as though one is desperately trying to fill a void... One is aware of having requisite conceptual structure" but the phonological structure is missing (1987, p. 291). He cites various other examples to show that thought is unconscious and that all we are conscious of is the phonetic imagery that expresses thought, often accompanied by nonverbal imagery. "The picture that emerges from these examples is that although language *expresses* thought, thought itself is a separate brain phenomenon" (1997, p. 185).

The Relation of Language to Thought

In spite of this disconnect between conscious phonetic imagery and unconscious thought, Jackendoff discusses three ways in which "language helps us think." First of all, language makes it possible to *communicate* thoughts:

> Without language, one may have abstract thoughts, but one has no way to communicate them (beyond a few stereotyped gestures such as head shaking for affirmation and the like).... Language permits us to have history and law and science and gossip.... As a result of our having language, vastly more of our knowledge is collective and cumulative than that of nonlinguistic organisms... Good ideas can be passed on much more efficiently (1997, p. 194).

So, even though thought itself is unconscious, language provides an important way of sharing thoughts.

Second, "having linguistic expressions in consciousness allows us to pay attention to them" (1997, p. 200). Jackendoff views

attention as a process for zeroing in on what consciousness makes available:

> I am claiming that consciousness happens to provide the basis for attention to pick out what might be interesting and thereby put high-power processing to work on it. In turn, the high-power processing resulting from attention is what does the intelligent work; and at the same time, as a byproduct, it enhances the resolution and vividness of the attended part of the conscious field (p. 200).

Furthermore, "without the phonetic form as a conscious manifestation of the thought, attention could not be applied, since attention requires some conscious manifestation as a 'handle'" (p. 201). Language is particularly useful because it "is the only modality of consciousness in which the abstract and relational elements of thought correspond even remotely to separable units" (p. 202). Units of that kind are not available to other components of consciousness, such as visual imagery.

Third, language gives access to what Jackendoff calls *valuations* of percepts. Valuations include judgments that something is novel or familiar, real or imagined, voluntary or involuntary, and the like. Language provides "words like *familiar, novel, real, imaginary, self-controlled, hallucination* that express valuations and therefore give us a conscious link to them. This conscious link permits us to attend to valuations and subject *them* to scrutiny" (p. 204). On awakening from a dream, for example, we can say, "It was just a dream," but a dog cannot do that – it cannot bring the valuation into consciousness in that way.

Summary

Jackendoff finds thought to be totally unconscious, but he suggests that it is manifested in consciousness by way of language, which itself enters consciousness only by way of phonetic imagery. Nevertheless, language enhances the power of thought in three ways: by allowing thought to be communicated, by making it possible to focus attention on selected aspects of thought (particularly on its relational and abstract elements), and by providing access to valuations of thought.

Jackendoff has presented a serious and responsible challenge to those who would like to believe that we are conscious of thought. If his suggestion that we are *not* conscious of thought seems on the face of it to conflict with ordinary experience, it is a conclusion that follows inevitably from these two propositions:

(1) Consciousness is limited to phonetic and nonverbal imagery.

(2) Thought is independent of those two kinds of imagery.

Behind these propositions lie particular ways of understanding consciousness, thought, and imagery, and the subjective nature of these phenomena leaves room for other interpretations. The remainder of this chapter explores other possibilities, based in large part on Chafe (1994, 1996a,b), with occasional references to William James (1890), whose views on "the stream of thought" are still worth taking seriously (Chafe, 2000).

Preliminaries to an Alternative View

Because *consciousness, thought,* and *imagery* do refer to subjective experiences, further discussion can benefit from specifying how these words are used here. Consciousness is notoriously difficult to define in an objective way, but some of its properties will emerge as we proceed.

Some Properties of Consciousness

There is agreement by Jackendoff, Chafe, and others that conscious experiences have two obvious components that may be present simultaneously. One of them is related to sensory experience, and the other is affect. A case could be made for the affective component being in some ways the more basic. It is certainly the oldest in terms of evolution, and it still underlies much of human behavior. It is reflected in language

in ways that have not been sufficiently studied (but see Chafe, 2002; Wierzbicka, 1999), and it is mentioned only in passing below.

It should also be apparent that consciousness may be focused on the environment immediately surrounding the conscious self, in which case we can speak of an *immediate* consciousness. However, it may also be focused on experiences remembered or imagined or learned from others, in which case we can characterize it as a *displaced* consciousness. Immediate consciousness involves direct perception, whereas displaced consciousness takes the form of imagery – an attenuated experiencing of visual, auditory, and/or other sensory information. Immediate and displaced consciousness are qualitatively different (Chafe, 1994).

Consciousness is dynamic, constantly changing through time, and it resembles vision in possessing both a focus and a periphery – a fully active and a semiactive range – analogous to foveal and peripheral vision. Its focus is severely limited in content and duration, typically being replaced every second or two, whereas its periphery changes at longer, more variable intervals. In that respect consciousness shares the properties of eye movements as they are monitored, for example, while people look at pictures (Buswell, 1935) and also while they talk about them (Holšánová, 2001). Language reflects the foci of active consciousness in prosodic phrases, whereas larger coherences of semiactive consciousness appear in hierarchically organized topics and subtopics (Chafe, 1994). This view sees the process termed *attention* as simply the process by which consciousness is deployed.

The Nature of Imagery

It is well known that direct perception of the environment is not a matter of simply registering what is "out there." Information that enters the eyes and ears is always interpreted in ways that are shaped in part by genetic endowments, in part by cultural and individual histories. Imagery is no different. It is not an attenuated replaying or imagining of raw visual, auditory, or other sensory input. Sensory experiences do not appear in that form even in immediate consciousness, and images are subject to considerably more interpretive processing. Experiencing imagery is not like looking at a picture. But even pictures are interpreted as containing particular people, structures, trees, or whatever, which are oriented and related in particular ways.

Although images always involve interpretations, there may be some circumstances under which it is possible to be conscious of interpretive phenomena in the absence of accompanying sensory experience. It is thus useful to distinguish these two aspects of consciousness. The word *imagery* is restricted here to sense-related phenomena, real or imagined, whereas the interpretive experiences that are often (but need not be) accompanied by imagery are termed *ideational*.

The imagistic component of consciousness may or may not include the sounds of language. On that basis one can distinguish verbal from non-verbal consciousness, the latter being focused on non-verbal aspects of experience. One may experience non-verbal imagery without language, one may experience language as well as non-verbal imagery, or one may experience language alone, either overtly or covertly. There are evidently individual differences in this regard (Poltrock & Brown, 1984). William James, having asked people about the images they had of their breakfast table, reported that

> an exceptionally intelligent friend informs me that he can frame no image whatever of the appearance of his breakfast-table. When asked how he then remembers it at all, he says he simply 'knows' that it seated four people, and was covered with a white cloth on which were a butter-dish, a coffee-pot, radishes, and so forth. The mind-stuff of which this 'knowing' is made seems to be verbal images exclusively (James, 1890, p. 265).

There are two possible interpretations of the phrase *verbal images* in this quote. James probably concluded that his friend experienced the sounds of language and nothing more. More interesting is the possibil-

ity that his friend was not restricted to the sounds of language, but had conscious access to ideational interpretations of those sounds devoid of sensory accompaniments. That is the more interesting interpretation because it suggests that one can indeed experience ideational consciousness while at the same time imagery is restricted (in some people) to the sounds of language. In other words, an absence of non-verbal imagery need not deprive individuals like James's friend of a consciousness of ideas. This consciousness of ideas, with or without accompanying imagery, can plausibly be considered a major component of thought.

Components of Language

Figure 13.1 lays out some basic stages that intervene between a person's interaction with the outside world and the utterance of linguistic sounds. These phenomena interact in ways that are obscured by their assignment to separate boxes. In the final analysis they are realized in structures and processes within the brain, distributed in ways that are surely not separated so neatly. Nevertheless, there are certain distinguishable principles of organization that do lend themselves to discussion in these terms.

The boxes on the far left and right, labeled *reality* and *sound*, represent phenomena external to the human mind. We need not concern ourselves with problems that might be associated with the word *reality*; here it is shorthand for whatever people think and talk about. It includes events and states and people and objects encountered in the course of living that may in some way affect a person's thoughts, but that would exist whether they were processed by a mind or not. *Sound* on the right represents external, physical manifestations of the sounds of language: their articulation by the vocal organs, their acoustic properties outside the human body, and their reception in the ears of a listener.

The boxes labeled *thought* on the left and *phonology* on the right represent immediate results of the interpretive processes that the mind applies to those external phenomena. Each has its own patterns of organization.

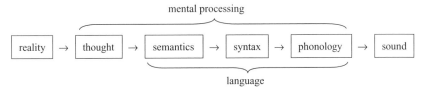

Figure 13.1. Stages in the production of language.

Thought need not be as directly related to external reality as Figure 13.1 suggests, because a great deal of it involves remembering one's own earlier experiences or experiences learned from others, or imagining things for which no direct contact with reality ever existed. Linguists have devoted a great deal of time and effort to understanding phonological organization, but have concerned themselves much less with the organization of thought, for reasons that have more to do with the history of the discipline than with the ultimate relevance of thought to language.

The two remaining boxes, labeled *semantics* and *syntax*, represent ways in which elements of thought are adjusted to fit the requirements of language so that they can be associated with sounds, manipulated symbolically, and communicated to other minds. If languages never changed, semantic structures could be submitted directly to phonology. But languages do change, and semantic structures are reshaped through processes of lexicalization and grammaticalization to form syntactic structures that are no longer related to thoughts fully or directly. It is these syntactic structures that then proceed to be associated with sounds (Chafe, 2005). Missing from Figure 13.1 is consciousness, and its place in this picture is our chief concern.

Consciousness of Phonology

It can be instructive to consider briefly what is involved in consciousness of the sounds of language, because what happens on the right side of Figure 13.1 may be simpler and easier to comprehend than what happens on the left. The important lesson is that the mind does not operate exclusively with raw sound. Jackendoff describes con-

sciousness of what he calls either phonological structure or phonetic form, pointing out that "we experience the inner speech stream as segmented into words and possibly further into syllables or individual segments. In addition, the rhythm, stress pattern, and intonation of inner speech must come from phonological units as well" (1987, p. 288). In educational psychology there have been numerous studies of children's awareness of segments ("phonemes") and syllables and the relevance of such awareness to the acquisition of reading (e.g., Anthony & Lonigan, 2004; Castles & Coltheart, 2004). It is clear that we are conscious of *interpreted* sounds, not physical sounds alone. Sounds are organized by the mind into linguistically relevant elements of which we can be conscious, although their physical manifestations can have a place in consciousness too. We organize sound into syllables, words, intonational patterns, and the rest, in association with their sensory manifestations. The point is that phonological consciousness has both imagistic and interpretive components. Can the same be said of thought, our focus in this chapter?

Consciousness of Thought

It is helpful at this point to consider an example of actual speech. The three lines below were taken from a conversation among three women, in the course of which they discussed some local forest fires. As they developed this topic, one of them said,

(a) You'd look at the sun,
(b) it just looked red;
(c) I mean you couldn't see the sun.

She was talking about something she had experienced 2 days earlier, when she had direct access to the unusual appearance of the sun. At that time her perception of it was in her immediate consciousness. It must have been primarily a visual experience, but it was probably accompanied by a feeling of awe or wonder at this rather extreme departure from normality. It was not just a registering of sensory information, but an interpretation that included a selection of certain salient ideas from those that must have been potentially available. Among them was the idea of an event she verbalized in line (a) as *look* and an object she verbalized as *the sun*. The visual input to her eyes had been interpreted by her mind, and she was conscious of both the interpretation and its sensory correlates. If the word *thought* means anything at all, this immediate experience, with its ideational and imagistic components, was at that moment present in her thought. It was an immediate perceptual experience, it had both ideational and imagistic components, she was conscious of it, and she was thinking about it.

When, 2 days later, she uttered the language above, the earlier experience was once more active in her consciousness. This time, however, it was no longer immediate but displaced. It was probably experienced in part as imagery, but her language expressed an interpretation in terms of ideas. By uttering this language she must have intended to activate a partially similar experience in the consciousness of her listeners. They, for their part, must have experienced their own displaced consciousness, but for them it was twice displaced. We can note a difference between the relative success of communicating the ideational elements and communicating their sensory accompaniments. The speaker's ideas as such could be communicated more or less intact, but their sensory accompaniments necessarily differed for her listeners from what she was experiencing. The ideas expressed as *the sun* and *looked red* could survive the communication process, but their sensory manifestations could only be reshaped by the listeners' imaginations.

Experiential and communicative events of this kind are ubiquitous in everyday speech, and indeed in everyday life. They are so common as to seem trivial, but they shed light on the basic nature of consciousness, thought, imagery, and communication by providing evidence for properties of immediate and displaced consciousness, for the mutually supportive roles of ideational and imagistic consciousness, and for the relation of consciousness to thought.

The Organization of Thought

The dynamic quality of consciousness is evident in the constantly changing content of its focus. The prosody of language divides speech into a sequence of prosodic phrases, each expressing a focus of the speaker's consciousness. Each focus is replaced by another at intervals in a typical range of 1 or 2 s (cf. Pöppel, 1994). This progression through time was described by James in his often-quoted statement regarding the stream of thought, where, it may be noted, he equated thought and consciousness:

> As we take, in fact, a general view of the wonderful stream of our consciousness, what strikes us first is this different pace of its parts. Like a bird's life, it seems to be made of an alternation of flights and perchings. The rhythm of language expresses this, where every thought is expressed in a sentence, and every sentence closed by a period. The resting-places are usually occupied by sensorial imaginations of some sort, whose peculiarity is that they can be held before the mind for an indefinite time, and contemplated without changing; the places of flight are filled with thoughts of relations, static or dynamic, that for the most part obtain between the matters contemplated in the periods of comparative rest (James, 1890, p. 243).

The example cited above shows three foci of consciousness expressed by the prosodic phrases transcribed in the three lines:

(a) You'd look at the sun,

(b) it just looked red;

(c) I mean you couldn't see the sun.

Within these foci, language shows the mind organizing experience into elements that can be called *ideas*, among which are ideas of events and states, typically expressed as clauses. This woman expressed first the idea of a remembered event, *you'd look at the sun*, including the idea of the looking event itself along with ideas of its participants – unspecified individuals expressed by the word *you* and the object expressed as *the sun*. She then proceeded to verbalize the idea of a state with *it just looked red*, including the idea of looking red and once more the sun, this time expressed as *it*. Finally, in *I mean you couldn't see the sun* she rephrased her experience. Language provides copious evidence that the processing of experience into ideas of events and states and their participants is fundamental to the mind's organization of thought. Outside linguistics the segmentation of experience into ideas of events has been investigated experimentally by Newtson, Engquist, and Boyd (1977) and more recently with brain imaging (Zacks et al., 2001).

The thoughts of this woman may have focused on these ideas, but there was clearly an affective accompaniment that was in fact foreshadowed by an earlier statement describing *the most weird day I've ever seen in my entire adult life*. In the above, affect is most noticeable in line (b) in a rise-fall pitch contour on the word *red*, expressive of a feeling engendered by the striking quality of the sun's appearance, and in line (c) in a rise-fall contour on *see*, conveying an emotionally laden contrast with what one would normally see.

Language, in summary, shows thought being organized into successive foci of consciousness, each typically activating ideas of events and states and their participants, often with accompanying affect. It is at least plausible to suppose that people are conscious of these ideational elements together with their imagistic correlates and that both the ideas and the images contribute to the flow of thought.

Pronouns

The idea of the sun was verbalized in three different ways in this example, although only two are visible in the transcription.

In line (a), *you'd look at the sun*, it was expressed with the words *the sun*, which were given prosodic prominence. They were spoken slowly, relatively loudly, and with a high falling pitch. In line (b), *it just looked red*, the same idea was expressed with the pronoun *it*, which was spoken rapidly with low volume and low pitch. The prosodically most prominent word in (b) was *red*. In line (c), *I mean you couldn't see the sun*, the same idea was expressed once more as *the sun*, but this time these words were spoken softly with the pitch deteriorating into creaky voice. The most prominent words in (c) were *couldn't see*.

The function of pronouns like the *it* in line (b) is well explained in terms of consciousness. Pronouns are used when an idea (like the idea of the sun) is in a speaker's fully active consciousness and is assumed to be in the listeners' fully active consciousness as well. This idea was activated for the listeners during the utterance of line (a). Because in (b) it was assumed to be already active in their consciousness, it could be expressed with a minimum of phonological material. There was no need to assign it the prominence it had in (a). English and many other languages typically express such already conscious ideas with unaccented pronouns. In Asian languages there is a tendency to give such ideas no phonological representation whatsoever.

In line (c) there was a reversion to the words *the sun*, but this time they were spoken without the prominence they had in (a). Because the idea of the sun was presumably still active in the consciousness of the speaker and listeners, why was it not again expressed with *it*? Line (c) is discussed further below, but here it can be noted that it involved a second attempt at verbalizing the speaker's consciousness, a kind of starting over. If she had said *I mean you couldn't see it*, she would have tied this act of verbalization too closely to what preceded. With its lack of prominence the idea of the sun was presented as still in active consciousness, but with the words *the sun*, rather than *it*, it was presented as part of a new attempt at verbalizing this experience.

Harry's Death Revisited

We can now return to reasons cited by Jackendoff for excluding imagery and consciousness from thought. As noted, he imagined a situation in which he said to someone, *Bill killed Harry*. (Linguists often use violent examples like this because they highlight in the starkest terms the properties of transitive verbs.) It is an example that conflicts with observations of actual speech, where it is only under special circumstances that nouns like *Bill* and *Harry* are spelled out in this way. In a more realistic context one might have said, for example, *he killed him*, with pronouns conveying an assumption that the ideas of Bill and Harry were already in the consciousness of the speaker and listener.

But let us suppose that this sentence was actually uttered and that the speaker and listener both experienced their own images of the event in question. The question is whether those images belonged to the speaker's and listener's *thoughts*. Jackendoff says they did not, because an image would have to be particular. It would have to "depict Bill stabbing or strangling or shooting or poisoning or hanging or electrocuting Harry.... And Harry had to fall down, or expire sitting down, or die hanging from a rope" (1997, p. 188). How could any of those particular images be the general concept of killing? But of course the thought expressed by this sentence was not a thought of killing in general; it was a thought of a particular event for which a particular image was entirely appropriate. The thought and the image were thus not at odds.

Jackendoff's question, however, goes beyond the relation of a particular image to a particular thought to ask how a listener would know Harry was dead, knowledge that would depend on a general knowledge of killing and its results. It is important at this point to distinguish between the *idea* of an event, an element of thought, and the way an idea is *categorized* for expression in language. That distinction is captured in Figure 13.1 by the placement of *thought* and *semantics* in separate boxes. Whoever said *Bill killed Harry* decided that the idea

of the event could be appropriately verbalized as an instance of the *kill* category. He might have decided to categorize it differently – as an instance of the *murder, stab*, or *poison* categories, for example – each with its own entailments. Choosing the *kill* category accomplished two things: It allowed the speaker to use the word *kill*, but at the same time it associated the idea of the event with expectations that would apply to instances of the category, and among them was the expectation that the victim would be dead. Categories give speakers words for their ideas, but they also carry expectations that are thereby associated with those ideas. Categorization is an essential step in the conversion of thoughts into sounds because of the obvious impossibility of associating every unique thought with a unique sound, but categories are also the locus of entailments.

Jackendoff asks further how a particular image could allow one to know the identities of Bill and Harry. That question, however, seems to be based on the view that an image resembles an uninterpreted picture. If images are always accompanied by interpretations, the identities of Bill and Harry would necessarily accompany the sense-related experience.

The Priority of Thought over Phonology

Let us suppose that one can be conscious of both thoughts and sounds. Language provides evidence of several kinds that consciousness of thoughts has priority over consciousness of sounds in ordinary mental life.

Familiar and Unfamiliar Languages

It is instructive to compare the experience of listening to one's own language with that of listening to an unfamiliar language. In the latter case it is only the sounds of which one *can* be conscious. They may be recognized as the sounds of a language, but that is all. Listening to one's own language is a very different experience. Normally one is hardly conscious of the sounds at all, but rather of the thoughts the language conveys, thoughts that may or may not appear in consciousness as imagery but that always have an ideational component.

Spoken language provides the best examples of this distinction, but it can be mimicked with written symbols. To anyone who is not familiar with the Japanese language and writing system the symbols below may at best be recognized as examples of such writing, but otherwise they are incomprehensible marks. To a literate Japanese they elicit consciousness of the sounds *ame ga furu*, but consciousness is primarily focused on a thought, a thought that might be expressed in English as *it's raining*.

雨 が 降 る

Linguists who conduct fieldwork with little-studied languages sometimes ask a consultant to repeat a certain word so they can focus on its phonetic properties. It is not unusual for the consultant to fail to cooperate, preferring to discuss at length what the word means. Uppermost in the consultant's consciousness is the thought behind the word, and questions regarding its sound are regarded as irrelevant and intrusive. This same priority in consciousness of thoughts over sounds may explain why it is difficult to teach writing to speakers of previously unwritten languages. To write accurately it is necessary to shift one's consciousness from thoughts to sounds, and that is not always an easy thing to do.

The same preference for thoughts can be instructive in another way. Although thoughts may be uppermost in consciousness, they can with prodding and effort be replaced by consciousness of sounds. Consciousness thus has priorities that are presumably established by their salience within the manifold varieties of human experience. Some experiences enter consciousness more readily or more naturally than others. We are not usually conscious of breathing or blinking our eyes, but we can become so. It follows that questions regarding the content of consciousness should not be phrased categorically. Availability to consciousness can be a graded matter, as people are conscious more easily, immediately, or readily of some things than others, but are able under the right circumstances to shift consciousness to less accustomed phenomena.

Rote Learning

As mentioned by Jackendoff (1996, pp. 6–7), one may have learned "by heart" the sounds of a poem, ritual, or song with little or no consciousness of thoughts associated with those sounds. In such rote learning consciousness of thought is excluded, and consciousness of sound is all that is available. This experience has something in common with listening to an unfamiliar language, but in this case one is, oneself, actually speaking. A basic element of linguistic processing is missing, however, and one recognizes that it is unusual to produce sounds with no accompanying thoughts. The fact that we have such experiences is indirect evidence that we are, under normal circumstances, conscious of thoughts and know when they are absent.

Ambiguity

One other linguistic phenomenon that suggests a consciousness of thoughts is ambiguity: the fact that certain words can be phonologically identical but associated with different thoughts. Chafe (1996b, p. 184) mentions the word *discipline*, which may categorize an idea similar to that categorized as *academic field* or may alternatively involve harsh training to obey a set of rules. Because the sound and spelling are the same, there must be consciousness of a difference in thought. Beyond that, one can consciously compare one of the ideas expressed as *discipline* with the idea expressed as *academic field* and judge the closeness of fit, a judgment that can only be accomplished in the realm of thought. Ambiguity can extend beyond lexical expressions like these to include aspectual distinctions, as when *I'm flying to Washington* may mean that the speaker is in the middle of the flight, is planning to undertake it, or is doing it generically these days. Consciousness is capable of focusing on such distinctions. Without conscious access to thought, the experiences mentioned in this paragraph would be difficult to explain.

Distinguishing Thought Organization From Semantic Organization

In Figure 13.1 thought and semantics were assigned to separate boxes, with the semantics box representing ways in which thoughts are organized to fit the requirements of language. Language often shows a consciousness of this distinction, a fact which suggests that thought and its semantic organization are both consciously available.

Inadequacies of Language as an Expression of Thought

We can return to our example:

(a) You'd look at the sun,

(b) it just looked red;

(c) I mean you couldn't see the sun.

In line (c) the phrase *I mean* is a device made available in the English language to show that one is having difficulty expressing thoughts with available semantic resources. All three lines of this example recorded the speaker's attempt to verbalize her memory of what she had experienced 2 days earlier, and evidently by the end of line (b) she was not fully satisfied with what she had said. Line (c) was a further attempt to put what she was thinking into words. In some logical sense, line (c) contradicted what she said in (a) and (b), but the total effect of all three lines was to convey in different ways the manner in which the sun was obscured by smoke, the larger idea on which her thoughts were focused. Line (c) provides one kind of evidence of a mismatch between thought and possible linguistic choices.

When people talk, their speech often exhibits disfluencies: hesitations, false starts, and rewordings that are evidence that people experience difficulty "turning thoughts into words." People are sometimes quite explicit

about this difficulty: *I don't know quite how to say it*, or *that's not exactly what I meant.* Noam Chomsky wrote,

> Now what seems to me obvious by introspection is that I can think without language. In fact, very often, I seem to be thinking and finding it hard to articulate what I am thinking. It is a very common experience at least for me and I suppose for everybody to try to express something, to say it and to realize that is not what I meant and then to try to say it some other way and maybe come closer to what you meant; then somebody helps you out and you say it in yet another way. That is a fairly common experience and it is pretty hard to make sense of that experience without assuming that you think without language. You think and then you try to find a way to articulate what you think and sometimes you can't do it at all; you just can't explain to somebody what you think (Chomsky, 2000, p. 76).

This kind of experience implies an ability to compare what one is thinking with possible ways of organizing it linguistically, ways that depend in the first instance on the semantic resources of one's language. Again, it seems that people are conscious of both thoughts and semantic options because they are able to evaluate differences between them.

The Tip-of-the-Tongue Experience

In the familiar tip-of-the-tongue phenomenon (A. S. Brown, 1991; Brown & McNeill, 1966; Caramazza & Miozzo, 1997), one experiences a thought and its categorization, but has difficulty accessing a word or name. What is missing is the connection to phonology. Suppose one is thinking of a relatively unfamiliar object like an *astragal* but is unable to retrieve that sound. One can reflect on many aspects of the idea, categorize it, and thus attribute to it a variety of traits, but the phonological representation that is usually provided by categorization is absent. Jackendoff (1987, p. 291) mentions this experience as evidence for the inability to be conscious of thought, but it can easily be seen as evidence for just the opposite: consciousness of a thought but only a glimmering of phonology at best. The experience may or may not include imagery, but it always has an ideational component. Chafe (1996b, p. 184) mentions temporary consciousness of a thought expressed by the word *inconclusiveness* without access to that sound, and probably in that case without imagery. This experience, when imagery is lacking, can be the purest kind of evidence for "imageless thought," a major issue for the Würzburg school a century ago (Humphrey, 1951).

Categories Lacking a Sound Altogether

There are certain categories that play a useful role in the organization of thought but lack any phonological representation. In some cases a word may be available to specialists, but it is a word of which most people are ignorant. An example might be the small sheath on the end of a shoelace that allows the lace to be passed through a small hole. One might or might not learn the word *aglet* sooner or later, but probably most who are totally familiar with both the thought and its categorization have never done so. There is a resemblance here to the tip-of-the-tongue experience, but in this case the phonological representation is wholly unavailable, not simply difficult to retrieve.

Repeated Verbalizations

One promising way to compare thoughts with their semantic organization is to examine repeated verbalizations of what can be assumed to be more or less the same thoughts experienced by the same person on different occasions (Chafe, 1998). Data of this kind arise only fortuitously in the recording of actual speech, but instances can be elicited by giving people something to talk about and recording what they say at different times. Bartlett (1932) pioneered this method with a written stimulus and written responses. A similar procedure was followed by Chafe and his associates using a short film and spoken reponses (Chafe, 1980). Descriptions of what happened in the film were recorded shortly after it was viewed, and

some of the viewers returned on one or more occasions to talk about it again (Chafe, 1991). The film depicted a theft of pears, and the following excerpts show how one person talked about certain events in three successive versions:

Version 1 (after approximately 15 minutes)

(a) And he ended up swiping one of his baskets of pears,
(b) and putting it on his bicycle.
(c) On the front of his bicycle,
(d) and riding off.

Version 2 (after 6 weeks)

(e) And so,
(f) he finally gets it,
(g) on his bike,
(h) and he starts riding away.

Version 3 (after a year)

(i) And just put it right on his...on the front of his bicycle,
(j) and rode off with it.

One cannot expect thoughts to remain constant over time, of course, but these three versions have enough in common to suggest the retention of certain ideas in contrast to the rather different language that was chosen to express those ideas each time. All three versions conveyed ideas of two events: the boy's placing a basket of pears on his bicycle followed by his departure from the scene. The participants in those events included the boy, verbalized as *he* or simply omitted; the basket of pears, verbalized as *it*; and the bicycle, verbalized as *his bicycle* or *his bike*. Probably the speaker experienced imagery each time, most vividly in version 1 and least vividly in version 3. A listener (or reader of the above) might experience imagery too, but it would necessarily be different from that of someone who saw the film.

Data of this kind highlight the distinction between relatively constant thoughts and the less constant language used to express them. The idea of positioning the basket of pears was expressed as *put it on his bicycle* or *put it on the front of his bicycle* in versions 1 and 3, but *get it on his bike* in version 2. The idea of the boy's departure was expressed as *ride off* or *start riding away* or *ride off with it*. These are not just partially different words, but partially different ways of organizing thoughts semantically.

As with the pronoun *it* that expressed the idea of the sun in the earlier example, the pronouns *he* and *it* in this example show again that speakers are conscious not only of imagery but also of ideas. One may experience imagery of a boy placing a basket of pears on his bicycle, but it is interpreted in terms of ideas of the boy, the basket, and the bicycle, and consciousness of those ideas is essential for the production of language. In this case the ideas themselves were relatively constant across time and across the communicative act. Their imagistic accompaniments may have had some constancy for the speaker, but they were left to the listeners' imaginations.

Language Differences

Different languages provide their speakers with different semantic resources, including different inventories of categories, different orientations, and different combinatory patterns. It is possible for thoughts to be more or less the same regardless of the language used to verbalize them, but they can be molded differently by different semantic resources. Semantic choices may then feed back on the thoughts themselves.

The film just mentioned was shown to a number of German speakers, one of whom expressed her thoughts concerning the events described above as follows:

(a) er wuchtet den fast so grossen Korb wie er selbst es auch ist,

(b) auf das grosse Fahrrad,

(c) und fährt dann davon.

German provides a semantic category that allows the idea of an event to be verbalized with the verb *wuchten*. That choice associates the idea of lifting with weight, entailing in this case that the weight of the basket caused the boy to have difficulty lifting it onto his bicycle. There is no corresponding category in English. One could say *he lifted it with difficulty* but the effect is not the same, lacking the association with weight and with a broader range of circumstances under which the German category might be employed. Line (a), furthermore, combines its elements in ways that are foreign to English. The entire sequence might be translated *he has trouble lifting the basket, which is almost as big as he is, onto his big bicycle, and rides off*, but neither this nor any other translation can capture the effect of the original with any precision.

Translation is an attempt to join two languages in the area of thought, and a completely successful translation would be one in which exactly the same thoughts were conveyed by both the source and target languages. Because the semantic resources of different languages are never identical, it is a goal that can never be fully achieved. Because the goal is to connect the languages in the realm of thought, translating cannot be accomplished at all without a consciousness of thoughts. One does the best one can to express the thoughts that were originally expressed with the semantic resources of one language while being unavoidably constrained by the semantic resources of another.

This German example provides a further illustration of the way repeated tellings can triangulate on constancies of thought. As this speaker watched the film she was evidently impressed with how difficult it was for the boy to transfer the basket from the ground to his bicycle. With the language quoted above she chose the *wuchten* category to express that difficulty. Later she used the following language:

(d) (er) nahm einen der Körbe,

(e) und hiefte ihn mit großer Anstrengung auf sein Fahrrad,

(f) und fuhr davon.

A possible translation is *he took one of the baskets, and heaved it with great effort onto his bicycle, and rode off*. In line (e) the idea of lifting was expressed with the verb *hiefte*, similar to English *heaved*, capturing again an impression of great effort that was then made explicit with the phrase *mit großer Anstrengung*. But this time her choice focused on the difficulty that was suggested by the boy's way of moving, not by the basket's weight. Every choice of a semantic category is a way of molding thought with a unique complex of associations, using resources that often differ from language to language.

Manipulations of Consciousness in Literature

Examining how people talk is not the only linguistic avenue to an understanding of consciousness. Authors of fiction have discovered various ways to involve their readers in a fictional consciousness, and studying such devices can lead to understandings of consciousness that might otherwise be difficult to achieve (Chafe, 1994; Cohn, 1978). The examples below are taken from Edith Wharton's novel *The House of Mirth*, first published in 1905 (Wharton, 1987).

There are several ways in which literature highlights qualitative differences between an immediate and a displaced consciousness. The most obvious difference may be in the richness of detail that is available to immediate consciousness. When something is available to direct perception, even though consciousness can focus on only a small portion at a time, a wealth of information is potentially available. With a displaced consciousness, as with imagery, detail is necessarily impoverished. The act of writing gives writers a freedom to verbalize details of a kind appropriate to an immediate consciousness, allowing readers to share in a fictional immediacy:

Seating herself on the upper step of the terrace, Lily leaned her head against the honeysuckles wreathing the balustrade. The fragrance of the late blossoms seemed an emanation of the tranquil scene, a landscape tutored to the last degree of rural elegance. In the foreground glowed the warm

tints of the gardens. Beyond the lawn, with its pyramidal pale-gold maples and velvety firs, sloped pastures dotted with cattle; and through a long glade the river widened like a lake under the silver light of September (p. 79).

Language like this allows readers to experience vicariously what was passing through the consciousness of the protagonist at the very time she was sitting and leaning her head, with a succession of olfactory and visual experiences. The impression conveyed by such language is that these experiences were not being reported from the perspective of a later displaced consciousness, but that they were immediate.

They were, nevertheless, presented in the past tense, and in ordinary speech the past tense is compatible with a displaced consciousness, with experiences recalled from a time preceding the time the language was produced. Its use here, as well as the third-person references to *herself* and *her*, imply the existence of a narrating consciousness that is separate from the protagonist's. With relation to that consciousness the time of Lily's experiences and her identity were displaced – thus the past tense and third person. Chafe (1994) termed this artifice *displaced immediacy*. The experiences of the protagonist, although displaced with tense and person, achieve immediacy through Lily's actions and the sensory detail. Her consciousness is available to the reader as an immediate consciousness while the narrating consciousness responsible for the tense and person remains unacknowledged, providing little more than a tense and person baseline.

There was also a consciousness of affect-laden judgments and comparisons:

Lily smiled at her classification of her friends. How different they had seemed to her a few hours ago! Then they had symbolized what she was gaining, now they stood for what she was giving up. That very afternoon they had seemed full of brilliant qualities; now she saw that they were merely dull in a loud way. Under the glitter of their opportunities she saw the poverty of their achievement. It was not that she wanted them to be more disinterested; but she would have liked them to be more picturesque. And she had a shamed recollection of the way in which, a few hours since, she had felt the centripetal force of their standards (pp. 88–89).

This passage, expressing thoughts that passed through Lily's consciousness, retains the quality of an immediate consciousness combined with the displacement expressed by the past tense and the third-person *she*. But the passage is noteworthy, in addition, for the fact that its adverbial expressions – *a few hours ago, then, now, that very afternoon* – have their baseline in the time of the immediate consciousness, not of the displaced consciousness responsible for tense and person. The *now*, for example, was the now of Lily's immediate experiences, not the now of the language production. Although tense and person are anchored in what Chafe (1994) has called the *representing* consciousness – the consciousness producing the language – temporal adverbs like *now* are anchored in the *represented* immediate consciousness. In their treatments of consciousness novelists thus manage to throw light on the separate functioning of tense and person as opposed to the functioning of adverbs, a distinction that might not otherwise be apparent.

Is There Thought Outside of Consciousness?

If we are conscious of what we are thinking in ways suggested above, that need not imply that *all* of thought is conscious. Whether there is unconscious thought is a question that calls first for agreement on the meaning of *thought*. To consider and reject one extreme possibility, it would not be useful for this word to encompass everything the brain does, including totally unconscious processes like those involved in the regulation of body chemistry, or semi-involuntary processes like breathing, none of which would belong within the domain of thought as generally conceived. At the other extreme the word could be restricted arbitrarily to conscious experiences alone, so that thought would be conscious by definition. That alternative need not be rejected out of hand, but it excludes various phenomena that many would prefer to include within the realm of thought. We can briefly examine three of them.

Reasoning

One such phenomenon is *reasoning*. Jackendoff (1997), in fact, presents reasoning as a core ingredient of thought and uses its supposed unavailability to consciousness as crucial evidence that thought is unconscious. The form that reasoning takes in ordinary experience, however, is far from well understood, and traditional logic is of little help. People do very often take advantage of things they have experienced in order to make inferences about things they have not experienced, such as distal events that have occurred or might hypothetically occur. All languages have devices of some sort for expressing the inferential nature of ideas, although different languages do it in different ways (Aikhenvald & Dixon, 2003; Chafe & Nichols, 1986; Palmer, 2001). A simple example from English is the use of *must* as in *you must have had a haircut*, where direct experience of your appearance has led to the idea of a displaced event. Whether inferential reasoning of this sort operates outside of consciousness is an open question, but it does seem that people use words like *must* without any primary awareness of what they are doing.

Orientations

Within the realm of thought, ideas are positioned in a multidimensional matrix of orientations. They may be positioned, for example, in time, space, epistemology (as above with *must*), affect, social interaction, and with relation to the context provided by neighboring ideas. These orientations affect the shape of languages in many ways, and the semantic resources of different languages give different prominence to different ones. English, for example, pays a great deal of attention to tense. In the English retelling quoted earlier, the first version was in the past tense:

(a) And he ended up swiping one of his baskets of pears,

(b) and putting it on his bicycle.

(c) On the front of his bicycle,

(d) and riding off.

whereas the second was in the present:

(e) And so,

(f) he finally gets it,

(g) on his bike,

(h) and he starts riding away.

Although English is semantically constrained to orient events in this way and so to anchor ideas with relation to the time the language is produced, these examples show that the choice of a particular tense varies easily from one telling to the next. It thus seems to be a choice that is made during the act of producing language, not a property of underlying thought. The thoughts in these two excerpts may have been more or less the same, but the speaker chose to orient them with two different tenses as she adjusted them to the semantic constraints of English. Other languages may pay less attention to tense and be more preoccupied, say, with aspectual or epistemological distinctions. But whatever a language does, such choices are not likely to be in the forefront of consciousness.

As another example, the ubiquitous English word *the*, which orients an idea as identifiable to the listener, has been responsible for numerous articles and books and is still an object of controversy (e.g., Lyons, 1999). If its semantic contribution has proved so difficult to specify and if, furthermore, it is so hard for Japanese, Korean, and other learners of English as a second language to assimilate, its availability to consciousness may be questioned.

The general question is whether or to what extent people are conscious, not just of ideas, but also of the ways in which those ideas are oriented. On the one hand, if specific orientations express variable semantic choices and not elements of thought per se, they may not bear directly on consciousness of thought but only on the semantic, linguistically imposed organization of thought. On the other hand, semantic choices may often feed back into thought itself, so that rigidly separating semantics from thought may in the end be misleading. Whether people are or can be conscious of orientations may turn out to depend on the particular orientations involved – some being more available to consciousness than others – and even perhaps on the varying semantic sensitivities of different individuals.

Relations

The elements of consciousness are not independent of each other, but are interrelated in a variety of ways, and there is a question as to whether at least some of these relations lie outside of consciousness. A simple example is provided by the first two lines of the example quoted above:

(a) You'd look at the sun,

(b) it just looked red.

The foci of consciousness expressed in lines (a) and (b) bear a relation that might be described as conditionality. There is an understanding that the event that was verbalized in (a) took place one or more times and that each time it occurred it was a necessary condition for the state that was verbalized in (b). For this person to experience the appearance of the sun, she first had to look at it. Relations like this are often verbalized overtly with little words like *if* and *when*, but in this case the conditional relation was only implied (Chafe, 1989). As with orientations, the question of whether speakers of a language are conscious of such relations, marked or not, remains open. Are they so integral to the succession of conscious ideas that they are conscious too, or do speakers and thinkers employ them without being conscious they are doing so? Language itself does not provide clear answers to such questions.

Summary

This chapter has focused on two different approaches to the relation between language and consciousness, both linguistically oriented. Both agree that this relation cannot be explored without taking other mental phenomena into account, in particular thought and imagery. They agree, furthermore, that conscious experience includes both imagery and affect, whether or not those experiences can be considered elements of thought.

Jackendoff sees consciousness as limited to uninterpreted imagery, whose qualities mirror those of uninterpreted visual, auditory, or other raw sensory information. He presents evidence that such imagery is external to thought, in part because it is too particular, in part because it does not allow the identification of individuals, and in part because it fails to support reasoning. If all we are conscious of is imagery and imagery does not belong to thought, it follows that we are not conscious of thought.

Chafe distinguishes between immediate and displaced consciousness, the former engaged in direct perception and the latter in experiences that are recalled or imagined. Immediate consciousness includes not only sensory experiences but also their interpretation in terms of ideas, which are positioned within a complex web of orientations and relations. Displaced consciousness includes sensory imagery that is different in quality from immediate sensory experience, but it is always accompanied by ideational interpretations that resemble those of immediate experience. Both the imagistic and the ideational components of consciousness are held to be central components of thought, as thought is ordinarily understood.

Acknowledgments

I am especially grateful to Ray Jackendoff and the editors of this volume for their helpful comments on this chapter. If Jackendoff and I do not always agree, his work has always provided a stimulating balance to tendencies that might otherwise have been weighted too strongly in a different direction.

References

Aikhenvald, A. Y., & Dixon, R. M. W. (Eds.). (2003). *Studies in evidentiality.* Amsterdam: John Benjamins.

Anthony, J. L., & Lonigan, C. J. (2004). The nature of phonological awareness: Converging evidence from four studies of preschool and early grade school children. *Journal of Educational Psychology, 96,* 43–55.

Bartlett, F. C. (1932). *Remembering: A study in experimental and social psychology.* Cambridge: Cambridge University Press.

Bloomfield, L. (1931). Obituary of Albert Paul Weiss. *Language, 7,* 219–221.

Brown, A. S. (1991). A review of the tip-of-the-tongue experience. *Psychological Bulletin, 109,* 204–223.

Brown, R., & McNeill, D. (1966). The "tip of the tongue" phenomenon. *Journal of Verbal Learning and Verbal Behavior, 5,* 325–337.

Buswell, G. T. (1935). *How people look at pictures: A study of the psychology of perception in art.* Chicago: University of Chicago Press.

Caramazza, A., & Miozzo, M. (1997). The relation between syntactic and phonological knowledge in lexical access: Evidence from the "tip-of-the-tongue" phenomenon. *Cognition, 64,* 309–343.

Castles, A., & Coltheart, M. (2004). Is there a causal link from phonological awareness to success in learning to read? *Cognition, 91,* 77–111.

Chafe, W. (Ed.). (1980). *The pear stories: Cognitive, cultural, and linguistic aspects of narrative production.* Norwood, NJ: Ablex.

Chafe, W. (1989). Linking intonation units in spoken English. In J. Haiman & S. A. Thompson (Eds.), *Clause combining in grammar and discourse* (pp. 1–27). Amsterdam: John Benjamins.

Chafe, W. (1991). Repeated verbalizations as evidence for the organization of knowledge. In W. Bahner, J. Schildt, & D. Viehweger (Eds.), *Proceedings of the Fourteenth International Congress of Linguists, Berlin 1987* (pp. 57–68). Berlin: Akademie-Verlag.

Chafe, W. (1994). *Discourse, consciousness, and time: The flow and displacement of conscious experience in speaking and writing*. Chicago: University of Chicago Press.

Chafe, W. (1996a). How consciousness shapes language. *Pragmatics and Cognition, 4*, 35–54.

Chafe, W. (1996b). Comments on Jackendoff, Nuyts, and Allwood. *Pragmatics and Cognition, 4*, 181–196.

Chafe, W. (1998). Things we can learn from repeated tellings of the same experience. *Narrative Inquiry, 8*, 269–285.

Chafe, W. (2000). A linguist's perspective on William James and the stream of thought. *Consciousness and Cognition, 9*, 618–628.

Chafe, W. (2002). Prosody and emotion in a sample of real speech. In P. Fries, M. Cummings, D. Lockwood, & W. Sprueill (Eds.), *Relations and functions within and around language* (pp. 277–315). London: Continuum.

Chafe, W. (2005). The relation of grammar to thought. In C. S. Butler, M. de losdr Ángeles Gómez-González, & S. M. Doval-Suárez (Eds.), *The dynamics of language use: Functional and contrastive perspectives*. Amsterdam: John Benjamins.

Chafe, W., & Nichols, J. (Eds.). (1986). *Evidentiality: The linguistic coding of epistemology*. Norwood, NJ: Ablex.

Chomsky, N. (2000). *The architecture of language*. New York: Oxford University Press.

Cohn, D. (1978). *Transparent minds: Narrative modes for presenting consciousness in fiction*. Princeton, NJ: Princeton University Press.

Holšánová, J. (2001). *Picture viewing and picture description: Two windows on the mind*. Lund University Cognitive Studies 83. Lund: Lund University Cognitive Science.

Humphrey, G. (1951). *Thinking*. New York: Wiley.

Jackendoff, R. (1987). *Consciousness and the computational mind*. Cambridge, MA: MIT Press.

Jackendoff, R. (1996). How language helps us think. *Pragmatics and Cognition, 4*, 1–34.

Jackendoff, R. (1997). *The architecture of the language faculty*. Cambridge, MA: MIT Press.

James, W. (1890). *The principles of psychology*. New York: Henry Holt.

Langacker, R. W. (1997). Consciousness, construal, and subjectivity. In M. I. Stamenov (Ed.), *Language structure, discourse and the access to consciousness* (pp. 49–75). Amsterdam: John Benjamins.

Lyons, C. (1999). *Definiteness*. Cambridge: Cambridge University Press.

Natsoulas, T. (1987). The six basic concepts of consciousness and William James's stream of thought. *Imagination, Cognition and Personality, 6*, 289–319.

Newtson, D., Engquist, G., & Bois, J. (1977). The objective basis of behavior units. *Personality and Social Psychology, 35*, 847–862.

Palmer, F. R. (2001). *Mood and modality* (2nd ed.). Cambridge: Cambridge University Press.

Piaget, J. (1967). *Six psychological studies*. (D. Elkind, Ed. & A. Tenzer, Trans.). New York: Vintage. (Original work published 1964)

Poltrock, S. E., & Brown, P. (1984). Individual differences in visual imagery and spatial ability. *Intelligence, 8*, 93–138.

Pöppel, E. (1994). Temporal mechanisms in perception. In O. Sporns & G. Tononi (Eds.), *Selectionism and the brain: International review of neurobiology* (Vol. 37, pp. 185–201). San Diego: Academic Press.

Russell, B. (1921). *Analysis of mind*. London: Allen & Unwin.

Stamenov, M. I. (Ed.). (1997). *Language structure, discourse and the access to consciousness*. Amsterdam/Philadelphia: John Benjamins.

Wharton, E. (1987). *The house of mirth*. New York: Macmillan. (Original work published 1905)

Wierzbicka, A. (1999). *Emotions across language and cultures: Diversity and universals*. Cambridge: Cambridge University Press.

Zacks, J. M., Braver, T. S., Sheriden, M. A., Donaldson, D. I., Snyder, A. Z., Ollinger, J. M., Buckner, R. L., & Raichle, M. E. (2001). Human brain activity time-locked to perceptual event boundaries. *Nature Neuroscience, 4*, 651–655.

CHAPTER 14

Narrative Modes of Consciousness and Selfhood

Keith Oatley

Abstract

Beyond mere awareness, human consciousness includes the reflexive idea of consciousness of self as a centre of agency and experience. This consciousness of self has been thought to involve narrative: a distinct mode of thinking about the plans and actions of agents (self and others), about vicissitudes encountered, about attempts to solve problems posed by these vicissitudes, and about the emotions that arise in these attempts. Philosophical discussion of this idea has included the question of to what extent this narrative-of-consciousness is epiphenomenal and to what extent it may have causal effects on action. To the extent that the self takes narrative forms and is constructive, it will tend to assimilate narratives encountered in the public space: stories that occur in conversation and elsewhere. Both the style and content of stories that circulate in a culture will potentially contribute to the extent and contents of consciousness, and therefore to the development of selfhood. A narratizing consciousness, in which self is a unifying centre of agency in relation to others, has emerged gradually during evolution, during cultural development, and during individual development. It functions importantly in social interaction and allows integrative understanding both of oneself and of others.

Introduction

Consciousness of the kind we value – of our surroundings, of our thoughts and emotions, of our selves, and of other people – often takes narrative forms. However, there is debate about how to define narrative. A recent discussion of the question is given by Wilson (2003). A minimalist definition is that narrative must include at least two events with some indication of their temporal ordering. The difficulty with such definitions is that on the one hand they are unenlightening, and on the other that even the seemingly unobjectionable ones seem to invite contention and counter-example. I do not base this chapter, therefore, on a definition of narrative. Instead, I adopt the more psychological stance of Bruner (1986) who writes that narrative "deals in human or human-like intention and action and the vicissitudes and consequences that mark their course" (p. 13).

The theory of narrative is known as narratology (Bal, 1997; Groden & Kreiswirth, 1994). Literary theorists such as Booth (1988), as well as cognitive scientists such as Rumelhart (1975) and Schank (1990), have contributed to it, as have theorists of identity and biography, such as Brockmeier & Carbaugh (2001). Following Bruner's proposal, here is a sketch of prototypical narrative and its elements. I label some as interaction-type elements. They are typical of narrated sequences of intended social interaction. I label a further set as story-type elements that are typical of those additional features that make narratives stories.

Interaction-Type Elements of Narrative

Interaction-type elements include the following:

- There are agents who may be called characters.
- There is a focus on intentions of the characters.
- Events occur in a causal, time-ordered sequence. These events include mental, interpersonal, and physical actions, some of which flow from the characters' emotions and intentions.
- Vicissitudes of intentions and actions occur and affect characters emotionally.
- Outcomes include further physical, mental, and social events, which affect characters emotionally.

Story-Type Elements of Narrative

Story-type elements of narrative include the following:

- A story is a narrative account that uses interaction-type elements (as indicated above), and that is related or depicted by an explicit or implicit narrator in some medium (talk, text, film, etc.).

- Characters have conscious awareness of vicissitudes – that is to say, problems – as well as of their own problem-solving attempts and outcomes.
- Readers and listeners are affected by the characters' problem-solving attempts and by the inferred experiences of the characters (emotional and otherwise).
- A story offers implications of meanings, often moral meanings, in relation to the culture in which the story arose.

Narratives include utterances of one person telling another what happened at the office that day. Stories are structured more consciously. They include anecdotes that may be told to friends, newspaper articles, films, novels, and so forth. When I use the term "narrative framework," I mean the kind of prototype indicated above, with or without characteristics of a story. One may notice that such frameworks are not purely syntactic. They include both structure and content.

The analyses I offer here are Western in their provenance. Although I believe that many of the themes I discuss are universal (see, e.g., Hogan, 2003), there would be differences in this kind of argument if it were elaborated within, say, Chinese or Indian culture.

One must of course distinguish between narratives as cultural objects and narrative thinking (see, e.g., Goldie, 2003). One must also distinguish between a life lived and a life thought about in narrative terms as elaborated, for instance, by a biographer. Given these distinctions, however, an advantage of adopting Bruner's (1986) view of narrative as a specific mode of thought about agents and their intentions is that it is accompanied by his parallel proposal of the mode of thought that he calls paradigmatic, which "attempts to fulfill the ideal of a formal, mathematical system of description and explanation. It employs categorization or conceptualization and the operations by which categories are established, instantiated, idealized, and related one to another to form a system" (p. 12). Bruner's starting point is helpful for this chapter because narrative seems to be the mode in which important aspects of human consciousness occur and because it offers a basis for making meaningful sense of ourselves and of our interactions with others. By contrast the paradigmatic mode is that by which science, including a science of consciousness, is expressed most typically.

Although consciousness used to be regarded almost as a non-topic because it was unanalyzable, it has recently become the object of considerable interest; witness this handbook. Likewise, the topic of narrative is drawing increasing scholarly attention not just within narratology but also, for instance, in narrative analyses of people's lives and identities, with the idea that thinking within narrative frameworks in the social sciences amounts to a paradigm shift (Brockmeier & Harré, 2001).

The idea of specifically narrative consciousness is also growing (see, e.g., Fireman, McVay, & Flanagan, 2003) and can be thought of as the intersection between interest in consciousness and interest in narrative. In itself this intersection is by no means new; in the theory of literary narratives, for instance, consciousness and its transformations have been topics of scholarly attention for many years (see Auerbach, 1953; Watt, 1957). In addition, for a hundred years, in areas touched by psychoanalysis, this intersection has been central as the formative idea of psychoanalysis is that consciousness is reclaimed from the unconscious precisely by turning it into language within narrative frameworks (see, e.g., Edelson, 1992; Spence, 1982). What is relatively new is that this intersection has become of interest for cognitive psychology and for the philosophical theory of mind. It is within these frameworks that this chapter is written, although with links to other disciplinary areas.

Given that this is a handbook, a reader's expectation will properly be of a system of categories and explanations in what Bruner has called the paradigmatic mode. A list of section headings is therefore given below. The clauses that succeed the main headings in this list are pointers to the contents of each

categorized section. Those readers who wish to see what work has been done in a particular area may turn to the corresponding section for discussion of representative work and references.

- **The question of whether consciousness has causal properties:** Does consciousness affect action, or does it occur only as retrospective commentary?
- **Four aspects of consciousness:** (i) Simple awareness, (ii) the stream of inner consciousness, (iii) conscious thought as it may affect decisions and action, (iv) consciousness of self-with-other.
- **Narrative and mutuality:** Personal and interpersonal functions of consciousness in humans as highly social beings who depend on mutuality with others.
- **The evolution of narrative:** Thinking and consciousness in hominid species and humans among whom both self and others are known as individuals with intentions; questions of mental models, emotions, and imagination.
- **The developmental psychology of narrative consciousness:** Individual development of narratizing consciousness in children, the role of language, and the idea of narrative consciousness in psychotherapy.
- **The rise of consciousness in Western imaginative literature:** Changes that have occurred in the depiction of consciousness from the earliest narrative writings to the present.
- **Coda:** The relation of conscious to unconscious actions and thoughts.

For those who want something more like a story, please read on. I have argued elsewhere (Oatley, 1992a) that psychology is a subject in which we expect both an approach directed to the attainment of insight (characteristic of the narrative mode) and information of the technical kind (in the paradigmatic mode). Styles of writing in psychology need typically to address both these expectations. In something more like a story framework, therefore, I have conceived this chapter partly as a debate of a protagonist (me) and an antagonist. The protagonist puts forth the idea that consciousness has causal properties. The antagonist is sceptical of this claim. At the same time, I tell a story (a true story I hope) about the evolution and development of consciousness.

The Question of Whether Consciousness Has Causal Properties

I propose that narrative consciousness has functions. Each of us is, at least in part, a centre of consciousness: a unified narrative agent. Many though not all of our decisions, thoughts, and actions flow from this centre. By means of a narrative consciousness, we can begin to understand ourselves and others in relation to the societies in which we live and to make sense of what would otherwise be disconnected. My proposal derives from the idea that, to understand anything satisfactorily in psychology, one must understand its functions. In this chapter I begin to answer the question of what the functions of narrative consciousness might be.

Intuitively, we think that we act on our conscious perceptions, beliefs, and desires. But this intuition that consciousness is functional is an expression of folk theory. The opposition in the debate is provided by a sceptic, such as Daniel Dennett (e.g., 1991). Dennett is representative of many cognitive scientists who believe that scientific understandings of the brain have replaced, or will replace, explanations based in folk theory. Neurons cause behavior, they say. Conscious thoughts do not. Folk theory – which includes ideas of beliefs, desires, and emotions; the idea that we act for reasons; and the idea of a conscious self that functions as a unified agent – is false, say such scientists and philosophers (e.g., Churchland, 1986). It is false not just in its details but altogether, just as were notions that stars and planets revolve in perfect circles round the earth because they were stuck to crystalline spheres. Although Churchland's brand of radical eliminativism (elimination of all folk-theoretical terminology from cognitive science) is on the wane, scep-

ticism about the functionality of consciousness remains strong.

Thus, although emotions are salient in consciousness (as discussed below), LeDoux (1996), prominent for his work on emotions and the amygdala, has written, "The brain states and bodily responses are the fundamental facts of an emotion, and the conscious feelings are the frills that have added icing to the emotional cake" (p. 302). This is the kind of view that is represented by Dennett, not just for emotional consciousness, but for consciousness generally. In this view the brain computes what it needs to compute. It recruits the neurons necessary to produce behavior. What we experience as consciousness is an extra, with no causal effects. Human behavior could occur without it. Consciousness is a rather narrow summary in narrative form of what has already happened. The real workings of mind occur elsewhere.

All varieties of perception – indeed all varieties of thought or mental activity – are accomplished in the brain by parallel, multitrack processes of interpretation of sensory inputs (Dennett, 1991, p. 111).

Humphrey and Dennett (2002) offer an analogy with a termite colony, which "builds elaborate mounds, gets to know its territory, organizes foraging expeditions" (p. 28). But for all this apparent purposefulness, it is just a collection of termites with various roles, influenced by each other but not by any master plan.

Dennett calls the idea of a unifying spectacle that constitutes our point of view the Cartesian Theater. The epithet comes from Descartes' (1649/1911) idea of a soul housed in the brain. The idea of a soul witnessing and forming meanings is too thoroughly old fashioned. There is no Cartesian Theater, says Dennett, no "Oval Office in the brain, housing a Highest Authority" (1991, p. 428). The conscious narratizing process is mistaken about how the mind works. Instead, Dennett says, think of the conscious self as "a center of narrative gravity" (1991, p. 418). He wants us to realize that a centre of gravity is an abstraction, not real. He writes,

Our tales are spun, but for the most part we don't spin them; they spin us. Our human consciousness, and our narrative selfhood, is their product, not their source (p. 418).

I suppose Dennett wants us to understand the terms "spun" and "spin" in the foregoing quotation as the output of a spin doctor. In another paper he has extended this idea: Not only does consciousness have no causal status but it is also mischievously misleading:

[W]e are virtuoso novelists, who find ourselves engaged in all sorts of behavior, more or less unified, but sometimes disunified, and we always put the best "faces" on it we can. We try to make all of our material cohere into a single good story. And that story is our autobiography (Dennett, 1986, p. 114).

The chief fictional character at the centre of that autobiography is one's *self*. And if you still want to know what the self *really* is, you are making a category mistake (Dennett, 1992, p. 114).

So a narratizing consciousness does not just happen after the fact; it's a phoney. Compelling, for Dennett, are the data of simultaneous but disparate brain processes. For instance, in a group of people who have had operations to sever their left and right hemispheres to relieve epilepsy (split-brain patients), the hemispheres can know contradictory things (Gazzaniga, 1998). Only the left side has language, and this side can also recount narratives. The right side is silent. Gazzaniga (1992) says his favorite split-brain phenomenon was illustrated by flashing to the left hemisphere of a split-brain patient, PS, a picture of a chicken claw and to the right hemisphere a picture of a snow scene. Then PS was asked to choose by hand which of a set of pictures in full and continuous view was associated with the pictures he had seen flashed previously. His left hand (activated by the right side of his brain and prompted by the snow scene) chose a picture of a shovel, and the right hand (activated by the left side of the brain) chose a picture of a chicken. When asked why he made these choices, he said. "Oh, that's simple. The chicken claw goes with the chic- ken, and you need a shovel to clean out the chicken shed" (p. 90). The left (language-equipped) side of the brain had seen the claw and chose the chicken picture. But this same left side had no consciousness of the snow scene; instead it saw the left hand choosing the shovel and it produced a reason without knowing it was – as one might say – a piece of fiction to fit what it knew. Also there are people who, because of brain damage, say they see nothing on one side of the visual field and yet react perfectly well to objects there. The phenomenon is called blindsight. Humphrey (2002) writes, "I have met such a case: a young man who maintained that he could see nothing at all to the left of his nose, and yet could drive a car through busy traffic without knowing how he did it" (p. 69). And, in multiple personality disorders there is not one self but several (Humphrey & Dennett, 2002).

Further along the spectrum of doubters of the value of narrativity is Galen Strawson (2004), who argues that the idea of a narrative self is regrettable. There are plenty of people, he says, whose selves are what he calls "episodic," with episodes being separate rather than bound together in any narrative way. He remembers, for instance, having fallen out of a boat into the water when he was younger and can recall details of this incident, but claims that this did not happen to the self who was writing his article. Strawson's intuition of disconnectedness in life's episodes is accompanied by the claim that to argue for narrative selves is to endorse falsehood: to tell stories is (as Dennett and Gazzaniga also argue) invariably to select, to revise, to confabulate, and thereby to falsify. Because of this falsification, the idea that we live narrative lives is therefore not just fallacious but ethically flawed.

Should the idea of a self with causal powers that involve a narratizing consciousness therefore be replaced? I argue that it should not. If we may take Dennett, again, as the central antagonist to the idea of a functional narrative consciousness, we can say that although he is thoroughly immersed in cognitive science, the adjacent area of human-computer interaction is also important. In that area there occurs the idea of the interface. In personal computers nowadays we are offered the interface of a simulated desktop, which is supported by layers of computer programs. Although computers work by means of electron flows and semiconductors or at a another level by binary operations, users would not find any inspection of them useful. They want to do such things as create documents and spreadsheets, make mathematical calculations, compose musical collections, or look at their photographs. Modern interfaces offer interfaces in such forms as enhanced virtual papers and other objects on a virtual desk, which enable them to do such things easily. Similarly, as users of our bodies, we do not want to know what our neurons are up to, nor yet the state of our hippocampus. We live in a world of agents somewhat like ourselves with whom we interact. We want to know what and who is in the world in terms of possibilities of interactions with them. We need an interface on our brain states in terms of intentions, beliefs, and emotions. That is what consciousness offers us: a functional conception of ourselves as agents, with certain memories, plans, and commitments. Narrative is, as Bruner has proposed, that way of thinking that connects actions to agents and their plans.

Confabulations certainly occur, and not just by split-brain patients. But one can also demonstrate the experience of light when one presses the side of the closed eye in the dark. The pressure triggers receptors in the retina. This does not mean that a world seen via light rays detected by the light-sensitive retina is an illlusion. Certainly human consciousness has some properties of post-hoc rationalization, as Dennett claims. Certainly its properties are generated by brain processes of which, in the ordinary course of events, we know nothing, just as the interface on the computer on which I am writing this chapter is produced by semiconductors whose workings I do not know in detail. But the conclusion is not that consciousness is a fraud, any more than the icons on my computer screen are hallucinations. A conscious understanding of self is the means by which

I keep track of my memories, my plans, my commitments, and my interactions with others. With it, I know about those activities that make me member of the society in which I live.

In this chapter I propose that we accept not only Dennett's metaphor of self-as-novelist but also that, as proposed by Richard Velleman (2002), different conclusions may be drawn than those offered by Dennett. Following Velleman's argument, I explore the idea of a conscious unitary self, based on functional properties of narrative.

Four Aspects of Consciousness

Consciousness has many meanings. To bring out some of the properties of consciousness that we value, I propose four aspects (Oatley, 1988), each named after an originator: Helmholtz, Woolf, Vygotsky, and Mead.

Helmholtzian Consciousness

The first and most basic conception of consciousness in modern cognitive science was formulated by Hermann von Helmholtz (1866). He proposed that perception was the drawing of unconscious conclusions by analogy (see, e.g., Oatley, Sullivan, & Hogg, 1988). He pointed out that we are not conscious of the means by which we reach cognitive conclusions (neural and cognitive computations). We are only conscious of the conclusions themselves.

Dennett's (1991) theory is a version of Helmholtz's idea of perception as unconscious inference to reach certain conscious conclusions. Dennett says distributed processes of neural computation deliver such perceptual and other mental conclusions, which are not necessarily veridical nor authoritative. Instead, as he argues, it is as if iterative drafts are produced of such conclusions, which change in certain respects as a function of other input.

So far so good. I agree. Helmholtz's proposal is, I believe, a deep truth about how the brain works. Information flows from sensory systems to perceptual and other kinds of interpretation, and from the operations of neural systems to experience. Although I did not include this aspect in my 1988 article, I think one must include in this proposal the consciousness of emotions (Panksepp, 2005), which I discuss further below. Much of Helmholtzian awareness is a one-way flow. For example, when one is looking at a visual illusion, even when one knows that it is an illusion, one cannot, by taking thought, alter the conclusion our visual processes reach.

Woolfian Consciousness

Helmholtz's theory is applied principally to perception, in which we receive input from excitations of the sense organs that provide cues to objects and events in the world that produce these excitations. We are, however, also conscious of images that occur verbally and visually, with no perceptual input. These images can be thought of as described by William James (1890) in his metaphor, the "stream of consciousness," or as the states depicted by Virginia Woolf in *Mrs Dalloway* (1925): a changing kaleidoscope of thoughts, ideas, and images. The verbal and visual images depicted by Woolf have as much to do with preoccupations, memories, emotions, and trains of inward thought as they do with perceptual input.

As with Helmholtzian consciousness, in Woolfian consciousness there is a principal direction of flow: from neural process to mental image. What Woolf did, starting with her novel *Mrs Dalloway*, was to make inner consciousness recognizable in the form of a narrative, a novel. Here we are, for instance, inside the mind of Clarissa Dalloway as she walks up Bond Street in London on a June morning, a year or two after the end of World War I.

>. . . a roll of tweed in the shop where her father had bought his suits for fifty years; a few pearls; salmon on an iceblock.

>"That is all," she said, looking at the fishmongers. "That is all," she repeated, pausing for a moment at the window of a glove shop where, before the War, you could buy almost perfect gloves. And her old Uncle

>William used to say a lady is known by her shoes and her gloves. He had turned on his bed one morning in the middle of the War. He had said, "I have had enough." Gloves and shoes; she had a passion for gloves, but her own daughter, Elizabeth, cared not a straw for either of them (p. 12).

No longer based in perception of the purely Helmholtzian kind, Mrs Dalloway does not just see a tailor's shop and fishmongers. Her consciousness is an admixture of perceptions, memories (where her father bought his suits), and judgements ("That is all"). Associations occur. Gloves remind her of her uncle, and they prompt memories. And "That is all," has a mental association with her uncle saying, "I have had enough." The thought of gloves also stirs her preoccupation with her daughter Elizabeth, from whom she is on the verge of painful estrangement. Underlying this are other emotional themes: her relationship with her father, her status as a lady, repercussions of the war, the fact of death.

In Woolfian consciousness, thought breaks free of the immediacy of perception. No doubt Dennett would be pleased to acknowledge the hints in Woolf's depiction that consciousness is not entirely unified.

Vygotskyan Consciousness

A third aspect is the influence of consciousness on thoughts, decisions, and actions. *Mrs Dalloway* is about a single day on which Clarissa Dalloway gives a party. The novel's opening line is, "Mrs Dalloway said she would buy the flowers herself." If Clarissa Dalloway were a real person, Dennett would say a set of neurocomputational processes generated her utterance: "I'll buy the flowers myself." She gives a reason: "For Lucy [her servant] had her work cut out for her," preparing for the party. Part of that work included arrangements with Rumpelmayer's men who were coming to take the doors off their hinges to allow the guests at the party to move about more freely. According to Dennett, all such thoughts of reasons for going out to buy the flowers would be post-hoc elaborations, perhaps confabulations.

Lev Vygotsky (a literary theorist before he became a psychologist) proposed that thoughts could affect actions. His basic conception was of children developing until about the age of 2 years much as apes develop, immersed in their relationships with parents and siblings and solving as well as they might the problems that confront them. But then, with the entry of each child into language, individual resources are augmented by the resources of culture. Vygotsky says the social world becomes internalized as mind. So it is not that the mind is a container that holds thoughts or that conscious thoughts are solely the output of neural processes. Rather, the mind is an internal social world, which one can consult and in which one can take part.

A typical example of Vygotsky's thinking is from a study by his colleague Levina (Vygotsky, 1930). She was studying a little girl who had been given the task of trying to retrieve some candy, with potential tools of a stool and a stick available. The child talks to herself. But she does not just say aloud what she has done, as one might think if one had been reading Dennett. She makes suggestions to herself: "'No that doesn't get it,'" she says. "'I could use the stick.' (Takes stick, knocks at the candy.) 'It will move now.' (Knocks candy.)" Moreover the child reflects on the problem and analyses its solution: "'It moved. I couldn't get it with the stool, but the, but the stick worked'" (p. 25).

Consciousness, here, is not an equivocal post-hoc account, but a mobilization of the resources of human culture, which become potentially available to each of us. In this case the child instructs herself as she has been instructed by adults. According to Vygotsky, this is how mind becomes mind. Consciousness is not just a result; it can be a cause.

Among the most interesting proposals about the functions of a unifying consciousness is one from the early days of artificial intelligence: a program called Hacker (Sussman, 1975), which would learn skills of building structures with (virtual) children's building blocks. (The name "Hacker" comes from a time that seems now almost prehistoric when it meant something like "computer nerd.") When it makes mistakes, the

program learns from them and rewrites parts of itself. For instance it might want to put a block on top of one that is on the floor. But say the block on the floor already has something on it. The program cannot complete its plan. Prompted by the discrepancy (the problem) between its current state and its goal, it constructs a new piece of plan (program). It draws from a library of mistakes (bugs) and tries to generalize: For instance, it might conclude, "If I want to put a block on another block which is on the floor, I must always clear off anything that is on the top of the block on the floor."

Sussman's program has two kinds of code. The first is code comparable to that in any program: detailed plans made up of sequences of actions that will achieve goals. The second kind is not represented explicitly in most programs. It is an explicit account of the goals of each procedure (e.g., to put one block on top of another). Only with such a representation could a program analyze a mismatch between an intended plan and an outcome that was not intended. With such a representation the program can reason backwards about the effects of each action in relation to a goal. With such a representation it can write new pieces of program – patches – to solve problems that are encountered and thereby achieve the goal.

Here is the analogy with consciousness. When introducing a patch to the program (itself), Hacker runs in what Sussman calls "careful mode" in which the patch is compared line by line with the range of possibly interacting subgoals and goals. Here is a unified agency, trying out imagined actions in a model of the world before committing to action. Hacker itself is not conscious. But Sussman's account contains the idea that consciousness is a unifying process that includes a model of goals and the possible results of our actions in relation to them. A unifying consciousness is needed to learn anything new that will change the substance of self.

Dennett (1992) compares a storytelling self with a character whose first words, in Melville's *Moby Dick*, are "Call me Ishmael." But says, Dennett, Ishmael is no more the author of that novel than we are the authors of stories we tell about ourselves. Dennett develops the idea further by imagining a robot, Gilbert:

> "Call me Gilbert," it says. What follows is the apparent autobiography of this fictional Gilbert. Now Gilbert is a fictional, created self, but its creator is no self. Of course there were human designers who designed the machine, but they did not design Gilbert. Gilbert is a product of a process in which there are no selves at all...the robot's brain, *the robot's computer, really knows nothing about the world; it is not a self. It's just a clanky computer. It doesn't know what it's doing. It doesn't even know that it's creating this fictional character. (The same is just as true of your brain: it doesn't know what it's doing either.) (pp.* 107–108).

Velleman (2002) has contested these points. Imagine Gilbert getting locked in a closet by mistake. It has to call for help to be released. The narratizing robot could then give an account of these matters. Velleman takes two important steps. In the first, he argues that such a robot as Gilbert would have subroutines that enabled him to avoid and escape from danger. Being locked in a closet would be such a danger, and if it occurred, subroutines would be activated. Let us suppose these subroutines were labeled "fear." Balleine and Dickinson (1998) argue that access to such affective states is a core process in identity.

Velleman says that if Gilbert were to make an attribution to such a state, his narrative autobiography might include the statement: "I'm locked in the closet and I'm starting to get frightened" (Velleman, p. 7). If the fear module recommended breaking down the door, then in his autobiographical narrative he might say, "I broke down the door, because I was frightened of being locked in for the whole weekend." Gilbert thereby would have taken a step to being an autonomous agent. He would be acting for a reason (his fear) and in a way that was intelligible to other people (us). Notice too, that, to act for a reason, the robot must be not just responsive to stimuli (internal or external) that prompt it to do this or that. It must have a representation of goal states (such as avoiding danger) of the kind that Sussman's

program had. A narrative processor – based on goals that can be represented explicitly and that can generate plans of action – is exactly the kind of representation needed by an autonomous self, able to explain action in terms of goals and other reasons.

Claparède's (1934) law of awareness is that people become conscious of an action when it is disrupted. Then consciousness is flooded with emotion. Why should this be? It is because emotions occur with the unexpected, when what is familiar, what is habitual, what is well practiced, no longer works. Negative emotions occur, as Peterson (1999) has proposed, when an anomaly occurs or, in narrative terms, when a vicissitude arises.

Emotions are central to narrative because they are the principal processes in which selfhood is constructed. One falls in love, and the self expands to include the new person. One is thwarted, and one forms vengeful plans to overcome the purposes of the antagonist. One suffers a severe loss, and one's consciousness searches to find what in one's theory of self was mistaken, perhaps perseverating in denial and blaming others or perhaps recognizing what should be changed in oneself. Consciousness of this urgent problem-solving kind functions in the kind of way that Sussman has proposed. If we are to learn from mistakes and change implicit theories in which we are lodged, a unifying consciousness is necessary.

The second step in Velleman's argument is that Gilbert's very abilities at telling stories also allow him to plan actions. Suppose Gilbert works in a university: He does useful things to achieve goals that he is given by members of the faculty. He might have been given the goal of going to library to fetch Dennett's book, *Consciousness Explained*. If at the same time his batteries had started to run down, Gilbert might notice this internal state and plan to go to the closet to get some new batteries. He might say, "I'm going into the closet." Then, argues Velleman, balanced between the possibilities of the library and the closet, "the robot now goes into the closet partly because of having said so" (2002, p. 6; see also Velleman, 2000).

Narrative is based on plans that flow from intentions. A computer sophisticated enough to construct its autobiography could run the narrative processor either forward in planning mode or backward in autobiographical mode. It would, in other words, achieve what I have called the Vygotskyan state of consciousness, of being able to direct its own actions. Gilbert is able to act not only in terms of reasons such as internal states but also – running the narrative/planning processor forward – to plan to act in coherence with the story he is telling about himself.

Velleman's idea, here, is that with coherence-making processes a central organizing agency comes into being. Oatley (1992b) has argued that narrative is a mode by which we humans give meaning to life events beyond our control, to our human limitations, to mortality. It would be an illusion to think that all such matters can be made meaningful, but we become human in the ways that we value by making some such matters so, and these we share with others in a meaning-drenched community. We are meaning-making beings who, by means of narrative, make some aspects of disorderly reality comprehensible, and in some ways tractable. Coherence in the computer generation of stories has been achieved by Turner (1994), and Oatley (1999) has argued that coherence is a principal criterion of successful narrative. By adhering to this criterion, then, the narratizing agency becomes capable of influencing action and creating a self who, in retrospect, could achieve an autobiography that has some meaningful coherence. Art stops merely imitating life. Life starts to imitate art. The Woolfian storyteller, aware of inner processes, becomes Vygotskyan. Coherent with the story in which she is the principal character, Mrs Dalloway instructs herself, "I'll buy the flowers myself." Having said so, she does.

Meadean Consciousness

The fourth aspect of consciousness is social. As described by George Herbert Mead (1913), it is a consciousness of voices in debate: "If I were to say this, she might say

that." This form of consciousness rests on an awareness of self and other. It is in this form that the possibility arises of being able to know what other people are thinking.

Mead describes how children at about the age of 4 years play games that require them to take roles and to experiment with changing these roles. In hide-and-seek, you can't have much fun hiding unless you imagine seekers looking for you. Developmental psychologists have discovered that, about the age of 4, children develop a theory of mind (Astington, Harris, & Olson, 1988). They begin to understand that other people might know quite different things than they do. The hider has a representation of herself; she knows who and where she is. She knows, too, that the seeker does know who she is but does not know where she is.

Once a person has reached this stage of consciousness, the idea of self as narrator comes fully into its own. Not many stories are autobiographies. The fully developed narrator does not simply offer output of some autobiographical module. Nor does he or she only use the narrating module to instruct him- or herself. Such a narrator has a theory of other minds and a theory of his or her own mind persisting through time. Such a narrator is able thereby to act in a world with other beings constituted in a similar way. Saying "I will do x," counts as a commitment to other people to do x, and other people organize their actions around this commitment. So if I were to extend the story of Gilbert begun by Dennett, and continued by Velleman, to include interaction with others, it would stop being autobiography. It would become more like an episode in a story, something like this:

Gilbert was nearing the end of the day, but like all good robots he was conscientious. He was about to set off to the library to fetch Consciousness Explained, *when he noticed his batteries were low. He felt anxious. If there were too long a wait at the library elevator, he might not make it back to the Department.*

"I'll go to the library to get the Dennett book in a few minutes," he said to Keith, "First

I have to go to the closet for some new batteries."

Keith was staring at his computer screen. "OK," he said, without paying much attention.

The phone rang. It was a teacher at his daughter's school. His daughter had had an accident while playing basketball. Could he come immediately? Keith had a sudden image of his daughter lying on the floor, immobile. He quickly put his stuff in his book bag, shut down his computer, locked the door to the closet, and ran down the hallway.

Gilbert heard the closet door being locked. In the middle of changing his batteries, he couldn't move and didn't have enough power to call out.

"Carbon-based life forms," he thought.

In his writings on consciousness, Dennett has worried about whether a conscious self might really be autonomous. Perhaps he should set aside his worries. The self is much more. It is a model of self-with-others: first the self-with-parent or other caregiver, then self-with-friends and suchlike others, then self with the generalized other of a certain society, then perhaps self with significant other, and so forth, each with a basis of emotions. Self is not just a kernel of autonomy. Self is self-in-relation-to-other, an amalgam of the implicit theories we inhabit, suffused with the emotions that prompt our lives and are generative of our actions in the social world. The very processes that allow us to make inferences about others' minds, about what another person may be thinking and feeling, that allow us to give a coherent account of that person as an autonomous agent, are the same as those that enable us to form models of our own selfhood, goals, and identity and to project ideas of our ourselves into the future.

Narrative and Mutuality

Having reviewed the aspects of consciousness that I proposed (Oatley, 1988;

Helmholtzian, Woolfian, Vygotskyan, and Meadean) and their role in the construction of narratives, let me turn to the crux of why consciousness is a narratizing process that must be based in folk theory. Selves are social. In our species we as individuals can't manage much on our own. Together we have built the communities in which we live and all the accoutrements of the modern world. Our accomplishments depend on culture, on being able to propose and carry out mutual plans in which people share objectives and do their parts to ensure they are accomplished, and then converse in a narrative way about outcomes. Oatley and Larocque (1995) have found that people typically initiate something of the order of ten explicitly negotiated new joint plans each day. We (Oatley & Larocque, 1995; Grazzani-Gavazzi & Oatley, 1999) had people keep diaries of joint plans that went wrong. Errors occurred in only about 1 in 20 new joint plans. People succeed in meeting friends for coffee, succeed in working together on projects, succeed in fulfilling contractual arrangements. If it were not for an interface of folk theory that enables each of us to discuss and adopt goals, exchange relevant beliefs about the world, and elaborate parts of plans to ensure mutual goals are reached (Power, 1979), joint plans could not be constructed. And if we were not able to narrate them to each other afterward, we could scarcely understand each other. If those psychologists, neuroscientists, and philosophers were correct who maintain that beliefs, desires, and emotions are figments of a radically false folk theory, we would not find that 19 out of 20 joint plans were accomplished. The number would be zero. And when things went wrong, confabulating narrators could never know why. Humans would be able to do certain things together, but we would perhaps live in much the same way as do the chimpanzees.

When joint plans go wrong, errors occur for such reasons as memory lapses or because a role in a joint plan has been specified inexactly. When such a thing occurs the participants experience a strong consciousness of emotion, most frequently anger but sometimes anxiety or sadness. People typically give narrative accounts of their own intentions and often of the failure of the other. When a person who has not showed up for a meeting is a loved one, vivid fears of accidental death may occur; but if there is a failure of a plan made with someone who is not an intimate, a mental model is elaborated of that person as unreliable and untrustworthy. Here is a piece of narrative recorded in a joint error diary (from Oatley & Larocque, 1995):

> My co-worker was measuring some circumferences of pipes, converting them to diameters and reporting them to me. I recorded the figures and used them to drill holes later. The drilled holes were incorrect for diameters. It could have been the conversion or measurement. I had to modify the holes.

Continuing the story, our participant elaborated a mental model of his co-worker and formulated a plan that was coherent with what had happened, in a way that depended on his analysis: "My co-worker is not as careful about numbers as I am – maybe I should do this kind of task with someone else." Further plans were elaborated – continuing the narrative in the forward direction – concerning the relationship with the co-worker: "I need to and want to do something about this kind of thing with him."

Personal and Interpersonal Functions of Consciousness

The novelist constructs characters as virtual people who typically have an ensemble of emotion-based goals (intentions), from which flow plans of interaction (Oatley, 2002). In daily life, we each construct our actions (actions, not just behavior) in a similar way, in the light of what is possible, by coherence with a mental model of our goals, of our resources, and of our commitments. The person (character) whom each of us constructs, improvising as we go along, is not virtual, but embodied. This person accomplishes things in the world and interacts with others whom we assume are constituted in a way that is much like our self.

The functions of consciousness include an ability to follow, to some extent, the injunction written long ago in the temple at Delphi: "Know thyself." In doing so, we each form a mental model of our goals, inner resources, limitations, emotions, commitments, and values that is no doubt inaccurate, but that is somewhat serviceable. In the course of life, we come to know how far and in what ways we can rely on ourselves. With such knowledge we can then also be dependable for others.

Humphrey (1976, 2002) has argued that a principal function of introspective consciousness of ourselves is the understanding of others as having selfhood and attributes that are similar to own. By using our model of ourselves to imagine what others are thinking and feeling, we become what Humphrey calls "natural psychologists." Although this method is not very accurate, it equips us far better to undertake social interaction than if we were to rely solely on behavioral methods. By elaborating mental models of others based on our own introspection, on our experience with them in joint plans, and on what they and others say in conscious narrative accounts about them, we come to know how far and in what ways we can rely on them in the joint plans of our extended relationships.

Here, then, I believe is the principal reason for thinking narrative consciousness to be functional. It is a reason that Dennett neglects because he, like most of us Westerners who work in the brain and behavioral sciences, tends to think in terms of individual selves, individual minds, and individual brains. But if our species is predominantly social and depends for its being on mutuality and joint planning, we need to consider also such interfaces as the interface of language along with its conscious access to what we take to be our goals and plans, by which we arrange our lives with others. The language is not just of describing, in the fashion of post-hoc autobiography, as Dennett suggests. It is based in what one might call a language of action (mental models, goals, plans, outcomes), of speech acts to others (see, e.g., Searle, 1969) as we establish mutuality, create joint plans, and subsequently analyze outcomes in shared narrative terms. The language is also one of explanation in terms of agents' intentions and the vicissitudes they meet. Narrative is an expression of this language.

The Evolution of Narrative

For the period up to about 30,000 years ago, the palaeontological record of hominid evolution is largely of fossilized bone fragments and stone tools, with nothing in writing until 5,000 years ago. Judicious comparisons with evidence of our living primate relatives have allowed a number of important inferences.

Intentions and Consciousness of Intentions

Narrative is about intentions. Its sequences involve chains of both human and physical causation (Trabasso & van den Broek, 1985). A surprising finding from primatology is that our closest relatives, chimpanzees and bonobos, have only a very limited understanding of causality in both the physical and the social world. Although they certainly have intentions, they do not seem conscious that they have them. Although they are good at interacting with others, they do not seem conscious, in the way that we are, that other primates have intentions. These conclusions have been reached independently by two research groups who have conducted extensive series of experiments with chimpanzees: Tomasello (1999) and Povinelli (2000).

Chimpanzees are successful instrumentally in the wild, and they are very social. Their brains generate intentions, which they carry out. If they were equipped with post-hoc autobiography constructors they would be the creatures whom Dennett describes. They seem to have no autonomous selves. Although they solve problems and even use primitive tools such as sticks and leaves, their lack of any sense of their own intentions, or of plans mediated by tools, makes them incapable of instructing other animals in a new technique or, in the wild at least, of receiving technical instruction. The occurrence of sticks near termite mounds, together with chimpanzees' interest in food and in manipulating objects, had led some groups of them

in eastern Africa to use sticks as tools to poke into termite mounds to fish out termites, which they eat (McGrew, 1992). A stick left near a termite mound by a mother chimpanzee may suggest to her daughter that she pick it up and poke it into the mound. What chimpanzees don't do – can't do according to Tomasello (1999) – is for one (say the mother) to show another (say her daughter) how by using a stick she can fish for termites. The daughter, although she may see from the mother's activity that there is something interesting to look at, and although she may work out herself how to fish for termites with a stick, does not understand that her mother is intentionally using a tool. She does not thereby see quickly how to use it herself. Chimpanzees thus lack an essential step for forming true cultures, in which useful technical innovations are preserved and passed on, in a ratchet-like process.

In an experiment by Povinelli and O'Neill (2000), two of a group of seven chimpanzees were each trained separately by the usual techniques of reinforcement-based learning to pull on a rope to bring toward them a weighted box with fruit on it. When they had become proficient at this task, their training changed. The box was made heavier so that one chimpanzee could not move it. Now, both chimpanzees were trained by reinforcement techniques to work together to pull the box and retrieve the food. All seven of the chimpanzees knew each other well, and all had previously taken part in other experiments that involved lone pulling on ropes to retrieve food. Here is the question. If, now, one who had not been taught to pull the rope in this apparatus were paired with a chimpanzee who was experienced in cooperative pulling, would the experienced one show the naïve one what to do? The answer was no. The experienced chimpanzee would pick up its rope, perhaps pull, and wait for a bit, looking over toward the other. One of the five naïve chimpanzees, Megan, discovered how to pull the rope independently of her experienced partner. She thereby managed to work with both of the experienced animals to retrieve the heavy box with the food on it. But for the most part the experienced and the other naïve partners failed in the joint task. On no occasion did either of the experienced chimpanzees make a gesture or attempt to direct the naïve one's attention to relevant features of the task. On no occasion did the experienced animal pick up and offer the rope to the naïve one. The experienced chimpanzee did not seem to infer that the naïve chimpanzee lacked the proper intentions or knowledge in the task.

Another striking finding is that neurons have been discovered in the premotor area of monkeys' brains that respond both when a human hand is seen picking up a raisin and when the monkey itself reaches intentionally to pick up a raisin. Rizzolatti, Fogasse, and Gallese (2001) call them "mirror neurons." They do not respond to a human hand when it is moving without any intention to pick up the raisin. They do not respond when a human hand picks up the raisin with a pair of pliers. Rizzolatti et al. argue that the brain recognizes action not in terms of a purely visual analysis, but in a process of analysis by synthesis, by means of its own motor programs of carrying out the action. Rizzolatti and Arbib (1998) have further suggested that this discovery is a preadaptation for learning language based on a case grammar (Fillmore, 1968) around verbs of intention. Gallese, Keysers, and Rizzolatti (2004) have proposed that mirror neurons enable simulation of intentions and emotions of other individuals in the social world, and hence afford a neural basis of social cognition.

The issue remains mysterious, as indicated by recent experiments by Tomasello and his group. For instance Behne et al. (2005) found that 18-month-old human infants, but not 6-month-olds, could tell the difference between an experimenter who was able but unwilling to give them a toy (teasing) and one who was willing but unable (e.g. because the toy dropped out of reach). Call et al. (2004) found that chimpanzees could also make this same distinction, thus demonstrating that they know more about others' intentions than had previously been thought. We might say that monkeys under-stand a bit about intention (in terms of mirror neurons) and that chimpanzees half-understand it in a more explicit way. They still, however, lack of grasp of full mutual intention, which is the centre of narrative consciousness.

Although they intend and feel, monkeys and apes do not fully know that they and their fellows are beings who can intend and feel. As John Donne put it: "The beast does but know, but the man knows that he knows" (1615–1631/1960, p. 225). This seemingly small extra step has made a great difference. It is an essential step to culture, to narrative consciousness, and to selfhood.

Mental Models of Others

In her ethological work with chimpanzees in the wild, Jane Goodall (1986) learned to recognize each one as an individual. Chimpanzees recognize each other as individuals, and this is the basis for their elaborate social life. They know who the alpha animal is, who everyone's friends and allies are. Because chimpanzees are promiscuous in their mating, no one knows who the father is of any youngster, but everyone knows other aspects of kinship. Only when Goodall had started to recognize individuals did the social lives and actions of the chimpanzees start to make sense.

Chimpanzees know everyone in their social group, which can reach a maximum size of about 50 individuals. Each one forms a mental model of each other one, which includes something of that one's history, habits, and allies. Dunbar (1993, 2003) and Aiello and Dunbar (1993) have found that the size of the brain in primate species has a close correlation with the maximum size of its social group.

Each chimpanzee spends some 20% of its time sitting with others, one at a time, and grooming: taking turns in sorting through their fur, removing twigs and insects. It is a relaxed activity. It is the way primates sustain affectionate friendships with each other. Dunbar (1996) shows a graph in which the data points are separate hominid species (*australopithecus*, *homo erectus*, etc.) with an x-axis of time over the past 3 million years and a y-axis of amount of grooming time required according to the species' brain size and the inferred size of its social group. Humans maintain individual mental models of about 150 others. If we used the same procedures as chimpanzees, we would have to spend about 40% of our time grooming to maintain our friendships. As group size increased, a threshold was reached, according to Dunbar, between 250,000 and 500,000 years ago, of about 30% of time spent grooming. This is the maximum any primate could afford and still have time for foraging and sleeping. It was at this point, argues Dunbar, that language emerged as conversation: a kind of verbal grooming.

Conversation is something one can do while gathering food or performing other tasks, and one can do it with several others. What do we human beings talk about in friendly conversation? Dunbar (1996) has found that, in a university refectory, about 70% of talk is about the doings of ourselves and others: conversation, including gossip, most typically the elaboration of mental models of self and others and of people's goals in the social group. Dunbar might have added that the incidents about which people talk are recounted in narrative form.

Consciousness and Emotions

Before conversation and narrative consciousness could emerge, preadapations were necessary. I have mentioned one suggested by the findings of Rizzolatti and his colleagues. In this subsection and in the next I sketch two more preadaptations, the first of which concerns emotions. Panksepp (1998, 2001, 2005) has argued that the most parsimonious explanation of a range of data is that emotion is the basic form of consciousness. He calls it primary process affective consciousness. We share it with other mammals, and it is subserved by a homologous region of the brain, the limbic system, in different mammalian species. Thus when a baby mammal is separated from its mother, it utters distress calls. This behavior is generated in a specific limbic area, and according

to Panksepp's conjecture, the animal's distress is much the same as a human infant feels when separated from its mother. It is also the core of the distress that we might feel as adults if we had arranged to meet our partner, and after a half-hour he or she did not show up, and we start to worry that he or she had suffered an accident. Notice that the consciousness involved is vividly salient. Its concern is interpersonal.

Consider another emotion: interpersonal fear. De Waal (1982) describes how, in the group of 25 or so chimpanzees who lived in a park-like enclosure at Arnheim Zoo, Yeroen was an alpha male until he was deposed by the then-beta male, Luit. As alpha, Yeroen received between 75% and 90% of the ritual submissive greetings made by individuals in the troop. This submissive greeting is well marked in chimpanzees. Typically it includes bowing, making short panting grunts, sometimes making offerings such as a leaf or stick, or sometimes giving a kiss on the feet or neck. In the early summer of 1976 Luit stopped making this kind of greeting to Yeroen. On 12 June, he mated with a female just 10 metres from Yeroen, something of which Yeroen was normally extremely intolerant. On this occasion Yeroen averted his eyes. Later that afternoon, Luit made angry aggressive displays toward Yeroen. De Waal said he thought at first that Yeroen was ill. But this was not so. Only later did he realize that these were the first moves of a take-over that took 2 1/2 months to accomplish and required much interindividual manoeuvering. It involved Luit inducing the adult females in the group to abandon their allegiance to Yeroen and enter an alliance with him. The take-over was completed on day 72 of the sequence when Yeroen made his first submissive greeting to Luit. When de Waal describes the events of this dominance take-over, he recounts a narrative that imposes meaning on the events for us humans. It is not, of course, a narrative that the chimpanzees could construct. De Waal says that 12 June was the first time he ever saw Yeroen scream and yelp and the first time he saw him seek support and reassurance. We may imagine that on that day, Luit felt angry toward Yeroen – his hair stood on end, and though he had normally looked small, he now looked the same size as the alpha male Yeroen. We may imagine too, that this was the first time Yeroen felt afraid of him. The Panksepp conjecture is that Luit did indeed feel angry and Yeroen did indeed feel afraid in the way that we humans would when our position was threatened.

What we may say about this in terms of consciousness is that, for the chimpanzees in this group, events and emotions would have unfolded in a sequence of present-tense happenings. Among them only what I have called the interaction-type elements of narrative would be present. My conjecture is that immediate emotions – anger, fear, friendly alliance, deference – conferred the structure on each episode of interaction, but the whole sequence would not have, could not have, a plot of the kind one expects in a story (either prospectively or retrospectively) as far as the animals were concerned.

Among humans, however, sequences of such events not only lend themselves to narratization but we are also unable to avoid turning them into story form (Oatley & Yuill, 1985). At some time since the line that would lead to humans split from that which would lead to the chimpanzees some 6 million years ago, the perception of interaction-type elements of narrative added the elements of story-type narratization. Thus when de Waal (1982) describes the events of Luit taking over the alpha position from Yeroen in 1976, he can only do so in terms of a humanly recognizable story told, inevitably, by a narrator, a kind of novelist not of the self as Dennett has postulated, but of others.

My hypothesis, then, is that first, as Panksepp has proposed, emotion is a primary form of Helmholtzian consciousness (with sensory awareness being another). Second, emotions are frames or scripts for interindividual relationships. Anger (such as Luit's when he displayed aggressively to Yeroen) sets up a script for conflict. Emotions structure relationships so that sequences of inter-action are prompted. Third, as Paulhan (1887/1930) proposed, emotions are caused by disruptions of action or expectancy (vicis-situdes), and they can completely fill consciousness. Fourth, only with the coming of language (or perhaps the concepts of prelanguage) do the interindividual scripts or frames of emotions become the bases of episodes in stories. At this point, a new kind of consciousness can emerge that sees itself and others as instigators of intended actions and as experiencers of the emotions that result from these actions. Oatley and Mar (2005) have argued that social cognition is based on narrative-like simulations, the conclusions of which can (as Helmholtz insisted) become conscious. The elaborated story-type consciousness, in which agents act for reasons and are responsible for their actions, is built on preadapted bases (including those of mirror neurons and emotion-based relating) that were in place in hominid ancestors.

Mimesis, Metaphor, and Imagination

Homo erectus emerged about 1.9 million years ago, and was our first ancestor to look more humanlike than apelike. Although simple stone tools pre-existed this species, it was with these beings that elaboration of such tools began. With them, also, came the first strong evidence for the importance of meat in the diet, and perhaps even according to Wrangham (2001), the control of fire and hence cooking. With them came a second important preadaptation to language (following that of consciousness of emotions). Donald (1991) calls it mimesis: a non-verbal representation of action and an ability to reproduce actions. It enabled fundamental cognitive developments of cultural forms of group enactment, some of which are still with us, such as dance and ritual.

Donald says that the next important evolutionary transformation did involve language. It was to myth, which I take to derive from an early form of narrative consciousness. He dates myth as far back as the time that Dunbar has postulated for the emergence of conversation, but his emphasis is on narrative aspects. Myth, says Donald, is the preliterate verbal way of understanding how the world works. It can pervade every aspect of people's lives. For instance among the !Kung of the Kalahari (Lee, 1984), illnesses are typically seen as caused by people who died a short time before (parents and grandparents). While they were alive these people were good, but many say that once dead they generally became malevolent (notice the narrative structure). Others say they are harmful only when the living don't behave properly. Living people are by no means powerless, however. The means of maintaining health, and healing the sick, have to do with interpreting the interventions of these spirits and sometimes combating them. So, says Donald,

> Myth is the authoritative version, the debated, disputed, filtered product of generations of narrative interchange about reality ... the inevitable outcome of narrative skill and the supreme organizing force in Upper Paleolithic society (p. 258).

Myth is a narrative form of social exchange, used for thinking and arguing about how the world works. It is active today, and not just in the Kalahari. "We are on the side of good, dedicated to the fight against evil," for instance, and "You can do whatever you really want to do," are mythic sentiments of some vitality in North America. (Notice, again, the narrative elements of goals and actions.) Myths have pragmatically important properties. By casting a matter into a symbolic form they make it potentially conscious and an object of cultural consideration. It becomes a potent means of organizing both individual and societal behavior.

It was between 50,000 and 30,000 years ago that the first art began to appear in the human record. Caves in southeast France contain paintings of animals on their walls from 31,000 years ago (Chauvet, Deschamps, & Hillaire, 1996). Several cultural developments, in addition to paintings and the production of ornamental artifacts, occurred around the same time. One was treating the dead in a special way, burying them with ceremony. Another was a sudden proliferation in the types of tools. Mithen (1996) has proposed that these develop-

ments were related. Rather than simply having separate domain-specific areas of knowledge – social knowledge of the group, technical knowledge of how to make stone tools, natural historical knowledge of plants and animals – the people of those times began to relate one kind of knowledge to another. Here began imagination and metaphor: A this (in one domain) is a that (in another domain). This charcoal mark on the wall of a cave is a rhinoceros, this person who is dead lives on in another kind of existence, this animal bone can be shaped to become a harpoon tip. During this period, argues Mithen, human culture began to accelerate. Imagination is the type of consciousness that makes narrative possible. It offers us stories of possibility and of people not currently present in situations that are not directly visible.

The Developmental Psychology of Consciousness

Although ontogeny may not exactly recapitulate phylogeny, there are parallels between the rise of narrative consciousness during hominid evolution and the development of narrative skills and consciousness in children. Zelazo and Sommerville (2001) and Zelazo (2004) have proposed a set of levels of consciousness, reached progressively during the preschool years (see Chapter 15). The earliest, which they call minimal consciousness, corresponds to Helmholtzian consciousness (described above). Subsequent levels include recursive representations. The second level includes minimal consciousness of a thing plus the name of that thing. Higher levels include further recursions. So reflective consciousness of the kinds I have called Woolfian and Vygotskyan (discussed above) include not just actions but also the consciousness of self-in-action. Finally a level is reached at about the age of 4 years that includes the social attributes of theory of mind (Astington, Harris, & Olson, 1988) in which one can know what another knows, even when the other person's knowledge is different from what one knows oneself. It corresponds to Meadean consciousness (discussed above), in which the social self can be explicitly represented and thought about. Tomasello and Rakoczy (2003), however, argue that at a much earlier stage, occurring about the age of 1 year, children come to understand themselves and others as intentional agents. They call this the "real thing": It is what separates us from other animals. They argue that it enables skills of cultural learning and shared intentions to occur and that this stage must precede any acquisition of theory of mind that would need to be based recursively on this ability.

Recursion also occurs in a way that extends the scheme proposed by Zelazo. Dunbar (2004) points out that from school age onward a person who takes part in a conversation or who tells a story must know (level 1) that a listener can know (level 2) what a person depicted in the conversation or story knows (level 3). Dunbar argues that skilled storytellers can work with about five recursive levels of consciousness. Thus in *Othello*, Shakespeare writes (level 1) so that audience members know (level 2) that Iago contrives (3) that Othello believes (4) that Desdemona is in love with (5) Cassio. All this, argues Dunbar, depends on neural machinery present in human brains that is not present in chimpanzee brains.

Recursion is an idea that became important in cognitive science in the 1960s. It is that representations may include representations of themselves. Productively, then, the idea of successive steps of recursion has been proposed by Zelazo as successive levels of consciousness, achieved in successive stages of development. Although each level of consciousness depends on a previous one, and each emerges at a certain stage during development, the earlier level it is not superceded. It continues to be available.

Tomasello's (1999) studies of the development of language indicate that soon after single words (at Zelazo's second level) come verb islands, in which different words can be put into slots for agent of the action, for object, and for outcome. Thus in the verb island of "throw" we get "Sam throws the ball." This is close to the idea of case

grammar, as postulated by Fillmore (1968), for which the preadaptation suggested by Rizzolatti and Arbib (1998) is the basis. As Tomasello points out, the child symbolizes exactly the kind of intention that chimpanzees enact, but do not know that they know. The symbolization can then be used as a tool to affect the attention of the person to whom the communication is made. Infant communications are sometimes requests, like "more," or even "more juice," but conversational priorities early become evident: Parents and children draw each others' attention, in conversation, to things in the world.

Then in development comes a phase that, on palaeontological grounds, would be unexpected: the appearance of monologue. Children start talking out loud to themselves. Nelson (1989) arranged for the parents of a small child, Emily, to place a tape recorder by her bed before she went to sleep. After some bedtime conversation with a parent, the parent would leave and Emily would often enter into monologues that, with the help of her mother, have been transcribed.

Nelson (1996) has argued that narrative binds memories of autobiographical events together in the meaningful form that we think of as selfhood. Here is an example from Emily aged 21 months: "The broke. Car broke, the . . . Emmy can't go in the car. Go in green car" (Nelson, 1989, p. 64). This monologue illustrates verb island constructions of the kind identified by Tomasello around the verbs "break" and "go." It also offers an agent, "Emmy," and the narrative structuring of an autobiographical event. The car was broken, and therefore Emmy had to go in a different car. Here, already, we see some of the elements of story-type narration: the telling of a story by a narrator, a self (character) persisting through time, a vicissitude, and the overall possibility of making meaningful sense of events (although not yet with a theory of other minds).

From the age of 2 or so, children are able to run the narrative process not just backward to link memories with an agent but also forward. Here is Emily in another monologue at the age of 2 years and 8 months.

Tomorrow when we wake up from bed, first me and Daddy and Mommy, you . . . eat breakfast eat breakfast, like we usually do and then we're going to p-l-a-y, and then soon as Daddy comes, Carl's going to come over, and then we're going to play a little while. And then Carl and Emily are both going down the car with somebody, and we're going to ride to nursery school . . . (Nelson, 1989, pp. 68–69).

Here, again, is a recognizable self, "Emily," who is a protagonist in a plan-like account with many of the attributes of a narrative structure in story form.

Fivush (2001), in pursuit of similar questions, has studied children discussing pieces of autobiographical narrative with their parents and other adults. Children as young as 3 years make such discussion an important part of their social activity. They use it to evaluate experience. For instance, a child of 3 years and 4 months said to an interviewer, "There was too much music, and they play lots of music, and when the circus is over we went to get some food at the food place" (p. 40). Part of the autobiographical point is to assert selfhood and subjectivity via things that the narrator liked or didn't like ("too much music"). By the age of 4 children beome aware, in a further step to individuality, that their experience might be different from that of others.

Nelson's narratives from the crib suggest how the inner chattering that is a feature of everyday Woolfian consciousness develops from spoken monologue. This idea is strengthened by Baddeley's (1993) account of PET scanning of his own brain when he was engaged in quiet inner speech. It showed involvement of those brain areas that are typically involved both in speech production and speech understanding.

Nelson (2003) concludes that consciousness is one of the functions that develops as an emergent property with the development of language, and most specifically with the development of narrative language. It is with this ability that a move occurs from simple Helmholtzian awareness of the here and now to the idea of a self. Several things are accomplished in this move. The

self is experienced as unified, not merely as a disparate bundle of reflexes. From psychoanalytic thought, the somewhat ironic but nonetheless suggestive idea comes that the moment of this realization occurs as a child can recognize him- or herself in a mirror (Lacan, 1949/1977). Other, more empirically minded psychologists have taken the infant's ability to touch a patch of rouge on his or her forehead, when the image of the infant bearing the patch of rouge is seen by him- or herself in the mirror, as an indication of the dawning of selfhood (Lewis et al., 1989). Nelson's proposal is that, with the dawning of narrative consciousness, the self is experienced in a world of widening possibilities, of other people and of other minds. Zelazo's (2004) proposal is that this ability to represent the self explicitly is fundamental to the development of consciousness and of a unified as opposed to a fragmented control of action.

Harris (2000) has argued that a major developmental accomplishment for children occurs when they start to construct, in their imagination, things that are not immediately present. They make such constructions not just in stories but also in pretend role play (discussed above). They start imagining what others might know (other minds). The idea of specifically narrative consciousness has been extended in the recent work of developmental psychologists on the question of how children conceptualize a self as persisting through time. Barresi (2001) and Moore and Macgillivray (2004) have shown that the imagination by which one can anticipate future experiences of the self (which they call prudence) is likely to involve the same processes as those in which one can become interested in others (prosocial behavior). This same ability of the imagination is the central core of understanding narrative. Arguably stories nurture it. As Vygotsky (1962) has proposed, language-based culture offers children resources that they do not innately possess, but also do not have to invent for themselves. Children in modern times aged 4 and 5 years have reached the point of the imagination that can take wing in the way that Woolf depicted and that Mithen (2001) argued had been reached in evolution by our ancestors, 30,000 years ago, when one may suppose with Donald (1991) that story-type accounts of meaning-making had become routine.

Conscious selfhood, in these kinds of accounts, is a meaning-making function that depends on, but has properties beyond, those of the separate neural processes and modalities of the kind on which Dennett concentrates. Although in this new field, there is debate about how best to characterize phases of child development, it seems that the systems pass through emergent stages of consciousness similar to those I have postulated – Helmholzian, Woolfian, Vygotskyan, and Meadean – or through those that Zelazo and Sommerville write of in terms of progressively recursive representations. By adulthood, consciousness can often be of the minimal Helmholtzian perceptual kind, or consciousness of an emotion, but it can also easily switch to narrative consciousness of self and of self in relation to others.

What developmental psychologists have shown is that, with each level of emergence of new abilities, there arrives a set of functions that these abilities subserve that are unavailable to creatures without these abilities. So, from the first movements of naming and drawing attention of others to things, infants enter into a world of a shared folk-theoretical understanding. They become creatures of different kinds than any wild-living chimpanzee. They have taken the first step toward constructing a narrative consciousness of themselves and others as actors in the world, who cause intended effects and struggle with the vicissitudes of life.

A kind of culmination to the development of narrative by Nelson, Fivush, and others has been offered by Pennebaker et al. (Pennebaker, Kiecolt-Glaser, & Glaser, 1988; Pennebaker & Seagal, 1999). The basic finding is that adults who wrote narratives for as little as 20 minutes a day for 3 days on topics that were emotionally important to them (vicissitudes), as compared with people who wrote about neutral subjects, made fewer

visits to doctors' offices subsequently. They also underwent improvements in immune function. The argument is that traumatic and stressful events that are not integrated by the meaning-making processes of narrative can impair health. Making such events conscious and integrating them in story form has beneficial effects.

The Rise of Consciousness in Western Imaginative Literature

Writers have been fascinated by consciousness. The great book on the subject in Western literature is by Auerbach (1953). Its 20 chapters span 3,000 years, from *Genesis* to Virginia Woolf. On the one hand Western literature involves the "representation of reality." On the other it offers chronicles at successive moments in a history of mind turning round, recursively, to reflect upon itself. Each chapter in Auerbach's book starts with a quotation, ranging in length from a paragraph to several pages, from a particular writer in a particular time and society. For each, Auerbach analyzes the subject matter, the words, and the syntax. Immediately the reader is in the middle of a scene, with knights in medieval times, or with Dante and Virgil descending into the Inferno, or in La Mancha with Don Quixote, or in Paris with Proust's narrator Marcel. In each there is a society with certain understandings. In each, the characters inhabit a certain implicit theory of consciousness.

The opening sequences of the *Bible*, written by the Hebrews about 3,000 years ago, narrate the story of God's creation of the world. When the first human beings, Adam and Eve, enter the scene (attributed to the writer J., *Genesis*, Chapter 3), they eat of the fruit of the tree of knowledge of good and evil, and they become ashamed. It is hard to avoid the interpretation that in the moment of becoming conscious of good and evil they became self-conscious.

In the Greek tradition, *The Iliad* (Homer, 850 BCE/1987) was written from previously oral versions about the same time as *Genesis*. Jaynes (1976) has made several provocative proposals that further Auerbach's idea that a different kind of consciousness from our own is found in *Genesis* and *The Iliad*. His theory is that consciousness is not only a narrative and unifying agency, the basis for modern selfhood, but that in early writings such as *The Iliad* one sees the fading of an older mentality. He argues that before about 3,000 years ago, human beings had what he called bicameral minds. Bicameral means having two chambers, like two chambers of government, a senate and a house of representatives. One chamber was of species-typical behavior: mating, attacking if one is attacked, and so on. The second was of obedience to the injunctions of a ruler. These injunctions tended to be heard in acoustic form – do this, don't do that – and they allowed hierarchical societies to live in cities beyond the immediacy of face-to face contact. One feature of this second chamber of government, argued Jaynes, was that when a ruler died, his injunctions could still be heard. The phenomena were referred to in terms of gods. Each new ruler would take on the mantle of command and be translated into the role of god. So it was not that the figurines that archaeologists have unearthed from Mesopotamia were statues of gods. They were gods. When one visited their shrines in a house or public building and looked at a god, one could hear his or her words in one's mind's ear.

Modern narratizing consciousness arose, argued Jaynes, as people started to travel beyond the rather simply governed city-states and began to encounter others, to take part in trade, and in wars. The simple two-chamber mental government broke down. It was inadequate for dealing with people from different cultures. At first a few and then more individuals started to entertain thoughts and reasons that were neither instinctive responses nor obedience to authority. They began to tell more elaborate stories about themselves and to reason in inner debate.

In the opening sequences of *The Iliad* Achilles draws his sword in anger. He is responding instinctively to an insult from the Greek army's commander-in-chief, Agam-

emnon. At that moment a goddess appears to Achilles. No one else sees her. It is the goddess Athene, who utters to Achilles the tribal injunction: "Do not kill the commander-in-chief." The two chambers of mental government are here in conflict. The outcome: Achilles obeyed Athene, but went into a sulk. His refusal to fight resulted in the Greeks almost losing the Trojan War. In *The Iliad*, Jaynes and a number of other scholars have noted that there is no word for mind. Emotions occur not as conscious preoccupations prompting actions, but as physiological perturbations: *thumos* (livingness, which may include agitation), *phrenes* (breathing, which can become urgent), *kradie* (the heart, which may pound), and *etor* (guts, which may churn). In *The Iliad* the word *psuche* (from which later derived such concepts as soul and mind) was an insubstantial presence that may persist after death. The word *noos* did not mean mind, but was an organ of visual images.

For the preclassical Greeks, there were bodily agitations of *thumos*, *phrenes*, and so on, and there were voices of gods offering tribal injunctions but – according to Jaynes – no narrative self-consciousness. Plans were not decided by mortals but by immortals. In the opening sequence the question is asked by the narrator: Whose plan (*boule*) set Achilles and Agamemnon to contend? The answer: the plan of a god, Zeus. The readers of this chapter might sense something familiar. Here were people whose important actions were determined not by themselves but in some other way, by what they called gods. The familiarity is that Dennett offers an echo of this same idea. For him the actions of all of us are determined not by human agents qua agents, but by something impersonal: brain processes.

By the time of *The Odyssey*, something else was beginning to enter mental life. It was human cunning. But still the conscious, reflective mind had not emerged or at least had not emerged in its modern form. It had, as Snell (1953/1982) put it, to be invented. Its invention perhaps began 200 years after Homer with the poet Sappho, as she began to reflect on the idea that her continual falling in love with young women had something repetitive about it. It was brought more fully into being by Aeschylus and Sophocles in their narrative plays about how we human beings are responsible for our actions, although we cannot foresee and do not necessarily intend all their consequences. It reached fully modern form with Socrates in his teachings about how we can choose to think and decide how to act for the good.

Not all scholars agree that large-scale changes of the kind described by Jaynes and Snell did occur (see, e.g., Williams, 1993) in a progression of consciousness from Homeric to classical times. If they did, however, it seems likely that they were cultural changes, rather than the neurological ones postulated by Jaynes.

The beginnings of the modern world are set by many scholars (following Burckhardt, 1860/2002) with Dante and the Renaissance. At this time the literary idea came into its own of character that included the concept that some of it is hidden: People not only act as they did in Homer, but reflect consciously on what kind of person they would be to act in such and such a way. In the 20th century, literary consciousness took an inward turn. Now we read to recognize the images and thought-sequences of our own minds, of the kind that Woolf portrayed.

Following Auerbach, Watt (1957) traced some of the movements of consciousness in English novels of the 18th century in response to social and economic changes. So Defoe's (1719) *Robinson Crusoe* emphasizes the individualism of the times, particularly in economic matters, as well as the trait that would be characteristic of the novel, the reflective examination of the self and its doings, which Watt traces to Puritanism.

Romanticism, the literary era that we still inhabit, with its emphases on emotions and on style, started around 1750. Although there has been postmodern debate about whether language can represent anything at all outside itself, Abrams (1953) makes clear that throughout the Romantic period such representation has not really been the intention of literary writers. The dominant

metaphor has not been the mirror held up to nature, but the lamp that illuminates. Just as the young child by pointing and saying "fire truck" is directing the attention of her or his companion, so dramatists and novelists direct the attention of their readers.

It is appropriate, perhaps, that the growing elaboration of consciousness in the great bourgeois European novels of the 19th century should reach a kind of culmination with Freud's cases, in which the gaps in the subject's consciousness of intentions are filled precisely by elaborating a story (see Freud, 1905/1979; Marcus, 1974; Oatley, 1990).

In recent times, the most influential literary theorist has been Bakhtin (1963/1984), who has moved beyond analyses of single narrators, such as Robinson Crusoe. With the fully developed novel, for which Bakhtin takes Dostoyevsky as the paradigmatic author, we do not so much listen to the monological voice of an author or narrator. We take part in something more like a conversation. In such a novel, there are several centres of consciousness, and if the author does it right, one of these is the reader's.

Bakhtin's idea of the dialogical basis of social life as depicted in the novel is present in practical affairs in the West in the elaborate procedures by which justice is administered in courts of law (Bruner, 2002). In a criminal trial, two narratives are related, one by the prosecution and one by the defense. The critical narrative, however, is constructed by others (judge and jury) who have listened and supplied a narrative ending in terms of one of a small number of prescribed outcomes of morality stories that have been told and retold in our society. Such completions are known as verdicts (Pennington & Hastie, 1991).

There are universals in the telling of stories. All cultures use narrative for purposes that are somewhat didactic (Schank & Berman, 2002). That is to say, all stories have attributes that Donald attributed to myths. They explain human relationships to a problematic world, to the gods, to society, as well as to individual emotions and the self. Some kinds of stories are universal (Hogan, 2003), the love story for instance.

Its typical plot is of two lovers who long to be united. Their union is prevented, typically by a father. In the comic version, after vicissitudes the lovers are united. They live happily together, and the previously oppositional father rejoices in the union. In the tragic version, the union is prevented and the lovers die, perhaps to unite on some non-material plane.

In Western literature, something changes as we move from the mentality of Achilles and Abraham to that of Mrs Dalloway just after World War I or more recently to that of Jacques Austerlitz, whose life was fractured by World War II (Sebald, 2001). Perhaps literature has changed in response to changes in society. In the West, these changes have included a growing individualism and a growing faculty of inwardness and reflection. Perhaps, too, literary narrative has itself been partly responsible for some of these changes: a workshop of the mind. We can link Dennett to this series. To be thoroughly Western, thoroughly modern (perhaps postmodern) he says, we must give up the idea of mind and accept that there is only the brain. Meanwhile, however, others, such as Flanagan (2002), reject the dichotomy of mind and brain: Perhaps we can accept brain science and still retain the idea of a soul.

A recent addition to the series of literary analyses begun by Auerbach is by novelist and literary theorist David Lodge, who has become interested in the comparison of literary and scientific approaches to consciousness. In the title essay of *Consciousness and the Novel* (2002), Lodge describes how, while writing *Consciousness Explained*, Dennett came across one of Lodge's novels, *Nice Work* (1988), and found in it a satirical portrait of literary postmodernism very like the idea of the absent self that Dennett was proposing.

Lodge concludes that, although cognitive scientists have started to devote themselves to the question of consciousness, they may neglect both the substance of what has been discovered by writers of literature – which allows us to explore and understand our consciousness – and the human-

ism that is thereby promoted. In Lodge's (2001) novel, *Thinks*, the literary idea is represented in a talk given by the female protagonist, novelist Helen Reed, at a cognitive science conference on consciousness. She presents Marvell's (1637–1678/1968) poem, "The Garden," and ends her talk with the stanza in which occur these lines:

> *My soul into the boughs does glide:*
> *There like a Bird, it sits, and sings…*
>   *(p. 50)*

We can smile at Descartes' or Marvell's pre-scientific idea of the soul. Or we can see it as a metaphor of what is most human in us: Perhaps like a bird, we are able to take to the wings of imagination toward what may yet be possible for our species.

No matter how we conceptualize these issues, we might agree that stories depend on mental simulation, which in Victorian times was spoken of in terms of imagination and of dreams. To simulate, make models, derive analogies, project metaphors, form theories … this is what mind does. The concept of simulation is used in several senses in psychology. In one sense, the idea of simulation is used by Barsalou (2003) to conceptualize how multimodal and multisensory mappings between conceptualization and situated action are unified. A second sense is that of Harris (2000), who argues principally in the context of child development for simulation as the means by which we may read another mind and more generally project ourselves into situations not immediately present. I describe a third, related sense (Oatley, 1999): that stories are simulations that run not on computers but on minds. Although our human minds are good at understanding single causes and single intentions, we are not good at understanding several of them interacting. A simulation (in Oatley's sense) is a means we use to understand such complex interactions: It can be run forward in time for planning and backward for understanding. In their constructions of characters' intentions and actions, novels and dramas explore the what-if of problems we humans face (vicissitudes) when repercussions of our actions occur beyond the horizon of habitual understanding. Multiple centres of consciousness can be set up in literary simulations and enable us to enter the dialogues they afford.

Coda

If selfhood and the conscious understanding of ourselves and others are the work of the novelist in each of us, we may have learned some of this work from writers. If, furthermore, we take Vygotsky's view, stories are conduits by which thinking about the self, about human plans with others and their vicissitudes, and about human emotions has become explicitly available for our use via culture. Imaginative literature is a means by which a range of human situations and predicaments are explored so that they can be made part of ourselves. It is a range we could not hope to encounter directly.

I have argued that some of who we are flows from a unifying sense of ourselves as a character whom we improvise. Within narrative-like constraints we come to accept who we are and consciously to create ourselves to be coherent with it. We commit ourselves to certain others, and to a certain kind of life. But Dennett is also right. Plenty of our brain processes – those that produce an emotion or mood here, a lack of attention there, a piece of selfishness when we ought to be thinking of someone else – can proceed not from any conscious or narratively coherent self, but from ill-understood brain processes and unintegrated impulses. At present we have few estimates of what proportion of our acts and thoughts is, in the terms of this chapter, consciously decided within a unifying narrative frame and what proportion derives from unintegrated elements of what one might call the Dennettian unconscious. In terms of making arrangements with other people, it looks as if as many as 95% of actions based on explicitly mutual plans can be made as consciousness decides, based on folk-theoretical categories of goals and beliefs. In terms of

certain emotional processes, however, we may be closer to the unconscious end of the spectrum. Certainly Shakespeare, that most accomplished of all narrators and one who has perhaps prompted more insightful consciousness than any other, put it to us that a fair amount of our judgement may not be as conscious as we might like to believe, especially when we are in the grip of an emotion. In *A Midsummer Night's Dream*, love induced by the administration of juice of "a little western flower " (a mere neurochemical substance as one might nowadays say) is followed not so much by conscious rationality as by rationalization. It is the emotion rather than any consciously narrated choice that sets the frame of relationship, as it did I think among our hominid ancestors. The one so dosed with the juice gazes upon the new loved one, and language comes from the love, not love from the language-based decisions. Here in such a condition is Titania as she speaks to Bottom (the weaver) who has been changed into an ass. He is the first individual she sees when she opens her eyes after sleeping.

> I pray thee gentle mortal sing again.
> Mine ear is much enamoured of thy note;
> So is mine eye enthrallèd to thy shape;
> And thy fair virtue's force perforce doth move me
> On the first view, to say, to swear, I love thee (3, 1, 124–128).

The question for us humans is how to integrate the various phenomena, caught as we are between emotional urgencies and a meaning-making consciousness. Such integrative capacities are a recent emergence in human beings. Perhaps they are not yet working as well as they might.

Acknowledgments

I am very grateful to Robyn Fivush, Keith Stanovich, Richard West, Philip Zelazo, and two anonymous referees whose suggestions much helped my thoughts and understanding in revising this chapter.

References

Abrams, M. H. (1953). *The mirror and the lamp: Romantic theory and the critical tradition*. Oxford: Oxford University Press.

Aiello, L. C., & Dunbar, R. I. M. (1993). Neocortex size, group size, and the evolution of language. *Current Anthropology, 34*, 184–193.

Astington, J. W., Harris, P. L., & Olson, D. R. (Eds.). (1988). *Developing theories of mind*. New York: Cambridge University Press.

Auerbach, E. (1953). *Mimesis: The representation of reality in Western literature* (W. R. Trask, Trans.). Princeton, NJ: Princeton University Press.

Baddeley, A. D. (1993). Verbal and visual subsystems of working memory. *Current Biology, 3*, 563–565.

Bakhtin, M. (1984). *Problems of Dostoevsky's poetics* (C. Emerson, Trans.). Minneapolis: University of Minneapolis Press (Original work published 1963).

Bal, M. (1997). *Narratology: Introduction to the theory of narrative* (2nd ed). Toronto: University of Toronto Press.

Balleine, B., & Dickinson, A. (1998). Consciousness – the interface between affect and cognition. In J. Cornwell (Ed.), *Consciousness and human identity* (pp. 57–85). Oxford: Oxford University Press.

Barresi, J. (2001). Extending self-consciousness into the future. In C. Moore & K. Lemmon (Eds.). *The self in time: Developmental perspectives* (pp. 141–161). Mahwah, NJ: Erlbaum.

Barsalou, L. W. (2003). Situated simulation in the human conceptual system. *Language and Cognitive Processes, 18*, 513–562.

Behne, T., Carpenter, M., Call, J., & Tomasello, M. (2005). Unwilling versus unable: Infants' understanding of intentional action. *Developmental Psychology, 41*, 328–337.

Booth, W. C. (1988). *The company we keep: An ethics of fiction*. Berkeley, CA: University of California Press.

Brockmeier, J., & Carbaugh, D. (2001). Introduction. In J. Brockmeier & D. Carbaugh (Eds.), *Narrative and identity: Studies in autobiography, self, and culture* (pp. 1–22). Amsterdam: Benjamins.

Brockmeier, J., & Harré, R. (2001). Problems and promises of an alternative paradigm. In J. Brockmeier & D. Carbaugh (Eds.), *Narrative and identity: Studies in autobiography, self, and culture* (pp. 39–58). Amsterdam: Benjamins.

Bruner, J. (1986). *Actual minds, possible worlds*. Cambridge, MA: Harvard University Press.

Bruner, J., S. (2002). *Making stories: Law, literature, life*. New York: Farrar, Straus and Giroux.

Burckhardt, J. (2002). *The civilization of the Renaissance in Italy* (S. G. C Middlemore, Trans.). New York: Random House.

Call, J., Hare, B., Carpenter, M., & Tomasello, M. (2004). 'Unwilling' versus 'unable': Chimpanzees' understanding of human intentional action. *Developmental Science, 7*, 488–498.

Chauvet, J.-M., Deschamps, E. , & Hillaire, C. (1996). *Dawn of art: The Chauvet cave*. New York: Abrams.

Churchland, P. S. (1986). *Neurophilosophy*. Cambridge, MA: MIT Press.

Claparède, E. (1934). *La genèse de la hypothèse*. Geneva: Kundig.

Defoe, D. (1719). *Robinson Crusoe*. London: Penguin.

Dennett, D. C. (1991). *Consciousness explained*. Boston: Little, Brown & Co.

Dennett, D. C. (1992). The self as a center of narrative gravity. In F. S. Kessel, P. M. Cole, & D. L. Johnson (Eds.), *Self and consciousness: Multiple perspectives* (pp. 103–115). Hillsdale, NJ: Erlbaum.

Descartes, R. (1911). *Passions of the soul*. In E. L. Haldane & G. R. Ross (Eds.), *The philosophical works of Descartes*. New York: Dover (Original work published 1649).

de Waal, F. (1982). *Chimpanzee politics*. New York: Harper & Row.

Donald, M. (1991). *Origins of the modern mind*. Cambridge, MA: Harvard University Press.

Donne, J. (1960). *The sermons of John Donne, Vol. 8*. (G. R. Potter & E. M. Simpson, Eds.). Berkeley: University of California Press (Original work published 1615-1631).

Dunbar, R. I. M. (1993). Coevolution of neocortical size, group size, and language in humans. *Behavioral and Brain Sciences, 16*, 681–735.

Dunbar, R. I. M. (1996). *Grooming, gossip and the evolution of language*. London: Faber & Faber.

Dunbar, R. I. M. (2003). The social brain: Mind, language, and society in evolutionary perspective. *Annual Review of Anthropology, 32*, 163–181.

Dunbar, R. I. M. (2004). *The human story: A new history of mankind's evolution*. London: Faber.

Edelson, M. (1992). Telling and enacting stories in psychoanalysis. In J. W. Barron, M. N. Eagle, & D. L. Wolitzsky (Eds.), *Interface of psychoanalysis and psychology* (pp. 99–123). Washington, DC: American Psychological Association.

Fillmore, C. J. (1968). The case for case. In E. Bach & R. T. Harms (Eds.), *Universals in linguistic theory* (pp. 1–88). New York: Holt, Rinehart & Winston.

Fireman, G. D., McVay, T. E., & Flanagan, O. J. (Eds.). (2003). *Narrative and consciousness: Literature, psychology, and the brain*. New York: Oxford University Press.

Fivush, R. (2001). Owning experience: Developing subjective perspective in autobiographical narratives. In C. Moore & K. Lemmon (Eds.), *The self in time: Developmental perspectives* (pp. 35–52). Mahwah, NJ: Erlbaum.

Flanagan, O. (2002). *The problem of the soul: Two visions of mind and how to reconcile them*. New York: Basic Books.

Freud, S. (1979). Fragment of an analysis of a case of hysteria (Dora). In J. Strachey & A. Richards (Eds.), *The Pelican Freud library, Vol. 9: Case histories, II* (Vol. 7, pp. 7–122). London: Penguin.

Gallese, V., Keysers, C., & Rizzolatti, G. (2004). A unifying view of the basis of social cognition. *Trends in Cognitive Sciences*, 8, 396–403.

Gazzaniga, M. S. (1992). Brain modules and belief formation. In F. S. Kessel, P. M. Cole, & D. L. Johnson (Eds.), *Self and consciousness: Multiple perspectives* (pp. 88–102). Hillsdale, NJ: Erlbaum.

Gazzaniga, M. S. (1998). The split brain revisited. *Scientific American*, 279(1), 35–39.

Goldie, P. (2003). One's remembered past: Narrative thinking, emotion, and the external perspective. *Philosophical Papers*, 32, 301–309.

Goodall, J. (1986). *The chimpanzees of Gombe: Patterns of behavior*. Cambridge, MA: Harvard University Press.

Grazzani-Gavazzi, I., & Oatley, K. (1999). The experience of emotions of interdependence and independence following interpersonal errors in Italy and Anglophone Canada. *Cognition and Emotion*, 13, 49–63.

Groden, M., & Kreisworth, M. (1994). *The Johns Hopkins guide to literary theory and criticism*. Baltimore: Johns Hopkins University Press.

Harris, P. L. (2000). *The work of the imagination*. Oxford: Blackwell.

Helmholtz, H. (1962). *Treatise on physiological optics, Vol 3*. New York: Dover (Original work published 1866).

Hogan, P. C. (2003). *The mind and its stories*. Cambridge: Cambridge University Press.

Homer (1987). *The Iliad* (M. Hammond, Ed. & Trans.). Harmondsworth: Penguin (Original work in 850 BCE).

Humphrey, N. (1976). The social function of the intellect. In P. Bateson & R. Hinde (Eds.), *Growing points in ethology*. Cambridge: Cambridge University Press.

Humphrey, N. (2002). *The mind made flesh: Frontiers of psychology and evolution*. Oxford: Oxford University Press.

Humphrey, N., & Dennett, D. (2002). Speaking for ourselves: An assessment of multiple personality disorder. In N. Humphrey (Ed.), *The mind made flesh: Frontiers of psychology and evolution* (pp. 19–48). Oxford: Oxford University Press.

James, W. (1890). *The principles of psychology*. New York: Holt.

Jaynes, J. (1976). *The origin of consciousness in the breakdown of the bicameral mind*. London: Allen Lane.

Lacan, J. (1977). The mirror stage as formative of the function of the I as revealed in psychoanalytic experience. In A. Sheridan (Ed.), *Jacques Lacan: Ecrits, a selection* (pp. 1–7). London: Tavistock. (Original work published 1949.)

LeDoux, J. (1996). *The emotional brain: The mysterious underpinnings of emotional life*. New York: Simon & Schuster.

Lee, R. B. (1984). *The Dobe !Kung*. New York: Holt, Rinehart & Winston.

Lewis, M., Sullivan, M. W., Stanger, C., & Weiss, M. (1989). Self development and self-conscious emotions. *Child Development*, 60, 146–156.

Lodge, D. (1988). *Nice work*. London: Secker & Warburg.

Lodge, D. (2001). *Thinks*. London: Secker & Warburg.

Lodge, D. (2002). *Consciousness and the novel*. Cambridge, MA: Harvard University Press.

Marcus, S. (1984). Freud and Dora: Story, history, case history. In S. Marcus (Ed.), *Freud and the culture of psychoanalysis* (pp. 42–86). New York: Norton.

Marvell, A. (1968). *Complete poetry* (George deF. Lord, Ed.). New York: Modern Library. (Original work 1637–1678).

McGrew, W. (1992). *Chimpanzee material culture.* Cambridge: Cambridge University Press.

Mead, G. H. (1913). The social self. *Journal of Philosophy, Psychology and Scientific Methods, 10,* 374–380.

Mithen, S. (1996). *The prehistory of the mind: The cognitive origins of art and science.* London: Thames and Hudson.

Mithen, S. (2001). The evolution of imagination: An archaeological perspective. *SubStance,* #94–95, 28–54.

Moore, C., & Macgillivray, S. (2004). Social understanding and the development of prudence and prosocial behavior. In J. Baird & B. Sokol, (Eds.). *New directions for child and adolescent development.* New York: Jossey Bass.

Nelson, K. (1989). *Narratives from the crib.* New York: Cambridge University Press.

Nelson, K. (1996). *Language in cognitive development: Emergence of the mediated mind.* New York: Cambridge University Press.

Nelson, K. (2003). Narrative and the emergence of consciousness of self. In G. D. Fireman, T. E. McVay, & O. Flanagan (Eds.), *Narrative and consciousness: Literature, psychology, and the brain* (pp. 17–36). New York: Oxford University Press.

Oatley, K. (1988). On changing one's mind: A possible function of consciousness. In A. J. Marcel & E. Bisiach (Ed.), Consciousness in contemporary science (pp. 369–389). Oxford: Oxford University Press.

Oatley, K. (1990). Freud's psychology of intention: The case of Dora. *Mind and Language, 5,* 69–86.

Oatley, K. (1992a). *Best laid schemes: The psychology of emotions.* New York: Cambridge University Press.

Oatley, K. (1992b). Integrative action of narrative. In D. J. Stein & J. E. Young (Eds.), *Cognitive science and clinical disorders* (pp. 151–170.). San Diego: Academic Press.

Oatley, K. (1999). Why fiction may be twice as true as fact: Fiction as cognitive and emotional simulation. *Review of General Psychology, 3,* 101–117.

Oatley, K. (2002). *Character.* Paper presented at the Society for Personality and Social Psychology Annual Convention, Savannah, GA.

Oatley, K., & Larocque, L. (1995). Everyday concepts of emotions following every-other-day errors in joint plans. In J. Russell, J.-M. Fernandez-Dols, A. S. R. Manstead, &

J. Wellenkamp (Eds.), *Everyday conceptions of emotions: An introduction to the psychology, anthropology, and linguistics of emotion. NATO ASI Series D 81* (pp. 145–165). Dordrecht: Kluwer.

Oatley, K., & Mar, R. A. (2005). Evolutionary pre-adaptation and the idea of character in fiction. *Journal of Cultural and Evolutionary Psychology, 3,* 181–196.

Oatley, K., Sullivan, G. D., & Hogg, D. (1988). Drawing visual conclusions from analogy: A theory of preprocessing, cues and schemata in the perception of three dimensional objects. *Journal of Intelligent Systems 1,* 97–133.

Oatley, K., & Yuill, N. (1985). Perception of personal and interpersonal actions in a cartoon film. *British Journal of Social Psychology, 24,* 115–124.

Panksepp, J. (1998). *Affective neuroscience: The foundations of human and animal emotions.* Oxford: Oxford University Press.

Panksepp, J. (2001). The neuro-evolutionary cusp between emotions and cognitions: Implications for understanding consciousness and the emergence of a unified mind science. *Evolution and Cognition, 7,* 141–163.

Panksepp, J. (2005). Affective consciousness: Core emotional feelings in animals and humans. *Consciousness and Cognition, 14,* 30–80.

Paulhan, F. (1930). *The laws of feeling.* London: Kegan-Paul, French, Trubner & Co. (Original work published 1887).

Pennebaker, J. W., Kiecolt-Glaser, J. K., & Glaser, R. (1988). Disclosure of traumas and immune function: Health implications of psychotherapy. *Journal of Consulting and Clinical Psychology, 56,* 239–245.

Pennebaker, J. W., & Seagal, J. D. (1999). Forming a story: The health benefits of narrative. *Journal of Clinical Psychology, 55,* 1243–1254.

Pennington, N., & Hastie, R. (1991). A cognitive theory of juror decision making: The story model. *Cardozo Law Review, 13,* 519–557.

Peterson, J. (1999). *Maps of meaning.* New York: Routledge.

Povinelli, D. J. (2000). *Folk physics for apes: The chimpanzee's theory of how the world works.* New York: Oxford University Press.

Povinelli, D. J., & O'Neill, D. K. (2000). Do chimpanzees use their gestures to instruct each other? In S. Baron-Cohen, H. Tager-Flusberg, & D. Cohen (Eds.), *Understanding other minds: Perspectives from developmental cognitive neuroscience* (pp. 459–487). Oxford: Oxford University Press.

Power, R. (1979). The organization of purposeful dialogues. *Linguistics*, 17, 107–152.

Rizzolatti, G., & Arbib, M. A. (1998). Language within our grasp. *Trends in Neuroscience*, 21, 188–194.

Rizzolatti, G., Fogassi, L., & Gallese, V. (2001). Neurophysiological mechanisms underlying the understanding and imitation of action. *Nature Reviews: Neuroscience*, 2, 661–670.

Rumelhart, D. E. (1975). Notes on a schema for stories. In D. G. Bobrow & A. M. Collins (Eds.), *Representation and understanding: Studies in cognitive science*. New York: Academic Press.

Schank, R. C. (1990). *Tell me a story: A new look at real and artificial memory*. New York: Scribner.

Schank, R. C., & Berman, T. R. (2002). The pervasive role of stories. In M. C. Green, J. J. Strange, & T. C. Brock (Eds.), *Narrative impact: Social and cognitive foundations* (pp. 287–313). Mahwah, NJ: Erlbaum.

Searle, J. R. (1969). *Speech acts: An essay in the philosophy of language*. Cambridge: Cambridge University Press.

Sebald, W. G. (2001). *Austerlitz*. Toronto: Knopf Canada.

Shakespeare, W. (1997). *The Norton Shakespeare* (S. Greenblatt, Ed.). New York: Norton. (Original work published 1623).

Snell, B. (1982). *The discovery of the mind in Greek philosophy and literature*. New York: Dover. (Original work published 1953).

Spence, D. P. (1982). *Historical truth and narrative truth*. New York: Dover.

Strawson, G. (2004). Against narrativity. *Ratio*, 17, 428–452.

Sussman, G. J. (1975). *A computer model of skill acquisition*. New York: American Elsevier.

Tomasello, M. (1999). *The cultural origins of human cognition*. Cambridge, MA: Harvard University Press.

Tomasello, M., & Rakoczy, H. (2003). What makes human cognition unique? From individual to shared to collective intentionality. *Mind and Language*, 18, 121–147.

Trabasso, T., & van den Broek, P. (1985). Causal thinking and the representation of narrative events. *Journal of Memory and Language*, 24, 612–630.

Turner, S. R. (1994). *The creative process: A computer model of storytelling and creativity*. Hillsdale, NJ: Erlbaum.

Velleman, J. D. (2000). *The possibility of practical reason*. Oxford: Oxford University Press.

Velleman, J. D. (2002). *The self as narrator*. First of the Jerome Simon Lectures in Philosophy, October 2002 University of Toronto. Retrieved from www-personal.umich.edu/~velleman/Work/Narrator.html.

Vygotsky, L. (1962). *Thought and language* (E. H. G. Vakar, Trans.). Cambridge, MA: MIT Press.

Vygotsky, L. (1978). Tool and symbol in child development. In M. Cole, V. John-Steiner, S. Scribner, & E. Souberman (Eds.), *Mind in society: The development of higher mental processes* (pp. 19–30). Cambridge, MA: Harvard University Press. (Original work published 1930).

Watt, I. (1957). *The rise of the novel: Studies in Defoe, Richardson, and Fielding*. London: Chatto & Windus.

Willams, B. (1993). *Shame and necessity*. Berkeley, CA: University of California Press.

Wilson, G. M. (2003). Narrative. In J. Levinson (Ed.), *The Oxford handbook of aesthetics* (pp. 392–407). New York: Oxford University Press.

Woolf, V. (1925). *Mrs. Dalloway*. London: Hogarth Press.

Wrangham, R. (2001). Out of the *Pan*, into the fire: How our ancestors' evolution depended on what they ate. In F. B. M. de Waal (Ed.), *Tree of origin: What primate behavior can tell us about human social evolution* (pp. 121–143). Cambridge, MA: Harvard University Press.

Zelazo, P. D. (2004). The development of conscious control in childhood. *Trends in Cognitive Sciences*, 8, 12–17.

Zelazo, P. D. , & Sommerville, J. A. (2001). Levels of consciousness of the self in time. In C. Moore & K. Lemmon (Eds.). *The self in time: Developmental perspectives* (pp. 229–252). Mahwah, NJ: Erlbaum.

E. Developmental Psychology

CHAPTER 15

The Development of Consciousness

Philip David Zelazo, Helena Hong Gao, and Rebecca Todd

Abstract

This chapter examines the extent to which consciousness might develop during ontogeny. Research on this topic is converging on the suggestion that consciousness develops through a series of levels, each of which has distinct consequences for the quality of subjective experience, the potential for episodic recollection, the complexity of children's explicit knowledge structures, and the possibility of the conscious control of thought, emotion, and action. The discrete levels of consciousness identified by developmental research are useful for understanding the complex, graded structure of conscious experience in adults, and they reveal a fundamental dimension along which consciousness varies: the number of iterations of recursive reprocessing of the contents of consciousness.

Introduction

Despite the explosion of scientific interest in consciousness during the past two decades, there is a relative dearth of research on the way in which consciousness develops during ontogeny. This may be due in part to a widespread belief that it goes without saying that children are conscious in same way as adults. Indeed, most people probably believe that newborn infants – whether protesting their arrival with a vigorous cry or staring wide-eyed and alert at their mother – are conscious in an essentially adult-like fashion. So, although there are dramatic differences between infants and toddlers and between preschoolers and adolescents, these differences are often assumed to reflect differences in the contents of children's consciousness, but not in the nature of consciousness itself.

There is currently considerable debate, however, concerning when a fetus first becomes capable of conscious experience (including pain). This debate has been instigated by proposed legislation requiring physicians in the United States to inform women seeking abortions after 22 weeks gestational age (i.e., developmental age plus 2 weeks) that fetuses are able to experience pain (Arkansas, Georgia, and

Minnesota have already passed similar laws). Professor Sunny Anand, a paediatrician and an expert on neonatal pain, recently testified before the U.S. Congress (in relation to the Unborn Child Pain Awareness Act of 2005; Anand, 2005) that the "substrate and mechanisms for conscious pain perception" develop during the second trimester. Others (e.g., Burgess & Tawia, 1996; Lee et al., 2005) have suggested that consciousness develops later, during the third trimester (at around 30 weeks gestational age) – because that is when there is first evidence of functional neural pathways connecting the thalamus to sensory cortex (see Chapter 27).

Inherent in these claims is the assumption that consciousness is an "all-or-nothing" phenomenon – one is either conscious or not, and capable of consciousness or not (cf. Dehaene & Changeux, 2004). This assumption is also reflected, for example, in information-processing models (e.g., Moscovitch, 1989; Schacter, 1989) in which consciousness corresponds to a single system and information is either available to this system or not. From this perspective, it is natural to think of consciousness as something that *emerges* full-blown at a particular time in development, rather than something that itself undergoes transformation – something that *develops*, perhaps gradually. Although the current debate concerning pain and abortion has centered on the prenatal period, there are those who believe that consciousness emerges relatively late. Jerome Kagan (1998), for example, writes that "sensory awareness is absent at birth but clearly present before the second birthday" (p. 48). It should be noted that Kagan believes that consciousness does develop beyond the emergence of sensory awareness, but if you've ever met a toddler (say, a 14-month-old), it may be difficult to imagine that children at this age lack sensory awareness – which Kagan (1998) defines as "awareness of present sensations" (p. 46).

The implications of Kagan's claim are profound. For example, if we follow Nagel (1974), who asserts that the essence of subjective experience is that it is "like something" to have it (see Chapter 3), we might conclude, as Carruthers (1989) does, that it

does not feel like anything to be an infant. Carruthers (1996) further tests our credulity when he argues that children are not actually conscious until 4 years of age (because it is not until then that children can formulate beliefs about psychological states). Kagan and Carruthers characterize infants and/or young children essentially as unconscious automata or zombies (cf. Chalmers, 1996; see Chapter 3) – capable of cognitive function but lacking sentience.

Although many theorists treat consciousness as a single, all-or-nothing phenomenon, others distinguish between first-order consciousness and a meta-level of consciousness. For example, they may distinguish between consciousness and meta-consciousness (Schooler, 2002), primary consciousness and higher-order consciousness (Edelman & Tononi, 2000), or core consciousness and extended consciousness (Damasio, 1999). In the developmental literature, this dichotomous distinction is usually described as the difference between consciousness and self-consciousness (e.g., Kagan, 1981; Lewis, 2003). In most cases, the first-order consciousness refers to awareness of present sensations (e.g., an integrated multimodal perceptual scene; Edelman & Tononi, 2000), whereas the meta-level consciousness is generally intended to capture the full complexity of consciousness as it is typically experienced by healthy human adults. Edelman and Tononi (2000), for example, suggest that higher-order consciousness is, according to their model, "accompanied by a sense of self and the ability ... explicitly to construct past and future scenes" (p. 102). Developmentally, the implication is that infants are limited to relatively simple sensory consciousness until an enormous transformation (usually presumed to be neurocognitive in nature and involving the acquisition of language or some degree of conceptual understanding) occurs that simultaneously adds multiple dimensions (e.g., self-other, past-future) to the qualitative character of experience. This profound metamorphosis has typically been hypothesized to occur relatively early in infancy (e.g., Stern, 1990; Trevarthen & Aitken, 2001) or some time during the second year (e.g.,

Kagan, 1981; Lewis, 2003; Wheeler, 2000), depending on the criteria used for inferring higher-order self-consciousness.

In this chapter, we propose that discussions of the development of consciousness have been hampered by a reliance on relatively undifferentiated notions of consciousness. Indeed, we argue that developmental data suggest the need for not just two, but *many* dissociable levels of consciousness; information may be available at one level but not at others (see Morin, 2004, 2006, for a review of recent models of consciousness that rely on the notion of levels; see also Cleeremans & Jiménez, 2002, for a related perspective on consciousness as a graded phenomenon). Consideration of these levels and of their utility in explaining age-related changes in children's behavior has implications for our understanding of consciousness in general, including individual differences in reflectivity and mindfulness (see Chapter 19), but the focus here is on development during childhood. Many of the arguments regarding *when* consciousness emerges – for example, at 30 months gestational age (e.g., Burgess & Tawia, 1996), at 12 to 15 months after birth (Perner & Dienes, 2003), at the end of the second year (Lewis, 2003), or around the fourth birthday (Carruthers, 2000) – have merit, and we propose that some of the most salient discrepancies among these accounts can be reconciled from the perspective that consciousness has several levels. Different theorists have directed their attention to the emergence of different levels of consciousness; a developmental perspective allows us to integrate these levels into a more comprehensive model of consciousness as a complex, dynamic phenomenon.

Early Accounts of the Development of Consciousness

For early theorists such as Baldwin (e.g., 1892), Piaget (1936/1952), and Vygotsky (1934/1986), consciousness was *the* problem to be addressed by the new science of psychology, and these theorists made major contributions by showing how children's consciousness, including the way in which children experience reality, is changed during particular developmental transformations. That is, they all understood that the structure of consciousness itself – and not just the contents of consciousness – develops over the course of childhood. For Baldwin, infants' experience can initially be characterized as a state of adualism – meaning that they are unaware of any distinctions that might be implicit in the structure of experience (e.g., subject vs. object, ego vs. alter; e.g., Baldwin, 1906). During the course of development, however, children proceed through a series of "progressive differentiations between the knower and the known" (Cahan, 1984, p. 131) that culminates in transcending these dualisms and recognizing their origin in what Baldwin calls the dialectic of personal growth (by *personal*, Baldwin refers both to oneself and to persons). Baldwin, therefore, suggests that consciousness develops through a circular process of differentiation and then integration (cf. Eliot's poem, "Little Gidding": "And the end of all our exploring/ Will be to arrive where we started/ And know the place for the first time.").

Imitation plays a key role in this dialectic, which starts when an infant observes behavior that is (at least partially) outside of his or her behavioral repertoire. At this point, the infant cannot *identify* with the behavior or the agent of the behavior, so the behavior is viewed solely in terms of its outward or *projective* aspects. By imitating this behavior, however, the infant discovers the subjective side of it, including, for example, the feeling that accompanies it. Once this happens, the infant automatically *ejects* this newly discovered subjectivity back into his or her understanding of the original behavior. Baldwin (1894) gives the example of a girl who watches her father prick himself with a pin. Initially, she has no appreciation of its painful consequence. When she imitates the behavior, however, she will feel the pain and then immediately understand that her father felt it too. Subsequently, she will view the behavior of pin pricking in a different light; her understanding of the behavior will have been transformed from *projective* to *subjective* to *ejective*. In effect, she will have brought the behavior into the scope of her self- and social-understanding, expanding the range of human behavior with which she can identify. Baldwin (1897, p. 36) writes, "It is not I, but I am to become it," a formulation that seems to capture the same fundamental insight about the development of consciousness as Freud's (1933/1940, p. 86) famous "Wo Es war, soll Ich werden." ("Where it was, there I shall be").

Piaget similarly saw "increasing self-awareness of oneself as acting subject" (Ferrari, Pinard, & Runions, 2001, p. 207) – or decreasing egocentrism – as one of the major dimensions of developmental change, and he tied this development to the emergence of new cognitive structures that allowed for new ways of knowing or experiencing reality. Indeed, for Piaget, consciousness (the experience of reality) is dependent on one's cognitive structures, which are believed to develop through a series of stages primarily as a result of a process of equilibration, whereby they become increasingly abstract (from practical to conceptual) and reflect more accurately the logic of the universe. Consciousness also develops in a characteristic way regardless of children's developmental stage; at all stages, from practical to conceptual, consciousness "proceeds from the periphery to the center" (Piaget, 1974/1977, p. 334), by which Piaget meant that one first becomes aware of goals and results and then later comes to understand the means or intentions by which these results are accomplished. For older (formal operational) children, Piaget (1974/1977) noted, this development from periphery to center can occur quite quickly via the *reflexive abstraction* of practical sensorimotor knowledge. This process, which corresponds to conceptualization or reflective redescription, allows children more rapidly to transform knowledge-in-action into articulate conceptual understanding. In all cases, however, we see consciousness developing from action to conceptualization. Piaget's (1974/1977) emphasis on the role of action in the development of consciousness was summarized concisely at the end of his key volume on the topic, *The Grasp of Consciousness*, where he wrote, "The study of cognizance [i.e., consciousness] has led us to place it in the general perspective of the circular relationship between subject and object. The subject only learns to know himself when acting on the object, and the latter can become known only as a result of progress of the actions carried out on it" (p. 353).

Vygotsky (1934/1986), in contrast to both Baldwin and Piaget, noted that children's consciousness was transformed mainly via the appropriation of cultural tools, chiefly language. Vygotsky, and then Luria (e.g., 1959, 1961), proposed that thought and speech first develop independently but then become tightly intertwined as a result of internalization – a process whereby the formal structure inherent in a cultural practice, such as speaking, is first acquired in overt behavior and then reflected in one's private thinking. Initially, speech serves a communicative purpose, but later it also acquires semantic, syntactic, and regulatory functions. The emergent regulatory function of speech is inherently self-conscious, and it allows children to organize and plan their behavior, essentially rendering them capable of consciously controlled behavior (Luria, 1961; Vygotsky, 1934/1986). Vygotsky (1978) wrote, "With the help of speech children, unlike apes, acquire the capacity to be both the subjects and objects of their own behavior" (p. 26). For Vygotsky, then, consciousness was transformed by language, with important consequences for action.

Contemporary theorists have elaborated on some of these seminal ideas about the development of consciousness – although they have not always explicitly addressed the implications for the character of children's subjective experience. Barresi and Moore (1996), for example, offered a model of the development of perspective taking that builds on Baldwin's (1897) dialectic of personal growth. According to Barresi and Moore, young children initially take a first-person, present-oriented perspective on their own behavior (e.g., "I want candy now") and a third-person perspective on the behavior of others – seeing that behavior from the outside, as it were. Because simultaneous consideration of first- and third-person perspectives is required for a representational understanding of mental states (e.g., "I know there are sticks in the box, but he thinks there is candy"), young children have difficulty understanding false beliefs – both their own and those of others (see Wellman, Cross, & Watson, 2001, for a review). With development, however, children are better able to adopt a third-person perspective on their own behavior, imagine a first-person perspective on the behavior of others, and coordinate these perspectives into a single schema.

As another example, Karmiloff-Smith (1992) builds on Piaget's (1974/1977) idea of reflexive abstraction with her model of Representational Redescription, in which consciousness develops as a function of domain-specific experience. According to this model, knowledge is originally represented in an implicit, procedural format (Level I), but, with sufficient practice, behavioral mastery of these procedures is achieved and the knowledge is automatically redescribed into a more abstract, explicit format (Level E1). This representational format reveals the structure of the procedures, but is still not conscious: Consciousness comes with yet additional levels of redescription or 'explicitation,' which occur "spontaneously as part of an internal drive toward the creation of intra-domain and inter-domain relationships" (1992, p. 18). Level E2 is conscious but not verbalizable, whereas Level E3 is both conscious and verbalizable.

Finally, Zelazo and his colleagues have expounded a model of consciousness, the Levels of Consciousness (LOC) model (e.g., Zelazo, 1999, 2004; Zelazo & Jacques, 1996; Zelazo & Zelazo, 1998) that builds on the work of Baldwin, Piaget, and Vygotsky and Luria – but especially Vygotsky and Luria. Because this model is relatively comprehensive and addresses explicitly the potential implications of neurocognitive development for children's subjective experience, we describe it in some detail. In what follows, we first provide an overview of the model and then show how it aims to provide an account of the way in which consciousness develops during the first 5 years of life (and potentially beyond). Empirical and theoretical contributions to our understanding of the development of consciousness are reviewed in the context of the LOC model.

Overview of the Levels of Consciousness (LOC) Model

The Levels of Consciousness (LOC) model describes the structure of consciousness and attempts to show the consequences that reflection has on the structure and functions of consciousness, including the key role that reflection plays in the conscious control of thought, action, and emotion via explicit rules. In what follows, we consider the implications of the LOC model for (1) the structure of consciousness, (2) cognitive control via the use of rules at different levels of complexity, (3) the functions of prefrontal cortex, and (4) the development of consciousness in childhood.

The Structure of Consciousness

According to the LOC model, consciousness can operate at multiple discrete levels, and these levels have a hierarchical structure – they vary from a first-order level of consciousness (minimal consciousness) to higher-order reflective levels that subsume lower levels. Higher levels of consciousness are brought about through an iterative process of reflection, or the recursive reprocessing of the contents of consciousness via thalamocortical circuits involving regions of prefrontal cortex. Each degree of reprocessing results in a higher level of consciousness, and this in turn allows for the integration of more information into an experience of a stimulus before a new stimulus is experienced; it allows the stimulus to be considered relative to a larger interpretive context. In this way, each additional level of consciousness changes the structure of experience, and the addition of each level has unique consequences for the quality of subjective experience: The addition of higher levels results in a richer, more detailed experience and generates more "psychological distance" from stimuli (e.g., Carlson, Davis, & Leach, 2005; Dewey, 1931/1985; Sigel, 1993). But the addition of new levels also has implications for the potential for episodic recollection (because information is processed at a deeper level; Craik & Lockhart, 1972), the complexity of children's explicit knowledge structures, and the possibility of the conscious control of thought, emotion, and action.

Control by Rules at Various Levels of Complexity

According to the LOC model, conscious control is accomplished, in large part, by the ability to formulate, maintain in working memory, and then act on the basis of explicit rule systems at different levels of complexity – from a single rule relating a stimulus to a response, to a pair of rules, to a hierarchical system of rules that allows one to select among incompatible pairs of rules, as explained by the Cognitive Complexity and Control (CCC) theory (e.g., Frye, Zelazo, & Palfai, 1995; Zelazo, Müller, Frye, & Marcovitch, 2003). On this account, rules are formulated in an ad hoc fashion in potentially silent self-directed speech. These rules link antecedent conditions to consequences, as when we tell ourselves, "If I see a mailbox, then I need to mail this letter." When people reflect on the rules they represent, they are able to consider them in contradistinction to other rules and embed them under higher-order rules, in the same way that we might say, "If it's before 5 p.m., then if I see a mailbox, then I need to mail this letter, otherwise, I'll have to go directly to the post office." In this example, the selection of a simple conditional statement regarding the mailbox is made dependent on the satisfaction of another condition (namely, the time). More complex rule systems, like the system of embedded if-if-then rules in this example, permit the more flexible selection of certain rules for acting when multiple conflicting rules are possible. The selection of certain rules then results in the amplifica-tion and diminution of attention to potential influences on thought (inferences) and action when multiple possible influences are present.

According to the LOC model, increases in rule complexity – whether age-related (see below) or in response to situational demands – are made possible by corresponding increases in the extent to which one reflects on one's representations: They are made possible by increases in level of consciousness. Rather than taking rules for granted and simply assessing whether their antecedent conditions are satisfied, reflection involves making those rules themselves an object of consideration and considering them in contradistinction to other rules at that same level of complexity.

Figure 15.1 contrasts relatively automatic action at a lower level of consciousness (a) with relatively deliberate action at a higher level of consciousness (b). The former type of action (a) is performed in response to the most salient, low-resolution aspects of a situation, and it is based on the formulation of a relatively simple rule system – in this case, nothing more than an explicit representation of a goal maintained in working memory. The more deliberate action (b) occurs in response to a more carefully considered construal of the same situation, brought about by several degrees of reprocessing the situation. The higher level of consciousness depicted in Figure 15.1b allows for the formulation (and maintenance in working memory) of a more complex and more flexible system of rules or inferences (in this case, a system of embedded rules considered against the backdrop of the goal that occasions them).

The tree diagram in Figure 15.2 illustrates the way in which hierarchies of rules can be formed through reflection – the way in which one rule can first become an object of explicit consideration at a higher level of consciousness and then be embedded under another higher-order rule and controlled by it. Rule A, which indicates that response 1 (r_1) should follow stimulus 1 (s_1), is incompatible with rule C, which connects s_1 to r_2. Rule A is embedded under, and

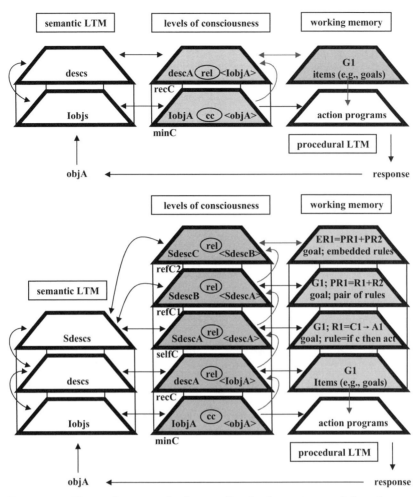

Figure 15.1. The implications of reflection (levels of consciousness) for rule use. (a, top): Relatively automatic action on the basis of a lower level of consciousness. An object in the environment (objA) triggers an intentional representation of that object (IobjA) in semantic long-term memory (LTM); this IobjA, which is causally connected (cc) to a bracketed objA, becomes the content of consciousness (referred to at this level as minimal consciousness or minC). The contents of minC are then fed back into minC via a re-entrant feedback process, producing a new, more reflective level of consciousness referred to as recursive consciousness or recC. The contents of recC can be related (rel) in consciousness to a corresponding description (descA) or label, which can then be deposited into working memory (WM) where it can serve as a goal (G1) to trigger an action program from procedural LTM in a top-down fashion. (b, bottom): Subsequent (higher) levels of consciousness, including self-consciousness (selfC), reflective consciousness 1 (refC1), and reflective consciousness 2 (refC2). Each level of consciousness allows for the formulation and maintenance in WM of more complex systems of rules. (Reprinted with permission from Zelazo, P. D. (2004). The development of conscious control in childhood. *Trends in Cognitive Sciences, 8,* 12–17.) (See color plates.)

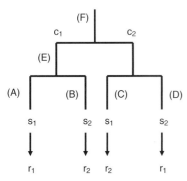

Figure 15.2. Hierarchical tree structure depicting formal relations among rules. *Note:* c_1 and c_2 = contexts; s_1 and s_2 = stimuli; r_1 and r_2 = responses. (Adapted from Frye, D., Zelazo, P. D., & Palfai, T. (1995). Theory of mind and rule-based reasoning. *Cognitive Development, 10*, 483–527).

controlled by, a higher- order rule (rule E) that can be used to select rule A or rule B, and rule E, in turn, is embedded under an even higher-order rule (rule F) that can be used to select the discrimination between rules A and B as opposed to the discrimination between rules C and D. This higher-order rule makes reference to setting conditions or contexts (c_1 and c_2) that condition the selection of lower-order rules, and that would be taken for granted in the absence of reflection. Higher-order rules of this type (F) are required in order to use bivalent rules in which the same stimulus is linked to different responses (e.g., rules A and C). Simpler rules like E suffice to select between univalent stimulus-response associations – rules in which each stimulus is uniquely associated with a different response, as when making discriminations *within* a single stimulus dimension.

To formulate a higher-order rule such as F and deliberate between rules C and D, on the one hand, and rules A and B, on the other, one has to be aware of the fact that one knows both pairs of lower-order rules. Figuratively speaking, one has to view the two rule pairs from the perspective of (F). This illustrates how increases in reflection on lower-order rules are required for increases in embedding to occur. Each level of consciousness allows for the formulation

and maintenance in working memory of a more complex rule system. A particular level of consciousness (SelfC) is required to use a single explicit rule such as (A); a higher level of consciousness (refC1) is required to select between two univalent rules using a rule such as (E); a still higher level (refC2) is required to switch between two bivalent rules using a rule such as (F).

The Role of Prefrontal Cortex in Higher Levels of Consciousness

The potential role of prefrontal cortex in reflection is arguably revealed by work on the neural correlates of rule use (see Bunge, 2004). Bunge and Zelazo (2006) summarized a growing body of evidence that prefrontal cortex plays a key role in rule use and that different regions of prefrontal cortex are involved in representing rules at different levels of complexity – from learned stimulus-reward associations (orbitofrontal cortex; Brodmann's area [BA] 11), to sets of conditional rules (ventrolateral prefrontal cortex [BA 44, 45, 47] and dorsolateral prefrontal cortex [BA 9, 46]), to an explicit consideration of task sets (rostrolateral prefrontal cortex [or frontopolar cortex; BA 10]; see Figure 15.3).

Figure 15.3 illustrates the way in which regions of prefrontal cortex correspond to rule use at different levels of complexity. Notice that the function of prefrontal cortex is proposed to be hierarchical in a way that corresponds, roughly, to the hierarchical complexity of the rule use underlying conscious control. As individuals engage in reflective processing, ascend through levels of consciousness, and formulate more complex rule systems, regions of lateral prefrontal cortex are recruited and integrated into an increasingly elaborate hierarchy of prefrontal cortical function via thalamo-cortical circuits. As the hierarchy unfolds, information is first processed via circuits connecting the thalamus and orbitofrontal cortex. This information is then reprocessed and fed forward to ventrolateral prefrontal

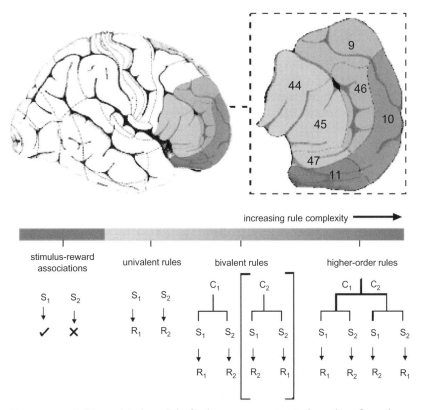

Figure 15.3. A hierarchical model of rule representation in lateral prefrontal cortex. A lateral view of the human brain is depicted at the top of the figure, with regions of prefrontal cortex identified by the Brodmann areas (BA) that comprise them: Orbitofrontal cortex (BA 11), ventrolateral prefrontal cortex (BA 44, 45, 47), dorsolateral prefrontal cortex (BA 9, 46), and rostrolateral prefrontal cortex (BA 10). The prefrontal cortex regions are shown in various colors, indicating which types of rules they represent. Rule structures are depicted below, with darker shades of blue indicating increasing levels of rule complexity. The formulation and maintenance in working memory of more complex rules depend on the reprocessing of information through a series of levels of consciousness, which in turn depends on the recruitment of additional regions of prefrontal cortex into an increasingly complex hierarchy of prefrontal cortex activation. *Note*: S = stimulus; check = reward; cross = nonreward; R = response; C = context, or task set. Brackets indicate a bivalent rule that is currently being ignored. (Reprinted with permission from Bunge, S., & Zelazo, P. D. (2006). A brain-based account of the development of rule use in childhood. *Current Directions in Psychological Science 15*, 118–121.) (See color plates.)

cortex via circuits connecting the thalamus and ventrolateral prefrontal cortex. Further processing occurs via circuits connecting the thalamus to dorsolateral prefrontal cortex. Thalamocortical circuits involving rostrolateral prefrontal cortex play a transient role in the explicit consideration of task sets at each level in the hierarchy.

Developmental Increases in Children's Highest Level of Consciousness

According to the LOC model, there are four major age-related increases in the highest level of consciousness that children are able to muster (although children may operate at different levels of consciousness in different situations). These age-related increases in children's highest level of consciousness correspond to the growth of prefrontal cortex, which follows a protracted developmental course that mirrors the development of the ability to use rules at higher levels of complexity. In particular, developmental research suggests that the order of acquisition of rule types shown in Figure 15.3 corresponds to the order in which corresponding regions of prefrontal cortex mature. Gray matter volume reaches adult levels earliest in orbitofrontal cortex, followed by ventrolateral prefrontal cortex, and then by dorsolateral prefrontal cortex (Giedd et al., 1999; Gogtay et al., 2004). Measures of cortical thickness suggest that dorsolateral prefrontal cortex and rostrolateral prefrontal cortex (or frontopolar cortex) exhibit similar, slow rates of structural change (O'Donnell, Noseworthy, Levine, & Dennis, 2005). With development, children are able to engage neural systems involving the hierarchical coordination of more regions of prefrontal cortex – a hierarchical coordination that develops in a bottom-up fashion, with higher levels in the hierarchy operating on the products of lower levels through thalamocortical circuits.

Minimal consciousness. The LOC model starts with the assumption that simple sentience is mediated by *minimal consciousness* (minC; cf. Armstrong, 1980), the first-order consciousness on the basis of which more complex hierarchical forms of consciousness are constructed (through degrees of reprocessing). MinC is intentional in Brentano's (1874/1973) sense – any experience, no matter how attenuated, is experience *of* something (see Brentano's description of presentations, p. 78 ff.), and it motivates approach and avoidance behavior, a feature that is essential to the evolutionary emergence of minC (e.g., Baldwin, 1894; Dewey, 1896; Edelman, 1989). However, minC is unreflective and present-oriented and makes no reference to an explicit sense of self; these features develop during the course of childhood. While minimally conscious, one is conscious of *what* one sees (the object of one's experience) as pleasurable (approach) or painful (avoid), but one is not conscious of *seeing* what one sees or that *one* (as an agent) is seeing what one sees. And because minC is tied to ongoing stimulation, one cannot recall seeing what one saw. MinC is hypothesized to characterize infant consciousness prior to the end of the first year of life.

In adults, this level of consciousness corresponds to so-called implicit information processing, as when we drive a car without full awareness, perhaps because we are conducting a conversation at a higher level of consciousness (in this example, we are operating at two different levels of consciousness simultaneously). Our behavioral routines are indeed elicited directly and automatically, but they are elicited as a function of consciousness of immediate environmental stimuli (cf. Perruchet & Vinter, 2002). It follows that implicit processing does not occur in a zombie-like fashion; it is simply unreflective (because the contents of minC are continually replaced by new stimulation) and, as a result, unavailable for subsequent recollection.

Consider how minC figures in the production of behavior according to the LOC model (Fig. 15.1a). An object in the environment (objA) triggers a "description" from semantic long-term memory. This particular description (or IobjA, for "intentional object") then becomes an intentional object of minC and automatically triggers an associated action program that is coded in procedural long-term memory. A telephone, for example, might be experienced by a minC baby as 'suckable thing,' and this description might trigger the stereotypical motor schema of sucking. Sensorimotor schemata are modified through practice and accommodation (i.e., learning can occur; e.g., DeCasper et al., 1994; Kisilevsky et al., 2003; Siqueland & Lipsitt, 1966; Swain, Zelazo, & Clifton, 1993), and they can be coordinated into higher-order units (e.g., Cohen, 1998; Piaget, 1936/1952), but a minC infant cannot represent these schemata in minC (the infant is only aware of the stimuli that trigger them). In the absence of reflection and a higher level of consciousness, the contents of minC are continually replaced by new intero- and exteroceptor stimulation and cannot be deposited into working memory.

Thus, minC infants exhibit learning and memory and may well perceive aspects of themselves and their current state implicitly, but they have no means by which they can consciously represent past experiences or states or entertain future-oriented representations. That is, they cannot engage in conscious recollection, although they provide clear behavioral evidence of memory, and they cannot entertain conscious expectations or plans, although their behavior is often future-oriented (e.g., Haith, Hazan, & Goodman, 1988; see Reznick, 1994, for a discussion of different interpretations of future-oriented behavior). At present, there is no behavioral evidence that young infants are capable of conscious recollection (as opposed to semantic memory; Tulving 1985) or explicit self awareness; their experience of events seems to be restricted to the present (see Figure 15.4a) – including objects in the immediate environment and current physical states.

Within the constraints of minC, however, infants may come to learn quite a bit about their bodies in relation to the world (e.g., Gallagher, 2005; Meltzoff, 2002; Rochat, 2001). Rochat (2003), for example, proposes five levels of self-understanding that, from the perspective of the LOC model, can be seen to unfold within particular levels of consciousness. The levels of self-understanding that develop in early infancy are characterized by somatic sensation and expectancies about the world, but they are not accompanied by explicit, higher-order representations of self and other. For example, the emergence of *level 1*, or the *differentiated self*, begins at birth, as infants learn to distinguish their own touch from that of another. *Level 2*, which refers to what Rochat calls the *situated self*, emerges at around 2 months and involves implicit awareness of the self as an agent situated in space. In this model, the differentiated and situated selves emerge from the development of (a) expectations of contingency between different sensory modalities (*intermodal contingency*)

and (b) a sense of *self-agency* that arises from interaction with the world.

Rochat has emphasized the role of proprioception in the experience of self, and several studies have explored the role of contingency between visual and proprioceptive information in the process of distinguishing self from the world between the ages of 2 and 5 months (Rochat & Morgan, 1995). For example, in one study, infants were shown split-screen images of their legs that were either congruent or incongruent with the view they would normally have of their own legs (i.e., the incongruent images were shown from a different angle). They looked significantly longer at the unfamiliar, incongruent view of their own legs, especially if the general direction of depicted movement conflicted with the direction of the actual, felt movement. The authors concluded that the infants have expectancies about what constitutes self-movement, that self is specified by the temporal and dynamic contingency of sensory information in different modalities, and that by 3 months of age, infants have an *intermodal body schema* that constitutes an *implicit bodily self*.

Based on a series of empirical studies examining infants' actions, then, Rochat has described the self-differentiation process as the systematic exploration of perceptual experience, scaffolded by dyadic interaction, that allows the emergence of an implicit sense of self and other (Rochat & Striano, 2000). For Rochat, such an implicit, interactive, and somatically based sense of self provides the foundation for the more explicit integration of first- and third-person information that will come later in childhood (see below). And in terms of the LOC model, all of this implicit learning about the self takes place at the level of minC.

Given this characterization of minC – as the simplest, first-order consciousness on the basis of which more complex consciousness is constructed, but one that allows an implicit understanding of self, we might return to the question of first emergence: When does minC emerge? According to this account, the onset of minC may be tied to a series of anatomical and behavioral changes

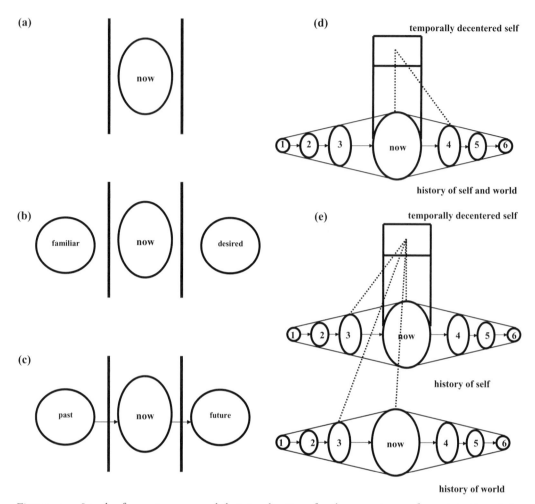

Figure 15.4. Levels of consciousness and their implications for the experience of events in time. (a) MinC. The contents of minimal consciousness are restricted to present intero- and exteroreceptor stimulation (Now). (b) RecC. Past and future events can now be considered but toddlers cannot simultaneously represent the present when representing past or future events. When descriptions of past experiences become the contents of recursive consciousness, they will feel familiar. Future-oriented states (goals) may be accompanied by a feeling of desire. (c) SelfC. Children can consider descriptions of past or future-oriented events in relation to a present experience. For example, while conscious of their current state (Now), 2-year-olds can appreciate that Yesterday they went to the zoo. This creates the conditions for a subjective experience of self-continuity in time, but it does not allow simultaneous consideration of events occurring at two different times. (d) RefC1. From this higher level of consciousness, which allows for a temporally decentered perspective, children can consider two events occurring at two different times, including an event occurring in the present. For example, they can consider that Now, EventA is occurring, but Yesterday, EventB occurred. This is an important advance in the development of episodic memory, but at this point, the history of own's own subjective experiences (history of self) and the history of the world are confounded – there is no means of conceptualizing the history of the world as independent of one's own experiences of the world. (e) RefC2. From a temporally decentered perspective, children can coordinate two series, the history of the self and the history of the world. (Reprinted from Zelazo, P.D., & Sommerville, J. (2001). Levels of consciousness of the self in time. In C. Moore & K. Lemmon (Eds.), *Self in time: Developmental issues* (pp. 229–252). Mahwah, NJ: Erlbaum.)

that occur during the third trimester of pre-natal development – between about 24 and 30 weeks gestational age. First, and perhaps foremost, is the development of thalamo-cortical fibres that show synaptogenesis in sensory cortex (and not in prefrontal cortex – the provenance of higher levels of consciousness). These thalamocortical connections are established as early as 24 weeks gestational age, but the first evidence of functionality does not occur until about 30 weeks, as indicated by sensory-evoked potentials recorded in preterm infants (Hrbek, Karlberg, & Olsson, 1973; Klimach & Cooke, 1988). A number of other neural events also occur at this time, including the emergence of bilaterally synchronous electroencephalographic (EEG) patterns of activation (bursts) and the emergence of EEG patterns that distinguish between sleep and wakefulness (Torres & Anderson, 1985). Fetal behavior also changes at this age in ways that may indicate the onset of minC. For example, fetuses begin to show clear heart rate increases to vibroacoustic stimuli (Kisilevsky, Muir, & Low, 1992), evidence of habituation to vibroacoustic stimuli (Groome, Gotlieb, Neely, & Waters, 1993), and sharp increases in coupling between their movement and their heart rate (DiPietro, Caulfield, Costigan, et al., 2004). There are also good reasons to believe that fetuses at this age are capable of pleasure and pain (e.g., Anand & Hickey, 1987; Lipsitt, 1986). So, on this account, we agree with those who hold that consciousness first emerges during the third trimester of fetal development, but we emphasize the relatively simple nature of this initial level of consciousness.

According to this account, attribution of minC manages to explain infant behavior until the end of the first year, when numerous new abilities appear within just a few months, from about 9 to 13 months of age. For example, during this period, most infants speak their first words, begin to use objects in a functional way, point proto-declaratively, and start searching in a more flexible way for hidden objects (e.g., passing Piaget's A-not-B task), among other milestones. According to the LOC model, these changes can all be explained by the emergence of the first new level of consciousness – *recursive consciousness* (recC). This new level of consciousness allows for recollection and the maintenance of a goal in working memory, key functional consequences.

Recursive consciousness. The term 'recursive' is used here in the sense of a computer program that calls itself (see Chapter 21). In recC (see Fig. 15.1a), the contents of minC at one moment are combined with the contents of minC at another moment via an identity relation (rel), allowing the toddler to *label* the initial object of minC. The 1-year-old toddler who sees a dog and says, "dog," for example, combines a perceptual experience of a dog with a label from semantic long-term memory, effectively indicating, "That [i.e., the object of minC] *is a* dog." Similarly, pointing effectively indicates, "That *is* that." There must be two things, the experience and the label, for one of them, the experience interpreted in terms of the label, to become an object of recC.

Whereas the contents of minC are continually replaced by new perceptual stimulation, recC allows for conscious experience in the *absence* of perceptual stimulation. Because a label can be decoupled from the experience labelled, the label provides an enduring trace of that experience that can be deposited into both long-term memory and working memory. The contents of working memory (e.g., representations of hidden objects) can then serve as explicit goals to trigger action programs indirectly so that the toddler is no longer restricted to responses triggered directly by minC of an immediately present stimulus. Now when objA triggers IobjA (see Figure 15.1a) and becomes the content of minC, IobjA does not trigger an associated action program directly, but rather IobjA is fed back into minC (called recC after one degree of reflection) where it can be related to a label (descA) from semantic long-term memory. This descA can then be decoupled and deposited in working memory where it can serve as a goal (G1) that triggers an action program even in the absence of objA and even if IobjA would otherwise trigger a different action program. For example, when presented with a telephone, the recC toddler may activate a specific semantic association and put the telephone to her ear (functional play) instead of putting the telephone in her mouth (a generic, stereotypical response). The toddler responds *mediately* to the label in working memory rather than *immediately* to an initial, minC gloss of the situation.

Despite these advances, recursively conscious toddlers still cannot explicitly consider the relation between a means and an end (e.g., Frye, 1991) and hence cannot follow arbitrary rules (i.e., rules linking means and ends or conditions and actions). Moreover, although they are no longer exclusively present-oriented, their experience of events in time is limited because they have no way to consider relations among two or more explicit representations. As a result, they cannot consider past- or future-oriented representations from the perspective of the present (i.e., from the perspective of an explicit representation of the present, or Now), because this would require an additional element to be represented (namely, a description of Now). Therefore, it should be impossible for these toddlers to appreciate past or future representations *as such* because the concepts of both past and future are only meaningful when considered in relation to a perception of the present circumstances. This situation is depicted in Figure 15.4b. As shown in the figure, recursively conscious infants are no longer restricted to Now, but they cannot explicitly consider events as occurring in the future from the perspective of the present. Similarly, they cannot explicitly consider past events as occurring in the past from the perspective of the present.

Perner and Dienes (2003) present an account of the emergence of consciousness (i.e., when children "become consciously aware of events in the world," p. 64) that seems to be congruent with this account of recC. These authors first distinguish between "unconsciousness awareness" and "conscious awareness" and illustrate the distinction in terms of blindsight (e.g., Weiskrantz, Sanders, & Marshall, 1974).

Patients with lesions to striate cortex may deny that they can see anything in a particular part of their visual field. Nonetheless, if they are asked to guess, they are often quite good at locating objects in that field or even describing features of the objects. Perner and Dienes suggest that the normal healthy visual perception of objects involves conscious awareness, whereas the impaired perception displayed by blindsight patients involves unconscious awareness. In terms of the LOC model, this distinction would seem to map onto the distinction between minC and recC.

Given this distinction, Perner and Dienes (2003) then consider three behaviors for which consciousness seems necessary in adults: verbal communication, executive function (or voluntary control over action), and explicit memory (i.e., conscious recollection). They note that most babies say their first words at about 12 to 13 months of age and that the earliest signs of executive function also appear at about this age. They also argue, on the basis of work with amnesic patients (McDonough, Mandler, McKee, & Squire, 1995), that delayed imitation requires explicit memory. Meltzoff's work (1985, 1988) suggests that infants first exhibit delayed imitation sometime between 9 and 14 months (although see Meltzoff & Moore, 1994).

In addition to these potential behavioral indices of consciousness, Perner and Dienes (2003) consider when children might be said to possess the cognitive capabilities that would allow them to entertain higher-order thoughts about their experiences – consistent with higher-order thought theories of consciousness (e.g., Armstrong, 1968; Rosenthal, 1986; see Chapter 3). Higher-order thought theories claim that consciousness consists in a belief about one's psychological states (i.e., a psychological state is conscious when one believes that one is in that state), which would seem to require a fairly sophisticated conceptual understanding of one's own mind. According to one version of higher-order thought theory (Rosenthal, 2005), however, the relevant higher-order thoughts may be relatively simple thoughts that just happen to be about one's psychological state. Perner and Dienes observe that children start referring to their own mental states between about 15 and 24 months of age, but they caution that reliance on a verbal measure may lead us to underestimate the abilities of younger children.

Another version of these theories (Carruthers, 2000) holds fast to the suggestion that children will not be conscious until they are capable of meta-representation – in particular appreciating the distinction between appearance and reality, or the notion of subjective perspective on independent reality, as assessed by measures of false belief understanding. It is fairly well established that children do not understand these concepts explicitly until about 4 years of age (e.g., Flavell, Flavell, & Green, 1983; Wellman, Cross, & Watson, 2001), and it is on these grounds that Carruthers (2000) suggests that children do not have consciousness until this age. Perner and Dienes, however, raise the intriguing possibility that perhaps higher-order thoughts do not require an explicit understanding of subjective perspective, but rather simply a procedural grasp of the notion – as might be manifested in children's pretend play during the second year of life (e.g., Harris & Kavanaugh, 1993).

Evidently, it remains unclear exactly what kinds of higher-order thoughts might be required for conscious experience. Perner and Dienes attempt to clarify this issue in terms of Dienes and Perner's (1999) framework of explicit knowledge, and they end up adopting a stance that resembles Carruthers' (2000) view more than Rosenthal's (2000) view. According to Perner and Dienes (2003), "If one saw [an] object as a circle, but only unconsciously, one might minimally represent explicitly only a feature, e.g., 'circle.' A minimal representation, 'circle' would not provide conscious awareness or conscious seeing since it does not qualify as a full constituent of a higher order thought" (p. 77). Other explicit representations that capture some fact about the object also fail to qualify: "The object in front of me is a circle" and "It is a fact that the object

in front of me is a circle." Rather, to be consciously aware of the circle, on this view, one must represent one's psychological *attitude* toward the factuality of the representation: "'I see that [it's a fact that (the object in front of me is a circle)]'" (p. 78).

This version of a higher-order thought theory is hardly compelling from a developmental perspective, however. For example, it is by no means inconceivable that a 3-year-old could be conscious of a fact ("There are pencils in the Smarties box") without being conscious of her attitude (belief) or being conscious that she herself is entertaining the attitude toward the fact. Indeed, this is exactly what the LOC model maintains: RecC allows for conscious experiences that can persist in the absence of perceptual stimulation, but this conscious experience is still simpler than the complex conscious state described by Perner and Dienes. From the perspective of the LOC model, a relatively high level of consciousness (see below), effected by several degrees of reflection, is required to represent one's psychological attitude toward a fact about an object.

As Perner and Dienes (2003) imply, the developmental conclusions to be drawn on the basis of higher-order thought theories are not entirely clear. These authors suggest, however, that the balance of the evidence suggests that children become consciously aware between 12 and 15 months (plus or minus 3 months). In terms of the LOC model, the changes occurring in this age range (or slightly earlier) do not correspond to the emergence of consciousness per se, but they do correspond to an important developmental change in the character of experience – one that allows the (singular) contents of consciousness to be made available to the child in more explicit fashion. Consider again the example of long-distance driving. The difference between MinC and RecC is the difference between the fleeting, unrecoverable awareness of a stop sign that is responded to in passing (without any elaborative processing) and the recoverable awareness that occurs when one not only sees the stop sign but also labels it as such.

Although the neural correlates of the behavioral changes at the end of the first year are still relatively unknown, there are several reasons to believe that these changes correspond to important developments in prefrontal cortical function. For example, in a pioneering study using positron emission tomography (PET), Chugani and Phelps (1986) assessed resting glucose metabolism in the brains of nine infants. Although there was activity in primary sensorimotor cortex in infants as young as 5 weeks of age, and there were increases in glucose metabolism in other areas of cortex at about 3 months of age, it was not until about 8 months of age that increases were observed in prefrontal cortex.

As another example, Bell and Fox (1992) measured EEG activity longitudinally in infants between 7 and 12 months of age and found a correlation between putative measures of frontal function and performance on Piaget's A-not-B task. In the A-not-B task, infants watch as an object is hidden at one location (location A), and then they are allowed to search for it. Then infants watch as the object is hidden at a new location (location B). When allowed to search, many 9-month-old infants proceed to search at A, but performance on this task develops rapidly at the end of the first year of life and seems to provide a good measure of keeping a goal in mind and using it to control behavior despite interference from prepotent response tendencies (see Marcovitch & Zelazo, 1999, for a review). The putative measures of frontal function were frontal EEG power (in the infant "alpha" range; 6–9 Hz) and frontal/parietal EEG coherence. Frontal EEG power reflects the amount of cortical neuronal activity as measured at frontal sites on the scalp, whereas EEG coherence reflects the correlation between signals within a particular frequency band but measured at difference scalp sites. Bell and Fox (1992, 1997) have suggested that changes in power may be associated with increased organization and excitability in frontal brain regions and that increases in coherence may indicate that more poste-rior regions are coming to be controlled by frontal function.

More recently, Baird and colleagues (2002) used near infrared spectroscopy (NIRS) to compare blood flow in prefrontal cortex in infants who reliably searched for hidden objects (i.e., keeping a goal in mind) and those who did not. These authors found that infants who reliably searched for hidden objects showed an increase in frontal blood flow after the hiding of the object, whereas those who failed to search showed a decrease.

Self-consciousness. Although a 12-month-old behaves in a way that is considerably more controlled than, say, a 6-month-old, there is currently no convincing evidence that children are explicitly self-conscious (e.g., at Rochat's third level of self-awareness) until midway through the second year of life, at which point they begin use personal pronouns, first appear to recognize themselves in mirrors, and first display self-conscious emotions like shame and embarrassment (see Kagan, 1981, and Lewis & Brooks-Gunn, 1979, for reviews). In the famous mirror self-recognition paradigm, an experimenter may surreptitiously put rouge on a toddler's nose and then expose children to a mirror. It is well established that most children first exhibit mark-directed behavior in this situation between about 18 and 24 months of age (e.g., Amsterdam, 1972; Lewis & Brooks-Gunn, 1979), and this has been taken to reflect the development of an objective self-concept (e.g., Lewis & Brooks-Gunn, 1979) or the sense of a 'me' as opposed to the sense of an 'I' (James, 1890/1950).

Kagan (1981) also noted the way in which 2-year-olds respond when shown a complex series of steps in the context of an imitative routine. Kagan found that infants at this age (but not before) sometimes exhibited signs of distress, as if they knew that the series of steps was beyond their ken and was not among the means that they had at their disposal. According to Kagan, this implies that children are now able to consider their own capabilities (i.e., in the context of a goal of imitating the experimenter). Consideration of a means relative to the goal that occasions it is a major advance that allows children consciously to follow rules linking means to ends. According to the LOC model, the further development of prefrontal cortex during the second year of life allows children to engage in a higher level of consciousness – referred to as SelfC. This new level of consciousness is what allows children to use a single rule to guide their behavior.

As shown in Figure 15.1b, a self-conscious toddler can take as an object of consciousness a conditionally specified self-description (SdescA) of their behavioral potential – they can consider conditionally specified means to an end. This SdescA can then be maintained in working memory as a single rule (R1, including a condition, C, and an action, A), considered against the background of a goal (G1). Keeping a rule in working memory allows the rule to govern responding regardless of the current environmental stimulation, which may pull for inappropriate responses.

Among the many changes in children's qualitative experience will be changes in their experience of themselves, and of themselves in time – changes in conscious recollection. Unlike recursively conscious infants, self-conscious children can now consider descriptions of events as past- or future-oriented, relative to a present experience (see Fig. 15.4c). For example, while conscious of their current state (Now), 2-year-olds can appreciate that yesterday they went to the zoo (Friedman, 1993). The concepts *yesterday* and *tomorrow* are intrinsically relational because they are indexed with respect to *today*. Thus, for children to comprehend that an event occurred yesterday (or will occur tomorrow), children must be conscious of Now and consider two linked descriptions: a description of the event and a further description of the event as occurring yesterday (or tomorrow). Doing so corresponds in complexity to the use of a single rule considered against the backdrop of a goal that occasions its use. That is, G1;

C1 → A1, from Figure 15.1b, is instantiated as follows: Now; Tomorrow → EventA.

When children can consider past or future events *as such*, they will have a subjective experience of self-continuity in time. As a result, they should now be able to engage in episodic recollection, which, according to Tulving (e.g., 1985), involves consciously recalling having experienced something in the past and so depends, by definition, on self-consciousness (or autonoetic [self-knowing] consciousness, in Tulving's terms). The close relation between the changes in children's self-consciousness that are indexed, for example, by mirror self-recognition, and the onset of episodic recollection has been noted by several authors (e.g., Howe & Courage, 1997; Wheeler, 2000), although others, such as Perner and Ruffman (1995), believe that genuine episodic recollection does not emerge until later, coincident with changes in children's theory of mind (see below).

Although the changes occurring during the second half of the second year are remarkable – so remarkable that Piaget (1936/1952) imagined they reflected the emergence of symbolic thought – there continues to be considerable room for development. For example, an additional degree of recursion is required for children to consider simultaneously two different events occurring at two different times (e.g., EventA, further described as occurring Now, considered in contradistinction to EventB, further described as occurring Tomorrow).

This characterization of the limitations on 2-year-old children's sense of themselves in time is similar in some respects to that offered by Povinelli (1995, 2001) and McCormack and Hoerl (1999, 2001), although it differs in others. Povinelli (1995) suggests that, although children between 18 and 24 months of age can pass mirror self-recognition tasks (e.g., Amsterdam, 1972; Lewis & Brooks-Gunn, 1979), they do not yet possess an objective and enduring self-concept. Instead, Povinelli (1995) suggests that children at this age maintain a succession of present-oriented representations of self (termed present selves; Povinelli, 1995, p. 165), and they cannot compare these representations or "integrate previous mental or physical states with current ones" (p. 166). Consequently, their sense of self-continuity in time is temporally restricted, and they might still be said to live in the present. In support of these claims, Povinelli and colleagues (1996) found that even 3-year-olds perform poorly on measures of delayed self-recognition. In their studies, children played a game during which an experimenter surreptitiously placed a sticker on their heads. About 3 minutes later, children were presented with a video image of the marking event. Whereas the majority of older children (4-year-olds) reached up to touch the sticker, few of the younger children (2- and 3-year-olds) did so.

Zelazo, Sommerville, and Nichols (1999) argued that children perform poorly on measures of delayed self-recognition not because they lack a subjective experience of self-continuity in time, but rather because they have difficulty adjudicating between conflicting influences on their behavior (which requires the use of higher-order rules and a higher level of consciousness). More specifically, children in Povinelli et al.'s (1996) experiment have a strong expectation that they do not have a sticker on their head (because they do not see it placed there and cannot see it directly at the time of testing). When they are provided with conflicting information via a dimly understood representational medium (e.g., video; Flavell, Flavell, Green, & Korfmacher, 1990), the new, conflicting information may be ignored or treated as somehow irrelevant to the situation. Empirical support for this suggestion comes from a study showing that although 3-year-olds can use delayed-video (and delayed-verbal) representations to guide their search for a hidden object in the absence of a conflicting expectation about the object's location, they have difficulty doing so in the presence of a conflicting expectation (Zelazo et al., 1999, Exp. 3). Because children have difficulty managing conflicting delayed representations in general, poor performance on tests of delayed self-recognition does not necessarily indicate an immature self-concept, although it may well reflect more general limitations on the highest level of consciousness that children are able to adopt.

Reflective consciousness 1. The LOC model holds that, in contrast to 2-year-olds, 3-year-olds exhibit behavior that suggests an even higher LOC, *reflective consciousness 1* (refC1). For example, they can systematically employ a pair of arbitrary rules (e.g., things that make noise vs. are quiet) to sort pictures – behavior hypothesized to rely on lateral prefrontal cortex. According to the model, 3-year-olds can now reflect on a SdescA of a rule (R1) and consider it in relation to another Sdesc (SdescB) of another rule (R2). Both of these rules can then be deposited into working memory where they can be used contrastively (via a rule like E in Figure 15.2) to control the elicitation of action programs. As a result, unlike 2-year-olds, 3-year-olds do not perseverate on a single rule when provided with a pair of rules to use (Zelazo & Reznick, 1991).

Of course, there are still limitations on 3-year-olds' executive function, as seen in their perseveration in the Dimensional Change Card Sort (DCCS). In this task, children are shown two bivalent, bidimensional target cards (e.g., depicting a blue rabbit and a red boat), and they are told to match a series of test cards (e.g., red rabbits and blue boats) to these target cards first according to one dimension (e.g., color) and then according to the other (e.g., shape). Regardless of which dimension is presented first, 3-year-olds typically perseverate by continuing to sort cards by the first dimension after the rule is changed. In contrast, 4-year-olds seem to know immediately that they know two different ways of sorting the test cards. Zelazo et al. (2003) have argued that successful performance on this task requires the formulation of a higher-order rule like F in Figure 15.2 that integrates two incompatible pairs of rules into a single structure.

Performance on measures such as the DCCS is closely related to a wide range of metacognitive skills studied under the rubric of theory of mind (e.g., Carlson & Moses, 2001; Frye et al., 1995). In one standard task, called the representational change task (Gopnik & Astington, 1988), children are shown a familiar container (e.g., a Smarties box) and asked what it contains. Subsequently, the container is opened to reveal something unexpected (e.g., string), and children are asked to recall their initial incorrect expectation about its contents: "What did you think was in the box before I opened it?" To answer the representational change question correctly, children must be able to recollect (or reconstruct) their initial false belief. Most 3-year-olds respond incorrectly, stating (for example) that they initially thought that the box contained string.

Three-year-old children's difficulty on this type of task has proven remarkably robust. Zelazo and Boseovksi (2001), for example, investigated the effect of video reminders on 3-year-olds' recollection of their initial belief in a representational change task. Children in a video support condition viewed videotapes of their initial, incorrect statements about the misleading container immediately prior to being asked to report their initial belief. For example, they watched a videotape in which they saw a Smarties box for the first time and said, "Smarties." They were then asked about the videotape and about their initial belief. Despite correctly acknowledging what they had said on the videotape, children typically failed the representational change task. When asked what they initially thought was in the box (or even what they initially said), they answered, "String."

At 3 years of age, then, children are able to consider two rules in contradistinction (i.e., they can consider a single pair of rules) from a relatively distanced perspective – even if they still cannot adopt the level of consciousness required for such measures as the DCCS and the representational change task. The relatively psychologically distanced perspective made possible by RefC1 and the consequent increase in the complexity of children's rule representations allow for a richer qualitative experience than

was possible at SelfC. For example, children can now conceptualize Now from a temporally decentered perspective (McCormack & Hoerl, 1999, 2001; see Figure 15.4d). From this perspective, children are now able to consider two events occurring at two different times. For example, they can consider that Now, EventA is occurring, but Yesterday, EventB occurred.

This important developmental advance allows children to make judgments about *history* (e.g., now vs. before). For example, in a control task used by Gopnik and Astington (1988, Exp. 1), most 3-year-olds were able to judge that *Now* there is a doll in a closed toy house but *Before* there was an apple. At this level of consciousness, however, children cannot differentiate between the history of the world and the history of the self. That is, the objective series and the subjective series remain undifferentiated; the two series are conflated in a single dimension. As a result, 3-year-olds typically fail Gopnik and Astington's (1988) representational change task, where they must appreciate that they themselves changed from thinking Smarties to thinking string, even while the contents of the box did not change. According to the LOC model, this failure to differentiate between the history of the world and the history of the self occurs because children who are limited to refC1 are only able to use a single pair of rules, which allows them to make a discrimination *within* a single dimension, but prevents them from making comparisons *between* dimensions (e.g., between shape and color in the DCCS).

Reflective consciousness 2. Research has revealed that between 3 and 5 years of age, there are important changes in children's executive function and theory of mind, assessed by a wide variety of measures, and these changes tend to co-occur in individual children (e.g., Carlson & Moses, 2001; Frye et al., 1995; Perner & Lang, 1999). For the measures of executive function and theory of mind that show changes in this age range, children need to understand how two incompatible perspectives are related (e.g., how it is possible to sort the same cards first by shape and then by color; how it is possible for someone to believe one thing when I know something else to be true). According to the LOC model, this understanding is made possible by the further growth of prefrontal cortex and the development of the ability to muster a further level of consciousness – reflective consciousness 2 (refC2). At refC2, the entire contents of refC1 can be considered in relation to a Sdesc of comparable complexity. This perspective allows children to formulate a higher-order rule that integrates the two incompatible perspectives (e.g., past and present self-perspectives in the representational change task or color vs. shape rules in the DCCS) into a single coherent system and makes it possible to select the perspective from which to reason in response to a given question. (In the absence of the higher-order rule, children will respond from the prepotent perspective.) In terms of Figure 15.3, RefC2 allows children to formulate and use a rule like F.

Being able to reflect on their discriminations within a dimension (e.g., shape) and considering two (or more) dimensions in contradistinction, allows children to conceptualize dimensions qua dimensions (see also Smith, 1989). In terms of their understanding of the self in time, this ability to consider dimensions qua dimensions (or series qua series) allows children to differentiate and coordinate two series, the history of the self and the history of the world, from a temporally decentered perspective (see Figure 15.4e). As Bieri (1986) notes, to have a genuine temporal awareness, one must differentiate the progression of the self from the progression of events in the world and then understand the former relative to the latter. (The latter corresponds to the objective series, which ultimately serves as the unifying temporal framework.) In Bieri's (1986, p. 266, italics in the original) words: "In order to have a genuine temporal awareness, a being must be able to distinguish between the history of the world and the history of its *encounters* with this world. And the continuously changing temporal perspective . . . is nothing but the continuous process of connecting these two series of events within a representation of one unified time."

Behavioral evidence of children's ability to differentiate and yet coordinate the history of the self and the history of the world can be seen in 4- and 5-year-olds' success on Gopnik and Astington's (1988) representational change task. In this task, children now appreciate that they themselves changed from thinking Smarties to thinking string, but that the contents of the box did not change. Thus, against the backdrop of Now, children appreciate the history of the world, on the one hand; that is, they appreciate that in the past, EventA (string in the box) occurred and Now, EventA is still occurring. However, they also appreciate the history of the self, on the other hand: In the past, EventA (believed Smarties in the box) occurred, and Now, EventB is occurring (believe string in the box).

Because refC2 allows children to integrate two incompatible pairs of rules within a single system of rules, it allows them to understand that they can conceptualize a single thing in two distinct ways. For example, they understand that they can conceptualize a red rabbit as a red thing and as a rabbit in the DCCS, and they understand that they can acknowledge that a sponge rock looks like a rock even though it is really a sponge (Flavell, Flavell, & Green, 1983). When applied to *time*, this understanding permits children potentially to appreciate multiple temporal perspectives on the same event (e.g., that time present is time past in time future). This acquisition, at about 4 or 5 years of age, corresponds to the major developmental change identified in McCormack and Hoerl's (1999) account of temporal understanding: At a higher level of temporal decentering, children appreciate that multiple temporal perspectives are perspectives onto the same temporal reality, and they acquire the concept of particular times (i.e., that events occur at unique, particular times).

Children's ability to conceptualize a single thing in multiple ways can also be applied to their understanding of *themselves* in time, where it allows children potentially to conceptualize themselves from multiple temporal perspectives – to understand themselves as exhibiting both continuity and change in time. Müller and Overton (1998) discuss this understanding in terms of Stern's (1934/1938) notion of *mnemic continuity*: "I am the *same one* who *now* remembers what I *then* experienced" (p. 250; italics in the original), and they note that Stern described this understanding as emerging around the fourth year of life.

Work with children during this period of development – the transition to refC2 – has been useful in revealing one of the key roles that language can play in fostering the adoption of higher levels of consciousness; namely, that it can promote reflection within developmental constraints on the highest level of consciousness that children are able to obtain. In particular, labeling one's subjective experiences helps make those experiences an object of consideration at a higher level of consciousness. Increases in level of consciousness, in turn, allow for the flexible selection of perspectives from which to reason. Therefore, for children who are capable in principle of adopting a particular higher level of consciousness, labeling perspectives at the next lower level will increase the likelihood that they will in fact adopt this higher level of consciousness, facilitating cognitive flexibility.

The effect of labeling on levels of consciousness and flexibility can be illustrated by work by Jacques, Zelazo, Lourenco, and Sutherland (2007), using the Flexible Item Selection Task (see also Jacques & Zelazo, 2005). On each trial of the task, children are shown sets of three items designed so one pair matches on one dimension, and a different pair matches on a different dimension (e.g., a small yellow teapot, a large yellow teapot, and a large yellow shoe). Children are first told to select one pair (i.e., Selection 1), and then asked to select a different pair (i.e., Selection 2). To respond correctly, children must represent the pivot item (i.e., the large yellow teapot) according to both dimensions. Four-year-olds generally perform well on Selection 1 but poorly on Selection 2, indicating inflexibility (Jacques & Zelazo, 2001). According to the LOC model, although 4-year-olds may not do so

spontaneously, they should be *capable* of comprehending two perspectives on a single item (as indicated, e.g., by successful performance on the Dimensional Change Card Sort and a variety of measures of perspective taking (Carlson & Moses, 2001; Frye et al., 1995). Therefore, the model predicts that asking 4-year-old children to label their perspective on Selection 1 (e.g., "Why do those two pictures go together?") should cause them to make that subjective perspective an object of consciousness, necessarily positioning them at a higher level of consciousness from which it is possible to reflect on their initial perspective. From this higher level of consciousness (i.e., the perspective of Rule F in Figure 15.2), it should be easier to adopt a different perspective on Selection 2, which is exactly what Jacques et al. (2006) found. This was true whether children provided the label themselves or whether the experimenter generated it for them.

In general, the adoption of a higher-order perspective allows for both greater influence of conscious thought on language and greater influence of language on conscious thought. On the one hand, it allows for more effective selection and manipulation of rules (i.e., it permits the control of language in the service of thought). On the other hand, it permits children to respond more appropriately to linguistic meaning despite a misleading context – allowing language to influence thought. An example comes from a recent study of 3- to 5-year-olds' flexible understanding of the adjectives "big" and "little" (Gao, Zelazo, & DeBarbara, 2005). When shown a medium-sized square together with a larger one, 3-year-olds had little difficulty answering the question, "Which one of these two squares is a *big* one?" However, when the medium square was then paired with a smaller one, and children were asked the same question, only 5-year-olds reliably indicated that the medium square was now the big one. This example shows an age-related increase in children's sensitivity to linguistic meaning when it conflicts with children's immediate experience, and it reveals that interpretation becomes decoupled, to some degree, from stimulus properties.

Another example of the same phenomenon comes from a study by Deák (2000), who examined 3- to 6-year-olds' use of a series of different predicates ("looks like a...," "is made of...," or "has a...") to infer the meanings of novel words. He found that 3-year-olds typically used the first predicate appropriately to infer the meaning of the first novel word in a series, but then proceeded to use that same predicate to infer the meanings of subsequent words despite what the experimenter said. In contrast, older children used the most recent predicate cues. Again, children are increasingly likely to use language to restrict their attention to the appropriate aspects of a situation (or referent).

Notice that language and conscious thought become increasingly intertwined in a complex, reciprocal relation, as Vygotsky (1934/1986) observed. Thus, language (e.g., labeling) influences thought (e.g., by promoting a temporary ascent to a higher level of consciousness), which in turn influences language, and so on. This reciprocal relation can be seen in the growing richness of children's semantic understanding and in the increasing subtlety of their word usage. Consider, for instance, children's developing understanding of the semantics of the verb *hit*. Children first understand *hit* from its use to depict simple accidental actions (e.g., an utterance by a child at 2;4.0: *Table hit head;* Gao, 2001, pp. 220). Usage is initially restricted to particular contexts. Eventually, however, reflection on this usage allows children to employ the word in flexible and creative ways (e.g., *I should hit her with a pencil and a stick* uttered metaphorically by the same child at 3;8.6; Gao, 2001, pp. 219).

Summary and Topics for Future Research

According to the LOC model, there are at least four age-related increases in the highest level of consciousness that children can

muster, and each level has distinct consequences for the quality of subjective experience, the potential for episodic recollection, the complexity of children's explicit knowledge structures, and the possibility of the conscious control of thought, emotion, and action. Higher levels of consciousness in this hierarchical model are brought about by the iterative reprocessing of the contents of consciousness via thalamocortical circuits involving regions of prefrontal cortex. Each degree of reprocessing recruits another region of prefrontal cortex and results in a higher level of consciousness, and this in turn allows for a stimulus to be considered relative to a larger interpretive context.

This model aims to provide a comprehensive account of the development of consciousness in childhood that addresses extant data on the topic and establishes a framework from which testable predictions can be derived. Naturally, however, there is considerable work to be done. Among the many questions for future research, a few seem particularly pressing. First, future research will need to explore the possibility that there are further increases in children's highest level of consciousness beyond the refC2 level identified in the LOC model. Compared to early childhood, relatively little is known about the development of consciousness in adolescence, although it is clear that the conscious control of thought, action, and emotion shows considerable development in adolescence. Indeed, to the extent that these functions are dependent on prefrontal cortex, which continues to develop into adulthood (e.g., Giedd et al., 1999), further age-related increases in the highest level of consciousness seem likely.

Second, future research should continue to search for more precise neural markers of the development of consciousness. Among the possible indices are increases in neural coherence, dimensional complexity, and/or the amount or dominant frequency of gamma EEG power. Such increases could be associated with the binding together of the increasingly complex hierarchical networks of prefrontal cortical regions that we have proposed are associated with higher levels of consciousness. Dimensional complexity (DCx), for example, is a nonlinear measure of global dynamical complexity (for review see Anokhin et al., 2000) that can be derived from EEG data. In a cross-sectional study of children and adults (ages 7 to 61 years), Anokhin et al. (1996) found that whereas raw alpha and theta power only changed until early adulthood, structural DCx continued to increase across the life span. Other research indicates that DCx may show particularly prominent increases during adolescence (Anokhin et al., 2000; Farber & Dubrovinskaya, 1991; Meyer-Lindenberg, 1996). In a study comparing children and adolescents (mean ages, 7.5, 13.8, 16.4 years), Anokhin et al. (2000) found that both resting and task-related complexity (in visual and spatial cognitive tasks) increased with age, as did the difference between resting and task-related DCx.

Finally, although formulated to explain developmental data, the LOC model suggests a framework for understanding the vagaries of human consciousness across the life span, and future research should explore the extent to which this framework is useful for understanding the role of consciousness in adult behavior. One application is to research on mindfulness (e.g., Brown & Ryan, 2003; see Chapter 19). Acting mindfully (and "super-intending" one's behavior) may involve adopting higher levels of consciousness and coordinating these levels so that they are all focused on a single thing – a single object of consciousness. This coordination of levels of consciousness on a single object would result in an experience that differs dramatically from the kind of multitasking observed, for example, when driving a car at the level of MinC but carrying on a conversation at a higher level of consciousness. Conceptualising mindfulness in terms of the LOC model yields predictions regarding the effects of mindfulness meditation on behavior (e.g., attentional control) and neural function (e.g., increasingly elaborated hierarchies of prefrontal cortical regions). From this perspective, mindfulness meditation practice can be seen as a type of training that may increase an individual's ability to enter a more coherent (coordinated) hierarchy of levels of consciousness.

Conclusion

Discussions regarding the development of consciousness have focused on the question of *when* consciousness emerges, with different authors relying on different notions of consciousness and different criteria for determining whether consciousness is present. In this chapter, we presented a comprehensive model of consciousness and its development that we believe helps clarify the way different aspects of consciousness do indeed emerge at different ages. Our hope is that this model provides a useful framework for thinking about consciousness as a complex, dynamic phenomenon that is closely tied to neural function, on the one hand, and cognitive control, on the other.

Acknowledgments

Preparation of this article was supported by grants from the Natural Sciences and Engineering Research Council (NSERC) of Canada and the Canada Research Chairs Program.

References

Amsterdam, B. (1972). Mirror self-image reactions before age two. *Developmental Psychobiology*, 5, 297–305.

Anand, K. J. S. (2005). *A scientific appraisal of fetal pain and conscious sensory perception*. Report to the Constitution Subcommittee of the U.S. House of Representatives (109th United States Congress).

Anand, K. J. S., & Hickey, P. R. (1987). Pain and its effects in the human neonate and fetus. *New England Journal of Medicine*, 317, 1321–1329.

Anokhin, A. P., Birnbaumer, N., Lutzenberger, W., Nikolaev, A., & Vogel, F. (1996). Age increases brain complexity. *Electroencephalography and Clinical Neurophysiology*, 99, 63–68.

Anokhin, A. P., Vedeniapin, A. B., Sirevaag, E. J., Bauer, L. O., O'Conner, S. J., Kuperman, S., Porjesz, B., Reich, T., Begleiter, H., Polich, J., & Rohrbaugh, J. W. (2000). The P300 brain potential is reduced in smokers. *Psychopharmacology, 149,* 409–413.

Armstrong, D. M. (1968). *A materialist theory of the mind.* London: Routledge.

Armstrong, D. M. (1980). *The nature of mind and other essays.* Ithaca, NY: Cornell University Press.

Baird, A. A., Kagan, J., Gaudette, T., Walz, K. A., Hershlag, N., & Baos, D. A. (2002). Frontal lobe activation during object permanence: Data from near-infrared spectroscopy. *NeuroImage, 16,* 1120–1126.

Baldwin, J. M. (1892). Origin of volition in childhood. *Science 20,* 286–288.

Baldwin, J. M. (1894). Imitation: A chapter in the natural history of consciousness. *Mind, 3,* 25–55.

Baldwin, J. M. (1897). *Social and ethical interpretations in mental development: A study in social psychology.* New York: Macmillan.

Baldwin, J. M. (1906). *Thought and things: A study of the development and meaning of thought, or genetic logic, Vol. 1.* London: Swan Sonnenschein & Co.

Barresi, J., & Moore, C. (1996). Intentional relations and social understanding. *Behavioral and Brain Sciences, 19,* 104–154.

Bell, M. A., & Fox, N. A. (1992). The relations between frontal brain electrical activity and cognitive development during infancy. *Child Development, 63,* 1142–1163.

Bell, M. A., & Fox, N. A. (1997). Individual differences in object permanence performance at 8 months: Locomotor experience and brain electrical activity. *Developmental Psychology, 31,* 287–297.

Bieri, P. (1986). Zeiterfahrung und Personalität. In H. Burger (Ed.), *Zeit, natur und mensch* (pp. 261–281). Berlin: Arno Spitz Verlag.

Brentano, F. (1973). *Psychology from an empirical standpoint.* London: Routledge & Kegan Paul. (Original work published 1874)

Brown, K. W., & Ryan, R. M. (2003). The benefits of being present: The role of mindfulness in psychological well-being. *Journal of Personality and Social Psychology, 84,* 822–848.

Bunge, S. A. (2004). How we use rules to select actions: A review of evidence from cognitive neuroscience. *Cognitive, Affective, and Behavioral Neuroscience, 4,* 564–579.

Bunge, S. A., & Zelazo, P. D. (2006). A brain-based account of the development of rule use in childhood. *Current Directions in Psychological Science, 15,* 118–121.

Burgess, J. A., & Tawia, S. A. (1996). When did you first begin to feel it? Locating the beginning of consciousness. *Bioethics, 10,* 1–26.

Cahan, E. (1984). The genetic psychologies of James Mark Baldwin and Jean Piaget. *Developmental Psychology, 20,* 128–135.

Carlson, S. M., Davis, A. C., & Leach, J. G. (2005). Less is more: Executive function and symbolic representation in preschool children. *Psychological Science, 16,* 609–616.

Carlson, S. M., & Moses, L. J. (2001). Individual differences in inhibitory control and theory of mind. *Child Development 72,* 1032–1053.

Carruthers, P. K. (1989). Brute experience. *Journal of Philosophy, 86,* 258–269.

Carruthers, P. K. (1996) *Language, thought, and consciousness: An essay in philosophical psychology.* New York: Cambridge University Press.

Carruthers, P. K. (2000). *Phenomenal consciousness: A naturalistic theory.* New York: Cambridge University Press.

Chalmers, D. J. (1996). *The conscious mind.* Oxford: Oxford University Press.

Chugani, H. T., & Phelps, M. E. (1986). Maturational changes in cerebral function in infants determined by [18]FDG positron emission tomography. *Science, 231,* 840–843.

Cleeremans, A., & Jiménez, L. (2002). Implicit learning and consciousness: A graded, dynamic perspective. In R. M. French & A. Cleeremans (Eds.), *Implicit learning and consciousness: An empirical, philosophical and computational consensus in the making* (pp. 1–40). Hove, England: Psychology Press.

Cohen, L. B. (1998). An information-processing approach to infant perception and cognition. In F. Simion & G. Butterworth (Eds.), *The development of sensory, motor, and cognitive capacities in early infancy* (pp. 277–300). East Sussex: Psychology Press.

Craik, F., & Lockhart, R. (1972). Levels of processing: A framework for memory research. *Journal of Verbal Learning and Verbal Behavior, 11,* 671–684.

Damasio, A. R. (1999). *The feeling of what happens.* New York: Harcourt Press.

Deák, G. O. (2000). The growth of flexible problem-solving: Preschool children use changing verbal cues to infer multiple word meanings. *Journal of Cognition and Development*, 1, 157–192.

DeCasper, A., Lecanuet, J-P., Busnel, M-C., Granier-Deferre, C., & Mangeais, R. (1994). Fetal reactions to recurrent maternal speech. *Infant Behavior and Development*, 17, 159–164.

Dehaene, S., & Changeux, J.-P. (2004). Neural mechanisms for access to consciousness. In M. Gazzaniga (Ed.), *The cognitive neurosciences* (3rd ed., pp. 1145–1157). Cambridge, MA: MIT Press.

Dewey, J. (1896). Review of studies in the evolutionary psychology of feeling. *Philosophical Review*, 5, 292–299.

Dewey, J. (1985). Context and thought. In J. A. Boydston (Ed.) & A. Sharpe (Textual Ed.), *John Dewey: The later works, 1925–1953* (Vol. 6 1931–1932, pp. 3–21). Carbondale, IL: Southern Illinois University Press. (Original work published 1931)

Dienes, Z., & Perner, J. (1999). A theory of implicit and explicit knowledge (target article). *Behavioral and Brain Sciences*, 22, 735–755.

DiPietro, J. A., Caulfield, L. E., Costigan, K. A., Merialdi, M., Nguyen, R. H., Zavaleta, N., & Gurewitsch, E. D. (2004). Fetal neurobehavioral development: A tale of two cities. *Developmental Psychology*, 40, 445–456.

Edelman, G. M. (1989). *Neural Darwinism: The theory of group neuronal selection*. Oxford University Press, Oxford.

Edelman, G. M., & Tononi, G. (2000). *A universe of consciousness*. New York: Basic Books.

Farber, D. A., & Dubrovinskaya, N. V. (1991). Organization of developing brain functions: Age-related differences and some general principles. *Human Physiology*, 19, 326–335.

Ferrari, M., Pinard, A., & Runions, K. (2001). Piaget's framework for a scientific study of consciousness. *Human Development*, 44, 195–213.

Flavell, J. H., Flavell, E. R., & Green, F. L. (1983). Development of the appearance-reality distinction. *Cognitive Psychology*, 17, 99–103.

Flavell, J. H., Flavell, E. R., Green, F. L., & Korfmacher, J. E. (1990). Do young children think of television images as pictures or real objects? *Journal of Broadcasting and Electronic Media*, 34, 399–419.

Freud, S. (1940). Neue folge der Vorlesungen zur Einführung in die Psychoanalyse [New introductory lectures on psychoanalysis]. In A. Freud, E. Bibring, & E. Kris (Eds.), *Gesammelte werke: XV (Whole volume)*. London: Imago Publishing. (Original work published 1933)

Friedman, W. J. (1993). Memory for the time of past events. *Psychological Bulletin*, 113, 44–66.

Frye, D. (1991). The origins of intention in infancy. In D. Frye & C. Moore (Eds.), *Children's theories of mind: Mental states and social understanding* (pp. 15–38). Hillsdale, NJ: Erlbaum.

Frye, D., Zelazo, P. D., & Palfai, T. (1995). Theory of mind and rule-based reasoning. *Cognitive Development*, 10, 483–527.

Gallagher, S. (2005). *How the body shapes the mind*. Oxford: Oxford University Press/Clarendon Press.

Gao, H. (2001). *The physical foundation of the patterning of physical action verbs*. Lund, Sweden: Lund University Press.

Gao, H. H., Zelazo, P. D., & DeBarbara, K. (2005, April). *Beyond early linguistic competence: Development of children's ability to interpret adjectives flexibly*. Paper presented at the 2005 Biennial Meeting of Society for Research in Child Development, Atlanta, GA.

Giedd, J. N., Blumenthal, J., Jeffries, N. O., Castellanos, F. X., Liu. H, Zijdenbos, A., Paus, T., Evans, A. C., & Rapoport, J. L. (1999). Brain development during childhood and adolescence: adolescence: A longitudinal MRI study. *Nature Neuroscience*, 2, 861–863.

Gogtay, N., Giedd, J. N., Lusk, L., Hayashi, K. M., Greenstein, D., Vaituzis, A. C., et al. (2004). Dynamic mapping of human cortical development during childhood through early adulthood. *Proceedings of the National Academy of Sciences U S A*, 101(21), 8174–8179.

Gopnik, A., & Astington, J. W. (1988). Children's understanding of representational change and its relation to the understanding of false belief and the appearance-reality distinction. *Child Development*, 59, 26–37.

Groome, L. J., Gotlieb, S. J., Neely, C. L., Waters, M. D. (1993). Developmental trends in fetal habituation to vibroacoustic stimulation. *American Journal of Prerinatology*, 10, 46–49.

Haith, M. M., Hazan, C., & Goodman, G. S. (1988). Expectation and anticipation of dynamic visual events by 3.5-month-old babies. *Child Development*, 59, 467–479.

Harris, P. L., & Kavanaugh, R. D. (1993). Young children's understanding of pretence. *Monographs of the Society for Research in Child Development* (Serial No. 237).

Howe, M., & Courage, M. (1997). The emergence and early development of autobiographical memory. *Psychological Review 104*, 499–523.

Hrbek, A., Karlberg, P., & Olsson, T. (1973). Development of visual and somatosensory responses in pre-term newborn infants. *Electroencephalography and Clinical Neurophysiology, 34*, 225–232.

Jacques, S., & Zelazo, P. D. (2001). The flexible item selection task (FIST): A measure of executive function in preschoolers. *Developmental Neuropsychology, 20*, 573–591.

Jacques, S., & Zelazo, P. D. (2005). Language and the development of cognitive flexibility: Implications for theory of mind. In J. W. Astington & J. A. Baird (Eds.), *Why language matters for theory of mind* (pp. 144–162). New York: Oxford University Press.

Jacques, S., Zelazo, P. D., Lourenco, S. F., & Sutherland, A. E. (2007). The roles of labeling and abstraction in the development of cognitive flexibility. Manuscript submitted for publication.

James, W. (1950). *The principles of psychology* (Vol. 1). New York: Dover. (Original work published 1890)

Kagan, J. (1981). *The second year: The emergence of self-awareness*. Cambridge, MA: Harvard University Press.

Kagan, J. (1998). *Three seductive ideas*. Cambridge, MA: Harvard University Press.

Karmiloff-Smith, A. (1992). *Beyond modularity: A developmental perspective on cognitive science*. Cambridge, MA: MIT Press.

Kisilevsky, B. S., Hains, S. M. J., Lee, K., Xie, X., Huang, H., Ye, H. H., Zhang K., & Wang, Z. (2003). Effects of experience on fetal voice recognition. *Psychological Science, 14*, 220–224.

Kisilevsky, B. S., Muir, D. W., & Low, J. A. (1992). Maturation of human fetal responses to vibroacoustic stimulation. *Child Development, 63*, 1497–1508.

Klimach, V. J., & Cooke, R. W. I. (1988). Maturation of the neonatal somatosensory evoked response in preterm infants. *Developmental Medicine & Child Neurology, 30*, 208–214.

Lee, S. J., Ralston, H. J. P., Drey, E. A., Partridge, J. C., & Rosen, M. A. (2005). Fetal pain: A systematic multidisciplinary review of the evidence. *Journal of the American Medical Association, 294*, 947–954.

Lewis, M. (2003). The development of self-consciousness. In J. Roessler & N. Eilan (Eds.), *Agency and self-awareness* (pp. 275–295). Oxford: Oxford University Press.

Lewis, M., & Brooks-Gunn, J. (1979). *Social cognition and the acquisition of self*. New York: Plenum.

Lipsitt, L. P. (1986). Toward understanding the hedonic nature of infancy. In L. P. Lipsitt & J. H. Cantor (Eds.), *Experimental child psychologist: Essays and experiments in honor of Charles C. Spiker* (pp. 97–109). Hillsdale, NJ: Erlbaum.

Luria, A. R. (1959). The directive function of speech in development and dissolution. Part I. Development of the directive function of speech in early childhood. *Word, 15*, 341–352

Luria, A. R. (1961). *Speech and the regulation of behaviour*. London: Pergamon Press.

Marcovitch, S., & Zelazo, P. D. (1999) The A-not-B error: Results from a logistic meta-analysis. *Child Development, 70*, 1297–1313.

McCormack, T., & Hoerl, C. (1999). Memory and temporal perspective: The role of temporal frameworks in memory development. *Developmental Review, 19*, 154–182.

McCormack, T., & Hoerl, C. (2001). The child in time: Episodic memory and the concept of the past. In C. Moore & K. Lemmon (Eds.), *Self in time: Developmental issues* (pp. 203–227). Mahwah, NJ: Erlbaum.

McDonough, L., Mandler, J. M., McKee, R. D., & Squire, L. R. (1995). The deferred imitation task as a nonverbal measure of declarative memory. *Proceedings of the National Academy of Sciences USA, 92*, 7580–7584.

Meltzoff, A. N. (1985). Immediate and deferred imitation in 14- and 24-month-old infants. *Child Development, 56*, 62–72.

Meltzoff, A. N. (1988). Infant imitation and memory: Nine month olds in immediate and deferred tests. *Child Development, 59*, 217–225.

Meltzoff, A. (2002). Imitation as a mechanism of social cognition: Origins of empathy, theory of mind, and the representation of action. In U. Goswami (Ed.), *Handbook of childhood cognitive development* (pp. 6–25). London: Blackwell.

Meltzoff, A. N., & Moore, M. K. (1994). Imitation, memory, and the representation of persons. *Infant Behavior and Development, 17,* 83–99.

Meyer-Lindenberg, A. (1996). The evolution of complexity in human brain development: An EEG study. *Electroencephalography and Clinical Neurophysiology, 99,* 405–411.

Morin, A. (2004, August). Levels of consciousness. *Science & Consciousness Review, 2.*

Morin, A. (2006). Levels of consciousness and self-awareness: A comparison and integration of various neurocognitive views. *Consciousness and Cognition, 15,* 358–371.

Moscovitch, M. M. (1989) Confabulation and the frontal systems: Strategic versus associative retrieval in neuropsychological theories of memory. In H. L. Roediger & F. I. M. Craik (Eds.), *Varieties of memory and consciousness: Essays in honour of Endel Tulving* (pp. 133–160). Mahwah, NJ: Erlbaum.

Müller, U., & Overton, W. F. (1998). How to grow a baby: A reevaluation of image-schema and Piagetian action approaches to representation. *Human Development, 41,* 71–111.

Nagel, T. (1974). What is it like to be a bat? *The Philosophical Review, 83,* 435–450.

O'Donnell, S., Noseworthy, M. D., Levine, B., & Dennis, M. (2005). Cortical thickness of the frontopolar area in typically developing children and adolescents. *NeuroImage, 24,* 948–954.

Perner, J., & Dienes, Z. (2003). Developmental aspects of consciousness: How much of a theory of mind do you need to be consciously aware? *Consciousness and Cognition, 12,* 63–82.

Perner, J., & Lang, B. (1999). Development of theory of mind and executive control. *Trends in Cognitive Sciences, 3,* 337–344.

Perner, J., & Ruffman, T. (1995). Episodic memory and autonoetic consciousness: Developmental evidence and a theory of childhood amnesia. *Journal of Experimental Child Psychology, 59,* 516–548.

Perruchet, P., & Vinter, A. (2002). The self-organizing consciousness. *Behavioral and Brain Sciences, 25,* 297–388.

Piaget, J. (1952). *The origins of intelligence in children.* (M. Cook, Trans.). New York: Vintage. (Original work published 1936)

Piaget, J. (1977). *The grasp of consciousness* (S. Wedgewood, Trans.). Cambridge, MA: Harvard University Press. (Original work published 1974.)

Povinelli, D. J. (1995). The unduplicated self. In P. Rochat (Ed.), *The self in infancy: Theory and research* (pp. 161–192). New York: Elsevier.

Povinelli, D. J. (2001). The Self: Elevated in consciousness and extended in time. In C. Moore & K. Lemmon (Eds.), *The self in time: Developmental perspectives* (pp. 73–94). New York: Cambridge University Press.

Povinelli, D. J., Landau, K. R., & Perilloux, H. K. (1996). Self-recognition in young children using delayed versus live feedback: Evidence of a developmental asynchrony. *Child Development, 67,* 1540–1554.

Reznick, J. S. (1994). In search of infant expectation. In M. Haith, J. Benson, B. Pennington, & R. Roberts (Eds.), *The development of future-oriented processes* (pp. 39–59). Chicago: University of Chicago Press.

Rochat, P. (2001). *The infant's world.* Cambridge, MA: Harvard University Press.

Rochat, P. (2003). Five levels of self-awareness as they unfold early in life. *Consciousness and Cognition, 12,* 717–731.

Rochat, P., & Morgan, R. (1995). Spatial determinants in the perception of self-produced leg movements in 3- to 5-month-old infants. *Developmental Psychology, 31,* 626–636.

Rochat, P., & Striano, T. (2000). Perceived self in infancy. *Infant Behavior and Development, 23,* 513–530.

Rosenthal, D. M. (1986). Two concepts of consciousness. *Philosophical Studies, 49,* 329–359.

Rosenthal, D. (2000). Consciousness, content, and metacognitive judgements. *Consciousness and Cognition, 9,* 203–214.

Rosenthal, D. M. (2005). Consciousness, interpretation, and higher-order thought. In P. Giamperie-Deutsch (Ed.), *Psychoanalysis as an empirical, interdisciplinary science: Collected papers on contemporary psychoanalytic research* (pp. 119-142). Vienna: Verlag der Österreichischen Akademie der Wissenschaften (Austrian Academy of Sciences Press).

Schacter, D. L. (1989). On the relation between memory and consciousness: Dissociable interactions and conscious experience. In H. L. Roediger & F. I. M. Craik (Eds.), *Varieties of memory and consciousness: Essays in honour of Endel Tulving* (pp. 355–389). Mahwah, NJ: Erlbaum.

Schooler, J. W. (2002). Re-presenting consciousness: dissociations between experience and meta-consciousness. *Trends in Cognitive Sciences*, 6, 339–344.

Sigel, I. (1993). The centrality of a distancing model for the development of representational competence. In R. R. Cocking & K. A. Renninger (Eds.), *The development and meaning of psychological distance* (pp. 91–107). Hillsdale, NJ: Erlbaum.

Siqueland, E. R., & Lipsitt, L. P. (1966). Conditioned head-turning in human newborns. *Journal of Experimental Child Psychology*, 3, 356–376.

Smith, L. B. (1989). From global similarities to kinds of similarities: The construction of dimensions in development. In S. Vosriadou & A. Ortony (Eds.), *Similarity and analogical reasoning* (pp. 146–178). Cambridge: Cambridge University Press.

Stern, D. (1990). *Diary of a baby*. New York: Basic Books.

Stern, W. (1938). *General psychology from the personalistic standpoint*. New York: Macmillan. (Original work published 1934.)

Swain, I. U., Zelazo, P. R., & Clifton, R. K. (1993). Newborn infants' memory for speech sounds retained over 24 hours. *Developmental Psychology*, 29, 312–323.

Torres, F., & Anderson, C. (1985). The normal EEG of the human newborn. *Journal of Clinical Neurophysiology*, 2, 89–103.

Trevarthen, C., & Aitken, K. J. (2001). Infant intersubjectivity: Research, theory, and clinical applications. *Journal of Child Psychology & Psychiatry* 42, 3–48.

Tulving, E. (1985). Memory and consciousness. *Canadian Psychology*, 25, 1–12.

Vygotsky, L. S. (1978). *Mind in society*. Cambridge, MA: Harvard University Press.

Vygotsky, L. S. (1986). *Thought and language* (A. Kozulin, Ed.). Cambridge, MA: MIT Press. (Original work published 1934.)

Weiskrantz, L., Sanders, M. D., & Marshall, J. (1974). Visual capacity in the hemianopic field following a restricted occipital ablation. *Brain*, 97, 709–728.

Wellman, H. M., Cross, D., & Watson, J. (2001). Meta-analysis of theory-of-mind development: The truth about false belief. *Child Development* 72, 655–684.

Wheeler, M. (2000). Varieties of consciousness and memory in the developing child. In E. Tulving (Ed.), *Memory, consciousness, and the brain: The Tallinn conference* (pp. 188–199). London: Psychology Press.

Zelazo, P. D. (1999). Language, levels of consciousness, and the development of intentional action. In P. D. Zelazo, J. W. Astington, & D. R. Olson (Eds.), *Developing theories of intention: Social understanding and self-control* (pp. 95–117). Mahwah, NJ: Erlbaum.

Zelazo, P. D. (2004). The development of conscious control in childhood. *Trends in Cognitive Sciences*, 8, 12–17.

Zelazo, P. D., & Boseovski, J. (2001). Video reminders in a representational change task: Memory for cues but not beliefs or statements. *Journal of Experimental Child Psychology*, 78, 107–129.

Zelazo, P. D., & Jacques, S. (1996). Children's rule use: Representation, reflection and cognitive control. *Annals of Child Development*, 12, 119–176.

Zelazo, P. D., Müller, U., Frye, D., & Marcovitch, S. (2003). The development of executive function in early childhood. *Monographs of the Society for Research in Child Development*, 68(3), Serial No. 274.

Zelazo, P. D., & Reznick, J. S. (1991). Age-related asynchrony of knowledge and action. *Child Development*, 62, 719–735.

Zelazo, P. D., & Sommerville, J. (2001). Levels of consciousness of the self in time. In C. Moore & K. Lemmon (Eds.), *Self in time: Developmental issues* (pp. 229–252). Mahwah, NJ: Erlbaum.

Zelazo, P. D., Sommerville, J. A., & Nichols, S. (1999). Age-related changes in children's use of representations. *Child Development*, 35, 1059–1071.

Zelazo, P. R., & Zelazo, P. D. (1998). The emergence of consciousness. *Advances in Neurology*, 77, 149–165.

F. Alternative States of Consciousness

CHAPTER 16

States of Consciousness: Normal and Abnormal Variation

J. Allan Hobson

Abstract

The goal of this chapter is to give an account of the phenomenology of the variations in conscious state, and to show how three mediating brain processes – activation, input-output gating, and modulation – interact over time so as to account for those variations in a unified way.

The chapter focuses on variations in consciousness during the sleep-wake cycle across species and draws on evidence from lesion, electrophysiological, and functional neuroimaging studies. A four-dimensional model called AIM pictorializes both normal and abnormal changes in brain state and provides a unified view of the genesis of a wide variety of normal and abnormal changes in conscious experience.

Introduction

The changes in brain state that result in normal and abnormal changes in the state of the mind all share a common process: an alteration in the influence of lower centers, principally located in the brainstem, upon the thalamus and cortex located in the upper brain. This means that consciousness is state dependent and that understanding the mechanisms of brain state control contributes indirectly to a solution of the mind-brain problem.

The normal and abnormal variations in conscious state operate through three fairly well-understood physiological processes: activation (A), input-output gating (I), and modulation (M) (see Figure 16.1).

Definition and Components of Consciousness

Consciousness may be defined as our awareness of our environment, our bodies, and ourselves. Awareness of ourselves implies an awareness of awareness; that is, the conscious recognition that we are conscious beings. Awareness of oneself implies meta-awareness.

To develop an experimental, scientific approach to the study of consciousness, it is convenient to subdivide the mental

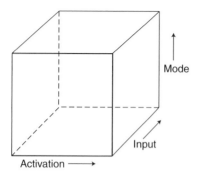

Figure 16.1. The AIM model.

elements that constitute consciousness. We may discern at least the ten distinct capacities of mind defined in Table 16.1. These are the faculties of the mind that have been investigated by scientific psychologists since their formulation by William James in 1890. From an examination of this table, it can be appreciated that consciousness is componential. That is to say, consciousness is made up of the many faculties of mind, which are seamlessly integrated in our conscious experience. It should be noted that all of these functions are also mediated unconsciously or implicitly.

Only human beings fulfill all of the demands of the definition of consciousness given above and the components listed in Table 16.1. And humans are only fully conscious when they are awake. It is evident that higher mammals have many of the components of consciousness and may thus be considered to be partially conscious. Consciousness is thus graded in both the presence and intensity of its components.

In Edelman's terms (1992), animals possess primary consciousness, which comprises sensory awareness, attention, perception, memory (or learning), emotion, and action. This point is of more than theoretical interest because so much that we know about the brain physiology upon which consciousness depends comes from experimental work in animals. In making inferences about how our own conscious experience is mediated by the brain, the attribution of primary consciousness to animals is not only naturalistic but also strategic.

What differentiates humans from their fellow mammals and gives humans what Edelman calls secondary consciousness depends upon language and the associated enrichment of cognition that allow humans to develop and to use verbal and numeric abstractions. These mental capacities contribute to our sense of self as agents and as creative beings. It also determines the awareness of awareness that we assume our animal collaborators do not possess.

Because the most uniquely human cognitive faculties are likely to be functions of our massive cerebral cortex, it is unlikely that the study of animal brains will ever tell us what we would like to know about these aspects of consciousness. Nonetheless, animals can and do tell us a great deal about how other components of consciousness change with changes in brain physiology. The reader who wishes to learn more about the brain basis of consciousness may wish to consult Hobson (1998).

It is obvious that when we go to sleep we lose sensation and the ability to act upon the world. In varying degrees, all the components of consciousness listed in Table 16.1 are changed as the brain changes state. According to the conscious state paradigm, consciousness changes state in a repetitive and stereotyped way over the sleep-wake cycle. These changes are so dramatic that we can expect to make strong

Table 16.1. Definition of components of consciousness

Attention	Selection of input data
Perception	Rpresentation of input data
Memory	Retrieval of stored representations
Orientation	Representation of time, place, and person
Thought	Reflection upon representations
Narrative	Linguistic symbolization of representations
Emotion	Feelings about representations
Instinct	Innate propensities to act
Intention	Representations of goals
Volition	Decisions to act

inferences about the major physiological underpinnings of consciousness.

Two conclusions stem from this recognition: The first is that consciousness is graded within and across individuals and species. The second is that consciousness is altered more radically by diurnal changes in brain state than it has been by millions of years of evolution. We take advantage of these two facts by studying normal sleep in humans and in those subhuman species with primary consciousness.

The Sleep-Waking Cycle

When humans go to sleep they rapidly become less conscious. The initial loss of awareness of the external world that may occur when we are reading in bed is associated with the slowing of the EEG that is called Stage 1 (see Fig. 16.2). Frank sleep onset is defined by the appearance of a characteristic EEG wave, the sleep spindle, which reflects independent oscillation of the thalamocortical system.

Consciousness is altered in a regular way at sleep onset. Although awareness of the outside world is lost, subjects may continue to have visual imagery and associated reflective consciousness. Sleep-onset dreams are short-lived, and their content departs progressively from the contents of previous waking consciousness. They are associated with Stage I EEG, rapidly decreasing muscle tone, and slow rolling eye movements. As the brain activation level falls further, consciousness is further altered and may be obliter-

ated as the EEG spindles of Stage II NREM sleep block the thalamocortical transmission of both external and internal signals within the brain. When the spindles of Stage II are joined by high-voltage slow waves in over half the record, the sleep is called NREM Stage III; it is called NREM Stage IV when the whole record comes to be dominated by the slow waves.

Arousal from Stage NREM IV is difficult, often requiring strong and repeated stimulation. On arousal, subjects evince confusion and disorientation that may take minutes to subside. The tendency to return to sleep is strong. This process, which is called sleep inertia, is enhanced in recovery sleep following sleep deprivation (Dinges et al., 1997).

As the activation level is falling, resulting in the sequence of sleep Stages I to IV, muscle tone continues to abate passively and the rolling eye movements cease. In Stage IV, the brain is maximally deactivated, and responsiveness to external stimuli is at its lowest point. Consciousness, if it is present at all, is limited to low-level, non-progressive thought. It is important to note three points about these facts. The first is that, because consciousness rides on the crest of the brain activation process, even slight dips in activation level lead to lapses in waking vigilance. The second is that even in the depths of Stage IV NREM sleep when consciousness appears to be largely obliterated, the brain remains highly active and is still capable of processing its own information. From PET and single neurone studies, it can safely be concluded that the brain remains about 80% active in the depths of sleep.

These conclusions not only emphasize the graded and state-dependent nature of consciousness. They also indicate how small a fraction of brain activation is devoted to consciousness and that most brain activity is *not* associated with consciousness. From this it follows that consciousness, being evanescent, is not only a very poor judge of its own causation and of information processing by the brain. It is evident that consciousness requires a very specific set of neurophysiological conditions for its occurrence.

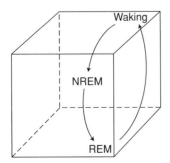

Figure 16.2. The sleep-wake cycle.

REM Sleep

In 1953, Aserinsky and Kleitman reported that the sleep EEG was periodically activated to near waking levels and that rapid eye movements (REMs) could then be recorded. When aroused from this REM sleep state, subjects frequently reported hallucinoid dreaming (Dement & Kleitman, 1957). It was later discovered by Jouvet and Michel (1959) that the EMG of the cat was actively inhibited as the brain was sleep activated and that the same inhibition of motor output occurs in humans during REM sleep (Hodes & Dement, 1964).

The overnight tendency is for the periods of Stage I–IV brain deactivation to become shorter and less deep while the REM periods become longer and more intense. As the brain is activated more and more, the differentiation in consciousness is correspondingly less marked, with reports from early morning Stage II coming more and more to resemble those of Stage I. Dreaming, it can thus be reasonably concluded, is our conscious experience of brain activation in sleep. Because brain activation is most intense in REM sleep, dreaming is most highly correlated with that brain state.

Waking and dreaming consciousness contrast along many of the dimensions shown in Table 16.2. It can be seen that, although dreaming constitutes a remarkable perceptual and emotional simulacrum of waking, it has equally remarkable cognitive deficiencies. The internally generated visual percepts of dreaming are so rich and vivid that they regularly lead to the delusion that we are awake. When they are associated with strong emotions (principally joy-elation, fear-anxiety, and anger), they can even be surreal.

"Why Does the Eye See a Thing More Clearly in Dreaming Than When We Are Awake?"

As Leonardo da Vinci pointed out, dream consciousness may be even more intense than that of normal waking. Such phenomenology suggests that perception and emotion centers of the brain are activated (or even hyperactivated) in REM sleep, and indeed, we have found that this is the case.

At the same time that the perceptual and emotional components of consciousness are enhanced in dreams, such cognitive functions as memory, orientation, and insight are impaired. It is difficult upon awakening to remember one's dreams but also previous scenes may be lost even as the dream unfolds (M. Fosse et al., 2002). It has recently been shown that even well-remembered dreams do not faithfully reproduce waking experience (M. Fosse et al., 2002). Perhaps related to the memory defect is the microscopic disorientation called dream bizarreness, which results in extreme inconstancy of the unities of time, place, person, and action (R. Fosse et al., 2001). It is these unities that constitute the anchors of waking consciousness.

Reports of thinking are rare on arousal from REM sleep, and the thinking that is reported, although logical within the fanciful assumptions of the dream, is almost wholly lacking in insight as to the true state of the mind (R. Fosse et al., 2001). Thus, in dreams, we typically assume we are awake when we are, in fact, asleep. The converse almost never occurs, weakening the thesis of such skeptical philosophers as Malcolm (1956), who hold that we never know certainly what state we are in and that reports of dreaming are fabricated upon awakening.

The Neurophysiology of Sleep with Special Reference to Consciousness

The deactivation of the brain at sleep onset is seen as the characteristic EEG change and is experienced as an impairment of consciousness. It is related to decreases in activity of the neurones that constitute the brainstem reticular formation. This finding is in concordance with the classical experiments of Moruzzi and Magoun (1949) who showed that arousal and EEG activation were a function of the electrical impulse traffic in the brainstem core.

Since 1949, the reticular activating system has been shown to be anything but

Table 16.2. Contrasts in the phenomenology of waking and dreaming consciousness

Function	Nature of Difference	Causal Hypothesis
Sensory input	Blocked	Presynaptic inhibition
Perception (external)	Diminished	Blockade of sensory input
Perception (internal)	Enhanced	Disinhibition of networks storing sensory representations
Attention	Lost	Decreased aminergic modulation causes a decrease in signal to noise ratio
Memory (recent)	Diminished	Because of aminergic demodulation, activated representations are not restored in memory
Memory (remote)	Enhanced	Distinhibition of networks storing mnemonic representations increases access to consciousness
Orientation	Unstable	Internally inconsistent orienting signals are generated by cholinergic system
Thought	Reasoning ad hoc, logical rigor weak, processing, hyperassociative	Loss of attention memory and volition leads to failure of sequencing and rule inconstancy; analogy replaces analysis
Insight	Self-reflection lost (failure to recognize state as dreaming)	Failure of attention, logic, and memory weaken second (and third) order representations
Language (internal)	Confabulatory	Aminergic demodulation frees narrative synthesis from logical restraints
Emotion	Episodically strong	Cholinergic hyperstimulation of amygdala and related temporal lobe structures triggers emotional storms, which are unmodulated by aminergic restraint
Instinct	Episodically strong	Cholinergic hyperstimulation of hypothalamus and limbic forebrain triggers fixed action motor programs, which are experienced fictively but not enacted
Volition	Weak	Top-down motor control and frontal executive power cannot compete with disinhibited subcortical network activation
Output	Blocked	Postsynaptic inhibition

non-specific (Hobson & Brazier, 1980). Instead, it consists of highly specific interneurones that project mainly locally but also reach upward to the thalamus and downward to the spinal cord. By means of these connections, reticular formation neurones regulate muscle tone, eye movements, and other sensorimotor functions necessary to waking consciousness.

The reticular formation also contains chemically specific neuronal systems whose axons project widely throughout the brain where they secrete the so-called neuromodulators: dopamine, norepinephrine, and serotonin (on the aminergic side) and acetyl-choline (on the cholinergic side). The state of the brain and consciousness is thus determined not only by its activation level but also by its mix of neuromodulators.

Sngle-cell recording studies in cats have revealed that in REM sleep, when global brain activation levels are as high as in waking, the firing of two aminergic groups is shut off (Hobson, McCarley, & Wyzinski, 1975; McCarley & Hobson, 1975). Thus the activated brain of REM sleep is aminergically demodulated with respect to norepinephrine and serotonin. Because norepinephrine is known to be necessary for attention (Foote, Bloom, & Aston-Jones,

1983) and serotonin is necessary for memory (Martin et al., 1997), we can begin to understand the cognitive deficiencies of dreaming consciousness in physiological terms.

What about the enhancement of internal perception and emotion that characterizes dream consciousness? Could it be related to the persistence of the secretion of dopamine and the increase in output of the cholinergic neurones of the brainstem? It turns out that the cholinergic neurones of the reticular formation are indeed hyperexciteable in REM; in fact, they fire in bursts that are tightly linked in a directionally specific way to the eye movements that give REM sleep its name. The result is that such forebrain structures as the amygdala (in the limbic, emotion-mediating brain) and the posterolateral cortex (in the multimodal sensory brain) are bombarded with cholinergically mediated internal activation waves during REM.

In the transition from waking to REM, consciousness has shifted from exteroceptive perception to interoceptive and from moderated to unmoderated emotion. To explain this shift, cholinergic hypermodulation together with persistent dopaminergic modulation is a candidate mechanism. The mind has simultaneously shifted from oriented to disoriented and from mnemonic to amnesic cognition. To explain this shift, aminergic demodulation is the best current candidate mechanism.

Input-Ouput Gating

If the brain is activated in sleep, why don't we wake up? One reason is the aminergic demodulation. Another powerful reason is that in REM sleep sensory input and motor output are actively blocked. This closing of the input and output gates is an active inhibitory process in the spinal and the motor neurones that convey movement commands to the muscles. Sensorimotor reticular formation neurones inhibit the sensory afferent sensory fibers coming from the periphery.

The net result is that in dreams we are not only perceptually and emotionally hyperconscious but also cognitively deficient and

off-line to sensory inputs and motor outputs. That is to say, we are anesthetized and paralyzed in addition to experiencing hallucinated emotion and being disoriented and amnesic. This is the activation-synthesis theory of dreaming (Hobson & McCarley, 1977). What other evidence can be brought to test these hypotheses?

A Four-Dimensional Model of Conscious State

Three factors – activation level (A), input-output gating (I), and neuromodulation ratio (M) – determine the normal changes in the state of the brain that give rise to changes in the state of consciousness that differentiate waking, sleeping, and dreaming. Because these three variables can be measured in animals, it is appropriate and heuristically valuable to model them. In so doing, we replace the traditional two-dimensional model with the four-dimensional model in Figure 16.1.

In the AIM model, time is the fourth dimension because the instantaneous values of A, I, and M are points that move in the three-dimensional state space. They form an elliptical trajectory that represents the sleep-wake sequence as a cyclical function, rather than as the stairway that is represented in the traditional two-dimensional model in which activation is plotted against time (look again at Figures 16.1 and 16.2).

To understand the AIM model, it is helpful to grasp the fact that the waking domain is in the back upper right corner of the state space. It is there, and only there, that activation (A) level is high, input-output gates (I) are open, and the modulatory mix (M) measured as the aminergic/cholinergic ratio is also high. Because all three measures change from moment to moment, the AIM points form a cloud in the waking domain of the state space.

When sleep supervenes, all three AIM variables fall. The net result is that the NREM (N) sleep domain is the center of the state space. With the advent of REM, the activation level rises again to waking levels, but the input-output gates are actively closed and aminergic neurones are shut off. Factors I and M therefore fall to their lowest possible levels. The REM sleep domain (R) is thus in the right anterior lower corner of the state space. The AIM model clearly differentiates REM sleep from waking. It also affords a valuable picture of how and why the conscious states of waking and dreaming differ in the way that they do.

As shown by the dashed line forming an elliptical trajectory through the state space, the sleep-wake cycle is represented as a recurrent cycle. Actually the sequential cycles of sleep move to the right (as the activation level increases overnight) and downward as the brain comes to occupy the REM domain for longer and longer periods of time.

Lucid dreaming is a normal variation in conscious state that serves to illustrate and emphasize the value of the AIM model. When subjects learn to recognize that they are dreaming while they are dreaming, they obviously have elements of both REM and waking consciousness. They can continue to hallucinate, but they are no longer deluded about the provenance of the imagery.

Lucid dreamers typically report that, although they may learn to watch and consciously influence the course of their dreams and even to voluntarily awaken to enhance recall, lucidity is difficult to maintain. Often, they are either pulled back down into nonlucid dreaming or wake up involuntarily. The lucid dreaming domain lies between REM and wake in the middle of the state space near the right side wall. Subjects normally cross the REM-wake transition zone rapidly, suggesting that lucid dreaming is a forbidden zone of the state space. Such unwelcome processes as sleep paralysis and hypnopompic hallucinations occur when subjects wake up but one or another REM process persists.

Brain Imaging and Lesion Studies in Humans

Over the past decade, two parallel lines of scientific inquiry have contributed striking insights to the brain basis of conscious experience via the conscious state paradigm.

Brain Imaging

Taking advantage of PET technology, three separate independent groups have imaged the human brain in normal waking and sleep (Braun et al., 1997; Maquet, 2000; Nofzinger et al., 1997). At sleep onset, the blood flow to all regions of the brain declines. When REM sleep supervenes most brain regions resume the wake state brain perfusion levels (from which we infer a restored activation level compared to waking). But several brain regions are selectively hyperactivated in REM. They include the pontine reticular formation (which previous animal studies have shown to regulate REM sleep), the amygdala and the deep basal forebrain (which are thought to mediate emotion), the parietal operculum (which is known to be involved in visuospatial integration), and the paralimbic cortices (which integrate emotion with other modalities of conscious experience).

Spontaneous Brain Damage

Patients who have suffered brain damage due to stroke report a complete cessation of dreaming when their lesion impairs either the parietal operculum or the deep frontal white matter (Solms, 1997). This finding suggests that those structures mediate connections that are essential to dream consciousness. When damage is restricted to the visual brain, subjects continue to dream vividly, but they lack visual imagery.

Intentional Lobotomy

The clinical histories of patients with mental illness who had undergone frontal lobotomy in the 1950s revealed an effect on dreaming. This surgical procedure was designed to cut the fibers connecting the frontal lobes to other parts of the limbic lobe on the assumption that the emotion that was thought to be driving the patient's psychosis was mediated by these fibers. Some patients did indeed benefit from the surgery, but many reported a loss of dreaming, again suggesting that fronto-limbic connections were as essential to that normal hallucinatory process as they were to psychosis.

Other Abnormal Conditions

When traumatic brain damage or stroke affects the brainstem, the resulting injury to neurones mediating activation, input-output gating, and modulation can render subjects comatose for long periods of time. Such subjects may be unable to wake or to sleep normally, in which case they are said to be in a chronic vegetative state. They have been permanently moved to the left half of the AIM state space. As they move further and further to the left, they may lose the capacity to activate their thalamocortical system even to the NREM sleep level. A flat EEG indicates a complete absence of activation and intrinsic oscillation.

LOCKED-IN SYNDROME

Patients with amytrophic lateral sclerosis (popularly known as Lou Gehrig's Disease) remain conscious during waking, but are unable to signal out because of motor neuronal death. Recent research suggests that they can be taught to signal out and say "yes" or "no" by raising or lowering their cortical DC potentials (Hinterberger et al., 2004). It is not known whether these subjects have normal sleep cycles, but the assumptions of the AIM model predict that they should.

TEMPORAL LOBE EPILEPSY AND
"DREAMY STATES"

When neuronal excitability is locally altered (as in temporal lobe epilepsy), patients sometimes experience the intrusion of dream-like states into waking consciousness. This phenomenon serves to illustrate both the value and the limitations of the AIM model.

If the abnormal discharge of the epileptic focus in the temporal lobe is strong enough, it can come to dominate the rest of the brain and cause it to enter an altered state of waking consciousness akin to dreaming. This shift, which is caused by an increase in internal stimulus strength, causes a change in the I

dimension of AIM in the direction of REM. Such a formulation is compatible with the PET finding of selective temporal lobe activation in normal REM sleep. It is reasonable to propose that the kinship of temporal lobe epilepsy "dreamy" states and normal dreaming is due to a shared selective activation of limbic structures.

However, this local excitability change cannot be easily modeled by AIM because the activation measure is global, and as PET studies indicate, the activation of REM (and TLE) is regionally selective, there being some brain areas (like the limbic lobe) that are turned on and others (like the dorsolateral prefrontal cortex) that are turned off.

The only way to deal with this reality is to add brain regions as a fifth dimension to the AIM model. Because it is impossible to represent brain regions within the state space of AIM, the easiest way to represent and visualize this modification is to see the brain as a regionally diverse set of AIM models. Thus the value of the AIM may be locally altered with profound effects upon consciousness.

Conclusions

By studying the way that consciousness is normally altered when we fall asleep and when we dream, it is possible to obtain insights about how the brain mediates consciousness. So stereotyped and so robust are the corresponding changes in brain and conscious state as to assure the following conclusions:

1. Consciousness is componential. It comprises many diverse mental functions that, in waking, operate in a remarkably unified fashion to mediate our experience of the world, our bodies, and ourselves.

2. Consciousness is graded. Within and across species, animals are continually more or less conscious depending upon the componential complexity and the state of their brains.

3. Consciousness is state dependent. During normal sleep, consciousness undergoes both global and selective componential

differentiation as the brain regions mediating the components of consciousness are globally or selectively activated and deactivated.

4. Conscious state is a function of brain state. Experimental studies of sleep have identified three factors that determine brain state: activation level (A), input-output gating (I), and modulation (M). With time as a fourth dimension, the resulting AIM model represents the sleep cycle as an ellipse and more clearly differentiates waking and REM as the substrate of the conscious states of waking and dreaming.

5. Recent brain imaging and brain lesion studies in humans indicate that activation (A) is not only global but also regional and that selective activations and inactivations of specific brain subregions contribute to differences in conscious experience. A fifth dimension may therefore have to be added to the AIM model.

6. Armed with the AIM model, it is possible to obtain a unified view of the genesis of a wide variety of normal and abnormal changes in conscious experience.

Acknowledgements

The author gratefully acknowledges the following sponsors of his research: the National Institutes of Health; the National Science Foundation; the John D. and Catherine T. MacArthur Foundation; and the Mind Science Foundation. Technical assistance was provided by Katerina di Perri and Nicholas Tranguillo.

References

Aserinsky, E., & Kleitman, N. (1953). Regularly occurring periods of eye motility and concomitant phenomena during sleep. *Science*, 118, 273–274.

Braun, A. R., Balkin, T. J., Wesenten, N. J., Carson, R. E., Varga, M., Baldwin, P., Selbie, S., Belenky, G, & Herscovitch, P. (1997). Regional cerebral blood flow throughout the sleep-wake cycle. An H2(15)O PET study. *Brain*, 120(7), 1173–1197.

Dement, W. C., & Kleitman, N. (1957). The relation of eye movements during sleep to dream activity: An objective method for the study of dreaming. *Journal of Experimental Psychology*, 53(3), 339–346.

Dinges, D. F., Pack, F., Williams, K., Gillen, K. A., Powell, J. W., Ott, G. E., Aptowicz, C., & Pack, A. I. (1997). Cumulative sleepiness, mood disturbance, and psychomotor vigilance performance decrements during a week of sleep restricted to 4–5 hours per night. *Sleep*, 20(4), 267–277.

Edelman, G. M. (1992). *Bright air, brilliant fire: On the matter of the mind.* New York: Basic Books.

Foote, S. L., Bloom, F. E., & Aston-Jones, G. (1983). Nucleus locus coeruleus: New evidence of anatomical physiological specificity. *Physiological Review*, 63, 844–914.

Fosse, M. J., Fosse, R., Hobson, J. A., & Stickgold, R. (2002). Dreaming and episodic memory: A functional dissociation? *Journal of Cognitive Neuroscience*, 15(1), 1–9.

Fosse, R., Stickgold, R., & Hobson, J. (2001). A. Brain-mind states: Reciprocal variation in thoughts and hallucinations. *Psychological Science*, 12(1), 30–36.

Hinterberger, T., Neumann, N., Pham, M., Kubler, A., Grether, A., Hofmayer, N., Wilhelm, B., Flor, H., & Birbaumer, N. (2004). A multimodal brain-based feedback and communication system. *Experimental Brain Research*, 154(4), 521–526.

Hobson, J. A. (1998). *Consciousness.* New York: W. H. Freeman.

Hobson, J. A., & Brazier, M. A. B. (Eds.). (1980). *The reticular formation revisited: Specifying function for a nonspecific system.* New York: Raven Press.

Hobson, J. A., & McCarley, R. W. (1977). The brain as a dream state generator: An activation synthesis hypothesis of the dream process. *American Journal of Psychiatry*, 134(12), 1335–1348.

Hobson, J. A., McCarley, R. W., & Wyzinski, P. W. (1975). Sleep cycle oscillation: Reciprocal discharge by two brain stem neuronal groups. *Science*, 189, 55–58.

Hodes, R., & Dement, W. C. (1964). Depression of electrically induced reflexes ("H-reflexes") in man during low voltage EEG sleep. *Electroencephalography and Clinical Neurophysiology*, 17, 617–629.

Jouvet, M. (1962). Recherches sur les structures nerveuses et les mecanismes responsables des differentes phases du sommeil physiologique. *Archives Italiennes de Biologie*, 100, 125–206.

Jouvet, M. (1969). Biogenic amines and the states of sleep. *Science*, 163 (862), 32–41.

Jouvet, M., & Michel, F. (1959). Correlation electromyographiques du sommeil chez le chat decortique mesencephalique chronique. *Comptes Rendues des Seances de la Societe de Biologie et de Ses Filiales*, 153, 422–425.

Malcolm, N. (1956). Dreaming and skepticism. *Philosophical Review*, 65, 14–37.

Maquet, P. (2000). Functional neuroimaging of sleep by positron emission tomography. *Journal of Sleep Research*, 9, 207–231.

Martin, K. C., Casadio, A., Zhu, H., Yaping, E., Rose, J. C., Chen, M., Bailey, C. H., &

Kandel, E. R. (1997). Synapse-specific, long-term facilitation of aplysia sensory to motor synapses: A function for local protein synthesis in memory storage. *Cell*, 91(7), 927–938.

McCarley, R. W., & Hobson, J. A. (1975). Neuronal excitability modulation over the sleep cycle: A structural and mathematical model. *Science*, 189, 58–60.

Moruzzi, G., & Magoun, H W. (1949). Brainstem reticular formation and activation of the EEG. *Electroencephalography and Clinical Neurophysiology*, 1, 455–473.

Nofzinger, E. A., Mintun, M. A., Wiseman, M., Kupfer, D. J., & Moore, R. Y. (1997). Forebrain, activation in REM sleep: An FDG PET study. *Brain Research*, 770(1–2), 192–201.

Solms, M. (1997). *The neuropsychology of dreams*. Hillsdale, NJ: Erlbaum.

CHAPTER 17

Consciousness in Hypnosis

John F. Kihlstrom

Abstract

In hypnosis, subjects respond to suggestions for imaginative experiences that can involve alterations in conscious perception, memory, and action. However, these phenomena occur most profoundly in those subjects who are highly hypnotizable. The chapter reviews a number of these phenomena, including posthypnotic amnesia; hypnotic analgesia; hypnotic deafness, blindness, and agnosia; and emotional numbing, with an eye toward uncovering dissociations between explicit and implicit memory, perception, and emotion. These dissociative phenomena of hypnosis bear a phenotypic similarity to the "hysterical" symptoms characteristic of the dissociative and conversion disorders. The experience of involuntariness in hypnotic response is considered in light of the concept of automatic processing. Hypnosis may be described as an altered state of consciousness based on the convergence of four variables: induction procedure, subjective experience, overt behavior, and psychophysiological indices – including neural correlates of hypnotic suggestion revealed by brain imaging.

Consciousness in Hypnosis

Hypnosis is a process in which one person (commonly designated the subject) responds to suggestions given by another person (designated the hypnotist) for imaginative experiences involving alterations in perception, memory, and the voluntary control of action. Hypnotized subjects can be oblivious to pain; they hear voices that aren't there and fail to see objects that are clearly in their field of vision; they are unable to remember the things that happened to them while they were hypnotized; and they carry out suggestions after hypnosis has been terminated, without being aware of what they are doing or why. In the classic case, these experiences are associated with a degree of subjective conviction bordering on delusion and an experience of involuntariness bordering on compulsion.

The Importance of Individual Differences

The phenomena of hypnosis can be quite dramatic, but they do not occur in everyone. Individual differences in hypnotizability are measured by standardized psychological tests, such as the Harvard Group Scale of Hypnotic Susceptibility, Form A (HGSHS:A) or the Stanford Hypnotic Susceptibility Scale, Form C (SHSS:C). These psychometric instruments are essentially work samples of hypnotic performance, consisting of a standardized induction of hypnosis accompanied by a set of 12 representative hypnotic suggestions. For example, on both HGSHS:A and SHSS:C, subjects are asked to hold out their left arm and hand, and then it is suggested that there is a heavy object in the hand, growing heavier and heavier, and pushing the hand and arm down. The subject's response to each suggestion is scored according to objective behavioral criteria (for example, if the hand and arm lower at least 6 inches over a specified interval of time), yielding a single score representing his or her hypnotizability, or responsiveness to hypnotic suggestions. Hypnotizability, so measured, yields a quasi-normal distribution of scores in which most people are at least moderately responsive to hypnotic suggestions, relatively few people are refractory to hypnosis, and relatively few fall within the highest level of responsiveness (Hilgard, 1965).

Although most people can experience hypnosis to at least some degree, the most dramatic phenomena of hypnosis – the ones that really count as reflecting alterations in consciousness – are generally observed in those "hypnotic virtuosos" who comprise the upper 10 to 15% of the distribution of hypnotizability. Accordingly, a great deal of hypnosis research involves a priori selection of highly hypnotizable subjects, to the exclusion of those of low and moderate hypnotizability. An alternative is a mixed design in which subjects stratified for hypnotizability are all exposed to the same experimental manipulations, and the responses of hypnotizable subjects are compared to those who are insusceptible to hypnosis. In any case, measurement of hypnotizability is crucial to hypnosis research: There is no point in studying hypnosis in individuals who cannot experience it.

Some clinical practitioners believe that virtually everyone can be hypnotized, if only the hypnotist takes the right approach, but there is little evidence favoring this point of view. Similarly, some researchers believe that hypnotizability can be enhanced by developing positive attitudes, motivations, and expectancies concerning hypnosis (Gorassini & Spanos, 1987), but there is also evidence that such interventions are heavily laced with compliance (Bates & Kraft, 1991). As with any other skilled performance, hypnotic response is probably a matter of both aptitude and attitude: Negative attitudes, motivations, and expectancies can interfere with performance, but positive ones are not by themselves sufficient to create hypnotic virtuosity.

Hypnotizability is not substantially correlated with most other individual differences in ability or personality, such as intelligence or adjustment (Hilgard, 1965). However, in the early 1960s, Ronald Shor (Shor, Orne, & O'Connell, 1962), Arvid As (As, 1962), and others found that hypnotizability was correlated with subjects' tendency to have hypnosis-like experiences outside of formal hypnotic settings, and an extensive interview study by Josephine Hilgard (1970) showed that hypnotizable subjects displayed a high level of imaginative involvement in such domains as reading and drama. In 1974, Tellegen and Atkinson developed a scale of *absorption* to measure the disposition to have subjective experiences characterized by the full engagement of attention (narrowed or expanded), and blurred boundaries between self and object (Tellegen & Atkinson, 1974). Episodes of absorption and related phenomena such as "flow" (Csikszentmihalyi, 1990; Csikszentmihalyi & Csikszentmihalyi, 1988) are properly regarded as altered states of consciousness in their own right, but they are not the same as hypnosis and so are not considered further in this chapter.

Conventional personality inventories, such as the Minnesota Multiphasic Personality Inventory and California Psychological Inventory, do not contain items related to absorption, which may explain their failure to correlate with hypnotizability (Hilgard, 1965). However, absorption is not wholly unrelated to other individual differences in personality. Recent multivariate research has revealed five major dimensions – the "Big Five" – which provide a convenient summary of personality structure: neuroticism (emotional stability), extraversion, agreeableness, conscientiousness, and openness to experience (John, 1990; Wiggins & Trapnell, 1997). Absorption and hypnotizability are correlated with those aspects of openness that relate to richness of fantasy life, aesthetic sensitivity, and awareness of inner feelings, but not those that relate to intellectance or sociopolitical liberalism (Glisky & Kihlstrom, 1993; Glisky, Tataryn, Tobias, & Kihlstrom, 1991).

Absorption is the most reliable correlate of hypnotizability; by contrast, vividness of mental imagery is essentially uncorrelated with hypnosis (Glisky, Tataryn, & Kihlstrom, 1995). However, the statistical relations between hypnotizability and either absorption or openness are simply too weak to permit confident prediction of an individual's actual response to hypnotic suggestion (Roche & McConkey, 1990). So far as the measurement of hypnotizability is concerned, there is no substitute for performance-based measures such as the Stanford and Harvard scales.

The Controversy over State

Consciousness has two principal aspects: *monitoring* ourselves and our environment, so that objects and events are accurately represented in phenomenal awareness, and *controlling* ourselves and the environment through the voluntary initiation and termination of thought and action (Kihlstrom, 1984). From this point of view, the phenomena that mark the domain of hypnosis (Hilgard, 1973a) seem to reflect alter-

ations in consciousness. The sensory alterations exemplified by hypnotic analgesia or deafness, as well as posthypnotic amnesia, are disruptions in conscious awareness: The subject seems to be unaware of percepts and memories that ought to be accessible to phenomenal awareness. Similarly, posthypnotic suggestion, as well as the experience of involuntariness that frequently accompanies suggested hypnotic experiences, reflects a loss of control over cognition and behavior.

Despite these considerations, the status of hypnosis as an altered state of consciousness has been controversial (e.g., Gauld, 1992; Hilgard, 1971; Kallio & Revensuo, 2003; Kirsch & Lynn, 1995; Shor, 1979a).[1] For example, psychoanalytically inclined theorists classified hypnosis as an instance of adaptive regression, or regression in the service of the ego (Fromm, 1979; Gill & Brenman, 1959). Orne believed that the essence of hypnosis was to be found in "trance logic" (Orne, 1959), whereas Hilgard argued that the phenomena of hypnosis were essentially dissociative in nature (Hilgard, 1973b, 1977). By contrast, Sarbin and Coe described hypnosis as a form of role-enactment (Sarbin & Coe, 1972); Barber asserted that the phenomena of hypnosis could be produced by anyone who held appropriate attitudes, motivations, and expectancies (Barber, 1969).

More recently, both Woody and Bowers (Woody & Bowers, 1994; Woody & Sadler, 1998) and Kihlstrom (Kihlstrom, 1984, 1992a, 1998) embraced some version of Hilgard's neodissociation theory of divided consciousness. By contrast, the "sociocognitive" approach offered by Spanos (1986a, 1991) emphasized the motivated subject's attempt to display behavior regarded as characteristic of a hypnotized person and the features of the social context that shaped these displays. Kirsch and Lynn (Kirsch, 2001a,b; Kirsch & Lynn, 1998a,b) offered a "social cognitive" theory of hypnosis that attributed hypnotic phenomena to the automatic effect of subjects' response expectancies. Following Kuhn (1962), the "state" and "nonstate" views of hypnosis have sometimes been construed as competing paradigms (e.g., Spanos & Chaves, 1970, 1991).

Consciousness and Social Influence

Part of the problem is the multifaceted nature of hypnosis itself. Hypnosis entails changes in conscious perception, memory, and behavior, to be sure, but these changes also occur following specific suggestions made by the hypnotist to the subject. As White (1941) noted at the dawn of the modern era of hypnosis research, hypnosis is a state of altered consciousness that takes place in a particular motivational context – the motivation being to behave like a hypnotized subject. Orne (1959), who was White's protege as both an undergraduate and a graduate student at Harvard, famously tried to distinguish between artifact and essence of hypnosis, but a careful reading of his work makes it clear that the demand characteristics that *surround* hypnosis are as important as any "trance logic" that arises *in* hypnosis.

Similarly, at the dawn of what might be called the "golden age" of hypnosis research, Sutcliffe published a pair of seminal papers that contrasted a credulous view of hypnosis, which holds that the mental states instigated by suggestion are identical to those that would be produced by the actual stimulus state of affairs implied in the suggestions, with a skeptical view that holds that the hypnotic subject is acting *as if* the world were as suggested (Sutcliffe, 1960, 1961). This is, of course, a version of the familiar state-nonstate dichotomy, but Sutcliffe also offered a third view: that hypnosis involves a quasi-delusional alteration in self-awareness – an altered state of consciousness that is constructed out of the interaction between the hypnotist's suggestions and the subject's interpretation of those suggestions.

Thus, hypnosis is simultaneously a state of (sometimes) profound cognitive change, involving basic mechanisms of perception, memory, and thought, and a social interaction, in which hypnotist and subject come together for a specific purpose within a wider sociocultural context. A truly adequate, comprehensive theory of hypnosis will seek understanding in both cognitive and interpersonal terms. We do not yet have such a theory, but even if we did individual investigators would naturally emphasize one aspect, whether altered consciousness or social context, over the other in their work. The interindividual competition that is part and parcel of science as a social enterprise often leads investigators to write as if alterations in consciousness and social influence were mutually exclusive processes – which they simply are not.

Taken together with the null-hypothesis statistical tests that remain part and parcel of the experimental method, and a propensity for making strong rather than weak inferences from experimental data, investigators will often present evidence for one process as evidence against the other. But if there is one reason why hypnosis has fascinated successive generations of investigators, since the very dawn of psychology as a science, it is that hypnosis exemplifies the marvelous complexity of human experience, thought, and action. In hypnosis and elsewhere, comprehensive understanding will require a creative synthesis in the spirit of discovery, rather than the spirit of proof – a creative synthesis of *both-and*, as opposed to a stance of *either-or*.

Defining an Altered State

Part of the problem as well are the difficulties of defining precisely what we mean by an altered state of consciousness (Ludwig, 1966). Some theorists have argued that every altered state should be associated with a unique physiological signature, much as dreaming is associated with the absence of alpha activity in the EEG and the occurrence of rapid eye movements (REM). The lack of a physiological indicator for hypnosis, then, is taken as evidence that hypnosis is not a special state of consciousness after all. But of course, this puts the cart before the horse. Physiological indices are validated against self-reports: Aserinsky and Kleitman (1953) had to wake their subjects up during periods of REM and ask them if they were dreaming. As such, physiological correlates have no privileged status over introspective self-reports: Aserinsky and Kleitman were in no position to contradict subjects who said "no." It is nice when our altered states have distinct physiological correlates, but our present knowledge of mind-body relations is simply not sufficient to make such correlates a necessary part of the definition. After all, cognitive neuroscience has made very little progress in the search for the neural correlates of ordinary waking consciousness (Metzinger, 2000). How far in the future do the neural correlates of altered states of consciousness, like hypnosis, await?

In the final analysis, it may be best to treat hypnosis and other altered states of consciousness as *natural concepts*, represented by a prototype or one or more exemplars, each consisting of features that are only probabilistically associated with category membership, with no clear boundaries between one altered state and another, or between altered and normal consciousness (Kihlstrom, 1984). And because we cannot have direct knowledge of other minds, altered states of consciousness must also remain *hypothetical constructs*, inferred from a network of relations among variables that are directly observable (Campbell & Fiske, 1959; Garner, Hake, & Eriksen, 1956; Stoyva & Kamiya, 1968), much in the manner of a psychiatric diagnosis. From this point of view the diagnosis of an altered state of consciousness can be made with confidence to the extent that there is convergence among four kinds of variables:

1. *Induction Procedure*: Operationally, a special state of consciousness can be defined, in part, by the means employed to induce it – or, alternatively, as the output resulting from a particular input. Barber (1969) employed such an input-output definition as the sole index of hypnosis, largely ignoring individual differences in hypnotizability. At the very least, hypnosis would seem to require *both* a hypnotic induction *and* a hypnotizable individual to receive it. But in the case of very highly hypnotizable subjects, even the induction procedure may be unnecessary.

2. *Subjective Experience*: Introspective self-reports of changes in subjective experience would seem to be central to any altered state of consciousness. As noted earlier, the domain of hypnosis is defined by changes in perception, memory, and the voluntary control of behavior – analgesia, amnesia, the experience of involuntariness, and the like. If the hypnotist gives a suggestion – for example, that there is an object in the subject's outstretched hand, getting heavier and heavier – and the subject experiences nothing of the sort, it is hard to say that he or she has been hypnotized.

3. *Overt Behavior*: Of course, a reliance on self-reports has always made psychologists nervous, so another residue of radical behaviorism (the first was the reliance on operational definitions) is a focus on overt behavior. If a subject hallucinates an object in his outstretched hand, and feels it grow heavier and heavier, eventually his arm ought to drop down to his side. As noted earlier, individual differences in hypnotizability are measured in terms of the subject's publicly observable, overt, behavioral response to suggestions. But in this instance, the overt behavior is, to borrow a phrase from the *Book of Common Prayer*, an outward and visible sign of an inward and spiritual grace: It is a consequence of the subject's altered subjective experience. Behavioral response is of no interest in the absence of corresponding subjective experience. For this reason, requests for "honesty reports" (Bowers, 1967; Spanos & Barber, 1968) or other appropriate postexperimental interviews (Orne, 1971; Sheehan & McConkey, 1982) can help clarify subjects' overt behavior and serve as correctives for simple behavioral compliance.

4. *Psychophysiological Indices*: Because both self-reports and overt behaviors are under voluntary control, and thus subject to distortion by social-influence processes, hypnosis researchers have been interested in

psychophysiological indices of response – including, of course, various brain imaging techniques. Over the years, a number of such indices have been offered, including skin conductance and alpha activity, but these have usually proved to be artifacts of relaxation and not intrinsic to hypnosis. In retrospect, it was probably a mistake to expect that there would be any physiological correlates of hypnosis in general, following an induction procedure but in the absence of any specific suggestions (Maquet et al., 1999), because subjects can have a wide variety of experiences while they were hypnotized. Progress on this issue is more likely to occur when investigators focus on the physiological correlates of specific hypnotic suggestions – as in brain imaging work that shows specific changes in brain activity corresponding to hypnotic visual hallucinations (Kosslyn, Thompson, Costantini-Ferrando, Alpert, & Spiegel, 2000) or analgesia (Rainville, Hofbauer, Bushnell, Duncan, & Price, 2002).

Hypnosis and Hysteria

At least since the late 19th century, interest in hypnosis has had its roots in the medical and psychiatric phenomenon known as *hysteria* (for historical overviews and detailed references, see Kihlstrom, 1994a; Veith, 1965). This term originated some 4,000 years ago in ancient Egyptian (and later Greek) medicine to refer to a variety of diseases thought to be caused by the migration of the uterus to various parts of the body. In the 17th century, the English physician Thomas Sydenham reformulated the diagnosis so that hysteria referred to physical symptoms produced by non-organic factors. In the 19th century, the concept of hysteria was refined still further, by Briquet, a French neurologist, to include patients with multiple, chronic physical complaints with no obvious organic basis (Briquet, 1859). Sometime later, Charcot noticed that the symptoms of hysteria mimicked those of certain neurological illnesses, especially those affecting tactile sensitivity, "special senses" such as vision and audition, and motor function. Charcot held that these symptoms, in turn, were the products of "functional" lesions in the nervous system produced by emotional arousal and suggestion.

Charcot's interest in hysteria passed to his protégé Pierre Janet, who held that the fundamental difficulty in hysteria was a restriction in awareness – such that, for example, hysterically deaf patients were not aware of their ability to hear and hysterically paralyzed patients were not aware of their ability to move (Janet, 1907). Like Charcot, Janet was particularly impressed by the apparently paradoxical behavior of hysterical patients, as exemplified by ostensibly blind individuals who nevertheless displayed visually guided behavior. Janet argued that these behaviors were mediated by mental structures called *psychological automatisms*. In his view, these complex responses to environmental events were normally accessible to conscious awareness and control, but had been "split off" from the normal stream of conscious mental activity by traumatic stress – a situation that Janet called *desaggregation*, or, in English translation, "dissociation."

Although the hegemony of Freudian psychoanalysis in psychiatry during the first half of the 20th century led to a decline of interest in the classical syndromes of hysteria, the syndrome as such was listed in the early (1952 and 1968) editions of the *Diagnostic and Statistical Manual for Mental Disorders* (*DSM*) published by the American Psychiatric Association. Beginning in 1980, more recent versions of *DSM* dropped the category "hysteria" in favor of separate listings of *dissociative disorders* – including psychogenic amnesia and multiple personality disorder – and *conversion disorder*, listed under the broader rubric of the somatoform disorders (Kihlstrom, 1992b, 1994a). As the official psychiatric nosology is currently constituted, only the functional disorders of memory (Kihlstrom & Schacter, 2000; Schacter & Kihlstrom, 1989) are explicitly labeled as dissociative in nature. However, it is clear that the conversion disorders also involve disruptions in conscious awareness and control (Kihlstrom, 1992b, 1994a; 2001a; Kihlstrom & Schacter, 2000; Kihlstrom, Tataryn, & Hoyt, 1993; Schacter & Kihlstrom, 1989). Renewed interest in the syndromes of hysteria, reconstrued in terms of dissociations affecting conscious awareness, was foreshadowed by Hilgard's "neodissociative" theory of divided consciousness, which re-established the link between hypnosis and hysteria (Hilgard, 1973b, 1977; see also Kihlstrom, 1979, 1992a; Kihlstrom & McGlynn, 1991).

Viewed from a theoretical perspective centered on consciousness, the dissociative disorders include a number of different syndromes all involving disruptions in the monitoring and/or controlling functions of consciousness that are not attributable to brain insult, injury, or disease (Kihlstrom, 1994a, 2001a). These syndromes are reversible, in the sense that it is possible for the patient to recover the lost functions. But even during the symptomatic phase of the illness, the patient will show evidence of intact functioning in the affected system, outside awareness. Thus, patients with psychogenic (dissociative) amnesia, fugue, and multiple personality disorder may show impaired explicit memory but spared implicit memory (Kihlstrom, 2001a; Schacter & Kihlstrom, 1989). In the same way, patients with conversion disorders affecting vision and hearing may show impaired explicit perception but spared implicit perception (Kihlstrom, 1992b; Kihlstrom, Barnhardt, & Tataryn, 1992). In light of these considerations, a more accurate taxonomy of dissociative disorders (Kihlstrom, 1994a) would include three subcategories of syndromes:

1. those affecting memory and identity (e.g., functional amnesia, fugue, and multiple personality disorder);
2. those affecting sensation and perception (e.g., functional blindness and deafness, analgesia, and tactile anesthesia);
3. those affecting voluntary action (e.g., functional weakness or paralysis of the limbs, aphonia, and difficulty swallowing).

Dissociative Phenomena in Hypnosis

As intriguing and historically important as the syndromes of hysteria and dissociation are, it is also true that they are very rare and for that reason (among others) have rarely been subject to controlled experimental investigation. However, beginning with Charcot's observation that hysterical patients are highly suggestible, a number of theorists have been impressed by the phenotypic similarities between the symptoms of hysteria and the phenomena of hypnosis. Accordingly, it has been suggested that hypnosis might serve as a laboratory model for hysteria (Kihlstrom, 1979; Kihlstrom & McGlynn, 1991; see also Oakley, 1999). In this way, study of alterations in consciousness in hypnosis might not just help us understand hypnosis, but also hysteria and the dissociative and conversion disorders as well. In this regard, it is interesting to note that hypnotically suggested limb paralysis seems to share neural correlates, as well as surface features, with conversion hysteria (Halligan, Athwal, Oakley, & Frackowiak, 2000; Halligan, Oakley, Athwal, & Frackowiak, 2000; Terao & Collinson, 2000).

Implicit Memory in Posthypnotic Amnesia

Perhaps the most salient alteration in consciousness observed in hypnosis is the one that gave hypnosis its name: posthypnotic amnesia. Upon termination of hypnosis, some subjects find themselves unable to remember the events and experiences that transpired while they were hypnotized – an amnesia that is roughly analogous to that experienced after awakening from sleeping. Posthypnotic amnesia does not occur in the absence of direct or implied suggestions (Hilgard & Cooper, 1965), and the forgotten memories are not restored when hypnosis is reinduced (Kihlstrom, Brenneman, Pistole, & Shor, 1985). Posthypnotic amnesia is so named because the subject's memory is tested in hypnosis, but hypnotic amnesia, in which both the suggestion and the test occur while the subject is hypnotized, has the same properties. Although posthypnotic amnesia typically covers events and experiences that transpired during hypnosis, it is also possible to suggest amnesia for events that occurred while the subject was not hypnotized (Barnier, 1997; Bryant, Barnier, Mallard, & Tibbits, 1999). Both features further distinguish posthypnotic amnesia from state-dependent memory (Eich, 1988).

In contrast to the amnesic syndrome associated with hippocampal damage, posthypnotic amnesia is temporary: On administration of a prearranged cue, the amnesia is reversed and the formerly amnesic subject is now able to remember the previously forgotten events (Kihlstrom & Evans, 1976; Nace, Orne, & Hammer, 1974) – although there is some evidence that a small residual amnesia may persist even after the reversibility cue has been given (Kihlstrom & Evans, 1977). Reversibility marks posthypnotic amnesia as a disruption of memory retrieval, as opposed to encoding or storage, somewhat like the temporary retrograde amnesias observed in individuals who have suffered concussive blows to the head (Kihlstrom, 1985; Kihlstrom & Evans, 1979). The difference, of course, is that posthypnotic amnesia is a functional amnesia – an abnormal amount of forgetting that is attributable to psychological factors, rather than to brain insult, injury, or disease (Kihlstrom & Schacter, 2000). In fact, as noted earlier, posthypnotic amnesia has long been considered to be a laboratory model of the functional amnesias associated with hysteria and dissociation (Barnier, 2002; Kihlstrom, 1979; Kihlstrom & McGlynn, 1991).

Probably the most interesting psychological research concerning posthypnotic amnesia concerns dissociations between explicit and implicit memory (Schacter, 1987), and posthypnotic amnesia is no exception. Following Schacter (1987), we can identify explicit memory with conscious recollection, as exemplified by performance on traditional tests of recall and recognition. By contrast, implicit memory refers to the influence of some past event on current experience, thought, and action in the absence of (or independent of) conscious recollection. Implicit memory, as exemplified by

various sorts of priming effects observed in amnesic patients, is for all intents and purposes unconscious memory.

Early evidence that posthypnotic amnesia impaired explicit memory but spared implicit memory came from a pair of experiments by Kihlstrom (1980), which were in turn inspired by an earlier investigation by Williamsen and his colleagues (see also Barber & Calverley, 1966; Williamsen, Johnson, & Eriksen, 1965). Kihlstrom found that hypnotizable subjects, given an amnesia suggestion, were unable to recall the items in a word list that they had memorized during hypnosis. However, they remained able to use these same items as responses on free-association and category instance-generation tasks. Kihlstrom originally interpreted this as reflecting a dissociation between episodic and semantic memory – as did Tulving (1983), who cited the experiment as one of four convincing demonstrations of the episodic-semantic distinction. However, Kihlstrom also noted a priming effect on the production of list items as free associations and category instances, compared to control items that had not been learned; furthermore, the level of priming observed was the same as that shown by insusceptible subjects who were not amnesic for the word list.[2]

Spared priming during posthypnotic amnesia was subsequently confirmed by Spanos and his associates (Bertrand, Spanos, & Radtke, 1990; Spanos, Radtke, & Dubreuil, 1982), although they preferred to interpret the results in terms of the demands conveyed by test instructions rather than dissociations between explicit and implicit memory. Later, Dorfman and Kihlstrom (1994) bolstered the case for spared priming by correcting a methodological oversight in the earlier studies: The comparison of priming with free recall confounded explicit and implicit memory with the cue environment of the memory test. The dissociation between explicit and implicit memory was confirmed when a free-association test of priming was compared to a cued-recall test of explicit memory. Similarly, Barnier and her colleagues extended the dissociation to explicit and implicit memory for material learned outside as well as within hypnosis (Barnier, Bryant, & Briscoe, 2001).

Whereas most studies of implicit memory in the amnesic syndrome employ tests of repetition priming, such as stem and fragment completion, the studies just described employed tests of semantic priming, which cannot be mediated by a perceptual representation of the stimulus materials. However, David and his colleagues (David, Brown, Pojoga, & David, 2000) found that posthypnotic amnesia spared repetition priming on a stem-completion task. Similar results were obtained by Barnier et al. (2001). In an especially important twist, David et al. employed Jacoby's process dissociation paradigm (Jacoby, 1991) to confirm that the priming spared in posthypnotic amnesia is a reflection of involuntary unconscious memory, rather than either involuntary or voluntary conscious memory.[3] That is to say, the spared priming is a genuine reflection of implicit, or unconscious, memory.

With the benefit of hindsight, we can trace studies of implicit memory in posthypnotic amnesia at least as far as the classic work of Hull (Hull, 1933; Kihlstrom, 2004a), who demonstrated that posthypnotic amnesia impaired recall but had no effect on practice effects, savings in relearning, or retroactive interference (see further discussion below). Hull concluded merely that the forgetting observed in posthypnotic amnesia was "by no means complete" (p. 138) – much as Gregg (1979, 1982) later interpreted the evidence as reflecting the distinction dissociation between optional and obligatory aspects of memory performance. But we can now interpret the same evidence as illustrating a strong dissociation between explicit and implicit memory.

In addition to priming, the dissociation between explicit and implicit memory is revealed by the phenomenon of *source amnesia*, in which the subject retains knowledge acquired through some learning experience while forgetting the learning experience itself (Schacter, Harbluk, & McClachlan, 1984; Shimamura & Squire,

1987). Interestingly, source amnesia was first identified in the context of hypnosis (Cooper, 1966; Evans, 1979a,b, 1988; Evans & Thorne, 1966). Evans and Thorne (1966) found that some amnesic subjects retained world-knowledge that had been taught to them during hypnosis, (e.g., the color an amethyst turns when exposed to heat or the difference between the antennae of moths and butterflies), although they did not remember the circumstances in which they acquired this information. In a later study, Evans (1979a) showed that source amnesia did not occur in insusceptible subjects who simulated hypnosis and posthypnotic amnesia. Although the methodology of Evans' study has been criticized (Coe, 1978; Spanos, Gwynn, Della Malva, & Bertrand, 1988), most of these criticisms pertain to the real-simulating comparison and do not undermine the phenomenon itself. Along with the notion of demand characteristics (Kihlstrom, 2002a; Orne, 1962, 1973), source amnesia is one of the most salient examples of a concept developed in hypnosis research that has become part of the common parlance of psychological theory.[4]

Source amnesia might be interpreted as a form of implicit learning (Berry & Dienes, 1993; Reber, 1967, 1993; Seger, 1994). In line with the traditional definition of learning, as a relatively permanent change in behavior that occurs as a result of experience, we may define implicit learning as the acquisition of new knowledge in the absence *either* of conscious awareness of the learning experience *or* conscious awareness of what has been learned, *or* both. Although evidence for implicit learning can be construed as evidence for implicit memory as well (Schacter, 1987), we may distinguish between the two phenomena with respect to the sort of knowledge affected. In implicit memory, the memories in question are *episodic* in nature, representing more or less discrete episodes in the life of the learner. Memories are acquired in implicit learning as well, of course, but in this case we are concerned with new *semantic* and *procedural* knowledge acquired by the subject. When implicit and explicit learning are dissociated, subjects have no conscious access to the knowledge – in which case implicit learning counts as a failure of metacognition (Flavell, 1979; Metcalfe & Shimamura, 1994; Nelson, 1992,1996; Nelson & Narens, 1990; Reder, 1996; Yzerbyt, Lories, & Dardenne, 1998). Because the subjects in Evans' experiments were aware of what they had learned, though they were amnesic for the learning experience, source amnesia is better construed as an example of implicit memory.

Preserved priming on free-association and category-generation tasks, in the face of impaired recall, is a form of dissociation between explicit and implicit memory. Preserved learning, in the face of amnesia for the learning experience, is also a form of dissociation between explicit and implicit memory. But the case of posthypnotic amnesia is different, in at least three respects, from other amnesias in which these dissociations are observed. First, in contrast to the typical explicit-implicit dissociation, the items in question have been deeply processed at the time of encoding. In the priming studies, for example, the critical targets were not just presented for a single trial, but rather were deliberately memorized over the course of several study-test cycles to a strict criterion of learning (Dorfman & Kihlstrom, 1994; Kihlstrom, 1980). Second, the priming that is preserved is *semantic* priming, which relies on the formation during encoding and preservation at retrieval of a semantic link between cue and target. This priming reflects deep, semantic processing of a sort that cannot be mediated by a perceptual representation system. Third, the impairment in explicit memory is reversible: Posthypnotic amnesia is the only case I know where implicit memories can be restored to explicit recollection.

Taken together, then, these priming results reflect the unconscious influence of semantic representations formed as a result of extensive attentional activity at the time of encoding. The priming itself may be an automatic influence, but again it is not the sort that is produced by automatic processes mediated by a perceptual representation system.

Implicit Perception in Hypnotic Analgesia

In addition to their effects on memory, hypnotic suggestions can have very dramatic effects on the experience of pain (Hilgard & Hilgard, 1975; Montgomery, DuHamel, & Redd, 2000). Although hypnotic analgesia was supplanted by more reliable chemical analgesia almost as soon as its efficacy was documented in the mid-19th century, modern psychophysical studies confirm that hypnotizable subjects given suggestions for analgesia can experience considerable relief from laboratory pain (Faymonville et al., 2000; Hilgard, 1969; Knox, Morgan, & Hilgard, 1974). In fact, a comparative study found that, among hypnotizable subjects, hypnotic analgesia was superior not just to placebo but also to morphine, diazepam, aspirin, acupuncture, and biofeedback (Stern, Brown, Ulett, & Sletten, 1977). Although hypnosis can serve as the sole analgesic agent in surgery, it is probably used more appropriately as an adjunct to chemical analgesics, where it has been shown to be both effective and cost effective in reducing actual clinical pain (Lang, Benotsch et al., 2000; Lang, Joyce, Spiegel, Hamilton, & Lee, 1996).[5]

Hypnotic analgesia is not mediated by relaxation, and the fact that it is not reversed by narcotic antagonists would seem to rule out a role for endogenous opiates (Barber & Mayer, 1977; Goldstein & Hilgard, 1975; Moret et al., 1991; Spiegel & Albert, 1983). There is a placebo component to all active analgesic agents, and hypnosis is no exception; however, hypnotizable subjects receive benefits from hypnotic suggestion that outweigh what they or their insusceptible counterparts achieve from plausible placebos (McGlashan, Evans, & Orne, 1969; Stern et al., 1977). It has also been argued that hypnotized subjects employ such techniques as self-distraction, stress inoculation, cognitive reinterpretation, and tension management to reduce pain (Nolan & Spanos, 1987; Spanos, 1986b). Although there is no doubt that cognitive strategies can reduce pain, their success, unlike the success of hypnotic suggestions, is not correlated with hypnotizability and thus is unlikely to be responsible for the effects observed in hypnotizable subjects (Hargadon, Bowers, & Woody, 1995; Miller & Bowers, 1986, 1993).

Rather, Hilgard suggested that hypnotic analgesia entails a division of consciousness that prevents the perception of pain from being represented in conscious awareness (Hilgard, 1973b, 1977). In other words, verbal reports of pain and suffering reflect the conscious perception of pain, whereas physiological responses reflect the processing of pain processed outside of conscious awareness. Hilgard's "hidden observer" is both a metaphor for the subconscious perception of pain and a label for a method by which this subconscious pain can be accessed (Hilgard, Morgan, & Macdonald, 1975; Knox et al., 1974). Although it has been suggested that hidden observer reports are artifacts of experimental demands (Spanos, 1983; Spanos, Gwynn, & Stam, 1983; Spanos & Hewitt, 1980), Hilgard showed that both the overt and covert pain reports of hypnotized subjects differed from those given by subjects who are simulating hypnosis (Hilgard, Hilgard, Macdonald, Morgan, & Johnson, 1978; Hilgard, Macdonald, Morgan, & Johnson, 1978; see also Laurence, Perry, & Kihlstrom, 1983).

The division in consciousness in hypnotic analgesia, as proposed by Hilgard, would help explain one of the paradoxes of hypnotic analgesia, which is that it alters subjects' self-reports of pain but has little or no effect on reflexive, physiological responses to the pain stimulus (e.g., Hilgard & Morgan, 1975; Hilgard et al., 1974). One interpretation of this difference is that hypnotized subjects consciously feel the pain after all. However, we know on independent grounds that physiological measures are relatively unsatisfactory indices of the subjective experience of pain (Hilgard, 1969). From the perspective of neodissociation theory, the diminished self-ratings are accurate reflections of the subjects' conscious experience of pain, whereas the physiological measures show that the pain stimulus has been registered and processed outside of awareness – a reg-

istration that can be tapped by the hidden observer method.

The paradox of hypnotic analgesia can also be viewed through an extension of the explicit-implicit distinction from learning and memory to perception (Kihlstrom, 1996; Kihlstrom et al., 1992). Explicit perception refers to the conscious perception of a stimulus event, whereas implicit perception refers to the effect of such an event on the subject's ongoing experience, thought, and action in the absence of, or independent of, conscious awareness. Just as explicit and implicit memory can be dissociated in the amnesic syndrome and in posthypnotic amnesia, so explicit and implicit perception can be dissociated in "subliminal" perception (Marcel, 1983) or prosopagnosia (Bauer, 1984). In the case of hypnotic analgesia, explicit perception of the pain stimulus is reflected in subjects' self-reports of pain, whereas implicit perception is reflected in their physiological responses to the pain stimulus.

Implicit Perception in Hypnotic Deafness

Dissociations between explicit and implicit perception can also be observed in two other classes of hypnotic phenomena. In hypnotic *esthesia*, the subject experiences a marked reduction in sensory acuity: Examples include hypnotic deafness, blindness, and tactile anesthesia. In *hypnotic negative hallucinations*, the subject fails to perceive a particular object (or class of objects) in the environment, but otherwise retains normal levels of sensory function (hypnotized subjects can experience positive hallucinations as well, perceiving objects that are not actually present in their sensory fields). Although the hypnotic esthesias mimic sensory disorders, the content-specificity of the negative hallucinations marks them as more perceptual in nature.

Careful psychophysical studies, employing both magnitude-estimation (Crawford, Macdonald, & Hilgard, 1979) and signal-detection (Graham & Schwarz, 1973) paradigms, have documented the loss of auditory acuity in hypnotic deafness.

Nevertheless, as is the case in posthypnotic amnesia and hypnotic analgesia, subjects experiencing these phenomena show through their behavior that stimuli in the targeted modality continue to be processed, if outside of awareness. For example, Hilgard's hidden observer has also been observed in hypnotic deafness (Crawford et al., 1979). Hypnotically deaf subjects continue to manifest speech dysfluencies when subjected to delayed auditory feedback (Scheibe, Gray, & Keim, 1968; Sutcliffe, 1961) and in the case of unilateral deafness show substantial numbers of intrusions from material presented to their deaf ear (Spanos, Jones, & Malfara, 1982). Nor does hypnotic deafness abolish the "beats" produced by dissonant tones (Pattie, 1937) or cardiovascular responses to an auditory conditioned stimulus (Sabourin, Brisson, & Deschamb, 1980).

Spanos and Jones (Spanos et al., 1982) preferred to interpret their findings as revealing that hypnotically deaf subjects heard perfectly well, but Sutcliffe (1960, 1961) offered a more subtle interpretation. In his view, the persisting effects of delayed auditory feedback certainly contradicted the "credulous" view that hypnotic deafness was identical to the actual stimulus state of affairs that might arise from damage to the auditory nerve or lesions in the auditory projection area – or, for that matter, the simple absence of an auditory stimulus (Erickson, 1938a,b). But instead of drawing the "skeptical" conclusion that hypnotized subjects were engaged in mere role-playing activity, Sutcliffe suggested that they were deluded about their experiences – that is, that they believed that they heard nothing, when in fact they did. Sutcliffe's emphasis on delusion can be viewed as an anticipation of Hilgard's (1977) neodissociation theory of divided consciousness, where the subjects' delusional beliefs reflect their actual phenomenal experience, and the evidence of preserved hearing reflects something like implicit perception.

Only one study has used priming to examine implicit perception in hypnotic deafness. Nash and his colleagues found that hypnotic deafness reduced the likelihood that subjects would select, from a visually presented array, words that were phonetically (but not semantically) similar to words that had been spoken to them (Nash, Lynn, Stanley, & Carlson, 1987). Because the hypnotic subjects selected *fewer* such words compared to baseline control subjects, this counts as an instance of negative phonological priming, and thus of implicit perception as well.

Implicit Perception in Hypnotic Blindness

Similar paradoxes are observed in the visual domain. Inspired by an earlier experimental case study of hypnotic blindness (Brady, 1966; Brady & Lind, 1961; see also Bryant & McConkey, 1989d; Grosz & Zimmerman, 1965), Sackeim and his colleagues (Sackeim, Nordlie, & Gur, 1979) asked a hypnotically blind subject to solve a puzzle in which the correct response was indicated by the illumination of a lamp. Performance was significantly *below* chance. Bryant and McConkey (1989a,b) conducted a similar experiment, with a larger group of subjects, generally finding *above*-chance performance. The difference in outcomes may reflect a number of factors, including the subjects' motivation for the experiment and individual differences in cognitive style (Bryant & McConkey, 1990a,b,c), but either outcome shows that the visual stimulus was processed by the hypnotically blind subjects.

Dissociations between explicit and implicit perception are also suggested by a series of studies by Leibowitz and his colleagues, who found that ablation of the background did not affect perception of the Ponzo illusion (Miller, Hennessy, & Leibowitz, 1973) and that suggestions for tubular (tunnel) vision had no effect on the size-distance relation (Leibowitz, Lundy, & Guez, 1980) or on illusory feelings of egomotion (roll vection) induced by viewing a rotating object (Leibowitz, Post, Rodemer, Wadlington, & Lundy, 1980). These experiments are particularly interesting because they make use of a class of perceptual phenomena known as *perceptual couplings*, which are apparently inviolable links between one perceptual organization and another (Epstein, 1982; Hochberg, 1974; Hochberg & Peterson, 1987; Peterson & Hochberg, 1983). If an observer sees two lines converging in a distance, he or she must see two identical horizontal bars arranged vertically along these lines as differing in length. In the Miller et al. study, ablation of the converging lines is a failure of explicit perception, but the persistence of the perceptually coupled Ponzo illusion indicates that they have been perceived implicitly.

Perceptual couplings also seem to be involved in the finding of Blum and his colleagues that hypnotic ablation of surrounding stimuli did not alter either the magnitude of the Titchener-Ebbinghaus illusion (Blum, Nash, Jansen, & Barbour, 1981) or the perception of slant in a target line (Jansen, Blum, & Loomis, 1982). They are also implicated in the observation that hypnotic anesthesia of the forearm does not affect perceptual adaptation of the pointing response to displacing prisms (Spanos, Dubreuil, Saad, & Gorassini, 1983; Spanos, Gorassini, & Petrusic, 1981; Spanos & Saad, 1984). The subjects may not feel their arms moving during the pointing trials, but the fact that adaptation occurs indicates that the kinesthetic information has been processed anyway.[6]

Although the evidence from perceptual couplings is consistent with the notion of spared implicit perception, only two studies have used priming methodologies to seek evidence of unconscious vision in hypnotic blindness. Bryant and McConkey (1989a) showed subjects pairs of words consisting of a homophone and a disambiguating context word (e.g., *window-pane*), half under conditions of ordinary vision and half during hypnotically suggested blindness. On a later memory test, the subjects generally failed to recall words they had been shown while blind. On a subsequent test, however, when the words were presented auditorially, they tended to spell them in line with their earlier visual presentation (e.g., *pane* rather than *pain*). A subsequent study found a similar priming effect on word-fragment completion (Bryant & McConkey, 1994). In both cases, priming was diminished somewhat by

hypnotic blindness compared to trials where the subjects saw the primes clearly, but any evidence of priming counts as evidence of implicit perception – and the magnitude of priming in both studies was substantial by any standards.

Color, Meaning, and the Stroop Effect

In addition to total (binocular or uniocular) or tubular blindness, hypnotic subjects can also be given suggestions for color blindness. Although some early research indicated that hypnotic colorblindness affected performance on the Ishihara test and other laboratory-based tests of color perception (Erickson, 1939), the claim has long been controversial (Grether, 1940; Harriman, 1942a,b), and the most rigorous study of this type found no effects (Cunningham & Blum, 1982). Certainly, hypnotically colorblind subjects do not show patterns of test performance that mimic those of the congenitally colorblind. Nor do hypnotic suggestions for colorblindness abolish Stroop interference effects (Harvey & Sipprelle, 1978; Mallard & Bryant, 2001). All of these results are consistent with the hypothesis that color is processed implicitly in hypnotically induced colorblindness, even if it is not represented in the subjects' phenomenal awareness.

However, hypnotic suggestions of a different sort may indeed abolish Stroop interference. Instead of suggesting that subjects were colorblind, Raz and his colleagues suggested that the color words were "meaningless symbols ... like characters of a foreign language that you do not know ... gibberish" (Raz, Shapiro, Fan, & Posner, 2002, p. 1157). The focus on meaning, rather than color, makes this suggestion more akin to the hypnotic agnosia (or, perhaps, alexia) studied by Spanos and his colleagues in relation to hypnotic amnesia (Spanos, Radtke et al., 1982). In contrast to the effects of suggested colorblindness, suggested agnosia completely abolished the Stroop interference effect. Subsequent research, employing a drug to induce cycloplegia and thus eliminate accommodation effects, ruled out peripheral mechanisms, such as visual blurring or looking away from the stimulus (Raz et al., 2003). However, preliminary fMRI research suggests that the reduced Stroop interference reflects a nonspecific dampening of visual information processing (Raz, Fan, Shapiro, & Posner, 2002) – a generalized effect of visual information processing, rather than an effect mediated at linguistic or semantic levels. This generalized effect on visual information processing may explain why Stroop interference did not persist as an implicit expression of semantic processing, despite the conscious experience of agnosia.

Implicit Emotion

Hypnotic suggestions can alter conscious emotion as well as perception and memory. In fact, the suggested alteration of emotion has been a technique for psychotherapy at least since the time of Janet (Ellenberger, 1970), and has played a role in hypnotic studies of psychodynamic processes (Blum, 1961, 1967, 1979; Reyher, 1967). Aside from its inclusion in an advanced scale of hypnotic susceptibility (Hilgard, 1965), the phenomenon and its underlying mechanisms have not been subject to much empirical study. However, more recent studies leave little doubt that hypnotic suggestions can alter subjects' conscious feeling states, just as they can alter their conscious percepts and memories (Bryant & McConkey, 1989c; Weiss, Blum, & Gleberman, 1987).

As with perception and memory, however, special interest attaches to the question of whether the "blocked" emotional responses can nevertheless influence the person's ongoing experience, thought, and action outside of conscious awareness. Until recently, the idea of unconscious emotion has generally been seen as a holdover from an earlier, more psychodynamically oriented period in the history of psychology. However, in an era where dissociations between explicit and implicit perception and memory are widely accepted as evidence of unconscious cognitive processing, there seems little reason to reject out of hand the prospect of dissociations between explicit

and implicit emotion (Kihlstrom, Mulvaney, Tobias, & Tobis, 2000).[7] Kihlstrom et al. have proposed that, in the absence of self-reported emotion, behavioral and physiological indices of emotional response, such as facial expressions and heart rate changes, might serve as evidence of implicit, unconscious emotional responding. In fact, a study by Bryant and Kourch found that hypnotic suggestions for emotional numbing diminished self-reported emotional responses, but had no effect on facial expressions of emotion (Bryant & Kourch, 2001). Although this finding is suggestive of a dissociation between explicit and implicit expressions of emotion, two other studies found that emotional numbing diminished both subjective reports and facial expressions (Bryant & Mallard, 2002; Weiss et al., 1987). With respect to the dissociation between explicit and implicit emotion, then, the effects of hypnotically induced emotional numbing are currently uncertain.

Anomalies of Dissociation in Hypnosis

Most of the classic phenomena of hypnosis – amnesia, analgesia, and the like – appear to be dissociative in two related but different senses. In the first place, hypnotized subjects lack awareness of percepts and memories that would ordinarily be accessible to consciousness. This disruption in conscious awareness is the hallmark of the dissociative disorders encountered clinically, including "functional" amnesia and "hysterical" deafness. In the second place, these percepts and memories continue to influence the subject's ongoing experience, thought, and action outside awareness – creating dissociations between explicit and implicit memory, or explicit and implicit perception, similar to those that have now become quite familiar in the laboratory or neurological clinic. As Hilgard (1977) noted, it is as if consciousness has been divided, with one stream of mental life (e.g., a failure of conscious recollection) proceeding in phenomenal awareness while another stream (e.g., the implicit expression of memory encoding, storage, and retrieval) proceeds outside of awareness.

Co-Consciousness and Trance Logic

Sometimes, however, the suggested and actual state of affairs are both represented in conscious awareness, leading to a set of inconsistencies and paradoxes that Orne, in a classic paper, labeled "trance logic" (Orne, 1959). Orne defined trance logic as the "apparently simultaneous perception and response to both hallucinations and reality without any apparent attempts to satisfy a need for logical consistency" (p. 295) – or, as he often put it in informal conversation, "the peaceful coexistence of illusion and reality." For example, in the double hallucination, it is suggested that the subject will see and interact with a confederate sitting in a chair that is actually empty. When the subject's attention is drawn to the real confederate, who has been quietly sitting outside his or her field of vision, Orne reported that hypnotized subjects typically maintained both the perception of the real confederate and the hallucinations, exhibiting confusion as to which was the real confederate. Similarly, many subjects reported that they could see through the hallucinated confederate to the back of the armchair. Thus, the subjects were simultaneously aware of two mutually contradictory states of affairs, apparently without feeling the need to resolve the contradictions inherent in the experience.

Orne's initial report of trance logic was somewhat impressionistic in nature, but later investigators have attempted to study the phenomenon more quantitatively – with somewhat mixed results (Hilgard, 1972; R.F.Q. Johnson, 1972; Johnson, Maher, & Barber, 1972; McConkey, Bryant, Bibb, Kihlstrom, & Tataryn, 1990; McConkey & Sheehan, 1980; Obstoj & Sheehan, 1977; Sheehan, Obstoj, & McConkey, 1976). On the other hand, everyone who has ever worked with hypnotized subjects has seen the phenomenon. Although Orne (Orne, 1959) held the view that trance logic was a defining characteristic of hypnosis, this does not seem to be the case – not least because similar inconsistencies and anomalies of response can occur in ordinary imagination as well as in hypnosis (McConkey,

Bryant, Bibb, & Kihlstrom, 1991). Spanos (Spanos, DeGroot, & Gwynn, 1987) suggested that the occurrence of trance logic was an artifact of incomplete response to the suggestion on the part of the subject, but this proposal seems to be based on the assumption that a "complete" image or hallucination would be tantamount to "the real thing" – the actual perceptual state of affairs produced by an adequate environmental stimulus. On the other hand, it may well be that the hallucination is quite complete, in the sense of being subjectively compelling to the person who experiences it – but the accompanying division of consciousness might be incomplete. In this case, trance logic reflects a kind of co-consciousness in which two different and mutually contradictory streams of mental activity – one perceptual, one imaginary – are represented simultaneously in phenomenal awareness.

Making the Unconscious Conscious

In the case of posthypnotic amnesia and hypnotic analgesia, as well as the hypnotic esthesias and negative hallucinations, it seems that hypnotized subjects are able to become unaware of percepts and memories that would ordinarily be represented in phenomenal awareness. In contrast, it has sometimes been suggested that hypnosis also has the opposite capacity – to enable subjects to become aware of percepts and memories that would not ordinarily be accessible to conscious introspection. For example, in *hypnotic hypermnesia* subjects receive suggestions that they will be able to remember events that they have forgotten. In *hypnotic age regression*, it is suggested that they will relive a previous period in their lives – an experience that is often accompanied by the apparent recovery of long-forgotten childhood memories.

Hypermnesia suggestions are sometimes employed in forensic situations, with forgetful witnesses and victims, or in therapeutic situations, to help patients remember traumatic personal experiences. Although field studies have sometimes claimed that hypnosis can powerfully enhance memory, these reports are mostly anecdotal in nature and generally fail to seek independent corroboration of the memories produced during hypnosis. Moreover, they have not been supported by studies run under laboratory conditions. A report by the Committee on Techniques for the Enhancement of Human Performance, a unit of the U.S. National Research Council, concluded that gains in recall produced by hypnotic suggestion were rarely dramatic and were matched by gains observed when subjects are not hypnotized (Kihlstrom & Eich, 1994; Nogrady, McConkey, & Perry, 1985). In fact, there is some evidence from the laboratory that hypnotic suggestion can interfere with normal hypermnesic processes (Register & Kihlstrom, 1987). To make things worse, any increases obtained in valid recollection can be met or exceeded by increases in false recollections (Dywan & Bowers, 1983). Moreover, hypnotized subjects (especially those who are highly hypnotizable) may be vulnerable to distortions in memory produced by leading questions and other subtle, suggestive influences (Sheehan, 1988).

Similar conclusions apply to hypnotic age regression (Nash, 1987). Although age-regressed subjects may experience themselves as children and may behave in a child-like manner, there is no evidence that they actually undergo either abolition of characteristically adult modes of mental functioning or reinstatement of childlike modes of mental functioning. Nor do age-regressed subjects experience the revivification of forgotten memories of childhood. Hypnotic age regression can be a subjectively compelling experience for subjects, but it is first and foremost an imaginative experience. As with hypnotic hypermnesia, any memories recovered during hypnotic age regression cannot be accepted at face value, in the absence of independent corroboration.

Some clinical practitioners have objected to these conclusions, on the ground that laboratory studies of memory generally lack ecological validity (Brown, Scheflin, & Hammond, 1998). In fact, one diary-based study did find some evidence that hypno-sis enhanced the recovery of valid memory of actual personal experiences (Hofling, Heyl, & Wright, 1971). This study has not been replicated, however, and another study, also employing lifelike stimulus materials – a gangland assassination staged before an audience of law enforcement officers – found no advantage for hypnosis whatsoever (Timm, 1981). Perhaps not surprisingly, many legal jurisdictions severely limit the introduction of memories recovered through hypnosis, out of a concern that such memories may be unreliable and tainted by suggestion and inappropriately high levels of confidence. An abundance of caution seems to be appropriate in this instance, but in the present context it seems that hypnotic suggestion is better at making percepts and memories inaccessible to consciousness than it is at making unconscious percepts and memories accessible to phenomenal awareness.

Automaticity in Hypnosis

Even before the discovery of implicit memory and the rediscovery of "subliminal" perception, psychology's renewed interest in unconscious mental life was signalled by the general acceptance of a distinction between *automatic* and *controlled* mental processes. As a first approximation, automatic processes are executed unconsciously in a reflex-like fashion, whereas controlled processes are executed consciously and deliberately (Kihlstrom, 1987, 1994b). A popular example of automaticity is the Stroop color-word effect, in which subjects have difficulty naming the colors in which words are printed when the words themselves name a different color (MacLeod, 1991, 1992; Stroop, 1935). Despite the subjects' conscious intention to name the ink colors and to ignore the words, they automatically process the words anyway, and this processing activity interferes with the naming task.

According to traditional formulations (LaBerge & Samuels, 1974; Posner & Snyder, 1975; Schneider & Shiffrin, 1977; Shiffrin &

Schneider, 1977, 1984), automatic processes share five properties in common:

1. **Inevitable Evocation**: Automatic processes are necessarily engaged by the appearance of specific cues in the stimulus environment, independent of the person's conscious intentions.

2. **Incorrigible Execution**: Once invoked, automatic processes proceed unalterably to their conclusion and cannot be modified by conscious activity.

3. **Effortlessness**: The execution of an automatic process consumes little or no attentional resources and therefore does not interfere with other ongoing mental processes.

4. **Speed**: Automatic processes are executed rapidly, on the order of seconds or even fractions of a second – too quickly to be vulnerable to conscious control.

5. **Unavailability**: Perhaps because they consume no attentional resources, perhaps because they are fast, or perhaps because they are represented as procedural rather than declarative knowledge (Anderson, 1992), automatic processes are unconscious in the strict sense of being unavailable to conscious introspection *in principle*, and they can be known only by inference from performance data.

The Experience of Involuntariness in Hypnosis

As indicated at the outset of this chapter, there is much about hypnosis that appears to be automatic. Indeed, the experience of involuntariness – sometimes called the classic suggestion effect (Weitzenhoffer, 1974) – is part and parcel of the experience of hypnosis. Hypnotic subjects don't simply imagine heavy objects in their hands and allow their arms to lower accordingly. They outstretch their hands voluntarily, as an act of ordinary compliance with the hypnotist's instruction or request to do so, but when he or she starts giving the suggestion they *feel* the heaviness in their hands, their arms drop, as involuntary *happenings* rather than

as voluntary *doings* (Sarbin & Coe, 1972). Not all responses to hypnotic suggestion are experienced as completely involuntary, but the experience is strongest among those who are most highly hypnotizable (Bowers, 1982; Bowers, Laurence, & Hart, 1988).

Automaticity lies at the heart of the "social cognitive" theory of hypnosis proposed by Kirsch and Lynn (Kirsch, 2000; Kirsch & Lynn, 1997, 1998b), which asserts that hypnotic behaviors are generated automatically by subjects' expectancies that they will occur – much in the manner of a self-fulfilling prophecy (Rosenthal & Rubin, 1978; Snyder & Swann, 1978). This view, in turn, is rooted in James's (1890) theory of ideomotor action (see also Arnold, 1946), which held that motor behavior was generated automatically by the person's idea of it. Conscious control over behavior, then, is accomplished by exerting conscious control over one's cognitive and other mental states; but once a subject attends to a particular idea, the resulting behavior occurs naturally.

Kirsch and Lynn's social cognitive, ideomotor theory of hypnosis is distinct from Spanos's "sociocognitive" approach (Spanos, 1986b), which holds either that subjects fabricate reports of involuntariness to convince the hypnotist that they are, in fact, deeply hypnotized (Spanos, Cobb, & Gorassini, 1985) or that certain features of the hypnotic context lead subjects to misattribute their responses to the hypnotist's suggestions, instead of to their own voluntary actions (Spanos, 1986a). Spanos's latter view, that the hypnotic experience of involuntariness is illusory, was also embraced by Wegner (2002; but see Kihlstrom, 2004b). Working from a neuropsychological perspective, Woody and Bowers have suggested that the experience of involuntariness is a genuine reflection of the effects of hypnosis on frontal-lobe structures involved in executive functioning (Woody & Bowers, 1994; Woody & Sadler, 1998).

On the other hand, it is possible that the hypnotic experience of involuntariness is illusory after all – though not for the reasons suggested by Spanos and Wegner. After all, as Shor noted, "A hypnotized subject is not a will-less automaton. The hypnotist does not crawl inside a subject's body and take control of his brain and muscles" (Shor, 1979b, p. 127). From the framework of Hilgard's neodissociation theory of divided consciousness (Hilgard, 1977; see also Kihlstrom, 1992a), the experience of involuntariness reflects an amnesia-like barrier that impairs subjects' conscious awareness of their own role in producing hypnotic responses. In this view, the hypnotic subject actively imagines a heavy object in his outstretched hand, and actively lowers his hand and arm as if it were heavy, but is not aware of doing so. Thus, the subject's behavior is technically voluntary in nature, but is experienced as involuntary – as occurring automatically – because the subject is unaware of his or her own role as the agent of the behavior. In other words, the apparent disruption of conscious control actually occurs by virtue of a disruption of conscious awareness – a proposal that (perhaps) gains credence from the dissociations between explicit and implicit memory and perception discussed earlier.

Automaticity in Posthypnotic Suggestion

Perhaps the most dramatic demonstration of apparent automaticity in hypnosis is posthypnotic suggestion, in which the subject responds after the termination of hypnosis to a suggestion administered while he or she was still hypnotized. On the group-administered HGSHS:A, for example, it is suggested that when the subjects hear two taps, they will reach down and touch their left ankles, but forget that they were instructed to do so. After the termination of hypnosis, many highly hypnotizable subjects will respond quickly to such a prearranged cue – without knowing why they are doing so or confabulating a reason, such as that they feel an itch. They may even be unaware that they are doing anything unusual at all.

Any suggested experience that can occur during hypnosis can also occur posthypnotically, provided that the subject is sufficiently hypnotizable. For this reason, posthypnotic suggestion has always been problematic for

some views of hypnosis as an altered state of consciousness, because the phenomenon occurs after the hypnotic state has been ostensibly terminated. So far as we can tell, subjects do not re-enter hypnosis while they are responding to the posthypnotic suggestion. At least, they are not particularly responsive to other hypnotic suggestions during this time (Reyher & Smyth, 1971). We cannot say that hypnosis caused the behavior to occur, because the subjects are not hypnotized when they make their response. Nevertheless, some alteration of consciousness has occurred, because at the very least they are not aware of what they are doing or why (Sheehan & Orne, 1968).

In the present context, posthypnotic suggestion is of interest because it seems to occur automatically in response to the prearranged cue (Erickson & Erickson, 1941). Certainly posthypnotic suggestion differs from ordinary behavioral compliance. Damaser (Damaser, 1964; see also Orne, 1969) gave subjects a posthypnotic suggestion to mail the experimenter one postcard per day, a control group received an ordinary social request to perform the same behavior, and a third group received both the posthypnotic suggestion and the social request. Surprisingly, the subjects who received the social request mailed more postcards than did those who received only the posthypnotic suggestion (see also Barnier & McConkey, 1999b). Apparently, those who agreed to the social request felt that they were under some obligation to carry it out, but those who received the posthypnotic suggestion carried it out only so long as they felt the urge to do so. This urge can be powerful: Subjects who fail to respond to a posthypnotic suggestion on an initial test appear to show a persisting tendency to perform the suggested behavior at a later time (Nace & Orne, 1970). Posthypnotic behavior can persist for long periods of time (Edwards, 1963), even after the posthypnotic suggestion has been formally canceled (Bowers, 1975).

Nevertheless, close examination shows that posthypnotic behavior does not meet the technical definition of automaticity, as it has evolved within cognitive psychology (Barnier, 1999). In the first place, posthypnotic suggestion fails the test of *inevitable evocation*. Except under special circumstances (Orne, Sheehan, & Evans, 1968), response to a posthypnotic suggestion declines markedly outside the experimental context in which the suggestion is originally given (Barnier & McConkey, 1998; Fisher, 1954; Spanos, Menary, Brett, Cross, & Ahmed, 1987). Moreover, like all other aspects of hypnosis, posthypnotic behavior depends intimately on the both the subject's interpretation of the hypnotist's suggestion and the context in which the cue appears (Barnier & McConkey, 1999a, 2001). It is in no sense reflexive in nature. Moreover, posthypnotic suggestion is not *effortless*. Subjects respond to simple posthypnotic suggestions more frequently than to complex ones (Barnier & McConkey, 1999c), suggesting that the activity makes demands on the subject's information-processing capacity. Responding to a posthypnotic suggestion interferes with responding to a waking instruction, even when the response requirements of the two tasks do not conflict (Hoyt & Kihlstrom, 1986). Thus, responding to a posthypnotic suggestion seems to consume more information-processing capacity than would be expected of a truly automatic process.

Posthypnotic suggestion does not appear to be an instance of automaticity, but it does appear to be an instance of prospective memory (Einstein & McDaniel, 1990), in which subjects must remember to perform a specified activity at some time in the future. Awareness of the posthypnotic suggestion does not seem to interfere with posthypnotic behavior (Barnier & McConkey, 1999c; Edwards, 1956; Gandolfo, 1971). But when accompanied by posthypnotic amnesia, posthypnotic behavior takes on some of the qualities of implicit memory. Even though subjects may forget the suggestion, the fact that they carry out the suggestion on cue shows clearly that the prospective memory has been encoded

and influences subsequent behavior in the absence of conscious recollection.

Hypnosis in Mind and Body

Researchers have long been interested in biological correlates of hypnosis. In the 19th century, Braid likened hypnosis to sleep, whereas Pavlov considered it to be a state of cortical inhibition (Gauld, 1992). In the mid-20th century revival of interest in consciousness, some theorists speculated that hypnosis entailed an increase in high-voltage, low-frequency alpha activity in the EEG, though this proved to be an artifact of relaxation and eye closure (Dumas, 1977; Evans, 1979b). The discovery of hemispheric specialization, with the left hemisphere geared to analytic and the right hemisphere to non-analytic tasks, coupled with the notion that the right hemisphere is "silent" or unconscious," led to the speculation that hypnotic response is somehow mediated by right-hemisphere activity (Bakan, 1969). Studies employing both behavioral and electrophysiological paradigms (e.g., MacLeod-Morgan & Lack, 1982; Sackeim, 1982) have been interpreted as indicating increased activation of the right hemisphere among highly hypnotizable individuals, but positive results have proved difficult to replicate (e.g., Graffin, Ray, & Lundy, 1995; Otto-Salaj, Nadon, Hoyt, Register, & Kihlstrom, 1992), and interpretation of these findings remains controversial.

It should be understood that hypnosis is mediated by verbal suggestions, which must be interpreted by the subject in the course of responding. Thus, the role of the left hemisphere should not be minimized (Jasiukaitis, Nouriani, Hugdahl, & Spiegel, 1995; Rainville, Hofbauer, Paus, Bushnell, & Price, 1999). One interesting proposal is that hypnotizable individuals show greater flexibility in deploying the left and right hemispheres in a task-appropriate manner, especially when they are actually hypnotized (Crawford, 2001; Crawford & Gruzelier, 1992). Because involuntariness is so central to the experience of hypnosis, it has also been suggested that the frontal lobes (which organize intentional action) may play a special role in hypnosis, and especially in the experience of involuntariness (Woody & Bowers, 1994; Woody & Sadler, 1998). Along these lines, Farvolden and Woody have found that highly hypnotizable individuals perform relatively poorly on neuropsychological tasks that assess frontal-lobe functioning (Farvolden & Woody, 2004).

"Neutral" Hypnosis

Although most work on the neural correlates of hypnosis has employed psychophysiological measures such as the EEG and event-related potentials, it seems likely that a better understanding of the neural substrates of hypnosis may come from the application of brain imaging technologies (Barnier & McConkey, 2003; Killeen & Nash, 2003; Ray & Tucker, 2003; Woody & McConkey, 2003; Woody & Szechtman, 2003). One approach has been to scan subjects after they have received a hypnotic induction but before they have received any specific suggestions, on the assumption that such a procedure will reveal the neural correlates (if indeed any exist) of hypnosis as a generalized altered state of consciousness. For example, one PET study found that the induction of hypnosis generated widespread activation of occipital, parietal, precentral, premotor, and ventrolateral prefrontal cortex in the left hemisphere, and the occipital and anterior cingulate cortex of the right hemisphere – in other words, pretty much the entire brain (Maquet et al., 1999). At the same time, another PET study found that the induction of hypnosis was accompanied by increased activation of occipital cortex and decreases in the right inferior parietal lobule, left precuneus, and posterior cingulate (Rainville, Hofbauer et al., 1999). As is so often the case in brain imaging experiments, the difference in results may be due to differences in control conditions. Whereas Rainville et al. asked their hypnotized subjects simply to relax (Rainville, Hofbauer et al., 1999),

Maquet et al. asked their subjects to review a pleasant life experience (Maquet et al., 1999).

Although the concept of "neutral" hypnosis has had its proponents (Kihlstrom & Edmonston, 1971), in subjective terms the state, such as it is, differs little from eyes-closed relaxation (Edmonston, 1977, 1981) and bears little resemblance to the dissociative and hallucinatory experiences associated with specific hypnotic suggestions. Moreover, it is unlikely that imaging subjects who are merely in neutral hypnosis and not responding to particular hypnotic suggestions will tell us much about the neural correlates of hypnosis, because the experiences of hypnotic subjects are so varied, depending on the suggestion to which they are responding. A more fruitful tack will likely involve imaging subjects while they are responding to particular hypnotic suggestions. Just as the neural correlates of NREM sleep differ from those of REM sleep (Hobson, Pace-Schott, & Stickgold, 2000), so the neural correlates of neutral hypnosis will differ from those of specific, suggested hypnotic phenomena.

Hypnotic Analgesia

Perhaps because of the added interest value that comes with clinical application, most brain imaging studies of hypnotic suggestions have focused on analgesia. A pioneering study using the ^{133}Xe technique found bilateral increases in the activation of the orbitofrontal region, as well as in somatosensory cortex, during analgesia compared to resting baseline and a control condition in which subjects attended to the pain (Crawford, Gur, Skolnick, Gur, & Benson, 1993). They suggested that these changes reflected the increased mental effort needed to actively inhibit the processing of somatosensory information. A more recent PET study implicated quite different regions, particularly the anterior cingulate cortex (ACC). However, this later study also employed quite a different procedure, modulating pain perception through a pleasant autobiographical reverie instead of a specific suggestion for analgesia (Faymonville et al., 2000).

Because the specific wording of suggestions is so important in hypnosis, perhaps the most interesting brain imaging studies of analgesia compared suggestions targeting sensory pain, which relates to the location and physical intensity of the pain stimulus, with suggestions targeting suffering, or the meaning of the pain (Melzack, 1975). Standard hypnotic suggestions for analgesia affect both sensory pain and suffering (Hilgard & Hilgard, 1975), but these two dimensions can also be dissociated by altering the specific wording of the suggestion (Rainville, Carrier, Hofbauer, Bushnell, & Duncan, 1999). Using hypnotic suggestions, Rainville and his colleagues have found that suggestions that alter the unpleasantness of a pain stimulus, without altering its intensity, are associated with changes in ACC but not in somatosensory cortex (Rainville, Duncan, Price, Carrier, & Bushnell, 1997; Rainville et al., 2002).

Hallucinations and Imagery

Brain imaging studies also bear on the relation between hypnotic hallucinations and normal imagery. On the surface, at least, imagery would seem to be a cognitive skill relevant to hypnosis, and some theorists sometimes write as if hypnosis were only a special case of a larger domain of mental imagery (for reviews, see Bowers, 1992; Glisky et al., 1995; Kunzendorf, Spanos, & Wallace, 1996; Sheehan, 1982). On the contrary, Szechtman and his colleagues found that hypnotized subjects experiencing suggested auditory hallucinations showed activation of the right ACC; this area was also activated during normal hearing, but not during auditory imagery (Szechtman, Woody, Bowers, & Nahmias, 1998). Interestingly, a parallel study found that schizophrenic patients also showed right ACC activation during their auditory hallucinations (Cleghorn et al., 1992). They suggested that activation of this region might cause internally generated thoughts and images to be confused with those aris-

ing from the external stimulus environment (Woody & Szechtman, 2000a,b). Another interpretation, based on the role of ACC in emotion, is that the activity in this region reflects affective arousal to experiences, whether perceptual or hallucinatory, which surprise the subject; mental images, being deliberately constructed by the subject, would not have this surprise value.

In another study, Kosslyn and his colleagues studied the modulation of color perception through hypnotic suggestion (Kosslyn et al., 2000). After PET imaging identified a region (in the fusiform area) that was differentially activated by the presentation of chromatic and gray-scale stimuli, these investigators gave suggestions to highly hypnotizable subjects that they would perceive the colored stimulus in gray scale, and the gray-scale stimulus as colored. The result was that the fusiform region was activated in line with subjects' perceptions – actual and hallucinated color or actual and hallucinated gray scale, independent of the stimulus. In contrast to nonhypnotic color imagery, which appears to activate only the right fusiform region (Howard et al., 1998), hypnotically hallucinated color activated both the left and right hemispheres. Taken together with the Szechtman et al. study (1998), these results suggest that hypnotic hallucinations are in at least some sense distinct from mental images.

Brain States and States of Consciousness

The controversy over the very nature of hypnosis has often led investigators to seek evidence of neural and other biological changes to demonstrate that hypnosis is "real" – or, alternatively, to debunk the phenomenon as illusion and fakery. For example, the lack of reliable physiological correlates of hypnotic response has been interpreted by Sarbin as supporting his role-enactment interpretation of hypnosis (Sarbin, 1973; Sarbin & Slagle, 1979). On the other hand, Kosslyn and his colleagues argued that the activity of the fusiform color area in response to suggestions for altered color vision "support the claim that hypnosis is a psychological state with distinct neural correlates and is not just the result of adopting a role" (Kosslyn et al., 2000, p. 1279).

Neither position is quite correct. Physiological correlates are nice when they exist, and they may enable otherwise skeptical observers to accept the phenomena of hypnosis as real. But such correlates are neither necessary nor sufficient to define an altered state of consciousness. In the final analysis, consciousness is a psychological construct, not a biological one, and can only be defined at a psychological level of analysis. The phenomena of hypnosis – amnesia, analgesia, positive and negative hallucinations, and the like – obviously represent alterations in conscious perception and memory. The neural correlates of these phenomena are a matter of considerable interest, but they are another matter entirely.

At the same time, the phenomena of hypnosis seem to offer a unique vantage point from which consciousness and its neural correlates can be studied, because they remind us that consciousness is not just a matter of attention and alertness. Mental states are also a matter of *aboutness*: They have intentionality, in that they refer to objects that exist and events that occur in the world outside the mind. Hypnotized subjects are conscious, in the sense of being alert and attentive, but when certain suggestions are in effect they are not conscious *of some things* – of some event in the past or some object in their current environment. The fact that percepts and memories can be explicit or implicit means that mental states themselves can be conscious or unconscious.

The phenomena of hypnosis remind us that there is a difference between being aware of something explicitly and being unaware of something that nonetheless, implicitly influences our ongoing experience, thought, and action. Almost uniquely, hypnosis allows us to create, and reverse, dissociations between the explicit and the implicit – between the conscious and the unconscious – at will in the laboratory. The difference between implicit and explicit percepts and memories, then, is the difference

that makes for consciousness. And the neural correlates of that difference are the neural correlates of consciousness.

Acknowledgements

The point of view represented in this paper is based on research supported by Grant #MH-35856 from the National Institute of Mental Health.

Notes

1. This was true even before hypnosis received its name (Braid, 1843; Gravitz & Gerton, 1984; Kihlstrom, 1992c) – and for that matter even before that, the status of hypnosis as an altered organismal state was controversial. In the 18th century, Mesmer thought his "crises" were induced by animal magnetism, but the Franklin Commission chalked them up to mere imagination (Kihlstrom, 2002b). In the 19th century, Charcot thought that hypnosis was closely related to hysteria and to neurological disease, whereas Liebeault and Bernheim attributed its effects to simple suggestion. Perhaps because he was writing in the heyday of functional behaviorism, Hull (1933) did not confront the "state-nonstate" issue: For him, hypnosis was an intrinsically interesting phenomenon that psychology ought to be able to explain (Kihlstrom, 2004a).

2. Lacking the explicit-implicit distinction subsequently introduced by Schacter (see also Graf & Schacter, 1985; Schacter, 1987; Schacter & Graf, 1986), Kihlstrom noted simply that the priming represented "a residual effect of the original learning episode on a subsequent task involving retrieval from 'semantic' memory" (p. 246), that it "took place outside of phenomenal awareness," and that it was "similar to one which occurs in patients diagnosed with the amnesic syndrome" (p. 246). A similar interpretation appeared in 1985 (Kihlstrom, 1985), in a paper that had been written in 1984, and the relevance of the explicit-implicit distinction was made explicit (sorry) in 1987 (Kihlstrom, 1987).

3. Interestingly, David et al. obtained a similar pattern of results for directed forgetting in the normal waking state. Posthypnotic amnesia and directed forgetting are both examples of retrieval inhibition (Anderson & Green,

2001; Anderson et al., 2004; Geiselman, Bjork, & Fishman, 1983; Levy & Anderson, 2002), but the two paradigms generally differ greatly in other respects (Kihlstrom, 1983); for example, the role of incidental or intentional learning, the amount of study devoted to the items, the temporal location of the cue to forget. the retention interval involved, and the means by which memory is measured – as well as the degree to which the to-be-forgotten items are actually inaccessible, whether the forgetting is reversible, and the extent of interference between to-be-forgotten and to-be-remembered items.

4. Source amnesia is a failure of source monitoring (Johnson, Hashtroudi, & Lindsay, 1993), a process that in turn is closely related to reality monitoring (Johnson & Raye, 1981). It probably lies at the heart of the experience of *déjà vu* (Brown, 2003). As noted by Evans and Thorne (1966), their work had been anticipated by Banister and Zangwill (1941a,b) who used hypnotic suggestion to produce visual and olfactory "paramnesias" in which subjects recognize a previously studied item but confabulate the context in which it has been studied.

5. A thorough discussion of experimental and clinical research on hypnotic analgesia is beyond the scope of this chapter. Interested readers may wish to consult Kihlstrom (2000, 2001b).

6. Note, however, Wallace and his colleagues have found that hypnotic anesthesia actually abolishes prism adaptation, so this finding remains in some dispute (Wallace, 1980; Wallace & Fisher, 1982, 1984a,b; Wallace & Garrett, 1973, 1975).

7. McClelland and his colleagues have made a distinction between explicit (conscious) and implicit (unconscious) motivation, as well (McClelland, Koestner, & Weinberger, 1989), but to date there have been no studies of hypnosis along these lines.

References

Anderson, J. R. (1992). Automaticity and the ACT* theory. *American Journal of Psychology*, 105(2), 165–180.

Anderson, M. C., & Green, C. (2001, March). Suppressing unwanted memories by executive control. *Nature*, 410(15), 366–369.

Anderson, M. C., Ochsner, K. N., Kuhl, B., Cooper, J., Robertson, E., Gabrieli, S. W.,

Glover, G. H., & Gabrieli, J. D. E. (2004). Neural systems underlying the suppression of unwanted memories. *Science*, 303, 232–235.

Arnold, M. B. (1946). On the mechanism of suggestion and hypnosis. *Journal of Abnormal and Social Psychology*, 41, 107–128.

As, A. (1962). Non-hypnotic experiences related to hypnotizability in male and female college students. *Scandinavian Journal of Psychology*, 3, 112–121.

Aserinsky, E., & Kleitman, N. (1953). Regularly occurring periods of eye motility, and concomitant phenomena, during sleep. *Science*, 118, 273–274.

Bakan, P. (1969). Hypnotizability, laterality of eye movements and functional brain asymmetry. *Perceptual and Motor Skills*, 28, 927–932.

Banister, H., & Zangwill, O. L. (1941a). Experimentally induced olfactory paramnesia. *British Journal of Psychology*, 32, 155–175.

Banister, H., & Zangwill, O. L. (1941b). Experimentally induced visual paramnesias. *British Journal of Psychology*, 32, 30–51.

Barber, J., & Mayer, D. (1977). Evaluation of efficacy and neural mechanism of a hypnotic analgesia procedure in experimental and clinical dental pain. *Pain*, 4, 41–48.

Barber, T. X. (1969). *Hypnosis: A scientific approach*. New York: Van Nostrand Reinhold.

Barber, T. X., & Calverley, D. S. (1966). Toward a theory of "hypnotic" behavior: Experimental analyses of suggested amnesia. *Journal of Abnormal Psychology*, 71, 95–107.

Barnier, A. J. (1997). *Autobiographical amnesia: An investigation of hypnotically created personal forgetting*. Proposal to Australian Research Council.

Barnier, A. J. (1999). Posthypnotic suggestion: Attention, awareness, and automaticity. *Sleep & Hypnosis*, 1, 57–63.

Barnier, A. J. (2002). Posthypnotic amnesia for autobiographical episodes: A laboratory model of functional amnesia? *Psychological Science*, 13(3), 232–237.

Barnier, A. J., Bryant, R. A., & Briscoe, S. (2001). Posthypnotic amnesia for material learned before or during hypnosis: Explicit and implicit memory effects. *International Journal of Clinical and Experimental Hypnosis*, 49(4), 286–304.

Barnier, A. J., & McConkey, K. M. (1998). Posthypnotic responding: Knowing when to stop helps to keep it going. *International Journal of Clinical & Experimental Hypnosis*, 46, 204–219.

Barnier, A. J., & McConkey, K. M. (1999a). Hypnotic and posthypnotic suggestion: Finding meaning in the message of the hypnotist. *International Journal of Clinical & Experimental Hypnosis, 47*, 192–208.

Barnier, A. J., & McConkey, K. M. (1999b). Posthypnotic responding away from the hypnotic setting. *Psychological Science, 9*, 256–262.

Barnier, A. J., & McConkey, K. M. (1999c). Posthypnotic suggestion, response complexity, and amnesia. *Australian Journal of Psychology, 51*(1), 1–5.

Barnier, A. J., & McConkey, K. M. (2001). Posthypnotic responding: The relevance of suggestion and test congruence. *International Journal of Clinical and Experimental Hypnosis, 49*, 207–219.

Barnier, A. J., & McConkey, K. M. (2003). Hypnosis, human nature, and complexity: Integrating neuroscience approaches into hypnosis research. *International Journal of Clinical and Experimental Hypnosis, 51*(3), 282–308.

Bates, B. L., & Kraft, P. M. (1991). The nature of hypnotic performance following administration of the Carleton Skills Training Program. *International Journal of Clinical & Experimental Hypnosis, 39*, 227–242.

Bauer, R. M. (1984). Autonomic recognition of names and faces in prosopagnosia: A neuropsychological application of the guilty knowledge test. *Neuropsychologia, 22*, 457–469.

Berry, D. C., & Dienes, Z. (1993). *Implicit learning: Theoretical and empirical issues.* Hove, UK: Erlbaum.

Bertrand, L. D., Spanos, N. P., & Radtke, H. L. (1990). Contextual effects on priming during hypnotic amnesia. *Journal of Research in Personality, 24*, 271–290.

Blum, G. S. (1961). *A model of the mind: Explored by hypnotically controlled experiments and examined for its psychodynamic implications.* New York: Wiley.

Blum, G. S. (1967). Hypnosis in psychodynamic research. In J. E. Gordon (Ed.), *Handbook of clinical and experimental hypnosis* (pp. 83–109). New York: Macmillan.

Blum, G. S. (1979). Hypnotic programming techniques in psychological experiments. In E. Fromm & R. E. Shor (Eds.), *Hypnosis: Developments in Research and new perspectives* (pp. 457–481). New York: Aldine.

Blum, G. S., Nash, J. K., Jansen, R. D., & Barbour, J. S. (1981). Posthypnotic attenuation of a visual illusion as reflected in perceptual reports and cortical event related potentials. *Academic Psychology Bulletin, 3*, 251–271.

Bowers, K. S. (1967). The effect for demands of honesty upon reports of visual and auditory hallucinations. *International Journal of Clinical and Experimental Hypnosis, 15*, 31–36.

Bowers, K. S. (1975). The psychology of subtle control: An attributional analysis of behavioural persistence. *Canadian Journal of Behavioral Science, 7*, 78–95.

Bowers, K. S. (1992). Imagination and dissociation in hypnotic responding. *International Journal of Clinical & Experimental Hypnosis, 40*, 253–275.

Bowers, P. (1982). The classic suggestion effect: Relationships with scales of hypnotizability, effortless experiencing, and imagery vividness. *International Journal of Clinical and Experimental Hypnosis, 30*, 270–279.

Bowers, P., Laurence, J. R., & Hart, D. (1988). The experience of hypnotic suggestions. *International Journal of Clinical and Experimental Hypnosis, 36*, 336–349.

Brady, J. P. (1966). Hysteria versus malingering: A response to Grosz & Zimmerman Bound with Brady & Lind. *Behavior Research & Therapy, 4*, 321–322.

Brady, J. P., & Lind, D. I. (1961). Experimental analysis of hysterical blindness. *Archives of General Psychiatry, 4*, 331–339.

Braid, J. (1843). *Neurypnology: or the rationale of nervous sleep considered in relation to animal magnetism.* London: Churchill.

Briquet, P. (1859). *Traite clinque et therapeutique à l'hysterie.* Paris: Balliere et Fils.

Brown, A. S. (2003). A review of the *déjà vu* experience. *Psychological Bulletin, 129*, 394–413.

Brown, D., Scheflin, A. W., & Hammond, D. C. (1998). *Memory, trauma treatment, and the law.* New York: W.W. Norton.

Bryant, R. A., Barnier, A. J., Mallard, D., & Tibbits, R. (1999). Posthypnotic amnesia for material learned before hypnosis. *International Journal of Clinical & Experimental Hypnosis, 47*, 46–64.

Bryant, R. A., & Kourch, M. (2001). Hypnotically induced emotional numbing. *International Journal of Clinical and Experimental Hypnosis, 49*(3), 220–230.

Bryant, R. A., & Mallard, D. (2002). Hypnotically induced emotional numbing: A real-simulating analysis. *Journal of Abnormal Psychology*, 111, 203–207.

Bryant, R. A., & McConkey, K. M. (1989a). Hypnotic blindness, awareness, and attribution. *Journal of Abnormal Psychology*, 98, 443–447.

Bryant, R. A., & McConkey, K. M. (1989b). Hypnotic blindness: A behavioral and experiential analysis. *Journal of Abnormal Psychology*, 98, 71–77.

Bryant, R. A., & McConkey, K. M. (1989c). Hypnotic emotions and physical sensations: A real-simulating analysis. *International Journal of Clinical and Experimental Hypnosis*, 37, 305–319.

Bryant, R. A., & McConkey, K. M. (1989d). Visual conversion disorder: A case analysis of the influence of visual information. *Journal of Abnormal Psychology*, 98, 326–329.

Bryant, R. A., & McConkey, K. M. (1990a). Hypnotic blindness and the relevance of attention. *Australian Journal of Psychology*, 42, 287–296.

Bryant, R. A., & McConkey, K. M. (1990b). Hypnotic blindness and the relevance of cognitive style. *Journal of Personality & Social Psychology*, 59, 756–761.

Bryant, R. A., & McConkey, K. M. (1990c). Hypnotic blindness: Testing the influence of motivation instructions. *Australian Journal of Clinical & Experimental Hypnosis*, 18, 91–96.

Bryant, R. A., & McConkey, K. M. (1994). Hypnotic blindness and the priming effect of visual material. *Contemporary Hypnosis*, 12, 157–164.

Campbell, D. T., & Fiske, D. W. (1959). Convergent and discriminant validation by the multitrait-multimethod matrix. *Psychological Bulletin*, 56, 82–105.

Cleghorn, J. M., Franco, S., Szechtman, H., Brown, G. M., Nahmias, C., & Garnett, E. S. (1992). Toward a brain map of auditory hallucinations. *American Journal of Psychiatry*, 149, 1062–1069.

Coe, W. C. (1978). Credibility of post-hypnotic amnesia – a contextualist's view. *International Journal of Clinical and Experimental Hypnosis*, 26, 218–245.

Cooper, L. M. (1966). Spontaneous and suggested posthypnotic source amnesia. *International Journal of Clinical & Experimental Hypnosis*, 2, 180–193.

Crawford, H. J. (2001). Neuropsychophysiology of hypnosis: Towards an understanding of how hypnotic interventions work. In G. D. Burrows,

R. O. Stanley, & P. B. Bloom (Eds.), *Advances in clinical hypnosis* (pp. 61–84). New York: Wiley.

Crawford, H. J., & Gruzelier, J. H. (1992). A midstream view of the neuropsychophysiology of hypnosis: Recent research and future directions. In E. Fromm & M. R. Nash (Eds.), *Contemporary hypnosis research* (pp. 227–266). New York: Guilford.

Crawford, H. J., Gur, R. C., Skolnick, B., Gur, R. E., & Benson, D. M. (1993). Effects of hypnosis on regional cerebral blood flow during ischemic pain with and without suggested hypnotic analgesia. *International Journal of Psychophysiology*, 15, 181–195.

Crawford, J. H., Macdonald, H., & Hilgard, E. R. (1979). Hypnotic deafness – psychophysical study of responses to tone intensity as modified by hypnosis. *American Journal of Psychology*, 92, 193–214.

Csikszentmihalyi, M. (1990). *Flow: The psychology of optimal experience*. New York: Harper & Row.

Csikszentmihalyi, M., & Csikszentmihalyi, E. S. (Eds.). (1988). *Optimal experience: Psychological studies of flow in consciousness*. New York: Cambridge University Press.

Cunningham, P. V., & Blum, G. S. (1982). Further evidence that hypnotically induced color blindness does not mimic congenital defects. *Journal of Abnormal Psychology*, 91, 139–143.

Damaser, E. (1964). *An experimental study of long-term post-hypnotic suggestion*. Unpublished doctoral dissertation, Harvard University, Cambridge, MA.

David, D., Brown, R., Pojoga, C., & David, A. (2000). The impact of posthypnotic amnesia and directed forgetting on implicit and explicit memory: New insights from a modified process dissociation procedure. *International Journal of Clinical and Experimental Hypnosis*, 48(3), 267–289.

Dorfman, J., & Kihlstrom, J. F. (1994, November). *Semantic priming in posthypnotic amnesia*. Paper presented at the Psychonomic Society, St. Louis, MO.

Dumas, R. A. (1977). EEG alpha-hypnotizability correlations: A review. *Psychophysiology*, 14, 431–438.

Dywan, J., & Bowers, K. (1983). The use of hypnosis to enhance recall. *Science*, 222, 184–185.

Edmonston, W. E., (1977). Neutral hypnosis as relaxation. *American Journal of Clinical Hypnosis*, 20, 69–75.

Edmonston, W. E. (1981). *Hypnosis and relaxation: Modern verification of an old equation.* New York: Wiley.

Edwards, G. (1956). Post-hypnotic amnesia and post-hypnotic effect. *British Journal of Psychiatry*, 11, 316–325.

Edwards, G. (1963). Duration of post-hypnotic effect. *British Journal of Psychiatry*, 109, 259–266.

Eich, E. (1988). Theoretical issues in state dependent memory. In H. L. Roediger & F. I. M. Craik (Eds.), *Varieties of memory and consciousness: Essays in honor of Endel Tulving* (pp. 331–354). Hillsdale, NJ: Erlbaum.

Einstein, G. O., & McDaniel, M. A. (1990). Normal aging and prospective memory. *Journal of Experimental Psychology: Learning, Memory, & Cognition*, 16, 717–726.

Ellenberger, H. F. (1970). *The discovery of the unconscious: The history and evolution of dynamic psychiatry.* New York: Basic Books.

Epstein, W. (1982). Percept-percept couplings. *Perception*, 11, 75–83.

Erickson, M. H. (1938a). A study of clinical and experimental findings on hypnotic deafness: I. Clinical experimentation and findings. *Journal of General Psychology*, 19, 127–150.

Erickson, M. H. (1938b). A study of clinical and experimental findings on hypnotic deafness: II. Experimental findings with a conditioned response technique. *Journal of General Psychology*, 19, 151–167.

Erickson, M. H. (1939). The induction of color blindness by a technique of hypnotic suggestion. *Journal of General Psychology*, 20, 61–89.

Erickson, M. H., & Erickson, E. M. (1941). Concerning the nature and character of posthypnotic suggestion. *Journal of General Psychology*, 24, 95–133.

Evans, F. J. (1979a). Contextual forgetting: Posthypnotic source amnesia. *Journal of Abnormal Psychology*, 88, 556–563.

Evans, F. J. (1979b). Hypnosis and sleep: Techniques for exploring cognitive activity during sleep. In E. Fromm & R. E. Shor (Eds.), *Hypnosis: Developments in research and new perspectives* (pp. 139–183). New York: Aldine.

Evans, F. J. (1988). Posthypnotic amnesia: Dissociation of context and context. In H. M. Pettinati (Ed.), *Hypnosis and memory* (pp. 157–192). New York: Guilford.

Evans, F. J., & Thorne, W. A. F. (1966). Two types of posthypnotic amnesia: Recall amnesia and source amnesia. *International Journal of Clinical and Experimental Hypnosis*, 14(2), 162–179.

Farvolden, P., & Woody, E. Z. (2004). Hypnosis, memory, and frontal executive functioning. *International Journal of Clinical & Experimental Hypnosis*, 52, 3–26.

Faymonville, M. E., Laureys, S., Degueldre, C., Del Fiore, G., Luxen, A., Franck, G., Lamy, M., & Maquet, P. (2000). Neural mechanisms of antinociceptive effects of hypnosis. *Anesthesiology*, 92(5), 1257–1267.

Fisher, S. (1954). The role of expectancy in the performance of posthypnotic behavior. *Journal of Abnormal & Social Psychology*, 49, 503–507.

Flavell, J. H. (1979). Metacognition and cognitive monitoring: A new area of cognitive-developmental inquiry. *American Psychologist*, 34(10), 906–911.

Fromm, E. (1979). The nature of hypnosis and other altered states of consciousness: An ego psychological theory. In E. Fromm & R. E. Shor (Eds.), *Hypnosis: Developments in research and new perspectives* (pp. 81–103). New York: Aldine.

Gandolfo, R. L. (1971). Role of expectancy, amnesia, and hypnotic induction in the performance of posthypnotic behavior. *Journal of Abnormal Psychology*, 77, 324–328.

Garner, W. R., Hake, H. W., & Eriksen, C. W. (1956). Operationism and the concept of perception. *Psychological Review*, 63, 149–159.

Gauld, A. (1992). *A history of hypnotism.* New York: Cambridge University Press.

Geiselman, R. E., Bjork, R. A., & Fishman, D. L. (1983). Disrupted retrieval in directed forgetting: A link with posthypnotic amnesia. *Journal of Experimental Psychology: General*, 112, 58–72.

Gill, M. M., & Brenman, M. (1959). *Hypnosis and related states: Psychoanalytic studies* (Vol. 2). New York: International Universities Press.

Glisky, M. L., & Kihlstrom, J. F. (1993). Hypnotizability and facets of openness. *International Journal of Clinical & Experimental Hypnosis*, 41(2), 112–123.

Glisky, M. L., Tataryn, D. J., & Kihlstrom, J. F. (1995). Hypnotizability and mental imagery. *International Journal of Clinical & Experimental Hypnosis*, 43(1), 34–54.

Glisky, M. L., Tataryn, D. J., Tobias, B. A., & Kihlstrom, J. F. (1991). Absorption, openness to experience, and hypnotizability. *Journal of Personality & Social Psychology*, 60(2), 263–272.

Goldstein, A. P., & Hilgard, E. R. (1975). Lack of influence of the morphine antagonist naloxone on hypnotic analgesia. *Proceedings of the National Academy of Sciences USA*, 72, 2041–2043.

Gorassini, D. R., & Spanos, N. P. (1987). A social cognitive skills approach to the successful modification of hypnotic susceptibility. *Journal of Personality and Social Psychology*, 50, 1004–1012.

Graf, P., & Schacter, D. L. (1985). Implicit and explicit memory for new associations in normal and amnesic subjects. *Journal of Experimental Psychology: Learning, Memory, and Cognition*, 11, 501–518.

Graffin, N. F., Ray, W. J., & Lundy, R. (1995). EEG concomitants of hypnosis and hypnotic susceptibility. *Journal of Abnormal Psychology*, 104, 123–131.

Graham, K. R., & Schwarz, L. M. (1973, August). *Suggested deafness and auditory signal detectability*. Paper presented at the annual meeting of the American Psychological Association, Montreal.

Gravitz, M. A., & Gerton, M. I. (1984). Origins of the term hypnotism prior to Braid. *American Journal of Clinical Hypnosis*, 27, 107–110.

Gregg, V. H. (1979). Posthypnotic amnesia and general memory theory. *Bulletin of the British Society for Experimental and Clinical Hypnosis*, 1979(2), 11–14.

Gregg, V. H. (1982). Posthypnotic amnesia for recently learned material: A comment on the paper by J. F. Kihlstrom (1980). *Bulletin of the British Society of Experimental & Clinical Hypnosis*, 5, 27–30.

Grether, W. F. (1940). A comment on "The induction of color blindness by a technique of hypnotic suggestion". *Journal of General Psychology*, 23, 207–210.

Grosz, H. J., & Zimmerman, J. (1965). Experimental analysis of hysterical blindness: A follow-up report and new experimental data. *Archives of General Psychiatry*, 13, 255–260.

Halligan, P. W., Athwal, B. S., Oakley, D. A., & Frackowiak, R. S. J. (2000, March 18). Imaging hypnotic paralysis: Implications for conversion hysteria. *Lancet*, 355, 986–987.

Halligan, P. W., Oakley, D. A., Athwal, B. S., & Frackowiak, R. S. J. (2000). Imaging hypnotic paralysis – Reply. *Lancet*, 356(9224), 163.

Hargadon, R., Bowers, K. S., & Woody, E. Z. (1995). Does counterpain imagery mediate hypnotic analgesia? *Journal of Abnormal Psychology*, 104(3), 508–516.

Harriman, P. L. (1942a). Hypnotic induction of color vision anomalies: I. The use of the Ishihara and the Jensen tests to verify the acceptance of suggested color blindness. *Journal of General Psychology*, 26, 289–298.

Harriman, P. L. (1942b). Hypnotic induction of color vision anomalies: II. Results on two other tests of color blindness. *Journal of General Psychology*, 27, 81–92.

Harvey, M. A., & Sipprelle, C. N. (1978). Color blindness, perceptual interference, and hypnosis. *American Journal of Clinical Hypnosis*, 20, 189–193.

Hilgard, E. R. (1965). *Hypnotic susceptibility*. New York: Harcourt, Brace, & World.

Hilgard, E. R. (1969). Pain as a puzzle for psychology and physiology. *American Psychologist*, 24, 103–113.

Hilgard, E. R. (1971, September). *Is hypnosis a state, trait, neither?* Paper presented at the American Psychological Association, Washington, DC.

Hilgard, E. R. (1972). A critique of Johnson, Maher, and Barber's "Artifact in the 'essence of hypnosis: An Evaluation of trance logic", with a recomputation of their findings. *Journal of Abnormal Psychology*, 79, 221–233.

Hilgard, E. R. (1973a). The domain of hypnosis, with some comments on alternative paradigms. *American Psychologist*, 28, 972–982.

Hilgard, E. R. (1973b). A neodissociation interpretation of pain reduction in hypnosis. *Psychological Review*, 80, 396–411.

Hilgard, E. R. (1977). *Divided consciousness: Multiple controls in human thought and action*. New York: Wiley-Interscience.

Hilgard, E. R., & Cooper, L. M. (1965). Spontaneous and suggested posthypnotic amnesia. *International Journal of Clinical & Experimental Hypnosis*, 13, 261–273.

Hilgard, E. R., & Hilgard, J. R. (1975). *Hypnosis in the relief of pain*. Los Altos, CA: Kaufman.

Hilgard, E. R., Hilgard, J. R., Macdonald, H., Morgan, A. H., & Johnson, L. S. (1978). Covert pain in hypnotic analgesia: Its reality as tested by the real-simulator paradigm. *Journal of Abnormal Psychology*, 87, 655–663.

Hilgard, E. R., Macdonald, H., Morgan, A. H., & Johnson, L. S. (1978). The reality of hypnotic analgesia: A comparison of highly hypnotizables with simulators. *Journal of Abnormal Psychology*, 87, 239–246.

Hilgard, E. R., & Morgan, A. H. (1975). Heart rate and blood pressure in the study of laboratory pain in man under normal conditions and as influenced by hypnosis. *Acta Neurobiologica Experimentalis*, 35, 741–759.

Hilgard, E. R., Morgan, A. H., Lange, A. F., Lenox, J. R., Macdonald, H., Marshall, G. D., & Sachs, L. B. (1974). Heart rate changes in pain and hypnosis. *Psychophysiology*, 11, 692–702.

Hilgard, E. R., Morgan, A. H., & Macdonald, H. (1975). Pain and dissociation in the cold pressor test: A study of hypnotic analgesia with "hidden reports" through automatic key pressing and automatic talking. *Journal of Abnormal Psychology*, 84, 280–289.

Hilgard, J. R. (1970). *Personality and hypnosis: A study in imaginative involvement.* Chicago: University of Chicago Press.

Hobson, J. A., Pace-Schott, E., & Stickgold, R. (2000). Dreaming and the brain: Towards a cognitive neuroscience of conscious states. *Behavioral & Brain Sciences*, 23(6).

Hochberg, J. (1974). Higher-order stimuli and interresponse coupling in the perception of the visual world. In R. B. MacLeod & H. L. Pick (Eds.), *Perception: Essays in honor of James J. Gibson* (pp. 17–39). Ithaca, NY: Cornell University Press.

Hochberg, J., & Peterson, M. A. (1987). Piecemeal organization and cognitive components in object perception: Perceptually coupled responses to moving objects. *Journal of Experimental Psychology: General*, 116, 370–380.

Hofling, C. K., Heyl, B., & Wright, D. (1971). The ratio of total recoverable memories to conscious memories in normal subjects. *Comprehensive Psychiatry*, 12, 371–379.

Howard, R. J., Ffytche, D. H., Barnes, J., McKeefry, D., Ha, Y., Woodruff, P. W., Bullmore, E. T., Simmons, A., Williams, S. C. R., David, A. S., & Brammer, M. (1998). The functional anatomy of imagining and perceiving colour. *Neuroreport*, 9, 1019–1023.

Hoyt, I. P., & Kihlstrom, J. F. (1986, August). *Posthypnotic suggestion and waking instruction.* Paper presented at the 94th annual meeting of the American Psychological Association, Washington, DC.

Hull, C. L. (1933). *Hypnosis and suggestibility: An experimental approach.* New York: Appleton.

Jacoby, L. L. (1991). A process dissociation framework: Separating automatic from intentional uses of memory. *Journal of Memory & Language*, 30, 513–541.

James, W. (1890). *Principles of psychology.* New York: Holt.

Janet, P. (1907). *The major symptoms of hysteria.* New York: Macmillan.

Jansen, R. D., Blum, G. S., & Loomis, J. M. (1982). Attentional alterations of slant specific interference between line segments in eccentric vision. *Perception*, 11, 535–540.

Jasiukaitis, P., Nouriani, B., Hugdahl, K., & Spiegel, D. (1995). Relateralizing hypnosis; or have we been barking up the wrong hemisphere? *International Journal of Clinical & Experiemental Hypnosis*, 45, 158–177.

John, O. P. (1990). The "big five" factor taxonomy: Dimensions of personality in the natural language and in questionnaires. In L. A. Pervin (Ed.), *Handbook of personality: Theory and research* (pp. 66–100). New York: Guilford.

Johnson, M. K., Hashtroudi, S., & Lindsay, D. S. (1993). Source monitoring. *Psychological Bulletin*, 114(1), 3–28.

Johnson, M. K., & Raye, C. L. (1981). Reality monitoring. *Psychological Review*, 88, 67–85.

Johnson, R. F. Q. (1972). Trance logic revisited: A reply to Hilgard's critique. *Journal of Abnormal Psychology*, 79, 234–238.

Johnson, R. F. Q., Maher, B. A., & Barber, T. X. (1972). Artifact in the "essence of hypnosis": An evaluation of trance logic. *Journal of Abnormal Psychology*, 79, 212–220.

Kallio, S., & Revensuo, A. (2003). Hypnotic phenomena and altered states of consciousness: A multilevel framework of description and explanation. *Contemporary Hypnosis*, 20, 111–164.

Kihlstrom, J. F. (1979). Hypnosis and psychopathology: Retrospect and prospect. *Journal of Abnormal Psychology*, 88(5), 459–473.

Kihlstrom, J. F. (1980). Posthypnotic amnesia for recently learned material: Interactions with "episodic" and "semantic" memory. *Cognitive Psychology*, 12, 227–251.

Kihlstrom, J. F. (1983). Instructed forgetting: Hypnotic and nonhypnotic. *Journal of Experimental Psychology: General*, 112(1), 73–79.

Kihlstrom, J. F. (1984). Conscious, subconscious, unconscious: A cognitive perspective. In K. S. Bowers & D. Meichenbaum (Eds.), *The unconscious reconsidered* (pp. 149–211). New York: Wiley.

Kihlstrom, J. F. (1985). Posthypnotic amnesia and the dissociation of memory. *Psychology of Learning and Motivation, 19*, 131–178.

Kihlstrom, J. F. (1987). The cognitive unconscious. *Science, 237*(4821), 1445–1452.

Kihlstrom, J. F. (1992a). Dissociation and dissociations: A comment on consciousness and cognition. *Consciousness & Cognition: An International Journal, 1*(1), 47–53.

Kihlstrom, J. F. (1992b). Dissociative and conversion disorders. In D. J. Stein & J. Young (Eds.), *Cognitive science and clinical disorders* (pp. 247–270). San Diego: Academic Press.

Kihlstrom, J. F. (1992c). Hypnosis: A sesquicentennial essay. *International Journal of Clinical & Experimental Hypnosis, 40*(4), 301–314.

Kihlstrom, J. F. (1994a). One hundred years of hysteria. In S. J. Lynn & J. W. Rhue (Eds.), *Dissociation: Clinical and theoretical perspectives* (pp. 365–394). New York: Guilford Press.

Kihlstrom, J. F. (1994b). The rediscovery of the unconscious. In H. Morowitz & J. L. Singer (Eds.), *The mind, the brain, and complex adaptive systems* (pp. 123–143). Reading, MA: Addison-Wesley.

Kihlstrom, J. F. (1996). Perception without awareness of what is perceived, learning without awareness of what is learned. In M. Velmans (Ed.), *The science of consciousness: Psychological, neuropsychological and clinical reviews* (pp. 23–46). London: Routledge.

Kihlstrom, J. F. (1998). Dissociations and dissociation theory in hypnosis: Comment on Kirsch and Lynn (1998). *Psychological Bulletin, 123*(2), 186–191.

Kihlstrom, J. F. (2000, November 2). *Hypnosis and pain: Time for a new look.* Paper presented at the Annual meeting of the American Pain Society, Atlanta, GA.

Kihlstrom, J. F. (2001a). Dissociative disorders. In P. B. Sutker & H. E. Adams (Eds.), *Comprehensive handbook of psychopathology* (3rd ed., pp. 259–276). New York: Plenum.

Kihlstrom, J. F. (2001b, August). *Hypnosis in surgery: Efficacy, specificity, and utility.* Paper presented at the the annual meeting of the American Psychological Association, San Francisco.

Kihlstrom, J. F. (2002a). *Demand characteristics in the laboratory and the clinic: Conversations and collaborations with subjects and patients.* Retrieved from http://journals.apa.org/prevention/volume5/pre0050036c.html.

Kihlstrom, J. F. (2002b). Mesmer, the Franklin Commission, and hypnosis: A counterfactual essay. *International Journal of Clinical & Experimental Hypnosis, 50*, 408–419.

Kihlstrom, J. F. (2004a). Clark L. Hull, hypnotist [Review of Hypnosis and Suggestibility: An Experimental Approach by C. L. Hull]. *Contemporary Psychology, 49*, 141–144.

Kihlstrom, J. F. (2004b). "An unwarrantable impertinence" [Commentary on *The Illusion of Conscious Will* by D.M.Wegner]. *Behavioral & Brain Sciences, 27*, 666–667,

Kihlstrom, J. F., Barnhardt, T. M., & Tataryn, D. J. (1992). Implicit perception. In R. F. Bornstein & T. S. Pittman (Eds.), *Perception without awareness: Cognitive, clinical, and social perspectives* (pp. 17–54). New York: Guilford Press.

Kihlstrom, J. F., Brenneman, H. A., Pistole, D. D., & Shor, R. E. (1985). Hypnosis as a retrieval cue in posthypnotic amnesia. *Journal of Abnormal Psychology, 94*(3), 264–271.

Kihlstrom, J. F., & Edmonston, W. E. (1971). Alterations in consciousness in neutral hypnosis: Distortions in semantic space. *American Journal of Clinical Hypnosis, 13*(4), 243–248.

Kihlstrom, J. F., & Eich, E. (1994). Altering states of consciousness. In D. Druckman & R. A. Bjork (Eds.), *Learning, remembering, and believing: Enhancing performance* (pp. 207–248). Washington, DC: National Academy Press.

Kihlstrom, J. F., & Evans, F. J. (1976). Recovery of memory after posthypnotic amnesia. *Journal of Abnormal Psychology, 85*(6), 564–569.

Kihlstrom, J. F., & Evans, F. J. (1977). Residual effect of suggestions for posthypnotic amnesia: A reexamination. *Journal of Abnormal Psychology, 86*(4), 327–333.

Kihlstrom, J. F., & Evans, F. J. (1979). Memory retrieval processes in posthypnotic amnesia. In J. F. Kihlstrom & F. J. Evans (Eds.), *Functional disorders of memory* (pp. 179–218). Hillsdale, NJ: Erlbaum.

Kihlstrom, J. F., & McGlynn, S. M. (1991). Experimental research in clinical psychology. In M. Hersen, A. E. Kazdin, & A. S. Bellack (Eds.), *The clinical psychology handbook* (2nd ed., pp. 239–257). New York: Pergamon Press.

Kihlstrom, J. F., Mulvaney, S., Tobias, B. A., & Tobis, I. P. (2000). The emotional unconscious. In E. Eich, J. F. Kihlstrom, G. H. Bower, J. P. Forgas, & P. M. Niedenthal (Eds.), *Cognition and emotion* (pp. 30–86). New York: Oxford University Press.

Kihlstrom, J. F., & Schacter, D. L. (2000). Functional amnesia. In F. Boller & J. Grafman (Eds.), *Handbook of neuropsychology* (2nd ed., Vol. 2, pp. 409–427). Amsterdam: Elsevier.

Kihlstrom, J. F., Tataryn, D. J., & Hoyt, I. P. (1993). Dissociative disorders. In P. J. Sutker & H. E. Adams (Eds.), *Comprehensive handbook of psychopathology* (2nd ed., pp. 203–234). New York: Plenum Press.

Killeen, P. R., & Nash, M. R. (2003). The four causes of hypnosis. *International Journal of Clinical and Experimental Hypnosis*, 51(3), 195–231.

Kirsch, I. (2000). The response set theory of hypnosis. *American Journal of Clinical Hypnosis*, 42(3–4), 274–292.

Kirsch, I. (2001a). The altered states of hypnosis. *Social Research*, 68(3), 795–807.

Kirsch, I. (2001b). The response set theory of hypnosis: Expectancy and physiology. *American Journal of Clinical Hypnosis*, 44(1), 69–73.

Kirsch, I., & Lynn, S. J. (1995). Altered state of hypnosis: Changes in the theoretical landscape. *American Psychologist*, 50(10), 846–858.

Kirsch, I., & Lynn, S. J. (1997). Hypnotic involuntariness and the automaticity of everyday life. *American Journal of Clinical Hypnosis*, 40(1), 329–348.

Kirsch, I., & Lynn, S. J. (1998a). Dissociation theories of hypnosis. *Psychological Bulletin*, 123(1), 100–115.

Kirsch, I., & Lynn, S. J. (1998b). Social-cognitive alternatives to dissociation theories of hypnotic involuntariness. *Review of General Psychology*, 2(1), 66–80.

Knox, V. J., Morgan, A. H., & Hilgard, E. R. (1974). Pain and suffering in ischemia: The paradox of hypnotically suggested anesthesia as contradicted by reports from the "hidden observer." *Archives of General Psychiatry*, 30, 840–847.

Kosslyn, S. M., Thompson, W. L., Costantini-Ferrando, M. F., Alpert, N. M., & Spiegel, D. (2000). Hypnotic visual hallucination alters brain color processing. *American Journal of Psychiatry*, 157(8), 1279–1284.

Kuhn, T. (1962). *The structure of scientific revolutions*. Chicago: University of Chicago Press.

Kunzendorf, R., Spanos, N., & Wallace, B. (Eds.). (1996). *Hypnosis and imagination*. New York: Baywood.

LaBerge, D., & Samuels, S. J. (1974). Toward a theory of automatic information processing in reading. *Cognitive Psychology*, 6, 293–323.

Lang, E. V., Benotsch, E. G., Fick, L. J., Lutgendorf, S., Berbaum, M. L., Berbaum, K. S., Logan, H., & Spiegel, D. (2000, April 29). Adjunctive non-pharmacological analgesia for invasive medical procedures: A randomised trial. *Lancet*, 355, 1486–1500.

Lang, E. V., Joyce, J. S., Spiegel, D., Hamilton, D., & Lee, K. K. (1996). Self-hypnotic relaxation during interventional radiological procedures: Effects on pain perception and intravenous drug use. *International Journal of Clinical & Experimental Hypnosis*, 44, 106–119.

Laurence, J. R., Perry, C., & Kihlstrom, J. F. (1983). Hidden observer phenomena in hypnosis: An experimental creation? *Journal of Personality and Social Psychology*, 44, 163–169.

Leibowitz, H. W., Lundy, R. M., & Guez, J. R. (1980). The effect of testing distance on suggestion induced visual field narrowing. *International Journal of Clinical and Experimental Hypnosis*, 28, 409–420.

Leibowitz, H. W., Post, R. B., Rodemer, C. S., Wadlington, W. L., & Lundy, R. M. (1980). Roll vection analysis of suggestion induced visual field narrowing. *Perception and Psychophysics*, 28, 173–176.

Levy, B. L., & Anderson, M. C. (2002). Inhibitory processes and the control of memory retrieval. *Trends in Cognitive Sciences*, 6, 299–305.

Ludwig, A. M. (1966). Altered states of consciousness. *Archives of General Psychiatry*, 15, 225–234.

MacLeod, C. M. (1991). Half a century of research on the Stroop effect: An integrative review. *Psychological Bulletin*, 109(2), 163–203.

MacLeod, C. M. (1992). The Stroop task: The "gold standard" of attentional measures. *Journal of Experimental Psychology: General*, 121(1), 12–14.

MacLeod-Morgan, C., & Lack, L. (1982). Hemispheric specificity: A physiological concomitant of hypnotizability. *Psychophysiology*, 19, 687–690.

Mallard, D., & Bryant, R. A. (2001). Hypnotic color blindness and performance on the Stroop test. *International Journal of Clinical and Experimental Hypnosis*, 49, 330–338.

Maquet, P., Faymonvi., M. E., DeGuelder, C., DelFiore, G., Franck, G., Luxen, A., & Lamy, M. (1999). Functional neuroanatomy of hypnotic state. *Biological Psychiatry*, 45, 327–333.

Marcel, A. J. (1983). Conscious and unconscious perception: Experiments on visual masking and word recognition. *Cognitive Psychology*, 15, 197–237.

McClelland, D. C., Koestner, R., & Weinberger, J. (1989). How do self-attributed and implicit motives differ?*Psychological Review*, 96, 690–702.

McConkey, K. M., Bryant, R. A., Bibb, B. C., & Kihlstrom, J. F. (1991). Trance logic in hypnosis and imagination. *Journal of Abnormal Psychology*, 100(4), 464–472.

McConkey, K. M., Bryant, R. A., Bibb, B. C., Kihlstrom, J. F., & Tataryn, D. J. (1990). Hypnotically suggested anaesthesia and the circle-touch test: A real-simulating comparison. *British Journal of Experimental & Clinical Hypnosis*, 7, 153–157.

McConkey, K. M., & Sheehan, P. W. (1980). Inconsistency in hypnotic age regression and cue structure as supplied by the hypnotist. *International Journal of Clinical and Experimental Hypnosis*, 38, 394–408.

McGlashan, T. H., Evans, F. J., & Orne, M. T. (1969). The nature of hypnotic analgesia and placebo response to experimental pain. *Psychosomatic Medicine*, 31, 227–246.

Melzack, R. (1975). The McGill Pain Questionnaire: Major properties and scoring methods. *Pain*, 1, 277–299.

Metcalfe, J., & Shimamura, A. P. (1994). *Metacognition: Knowing about knowing*. Cambridge, MA: MIT Press.

Metzinger, T. (Ed.). (2000). *Neural correlates of consciousness*. Cambridge, MA: MIT Press.

Miller, M. E., & Bowers, K. S. (1986). Hypnotic analgesia and stress inoculation in the reduction of pain. *Journal of Abnormal Psychology*, 95, 6–14.

Miller, M. E., & Bowers, K. S. (1993). Hypnotic analgesia: Dissociated experience or dissociated control?*Journal of Abnormal Psychology*, 102, 29–38.

Miller, R. J., Hennessy, R. T., & Leibowitz, H. W. (1973). The effect of hypnotic ablation of the background on the magnitude of the Ponzo perspective illusion. *International Journal of Clinical and Experimental Hypnosis*, 21, 180–191.

Montgomery, G. H., DuHamel, K. N., & Redd, W. H. (2000). A meta-analysis of hypnotically induced analgesia: How effective is hypnosis?*International Journal of Clinical and Experimental Hypnosis*, 48(2), 138–153.

Moret, V., Forster, A., Laverriere, M.-C. , Gaillard, R. C., Bourgeois, P., Haynal, A., Gemperle, M., & Buchser, E. (1991). Mechanism of analgesia induced by hypnosis and acupuncture: Is there a difference? *Pain*, 45, 135–140.

Nace, E. P., & Orne, M. T. (1970). Fate of an uncompleted posthypnotic suggestion. *Journal of Abnormal Psychology*, 75, 278–285.

Nace, E. P., Orne, M. T., & Hammer, A. G. (1974). Posthypnotic amnesia as an active psychic process. *Archives of General Psychiatry*, 31, 257–260.

Nash, M. (1987). What, if anything, is regressed about hypnotic age regression: A review of the empirical literature. *Psychological Bulletin*, 102, 42–52.

Nash, M. R., Lynn, S. J., Stanley, S., & Carlson, V. (1987). Subjectively complete hypnotic deafness and auditory priming. *International Journal of Clinical and Experimental Hypnosis*, 35, 32–40.

Nelson, T. O. (1992). *Metacognition: Core readings*. Boston: Allyn and Bacon.

Nelson, T. O. (1996). Consciousness and metacognition. *American Psychologist*, 51(2), 102–116.

Nelson, T. O., & Narens, L. (1990). Metamemory: A theoretical framework and some new findings. In G. H. Bower (Ed.), *The psychology of learning and motivation* Vol. 26 (pp. 125–173). New York: Academic Press.

Nogrady, H., McConkey, K. M., & Perry, C. (1985). Enhancing visual memory: Trying hypnosis, trying imagination, and trying again. *Journal of Abnormal Psychology*, 94, 195–204.

Nolan, R. P., & Spanos, N. P. (1987). Hypnotic analgesia and stress inoculation: A critical reexamination of Miller and Bowers. *Psychological Reports*, 61, 95–102.

Oakley, D. A. (1999). Hypnosis and conversion hysteria: A unifying model. *Cognitive Neuropsychiatry*, 4, 243–265.

Obstoj, I., & Sheehan, P. W. (1977). Aptitude for trance, task generalizability, and incongruity response in hypnosis. *Journal of Abnormal Psychology*, 86, 543–552.

Orne, M. T. (1959). The nature of hypnosis: Artifact and essence. *Journal of Abnormal and Social Psychology*, 58, 277–299.

Orne, M. T. (1962). On the social psychology of the psychological experiment: With particular reference to demand characteristics and their implications. *American Psychologist*, 17, 776–783.

Orne, M. T. (1969). On the nature of the posthypnotic suggestion. In L. Chertok (Ed.), *Psychophysiological mechanisms of hypnosis* (pp. 173–192). Berlin: Springer-Verlag.

Orne, M. T. (1971). The simulation of hypnosis: Why, how, and what it means. *International Journal of Clinical and Experimental Hypnosis*, 19, 183–210.

Orne, M. T. (1973). Communication by the total experimental situation: Why it is important, how it is evaluated, and its significance for the ecological validity of findings. In P. Pliner, L. Krames, & T. Alloway (Eds.), *Communication and affect* (pp. 157–191). New York: Academic.

Orne, M. T., Sheehan, P. W., & Evans, F. J. (1968). Occurrence of posthypnotic behavior outside the experimental setting. *Journal of Personality & Social Psychology*, 9, 189–196.

Otto-Salaj, L. L., Nadon, R., Hoyt, I. P., Register, P. A., & Kihlstrom, J. F. (1992). Laterality of hypnotic response. *International Journal of Clinical & Experimental Hypnosis*, 40, 12–20.

Pattie, F. A. (1937). The genuineness of hypnotically produced anesthesia of the skin. *American Journal of Psychology*, 49, 435–443.

Peterson, M. A., & Hochberg, J. (1983). Opposed set measurement procedure: A quantitative analysis of the role of local cues and intention in form perception. *Journal of Experimental Psychology: Human Perception and Performance*, 9, 183–193.

Posner, M. I., & Snyder, C. R. R. (1975). Attention and cognitive control. In R. L. Solso (Ed.), *Information processing and cognition: The Loyola Symposium* (pp. 55–85). New York: Wiley.

Rainville, P., Carrier, B., Hofbauer, R. K., Bushnell, M. C., & Duncan, G. H. (1999). Dissociation of sensory and affective dimensions of pain using hypnotic modulation. *Pain*, 82(2), 159–171.

Rainville, P., Duncan, G. H., Price, D. D., Carrier, B., & Bushnell, M. C. (1997, August 15). Pain affect encoded in human anterior cingulate but not somatosensory cortex. *Science*, 277, 968–971.

Rainville, P., Hofbauer, R. K., Bushnell, M. C., Duncan, G. H., & Price, D. D. (2002). Hypnosis modulates the activity in cerebral structures involved in the regulation of consciousness. *Journal of Cognitive Neuroscience*, 14(Suppl), 887–901.

Rainville, P., Hofbauer, R. K., Paus, T., Bushnell, M. C., & Price, D. D. (1999). Cerebral mechanisms of hypnotic induction and suggestion. *Journal of Cognitive Neuroscience*, 11, 110–125.

Ray, W. J., & Tucker, D. M. (2003). Evolutionary approaches to understanding the hypnotic experience. *International Journal of Clinical and Experimental Hypnosis*, 51(3), 256–281.

Raz, A., Fan, J., Shapiro, T., & Posner, M. I. (2002, November). *fMRI of posthypnotic suggestion to modulate reading of Stroop words.* Paper presented at the Society for Neuroscience, Washington, DC.

Raz, A., Landzberg, K. S., Schweizer, H. R., Zephrani, Z., Shapiro, T., Fan, J., & Posner, M. I. (2003). Posthypnotic suggestion and the modulation of Stroop interference under cycloplegia. *Consciousness & Cognition*, 12, 332–346.

Raz, A., Shapiro, T., Fan, J., & Posner, M. I. (2002). Hypnotic suggestion and the modulation of Stroop interference. *Archives of General Psychiatry*, 59, 1155–1161.

Reber, A. S. (1967). Implicit learning of artificial grammars. *Journal of Verbal Learning & Verbal Behavior*, 6, 855–863.

Reber, A. S. (1993). *Implicit learning and tacit knowledge: An essay on the cognitive unconscious.* Oxford: Oxford University Press.

Reder, L. M. (1996). *Implicit memory and metacognition.* Mahwah, NJ: Erlbaum.

Register, P. A., & Kihlstrom, J. F. (1987). Hypnotic effects on hypermnesia. *International Journal of Clinical & Experimental Hypnosis*, 35(3), 155–170.

Reyher, J. (1967). Hypnosis in research on psychopathology. In J. E. Gordon (Ed.), *Handbook of clinical and experimental hypnosis* (pp. 110–147). New York: Macmillan.

Reyher, J., & Smyth, L. (1971). Suggestibility during the execution of a posthypnotic suggestion. *Journal of Abnormal Psychology*, 78, 258–265.

Roche, S. M., & McConkey, K. M. (1990). Absorption: Nature, assessment, and correlates. *Journal of Personality and Social Psychology*, 59, 91–101.

Rosenthal, R., & Rubin, D. B. (1978). Interpersonal expectancy effects: The first 345 studies. *Behavioral & Brain Sciences*, 3, 377–415.

Sabourin, M., Brisson, M. A., & Deschamb, A. (1980). Evaluation of hypnotically suggested selective deafness by heart-rate conditioning and reaction time. *Psychological Reports*, 47, 995–1002.

Sackeim, H. A. (1982). Lateral asymmetry in bodily response to hypnotic suggestions. *Biological Psychiatry, 17,* 437–447.

Sackeim, H. A., Nordlie, J. W., & Gur, R. C. (1979). A model of hysterical and hypnotic blindness: Cognition, motivation, and awareness. *Journal of Abnormal Psychology, 88,* 474–489.

Sarbin, T. R. (1973). On the recently reported physiological and pharmacological reality of the hypnotic state. *Psychological Record, 23,* 501–511.

Sarbin, T. R., & Coe, W. C. (1972). *Hypnosis: A social psychological analysis of influence communication.* New York: Holt, Rinehart, & Winston.

Sarbin, T. R., & Slagle, R. W. (1979). Hypnosis and psychophysiological outcomes. In. In E. Fromm & R. E. Shor (Eds.), *Hypnosis: Developments in research and new perspectives* (pp. 273–303). New York: Aldine.

Schacter, D. L. (1987). Implicit memory: History and current status. *Journal of Experimental Psychology: Learning, Memory, and Cognition, 13,* 501–518.

Schacter, D. L., & Graf, P. (1986). Effects of elaborative processing on implicit and explicit memory for new associations. *Journal of Experimental Psychology: Learning, Memory, and Cognition, 12.*

Schacter, D. L., Harbluk, J. L., & McClachlan, D. R. (1984). Retrieval without recollection: An experimental analysis of source amnesia. *Journal of Verbal Learning and Verbal Behavior, 23,* 593–611.

Schacter, D. L., & Kihlstrom, J. F. (1989). Functional amnesia. In F. Boller & J. Graffman (Eds.), *Handbook of neuropsychology* (Vol. 3, pp. 209–231). Amsterdam: Elsevier.

Scheibe, K. E., Gray, A. L., & Keim, C. S. (1968). Hypnotically induced deafness and delayed auditory feedback: A comparison of real and simulating subjects. *International Journal of Clinical & Experimental Hypnosis, 16,* 158–164.

Schneider, W., & Shiffrin, R. M. (1977). Controlled and automatic human information processing: I. Detection, search, and attention. *Psychological Review, 84*(1), 1–66.

Seger, C. A. (1994). Criteria for implicit learning: De-emphasize conscious access, emphasize amnesia. *Behavioral & Brain Sciences, 17,* 421–422.

Sheehan, P. W. (1982). Imagery and hypnosis: Forging a link, at least in part. *Research Communications in Psychology, Psychiatry & Behavior, 7,* 357–272.

Sheehan, P. W. (1988). Memory distortion in hypnosis. *International Journal of Clinical and Experimental Hypnosis, 36,* 296–311.

Sheehan, P. W., & McConkey, K. M. (1982). *Hypnosis and experience: The exploration of phenomena and process.* Hillsdale, NJ: Erlbaum.

Sheehan, P. W., Obstoj, I., & McConkey, K. M. (1976). Trance logic and cue structure as supplied by the hypnotist. *Journal of Abnormal Psychology, 85,* 459–472.

Sheehan, P. W., & Orne, M. T. (1968). Some comments on the nature of posthypnotic behavior. *Journal of Nervous & Mental Disease, 146,* 209–220.

Shiffrin, R. M., & Schneider, W. (1977). Controlled and automatic human information processing: II. Perceptual learning, automatic attending and a general theory. *Psychological Review, 84*(2), 127–190.

Shiffrin, R. M., & Schneider, W. (1984). Automatic and controlled processing revisited. *Psychological Review, 91*(2), 269–276.

Shimamura, A. P., & Squire, L. R. (1987). A neuropsychological study of fact memory and source amnesia. *Journal of Experimental Psychology: Learning, Memory, and Cognition, 13,* 464–473.

Shor, R. E. (1979a). The fundamental problem in hypnosis research as viewed from historic perspectives. In E. Fromm & R. E. Shor (Eds.), *Hypnosis: Developments in research and new perspectives.* New York: Aldine.

Shor, R. E. (1979b). A phenomenological method for the measurement of variables important to an understanding of the nature of hypnosis. In E. Fromm & R. E. Shor (Eds.), *Hypnosis: Developments in research and new perspectives* (pp. 105–135). New York: Aldine.

Shor, R. E., Orne, M. T., & O'Connell, D. N. (1962). Validation and cross-validation of a scale of self-reported personal experiences which predicts hypnotizability. *Journal of Psychology, 53,* 55–75.

Snyder, M., & Swann, W. B. (1978). Behavioral confirmation in social interaction: From social perception to social reality. *Journal of Experimental Social Psychology, 14,* 148–162.

Spanos, N. P. (1983). The hidden observer as an experimental creation. *Journal of Personality and Social Psychology, 44,* 170–176.

Spanos, N. P. (1986a). Hypnosis, nonvolitional responding, and multiple personality: A social psychological perspective. In B. A. Maher & W. B. Maher (Eds.), *Progress in experimental personality research* (pp. 1–62), New York: Academic Press.

Spanos, N. P. (1986b). Hypnotic behavior: A social psychological interpretation of amnesia, analgesia, and trance logic. *Behavioral and Brain Sciences*, 9, 449–467.

Spanos, N. P. (1991). A sociocognitive approach to hypnosis. In S. J. Lynn & J. W. Rhue (Eds.), *Theories of hypnosis: Current models and perspectives* (pp. 324–361). New York: Guilford Press.

Spanos, N. P., & Barber, T. X. (1968). "Hypnotic" experiences as inferred from auditory and visual hallucinations. *Journal of Experimental Research in Personality*, 3, 136–150.

Spanos, N. P., & Chaves, J. F. (1970). Hypnosis research: A methodological critique of experiments generated by two alternative paradigms. *American Journal of Clinical Hypnosis*, 13(2), 108–127.

Spanos, N. P., & Chaves, J. F. (1991). History and historiography of hypnosis. In S.J. Lynn & J.W. Rhue (Eds.), *Theories of hypnosis: Current models and perspectives* (pp. 43–78). New York: Guilford Press.

Spanos, N. P., Cobb, P. C., & Gorassini, D. R. (1985). Failing to resist hypnotic test suggestions: A strategy for self-presenting as deeply hypnotized. *Psychiatry*, 48, 282–292.

Spanos, N. P., DeGroot, H. P., & Gwynn, M. I. (1987). Trance logic as incomplete responding. *Journal of Personality and Social Psychology*, 53, 911–921.

Spanos, N. P., Dubreuil, D. L., Saad, C. L., & Gorassini, D. (1983). Hypnotic elimination of prism-induced aftereffects: Perceptual effect or responses to experimental demands. *Journal of Abnormal Psychology*, 92, 216–222.

Spanos, N. P., Gorassini, D. R., & Petrusic, W. (1981). Hypnotically induced limb anesthesia and adaptation to displacing prisms: A failure to confirm. *Journal of Abnormal Psychology*, 90, 329–333.

Spanos, N. P., Gwynn, M. I., et al. (1988). Social psychological factors in the genesis of posthypnotic source amnesia. *Journal of Abnormal Psychology* 97, 322–329.

Spanos, N. P., Gwynn, M. I., & Stam, H. J. (1983). Instructional demands and ratings of overt and hidden pain during hypnotic analgesia. *Journal of Abnormal Psychology*, 92, 479–488.

Spanos, N. P., & Hewitt, E. C. (1980). The hidden observer in hypnotic analgesia: Discovery or experimental creation. *Journal of Personality & Social Psychology*, 39, 1201–1214.

Spanos, N. P., Jones, B., & Malfara, A. (1982). Hypnotic deafness: Now you hear it – Now you still hear it. *Journal of Abnormal Psychology*, 91, 75–77.

Spanos, N. P., Menary, E., Brett, P. J., Cross, W., & Ahmed, Q. (1987). Failure of posthypnotic responding to occur outside the experimental setting. *Journal of Abnormal Psychology*, 96, 52–57.

Spanos, N. P., Radtke, H. L., & Dubreuil, D. L. (1982). Episodic and semantic memory in posthypnotic amnesia: A reevaluation. *Journal of Personality and Social Psychology*, 43, 565–573.

Spanos, N. P., & Saad, C. L. (1984). Prism adaptation in hypnotically limb-anesthetized subjects: More disconfirming data. *Perceptual and Motor Skills*, 59, 379–386.

Spiegel, D., & Albert, L. H. (1983). Naloxone fails to reverse hypnotic alleviation of chronic pain. *Psychopharmacology*, 81, 140–143.

Stern, J. A., Brown, M., Ulett, G. A., & Sletten, I. (1977). A comparison of hypnosis, acupuncture, morphine, valium, aspirin, and placebo in the management of experimentally induced pain. *Annals of the New York Academy of Science*, 296, 175–193.

Stoyva, J., & Kamiya, J. (1968). Electrophysiological studies of dreaming as the prototype of a new strategy in the study of consciousness. *Psychological Review*, 75, 192–205.

Stroop, J. R. (1935). Studies of interference in serial verbal reactions. *Journal of Experimental Psychology*, 18, 643–662.

Sutcliffe, J. P. (1960). "Credulous" and "skeptical" views of hypnotic phenomena: A review of certain evidence and methodology. *International Journal of Clinical and Experimental Hypnosis*, 8, 73–101.

Sutcliffe, J. P. (1961). "Credulous" and "skeptical" views of hypnotic phenomena: Experiments in esthesia, hallucination, and delusion. *Journal of Abnormal & Social Psychology*, 62, 189–200.

Szechtman, H., Woody, E., Bowers, K. S., & Nahmias, C. (1998). Where the imaginal appears real: A positron emission tomography study of auditory hallucination. *Proceedings of the National Academy of Sciences USA, 95*, 1956–1960.

Tellegen, A., & Atkinson, G. (1974). Openness to absorbing and self-altering experiences ("absorption"), a trait related to hypnotic susceptibility. *Journal of Abnormal Psychology, 83*, 268–277.

Terao, T., & Collinson, S. (2000). Imaging hypnotic paralysis. *Lancet, 356*(9224), 162–163.

Timm, H. W. (1981). The effect of forensic hypnosis techniques on eyewitness recall and recognition. *Journal of Police Science, 9*, 188–194.

Tulving, E. (1983). *Elements of episodic memory*. Oxford: Oxford University Press.

Veith, I. (1965). *Hysteria: The history of a disease*. Chicago: University of Chicago Press.

Wallace, B. (1980). Factors affecting proprioceptive adaptation to prismatic displacement. *Perception & Psychophysics, 28*, 550–554.

Wallace, B., & Fisher, L. E. (1982). Hypnotically induced limb anesthesia and adaptation to displacing prisms: Replication requires adherence to critical procedures. *Journal of Abnormal Psychology, 91*, 390–391.

Wallace, B., & Fisher, L. E. (1984a). Prism adaptation with hypnotically induced limb anesthesia: The critical roles of head position and prism type. *Perception and Psychophysics, 36*, 303–306.

Wallace, B., & Fisher, L. E. (1984b). The roles of target and eye motion in the production of the visual shift in prism adaptation. *Journal of General Psychology, 110*, 251–262.

Wallace, B., & Garrett, J. B. (1973). Reduced felt arm sensation effects on visual adaptation. *Perception and Psychophysics, 14*, 597–600.

Wallace, B., & Garrett, J. B. (1975). Perceptual adaptation with selective reductions of felt sensation. *Perception, 4*, 437–445.

Wegner, D. M. (2002). *The illusion of conscious will*. Cambridge, MA: MIT Press.

Weiss, F., Blum, G. S., & Gleberman, L. (1987). Anatomically based measurement of facial expressions in simulated versus hypnotically induced affect. *Motivation and Emotion, 11*, 67–81.

Weitzenhoffer, A. M. (1974). When is an "instruction" an "instruction"? *International Journal of Clinical & Experimental Hypnosis, 22*, 258–269.

White, R. W. (1941). A preface to the theory of hypnotism. *Journal of Abnormal & Social Psychology, 36*, 477–505.

Wiggins, J. S., & Trapnell, P. D. (1997). Personality structure: The return of the big five. In R. Hogan, J. A. Johnson, & S .R.dr Briggs (Eds.), *Handbook of personality psychology* (pp. 737–765). San Diego: Academic Press.

Williamsen, J. A., Johnson, H. J., & Eriksen, C. W. (1965). Some characteristics of posthypnotic amnesia. *Journal of Abnormal Psychology, 70*, 123–131.

Woody, E. Z., & Bowers, K. S. (1994). A frontal assault on dissociated control. In S. J. Lynn & J. W. Rhue (Eds.), *Dissociation: Clinical and theoretical perspectives* (pp. 52–79). New York: Guilford Press.

Woody, E. Z., & McConkey, K. M. (2003). What we don't know about the brain and hypnosis, but need to: A view from the Buckhorn Inn. *International Journal of Clinical and Experimental Hypnosis, 51*(3), 309–337.

Woody, E. Z., & Sadler, P. (1998). On reintegrating dissociated theories: Commentary on Kirsch and Lynn (1998). *Psychological Bulletin, 123*, 192–197.

Woody, E. Z., & Szechtman, H. (2000a). Hypnotic hallucinations and yedasentience. *Contemporary Hypnosis, 17*(1), 26–31.

Woody, E. Z., & Szechtman, H. (2000b). Hypnotic hallucinations: Towards a biology of epistemology. *Contemporary Hypnosis, 17*(1), 4–14.

Woody, E. Z., & Szechtman, H. (2003). How can brain activity and hypnosis inform each other? *International Journal of Clinical and Experimental Hypnosis, 51*(3), 232–255.

Yzerbyt, V., Lories, G., & Dardenne, B. (1998). *Metacognition: Cognitive and social dimensions*. Thousand Oaks, CA: Sage Publications.

CHAPTER 18

Can We Study Subjective Experiences Objectively? First-Person Perspective Approaches and Impaired Subjective States of Awareness in Schizophrenia

Jean-Marie Danion and Caroline Huron

Abstract

One of the main challenges of scientific research in psychiatry and clinical psychology is to take account of subjectivity, as defined by the experiential sense of existing as a subject of experience, or the first-person perspective of the world (Sass & Parnas, 2003). Such clinical symptoms as hallucinations, delusions of alien control, feelings of guilt, thoughts of worthlessness, derealization, and depersonalization are subjective experiences that have to be studied in themselves if research in clinical psychology and psychiatry is not to be excessively simplistic. First-person approaches, such as the remember/know procedure (Tulving, 1985), make it possible to study subjective experiences objectively. We show how results from studies exploring conscious awareness in schizophrenia using first- and third-person perspective approaches provide new evidence for the validity of using first-person perspective approaches.

All this I do within myself, in that huge hall of my memory. [. . .]. There also I meet myself and recall myself – what, when, or where I did a thing, and how I felt when I did it. There are all the things that I remember, either having experienced them myself or been told about them by others. Out of the same storehouse, with these past impressions, I can construct now this, now that, image of things that I either have experienced or have believed on the basis of experience – and from these I can further construct future actions, events, and hopes; and I can meditate on all these things as if they were present. [. . .]. I speak to myself in this way; and when I speak, the images of what I am speaking about are present out of the same store of memory; and if the images were absent I could say nothing at all about them. [. . .]. Here also is all, learnt of the liberal sciences and as yet unforgotten; removed as it were to some inner place, which is yet no place: nor are they the images thereof, but the things themselves.
St Augustine, Confessions, Book X

First-Person Perspective Approaches to Conscious Awareness

Since it became an object of scientific investigation, conscious awareness has been studied using the so-called third-person perspective approaches. Typically, these approaches contrast performance in tasks that rely heavily on conscious processes to that in tasks that do not rely, or rely less, on conscious processes. Demonstration of an impaired performance only in tasks that rely heavily on conscious processes is taken as evidence of a specific impairment of these conscious processes. These approaches to conscious awareness are described as third-person perspective approaches because the workings of consciousness are inferred by investigators from performance patterns in selected tasks. However, as the investigator's interpretation is based on indirect data, alternative explanations sometimes have to be considered. Indeed, the two selected tasks may differ in terms of parameters other than the involvement of conscious processes, in which case these different parameters may account for the dissociation of performance.

First-person perspective approaches have been developed recently by cognitive scientists as a means of studying consciousness directly as a subjective experience, rather than indirectly as a function. These approaches are not aimed at explaining the individual subjective experience of a particular subject, a goal that remains beyond the realms of science. Rather, the goal is to account for populations of subjective experiences that may be experienced by numerous subjects. Thus, first-person perspective approaches are aimed at defining these populations of subjective experiences as precisely as possible and measuring them in a reproducible way (Gardiner, 2000).

First-person Perspective Approaches to Recognition Memory: The Distinction Between Autonoetic and Noetic Awareness

All of us, at least once in our lives, have recognized someone as being familiar but have not been able to remember who he or she was or been able to recollect anything about the person and our previous encounter with him or her. Similarly, we can know that we have read a book or watched

a film but fail to remember anything else about it. These examples from everyday life suggest that recognition memory may be based either on feelings of familiarity accompanied by no recollection of contextual information or alternatively on the conscious recollection of details from a past event. Tulving (1985) was the first to propose a first-person perspective approach to measure these two subjective experiences (see Chapter 10). This approach hypothesizes that consciousness is not a unitary phenomenon and it has to be fragmented to be accessible to experiments. Thus, Tulving (1985) distinguishes two subjective experiences, referred to as autonoetic and noetic awareness, which are characterized by distinct phenomenological attributes. Autonoetic awareness is the kind of conscious awareness that is experienced by normal subjects who consciously recollect personal events by reliving them mentally. It makes it possible to be aware of one's own experiences across subjective time and to have a feeling of individuality, uniqueness, and self-direction. It is intimately associated with our awareness of ourselves as persons with a past and a future. Noetic awareness, on the other hand, corresponds to the knowledge that an event occurred but without any conscious recollection. It conveys a more abstract sense of the past and future, based on feelings of familiarity (Tulving, 1985). It does not entail time travel but awareness of knowledge that one has about the world in which one lives. Unlike autonoetic awareness, noetic awareness does not enable us to re-experience personal events in a self-reflective way (Gardiner, 2000). Tulving suggests that memory systems should be redefined in accordance with the related subjective experience at retrieval. In this context, autonoetic awareness stems from an episodic system, whereas noetic awareness stems from a semantic system.

The Remember/Know Procedure

To investigate the distinction between autonoetic and noetic awareness experimentally, Tulving (1985) developed the remember/

know procedure, an experiential procedure in which the states of awareness related to memory recognition are measured. Typically, participants are asked to report their subjective state of awareness at the time they recognize each individual item. They make a remember response if recognition is accompanied by the conscious recollection of some specific feature of the item's presentation (where it was, what they thought, etc.). Thus, remember responses are associated with a qualitatively rich mental experience, including perceptual, spatial, temporal, semantic, emotional, and other details that are attributed to the past learning phase (Johnson, Hashtroudi, & Lindsay, 1993). These remember responses index autonoetic awareness. Participants make a know response if recognition is associated with feelings of familiarity in the absence of conscious recollection. Thus, know responses are associated with the simple knowledge that an item has been seen previously. They index noetic awareness.

Recent studies using the remember/know procedure suggest that some know responses are not in fact based on feelings of familiarity but are simply guesses (Gardiner, Java, & Richardson-Klavehn, 1996): Participants guess that they studied an item previously but do not experience familiarity (knowing) or recollect any details from the learning phase (remembering). To distinguish between knowing and guessing, a third category of responses, namely guess responses, has been added in some studies.

Following the first study by Tulving in 1985, the remember/know procedure has been used widely in numerous recognition memory studies. Findings from these studies provide evidence that the scientific study of subjective experiences is relevant. The first type of evidence comes from reports of systematic and replicable dissociations and associations between remember and know responses as a function of various experimental manipulations. A fourfold patterns of outcomes has been observed: Some variables influence remember but not know responses, some variables influence know but not remember responses, some variables

influence remember and know responses in an opposite way, and finally, some variables influence remember and know responses in a parallel way (for a review, see Gardiner & Richardson-Klavehn, 2000). These results show that remember and know responses are not only dissociable but also functionally independent. They indicate that remember responses involve strategic, intentional, and goal-directed processes, whereas know responses are based on more perceptual processes.

The second type of evidence comes from studies carried out in brain-damaged patients and neuroimaging studies. These studies show that remember and know responses are associated with the activation of distinct neural substrates (Eldridge et al., 2000; Henson et al., 1999; Yonelinas, 2002). Broadly speaking, remember responses are associated with activations of left prefrontal and hippocampal regions, whereas know responses are associated with activations of right prefrontal and parahippocampal regions. Taken together, these findings lend much weight to the view that remember and know responses index two distinct subjective states of conscious awareness.

First-Person Perspective Approaches to Conscious Awareness in Schizophrenia

Henry Ey (1963) was the first person to postulate that schizophrenia is primarily a disorder of consciousness. He argued that an impairment of consciousness is associated with the typical impairment of the self in patients with schizophrenia. However, his view of schizophrenia as a disorder of consciousness was based on a philosophical premise, and concepts and methods to assess consciousness empirically did not exist at the time. Recently, several theoretical models of schizophrenia have reformulated the hypothesis of schizophrenia as a disorder of consciousness with reference to the conceptualization of consciousness as a function. Nancy Andreasen (1999) argues that the disruption of the fluid, coordinated sequences of thought and action that underlie consciousness in normal subjects is the fundamental deficit in schizophrenia. Frith (1992) regards schizophrenia as a disorder of consciousness, impairing the ability to think using metarepresentations, which are representations of mental states.

Several studies using third-person perspective approaches to consciousness provide consistent experimental evidence for an impairment of consciousness in schizophrenia. Patients with schizophrenia exhibit a dissociation between impaired performance in explicit tasks, such as recall and recognition ones, in which participants are required to retrieve information from memory consciously (Clare, McKenna, Mortimer, & Baddeley, 1993; Gras-Vincendon et al., 1994), and preserved performance in implicit tasks, such as perceptual priming tasks (Gras-Vincendon et al., 1994) and procedural memory tasks (Goldberg, Saint-Cyr, & Weinberger, 1990; Michel, Danion, Grange, & Sandner, 1998), for which subjects are not required to retrieve material consciously. Performance of patients with schizophrenia is also intact in implicit learning tasks in which the acquisition of knowledge is also implicit (Danion, Gokalsing, Robert, Massin-Krauss, & Bacon, 2001). Furthermore, patients with schizophrenia experience a dissociation between preserved automatic subliminal priming and impaired conscious control (Dehaene et al., 2003).

Together with evidence of impaired awareness of self-generated action (Franck et al., 2001), these results converge to suggest that an impairment of conscious awareness might be a core deficit in schizophrenia. However, this assumption is drawn from an inference based on indirect evidence, and the use of first-person perspective approaches in patients with schizophrenia to measure conscious awareness directly might be a particularly relevant and informative way of finding out more about the cognitive mechanisms of this mental disease.

But if it is conceded that mental disorders may impair not only subjective experiences but also the ability of patients to assess these subjective experiences, the question of

the validity of using first-person perspective approaches seems to be especially critical in these patients. This question is so crucial that some psychiatrists and psychologists deny the scientific interest of these approaches in schizophrenia. It has to be said, though, that this denial seems somewhat paradoxical as it implies that first-person perspective approaches should not be applied to subjects for which they are the most likely to be interesting. We argue that the only way to deal satisfactorily with the issue of the validity of using first-person perspective approaches in patients with schizophrenia is to examine available empirical data. In the next part of the chapter, we present the results of our studies using the remember/know procedure in patients with schizophrenia.

Impairment of Autonoetic Awareness in Schizophrenia

A set of studies using the remember/know procedure to assess subjective states of awareness in patients with schizophrenia showed that autonoetic awareness is impaired.

IMPAIRMENT OF WORD FREQUENCY
EFFECT IN REMEMBER RESPONSES
Huron et al. (1995) used a recognition memory task including high- and low-frequency words. The results show that the level of remember responses is reduced for low-frequency words in patients with schizophrenia, whereas the number of remember responses for high-frequency words and the number of know responses for both high- and low-frequency words do not differ between groups. Therefore, patients with schizophrenia do not exhibit the word frequency effect (more remember responses for low-frequency than high-frequency words) observed in normal subjects (see also Gardiner & Java, 1990). The word frequency effect has been accounted for in normal subjects by encoding differences in information processing that appear during the study phase: The distinctive low-frequency words undergo more strategic processing than the less distinctive

high-frequency words. Therefore, the absence of a word frequency effect on remember responses in patients with schizophrenia suggests that the impairment of autonoetic awareness may be attributed to a failure of strategic processes engaged at encoding.

IMPAIRMENT OF FALSE MEMORIES ASSOCIATED WITH REMEMBER RESPONSES

We have also studied subjective states of awareness associated with false memories – that is, memories for events that never happened – in schizophrenia. The most widely used experimental procedure to induce false memories in normal subjects is that initially introduced by Deese and subsequently modified by Roediger and McDermott (1995). In this procedure, subjects study lists of 15 words that are semantically related to a non-presented theme word or critical lure. For instance, the words presented for the critical word *mountain* are *hill, valley, climb, summit, top, molehill, peak, plain, glacier, goat, bike, climber, range, steep, ski.* A subsequent recognition test includes both previously presented words and non-presented critical words, along with unrelated new items. In normal subjects, this procedure induces a robust false recognition effect for the critical lures (*mountain,* in this case). Moreover, when subjects are asked to report, for each item they identify as being old, whether they remember or know that the item was on the list they studied, the false recognition of critical lures is most often accompanied by an experience of remembering. It has been hypothesized that this false recollection involves strategic processes (Holmes et al., 1998; Mather et al., 1997). On the whole, studies of false memories in normal subjects provide direct evidence that memories and associated awareness are not a literal reproduction of the past but depend instead on constructive and reconstructive processes that are sometimes prone to errors and distortions (Conway, 1997; Holmes et al., 1998; Schacter et al., 1998).

We used the Deese/Roediger-McDermott approach to investigate false recog-

nition and related states of awareness in schizophrenia (Huron & Danion, 2002). The results show that patients with schizophrenia recognize fewer critical lures (false recognition) and studied words (correct recognition) than normal subjects. This deficit is restricted to items associated with remember responses. The proportion of know responses does not differ between groups. The results confirm the selective impairment of autonoetic awareness associated with true memories and extend these findings to false memories. They are consistent with an impairment of strategic processes in schizophrenia. They also indicate that the mere construction of memories and autonoetic awareness is defective in this pathology.

IMPAIRMENT OF CONTENTS OF AUTONOETIC AWARENESS

As well as studying the frequency of autonoetic awareness in schizophrenia, we investigated the content of autonoetic awareness (Sonntag et al., 2003). More precisely, we used a remember/know procedure together with a directed forgetting paradigm to investigate the contents of awareness at retrieval depending on whether information has been identified as relevant or irrelevant at encoding. In this paradigm, patients with schizophrenia and comparison subjects are presented with words and instructed to learn half of them and forget the other half. The instruction "to be learned" or "to be forgotten" occurs just after each word is presented during the study phase. The recognition task is carried out on all the words presented previously, mixed with new words. Participants are instructed to identify all the words from the study list irrespective of whether the words were to be learned or forgotten and to report their subjective state of awareness at the time they recognize a word. This approach tells us about the strategic regulation of the content of awareness for relevant information, which is beneficial to recollect, and irrelevant information, which is beneficial to forget. The results show that both normal subjects and patients with schizophrenia recognize more to-be-learned than to-be-forgotten words, indicating that both groups exhibited a directed forgetting effect. However, whereas the effect was observed both for remember and know responses in comparison subjects, it was observed for know, but not for remember, responses in patients. This experiment provides evidence that schizophrenia impairs the relevance of the content of autonoetic awareness. It is possible that patients, unlike comparison subjects, fail to engage the strategic regulation of encoding that makes the relevant information easier to retrieve than the irrelevant information.

Is the Remember/Know Procedure Valid in Schizophrenia?

Evidence for the validity of using the remember/know procedure in schizophrenia is provided by checking that patients with schizophrenia properly understand and apply the task instructions, demonstrating that some experimental variables induce the same patterns of responses in patients and in controls, and showing the consistency of findings from first-person and third-person perspective approaches to recognition memory.

DO PATIENTS WITH SCHIZOPHRENIA PROPERLY UNDERSTAND AND APPLY INSTRUCTIONS DURING THE REMEMBER/KNOW PROCEDURE?

When using the remember/know procedure in patients with schizophrenia, it is particularly important to check carefully that patients fully understand the instructions given for the task and apply them properly. Because a proper understanding of the distinction among remember, know, and guess responses is critical to the task, we took numerous precautions to ensure that the subjects fully understood the meanings of these responses in all our studies using this procedure in patients with schizophrenia. Instructions were presented orally and then in written form. Some examples from everyday life were described, and subjects were asked whether they would choose a remember, know, or guess response for each instance. Corrections were made by the

investigator when necessary. All participants performed a practice test on 10 items, 5 of which were presented just after the items to be studied in the main test and 5 of which were new items. For each item, subjects were asked whether they recognized it as having been presented previously or not. When they recognized an item, they were asked to select a remember, know, or guess response. At the end of the practice test, they were asked to explain each response to check that they had correctly interpreted the instructions. Throughout all of this, there was no indication that patients had any difficulty understanding or remembering the instructions. The very few participants who failed to perform the practice test properly were left out of the experiment. They represent less than 5% of the overall participants in our studies and include both patients with schizophrenia and normal subjects. These findings confirm that the remember/know distinction is psychologically relevant not only in normal subjects (Gardiner, 2000) but also in patients with schizophrenia.

Another possibility is to ask participants, at the end of the main recognition task, to explain their remember responses by reporting exactly what they remembered. Like comparison subjects, patients with schizophrenia explain these responses by the recollection of highly specific details from the learning phase. However, a more precise analysis of these explanations shows that, in some experimental conditions, patients with schizophrenia report fewer associations between words from the study list than comparison subjects, whereas they recollect as many associations with personal events (Huron et al., 1995). This finding does not raise any doubts about the accuracy of the remember responses reported by patients with schizophrenia. Indeed, it is likely that these differences reflect the failure of strategic processes in schizophrenia: Associations between studied words require intentional, strategic organization of the information to be learned, whereas the spontaneous evocation of a personal event may be triggered automatically by a studied word. This interpretation is consistent with the view expressed by Yonelinas (2002) that autonoetic awareness sometimes depends on strategic processes and sometimes depends on more automatic processes. Thus, schizophrenia might specifically impair autonoetic awareness based on strategic processes, but appears to spare autonoetic awareness involving more automatic processes.

A further way of assessing the validity of using remember, know, and guess responses is to compare patients with schizophrenia and comparison subjects in terms of the qualitative characteristics or, in other words, the perceptual, spatial, temporal, semantic, and emotional attributes of the subjective experience for each reported response. This kind of assessment has been performed in a study of the picture superiority effect, in which participants were instructed not only to report a remember, know, and guess response for each recognized item but also to rate the specific qualitative characteristics of their memory on visual analog scales (Huron et al., 2003). The picture superiority effect describes the finding that it is typical for normal subjects to recognize pictures more readily than words in a subsequent recognition memory task. Moreover, this effect is mainly related to recognition accompanied by remember responses. Our results show that patients with schizophrenia exhibit a lower picture superiority effect selectively related to remember responses than comparison subjects. Most importantly, they show that the qualitative characteristics of memories do not differ between patients with schizophrenia and controls. Despite the lower frequency of remember responses in patients with schizophrenia, when they report a remember response, the qualitative characteristics of this subjective state of awareness seem to be similar to those reported by comparison subjects. Moreover, in both groups the qualitative characteristics of subjective experiences associated with remember responses are quite different from those associated with know and guess responses. These findings suggest that the remember and know responses of patients with schizophrenia index two distinct subjective experiences of awareness that are qualitatively similar to those experienced by comparison subjects.

Evidence that the memory of the source of an item and, more generally, the memory of an association is better for a consciously recollected item than for a familiar item also seems to demonstrate the validity of using remember and know responses (Conway & Dewhurst, 1995; Perfect, Mayes, Downes, & Van Eijk, 1996). Such evidence has been found in patients with schizophrenia (Danion et al., 1999). We have used a source recognition memory task to measure the relation between defective autonoetic awareness and impaired source memory in schizophrenia. During the study phase, participants are presented with a set of common objects (e.g., a candle, a toothbrush, a handkerchief, a battery, and a tire pump). They are instructed to make pairs of objects by positioning an object next to another (e.g., the subject has to put the candle next to the tire pump) or to watch the experimenter perform the action (e.g., the experimenter puts the toothbrush next to the battery). In this way, participants have to study complex events, which each consist of target information (a pair of objects) and source contextual information (who paired the two objects).

In a recognition task, participants are presented with pairs of objects. All the objects have been presented during the study phase, so that the recognition of objects has no influence on the recognition of pairs. As presented, the pairs consist of old pairs of two old objects occurring in their previous combination and new pairs of two old objects occurring in a new combination. Accordingly, correct recognition of old pairs depends on specific associations between objects made by participants during the study session, which make the pairs distinctive. Participants are asked to identify old pairs (recognition of pairs of objects) and to make a remember or know response for the pair. They then have to say whether they performed the action or watched it (source recognition) and to make a remember or know response for the action.

The performance of patients with schizophrenia is particularly impaired in observed actions, as both recognition of pairs of objects and recognition of source are impaired. This impairment is associated with a reduction in the frequency of remember, but not know, responses. Comparison subjects make few errors in source recognition when recognition of pairs of objects is accompanied by remember responses. They make significantly more errors when recognition is accompanied by know responses. Patients with schizophrenia make numerous source recognition errors. However, their performance is better for remember responses than for know responses, albeit to a lesser degree than in comparison subjects. Both groups perform better when they paired the objects themselves: Pair recognition, source recognition, and the frequency of remember responses increase. Source recognition performance improves when recognition of pairs of objects is accompanied by remember, but not know, responses. Therefore, in patients with schizophrenia, as in comparison subjects, subjective reports of awareness and objective measures of memory (recognition of pairs of objects and source recognition) are consistent in all experimental conditions. Evidence that source recognition is higher for consciously recollected pairs of objects than for familiar pairs provides a powerful argument for the validity of using remember and know responses in schizophrenia. Moreover, these results indicate that patients with schizophrenia are less able than comparison subjects to link the separate aspects of events together into a cohesive, memorable, and distinctive whole.

DO SOME EXPERIMENTAL VARIABLES
INDUCE THE SAME PATTERN OF
REMEMBER/KNOW RESPONSES IN
PATIENTS WITH SCHIZOPHRENIA
AS IN CONTROLS?

Most of the studies that have used the remember/know procedure in schizophrenia have shown that the effect on remember responses of an experimental variable (i.e., word frequency, picture) differs between patients and controls. Evidence that an experimental variable has the same impact on remember responses in both groups would show that patients with schizophrenia and comparison subjects behave similarly during this first-person perspective task. Such evidence has been provided in a study in which the effect of the affective valence (positive, negative, or neutral) of words on subjective states of awareness was compared between patients with schizophrenia and comparison subjects. The results show lower levels of remember responses in patients. However, like comparison subjects, patients report more remember responses for emotional words than for neutral words. In contrast, the level of know responses is not influenced by emotional words. Evidence that both patients and comparison subjects consciously recollect emotional words better than neutral words suggests that the impact of the emotional valence of words on autonoetic awareness is preserved in schizophrenia.

Are the Results from First-Person and Third-Person Perspective Approaches to Recognition Memory Consistent in Schizophrenia?

The distinction between two subjective states of consciousness proposed by Tulving (1985) is similar to the distinction between two types of memory processes or systems, generally referred to as conscious recollection and familiarity,[1] reported in dual recognition memory models. These models, which have been developed mainly by Atkinson and colleagues, Mandler, Jacoby, and Yonelinas (reviewed in Yonelinas, 2002), have been tested using a variety of third-person perspective methods, including recall/recognition comparisons, item/associative recognition comparisons and the process-dissociation procedure. Yonelinas (2002) took advantage of the similarity between the remember/know and the conscious recollection/familiarity distinctions to compare findings from first-person and third-person perspective approaches to recognition memory in normal subjects and

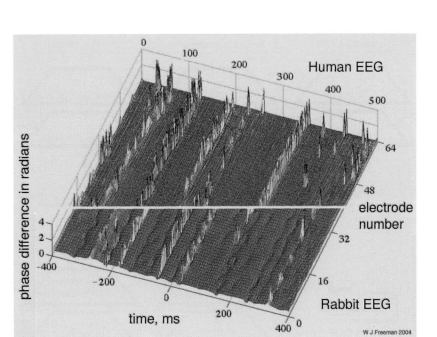

Plate 8.5. A Hilbert analysis of analytic phase differences in EEG across cortical surface measured over 400 ms in rabbit and human conscious processing. Phase differences are calculated in the beta band (12–30 Hz) for human EEG and in the gamma band (20–50 Hz) for the rabbit EEG. (With permission of the author.)

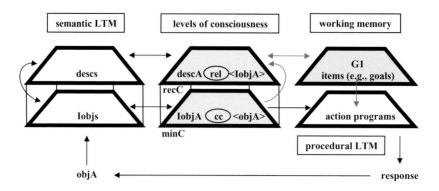

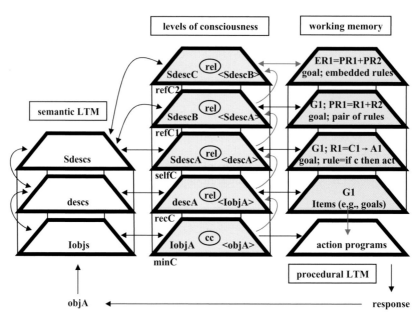

Plate 15.1. The implications of reflection (levels of consciousness) for rule use. (a, top): Relatively automatic action on the basis of a lower level of consciousness. An object in the environment (objA) triggers an intentional representation of that object (IobjA) in semantic long-term memory (LTM); this IobjA, which is causally connected (cc) to a bracketed objA, becomes the content of consciousness (referred to at this level as minimal consciousness or minC). The contents of minC are then fed back into minC via a re-entrant feedback process, producing a new, more reflective level of consciousness referred to as recursive consciousness or recC. The contents of recC can be related (rel) in consciousness to a corresponding description (descA) or label, which can then be deposited into working memory (WM) where it can serve as a goal (G1) to trigger an action program from procedural LTM in a top-down fashion. (b, bottom): Subsequent (higher) levels of consciousness, including self-consciousness (selfC), reflective consciousness 1 (refC1), and reflective consciousness 2 (refC2). Each level of consciousness allows for the formulation and maintenance in WM of more complex systems of rules. (Reprinted with permission from Zelazo, P. D. (2004). The development of conscious control in childhood. *Trends in Cognitive Sciences*, 8, 12–17.)

brain-lesioned patients. He showed that findings from the remember/know procedure are consistent with those from third-person perspective approaches, providing evidence to support the validity of using first-person perspective approaches in these populations. In keeping with this line of reasoning, we review the studies that used these third-person perspective approaches to recognition memory in schizophrenia. Doing so enables us to draw inferences about recollection and familiarity in schizophrenia and to compare the results from these studies with those from first-person perspective studies. Consistent findings will provide further arguments for the validity of using first-person perspective approaches to recognition memory in patients with schizophrenia.

RECALL/RECOGNITION COMPARISON

The rationale underlying third-person perspective approaches to conscious recognition is similar to that underlying the above-mentioned third-person perspective approaches to conscious awareness. However, instead of using tasks selected to compare conscious and unconscious processes, these approaches use tasks selected to compare recollection and familiarity. They compare performance in task conditions assumed to require one of the two recognition memory processes more than the other. For instance, performance in a recall task is assumed to rely more on conscious recollection than on familiarity. On the other hand, whereas familiarity has few effects on recall performance, it contributes to performance in an item recognition task to a greater extent. Accordingly, recall performance is taken as an index of conscious recollection, whereas item recognition performance is taken as an index of familiarity. If a condition influences recall performance to a greater extent than recognition performance, this condition is assumed to influence conscious recollection more than familiarity.

On the whole, studies on recall in schizophrenia show defective performance: Patients with schizophrenia consistently recall fewer items than control subjects (Culver et al., 1986; Gerver, 1967; Koh & Kayton, 1974; Koh et al., 1973, 1980; McClain, 1983; Russel & Beekhuis, 1976; Sengel & Lovallo, 1973; Truscott, 1970). The robustness of this deficit has been confirmed by a recent meta-analysis (Aleman et al., 1999) including 70 studies on long-term memory in schizophrenia that reported a large effect size for recall. This deficit occurs for verbal and non-verbal stimuli.

In studies using recognition tasks, it is sometimes reported that patients with schizophrenia perform worse than normal controls (Barch et al., 2002; Russel et al., 1975; Sullivan et al., 1997; Traupman, 1975), but sometimes there seems to be no difference (Koh et al., Exp. 2, 1973; Rushe et al., 1999). A meta-analysis by Aleman et al. (1999) indicates that recognition is less impaired than recall. Studies that assess both recall and recognition performance in the same patients with schizophrenia lead to the same conclusion. Some of these studies found impaired recall along with normal recognition in patients compared to controls (Bauman, 1971; Bauman & Muray, 1968; Beatty et al, 1993; Koh & Peterson, 1978; Nachmani & Cohen, 1969). Other studies have shown that, even if patients with schizophrenia exhibit a recognition deficit, they are nevertheless more impaired in recall tasks than in recognition memory tasks (Brébion et al., 1997; Calev, 1984; Calev et al., 1983; Chan et al., 2000; Gold et al, 1992; Goldberg et al., 1989; Paulsen et al., 1995; Russel et al., 1975). In the few studies in which recognition and recall tasks have been matched for difficulty (e.g., Calev, 1984), it has also been reported that performance is less impaired in recognition than in recall. Because conscious recollection is assumed to contribute more to recall than to recognition performance, a greater impairment in recall provides evidence for a deficit in recollection.

ITEM/ASSOCIATIVE RECOGNITION COMPARISON

A complementary third-person perspective approach contrasts performance in a single-item recognition task and an associative recognition task. In an associative recognition task participants have to recollect a specific association between a target information and contextual information. Performance depends mainly on a conscious recollection process because this process requires the binding together of the distinct aspects of an event to be remembered. Conversely, performance in an item-recognition task relies more on familiarity. Several studies have compared the performance of patients with schizophrenia in a single-item recognition task and an associative recognition task requiring memory of contextual information. They have shown that patients with schizophrenia exhibit disproportionate deficits in associative recognition tests compared to item-recognition tests. This finding has been confirmed by a meta-analysis (Achim & Lepage, 2005) of 23 studies of recognition memory in schizophrenia that observed an impairment 20% greater for associative recognition relative to item recognition. In comparison to single-item recognition tests, patients perform poorly in tests that require them to remember when or where an item was presented (Rizzo et al., 1996a,b; Schwartz et al., 1991; Sullivan et al., 1997; Waters et al, 2004; but see Shoqueirat & Mayes, 1998), which modality it was presented in (for instance, verbally or visually; Brébion et al., 1997), or how frequently it was presented (Gold et al., 1992; Gras-Vincendon et al., 1994). Patients with schizophrenia have also been found to exhibit deficits in reality-monitoring tasks in which they have to discriminate (1) self-generated information from information generated by an external source (Brébion et al., 1997; Harvey, 1985; Keefe et al., 1999; Moritz et al., 2003; Vinogradov et al., 1997; Waters et al, 2004), (2) information from two external sources – a male and a female voice, and (3) information from two internal sources – i.e., words they imagine themselves saying and words they imagine the experimenter saying (Keefe et al., 1999) or imagined answers and verbalized answers (Henquet et al., 2005). These results suggest a greater deficit in associative recognition memory, which is assumed

to rely primarily on recollection, than in item recognition, which may reflect both recollection and familiarity. They are consistent with an impairment of conscious recollection in schizophrenia. Direct evidence of a link between defective associative recognition memory and impaired conscious recollection has been provided by the study by Danion et al. (1999) referred to above using a combination of the remember/know procedure and source judgements in schizophrenia.

PROCESS-DISSOCIATION PROCEDURE

Both recall/recognition and item/associative recognition comparisons provide consistent findings about conscious recollection in schizophrenia. However, these third-person perspective approaches are not designed to estimate quantitatively the respective contribution of conscious recollection and familiarity processes. Jacoby (1991) has developed the process-dissociation procedure to overcome this limitation (see Chapter 10). This procedure was devised to separate mathematically the respective contributions of consciously controlled and automatic memory processes to performance in a single memory task by combining inclusion and exclusion test conditions. The procedure initially proposed by Jacoby involves a source memory task. During the study phase, subjects are shown words that they are not instructed to learn and then asked to learn words that they hear. During the test phase, under the inclusion condition, participants are instructed to give a yes response to all previously presented words; that is, both to words they have seen and to words they have heard. Under this condition, consciously controlled and automatic memory processes act in concert to facilitate performance. Under the exclusion condition, participants are instructed to give a yes response only to words that they have heard. Under this condition, consciously controlled and automatic memory processes act in opposition: The controlled use of memory both increases the number of correct yes responses (yes responses to words heard) and decreases the number of false alarms (yes responses to words seen), whereas automatic influences increase the number of false alarms. Estimates of recollection and familiarity are derived from equations based on performance (correct responses and false alarms) under each condition.

Two studies (Kazès et al., 1999; Linscott & Knight, 2001) have used the process-dissociation procedure to assess recollection and familiarity in schizophrenia directly. In a source memory task, Linscott and Knight (2001) reported lower estimates of conscious recollection in patients with schizophrenia than in comparison subjects, but no difference between groups for the estimates of familiarity. Using a version of the process-dissociation procedure that involves a word-stem completion task, both Kazès et al. (1999) and Linscott and Knight observed reduced levels of conscious recollection in schizophrenia. This impaired conscious recollection was associated with a spared familiarity in the study by Kazès et al. (1999) and an increased familiarity in Linscott and Knight's study (2001). These two studies confirm the impairment of conscious recollection and do not provide any evidence of a deficit in familiarity.

To summarize, findings from studies of schizophrenia using first- and third-person perspective approaches are concordant, showing a consistent impairment of autonoetic awareness and the underlying process of conscious recollection. In combination with empirical evidence that patients with schizophrenia properly understand and use task instructions, and that some experimental variables induce the same response patterns in patients and in comparison subjects, these findings provide substantial evidence of the validity of using the remember/know procedure in schizophrenia.

Does Schizophrenia Impair Noetic Awareness and Familiarity?

Whereas there is converging evidence that autonoetic awareness and conscious recollection are consistently impaired in schizophrenia, the results from both first- and third-person perspective studies of noetic awareness and the underlying process of familiarity are less clear. Evidence from third-person perspective approaches that recognition memory is sometimes intact in schizophrenia is consistent with preserved familiarity. However, some studies have shown lowered recognition performance, and the two studies in which the process-dissociation-procedure was used to measure familiarity directly have produced discrepant findings: Familiarity is preserved in one of these studies and increased in the other. Studies using the remember/know procedure show no impairment of noetic awareness as measured by know responses. However, results from studies by Danion et al. (2003) show a decrease in familiarity when familiarity is estimated using an independence model applied to the proportions of remember and know responses (Yonelinas et al., 1998).

These discrepancies prompted us to review the results of all our remember/know studies using the framework of the independence model devised by Yonelinas et al. (1998). The underlying assumption of this model is that conscious recollection and familiarity are independent processes, whereas the typical remember/know procedure is based on a mutually exclusive relation. The results of these reviews, which are presented in Table 18.1, show that familiarity decreases in two studies (Danion et al., 2003; Huron et al., 1995), but not in all the others.

Overall, when results from both first-person perspective and third-person perspective approaches in schizophrenia are considered, there is no evidence of a deficit in noetic awareness as measured by know responses and little evidence of an impairment in the process of familiarity. Therefore, we can conclude that, although a deficit in familiarity may be observed under certain experimental conditions, this deficit is much less pronounced than the deficit of conscious recollection. However, this conclusion cannot be regarded as definitive because no study to date has taken the experimental variables that are known to influence know responses specifically in normal subjects and applied them to patients with schizophrenia.

Table 18.1. Mean values of recollection (R) and familiarity (F) of patients with schizophrenia and comparison subjects, condition by condition, computed from individual values

	Patients with Schizophrenia								Comparison Subjects							
	Remember		Know		Guess		R^1	F^2	Remember		Know		Guess		R^1	F^2
	Old	New	Old	New	Old	New			Old	New	Old	New	Old	New		
Word frequency (Huron et al., 1995)																
High-frequency words	0.22	0.03	0.28	0.04			0.20	0.32	0.29	0.02	0.34	0.05			0.28	0.45
Low-frequency words	0.22	0.01	0.33	0.02			0.21	0.42	0.39	0.002	0.33	0.03			0.39*	0.51
False recognition (Huron et al., 2002a)																
Studied	0.33	0.02	0.19	0.03	0.14	0.09	0.32	0.37	0.47	0.02	0.18	0.16	0.10	0.07	0.46*	0.41
Critical lures	0.37	0.07	0.13	0.06	0.13	0.08	0.32	0.29	0.43	0.03	0.02	0.03	0.17	0.10	0.32	0.46
Directed forgetting paradigm (Sonntag et al., 2003)																
To-be-learned items	0.26	0.04	0.19	0.05	0.07	0.04	0.23	0.20	0.36	0.01	0.14	0.02	0.09	0.07	0.35*	0.19
To-be-forgotten items	0.24		0.14		0.07		0.21	0.13	0.25		0.11		0.10		0.24	0.12
The picture superiority effect (Huron et al., 2003)																
Words	0.14	0.01	0.07	0.01	0.06	0.01	0.15	0.22	0.17	0.01	0.10	0.01	0.13	0.05	0.13	0.13
Pictures	0.56		0.16		0.07		0.73	0.45	0.74		0.11		0.04		0.56*	0.42
Affective valence (Danion et al., 2003)																
Positive	0.31	0.01	0.36	0.03			0.31	0.48	0.68	0.02	0.18	0.02			0.67	0.52
Neutral	0.20	0.01	0.40	0.02			0.19	0.50	0.50	0.002	0.36	0.02			0.49*	0.66
Negative	0.26	0.01	0.38	0.04			0.25	0.49	0.56	0.02	0.29	0.03			0.55*	0.64

* Significant differences between patients with schizophrenia and comparison subjects, $p < .05$.

[1] For each participant, recollection (R) was calculated by subtracting the proportion of remember responses for new items (R_{new}) from the proportion of remember responses for old items (R_{old}) and then dividing by the opportunity to assign a remember response to old items ($1-R_{new}$).

[2] For each participant, estimates of familiarity were computed separately for old and new items. For old items, F_{old} was estimated by the proportions of know responses to old items divided by the probability that an old item did not receive a remember response ($1-R_{old}$). Similarly, for new items, F_{new} was estimated by the proportions of know responses to new items divided by the probability that a new item did not receive a remember response ($1-R_{new}$). To calculate familiarity (F), F_{new} was subtracted from F_{old}. It has to be noted that when the studies allow both know and guess responses, the proportion of know responses was replaced by the sum of the proportions of know and guess responses.

Conclusions

Throughout this chapter, we have argued that the concepts and methods needed to study some subjective experiences objectively are already available. For instance, the first-person perspective approach proposed by Tulving to assess subjective states of conscious awareness at retrieval seems to be valid not only in normal subjects (Yonelinas, 2002) but also in patients with schizophrenia. The distinction between remember and know responses is relevant from a psychological viewpoint and is, more often than not, appropriately applied by normal subjects and by patients with schizophrenia. Moreover, as is indicated by numerous experimental and neuropsychological dissociations, remember and know responses index two distinct subjective states of awareness: autonoetic and noetic awareness. These subjective states are not a literal reproduction of the past but instead a reconstruction of the past, which takes into account the present time. Finally, this review shows a strong consistency of results from first-person and third-person perspective approaches. In the future, it will be of interest to develop integrative and multidisciplinary approaches that combine first-person and third-person perspective methods in the same studies. First-person perspective approaches combined with brain imaging (e.g., fMRI) will also be required.

The use of the remember/know procedure in patients with schizophrenia provides a better understanding of the cognitive impairments associated with the disease. It makes it possible to present a coherent and accurate picture of the various recall and recognition disturbances that have been reported in these patients. Schizophrenia seems to be characterized by an impairment of autonoetic awareness and its underlying conscious recollection process. This impairment results from a failure of strategic processing at encoding (e.g., Brebion et al., 1997; Gold et al., 1992; Koh & Peterson, 1978), but an impairment of strategic processing at retrieval cannot be ruled out. The impairment of autonoetic awareness and conscious recollection might explain some behavioral abnormalities associated with schizophrenia, notably inadequate functional outcomes in everyday life. Because autonoetic awareness is severely disrupted in schizophrenia, a past event cannot be used with great flexibility to guide and control behavior, affects, and beliefs, which in turn are likely to be inappropriate inasmuch as they can be driven only by noetic awareness or implicit memory. This probably explains why memory impairments of patients with schizophrenia are so consistently related to inadequate functional outcome in their daily lives (Green, 1996).

Future Prospects

We conclude this chapter by looking at some of the outstanding questions that first-person perspective approaches have opened up in the research field of psychiatry and clinical psychology. From a clinical viewpoint, patients with schizophrenia frequently experience perplexity about their own identity, which can take the form of derealization and depersonalization. These symptoms are taken to be a disturbance of the subjective sense of self. It has been argued that the sense of self is supported by autobiographical events associated with autonoetic awareness (Conway & Pleydell-Pearce, 2000). Therefore, the use of the remember/know procedure to study subjective states of awareness associated with autobiographical memories makes it possible to study the subjective sense of the self. However, until now, studies using the remember/know procedure in patients with schizophrenia have been performed under conditions that have had little to do with real life and so prevent the generalization of their conclusions to autobiographical memory. Indeed, the stimuli have been words and pictures, and the learning and test phases have been measured in minutes or hours. These stimuli are not comparable with complex and meaningful autobiographical events that have retention intervals measured in weeks, months, and years. Using an autobiographical memory inquiry in combination with the remember/know procedure, we showed a lower frequency and consistency among patients of remember responses associated with autobiographical memories (Danion et al., 2005). This finding is consistent with the impairment of the sense of self reported by patients. There is preliminary evidence that this impairment might result from a defective construction of personal identity occurring during adolescence or early adulthood (Riutort, Cuervo, Danion, Peretti, & Salame, 2003).

First-person perspective approaches have also been developed to investigate metamemory; that is, subjects' knowledge about their own memory capabilities. They make it possible to study subjective experiences related to the knowledge that subjects possess about the functioning of their memory. These experiences can be evaluated either qualitatively, such as the phenomenon of something being on the tip of the tongue, or quantitatively, such as the Feeling of Knowing or the Judgment of Confidence. Applying these approaches to the study of schizophrenia or other mental diseases opens up a new field of research, which is still virtually unexplored (but see Bacon, Danion, Kauffmann-Muller, & Bruant, 2001; Danion et al., 2001).

From a more theoretical point of view, because first-person perspective methods focus on the subjective dimension of psychopathological manifestations, they may be the first step in a major conceptual change that would modify our understanding of these manifestations. Behrendt and Young (2004) point out that psychiatry has usually adopted a philosophical position of realism that assumes that the world that we perceive is an objective reality. This world is thought to exist independently of those who perceive it and not to be a product of their mind. In contrast, Gestalt psychologists, in keeping with the philosophical position of transcendental idealism of Kant, consider that a clear distinction has to be made between the world that we subjectively perceive and the external physical world with which we interact. The world subjectively experienced is distinct from the external physical world. It is an active construction arising from our mind that we project outside it. This subjective representation of the world has to be constrained by external physical realities in order to be adaptive. Realism and idealism lead to diametrically opposed views of psychopathological manifestations, as illustrated by hallucinations. According to the realism point of view, hallucinations are false perceptions that arise in the absence of an external object or event. According to transcendental idealism, both normal perceptions and hallucinations are subjective experiences subserved by the same internal process. They only differ in respect to the extent to which they are constrained by sensory input from the external world. Such a position might open up new prospects for the understanding of hallucinations (Behrendt & Young, 2004), and more generally of the subjectivity impairments associated with mental disorders.

Note

1. Conscious recollection and familiarity are sometimes used to describe subjective states of awareness, as well as cognitive processes underlying recognition memory. The use of the same terms to describe separate concepts is confusing. Indeed, in the former case, conscious recollection and familiarity refer to experimental data in the form of remember and know responses, whereas in the latter case, they refer to hypothetical constructs – processes – arising from a theoretical model and its underlying hypotheses. To avoid any confusion, we use autonoetic and noetic awareness to qualify subjective states of awareness associated with recognition memory and conscious recollection and familiarity to qualify cognitive processes underlying recognition memory.

References

Achim, A. M., & Lepage, M. (2005). Episodic memory-related activation in schizophrenia: meta-analysis. *British Journal of Psychiatry*, *187*(12), 500–509.

Aleman, A., Hijman, R., de Haan, E. H., & Kahn, R. S. (1999). Memory impairment in schizophrenia: a meta-analysis. *American Journal of Psychiatry*, 156(9), 1358–1366.

Andreasen, N. C. (1999). A unitary model of schizophrenia: Bleuler's "fragmented phrene" as schizencephaly. *Archives of General Psychiatry*, 56(9), 781–787.

Bacon, E., Danion, J. M., Kauffmann-Muller, F., & Bruant, A. (2001). Consciousness in schizophrenia: A metacognitive approach to semantic memory. *Consciousness and Cognition*, 10(4), 473–484.

Barch, D. M., Csernansky, J. G., Conturo, T., & Snyder, A. Z. (2002). Working and long-term memory deficits in schizophrenia: Is there a common prefrontal mechanism? *Journal of Abnormal Psychology*, 111(3), 478–494.

Bauman, E. (1971). Schizophrenic short-term memory: A deficit in subjective organization. *Canadian Journal of Behavioral Sciences*, 3(1), 55–65.

Bauman, E., & Murray, D. J. (1968). Recognition versus recall in schizophrenia. *Canadian Journal of Psychology*, 22(1), 18–25.

Beatty, W. W., Jocic, Z., Monson, N., & Staton, R. D. (1993). Memory and frontal lobe dysfunction in schizophrenia and schizoaffective disorder. *Journal of Nervous and Mental Diseases*, 181(7), 448–453.

Behrendt, R. P., & Young, C. (2004). Hallucinations in schizophrenia, sensory impairment and brain disease: A unifying model. *Behavioral & Brain Sciences*, 27(6), 771–787.

Brebion, G., Amador, X., Smith, M. J., & Gorman, J. M. (1997). Mechanisms underlying memory impairment in schizophrenia. *Psychological Medicine*, 27(2), 383–393.

Calev, A. (1984). Recall and recognition in mildly disturbed schizophrenics: the use of matched tasks. *Psychological Medicine*, 14(2), 425–429.

Calev, A., Venables, P. H., & Monk, A. F. (1983). Evidence for distinct verbal memory pathologies in severely and mildly disturbed schizophrenics. *Schizophrenia Bulletin*, 9(2), 247–264.

Chan, A. S., Kwok, I. C., Chiu, H., Lam, L., Pang, A., & Chow, L. Y. (2000). Memory and organizational strategies in chronic and acute schizophrenic patients. *Schizophrenia Research*, 41(3), 431–445.

Clare, L., McKenna, P. J., Mortimer, A. M., & Baddeley, A. D. (1993). Memory in schizophrenia: What is impaired and what is preserved? *Neuropsychologia*, 31(11), 1225–1241.

Conway, M. A. (1997). Past and present: Recovered memories and false memories. In M. A. Conway (Ed), *Recovered memories and false memories*. (pp. 150–191). New York: Oxford University Press.

Conway, M. A., & Dewhurst, S. A. (1995). Remembering, familiarity, and source monitoring. *The Quarterly Journal of Experimental Psychology A, Human Experimental Psychology*, 48(1), 125–140.

Conway, M. A., & Pleydell-Pearce, C. W. (2000). The construction of autobiographical memories in the self-memory system. *Psychological Review*, 107(2), 261–288.

Culver, L. C., Kunen, S., & Zinkgraf, S. A. (1986). Patterns of recall in schizophrenics and normal subjects. *Journal of Nervous and Mental Diseases*, 174(10), 620–623.

Danion, J. M, Cuervo, C., Piolino, P., Huron, C., Riutort, M., Peretti, S., et al. (2005). Abnormal subjective sense of self in patients with schizophrenia. *Consciousness and Cognition*, 14(3), 535–47.

Danion, J. M., Gokalsing, E., Robert, P., Massin-Krauss, M., & Bacon, E. (2001). Defective relationship between subjective experience and behavior in schizophrenia. *American Journal of Psychiatry*, 158(12), 2064–2066.

Danion, J. M., Kazès, M., Huron, C., & Karchouni, N. (2003). Do patients with schizophrenia consciously recollect emotional events better than neutral events? *American Journal of Psychiatry*, 160(10), 1879–1881.

Danion, J. M., Rizzo, L., & Bruant, A. (1999). Functional mechanisms underlying impaired recognition memory and conscious awareness in patients with schizophrenia. *Archives of General Psychiatry*, 56(7), 639–644.

Dehaene, S., Artiges, E., Naccache, L., Martelli, C., Viard, A., Schurhoff, F., et al. (2003). Conscious and subliminal conflicts in normal subjects and patients with schizophrenia: The role of the anterior cingulate. *Proceedings of the National Academy of Science USA*, 100(23), 13722–13727.

Eldridge, L. L., Knowlton, B. J., Furmanski, C. S., Bookheimer, S. Y., & Engel, S. A. (2000). Remembering episodes: a selective role for the hippocampus during retrieval. *Nature Neuroscience*, 3(11), 1149–1152.

Ey, H. (1963). *La conscience* [*Consciousness*]. Oxford: Presses Universitaires France.

Franck, N., Farrer, C., Georgieff, N., Marie-Cardine, M., Dalery, J., d'Amato, T., et al. (2001). Defective recognition of one's own actions in patients with schizophrenia. *American Journal of Psychiatry*, 158(3), 454–459.

Frith, C. D. (1992). *The cognitive neuropsychology of schizophrenia*. Hove: Lawrence Erlbaum Associates.

Gardiner, J. M. (2000). On the objectivity of subjective experiences of autonoetic and noetic consciousness. In E. Tulving (Ed.), *Memory, consciousness, and the brain: The Tallinn Conference* (pp. 159–172). Philadelphia: Psychology Press.

Gardiner, J. M., & Java, R. I. (1990). Recollective experience in word and nonword recognition. *Memory and Cognition*, 18(1), 23–30.

Gardiner, J. M., Java, R. I., & Richardson-Klavehn, A. (1996). How level of processing really influences awareness in recognition memory. *Canadian Journal of Experimental Psychology*, 50(1), 114–122.

Gardiner, J. M., & Richardson-Klavehn, A. (2000). Remembering and knowing. In E. Tulving & F. I. M. Craik (Eds.), *Handbook of memory*. Oxford: Oxford University Press.

Gerver, D. (1967). Linguistic rules and the perception and recall of speech by schizophrenic patients. *The British Journal of Social and Clinical Psychology*, 6(3), 204–211.

Gold, J. M., Randolph, C., Carpenter, C. J., Goldberg, T. E., & Weinberger, D. R. (1992). Forms of memory failure in schizophrenia. *Journal of Abnormal Psychology*, 101(3), 487–494.

Goldberg, T. E., Saint-Cyr, J. A., & Weinberger, D. R. (1990). Assessment of procedural learning and problem solving in schizophrenic patients by Tower of Hanoi type tasks. *Journal of Neuropsychiatry and Clinical Neuroscience*, 2(2), 165–173.

Goldberg, T. E., Weinberger, D. R., Pliskin, N. H., Berman, K. F., & Podd, M. H. (1989). Recall memory deficit in schizophrenia. A possible manifestation of prefrontal dysfunction. *Schizophrenia Research*, 2(3), 251–257.

Gras-Vincendon, A., Danion, J. M., Grange, D., Bilik, M., Willard-Schroeder, D., Sichel, J. P., et al. (1994). Explicit memory, repetition priming and cognitive skill learning in schizophrenia. *Schizophrenia Research*, 13(2), 117–126.

Green, M. F. (1996). What are the functional consequences of neurocognitive deficits in schizophrenia? *American Journal of Psychiatry*, 153(3), 321–330.

Harvey, P. D. (1985). Reality monitoring in mania and schizophrenia. The association of thought disorder and performance. *Journal of Nervous and Mental Diseases*, 173(2), 67–73.

Henquet, C., Krabbendam, L., Dautzenberg, J., Jolles, J., Merckelbach, H. (2005). Confusing thoughts and speech: source monitoring and psychosis. *Psychiatry Research*, 133(1), 57–63.

Henson, R. N., Rugg, M. D., Shallice, T., Josephs, O., & Dolan, R. J. (1999). Recollection and familiarity in recognition memory: an event-related functional magnetic resonance imaging study. *Journal of Neurosciences*, 19(10), 3962–3972.

Holmes, J. B., Waters, H. S., Rajaram, S. (1998). The phenomenology of false memories: episodic content and confidence. *Journal of Experimental Psychology: Learning, Memory, and Cognition*, 24(4), 1026–40.

Huron, C., & Danion, J. M. (2002). Impairment of constructive memory in schizophrenia. *International Clinical Psychopharmacology*, 17(3), 127–133.

Huron, C., Danion, J. M., Giacomoni, F., Grangé, D., Robert, P., & Rizzo, L. (1995). Impairment of recognition memory with, but not without, conscious recollection in schizophrenia. *American Journal of Psychiatry*, 152(12), 1737–1742.

Huron, C., Danion, J. M., Rizzo, L., Killofer, V., & Damiens, A. (2003). Subjective qualities of memories associated with the picture superiority effect in schizophrenia. *Journal of Abnormal Psychology*, 112(1), 152–158.

Huron, C., Giersch, A., & Danion, J. M. (2002). Lorazepam, sedation, and conscious recollection: a dose-response study with healthy volunteers. *International Clinical Psychopharmacology*, 17(1), 19–26.

Jacoby, L. L. (1991). A process dissociation framework – separating autonomic from intentional uses of memory. *Journal of Memory and Language*, 30, 513–541.

Johnson, M. K., Hashtroudi, S., & Lindsay, D. S. (1993). Source monitoring. *Psychological Bulletin*, 114(1), 3–28.

Kazès, M., Berthet, L., Danion, J. M., Amado, I., Willard, D., Robert, P., et al. (1999). Impairment of consciously controlled use of memory in schizophrenia. *Neuropsychology*, 13(1), 54–61.

Keefe, R. S., Arnold, M. C., Bayen, U. J., & Harvey, P. D. (1999). Source monitoring deficits in patients with schizophrenia: a multinomial modelling analysis. *Psychological Medicine*, 29(4), 903–914.

Koh, S. D., & Kayton, L. (1974). Memorization of "unrelated" word strings by young nonpsychotic schizophrenics. *Journal of Abnormal Psychology*, 83(1):14–22.

Koh, S. D., Kayton, L., & Berry, R. (1973). Mnemonic organization in young nonpsychotic schizophrenics. *Journal of Abnormal Psychology*, 81(3), 299–310.

Koh, S. D., Marusarz, T. Z., & Rosen, A. J. (1980). Remembering of sentences by schizophrenic young adults. *Journal of Abnormal Psychology*, 89(2), 291–294.

Koh, S. D., & Peterson, R. A. (1978). Encoding orientation and the remembering of schizophrenic young adults. *Journal of Abnormal Psychology*, 87(3), 303–313.

Linscott, R. J., & Knight, R. G. (2001). Automatic hypermnesia and impaired recollection in schizophrenia. *Neuropsychology*, 15(4), 576–585.

Mather, M., Henkel, L. A., & Johnson, M. K. (1997). Evaluating characteristics of false memories: Remember/know judgments and memory characteristics questionnaire compared. *Memory and Cognition*, 25(6), 826–837.

McClain, L. (1983). Encoding and retrieval in schizophrenics' free recall. *Journal of Nervous and Mental Diseases*, 171(8), 471–479.

Michel, L., Danion, J. M., Grange, D., & Sandner, G. (1998). Cognitive skill learning and schizophrenia: Implications for cognitive remediation. *Neuropsychology*, 12(4), 590–599.

Moritz, S., Woodward, T. S., & Ruff, C. C. (2003). Source monitoring and memory confidence in schizophrenia. *Psychological Medicine*, 33(1), 131–139.

Nachmani, G., & Cohen, B. D. (1969). Recall and recognition free learning in schizophrenics. *Journal of Abnormal Psychology*, 74(4), 511–516.

Paulsen, J. S., Heaton, R. K., Sadek, J. R., Perry, W., Delis, D. C., Braff, D., et al. (1995). The nature of learning and memory impairments in schizophrenia. *Journal of the International Neuropsychological Society*, 1(1), 88–99.

Perfect, T. J., Mayes, A. R., Downes, J. J., & Van Eijk, R. (1996). Does context discriminate recollection from familiarity in recognition memory? *The Quarterly Journal of Experimental Psychology A, Human Experimental Psychology*, 49(3), 797–813.

Riutort, M., Cuervo, C., Danion, J. M., Peretti, C. S., & Salame, P. (2003). Reduced levels of specific autobiographical memories in schizophrenia. *Psychiatry Research*, 117(1), 35–45.

Rizzo, L., Danion, J. M., Van Der Linden, M., & Grangé, D. (1996a). Patients with schizophrenia remember that an event has occurred, but not when. *British Journal of Psychiatry*, 168(4), 427–431.

Rizzo, L., Danion, J. M., Van Der Linden, M., Grangé, D., & Rohmer, J. G. (1996b). Impairment of memory for spatial context in schizophrenia. *Neuropsychology*, 10(3), 376–384.

Roediger, H. L., & McDermott, K. B. (1995). Creating false memories: Remembering words not presented in lists. *Journal of Experimental Psychology: Learning, Memory, and Cognition*, 21(4), 803–814.

Rushe, T. M., Woodruff, P. W., Murray, R. M., & Morris, R. G. (1999). Episodic memory and learning in patients with chronic schizophrenia. *Schizophrenia Research*, 35(1), 85–96.

Russell, P. N., Bannatyne, P. A., & Smith, J. F. (1975). Associative strength as a mode of organization in recall and recognition: a comparison of schizophrenics and normals. *Journal of Abnormal Psychology*, 84(2), 122–128.

Russell, P. N., & Beekhuis, M. E. (1976). Organization in memory: a comparison of psychotics and normals. *Journal of Abnormal Psychology*, 85(6), 527–534.

Sass, L. A., & Parnas, J. (2003). Schizophrenia, consciousness, and the self. *Schizophrenia Bulletin*, 29(3), 427–444.

Schacter, D. L., Norman, K. A., & Koutstaal, W. (1998). The cognitive neuroscience of constructive memory. *Annual Review of Psychology*, 49, 289–318.

Schwartz, B. L., Deutsch, L. H., Cohen, C., Warden, D., & Deutsch, S. I. (1991). Memory for temporal order in schizophrenia. *Biological Psychiatry*, 29(4), 329–339.

Sengel, R. A., & Lovallo, W. R. (1983). Effects of cueing on immediate and recent memory in schizophrenics. *Journal of Nervous and Mental Diseases*, 171(7), 426–430.

Shoqeirat, M. A., & Mayes, A. R. (1988). Spatiotemporal memory and rate of forgetting in acute schizophrenics. *Psychological Medicine*, 18(4), 843–853.

Sonntag, P., Gokalsing, E., Olivier, C., Robert, P., Burglen, F., Kauffmann-Muller, F., et al. (2003). Impaired strategic regulation of contents of conscious awareness in schizophrenia. *Consciousness and Cognition*, 12(2), 190–200.

Sullivan, E. V., Shear, P. K., Zipursky, R. B., Sagar, H. J., & Pfefferbaum, A. (1997). Patterns of content, contextual, and working memory impairments in schizophrenia and nonamnesic alcoholism. *Neuropsychology*, 11(2), 195–206.

Traupmann, K. L. (1975). Effects of categorization and imagery on recognition and recall by process and reactive schizophrenics. *Journal of Abnormal Psychology*, 84(4), 307–314.

Truscott, I. P. (1970). Contextual constraint and schizophrenic language. *Journal of Consulting and Clinical Psychology*, 35(2), 189–194.

Tulving, E. (1985). Memory and consciousness. *Canadian Psychology*, 26(1), 1–12.

Vinogradov, S., Willis-Shore, J., Poole, J. H., Marten, E., Ober, B. A., & Shenaut, G. K. (1997). Clinical and neurocognitive aspects of source monitoring errors in schizophrenia. *American Journal of Psychiatry*, 154(11), 1530–1537.

Waters, F. A. V., Maybery, M. T., Badcock, J. C., Michie, P. T. (2004). Context memory and binding in schizophrenia. *Schizophrenia Research*, 68(2-3), 119–125.

Yonelinas, A. P. (2002). The nature of recollection and familiarity: A review of 30 years of research. *Journal of Memory & Language*, 46(3), 441–517.

Yonelinas, A. P., Kroll, N. E. A., Dobbins, I., Lazzara, M., & Knight, R. T. (1998). Recollection and familiarity deficits in amnesia: Convergence of remember-know, process dissociation, and receiver operating characteristic data. *Neuropsychology*, 12(3), 323–339.

CHAPTER 19

Meditation and the Neuroscience of Consciousness: An Introduction

Antoine Lutz, John D. Dunne, and Richard J. Davidson

Abstract

The overall goal of this chapter is to explore the initial findings of neuroscientific research on meditation; in doing so, the chapter also suggests potential avenues of further inquiry. It has three sections that, although integral to the chapter as a whole, may also be read independently. The first section, "Defining Meditation," notes the need for a more precise understanding of meditation as a scientific explanandum. Arguing for the importance of distinguishing the particularities of various traditions, the section presents the theory of meditation from the paradigmatic perspective of Buddhism, and it discusses the difficulties encountered when working with such theories. The section includes an overview of three practices that have been the subject of research, and it ends with a strategy for developing a questionnaire to define more precisely a practice under examination. The second section, "The Intersection of Neuroscience and Meditation," explores some scientific motivations for the neuroscientific examination of meditation in terms of its potential impact on the brain and body of long-term practitioners. After an overview of the mechanisms of mind-body interaction, this section addresses the use of first-person expertise, especially in relation to the potential for research on the neural counterpart of subjective experience. In general terms, the section thus points to the possible contributions of research on meditation to the neuroscience of consciousness. The final section, "Neuroelectric and Neuroimaging Correlates of Meditation," reviews the most relevant neuroelectric and neuroimaging findings of research conducted to date, including some preliminary correlates of the previously discussed Buddhist practices.

Introduction

This chapter discusses possible contributions of meditation to the neurobiological study of consciousness and to cognitive and affective neurosciences in general. Empirical research on meditation started in the 1950s, and as much as 1,000 publications on meditation already exist.[1] Despite such a high number of scientific reports and inspiring theoretical proposals (Austin, 1998; Shapiro & Walsh, 1984; Varela, Thompson, & Rosch, 1991; Wallace, 2003; West, 1987), one still needs to admit that little is known about the neurophysiological processes involved in meditation and about its possible long-term impact on the brain. The lack of statistical evidence, control populations, and rigor of many of the early studies; the heterogeneity of the studied meditative states; and the difficulty in controlling the degree of expertise of practitioners can in part account for the limited contributions made by neuroscience-oriented research on meditation. Thus, instead of providing a complete review of this empirical literature (Austin, 1998; Cahn & Polich, 2006; Delmonte, 1984, 1985; Fenwick, 1987; Holmes, 1984; Pagano & Warrenburg, 1983) we choose to address our central question from three directions.

The purpose of this first section is to clarify conceptually what the term "meditation" means and to propose an operational definition. We focus on Buddhist meditative practices as a canonical example. We provide a short presentation of the main tenets of Buddhist psychology and epistemology, as well as a description of the standard techniques used in many Buddhist practices. From these standard claims, we then derive the possible contributions of meditation to neurosciences and develop tentative proposals for a neuroscientific understanding of the cognitive and affective processes that are altered by training in meditation. In the last section, we review existing neuroelectric and neuroimaging findings on meditation, as well as some preliminary correlates of these Buddhist practices.

1. Defining Meditation

Although widely used, the term "meditation" is often employed in a highly imprecise sense such that its descriptive power is greatly decreased. One underlying reason for the term's inadequacy is that, in its typical usage, it refers generically to an extremely wide range of practices. Thus, in a typical discussion of this kind, West (1987) argues that practices as diverse as the ritual dances of some African tribes, the spiritual exercises of the desert fathers, and the tantric practices of a Tibetan adept are all forms of meditation. Historically, this attempt to categorize diverse practices under the same rubric reflects some intellectual trends in the early 20th century, most especially "perennialism," that argue unequivocally for a certain genre of mystical experience as the essence of religion (Proudfoot, 1985; Sharf, 1998). From the standpoint of the neurosciences, the problem with such a position is that it begins from a set of hypotheses that are difficult to test because they assume that the common element in mystical experience necessarily transcends thought, language, reason, and ordinary perception – most of which are required for any reliable neuroscientific procedure to test the hypotheses.

In addition to the problem of unverifiable hypotheses, the generic use of meditation as applying to such a wide range of diverse practices inevitably trivializes the practices themselves. For example, the unique techniques and context of Sufi *zikr* must be ignored if they are to be considered the same as the Taoist practice of T'ai Chi. In short, to make *zikr* and T'ai Chi describable with the same term, one must ignore a good deal of what makes them radically different from each other. This would be akin to the use of the word "sport" to refer to all sports as if they were essentially the same. A typical result of such an approach is the extremely general model proposed by Fischer (1971) in which all forms of meditation – exemplified by Zazen and some unspecified "Yoga" practice – fall along the same trophotropic scale of hypoarousal, even though attention to the details of many Buddhist practices, including Zazen (Austin, 1998), makes a description in terms of hypoarousal extremely problematic.

An alternative approach to research on meditation is to attend more closely to the particularity of the individual practices in question. An apt metaphor in this case might be the interaction between traditional medical systems and researchers seeking to develop new pharmaceuticals. In their search for plants whose active ingredients might yield effective new medications, some researchers have begun examining traditional medical systems in various cultures in order to narrow their search based on traditional claims about the medicinal properties of local plants (Jayaraman, 2003; Schuster, 2001). In that collaboration, attention to the particularity of the healing tradition is crucial, for it is the local knowledge about specific, local plants that will aid the search for new medications. Clearly, such a project would be gravely hindered if researchers were to assume that, for example, an Amazonian healer's traditional herbal lore would somehow amount to the same traditional knowledge about medicinal herbs that one would hear from a Himalayan healer. The value of consulting a specific tradition is precisely that – through accident or expertise – the tradition may have gleaned some valuable knowledge or developed some practice that is not found elsewhere. This importance of particularity supports the need to preserve local traditions, but it also speaks to the need to heed their boundaries. A common problem with the literature on meditation is a tendency to ignore those boundaries in order to emphasize some vague universality in human experience.

This attention to the particularity of contemplative traditions is related to another aspect of the approach we adopt; namely, that it is also strongly consistent with our knowledge of the neurosciences. Specifically, cognitive and affective neuroscience has matured over the past decade, and we now understand something about the brain mechanisms that subserve different attentional and affective processes. Meditation techniques that target specific underlying processes are thus likely to engage different neural circuitry. If, however, the particularity of a tradition's claims and practices are not examined, the possibility that a practice targets a specific process will not be noted.

Sorting Claims and Descriptions

In emphasizing the particularity of each tradition's approach to meditation, one need not discount the possibility that highly disparate traditions may have independently developed techniques that lead to similar and measurable outcomes.[2] Nevertheless, it seems best not to begin with an assumption about any such innate similarity in disparate meditative traditions. One reason for avoiding such assumptions is the issue of particularity above, but another reason is that similarities among traditions tend to appear primarily in claims about the ultimate meaning or nature of the state attained (e.g., "pure consciousness") or in metaphysically charged phenomenological descriptions (e.g., ineffability) that do not lend themselves to easy measurement or interpretation.

Because similarities among traditions often rest on such issues, an emphasis on those similarities tends to exaggerate a problem that all researchers on meditation must face; namely, the need to discern which parts of a traditional account of meditation are useful in formulating a neuroscientific research strategy, as opposed to parts of an account that are not suitable for that purpose. The problem here is the need to interpret traditional discourse about meditation, especially in terms of meditative techniques and resultant states. In short, traditional accounts often describe techniques and resultant states that are measurable and repeatable; nevertheless, parts of the same account may also focus on issues that can neither be measured nor repeated. In many traditions, the distinction between these parts of an account reflects a tension between (1) close descriptions of meditative techniques and states and (2) the metaphysical or soteriological requirements that must be met by those states, often expressed in textual sources that the tradition considers inviolable.

Let us take as an example the Tibetan practice of "Open Presence," which we discuss further below. In describing Open Presence, traditional authors, such as Wangchug

Dorjé (1989) and Thrangu (Thrangu & Johnson, 2004), offer typically detailed descriptions both of the techniques that induce that state and also of the experiences that should occur when the techniques are applied properly.[3] For example, discursive techniques for de-emphasizing the objectification of sensory content are described in detail, and in terms of resultant states, the consequent loss of a sense of subject-object duality is also articulated clearly. These parts of the traditional account lend themselves to investigation, inasmuch as they describe techniques and results for which neural correlates may be plausibly postulated and tested. At the same time, however, Buddhist philosophical concerns also demand that the state of open presence reflects the ontological foundation of all reality, and Buddhist notions of nirvāṇa also require that the realization of that state will lead the adept to attain inconceivable physical and mental powers. Such claims often occur in texts that traditional scholars are obliged to defend under all circumstances. From a neuroscientific perspective, however, these claims do not lend themselves readily to analysis or description. Thus, from the vantage point of the researcher who stands outside the tradition, it is crucial to separate the highly detailed and verifiable aspects of traditional knowledge about meditation from the transcendental claims that form the metaphysical or theological context of that knowledge.

Meditation as Explanandum

Attention to the particularity of each tradition and the careful examination of traditional knowledge about meditation both contribute to a main concern of this chapter: the notion of meditation as an explanandum. Or, to put the issue another way, how does one define "meditation" in the context of neuroscientific study? This question is not answered easily in part because of the extremely wide variety of human activities to which the term "meditation" might be applied. And the situation may not be much improved even if one focuses on just one tradition. In the case of Buddhism, most traditions use a term for meditation that correlates with the Sanskrit term bhāvanā, literally, "causing to become." In Tibetan traditions, the usual translation for bhāvanā is gôm (sgom), which roughly means "to become habituated to" or "to become familiar with." The meditative traditions of Tibetan Buddhism often employ the term in a generic fashion, and as a result, it is often translated into English with the equally generic term "meditation." The generic usage of gôm or "meditation" reflects its application to a remarkably wide range of contemplative practices: For example, the visualization of a deity, the recitation of a mantra, the visualization of "energy" flowing in the body, the focusing of attention on the breath, the analytical review of arguments or narratives, and various forms of objectless meditations would all be counted as "meditation."

Nevertheless, despite this variety, it is possible to identify some relevant features common to the traditional descriptions of these Buddhist practices, especially when one separates those descriptions from metaphysical arguments or exigencies that stem from defending a textual tradition. First, it is assumed that each such practice induces a predictable and distinctive state (or set of states) whose occurrence is clearly indicated by certain cognitive or physical features or events phenomenally observable to the practitioner. Second, the state induced is said to have a predictable effect on both mind and body in such a way that, by inducing that state repeatedly, a practitioner can allegedly use it to enhance desirable traits and inhibit undesirable ones. Third, the practices are gradual in the sense that the ability to induce the intended state is supposed to improve over time, such that an experienced practitioner should meditate in a manner that is superior to a novice. From the traditional standpoint, this improvement is marked especially by two phenomenally reportable features: the acquisition of certain traits (cognitive, emotional, or physical) and/or the occurrence of certain events (cognitive, emotional, or physical). Finally, the practice used to induce the state must be learned, usually from a meditation teacher who is said to be a virtuoso in the practice. That teacher will also serve as a guide to the practice so as to assist the practitioner in improving his or her ability to produce the state.

Based on these features, these diverse forms of Buddhist meditation may be taken as explananda in regard to three general issues: (1) the claimed production of a distinctive and reproducible state that is phenomenally reportable, (2) the claimed relationship between that state and the development of specific traits, and (3) the claimed progression in the practice from the novice to the virtuoso. Although initially formulated in terms of Tibetan practices, these features seem to be a useful way of understanding how meditative practices in most contemplative traditions may be construed as neuroscientific explananda.

A Paradigmatic Framework: Buddhist Meditative Techniques

Our use of Buddhist contemplative traditions to develop a theoretical framework for understanding meditation is not merely a product of historical accident; rather, Buddhist contemplative traditions are particularly well suited to the development of this kind of theoretical model. The reason, in brief, is that unlike many contemplative traditions, Buddhist traditions tend to offer extensive, precisely descriptive, and highly detailed theories about their practices in a manner that lends itself readily to appropriation into a neuroscientific context. This emphasis on descriptive precision stems from the central role that various forms of meditation play in Buddhist practice. That is, from the standpoint of nearly every Buddhist tradition, some type of meditative technique *must* be employed if one is to advance significantly on the Buddhist spiritual path, and because Buddhism initially developed in a cultural context where a wide range of such techniques were available, Buddhist theoreticians recognized the need to specify exactly the preferred techniques. Their analyses eventually develop

into a highly detailed scholastic tradition known in Sanskrit as the *Abhidharma* – a type of Buddhist "psychology" that also includes discussions of epistemology, philosophy of language, the composition of the material world, and cosmology.[4]

Despite the variety of Buddhist traditions, they share two axioms articulated in *Abhidharma* texts: A central goal of Buddhist practice is the elimination of suffering, and any effective method to eliminate suffering must involve changes in one's cognitive and emotional states, because the root cause of suffering is a set of correctable defects that affect all the mental states of an untrained person (Gethin, 1998). Thus, any practice that is considered by the tradition to be an effective method must involve the features noted above, including some set of reliable techniques that induce mental states that will induce the desired changes in behavioral and psychological traits. In this regard, the Buddhist contemplative traditions exhibit considerable diversity, because they hold divergent opinions about the precise nature of the defects to be eliminated, the traits to be induced, and the best methods for accomplishing all this. At the same time, both the diversity and the continuity of Buddhist contemplative practices also stem from the rich cultural context in which Buddhism initially flourished.

EARLY HISTORY AND BASIC FORMS
When the historical Buddha Śākyamuni first set out on the religious life (ca. 500 BCE), he apparently encountered a large number of meditative techniques that were already being practiced by various contemplative traditions in South Asia. Although historical sources from this period are generally vague in their descriptions of contemplative practices, one can identify some common trends. Broadly speaking, these traditions maintained that the contemplative life should be focused on the search for one's true self (often called the *ātman*), and because this true self was generally assumed to be somehow obscured by one's involvement in the world of the senses, many contemplative techniques involved an inward

focus whereby one's mind was retracted from the senses. In addition to this inward focus, most techniques from this period probably sought to reduce the occurrence of other types of mental content – generically called "conceptuality" *(kalpanā)* – that were also thought to obscure one's vision of the true self. Distractions caused by the fluctuation of the mind were commonly thought to be linked to the fluctuation of the breath, and meditative techniques therefore often involved either breath control *(prāṇāyāma)* or at least some attention to the disposition of the breath. And because the mind was thought to be strongly influenced by the body, contemplative practices involved specific postures or corporeal exercises (Bronkhorst, 1986; Gethin, 1998).

When these practices were appropriated by the historical Buddha Śākyamuni, their overall context was altered, inasmuch as the Buddha maintained that the belief in a "true self" *(ātman)* was completely mistaken. Indeed, from the earliest days a central goal of Buddhist contemplative practice is precisely to demonstrate to the practitioner that no such fixed or absolute identity could ever be possible (Gethin, 1998). Nevertheless, although the Buddha altered the context of the contemplative practices that he encountered, the Buddhist meditative techniques that he and his followers developed retained some of the same basic principles of inward focus, reduction of conceptuality, the importance of the breath, and the relevance of the body.

Perhaps the most ubiquitous style of Buddhist meditation that exhibits these features is meditation aimed at improving concentration – a style of meditation that is rooted in practices aimed at obtaining *śamatha.* Translatable literally as "quiescence," *śamatha* is a state in which the practitioner is able to maintain focus on an object for a theoretically unlimited period of time. As a term, *śamatha* therefore can also describe one of the historically earliest and most basic styles of Buddhist meditation that aims at attaining that state. In such a practice, the practitioner augments especially a mental faculty known as *smṛti,* confusingly trans-

lated as both "mindfulness" and "awareness"; in simple terms, it is the mental function *(caittāsika)* that focuses the mind on an object. At the same time, the meditation involves a faculty that checks to see whether the *smṛti* is focused on the intended object or whether it has lost the object. Thus, this other faculty, often called *samprajanya,* involves a type of meta-awareness that is not focused on an object per se, but rather is an awareness of that intentional relation itself (Gethin, 1998; Silananda, 1990; Wallace, 1999).

Both as a state and as a style of practice, *śamatha* provides the practical and theoretical underpinnings of many other Buddhist practices, especially because it constitutes the basic paradigm for any practice that involves one-pointed concentration *(ekāgratā)* on a specific object. At the same time, however, Buddhist theorists who discuss *śamatha* generally do not consider it to be in and of itself Buddhist. That is, practices oriented toward attaining *śamatha* must create a highly developed ability to sustain intense focus on an object, and whereas the development of that ability does lead to some trait changes, it does not lead to all of the changes that Buddhists seek, most especially in regard to the regulation of emotions. Hence, although a *śamatha*-oriented practice may be a necessary ingredient of most Buddhist contemplative traditions, it must be accompanied by another fundamental style of Buddhist practice; namely *vipaśyanā* or "insight." (Gethin, 1998; Silananda, 1990; Wallace, 1999).

As with the *śamatha* style of practice, *vipaśyanā* is also one of the earliest and most fundamental forms of meditation. For Buddhist theorists, *vipaśyanā* is a style of meditation that, in combination with the focus or stability provided by cultivating *śamatha,* enables the practitioner to gain insight into one's habits and assumptions about identity and emotions. In general, this insight includes especially the realization of "selflessness" *(nairātmya)* – that is, realizing that one's belief in a fixed, essential identity is mistaken and hence that the emotional habits that reflect that belief are baseless (Dalai Lama XIV, 1995; Gethin, 1998; Silananda, 1990). Nevertheless, although every Buddhist contemplative tradition would agree that such a realization must be part of *vipaśyanā*, one again encounters considerable diversity in the precise way in which *vipaśyanā* is defined and the way it is developed in practice. For example, in some traditions reasoning and a type of internal conceptual discourse are critical to the practice, but other traditions maintain that reason and concepts are of only limited use in obtaining *vipaśyanā*. Likewise, some traditions maintain that a *vipaśyanā* meditation must have an object toward which some type of analysis is brought to bear (Dalai Lama XIV, 1995; Silananda, 1990), whereas others maintain that the meditation must eventually become completely objectless (Wangchug Dorjé, 1989). Perhaps the sole theme that runs throughout all Buddhist traditions is that, in *vipaśyanā* meditation, the type of meta-awareness mentioned earlier plays an especially important role – an issue that we examine in the section on the theory of meditation.

FURTHER HISTORICAL DEVELOPMENTS
Although the basic combination of *śamatha* and *vipaśyanā* provides both a theoretical and historical touchstone for the development of Buddhist contemplative practices, a number of other forms of meditation were developed in the various Buddhist communities of Asia. Three practices initially developed in India are especially emblematic of the range of developments: "Recollection of the Buddha" meditations *(buddhānusmṛti)*, Lovingkindness meditation *(maitrībhāvanā)*, and tantric "Wind" *(vāyu)* meditations.

The practice of Recollection of the Buddha is probably, along with Lovingkindness meditation, one of the oldest Buddhist practices. Recollection involves the recitation of the Buddha's attributes, and in its earliest form it may have involved nothing more than that. At some point, however, the recitation of the Buddha's physical attributes was linked with the visualization of the Buddha in the space in front of the prac-

titioner. This basic technique of recitation and visualization is representative of a wide range of similar Buddhist practices that evolved during the first millennium. Chief among these is the practice of visualizing deities and paradisiacal environments, a technique especially important in most forms of Buddhist tantra (Beyer, 1977).

Alongside Recollection (and later, visualization) practices, Lovingkindness meditation was also a widespread practice in both early and later Buddhism, where it is thematized as the cultivation of "great compassion" *(mahākaruṇā)*. The practice aims to cultivate an emotional state; namely, a sense of love and compassion toward all living things. Representative of a wide range of practices that promote or inhibit traits by repeatedly inducing a particular emotional state, some forms of the practice involve the recitation/visualization techniques employed in Recollection meditation. Some discursive strategies, such as thinking through the steps of an argument for compassion, may also be employed (Dalai Lama XIV, 1991; P. Williams, 1989).

Last to develop (toward the end of the first millennium in India) are a variety of practices that may be called tantric Wind meditations. These practices aim to manipulate the various forms of energy, metaphorically called Wind *(vāyu)*, that are alleged to flow in channels throughout the body. This model is roughly analogous to the contemporary understanding of the nervous system, where the notion of Wind is analogous to the propagation of neural impulses. In the Buddhist model, the mind itself is thought to consist of such Wind energy, and practices that manipulated that energy were therefore intended to induce or inhibit mental states or traits. The many techniques employed include the visualization of various syllables or other items at specific points in the body as a means to alter the flow of mental energy; physical exercises, including breathing exercises; and an array of other techniques, including manipulation of the diet. An example of this style of practice that later becomes important in Tibet is the "Tummo" *(gtum mo)* practice – a method that, in manipulating the Wind, is also said to generate considerable body heat as a byproduct (Cozort, 1986; Dalai Lama XIV, 1995; English, 2002; Snellgrove, 2002).

As Buddhism spread from its initial location in the Gangetic plain, Buddhist practitioners developed and enhanced the above practices, along with many other related forms of meditation. Eventually, Buddhism spread to other regions of Asia, and various traditions arose that persist to this day. Each tradition elaborated its own particular interpretation of techniques that, although likely inherited from Indian Buddhist traditions, always acquired a local flavor. Nevertheless, most extant practices reflect the various styles of meditation noted above.

ANALYSIS OF MEDITATION: ŚAMATHA AND VIPAŚYANĀ AS PARADIGM

To aid in the mastery of meditative techniques – and also to respond to critics outside their traditions – Buddhist theoreticians in India and elsewhere developed detailed accounts of their contemplative practices. These accounts are often extremely complex, and as noted above, they sometimes raise metaphysical issues that are not easily addressed in neuroscience. Likewise, to some degree the accounts are shaped by the need to defend a particular textual tradition or line of argumentation, and as a result, some statements that seem to be descriptive are not known to be exemplified by any actual Buddhist practice. Nevertheless, other aspects of the accounts seem more empirical in their approach, and attention to those aspects may prove useful when examining meditation in a laboratory context. With this in mind, we have sketched the following practical and simplified account of Buddhist meditation theory, aimed especially at researchers interested in studying contemplative practices in Buddhism and other traditions. As one might expect, the numerous forms of Buddhist meditation are accompanied by an equally wide range of theoretical accounts. Nevertheless, the central issues can be addressed in terms of the theories that undergird *śamatha* and *vipaśyanā*, especially when these styles of meditation are under-

stood to describe *two aspects of the same meditative state*. In the interest of both applicability and simplicity, we derive our account primarily from a specific and living contemplative tradition: Tibetan Buddhism.

Drawing on a maxim developed by their Indian predecessors, Tibetan theorists maintain that the highest forms of Buddhist meditation must integrate the qualities of *śamatha* and *vipaśyanā* into a single practice. As described by the most common traditional metaphor, the practitioner cannot make significant spiritual advancement without the combination of *śamatha* and *vipaśyanā*, just as a cart cannot move without two wheels. Another traditional metaphor is perhaps more descriptive: When attempting to see the murals on the wall of a dark cave, one must use a lamp that is both well shielded and bright. If the lamp is not well shielded, then its flame will flicker or even become extinguished, and if its flame is not sufficiently intense, the lamp's light will be insufficient for the task at hand (Tsongkhapa, 2002). This very basic metaphor describes the qualities that are indicated by the terms *śamatha* and *vipaśyanā*: The former primarily concerns the stability *(gnas cha)* of the meditative state, whereas the latter concerns that state's phenomenal or subjective intensity *(gsal cha)* (Thrangu & Johnson, 2004).

To state these features more precisely, in meditations that involve an object, stability refers to the degree to which the practitioner is able to retain focus on the object without interruption. In such meditations, clarity refers to the sharpness or vividness of the appearance of the object in awareness. For example, in the visualization of a colored disc, a completely stable meditation would be one in which the meditator's focus on the object is not perturbed at all by other phenomenal events, such as emotions, thoughts, or sensory perceptions. In such a meditation, the clarity would be constituted by the disc's vividness of color and sharpness of shape.

Generally, these two aspects of a meditative state are understood to work somewhat at odds with each other in the case of novice meditators. That is, in the case of a novice, the greater the stability of the meditative state, the more likely is it to lack intensity. And the greater its intensity, the more likely is its lack of stability. This tension between stability and clarity is expressed in the two main flaws that hinder a meditation: "dullness" (Tib., *bying ba*) and "excitement" (Tib., *rgod pa*). When dullness first arises, the focus on the object will be retained, but as dullness progresses, the clarity of the object becomes progressively hindered, and a sensation of drowsiness overtakes the meditator. If dullness continues, the dimness of the object will cause the meditator to lose focus on it, or in the case of gross dullness, the meditator will simply fall asleep. In contrast, when excitement occurs, the clarity of the object will often increase, but the intensity of the mental state perturbs the meditation such that distractions easily arise and focus on the object is lost (Thrangu & Johnson, 2004; Tsongkhapa, 2002; Wangchug Dorjé, 1989).

In most practices, the ideal meditative state – one beyond the novice stage – is a state in which neither dullness nor excitement occurs; in short, stability and clarity are balanced perfectly. Hence, for the Tibetan contemplative traditions (and indeed, for nearly every other Buddhist tradition), it would be incorrect to interpret Buddhist meditation as "relaxation." This is not to deny the importance of mental and physical techniques that help the practitioner relax. Without such techniques, an excess of physical or mental tension may develop, and when such tension occurs, excitement will almost certainly arise. If, however, such relaxation techniques are overused, they are likely to propel the practitioner into dullness and hence hinder the meditation. Indeed, from a Buddhist perspective a practice that only relaxes the mind might eventually prove harmful. That is, such a practice would develop a great deal of dullness, and as a result the practitioner might become withdrawn, physically inactive, and mentally depressed. Overall, then, Buddhist meditations avoid an excess of relaxation, and it is for this reason that very few practices are done while lying down. It is also

worth noting that, just as the tradition contains techniques to ease mental or physical tension, it also espouses methods to counteract an excess of relaxation or dullness (Thrangu & Johnson, 2004; Tsongkhapa, 2002; Wangchug Dorjé, 1989).

Although the balance of clarity and stability as described above forms an overall paradigm for Tibetan Buddhist practices, it is important to recognize the ways in which that paradigm is modified for each practice. For example, novices hoping to develop the meditative state of *Rigpa Chôgzhag* or "Open Presence" may be taught to emphasize one or another feature in order to make initial headway in the practice. In short, they are encouraged to err on the side of clarity, because it is more important to avoid dullness than excitement in the early stages of that practice (Thrangu & Johnson, 1984; Wangchug Dorjé, 1989).

The practice of Open Presence raises another issue: the applicability of this model to meditations that do not focus on an object. In objectless practice, the loss of focus on the object or its degree of phenomenal vividness obviously cannot be taken as criteria for the degree of stability or clarity. Instead, stability becomes a marker for the ease and frequency with which the meditator is perturbed out of the state the meditation is intended to induce, and clarity refers to the subjective intensity of that induced state. Thus, after a session of Open Presence, a meditator who reports that the meditation was unstable but very clear would mean that, although the intended state was interrupted repeatedly, the subjective experience of the state was especially intense when it occurred.

A final aspect of the basic theory of meditation concerns the distinction between the actual meditative state (Tib., *dngos gzhi*) and the post-meditative state (Tib., *rjes thob*). In brief, the states developed in meditation are usually thought to create a post-meditative effect. In some cases, some phenomenal aspect of the meditation persists in the post-meditative state. For example, after a meditation in which one cultivates the experience of phenomenal content as seeming dreamlike, one's perceptions in the post-meditative state are also said to have a dreamlike quality for at least some period after arising out of meditation. In other cases, the post-meditative state involves a trait change. Meditation on love and compassion, for example, is alleged to inhibit the occurrence of anger between meditative sessions. From the Buddhist theoretical perspective, such post-meditative changes are often at least as important as the states induced during the meditation itself, and success in a practice is often measured by the strength of the effects that occur after meditation (Dalai Lama XIV, 1995; Thrangu & Johnson, 1984; Tsongkhapa, 2002; Wangchug Dorjé, 1989).

CONTEMPORARY PRACTICE AND
PROBLEMS OF TERMINOLOGY

In the laboratory setting neuroscientific researchers are likely to encounter Buddhists who engage in contemplative practices located in three overall traditions: the Vipassanā or Insight Meditation movement located within Theravāda Buddhism, the Zen tradition of Japan, and the Tibetan tradition. One might encounter practices from other Buddhist traditions, but the meditations of the aforementioned three traditions are by far the most widespread. They are also the most likely to be practiced by persons, such as Europeans and North Americans, who are not native to the cultures in which the practices have developed (Coleman, 2002). Of these three traditions, the style of meditation taught in the Vipassanā traditions is especially emblematic, because the basic meditative style of Vipassanā closely resembles some foundational practices in the Zen and Tibetan traditions.

The Vipassanā or Insight Meditation movement consists of several loosely allied institutions and individuals that teach a style of meditation rooted in the older contemplative traditions of Theravāda Buddhism in Myanmar, Thailand, and Śrī Laṅka. Although it draws on older traditions, the Vipassanā movement is "modern" in that it makes a somewhat simplified and regu-

larized set of meditation instructions available to a wide population that is not limited to celibate monastics (Coleman, 2002). In its most typical form, the early stage of Vipassanā practice consists largely of a basic *śamatha* style of meditation focused on the sensation made by the breath as it flows in and out of the nostrils, although sometimes another aspect of the breath may be taken as the object of meditation (Gunaratana, 2002). In the early stages, the aim of the meditation is to keep the attention focused on the breath without distraction – that is, without the attention wandering to some other object, such as a sensation or a memory. For beginners (and even for advanced practitioners), the attention inevitably wanders, and the usual instruction is to recognize that the mind has wandered – for example, to see that it is now focused on the pain in one's knee, rather than on one's breath – and then to "drop" or "release" the distraction (the knee pain) and return to the breath. Part of the aim is not only to develop focused attention on the breath but also to develop two other faculties: a meta-awareness that recognizes when one's attention is no longer on the breath and an ability to redirect the attention without allowing the meta-awareness to become a new source of distraction, as when one berates oneself for allowing the mind to wander (Gunaratana, 2002; Kabat-Zinn, 2005).

Given the description thus far, practices very similar to Vipassanā meditation are also found among contemporary practitioners of Zen and Tibetan Buddhism. Indeed, it is possible that the Vipassanā approach to meditation on the breath has led Zen and Tibetan practitioners to employ a similar style of breath-meditation to a much greater extent than they have in the past. Certainly, it is clear that in contemporary Zen and Tibetan practice, focusing the attention on the breath (or sometimes another static object) is often used as a means to develop the basic level of concentration required for more advanced forms of meditation. In many cases, these more advanced meditations aim to enhance the type of meta-awareness that is cultivated during the Vipassanā style of practice, and because the traditions have different ways of understanding and enhancing that meta-awareness, all three kinds of traditions – Vipassanā, Zen, and Tibetan Buddhism – diverge in their practices from this point forward.

Although Vipassanā meditation may be especially representative of a widespread and foundational style of practice in contemporary Buddhism, any discussion of Vipassanā meditation must address a problem of terminology: the often confusing use of the terms "mindfulness" and "awareness." In the Mindfulness-Based Stress Reduction (MBSR) designed by Jon Kabat-Zinn (2005), for example, the term "mindfulness" is used primarily to refer not to the focusing aspect of mind, but rather to the meta-awareness that surveys that focus and its relation to the intended object. Likewise, in MBSR the term "awareness" sometimes seems to stand primarily for attention or the focusing aspect of mind. In contrast, popular works on Tibetan Buddhist meditation, such as the work of Thrangu (Thrangu & Johnson, 2004), use these same two terms, but their meaning is reversed: "mindfulness" refers to attention or focus, whereas "awareness" refers to a faculty of mind that surveys the mental state at a meta-level.

The confusion in English terminology is in part due to some confusion in the proper usage of the Buddhist technical terms themselves. Strictly speaking, *smṛti* – literally, "memory" – is the focusing aspect of mind, and historically it is often translated as mindfulness when used in the context of meditation. An obvious case is the common technical term *smṛtyupasthāna* (in Pāli, *satipaṭṭhāna*), usually rendered as "foundation of mindfulness." The problem, however, is that even though *smṛti* should stand only for the focusing aspect of mind, in both popular and technical Buddhist literature on meditation it is not infrequently assimilated to the meta-awareness mentioned above. One reason for this is that in the Vipassanā tradition, meditations that initially emphasize *smṛti* as the focusing faculty are them-

selves used as a means to thoroughly develop meta-awareness *(samprajanya* or *prajñā)* at a later stage in the practice (Gunaratana, 2002). It is therefore not surprising that *smṛti* becomes closely associated with the meta-awareness, but this imprecise use of *smṛti* has contributed to the confusion concerning the English terms "mindfulness" and "awareness."

To restate the problem using the terms discussed earlier, we should note that such authors as Thrangu (Thrangu & Johnson, 2004) employ the term "mindfulness" to refer to the *śamatha* aspect of a meditative practice – that is, the stability of the meditation. And these authors then use "awareness" for the *vipaśyanā* aspect of the practice; that is, the meta-awareness that is especially associated with the clarity of the meditation. Turning then to its usage in, for example, MBSR, one finds that mindfulness refers primarily to the *vipaśyanā* aspect of the practice, not the *śamatha* aspect.

Although this problem is simply one of terminology, it can prove quite confusing in a laboratory setting. In the case of Open Presence practice, Tibetan meditators will usually deny that their practice is of mindfulness (i.e., *dran pa'i nyer gzhag*), whereas in fact, they mean to say that they are emphasizing the development of some meta-awareness in a way that has many parallels with the mindfulness practice of Vipassanā meditators or persons trained in MBSR. For the researcher, one solution to this problem is again to be attentive to the particularities of the practice in question while keeping track of the fact that we have yet to standardize the English lexicon of technical terms for the analysis of meditation.

Another problem of terminology comes with the use of the term *śamatha* itself, especially in its Tibetan context. Our discussion thus far has used the term *śamatha* in three basic meanings: (1) a particular state in which one can allegedly focus on an object for an unlimited period of time, (2) a style of practice aimed at attaining that state, and (3) the aspect of any meditative state that constitutes its maximal stability. Already, these three meanings can lead to considerable ambiguity, but the second meaning is particularly troublesome. One problem is simply that the expression "*śamatha* meditation" is not sufficiently clear. That is, when Buddhist theorists are being precise, they recognize that *śamatha* meditation should be rendered more properly as "meditation aimed at obtaining *śamatha*."

But even after this clarification, a problem remains: When one practices *śamatha* meditation, which kind of *śamatha* is one trying to obtain? In other words, is one attempting to cultivate the ability to concentrate on an object for an unlimited period? Or is one trying to cultivate some other kind of maximal stability? The main problem here is that, in the Tibetan context, the term *śamatha* is used to refer to stability in meditations that do not even have an object; hence, in those cases *śamatha* cannot relate to concentration on an object. To make the matter even more complicated, there are Tibetan practices in which *śamatha* is used in connection with both kinds of meditations (i.e., with an object and without an object). Finally, even when *śamatha* is related to practices with an object, the object in question may differ considerably; an example with neuroscientific import is the difference between focus on the breath and focus on a visualized object. Indeed, traditional scholars, such as Thrangu (Thrangu & Johnson, 2004, p. 21), with all these issues in mind, caution their students about the potential for confusion caused by the ambiguity of technical terms such as *śamatha*.

As with the case of mindfulness and awareness, the problems with the term "*śamatha*" should remind researchers that the particularities of a practice may be obscured by ambiguous terminology, whether in the source language or in English translation. As a practical matter, one may even wish to avoid the term *śamatha* as a description of a practice. This is not to say that the term should be abandoned: Clearly, for both historical and theoretical reasons, *śamatha* must remain in the lexicon on Buddhist meditation. But when seeking to specify exactly what a practitioner is doing during meditation, it may be more useful to use other Buddhist terms as labels for a particular practice – or perhaps researchers will develop new terms in dialogue with practitioners. Otherwise, if one is not careful, one may be misled into believing that a wide set of disparate practices are the same because, for one reason or another, they may all be called "*śamatha* meditation."

Three Meditative States in Tibetan Buddhism

We have mentioned repeatedly the importance of attending to the particularity of the contemplative tradition whose practices might become part of a research agenda, and with this in mind, we now discuss briefly three specific forms of meditation found in Tibetan Buddhism. Part of our aim is to set the ground for a discussion of these practices, because they have already been the subjects of some preliminary neuroscientific research, as is presented below.

All three styles of meditation come from a particular strand of contemplative practice in contemporary Tibetan Buddhism. In Tibetan, a term for this style of practice is *Chag-zôg (phyag rdzogs)*, a compound that refers to two traditions of meditation: the "Great Seal" or *Chag-chen (phyag chen;* Skt. *Mahāmudrā)* of the Kargyü *(bka' brgyud)* school and the "Great Perfection" or *Dzôg-chen* (Karma Chagmé, 2000) of the Nying-ma *(Rnying ma)* or "Ancient" school. Although historically and institutionally distinct, for the last 200 years the Great Seal and Great Perfection traditions have become allied so closely that it is now exceedingly rare to find a practitioner who employs the techniques of only one style in complete isolation from the techniques of the other style. This is not to say, however, that there are no important differences between these two traditions. They differ especially in the details of their most advanced practices, and they also propose slightly different techniques for the three meditations discussed below. Nevertheless, for the purposes of the brief descriptions below, they may be treated as constituting a single overall style of contemplative practice.

The three practices in question are *Tsé-cig Ting-ngé-dzin (rtse gcig ting nges 'dzin)* or Focused Attention, *Rig-pa Chôg-zhag (rig pa cog bzhag)* or Open Presence, *and Mig-mé Nying-jé (dmigs med snying rje)* or Non-Referential Compassion. All meditators in the *Chag-zôg* style receive at least some instruction in all three of these practices, and all advanced meditators will be thoroughly familiar with them.

FOCUSED ATTENTION (*TSÉ-CIG TING-NGÉ-DZIN*)

The Tibetan term *Tsé-cig Ting-ngé-dzin* or "Focused Attention" refers to a mental state in which the mind is focused unwaveringly and clearly on a single object. This state, which literally translates as "one-pointed concentration," occurs in many practices, and it is a typical goal for novices in the *Chag-zôg* traditions. The relevant Buddhist theories and techniques are usually drawn from a generic account of practices that seek to develop *śamatha* in the sense of the ability to focus on an object for an unlimited time. This generic account, sometimes called "common *śamatha*" *(thun mong gi zhi gnas)*, differs from the present context. That is, in actual practice, *Chag-zôg* practitioners of Focused Attention usually develop a lesser (and often unspecified) state of concentration before being instructed by their teachers to move on to other practices, which no longer involve focusing on an object (Thrangu & Johnson, 2004). Nevertheless, the practice of cultivating Focused Attention draws heavily on the theories and techniques of common *śamatha*. Perhaps the most important principles drawn from that generic account can be summarized under six overall issues: the setting, the body posture, the object, the flaws that hinder progress, the "antidotes" to the flaws, and the stages of development in meditation (Tsongkhapa, 2002).

Although sometimes neglected in scholarly work on Buddhist meditation, the setting for meditation is clearly considered by traditional authors to be an important element in developing the ability to concentrate on an object (Thrangu & Johnson, 2004; Tsongkhapa, 2002; Wangchug Dorjé, 1989). One aspect of setting is the context formed by the other practices in which a meditator is engaged. These practices include especially formal guidance received from one's preceptor, the study of Buddhist thought, a wide range of devotional practices, and the observance of a basic moral code based upon non-harm *(ahiṃsā)* and compassion. Another aspect of setting concerns the site where one is to meditate. In this regard, traditional accounts speak at length about the need for a quiet place with few distractions and adequate access to food and water. So too, the spot to be used for meditation is prepared by the meditator on a daily basis by cleaning it and preparing it through various ritual activities.

Once preparations for the session are complete, the meditator adopts the posture for meditation. Various styles of Tibetan meditation involve different postures, but in the context of developing Focused Attention, the general rule is that the spine must be kept straight and that the rest of the body must be neither too tense nor too lax (Thrangu & Johnson, 1984; Tsongkhapa, 2002; Wangchug Dorjé, 1989). At this point, another element of the setting – the use of memorized formulas to induce the proper conceptual attitude – is invoked, and depending on the practice in question, a number of other practices or ritual activities may precede the portion of the practice in which one seeks to develop Focused Attention.

When actually engaged in the practice of Focused Attention, the meditator focuses the mind on the object to be meditated upon. This object may be a sensory object, such as a visible object in front of the meditator, or it might be mental, such as a visualized image (Thrangu & Johnson, 2004; Wangchug Dorjé, 1989). In general, Tibetan practitioners do not use the breath as an object of meditation, except perhaps for relatively brief periods as a means to settle the mind (Thrangu & Johnson, 2004). This trend may be changing, however, in part because of the modern encounter with other Buddhist traditions. To a great extent, the particular object chosen depends largely on the particular practice (such as tantric visualization or Open Presence) that forms the overall context for the development of Focused Attention.

Having placed the attention on the object, the meditator then seeks to avoid two overall flaws: dullness and excitement. As mentioned above, in the early stages, these flaws manifest in a straightforward fashion. Dullness is detected by, for example, a dimming or blurring of the object and, in its most gross form, a sensation of drowsiness. The main symptom of excitement is distraction (i.e., the intensity of the focus causes one to be hyperaroused, and as a result, attention wanders to other mental content or phenomena; Thrangu & Johnson, 1984; Tsongkhapa, 2002; Wangchug Dorjé, 1989).

In practice, the usual technique to counteract excitement is to become aware of the occurrence of the distracting content or phenomenon – that is, one notes the fact that the mind is now attending to another object, and then one returns the mind to the intended object without allowing the original distraction to produce more mental distractions, such as the thought, "It is not good to be distracted" (Thrangu & Johnson, 2004). Sometimes excitement is also caused by physical or environmental factors – too much tension in the body or too much bright light in the meditation area, for example. Or, excitement may be caused by applying too much effort to the meditation (i.e., being too rigid in one's focus). Similarly, in the case of visualized objects, excitement might be caused by too much intensity or brightness in the visualized object. Sometimes an affective remedy is used; for example, the meditator might temporarily switch to a contemplation of suffering, and the affective impact of that contemplation will reduce excitement enough that one can return to the original object of meditation. Various visualizations – such as visualizing a small black drop behind the navel – may also be employed to counteract excitement and allow the meditator to return to the original object of meditation (Wangchug Dorjé, 1989).

In terms of dullness, methods to counteract it are often related to those that counteract excitement. For example, just as one might counteract excitement by meditating in a dimly lit room, one can counteract dullness by meditating in a brightly lit setting. So too, adding tension to the body or intensity to a visualized object can also counteract dullness. And in terms of affective methods, the meditator might temporarily contemplate joy or compassion (and sometimes even fear) so as to energize the mind enough to return to the original object. As with excitement, visualizations may also be employed; for example, one may visualize a white dot on one's forehead at the point between the eyes (Wangchug Dorjé, 1989).

For advanced meditators, many of the "antidotes" mentioned here are too coarse, and they would lead to an overcorrection in the meditation. For these practitioners, the subtle degree of dullness or excitement that they encounter is corrected by equally subtle adjustments to the clarity (for dullness) or the stability (for excitement) of the meditation state until both stability and clarity reach their maximal, balanced state.

The notion that advanced meditators employ different responses to flaws in meditation raises the final relevant issue in traditional accounts; namely, the theories about the progression of stages in meditation. Many contemplative traditions speak of ascending stages through which the practitioner passes; a typical account speaks of nine levels of progressively higher degrees of concentration along with corresponding changes in the meditator's response to dullness and excitement (Thrangu & Johnson, 1984; Tsongkhapa, 2002; Wangchug Dorjé, 1989). This schema, however, is far more complicated than it seems, and as Apple (2003) demonstrates, the Buddhist penchant for scholasticism makes this topic an extremely complicated one when it is considered in its fullest form. Without going into great detail, it is important to note that, according to these schemas, a single practice may progress gradually through a number of meditative states, but some of those states might differ significantly from each other both phenomenally and in terms of the appropriate technique to be applied. Likewise, the mental and physical effects of a practice may build gradually; for example, as one's level of concentration improves, mental and physical well-being is also said to increase But some effects occur only at some stages and do not progress further (Tsongkhapa, 2002).

In terms of the most relevant effects that are traditionally expected to arise from this practice, the main result of Focused Attention is a greater ability to concentrate and a concomitant decrease in susceptibility to being perturbed out of a concentrated state. The practice is also thought to increase not only the stability of one's concentration but also its intensity. At the higher levels of practice, this type of meditation is also said to reduce the need for sleep, and during the meditation it is thought to induce pleasurable sensations, including a lightness or pliancy of mind and body.

OPEN PRESENCE (*RIG-PA CHÔG-ZHAG*)

Open presence or *Rig-pa Chôg-zhag* is one of the main meditative states that practitioners following the *Chag-zôg* style of practice attempt to cultivate. The basic motivation for the practice is rooted in a Buddhist axiom mentioned earlier: Namely, that one's negative emotional habits and behaviors arise from a set of mental flaws that cause one to consistently misconstrue both one's identity and also the objects toward which those emotions and behaviors are directed. As noted above, those flaws are meant to be corrected by *vipaśyanā* meditation through which one cultivates an accurate understanding of the nature of one's identity and the nature of objects in the world. In this sense, Open Presence may be considered a particular version of *vipaśyanā*. *Chag-zôg* theorists, however, have a unique understanding of what it means to gain the understanding or "wisdom" (Tib. *ye shes*) that

counteracts flaws by seeing the true nature of identity and objects. And because the practice involves many discursive strategies that are based upon an underlying theory, one must have some sense of those theoretical underpinnings. Hence, even though our presentation aims to focus on empirical descriptions of what practitioners actually do, a brief foray into more abstract theory is necessary. Our theoretical discussion is based on three authors who are typical of the *Chag-zôg* traditions: Karma Chagmé (2000), Thrangu (Thrangu & Johnson, 2004), and Wangchug Dorjé (1989). Our concise and thematic presentation, however, might not be satisfactory to a strict traditionalist, in part because the issues involved are notoriously difficult to explain. Nevertheless, from an academic and anthropological standpoint, this presentation should suffice to convey the main theoretical issues relevant to this style of contemplation as it is practiced currently.

Theoretical Background. When justifying and explaining the types of practices that induce Open Presence, *Chag-zôg* theorists, such as Karma Chagmé (2000), Thrangu (Thrangu & Johnson, 2004), and Wangchug Dorjé (1989), argue that, properly speaking, objects are only known through experience; it is nonsensical to speak of objects separate from experience. Likewise, experience of an object necessarily involves a subject that experiences the object, and it is therefore nonsensical to speak of objects without speaking of a subject. The theoretical linchpin is that the nature of both objects and subjects is that which characterizes them under any circumstances – it must be essential to them, rather than accidental. And what is essential to them is that they always occur within experience. Hence, to know the nature of objects and subjects is to know the nature of experience (Thrangu & Johnson, 2004).

Whatever may be the philosophical merits of such an analysis, *Chag-zôg* practitioners are thus aiming to understand the nature of experience – that which is essential to any instance of experience, regardless of the accidental and changing features of the objects or subjectivities involved. To do so, they employ a set of techniques that are intended to make the practitioner aware of the invariable feature of all experiences. They speak of this invariable feature using various descriptions, including *Rigpa*, "Awareness," or, using the metaphor of light, *Selwa (gsal ba)*, "Luminosity" or "Clarity." But whether called Awareness, Clarity, or some other synonym, the point is that the invariant element in experience is that which, from a phenomenal standpoint, makes it possible for the subject-object relation to be presented in experience.

As the alleged invariant in all states of knowing, Awareness contrasts with features that are accidental (i.e., not essential) to any given cognition; namely, the particular features of the object and subject occurring within the cognition. What is accidental about the object are its characteristics, such as color or shape. And what is accidental about a subject is, for example, its temporal location in the narrative of personal identity or the particular emotional state that is occurring with the subjectivity. Hence, a meditative technique that enables the practitioner to know Awareness or Clarity must somehow avoid attending to the particularities of object and subject and grant access instead to the fact of knowing itself. The problem, according to *Chag-zôg* theorists, is that untrained persons are deeply entangled in the accidental features of experience; generally, they focus especially on the features of the object, and occasionally they are explicitly aware of themselves as subjects. But in either case, untrained persons are not aware of what is invariant in those experiences.

To overcome this problem, the various lineages of contemplative practice that fall under the rubric of *Chag-zôg* propose distinct techniques, but one common approach is based upon a move toward subjectivity in meditation. The notion here is that the invariant aspect of experience is closely tied to the reflexive awareness (Tib. *rang rig*) that enables one to have memories of oneself as an experiencing subject. On this theory, as an object is being presented to an experiencing subject, reflexive awareness also presents

the process or occurrence of that experience either passively or involuntarily. For *Chag-zôg* theorists, this faculty of apperceptive presentation is a derivative form of the more fundamental Awareness that is the basic nature or structure of consciousness itself. Hence, a meditative technique that removes the cognitive features that usually obscure the implicit reflexivity of experience is one that moves that practitioner closer to an understanding of that fundamental Awareness.

Above we noted that even the earliest forms of *vipaśyanā* meditation seem to involve some form of meta-awareness that surveys the meditative state in such a way that it enables one to know whether one has lost the focus on the object. Likewise, that same type of meta-awareness serves to determine whether or not dullness and excitement are occurring. Thus, even in these other forms of *vipaśyanā* practice, one encounters a type of reflexivity, inasmuch as the meditative state is meant to involve an awareness of the state itself. With this in mind, one can think of the *Chag-zôg* practice of cultivating Open Presence as emphasizing this aspect of *vipaśyanā* practice to its furthest possible point. This practice differs from other meditations, however, in that theoretically it is taking an implicit aspect of all cognitions – a fundamental form of reflexivity – and making it phenomenally accessible to the practitioner.

On this theoretical understanding of Open Presence, two features of the practice are especially salient. First, in other meditations that fall under the general rubric of *vipaśyanā*, one cultivates a faculty of mind that is best described as a meta-awareness; it is "meta" in that it is dependent upon the mindfulness *(smṛti)* that is focusing the mind on the object at hand. As noted above, this meta-awareness surveys the mind itself so as to determine, for example, whether it is dull or excited. Thus, inasmuch as it focuses on cognition itself, the meta-awareness is reflexive, and to this degree it resembles the type of state cultivated in the practice of Open Presence. The difference, however, is that in Open Presence the prefix "meta" would be inappropriate; instead, it is assumed that, rather then being attendant upon the basic faculty of mindfulness – i.e., the faculty that focuses on an object – the reflexive aspect of mind is actually more fundamental than mindfulness. In other words, mindfulness must occur with an object, but the possibility of objects being presented in experience is itself rooted in a more fundamental reflexivity.

The second distinctive aspect of Open Presence is that, unlike other meditations, at advanced stages of the practice there is no attempt either to suppress or to cultivate any particular mental content. One does not focus, for example, on a visualized image or on a sensory object, such as a sensation made by the breath. In this sense the state of Open Presence is objectless. Nevertheless, even though higher levels of the practice do not involve any particular content or object, it also is important for content to be occurring in the mind because to cultivate an awareness of the invariant nature of experience, one must be having experiences. Indeed, for beginners it is preferable that the experiences be especially striking or clear. Thus, even though the meditation is objectless, it is not a state of blankness or withdrawal. Sensory events are still experienced, sometimes even more vividly. In terms of technique, this facet of the meditation is indicated by the fact that one meditates with the eyes open and directed somewhat upward.

Basic Practice. The actual state of Open Presence is one in which the meditator is aware of the Clarity or Awareness that makes all cognitions possible. This state is a relatively advanced one, and even experienced practitioners may not be able to sustain it for more than a short period of time. There are, however, a series of practices that train inexperienced meditators to cultivate Open Presence, and even experienced practitioners sometimes modulate their practice so as to move up or down the scale of practices, depending on how well the particular session is proceeding.

Schematically, we use the diagram in Figure 19.1 to summarize the stages of the style of practice that leads to Open Presence:

Stage	Object	Subject	Reflexive Awareness
1	+	−	−
2	−	+	+
3	−	−	+
4	Ø	Ø	++

Legend: "−" = de-emphasis, "+" = emphasis, "Ø" = absent

Figure 19.1.

This diagram is based especially on the styles of *Chag-zôg* practice exemplified by Karma Chagmé (2000), Thrangu (Thrangu & Johnson, 2004), and Wangchug Dorjé (1989, and their works are the main textual sources for the presentation below. It is important to note, however, that the diagram suggests a trajectory of actual practice that, although clearly implicit in these authors' writings, is not explicit. Nevertheless, this way of presenting the flow of the practice has the advantage of being far less complicated than traditional presentations.

As Figure 19.1 illustrates, in this style of practice the overall trajectory begins with a meditation that develops concentration on an object. One then employs techniques that cultivate an awareness of subjectivity in a manner that de-emphasizes the object. In doing so, one gains phenomenal access to the reflexive awareness that is thought to be invariant in cognition. One then de-emphasizes subjectivity as well so as to further enhance that access to reflexivity, and finally one practices so as to move to the point where the invariant aspect of awareness is realized fully in meditation. Throughout this entire process the close guidance of an instructor is considered essential.

This style of practice generally begins with the development of Focused Attention (i.e., concentration on a particular object as described previously). Initially retaining some focus on the object, one then cultivates attention to the state of the subjectivity observing the object. This is in part accomplished by discursive strategies that are implemented after a certain level of concentration and mental calm has been reached. In one such strategy, one is instructed to ask questions about the object, such as, "Is it inside the mind or outside the mind?" Or, when an appearance arises, one observes it and asks, "Where did it arise from?" Or as it abides in the mind, one asks, "Where is it abiding?" Or as it disappears, one asks, "Where did it go?" These questions and similar discursive strategies are used to train one to see the object as just a phenomenal appearance and to create the subjective impression that the appearance is not something separate from one's mind. As a means to heighten one's awareness of subjectivity, the same types of questions are then applied to the phenomenal appearance as mind (with questions such as, "What color is the mind?" "What shape is the mind?"), which has the effect of pointing out the manner in which the phenomenal content is accidental to the experience. Along with or in lieu of such strategies, a deliberate perturbation – such as a sudden shout – may be introduced into the meditation so that the effects on subjectivity will be especially salient.

The move to an emphasis on subjectivity is further encouraged by dropping any deliberate focus on an object. As a sensory content or mental event occurs, one observes it (sometimes along with the momentary use of a discursive strategy), and then one releases any focus on it. This is similar to the Vipassanā practice discussed above, except that after releasing the content or event one does not return to any object. Instead, one releases the mind into its "natural state" (rang babs), which one understands to be the state reflecting only the invariant nature of consciousness and not the accidental properties of subject and object.

One is also repeatedly reminded by one's instructor that "grasping" ('dzin pa) – taking the mental content as an object – is to be avoided. Here, the gross symptoms of grasping include indications that one has begun to focus on or examine the content or event and then elaborate upon it – in a phrasing often employed in oral instructions, one is not to "follow along" (rjes su 'brang ba) a chain of thoughts. A much subtler indication of grasping, however, is simply the fact that, in phenomenal terms, the appearance or event seems separate from the subjectivity in the experience. Thus, when one "releases" objects, one must do so with the understanding that the objects actually are not separate from awareness itself, of which the subjectivity is also just a facet. This attitude is initially developed through discursive strategies, which seem to play a crucial role in developing Open Presence.

Having become adept at emphasizing subjectivity – attending to the state of one's awareness without construing its contents as separate from the subjectivity – the next stage of the practice involves techniques that de-emphasize subjectivity itself. Theoretically, this is accomplished in part by one's facility at releasing objects. That is, because awareness is construed as subjectivity in relation to objects, the practice of releasing objects will also erode subjectivity. But another important aspect of this stage of practice is not to grasp onto subjectivity itself as an object. That is, as one is attempting to abide in a state that is aware and yet not focused on an object, one may still have a sense of subjectivity that is caught up in an identity that extends beyond the particular moment – as such, that sense of an identity is considered an accidental feature of the state because it changes over time.

One of the many remedies employed here is the repeated (and somewhat paradoxical) instruction not to make an effort to meditate. In other words, for the meditator a persistent way that the sense of "I" manifests would be in the form of a thought, such as, "I am meditating." Such a thought involves conceptual and linguistic structures that connect to a sense of "I" located in the past and the future. And because that way of locating subjectivity – essentially as a narrative agent – changes from one cognitive context to the next, it is a type of subjectivity that is thought to obscure the invariant feature of consciousness. According to most traditional accounts, it is extremely difficult to de-emphasize subjectivity to this degree. As a result, most beginner and mid-range meditators engaged in the cultivation of open presence are likely to be actually meditating at the level below this stage; that is, the stage at which subjectivity is still emphasized.

Through the above techniques – along with other methods that involve visualizations and breathing exercises – advanced meditators are thought to eventually induce a particular phenomenal experience: The experience's content does not appear as an object over against a subject, and the experience also does not involve a sense of subjectivity that is articulated by conceptual or linguistic structures, even if those structures are only implicit. It is worth reiterating, however, that in de-emphasizing both object and subject, the aim of the practice is not to become withdrawn from experiences, whether perceptual or mental. Instead, the aim is for experiences to continue to occur even though the state de-emphasizes the particularity of the object and subject. It is in this way that, according to *Chag-zôg* theorists, one will become aware of the invariant feature of all states of consciousness.

Finally, at the highest level of practice, what we have described as a de-emphasis of both object and subject moves, at least theoretically, to a point where no elements of objectivity or subjectivity – whether in the form of conceptual structures, categories of time and space, or some other feature – remain in the experience. At this point, the invariant feature of cognition is said to be realized fully by the meditator, and this is the full-blown state of Open Presence. It seems that because this state is extremely advanced in each generation of practitioners the *Chag-zôg* traditions recognize only a small number of practitioners as having truly reached this level of practice.

In terms of the effects of the practice, one ability developed through cultivating Open Presence is the stability of the state – that is, one is not easily perturbed out of the state. The difference, however, is that unlike in Focused Attention, in Open Presence the stability is not constituted by the fact that other phenomena do not pull one away from the object on which one focuses. Instead, stability consists of one's ability to

continue to experience phenomena without objectifying them and, ideally, without having a sense of an agentive or narrative subjectivity. The state thus seems to cultivate a type of *ipseity* or bare awareness. After a session, for advanced meditators the objects of perception will phenomenally appear to be less fixed and more like appearances in a dream or a mirage for at least some period afterward. And as one advances further, the state between sessions begins to seem more like Open Presence itself. The relevant longer-term traits that are expected to arise from cultivating Open Presence include most prominently a facility to regulate one's emotions, such that one is disturbed less easily by emotional states. The mind is also said to be more sensitive and flexible, and the cultivation of other positive states and traits is therefore greatly facilitated. All three of our main traditional sources (Karma Chagmé, 2000; Thrangu & Johnson, 2004; Wangchug Dorjé, 1989) make it clear that these and other indications are thought to be observable in behavior, because it is through observing and interviewing students that the meditation master is able to guide them in this difficult practice.

NON-REFERENTIAL COMPASSION (*MÎG-MÉ NYING-JÉ*)

Unlike practices oriented toward generating Focused Awareness or Open Presence, the practice of Non-Referential Compassion aims to produce a specific emotional state; namely, an intense feeling of lovingkindness.[5] The state is necessarily other-centered, but it is non-referential *(dmigs med)* in that it does not have any specific object or focus *(dmigs pa)*, such as a specific person or group of persons. Thus, in effect this meditation has two aspects: the cultivation of compassion and the cultivation of objectless awareness (i.e., Open Presence). Hence, this practice may be considered a kind of variation on Open Presence, but it also differs somewhat from Open Presence. That is, except for the earliest stages of the practice, in Open Presence the meditator does not usually require any particular mental content or event as the context for the cultivation of Open Presence. But in the cultivation of Non-Referential Compassion, one does require a particular mental event – the emotion of compassion – that forms the context for the cultivation of the objectless awareness that is Open Presence.

The two aspects of Non-Referential Compassion – compassion and Open Presence – must occur together for the meditation to be successful (Wangchug Dorjé, 1989), but although precise descriptions of this practice are not readily available, it appears that for many practitioners this practice requires a sequence within the session. In some cases, a meditator may first cultivate Open Presence and then cultivate compassion while retaining the state of Open Presence to the greatest degree possible. After compassion has been evoked, the meditator may then emphasize Open Presence once again, because the techniques for cultivating compassion may have led the meditator to stray from an objectless state. In other cases, a meditator may begin by first evoking compassion, and then, while the mind is suffused with compassion, the meditator will cultivate Open Presence.

The sequentiality of the practice, which does not apply to the most advanced practitioners, stems largely from the methods that are initially used to evoke a compassionate mental state. These methods often combine multiple techniques, most especially a discursive strategy (usually the steps of a memorized argument), a set of visualizations, and sometimes a litany or other recitation. In all the Tibetan traditions, three such meditations are widely practiced: the "Sevenfold Causal Instructions" *(sems bskyed rgyu 'bras man ngag bdun)*, the "Equanimous Exchange of Self and Other" *(bdag bzhan mnyam brjes)*, and the practice of "Giving and Taking" *(gtong len)* (Dalai Lama XIV, 1991, 1995).

All three of these practices, which themselves may be combined in various ways, typically begin with an evocation of equanimity *(btang snyoms,* Skt, *upekṣā)*. Often a visualization of three persons is used: a beloved person (most especially one's mother), a person for whom one has some enmity, and

a person toward whom one feels indifference. With a visualization of these persons in place, one then employs discursive strategies – such as the argument that all beings are equal in wanting to be happy and wishing to avoid suffering – that are designed to eliminate one's biases toward these persons. In the Sevenfold Causal Instructions, one is then encouraged not only to see all beings as equal but also to take one's mother as paradigmatic of all beings. Another set of discursive contemplations – sometimes including specific visualizations – are then used to displace one's preferential treatment of oneself over others. One contemplates, for example, how despicable one would be to prefer one's own happiness over the well-being of one's mother; here, the practitioner might recall a memorized aphorism or the admonitions of his or her teacher. Finally, by recalling or visualizing the intense suffering experienced by others – i.e., "all sentient beings who are as if one's mother" *(ma sems can thams cad)* – one becomes motivated empathetically to eliminate that suffering. Toward the endpoint of this process one experiences a visceral, emotional reaction that is said to involve especially a feeling of opening at the center of the chest, sometimes accompanied by horripilation and the welling of tears in the eyes. This state involves both love *(matrī)* – the aspiration that other beings be happy – and compassion *(karuṇā)* – the aspiration that other beings be free of suffering. At this point the state might involve a degree of sentimentality, and the final phase of developing compassion is meant to go beyond that state to one that is both more stable and also more engaged with aiding others (Dalai Lama XIV, 1991).

Most Tibetan practitioners are trained intensively in this type of contemplation for generating compassion. It is evident, however, that these techniques for inducing compassion are not objectless, inasmuch as they involve visualizations, arguments, aphorisms, litanies, and so on that are focused on objects of one kind or another. Nevertheless, having generated compassion, the practitioner can then cultivate Open Presence from within that state. Indeed, as a phenomenally intense state, compassion is well suited to the early stages of cultivating Open Presence, because compassion's intensity lends itself well to an awareness of subjectivity and, hence, reflexivity. And if the emotional state of compassion can be sustained even while one is cultivating Open Presence, the meditator is in the state of Non-Referential Compassion. As a meditator becomes more adept at cultivating compassion through the various techniques mentioned above, the mind becomes more habituated to the state such that an advanced practitioner can induce the state of compassion almost effortlessly. At this stage the practice would no longer require a sequence; that is, compassion can be cultivated directly within a state of Open Presence itself (Wangchug Dorjé, 1989).

In general the cultivation of compassion is thought to grant the meditator numerous beneficial effects between sessions, such as creating a general sense of well-being and aiding in counteracting anger or irritation. Long-term practitioners of this practice are also said to have an effect on others around them, in that other persons nearby may also feel a greater sense of well-being and happiness. Compassion is also thought to provide benefits when one is in a meditative session involving other practices. It is especially useful for counteracting torpor in meditation; that is, it is a considered a strong antidote for dullness, as mentioned earlier. Likewise, because compassion is other-centered, it is considered to develop traits that are essential for the successful cultivation of Open Presence. That is, in developing Open Presence one must eliminate the mind's "grasping" directed toward objects and also toward subjectivity itself. Grasping, moreover, is rooted in a persistent trait within the mind that absolutizes the standpoint of the subject. By persistently orienting the meditator toward others, compassion lessens this fixation on self and makes it possible for grasping to be eliminated through the practice of Open Presence. In this way, the cultivation of compassion is thought to train the mind in a way that is essential to the success of some practices (Dalai Lama XIV, 1991, 1995; Karma Chagmé, 2000; Thrangu & Johnson, 2004; Wangchug Dorjé, 1989).

Generating a Description

As the discussion above indicates, even within Buddhism a large number of distinct contemplative practices continue to be practiced in living traditions. For this reason, significant changes in meditative style are found even for a basic *samatha* style of meditation focused on the sensation made by the breath. For instance, practitioners from the Vipassanā or Insight Meditation movement may practice this meditation with the eyes closed so as to de-emphasize the importance of the visual modality. In contrast, closing the eyes is rarely encouraged in the Zen and Tibetan traditions, in part because it is assumed to induce dullness or drowsiness.

The difference of opinion concerning the closing of the eyes is illustrative of the difficulties that researchers face when specifying the exact nature of a meditation to be studied. One main problem is that the traditional accounts of these practices move far beyond the sketches given here; instead, those accounts are usually highly detailed and extremely complex. Likewise, the terminology used to describe the practices is sometimes unreliable, either because of ambiguities in the traditions themselves or problems in translation. Practices from different traditions may in fact overlap significantly – the overlap between contemporary Mindfulness practice and Open Presence meditation is one case in point. Finally, subjects from traditionally Buddhist cultures sometimes are reluctant to depart from textual descriptions of meditative practices. To do so would require a practitioner to assert some authoritative experience as a meditator, and it is usually thought to be inappropriate to claim that degree of accomplishment in meditation.

Researchers may also encounter problems when attempting to assess the degree of training and practice over the life of a particular practitioner. One of the main difficulties is that, traditionally, contemplative practice involves many varieties of meditation, each of which mutually influence each other and differentially affect the mind. The quantification of the total hours of meditation throughout a practitioner's life is thus not straightforward and will require further methodological development.

In any case, before tackling the problem of quantification, an important task for any researcher is generating a precise and concrete account of the practices in which meditating subjects claim to be engaged. The best way to proceed is probably to develop a list of questions that can be used to help prompt descriptions from practitioners without getting caught either in traditional categories or issues of cultural translation. To assist researchers in this task, we close this section on Buddhist meditation with a practical series of sample questions that would aid both the meditator and researcher in defining more clearly the relevant facets of the practice to be studied. The questions address five overall issues: (1) the relative degree of stability and clarity appropriate to the practice; (2) the "intentional modality" (i.e., whether the meditation has an object); (3) the techniques, such as breath manipulation, that are employed; (4) the expected effects of the practice during meditation; and (5) the expected effects after a session. Although based especially on the practice and theory of meditation found in Tibetan Buddhism, questions of this type are likely to be useful when examining other contemplative traditions.

1. *Concerning stability and clarity, one may ask the following*:
   - In view of the practitioner's level, should the meditation favor stability, clarity, or a balance?
     - What are the indications that stability needs adjustment?
     - What are the indications that clarity needs adjustment?

2. *Concerning intentional modality, one may ask the following*:
   - If the meditation includes an object, then,
     - Is there one object or many objects in the meditation?
     - For each object, is the object dynamic or static?
     - If the object includes or consists of a visual form, a sound, or a sensation, then is the object perceived through the senses, or is it imagined in the mind through visualization or another technique?
   - If the meditation does not include an object, then does one direct one's attention to something else?

3. *Concerning meditative techniques, one may ask the following*:
   - Is the practice done with the eyes opened or closed?
   - Does the practice employ any discursive strategies, such as recitations, memorized descriptions, or arguments that one reviews?
   - Does the practice use breath manipulation?
   - Does the meditation involve focusing on different parts of the body by means of a visualization or some other technique?
   - Does the practice require a specific posture or set of physical exercises?

4. *Concerning expected effects during meditation, one may ask the following*:
   - Is the meditation expected to produce any physical sensations or mental events, either constantly or intermittently?
   - Does one expect the meditation to produce subjectively noticeable alterations in cognition, either constantly or intermittently? One example would be the impression that one's perceptions seem to be like the appearances in a dream.
   - Is the meditation expected to cause any emotions, either constantly or intermittently?

5. *Concerning expected effects after meditation, one may ask the following*:
   - Does one expect the meditation to alter one's cognitions? One example would be the impression that one's perceptions are more vivid.
   - Does one expect the meditation to alter one's behavior? One example would be a tendency to sleep less.
   - Does one expect the meditation to alter one's emotions? One example would be the tendency to recover more quickly from emotional disturbances.

By adapting or adding to this list of questions for the particular practice in question, meditators and researchers may be able to collaborate more readily so as to describe in a straightforward way the major features of a practice that are relevant to a particular neuroscientific research agenda. With such descriptions in place, the dialogue between meditators and researchers can be far more precise, and the interaction between neuroscience and meditation is therefore likely to be more fruitful.

The Intersection of Neuroscience and Meditation

This section briefly explores some possible scientific motivations for the neuroscientific examination of meditative practices and their possible impact on the brain and body in advanced practitioners. The aim here is to clarify further the distinguishing features of this approach compared to other empirical strategies described in this handbook. Before we move forward with this discussion, however, two points of clarification need to be made. First, because of the relative paucity of currently available empirical data in this field, this section remains largely programmatic. Second, we discuss some studies that involve novice meditators, but the set of issues examined here are most relevant to advanced practitioners of meditation. Nevertheless, emphasis on advanced practitioners should not minimize the importance of studying meditation in less practiced individuals. Indeed, some of us have already done so (see, e.g. Davidson et al., 2003). For progress in this general area to advance, we believe that research on practitioners at all levels should be encouraged, but one must also recognize that the goals of studying individuals at different levels of accomplishment differ somewhat.

Turning now to the question of advanced practitioners, we begin by noting three frequently advanced hypotheses:

1. Advanced practitioners can generate *new data* that would not exist without sustained mental training. These data encompass either *meditative states* or *traits* induced by meditation. Meditative states refer to the transient alterations of experience voluntarily cultivated by a given meditation practice (i.e., bodily awareness, relaxation, emotions, and so on). Traits refer to the lasting changes in these dimensions that persist in the practitioner's daily experience irrespective of being actively engaged in meditation.

2. Advanced practitioners can robustly *reproduce* specific features in experience as cultivated in given meditative practice. This reproducibility makes those features scientifically tractable.

3. Advanced practitioners provide more *refined first-person descriptions* of their experiences than naïve subjects. Thus, the neurophysiological counterpart of these first-person accounts can be defined, identified, and interpreted more easily by the experimentalist.

We now discuss these claims in relation to three neuroscientific agendas: neuroplasticity, the interaction of mind and body, and the possibility of neural counterparts to subjective experience. In the course of this discussion, specific techniques from the Buddhist tradition serve as illustrations.

Transforming the Mind and Brain Neuroplasticity

From a neuroscientific perspective, the first promising claim made by Buddhist contemplative traditions is that experience is not a rigid, predetermined, and circumscribed entity, but rather a flexible and transformable process. On this view, emotions, attention, and introspection are ongoing and labile processes that need to be understood and studied as skills that can be trained, similar to other human skills like music, mathematics, or sports. This principle is foundational for Buddhist contemplative practice, because such practices are based upon the notion that the mind is malleable in this way. As a result, the methods employed by Buddhist contemplative practices resonate with widely accepted developmental models of basic cognitive processes; according to these models, cognitive functions are skills that critically depend upon learning from environmental input (e.g., McClelland & Rogers, 2003; Saffran, Aslin, & Newport, 1996). This basic stance reflects another well-accepted and well-documented theory; namely, that experience changes the brain. Interest in this feature, known as neuroplasticity, has prompted an explosion of research over the past decade.

As a result of ongoing research on neuroplasticity, we now have a detailed understanding of many of the molecular and system-level changes that are produced by specific types of experiential input. For example, neonatal rodents exposed to varying levels of maternal licking and grooming develop very different behavioral phenotypes. Those animals that receive high levels of licking and grooming (the rodent equivalent of highly nurturing parenting) develop into more adaptable and relaxed adults. Of great interest is the fact that the brains of the animals are critically affected by this differential rearing. Indeed, gene expression for the gene that codes for the glucocorticoid receptor is actually changed by this experience, and the detailed molecular pathways by which experience can alter gene expression have now been worked out in this model (Meaney, 2001). This program of research illustrates the profound ways in which neuroplasticity can unfold, and it demonstrates that experience-induced alterations in the brain can occur all the way down to the level of gene expression.

Meaney's work on alterations in brain gene expression implies that similar experience-induced alterations might occur in humans. Currently, however, there are no direct measures of localized neuronal gene expression that can be non-invasively obtained in humans. Nevertheless, other research suggests that such changes do indeed occur. For instance, the brain of an expert, such as a chess player, a taxi driver, or a musician, is functionally and structurally different from that of a nonexpert. London taxi cab drivers have larger hippocampi than matched controls, and the amount of time the individual has worked

as a cab driver predicted the size of the posterior hippocampus (Maguire et al., 2000). Further work by this group suggests that these differences in hippocampal size are the results of experience and training as a cab driver and not a consequence of pre-existing differences in hippocampal structure (Maguire et al., 2003).

Whether similar structural alterations in different regions of the brain occur also as a consequence of affective – rather than sensorimotor – experience is not definitively known, but all of the extant work at both the animal and human levels indicates that it does. Certainly there are good animal data to suggest that such changes occur, as indicated by the study on neonatal rodents. In humans, a variety of research indicates that deleterious conditions, such as chronic stress, neglect, and abuse, produce functional changes in the brain that are likely subserved by structural alterations (Glaser, 2000). Likewise, research on depression indicates that patients with mood disorders exhibit structural differences in several brain regions, including the hippocampus and territories with the prefrontal cortex; significantly, at least some of these differences are associated strongly with the cumulative number of days of depression in the patients' lifetimes (Sheline, 2003).

These findings raise the possibility that training and practices that are specifically designed to cultivate positive qualities, such as equanimity and lovingkindness, will produce beneficial alterations in brain function and structure. Presumably, these alterations would be most prominent in long-term, advanced practioners, but we have already shown that even very brief short-term training (30 minutes) in emotion regulation can produce reliable alterations in brain function (Urry et al., 2003). So too, we have observed that a 2-month course in Mindfulness-Based Stress Reduction (MBSR) can produce alterations in patterns of prefrontal brain activity that we have previously found to accompany positive affect (Davidson et al., 2003).

The findings concerning MBSR may be especially relevant, because MBSR is likely to provide a large pool of persons for the study of neuroplasticity and meditation. An 8-week program that was originally developed in a hospital setting for patients with chronic illnesses, MBSR is now applied across an extremely wide range of populations (Kabat-Zinn & Chapman-Waldrop, 1988; Kabat-Zinn, Lipworth, & Burney, 1985). The method, based primarily on Buddhist practices, seems to be effective for chronic pain, anxiety disorders, general psychological well-being, psoriasis, and recurrent depression (Grossman, Niemann, Schmidt, & Walach, 2004). The program seems to work by helping the patient distinguish primary sensory experience (e.g., chronic pain, physical symptoms of anxiety) from the secondary emotional or cognitive processes created in reaction to the primary experience. Individuals are trained to use the mindfulness practice to elicit the details of their experience and to directly perceive the unstable and contingent nature of the feelings and sensations that are associated with aversion and withdrawal; as a result, individuals are better able to counter any propensity toward withdrawal and aversion in response to physical or psychological pain.

From a neuroscientific perspective, the apparent effectiveness of MBSR practice raises the question of neuroplasticity – that, is, does it produce alterations in brain function and structure? Recent data indicate a possible relationship between meditation training and changes in brain structure (Lazar et al., 2005). In this study, cortical thickness was assessed using magnetic resonance imaging. Increased cortical thickness could be caused by greater arborization per neuron, increased glial volume, or increased regional vasculature, all of which are important for neural function. Cortical brain regions associated with attention, interoceptive, and sensory processing were found to be thicker for a group of mid-range practitioners than for matched controls (the meditator participants had, on average, 40 minutes of daily practice of Insight meditation for an average of 9 years). We anticipate that research conducted over the next 2 years by several groups will further examine possible anatomical changes induced by meditation.

Mechanisms of Mind-Body Interaction

In addition to the study of neuroplasticity, one of the most potentially fruitful questions in the study of meditation is the impact of training the mind on peripheral biological processes that are important for physical health and illness. Quite literally, the question here is whether mental training can affect the body in a way that will have a significant impact on physical health. Although there are many popular claims about the health benefits of meditation and contemplative practice, there is relatively little that is solidly known about this potentially crucial issue. Even more importantly, there are preciously few attempts to mechanistically link the changes that are occurring in the brain with alterations that may be produced in peripheral biology. It is beyond the scope of this chapter to review the basic research relevant to these questions, but it provides some general guidelines and examples.

It is established that there is bidirectional communication between the brain and the periphery and that this communication proceeds along three basic routes: the autonomic nervous system, the endocrine system, and the immune system. In each of these systems, specific pathways and signaling molecules enable this bidirectional communication to occur. These structural characteristics are highly relevant to the possibility that meditation may influence physical health. That is, some conditions of peripheral biology may be potentially affected by meditative practices because those conditions – such as an illness – are susceptible to modulation by the autonomic, endocrine, and/or immune pathways involved in brain-periphery communication. Thus, because there is bidirectional communication between the brain and periphery, it is theoretically possible to affect those types of conditions by inducing changes in the brain through meditation. At the same time, however, other conditions or illnesses may not be influenced in this way by

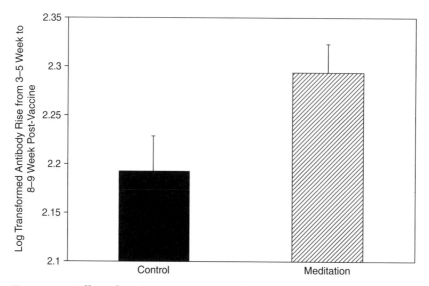

Figure 19.2. Effect of meditation training on the immune system during a Mindfulness-Based Stress Reduction program (8-week program) with novice practitioners. Means ± SE antibody increase from the 3- to 5-week to the 8- to 9-week blood draw in the Meditation and Control groups. The ordinate displays the difference in the log-transformed antibody rise between the 3- to 5-week and the 8- to 9-week blood draws derived from the hemagglutination inhibition array. (From Davidson et al., 2003.)

meditation because the peripheral biological processes in question cannot be affected by any pathway involved with brain-periphery communication.

With this in mind, the strategy that we have adopted in some of our work is to examine a proxy measure that we know can be modulated by central nervous changes and that is health-relevant. In a seminal study, Kiecolt-Glaser, Glaser, Gravenstein, Malarkey, and Sheridan (1996) reported that caregivers of dementia patients had an impaired response to influenza vaccine compared with a matched control group. Several groups have now independently replicated this basic finding and have examined some of the details regarding the mechanism by which stress might impair humoral immunity (e.g., Miller et al., 2004).

In our group, we have investigated whether individual differences in patterns of prefrontal brain activity that we have previously found to be associated with affective style (i.e., individual differences in profiles of affective reactivity and regulation) are also associated with differences in anti-body response to the influenza vaccine. We found that individuals with high levels of left prefrontal activation, a pattern that we have previously found to predict more positive dispositional mood, had higher levels of antibody titers in response to the vaccine (Rosenkranz et al., 2003). The specific question of whether mental training could improve the immune response was addressed in our study of MBSR (Davidson et al., 2003; Figure 19.2). In this study, individuals who had been randomly assigned to an MBSR group were compared to a wait-list control group. Subjects were tested just after the MBSR group had completed their 8-week training. We found that the meditators exhibited a significantly greater antibody response to the influenza vaccine. Of most importance in this study was an analysis we conducted that examined relations between brain and immune function changes with meditation. We found that for the individuals assigned to the meditation group, those who showed the greatest shift toward left-sided activation also exhibited the largest increase in antibody titers to the

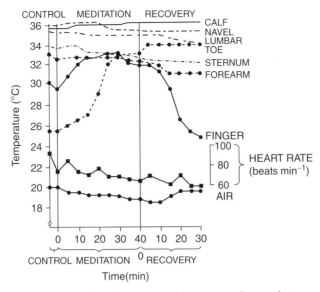

Figure 19.3. Effect of Tummo meditation on the regulation of body temperature. Skin and air temperature and heart rate changes before, during, and after the meditation of long-term practitioner L.T. (adapted from Benson et al., 1982).

vaccine. These findings suggest some association between the magnitude of neural and immune changes.

A variety of other findings in the literature suggest that autonomic changes occur during specific types of meditation. As noted in the first part of this chapter, the Tibetan Tummo practice has as its byproduct the production of heat. Benson and his colleagues reported on three practitioners and found that, by using this practice, they were indeed able to voluntarily increase temperature in their toes and fingers by as much as 8°C (Figure 19.3; Benson et al., 1982). Takahashi et al. in a study of Zen meditation in a fairly large sample (N = 20) found changes in heart rate variability (reflecting parasympathetic nervous system activity) that were associated with changes in specific EEG frequencies (Takahashi et al., 2005). In future studies, the combination of both brain and peripheral measures will be important in helping understand the mechanisms by which such peripheral changes may be occurring. This type of data will be especially useful as research moves forward on the practical question of whether meditative

practices can affect the body in a way that improves health.

Using First-Person Expertise to Identify the Neural Counterpart of Subjective Experience

As discussed in the first section of this chapter, various meditative practices induce a wide variety of altered states of consciousness. It is thus frequently claimed that the study of meditation will contribute to our general understanding of the neural basis of consciousness. Here we aim to move beyond this general claim and illustrate how specific Buddhist practices might provide research opportunities to glean new insights about some of the brain mechanisms contributing to consciousness. More precisely, we discuss how the collaboration with long-term Buddhist practitioners is of great interest in the study of (1) the physical substrate of subjectivity or the self, (2) the physical principles underlying the emergence of coherent conscious states from unconscious brain processes, and (3) the functional role of the spontaneous brain baseline.

STUDYING THE SUBSTRATE
OF SUBJECTIVITY

One of the useful points of intersection between Buddhist contemplative practice and the neuroscience of consciousness is the emphasis on understanding the nature of the self. A comparison between Buddhist and neuroscientific models of the self is beyond the scope of this chapter, but it is important to note that both traditions distinguish between a minimal subjective sense of "I-ness" in experience, or ipseity, and a narrative or autobiographical self. Ipseity is the minimal subjective sense of I-ness in experience, and as such, it is constitutive of a minimal or core self. By contrast, a narrative or autobiographical self (Legrand, 2005) encompasses categorical or moral judgment, emotions, anticipation of the future, and recollections of the past. This explicit sense of narrative or autobiographical self is often characterized as occurring in correlation with an explicit content, or object, of experience. It also appears to be dependent in some fashion on ipseity, inasmuch as the narrative self is in part based upon that minimal subjective sense of I-ness.

The notion of ipseity is further explained through Western phenomenological theory, according to which one can speak of experience in terms of both transitive and intransitive modes of consciousness. Any experience "intends" (i.e., refers to) its intentional object; this is its transitive aspect. At the same time, the experience is also reflexively manifest to itself, and this is its intransitive aspect. On this theory, the intransitive aspect of experience is a form of self-consciousness that is primitive inasmuch as it (1) does not require any subsequent act of reflection or introspection, but occurs simultaneously with awareness of the object; (2) does not consist of forming a belief or making a judgment; and (3) is passive in the sense of being spontaneous and involuntary (Zahavi & Parnas, 1998). For instance, when one consciously sees an object, one is also at the same time aware of one's seeing; similarly, when one visualizes a mental image, one is also aware of one's visualizing. This tacit self-awareness has often been

explained as involving a reflexive awareness of one's lived body or embodied subjectivity correlative to the experience of the object (Mearleau-Ponty, 1962; Wider, 1997). It is, in short, another way of speaking about ipseity.

If the above model is correct, then in giving an account of consciousness, neuroscience needs to explain both "how the brain engenders the mental patterns we experience as the images of an object" and "how, in parallel . . . the brain also creates a sense of self in the act of knowing . . ." In other words, to give an account of consciousness, neuroscience must show how it is that one has a "sense of me" by demonstrating "how we sense that the images in our minds are shaped in our particular perspective and belong to our individual organism" (Damasio, 1999, pp. 136–137). As a number of cognitive scientists have emphasized, this primitive self-consciousness might be fundamentally linked to bodily processes of life regulation (Damasio, 1999; Panksepp, 1988).

This approach to the question of consciousness suggests a research strategy that might be aided by the use of experienced meditators. That is, to understand consciousness, it is presumably best to begin by examining it in its simplest form. And on this theory, the simplest form of a conscious state is reducible to ipseity, which is required for or is prior to the narrative self. One experimental strategy would be to involve long-term practitioners of a practice such as Open Presence that allegedly induces a state in which ipseity is emphasized and the narrative self is lessened or eliminated. By examining such practices, one may be able to find neural correlates of a bare subjectivity, which in turn may yield some insight into the neural correlates of the most basic type of coherent states that we call consciousness.

STUDYING THE SUBSTRATE
OF CONSCIOUSNESS

Empirical evidence clearly indicates that only a selective set of neurons in the brain participates in any given moment of consciousness. In fact many emotional, motor, perceptual, and semantic processes occur unconsciously. These unconscious processes are usually circumscribed brain activities in local and specialized brain areas (Dehaene & Naccache, 2001). This result suggests that, when a stimulus is phenomenally reportable from the standpoint of experience, it is the result of translocal, large-scale mechanisms that somehow integrate local functions and processes. In other words, it has been hypothesized that the neural activity crucial for consciousness most probably involves the transient and continual orchestration of scattered mosaics of functionally specialized brain regions, rather than any single, highly localized brain process or structure (Dehaene & Naccache, 2001; Llinas, Ribary, Contreras, & Pedroarena, 1998; W. Singer, 2001; Tononi & Edelman, 1998).

The issue at stake here can be illustrated by the example of binocular rivalry. When the right eye and the left eye are presented with competing, dissimilar images, the observer does not experience a stable superimposed percept of the images presented to the two eyes, but instead perceives an ongoing alternation between the images seen by each eye every couple of seconds. When one percept is consciously perceived, the other remains unconscious. Yet, even if a stimulus is not reportable, there is evidence it is still processed by the brain in various ways. Activity in the amygdala, which is known to increase during the presentation of facial expressions of fear and anger, is still detectable even when the emotional face is suppressed because of binocular rivalry (Williams, Morris, McGlone, Abbott, & Mattingley, 2004).

Binocular rivalry suggests that local neural processes – such as those involved in the processing of visual stimuli – are not in themselves sufficient to account for consciousness. In other words, the neural process occurs, but may or may not be consciously experienced. Some other process or mechanism must be involved. It is in response to this type of issue that contemporary researchers (Llinas et al., 1998; Singer, 2001; Tononi & Edelman, 1998) have hypothesized some kind of integrative mechanisms or processes that, although transient, are able to orchestrate or coordinate function-

ally specialized brain regions. A common theoretical proposal is that each moment of conscious awareness involves the transient selection of a distributed neural population that is both integrated or coherent, and differentiated or flexible, and whose members are connected by reciprocal and transient dynamic links. As we show in the next section, neural synchronization and de-synchronization between oscillating neural populations at multiple frequency bands are popular indicators of this large-scale integration (Engel, Fries, & Singer, 2001; Varela, et al. 2001). For instance, during the binocular rivalry discussed above the alternation of perceptual dominance correlates with different ongoing patterns of distributed synchronous brain patterns (Cosmelli et al., 2004; Srinivasan, Russell, Edelman, & Tononi, 1999).

Thus it is hypothesized that large-scale integrative mechanisms play a role in conscious processes. However, these large-scale brain processes typically display endogenous, self-organizing behaviors that cannot be controlled fully by the experimenter and are highly variable both from trial to trial and across subjects. Linking these brain patterns to the experiential domain is notoriously difficult in part because the first-person reports are readily inaccurate or biased (Nisbett & Wilson, 1977). The problem, in a nutshell, is that the experimenter is led to treat as noise the vast majority of the large-scale brain activity, as he or she can neither interpret it nor control it.

It is in this context that meditation becomes relevant. We hypothesize that long-term practitioners of meditation can generate more stable and reproducible mental states than untrained subjects and that they can also describe these states more accurately than naïve subjects. The practitioners' introspective skills could provide a way for experimenters to better control, identify, and interpret the large-scale integrative processes in relation to the subjective experience.

This "neurophenomenology" approach (Varela, 1996) was tested in the context of a visual protocol with naïve subjects. On the day of the experiment, participants were first trained during a practice session to be aware of subtle fluctuations from trial to trial in their cognitive context as defined by their attentive state, spontaneous state processes, and the strategy used to carry out the task. During the visual task, their electrical brain activity and their own report about their cognitive context were recorded. Trials were clustered according to the acquired first-person data, and separate, dynamical analyses were conducted for each cluster. Characteristic patterns of synchrony in the frontal electrodes were found for each cluster, depending in particular on the stability of attention and the preparation to do the task (Lutz, Lachaux, Martinerie, & Varela, 2002).

As discussed in the report by Lutz and Thompson (2003), the collaboration with long-term practitioners will be particularly relevant to the further extension of this research strategy. Let us return again to the binocular rivalry paradigm. The perceptual selection in rivalry is not completely under the control of attention, but can be modulated by selective attention (Ooi & He, 1999). Evidence suggests in particular that the frequencies of the perceptual switch can be controlled voluntarily (Lack, 1978). It is possible that long-term practitioners of Focused Attention meditation can gain a more thorough control of the dynamic of perceptual switch than naïve subjects and that they can also refine their descriptions of the spontaneous flow of perceptual dominance beyond the mere categories of being conscious of one or another percept, thereby leading possibly to new brain correlates. Carter et al. (2005) recently provided behavioral evidence that long-term practitioners can indeed change the rivalry rate during meditation. They reported differential effects on visual switching accompanying rivalry during Non-Referential Compassion meditation and Focused Attention meditation (see the earlier discussion on meditative states in Tibetan Buddhism) among 23 Tibetan Buddhist monks varying in experience from 5 to 54 years of training. Compassion meditation led to no modifica-

tion in rivalry rate, in contrast with Focused Attention meditation, which led to extreme increases in perceptual dominance durations that were reported by 50% of monks after a period of single-pointed meditation. The monks reported additional stabilization of the visual switching when they did the visual task during Focused Attention meditation.

In sum, the capacity of long-term practitioners to examine, modulate, and report their experience might provide a valuable heuristic to study large-scale synchronous brain activity underlying conscious activity in the brain.

MEDITATION AND PHYSIOLOGICAL BASELINES

A central goal of the practice of meditation is to transform the baseline state of experience and to obliterate the distinction between the meditative state and the post-meditative state. The practice of Open Presence, for instance, cultivates increased awareness of a more subtle baseline (i.e., ipseity) during which the sense of an autobiographical or narrative self is de-emphasized. Long-term training in Compassion meditation is said to weaken egocentric traits and change the emotional baseline. Practitioners of Mindfulness/Awareness meditation aim to experience the present nowness, and this type of meditation affects the "attentional baseline" by lessening distractions or daydreamlike thoughts. In this way, meditative practices are generally designed to cultivate specific qualities or features of experience that endure through time relatively independent of ongoing changes in somatosensory or external events. These qualities are thought to gradually evolve into lasting traits.

From an empirical standpoint, one way to conceptualize these various meditative traits is to view them as developmental changes in physiological baselines in the organism. Finding ways of systematically characterizing these baselines before, during, and after mental training is thus crucial for the empirical examination of the long-term impact of meditation. A systematic characterization of baselines in the context of meditation is also an important methodological issue because an essential aspect of experimental research is the identification and control of a baseline against which the condition of interest can be contrasted. Underestimating this issue is a potential source of confusion when studying meditation practitioners, particularly long-term practitioners, because the contrast between the initial baseline and the meditative state might be biased by a baseline difference between groups (i.e., novices versus adepts).

When conceptualizing the notion of a baseline, perhaps the most useful approach is to consider a baseline in terms of the capacity for living systems to maintain their identity despite the fluctuations that affect them. Indeed, for many theorists this ability is one of the most fundamental biological roots of individuality, if not subjectivity itself (Maturana & Varela, 1980). This basic notion of homeostatic identity is the intuition that underlies the concept of a baseline in various domains. In the context of meditation, the notion of a baseline is clearly meaningful in relation to "raising the baseline" by developing traits that persist outside of any meditative state. In the scientific context, the concept of a baseline plays an important role in characterizing a broad variety of biological phenomena. Similarly, in psychology a baseline state is defined as a resting state by comparison to a task-specific state (say the task of remembering a succession of numbers). In an even broader, ecological context, psychologists attempt also to identify regularities or traits in the average ongoing states of an individual (e.g., mood and personality). Areas of biology that study living processes at a systemic level – such as the level of the cell, the organism, or the immune system – also use the notion of the baseline to convey the idea that something remains constant in the system through time. Such features would include, for example, the electrical charges of the neuron, the glucose level in the blood system, and body temperature. It is important to note that, in all these contexts, the functional invariance of a given baseline provides information about the homeostatic mechanisms that regulate and maintain the organization of the

system even amid environmental perturbations. It is in this sense that the notion of a baseline is related to the ongoing identity of an organism. And given the sensitivity that most contemplative traditions show to this type of issue, the search for baseline changes throughout the continuum of mental training is a general strategy that can potentially be applied to clarify mind-brain-body interactions at many explanatory levels, including brain chemical, metabolic, or electrical activity; the immune system; the cardiovascular system; and the hormonal system.

This idea can be illustrated with the case of metabolic and electrical brain baselines. Investigation of the metabolic brain baseline began following the finding that in an awake resting state, the brain consumes about 20% of the total oxygen used by the body, despite the fact that it represents only 2% of the total body weight (Clark & Sokoloff, 1999). This finding raises the question of the functional significance of this ongoing consumption of energy by the brain. Interestingly, brain imaging techniques that permit an examination of baseline levels of brain activity have suggested that this global activation at rest is not homogeneously localized in the brain. There are a consistent set of brain areas active at rest with eyes closed, as well as during visual fixation and the passive viewing of simple visual stimuli. The role of these activated areas is revealed from the attenuation of their activity during the performance of various goal-directed actions. Because the activity in these areas is associated with the baseline activity of the brain in these passive conditions, Raichle and colleague have suggested that they are functionally active, although they are not "activated" (Gusnard & Raichle, 2001). In contrast to the transient nature of typical activations, the presence of this functional activity in the baseline implies the presence of sustained information processing.

Our current understanding of the functional role of these tonically active networks is still limited. Evidence from brain imaging indicates that the posterior part of this tonically activated network (posterior cingulate cortex, precuneus, and some lateral posterior cortices) is important for the continuous gathering of information about the world around and possibly within us, whereas the anterior part (ventro- and dorsoventral prefrontal cortices) is important for the ongoing association among sensory, emotional, and cognitive processes that participate in spontaneous self-referential or introspectively oriented mental activity (Gusnard & Raichle, 2001). One can speculate that, given the nature of many meditations, these brain areas activated in the resting brain will be functionally affected by long-term meditative practices.

Similarly, the awake, resting brain is associated with a well-defined neuroelectric oscillatory baseline different from the one during sleep, anesthesia, or active mental activity. Changes in this baseline index are implicated in developmental processes in children, aging, cognitive IQ, and mental disorders (Klimesch, 1999). Along these same lines, we found a group difference in the initial premeditation baseline between long-term Buddhist practitioners and novices, suggesting some impact of long-term mental training (Lutz, Greischar, Rawlings, Ricard, & Davidson, 2004). The number of hours of formal meditation during the lifetime of long-term Buddhist practitioners correlates with some oscillatory properties of the brain electrical baselines. Furthermore, we showed that the post-meditation baseline was affected by the meditation session, and this suggests a short-term effect of meditation on the EEG baseline (Figure 19.4). In any case, this question of a neuroelectric baseline and its relation to mental training is a fruitful one, and it is currently being investigated, as is discussed in more detail in the next section.

To summarize, our functional understanding of the brain and body baselines remains largely incomplete, and given the importance played by some notion of a baseline in most meditative traditions, it is likely that our understanding will be significantly advanced by understanding those meditative practices that, above all else, aim to transform the "baseline of the mind."

Neuroelectric and Neuroimaging Correlates of Meditation

The search for the physiological correlates of meditation has been centered essentially on three groups: Yogis and students of Yoga in India, adherents of Transcendental Meditation (TM; Becker & Shapiro, 1981) in the United States, and practitioners of Zen and Tibetan Buddhism in Japan, the United States, and South Asia (India, Nepal). Historically, the first studies took place in Asia in the 1950s with advanced yogic practitioners in India (Das & Gastaut, 1955) and with long-term Zen practitioners in Japan (Kasamatsu & Hirai, 1966). Since the 1970s, meditation research has been done almost exclusively in the United States on practitioners of TM (Becker & Shapiro, 1981); over 500 studies have been conducted to date. Compared to the degree and sophistication of the training of practitioners in the early studies conducted in Asia, TM research relied mainly on the experience of relatively novice Western practitioners using mostly a single standard relaxation technique.

Since the late 1990s, we have witnessed a renewed interest in research on meditation. Various researchers have begun the exploration of a broad range of meditative practices inspired by various traditions – such as Zen, Tibetan Buddhism, Yoga, and Qigong – involving novices, patients, or long-term practitioners. Academic research institutions are starting to express an interest in this area as epitomized by the Mind and Life meetings at MIT in 2003 and a meeting co-sponsored by the John Hopkins School of Medicine and the Georgetown School of Medicine in November 2005 between the Dalai Lama, along with other Buddhist scholars, and neuroscientists (Barinaga, 2003).

This new, broad interest has been fostered by several factors. First, the neurobiology of consciousness and cognitive, affective, and social neuroscience have become central and accepted areas of research in neurosciences over the last two decades, which lends legitimacy to the research on meditation.

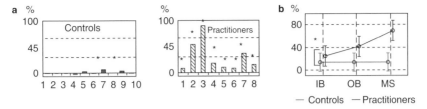

Figure 19.4. Relative EEG gamma power during non-referential compassion meditation in a group of novices and a group of long-term Buddhist practitioners. a–b. Intra-individual analysis on the ratio of gamma (25–42 Hz) to slow oscillations (4–13 Hz) averaged through all electrodes. a. The abscissa represents the subject numbers, the ordinate represents the difference in the mean ratio between the initial state and meditative state, and the black and red stars indicate that this increase is greater than two and three times, respectively, the baseline standard deviation. b. Interaction between the subject and the state factors for this ratio (ANOVA, $F_{(2,48)} = 3.5$, $p < .05$). IB (initial baseline), OB (ongoing baseline) and MS (Fischer, 1971 #68). The relative gamma increase during meditation is higher in the post-meditation session. In the initial baseline, the relative gamma is already higher for the practitioners ($p < .02$) than the controls and correlates with the length of the long-term practitioners' meditation training through life (adapted from Lutz et al. 2004).

Second, because meditative practices, such as Yoga or Mindfulness-Based Stress Reduction (MBSR), are now used routinely in the medical environment, clinicians recognize the need to validate its impact on the brain and the body.

Neuroelectric Correlates of Meditative States

Since the 1950s, the electrophysiological measure of brain or autonomic system has been the most popular imaging tool with which to study meditation.

Electroencephalography (EEG: Cooper et al., 2003) is a non-invasive technique that measures the electrical potentials on the scalp. EEG has an excellent temporal resolution in the millisecond range that allows the exploration of the fine temporal dynamic of neural processes. Below we discuss some basic findings about the nature and function of brain oscillatory processes as measured by electrophysiology, present some common theoretical assumptions about the neurodynamic basis of consciousness, and review the neuroelectric correlates of various meditative styles.

OSCILLATORY NEURAL SYNCHRONY AND CONSCIOUSNESS

In 1929, Hans Berger recorded for the first time a human brain's EEG and reported the presence of several brain rhythms in these signals (Berger, 1929). Since Berger's first observation, the various ongoing brain oscillations have been used successfully to characterize mental states, such as sleep, the waking state, or vigilance, and mental pathologies, such as epilepsy. Sensory evoked potentials (EEG signals triggered by an external stimulation) or the Bereitschaftpotential (a "readiness EEG potential" that can be recorded over motor areas up to 1 s before the execution of a movement) have demonstrated that such mental factors as sensation, attention, intellectual activity, and the planning of movement all have distinctive electrical correlates at the surface of the skull (Zeman, 2001).

Even though EEG results may be also contaminated by muscle activity, EEG oscillations are believed to reflect mostly the post-synaptic activity of neurons, in particular from the neocortex. More precisely, when a large population of neurons recorded by a single electrode transiently oscillates at the same frequency with a common phase, their local electric fields add up to produce a burst of oscillatory power in the signal reaching the electrode (Nunez, Wingeier, & Silberstein, 2001). The amplitude, or power, of these EEG oscillations thus provides a coarse way to quantify the synchronization of a large population of oscillating neurons below an electrode.

Oscillatory neural synchrony is a fundamental mechanism for implementing coordinated communication among spatially distributed neurons. Synchrony occurs in the brain at multiple spatial and temporal scales in local, regional, and long-range neural networks. At the cellular level, oscillatory synchrony, or phase synchrony, refers to the mechanism by which a population of oscillating neurons fires their action potentials in temporal synchrony with a precision in the millisecond range. At the population level, neuronal synchrony is best analyzed by looking at the common average oscillatory neural activity among the population. This oscillatory activity can be measured either from the local field potentials (the summated dendritic current of local neural groups) or from the macroscale of scalp recordings in EEG (Becker & Shapiro, 1981) and magnetoencephalography (MEG); Srinivasan et al., 1999). The emergence of synchrony in a neural population depends on the intrinsic rhythmic properties of individual neurons, on the properties of the network (Llinas et al., 1998), and on the inputs delivered to the network. As a general principle, synchrony has been proposed as a mechanism to "tag" the spatially distributed neurons that participate in the same process and, consequently, to enhance the salience of their activity compared to other neurons (Singer, 1999).

The functional and causal roles of synchrony are still an active area of research and depend on the spatial scale at which these phenomena are analyzed. In particular, it is useful to distinguish between two main scales, short range and long range. Short-range integration occurs over a local network (e.g., columns in the primary visual cortex), distributed over an area of approx-

imately 1 cm, through monosynaptic connections with conduction delays of 4 to 6 ms. Most electrophysiological studies in animals have dealt with short-range synchronies or synchronies between adjacent areas corresponding to a single sensory modality. These local synchronies have usually been interpreted as a mechanism of perceptual binding – the selection and integration of perceptual features in a given sensory modality (e.g., visual Gestalt features).

Large-scale integration concerns neural assemblies that are farther apart in the brain and are connected through polysynaptic pathways with transmission delays longer than 8 to 10 ms (Schnitzler & Gross, 2005; Varela et al., 2001). In this case, synchrony cannot be based on the local cellular architecture, but must instead reside in distant connections (cortico-cortical fibers or thalamocortical reciprocal pathways). These pathways correspond to the large-scale connections that link different levels of the network in different brain regions to the same assembly. The underlying mechanism of long-range synchrony is still poorly understood (for a model see Bibbig, Traub, & Whittington, 2002). Long-range synchronization is hypothesized to be a mechanism for the transient formation of a coherent macroassembly that selects and binds multimodal networks, such as assemblies between occipital and frontal lobes, or across hemispheres, which are separated by dozens of milliseconds in transmission time. The phenomenon of large-range synchrony has received considerable attention in neuroscience because it could provide new insights about the emergent principles that link the neuronal and the mental levels of description. Several authors have proposed that these mechanisms mediate several generic features of consciousness, such as unity (Varela & Thompson, 2001), integration and differentiation (Tononi & Edelman, 1998), transitoriness and temporal flow (Varela, 1999), and awareness of intentional action (Freeman, 1999). In this view, the emergence of a specific coherent global assembly underlines the operation of any moment of experience. The transition from one moment to the next would be subserved by desynchronization of some coherent assemblies and the synchronization of new ones. It has also been hypothesized that whether a local process participates directly in a given conscious state depends on whether it participates in a coherent, synchronous global assembly (Dehaene & Naccache, 2001; Engel et al., 2001).

Neural synchronies occur in a broad range of frequencies. Fast rhythms (above 15 Hz) in gamma and beta frequencies meet the requirement for fast neural integration and thus are thought to play a role in conscious processes on the time scale of fractions of a second (Tononi & Edelman, 1998; Varela, 1995). Fast-frequency synchronies have been found during such processes as attention, sensory segmentation, sensory perception, memory, and arousal.

Yet neural synchrony must also be understood in the context of the slower alpha and theta bands (4–13 Hz), which play an important role in attention, working memory (Fries, Reynolds, Rorie, & Desimone, 2001; von Stein, Chiang, & Konig, 2000), and sensorimotor integration (Burgess & O'Keefe, 2003; Rizzuto et al., 2003). This evidence supports the general notion that neural synchronization subserves not simply the binding of sensory attributes, but the overall integration of all dimensions of a cognitive act, including associative memory, affective tone and emotional appraisal, and motor planning.

So far, oscillatory synchrony has been investigated mostly on oscillatory signals having the same rhythms. More complex non-linear forms of cross-band synchronization, so-called generalized synchrony (Schiff, So, Chang, Burke, & Sauer, 1996), are also expected and may indeed prove more relevant in the long run to understanding large-scale integration than strict phase synchronization (Le Van Quyen, Chavez, Rudrauf, & Martinerie, 2003).

Considering the general importance of neural synchrony in brain processing, it is not surprising that scientists interested in meditation have tried to study its electrical brain correlates as early as the 1950s (Das & Gas-

taut, 1955; Wenger & Bagchi, 1961). Since then, more than 100 studies have investigated the tonic changes in the ongoing EEG from a restful state to a meditative state or the modulatory, or phasic, effect of meditation on the electrical brain responses to external sensory stimuli (for reviews, see Andresen, 2000; Davidson, 1976; Delmonte, 1984; Fenwick, 1987; Pagano & Warrenburg, 1983; Schuman, 1980; Shapiro & Walsh, 1984; West, 1980, 1987; Woolfolk, 1975).

The majority of these EEG studies focused on the change in the brain's oscillatory rhythms, particularly in the slow frequencies (alpha and theta rhythms). It is important to keep in mind that such measures reflect extremely blurred and crude estimates of the synchronous processes of the $\sim 10^{11}$ neurons in a human brain. Because slow oscillations have high electrical voltages that make them visually detectable, early studies only reported coarse visual descriptions of EEGs. Changes in fast-frequency oscillations during meditation have been rarely reported (with the notable exception of Das & Gastaut, 1955, and more recently Lutz et al., 2004) possibly because the lower voltage of these oscillations requires spectral analysis instead of simple visual inspection. The investigation of fast-frequency synchrony during meditation has become more common since the 1990s following a developing understanding of its functional role in the "binding problem."

In addition to spectral analysis, meditation has also been characterized with measures of coherence or long-distance phase synchrony (LDS) (Fries et al., 2001). These measures quantify the dynamic coupling between EEG channels over distant brain regions. Coherence is the frequency correlation coefficient, and it represents the degree to which the frequency profiles of two distant areas of the head, as reflected in the electrical signals detected by scalp electrodes, are similar. LDS measures the instantaneous phase relationship between signals at a given frequency (Lachaux, Rodriguez, Martinerie, & Varela, 1999). LDS provides a more direct measure of phase-locking than coherence because it can separate the effects of amplitude and phase in the interrelations between signals. Thus, LDS can test more precisely the assumption that phase synchrony is involved in long-distance neuronal integration. Because of the non-linear nature of brain processes, these linear analysis approaches are likely to characterize only partially the functional properties of synchronous activity. Yet, complementary non-linear analysis of brain dynamics during meditation has only just started to be explored (Aftanas & Golocheikine, 2002).

In the selective summary of the literature below, we review only those EEG studies published in top-tier journals and/or those that focused on the study of long-term practitioners.

TRANSCENDENTAL MEDITATION

TM is a passive meditation adapted for Westerners from the Vedic or Brahmanical traditions of India. The subject sits quietly, with the eyes closed, repeating a Sanskrit sound (mantra), while concentrating on nothing and letting the mind "drift" (Morse, Martin, Furst, & Dubin, 1977). The continued practice of TM supposedly is said to lead to an expansion of consciousness or the attainment of "cosmic" or "pure, self-referral consciousness" (Maharishi, 1969). The technique is described as "easy, enjoyable and does not involve concentration, contemplation or any type of control" (R. K. Wallace, 1970).

The standard EEG correlate of TM is an increase in alpha rhythm amplitude, frequently followed by a slowing in frequency by 1–3 Hz and a spreading of this pattern into the frontal channels (R. K. Wallace, 1970). An increase in bursts of theta oscillations (4–7 Hz) has also been reported. Global fronto-central increases in coherence in alpha (6–12 Hz), as well as in theta frequency ranges between baseline and TM practice, have been found frequently (for reviews and for a model of TM practice see Travis, Arenander, & DuBois, 2004)).

The dominant frequency in the scalp EEG of human adults is the alpha rhythm. It is manifest by a peak in spectral analysis around 10 Hz and reflects rhythmic alpha waves (Klimesch, 1999; Nunez et al., 2001).

Alpha oscillations are found primarily over occipital-parietal channels particularly when the eyes are closed, yet alpha activity can be recorded from nearly the entire upper cortical surface. During wakefulness, it is a basic EEG phenomenon that the alpha peak reflects a tonic large-scale synchronization of a very large population of neurons. This low-frequency global neural activity is thought to be elicited by reciprocal interactions among the cortex, the reticular nucleus, and the thalamocortical (Delmonte, 1985) cells in other thalamic nuclei (Klimesch, 1999; Nunez et al., 2001; Slotnick, Moo, Kraut, Lesser, & Hart, 2002) even if cortico-cortical mechanisms also play a possible role (Lopes da Silva, Vos, Mooibroek, & Van Rotterdam, 1980).

Because an overall decrease in alpha power has been related to increasing demands of attention, alertness, and task load, alpha activity is classically viewed as an "idling rhythm" reflecting a relaxed, unoccupied brain (Klimesch, 1999). Large-scale alpha synchronization blocks information processing because very large populations of neurons oscillate with the same phase and frequency; thus, it is a state of high integration but low differentiation. Within a bandwidth of perhaps 2 Hz near this spectral peak, alpha frequencies frequently produce spontaneously moderate to large coherence (0.3–0.8 over large interelectrode distance (Nunez et al., 1997). The alpha coherence values reported in TM studies, as a trait in the baseline or during meditation, belong to this same range. Thus a global increase of alpha power and alpha coherence might not reflect a more "ordered" or "integrated" experience, as frequently claimed in TM literature, but rather a relaxed, inactive mental state (Fenwick, 1987).

In contrast, alpha desynchronization reflects actual cognitive processes in which different neuronal networks start to oscillate locally at different frequencies – typically in higher frequencies (>15 Hz), as well as slower rhythms (4–15 Hz) – and with different phases, reflecting local processing of specialized neuronal circuitries, such as those for attention, vision, memory, emotion, and so on. Large-scale synchrony between distant neuronal assemblies oscillating at various frequencies reflects an active coordination of functionally independent networks; in short, it reflects a state of high integration and high differentiation. Thus, the slow frequency activity (<13 Hz) found during TM meditation, combined with the frequent finding of decreased autonomic activity, has been interpreted by many authors as reflecting hypoarousal or a relaxed state (Delmonte, 1984; Holmes, 1984; Pagano & Warrenburg, 1983).

Yet, the "idling" model of alpha activity has been extended recently to account for new findings. Alpha oscillation can, paradoxically, increase locally over specific regions or also across specific areas while the subject is actively focusing his or her attention on an object or while holding in mind information (memory load during retention, for instance). Slow rhythms (4–12 Hz) can thus also be involved in active mental states requiring attention, working memory, or semantic encoding (Ward, 2003). This alpha model still remains compatible with the idling model because on this view, alpha rhythms during mental activity reflect active inhibition of non-task-relevant cortical areas (Klimesch, 1999).

Because TM is described as a passive meditation without active control or concentrative effort, the EEG picture found during TM meditation can still be interpreted as reflecting mainly hypoarousal or a relaxed state. Yet, it is also possible that the ongoing repetition of the mantra, which involves, for instance, some form of attention and working memory, can lead to an active exclusion of some brain processes compatible with an increase in alpha activity in non-task-related cortical territories.

TM researchers further view this EEG picture as reflecting a single and original state of "Transcendental pure consciousness" (Maharishi, 1969; Travis et al., 2004). The transcendental state is conceptualized as a "fourth state of consciousness," a "wakeful hypometabolic state" that differs from hypnosis and ordinary or sleep states (R. K. Wallace, 1970). Although these descriptions might best be interpreted as metaphysical assertions rather than first-person descriptions, they do suggest that this state of absorption could also involve some form of meta-awareness. Nevertheless, despite the possibility of a more sophisticated phenomenological interpretation and the need to relate physiological data to subjective data, it is still unclear whether and how TM meditation practices produce increased alpha activity beyond a general arousal effect or an inhibition of task-irrelevant cortical zones. Other relaxation techniques have led to the same EEG profile, and studies that employed counter-balanced control relaxation conditions consistently found a lack of alpha power increases or even decreases when comparing relaxation or hypnosis to TM meditation (Morse et al., 1977; Tebecis, 1975; Warrenburg, Pagano, Woods, & Hlastala, 1980). Similarly, the initial claim that TM produces a unique state of consciousness different from sleep has been refuted by several EEG meditation studies that reported sleep-like stages during this technique with increased alpha and then theta power (Pagano, Rose, Stivers, & Warrenburg, 1976; Younger, Adriance, & Berger, 1975).

To summarize, alpha global increases and alpha coherence mostly over frontal electrodes are associated with TM practice when meditating compared to baseline (Morse, Martin, Furst, & Dubin, 1977). This global alpha increase is similar to that produced by other relaxation techniques. The passive absorption during the recitation of the mantra, as practiced in this technique, produces a brain pattern that suggests a decrease of processing of sensory or motor information and of mental activity in general. Because alpha rhythms are ubiquitous and functionally non-specific, the claim that alpha oscillations and alpha coherence are desirable or are linked to an original and higher state of consciousness seem quite premature.

ATTENTION MEDITATION WITH AN OBJECT

This section regroups EEG studies on meditative practices having a component of attention regulation. In all these practices, the intentional structure of a subject/object remains. As mentioned earlier these techniques lie somewhere on a continuum between two poles of practices: On the one hand, one-pointed attention techniques cultivate a form of voluntary, effortful, and sustained attention on an object, and on the other hand, *vipaśyanā* meditation cultivates a more broadly focused, non-judgmental mode of bare attention. These meditations differ from relaxation techniques because they cultivate a balance between hypoarousal (Becker & Shapiro, 1981) and excitation. This balance is required, in particular, to maintain a sufficient clarity or meta-awareness throughout the meditative session. These practices encompass, for instance, Zazen meditation, Indian yogic concentration, meditation in MBSR, and one-pointed focused attention. The emphasis on stabilizing the mind on an object or on the awareness of the intentional relation itself depends not only on the given technique but also likely on the degree of the practitioner's accomplishment in a given practice.

With some important exceptions, most studies on Zazen or India yogic concentration practices have revealed an EEG signature similar to TM as characterized by lowered autonomic arousal and slow-frequency EEG patterns (either an increase in alpha or an increase in theta activity; Austin, 1998; Delmonte, 1984; Fenwick, 1987; Shapiro & Walsh, 1984). This pattern was reported as a state and sometimes also a trait. For instance, Kasamatsu and Hirai measured the EEG signals of 48 priests and disciples during Zazen practices (Kasamatsu & Hirai, 1966). All subjects exhibited visually an increase in alpha activity mostly over central and frontal electrodes immediately after beginning meditation. Less experienced subjects tended to maintain high-amplitude alpha activity throughout the meditative session, whereas the EEGs of those with more years of Zazen practice showed a rhythmical theta wave pattern during the later stage of Zazen. Anand, Chhina, and Singh (1961) visually compared the EEG activity of four advanced yogis during rest and during meditation. All subjects displayed large alpha activity during periods of rest and increases during meditation (Anand et al., 1961).

Yet, several exceptions deserve scrutiny. Two early field studies of Yoga in India by Das and Gastaut (1955) and Wenger and Bagchi (1961), reported a clear sign of autonomic arousal with increased heart rate and skin conductance when advanced yogis meditate. High-amplitude high-frequency EEG oscillations (beta and gamma) were found and were more pronounced during deep meditation (Das & Gastaut, 1955). In a well-controlled study, Corby et al. (1978) studied a form of Tantric Yoga meditation where the practitioners and controls focused on their breath and on the mantra. Unlike previously reported studies, proficient meditators demonstrated increased autonomic activation during meditation, whereas unexperienced meditators demonstrated autonomic relaxation. During meditation, proficient meditators showed an increase in alpha and theta power, minimal evidence of EEG-defined sleep, and a decrease in autonomic orienting to external stimulation.

These findings are consistent with the view described above that alpha and theta activation can also index attentional processes. Because one major feature of attention is selection, it is likely that the localized increases in slow frequencies reflect cortical tuning such that those cortical zones that are not required for task engagement are selectively inhibited to facilitate task performance (see e.g., Cooper et al., 2003). Also consistent with this formulation are data on attentional anticipation. Foxe, Simpson, and Ahlfors (1998) demonstrated that a cue indicating an upcoming auditory stimulus induced increased alpha power over parieto-occipital (Blake & Logothetis, 2002) cortex, compared when the cue indicated an upcoming visual stimulus. These findings are all consistent with the idea that alpha synchronization during attentional processes reflects inhibition of non-relevant areas or process (Klimesch, 1999).

It would be misguided to identify alpha or theta activity as the sole index of mindfulness/awareness meditation. Numerous data suggest that synchronized gamma activity is also specifically involved in selective attention. In the literature on meditation, one early study on advanced yogic practitioners reported spectacular generalized high-amplitude beta/gamma oscillations during intense internal concentration of attention (Das & Gastaut, 1955). We also found an increase in fast-frequency oscillations during *samatha* practice (unpublished data). Numerous studies of humans, as well as animals, have demonstrated an enhancement of the gamma activity when subjects were actively attending to a certain stimulus or simply perceived an object (Tallon-Baudry & Bertrand, 1999). Such synchronized gamma activity during attention participates not only in bottom-up processes (e.g., sensory segmentation, feature extraction) but also in top-down processes (Engel et al., 2001).

Slow and fast-frequency rhythms interact in the brain. For instance, in intracranial recordings from area V_4 in monkeys, increased gamma range synchronization but reduced low-frequency synchronization is observed among neurons activated by the attended stimulus as compared to neurons activated by an identical but non-attended stimulus (Fries et al., 2001). These important results, as well as event-related data, lead to the notion of a *surround inhibition* wherein active cortical areas, indexed by alpha desynchronization and/or fast-frequency synchronies, are surrounded by a "doughnut" of alpha synchronization or inhibition (Suffczynski, Kalitzin, Pfurtscheller, & Lopes da Silva, 2001). This balance between slow and fast frequencies can be detected under specific experimental conditions, such as intracranial recording or simple event-related tasks, over motor or sensory areas. Yet, this distinction is likely to be blurred in general while recording ongoing EEG signals because of volume conduction (i.e., a single neural source is likely to influence the signal in many recording channels). Despite this limitation, the combined characterization of fast-frequency synchronies, in addition to the slow frequencies, over various topographical regions of the scalp is likely to provide increased understanding of the specific neural processes that are altered by these practices.

Finally there is some evidence that alpha/theta oscillations during Zazen or Samadhi practices differ functionally from the alpha/theta activity during a relaxed non-meditative state. An early model of meditation proposed that "de-automization" was induced, such that each stimulus trial was perceived as "fresh" during meditative states cultivating a receptive and open awareness (Deikman, 1966; Kasamatsu & Hirai, 1966). A possible indication of this process is EEG alpha blocking, which is defined as a decrease in ongoing alpha (8–12 Hz) power when comparing prestimulus to post-stimulus activity. Typically alpha activity is reduced from closed eyes to open eyes or when discrete stimuli are presented and is thought to reflect cortical processing. This response habituates after repetitive stimulus presentations (Morrell, 1966). Early field studies on yogis reported no alpha blocking in response to auditory, thermal, and visual stimuli (Anand et al., 1961; Das & Gastaut, 1955; Wenger & Bagchi, 1961). Subsequent Zen studies found alpha blocking to auditory sounds but without habituation (Kasamatsu & Hirai, 1966). Early TM studies produced conflicting results, with one finding an absence of alpha blocking whereas the other reported habituation of alpha blocking to auditory stimuli (Banquet, 1973; R. K. Wallace, 1970).

A replication and extension of these findings were attempted (Becker & Shapiro, 1981). Experienced Zen, Yoga, and TM meditators, and "attend" and "ignore" groups of controls were presented with auditory clicks during mediation. The attend group was asked to "pay strong attention" to each click, notice all of its sound qualities and subtleties, and count the number of clicks; the ignore group was told "try not to let the clicks disturb your relaxed state." EEG alpha suppression and skin conductance response both showed clear habituation, which did not differ among groups, thus failing to replicate the earlier studies.

As a summary, these meditation practices that feature focused attention on objects most frequently are accompanied by increases in alpha and theta power, but also by fast frequencies (beta and gamma) during deep meditation. The slow-frequency activity overlaps notably with early drowsiness and sleep stages even if these oscillations potentially differ functionally. The neuroelectric signatures of these various meditative techniques (Focus Attention, Zazen, Vipaśyanā meditation) have not yet been firmly established. Our current understanding of attention suggests that the selection or the exclusion from attention of particular contents (sensory, motor, internal tasks) is correlated with the activation or inhibition of specific brain areas, as indexed by specific changes in selective brain oscillatory patterns. The combination of topographical information with spectral information seems a promising method by which to delineate further these various meditative techniques.

OBJECTLESS MEDITATION

During objectless meditation, such as Open Presence or Non-Referential Compassion meditation, it is said that the practitioner does not focus on a particular object but rather cultivates a state of being. Objectless meditation does so in such a way that, according to reports given after meditation, the intentional or object-oriented aspect of experience appears to dissipate in meditation along with the explicit sense of being a perceiver or an agent (autobiographical self). One working hypothesis is that some form of meta-awareness or, more precisely, of some mere ipseity still remains or is enhanced during these states.

These types of meditation have been poorly investigated so far. We studied a group of long-term practitioners who underwent mental training in the same Tibetan Nyingmapa and Kargyupa traditions for 10,000 to 50,000 hours over time periods ranging from 15 to 40 years. We found that these long-term Buddhist practitioners self-induced sustained EEG high-amplitude gamma-band oscillations and phase synchrony during Non-Referential Compassion meditation (Lutz et al., 2004, Figure 19.5). These fast-frequency oscillations (>20 Hz)

had a peak-to-peak amplitude of the order of dozens of microvolts for several practitioners. High-amplitude oscillations were continuous during the meditation over several dozens of seconds and gradually increase during the practices. These EEG patterns differ from those of controls, in particular over lateral fronto-parietal electrodes. Some preliminary data further suggest that these ongoing high-amplitude gamma oscillations are correlated with self-reports of the clarity (see the section on *samatha* and *vipaśyanā* as paradigms of meditation; Lutz et al., 2005).

These new findings are similar to the early report of Das and Gastaut (1955) during the Samadhi of advanced Indian Yogis. Samadhi was defined as a state during which "the perfectly motionless subject is insensible to all that surrounds him and is conscious of nothing but the subject of his meditation." Das and Gastaut (1955) reported an acceleration of the cardiac rhythm during meditation almost perfectly parallel to that of the EEG. The EEG showed progressive and spectacular modifications during the deepest meditations in those subjects who had the longest training: acceleration of the alpha rhythm and decrease in the amplitude and appearance of faster oscillations (>20 Hz). These fast frequencies (beta (25–30 Hz) and sometimes even gamma activity (40–45 Hz) became generalized during the Samadhi meditation, with high amplitude reaching between 30–50 mV.

In our study (Lutz et al., 2004), we further showed that during this objectless meditation the ratio of fast-frequency activity (25–42 Hz) to slow oscillatory activity (4–13 Hz) over medial fronto-parietal electrodes is initially higher in the resting baseline before meditation for the practitioners than controls (Figure 19.4). During meditation, this difference increases sharply over most of the scalp electrodes and remains higher than the initial baseline in the post-meditative baseline. The functional and behavioral consequences of sustained gamma activity during objectless meditation are not currently known, and such effects clearly need further study.

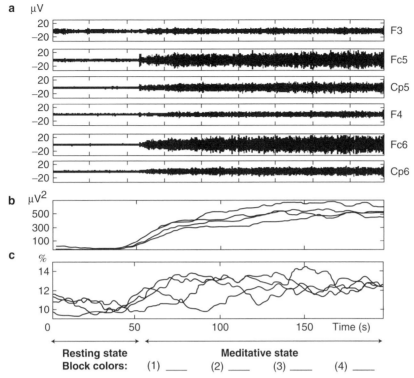

Figure 19.5. Example of high-amplitude gamma activity during the non-referential compassion meditation of long-term Buddhist practitioners. **a**. Raw electroencephalographic signals. At t = 45 s, practitioner S4 started generating a state of non-referential compassion, block 1. **b**. Time course of gamma activity power over the electrodes displayed in "a" during four blocks computed in a 20-s sliding window every 2 s and then averaged over electrodes. c. Time course of their cross-hemisphere synchrony between 25–42 Hz. The density of long-distance synchrony above a surrogate threshold was calculated in a 20-ssliding window every 2 s and for each cross-hemisphere electrode pairs and, then, was averaged across electrode pairs (adapted from Lutz et al. 2004).

Neuroimaging Correlates of Meditation

At this stage neuroimaging studies on meditation are typically more exploratory than hypothesis driven. Nevertheless, some progress has been made in the identification of structural-functional brain relationships of meditative states and traits using a variety of neuroimaging modalities. In particular, some theoretical efforts have been made to localize the neural circuitry selectively engaged during a meditative state. Austin (1998), for instance, elegantly combined his insight as a Zen practitioner with his neuroanatomical knowledge of the brain as a medical doctor to speculate about the

neural basis of the peak experience of a meditative state termed "kensho" or "satori" in Japanese Zen Buddhism. In this state, the sense of selfhood is allegedly dissolved and an "unattached, self-less, impersonal" awareness remains (this state shares a strong, descriptive similarity with the Open Presence state discussed above). After examining the precise experiential changes induced by this state, he reviewed the various physiological subsystems that might participate in this state. Austin specifically introduces the distinction between "egocentric" neural networks involved in the generation of a multifaceted self situated in time and space and "allocentric" neural networks involved in the mere processing of the external environment. For Austin, neural networks participating in the construction of the narrative self could be shut down during Kensho, specifically through thalamic gating originating from the reticular formation. At the same time, he proposes that the state of hyperawareness during this practice is mediated by intralaminar nuclei of the thalamus that can increase the fast-frequency synchrony in other cortical regions. These nuclei could shape the resonance of the cortico-thalamo-cortical loops and functionally alter the neural processing in these egocentric/allocentric networks. These proposals (Austin, 1998, 2006) are clearly speculative, and further discussion is beyond the scope of this review. Nevertheless, Austin's work amply illustrates the potential benefits that may come when the neuroscience of meditation and first-person descriptions are brought into a dynamic dialogue that combines their findings in a manner that places fruitful constraints on each.

Although there is considerable potential for advancement in neuroscience through neuroimaging studies of meditation, the number of published studies remains sparse. To illustrate the range of methods and questions utilized thus far, we now review briefly the published research in this area.

BRAIN IMAGING TECHNIQUES USED
IN MEDITATION RESEARCH
Positron emission tomography (PET; Blake & Logothetis, 2002) and functional magnetic resonance imaging (fMRI) are two functional brain imaging methods that have been used to study meditation. PET measures emissions from radioactively labeled chemicals that have been injected into the bloodstream and uses the data to produce two- or three-dimensional images of the distribution of the chemicals throughout the brain and body. Using different tracers, PET can reveal blood flow, oxygen and glucose metabolism, and neurotransmitter concentrations in the tissues of the working brain. Blood flow and oxygen and glucose metabolism reflect the amount of brain activity in different regions, and this type of data enables scientists to characterize the physiology and neurochem-

istry of the working brain. SPECT (single photon emission computed tomography) is another neuroimaging method that is similar to, though less sophisticated than, PET, and it produces images of neurochemical function that have less spatial resolution than PET. MRI uses magnetic fields and radio waves to produce high-quality two- or three dimensional images of brain structures without injecting radioactive tracers. Using MRI, scientists can see both surface and deep brain structures with a high degree of anatomical detail (millimeter resolution). MRI techniques can also be used to image the brain as it functions.

Functional MRI (fMRI) relies on the magnetic properties of blood to enable the researcher to measure the blood flow in the brain as it changes dynamically in real time. Thus researchers can make maps of changes in brain activity as participants perform various tasks or are exposed to various stimuli. An fMRI scan can produce images of brain activity as fast as every second or two, whereas PET usually takes several dozens of seconds to image brain function. Thus, with fMRI, scientists can determine precisely when brain regions become active and how long they remain active. As a result, they can see whether brain activity occurs simultaneously or sequentially in different brain regions as a participant thinks, feels, or reacts to external stimuli. An fMRI scan can also produce high-quality images that can identify more accurately than PET which areas of the brain are being activated. In summary, fMRI offers better image clarity along with the ability to assess blood flow and brain function in seconds. So far, however, PET retains the advantage of being able to pinpoint which neurochemicals are involved in functional brain alterations.

EARLY NEUROIMAGING STUDIES ON
RELAXATION PRACTICE AND MEDITATION
The studies from Lou et al. (1999) and Newberg et al. (2001) provide the first evidence of functional brain changes using PET or SPECT during a relaxation practice and a meditative practice, respectively. Even if these studies offer new insights about these states, they speak also for the need to more

precisely develop descriptions of the practices to better understand just what the functional neural changes are reflecting.

Yoga Nidrā, literally "Yoga-Sleep," is a state in the Yoga tradition in which consciousness of the world and consciousness of action are meant to be dissociated: The mind "withdraws" from wishing to act and is not associated with emotions or the power of will. The practitioner allegedly becomes a neutral observer who experiences the loss of conscious control, concentration, or judgment, yet maintains an equal and impartial attention to sensory awareness, which is said to be enhanced. A PET (^{15}O-H$_2$O) study of blood flow changes during Yoga Nidrā practice was carried out while subjects listened to a tape recording, with guided instructions on the different phases of the practice (Lou et al., 1999). The relaxation tape contained focusing exercises on body sensation, abstract joy, visual imagery of a summer landscape, and symbolic representation of the self. Participants listened to the tape and followed the instructions of the guided meditation. The baseline condition was obtained by replaying the tape while participants remained neutral (i.e., they did not follow the instructions). Each of the guided meditation phases was associated with different regional activations during meditation relative to the control conditions. Yet, during all meditative phases, overall increases in bilateral hippocampus, parietal, and occipital sensory and association regions were found compared to control conditions. This pattern suggests an increase of activity in areas involved in imagery.

Deactivation was found during meditation in orbitofrontal, dorsolateral prefrontal, anterior cingulate cortices, temporal and inferior parietal lobes, caudate, thalamus, pons, and cerebellum. This differential activity was interpreted as reflecting a "tonic" activity during normal consciousness in the baseline condition. The areas decreasing during the meditation state are known to participate in executive function or control of attention. More particularly, dorsolateral prefrontal cortex participates in working memory and the preparation for voluntary movement, the anterior cingulate plays a role not only in motivation and resolution of conflict but also skeleto-motor control and executive attention, and the cerebellum is implicated in cognitive functions such as attention.

Lou et al. (1999) interpreted these results as reflecting dissociation between two complementary aspects of consciousness: the conscious experience of the sensory world and the "fact or illusion of voluntary control, with self regulation." Unfortunately, the lack of a control population makes it difficult to interpret whether the brain patterns reflect specific meditative qualities or the cognitive processes induced by the instructions.

Using SPECT Newberg et al. (2001) measured changes in regional blow flow (rCBF) while eight relatively experienced Tibetan Buddhist practitioners meditated. The practitioners practiced daily for at least 15 years and underwent several 3-month retreats. In the scanner, the practitioners were instructed to "focus their attention on a visualized image and maintained that focus with increasing intensity." In contrast to Lou et al. (1999), Newberg and colleagues (2001) reported an increase in activity in orbital frontal cortex, dorsolateral prefrontal cortex (DLPFC), and thalamus. They also found a negative correlation between the DLPFC and the superior parietal lobe, which was interpreted as reflecting an altered sense of space experienced during meditation. The difference in the frontal areas between their finding and that of Lou et al. (1999) was viewed as reflecting a difference between an active and a passive form of meditation.

In addition to the fact that no control participants were involved in the Newberg study, there is regrettably a lack of descriptive precision of the meditative state that was studied. This limitation will hamper the future comparison of this study with others. More precisely, a broad variety of Tibetan meditative techniques could encompass the provided meditative descriptions. These practices include, for instance, Focused Attention on a mental object, or any meditation on the visualization of a deity, or indeed the visualization of one's guru. Unfortunately, these practices can differ or even be opposite in terms of their motivations or emotional qualities. For instance, the visualization of deities could involve some invocation of anger or lust, whereas the visualization of the guru is meant to induce a strong devotional affect in the meditator. Because the independent variable (i.e., the specific meditative practice) was only vaguely described in this study, its impact is limited.

FOCUSED ATTENTION/MINDFULNESS-AWARENESS MEDITATION

A form of Kundalini Yoga using mantra repetition combined with breath awareness was assessed with fMRI (Lazar et al., 2000). The control state entailed the mental enunciation of animal names. Five Yoga adepts who had practiced Kundalini Yoga for at least 4 years served as subjects. An increase in the Blood Oxygenation Level Dependent (BOLD) signal was found from baseline to meditation in the putamen, midbrain, anterior cingulate cortex, and the hippocampal/parahippocampal formation, as well as in regions in the frontal and parietal cortices. The comparison of early versus late meditation states showed activity increase in these regions, but within a greater area and with larger signal changes later in the practice. Because the pattern of brain activity increased with meditation time, it may index the gradual changes induced by meditation. This pattern of activity encompassed areas subserving attention (fronto-parietal cortices) and areas subserving arousal and autonomic control (limbic regions, midbrain, and anterior cingulate cortex).

In another attention-related study, we recently studied experienced Buddhist meditators (>10,000 hours of cumulative meditation practice) and newly trained control subjects while they performed a Focused Attention meditation (Tsé-cig Ting-ngé-dzin; see the section on Focused Attention), alternating with a passive state, while undergoing block-design fMRI (Brefczynski-Lewis, Lutz, & Davidson, 2004). During this standard meditation, the participants concentrated their attention on an external visual object (a white dot on the screen), gently bringing attention back to the object if they

became distracted or sleepy. Control subjects with no prior meditative training were given instruction in concentration meditation with daily practice a week before the fMRI scan. fMRI of concentration meditation in both the experienced meditators and the controls showed common areas of activation in the traditional attention network, including such areas as the intraparietal sulci, frontal eye fields (FEF), thalamus, insula, lateral occipital, and basal ganglia. However, experienced meditators showed more activation, especially in the frontal-parietal network. The increased activation in these regions for experienced practitioners may represent a neural correlate for these subjects' expertise in sustained attention. The fact that controls show greater activation in the anterior cingulate compared with the adepts may reflect greater error proneness (i.e., distraction) and conflict monitoring in the controls than the adepts; the conflict would be between the instructions to focus and the difficulty of complying with such instructions.

Taken together these two brain imaging studies show that concentration meditation enhances processing in regions similar to those found in other attentional paradigms. The group differences between long-term practitioners and novices support the view that attention processing could be affected by mental training.

PURE COMPASSION AND LOVINGKINDNESS MEDITATION

Using functional imaging, we assessed brain activity while novice and long-term practitioners generated a Lovingkindness-Compassion meditation, alternating with a resting state (Brefczynski-Lewiset et al., 2004). As described in the section on Non-Referential Compassion meditation, this standard Buddhist meditation involves the generation of a state in which an unconditional feeling of lovingkindness and compassion pervades the whole mind as a way of being, with no other consideration, reasoning, or discursive thoughts. This state is called in Tibetan "pure" or "non-referential" compassion, as the practitioner is not focused upon particular objects during this state. In the resting state the subjects were asked to be in the most ordinary state without being engaged in an active mental state or being in a pleasant or unpleasant emotional state. Subjects were eight long-term Buddhist practitioners and eight age-matched healthy control volunteers who were interested in learning to meditate. Buddhist practitioners underwent mental training in the Tibetan Nyingmapa and Kargyupa traditions for 10,000 to 50,000 hours over time periods ranging from 15 to 40 years. During the meditative state, we found a common activation in the striatum, anterior insula, somatosensory cortex, anterior cingulate cortex, and left-prefontal cortex and a deactivation in the right interior parietal. This pattern was robustly modulated by the degree of expertise, with the adepts showing considerably more enhanced activation in this network compared with the novices.

These data provide evidence that this altruistic state involved a specific matrix of brain regions that are commonly linked to feeling states, planning of movements, and positive emotions. Maternal and romantic love have been linked in humans to the activation of the reward and attachment circuitries, such as the substantia nigra and the striatum (caudate nucleus, putamen, globus pallidus; Bartels & Zeki, 2004). Positive and negative emotions are expected to differentially activate the left and right prefrontal cortices, respectively, as suggested by lesion and electrophysiological data (Davidson, 2000). More generally, feeling states are thought to be mediated by structures that receive inputs regarding the internal milieu and musculoskeletal structures and include the brainstem tegmentum, hypothalamus, insula, and somatosensory and cingulate cortices (Damasio, 1999). This view has received some neuroimaging support in a task where subjects self-generate emotional states and more recently in studies using pain experience or interoceptive tasks (Craig, 2002).

Finally, love and compassion require an understanding of the feelings of others; hence, a common view is that the very regions subserving one's own feeling states also instantiate one's empathic experience of other's feelings. This framework derives from perception-action models of motor behavior and imitation. The key proposal is that the observation and imagination of another person in a particular emotional state automatically activate a similar affective state in the observer, with its associated autonomic and somatic responses. Thus, experienced and empathic pain commonly activated the anterior insula and rostral anterior cingulate cortex (Singer et al., 2004). The activation in the anterior insula was stronger for the practitioners, an area that some scientists have found to be involved in feelings. These data are consistent with the view that our experience of another's suffering is mediated by the same brain regions involved in the experience of our own pain.

We further found that brain activity for the long-term practitioners was greater than the novices in several of the commonly activated regions. These analyses indicate that the degree of training, as reflected in the hours of cumulative meditation experience, modulates the amplitude of activation in the brain areas commonly involved in this state.

To summarize, our study of Compassion meditation found activation in brain regions thought to be responsible for monitoring one's feeling state, planning of movements, and positive emotions. This pattern was robustly modulated by the degree of expertise. These data suggest that emotional and empathic processes are flexible skills that can be enhanced by training and that such training is accompanied by demonstrable neural changes.

General Conclusion

Overall, this chapter aimed to summarize the state of knowledge in neuroscientific research on meditation and to suggest potential avenues of inquiry illuminated by these initial findings. The first section discussed the need for more precise descriptions of meditative practices so as to define properly the practices that are the objects of scientific study. Following this recommendation, the Buddhist contemplative tradition was presented in detail as a canonical example. The main Buddhist theories of meditation were reviewed as well as the basic parameters that define most forms of Buddhist contemplative practice. In addition to suggesting an approach to defining and categorizing meditation, this section also aimed to underscore the difficulty of separating well-defined first-person descriptions of meditative states from other claims that, although apparently descriptive, are best understood as reflecting particular cultural or religious exigencies that are not strictly rooted in scientifically tractable observations. The choice to view a Buddhist claim as a first-person description of an actual state or as primarily a product of some religious and cultural rhetoric is certainly subject to debate and interpretation. Further developments will definitely be needed to delineate these distinctions. With these difficulties in mind, three standard Buddhist meditative states were described in detail, as well as the rationale for the cultivation of these states and the expected post-meditative effects. Some general guidelines were then proposed for developing a questionnaire to define more precisely a practice under examination. It is our hope that this first section will provide researchers with some theoretical and methodological principles to clarify and enhance future research on meditation.

The second section explored some scientific motivations for the neuroscientific examination of meditation in terms of its potential impact on the brain and body of long-term practitioners or its possible role in the neuroscientific study of subjective experience. After an overview of the mechanisms of neuroplasticity and mind-body interaction, we argued that mental training might have a long-term impact on the brain and body in a way that is beneficial for physical health, illness, and possibly well-being. We then suggested how the use of first-person expertise might foster our understanding of

the neural counterpart of subjective experience. These intersections between neuroscience and meditation were separated here mainly for analytical purposes, but these heuristic distinctions implicitly suggest an important area of further research; namely, the interactions among the various themes of research. For instance, one question of interest will be to explore whether it is meaningful to study the alleged therapeutic or healing virtues of meditation as a variable of research in isolation from other issues. The interest in this question stems from the possibility that the beneficial changes found in practitioners of meditation are intrinsically dependent on other practices or virtues cultivated in their tradition, such as compassion, ethical behavior, or a first-person exploration of the nature of the self and external perception. Having suggested, in any case, the potentially fruitful exploration of meditation from a neuroscientific perspective, in the final section, we reviewed the most relevant neuroelectric and neuroimaging findings of research conducted to date. We anticipate that the renewed interest in research on meditation will probably extend and possibly modify this section within the near future.

As noted earlier, we chose to emphasize the practice of long-term Buddhist practitioners, in part because of the potential that a study of such practitioners might have to enhance our understanding of consciousness. Already we have some indication that experienced practitioners are able to provide repeatable subjective reports that are more reliable than those from untrained persons, and this opens the door to wide-ranging research into the neural correlates of those reportable states. More particularly, the possibility that some meditators may be able to induce a state approaching some form of bare consciousness or ipseity raises the tantalizing (if contentious) hypothesis that the neural correlates of such a state would bring us closer to understanding what we mean by consciousness from a neuroscientific perspective.

Our decision to focus on long-term Buddhist practitioners, however, should not diminish the importance of future research on novices, of longitudinal studies of changes over time in novice or mid-range practitioners, or of research involving other contemplative traditions. This point is crucial if one believes that some of these meditative practices have the potential to evolve into a more secular form of mental training, with alleged therapeutic, pedagogical, and/or health value. Most importantly, the collective evidence showcased in this review underscores the fact that many of our core mental processes, such as awareness and attention and emotion regulation, including our very capacity for happiness and compassion, should best be conceptualized as trainable skills. The meditative traditions provide a compelling example of strategies and techniques that have evolved over time to enhance and optimize human potential and well-being. The neuroscientific study of these traditions is still in its infancy, but the early findings promise both to reveal the mechanisms by which such training may exert its effects and underscore the plasticity of the brain circuits that underlie complex mental functions. It is our fervent hope that this review will stimulate additional research and will lead to the increased use of these practices in a wide range of everyday contexts.

Acknowledgments

Support for writing this chapter and the research from the authors' lab that is reported herein was provided by NIMH P50-MH069315 to RJD, gifts from Adrianne and Edwin Cook-Ryder and from Bryant Wangard, NCCAM U01AT002114-01A1 and the Fyssen Foundation to A. L.

Notes

1. Number of articles indexing the term "meditation" in Medline in 2005.
2. For a fruitful and pragmatic development of this hypothesis see Depraz, Varela, & Vermersch (2003).

3. To facilitate further inquiry by readers unfamiliar with the relevant Asian languages, only sources available in English have been used to present the pertinent Buddhist theories and practices. It is important to note, however, that many of the most relevant Tibetan texts in particular have yet to be translated reliably into any European language.
4. Gethin (1998) provides an excellent overview of the *Abhidharma* and its context. It is important to note that the two classical South Asian languages most relevant to the history of living Buddhist traditions are Sanskrit and Pāli. Sanskrit is relevant especially to Tibetan, Chinese, Japanese, and Korean Buddhism. Pāli is still a scholarly language of the Theravāda Buddhist traditions that are active, especially in Śrī Laṅka, Thailand, and Myanmar. For consistency, we have used Sanskrit for technical terms that apply generally to Buddhist traditions, but some academic sources will favor the Pāli equivalents. In such sources, *Abhidharma* would be rendered as *Abhidhamma*.
5. In English, the term "lovingkindness" is often used in lieu of "compassion" because it more accurately translates the Sanskrit compund, *maitrīkaruṇā*. This compound consists of two terms: *maitrī*, translated as "loving," is defined as the aspiration for another to be happy, and *karuṇā*, translated as "kindness," is defined as the aspiration that another be free of suffering. The term *karuṇā* is also translated as "compassion," and in Tibetan it is rendered as *snying rje*, the term that occurs in "non-referential compassion" *(dmigs med snying rje*; Skt., *niralambanakaruṇā)*. Nevertheless, even though the most accurate translation of this compound should include only the word "compassion," the actual practice of generating this state involves both love and compassion; that is, both maitrī and karuṇā.

References

Aftanas, L. I., & Golocheikine, S. A. (2002). Non-linear dynamic complexity of the human EEG during meditation. *Neuroscience Letters*, 330(2), 143–146.

Anand, B., Chhina, G., & Singh, B. (1961). Some aspects of electroencephalographic studies in yogis. *Electroencephalography and Clinical Neurophysiology*, 13, 452–456.

Andresen, J. (2000). Meditation meets behavioural medicine: The story of experimental research on meditation. *Journal of Consciousness Studies*, 7, 17–73.

Apple, J. (2003). Twenty varieties of the Samgha: A typology of noble beings (ārya) in Indo-Tibetan scholasticism. Part 1. *Journal of Indian Philosophy*, 31(5–6), 503–592.

Austin, J. H. (1998). *Zen and the brain: Toward an understanding of meditation and consciousness* (2nd ed.). Cambridge, MA: MIT Press.

Austin, J. H. (2006). *Zen-brain reflections. Reviewing recent developments in meditation and consciousness*. Cambridge, MA: MIT Press.

Banquet, J. P. (1973). Spectral analysis of the EEG in meditation. *Electroencephalography & Clinical Neurophysiology*, 35(2), 143–151.

Barinaga, M. (2003). Buddhism and neuroscience. Studying the well-trained mind. *Science*, 302(5642), 44–46.

Bartels, A., & Zeki, S. (2004). The neural correlates of maternal and romantic love. *Neuroimage*, 21(3), 1155–1166.

Becker, D. E., & Shapiro, D. (1981). Physiological responses to clicks during Zen, Yoga, and TM meditation. *Psychophysiology*, 18(6), 694–699.

Benson, H., Lehmann, J. W., Malhotra, M. S., Goldman, R. F., Hopkins, J., & Epstein, M. D. (1982). Body temperature changes during the practice of Tum-mo yoga. *Nature*, 295(5846), 234–236.

Berger, H. (1929). Uber das Elektrenkelaphogramm des Menschen. *Archiv für Psychiatrie und Nervenkrankheiten*, 87, 527–570.

Beyer, S. (1977). Notes on the vision quest in early Mahāyāna. In L. Lancaster (Ed.), *Prajñāpāramitā and related systems* (pp. 329–340). Berkeley, CA: University of California Press.

Bibbig, A., Traub, R. D., & Whittington, M. A. (2002). Long-range synchronization of gamma and beta oscillations and the plasticity of excitatory and inhibitory synapses: A network model. *Journal of Neurophysiology*, 88(4), 1634–1654.

Blake, R., & Logothetis, N. K. (2002). Visual competition. *Nature Reviews Neuroscience*, 3(1), 13–21.

Brefczynski-Lewis, J. A., Lutz, A., & Davidson, R. J. (2004). *A neural correlate of attentional expertise in long-time Buddhist practitioners*. (Report no. 715.8.). San Diego: Society for Neuroscience.

Bronkhorst, J. (1986). *The two traditions of meditation in ancient India* (28th ed.). Stuttgart: F. Steiner Verlag Wiesbaden.

Burgess, N., & O'Keefe, J. (2003). Neural representations in human spatial memory. *Trends in Cognitive Science*, 7(12), 517–519.

Cahn, R., & Polich, J. (2006). Meditation states and traits: EEG, ERP, and neuroimaging studies. *Psychological Bulletin*, 132, 180–211.

Carter, O. L., Presti, D. E., Callistemon, C., Ungerer, Y., Liu, G. B., & Pettigrew, J. D. (2005). Meditation alters perceptual rivalry in Tibetan Buddhist monks. *Current Biology*, 15(11), R412–413.

Clark, D. D., & Sokoloff, L. (1999) Circulation and energy metabolism of the brain. In G. J. Siegel, B. W. Agranoff, R. W. Albers, S. K. Fisher, & M. D. Uhler (Eds.), *Basic neurochemistry. Molecular, cellular and medical aspects*. Philadelphia: Lippincott-Raven.

Coleman, J. W. (2002). *The new Buddhism: The Western transformation of an ancient tradition*. New York: Oxford University Press.

Cooper, N. R., Croft, R. J., Dominey, S. J., Burgess, A. P., & Gruzelier, J. H. (2003). Paradox lost? Exploring the role of alpha oscillations during externally vs. internally directed attention and the implications for idling and inhibition hypotheses. *International Journal of Psychophysiology*, 47(1), 65–74.

Corby, J. C., Roth, W. T., Zarcone, V. P., Jr., & Kopell, B. S. (1978). Psychophysiological correlates of the practice of Tantric Yoga meditation. *Archives of General Psychiatry*, 35, 571–577.

Cosmelli, D., David, O., Lachaux, J. P., Martinerie, J., Garnero, L., Renault, B., & Varela, F. (2004). Waves of consciousness: Ongoing cortical patterns during binocular rivalry. *Neuroimage*, 23(1), 128–140.

Cozort, D. (1986). *Highest yoga tantra: An introduction to the esoteric Buddhism of Tibet*. Ithaca, NY: Snow Lion Publications.

Craig, A. D. (2002). How do you feel? Interoception: The sense of the physiological condition of the body. *Nature Reviews Neuroscience*, 3(8), 655–666.

Dalai Lama XIV [= Bstan-'dzin-rgya-mtsho]. (1991). *Path to bliss*. Ithaca, NY: Snow Lion Publications.

Dalai Lama XIV [= Bstan-'dzin-rgya-mtsho]. (1995). *The world of Tibetan Buddhism: An overview of its philosophy and practice*. Boston: Wisdom Publications.

Damasio, A. R. (1999). *The feeling of what happens: Body and emotion in the making of consciousness.* New York: Harcourt Brace.

Das, N. N., & Gastaut, H. C. (1955). Variations de l'activite electrique du cerveau, du coeur et des muscles squelletiques au cours de la meditation et de l'extase yogique. *Electroencephalography & Clinical Neurophysiology, 6(suppl.)*, 211–219.

Davidson J. M. (1976). The physiology of meditation and mystical states of consciousness. *Perspect Biol Med.* 19(3):345–79.

Davidson, R. J. (2000). Affective style, psychopathology, and resilience: Brain mechanisms and plasticity. *American Psychologist*, 55(11), 1196–1214.

Davidson, R. J., Kabat-Zinn, J., Schumacher, J., Rosenkranz, M., Muller, D., Santorelli, S. F., Urbanowski, F., Harrington, A., Bonus, K., & Sheridan, J. F. (2003). Alterations in brain and immune function produced by mindfulness meditation [see comment]. *Psychosomatic Medicine*, 65(4), 564–570.

Dehaene, S., & Naccache, L. (2001). Towards a cognitive neuroscience of consciousness: Basic evidence and a workspace framework. *Cognition*, 79(1–2), 1–37.

Deikman, A. J. (1966). Implication of experimentally induced contemplative meditation. *Journal of Nervous and Mental Disease.* 142(2):101–16.

Delmonte, M. M. (1984). Electrocortical activity and related phenomena associated with meditation practice: A literature review. *International Journal of Neuroscience*, 24, 217–231.

Delmonte, M. M. (1985). Biochemical indices associated with meditation practice: A literature review. *Neuroscience & Biobehavioral Reviews*, 9(4), 557–561.

Depraz, N., Varela, J. F., & Vermersch, P. (2003). *On becoming aware: A pragmatics of experiencing.* Amsterdam: John Benjamins.

Engel, A. K., Fries, P., & Singer, W. (2001). Dynamic predictions: Oscillations and synchrony in top-down processing. *Nature Reviews Neuroscience*, 2(10), 704–716.

English, E. (2002). *Vajrayoginī, a study of her visualizations, rituals & forms: A study of the cult of Vajrayoginī in India.* Boston: Wisdom Publications.

Fenwick, P. B. (1987). Meditation and the EEG. In A. West (Ed.), *The psychology of meditation* (pp. 104–117). New York: Clarendon Press.

Fischer, R. (1971). A cartography of the ecstatic and meditative states. *Science*, 174(12), 897–904.

Foxe, J. J., Simpson, G. V., & Ahlfors, S. P. (1998). Parieto-occipital approximately 10 Hz activity reflects anticipatory state of visual attention mechanisms. *Neuroreport*, 9(17), 3929–3933.

Freeman, W. (1999). Consciousness, intentionality, and causality. *Journal of Consciousness Studies*, 6, 143–172.

Fries, P., Reynolds, J. H., Rorie, A. E., & Desimone, R. (2001). Modulation of oscillatory neuronal synchronization by selective visual attention [see comment]. *Science*, 291(5508), 1560–1563.

Fries, P., Roelfsema, P. R., Engel, A. K., Konig, P., & Singer, W. (1997). Synchronization of oscillatory responses in visual cortex correlates with perception in interocular rivalry. *Proceedings of the National Academy of Sciences USA*, 94(23), 12699–12704.

Gethin, R. (1998). *The foundations of Buddhism.* Oxford: Oxford University Press.

Glaser, D. (2000). Child abuse and neglect and the brain – a review. *Journal of Child Psychology & Psychiatry & Allied Disciplines*, 41(1), 97–116.

Grossman, P., Niemann, L., Schmidt, S., & Walach, H. (2004). Mindfulness-based stress reduction and health benefits. A meta-analysis. *Journal of Psychosomatic Research*, 57(1), 35–43.

Gunaratana, H. (2002). *Mindfulness in plain English.* Boston: Wisdom Publications.

Gusnard, D. A., & Raichle, M. E. (2001). Searching for a baseline: Functional imaging and the resting human brain. *Nature Reviews Neuroscience*, 2(10), 685–694.

Holmes, D. S. (1984). Meditation and somatic arousal reduction. A review of the experimental evidence. *American Psychologist*, 39, 1–10.

Jayaraman, K. S. (2003). Technology, tradition unite in India's drug discovery scheme. *Nature Medicine*, 9(8), 982.

Kabat-Zinn, J. (2005). *Wherever you go, there you are: Mindfulness meditation in everyday life.* New York: Hyperion.

Kabat-Zinn, J., & Chapman-Waldrop, A. (1988). Compliance with an outpatient stress reduction program: Rates and predictors of program completion. *Journal of Behavioral Medicine*, 11(4), 333–352.

Kabat-Zinn, Lipworth, & Burney (1985). The clinical use of mindfulness meditation for the self-regulation of chronic pain. *J Behav Med.* 8(2):163–90.

Kabat-Zinn, J., Massion, A. O., Kristeller, J., Peterson, L. G., Fletcher, K. E., Pbert, L., Lenderking, W. R., & Santorelli, S. F. (1992). Effectiveness of a meditation-based stress reduction program in the treatment of anxiety disorders. *American Journal of Psychiatry, 149*(7), 936–943.

Karma Chagmé [= Karma-chags-med]. (2000). *Naked awareness: Practical instructions on the union of Mahamudra and Dzogchen. With commentary by Gyatrul Rinpoche* (A. B. Wallace, Trans.). Ithaca, NY: Snow Lion Publications.

Kasamatsu, A., & Hirai, T. (1966). An electroencephalographic study of Zen meditation (Zazen). *Folia Psychiatrica et Neurologica Japonica, 20*, 315–336.

Kiecolt-Glaser, J. K., Glaser, R., Gravenstein, S., Malarkey, W. B., & Sheridan, J. (1996). Chronic stress alters the immune response to influenza virus vaccine in older adults. *Proceedings of the National Academy of Sciences USA, 93*(7), 3043–3047.

Klimesch, W. (1999). EEG alpha and theta oscillations reflect cognitive and memory performance: A review and analysis. *Brain Research – Brain Research Reviews, 29*(2–3), 169–195.

Lachaux, J. P., Rodriguez, E., Martinerie, J., & Varela, F. J. (1999). Measuring phase synchrony in brain signals. *Human Brain Mapping, 8*(4), 194–208.

Lack, L. C. (1978). *Selective attention and the control of binocular rivalry.* Adelaide, The Flinders University of South Australia.

Lazar, S., Bush, G., Gollub, R. L., Fricchione, G. L., Khalsa, G., & Benson, H. (2000). Functional brain mapping of the relaxation response and meditation. *Neuroreport, 11*(7), 1581–1585.

Lazar, S., Kerr, C., Wasserman, R., Gray, J., Greve, D., Treadway, M., McGarvey, M., Quinn, B., Dusek, J., Benson, H., Rauch, S., Moore, C., & Fischl, B. (2005). Meditation experience is associated with increased cortical thickness. *Neuroreport, 16*(17):1893–7.

Legrand, D. (2005). The bodily self: The sensorimotor roots of pre-reflexive self-consciousness. *Phenomenology and the Cognitive Sciences, 5*(1): 89–118.

Le Van Quyen, M., Chavez, M., Rudrauf, D., & Martinerie, J. (2003). Exploring the nonlinear dynamics of the brain. *Journal of Physiology, Paris, 97*(4–6), 629–639.

Llinas, R., Ribary, U., Contreras, D., & Pedroarena, C. (1998). The neuronal basis for consciousness. *Philosophical Transactions of the Royal Society of London – Series B: Biological Sciences, 353*(1377), 1841–1849.

Lopes da Silva, F. H., Vos, J. E., Mooibroek, J., & Von Rotterdam, A. (1980). Relative contributions of intracortical and thalamo-cortical processes in the generation of alpha rhythms, revealed by partial coherence analysis. *Electroencephalography and Clinical Neurophysiology, 50*(5–6), 449–456.

Lou, H. C., Kjaer, T. W., Friberg, L., Wildschiodtz, G., Holm, S., & Nowak, M. (1999). A 15O-H2O PET study of meditation and the resting state of normal consciousness. *Human Brain Mapping, 7*(2), 98–105.

Lutz & Davidson 2005.

Lutz, A., Greischar, L. L., Rawlings, N. B., Ricard, M., & Davidson, R. J. (2004). Long-term meditators self-induce high-amplitude gamma synchrony during mental practice. *Proceedings of the National Academy of Sciences USA, 101*(46), 16369–16373.

Lutz, A., Lachaux, J. P., Martinerie, J., & Varela, F. J. (2002). Guiding the study of brain dynamics by using first-person data: Synchrony patterns correlate with ongoing conscious states during a simple visual task. *Proceedings of the National Academy of Sciences USA, 99*(3), 1586–1591.

Lutz, A., Rawlings, N., & Davidson, R. J. (2005). *Changes in the tonic high-amplitude gamma oscillations during meditation correlates with long-term practitioners' verbal reports.* Paper presented at the Society for Neuroscience, Washington, DC.

Lutz, A., & Thompson, E. (2003). Neurophenomenology: Integrating subjective experience and brain dynamics in the neuroscience of consciousness. *Journal of Consciousness Studies, 10*(9–10), 31–52.

Maguire, E. A., Gadian, D. G., Johnsrude, I. S., Good, C. D., Ashburner, J., Frackowiak, R. S., & Frith, C. D. (2000). Navigation-related structural change in the hippocampi of taxi drivers [see comment]. *Proceedings of the National Academy of Sciences USA, 97*(8), 4398–4403.

Maguire, E. A., Spiers, H. J., Good, C. D., Hartley, T., Frackowiak, R. S., & Burgess, N.

(2003). Navigation expertise and the human hippocampus: A structural brain imaging analysis. *Hippocampus*, 13(2), 250–259.

Maharishi, M. Y. (1969). *Maharishi Mahesh Yogi on the Bhagavad Gita*. New York: Penguin.

Maturana, H. R., & Varela, F. J. (1980). *Autopoiesis and cognition: The realization of the living*, Vol. 42. Dordrecht: D. Reidel.

McClelland, J. L., & Rogers, T. T. (2003). The parallel distributed processing approach to semantic cognition. *Nature Reviews Neuroscience*, 4(4), 310–322.

Meaney, M. J. (2001). Maternal care, gene expression, and the transmission of individual differences in stress reactivity across generations. *Annual Review of Neuroscience*, 24, 1161–1192.

Merleau-Ponty, M. (1962). *Phenomenology of perception* (C. Smith, Trans.). London: Routledge.

Miller, G. E., Cohen, S., Pressman, S., Barkin, A., Rabin, B. S., & Treanor, J. J. (2004). Psychological stress and antibody response to influenza vaccination: When is the critical period for stress, and how does it get inside the body? *Psychosomatic Medicine*, 66(2), 215–223.

Morrell, L. K. (1966). Some characteristics of stimulus-provoked alpha activity. *Electroencephalography & Clinical Neurophysiology*, 21(6), 552–561.

Morse, D. R., Martin, J. S., Furst, M. L., & Dubin, L. L. (1977). A physiological and subjective evaluation of meditation, hypnosis, and relaxation. *Psychosomatic Medicine*, 39(5), 304–324.

Newberg, A., Alavi, A., Baime, M., Pourdehnad, M., Santanna, J., & d'Aquili, E. (2001). The measurement of regional cerebral blood flow during the complex cognitive task of meditation: A preliminary SPECT study. *Psychiatry Research*, 106(2), 113–122.

Nisbett, R. E., & Wilson, T. D. (1977). Telling more than we can know: Verbal reports on mental processes. *Psychological Review*, 84, 231–259.

Nunez, P. L., Srinivasan, R., Westdorp, A. F., Wijesinghe, R. S., Tucker, D. M., Silberstein, R. B., & Cadusch, P. J. (1997). EEG coherency. I: Statistics, reference electrode, volume conduction, Laplacians, cortical imaging, and interpretation at multiple scales. *Electroencephalography & Clinical Neurophysiology*, 103(5), 499–515.

Nunez, P. L., Wingeier, B. M., & Silberstein, R. B. (2001). Spatial-temporal structures of human alpha rhythms: Theory, microcurrent sources, multiscale measurements, and global binding of local networks. *Human Brain Mapping*, 13(3), 125–164.

Ooi, T. L., & He, Z. J. (1999). Binocular rivalry and visual awareness: The role of attention. *Perception*, 28(5), 551–574.

Pagano, Rose, Stivers, & Warrenburg, (1976) Sleep during transcendental meditation. Science. 23;191(4224):308–10.

Pagano, R. R., & Warrenburg, S. (1983). Meditation: In search of a unique effect. In R. J. Davidson, G. E. Schwartz, & D. Shapiro (Eds.), *Consciousness and self-regulation* (Vol. 3). New York: Plenum Press.

Panksepp, J. (1988). *Affective neuroscience: The foundations of human and animal emotions.* Oxford: Oxford University Press.

Proudfoot, W. (1985). *Religious experience*. Berkeley: University of California Press.

Rizzuto, D. S., Madsen, J. R., Bromfield, E. B., Schulze-Bonhage, A., Seelig, D., Aschenbrenner-Scheibe, R., & Kahana, M. J. (2003). Reset of human neocortical oscillations during a working memory task. *Proceedings of the National Academy of Sciences USA*, 100(13), 7931–7936.

Rosenkranz, M. A., Jackson, D. C., Dalton, K. M., Dolski, I., Ryff, C. D., Singer, B. H., Muller, D., Kalin, N. H., & Davidson, R. J. (2003). Affective style and in vivo immune response: Neurobehavioral mechanisms. *Proceedings of the National Academy of Sciences USA*, 100(19), 11148–11152.

Saffran, J. R., Aslin, R. N., & Newport, E. L. (1996). Statistical learning by 8-month-old infants. *Science*, 274(5294), 1926–1928.

Schiff, S. J., So, P., Chang, T., Burke, R. E., & Sauer, T. (1996). Detecting dynamical interdependence and generalized synchrony through mutual prediction in a neural ensemble. *Physical Review. E. Statistical Physics, Plasmas, Fluids, and Related Interdisciplinary Topics*, 54(6), 6708–6724.

Schnitzler, A., & Gross, J. (2005). Normal and pathological oscillatory communication in the brain. *Nature Review Neuroscience*, 6(4), 285–296.

Schuman, M. (1980). The psychophysiological model of meditation and altered states of consciousness: A critical review. In J. M. Davidson & R. J. Davidson (Eds.), *The psychobiology of consciousness*, 333–378. New-York: Plenum.

Schuster, B. G. (2001). A new integrated program for natural product development and the value of an ethnomedical approach. *Journal of Alternative & Complementary Medicine*, 7(6), 61–72.

Shapiro, D. H., & Walsh, R. N. (Eds.). (1984). *Meditation: Classical and contemporary perspectives*. New York: Aldine.

Sharf, R. H. (1998). Experience. In M. Taylor (Ed.), *Critical terms for religious studies* (pp. 94–116). Chicago: University of Chicago Press.

Sheline, Y. I. (2003). Neuroimaging studies of mood disorder effects on the brain. *Biological Psychiatry*, 54(3), 338–352.

Silananda, U. (1990). *The four foundations of mindfulness*. Boston: Wisdom Publications.

Singer, T., Seymour, B., O'Doherty, J., Kaube, H., Dolan, R. J., & Frith, C. D. (2004). Empathy for pain involves the affective but not sensory components of pain. *Science*, 303(5661), 1157–1162.

Singer, W. (2001). Consciousness and the binding problem. *Annals of the New York Academy of Sciences*, 929, 123–146.

Singer, W. (1999). Neuronal synchrony: A versatile code for the definition of relations? *Neuron*, 24(1), 49–65, 111–125.

Slotnick, S. D., Moo, L. R., Kraut, M. A., Lesser, R. P., & Hart, J., Jr. (2002). Interactions between thalamic and cortical rhythms during semantic memory recall in human. *Proceedings of the National Academy of USA*, 99(9), 6440–6443.

Snellgrove, D. L. (2002). *Indo-Tibetan Buddhism: Indian Buddhists and their Tibetan successors*. Boston: Shambhala.

Srinivasan, R., Russell, D. P., Edelman, G. M., & Tononi, G. (1999). Increased synchronization of neuromagnetic responses during conscious perception. *Journal of Neuroscience*, 19(13), 5435–5448.

Suffczynski, P., Kalitzin, S., Pfurtscheller, G., & Lopes da Silva, F. H. (2001). Computational model of thalamo-cortical networks: Dynamical control of alpha rhythms in relation to focal attention. *International Journal of Psychophysiology*, 43(1), 25–40.

Takahashi, T., Murata, T., Hamada, T., Omori, M., Kosaka, H., Kikuchi, M., Yoshida, H., & Wada, Y. (2005). Changes in EEG and autonomic nervous activity during meditation and their association with personality traits. *International Journal of Psychophysiology*, 55(2), 199–207.

Tallon-Baudry, C., & Bertrand, O. (1999). Oscillatory gamma activity in humans and its role in object representation. *Trends in Cognitive Science*, 3(4), 151–162.

Tebecis, A. K. (1975). A controlled study of the EEG during transcendental meditation: Comparison with hypnosis. *Folia Psychiatrica et Neurologica Japonica*, 29(4), 305–313.

Thrangu, & Johnson, C. (2004). *Essentials of Mahamudra: Looking directly at the mind*. Boston: Wisdom Publications.

Tononi, G., & Edelman, G. M. (1998). Consciousness and complexity. *Science*, 282(5395), 1846–1851.

Travis, F., Arenander, A., & DuBois, D. (2004). Psychological and physiological characteristics of a proposed object-referral/self-referral continuum of self-awareness. *Consciousness & Cognition*, 13(2), 401–420.

Tsongkhapa [= Tsong kha pa blo bzang grags pa]. (2002). *The great treatise on the stages of the path to enlightenment* (31st ed.). Ithaca, NY: Snow Lion Publications.

Urry, H. L., van Reekum, C. M., Johnstone, T., Thurow, M. E., Burghy, C. A., Mueller, C. J., & Davidson, R. J. (2003). *Neural correlates of voluntarily regulating negative affect*. (Report no. 725.18.). San Diego: Society for Neuroscience.

Varela, F. (1995). Resonant cell assemblies: A new approach to cognitive functions and neuronal synchrony. *Biological Research*, 28(1), 81–95.

Varela, F. (1996). Neurophenomenology: A methodological remedy to the hard problem. *Journal of Consciousness Studies*, 3, 330–350.

Varela, F. (1999). The specious present: A neurophenomenology of time consciousness. In J. Petitot, F. J. Varela, J.-M. Roy, & B. Pachoud (Eds.), *Naturalizing phenomenology* (pp. 266–314). Stanford, CA: Stanford University Press.

Varela, F., Lachaux, J. P., Rodriguez, E., & Martinerie, J. (2001). The brainweb: Phase synchronization and large-scale integration. *Nature Reviews Neuroscience*, 2(4), 229–239.

Varela, F., & Thompson, E. (2001). Radical embodiment: Neural dynamics and consciousness. *Trends in Cognitive Science*, 5(10), 418–425.

Varela, F. J., Thompson, E., & Rosch, E. (1991). *The embodied mind*. Cambridge, MA: MIT Press.

von Stein, A., Chiang, C., & Konig, P. (2000). Top-down processing mediated by interareal synchronization. *Proceedings of the National Academy of Sciences USA*, 97(26), 14748–14753.

Wallace, A. B. (Ed.). (2003). *Buddhism and science*. New York: Columbia University Press.

Wallace, B. A. (1999). The Buddhist tradition of Samatha: Methods for refining and examining consciousness. *Journal of Consciousness Studies*, 6(2–3), 175–187.

Wallace, R. K. (1970). Physiological effects of transcendental meditation. *Science*, 167(926), 1751–1754.

Wangchug Dorjé [=Dbang-phyug-rdo-rje]. (1989). *The Mahamudra eliminating the darkness of ignorance* (3rd rev. ed.). Dharamsala, India: Library of Tibetan Works and Archives.

Ward, L. M. (2003). Synchronous neural oscillations and cognitive processes. *Trends in Cognitive Science*, 7(12), 553–559.

Warrenburg, Pagano, Woods, & Hlastala, (1980). A comparison of somatic relaxation and EEG activity in classical progressive relaxation and transcendental meditation. *J Behav Med*. 3(1):73–93.

Wenger, M. A., & Bagchi, B. K. (1961). Studies of autonomic functions in practitioners of Yoga in India. *Behavioral Sciences*, 6, 312–323.

West, M. A. (1980). Meditation and the EEG. *Psychological Medicine*, 10(2), 369–375.

West, M. A. (Ed.). (1987). *The psychology of meditation*. New York: Clarendon Press.

Wider, K. V. (1997). *The bodily basis of consciousness*. Ithaca, NY: Cornell University Press.

Williams, M. A., Morris, A. P., McGlone, F., Abbott, D. F., & Mattingley, J. B. (2004). Amygdala responses to fearful and happy facial expressions under conditions of binocular suppression. *Journal of Neuroscience*, 24(12), 2898–2904.

Williams, P. (1989). *Mahāyāna Buddhism: The doctrinal foundations*. London: Routledge.

Woolfolk R. L. (1975). Psychophysiological correlates of meditation. *Arch Gen Psychiatry*. 32(10):1326–33.

Younger, J., Adriance, W., & Berger, R. J. (1975). Sleep during Transcendental Meditation. *Perceptual & Motor Skills*, 40(3), 953–954.

Zahavi, D., & Parnas, J. (1998). Phenomenal consciousness and self-awareness: A phenomenological critique of representational theory. *Journal of Consciousness Studies*, 5, 687–705.

Zeman, A. (2001). Consciousness. *Brain*, 124(Pt 7), 1263–1289.

G. Anthropology/Social Psychology of Consciousness

CHAPTER 20

Social Psychological Approaches to Consciousness

John A. Bargh

Abstract

A central focus of contemporary social psychology has been the relative influence of *external* (i.e., environmental, situational) versus *internal* (i.e., personality, attitudes) forces in determining social judgment and social behavior. But many of the classic findings in the field – such as Milgram's obedience research, Asch's conformity studies, and Zimbardo's mock-prison experiment – seemed to indicate that the external forces swamped the internal ones when the chips were down. Where in the social psychological canon was the evidence showing the internal, intentional, rational control of one's own behavior? Interestingly, most models of a given phenomenon in social psychology have started with the assumption of a major mediational role played by conscious choice and intentional guidance of judgment and behavior processes. Then, empirical work focuses on the necessity or validity of this assumption. As a consequence there has been a greater research focus on the non-conscious than the conscious aspects of any given phenomenon. However, because these studies focus on the relative influence of both conscious and automatic processes, there has been a strong influence within social psychology of dual-process models that capture these distinctions (e.g., intentional versus unintentional, effortful versus efficient, aware versus unaware). Another reason that dual-process models became popular in social psychology is that the distinction nicely captured an important truth about social cognition and behavior: that people seem to process the identical social information differently depending on its relevance or centrality to their important goals and purposes.

Introduction

Historically, social psychology has been concerned with the determinants of social behavior; specifically, the relative influence of external (i.e., environmental, situational) versus internal (i.e., personality, attitudes) causal forces. Many of the most famous studies in social psychology focused on this issue of internal versus external determinants of behavior (Wegner & Bargh, 1998). For example, early attitude research was driven by the belief that attitudes would prove to be a strong predictor of actual behavior. Yet it wasn't long after Thurstone (1928) first demonstrated that internal, private attitudes could be measured that LaPiere (1934) caused great consternation by seeming to show that one's stated attitudes toward a social group did not predict one's actual behavior toward that group very well at all.

Asch's (1952) famous conformity studies were surprising at the time because they seemed to show that a person's publicly made judgments of the relative lengths of lines presented clearly on a chalkboard were swayed by the (stage-managed) opinions of the other "subjects" present in the experimental session. Thus even in cases where the judgment or behavior should have been determined entirely by internal perceptual experience, external forces still played a role. Milgram's (1963) obedience experiments, in which subjects believed they were administering painful shocks to another subject, were disturbing and controversial because they demonstrated the power of a situational influence over the subject's behavior (i.e., the experimenter's authority) to override presumed internal influences (i.e., the subject's presumed personal values not to cause pain or harm to another).

Darley and Latane's (1968) seminal studies of bystander intervention showed how the simple presence of other people in the situation seemed to inhibit individuals from helping another person in clear distress. And last but not least, the well-known Stanford Prison Study (Haney, Banks, & Zimbardo, 1973) provided a powerful demonstration of situational forces (social roles, as prisoner versus guard) swamping dispositional forces (values, good intentions) in determining the behavior of the participants in a realistic prison simulation.

Where oh where, in all of these findings, was the internal, intentional, rational control of one's own behavior?

Conscious by Default

These findings were surprising at the time (to social psychologists as well as to the general public) because they violated people's strongly held assumption that one's own behavior was under one's internal and intentional control. Compared with cognitive psychology or cognitive neuroscience, social psychology tends to focus on psychological processes of a relatively high order of complexity: for instance, judgment, goal pursuit over extended time periods, and behavior in social interaction. Going back at least to Descartes (1633) there is a deep philosophical tradition of assigning such complex processes to an agentic "mind" instead of the mechanical "body." That is, for any given process of such complexity, the initial assumption tends to be that the individual plays an active, agentic role in its instigation and operation, as opposed to it being a purely mechanical, determined phenomenon (see Bargh & Ferguson, 2000).

Perhaps as an inheritance or vestige of this long-standing philosophical stance, then, social psychology tends to begin its analysis of any complex, important phenomenon by assuming a central role for conscious (intentional, effortful, and aware; see next section) choice and monitoring processes. Research then has the effect of discovering the extent and role of *non-conscious* components of the process or phenomenon. Note how, in the classic studies above, the initial starting assumption is that the judgment or behavior is under internal, strategic (i.e., conscious) control. This pattern can be found in other traditional areas of social psychological inquiry as well. Early attribution theories began with a model of humans as rational scientists, using effortful and intentional "analysis-of-variance" methods to draw inferences of causality (Kelley, 1967). However as the research evidence started to come in, attribution theory then moved to a more automatic and less deliberative model (e.g., Gilbert, 1989; Taylor & Fiske, 1978). Similarly, the phenomena of stereotyping and prejudice were initially assumed to be driven by motivated, conscious processes (see Nisbett & Ross, 1980), but then were shown by a considerable amount of research to have a significant automatic, non-conscious component (Brewer, 1988; Devine, 1989).

This is how research related to issues of consciousness has proceeded in social psychology. The initial models start with the default assumption that the phenomenon under investigation involves conscious, aware, intentional appraisals or behavior on the part of the participants, and then this set of presumed necessary conditions is whittled down as the research findings warrant. As a consequence there has been a greater research focus on the non-conscious than the conscious aspects of any given phenomenon.

The main exceptions to this rule are models of self-regulation and goal pursuit (see Bandura, 1986; Carver & Scheier, 1981; Deci & Ryan, 1985; Locke & Latham, 1990; Mischel, Cantor, & Feldman, 1996), in which conscious choice and willpower are featured as mediating, explanatory variables. This is probably because, even among the relatively complex phenomena studied in social psychology, self-regulatory processes are the most complex, dynamic, and interactive with the shifting, uncertain environment (see Baumeister, 1998; Fitzsimons & Bargh, 2004). Because of the level of abstraction and complexity of these processes, it is understandable that it has taken longer to find and isolate their mechanisms and components. Yet even in the domain of self-regulation research, studies are beginning to identify non-conscious, automatic components (see Fitzsimons & Bargh, 2004). For example, complex goal pursuit can be put into motion by situational features instead of exclusively by consciously made intentions or choices, and it can operate in a flexible manner, interacting with the changing environment over time, just as can conscious goal pursuit (Chartrand & Bargh, 2002).

All of these domains of research, then, recognize the influence and importance of both conscious and automatic processes. It is not surprising then that there has been a strong influence within social psychology of

dual-process models that capture these distinctions (e.g., intentional versus unintentional, effortful versus efficient, aware versus unaware). Cognitive social psychology has emphasized the study of non-conscious processes, whereas motivational social psychology is still mainly the study of conscious processes. But clearly, conscious and non-conscious components of a complex psychological process are two sides of the same coin. By testing the default initial assumptions of a necessary and pivotal role for conscious processes – showing where conscious processes are needed versus where they are not – we learn a great deal about the role and function of consciousness. In this subtractive manner, the social psychological study of non-conscious judgment and behavioral phenomena adds to our understanding of the purpose of conscious processes.

Dual-Process Models: Automatic Versus Controlled Processes

Cognitive approaches to social psychology were greatly influenced by the dual-process models of the 1970s (Posner & Snyder, 1975; Shiffrin & Schneider, 1977) that distinguished between conscious and automatic modes of information processing (see Chaiken & Trope, 1999). Conscious or controlled processes were said to be *intentional, controllable, effortful*, and in *awareness*, whereas automatic processes were characterized by the opposite set of features: They were *unintended, uncontrollable, effortless*, and *outside of awareness* (Johnson & Hasher, 1987). However, at least for psychological processes of the level of complexity studied by social psychologists, these qualities did not seem to co-vary together in an all-or-nothing fashion (Bargh, 1989). For instance, stereotypes might become activated automatically (unintentionally and efficiently), but their influence on judgment was controllable (Devine, 1989; Fiske, 1989); making dispositional attributions might be the efficient and reflexive default process, but still required the intention to understand the causes of the person's behavior (Gilbert,

1989). Consequently, social psychologists have tended to study the separate and distinct aspects of automatic and controlled processes, and I have organized the brief review below in these lower-level terms (for more complete reviews see Bargh, 1994, 1996; Wegner & Bargh, 1998).

Effortful Processing: Only When it Matters

One reason that dual-process models became popular in social psychology is that the distinction nicely captured an important truth about social cognition and behavior: that people seem to process the identical social information differently depending on its relevance or centrality to their important goals and purposes. For example, people process a persuasive message differently if it concerns or affects them directly versus when it does not. If a proposed comprehensive exam requirement is allegedly to be instituted next year at a student's own university, she will spend more time and think more effortfully about the various arguments for versus against it; if it is to occur 5 years from now or at another university, she will not expend the same degree of effort. Instead she will tend to rely on heuristics or shortcuts – such as the attractiveness or expertise of the source of the message – to decide her position (Chaiken, 1980; Petty & Cacioppo, 1984).

People also were found to use shortcut heuristics in making causal attributions (Taylor & Fiske, 1978) and even behavioral choices in social interaction settings (Langer, Blank, & Chanowitz, 1978). Langer and colleagues argued that people develop mental representations of common situations ('scripts'; see Abelson, 1981) that then guide their behavior "mindlessly" within those situations. Heuristic cues such as the size of a request (e.g., for 1 minute versus 10 minutes of your time) determined whether people would assent to it, not the quality of the reason given for the request.

This basic principle – that the personal importance or goal relevance of target infor-

mation moderates whether the individual will deal with it in an effortful and systematic manner versus in an off-hand and efficient way – holds across many different social psychological phenomena. One of the most important is *impression formation*, in particular the degree to which the perceiver will pay attention to and be influenced in his or her judgment by the target person's individual characteristics, as opposed to more superficial (but less effort-requiring) features, such as race, gender, age, or ethnicity. If a person's own outcomes depend on the target person (i.e., there is goal relevance), a more individuated and less stereotype-based impression is formed (Erber & Fiske, 1984; Neuberg & Fiske, 1987) than if the target person does not have control over the perceiver's outcomes.

Taylor and Fiske (1978) coined the term "cognitive miser" to refer to this human tendency not to think effortfully about other people or attitude issues unless really necessary. Underlying this idea is the notion that effortful processing is limited in its capacity at any given moment and so should be used only sparingly, to be reserved for the most important stimuli and events. Consistent with this notion, recent research by Baumeister, Bratslavsky, Muraven, and Tice (1998) has confirmed the limited-capacity nature of effortful social-information processing: They found that using it in one domain – even just to make a simple choice – seems to severely limit its availability for other tasks, for some time thereafter.

Efficient Processing: Automatic Components of Social Perception

Another important variable moderating whether people will engage in effortful versus heuristic or superficial processing is whether they are able to do so under the current circumstances. Conscious, effortful processing is relatively slow and so takes time; often the individual does not have the time, as when under time pressure or when there are multiple people or events to attend to at once. Indeed, such *information overload* conditions are not unusual in the busy, noisy "real world" outside the psychology laboratory. Under these conditions, efficient, automatic forms of information processing have greater influence than usual, because they are not constrained as much by capacity or time limitations or by the current focus of conscious thought.

ATTITUDE ACTIVATION

An excellent example of this can be found in Fazio's (1986, 1990) model of the relation between attitudes and behavior. The extent to which one's attitudes determine one's behavior has long been a central research question in social psychology (see Eagly & Chaiken, 1993). Faced with evidence that the general correspondence between attitudes and behavior was weak at best (e.g., LaPiere, 1934; Wicker, 1969), attitude researchers began to look for the conditions that supported or fostered the relation. One such proposal was Fazio's (1986) *automatic attitude activation* model.

In this model he contended that attitudes varied in *strength*, or the degree of association between the representation of the attitude object and its evaluative tag (i.e., as good or bad). Strong attitudes are those characterized by a relatively automatic association, such that the mere perception of the attitude object in the environment was sufficient to also activate its associated attitude – no intentional, effortful thinking (such as about how one feels about the object) was necessary. Weak attitudes, on the other hand, did not possess this automatic association and so did not become active unless the person happened to think about his or her feelings toward the object.

In several studies, in which attitude strength was either manipulated or measured, automatic attitudes showed a more consistent influence on behavior than did weak attitudes. Indeed, Fazio and Williams (1986) showed that those participants who possessed strong, relatively automatic attitudes toward the candidates in the 1984 U.S. presidential contest (compared to those

who did not) showed much higher correspondence between those attitudes and their actual voting behavior (several months later) in the election.

CAUSAL ATTRIBUTION

Because of the immediacy and fluency of automatic forms of information processing, such as stereotyping, several researchers have proposed sequential or stage models of phenomena in which the first or default stage is relatively reflexive or automatic, with the second, more controlled stage occurring only if the person has both the ability (i.e., lack of time or overload constraints) and motivation to do so. Gilbert (e.g., 1989) argued that people have a default or automatic bias to locate causality for another person's behavior "in" that person him- or herself – in other words, making a *dispositional attribution* about the reason for that behavior. In his model, a causal attribution to situational factors is only made within a second, conscious processing stage – but that stage only occurs if the person has the time and processing resources available to engage in it.

In several studies, Gilbert and colleagues showed that people did not take clear situational influences into account when under conditions of distraction or attentional load. When watching a videotape of a woman being interviewed and being asked rather embarrassing questions, those participants under attentional overload (performing a secondary attention-demanding task while watching the tape) concluded she was a dispositionally shy and anxious person. People in the control condition, on the other hand, who watched the tape without having to do the secondary task, did not draw that conclusion – instead, they attributed the reason for her anxious behavior to the situation of having to answer embarrassing questions.

IMPRESSION FORMATION

Much research in social psychology has focused on the immediate or spontaneous effects of social stimuli – those that occur so efficiently that all it takes for the process to occur is the mere perception of the object, person, or event in the environment (Bargh, 2001). For example, in the case of Fazio's (1986) model of the attitude-behavior relation, discussed above, seeing a rose activates not only the associated concept "rose" but also one's feelings or attitude toward roses. The activation of the attitude occurs in an uncontrollable manner similar to how written words activate their meanings during reading.

When forming initial impressions of other people, certain forms of information about them appear to have a similarly privileged status; we tend to detect and be influenced by these features in the course of perception, in an automatic fashion, without being aware of it. For example, Higgins, King, and Mavin (1982) showed that each of us is chronically sensitive to certain kinds of social behavior but not others, with wide individual differences in the exact content of these chronic sensitivities. Bargh and Thein (1985) then showed that under information overload (rapid presentation) conditions that prevented people in a control group from being able to differentiate in their impressions between a mainly honest and a mainly dishonest target person, those participants who were chronically or automatically sensitive to the dimension of honesty were still able to differentiate the two target persons. This is because they were able to process and be influenced by the honest and dishonest behaviors in an automatic, efficient manner.

STEREOTYPING AND PREJUDICE

By far the most researched form of such spontaneous cognitive reactions to the social environment is social stereotyping (see Bargh, 1999; Brewer, 1988; Devine, 1989). In a now classic study, Devine (1989) found that even non-prejudiced people (at least by one fairly explicit paper-and-pencil measure of racism) show evidence of automatic stereotype activation. In one study (1989, Experiment 2), she presented participants subliminally with stimuli related to positive aspects of the African-American stereotype (e.g., musical, athletic) and showed that this caused the negative aspects (e.g., hostility)

to become active as well to influence impressions of a target person.

Devine's study stimulated a great deal of research into the conditions under which the automatic stereotype activation effect is more or less likely to occur (see review in Devine & Monteith, 1999). The bottom line seems to be that cultural stereotypes can be picked up at a quite early age and can exert a biasing influence on social perception, judgment, and even behavior (Fazio et al., 1995) without the person being aware of such influence (Bargh, 1999). Fortunately, however, racial and gender stereotyping is one form of unconscious bias that many people now seem to accept as a possibility (i.e., they have a correct "theory of influence" in this case; see next section) and so can adjust and correct for it if they have the motivation to do so.

Awareness and Control

People are often unaware of the reasons and causes of their own behavior. In fact, recent experimental evidence across several different areas of psychology points to a deep and fundamental dissociation between conscious awareness and the mental processes responsible for one's behavior; many of the wellsprings of behavior appear to be opaque to conscious access. Although that research has proceeded somewhat independently in social psychology (e.g., Dijksterhuis & Bargh, 2001; Wilson, 2002), cognitive psychology (e.g., Knuf, Aschersleber, & Prinz, 2001; Prinz, 1997), and neuropsychology (e.g., Frith, Blakemore, & Wolpert, 2000; Jeannerod, 1999), using quite different methodologies and guiding theoretical perspectives, all three lines of research have reached the same general conclusions.

In social psychology, awareness of sources of influence on judgment and social behavior has long been an important research topic. Beginning with the seminal work of Nisbett and Wilson (1977), researchers observed that people were often unaware of actual strong influences on their choices and behavior. In one study, for example, some experimental participants watched a job interview in which the interviewee spilled some coffee; others saw the identical tape without the spill incident. Although the former group rated the interviewee as significantly less qualified for the job, they also reported that the coffee spill (among a list of many possible influencing factors) did not affect their judgment.

Wilson (2002; Wilson & Brekke, 1994) has extended this line of research to document the many ways in which people seem out of touch with the actual determinants and influences of their judgments and behavior. An emergent principle from this research is that people have lay "theories" about what influences their feelings and decisions, or causes them (and others) to behave in certain ways, and often if not usually these theories do not accurately reflect the actual influences and causes.

Priming research, in which social concepts (e.g., traits and stereotypes) are first activated in an off-hand, subtle manner and then influence the person's subsequent judgments or behavior (see reviews in Bargh & Chartrand, 2000; Higgins, 1996), provides another example of the dissociation between important environmental influences and the person's awareness of those influences. Across many studies, the critical variable as to whether a person is able to control the external effect is not whether the person is aware of the influencing stimulus per se (i.e., whether it was subliminal or supraliminal), but rather whether the person is aware of the potential influence of that stimulus. Thus, priming stimuli presented subliminally have the same quality of effect as those presented supraliminally (i.e., visible, reportable), as long as the person does not believe or appreciate that the stimulus could have an effect on him or her (Bargh, 1992).

For example, in the popular scrambled sentence test method of priming (Srull & Wyer, 1979; see Bargh & Chartrand, 2000), experimental participants complete an ostensible language test in which they reorder strings of words into grammatically correct sentences. Embedded in this test are some words semantically related to a certain social concept; merely being exposed

to these stimuli is believed to "prime" or make that concept temporarily accessible in memory. In such experiments, participants are of course aware of the critical word stimuli at the time of working on the test, yet they have no awareness that such mere exposure to words could possibly influence their judgments or behavior (they can and do). However, when participants do become aware of a potential influence, such as when the priming stimuli are extreme and salient (e.g., "Dracula" as a prime for hostility; Herr, Sherman, & Fazio, 1986), the usual priming effects are no longer obtained. Thus, in social psychology, an important distinction is that between awareness of the stimulus versus awareness of its possible effects (Bargh, 1992). The latter and not the former appears to be the key moderator of whether unconscious influences of that stimulus will occur.

Intentionality: What We Do Without Meaning To

IMPRESSION FORMATION

Uleman and his colleagues (1989; Uleman, Newman, & Moskowitz, 1996; Winter & Uleman, 1984; see also Carlston & Skowronski, 1994) have documented a "spontaneous trait inference" effect, in which social perceivers tend to encode the behavior of others in trait-concept terms (e.g., as an *honest*, *intelligent*, or *selfish* behavior), automatically and without intending to do so. Using Tulving and Thompson's (1973) encoding specificity paradigm, these researchers showed that trait terms corresponding to the behavior (e.g., *generous* for "she donated her stock gains to charity") later served as effective retrieval cues for the behavior, even though the experimental participants had not been instructed to form impressions of the sentence actors (merely to remember the behaviors). Apparently, then, the trait term had been spontaneously encoded by the participants when reading that behavior.

Spontaneous attitude, trait-concept, and stereotype activation are three important ways in which people "go beyond the information given" (Bruner, 1957), such that semantic and affective information not actually present in the current environment becomes activated automatically in the course of perception to then exert an "unseen" influence on judgments and behavior.

IMITATIVE BEHAVIOR AND IDEOMOTOR ACTION

Two streams of research in social psychology have converged on the idea that complex social behavior tendencies can be triggered and enacted non-consciously. One line of research focuses on ideomotor action or the finding that mental content activated in the course of perceiving one's social environment automatically creates tendencies to behave the same way oneself (Prinz, 1997). Thus, for example, one tends to mimic, without realizing it, the posture and physical gestures of one's interaction partners (Chartrand & Bargh, 1999).

This "chameleon effect" has been found to extend even to the automatic activation of abstract, schematic representations of people and groups (such as social stereotypes) in the course of social perception (see Dijksterhuis & Bargh, 2001). For example, subtly activating (priming) the professor stereotype in a prior context causes people to score higher on a knowledge quiz (Dijksterhuis & van Knippenberg, 1998), and priming the elderly stereotype makes college students not only walk more slowly but have poorer incidental memory as well (Bargh, Chen, & Burrows, 1996). Thus, the passive activation of behavior (trait) concepts in the natural course of social perception (as experimentally simulated by priming manipulations) increases the person's tendency to behave in line with that concept him- or herself.

UNCONSCIOUS MOTIVATION AND AUTOMATIC GOAL PURSUIT

The second stream of research has shown that social and interpersonal goals can also be activated automatically through external means (as in priming manipulations). The individual then pursues that goal in the subsequent situation, but without consciously intending to or being aware of doing so (Bargh, 1990; Bargh, Gollwitzer, Lee-Chai, Barndollar, & Troetschel, 2001; Chartrand & Bargh, 1996).

For example, words related to achievement and high performance might be embedded along with other, goal-irrelevant words in a puzzle, or words related to cooperation might be presented subliminally in the course of an ostensible reaction time task. Just as with single forms of social behavior such as politeness or intelligence, presenting goal-related stimuli in this fashion causes the goal to become active and then operate to guide behavior over time toward that goal. People primed with achievement-related stimuli perform at higher levels on subsequent tasks than do control groups, those primed with cooperation-related stimuli cooperate more in a commons-dilemma game, and those primed with evaluation-related stimuli form impressions of other people while those in a control group do not (see reviews in Chartrand & Bargh, 2002; Fitzsimons & Bargh, 2004).

Neither the ideomotor action nor the automatic goal pursuit effects are restricted to the laboratory environment; for example, merely thinking about the significant other people in our lives (something we all do quite often) causes the goals we characteristically pursue when with them to become active and to then guide our behavior without our choosing or knowing it, even when those individuals are not physically present (Fitzsimons & Bargh, 2003). And the non-conscious ideomotor effect of perception on action becomes a matter of widespread social importance considering the mass exposure of people to violent behavior on television or in movies (see Anderson & Bushman, 2002; Berkowitz, 1984).

Dissociations Between Intention and Action

These findings within social psychological research of non-conscious control over higher mental processes, such as support behavior in social settings, may seem a bit magical or mysterious without a consideration of related recent findings in cognitive psychology and cognitive neuroscience. Together, though, these streams of research tell a coherent story about the non-conscious wellsprings and governing structures of social judgment, behavior, and goal pursuit.

Non-Conscious Action Control

Several lines of cognitive neuroscience research support the idea of a dissociation between conscious awareness and intention, on the one hand, and the operation of complex motor and goal representations on the other (Prinz, 2003). One major area of such research focuses on the distinct and separate visual input pathways devoted to perception versus action.

The first such evidence came from a study of patients with lesions in specific brain regions (Goodale, Milner, Jakobsen, & Carey, 1991). Those with lesions in the parietal lobe region could identify an object but not reach for it correctly based on its spatial orientation (such as a book in a horizontal versus vertical position), whereas those with lesions in the ventral-visual system could not recognize or identify the item but were nonetheless able to reach for it correctly, when asked in a casual manner to take it from the experimenter. In other words, the latter group showed appropriate action toward an object in the absence of conscious awareness or knowledge of its presence.

Decety and Grèzes (1999) and Norman (2002) concluded from this and related evidence that two separate cortical visual pathways are activated during the perception of human movement: a dorsal one for action tendencies based on that information, and a ventral one used for understanding and recognition of it. The dorsal system operates mainly outside of conscious awareness, whereas the workings of the ventral system are normally accessible to consciousness. Thus the dorsal stream (or activated pragmatic representation) could drive behavior in response to environmental stimuli in the absence of conscious awareness or understanding of that external information. It could, in principle, support a non-conscious basis for ideomotor action effects that are primed or driven by recent behavioral informational input from other people.

Additional support for non-conscious action initiation comes from the discovery of "mirror neurons" – first in macaque monkeys (Rizzolatti & Arbib, 1998) and then in humans (Buccino et al., 2001). In these studies, simply watching mouth, hand, and foot movements causes the activation of the same functionally specific regions of the premotor cortex as when performing those same movements oneself. These mirror neurons could be a neurological basis for the "chameleon effect" of non-conscious imitation of the behavior of one's interaction partners (Chartrand & Bargh, 1999).

Non-Conscious Operation of Working Memory During Goal Pursuit

Clearly, non-conscious goal pursuit must utilize the structures of working memory to guide behavior within the unfolding situation toward the desired goal (see Hassin, 2004). Such complex behavior, which is continually responsive to ongoing environmental events and coordinated with the behavior of others, has to involve the operation of the brain structures that support working memory – namely the frontal and prefrontal cortex. However, under the original concept of working memory as that portion of long-term memory that was currently in conscious awareness (e.g., Atkinson & Shiffrin, 1968), the idea of *non-conscious* operation of working memory structures is incoherent at best. If working memory was a single mental "organ" that held both the current goal and the relevant environmental information on which that goal was acting (selecting relevant information and transforming it according to the requirements of the current goal; see Cohen, Dunbar, & McClelland, 1990), then one should always be aware of the intention or goal that is currently residing in active, working memory.

The answer to this apparent paradox, of course, is that working memory is not a single unitary structure. This idea was originally proposed by Baddeley and Hitch (1974; see also Baddeley, 1986), who envisaged a system comprising multiple components, not just for the temporary storage of information (the phonological loop and visuospatial scratchpad) but also for the direction and allocation of limited attention (the "central executive"). In a parallel development, psychiatrists working with patients with frontal lobe damage – the frontal lobes being brain structures underlying the executive control functions of working memory (Baddeley, 1986) – were noting how the behavioral changes associated with frontal lobe damage were exceedingly complex and variable, depending on the exact locations of the damage (Mesulam, 1986, p. 320). This too was consistent with the notion that executive control was not a single resource but rather comprised several distinct specialized functions, located in different parts of the frontal and prefrontal cortex.

If so, then at least in theory it becomes possible that there are dissociations between consciously held intentions on the one hand and the goal-driven operation of working memory structures on the other. This is what is manifested in Lhermitte's (1986) syndrome; "an excessive control of behavior by external stimuli at the expense of behavioral autonomy" (p. 342). Lhermitte's patients had suffered a stroke which had produced lesions in the same (inferior prefrontal) location of the brain in both cases. The behavior of these patients became continually driven by cues in the environment and by little else. For example, bringing the man onto a stage in front of a small audience caused him to deliver an award acceptance speech; bringing the woman into the (medical) doctor's office caused her to give Dr. Lhermitte a physical exam complete with injections of vaccines. Across these and several other situations, neither patient noticed or remarked on anything unusual or strange about their behavior. Lhermitte (1986) concluded that they had suffered "a loss of autonomy: for the patient, the social and physical environments issue the order to use them, even though the patient himself or herself has neither the idea nor the intention to do so" (p. 341).

Subsequent research in cognitive neuroscience has largely supported Lhermitte's deductions that this area of the prefrontal cortex is critical for the planning and control of action. Frith et al. (2000) concluded from their review of this research that intended

movements are normally represented in the prefrontal and premotor cortex, but the representations actually used to guide action are in the parietal cortex. In other words, intentions and the motor representations used to guide behavior seem to be held in anatomically separate, distinct parts of the brain. This makes it possible for some patients to no longer be able to link their intentions to their actions if there is impairment in the location where intended movements are represented, but no impairment in the location where action systems actually operate.

The finding that, within working memory, representations of one's intentions (accessible to conscious awareness) are stored in a different location and structure from the representations used to guide action (not accessible) is of paramount importance to an understanding of the mechanisms underlying non-conscious social behavior and goal pursuit. If it had been the case that intentions and corresponding action plans were stored in the same location, so that awareness of one's intention was solely a matter of conscious access to the currently operative goal or behavior program, then it would be difficult to see how non-conscious control over social behavior could be possible. Instead, as Posner and DiGirolamo (2000) recently remarked, the information-processing and the neurophysiological levels of analysis of psychological processes have achieved a level of mutual support greater than previously imagined.

Implications for the Nature and Purpose of Consciousness

There is a baffling problem about what consciousness is for. It is equally baffling, moreover, that the function of consciousness should remain so baffling. It seems extraordinary that despite the pervasiveness and familiarity of consciousness in our lives, we are uncertain in what way (if at all) it is actually indispensable to us. (Frankfurt, 1988, p. 162)

Action tendencies can be activated and put into motion without the need for the individual's conscious intervention; even complex social behavior can unfold without an act of will or awareness of its sources. Evidence from a wide variety of domains of psychological inquiry is consistent with this proposition. Behavioral evidence from patients with frontal lobe lesions, behavior and goal-priming studies in social psychology, cognitive neuroscience studies of the structure and function of the frontal lobes as well as the separate actional and semantic visual pathways, cognitive psychological research on the components of working memory and on the degree of conscious access to motoric behavior – all of these converge on the conclusion that complex behavior and other higher mental processes can proceed independently of the conscious will. Indeed, the neuropsychological evidence suggests that the human brain is designed for such independence.

But this is not to say that consciousness does not exist or is merely an epiphenomenon. It just means that if all of these things can be accomplished without conscious choice or guidance, then the purpose of consciousness (i.e., why it evolved) probably lies elsewhere. And the research described above points to one prime candidate.

That is, although we do not yet know much about how non-conscious goal pursuit capabilities develop, the most plausible guess is that they develop much as other automatic processes develop – out of frequent and consistent experience (Bargh, 1990; Bargh & Gollwitzer, 1994; see Shiffrin & Dumais, 1981). This means in the case of automatic goal pursuit that the individual most likely *consciously chose* at one point to pursue that particular goal in that particular situation, then chose it again, and so on until that goal representation became associated so strongly with that situation representation that the former became automatically associated with the latter. Then, entering the situation from then on causes both the situation and the goal representations to become active, no longer with any need for conscious choice of that goal (see Bargh & Chartrand, 1999). As William

James (1890) argued, consciousness tends to drop out of those processes where it is no longer needed and thereby frees itself for where it is.

In a very real sense, then, the purpose of consciousness – why it evolved – may be for the assemblage of complex non-conscious skills. In harmony with the general plasticity of human brain development (see Donald, 2001), human beings – unlike even our nearest primate kindred – have the capability of building ever more complex automatic "demons" that sublimely fit their own idiosyncratic environment, needs, and purposes. Intriguingly, then, one of the primary objectives of conscious processing at the level of the individual person may be to eliminate the need for itself in the future as much as possible, freeing itself up for even greater things. It would be ironic indeed, given the juxtaposition of automatic and conscious processes in contemporary social psychology, if the evolved purpose of consciousness turned out to be the creation of ever more complex non-conscious processes.

Acknowledgments

Preparation of this chapter was supported in part by Grant MH60767 from the U.S. Public Health Service.

References

Abelson, R. P. (1981). Psychological status of the script concept. *American Psychologist*, 36, 715–729.

Anderson, C. A., & Bushman, B. J. (2002, March 29). The effects of media violence on society. *Science*, 295, 2377–2379.

Asch, S. E. (1952). Effects of group pressure on the modification and distortion of judgments. In G. E. Swanson, T. M. Newcomb, & E. L. Hartley (Eds.), *Readings in social psychology* (2nd ed., pp. 2–11). New York: Holt.

Atkinson, R. C., & Shiffrin, R. M. (1968). Human memory: A proposed system and its control processes. In K. W. Spence & J. T. Spence

(Eds.), *The psychology of learning and motivation: Advances in research and theory* (Vol. 2, pp. 89–195). New York: Academic Press.

Baddeley, A. D. (1986). *Working memory.* New York: Oxford University Press.

Baddeley, A. D., & Hitch, G. J. (1974). Working memory. In G. Bower (Ed.), *Recent advances in learning and motivation* (Vol. 8, pp. 47–90). New York: Academic Press.

Bandura, A. (1986). *Social foundations of thought and action.* Englewood Cliffs, NJ: Prentice-Hall.

Bargh, J. A. (1989). Conditional automaticity: Varieties of automatic influence in social perception and cognition. In J. S. Uleman & J. A. Bargh (Eds.), *Unintended thought* (pp. 3–51). New York: Guilford.

Bargh, J. A. (1990). Auto-motives: Preconscious determinants of social interaction. In E. T. Higgins & R. M. Sorrentino (Eds.), *Handbook of motivation and cognition* (Vol. 2, pp. 93–130). New York: Guilford.

Bargh, J. A. (1992). Why subliminality does not matter to social psychology: Awareness of the stimulus versus awareness of its influence. In R. F. Bornstein & T. S. Pittman (Eds.), *Perception without awareness* (pp. 236–255). New York: Guilford.

Bargh, J. A. (1994). The four horsemen of automaticity: Awareness, intention, efficiency, and control in social cognition. In R. S. Wyer & T. K. Srull (Eds.), *Handbook of social cognition* (2nd ed., Vol. 1, pp. 1–40). Hillsdale, NJ: Erlbaum.

Bargh, J. A. (1996). Principles of automaticity. In E. T. Higgins & A. W. Kruglanski (Eds.), *Social psychology: Handbook of basic principles* (pp. 169–183). New York: Guilford.

Bargh, J. A. (1999). The cognitive monster: The case against controllability of automatic stereotype effects. In S. Chaiken & Y. Trope (Eds.), *Dual process theories in social psychology* (pp. 361–382). New York: Guilford.

Bargh, J. A. (2001). The psychology of the mere. In J. A. Bargh & D. Apsley (Eds.), *Unraveling the complexities of social life: A Festschrift in honor of Robert B. Zajonc* (pp. 25–37). Washington, DC: American Psychological Association.

Bargh, J. A., & Chartrand, T. (1999). The unbearable automaticity of being. *American Psychologist, 54*, 462–479.

Bargh, J. A., & Chartrand, T. L. (2000). A practical guide to priming and automaticity research. In H. Reis & C. Judd (Eds.), *Handbook of research methods in social psychology* (pp. 253–285). New York: Cambridge University Press.

Bargh, J. A., Chen, M., & Burrows, L. (1996). Automaticity of social behavior: Direct effects of trait construct and stereotype priming on action. *Journal of Personality and Social Psychology, 71*, 230–244.

Bargh, J. A., & Ferguson, M. L. (2000). Beyond behaviorism: On the automaticity of higher mental processes. *Psychological Bulletin, 126*, 925–945.

Bargh, J. A., & Gollwitzer, P. M. (1994). Environmental control over goal-directed action. *Nebraska Symposium on Motivation, 41*, 71–124.

Bargh, J. A., Gollwitzer, P. M., Lee-Chai, A. Y., Barndollar, K., & Troetschel, R. (2001). The automated will: Nonconscious activation and pursuit of behavioral goals. *Journal of Personality and Social Psychology, 81*, 1014–1027.

Bargh, J. A., & Thein, R. D. (1985). Individual construct accessibility, person memory, and the recall-judgment link: The case of information overload. *Journal of Personality and Social Psychology, 49*, 1129–1146.

Baumeister, R. F. (1998). The self. In D. T. Gilbert, S. T. Fiske, & G. Lindzey (Eds.), *Handbook of social psychology* (4th ed., pp. 680–740). Boston: McGraw-Hill.

Baumeister, R. F., Bratslavsky, E., Muraven, M., & Tice, D. M. (1998). Ego-depletion: Is the active self a limited resource? *Journal of Personality and Social Psychology, 74*, 1252–1265.

Berkowitz, L. (1984). Some effects of thoughts on anti- and prosocial influences of media events: A cognitive-neoassociation analysis. *Psychological Bulletin, 95*, 410–427.

Brewer, M. B. (1988). A dual process model of impression formation. In T. K. Srull & R. S. Wyer, Jr. (Eds.), *Advances in social cognition* (Vol. 1, pp. 1–36). Hillsdale, NJ: Erlbaum.

Bruner, J. S. (1957). On perceptual readiness. *Psychological Review, 64*, 123–152.

Buccino, G., Binkofski, F., Fink, G. R., Fadiga, L,, Fogassi, L., Gallese, V., Seitz, R. J., Zilles, K., Rizzolatti, G., & Freund, H.-J. (2001). Action observation activates premotor and parietal areas in somatotopic manner: An fMRI study. *European Journal of Neuroscience, 13*, 400–404.

Carlston, D. E., & Skowronski, J. J. (1994). Savings in the relearning of trait information as evidence for spontaneous inference generation. *Journal of Personality and Social Psychology, 66*, 840–856.

Carver, C. S., & Scheier, M. F. (1981). *Attention and self-regulation: A control-theory approach to human behavior*. New York: Springer.

Chaiken, S. (1980). Heuristic versus systematic information processing and the use of source versus message cues in persuasion. *Journal of Personality and Social Psychology, 39*, 752–766.

Chaiken, S., & Trope, Y. (Eds.). (1999). *Dual process theories in social psychology*. New York: Guilford.

Chartrand, T. L., & Bargh, J. A. (1996). Automatic activation of social information processing goals: Nonconscious priming reproduces effects of explicit conscious instructions. *Journal of Personality and Social Psychology, 71*, 464–478.

Chartrand, T. L., & Bargh, J. A. (1999). The chameleon effect: The perception-behavior link and social interaction. *Journal of Personality and Social Psychology, 76*, 893–910.

Chartrand, T. L., & Bargh, J. A. (2002). Nonconscious motivations: Their activation, operation, and consequences. In A. Tesser, D. A. Stapel, & J. V. Wood (Eds.), *Self and motivation: Emerging psychological perspectives* (pp. 13–41). Washington, DC: American Psychological Association.

Cohen, J. D., Dunbar, K., & McClelland, J. (1990). On the control of automatic processes: A parallel distributed processing account of the Stroop effect. *Psychological Review, 97*, 332–361.

Darley, J. M., & Latane, B. (1968). Bystander intervention in emergencies: Diffusion of responsibility. *Journal of Personality and Social Psychology, 8*, 377–383.

Decety, J., & Grèzes, J. (1999). Neural mechanisms subserving the perception of human actions. *Trends in Cognitive Sciences, 3*, 172–178.

Deci, E. L., & Ryan, R. M. (1985). *Intrinsic motivation and self-determination in human behavior*. New York: Plenum.

Descartes, R. (1972). *Treatise of man* (T. S. Hall, Trans.). Cambridge, MA: Harvard University Press. (Work originally published 1633)

Devine, P. G. (1989). Stereotypes and prejudice: Their automatic and controlled components. *Journal of Personality and Social Psychology, 56*, 680–690.

Devine, P. G., & Monteith, M. J. (1999). Automaticity and control in stereotyping. In S. Chaiken & Y. Trope (Eds.), *Dual process theories in social psychology* (pp. 339–360). New York: Guilford.

Dijksterhuis, A., & Bargh, J. A. (2001). The perception-behavior expressway: Automatic effects of social perception on social behavior. In M. P. Zanna (Ed.), *Advances in experimental social psychology* (Vol. 33, pp. 1–40). San Diego: Academic Press.

Dijksterhuis, A., & van Knippenberg, A. (1998). The relation between perception and behavior, or how to win a game of Trivial Pursuit. *Journal of Personality and Social Psychology, 74*, 865–877.

Donald, M. (2001). *A mind so rare*. New York: Norton.

Eagly, A. H., & Chaiken, S. (1993). *The psychology of attitudes.* New York: Harcourt Brace Jovanovich.

Erber, R., & Fiske, S. T. (1984). Outcome dependency and attention to inconsistent information. *Journal of Personality and Social Psychology, 47*, 709–726.

Fazio, R. H. (1986). How do attitudes guide behavior? In R. M. Sorrentino & E. T. Higgins (Eds.), *Handbook of motivation and cognition* (Vol. 1, pp. 204–243). New York: Guilford.

Fazio, R. H. (1990). Multiple processes by which attitudes guide behavior: The MODE model as an integrative framework. In M. P. Zanna (Ed.), *Advances in experimental social psychology* (Vol. 23, pp. 75–109). San Diego, CA: Academic Press.

Fazio, R. H., Jackson, J. R., Dunton, B. C., & Williams, C. J. (1995). Variability in automatic activation as an unobtrusive measure of racial attitudes: A bona fide pipeline? *Journal of Personality and Social Psychology, 69*, 1013–1027.

Fazio, R. H., & Williams, C. J. (1986). Attitude accessibility as a moderator of the attitude-perception and attitude-behavior relations: An investigation of the 1984 presidential election. *Journal of Personality and Social Psychology, 51*, 505–514.

Fiske, S. T. (1989). Examining the role of intent: Toward understanding its role in stereotyping and prejudice. In J. S. Uleman & J. A. Bargh (Eds.), *Unintended thought* (pp. 253–283). New York: Guilford.

Fitzsimons, G. M., & Bargh, J. A. (2003). Thinking of you: Nonconscious pursuit of interpersonal goals associated with relationship partners. *Journal of Personality and Social Psychology, 83*, 148–164.

Fitzsimons, G. M., & Bargh, J. A. (2004). Automatic self-regulation. In R. Baumeister & K. Vohs (Eds.), *Handbook of self-regulation* (pp. 151–170). New York: Guilford.

Frankfurt, H. G. (1988). *The importance of what we care about*. New York: Cambridge University Press.

Frith, C. D., Blakemore, S.-J., & Wolpert, D. M. (2000). Abnormalities in the awareness and control of action. *Philosophical Transactions of the Royal Society of London*, 355, 1771–1788.

Gilbert, D. T. (1989). Thinking lightly about others: Automatic components of the social inference process. In J. S. Uleman & J. A. Bargh (Eds.), *Unintended thought* (pp. 189–211). New York: Guilford.

Goodale, M. A., Milner, A. D., Jakobsen, L. S., & Carey, D. P. (1991). Perceiving the world and grasping it: A neurological dissociation. *Nature*, 349, 154–156.

Haney, C., Banks, C., & Zimbardo, P. G. (1973). Interpersonal dynamics in a simulated prison. *International Journal of Criminology and Penology*, 1, 69–97.

Hassin, R. R. (2004). Implicit working memory. In R. R. Hassin, J. S. Uleman, & J. A. Bargh (Eds.), *The new unconscious*. New York: Oxford University Press.

Herr, P. M., Sherman, S. J., & Fazio, R. H. (1984). On the consequences of priming: Assimilation and contrast effects. *Journal of Experimental Social Psychology*, 19, 323–340.

Higgins, E. T. (1996). Knowledge activation: Accessibility, applicability, and salience. In E. T. Higgins & A. T. Kruglanski (Eds.), *Social psychology: Handbook of basic principles* (pp. 133–168). New York: Guilford.

Higgins, E. T., King, G. A., & Mavin, G. H. (1982). Individual construct accessibility and subjective impressions and recall. *Journal of Personality and Social Psychology*, 43, 35–47.

James, W. (1890). *Principles of psychology*. New York: Holt.

Jeannerod, M. (1999). To act or not to act: Perspectives on the representation of actions. *Quarterly Journal of Experimental Psychology*, 52A, 1–29.

Johnson, M. K., & Hasher, L. (1987). Human learning and memory. *Annual Review of Psychology*, 38, 631–668.

Kelley, H. H. (1967). Attribution theory in social psychology. In D. Levine (Ed.), *Nebraska Symposium on Motivation* (Vol. 15, pp. 192–241). Lincoln: University of Nebraska Press.

Knuf, L., Aschersleben, G., & Prinz, W. (2001). An analysis of ideomotor action. *Journal of Experimental Psychology: General*, 130, 779–798.

Langer, E. J., Blank, A., & Chanowitz, B. (1978). The mindlessness of ostensibly thoughtful action: The role of 'placebic' information in interpersonal interaction. *Journal of Personality and Social Psychology*, 36, 635–642.

LaPiere, R. T. (1934). Attitudes vs. actions. *Social Forces*, 13, 230–237.

Lhermitte, F. (1986). Human anatomy and the frontal lobes. Part II: Patient behavior in complex and social situations: The "environmental dependency syndrome." *Annals of Neurology*, 19, 335–343.

Locke, E. A., & Latham, G. P. (1990). *A theory of goal setting and task performance*. Englewood Cliffs, NJ: Prentice-Hall.

Mesulam, M.-M. (1986). Frontal cortex and behavior. *Annals of Neurology*, 19, 320–325.

Milgram, S. (1963). Behavioral study of obedience. *Journal of Abnormal and Social Psychology*, 67, 371–378.

Mischel, W., Cantor, N., & Feldman, S. (1996). Principles of self-regulation: The nature of willpower and self-control. In E. T. Higgins & A. W. Kruglanski (Eds.), *Social psychology: Handbook of basic principles* (pp. 329–360). New York: Guilford.

Neuberg, S. L., & Fiske, S. T. (1987). Motivational influences on impression formation: Outcome dependency, accuracy-driven attention, and individuating processes. *Journal of Personality and Social Psychology*, 53, 431–444.

Nisbett, R. E., & Ross, L. (1980). *Human inference: Strategies and shortcomings of social judgment*. Englewood Cliffs, NJ: Prentice-Hall.

Nisbett, R. E., & Wilson, T. D. (1977). Telling more than we can know: Verbal reports on mental processes. *Psychological Review*, 84, 231–259.

Norman, J. (2002). Two visual systems and two theories of perception: An attempt to reconcile the constructivist and ecological approaches. *Behavioral and Brain Sciences*, 24, 73–96.

Petty, R. E., & Cacioppo, J. T. (1984). The effects of involvement on responses to argument quantity and quality: Central and peripheral routes to persuasion. *Journal of Personality and Social Psychology*, 46, 69–81.

Posner, M. I., & DiGirolamo, G. (2000). Cognitive neuroscience: Origins and promise. *Psychological Bulletin*, 126, 873–889.

Posner, M. I., & Snyder, C. R. R. (1975). Attention and cognitive control. In R. L. Solso (Ed.), *Information processing and cognition: The Loyola symposium* (pp. 55–85). Hillsdale, NJ: Erlbaum.

Prinz, W. (1997). Perception and action planning. *European Journal of Cognitive Psychology, 9,* 129–154.

Prinz, W. (2003). How do we know about our own actions? In S. Maasen, W. Prinz, & G. Roth (Eds.), *Voluntary action: Brains, minds, and sociality* (pp. 21–33). New York: Oxford University Press.

Rizzolatti, G., & Arbib, M. A. (1998). Language within our grasp. *Trends in Neurosciences, 21,* 188–194.

Shiffrin, R. M., & Dumais, S. T. (1981). The development of automatism. In J. R. Anderson (Eds.), *Cognitive skills and their acquisition* (pp. 111–140). Hillsdale, NJ: Erlbaum.

Shiffrin, R. M., & Schneider, W. (1977). Controlled and automatic human information processing: II. Perceptual learning, automatic attending, and a general theory. *Psychological Review, 84,* 127–190.

Srull, T. K., & Wyer, R. S., Jr. (1979). The role of category accessibility in the interpretation of information about persons: Some determinants and implications. *Journal of Personality and Social Psychology, 37,* 1660–1672.

Taylor, S. E., & Fiske, S. T. (1978). Salience, attention, and attribution: Top of the head phenomena. In L. Berkowitz (Ed.), *Advances in experimental social psychology* (Vol. 11, pp. 249–288). New York: Academic Press.

Thurstone, L. L. (1928). Attitudes can be measured. *American Journal of Sociology, 33,* 529–554.

Tulving, E., & Thomson, D. M. (1973). Encoding specificity and retrieval processes in episodic memory. *Psychological Review, 80,* 352–373.

Uleman, J. S. (1989). A framework for thinking intentionally about unintended thoughts. In J. S. Uleman & J. A. Bargh (Eds.), *Unintended thought*(pp. 425–449). New York: Guilford.

Uleman, J. S., Newman, L. S., & Moskowitz, G. B. (1996). People as spontaneous interpreters: Evidence and issues from spontaneous trait inference. In M. P. Zanna (Ed.), *Advances in experimental social psychology* (Vol. 28, pp. 211–279). San Diego, CA: Academic Press.

Wegner, D. M., & Bargh, J. A. (1998). Control and automaticity in social life. In D. T. Gilbert, S. T. Fiske, & G. Lindzey (Eds.), *Handbook of social psychology* (4th ed., pp. 446–496). Boston: McGraw-Hill.

Wicker, A. W. (1969). Attitudes versus actions: The relationship of verbal and overt behavioral responses to attitude objects. *Journal of Social Issues, 25* (4), 41–78.

Wilson, T. D. (2002). *Strangers to ourselves.* Cambridge, MA: Harvard University Press.

Wilson, T. D., & Brekke, N. (1994). Mental contamination and mental correction: Unwanted influences on judgments and evaluations. *Psychological Bulletin, 116,* 117–142.

Winter, L., & Uleman, J. S. (1984). When are social judgments made? Evidence for the spontaneousness of trait inferences. *Journal of Personality and Social Psychology, 47,* 237–252.

CHAPTER 21

The Evolution of Consciousness

Michael C. Corballis

Abstract

It is likely that many other species are conscious of the physical world in much the same way that we humans are. It is often claimed, however, that only humans are self-conscious, or can represent the mental states of others, or can travel mentally through time. I argue that the embracing characteristic that distinguishes such aspects of human cognition from that of other species is recursion. This feature not only permits us to mentally represent the mental states of others but also underlies such activities as mental time travel, manufacture, and language. Recursive operations are themselves not necessarily conscious, but they permit a more advanced level of consciousness, providing virtually infinite flexibility and generativity. It is likely that recursion evolved with the increase in brain size in the genus *Homo* from about 2 million years ago, probably as a result of increasing social demands. Generative language probably evolved during the first million years of this period, and switched gradually from a manual to a vocal mode, culminating in autonomous speech
in our own species, *Homo sapiens*, perhaps around 100,000 years ago. This gave rise to the "human revolution," with dramatic advances in manufacture, art, and social behavior. These developments may not have altered the nature of consciousness itself, but they added to its content by vastly enriching our mental and physical lives.

Introduction

Consciousness has so far managed to escape any universally agreed definition. Most would agree that an earthworm is probably not conscious and that we normally consider ourselves to be conscious at least some of the time. This relies partly on subjective experience, from which we can conclude that we are not only conscious but that we actually exist, as Descartes famously deduced. The introspective certainty that we are conscious is of little help in understanding the evolution of consciousness, although Wilhelm Wundt (1894), who built an experimental psychology on the introspective method, nevertheless was able late in his career to make some pronouncements about the animal mind. Even so, the identification of consciousness in non-human species must surely be based largely on behavioral rather than introspective evidence, whatever conscious empathy we may experience through gazing into the soulful eyes of a chimpanzee.

Historically, though, animal behaviorists have not been much help since J. B. Watson's (1913) famous manifesto of the behaviorist revolution that banished all mention of consciousness, or even of mind. There was at least a whiff of consciousness, however, in the later distinction between instrumental or operant conditioning, on the one hand, and respondent or classical conditioning, on the other. A dog classically conditioned to salivate at the sound of a bell presumably makes no conscious decision to salivate, although it may arguably be consciously aware of its unseemly drool. A pigeon pressing a key to achieve a food reward, however, may well be aware of the contingency that leads it to peck, and there are well-articulated laws governing the rates of pecking under different reinforcement regimes (Davison & McCarthy, 1987; Ferster & Skinner, 1957).

Despite the traditional lack of interest in consciousness among behaviorists, there have been recent attempts to develop proxies for introspection in non-human animals. For example Logothetis (1998) studied bistable percepts in macaques by teaching them to give different responses to different stimuli and then placing the two stimuli in binocular rivalry. The animals then indicate which stimulus they perceive at any given time by giving the response to that stimulus, implying report of their own internal percepts. That is, the animals are indicating what they see, rather than simply responding to the presence or absence of a stimulus. Cowie and Stoerig (1995) have also developed a way of testing blindsight in monkeys that seems tantamount to subjective report. After unilateral removal of the striate cortex, monkeys were able to reach accurately for panels that were lit up in either visual field, thereby demonstrating blindsight – just as humans with striate-cortex lesions do (Weiskrantz, 1986). The interest-

ing question then, however, was whether the animals had the subjective experience of seeing the light in the blind field. When given the choice of three responses, one for a left light, one for a right light, and one for no light, the animals consistently chose "no light" when the light was in the blind field. That is, monkeys seem to be able to report on their own subjective experience of seeing nothing when a light was presented in the blind field, even though they were able to respond to it accurately.

There is also evidence that monkeys can perform such mental operations as mental rotation and memory scanning (Georgopoulos & Pellizzer, 1995). In his classic study of problem solving in chimpanzees, Köhler (1925) provided compelling evidence that the animals were able to solve problems mentally before demonstrating the solutions in practice. For example, a chimpanzee may understand that one can haul in a banana that is out of reach by using a rake, or even by extending the length of a rake by adding an extra piece to the handle. The chimpanzees often seemed to solve these problems suddenly, as though through insight rather than trial and error. Tomasello (1996) has demonstrated similar problem-solving abilities in chimpanzees, but notes that chimpanzees do not learn to solve problems by imitating others, whereas human children do. Povinelli (2001) suggests that chimpanzees are actually fairly limited in their ability to solve physical problems. In one experiment, chimpanzees were taught how to reach a hooked tool through holes in a plexiglass screen and retrieve a banana that was just out of reach. The banana was on a piece of wood with a vertical post at one end and a ring at the other, and the animals learned to hook the ring and haul in the banana. But when the ring was removed, they did not seem to understand that they could use the tool to hook the post and haul in the banana that way. Whatever the limitations of these thought-provoking experiments, there seems no reason to doubt that great apes, and probably other primates as well, have some internal computational abilities, and it is probably also reasonable to suppose that the implied mental activity is in some sense subjective – although we can never know for sure.

Nevertheless there seems good reason to believe that other primates, at least, are conscious of the physical world in much the same ways as we humans are and that they can also think consciously about operations on the world, even if in rather primitive fashion. It is sometimes suggested, however, that there are additional dimensions of consciousness that only humans possess. As we shall see, for example, it is claimed that only humans have an awareness of self or of the thoughts, perceptions, and feelings of others. The rest of this chapter is concerned with these more complex, social aspects of consciousness and the claim that at least some of these are uniquely human. Again, though, the problem is largely one of method. How can we know, for example, whether a chimpanzee or a bonobo can tell what another individual ape is thinking?

Of course, this problem applies as much to other people as to animals. How can I be sure that you, the reader, are subjectively aware of what I am trying to convey through these very words? How do I know that all my friends are not simply zombies, programmed to act intelligently in my presence? Part of the answer comes from the fact that we can interrogate people as to what is going on in their minds through language. Indeed, language is not only the principal access into the subjective lives of other people but it is also sometimes taken as integral to consciousness itself. Bickerton (1995), for example, proposed that "the peculiar properties of a distinctively human intelligence as such are derived from the possession of language" and went on to suggest that "consciousness as we know it may arise from an identical source" (p. 7). The idea that language distinguishes humans from other animals goes back at least to Descartes (1985/1647), who thought that non-human animals were mere machines, operating according to mechanical principles, whereas humans possessed a freedom of thought and action that set them apart. Language, in particular, had an open-endedness that defied any mechanical expla-

nation. This point was revived by Chomsky (1966), who similarly pointed out the generativity of language and emphasized its uniqueness to humans.

The emphasis on language as the entry into the consciousness of others, or even as a criterion of consciousness itself, and the Chomsky-inspired insistence that language is uniquely human may have at least temporarily closed off the possibility of admitting consciousness in non-human animals, although there was something of a challenge from those who tried to demonstrate language-like behaviors in apes (e.g., Gardner & Gardner, 1969; Miles, 1990; Patterson, 1978; Savage-Rumbaugh, Shanker, & Taylor, 1998) and dolphins (e.g., Herman, Richards, & Wolz, 1984). The possibilities of animal consciousness were revived somewhat, and broadened, when Premack and Woodruff (1978), frustrated by the lack of progress in the ape-language research, opened the door a little wider with the question: "Does the chimpanzee have a theory of mind?" (p. 515). Yet even if the answer is no, we might still be reluctant to deny some form of consciousness to our cat or dog, or to the New Caledonian crow that manufactures tools so skillfully to extract foodstuffs from holes (Hunt, 1996), or to the above-mentioned chimpanzees with their problem-solving exploits. The question then is whether we can gain a better understanding of an animal's behavior by attributing consciousness to it. How are we to do this?

The Intentional Stance

One approach is that of the *intentional stance*, which seems to offer a way out of radical behaviorism and its denial of consciousness without resorting to introspectionism and the implied inaccessibility to animal minds (Dennett, 1983). The characteristics that identify intentional as distinct from non-intentional systems, at least as presented by Dennett, may seem counter-intuitive and have to do with the nature of statements about the world. In most true statements, one can replace a term in the statement by another term that refers to exactly the same thing, and the statement remains true. For example, if Jack is the farmer's son, then the sentence "This is the house that Jack built" can be replaced by "This is the house that the farmer's son built." The truth or falsity of the first sentence is not altered by the substitution.

Statements of intentionality, in contrast, exhibit *referential opacity*, such that substituting a term with one that refers to the same thing can alter its truth or falsity. Dennett gives an example taken from Bertrand Russell (1905). Consider the sentence "George IV wondered whether Scott was the author of *Waverly*," and suppose it to be true. It is also true that Sir Walter Scott did write the novel *Waverly*, so one might consider substituting "Scott" for "the author of *Waverly*": "George IV wondered whether Scott was Scott." It is unlikely (though remotely possible) that George IV actually did wonder this, so in this case the substitution does change the sentence from a true one to a false one. In other words, referential opacity creates a barrier to logical analysis.

To down-to-earth scientists these considerations may seem far removed from consciousness, but referential opacity picks out precisely those clauses that include subjective terms like "believes (that)," "knows (that)," "expects (that)," "wants (it to be the case that)," "recognizes (that)," "wonders (whether)," "understands (that)," and so forth. The question then is, do we get a better account of some behavioral act if we include one of these terms, thereby creating referential opacity? For example, do we gain a better account of a pigeon's behavior if we conclude not just that it pecks a key and then receives food but also that it pecks the key in the *belief* that this will produce food?

By attributing subjective states, the intentional stance does not appeal to introspection – you don't actually ask the pigeon to introspect about its behavior and tell you what it thinks. The important tests are still behavioral, and the question is whether the attribution gives a more compelling account of observed behavior than would otherwise be the case. As Dennett recognized, more-

over, the intentional stance is not watertight because it is always possible to devise purely behavioral accounts that make no reference to subjective terms (or more formally, that do not exhibit referential opacity). For example, we may be willing to attribute belief to the egregious pigeon if it does not peck the key if it happens to notice that there is no food in the food hopper. It now does not believe that it will receive food if it pecks the key, and being a rational bird it stops. However, we could just as easily explain the behavior in terms of environmental contingencies. The bird pecks if the hopper contains food, but does not peck if the hopper is empty.

My guess is that it will always be possible to convert an intentional statement about an animal's behavior into a statement that does not include intentional clauses, but is expressed rather in terms of environmental contingencies. This means that there will always be those who reject claims of animal consciousness – from Watson (1913) to Skinner (1957) to Heyes (1998, 2001). The two points of view may remain as implacably opposed as the particle and wave theories of light. And there may never be a crucial experiment (*pace* Heyes, 1998) that can distinguish them.

Does that mean we should abandon the quest for animal consciousness? For the present, at least, I think it is worth taking the intentional stance, because it offers a vocabulary that can address the important issues and suggest interesting experiments. This is not to say that a purely behavioral account might not eventually do as well, if not better, but it is the intentional stance that seems to be making the running, perhaps beginning with Premack and Woodruff's (1978) famous question about theory of mind in the chimpanzee. Thanks to Dennett's formalism, the definition of intentional clauses removes the taint of introspectionism, and questions about believing, wanting, recognizing, etc, can be translated into objective experiments. The fact that such terms map onto introspective states can even be considered an advantage because we are accustomed to thinking in such terms, and this can help in setting up the important tests of animal consciousness. In this chapter I therefore continue to use subjective terms like *think, understand, feel,* and *imagine,* but for the philosophically pure it should be understood (*sic*) that these terms owe their special status to referential opacity, and not to whatever it is that we experience in our own heads. In other words, these terms should be un*qualia*fied (again, *sic*).

One major reason to prefer the intentional stance to the purely behavioral one is that it allows us to define different *orders* of intentionality. This may be helpful, if not crucial, in understanding what is different about the human mind and human consciousness and what may be different about the minds of the great apes relative to other primates.

Orders of Intentionality, and Recursion

Zero-order intentionality simply involves one subjective term, as in "Alice *wants* Fred to stop bugging her." First-order intentionality would involve two such terms, as in "Ted *thinks* Alice *wants* Fred to stop bugging her." And so to second-order: "Alice *believes* that Fred *thinks* she *wants* him to stop bugging her."

It should be clear from these examples that the different orders of intentionality involve recursion and can be continued indefinitely. There seems some reason to believe, though, that we humans run out of grunt at about the fifth or sixth order (Cargile, 1970), perhaps because of limited working memory capacity, rather than any intrinsic limit on recursion itself. We can perhaps just wrap our minds around propositions like "Ted *suspects* that Alice *believes* that he does indeed *suspect* that Fred *thinks* that she *wants* him (Fred) to stop bugging her." That's fourth-order, as you can tell by counting the italicized words and subtracting one. You could make it fifth-order by adding "George *imagines* that . . ." at the beginning.

More formally, recursion is a mathematical device for generating terms in a sequence, where the rule for generating the next term in a sequence involves one or more of the preceding terms. A simple example is the use of integers for counting. So long as we have rules that allow us to generate a number from the preceding number in a sequence, there is no limit to the number of objects we can count. The basic rule, of course, is simply to add 1 to the preceding number. This is not an entirely trivial exercise because there are subrules that tell you how to do this by starting with the rightmost digit, and dealing with the special case where the rightmost digit or digits equal 9. The point is that the procedure is recursive, and the sequence can be continued indefinitely. Counting is thus an example of what Chomsky (1988) has called "discrete infinity."

The example of counting illustrates that recursion is not restricted to intentional states – a computer can count without anyone suspecting it of consciousness. Consider also the following well-known children's story:

> *This is the house that Jack built.*
> *This is the malt that lay in the house that Jack built.*
> *This is the rat that ate the malt that lay in the house that Jack built.*
> *This is the cat that killed the rat that ate the malt that lay in the house that Jack built.*
> *This is the dog that worried the cat that killed the rat that ate the malt that lay in the house that Jack built.*

This increasingly recursive sequence does not involve intentional clauses, although in telling the story there is perhaps implicit intentionality. Bennett (1976) has argued that genuinely communicative speech requires at least three orders of intentionality. In telling you the story, I *intend* you to *recognize* that I *want* you to understand that "This is the house that Jack built," etc. Otherwise I might as well be talking to the moon.

It should be understood that stories like *The House that Jack Built* are not simply sequential events. It is not simply that a dog worried a cat, a cat killed a rat, and so forth; the recursion implies that we are specifying a rather specific dog. We are not referring to a dog that worried a cat that killed a rat that did *not* eat the malt that lay in the house that Jack built. In a line-up of suspects, such a dog would not do.

We can also express the story using embedded phrases, which allows us to focus on a particular actor in the story, such as the unfortunate malt:

> *The malt that the rat that the cat that the dog worried killed ate lay in the house that Jack built.*

And this, I think, again pushes the boundaries of human understanding, although I find that if I take it slowly I can get there.

In presenting these examples, I have also illustrated the recursiveness of language itself – we need recursive language to express recursive thoughts. In linguistics, the recursiveness is often expressed in terms of rewrite rules in which the same term can appear on either side of the expression defining a rule. For example, *The House that Jack Built* involves a succession of relative clauses into which we can substitute more relative clauses; thus

relative clause = relative clause

+ relative clause.

Or we could break it down into a more complex set of rules, as follows:

(Rule 1)	S	NP + VP
(Rule 2)	NP	article + noun + [RC]
(Rule 3)	RC	relative pronoun + VP
(Rule 4)	VP	verb + [NP]

where S = sentence, NP = noun phrase, RC = relative clause, and VP = verb phrase, and the bracketed items are optional. These rules are sufficient to generate sentences like "The dog that chased the cat killed the rat," as shown in Figure 21.1.

The Recursive Mind

Hauser, Chomsky, and Fitch (2002), discussing the evolution of language, have argued that recursion is a uniquely human mental accomplishment. People can count recursively, think recursively about the mental states of others (and of themselves), and use recursive syntax to tell stories. Our social lives involve a subtle calculus of cooperation

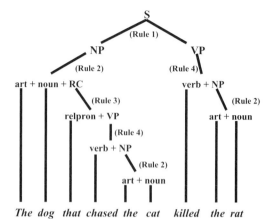

Figure 21.1. This tree diagram shows how the recursive use of rules can produce a sentence with an embedded clause.

and competition, of guess and second-guess. The recursive nature of social relations is well conveyed in literature and the theater. In Jane Austen's *Pride and Prejudice*, Elizabeth Bennet *thinks* that Darcy *thinks* that she *thinks* he *thinks* too harshly of her family. Or in Shakespeare's *Twelfth Night*, Maria *foresees* that Sir Toby will eagerly *anticipate* that Olivia will *judge* Malvolio absurdly impertinent to *suppose* that she *wishes* him to *regard* himself as her preferred suitor.[1] One might add a further order of recursion by prefixing each of these situations with the phrase, "The audience *understands* that . . ."

Recursion might be said to add a further dimension to consciousness (see Chapter 15). Tulving (2001) has distinguished noetic consciousness, which implies knowing, from what he calls autonoetic consciousness, which implies knowing that one knows. According to Tulving, autonoetic consciousness is uniquely human and underlies the concept of self. One example of autonoetic consciousness is episodic memory, which is memory for events in one's life that have specific locations in time and space. Episodic memory is distinguished from semantic memory, which is memory for generic facts, and is noetic rather than autonoetic. Episodic memory does seem to depend on a mental reconstruction or re-enactment of some earlier experience and implies first-order intentionality of the form *I experience that I experienced* X. One can remember that one saw something, remember that one felt ill, or even remember that one once remembered something now forgotten.

Episodic memory may be regarded as part of a more general ability to engage in *mental time travel*, which involves imagining the future, as well as the past (Suddendorf & Corballis, 1997). There is evidence, for example, that the loss of episodic memory due to brain injury also leads to a loss of the ability to engage in what has come to be called episodic future thinking, and which probably depends on the prefrontal cortex (Atance & O'Neill, 2001; Wheeler, Stuss, & Tulving, 1997). Although we tend to think of memory as factual and the future as hypothetical, both are probably constructed from a mixture of fact and fantasy. By including the future as well as the past, we essentially create an extended sense of self that allows us to create the entity that distinguishes us from others.

Yet recursion runs deeper than autonoetic consciousness and the concept of self. We can think recursively well beyond first-order intentionality, as explained earlier. Recursive thinking need not have anything to do with the self or even with levels of knowing. Our counting system is recursive, as is language itself. Human manufacture is also recursive, and in a review of evidence on toolmaking, Beck (1980, p. 218) noted, "Unquestionably man [*sic*] is the only animal that to date has been observed to use a tool to make a tool." In addition, we create objects, or components, that are then used in the manufacture of higher-order objects, which are then combined into yet higher-order ones. From bricks come houses, and from houses villages. And there are wheels within wheels.

Recursion in Other Species

The claim that only humans are capable of recursion does not mean that other animals don't possess consciousness. There seems no reason to deny at least some other animals pleasure or pain, or even belief, and we saw earlier that primates, at least, can apparently give overt reports on their own internal states. That is, we might easily concede zero-order intentionality, or noetic consciousness. It may well be reasonable to suppose that a pigeon in some sense "believes" that if it pecks a key it will receive food, but it is problematic as to whether it believes this of another pigeon. Much of the discussion and research effort has been essentially concerned with whether first-order intentionality can be demonstrated in any other species, and most particularly in the great apes.

Theory of Mind in Great Apes?

Premack and Woodruff (1978), who set the ball rolling, suggested a number of experiments that might demonstrate first-order intentionality and applied a few of them to Sarah, a captive chimpanzee. One of their techniques was to show videos of a human grappling with some problem and then offer Sarah a choice of photographs, one of which depicted a solution to the problem. One such test showed a woman trying to escape from a locked cage, and one of the photos showed a key, whereas others showed objects irrelevant to the task. Sarah performed quite well at choosing the appropriate photo, although as Premack and Woodruff recognized, this need not show that she appreciated what was going on in the mind of the person depicted. For example, the key might have been selected through simple association with the cage.

One researcher who has taken up Premack and Woodruff's challenge is Povinelli, who has tried further tests to determine whether a chimpanzee can understand what is going on in the mind of a person (see Povinelli, Bering, & Giambrone, 2000, for a summary). The results have been largely negative. Chimpanzees readily approach humans to beg for food, and this behavior provided an opportunity to check whether in so doing they are influenced by whether the person can see or not. But when offered the choice of two individuals to beg from, one with a blindfold over her eyes, the animals did not systematically choose the one who could see. The same was true when one of the people had a bucket over her head or covered her eyes with her hands. Only when one of the people was actually facing the other way did the chimpanzees easily choose the one facing toward the animal. Young children, on the other hand, quickly recognize that they should approach the person who can see them and understand that this depends on the eyes. The failure of the chimpanzee to appreciate this fact does not arise from failure to observe the eyes, because they readily follow the gaze of a person confronting them. Chimpanzees may eventually choose the person who can see them, but the behavior is more simply explained as being due to associative learning, and not due to the understanding that eyes are for seeing.

Another test depends on the chimpanzee's apparent understanding of pointing. If a person sits in front of a chimpanzee and points to one of two boxes on the left or right, the chimpanzee understands readily enough that if it wants food, it should go to the box that the person is pointing to. But the choice breaks down if the person points from some distance away and is systematically reversed if the person sits closer to the box that does not contain the food and points to the other one. It seems that chimpanzees respond on the basis of how close the pointing hand is to the box containing the food, and not on the basis of where the hand is actually pointing.

Yet chimpanzees do follow eye gaze (Tomasello, Hare, & Agnetta, 1999), just as humans do, and this may suggest that they have at least some understanding that others can see. Povinelli argues, though, that behaviors like following eye gaze have the same basis in humans as in other primates, but that we "reinterpret" these behaviors as being more sophisticated than they really are (Povinelli & Bering, 2002). For example, we may spontaneously follow the gaze of someone who seems to be gazing at something in the sky without going through an intellectual (and presumably conscious) exercise along the lines of the following: "That fellow must be able to see something up there that's interesting." Gaze following may simply be an adaptive response that alerts other animals to danger or reward, but we humans have intellectualized it, often after the fact.

There is some evidence, though, that the work of Povinelli and his colleagues underestimates the social intelligence of the chimpanzee. Chimpanzees are by nature competitive creatures, and one may wonder why they should trust what humans are trying to indicate. Dogs, in contrast, have been bred to cooperate with humans, and Hare and Tomasello (1999) have shown that dogs do seem to be able to choose food sources according to where either a person or another dog is looking or pointing. It is of course possible that some dogs, through selective breeding, have acquired an order of intentionality beyond that achieved by the chimpanzee, although it is perhaps more likely that they have simply learned a skill that does not involve any understanding of what goes on in the mind of the pointer. Hare, Call, Agnetta, and Tomasello (2000) have also shown that chimpanzees are aware of what other *chimpanzees* can see and modify their behavior accordingly. For example, a chimpanzee will approach food when a more dominant chimpanzee cannot see the food, but will be reluctant to do so when they can see that the dominant chimpanzee is watching.

This is an example of tactical deception. Deception itself is widespread in nature, whether in the camouflage of a butterfly wing or the uncanny ability of the Australian lyre bird to imitate the sounds of other species – including, it is said, the sound of a beer can being opened. Tactical deception, however, is that in which the deception is based on an appreciation of what the deceived animal is actually thinking or what it can see. From primate researchers working in field settings, Whiten and Byrne (1988) collected a database of anecdotal evidence suggesting tactical deception. They screened the reports to eliminate cases in which the animals might have learned to deceive through trial and error and concluded that only the four species of ape occasionally showed evidence of having deceived on the basis of an understanding of what the deceived animal could see or know. Even so, there were relatively few instances – only 12 from common chimpanzees and 3 each from bonobos, gorillas, and orangutans – so there remains some doubt as to whether tactical deception truly shows that great apes can "read the minds" of others.

Leslie (1994) distinguished between two levels of what he called the Theory of Mind Mechanism (ToMM). A child or a chimp with ToMM-1 can attribute goal directedness and self-generated motion to others, whereas a child with ToMM-2 attributes full-blown intentional states, such as believing, desiring, seeing, or remembering, to others. Tomasello and Rakoczy (2003) make a very similar distinction). ToMM-1 does not seem to enable recursion; attributing self-generated motion to another creature carries no implication that the other creature can also attribute self-generated motion. But once desires and beliefs are attributed, as in ToMM-2, then recursion can follow because one can attribute the attribution of such desires and beliefs. There seems no reason at present to suppose that the great apes can advance beyond ToMM-1 at most, and Hauser and Carey (1998) suggest that "the intellectual tie breaker between humans and nonhumans is likely to lie within the power of ToMM-2." A person with full recursive capabilities would bestow upon others all of the mental states that they themselves experience, and do so recursively.

Self-Awareness in Other Species?

It has been shown that great apes (with the possible exception of the gorilla) pass the so-called mirror test, implying self-awareness. A rigorous form of the test is first to anesthetize the animal and then apply red dye to an eyebrow ridge, and then, when the animal awakes, to allow it to see itself in a mirror. Chimpanzees with prior experience of mirrors reach up and touch the red marks on their faces, whereas those without experience with mirrors react as though there is another chimpanzee in the mirror, as do rhesus monkeys even after many years of experience (Gallup, 1998). (Gorillas, curiously, do not seem able to pass the test – see Gallup, 1997). But even this test need not imply more than ToMM-1. That is, a chim-

panzee who passes the test may recognize its mirror image as its own body, but still not attribute its mental states to that image.

What of mental time travel? Curiously, the main challenge to the idea that mental time travel is uniquely human has come, not from apes or even primates, but from birds. Clayton, Bussey, and Dickinson (2003) have shown that scrub jays cache food in different locations and then unerringly return to the appropriate locations to recover the food. Moreover, they calibrate food recovery according to how long it has been cached. For example, if they cache worms in one location and peanuts in another, after 4 hours they will return to the location containing the worms, which they prefer to peanuts. But if they have already learned that worms become inedible if left buried for too long, and if they are tested 24 hours later, they will recover the peanuts in preference to the worms. According to Clayton et al., this means that they remember *what* they have cached, *where* they have cached it, and *when* they cached – thereby passing what they call the "www test" for episodic memory. But are we really to believe that these birds travel mentally in time to re-enact the actual experience of caching food? It seems more likely that they have evolved simpler mechanisms for recovering cached food, perhaps attaching some internal timing device to each location that specifies how long ago food was stored there.

There is some evidence, reviewed by Schwarz and Evans (2001), that primates can also remember where specific events occurred. In one example, a chimpanzee taught to use lexigrams to represent objects was able to select a lexigram for a food item and then point to a location where that item had been hidden some time beforehand (Menzel, 1999). In a slightly more complicated example, Schwarz, Colon, Sanchez, Rodriguez, and Evans (2002) report evidence that a gorilla had encoded both a food item and the person who had previously given him the food. But in none of reviewed cases was there any evidence that the animals had coded the *time* of the past event, so the www criteria were not fully satisfied.

Social Behaviors

Whether or not apes have ToMM-2, or first-order intentionality, or mental time travel, there seems no need to deny them rich social lives. Most primates, with some exceptions such as the solitary orangutan, are social creatures with established hierarchies of dominance, who form coalitions and friend-ships, show empathy, and help each other in distress. Indeed, de Waal (1996) has claimed that the basic ingredients of morality can be discerned in the behavior not just of pri-mates but also of other animals, including marine animals and dogs. Animals have often been observed to perform acts of seeming generosity, in which there is a cost to the giver but a benefit to the receiver. Exam-ples include food sharing, especially promi-nent among chimpanzees, and alliances to ward off aggression, where one animal will come to the aid of another despite the risk of injury. The principle underlying such behavior is thought to be *reciprocal altruism*, such that the giver eventually receives a reciprocal benefit from the orig-inal receiver. An important feature of recip-rocal altruism is that the payback is not immediate. As de Waal points out, primates form friendships, just as humans do, with the effective guarantee of reciprocal altruism in future interactions.

Evolutionary accounts of reciprocal altru-ism had been assumed to apply only to genetically related animals, enhancing the survival of shared genes, until Trivers (1971) gave a plausible evolutionary account of reciprocal altruism among non-kin. Recipro-cal altruism may well underlie the increase in group size in primate evolution, culminating in the large groupings that we see in human societies – and making the perils of war that much more horrific. Yet reciprocal altruism need not imply intentionality. We humans form friendships, or go to the aid of strangers in distress, usually without thinking explic-itly of any future benefit – although there are of course exceptions, as in those who culti-vate the rich. In that respect, the behaviors that reflect reciprocal altruism may be like the response to pointing, referred to above –

a disposition that has been selected in evo-lution, but that need not imply any under-standing of what goes on in the minds of others.

The evidence on theory of mind in the great apes seems to have left researchers as divided as ever they have been on the issue of continuity and discontinuity. In the Introduction to a special issue of *Cogni-tive Science* devoted to primate cognition, Tomasello (2000) wrote as follows:

> H]uman cognition is a specific (in the literal meaning of the word) instance of primate cognition, and evolution by means of nat-ural selection is a mostly conservative pro-cess that preserves adaptations for as long as they work. Human cognition is thus not just similar to nonhuman primate cogni-tion, it is identical in many of its structures. The study of nonhuman primate cognition should therefore play a more important role in cognitive science than is currently the case (p. 351).

That says it for continuity, but it did not take long for the opposite view to emerge from other researchers in primate cogni-tion. Povinelli and Bering (2002) decry the overzealous attempts "to dismantle argu-ments of human uniqueness" while never-theless reaffirming the importance of com-parative psychology: "A true comparative science of animal minds . . . will recognize the complex diversity of the animal king-dom, and will thus view Homo sapiens as one more species with a unique set of adap-tive skills crying out to be identified and understood" (p. 115).

My guess is that it is indeed recursion that sets the human mind apart. The great apes may have evolved a limited repertoire of recursive thought processes, but these are largely situation-specific and perhaps more dependent on trial and error or on emo-tional traits than on logical reasoning. Chim-panzees may well have learned that it is a good idea to not to behave in particular ways when the dominant male is watching, and this is sometimes elevated (or degraded) into deliberate deception. But there is no con-vincing evidence, as far as I know, for levels of intentionality beyond zero-order intentionality and therefore no convincing evidence of recursive thought in any of the great apes, or indeed in any non-human species. But once recursive thinking is established, then the step beyond zero-order to higher orders of intentionality may follow quite easily, but it is a step that has massive implications. It is a bit like the discovery that, having learned to count to 10, one can then use recursion to carry on counting forever.

What does this have to do with consciousness itself? As we have seen, recursion itself does not imply consciousness. However, the ability to think recursively may have endowed our species with an extra dimension of consciousness that underlies much of our complex social behavior, including the ability to express that complexity in the form of language.

Evolution of the Recursive Mind

The question now arises as to how and when the mind began to take on this recursive aspect. If chimpanzees do not think recursively, then recursion must have evolved in the 6 or 7 million years since the hominids split from the line leading to modern chimpanzees and bonobos.

As noted earlier, it is often supposed that recursion was driven by language, and there is little doubt that language has a recursive structure. Yet there seems little reason to believe that recursive syntax evolved de novo. It must surely have evolved as a vehicle for the expression of recursive thought. Bickerton (2000) has argued that it evolved from reciprocal altruism, which requires keeping track of the variety of events that take place within an animal's social group. It implies a distinction between individuals (you need to know who your friends are), a recognition of actions, and a knowledge of payback structures. According to Bickerton, this leads to setting up the categories of *agent, theme,* and *goal.* As the complexity of social life increased the demands on these categories must have grown, so that they could be used flexibly, and ulti-

mately recursively, in the calculus of social relations.

When is this likely to have occurred? It was probably late in hominid evolution, because brain size remained approximately constant from the divergence from the chimpanzee line until around 2 million years ago. Further, there was little evidence for sophisticated tool use during that period. There are a number of reasons to believe that the progression from protolanguage and recursive thought may have begun with the emergence of *Homo erectus* some 2 million years ago. Around that time, hominids began to migrate out of Africa into Asia and later into Europe (Tattersall, 1998), and the Acheulian industry emerged, with large bifacial tools and handaxes that seemed to mark a significant advance over the simple flaked tools of the earlier Oldowan industry (Gowlett, 1992) – although, as we see, the advancement of manufacturing techniques remained relative slow until comparatively recently.

Brain size also began to increase dramatically (Deacon, 1997). Indeed Chomsky (1975) has suggested that language may have emerged simply as a consequence of possessing an enlarged brain, without the assistance of natural selection:

> We know very little about what happens when 10^{10} neurons are crammed into something the size of a basketball, with further conditions imposed by the specific manner in which this system developed over time. It would be a serious error to suppose that all properties, or the interesting structures that evolved, can be 'explained' in terms of natural selection (p. 59).

Although this seems to ignore the selective processes that must have led to the increase in brain size in the first place, it is plausible to suppose that an enlarged brain provided the extra circuitry required, if not for language alone, then for recursive thought generally.

Another factor may have been the prolongation of childhood, which was probably an indirect result of the increase in the size of the brain, and therefore of the head. To conform to the general primate pattern, human babies should be born at around 18 months, not 9 months (Krogman, 1972), but as any mother will know this would be impossible, given the size of the birth canal. The brain of a newborn chimpanzee is about 60% of its adult weight; that of a newborn human is only about 24%. This feature of prolonged childhood probably emerged in evolution with the increase in brain size, and there is evidence that it was present in *Homo erectus* by 1.6 million years ago (Brown, Harris, Leakey, & Walker, 1985). Our prolonged childhood means that the human brain undergoes most of its growth while exposed to external influences and is therefore tuned more finely to its environment.

There is some reason to believe that learning during growth may be the key to recursion. Elman (1993) has devised a network with recurrent loops that can apparently learn something resembling grammar. Given a partial sequence of symbols, analogous to a partial sentence, the network can learn to predict events that would follow according to rules of grammar. In a very limited way, then, the network "learns" the rules of grammar. At first, the network was unable to handle the recursive aspects of grammar, in which phrases are embedded in other phrases, so that words that go together may be separated by several other words. This problem was at least partially surmounted when Elman introduced a "growth" factor, which he simulated by degrading the system early on so that only global aspects of the input were processed, and then gradually decreasing the "noise" in the system so that it was able to process more and more detail. When this was done, the system was able to pick up some of the recursive quality of grammar and so begin to approximate the processing of true language (Elman, 1993; Elman, Bates, & Newport, 1996).

Language is not critical to consciousness, or even to recursive consciousness, but it surely enriches our conscious lives. The unboundedness of language means that there is no limit to the number of sentences we can create, and therefore no limit to the number of images and scenarios we can create in the minds of others. Consciousness thus becomes a shared experience. This also allows for the cumulative development of culture, because information can be transmitted verbally from generation to generation, bypassing the slow route of evolutionary change.

As suggested earlier, another possible manifestation of recursive consciousness is mental time travel. Perhaps it was this that led to an appreciation of impending death and the emergence of burial rituals. There is some evidence that the Neanderthals buried their dead (Smirnov, 1989), perhaps even with offerings of flowers (Solecki, 1975), although the evidence remains controversial (Noble & Davidson, 1996). There is also evidence of cut marks inflicted on the crania of the dead from the earliest *Homo* (Pickering, White & Toth, 2000) to early *Homo sapiens* (Clarke et al., 2003), suggesting defleshing, but it is not clear whether its purpose was decorative or cannibalistic. It may have more to do with hunger than with empathy. There is clear evidence of ritual burial, often involving the use of red ochre for decoration, dating from some 40,000 years ago in Europe and Australia (Wreschner, 1980).

Evolutionary Psychology and the Pleistocene

The four critical evolutionary markers mentioned above – migrations, enhanced manufacture, increased brain size, and prolongation of childhood – presumably took place slightly before or during the early part of the era known as the Pleistocene, which is usually dated from about 1.8 million years ago until about 10,000 years ago (e.g., Janis, 1993). The new-found discipline of evolutionary psychology (see Chapter 22) has typically emphasized the Pleistocene era, and the so-called hunter-gatherer phase of hominid evolution, as the source of most distinctively human characteristics (e.g., Barkow, Cosmides, & Tooby, 1992). The basic research strategy, as also popularized by Pinker (1994), is to "reverse engineer" present-day cognitive and social characteristics to discover their roots in the Pleistocene. This approach is allied with the view that the mind consists of independent, encapsulated "modules" (Fodor, 1983).

One example is the so-called cheater-detection module, inferred from performance on a test devised by Wason (1966), which runs as follows. You are shown four cards, bearing symbols such as A, C, 22, and 17. You are then asked which two cards you should turn over to test the truth of the following statement: "If a card has a vowel on one side, then it has an even number on the other side." Most people will choose the A, which is rational, because if there is an odd number on the other side, then the proposition is false. For their second choice, most people turn over the 22, but this is in fact not very revealing, because whatever is on the other side cannot disconfirm the statement. The better strategy is to turn over the 17, because the presence of a vowel on the other side would disconfirm the statement.

Suppose now that the task is translated so that A stands for *ale* and C for *coke*, the numbers stand for people's ages, and the statement to be verified is "If a person is drinking ale, then he or she must be over 20 years old." People still turn over the A to check the age of the drinker, but most now understand that they should turn over the 17, and if the kid is drinking ale he should be thrown out of the pub. In short, there is a module for detecting people who don't obey the rules, and its logic is better understood in social contexts than in an abstract formulation (after Cosmides, 1989).

The danger with this approach is that it becomes too easy to postulate modules and to tell "just so" stories as to how they evolved in the Pleistocene, so that there is a risk of returning to the instinct psychology of the early 20th century (e.g., McDougall, 1908). Instinct psychology perished under the sheer weight of numbers – the author of one text counted 1,594 instincts that had been attributed to animals and humans (Bernard, 1924) – and evolutionary psychology may also drown in a sea of modules, if not of mixed metaphors. Pinker (1997) suggests that we like potato chips because fatty foods were nutritionally valuable during the Pleistocene, but scarce enough that there

was no danger of obesity; we like landscapes with trees because trees provide shade and escape from dangerous carnivores on the Africa savanna; flowers please us because they are markers for edible fruits, nuts, or tubers amid the greenery of the savanna; and so on – "there are modules," he writes, "for objects and forces, for animate beings, for minds, and for natural kinds like animals, plants, and minerals" (p. 315).

Becoming Modern

Whether or not the mind is quite as modular as the evolutionary psychologists suggest, there can be little doubt that it was during the Pleistocene era that our forebears put away apish things and became human. Even so, developments were in many respects slow. Our own wise species, *Homo sapiens*, arrived late in the Pleistocene. Estimates based on mitochondrial DNA place the most recent common ancestor of modern humans at some 170,000 years ago (Ingman, Kaessmann, Pääbo, & Gyllensten, 2000), and there is fossil evidence that modern human cranial structure had emerged by at least 154,000 years ago (White et al., 2003). But so-called modern behavior may not have surfaced until even more recently. As Bickerton (2002) roguishly puts it, "For the first 1.95 million years after the emergence of *erectus* almost nothing happened: The clunky stone tools became less clunky and slightly more diversified stone tools, and everything beyond that, from bone tools to supercomputers, happened in the last one-fortieth of the period in question" (p. 104).

The "last one fortieth" refers to what has been called a "human revolution" (Mellars & Stringer, 1989), beginning a mere 40,000 years ago. That period heralded a number of developments suggestive of "modern" behavior. A sudden flowering of art and technology in Europe around 30,000 to 40,000 years ago includes a dramatic expansion of manufactured objects to include projectiles, harpoons, awls, buttons, needles, and ornaments (Ambrose, 2001). Cave drawings in France and Northern Italy, depicting a menagerie of horses, rhinos, bears, lions, and horses, date from the same period (Knecht, Pike-Tay, & White, 1993). The first unequivocal musical instruments are bird-bone flutes from the early Upper Paleolithic in Germany (Hahn & Münzel, 1995), and there is widespread evidence across Russia, France, and Germany for the weaving of fibers into clothing, nets, bags, and ropes, dating from some 29,000 years ago (Soffer, Adovasio, Illingworth, Amirkhanov, Praslov, & Street, 2000).

The suddenness of the human revolution may actually be somewhat illusory, because it may not have been entirely indigenous to Europe. The conventional view is that it was probably instigated by the arrival of a migratory wave of *H. sapiens* that began from Africa around 50,000 years ago, reaching Europe some 10,000 years later (Klein, 2001). This is consistent with a study of present-day variation in mitochondrial DNA (mtDNA), which confirms other evidence that *H. sapiens* dates from some 170,000 years ago in Africa and also indicates that non-Africans share a most recent common ancestor with Africans dated at an estimated 52,000 years ago (Ingman et al., 2000). This in turn is consistent with the idea that all present-day non-Africans are descended from people who migrated from Africa relatively late in the history of our species. These migrants replaced, to put it politely, the Neanderthals in Europe, who became extinct some 28,000 years ago, and may also have overlapped with, and eventually replaced, *Homo erectus* in Java (Swisher et al., 1996).

There is now reason to believe, however, that the exodus of *H. sapiens* from Africa that gave rise to all modern humans took place around 83,000 years ago, rather than 52,000 years ago (Macaulay et al., 2005; Oppenheimer, 2003). This claim is based in part on an analysis by Oppenheimer (2003) of the complete mtDNA sequences collected by Ingman et al. According to this more recent scenario, as constructed by Oppenheimer, the emigrants crossed the mouth of the Red Sea to the Yemen and proceeded round the coast to India, with one branch continuing on and eventually reaching Australia as early as 74,000 years ago. Another branch eventually turned northward from somewhere near western India to reach Europe some 46,000 to 50,000 years ago. According to Oppenheimer, this view makes better sense of the evolutionary trees based on mtDNA and Y-chromosome sequences than does the view that the migrants from Africa proceeded directly through the Levant to Europe (see also Macaulay et al., 2005).

The seeds of the human revolution may therefore have been sown in Africa and developed by the early emigrants well before they arrived in Europe. Stone tool industries from the Klasies River Mouth near the southern tip of Africa are very similar to those of the Upper Paleolithic in Europe, but have been provisionally dated at around 70,000 years ago (Mellars, 2002). Evidence for a bone-tool industry, as well as deliberate engraving of abstract forms in ochre and other artifacts indicative of "modern" behavior, has been discovered at Blombos Cave in South Africa and dated at around 70,000 years ago (Henshilwood, d'Errico, Marean, Milo, & Yates, 2001). An even earlier bone industry, which probably included the manufacture of harpoons to catch fish, has been discovered in the republic of Congo and dates from about 90,000 years ago (Yellen, Brooks, Cornelissen, Mehlman, & Stewart, 1995).

On the basis of such evidence, it has been argued that there was really no human revolution at all, but simply the accumulation of shared knowledge and expertise in Africa, perhaps originating as far back as 250,000 to 300,000 years ago (McBrearty. & Brooks, 2000). Stringer (2003) suggests, however, that "this may be too simple a story" (p. 28), and it is perhaps more likely that modern behavior evolved in Africa after the earlier migration of *H. sapiens* around 125,000 years ago. Stone tools discovered on the Red Sea coast of Eritrea and dated at around 125,000 years ago are characteristic of the Middle Stone Age and are more primitive than the African industries dated within the past 100,000 years (Walter et al., 2000).

The Eritrean tools were probably associated with a migration of early *H. sapiens* to coastal regions – a migration that may have led to subsequent coastal migrations into the Levant by 100,000 years ago (Grün & Stringer, 1991). These early migrants probably did not survive the Ice Age that descended from the north from about 90,000 years ago (Oppenheimer, 2003). The evidence from the earliest known remains of *H. sapiens* in Africa, dating from around 154,000 to 160,000 years ago, also suggests a tool culture that was a mix of Acheulian and Middle Stone Age cultures (Clarke et al., 2003).

The likely scenario, then, is that modern human behavior evolved in Africa some time within the period after the first expansion of *H. sapiens* out of Africa some 125,000 years ago, but before the later expansion of around 83,000 years ago, and was carried and developed in the coastal migrations to Asia and Australia and in the eventual migrations north to Europe and China. There is some dispute as to whether this development was seeded by some biological change or was purely cultural. Klein (2001) has argued that there was indeed some biological change, and White at al. (2003) suggest that the Ethiopian fossils dating from over 150,000 years ago represent an archaic form, which they label *H. sapiens idaltu*. Stringer (2003) disagrees, suggesting that these fossils are "the oldest definite record of what we currently think of as modern *H. sapiens*" (p. 693).

Whether biological or cultural, whatever it was that *H. sapiens* cooked up in Africa between 125,000 and 83,000 years ago was a powerful brew. Not only did it lead to the human revolution, but there was a darker side as well, resulting in the extinction of the other species of *Homo* – namely, the Neanderthals and *Homo erectus* – outside of Africa. It may have had to do simply with superior weaponry or advances in technology that allowed our forebears to adapt better to new environments – although it should be remembered that the conquerors were moving into a new environment, and one might have expected the indigenous Neanderthals to have held the home advantage,

as modern sports teams do. The invading sapiens may have been simply wiser, as their name suggests, although their ascendancy was probably not simply a matter of brain size, because the Neanderthal brain appears to have been slightly larger than the brain of *H. sapiens*. Tattersall (2003) refers to "the emergence of modern cognition – which, it is reasonable to assume, is equivalent to the advent of symbolic thought" (p. 27). Yet Kanzi, the bonobo, learned to use abstract symbols to refer to objects and actions (Savage-Rumbaugh et al., 1998), so it seems unlikely that symbol use per se was the decisive development.

The cognitive ingredient that distinguished modern *H. sapiens* from the Neanderthals, and even from earlier *sapiens*, is indeed one of the puzzles of human evolution. A common solution is simply to suppose that some capacity for complex thought, be it language or some deeper property of thought, was potentially present in large-brained hominids, but was not realized until the human revolution. In speculating about the emergence of syntax, for example, Bickerton (1995) suggests that the essential elements were already present, and all it took was a throw of a switch to get them up and running:

> *Imagine a newly constructed factory lying idle because someone neglected to make a crucial connection in the electric wiring. The making of that single connection is all that is needed to turn a dark and silent edifice into a pulsating, brilliantly lit workplace. This could have been how syntax evolved in the brain (p. 83).*

Similarly, Tattersall (2003) suggests that the modern human capacity "lay fallow until it was activated by a cultural stimulus of some kind" and goes on to suggest that this capacity was "the invention of language" (p. 27).

In evolutionary terms, it is difficult to understand how there could be natural selection for unrealized capacities, although it is of course possible that complex abilities in one domain might be generalized to another. Some humans perform prodigiously on the piano, for example, but this can scarcely have been a factor in the evolution of manual dexterity. But language seems too embed-ded biologically to be the result of a late invention, or the late throwing of a switch, or a generalization from some other ability – or even, as Chomsky (1975) proposed, an adventitious consequence of increased brain size. I think it more likely that recursive thought evolved over the past 2 million years as a consequence of social pressures and was selected in overt behavioral contexts involv-ing social dynamics, including language. In what follows, I want to suggest that the new ingredient that led to the dominance of our species was not language per se, nor the abil-ity to think recursively, but was the emer-gence of autonomous speech.

Did We *Talk* Our Way into Modernity?

Attempts over the past half-century to com-municate with the great apes have taught us at least one thing – these animals are a long way from being able to speak. For example Viki, the chimpanzee raised from infancy in a human household, was never able to utter more than about four indistinct words (Hayes, 1952). The limitation was at least partly articulatory, because much greater success was later achieved by teach-ing apes to communicate using manual ges-tures (e.g., Gardner & Gardner, 1969) or pointing to symbols displayed on a keyboard (e.g., Savage-Rumbaugh et al., 1998). Even then, though, their communicative abilities remained at the level of what Bickerton has called "protolanguage," which is essentially language without grammar.

The evidence suggests that the articula-tory and neural adaptations necessary for flu-ent speech emerged late in the evolution of *Homo* and may have been complete only with the emergence of our own species – and possibly even later still. According to P. Lieberman (1998; Lieberman, Crelin, & Klatt, 1972), the lowering of the larynx, an adaptation that increased the range of speech sounds, was incomplete even in the Neanderthals of 30,000 years ago. Their resultant poor articulation would have kept them separate from *H. sapiens*, leading to

their eventual extinction. This work remains controversial (e.g., Gibson & Jessee, 1999), but there is other evidence that the cranial structure underwent critical changes sub-sequent to the split between anatomically modern and earlier "archaic" *Homo*, such as the Neanderthals, *Homo heidelbergensis*, and *Homo rhodesiensis*. One such change is the shortening of the sphenoid, the central bone of the cranial base from which the face grows forward, resulting in a flattened face (D. E. Lieberman, 1998). D. E. Lieberman specu-lates that this is an adaptation for speech, contributing to the unique proportions of the human vocal tract, in which the hori-zontal and vertical components are roughly equal in length – a configuration, he argues, that improves the ability to produce acous-tically distinct speech sounds.

Articulate speech also required radical change in the neural control of vocalization. The species-specific and largely involuntary calls of primates depend on an evolutionar-ily ancient system that originates in the lim-bic system, but in humans this is augmented by a separate neocortical system operating through the pyramidal tract and synapsing directly with the brainstem nuclei for the vocal cords and tongue (Ploog, 2002). The evidence suggests that voluntary control of vocalization in the chimpanzee is extremely limited at best (Goodall, 1986). The devel-opment of cortical control must surely have occurred gradually, rather than in an all-or-none fashion, and may have reached its final level of development only in anatomi-cally modern humans. An adaptation unique to *H. sapiens* is neurocranial globularity, defined as the roundness of the cranial vault in the sagittal, coronal, and transverse planes, which is likely to have increased the relative size of the temporal and/or frontal lobes rela-tive to other parts of the brain (D. E. Lieber-man, McBratney, & Krovitz, 2002). These changes may reflect more refined control of articulation and/or more accurate percep-tual discrimination of articulated sounds.

One clue as to the recency of articulate speech comes from a speech and language disorder that afflicts a large family, known as the KE family, in England. Over three gen-erations, half of the members of this family have been affected by the disorder, which is evident from the affected child's first attempts to speak and persists into adulthood (Vargha-Khadem, Watkins, Alcock, Fletcher, & Passingham, 1995). The precise nature of the deficit remains somewhat controversial. Some have argued that the deficit is primarily linguistic, mainly (but not exclusively) affecting the ability to use inflectional morphosyntactic rules, such as changing the endings of words to mark tense or number (Gopnik, 1990; Gopnik & Goad, 1997; Pinker, 1994). Other, more recent work suggests that the core deficit is one of articulation rather than syntax, with morphosyntax a secondary casualty (Alcock, Passingham, Watkins, & Vargha-Khadem, 2000; Vargha-Khadem et al., 1998; Watkins, Dronkers, & Vargha-Khadem, 2002).

It is now known that the disorder is due to a point mutation on the *FOXP2* gene (forkhead box P2) on chromosome 7, and for normal speech to be acquired, two functional copies of this gene seem to be necessary (Fisher, Vargha-Khadem, Watkins, Monaco, & Pembrey, 1998). *FOXP2* has been sequenced in humans, chimpanzees, gorillas, orangutans, rhesus monkeys, and mice (Enard et al., 2002). The sequences reveal changes in amino-acid encoding and the pattern of nucleotide polymorphism that emerged after the split between human and chimpanzee lineages and were therefore probably selected for their beneficial effect on vocal communication.

In attempting to estimate the date of fixation of the mutated gene, Enard et al. (2002) obtained the surprising answer that the most likely date was *zero* years ago, but suggested that this should be adjusted by some 10,000 to 100,000 years to correct for rapid population growth. Although the estimated standard error was some 120,000 years, which could place the mutation as much as 200,000 years into the past, the most likely estimate places it closer to the present, and not implausibly in the window between the earlier exodus from Africa some 125,000 years ago and the more recent (and cataclysmic) exodus of 83,000 years ago. Enard et al. (2002) write that their dating of the *FOXP2* mutation "is compatible

with a model in which the expansion of modern humans was driven by the appearance of a more-proficient spoken language" (p. 871). That is, the *FOXP2* mutation may have been the most recent step in the evolution of articulate speech.

If recursive thinking and syntax emerged before articulate speech in the evolution of *Homo*, as suggested earlier in this chapter, then how did syntactic language itself evolve? There has been a long history of speculation that language evolved from manual gestures (e.g., Armstrong, 1999; Armstrong, & Wilcox, 1995; Corballis, 1992, 1999, 2002; Givón, 1995; Hewes, 1973; Rizzolatti & Arbib, 1998), and syntax may therefore have evolved in the context of manual gesture, not of speech. My own view is that the vocal component was introduced only gradually, perhaps culminating in the mutation of the *FOXP2* gene (Corballis, 2003) – and even today most people gesture as they speak (McNeill, 1985). Evidence for the gestural theory is necessarily indirect, but comes from a variety of sources. First, as we have seen, attempts to teach language to great apes have achieved much more success by using gestural or visual means than by using vocalization. Second, the homologue of Broca's area in the monkey includes so-called mirror neurons that respond both to the production and the perception of specific reaching and grasping movements, suggesting that the foundations for language were manual rather than vocal (Rizzolatti & Arbib, 1998). Broca's area is now considered part of a more general "mirror system" involved in the understanding of biological action (Rizzolatti, Fogassi, & Gallese, 2001). Third, it is now clear that the signed languages invented by the deaf have all the hallmarks of true language, including syntax (e.g., Armstrong et al., 1995; Neidle, Kegl, MacLaughlin, Bahan, & Lee, 2000). Fourth, the fact that the left hemisphere in most people plays the dominant role in both speech and manual praxis (as well as in signed languages) suggests a common neurological basis (Corballis, 1991, 2003).

The conversion from manual and facial gestures to vocal speech is perhaps best understood if speech itself is considered a gestural system, as a number of authors have proposed (Liberman & Whalen, 2000; Studdert-Kennedy & Goldstein, 2003). Browman and Goldstein (1991) developed a gestural theory of speech, based on "exactly the model used for controlling arm movements, with the articulators of the vocal tract simply substituted for those of the arm" (p. 314). The McGurk effect, with false dubbing of speech syllables onto videos of mouths uttering different syllables, illustrates that the perception of a speech sound depends as much on what is seen as on what is heard (McGurk & MacDonald, 1976), which explains the disturbing effect of movies in which the sound track is out of sync. Neuroimaging has also shown that both Broca's and Wernicke's areas are active when people "read" speech from facial gestures, consistent with the view that "the core perceptual processes for speech are embodied" (Calvert & Campbell 2003, p. 67).

A recent fMRI study suggests a link between the *FOXP2* mutation and the mirror system. Unaffected members of the KE family showed the expected activation of Broca's area while they covertly generated verbs, but affected members of the family showed *under*activation of Broca's area (Liégeois, Baldeweg, Connelly, Gadian, Mishkin, & Vargha-Khadem, 2003). This finding might be interpreted to mean that the mutation of the *FOXP2* gene some 100,000 years ago had to do with the incorporation of vocal control into the mirror system (Corballis, 2004). It provides further evidence that the *FOXP2* mutation was the final stage in a series of adaptations that allowed speech to become autonomous. It was the mutation, perhaps, that held the key to modernity.

What Advantages Did Speech Confer over Manual Gesture?

One possible scenario is that the development of manufacturing and tool use gave selective advantage to shifting the burden of communication from the hands to the face. Grunts associated with facial gestures may have been assimilated to add diversity to facial gestures, eventually creating the distinction between voiced and unvoiced speech sounds. Voicing would also have rendered accessible facial gestures that would otherwise be inaccessible, such as those involving the positioning of the tongue inside the mouth.

Speech confers other advantages. It allows communication in the dark or when obstacles intervene between sender and receiver. There is some evidence that the telling of stories, critical for the transmission of culture, may have been accomplished at night. In describing life among the San, a modern hunter-gatherer society, Konner (1982) writes,

> War is unknown. Conflicts within the group are resolved by talking, sometimes half the night or all the night, for nights, weeks on end. . . . When we slept in a grass hut in one of the villages, there were many nights when its flimsy walls leaked charged exchanges from the circle around the fire, frank expressions of feeling and contention beginning when the dusk fires were lit and running on until the dawn (p. 7).

Konner later notes that pedagogy is also a night-time activity among the San:

> Not only stories, but great stores of knowledge are exchanged around the fire among the !Kung and the dramatizations – perhaps best of all – bear knowledge critical to survival. A way of life that is difficult enough would, without such knowledge, become simply impossible (p. 171).

Pinker and Bloom (1990) suggest that vocal oratory (especially at night, one is tempted to think) might have been subject to sexual selection, citing Symons's (1979) observation that tribal chiefs are often both gifted orators and highly polygynous.

Speech would have freed the hands for other activities. In a species that increasingly made use of the hands and arms for manufacture, and probably also for carrying things (Lovejoy, 1981), there were surely advantages to shifting the communicative load to the face and ultimately to the vocal channel. Carrying would presumably have been important in an increasingly peripatetic existence, as exemplified in migrations from Africa well before the emergence of *H. sapiens*, beginning a little under 2 million years ago (Tattersall, 1998), perhaps leading to the pressure to add voicing. Speech and the freeing of the hands may have enhanced the development of technologies, enabling manual crafts to be at once demonstrated and verbally explained (Corballis, 2002). Moreover, the products of manufacture are cumulative, so that a slight initial advantage may have multiplied to the point that our African forebears were able to dominate and eventually replace all other hominids. Technology has continued to advance in exponential fashion, allowing us unprecedented dominion over and beyond the planet, but it may have been seeded by a simple mutation that enabled us to talk.

These arguments in favor of speech must of course be qualified by the growing evidence that the signed languages of the deaf have all of the semantic and syntactic sophistication of spoken languages. Powerful testimony to this is Gallaudet University, located in Washington DC – the only university in the world that caters exclusively for the deaf, with American Sign Language as the language of instruction. The advantages associated with vocal language were therefore probably to do with factors unrelated to language per se, but rather to the extended circumstances under which language could operate and the effects of freeing the hands for the various other activities that have changed the very nature of the physical world. Indeed, there must surely have been strong evolutionary pressure to add vocalization to the communicative repertoire, despite the fact that the lowering of the larynx increases the chances of death by choking.

The switch to autonomous speech probably did not alter the fundamental nature of consciousness itself. There is no reason to believe that deaf signers, or the affected members of the KE family, are incapable of recursive thought, whether conscious or not. Recursive thought is more likely to have evolved from 2 million years earlier, when brain size underwent its dramatic increase.

Homo erectus in Asia and the Neanderthals in Europe were probably capable of recursive thought, theory of mind, and grammatical language well before *Homo sapiens* burst onto the scene. But the final accomplishment of a form of language that could be purely vocal led to an explosion of art, manufacture, and creative accomplishment that would have added to the contents of consciousness, if not to its fundamental nature.

Conclusions

Consciousness itself is almost certainly not unique to humans. The ability to represent aspects of the world internally and to carry out mental manipulations, such as mental rotation and problem solving, probably evolved independently in mammals, cetaceans, and birds, driven in part by selection to survive in increasingly complex social worlds (although ants may have found an alternative solution). In the case of primates, especially, mental life would have included representations of conspecifics, and their dominance relations, moods, and the like. Their mental life may include at least zero-order intentionality, such that a chimpanzee may believe that another chimpanzee is angry or that chimpanzee A is dominant over chimpanzee B. There is little convincing evidence, that non-human primates – or indeed any non-human species – are capable of higher levels of intentionality.

Nevertheless, it is still something of an open question whether the great apes can achieve first-order intentionality. A gorilla well appreciates that another gorilla is angry, but this could be simply be based on the behavioral demeanor of the other animal, and not on the attribution of an emotional state comparable to its own state when angry. Similarly, a chimpanzee might avoid certain actions while a more dominant chimpanzee is watching, but it remains unclear whether this is simply a consequence of learning or whether the animal somehow understands what is going on in the mind of the other. It is clear, however, that humans can easily attribute mental states to others and do so recursively, so that I can understand that you understand what I am getting at, right? Recursive thought also allows us to imagine ourselves in the past or future, thus generating a sense of self as distinct from others.

Recursive thought may have evolved with the genus *Homo* from around 2 million years ago. The earliest selective pressures leading to recursive thought may have been primarily social. Evolutionary psychologists have speculated at length about social characteristics, such as cooperation, mate choice, parental investment strategies, and language itself, as having emerged in the Pleistocene (Barkow et al., 1992; for an updated review, see Barrett, Dunbar, & Lycett, 2002). Whereas evolutionary psychology is typically based on the premise that the mind is modular, recursion is a property that cuts across different mental attributes, including language, theory of mind, mental time travel, and manufacture.

Human activity took a "Great Leap Forward," to borrow Diamond's (1997) phrase, with the human revolution of around 40,000–50,000 years ago – although the dramatic events in Europe may have been the culmination of changes that took place prior to the exodus from Africa some 83,000 years ago and in the long trek into South Asia and then into Europe. These developments are generally considered to mark the beginnings of so-called modern human behavior. There is controversy as to whether they were due to some biological change or whether they were purely cultural innovations. One possibility is that syntactic language itself emerged during this period (Bickerton, 1995), either as a cultural invention or as the result of some structural change in the brain. In this chapter, I have argued instead that syntactic language emerged more gradually over the preceding 2 million years, in concert with the development of recursive thought. The revolutionary events of the past 100,000 years or so may have been instead a consequence of the emergence of autonomous speech as the primary vehicle for linguistic expression. The anatomical change that finally permitted speech to dominate may have been a mutation of the *FOXP2* gene.

It is probably safe to assume, however, that our forebears of 80,000 to 100,000 years ago were fully anatomically modern. Subsequent developments have been profound, but can be attributable to cultural invention and accurate transmission between generations rather than to changes in biology. Although chimpanzees display quite marked cultural variations (Whiten et al., 1999), transmission of culture is undoubtedly much more efficient in humans, creating a ratchet effect culminating in the complex lives we lead today. As Tomasello (1999) points out, "[The] key adaptation is one that enables individuals to understand other individuals as intentional agents like the self" (p. 509) – or in other words, first-order intentionality. It is not simply a question of language; young children have a capacity for joint attention that enables rapid cultural learning and effective imitation. We are wired to assimilate in a way that no other primate is.

Nevertheless changes in the medium of language have undoubtedly had a profound effect on cultural transmission. The emergence of speech would have permitted communication at night and enabled the oral transmission of culture that persists in many societies today. The invention of writing some 5,000 years ago would have greatly increased the precision and duration of transmitted culture (see Diamond, 1997) and contributed to the profound variation among human cultures. The invention of the Internet is likely to have equally profound implications. Another major factor in human cultural variation simply has to do with the pattern of migrations. Following the migrations out of Africa some 50,000 years ago, our forebears distributed themselves around the globe in vastly different conditions of climate and geography. Around 13,000 years ago, domestication of wild plants and animals in different regions, notably the Fertile Crescent, China, and Mesoamerica, began traditions of control over the environment and the eventual emergence of what we are pleased to call civilizations.

The growth of culture, especially in manufacturing societies, has vastly increased the number of material objects, ideas, and words to describe them, which has surely had a major impact on the contents of human consciousness, if not its essential nature. It is unlikely that the mechanisms of consciousness have changed much since the emergence of *Homo sapiens* some 170,000 years ago or even since the large-brained hominids of a million years ago, but the things we are conscious of have changed dramatically, at least in Western societies. Yet has civilization made us smarter? After working for 33 years among technologically primitive New Guineans, Diamond (1997) argues that they are in fact smarter than Westerners. It may be appropriate then to end this chapter with the question posed to Diamond by Yali, a local New Guinean: "Why is that you white people developed much cargo and brought it to New Guinea, but we black people had little cargo of our own?" The answer, as Diamond demonstrates so convincingly, has to do with geography, not biology, and Yali reminds us that we are all people beneath the veneer of culture.

Note

1. I am indebted to Brian Boyd for these examples. They are taken from a talk entitled "Evolution, Cognition, Narration, Fiction," which he presented at the Interdisciplinary Symposium on the Nature of Cognition, Tamaki Campus, University of Auckland, on October 13, 2001.

References

Alcock, K. J., Passingham, R. E., Watkins, K. E., & Vargha-Khadem, F. (2000). Oral dyspraxia in inherited speech and language impairment and acquired dysphasia. *Brain & Language, 75,* 17–33.

Ambrose, S. H. (2001). Paleolithic technology and human evolution. *Science, 291,* 1748–1753.

Armstrong, D. F. (1999). *Original signs: Gesture, sign, and the source of language.* Washington, DC: Gallaudet University Press.

Armstrong, D. F., Stokoe, W. C., & Wilcox, S. E. (1995). *Gesture and the nature of language.* Cambridge: Cambridge University Press.

Atance, C. M., & O'Neill, D. K. (2001). Episodic future thinking. *Trends in Cognitive Sciences, 5,* 533–539.

Barkow, J., Cosmides, L., & Tooby, J. (Eds.) (1992). *The adapted mind: Evolutionary psychology and the generation of culture.* New York: Oxford University Press.

Barrett, L., Dunbar, R., & Lycett, J. (2002). *Human evolutionary psychology.* New York: Palgrave.

Beck, B. B. (1980). *Animal tool behavior: The use and manufacture of tools by animals.* New York: Garland STPM Press.

Bennett, J. (1976). *Linguistic behavior.* Cambridge: Cambridge University Press.

Bernard, L. L. (1924). *Instinct: A study in social psychology.* New York: Holt.

Bickerton, D. (1995). *Language and human behavior.* Seattle, WA: University of Washington Press/UCL Press.

Bickerton, D. (2000). Reciprocal altruism as the predecessor of argument structure. In W. H. Calvin & D. Bickerton (Eds.), *Lingua ex machina: Reconciling Darwin and Chomsky with the human brain* (pp. 123–134). Cambridge, MA: MIT Press.

Bickerton, D. (2002). From protolanguage to language. In T. J. Crow (Ed.), *The speciation of modern Homo Sapiens* (pp. 103–120). Oxford: Oxford University Press.

Browman, C., & Goldstein, L. (1991). Gestural structures: Distinctiveness, phonological processes, and historical change. In I. G. Mattingly & M. Studdert-Kennedy (Eds.), *Modularity and the motor theory of speech perception* (pp. 313–338). Hillsdale, NJ: Erlbaum.

Brown, F., Harris, J., Leakey, R., & Walker, A. (1985). Early Homo erectus skeleton from west Lake Turkana, Kenya. *Nature, 316,* 788–792.

Calvert, G. A., & Campbell, R. (2003). Reading speech from still and moving faces: The neural substrates of visible speech. *Journal of Cognitive Neuroscience, 15,* 57–70.

Cargile, J. (1970). A note on "iterated knowings." *Analysis, 30,* 151–155.

Chomsky, N. (1966). *Cartesian linguistics: A chapter in the history of rationalist thought.* New York: Harper & Row.

Chomsky, N. (1975). *Reflections on language.* New York: Pantheon.

Chomsky, N. (1988). *Language and problems of knowledge: The Managua lectures.* Cambridge, MA: MIT Press.

Clarke, J. D., Beyenne, Y., WoldeGabriel, G., Hart, W. K., Renne, P. R., Gilbert, H., et al. (2003). Stratigraphic, chronological and behavioral contexts of Pleistocene *Homo sapiens* from Middle Awash, Ethiopia. *Nature, 423*, 747–752.

Clayton, N. S., Bussey, T. J., & Dickinson, A. (2003). Can animals recall the past and plan for the future? *Nature Reviews, 4*, 685–691.

Corballis, M. C. (1991). *The lopsided ape: Evolution of the generative mind*. Oxford: Oxford University Press.

Corballis, M. C. (1992). On the evolution of language and generativity. *Cognition, 44*, 197–226.

Corballis, M. C. (1999, March-April). The gestural origins of language. *American Scientist, 87*, 138–45.

Corballis, M. C. (2002). *From hand to mouth: The gestural origins of language*. Princeton, NJ: Princeton University Press.

Corballis, M. C. (2003). From hand to mouth: The gestural origins of language. In M. H. Christiansen & S. Kirby (Eds.), *Language evolution* (pp. 201–218). Oxford: Oxford University Press.

Corballis, M. C. (2004). FOXP2 and the mirror system. *Trends in Cognitive Sciences, 8*, 95–96.

Cosmides, L. (1989). The logic of social exchange: Has natural selection shaped how humans reason? Studies with the Wason selection task. *Cognition, 31*, 187–276.

Cowie, A., & Stoerig, P. (1995). Blindsight in monkeys. *Nature, 373*, 247–249.

Davison, M. C., & McCarthy, D. C. (1987). *The matching law: A research review*. Hillsdale, NJ: Erlbaum.

Deacon, T. (1997). *The symbolic species: The co-evolution of language and the brain*. New York: Norton.

Dennett, D. C. (1983). Intentional systems in cognitive ethology: The "Panglossian paradigm" defended. *Behavioral & Brain Science, 6*, 343–390.

Descartes, R. (1985). *The philosophical writings of Descartes* (J. Cottingham, R. Stoothoff, & D. Murdock, Eds. & Trans.). Cambridge: Cambridge University Press. (Work originally published 1647)

de Waal, F. B. M. (1996). *Good natured: The origins of right and wrong in humans and other animals*. Cambridge, MA: Harvard University Press.

Diamond, J. (1997). *Guns, germs, and steel*. New York: Norton.

Elman, J. (1993). Learning and development in neural networks: The importance of starting small. *Cognition, 48*, 71–99.

Elman, J., Bates, E., & Newport, E. (1996). *Rethinking innateness: A connectionist perspective on development*. Cambridge, MA: MIT Press.

Enard, W., Przeworski, M., Fisher, S. E., Lai, C. S., Wiebe, V., Kitano, T., et al. (2002). Molecular evolution of FOXP2, a gene involved in speech and language. *Nature, 418*, 869–872.

Ferster, C. B., & Skinner B. F. (1957). *Schedules of reinforcement*. New York, Appleton-Century-Crofts.

Fisher, S. E., Vargha-Khadem, F., Watkins, K. E., Monaco, A. P., & Pembrey, M. E. (1998). Localization of a gene implicated in a severe speech and language disorder. *Nature Genetics, 18*, 168–170.

Fodor, J. (1983). *The modularity of mind*. Cambridge, MA: MIT Press.

Gallup, G. G., Jr. (1997). The rise and fall of self-conception in primates. *Annals of the New York Academy of Sciences, 118*, 73–84.

Gallup, G. G., Jr. (1998). Self-awareness and the evolution of social intelligence. *Behavioural Processes, 42*, 239–247.

Gardner, R. A., & Gardner, B. T. (1969). Teaching sign language to a chimpanzee. *Science, 165*, 664–672.

Georgopoulos, A. P., & Pellizzer, G. (1995). The mental and the neural – psychological and neural studies of mental rotation and memory scanning. *Neuropsychologia, 33*, 1531–1547.

Gibson, K. R., & Jessee, S. (1999). Language evolution and expansions of multiple neurological processing areas. In B. J. King (Ed.), *The origins of language: What nonhuman primates can tell us*. Santa Fe, NM: School of American Research Press.

Givón, T. (1995). *Functionalism and grammar*. Philadelphia: Benjamins.

Goodall, J. (1986). *The chimpanzees of Gombe: Patterns of behavior*. Cambridge, MA: Harvard University Press.

Gopnik, M. (1990). Feature-blind grammar and dysphasia. *Nature, 344*, 715.

Gopkin, M., & Goad, H. (1997). What underlies inflectional error patterns in genetic dysphasia? *Journal of Neurolinguistics, 10*, 109–137.

Gowlett, J. A. J. (1992). Early human mental abilities. In S. Jones, R. Martin, & D. Pilbeam (Eds.), *The Cambridge encyclopedia of human evolution* (pp. 341–345). Cambridge: Cambridge University Press.

Grün, R., & Stringer, C. B. (1991). Electron spin resonance dating and the evolution of modern humans. *Archaeometry, 33*, 153–199.

Hahn, J., & Münzel, S. (1995). Knochenflöten aus dem Aurignacien des Geissenklösterle bei Blaubeuren, Alb-Donau-Kreis. *Fundberichte Aus Baden-Wurttemberg, 20*, 1–12.

Hare, B., Call, J., Agnetta, B., & Tomasello, M. (2000). Chimpanzees know what conspecifics do and do not see. *Animal Behaviour, 59*, 771–785.

Hare, B., & Tomasello, M. (1999). Domestic dogs (*Canis familiaris*) use human and conspecific cues to locate hidden food. *Journal of Comparative Psychology, 113*, 173–177.

Hauser, M., & Carey, S. (1998). Building a cognitive creature from a set of primitives. In D. D. Cummins & C. Allen (Eds.), *The evolution of mind* (pp. 51–106). New York: Oxford University Press.

Hauser, M. D., Chomsky, N., & Fitch, W. T. (2002). The faculty of language: What is it, who has it, and how did it evolve? *Science, 298*, 1569–1579.

Hayes, C. (1952). *The ape in our house*. London: Gollancz.

Henshilwood, C. S., d'Errico, F., Marean, C. W., Milo, R. G., & Yates, R. (2001). An early bone tool industry from the Middle Stone Age at Blombos Cave, South Africa: Implications for the origins of modern human behaviour, symbolism and language. *Journal of Human Evolution, 41*, 631–678.

Herman, L. M., Richards, D. G., & Wolz, J. P. (1984). Comprehension of sentences by bottle-nosed dolphins. *Cognition, 16*, 129–219.

Hewes, G. W. (1973). Primate communication and the gestural origins of language. *Current Anthropology, 14*, 5–24.

Heyes, C. M. (1998). Theory of mind in nonhuman primates. *Behavioral & Brain Sciences, 21*, 101–148.

Heyes, C. M. (2001). Theory of mind and other domain-specific hypotheses – Response. *Behavioral & Brain Sciences, 24*, 1143–1145.

Hunt, G. R. (1996). Manufacture and use of hook-tools by New Caledonian crows. *Nature, 379*, 249–251.

Ingman, M., Kaessmann, H., Pääbo, S., & Gyllensten, U. (2000). Mitochondrial genome variation and the origin of modern humans. *Nature, 408*, 708–713.

Janis, C. (1993). Victors by default: The mammalian succession. In S. J. Gould (Ed.), *The book of life* (pp. 169–217). New York: Norton.

Klein, R. G. (2001). Southern Africa and modern human origins. *Journal of Anthropological Research, 57*, 1–16.

Knecht, H., Pike-Tay, A., & White, R. (1993). *Before Lascaux: The complex record of the early Upper Paleolithic*. Boca Raton: CRC Press.

Köhler, W. (1925). *The mentality of apes*. New York: Routledge & Kegan Paul.

Konner, M. (1982). *The tangled wing: Biological constraints on the human spirit*. New York: Harper.

Krogman, W. M. (1972). *Child growth*. Ann Arbor: University of Michigan Press.

Leslie, A. M. (1994). ToMM, ToBY, and agency: Core architecture and domain specificity. In L. A. Hirschfeld & S. A. Gelman (Eds.), *Mapping the mind: Domain specificity in cognition and culture* (pp. 119–148). New York: Cambridge University Press.

Liberman, A. M., & Whalen, D. H. (2000). On the relation of speech to language. *Trends in Cognitive Sciences, 4*, 187–196.

Lieberman, D. E. (1998). Sphenoid shortening and the evolution of modern cranial shape. *Nature, 393*, 158–162.

Lieberman, D. E., McBratney, B. M., & Krovitz, G. (2002). The evolution and development of cranial form in Homo sapiens. *Proceedings of the National Academy of Sciences USA, 99*, 1134–1139.

Lieberman, P. (1998). *Eve spoke: Human language and human evolution*. New York: Norton.

Lieberman, P., Crelin, E. S., & Klatt, D. H. (1972). Phonetic ability and related anatomy of the new-born, adult human, Neanderthal man, and the chimpanzee. *American Anthropologist, 74*, 287–307.

Liégeois, F., Baldeweg, T., Connelly, A., Gadian, D. G., Mishkin, M., & Vargha-Khadem, F. (2003). Language fMRI abnormalities associated with FOXP2 gene mutation. *Nature Neuroscience, 6*, 1230–1237.

Logothetis, N. K. (1998). Single units and conscious vision. *Proceedings of the Royal Society of London, Series B, 353*, 1801–1818.

Lovejoy, O. C. (1981). The origin of man. *Science, 221*, 341–350

Macaulay, V., Hill, C., Achilli, A., Rengo, C., Clarke, D., Meehan, W., et al. (2005). Single, rapid coastal settlement of Asia revealed by analysis of complete mitochondrial genomes. *Science, 308*, 1034–1036.

McBrearty, S., & Brooks, A. S. (2000). The revolution that wasn't: A new interpretation of the origin of modern human behavior. *Journal of Human Evolution, 39*, 453–563.

McDougall, W. (1908). *An introduction to social psychology*. London: Methuen.

McGurk, H., & MacDonald, J. (1976). Hearing lips and seeing voices. *Nature, 264*, 746–748.

McNeill, D. (1985). So you think gestures are nonverbal?' *Psychological Review, 92*, 350–371.

Mellars, P. A. (2002). Archaeology and the origins of modern humans: European and African perspectives. In T. J. Crow (Ed.), *The speciation of modern Homo Sapiens* (pp. 31–47). Oxford: Oxford University Press.

Mellars, P. A., & Stringer, C. B. (Eds.) (1989). *The human revolution: Behavioral and biological perspectives on the origins of modern humans*. Edinburgh: Edinburgh University Press.

Menzel, C. R. (1999). Unprompted recall and reporting of hidden objects by a chimpanzee (Pan troglodytes) after extended delays. *Journal of Comparative Psychology, 113*, 1–9.

Miles, H. L. (1990). The cognitive foundations for reference in a signing orangutan. In S. T. Parker & K. Gibson (Eds.), *'Language' and intelligence in monkeys and apes: Comparative developmental perspectives* (pp. 511–539). New York: Cambridge University Press.

Neidle, C., Kegl, J., MacLaughlin, D., Bahan, B. & Lee, R. G. (2000). *The syntax of American Sign Language*. Cambridge, MA: MIT Press.

Noble, W., & Davidson, I. (1996). *Human evolution, language, and mind*. Cambridge: Cambridge University Press.

Oppenheimer, S. (2003). *Out of Eden: The peopling of the world*. London: Robinson.

Patterson, F. (1978). Conversations with a gorilla. *National Geographic, 154*, 438–465.

Pickering, T., White, T. D., & Toth, N. (2000). Cutmarks on a Plio-Pleistocene hominid from Sterkfontein, South Africa. *American Journal of Physical Anthropology, 111*, 579–584.

Pinker, S. (1994). *The language instinct*. New York: William Morrow.

Pinker, S. (1997). *How the mind works*. New York: Norton.

Pinker, S., & Bloom, P. (1990). Natural language and natural selection. *Behavioral & Brain Sciences, 13*, 707–784.

Ploog, D. (2002). Is the neural basis of vocalization different in non-human primates and *Homo sapiens*? In T. J. Crow (Ed.), *The speciation of Modern Homo Sapiens* (pp. 121–135). Oxford: Oxford University Press.

Povinelli, D. J. (2001). *Folk physics for apes*. New York: Oxford University Press.

Povinelli, D. J., & Bering, J. M. (2002). The mentality of apes revisited. *Current Directions in Psychological Science, 11*, 115–119.

Povinelli, D. J., Bering, J. M., & Giambrone, S. (2000). Toward a science of other minds: Escaping the argument by analogy. *Cognitive Science, 24*, 509–541.

Premack, D., & Woodruff, G. (1978). Does the chimpanzee have a theory of mind? *Behavioral & Brain Sciences, 4*, 515–526.

Rizzolatti, G., & Arbib, M. A. (1998). Language within our grasp. *Trends in Neuroscience, 21*, 188–194.

Rizzolatti, G., Fogassi, L., & Gallese, V. (2001). Neurophysiological mechanisms underlying the understanding and imitation of action. *Nature Reviews, 2*, 661–670.

Russell, B. (1905). On denoting. *Mind*, 479–493.

Savage-Rumbaugh, S., Shanker, S. G., & Taylor, T. J. (1998). *Apes, language, and the human mind*. New York: Oxford University Press.

Schwarz, B. L., Colon, M. R., Sanchez, I. C., Rodriguez, I. A., & Evans, S. (2002). Single-trial learning of 'what' and 'who' information in a gorilla (*gorilla gorilla gorilla*): Implications for episodic memory. *Animal Cognition, 5*, 85–90.

Schwarz, B. L., & Evans, S. (2001). Episodic memory in primates. *American Journal of Primatology, 55*, 71–85.

Skinner, B. F. (1957). *Verbal behavior*. New York: Appleton-Century-Crofts.

Smirnov, Y. (1989). Intentional human burial. *Journal of World Prehistory, 3*, 199–233.

Soffer, O. J. M., Adovasio, J. S., Illingworth, H. A., Amirkhanov, N. D., Praslov, N. D., & Street, M. (2000). Palaeolithic perishables made permanent. *Antiquity, 74*, 812–821.

Solecki, R. S. (1975). Shanidar IV, a Neanderthal flower burial in Northern Iraq. *Science, 190*, 880–881.

Stringer, C. (2003). Out of Ethiopia. *Nature, 423*, 692–695.

Studdert-Kennedy, M., & Goldstein, L. (2003). Launching language: The gestural origin of discrete infinity. In M. H. Christiansen & S. Kirby (Eds.), *Language evolution* (pp. 235–254). Oxford: Oxford University Press.

Suddendorf, T., & Corballis, M. C. (1997). Mental time travel and the evolution of the human mind. *Genetic, Social, and General Psychology Monographs, 123*, 133–167.

Swisher, C. C., III, Rink, W. J., Anton, H. P., Schwarcz, H. P., Curtis, G. H., Suprijo, A., & Widiasmoro (1996). Latest *Homo erectus* of Java: Potential contemporaneity with *Homo sapiens* in Southeast Asia. *Science, 274*, 1870–1874.

Symons, D. (1979). *The evolution of human sexuality*. Oxford: Oxford University Press.

Tattersall, I. (1998). *Becoming human: Evolution and human uniqueness*. New York: Harcourt Brace.

Tattersall, I. (2003). Once we were not alone. *Scientific American, 13*(2), 20–27.

Tomasello, M. (1996). Do apes ape? In J. Galef & C. Heyes (Eds.), *Social learning in animals: The roots of culture* (pp. 319–346). New York: Academic Press.

Tomasello, M. (1999). The human adaptation for culture. *Annual Review of Anthropology, 28*, 509–529.

Tomasello, M. (2000). Primate cognition: Introduction to the issue. *Cognitive Science, 24*, 351–361.

Tomasello, M. Hare, B., & Agnetta, B. (1999). Chimpanzees, *Pan troglodytes*, follow gaze direction geometrically. *Animal Behaviour, 58*, 769–777.

Tomasello, M., & Rakoczy, H. (2003). What makes human cognition unique? From individual to shared to collective intentionality. *Mind and Language, 18*, 121–147.

Trivers, R. L. (1971). The evolution of reciprocal altruism. *Quarterly Review of Biology, 46*, 35–57.

Tulving, E. (2001). Origin of autonoesis in episodic memory. In H. L. Roediger, III, J. S. Nairne, I. Neath, & A. M. Surprenant (Eds.), *The nature of remembering: Essays in honor of Robert G. Crowder* (pp. 17–34). Washington, DC: American Psychological Association.

Vargha-Khadem, F., Watkins, K. E., Alcock, K. J., Fletcher, P., & Passingham, R. (1995). Praxic and nonverbal cognitive deficits in a large family with a genetically transmitted speech and language disorder. *Proceedings of the National Academy of Sciences USA, 92*, 930–933.

Vargha-Khadem, F., Watkins, K. E., Price, C. J., Ashburner, J., Alcock, K. J., Connelly, A., et al. (1998). Neural basis of an inherited speech and language disorder. *Proceedings of the National Academy of Sciences USA, 95*, 12695–12700.

Walter, R. C., Buffler, R. T., Bruggemann, J. H., Guillaume, M. M. M., Berhe, S. M., Negassi, B., et al. (2000). Early human occupation of the Red Sea coast of Eritrea during the last interglacial. *Nature, 405*, 65–69.

Wason, P. (1966). Reasoning. In B. M. Foss (Ed.), *New horizons in psychology* (pp. 135–151). London: Penguin.

Watkins, K. E., Dronkers, N. F., & Vargha-Khadem, F. (2002). Behavioural analysis of an inherited speech and language disorder: Comparison with acquired aphasia. *Brain, 125*, 452–464.

Watson, J. B. (1913). Psychology as a behaviorist views it. *Psychological Review, 20*, 1–14.

Weiskrantz, L. (1986). *Blindsight. A case study and implications*. Oxford: Oxford University Press.

Wheeler, M. A., Stuss, D. T., & Tulving, E. (1997) Toward a theory of episodic memory: Autonoetic consciousness and the frontal lobes. *Psychological Bulletin, 121*, 331–354.

White, T. D., Asfaw, B., DeGusta, D., Gilbert, H., Richards, G. D., Suwa, G., et al. (2003). Pleistocene *Homo sapiens* from Middle Awash, Ethiopia. *Nature, 423*, 742–747.

Whiten, A., & Byrne, R. W. (1988). Tactical deception in primates. *Behavioral & Brain Sciences, 11*, 233–244.

Whiten, A., & Byrne, R. W. (1997). *Machiavellian intelligence II: Extensions and evaluations*. Cambridge: Cambridge University Press.

Whiten, A., Goodall, J., McGrew, W. C., Nishida, T., Reynolds, V., Sugiyama, Y., et al. (1999). Culture in chimpanzees. *Nature, 399*, 682–685.

Wreschner, E. E. (1980). Red ochre and human evolution. *Current Anthropology, 21*, 631–644.

Wundt, W. (1894). *Lectures on human and animal psychology*. London: Swan & Sonnenschein.

Yellen, J. E., Brooks, A. S., Cornelissen, E., Mehlman, M. J., & Stewart, K. (1995). A Middle Stone Age worked bone industry from Katanda, Upper Semliki Valley, Zaire. *Science, 268*, 553–556.

CHAPTER 22

The Serpent's Gift: Evolutionary Psychology and Consciousness

Jesse M. Bering and David F. Bjorklund

Abstract

As a higher-order cognitive system enabling access to intentional states, and one that few (if any) other species even marginally possess, consciousness or, more appropriately, self-consciousness has likely been both selectively advantageous and the source of adaptive conflict in human evolutionary history. Consciousness was likely advantageous to early human beings because it built on more ancient primate social adaptations. Individuals likely profited by having the capacity to track the intentions of the self and of social others in that consciousness permitted behavioral strategies involving deception and declarative communication. However, consciousness was likely also a source of adaptive conflict in that it interfered with the functioning of more ancient social adaptations, such as infanticide and male sexual coercion of females. Having access to the epistemic states of others meant that knowledge of social transgressions could be rapidly conveyed between parties. For many evolved psychological mechanisms, what was adaptive in human ancestral history suddenly became maladaptive when consciousness appeared.

The Serpent's Gift: Evolutionary Psychology and Consciousness

Consciousness or, more properly, self-consciousness (or self-awareness) has long been one of the features, along with culture, tool use, and language, that have been used to set human beings apart from other animals (at least in the minds of many *Homo sapiens*). Yet, the erection of a species barrier only serves as a target for others to topple (see, for example, evidence of tool use and cultural transmission in chimpanzees; Whiten et al., 1999), and consciousness is no exception. Although we have our own views about the possible uniqueness of human consciousness (see below), our primary task is this chapter is not a discussion of the *evolution of consciousness* per se as much as it is about the *role of consciousness* in determining particular human adaptations. Of course, we are concerned with the evolutionary origins of these adaptations, and we do not neglect this topic. Nonetheless, we see human beings as possessing a degree of self-awareness that has no parallel in the animal world and that, once evolved, drastically modified the nature of the beast, comparable to the effect that flight must have had on the biological line that led to birds. Consciousness, however, was a mixed blessing, for it provided not only new opportunities for the species that possessed it but also new challenges, and it required the seemingly rapid acquisition of a suite of cognitive adaptations to deal with this new level of self-awareness. In this chapter, we examine the role of consciousness in human functioning from the perspective of evolutionary psychology. As we demonstrate, evolutionary psychology has had relatively little to say about this role to date, but has the tools to contribute significantly to our understanding of this phenomenon.

As a first step, we feel it necessary to define consciousness in terms that are amenable to empirical science. There will therefore be no zombies joining us at the table nor qualia to occupy our thoughts (cf. Chalmers, 1996) Rather, we define consciousness as *that naturally occurring cognitive representational capacity permitting explicit and reflective accounts of the – mostly causative – contents of mind, contents harbored by the psychological frame of the self and, as a consequence, also the psychological frames of others.* Our view of consciousness is therefore not one of a solely autonoetic (cf. Tulving, 1985) nature, nor does it remove the self from consciousness, but rather seeks to integrate the concept into the empirical tradition of cognitive science by holding it as a system enabling higher-order representations of abstract causes of behaviors.

This definition of consciousness will almost certainly strike some readers as too narrow. Commonly, the topic of consciousness is handled by scholars in the fields of cognitive neuroscience, philosophy, and comparative psychology, and within these areas consciousness is frequently viewed in shades of increasing complexity both within and across species. This is certainly the right

approach for investigations of the anatomical and physiological aspects of consciousness, particularly if the goal of explanation is at, say, the level of sensory experience and motor planning (e.g., Cotterill, 2001; Humphrey, 2000; Jeannerod, 1999; Searle, 2000). But our goal in the current chapter is somewhat different – although we acknowledge the phylogenetic continuity of the biological substrates of consciousness, we believe that there is now sufficient evidence to show that human beings are operating with a mental representational system that can find no analogy in the central nervous systems of other species. Thus, our approach here is to highlight the likely consequences, both the good and the bad, of this evolutionary innovation on the lives of hominid ancestors. We further propose that modern humans have inherited behavioral propensities to act in ways that enabled these ancestors to capitalize on the consequences of this system's presence, and thus also the psychological mechanisms that made these behaviors likely to occur in an adaptive context.

In the sections that follow, we first introduce the reader to the basic concepts of evolutionary psychology. We then provide a brief description of human brain evolution, along with speculations as to how human consciousness emerged. We then examine a related topic; namely, evidence for higher-order cognition in our closest primate relatives, chimpanzees, which serve as imperfect models for what the common ancestor of apes and human beings may have been like. Finally, we discuss the impact that consciousness made on human evolution – an impact that was felt in three ways. First, consciousness, as a domain-general mechanism, provided direct benefits to the species because it expanded on more ancient primate adaptations (e.g., deception, cooperation, reciprocal altruism) that had evolved to cope with living in large social groups but were not necessarily dependent on an awareness of other minds. Second, the emergence of consciousness posed a new series of adaptive challenges because it disrupted fitness-maximizing categories of primate behavior, particularly social behaviors involving the adaptive exploitation of other members of the species (e.g., sexual coercion and infanticide). These conflicting challenges between more ancient adaptations and the new problems encountered by consciousness created new behavioral algorithms that served to reduce, but not eliminate, the incidence of socially proscribed behaviors in the species. And, third, we propose that human consciousness has been responsible for the evolution of a suite of novel psychological adaptations that are unshared, even in precursory form, with other species (e.g., the psychological mechanisms responsible for suicide).

Evolutionary Psychology

Underlying Assumptions of Evolutionary Psychology

For the past two decades, investigators have been carefully reconstructing the evolutionary history of specific human psychological systems (see e.g., Barkow, Tooby, & Cosmides, 1992; Buss, 1995, 2005; Daily & Wilson, 1988). Based on the central tenets of Darwinian natural selection, evolutionary psychology is a subfield of psychology that seeks to understand the *adaptive function* of the diverse universal cognitive abilities and human behaviors that were selected in the *environment of evolutionary adaptedness*, usually defined as the Pleistocene, the last 2 million years or so when humans emerged as a species. Evolutionary psychology is not concerned with how human beings are similar to or different from other species, but rather with how the human mind was shaped over the course of its recent evolution. Similar to the way evolutionary biologists attempt to explain the emergence and contemporary appearance of morphological structures, such as the human hand or digestive tract, evolutionary psychologists are concerned with the emergence and contemporary appearance of psychological structures, such as those involved in mateguarding or reciprocal altruism. That is, to what extent did those individuals who possessed psychological traits driving such

behaviors as mate-guarding and reciprocal altruism have greater *inclusive fitness* over those who lacked them? (Inclusive fitness not only refers to producing offspring, as in the case of the more traditional Darwinian concept of reproductive fitness, but also considers the influence that an individual may have in getting other copies of his or her genes into subsequent generations, through grandchildren or nieces and nephews, for example [Hamilton, 1964].)

A central assumption of evolutionary psychology is that the psychological structures that evolved are adaptive, information-processing mechanisms designed to deal with recurrent problems faced by our ancestors. According to evolutionary psychologists, "the causal link between evolution and behavior is made through psychological mechanisms" (Cosmides & Tooby, 1987, p. 277). Individuals who did not possess adaptive psychological traits were unable to reliably engage in behaviors that were adaptive in ancestral environments. As a result, they failed to disperse their genes as much as those who did engage in these adaptive behaviors, and eventually only those individuals whose behaviors were supported by these psychological systems were represented in the population. What get selected, according to this rationale, are not the adaptive behaviors per se, but rather those psychological systems undergirding and enabling these adaptive behaviors (e.g., Buss, 1995; Tooby & Cosmides, 1992).

Moreover, these mechanisms are domain-specific in nature. Human beings (and presumably other animals) did not evolve general learning or information-processing abilities that could be applied to the wide range of problems they encounter as they go about their lives. Instead, what evolved were a host of relatively specific mechanisms, each sculpted by natural selection to deal with relatively specific and recurring problems, such as language, detecting cheaters, or gaining and maintaining mates. As an analogy, the mind is compared to a Swiss Army Knife, with different tools designed for different tasks (Tooby & Cosmides, 1992), rather than a broad ax, which may be powerful but too wieldy to be useful for many complex problems. Despite claims to the contrary (e.g., Lickliter & Honeycutt, 2003), evolutionary psychology does not advocate a form of genetic determinism, but emphasizes that evolved, adaptive mechanisms are sensitive to environmental context (see Tooby, Cosmides, & Barrett, 2003). This is especially true for human beings, who live in diverse physical and social environments and require a flexible intelligence to survive.

Nevertheless, the plasticity of human thought and behavior is not infinite. Human infants are prepared by evolution for a structured world that includes sights and sounds, a lactating mother, social support, and language, among many other things. There are constraints on what they can process and how they will interpret experience. These *enabling constraints* (Gelman & Williams, 1998) should not be viewed negatively, for they make it easier for children to master the ways of a *human* world, facilitating the acquisition of language, for example, but making it impossible to learn to navigate via echolocation. Over the course of development, children's information-processing biases are modified by experience, but inevitably result in behaviors that are generally well suited to the social environments in which they live.

In an effort to disentangle such complex issues, evolutionary psychologists have established empirical programs with the explicit purpose of identifying and explaining the ultimate function of human thinking in different problem-solving domains, such as those found in the social, physical, and biological environments (see examples in Barkow et al., 1992; Buss, 2005). The unique metatheoretical perspective of evolutionary psychology has also contributed to an understanding of human behavior that goes well beyond that of solely proximate explanations proffered by many social learning theories. Importantly, evolutionary psychology argues that human behavior is motivated not by the conscious interests of people in infinitely malleable social environments, but rather by the genetic interests of human organisms living in complex socioecologies (e.g., Tooby & Cosmides, 1992).

Self-Consciousness as an Epiphenomenon

Still, the role of self-consciousness, which appears to be a very general mechanism permitting reflective awareness of the self's proximate motivational states, continues to remain very unclear in evolutionary models of human cognition. Many evolutionary psychologists consider consciousness to be an epiphenomenon that shadows the intuitive operations of psychological adaptations and that has played no important role in the evolutionary emergence of these adaptations. To support this position, such theorists cite people's naïve, explicit explanations for the causes of their own adaptive behaviors, explanations that are far removed from plausible selection-based explanations for their actions (French, Kamil, & Ledger, 2001). In addition, similar behaviors that occur under similar ecological conditions in different societies are often interpreted in very different ways (e.g., for an application of this principle to the subject of infanticide, see Daly & Wilson, 1988). This suggests that, although there was selection for cognitive programs that prompt specific types of responses when encountering particular environmental conditions, people's causal interpretations of these identical behaviors may vary considerably. Among those factors contributing to attributional differences between societies and between individuals are cultural traditions, narratives, religious indoctrination, and education.

The key point is that such causal interpretations of behavior matter little in the long run – so long as an adaptive behavior occurs, it makes no difference whether people believe that the gods made it so or that it was triggered by the state of the economy. This informs us that the cognitive systems supporting many human behaviors appeared earlier in evolutionary phylogeny than did the conscious awareness that currently oversees and interprets them. According to this rationale, if self-consciousness were integral in causing adaptive behaviors, then it is reasonable to expect that all individuals, irrespective of population or individual differences, would provide the same type of causal explanation when interpreting these behaviors. In this light, self-consciousness is rightly considered an epiphenomenon with respect to these strategies, in that it is ostensibly inconsequential to the standard operations of many psychological adaptations. As a general rule of thumb, whenever a behavior can be reliably predicted to arise in response to a definable set of environmental factors, and whenever post-hoc explanations for this identical response vary from person to person or from culture to culture, self-consciousness has served at most a peripheral role in the evolution of the psychological adaptation supporting this behavior. *Homo sapiens*, like any other extant species, has a deep history; in addition, it also has one that is characterized by only a recent split from the other primate clades. We therefore suspect that a significant proportion of human psychological adaptations fit into this category. That is, we believe that much of human behavior is likely governed by unconscious decision-making strategies that led to genetic fitness throughout the course of primate evolution. For such adaptations, self-consciousness principally serves a spectator role, allowing explanatory searches for the causes of adaptive behaviors but not inserting itself into the decision making in any meaningful way.

Research in evolutionary psychology has amassed considerable support for the idea that there exists an underlying genotypic structure in human beings that leads, in interaction with the environment over the course of development, to the phenotypic expression of psychological systems specially designed to solve recurrent environmental problems. Across human societies, and across the human life cycle, individuals encounter the same set of basic challenges in the social and physical environments – challenges that, if gone unmet, would directly threaten the successful propagation of their genes. One important impli-

cation of this fact is that, regardless of both cross-cultural and individualistic differences in how people explain the causes of their own behaviors, what ultimately determines behavior are the implicit, evolved psychological mechanisms that instantiate a given course of action whenever an individual is confronted with a problem that the human mind is designed to solve.

We also suspect, as do others (e.g., Crook, 1980; Donald, 2000; Humphrey, 1976), that this is only part of the picture and that self-consciousness in fact played an enormously important role in the evolution of psychological adaptations that are specific to human beings. This is because self-consciousness seems to have meaningfully disrupted many ancient psychological adaptations that human beings share with other species and to have presented a new series of challenges that our distant human ancestors were never forced to confront. These challenges, we believe, were initially focused in the social realm, with self-consciousness producing individuals who were more keenly aware of their own knowledge and motivations *and* those of others. Such awareness could have provided great advantages, but with it great problems. With an onslaught of new dynamical problems caused by consciousness, human beings evolved a fundamentally novel suite of adaptive solutions designed to redress these problems.

Along these lines, evolutionary psychology distinguishes the *proximate causes* of human behaviors from their *distal causes*. The proximate level of behavioral causation consists of motivational causes, such as affective, perceptual, and epistemic states that the individual experiences subjectively. In contrast, the ultimate level of behavioral causation consists of the intuitive, domain-driven psychological processes promoting adaptive behavior that are barred from the individual's conscious access. Because any given adaptive behavior has both a proximate cause that must gear the individual toward engaging in a specific course of action, as well as a distal cause that strives to ensure that this course of action is in the best interests of the individual's genes, these two levels of causation are inseparable. Psychological adaptations are complex, rule-driven processing systems that respond to domain-specific environmental factors.

Adaptations, Byproducts, Noise, and Exaptations

At this point, some comment should be made about evolutionary psychology's adoption of an "adaptationist program." Evolutionary psychology has often falsely been accused of assuming that any species-universal contemporary behavior must be an adaptation. But this is not so. Many features of the modern human mind and behavior are byproducts of other adaptations, or are simply noise. Some may actually be maladaptive, just not so maladaptive as to have caused the elimination of the genes underlying these features from the species' genome. David Buss and his colleagues (Buss, Haselton, Shackelford, Bleske, & Wakefield, 1998) defined *adaptations* as reliably developing, inherited characteristics, produced by natural selection, that served to solve recurrent problems in the environment of evolutionary adaptedness and resulted in greater inclusive fitness. Buss et al. used the umbilical cord as an example of an adaptation, as it solved the problem of how to get nutrients from a mammal mother to her fetus. In contrast, *byproducts* are features that have not been shaped by natural selection and did not solve some recurring problem, but are a consequence of being associated with some adaptation. The belly button would be an example of a byproduct. Finally, *noise* refers to random effects that may be attributed to mutations, changes in the environment, or variations of development, such as the shape of one's belly button. Thus, not all evolved characteristics should be viewed as adaptations. The belly button clearly evolved, but it cannot accurately be viewed as an adaptation. Moreover, some adaptations may have negative side effects (byproducts). For instance, the fetus's large skull is surely an adaptation, housing the large brain that resides within it. Yet, this

large head makes birth difficult, due to limits on how broad a woman's hips can be and still afford bipedality. As a result, many women and infants have died in childbirth. However, the cognitive benefits of a large brain must have been greater than the cost in maternal and neonatal mortality; otherwise selective factors would have worked against such costly anatomical constraints and alternative fitness-conferring mechanisms would likely have evolved.

A related concept popular with many evolutionary biologists (e.g., Tattersall, 1998) is that of *exaptation*, defined as "a feature, now useful to an organism, that did not arise as an adaptation for its present role, but was subsequently co-opted for its current function." Further, exaptations are "features that now enhance fitness, but were not built by natural selection for their current role" (Gould, 1991, p. 47). The classic example of an exaptation is the case of avian feathers, which evolved initially to serve a thermoregulatory function but were co-opted to facilitate flight in birds.

Although the concept of exaptations has not generally been accepted by evolutionary psychologists (Buss et al., 1998), we believe that the basic idea is solid – many of the products of evolution arose based on byproducts of other adaptations or features that, initially, had no inherent function for an organism. This is likely to be especially true for brain evolution, with parts of the brain being co-opted for functions they were not originally selected to perform. Yet, once co-opted, any new function must pass through the sieve of natural selection. For instance, although feathers may not have initially evolved for flight, they became necessary for birds to fly, making them an adaptation. Likewise, even if many human cognitive abilities are the products of the co-opting of brain tissue originally used for other purposes, it is reasonable to ask what new problems (if any) these abilities solved and if they, too, may be adaptations (albeit co-opted ones). We thus treat exaptations as special cases of adaptations. Because natural selection is not forward looking but serves only to adapt organisms to their local environments, it is likely that many contemporary and ancient adaptations may have been co-opted from other seemingly unrelated functions. This perspective may be of special importance to human intelligence and for functions associated with the expanding neocortex that characterized members of the hominid line over the past 5 million years. Consciousness may be the product of our big brain, but we can only guess at the selection pressures, if any, that generated this ability.

The Evolution of the Human Brain

Changes in Brain Size over Hominid Evolution

Human beings are noted for their big brains relative to their body size. Primates, in general, have large brain-to-body size ratios, but this trend is exaggerated in human beings (Jerrison, 1973; Rilling & Insel, 1999). Jerrison (1973) developed the *encephalization quotient* (EQ) to evaluate the expected brain weight/body weight ratio for animals within a family. For instance, given the typical pattern of changes in brain and body weight in mammals, brain weight should increase at a certain rate relative to increases in body weight. If a species' brain is smaller than that expected for its body weight, the encephalization quotient will be less than 1.0, and it will be greater than 1.0 if its brain is larger than expected for its body weight. Most primates have encephalization quotients greater than 1.0, with chimpanzees being 2.3, meaning their brains are, on average, more than twice the size expected for a mammal of their size. This impressive brain/body ratio is dwarfed by that of human beings, however, which is more than three times greater still (EQ = 7.6, Jerrison, 1973; Rilling & Insel, 1999).

Of course, human beings did not evolve from chimpanzees, but last shared a common ancestor with modern chimps between 5 and 7 million years ago. In between our chimp-like common ancestor[1] and contemporary people, paleoanthropologists descri-

be a series of species, some of which were surely our ancestors and others of which likely lead to evolutionary dead ends. Figure 22.1 presents one possible phylogeny for human evolution, dating back about 5 million years. These species differed in many physical characteristics (we can only guess at what their behavior might have been based on brain size and some artifacts), perhaps most prominently being brain size in relation to body size. Figure 22.2 presents the encephalization quotients for contemporary chimpanzees (*Pan troglodytes*), modern human beings (*Homo sapiens*), and three species believed to be ancestral to *Homo sapiens*: *Australopithecus afarensis*, which roamed Africa about 3 million years before present; *Homo habilis*, the first member of the *Homo* genus that first appears in the fossil record about 2.5 million years ago; and *Homo erectus*, who left Africa to populate Asia and Europe about 1.5 million years ago. As can be seen, the encephalization quotient of *Australopithecus afarensis* was only slightly greater than that of modern chimpanzees, with this value increasing sharply over the next 3 million years in the genetic line that presumably led to *Homo sapiens* (Tobias, 1987). The modern human brain, then, is a reflection of a more general pattern shown in primates and particularly in hominids, those big-brained, bipedal animals of which *Homo sapiens* is the only extant species.

Building bigger brains, at least in primates, seems to be the result of extending the time the brain can grow; delaying the offset of brain growth results in the production of more neurons (Finlay & Darlington, 1995; Finlay, Darlington, & Nicastro, 2001) and greater dendritic and synaptic growth. However, in human beings, the brain can only get so large before the skull that confines it becomes too big to fit through the birth canal. As a result, human infants are born prematurely, and much of brain development occurs postnatally. Were human gestation to correspond to what would be expected for their brain and body size, women would be pregnant between 18 and 24 months (Gould, 1977).

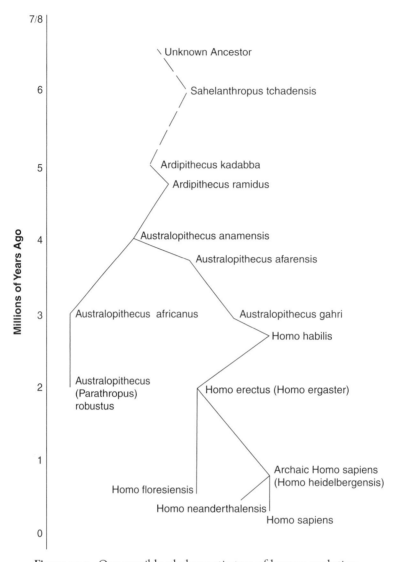

Figure 22.1. One possible phylogenetic tree of human evolution.

Although the canonical perspective of evolutionary psychology is that adaptive mechanisms are domain-specific in nature, a more parsimonious interpretation, we believe, is that increased brain size afforded greater general information-processing capacity that may have permitted the evolution or execution of more domain-specific mechanisms, particularly in the social realm (see Bjorklund & Harnishfeger, 1995; Bjorklund & Kipp, 2001; Bjorklund & Pellegrini, 2002; Geary, 2005). Consistent with this domain-general perspective is the claim that most of the increase in brain size over mam-

malian evolution can be attributed to delaying "neuronal birthdays" (when precursor nerve cells stop dividing symmetrically and begin their migration within the neural tube), and not to changes in specific areas of the brain associated with particular functions, which would be indicative of domain-specific selection pressures (Finlay et al., 2001). This is similar to claims made by Gould (1991), who argued that many aspects of modern human intelligence do not represent domain-specific evolved psychological mechanisms, but rather are the byproducts of an enlarged brain (see also Finlay

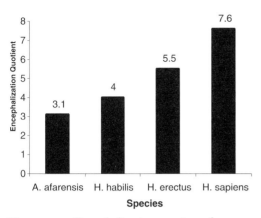

Figure 22.2. Encephalization quotients for several hominid species (from Tobias, 1987). Reprinted with permission.

et al., 2001). Although this argument suggests that not all features of the human brain and mind were specifically targeted for selection (see Geary, 2005; Geary & Huffman, 2002), it does not mean that differences between chimpanzees and human beings, for example, are due only to differences in the total volume of brain tissue between these species. There are many differences in the microcircuitry of many parts of the brains of monkeys, chimpanzees, and human beings, for example, suggesting that specific brain areas and cognitive functions have indeed undergone selective pressure (Preuss, 2001). This implies that, even if much of brain evolution within the hominid line can be attributed to a general mechanism associated with the delay of neuronal birthdays, subsequent specialization of brain and cognitive functions, which are relatively domain-specific in their application, could still have taken place (Geary, 2001).

Big Brains, Slow Development, and Social Complexity

What are big brains for? For one thing, large brains are greatly beneficial for learning. A species that lives in varied environments or requires sophisticated memory abilities to navigate its environment or to remember the location of hidden caches of food cannot achieve these feats with a brain that is barely large enough to control its basic bod-

ily functions. But if an animal is going to invest the time necessary to learn important aspects of its environment, it should be relatively long-lived. Brains are metabolically expensive (Aiello & Wheeler, 1995), and an animal whose existence on this earth is measured in weeks or months, rather than years or decades, would be better off investing its time and caloric resources in pursuits that do not require substantial learning. And the more an animal has to learn to achieve inclusive fitness, the longer its prereproductive period needs to be. Human beings, of course, fit this bill well, not reaching reproductive maturity until the teen years, with some anthropologists suggesting that this was likely closer to 20 years of age for our ancestors (e.g., Bogin, 1999; Kaplan, Hill, Lancaster, & Hurtado, 2000).

In particular, we, and others, have argued that big brains and slow development evolved in primates to deal with the complexity of their social group (e.g., Alexander, 1989; Bjorklund & Bering, 2003a; Bjorklund & Harnishfeger, 1995; Byrne & Whiten, 1988; Dunbar, 1992, 2001; Geary & Flinn, 2001; Humphrey, 1976). Our remarkable technological and abstract reasoning skills have been co-opted from the "intelligence" evolved to deal with cooperating, competing, and understanding conspecifics, and this is a trend observed in primates in general. This trend is seen in research by Dunbar (1992, 1995, 2001), who reported a significant relation between measures of brain size and social complexity among primates (correlation between size of neocortex and group size = .76). Moreover, larger brain size is also negatively associated with length of the juvenile period (Bonner, 1988), suggesting that both brain size and delayed development are important interdependent factors that are related to success in complex societies. This triadic relationship was empirically demonstrated by Joffe (1997), who reported that the proportion of the lifespan spent as a juvenile among 27 different species of primates was positively correlated with group size *and* the relative size of the nonvisual neocortex. We make no claims that any one of these factors is the *cause* for another; surely, brain size, length of juvenile period, and social complexity interacted synergistically, with large brains and an extended juvenile period being necessary for mastering the ways of one's group, and social complexity in turn exerting selection pressures for increased brain size and an extension of the juvenile period.

As suggested above, the increasing brain volume over the course of primate and hominid evolution likely is the result of constraints in neural development (e.g., Finlay et al., 2001). Yet, it seems that the increased computing power that larger brains afforded was put to good use, specifically to deal with the complexity of primate social groups. It also suggests that consciousness is not *necessary* for life in a complex primate social group. However, we believe that when neural organization produced consciousness, it did so in a context in which it could be put to good use, specifically in social cognition.

Precursors to Consciousness: The Comparative Psychology of Consciousness

If the common ancestor of human beings and contemporary members of the *Pan* genus were anything like extant chimpanzees, they lived a highly complex social life. For example, chimpanzees in the wild have been shown to possess at least crude culture, as reflected by the transmission from one generation to the next of complex behaviors involved in grooming, nut cracking, and termite fishing, for example (Whiten et al., 1999). Many of these behaviors are unique to a particular chimpanzee troop and so cannot be attributed to species-universal behavioral features. Human beings and chimpanzees also show considerable overlap when it comes to social behaviors, such as, among many others, status striving, coalition formation, reconciliation, and tit-for-tat strategies (e.g., de Waal, 1982, 1986; Goodall, 1986). But do chimpanzees achieve these complex social feats using higher-order cognition involving consciousness, or can their accomplishments be explained otherwise?

Higher-order cognition in great apes has been an area of great contention, with some scientists arguing that chimpanzees are "almost human," possessing, in rudimentary form, nearly all the intellectual abilities seen in *Homo sapiens* (e.g., Fouts, 1997; Goodall, 1986; de Waal, 1986); whereas others contend that chimpanzees are merely clever "behaviorists," able to accomplish feats of social and technological complexity without the need for abstract (i.e., self-conscious) cognition (e.g., Povinelli, 2000; Povinelli & Bering, 2002). Although a detailed discussion of this literature is beyond the scope of the present chapter (see Bjorklund & Pellegrini, 2002; Suddendorf & Whiten, 2001; Tomasello & Call, 1997, for reviews), we now present briefly some of the evidence for and against higher-order cognition in chimpanzees and the implications it may have for the evolution of human consciousness.

Mirror-Self-Recognition

Many comparative psychologists have argued that evidence of mirror "self-recognition" in great apes is diagnostic of self-consciousness, and this, in turn, has led them to infer that such species must have empathic social cognition as well (Gallup, 1982, 1985; Jolly, 1991). This position was initially advanced by Gallup (1979), whose original mirror self-recognition procedure of placing a dye mark on a hidden portion of an animal's body and then recording its responses to the mark when confronted with a mirror has become the litmus test for self-awareness in other species. If the animal reaches up to touch the mark, then it is said to understand that the mirror image is a representation of itself. If it does something else, however, such as touch the surface of the mirror or threaten its own image, then it is said to have "failed" the mark test and have shown no understanding of its own subjective existence.

To date, other than human beings, who show mirror self-recognition at about 18 months of age (see Brooks-Gunn & Lewis, 1984), only chimpanzees, orangutans, and a few gorillas have "passed" the mark test (see Suddendorf & Whiten, 2001; Swartz, Sarauw, & Evans, 1999), although variants of the test that have been devised for use with the anatomical constraints of dolphins (Reiss, & Marino, 2001) suggest that this species may demonstrate mirror self-recognition as well. Interpretation of these findings vary widely, however, with some researchers arguing that such mirror-contingent behaviors are clear evidence of self-consciousness and others arguing that they demand only an ability to learn how certain kinesthetic-proprioceptive experiences map onto a mirror image (for a review of this complex debate, see Parker, Mitchell, & Boccia, 2006).

Social Learning

The impressive social learning of chimpanzees, on the surface, would seem to involve an appreciation on the part of the observer of the goal, or intent, of the model, a form of secondary representation and seemingly a characteristic of conscious creatures. But not all social learning requires such mental representation. For instance, Tomasello and his colleagues (e.g., Tomasello, 1996, 2000; Tomasello, Kruger, & Ratner, 1993) have proposed that only *true imitation* requires an understanding of the goals, or intentions, of the model, in addition to replication of important aspects of the model's behavior. Such imitation requires the ability to take the perspective of another, apparently requiring conscious awareness. Although great apes often master complicated tasks after watching a model perform similar problems, such learning usually occurs over multiple trials and involves significant trial-and-error learning (e.g., Whiten, 1998; Whiten, Custance, Gómez, Teixidor, & Bard, 1996); in general, there is little evidence for true imitation of actions on objects in chimpanzees (e.g., Tomasello, Savage-Rumbaugh, & Kruger, 1993). The exception seems to be for great apes that have been enculturated by human caregivers (e.g., Bering, Bjorklund, & Ragan, 2000; Bjorklund, Yunger, Bering, & Ragan, 2002; Tomasello, Savage-Rumbaugh,

& Kruger 1993). However, it is still unclear whether such atypical rearing experiences endow these animals with an understanding of intentionality or whether they simply become more sensitive to human behavioral contingencies that co-occur with specific intentional states (Bering, 2004a; Bjorklund & Bering, 2003b; Bjorklund & Rosenberg, 2005; Call & Carpenter, 2003).

Boesch (1991, 1993) has argued that one phenomenon that would seemingly require conscious cognition is explicit teaching. He reasons that teaching requires the understanding of others as not possessing information, and thus behaviors that appear designed to change the epistemic content of others' minds would (in principle) be evidence of the instructor's metarepresentational capacities. There have been several observations of female chimpanzees in the wild teaching their young offspring how to crack nuts (e.g., Boesch, 1991, 1993; Greenfield, Maynard, Boehm, & Schmidtling, 2000). For example, mother chimps were observed to position the anvil and hammer rocks and the nut in such a way that all an infant had to do was strike the nut to open it. At other times, the female would move especially slowly in the presence of her infant. Although these are impressive demonstrations and consistent with the interpretation that mother chimpanzees actively teach their offspring complex technological skills, they have been observed only rarely and do not seem to be a common way in which "cultural" information is transmitted (see Tomasello et al., 1993).

Understanding the Perspective of Others

In other research, subordinate chimpanzees seem to realize when and when not a dominant chimp can see a valued food item and will only "compete" for the food when it is out of the dominant animal's sight (Hare, Call, Agentta, & Tomasello, 2000; Hare, Call, & Tomasello, 2001). This behavior implies that chimpanzees understand that "sight implies knowledge," a seemingly rudimentary (but valuable) ability in social cognition. Yet, research by Povinelli and his colleagues (e.g., Povinelli & Eddy, 1996a; Reaux, Theall, & Povinelli, 1999) questions this interpretation. In Povinelli's research, chimpanzees face two experimenters, one with her eyes open and the other with her eyes somehow occluded (e.g., her eyes are closed or she's wearing a mask). When given the opportunity to make a reaching response to either of the experimenters to get food located between them, the chimpanzees respond randomly. Unlike the apes in the food-competition studies of Hare and his colleagues (2000, 2001), they seem not to appreciate that the eyes are a source of knowledge.

With respect to complex social behavior, chimpanzees do occasionally seem to engage in deception; for example, females occasionally place a hand over a subordinate male's mouth during furtive mating, serving to prevent the male's screams from reaching the ears of a dominant male and alerting him to the behavior (see Whiten & Byrne, 1988, for other examples). Yet such deception does not necessarily require that an animal knows what another animal is thinking, but could have been acquired via processes of trial-and-error learning. In related research, when chimpanzees are given false-belief tasks under laboratory control, so that the only way to solve the problem is to appreciate what another individual knows, they fail (Call & Tomasello, 1999). Taken together, these findings and others from a variety of controlled investigations lend support to the idea that chimpanzees have, at best, a vastly impoverished understanding of intentionality (Bering & Povinelli, 2003; Povinelli & Bering, 2002; Tomasello & Call, 1997). They have failed to distinguish between ignorant and knowledgeable social partners (e.g., Call & Tomasello, 1999), to understand *seeing* as a psychological state (e.g., Povinelli & Eddy, 1996a), to distinguish between intentional and accidental actions (e.g., Povinelli, Perriloux, Reaux, & Bierschwale, 1998), to instruct a naïve conspecific on how to go about a novel task that requires cooperative effort (e.g., Povinelli & O'Neill, 2000), and to understand the psychological state of *attention* (e.g., Povinelli & Eddy, 1996b,c).

We cannot say that the primate literature paints an easily interpretable picture of higher-cognitive abilities in great apes. It seems that chimpanzee social cognition is, in many ways, very much like that of human beings. Yet, the understanding they demonstrate of the knowledge of others – perhaps *the* critical component in human social cognition and one for which self-consciousness is required – is limited at best. We feel comfortable saying that chimpanzees and the other great apes do not experience a sense of self-awareness and do not possess an understanding of belief/desire reasoning comparable to the degree characterizing nearly every normal 5-year-old human child. But the roots of such awareness may be visible, and in the absence of controlled conditions, one can easily misinterpret the actions of these animals as being based on an understanding of the knowledge and motivations of others (as we often do with our pets). Assuming that our common ancestor had a social organization and social learning abilities similar to those of extant chimpanzees, when consciousness did first appear, it was in a species and context that would readily capitalize on its attributes.

Evolutionary Psychology and Consciousness

Adaptive Information-Processing Mechanisms: The Assumption of Implicit Cognition

For the most part, when evolutionary psychologists talk about information-processing mechanisms or strategies used to solve specific problems (e.g., mate-selection strategies), they do so in the same way that evolutionary biologists speak of physiological mechanisms or behavioral strategies. Such "strategies" do not imply self-awareness. For example, the mating strategy of a smaller-than-average male fish to mingle among the females and mate inconspicuously with them is quite different from the strategy used by a larger, more dominant fish. Neither strategy, of course, is conscious. Neither animal has reflected upon the best way to get its genes into the next generation and chosen, after careful deliberation, which course to take. These are unconscious, implicit strategies and of the same sort that evolutionary psychologists propose underlie human behavior. Such an approach affords great explanatory benefits, for it permits psychologists to explain the actions of human beings in the same way that the actions of non-human animals are explained. No special pleading for the uniqueness of humans is necessary.

As a result, higher-order cognition, such as that requiring consciousness, is not a required topic for evolutionary-minded psychologists. This is reflected by examining the indexes of popular books on evolutionary psychology. For example, the term "consciousness" is not found in the indexes of Barkow, Tooby, and Cosmides's (1992) seminal edited volume *The Adapted Mind*, Buss's (1999) textbook *Evolutionary Psychology*, Cartwright's (2000) textbook *Evolution and Human Behavior*, or in Pinker's deservedly popular books *The Language Instinct* (1994) and *The Blank Slate* (2002). Yet the topic of consciousness receives considerable attention in other evolutionary psychology texts (e.g., Gaulin & McBurney, 2001; Palmer & Palmer, 2002) and in popular books such as Pinker's (1997) *How the Mind Works*, reflecting, we think, the recognition by some evolutionary psychologists of the central role consciousness plays in what it means to be human. But, in general, consciousness has been out of the mainstream of evolutionary psychology, and certainly conscious cognition is not necessary to explain adaptive behavior.

Although evolutionary psychologists need not postulate conscious cognition when trying to explain the adaptive value of some cognitive mechanisms, they cannot totally ignore it. Cognitive scientists have recognized for some time the complex interplay between consciousness and behavior. In human beings, the relation between higher-order thought and action is a complicated affair. As Cotterill (2001) writes, "We can think without acting, act without thinking, act while thinking about that act, and act while thinking about something

else" (p. 10). Clearly, any behaviors that are directly caused by consciousness can become targeted by natural selection. But a novel twist to this logic, and one we think should be underscored in discussions of human cognitive evolution, is that, in a gossiping society, the inhibition of selfish behaviors would also have become targeted by natural selection (Bering, 2004b; see also Bjorklund & Harnishfeger, 1995; Bjorklund & Kipp, 2001; Dunbar, 1993). That is, *not engaging* in a behavior that has been conditioned by natural selection to occur in response to specific environmental contingencies, but instead overriding this tendency through higher-order cognitive means, may under certain conditions be the more adaptive response. We argue that this is often the case for human beings, an organism whose genetic fitness hinges on social reputation, impression management, and the advertisement of its altruistic traits. The behavioral dispositions that we have inherited from our genetically gratuitous prehominid ancestors, ancestors that did not have to worry about the existence of other minds, must be suppressed very often. This is new psychology shaking hands with old psychology.

We also see an important overlap here between our definition of consciousness as a system permitting metarepresentational thought and the more conventional view of consciousness, and the one often referred to in evolutionary terms as having conferred a selective advantage, as a system that permits simulated outcomes on motoric planning. According to Cotterill (2001), "The adequately endowed system conjures up a simulated probable outcome of the intended motor pattern, and vetoes it if the motion is adverse" (p. 8). Indeed, Jeannerod (1999) presents evidence showing that overt movement and sheer imagery of these actions activate the same brain regions. Povinelli and Cant (1995) have speculated that a large-bodied arboreal primate, such as that envisioned as the common ancestor of humans and great apes, would have profited enormously from symbolic representational abilities enabling such foresight (a wrong move in the tree canopy could prove deadly.) We would simply extend this line of reasoning by arguing that mental simulations of the probable outcomes of intended actions would have given human beings significant strategic leverage in a variety of both physical *and* social contexts. Social simulations would instantiate alternative psychological construals that included representations not only of others' likely reactions to the self's behaviors but also mental state attributions to these behaviors. Actions can thus be tailored to the unique demands of the social situation. Although it may be the case that other primate species are capable of simulating behavioral outcomes of their actions in social contexts, we argue that only humans can simulate the way that their actions will be interpreted and understood by social others.

As we mentioned earlier, evolutionary psychology deals with both distal and proximate causes of behavior, expressed through adaptive information-processing mechanisms that are responsive to factors in the local environment. Because, in human beings, psychological adaptations occur in conscious agents, these rule-driven processing systems are also tethered to the subjective states of biological organisms. Environmental information that is detected and perceived by the human brain is handled in ways that maximize biological success by either stimulating or inhibiting specific behavioral responses. At least in human beings, however, the perception of these sources of information is often accessible to conscious awareness, and any behaviors occurring in response to environmental input may be closely monitored, if not controlled, by an executive cognitive system.

The Adaptive Benefits and Challenges of Consciousness

On the surface, the benefits of consciousness are self-evident. Self-consciousness and higher-order cognition are so integrated into the fabric of what it means (phenomenologically) to be human that there is no need to look for its benefits. Yet, although it is unquestionable that we'd be a very differ-

ent species than we are today without conscious awareness, that does not preclude the question of what adaptive benefits, if any, consciousness afforded our ancestors. Moreover, consciousness was a mixed blessing, perhaps producing as many problems as it solved. In this section, we look at some of the benefits and challenges brought about by consciousness.

The Benefits of Consciousness

KNOW THYSELF, AND KNOW OTHERS
Perhaps the dominant perspective of the "reason" for the evolution of consciousness was first presented by Nicholas Humphrey (1976), who argued that consciousness played a critical role when dealing with members of our own species. For animals living in complex social groups, the ability to predict, and possibly control, the behavior of others would provide great advantage. Social primates, which surely included our ancient ancestors, already formed coalitions, cooperated and competed with one another, and sometimes used deception to obtain valuable resources or to avoid detection when a social rule was broken. Consciousness arose in this arena and provided an immediate social, and therefore reproductive, advantage to its possessor.

Note that it is implicitly assumed here that the ability to attribute mental states to others is somehow linked to self-consciousness. This requires making the conceptual inference that one's privileged access to one's own proximate causal states feeds an understanding of others' causal states. Specifically, it is assumed that any evolved social algorithms in human beings that necessitate the representation of what others *do* or *do not* know first required the ability to reflect upon the epistemic contents of one's own mind. Indeed, we believe that the ability to detect the intentions of other agents, as well as their emotional, epistemic, and perceptual status, has likely been an enormously influential factor in the evolution of social adaptations in the human species. Such a general representational system, which falls under the rubric of "theory of mind" in the developmental and comparative psychological literatures, was capable of transforming already existing ancient primate adaptations in the social domain, such as reciprocal altruism and mate-guarding, into more complex adaptations demanding the rapid inferential processing of information dealing with mental states.

From this perspective, self-consciousness was first applied to social cognition and may have permitted the evolution of more domain-specific adaptations devoted to dealing with conspecifics. For example, Baron-Cohen (1995) proposed four separate modules involved with theory of mind. The first module, the *intentionality detector* (ID), permits one to infer that a moving object may have some intent toward the individual (it may be trying to catch me), and the *eye-direction detector* (EDD) interprets eye gaze. These modules develop by around 9 months in infancy and likely do not require full-blown consciousness. The *shared-attention mechanism* (SAD) module is involved in triadic interactions (e.g., person A and person B can each be looking at object C and understand that they see the same thing) and develops at around 18 months in human beings. The *theory-of-mind module* (TOMM) develops around age 4 in children and is similar to *belief-desire reasoning* as described by Wellman (1990), in which children understand that their behaviors are governed by what they believe, or know, and what they want, or desire, and so is the behavior of other people. Such reasoning requires secondary representation and what is conventionally referred to as self-awareness or self-consciousness. Theory of mind has been one of the most investigated topics in cognitive development over the past 20 years, in part because it is at the core of social functioning in any human society.

The most frequently used tasks to assess theory of mind involves children's understanding of false belief. In one version of the task, a child and a confederate watch as a treat is placed in one container (A). The confederate then leaves the room, and the treat is moved to a second container (B) while the child watches. The child is then asked where the confederate will think the treat is hidden. By age 4, most children solve the problem correctly, stating that the confederate will have the false belief that the treat is hidden in the first container. Most children much younger than this age, however, erroneously state that the confederate will believe the treat is hidden in container B. This, indeed, is where the treat is hidden, but this fact is known to the child and not the confederate. Results from experiments using this and other variants of false-belief tasks indicate that young children do not behave as if they possess belief-desire reasoning (see Wellman, Cross, & Watson, 2001). We would not want to declare these children to be unconscious, but they fail to be able to take the perspective of the confederate and to understand that other people have knowledge and desires different from their own that guide their behavior. People in all societies generally behave kindly toward preschool children, so their lack of belief-desire reasoning rarely causes them much trouble. But it is difficult to imagine any adult (or child beyond the age of 7 or 8) who lacks such reasoning functioning well in any human culture, modern or ancient.

CONSCIOUSNESS AND THE DEVELOPMENT OF TECHNOLOGICAL SKILLS

According to Humphrey's hypothesis, consciousness evolved to play a central role in social cognition. But human consciousness extends beyond the social realm into technology (e.g., tool making) and educability. Human beings are not the only tool makers in the animal kingdom, but the tools made by chimpanzees, for instance preparing sticks for use in termite fishing (e.g., McGrew, 1992), are simple, uncomplicated devices compared to the tools made by modern human beings (even those possessing "stone age" technology, see Stout, 2002). Moreover, *Homo sapiens* are the only species that make tools to make tools. Is consciousness required for these accomplishments, and if so, how did it evolve?

Mithen (1996) proposed that, with the advent of language, "social intelligence starts being invaded by non-social information, the non-social world becomes available for reflexive consciousness to explore" (p. 190). In other words, people are able to represent their thoughts and actions to themselves (or re-representation, following the arguments of Karmiloff-Smith, 1992). For Mithen, with consciousness, general intelligence now serves to integrate the various modules of the mind (e.g., social, technological, natural history) and, with this integration, permits the construction of tools and the transmission of knowledge in a way unprecedented in the animal world. With consciousness, our ancestors could reflect on what they knew, using information acquired in one domain to bring to bear on issues in other domains. Learning can extend beyond the immediate context and be applied to situations only imagined or in one's memory.

The extension of learning is likely an important consequence of consciousness. Self-awareness is, of course, not necessary for complex learning to occur. But much of what makes human beings unique is our educability, our ability to acquire information and procedures for solving problems that our ancestors never encountered (see Bjorklund & Bering, 2000). Relevant here is Geary's (1995) distinction between biologically primary and biologically secondary cognitive abilities. Biologically primary abilities refer to those cognitive mechanisms that have undergone selection pressure over the course of evolution. The abilities themselves and their developmental timetable are species universal, they are acquired via routine interaction with the environment, and children are highly motivated to execute them. Language is a prime example of a biologically primary ability. In contrast, biologically secondary abilities are those a culture "invents" to solve particular recurrent problems. They have not undergone selective pressure and thus are not universal; they are based on biologically primary abilities, but often require substantial practice to achieve, and children may need external motivation to execute them. Reading is a good example of a biologically secondary ability. Most of the cognitive accomplishments associated

with culture can be considered to be biologically secondary abilities.

As defined, human beings may not be the only species to display biologically secondary abilities; chimpanzees, as we noted previously, pass on unique cultural knowledge from one generation to the next (Whiten et al., 1999), and such accomplishments as nut cracking and termite fishing can be considered to reflect biologically secondary abilities (Bjorklund & Bering, 2003a). But it is human beings who have made the most of culturally acquired cognitions, and this has been achieved, we argue, through consciousness. The acquisition of such skills as reading, arithmetic, navigation, coordinated hunting, and external forms of memory (such as pictures, or even intentionally placed cues designed to prompt memory) all required a degree of self-regulation and secondary representation not available without consciousness. Self-awareness, by itself, may not be sufficient for the successful execution of biologically secondary abilities. Individuals required the ability to sustain attention and to avoid distraction (i.e., to stay "on task") and to have sufficient working memory to achieve many secondary skills. These are abilities that likely evolved with increased brain size (e.g., Bjorklund & Harnishfeger, 1995) and may have been necessary for the emergence of consciousness and higher-order cognition. But the consciousness initially applied to social intelligence was eventually applied to other domains, and the result was an animal that created a complex and rapidly changing culture, which affected its members' inclusive fitness more than its biology.

The Challenges of Consciousness

OTHER MINDS, NEW PROBLEMS

As we have commented earlier, however, possessing consciousness may have its drawbacks. For one thing, if consciousness provides a window to one's own thoughts and educated guesses to the thoughts of others, it is highly likely that those "others" possess the same insight. This makes social intercourse all the more complicated, particularly for one who may be less proficient at "mind reading" than others. Because intentional states are actually the causes of behavior, any ineffectiveness in taking these states into account when strategically interacting with others who are also able to detect intentionality would be highly detrimental. If other individuals do employ such knowledge effectively (i.e., to adaptive ends) while the self merely represents others' mental states and perseveres with its old unconscious devices, then unavoidably the self's genetic fitness would become reduced significantly. For the successful organism, however, the structured and organized use of intentionality – again, a categorically new brand of social information perhaps undetectable by any other species – may have elaborated these already existing psychological adaptations by applying strategic inferential mechanisms involved in assessing other agents' motives (Haslam, 1997).

COUNTER-INTUITIVE CHALLENGES OF CONSCIOUSNESS

In addition to the problems of dealing with other self-aware conspecifics, there may also be some counter-intuitive detriments of self-consciousness. According to Trivers (1981, 1985), being self-conscious of certain proximate, socially proscribed motivations could put someone at a disadvantage relative to those who were able to mask these intentions through either self-deception or through the targeted loss of conscious access to such motives. In effect, self-consciousness began to interfere with adaptive functioning in the social domain. The ability to represent one's own selfish intentions and motives can seriously disrupt the efficiency of adaptive behaviors because these motives must be well hidden from others for adaptive outcomes to occur. Because emotions are closely tied to intentions, the ability to engage in adaptive social behaviors may be affected negatively by having these selfish intentions "leak" through behavior (Ekman & Friesen, 1975). Social partners may be able to detect ulterior motives through a variety of subtle, affectively induced behavioral cues, such as a higher than normal tone of voice, avoid-

ance of eye contact, and defensive posturing. Because individuals who leaked these cues in the environment of evolutionary adaptedness were less able to deceive others in the interest of their own genetic fitness, individuals who were able to deceive *themselves* about their own selfish motives may have been at a select advantage. These latter individuals possessed a new type of psychological adaptation – self-deception – that essentially militated against the behavioral effects of having knowledge of their own socially maligned intentions. As a consequence, they could deceive others more effectively in the service of their own genes (Nesse & Llloyd, 1992; Trivers, 1981, 1985). Trivers (1981) therefore reasons that "the mind must be structured in a very complex fashion, repeatedly split into public and private portions, with complicated interactions between the subsections" (p. 35).

Interestingly, implicit in this rationale is the suggestion that the "unconscious" of the Freudian variety has a more recent phylogenetic history than does consciousness, essentially emerging to serve as a repository for those self-epistemological states that may seriously hazard people's biological success. In addition to Freud, the existential philosopher Kierkegaard (1946/1849) seemed to capture these ideas when he wrote in *The Sickness Unto Death* that "with every increase in the degree of consciousness, and in proportion to that increase, the intensity of despair increases: the more consciousness, the more intense the despair" (p. 345). For the contemporary evolutionary psychologist, this despair is probably defined in terms of intrusive higher-order thoughts that interfere with an individual's adaptive information processing. Although interpreting correlations is an inherently difficult task, neurobiological findings of shrinkage in hippocampus volume in adult women who experienced childhood sexual abuse *and* who have also been diagnosed with post-traumatic stress disorder may support hypotheses arguing for an adaptive role of unconscious processes (Bremner et al., 1999; but see Gilbertson et al., 2002). Repression of such traumatic experiences so that they are inaccessible to declarative memory may help sustain brain regions devoted to short-term and autobiographical memory.

In another hypothesis, Burley (1979) has argued that, with the onset of consciousness, women who could detect the physiological cues signaling ovulation in their own bodies might begin consciously regulating their birth cycles. The likely result of this purposeful regulation is fewer pregnancies, which, although satisfying the "egocentric" interests of individual women (e.g., avoiding pain, having a manageable family size, accruing enough resources before having children), would also be necessarily detrimental to the genetic fitness of these same women. Indeed, some women, according to Burley, would fully exploit these physiological indices and avoid pregnancy altogether by continually abstaining from intercourse near the time of ovulation. Natural selection might have therefore concealed ovulation from women's conscious awareness, eliminating estrus and sharply reducing their sensitivity to this critical reproductive period. In fact, evolutionary psychological research indicates that ovulating women, who are not taking oral contraceptives, are more sexually receptive, as reflected by their emotional ratings of the smell of androstenone (e.g., Grammer, 1993) and also their dress and social signals, than are nonovulating women.

What is interesting about these accounts is that consciousness is considered to pose adaptive challenges to human beings, rather than to facilitate their genetic fitness. This argument flies in the face of any theorist who has ever boasted that human consciousness represents the pinnacle of evolutionary achievement. In contrast, in many regards, self-consciousness seems to be a maladaptive trait, providing individuals with access to information that causes them to engage in biologically poor decision making that disrupts their ability to carry out adaptive behaviors. Because self-consciousness tampered with evolutionarily stable behavioral patterns, it is very possible that self-consciousness was an evolutionary byproduct of some other adaptive system or adaptive trend in the human brain, rather

than a trait that evolved directly through natural selection. As we have suggested previously, self-consciousness may, for example, have been an outgrowth of a dramatic expansion of the frontal cortex during hominid evolution, a highly adaptive trend that greatly increased the general intelligence and planning abilities of these species (Banyas, 1999; Luria, 1973). In line with this, self-consciousness may rightly be considered an "all or nothing" phenomenon, rather than appearing in stages and degrees over the course of phylogeny. As Humphrey (1992) puts it, "There must have been a threshold where consciousness quite suddenly appeared – just as there is a threshold that we ourselves cross in going from sleep to wakefulness" (p. 206).

If self-consciousness emerged as an unavoidable byproduct of such a cortical expansion, it may not have been easily "removed" by natural selection because such a reorganization of the brain might have come with costly adaptive tradeoffs. Instead, it may have been more economical for nature to have "allowed" human consciousness by keeping the species' evolved neural organization intact while hammering out a series of constrained, novel psychological adaptations that were specifically designed to handle the new adaptive problems of consciousness.

This approach to consciousness differs substantially from those who have been searching for an adaptive explanation for the presence of such a representational capacity. For instance, in a discussion on the adaptive value of introspection, McGuire and Troisi (1998) note,

> There are good theoretical and empirical reasons for doubting the accuracy of introspections; the workings of most infrastructural systems are not available to awareness despite often heroic efforts to make them so. Nevertheless, it is reasonable to argue that a capacity that can so influence how we think, feel, and act is unlikely to have appeared by chance. Most persons introspect; most give credence to their introspections; and introspections often trigger strong emotions (e.g., shame) (p. 125).

Consciousness as a Double-Edged Sword

As we noted above, consciousness had its advantages, despite its apparently considerable disadvantages. The evolution of consciousness might have been responsible for a fundamentally novel set of psychological adaptations – specialized cognitive systems that went through the sieve of natural selection and that made human beings qualitatively distinct from other closely related species, such as chimpanzees. Once armed with these psychological adaptations that were specially fitted to the problem of consciousness, human beings were poised to become an enormously successful species, ultimately capable of radiating widely across both hemispheres and easily outcompeting competitor species. To this end, consciousness was a "blessing in disguise" because it forced heritable potentialities in individual members of the species that, in concert with consciousness, enabled these organisms to harness fitness advantages that occurred at unprecedented evolutionary rates. That is, once consciousness became "manned" with an ensemble of psychological adaptations that were functionally designed to operate it, the information made accessible by self-consciousness (i.e., the proximate causes of behavior) could be systematically controlled and exploited by the species.

We believe that this interpretation of the evolution of consciousness can go some distance in answering the following important question posed by Pinker (1997, p. 132): "If consciousness is useless – if a creature without it could negotiate the world as well as a creature with it – why would natural selection have favored the conscious one?"

On the Reorganization of More Ancient Primate Adaptations

How Previously Adaptive Social Behaviors Became Socially Maladaptive in Modern Human Beings

We propose that new psychological adaptations emerging in response to the evolution of consciousness were woven into an ancestral tapestry containing more ancient psychological adaptations (Povinelli, Bering, & Giambrone, 2000). It is this synchronic existence of the old and the new that characterizes human behavior and the breakdown of which results in dysfunctional consequences. Failure to adequately defend the self from knowledge of its own biologically oriented intentional states may lead to psychopathy (Becker, 1974; Fábrega, 2002). For instance, human males appear to have inherited ancestral adaptations for female sexual coercion (Thornhill & Palmer, 2000), but these ancient adaptations must peacefully coexist with more recently evolved psychological systems that enable others to infer males' sexual intentions and to rapidly transmit information dealing with socially proscribed behaviors. Under these social conditions, the inhibition of certain ancestrally adaptive behaviors, such as sexual coercion, becomes adaptive, and the evolution of psychological mechanisms (e.g., moral emotions such as guilt and shame) capable of disengaging such phylogenetically older responses becomes essential. This coexistence of ancient primate adaptations with recent human psychological adaptations is not well understood, as demonstrated by the recent statements of primatologist de Waal (2002):

> A major problem with the strategy of singling out rape for evolutionary explanation is that the behavior is shown by only a small minority. The same criticism applies to Daly and Wilson's (1988) well-known work on infanticide by stepparents…If child abuse by stepfathers is evolutionarily explained, why do so many more stepfathers lovingly care for their children than abuse them? And if rape is such an advantageous reproductive strategy, why are there so many more men who do not rape than who do? (p. 189, italics in original).

In fact, the relative rate of sexual coercion *should* drop off substantially once encroached upon by a representational system capable of tracking the self's intentions and also the intentions of others. In other primate species, such behaviors as forced copulation and infanticide may lead to retaliatory attacks, sometimes lethal, by offended higher-status parties who have direct perceptual access to such incidents (de Waal, 1982; Goodall, 1986; Kummer, 1971). However, (a) the inability of potential "victims" to perceive the hidden, aggressive intentions of potential "perpetrators"; (b) the inability of perpetrators to track others' knowledge of their behaviors; and (c) the inability of observers to intentionally communicate the occurrence of these transgressions to naïve others who did not witness the event foster a high level of frequency of such behaviors in non-human primates. Indeed, by all accounts, such behaviors almost certainly will occur whenever the conditions are "right" – that is, when dominant animals, or those with connections to dominant animals who may recruit others to the event through various alarm displays, are absent, making retaliation unlikely to occur.

This changes dramatically, however, with a species such as *Homo sapiens*, for whom social information is capable of being transmitted rapidly between parties far removed from the actual behavioral incident (Dunbar, 1993), and individuals (any one of whom is a potential perpetrator) are knowledgeable to this extent. In such cases, retaliation for social transgressions is likely to ensue as a direct consequence of others gaining knowledge of the proscribed behavior. What is defined as a transgression is going to be determined by the various socioecologies of different groups. However, in general such judgments will be made for those behaviors that pose a clear and present danger to the fitness interests of individual members of a community such that group functioning is adversely affected and may not adequately sustain the needs of individuals within the group as long as the behavior is allowed to occur. It is difficult to imagine any human socioecology where rape, homicide, and child abuse would not meet these criteria. But the real confound is the fact that, for human beings, the possibility of retaliation is no longer just a matter of who was physically present at the time of the transgression but also who *else* knows what Agent A did to Agent B; what these others believe Agent A's intentions were in doing

so; whether others know about or what they believe about *Agent A* engaging in similar behavior in the past; whether others believe *Agent B* "deserved" such treatment; whether others believe *Agent B* experienced physical or psychological pain from *Agent A's* behavior; whether others believe *Agent A's* behavior is diagnostic of a stable personality characteristic and is thus likely to occur again; whether *Agent A* knows something of relevance about those who know about the behavior and can use this information strategically; whether others believe *Agent A's* behavior was caused by his own intrinsic traits or was governed by the circumstances surrounding the event; whether others believe *Agent A's* claims about the causes of his own behavior; whether others believe *Agent A's* displays of remorse over or regret about his behavior are sincere; whether others believe *Agent A* possesses specialized knowledge that makes him valuable; and whether *Agent B* might have possessed such knowledge. In contrast, individual members of non-human primate species may have "witnesses" to their social transgressions in the technical sense of the term, but such witnesses pose minimal risks to genetic fitness given their inability to represent the epistemic states of those who did not perceive the proscribed incident.

This functional synchrony between old and new psychological adaptations should not be terribly surprising when considering the species' recent phyletic history. In terms of their general morphological characteristics, human beings seem to have undergone what Mayr (2001) refers to as *mosaic evolution*, which is "evolutionary change that occurs in a taxon at different rates for different structures, organs, or other components of the phenotype" (p. 288). That is, aside from a handful of trademark characteristics, *Homo sapiens* has remained largely unchanged at the level of its structural appearance from the time it last shared a common ancestor with the great apes. Derived traits distinguishing the species from other primates evolved mostly independently of those ancestral traits – the "morphological bulk" – that are responsible for the taxonomic classification of human beings as primates. Human beings continue to share with the African apes a basic *bauplan*, or body plan, where the only distinctly human characteristics are differences in the proportions of the arms and legs, the mobility of the thumb, amount of body hair, skin pigmentation, the size of the central nervous system and, related to this, the reduction in prognathic facial features (Mayr, 2001). By all accounts, human beings are primates first and hominids second; some scholars have even argued that the molecular differences between human beings and chimpanzees are too minimal to warrant classification as separate genera (Diamond, 1992).

It is unlikely that gross similarities and a small subset of novel derivations are limited to physical characteristics, however. Consciousness-based psychological adaptations in human beings have continued to interact with many of the cognitive programs supporting adaptive behaviors in non-human primates. This explains why human beings share so many behavioral patterns with chimpanzees and the other great apes, as we noted above. According to Povinelli and his colleagues (Bering & Povinelli, 2003; Povinelli, 2000; Povinelli et al., 2000), the ability to represent the underlying intentional states promoting these adaptive behavioral patterns (e.g., those involved in reconciliation, coalition formation) enabled human beings to reinterpret the separable actions comprising them in fundamentally novel ways. This reinterpretation process in turn led human beings to adopt new sets of behaviors that were qualitatively different from the evolved action configurations upon which they were based.

For example, human beings share with chimpanzees a number of gestural displays that are morphologically identical between the two species (see Povinelli, Bering, & Giambrone, 2003). One of these displays is the holding-out-a-hand gesture that is used by chimpanzees to recruit allies, to solicit reconciliation, and to seek physical contact with conspecifics (Bygott, 1979; de Waal, 1982). Without an attending higher-order cognitive system that enables the representation of the intentional states causing such behavior, however, the gesture cannot take

on any referential meaning. That is, although it serves adaptive ends (e.g., promoting physical contact such as grooming and consequently allowing subordinate chimpanzees to avoid future conflict with rivals), those chimpanzees receiving this communicative sign will fail to recognize the "aboutness" of the gestural display. This can explain why chimpanzees in the wild have not been observed to engage in referential gesturing (e.g., Plooij, 1978). To understand the referential nature of communicative displays, organisms must first be capable of representing those unobservable causal states that are behind intentional actions (Baldwin, 1991, 1993).

For instance, the holding-out-a-hand gesture that human beings inherited from an ancestral primate species is reinterpreted as being an intentionally communicative display (Povinelli et al., 2003; see also Franco & Butterworth, 1996; Vygotsky, 1962). Adult caregivers, for example, who witness their young infants extending their hand toward an out-of-reach object on the ground will automatically attribute the gesture to the infant's *wanting* the object and will subsequently retrieve it for them. Some theorists have even speculated that indexical pointing naturally emerges in ontogeny because there is a differential extension of this finger in the human hand (Itakura, 1996; Povinelli & Davis, 1994). The index finger is essentially "pulled out" by parental response during the course of early reaching attempts; those reaches that contain more explicit indexical extensions are interpreted more readily by caregivers as communicatively meaningful. Such indexical extensions may then be co-opted to provide a more accurate referential trajectory when engaging in both imperative and declarative communicative attempts using pointing.

Comparative experimental analyses of chimpanzees' and human beings' comprehension of pointing provide support for Povinelli's reinterpretation hypothesis (Povinelli et al., 1998). Chimpanzees that are confronted with a human experimenter who is pointing to the correct location of a hidden food reward fail to understand the communicative intention of this action. Rather, they choose a location to which the experimenter's hand is physically nearest, even though the pointing gesture clearly references a distal location. In contrast, 2-year-old children easily interpret the referential intent of the experimenter and are able to find the hidden prize in the distal location.

This principle is captured by Dennett's (1987) concept of the *intentional stance*, which essentially describes human beings' intuitive causal reasoning about the underlying reason, or purpose, that the designer of the action had in mind. Specifically, human beings appeal to the mental states of others when attempting to explain their actions. There is an intentionality that underlies all purposeful behavior; this intentionality consists of the range of proximate causes (e.g., emotions, cognitions, perceptions) to which the agent in question has conscious access. Povinelli reasons that, with the evolution of human beings, an awareness of this underlying intentionality engendered a new way of thinking about others' behaviors, where explanatory searches are intuitively launched in pursuit of the proximate causes of behaviors. This explanatory drive is extremely powerful in human beings and seems to extend to the physical domain as well (Baillargeon, 1994; Spelke, Breinlinger, Macomber, & Jacobson, 1992). Gopnik (2000) has argued that the need to understand the causes of events is automatic, compulsive, and affectively based. This argument puts intuitive explanatory theorizing about the causes of events in line with Geary's biologically primary abilities. A biologically secondary ability in this domain might be scientific explanation, which builds on the natural explanatory drive but which is cognitively effortful, requires extensive practice and training, and is mastered by only a subset of the species' population (McCauley, 2000).

The Evolution of Qualitatively Unique Psychological Adaptations in Human Beings

In addition to adding increasing complexity to pre-existing adaptations, metarepresenta-tion seems to have also constructed several fundamentally novel psychological adaptations that are entirely based and dependent upon this competency. For instance, although there are several species, particularly insects, where individual organisms systematically increase their own risk of mortality in the face of threats of interspecies predation to their larger colonies (e.g., Andrade, 1996; Holmes & Bethel, 1972; McAllister, Roitberg, & Weldon, 1990; McAllister & Roitberg, 1987; O'Connor, 1978; Poulin, 1992), human beings seem to be the only species where individual members commit suicide in response to the negative social appraisal of conspecifics. Although suicide is a leading cause of death in human beings, it is completely unheard of in other primate species beyond highly questionable anecdotal accounts. According to some theorists, shame is both the best predictor of suicide and its primary determinant (Lester, 1997). The capacity to experience shame requires self-consciousness in that it is an emotional reaction to negative self-appraisal (Gilbert, 1998; Tangney, 2001). Indeed, Baumeister (1990) has even referred to suicide as "escape from self." In addition, shame assumes metarepresentational abilities because it is a *secondary social emotion*, centering on others' perceptions and knowledge about the self's negative traits (Tangney, 2001).

These factors are interesting in light of the current discussion because suicide has been implicated as a probable adaptation facilitating inclusive fitness. In his "mathematical model of self-destruction," de Catanazaro (1986, 1987, 1991, 1992; see also Brown, Dehlen, Mils, Rick, & Biblarz, 1999) has shown that suicide is positively correlated with genetic burdensomeness to close kin; individuals whose lives negatively affect the reproductive opportunities of family members are significantly more likely to commit suicide than others. Adaptations subserving inclusive fitness are fairly common among various species (Hamilton, 1964); however, psychological adaptations involving human suicide promote inclusive fitness in a qualitatively different manner because they are dependent on access to the informational reservoir of intentionality. Human beings seem to be unusual among other primates in that the representation of another conspecific's mere thoughts, or the misperception of their thoughts, can engender affective reactions in the self that are translated into actual behavior. One such behavior is suicide, and it is therefore difficult to reason that consciousness serves only the role of an epiphenomenon in this case.

The Evolutionary Significance of the Mechanism of Consciousness

To state that the mechanism of consciousness is responsible for certain psychological adaptations is to say that, without having the means to access the type of information we are calling intentionality, many human behavioral patterns could simply not have evolved. This is the position that we endorse and also one that, we believe, most evolutionary psychologists would accept as well. However, we make no claims that people's explanations for their own behaviors must be correct (i.e., biologically relevant) for self-consciousness to have been a meaningful component of natural selection. Because there is overwhelming evidence that people do not understand the biological relevance of their own adaptive behaviors (see Buss, 1999; French et al., 2001), evolutionary psychologists rightly reject this notion of *propositional veracity*. This is typically what evolutionary psychologists are referring to when they state that self-consciousness has had little to do with the evolution of adaptive human behaviors. People do not need to know why they do what they do in order to behave adaptively (e.g., "I find my wife sexually attractive because she possesses features that indicate our mutual offspring will likely be resistant to parasites"). The *capacity* to ascribe intentions and beliefs to the self and to others, however, is something altogether different from this use of the term "consciousness" and *is* a pivotal element that is required for many adaptive human behaviors to occur (e.g., "I don't think Kevin is sincere about his intentions to marry my sister,

so I'm going to discourage her from seeing him again").

Although there is disagreement over the precise developmental mechanisms by which children come to understand the existence of other minds (e.g., Wellman, 1990), it seems reasonable to assume that gaining access to the type of information provided by self-consciousness (i.e., the self's own intentions), at the very least, would *facilitate* an understanding that others' behaviors are caused by similar means. It seems implausible to us that an ensemble of adaptive heuristics concerning various relationships between other people's behaviors and the causal states generating them could be adequately developed by an organism that does not first have the intellectual device required to conceptualize the general category of causal states (i.e., intentionality) in question. Theories are only as useful as the concepts that they contain; without an ability to conceptualize those mental constructs that are correlated to specific types of behaviors (e.g., "Jakob opened the cabinet because he *thought* that's where the bananas were"), such theories, whether wrong or right, simply could not be constructed.

Children's conceptual knowledge about mental states might become progressively enriched through language (see Tomasello & Bates, 2001) and also through personal experience involving intuitive hypothesis testing (Gopnik & Meltzoff, 1997), but such elaboration can only build on a basic capacity to represent such states to begin with. As Bloom (1998) writes, "Language is a tool for the expression and storage of ideas, but not a mechanism that could give rise to the capacity to generate and appreciate these ideas" (p. 215). This is supported by strong evidence of preverbal infants' abilities to attribute goals and intentions (Carpenter, Akhtar, & Tomasello, 1998; Meltzoff, 1995; but see Huang, Heyes, & Charman, 2001). By 9 to 12 months of age, human beings seem to be sensitive to the fact that intentional agents engage in goal-directed actions, that their behavior is teleological, and that their actions are self-generated. Throughout early ontogeny, children's understanding of intentionality becomes increasingly enriched, so that by the age of 4 years, they are able to represent the beliefs and knowledge states of other individuals and predict and explain their behavior on these grounds (see Wellman et al., 2001). Although slight differences may exist among societies in the relative rate of acquisition of such social cognitive skills, as well as the emphasis that is placed on the types of mental state attributions that are made, the development of this "theory of mind" system runs a standard epigenetic track across human societies (Tardif & Wellman, 2000; Wellman et al., 2001; see also Lillard, 1998).

To help illustrate, consider a case where, unlike mental states, the ability to naturally detect adaptively relevant information is an impossibility for human beings. The human sensory system is unable to detect dangerous levels of carbon monoxide, an odorless, colorless, tasteless gas that results from the incomplete combustion of hydrocarbon fuels. Carbon monoxide binds with hemoglobin with an affinity about 250 times that of oxygen, interfering with oxygen transport, delivery, and utilization. At high levels of exposure, carbon monoxide can lead to loss of consciousness, coma, and death.

From an evolutionary perspective, hydrocarbon fuels are apparently too recent an innovation for human beings to have evolved sensory capabilities designed to detect high levels of carbon monoxide. As a result, victims receive no obvious sensory warning that dangerous levels are present in the environment. If such information were accessible (e.g., through olfaction) and also present in ancestral conditions, natural selection would have likely favored those individuals who responded to the presence of carbon monoxide in adaptive fashion. Without such ability, however, no adaptive mechanisms associated with such toxic environmental conditions have evolved, and contemporary individuals are seriously threatened by this poisonous gas.

Fortunately, human beings have developed fairly effective strategies of detecting high levels of carbon monoxide by artificial means. Electrochemical devices, for instance, contain platinum electrodes embedded in an electrolyte solution, the combination of which creates a sensor that is designed to react with carbon monoxide molecules and to sound an auditory alarm when the gas is present. There is also, of course, the proverbial canary in the coal mine, whose odd behavior or death in poorly ventilated mining shafts serves to alert workers of dangerous levels of carbon monoxide.

To some extent, self-consciousness is similar to this canary in the coal mine, in that it provides us with conceptual access to a hidden source of information that has consequences for our genetic fitness. The canary provides us with access to information (carbon monoxide) in the external environment (the coal mine), whereas self-consciousness provides us with access to information (proximate causal states) in the internal environment (the mind). What is adaptive is not simply having access to these types of information, however, but rather how that information is translated into the production of actual behavioral responses. Merely "being" self-conscious without having functional psychological adaptations designed to respond to and control the flow of information dealing with the self's proximate causal states is like ignoring the dead canary in the coal mine. Information is only as useful as the psychological adaptations that are designed to harness and exploit it (for complementary accounts of consciousness, see Damasio, 2002; Frank, 1988).

The analogy falls short, however, in that self-consciousness provides human beings with access to information without requiring an artificial means of detection. The detection mechanism is naturally entrenched in the human cognitive system and does not rely on metaphors or external devices. Rather, the same concepts that are used to construct adaptive theories about other peoples' behaviors are also the ones represented through first-order psychological experiences.

The Serpent's Gift

"But the serpent said to the woman, 'You will not die. For God knows that when you eat of it your eyes will be opened, and you will be like God, knowing good and evil.' So...she took of its fruit and ate; and she also gave some to her husband, and he ate. Then the eyes of both were opened, and they knew they were naked" (Genesis 3: 4–7, Revised Standard Version).

The serpent's gift was self-knowledge, and with it the knowledge of others and the ability to acquire a knowledge of right and wrong. Nature is amoral. We may shudder at the way chimpanzees tear apart a colobus monkey they have caught or feel revulsion that a male lion kills the cubs sired by another when it acquires a new mate. But those emotions are uniquely human, and we do not judge as immoral the chimpanzee or the lion for acting in its own best genetic interest. With consciousness, however, comes social proscriptions. Actions can now be right or wrong, moral or immoral, even if they are executed in, what in ancient times, would have been our own best interest. Stepfathers still murder their stepchildren at rates many times greater than that of biological fathers (see Daly & Wilson, 1988), something the male lion might understand (if he were conscious). But with the advent of consciousness this behavior is now wrong, and because it is not socially sanctioned, it is rare in an absolute sense. Theft, adultery, assault, and murder still happen with high frequency in all societies (although rates differ considerably among societies), and most societies have proscriptions against them and punishment for transgressors who are "caught in the act." Although most of us believe that there are some universal human rights, a look at the variety of behaviors that are judged as moral and immoral, legal and illegal, in cultures around the world suggests that this may not be so. For example, although modern Westerners are aghast by infanticide, it is expected, under some circumstances, in some cultures (see Hrdy, 1999); the treatment of women varies considerably across cultures and history, each culture believing that its view is the morally correct one. (According to Genesis, it was woman who first ate of the tree of knowledge, and this has influenced her status in many cultures over the past two millennia.)

So consciousness did not provide a moral code, but it did provide the ability to see things from another's perspective, and with it the knowledge of good and evil, at least as defined within a particular society.

Consciousness also provided a view of the mind of the gods. With consciousness comes the need for explanation. We look for causes, for intentionality, not only in the actions of others but also in the events that surround us. If Homer's behavior is motivated by his knowledge or his wishes, might not the behavior of lightning or rain be motivated similarly? There is a reason for everything, our consciousness tells us, and in prescientific days it was the gods or spirits that made things happen – gods or spirits we imbued with human-like motivation through our theory of mind.

The Role of Consciousness in Religion: Spirits, Gods, and Morality

Our ancestors' behaviors were mediated not only by the social forces that be, as are chimpanzees' behaviors, but also by the assumptions that people made about what was appropriate and inappropriate, moral and immoral, evil and righteous. These beliefs were supported by intuitions about fairness and injustice, but were also strongly enforced by the community's shared belief in supernatural agents who were envisioned as having a vested interest in moral affairs. Some of these deontological assumptions, such as "one should never steal," were universal in nature because they contravened the fitness interests of individual members of any social group. Other deontological assumptions, such as "one should never disobey one's maternal grandfather," were limited to individual cultures, because in some societies following such orders was adaptive whereas in other socioecologies it was either maladaptive or not sufficiently adaptive to be supported through custom (Reynolds & Tanner, 1995).

Although subscribing to these moral and conventional rules led to social harmony in the group, which ultimately subserved the individual interests of in-group members, people were easily tempted to go astray, especially when they felt that they were not being observed by social others and when they could benefit through transgressing. Unfortunately, human beings have never been especially good at avoiding detection, and they are prone to overestimating their ability to deceive others. Such errors can be genetically catastrophic, because the payoffs for a successful social transgression (e.g., stealing a neighbor's food) are not necessarily worth the risk of getting caught and facing the punitive actions of the other ingroup members.

Under conditions where individuals are uncertain of the presence of social others and are presented with opportunities to increase their own genetic fitness at the expense of others, there was likely selective pressure for a heuristic strategy leading to the inhibition of the socially proscribed behavior. If individuals are inclined to represent the presence of some supernatural agency that has "privileged" perceptual access to the transgressor's behaviors and that is also capable of responding to these actions in the form of aversive life events, then this might facilitate the inhibition of the social transgression, therefore promoting an adaptive outcome. In fact, Pascal Boyer (1994, 2001; also Atran, 2002; but see Bering, 2002) has shown that human cognition is naturally susceptible to supernatural agent concepts because such concepts violate people's intuitive ontological assumptions. For example, gods and spirits are represented as being essentially human and as such activate our folk psychology systems (e.g., they can see and hear and think), but gods and spirits also violate our intuitive assumptions about other agents (e.g., they are invisible). Such scholars as Boyer (2001) and Atran (2002) have argued that religious concepts gain their entrance to mundane cognitive mechanisms through such attention-grabbing properties.

Concluding Remarks

A central challenge for evolutionary approaches to consciousness is devising empirical procedures that address its functional role in various psychological adaptations. Although the works of Trivers on the origins of defense mechanisms and that of Burley on the loss of human estrus, for instance, are regarded as highly plausible, such models have yet to be validated through empirical means. Comparative analyses between human beings and closely related species, such as chimpanzees, can be extraordinarily informative in this regard.

Although there may be few classes of behavior that are truly unique to human beings, there are numerous categories of natural social behaviors that occur cross-culturally in human beings that are rarely observed, or altogether absent, in closely related species. Suicide is one such case, but feral chimpanzees have also not been observed to manufacture symbolic artifacts; to partake in non-functional, group-specific ritualistic behavior; to translate their developmentally canalized repertoire of vocalizations into new strings of communicative meaning unique to certain populations; to physically care for ill, maimed, or otherwise importuned conspecifics; to engage in juvenile pretend play; to construct material (i.e., clothing) designed to cover their anogenital region; to kill or conspire to kill others who possess damaging knowledge; or to cooperate to solve novel problems. Even pointing behavior (for either declarative or imperative purposes) and direct teaching of novel tasks have only rarely been observed in chimpanzees (e.g., Boesch, 1991), and even these have been questioned (see Povinelli et al., 2000).

All of these behaviors (and others) are considered standard fare in human groups, whether small hunter-gatherer societies or large industrialized nation-states. What is important is that each of these categories of adaptive behaviors requires the presence of a functionally organized intentionality system that not only provides individuals with access to the hidden causes of behavior but also leads them to engage in adaptive behaviors. We have proposed throughout this chapter that consciousness endowed human beings with information *sui generis* in the form of mental states, and that once consciousness became standardized in human cognition, a new suite of adaptive behaviors, such as those listed above, evolved to satisfy its unique demands. There are no "precursory forms" of such behaviors in other primates because human beings alone faced the adaptive challenges of consciousness that led to their regular appearance in the species.

Note

1. Paleontologists refer to chimpanzees as a "conservative species," suggesting that they have changed relatively little over the past 7 million years, making them a reasonably good model for what our common ancestor may have been like.

References

Aiello, L. C., & Wheeler, P. (1995). The expensive-tissue hypothesis: The brain and the digestive system in human and primate evolution. *Current Anthropology, 36,* 199–221.

Alexander, R. D. (1989). Evolution of the human psyche. In P. Mellers & C. Stringer (Eds.), *The human revolution: Behavioural and biological perspectives on the origins of modern humans* (pp. 455–513). Princeton, NJ: Princeton University Press.

Andrade, M. C. B. (1996). Sexual selection for male sacrifice in the Australian redback spider. *Science, 271,* 70–72.

Atran, S. (2002). *In gods we trust: The evolutionary landscape of religion.* Oxford: Oxford University Press.

Baillargeon, R. (1994). How do infants learn about the physical world? *Current Directions in Psychological Science, 3,* 133–140.

Baldwin, D. A. (1991). Infants' contribution to the achievement of joint reference. *Child Development, 62,* 875–890.

Baldwin, D. A. (1993). Early referential understanding: Infants' ability to recognize referential acts for what they are. *Developmental Psychology, 29,* 832–843.

Barkow, J. H., Cosmides, L., & Tooby, J. (Eds.). (1992). *The adapted mind: Evolutionary psychology and the generation of culture.* New York: Oxford University Press.

Banyas, C. A. (1999). Evolution and phylogenetic history of the frontal lobes. In B. L. Miller & J. L. Cummings (Eds.), *The human frontal lobes: Functions and disorders* (pp. 83–106). New York: Guilford Press.

Baron-Cohen, S. (1995). *Mindblindness: An essay on autism and theory of mind.* Cambridge, MA: MIT Press.

Baumeister, R. F. (1990). Suicide as escape from self. *Psychological Review, 97,* 90–113.

Becker, E. (1974). *The denial of death.* New York: The Free Press.

Bering, J. M. (2002). The existential theory of mind. *Review of General Psychology, 6,* 3–24.

Bering, J. M. (2004a). A critical review of the "enculturation hypothesis": The effects of human rearing on great ape social cognition. *Animal Cognition, 7,* 201–212.

Bering, J. M. (2004b). Consciousness was a trouble-maker: On the general maladaptiveness of unsupported higher-order mental representation. *Journal of Mind and Behavior, 25,* 33–56.

Bering, J. M., Bjorklund, D. F., & Ragan, P. (2000). Deferred imitation of object-related actions in human-reared juvenile chimpanzees and orangutans. *Developmental Psychobiology, 36,* 218–232.

Bering, J. M., & Povinelli, D. J. (2003). Comparing cognitive development. In D. Maestripieri (Ed.), *Primate psychology: Bridging the gap between the mind and behavior of human and nonhuman primates* (pp. 205–233). Cambridge, MA: Harvard University Press.

Bjorklund, D. F., & Bering, J. M. (2000). The evolved child: Applying evolutionary developmental psychology to modern schooling. *Learning and Individual Differences, 12,* 347–373.

Bjorklund, D. F., & Bering, J. M. (2003a). Big brains, slow development, and social complexity: The developmental and evolutionary origins of social cognition. In M. Brüne, H. Ribbert, & W. Schiefenhövel (Eds.). *The social brain: Evolutionary aspects of development and pathology* (pp. 113–151). New York: Wiley.

Bjorklund, D. F., & Bering, J. M. (2003b). The development of deferred imitation in juvenile chimpanzees. *Developmental Review, 23,* 389–412.

Bjorklund, D. F., & Harnishfeger, K. K. (1995). The role of inhibition mechanisms in the evolution of human cognition and behavior. In F. N. Dempster & C. J. Brainerd (Eds.), *New* perspectives on interference and inhibition in cognition (pp. 141–173). New York: Academic Press.

Bjorklund, D. F., & Kipp, K. (2001). Social cognition, inhibition, and theory of mind: The evolution of human intelligence. In R. J. Sternberg & J. C. Kaufman (Eds.), *The evolution of intelligence* (pp. 27–53). Mahwah, NJ: Erlbaum.

Bjorklund, D. F., & Pellegrini, A. D. (2002). *The origins of human nature: Evolutionary developmental psychology*. Washington, DC: American Psychological Association.

Bjorklund, D. F., & Rosenberg, J. S. (2005). The role of developmental plasticity in the evolution of human cognition: Evidence from enculturated, juvenile great apes. In B. Ellis & D. F. Bjorklund (Eds.), *Origins of the social mind: Evolutionary psychology and child development* (pp. 45–75). New York: Guilford.

Bjorklund, D. F., Yunger, J. L., Bering, J. M., & Ragan, P. (2002). The generalization of deferred imitation in enculturated chimpanzees (*Pan troglodytes*). *Animal Cognition, 5,* 49–58.

Bloom, P. (1998). Some issues in the evolution of language and thought. In D. Cummins & C. Allen (Eds.), *The evolution of mind* (pp. 204–223). New York: Oxford University Press.

Boesch, C. (1991). Teaching among wild chimpanzees. *Animal Behavior, 41,* 530–532.

Boesch, C. (1993). Toward a new image of culture in chimpanzees. *Behavioral and Brain Sciences, 16,* 514–515.

Bogin, B. (1999). *Patterns of human growth* (2nd ed.). Cambridge: Cambridge University Press.

Bonner, J. T. (1988). *The evolution of complexity by means of natural selection*. Princeton, NJ: Princeton University Press.

Boyer, P. (1994). *The naturalness of religious ideas: A cognitive theory of religion*. Berkeley: University of California Press.

Boyer, P. (2001). *Religion explained: The evolutionary origins of religious thought*. New York: Basic Books.

Bremner, J. D., Narayan, M., Staib, L. H., Southwick, S. M., McGlashan, T., & Charney, D. S. (1999). Neural correlates of childhood sexual abuse in women with and without posttraumatic stress disorder. *American Journal of Psychiatry, 156,* 1787–1795.

Brooks-Gunn, J., & Lewis, M. (1984). The development of early self-recognition. *Developmental Review, 4,* 215–239.

Brown, R. M., Dehlen, E., Mils, C., Rick, J., & Biblarz, A. (1999). Evaluation of an evolutionary model of self-preservation and self-destruction. *Suicide & Life-Threatening Behavior, 29,* 58–71.

Burley, N. (1979). The evolution of concealed ovulation. *American Naturalist, 114,* 835–838.

Buss, D. M. (1995). Evolutionary psychology. *Psychological Inquiry, 6,* 1–30.

Buss, D. M. (1999). *Evolutionary psychology: The new science of the mind*. Boston: Allyn and Bacon.

Buss, D. M. (Ed.) (2005). *Evolutionary psychology handbook*. New York: Wiley.

Buss, D. M., Haselton, M. G., Shackelford, T. K., Bleske, A. L., & Wakefield, J. C. (1998). Adaptations, exaptations, and spandrels. *American Psychologist, 53,* 533–548.

Bygott, J. D. (1979). Agonistic behavior, dominance, and social structure in wild chimpanzees of the Gombe National Park. In D. A. Hamburg & E. R. McCown (Eds.), *The great apes: Perspectives on human evolution* (Vol. 5, pp. 307–317). Menlo Park: Benjamin/Cummings.

Byrne, R., & Whiten, A. (Eds.) (1988). *Machiavellian intelligence: Social expertise and the evolution of intellect in monkeys, apes, and humans*. Oxford: Clarendon.

Call, J., & Carpenter, M. (2003) On imitation in apes and children. *Infancia y Aprendizaje, 26,* 325–349.

Call, J., & Tomasello, M. (1999). A nonverbal false belief task: The performance of children and great apes. *Child Development, 70,* 381–395.

Carpenter, M., Akhtar, N., & Tomasello, M. (1998). Fourteen- through 18-month-old infants differentially imitate intentional and accidental actions. *Infant Behavior & Development, 21,* 315–330.

Cartwright, J. (2000). *Evolution and human behavior: Darwinian perspectives on human nature*. Cambridge, MA: MIT Press.

Chalmers, D. J. (1996). *The conscious mind: In search of a fundamental theory*. New York: Oxford University Press.

Cosmides, L., & Tooby, J. (1987). From evolution to behavior: Evolutionary psychology as the missing link. In J. Dupre (Ed.), *The latest on the best essays on evolution and optimality* (pp. 277–306). Cambridge, MA: MIT Press.

Cotterill, R. M. J. (2001). Evolution, cognition and consciousness. *Journal of Consciousness Studies, 8,* 3–17.

Crook, J. M. (1980). *The evolution of human consciousness*. Oxford: Clarendon Press.

Daly, M., & Wilson, M. (1988). *Homicide*. New York: Aldine.

Damasio, A. R. (2002). A note on the neurobiology of emotions. In S. G. Post, L. G. Underwood, J. P. Schloss, & W. B. Hurlbut (Eds.), *Altruism and altruistic love: Science, philosophy, and religion in dialogue* (pp. 264–271). London: Oxford University Press.

de Catanazaro, D. (1986). A mathematical model of evolutionary pressures regulating self-preservation and self-destruction. *Suicide & Life-Threatening Behavior, 16*, 166–181.

de Catanzaro, D. (1987). Evolutionary pressures and limitations to self-preservation. In C. Crawford, M. Smith, & D. Krebs (Eds.), *Sociobiology and psychology* (pp. 311–333). Hillsdale, NJ: Erlbaum.

de Catanzaro, D. (1991). Evolutionary limits to self-preservation. *Ethology & Sociobiology, 12*, 13–28.

de Catanzaro, D. (1992). Prediction of self-preservation failures on the basis of quantitative evolutionary biology. In R. W. Maris, A. L. Berman, J. T. Maltsberger, & R. I. Yufit (Eds.), *Assessment and prediction of suicide* (pp. 607–621). New York: Guilford Press.

Dennett, D. (1987). *The intentional stance*. Cambridge, MA: Bradford Books/MIT Press.

de Waal, F. B. M. (1982). *Chimpanzee politics: Power and sex among apes*. London: Jonathan Cape.

de Waal, F. B. M. (1986). The integration of dominance and social bonding in primates. *Quarterly Review of Biology, 61*, 459–479.

de Waal, F. B. M. (2002). Evolutionary psychology: The wheat and the chaff. *Current Directions in Psychological Science, 11*, 187–191.

Diamond, J. M. (1992). *The third chimpanzee: The evolution and future of the human animal*. New York: Harper Collins.

Donald, M. (2000). The central role of culture in cognitive evolution: A reflection on the myth of the "isolated mind." In L. P. Nucci, G. B. Saxe, & E. Turiel (Eds.), *Culture, thought, and development* (pp. 19–38). Mahwah, NJ: Erlbaum.

Dunbar, R. I. M. (1992). Neocortex size as a constraint on group size in primates. *Journal of Human Evolution, 20*, 469–493.

Dunbar, R. I. M. (1993). Coevolution of neocortical size, group size and language in humans. *Behavioral and Brain Sciences, 16*, 681–735.

Dunbar, R. I. M. (1995). Neocortex size and group size in primates: A test of the hypothesis. *Journal of Human Evolution, 28*, 287–296.

Dunbar, R. I. M. (2001). Brains on two legs: Group size and the evolution of intelligence. In F. B. M. de Waal (Ed.), *Tree of origins: What primate behavior can tell us about human social evolution* (pp. 173–191). Cambridge, MA: Harvard University Press.

Ekman, P., & Friesen, W. V. (1975). *Unmasking the face*. Englewood Cliffs, NJ: Prentice-Hall.

Fábrega, H. (2002). *Origins of psychopathology: The phylogenetic and cultural basis of mental illness*. New Brunswick, NJ: Rutgers University Press.

Finlay, B. L., & Darlington, R. D. (1995, June 16). Linked regularities in the development and evolution of mammalian brains. *Science, 268*, 1579–1584.

Finlay, B. L., Darlington, R. B. , & Nicastro, N. (2001) Developmental structure in brain evolution. *Behavioral and Brain Sciences 24*, 263–308.

Fouts, R. (1997). *Next of kin: What chimpanzees have taught me about who we are*. New York: William Morrow.

Franco, F., & Butterworth, G. (1996). Pointing and social awareness: Declaring and requesting in the second year. *Journal of Child Language, 23*, 307–336.

Frank, R. H. (1988). *Passions with reason: The strategic role of the emotions*. New York: Norton.

French, J. A., Kamil, A. C., & Ledger, D. W. (2001). *Evolutionary psychology and motivation. Vol. 47 of the Nebraska Symposium on Motivation*. Lincoln, NE: University of Nebraska Press.

Gallup, G. G. Jr. (1979). *Self-recognition in chimpanzees and man: A developmental and comparative perspective*. New York: Plenum Press.

Gallup, G. G. Jr. (1982). Self-awareness and the emergence of mind in primates. *American Journal of Primatology, 2*, 237–248.

Gallup, G. G. Jr. (1985). Do minds exist in species other than our own? *Neuroscience & Biobehavioral Reviews, 9*, 631–641.

Gaulin, S. J. C., & McBurney, D. H. (2001). *Psychology: An evolutionary approach*. Upper Saddle River, NJ: Prentice Hall.

Geary, D. C. (1995). Reflections of evolution and culture in children's cognition: Implications for mathematical development and instruction. *American Psychologist, 50*, 24–37.

Geary, D. C. (2001). Sexual selection and sex differences in social cognition. In A. V. McGillicuddy-DeLisi & R. DeLisi (Eds.), *Biology, society, and behavior: The development of sex differences in cognition* (pp. 23–53). Greenwich, CT: Ablex.

Geary, D. C. (2004). *The origin of mind: Evolution of brain, cognition, and general intelligence*. Washington, DC: American Psychological Association.

Geary, D. C., & Flinn, M. V. (2001). Evolution of human parental behavior and the human family. *Parenting: Science and Practice*, 1, 5–61.

Geary, D. C., & Huffman, K. (2002). Brain and cognitive evolution: Forms of modularity and functions of mind. *Psychological Bulletin*, 128, 667–698.

Gelman, R., & Williams, E. M. (1998). Enabling constraints for cognitive development and learning: Domain-specificity and epigenesis. In D. Kuhn & R. S. Siegler (Eds.), *Cognition, perception, and language* (Vol. 2, pp. 575–630). New York: Wiley.

Gilbert, P. (1998). What is shame? Some core issues and controversies. In P. Gilbert & B. Andrews (Eds.), *Shame: Interpersonal behavior, psychopathology, and culture. Series in affective science* (pp. 3–38). New York: Oxford University Press.

Gilbertson, M. W., Shenton, M. E., Ciszewski, A., Kasai, K., Lasko, N. B., Orr, S. B., & Pittman, R. A. (2002). Smaller hippocampal volume predicts pathologic vulnerability to psychological trauma. *Nature Neuroscience*, 5, 1242–1247.

Goodall, J. (1986). *The chimpanzees of Gombe*. Cambridge, MA: Belknap.

Gopnik, A. (2000). Explanation as orgasm and the drive for causal knowledge: The function, evolution, and phenomenology of the theory formation system. In F. C. Keil & R. A. Wilson (Eds.), *Explanation and cognition* (pp. 299–323). Cambridge, MA: MIT Press.

Gopnik, A., & Meltzoff, A. N. (1997). *Words, thoughts, and theories*. Cambridge, MA: MIT Press.

Gould, S. J. (1977). *Ontogeny and phylogeny*. Cambridge, MA: Harvard University Press.

Gould, S. J. (1991). Exaptation: A crucial tool for evolutionary psychology. *Journal of Social Issues*, 47, 43–65.

Grammer, K. (1993). 5-!a-androst-16en-3!a-on: A male pheromone? A brief report. *Ethology & Sociobiology*, 14, 201–207.

Greenfield, P., Maynard, A., Boehm, C., & Schmidtling, E. Y. (2000). Cultural apprenticeship and cultural change: Tool learning and imitation in chimpanzees and humans. In S. T. Parker, J. Langer, & M. L. McKinney (Eds.), *Biology, brains, and behavior: The evolution of human development* (pp. 237–277). Santa Fe, NM: School of American Research Press.

Hamilton, W. D. (1964). The genetical theory of social behavior. *Journal of Theoretical Biology*, 7, 1–52.

Hare, B., Call, J., Agentta, B., & Tomasello, M. (2000). Chimpanzees know what conspecifics do and do not see. *Animal Behaviour*, 59, 771–785.

Hare, B., Call, J., & Tomasello, M. (2001). Do chimpanzees know what conspecifics know? *Animal Behaviour*, 61, 139–151.

Haslam, N. (1997). Four grammars for primate social relations. In J. A. Simpson & D. T. Kenrick (Eds.), *Evolutionary social psychology* (pp. 297–316). Mahwah, NJ: Erlbaum.

Holmes, J. C., & Bethel, W. M. (1972). Modification of intermediate host behavior by parasites. In E. U. Canning & C. A. Wrighs (Eds.), *Behavioural aspects of parasite transmission* (pp. 123–149). London: Academic Press.

Hrdy, S. B. (1999). *Mother Nature: A history of mothers, infants, and natural selection*. New York: Pantheon Books.

Huang, C.-T., Heyes, C., & Charman, T. (2002). Infants' behavioral reenactment of "failed attempts": Exploring the roles of emulation learning, stimulus enhancement, and understanding of intentions. *Developmental Psychology*, 38, 840–855.

Humphrey, N. K. (1976). The social function of intellect. In P. P. G. Bateson & R. A. Hinde (Eds.), *Growing points in ethology* (pp. 303–317). Cambridge: Cambridge University Press.

Humphrey, N. K. (1992). *A history of the mind: Evolution and the birth of consciousness*. New York: Simon & Schuster.

Humphrey, N. K. (2000). How to solve the mind-body problem. *Journal of Consciousness Studies*, 7, 5–20.

Itakura, S. (1996). Manual action in infant chimpanzees: A preliminary study. *Perceptual and Motor Skills*, 83, 611–614.

Jeannerod, M. (1999). To act or not to act: Perspectives on the representation of actions. *Quarterly Journal of Experimental Psychology*, 52, 1–29.

Jerrison, H. J. (1973). *Evolution of the brain and intelligence*. New York: Academic Press.

Joffe, T. H. (1997). Social pressures have selected for an extended juvenile period in primates. *Journal of Human Evolution, 32*, 593–605.

Jolly, A. (1991). Conscious chimpanzees? A review of recent literature. In C. A. Ristau (Ed.), *Cognitive ethology: The minds of other animals. Essays in honor of Donald R. Griffin: Comparative cognition and neuroscience* (pp. 231–252). Hillsdale, NJ: Erlbaum.

Kaplan, H., Hill, K., Lancaster, J., & Hurtado, A. M. (2000). A theory of human life history evolution: Diet intelligence, and longevity. *Evolutionary Anthropology, 9*, 156–185.

Karmiloff-Smith, A. (1992). *Beyond modularity: A developmental perspective on cognitive science*. Cambridge, MA: MIT Press.

Kierkegaard, S. (1946). *A Kierkegaard anthology* (R. Bretall, Ed.). New York: Modern Library. (Work originally published 1849)

Kummer, H. (1971). *Primate societies: Group techniques of ecological adaptation*. Chicago: Aldine.

Lester, D. (1997). The role of shame in suicide. *Suicide & Life Threatening Behavior, 27*, 352–361.

Lickliter, R., & Honeycutt, H. (2003). Developmental dynamics: Towards a biologically plausible evolutionary psychology. *Psychological Bulletin, 129*, 819–835.

Lillard, A. S. (1998). Ethnopsychologies: Cultural variations in theory of mind. *Psychological Bulletin, 123*, 3–32.

Luria, A. R. (1973). *The working brain: An introduction to neuropsychology*. New York: Basic Books.

Mayr, E. (2001). *What evolution is*. New York: Basic Books.

McAllister, M. K., & Roitberg, B. D. (1987). Adaptive suicidal behaviour in pea aphids. *Nature, 328*, 797–799.

McAllister, M. K., Roitberg, B. D., & Weldon, K. L. (1990). Adaptive suicide in pea aphids: Decisions are cost sensitive. *Animal Behaviour, 40*, 167–175.

McCauley, R. N. (2000). The naturalness of religion and the unnaturalness of science. In F. C. Keil & R. A. Wilson (Eds.), *Explanation and cognition* (pp. 61–85). Cambridge: Cambridge University Press.

McGrew, W. C. (1992). *Chimpanzee material culture: Implication for human evolution*. Cambridge: Cambridge University Press.

McGuire, M. T., & Troisi, A. (1998). *Darwinian psychiatry*. New York: Oxford University Press.

Meltzoff, A. N. (1995). Understanding the intentions of others: Re-enactment of intended acts by 18-month-old children. *Developmental Psychology, 31*, 838–850.

Mithen, S. (1996). *The prehistory of the mind: The cognitive origins of art, religion and science*. London: Thames and Hudson.

Nesse, R. M., & Lloyd, A. T. (1992). The evolution of psychodynamic mechanisms. In J. H. Barkow, L. Cosmides, & J. Tooby (Eds.), *The adapted mind* (pp. 601–624). New York: Oxford University Press.

O'Connor, R. J. (1978). Brood reduction in birds: Selection for fratricide, infanticide and suicide. *Animal Behaviour, 26*, 79–96.

Palmer, J. A., & Palmer, L. K. (2002). *Evolutionary psychology: The ultimate origins of human behavior*. Needham Heights, MA: Allyn & Bacon.

Parker, S. T., Mitchell, R. W., & Boccia, M. L. (2006). *Self-awareness in animals and humans: Developmental perspectives*. Cambridge, MA: Cambridge University Press.

Pinker, S. (1994). *The language instinct: How the mind creates language*. New York: Morrow.

Pinker, S. (1997). *How the mind works*. New York: Norton.

Pinker, S. (2002). *The blank slate: The modern denial of human nature*. New York: Viking Press.

Plooij, F. X. (1978). Some basic traits of language in wild chimpanzees? In A. Lock (Ed.), *Action, gesture and symbol* (pp. 111–131). London: Academic Press.

Poulin, R. (1992). Altered behaviour in parasitized bumblebees: Parasite manipulation or adaptive suicide? *Animal Behaviour, 44*, 174–176.

Povinelli, D. J. (2000). *Folk physics for apes*. New York: Oxford University Press.

Povinelli, D. J., Bering, J. M. (2002). The mentality of apes revisited. *Current Directions in Psychological Science, 11*, 115–119.

Povinelli, D. J., Bering, J. M., & Giambrone, S. (2000). Toward a science of other minds: Escaping the argument by analogy. *Cognitive Science, 24*, 509–541.

Povinelli, D. J., Bering, J., & Giambrone, S. (2003). Chimpanzee 'pointing': Another error of the argument by analogy? In S. Kita (Ed.), *Pointing: Where language, culture, and cognition meet* (pp. 35–68). Hillsdale, NJ: Erlbaum.

Povinelli, D. J., & Cant, J. G. H. (1995). Arboreal clambering and the evolution of self-conception. *Quarterly Review of Biology*, 70, 393–421.

Povinelli, D. J., Davis, D. R. (1994). Differences between chimpanzees (*Pan troglodytes*) and humans (*Homo sapiens*) in the resting state of the index finger: Implications for pointing. *Journal of Comparative Psychology*, 108, 134–139.

Povinelli, D. J., & Eddy, T. J. (1996a). What young chimpanzees know about seeing. *Monograph of the Society for Research in Child Development*, 61 (3), no. 247.

Povinelli, D. J., & Eddy, T. J. (1996b). Factors influencing chimpanzees' (*Pan troglodytes*) recognition of attention. *Journal of Comparative Psychology*, 110, 336–345.

Povinelli, D. J., & Eddy, T. J. (1996c). Chimpanzees: Joint visual attention. *Psychological Science*, 7, 129–135.

Povinelli, D. J., & O'Neill, D. K. (2000). Do chimpanzees use their gestures to instruct each other? In S. Baron-Cohen, H. Tager-Flusberg, & D. J. Cohen (Eds.), *Understanding other minds* (pp. 459–487). Oxford: Oxford University Press.

Povinelli, D. J., Perilloux, H. K., Reaux, J. E., & Bierschwale, D. T. (1998). Young and juvenile chimpanzees' (*Pan troglodytes*) reactions to intentional versus accidental and inadvertent actions. *Behavioural Processes*, 42, 205–218.

Preuss, T. M. (2001). The discovery of cerebral diversity: An unwelcome scientific revolution. In D. Falk & K. Gibson (Eds.), *Evolutionary anatomy of the primate cerebral cortex* (pp. 138–164). Cambridge: Cambridge University Press.

Reaux, J. E., Theall, L. A., & Povinelli, D. J. (1999). A longitudinal investigation of chimpanzee's understanding of visual perception. *Child Development*, 70, 275–290.

Reiss, D., & Marino, L. (2001). Mirror self-recognition in the bottlenose dolphin: A case of cognitive convergence. *Proceedings of the National Academy of Sciences USA*, 98, 5937–5942.

Reynolds, V., & Tanner, R. (1995). *The social ecology of religion*. New York: Oxford University Press.

Rilling, J. K., & Insel, T. R. (1999). The primate neocortex in comparative perspective using magnetic resonance imaging. *Journal of Human Evolution*, 37, 191–223.

Searle, J. R. (2000). Consciousness. *Annual Review of Neuroscience*, 23, 557–578.

Spelke, E. S., Breinlinger, K., Macomber, J., & Jacobson, K. (1992). Origins of knowledge. *Psychological Review*, 99, 605–632.

Stout, D, (2002). Skill and cognition in stone tool production: An ethnographic case study from Irian Jaya. *Current Anthropology*, 43, 693–722.

Suddendorf, T., & Whiten, A. (2001). Mental evolution and development: Evidence for secondary representation in children, great apes and other animals. *Psychological Bulletin*, 127, 629–650.

Swartz, K. B., Sarauw, D., & Evans, S. (1999). Cognitive aspects of mirror self-recognition in great apes. In S. T. Parker, R. W. Mitchell, & H. L. Miles (Eds.), *The mentalities of gorillas and orangutans: Comparative perspectives* (pp. 283–294). Cambridge: Cambridge University Press.

Tangney, J. P. (2001). Self-conscious emotions: The self as a moral guide. In A. Tesser, D. A. Stapel, & J. V. Wood (Eds.), *Self and motivation: Emerging psychological perspectives* (pp. 97–117). Washington, DC: American Psychological Association.

Tardif, T., & Wellman, H. M. (2000). Acquisition of mental state language in Mandarin- and Cantonese-speaking children. *Developmental Psychology*, 36, 25–43.

Tattersall, I. (1998). *Becoming human: Evolution and human uniqueness*. New York: Harcourt Brace.

Thornhill, R., & Palmer, C. T. (2000). *A natural history of rape: Biological bases of sexual coercion*. Cambridge, MA: MIT Press.

Tobias, P. V. (1987). The brain of *Homo habilis*: A new level of organization in cerebral evolution. *Journal of Human Evolution*, 16, 741–761

Tomasello, M. (1996). Do apes ape? In C. Heyes & B. Galef (Eds.), *Social learning in animals: The role of culture* (pp. 319–346). San Diego: Academic Press.

Tomasello, M. (2000). Culture and cognitive development. *Current Directions in Psychological Science*, 9, 37–40.

Tomasello, M., & Bates, E. (2001). *Language development: The essential readings*. Oxford: Blackwell.

Tomasello, M., & Call, J. (1997). *Primate cognition*. Oxford: Oxford University Press.

Tomasello, M., Kruger, A. C., & Ratner, H. H. (1993). Cultural learning. *Behavioral and Brain Sciences*, 16, 495–511.

Tomasello, M., Savage-Rumbaugh, S., & Kruger, A. C. (1993). Imitative learning of actions on objects by children, chimpanzees, and enculturated chimpanzees. *Child Development, 64*, 1688–1705.

Tooby, J., & Cosmides, L. (1992). The psychological foundations of culture. In J. H. Barkow, L. Cosmides, & J. Tooby (Eds.), *The adapted mind: Evolutionary psychology and the generation of culture* (pp. 19–139). New York: Oxford University Press.

Tooby, J., Cosmides, L., & Barrett, H. C. (2003). The second law of thermodynamics is the first law of psychology: Evolutionary developmental psychology and the theory of tandem, coordinated inheritances: Comment on Lickliter and Honeycutt (2003). *Psychological Bulletin, 129*, 858–865.

Trivers, R. (1981). Sociobiology and politics. In E. White (Ed.), *Sociobiology and human politics* (pp. 1–43). Lexington, MA: D. C. Health.

Trivers, R. (1985). *Social evolution*. Reading, MA: Benjamin/Cummings.

Tulving, E. (1985). How many memory systems are there? *American Psychologist, 40*, 385–398.

Vygotsky, L. S. (1962). *Thought and language*. Cambridge, MA: MIT Press.

Wellman, H. M. (1990). *The child's theory of mind.* Cambridge, MA: MIT Press.

Wellman, H. M., Cross, D., & Watson, J. (2001). Meta-analysis of theory-of-mind development: The truth about false belief. *Child Development, 72*, 655–684.

Whiten, A. (1998). Imitation of sequential structure of actions by chimpanzees (*Pan troglodytes*). *Journal of Comparative Psychology, 112*, 270–281.

Whiten, A., & Byrne, R. W. (1988). The manipulation of attention in primate tactical deception. In R. W. Byrne & A. Whiten (Eds.). *Machiavellian intelligence: Social expertise and the evolution of intellect in monkeys, apes, and humans* (pp. 211–223). Oxford: Clarendon Press.

Whiten, A., Custance, D. M., Gómez, J. C., Teixidor, P., & Bard, K. A. (1996). Imitative learning of artificial fruit processing in children (*Homo sapiens*) and chimpanzees (*Pan troglodytes*). *Journal of Comparative Psychology, 110*, 3–14.

Whiten, A., Goodall, J., McGrew, W. C., Nishida, T., Reynolds, V., Sugiyama, Y., Tutin, C. E. G., Wrangham, R. W., & Boesch, C. (1999). Cultures in chimpanzees. *Nature* 399, (Jun), 682–685.

CHAPTER 23

Anthropology of Consciousness

C. Jason Throop and Charles D. Laughlin

From the standpoint of human evolution, then, both a social matrix of conduct and the expansion of the cortex are among the necessary conditions for the emergence of a human mind or a human personality structure. Just as bodily evolution and mental evolution cannot be separated, neither can psychological structuralization and the social evolution of mankind. To behave humanly as an adult the individual must become psychologically organized in a socialization process. His biological equipment is only one of the conditions necessary for this. Social or sensory isolation is a fatal handicap. Hence, it seems reasonable to suppose that the emergence of culture as a prime attribute of human societies must be somehow connected with a novel psychological structure rooted in the social behavior of the gregarious primate that gave rise to man. It is at this point that organic evolution, behavioral evolution, and the old problem of mental evolution come to a common focus.
Irving Hallowell, *Culture and Experience* (1955)

Abstract

In this chapter we discuss the history of anthropological studies of consciousness since the mid-19th century. We cover the vision of an anthropology of consciousness apparent in the writings of some of the discipline's forefathers – including Adolph Bastian, Franz Boas, and Emile Durkheim, among others – before turning to examine the history of thought among anthropologists living during various eras up to and including the present. The development of consciousness studies is tracked through mid- to late-20th century structuralism, practice theory, neuroanthropology, and the symbolic-interpretative approaches. These developments are then shown to have culminated in contemporary consciousness-related approaches, including cognitive anthropology, psychocultural anthropology, cultural psychology, phenomenological anthropology, the anthropology of the senses, and cultural neurophenomenology. Among the issues discussed are: the structures and vicissitudes of human experience; the extent to which culture influences perception, emotion, categorization, etc.; the biocultural constraints upon development as manifest in different cultures; the relationship between the evolution of the human nervous system and subjective experience; and how different societies encourage, evoke, and interpret alternative states of consciousness.

Introduction

Anthropology is the study of humanity from the broadest possible scope across time and space. Anthropologists study our species, *Homo sapiens*, throughout its millions of years of evolution to the present and beyond. Anthropological research investigates the variety of sociocultural forms from a cross-cultural perspective, utilizing data from hundreds of the estimated 4,000-plus societies living either during the present or in the not-so-distant past. Hence the range of perspectives within the discipline encompasses both biological and cultural concerns. Moreover, the anthropological study of living peoples tends to be naturalistic – that is, anthropologists live with people for extended periods of time, observing and learning from them in the context of everyday interaction and, with but rare exceptions, seldom rely upon experimentation. Rather, anthropologists are interested in recording the way of life of a people going about their normal daily activities.

Examining consciousness through the broad lens of anthropology offers at least three major advantages to consciousness studies. First, by combining evidence from both the evolutionary/biological and the cultural points of view, we are able to eliminate the pernicious effects of mind-body dualism that infest much of social scientific thinking. Second, by maximizing our picture of the range of states and contents of consciousness occurring cross-culturally, we are able to counter our own ethnocentrism – that is, our natural tendency to experience and think about things from our own cultural point of view. And third, by considering consciousness within its natural and local context, we are better able to evaluate how states and contents of consciousness dynamically relate to social interaction and environmental adaptation.

In this chapter we discuss the history of anthropological studies of consciousness since the mid-19th century. We cover the vision of an anthropology of consciousness apparent in the writings of some of the discipline's forefathers, before turning to examine the history of thought among anthropologists living during various eras up to and including the present. Most of our coverage is of American anthropologists who, more than any of the other schools of anthropology, considered consciousness-related issues to be important. We show how these early practical and theoretical ruminations centered on questions of the evolution of human consciousness, the putative differences between primitive versus civilized mentalities, and the role of the group in establishing collective states of consciousness. We track the development of consciousness studies through mid- to late-20th century structuralism, practice theory, neuroanthropology, and the symbolic-interpretative approaches. We show how these developments have culminated in contemporary consciousness-related approaches, including cognitive anthropology, cultural psychology, phenomenological anthropology, the anthropology of the senses, and cultural neurophenomenology. We conclude by listing some of the major findings pertaining to consciousness provided by anthropological research and understanding to date. We believe the most crucial of these findings is that anthropological studies of consciousness have often set out to problematize theoretical orientations that proffer accounts based upon unidirectional flows of causation *either* from the external organization of socioeconomically determined activity patterns and cultural symbols to the formation of contents and structures of consciousness *or* from pregiven structures of consciousness to those social and cultural forms that are held to be their material externalizations.

In the first section of this chapter we chose to dwell upon a few leading anthropological thinkers in both theory and methods. This focus is easily achieved, for the number of practicing anthropologists was relatively small during the 19th and first half of the 20th centuries, and most field-workers followed the theories and methods of their mentors. Margaret Mead used to say that in pre-World War II meetings of the American Anthropological Association everyone would fit into two buses when they would go on excursions, and had the buses fallen off a bridge, there would have been no American anthropology left. But the discipline has grown rapidly during the last half-century, and theoretical and methodological issues have become much more diverse. For this reason, the latter portions of the chapter focus less upon influential individual thinkers and more upon general approaches to the study of consciousness.

What Do We Mean by Consciousness?

Before we proceed any further, however, it is necessary to examine just what the term "consciousness" means. For Western scholars without the broader cross-cultural perspective embraced in anthropology, this might be deemed to be less of a problem (but see Hunt 1995), and accordingly, cognitive scientists and philosophers today generally define consciousness in terms of such concepts as intentionality, qualia, and the like. The central problem for anthropologists is, however, that such definitions are extremely ethnocentric, and very few non-Western cultures would view the matter in the way that Western consciousness researchers might conceive of it. From the anthropological perspective, the term "consciousness" presents particular difficulties as an empirical term in science. This is because it is difficult to operationalize, perhaps especially in cross-cultural research (see Laughlin, McManus, & d'Aquili, 1990, pp. 76–82; Peacock, 1975, p. 6; Winkelman 2000, pp. 9–15 for the problems confronted in operationalizing consciousness cross-culturally). Few anthropologists before the late 20th century underwent fieldwork intending to research consciousness per se. Why? Because few peoples on the planet would explicitly recognize the concept as it has been developed in the context of Western philosophy and science, and their languages would have no words that neatly gloss with the English term. Even among Indo-European languages the term does not translate perfectly.

For instance, the Spanish word *consciencia* connotes both awareness and what we would call "conscience" or "social consciousness," whereas in German there are at least two words, *Bewusstsein* and *Erkenntnis*, that cover the semantic field covered by the English term. And depending upon how we define consciousness, many of the world's non-Indo-European languages would either have no word at all or a term or terms that would have to be transposed to make them fit. For example, it is far easier to find a gloss for awareness or of the sensory or moral aspects of consciousness than it would be to find an exact gloss for, say, intentionality (see Duranti 1993, 2006), which in both Western philosophy and science is such a critical component – or for consciousness defined either as a complex system of psychophysical functions (e.g., Baars, 1997) or as implying self-awareness as a necessary condition (Donald, 1991).

It is fair to say then that most anthropological research pertaining to consciousness focuses upon those contents and properties of consciousness commonly encountered in the field – including such aspects as sensation (Classen, 1997; Howes, 1991; Stoller, 1989), time perception (Adam, 1994, Gell, 1992; Munn, 1992), perception of space (Pinxton, Van Dooren, & Harvey, 1983), emotion (Hinton, 1999; Lutz & White, 1986, cognition (D'Andrade, 1995; Geertz, 1983), apperception (Hallowell, 1955), memory (Antze & Lambek, 1996; Garro 2000, 2001) and symbolization and meaning (Foster, 1994; Foster & Botscharow, 1990), as well as questions of picture and illusion perception (Segall, Campbell, & Herscovits, 1966), reason (Garro, 1998; Hamill, 1990; Tambiah, 1990) creative imagination (Dissanayake, 1992), sense of the self (Heelas & Lock, 1981; Morris, 1994; White & Kirkpatrick 1986), cultural influence on experience (Jackson, 1989; Throop 2003a,b; Turner & Bruner, 1986), dream states (Lincoln, 1935; O'Nell, 1976), and other alternative states of consciousness (visions, hallucinations, drug-induced alternative states of consciousness (Laughlin, McManus & d'Aquili, 1990; Winkelman, 2000). Such Western scientific and philosophical notions as stream of consciousness, qualia, sphere of consciousness, intentional field, and the like are far less operationalizable cross-culturally, and hence *direct* evidence about them is difficult to uncover in the ethnopsychologies and ethnophilosophies of other peoples, save for those societies with religions that specialize in one form of phenomenology or another (e.g., certain Buddhist and Hindu societies; see Chapter 5).

That said, keeping the problem of ethnocentricity squarely in mind and focusing our attention on those attributes of consciousness that are in fact represented in the reports of peoples in widely disparate parts of the world, we may say that the question of consciousness has in one way or another been central to the anthropological enterprise from its inception as a discipline. The domain of consciousness has been the focus of both temporal (historical or evolutionary) and spatial (cross-cultural) concerns for over a century and a half. We may say with surety that anthropologists have had much to say about how observed differences and similarities in the contents of consciousness cross-culturally should inform theorizing about the structures and processes of consciousness as they are conceived in the social and physical sciences today.

A Brief Note on Methodology in Anthropology

Anthropological research on consciousness has traditionally been broadly qualitative and descriptive, often relying on structured and semi-structured interviewing, observing (and more recently videotaping) real-time social interaction, and participant observation. To this end, anthropologists have tended to rely upon a variety of methodologies that integrate third-person (i.e., observing), second-person (i.e., interviewing), and first-person (i.e., participant observation) perspectives. Of all of these methodologies, participant observation is perhaps the

most uniquely anthropological. Participant observation is based on the assumption that, through participating in the day-to-day activities of a particular culture or social group, a researcher will be able to glean insights from the effects of such participation on his or her own subjective states while also being granted access to observing social actors from the perspective of a co-actor who is him- or herself enmeshed in the field of social action as it unfolds.

Through participating in the everyday activities of actors who are at times drawing from significantly different assumptions about self, intersubjectivity, and reality, anthropologists are thus often forced to confront directly many of the assumptions that they otherwise take for granted as "natural" attributes of human mentation, behavior, and social life. In addition to its function in highlighting the contours for what Edmund Husserl (1913/1962) would have termed the anthropologist's "natural attitude," this methodology further allows anthropologists to explore how human consciousness is manifest in the context of everyday interaction.

Although a great deal of anthropological research has been grounded primarily upon this qualitative/descriptive foundation, cognitive anthropologists, psychological anthropologists, and evolutionary psychological anthropologists have also, at times, incorporated standardized psychological testing (e.g., Rorschach; see Hallowell, 1955), systematic data collection (e.g., triad testing, free-listing, paired comparisons, etc., see D'Andrade, 1995), and in some rare cases experimental designs (see Barrett, 2004; Heinrich et al., 2004) in the context of their investigations into the structures and contents of consciousness cross-culturally.

Structure and Content I: A History of Early Anthropological Thought and Research

Anthropology has been concerned with both the structural underpinnings and content variation in consciousness since at least the mid-19th century. The linchpin idea that permeated much of 19th-century thinking about the origins of human culture and consciousness was the "cultural idealist" (idealism from Latin *idealis*, "idea"; belief that knowledge and experience about the world derive from certain inherent structures of mind) notion of the *psychic unity of humankind*. This was the presumption that there exists a single, overarching human nature that permeates all peoples in all places on the planet, regardless of the particularities of their sociocultural organization. All people everywhere are born with the same mental and physical potentialities, which will cause them, when presented with similar problems, to create similar solutions to those problems. However, because peoples are faced with quite unique circumstances by their locality and their history, their societies and cultures will diverge in time and appear, at least on the surface, to be quite different one from another. As we see in the context of this section, the interplay of similarity and difference that is inherent in the 19th-century understanding of psychic unity was itself, however, articulated quite differently in the context of those early anthropologists whose writings explored most explicitly both the structure and content of consciousness cross-culturally.

Adolf Bastian (1826–1905) and the Psychic Unity of Humankind

Adolph Bastian was one of the leading proponents of this cultural idealist view in ethnology during the mid- to late-19th century. This was a period when Germany was a major player in science, and Bastian was Germany's leading social anthropologist (Koepping, 1983; see also Lowie, 1937). Bastian (1881, 1887) is now credited with having developed the notion of the "psychic unity of mankind," which played a critical role in defining many of the anthropological theories of consciousness that are explored below.

Bastian proposed a straightforward project for the long-term development of a science of human culture and consciousness based upon this notion. He argued that the mental acts of all people are the products of physiological mechanisms characteristic of the human species (what today we might term the genetic loading on the organization and functioning of the brain). Every human mind inherits a complement of species-specific "elementary ideas" (*Elementargedanken*), and hence the minds of all people, regardless of their race or culture, operate in the same way. It is the contingencies of geographic location and historical background that we have to thank for the different elaborations of these elementary ideas, the different sociocultural traditions, and the various levels of sociocultural complexity. According to Bastian (1881, 1887), there also exists a lawful "genetic principle" by which societies develop over the course of their history from exhibiting simple sociocultural institutions to becoming increasingly complex in their organization.

These elementary, inherited psychological processes can be studied in a systematic, objective, and comparative way, Bastian taught. Accordingly, he argued that the ethnographic project had to proceed through a series of five analytical steps (see Koepping, 1983):

1. Fieldwork: Empirical description of cross-cultural data (as opposed to armchair philosophy). Bastian himself spent much of his adult life among non-European peoples.

2. Deduction of collective representations: From cross-cultural data we describe the collective representations in a given society.

3. Analysis of folk ideas: Collective representations are broken down into constituent folk ideas. Geographical regions often exhibit similar patterns of folk ideas – he called these "idea circles" that described the collective representations of particular regions.

4. Deduction of elementary ideas: Resemblances between folk ideas and patterns of folk ideas across regions indicate underlying elementary ideas.

5. Application of a scientific psychology: Study of elementary ideas defines the psychic unity of humankind, which is due to the underlying psychophysiological structure of the species.

What Bastian argued for was nothing less than what today we might call a psychobiologically grounded, cross-cultural social psychology. Through ethnographic research, he wrote, we can study the psychological laws of mental life as they reveal themselves in diverse geographical settings.

Franz Boas (1858–1942) and the Anthropology of Sensory Impressions

Although the investigation of consciousness per se may not have been an explicit object of attention for many anthropologists who followed Bastian in the context of their ethnographic research, practically since its inception as an organized field of study, anthropology has been vitally interested in questions concerning the cultural patterning of sensory impressions. Indeed, a careful reading of the history of the discipline reveals that much of modern anthropology was founded upon an active interest in the relation between culture and the differential organization of various modes of sensory experience. Beginning with Franz Boas, whose dissertation in physics at the University of Kiel was focused on problems concerning the color of seawater and who later spent time with Wilhelm Wundt at his laboratory in Leipzig studying the laws that account for the emergence, combination, and organization of elementary sensations in consciousness (Harkness, 1992; Laboratory of Comparative Human Cognition, 1983), we find an early and influential interest in investigating the relationship between culture and sensation. In fact, it was a growing dissatisfaction with the psychophysical approach of Wundt's laboratory that eventually led Boas to come "away convinced that 'even elementary sensations were influenced by their contexts of occurrence" (Harkness, 1992, p. 103). This focus on the cultural patterning of sensory experience also importantly fueled Boas's long-standing dialogue

with the psychic unity question – a dialogue that may very well have originated in the context of Boas's correspondences with Bastian during the early 1880s and his later studies under him in Berlin during 1886–1887 at the Royal Ethnographic Museum.

A key article highlighting some of Boas's views on culture and sensation is his "On Alternating Sounds" (1889/1974). In this article, Boas set out to demonstrate that most forms of sensory perception are forms of culturally mediated apperception – perception informed by some classificatory framework. Using the examples of "sound blindness" and color perception, Boas attempted to demonstrate the effects of linguistically mediated cultural categories on the patterning of auditory and visual sensations. The phenomena of sound blindness – a condition noted by the phonologists of the day wherein the sounds uttered by a speaker are either not perceived at all or are misperceived by a hearer – provided the means for Boas to lay the groundwork for a model of the cultural patterning of auditory sensations. This model was based on a suggestion that the probability that two resembling sounds will be perceived as identical for any one given hearer is tied directly to the extent to which the two sounds correspond to a pregiven classificatory frame (Boas, 1889/1974).

In the case of color perception, Boas noted the growing evidence for cross-cultural variability in color terminology and pointed to the fact that in languages where there are no terms for "green," the colors that fall within the spectrum of green become classified according to the two closest sensory frames; namely, blue and yellow. In the case of sound blindness, Boas focused upon how our culturally mediated apperceptive frames serve to selectively filter out differences between discrete instances of auditory sense impressions. In the case of color perception, he noted how similar apperceptive frames work to selectively code for differences between sense impressions that would otherwise display a significant amount of perceptual similarity. Borrowing from the Kantian tradition, Boas thus distinguished apperception (cognitively mediated mental representation of sense objects) from perception (immediate sensation). And to this extent, for "Boas, as Benedict put it, the seeing eye was the organ of tradition" (Sahlins, 2000, p. 152).

Boas is generally considered the father of cultural anthropology. His name and the methods he espoused are commonly associated with relativist notions of human nature – that is, with the idea that in some way our species transcended biological conditioning when it became fully cultural in its patterns of adaptation. The naïve assumption here is that there was some kind of saltative leap from "nature" to "nurture" during the evolution of humanity. But Boas himself was neither so naïve, nor was he completely comfortable with an extreme relativist (or purely constructivist) view of human consciousness. One need only consider Boas's discussion of psychic unity in his book, *The Mind of Primitive Man* (1910/1938), in which he wrestled with the tension between his conviction that all people everywhere are born with the same mind, and yet some cultures appear to be more "advanced" in terms of technological and social adaptation than others. His overwhelming concern methodologically was with recording the narratives of traditional peoples verbatim and in using these texts as data upon which to eventually ground a solid science of human nature and consciousness – a research strategy he in fact shared with Bastian.

The Torres Strait Expedition of 1898

Boas was not alone in his interest in exploring the relation between culture and sensation during this period. A year before the publication of Boas's pioneering discussion of the influence of culture on auditory and visual sensory modalities, the famous Cambridge Expedition to the Torres Strait (between Australia and New Guinea) set out to explore how culture affects "acuity for each of the basic senses" (Haddon, 1901; see also Cole, 1996; Richards, 1998; Kuklick, 1991). Here Boas's nascent interest in color perception and audition was extended to general visual acuity, spatial perception, auditory acuity, olfaction, taste, tactile sensitivity, pain threshold, weight discrimination, and perceptual illusions tied to abilities to perceive differences in the relation between size and weight. With W. H. R. Rivers in charge of the experiments on vision; C. S. Myers focusing on audition, olfaction, and gustation; and William McDougall investigating the haptic senses and sensitivity to pain, the team sought to test ongoing debates over Herbert Spencer's (1886) hypothesis regarding differences in the sensory acuity of "primitive" and "civilized" cultures (see Cole, 1996, p. 41; Richards, 1998, p. 137). As Richards (1998) notes, Spencer's hypothesis was "that 'primitives' surpassed 'civilized' people in psychophysical performance because more energy remained devoted to this level in the former instead of being diverted to 'higher functions,' a central tenet of late Victorian 'scientific racism'" (p. 137).

The orientation of these researchers was based upon the assumption, articulated by Myers, that so-called primitive peoples were predisposed to pay greater attention to the perception of "external stimuli" than Europeans (cited in Titchener 1916, p. 210). In line with this thesis, McDougall (1901) asserted that the people of Torres Strait showed greater sensitivity to the external impingement of two points applied to the skin while demonstrating a much greater insensitivity to the internal impingement of pain sensation than their European counterparts. Finding that the Torres Straight islanders subjects were not fooled by a variety of optical illusions, Rivers (1901a) argued that the islanders had greater visual acuity than Europeans. He also asserted that the islanders demonstrated a greater sensitivity to the color red and a slight insensitivity to the color blue, which was marked in terms of the discernible prevalence or lack of lexical items used to designate these particular ranges in the color spectrum. Myers found that, although there were some observational data suggesting that islanders had a greater ability to identify faint, imperceptible sounds, none of his tests on audition or olfaction proved conclusive in this regard. In fact, as Cole (1996) notes, Myers "found that auditory sensitivity was somewhat greater for European samples while there was no apparent difference in sensitivity to odors" (p. 43).

Although it seems that the expedition was able to garner some evidence supporting the extent to which culture might serve to pattern sensory experience, a number of questions concerning the accuracy and validity of the methods and findings of the expedition were raised in a critical article by Titchener (1916; see also Cole, 1996).

Emile Durkheim (1858–1918) and the Elementary Forms of Consciousness

The concern for the invariant properties of consciousness, which was first explicated in Bastian's project, continued through the history of the discipline. Although the overly simplistic, evolutionist notion of the "psychic unity of mankind" came into serious question in the early 20th century, researchers were still interested in pan-human regularities in sociocultural phenomena, as well as the variation in sensory experience influenced by culture. Well informed by these discussions, Emile Durkheim (1858–1918), a renowned father of contemporary social theory, argued that socially derived collective representations play an important role in patterning the individual's various sensory modalities. At the same time, he emphasized, in a critical dialogue with Immanuel Kant, that although all people come to know the world filtered through the categories of time, space, number, cause, class, person, and totality, these categories of understanding were empirically derived through social experience.

Emile Durkheim and his student, Marcel Mauss (1872–1950), worked on the relations among classificatory schemes, social organization, and spatial perception, an effort that can also be viewed as an early attempt at establishing the parameters for an anthropology of consciousness. In *Primitive Classification* (Durkheim & Mauss, 1903/1963), they suggested that it is forms of social organization that serve to shape the categorical schemes mediating an individual's perception of space. Expanding on some of these ideas in his magnum opus, *The Elementary Forms of Religious Life* (1912/1995), Durkheim argued further that socially derived collective representations play an important role in patterning the individual's various sensory modalities (see also Throop, 2003c). As Durkheim put it, collective representations "turn upon sensation a beam that lights, penetrates, and transforms it" (1912/1995, p. 437). Moreover, Durkheim demonstrated that collective representations are reinforced through rituals that pair the society's knowledge with certain altered states of consciousness – or what he called "collective effervescence." This strain of thinking in Durkheim influenced the fundamental structuralist notions perpetuated by Mauss and later by Mauss's own pupil, Claude Lévi-Strauss (1908-), founder of modern-day structuralism (see below).

Indeed, in his now famous essay, *Les techniques du corps* (1950), Mauss importantly extended some of these basic ideas regarding the relationship between culture and consciousness to questions concerning the ways in which culture influences body posture, balance, motility, and the kinesthetic sense. Using the term "habitus" to account for the acquired practical nexus that informs an individual's habitual use and perception of the body, Mauss viewed reproduction, consumption, care, movement, rest, and sleep as significant fields for investigating the various ways that culture can pattern techniques of somatic perception and action. As we see below, this insight informed later approaches in anthropology that sought to emphasize the significance of non-discursive, practical, and embodied aspects of consciousness.

Lévy-Bruhl (1857–1939) on Multiple Modes of Consciousness

Building upon Durkheim's earlier writings on collective representations, Lucien Lévy-Bruhl, both an influential and controversial figure in the history of the discipline, set out to further Durkheim's initial insight that "different mentalities will correspond to different social types" (1926, p. 27) by detailing what he argued to be the fundamental differences between "primitive" and "modern" mentalities (see Throop, 2003c). Where the latter were held to be organized according to logical modes of thought that were primarily grounded in cognitive functioning, the former were thought to be fundamentally "prelogical" and infused with imagination and emotional currents that often served to distort the stability and coherence of the world as first given to the senses. Careful not to follow Edward Tylor (1817/1958) and Herbert Spencer's (1886) view of primitive mentality as an antecedent and inferior stage to modern mentality, Lévy-Bruhl (1926) argued that both forms of mentality, although organized differently, were to be understood as equally valued.

In terms of the cultural patterning of conscious experience, Lévy-Bruhl (1926) asserted that, although for the modern mind mental representations are cognitive phenomena that are precise and well differentiated, for primitive mentality, mental representations are far more complex, undifferentiated, and infused with emotion, feeling, and passion. Furthermore, he held that, in addition to being suffused with such emotional and motor currents, the primitive mentality is directed almost exclusively by culturally constituted collective representations. Accordingly, it is "bound up with preperceptions, preconceptions, preconnections, and we might almost say with prejudgments" that alter the functioning of such mental capacities as reason, logic, and inference (p. 108).

Lévy-Bruhl believed that the primitive mentality, driven by an alternative kind of logic, operated such that an individual would confront a world constituted by collective representations that were largely "impervious to experience." As he put it, "Primitives see with eyes like ours, but they do not perceive with the same minds. We might almost say that their perceptions are made up of

a nucleus surrounded by a layer of varying density of representations which are social in their origin" (1926, p. 44). For Lévy-Bruhl, it was precisely this collectively generated representational saturation that accounted for the differential functioning of primitive logic that operated without regard to the law of contradiction: the idea that a statement and its negation cannot be true simultaneously. Because a "primitive's" collective representations directed his or her perception beyond immediate sensory data to the occult forces and the imperceptible elements thought to operate beyond the purview of our various sensory modalities, the primitive mind was understood by Lévy-Bruhl to be driven to see connections between otherwise logically disparate phenomena (e.g., between a man and his totem animal). In Lévy-Bruhl's (1926) estimation, therefore, categorical thought and instances of mutual exclusivity, which were the putative hallmark of logical thought, were abandoned in primitive mentality. By contrast, primitive mentality was held to be organized according to a "law of participation" whereby the mind is not merely presented with an object, but "communes with it and participates in it, not only in the ideological, but also in the physical and mystic sense of the word" (p. 362).

Although his perspective on putative differences between these differing mentalities was criticized quite rightfully by his peers and successors, in all fairness to Lévy-Bruhl, we should note that later on in his career he came to argue that all people, be they primitive or civilized, operate on both logical thought and the "participation mystique," depending upon social context (see Lévy-Bruhl, 1975). In other words, Lévy-Bruhl's description of the primitive mentality can be understood as an accurate description of all mentalities where cognitive, affective, and conative (i.e., volitional) elements are ever present and often interfused. Indeed, much of human experience is conditioned to a great extent by "preperceptions," "preconceptions," "preconnections," and "prejudgments."

Language, Consciousness, and the Sapir-Whorf Hypothesis

One of Boas's students, Edward Sapir (1884–1939), and one of Sapir's students, Benjamin Lee Whorf (1897–1941), are famous both within and beyond the discipline of anthropology for revisiting Boas's concern for cultural variation in consciousness. Each in their own way explored the effects of culture and language on the patterning of contents of consciousness. Throughout their careers, they attempted to highlight the various ways that cultural and linguistic systems serve to selectively direct individuals' attention to linguistically salient elements in the perceptual field. Although there is still much controversy over the extent to which Sapir (1929/1958) would have supported versions of linguistic relativity that postulated any simple correspondence among the structures of language, the structures of thought, and the patterning of sensation and perception (e.g., see Gumperz & Levinson, 1996), he did argue, however, that even "comparatively simple acts of perception are very much more at the mercy of social patterns called words than we might suppose. . . . We see and hear and otherwise experience very largely as we do because the language habits of our community predispose certain choices of interpretation" [emphasis in original] (p. 69).

Following Boas's and Sapir's lead, Benjamin Lee Whorf (1956) also examined the relations among language, thought, and experience. For instance, in an exploration of how punctual and segmentative aspects of Hopi verbs come to characterize phenomena according to "pulsative" and "vibrative" characteristics, Whorf (1956) pointed out that, although we tend to view language in terms of its expressive function, "language first of all is a classification and arrangement of the *stream of sensory experience* which results in a certain world-order, a certain segment of the world that is easily expressible by the type of symbolic means that language employs" (p. 55; emphasis ours). According to Whorf (1956), whether we are talking about visual perception, audition, or the temporal sense of "ever becoming later," streams of sensory input are organized or patterned by habitual language use and the often covert grammatical forms – "cryptotypes" – that serve to give structure to that usage. Indeed, Whorf argued that the punctual and segmentative aspects of Hopi verbs actually supply Hopi speakers with a grammatical system that is better equipped to describe vibratile phenomena than the terminology we find in modern-day physics. In this respect, Whorf (1956) argued that this "Hopi aspect-contrast which we have observed, being obligatory upon their verb forms, *practically forces the Hopi to notice and observe* vibratory phenomena, and furthermore encourages them to find names for and to classify such phenomena" (p. 56; emphasis ours).

The combined efforts of Sapir and Whorf to understand the influence of language upon experience came to be known as the Sapir-Whorf Hypothesis. The tradition in anthropology has been to speak of a hard and a soft version of the hypothesis. The hard version would read something like this: Language categories determine the organization of experience. However, virtually all of the empirical evidence over the last half-century garnered in both anthropology and psychology appears to disconfirm this version of the hypothesis. Moreover, neither Sapir, nor Whorf ever advocated such a simplistic and deterministic relationship between language and consciousness. What they did do, however, was to hold fast to the notion, common in their day, that the structure of language provides researchers with significant insight into an underlying cultural ontology for reality. Consider one of Sapir's (1931) statements: "The 'real world' is to a large extent unconsciously built up on the language habits of the group" (p. 580). Whorf (1956) took this a step further when he suggested that "the categories and types that we isolate from the world of phenomena we do not find there because they stare every observer in the face. On the contrary the world is presented in a kaleidoscopic flux of impressions which have to be organized in our minds. This means, largely, by the linguistic system in our minds" (p. 128).

Although the extent to which either thinker would have supported the "hard" version of the hypothesis is still much debated, it is safe to assume that both Sapir and Whorf would have definitely supported a softer version, which might go something like this: The way people learn to speak about things influences how they are conditioned to think about things (see Lucy, 1985; Rumsey, 1990). The weight of the evidence over the last half-century would support some form of this view (Gumperz & Levinson, 1996; Hunt & Agnoli, 1991; Kay & Kempton, 1984; Lucy, 1992).

Irving Hallowell (1892–1974) and the "Behavioral Environment"

Irving Hallowell is another important pioneering figure in anthropology's long-standing interest in the cultural patterning of sensation and consciousness. Much like Sapir and Whorf before him, Hallowell's approach to consciousness can be understood as an extension of the Boasian tradition. This is not surprising because Hallowell was a student of Boas's student, Frank Speck, at the University of Pennsylvania, and he also participated regularly in Boas's weekly seminars at Columbia (Bock, 1999). Moreover, although never officially a student of Sapir's, Hallowell was also clearly influenced by his writings (Regna Darnell, personal communication). Hallowell (1955) argued that much of what individuals take to be "direct perception" is in fact informed by personally and culturally constituted "nonsensory" symbolic forms. Citing Bruner's (1951) claim that perception must be understood as the expression of the entire personality structure and Bartlett's (1932) view that the mind's perceptual processes are organized according to an "effort after meaning," Hallowell explained that much of what we understand to be the transparent perception of an external world is guided by the psychophysical structure of the nervous system, which has developed in each individual member of society according to that individual's per-

sonal psychology and the influence of the culture in which he or she has been raised (1955, p. 40).

This understanding of the effects of culture on perceptual processes – particularly those perceptual processes subserving vision – further informs what is perhaps Hallowell's most famous contribution to anthropological theory; namely, the concept of the "behavioral environment." Borrowing the term from the Gestalt psychology of Koffka, Hallowell explained that the behavioral environment is not merely the generalized physical or geographical environment, but rather that culturally ordered environment that is experienced by an individual social actor. That is, according to Hallowell, the behavioral environment consists of an ordered world of objects, persons, and relations that is experienced by a social actor whose perceptual capacities effectively suffuse those objects, persons, and relations with personally and culturally constituted meanings, values, feelings, and motivations. That said, in accord with the ongoing dialogue in anthropology between the interplay of similarity and difference in the structure and content of consciousness cross-culturally, Hallowell (1955) also argued that it is possible to determine a number of basic orientations that provide the structural underpinnings for the constitution of an individual's world of experience, regardless of the historical, cultural, and/or personal factors that shape siginificantly each of these orientations in a multitude of ways. Outlining orientations for self, objects, space-time, motivation, and norms, Hallowell demonstrated how each orientation can be construed as a universal and necessary structure of human consciousness that is also patterned significantly according to unique cultural, social, and personal dictates. For instance, he pointed out that, although for all cultures it is necessary to classify and discriminate among objects in relation to a culturally constituted understanding of the self, the ways in which objects are conceived varies tremendously among different cultural systems. Hallowell explored this complex blend of psychophysical, personal, and cultural influences upon perception through the use of traditional anthropological methods as well as by administering Rorschach tests to subjects from Ojibwa and other societies (1955, pp. 32–74).

Structure and Content II: Modern Structuralism, Practice Theory, Hermeneutics, and the Anthropology of Experience

Many of the themes and orientations present in the early development of the anthropology of consciousness continued to be developed during the mid- to late 20th century. However, research techniques became more sophisticated, and there were many more ethnographers collecting data from among the myriad peoples on the planet. Among other things, the tension between universalist (orientation toward the ways peoples are alike) and relativist (orientation toward the ways people are different) perspectives became intensified. As we shall see, part of the tension is ideological, but part is also methodological – it is next to impossible to perceive the structures subserving human activity in the kind of naturalistic setting encountered by most ethnographers in the field. We return to this point in the conclusion of the chapter.

Claude Lévi-Strauss (1908–) and Structuralism

An important contribution to anthropological approaches to consciousness is found in the work of the famous French structuralist, Claude Lévi-Strauss. What was novel about Lévi-Strauss's approach to consciousness was that he set out to ground the generative source of particularistic cultural givens in the universal structures of the human brain (see Scholte, 1973; Throop, 2003c). He held that it was unconscious mental structures that gave rise to the experiential vicissitudes of culturally mediated consciousness. It was thus a movement

from empirical and experiential diversity to conceptual and intellectual simplicity that guided much of Lévi-Strauss's structuralist vision. In this paradigm, cultural products were therefore understood to be constrained by the limits imposed by the structural underpinnings of the human mind. These products were held to be expressions of the mind that generates them and were intelligible on that accord.

In this light, Lévi-Strauss argued that phenomenological appeals to lived experience in the context of anthropological explorations into the structures of consciousness are in and of themselves always inadequate. They are inadequate because Lévi-Strauss held that such an approach necessarily biases researchers to focusing exclusively on the particular, contingent, individual, and often inexpressible affective and sensorial realm. He paid little attention to this "superficial," "idiosyncratic" realm of individual consciousness, however, for although "ideas resulting from hazy and unelaborated attitudes ... have an experiential character for each of us. ... [t]hese experiences, however, remain intellectually diffuse and emotionally intolerable unless they incorporate one or another of the patterns present in the group's culture. The assimilation of such patterns is the only means of objectivizing subjective states, of formulating inexpressible feelings, and of integrating inarticulated experiences into a system" (Lévi-Strauss, 1958/1963, pp. 171–172).

In his analysis of myth, Lévi-Strauss (1964/1969, 1966/1973, 1968/1978, 1971/1981) attempted to show how, despite their seemingly non-linear, mystical, and irrational exposition, myths are governed by a logical structure of binary oppositions, mediators, and the reconciliation of the very logical contradictions (e.g. between nature and culture) that Lévy-Bruhl claimed to go unnoticed by thinkers immersed in a participatory consciousness. For Lévi-Strauss these seemingly irrational and culturally specific narratives are actually one of the best means of accessing the invariant structures of the human mind. Most simply put, Lévi-Strauss's project is predicated upon a model of consciousness and culture that is rooted in externalization. It is important to realize that Lévi-Strauss was not interested in personal externalization (i.e., creativity), but rather in a view that takes externalization to be tied primarily to the projection of the universal and invariant structures of the human mind into the tangible medium of cultural forms, in this case mythological texts (and elsewhere kinship systems; see Lévi-Strauss, 1949/1969).

Lévi-Strauss's (1958/1963) approach to consciousness has been faulted for failing to recognize the significance of emotion and motivation in all forms of mentality and for overemphasizing the importance of externalization in the patterning of cultural products such as myth. In addition, many critical assessments of Lévi-Strauss's work are grounded in the contention that he never systematically outlined a methodology for how he went about discovering binary oppositions, mediators, etc., in the context of his textual analysis of the underlying structural elements of myth. Although having important roots in Bastian's and Boas's research paradigms, Levi-Strauss's almost exclusive methodological reliance on texts to the exclusion of other research methodologies fueled many of the most trenchant critiques of structuralist approaches to consciousness in the discipline as a whole.

Clifford Geertz (1926–2006) and the Interpretivist/Hermeneutic Approach

In his now famous appropriation of philosopher Gilbert Ryle's (1949/1984) notion of the "thick description" of the behaviors that reputedly evidence the workings of internal/mental acts, Clifford Geertz's (1973) approach to consciousness was clearly rooted in his position that an "I-am-a-camera, 'phenomenalistic'" approach to anthropology is necessarily insufficient for any attempts to uncover the structures of signification that give meaning to observed phenomena (see Throop, 2003a). According to Geertz, "thick description" as a methodology is predicated on anthropologists turning their attention to a detailed description of

ongoing expressive behavior and the social context within which that behavior arises. This description of expressive behavior in the context of its occurrence is thus understood to serve as the foundation from which researchers are later able to build an understanding of the interpretive frameworks that actors use to give meaning to their action.

Following Max Weber (1864–1920), Geertz (1973) asserted that his vision of an "interpretive science," whose purpose is to explore the "webs of significance" that serve to constitute culture, is founded on the idea that culture is a public, ideational, and yet non-mentalistic system of construable signs. Again paraphrasing Ryle, Geertz held that it is precisely the inherently public nature of culture that makes problematic the notion that cultural symbols exist "in someone's head" – as operating within human consciousness. Accordingly, he strongly criticized the work of Goodenough (1971) and other "ethnoscientists" (e.g., Conklin, 1969; Frake, 1961; etc.) who have construed culture to be "composed of psychological structures by means of which individuals or groups of individuals guide their behavior" (p. 11).

In fact, Geertz (1973) believed with Ryle (1949/1984) that "mind" is a term that denotes most accurately not some privately accessible "ghost in the machine," but rather a publicly accessible "class of skills, propensities, capacities, tendencies and habits... [in short] an organized system of dispositions which finds its manifestation in some actions and some things" (p. 58). He argued that it is these "external" (i.e., public) symbolic manifestations of complexes of skills and habits that ultimately underlie all reflective modes of consciousness. Indeed, what many scholars assume to be mental processes are, according to Geertz, construed more accurately as processes of "matching... states and processes of [public] symbolic models against [equally public] states and processes of the wider world" (1973, p. 78).

Geertz also followed Ryle's lead in arguing that it is only by viewing symbols to be "material vehicles of thought" that allow individuals to impress meaning upon objects in experience that we can ever hope to legitimize the anthropological study of consciousness. Geertz believed that it is only this public view of symbols that can ensure the possibility that anthropologists may eventually discover properties of cultural and personal systems through systematic empirical analysis (1973). In Geertz's view then, his perspective provides anthropology with a way in which to uncover "what is given, what the conceptual structure embodied in the symbolic forms through which persons are perceived actually is" (1973, p. 364). It was his opinion that this potential "method of describing and analyzing the meaningful structure of experience" can therefore provide anthropology with the basis for establishing a valid scientific "phenomenology of culture" (1973, p. 364).

Building on Ryle, as well as on the work of George Herbert Mead, Geertz argued that the assumption that culture is both public and social leads inevitably to the insight that cultural processes do not "happen in the head," but, consist, in contrast, of a traffic of significant symbols that *"impose meaning upon experience"* (1973, p. 45; emphasis ours). In short, Geertz's view is that conscious experience is a cultural artifact. Without the medium of culturally infused significant symbols Geertz asserted that conscious experience would be relegated to incoherent and impenetrable behaviors and sensations. For Geertz then, the imposition of meaning on an otherwise chaotic stream of stimuli and responses is one of the key defining components of human existence as cultural beings. It is this externalized, socially infused understanding of culture as a coherent system of symbols serving to inform all moments of conscious experience that allows Geertz to later establish his memorable metaphor of culture as text (1973).

Pierre Bourdieu (1930–2002) and Practice Theory

Taking a significant step away from both Lévi-Straussian structuralism and Geertzian semiotics, Pierre Bourdieu may be credited with turning the attention of anthropologists (as well as philosophers and other social scientists) to the significance of exploring nonconceptual, embodied aspects of human consciousness (see Throop & Murphy, 2002). His perspective, which has inspired a long line of scholars interested in exploring consciousness from a practice theoretical approach, pivots on the concept of "habitus." According to Bourdieu, habitus is a durable set of culturally and socially inculcated proclivities to act, perceive, feel, appreciate, and generally inhabit the world. He argued that the concept of habitus enables him "to break away from the structuralist paradigm (see the above discussion of Lévi-Strauss) without falling back into the old philosophy of the subject or of consciousness" (Bourdieu, 1985, p. 13).

Bourdieu's (1977) understanding of habitus is based on the assumption that "agents are possessed by their habitus more than they possess it" (p. 18). It is thus not through conscious attention to predetermined "roles," "rules," or "models" that agents negotiate their interactions with the social world, but through the unintentional triggering of strategic patterns of thought and action produced by habitus in its mutually informing relation to structure. Here lies what Bourdieu labeled the "fallacy of the rule," which is based on the putatively false belief that agents are conscious of how their practice is "objectively governed." Instead, Bourdieu argued that agents always lack explicit cognizance of the "mechanisms producing this conformity in the absence of intention to conform" (1977, p. 29). According to Bourdieu, rules are only ever functional if they serve to "awaken . . . the schemes of perception and appreciation deposited, in their incorporated state, in every member of the group" (1977, p. 17). Rules are thus only ever intended to deal with "the collective enterprise of inculcation tending to produce habitus" (1977, p. 17).

Connected to the "fallacy of the rule," and also crucial to understanding his perspective on consciousness, is what Bourdieu terms the "finalist illusion." In Bourdieu's opinion, practices are produced by habitus, which serves as a generative principle allowing individuals to adjust and respond to ever-changing situations. He suggested that it is a mistake, however, to believe that these strategies are determined in accord with some future orientation that is explicitly accessible in conscious experience. Instead, he argued that habitus is "always tending to reproduce the objective structures of which they are a product, [as] they are determined by the past conditions which have produced the principle of their production" (1977, p. 72). In this light, habitus "is that presence of the past in the present which makes possible the presence in the present of the forth-coming" (2000, p. 210). Bourdieu therefore stresses the conservative nature of habitus and the unconscious basis for the patterning of human behavior, for he asserts that habitus is predisposed to defend its integrity, resisting change by avoiding or rejecting information that serves to contradict or question its previously acquired presuppositions (1977, pp. 60–61). As he puts it, "habitus tends to favor experiences likely to reinforce it by[protecting] itself from crises and critical challenges by providing itself with a milieu to which it is as pre-adapted as possible" (1990, p. 61). In this light, Bourdieu explained that habitus is implicated in processes of naturalizing the conventional in the service of producing taken-for-granted (i.e., doxic) orientations to social life. In his words, "schemes of thought and perception can produce the objectivity that they produce only by producing misrecognition of the limits of the cognition that they make possible, thereby founding immediate adherence, in doxic mode, to the world of tradition experienced as a 'natural world' and taken for granted" (1977, p. 164).

Bourdieu occasionally acknowledged, however, that we cannot in fact dispense completely with all forms of explicitness in consciousness, precisely because within the dialectical interaction of structure and disposition, the inscription of structure in habitus is seldom, if ever, a perfect match. Even with these occasional cautions he was not, however, always consistent in this regard. There are, in fact, a number of instances where we find Bourdieu defining

habitus as a set of mental, perceptual, cognitive, and behavioral dispositions that are inscribed in agents' individual bodies early in their lifespans while being "constantly reinforced by calls to order from the group, that is to say, from the aggregate of individuals endowed with the *same dispositions*, to whom each is linked by his dispositions and interests" (1977, p. 15; emphasis ours).

Bourdieu also stated that the unconscious patterning of perceptual, evaluative, and behavioral schemes functions in such a way that conscious "quasi theoretical reflection" in practice merely serves to conceal "the true nature of practical mastery" (1977, p. 19). Here we again find some inconsistencies in his position, however, for he also explained that pedagogy can be seen as a process of explication that entails the necessary distancing from the "natural" feel of practical mastery in the attempt to transfer skills from master to student (1977, p. 19). If it is indeed the case that the transmission of skills from an adept to a novice is often associated with direct explicit representation in consciousness that is thus distanced from the experience of "practical mastery," the question that may be asked of Bourdieu is why he devotes so little attention to exploring the relationship between representational and non-representational aspects of consciousness and why he focused so much attention on the unconscious acquisition of habitus. These questions and critiques aside, Boudieu's formulation of habitus helped to draw greater anthropological attention to the significance of non-reflective, embodied, and sensory aspects of consciousness as key sites for understanding social actors culturallly defined participation in everday life.

Victor Turner (1920–1983) and the Anthropology of Experience

Victor Turner has been held as one of the key figures in the development of both symbolic anthropology and the anthropology of experience, and his approach to consciousness has also influenced significantly many current approaches to the topic in the discipline (Peacock, 1975; Throop 2002,

2003a). In his earliest works, Victor Turner's account of consciousness attempted to integrate symbolic, physiological, bodily, sensory, and emotional dimensions of human existence. His distinction between the ideological/normative and sensory/orectic poles of meaning serves as a good case in point. In Turner's (1969) framework, ritual symbols are understood to be conventionalized, multivocal (i.e., multi-referential) signs that instigate action and that share three basic properties: (1) the condensation of multiple percepts, thought objects, and actions within a "single formation"; (2) the unification of disparate significata by means of "analogous qualities or by association in fact or thought"; and (3) the polarization of meaning into ideological (i.e., structurally normative) and sensory (i.e., physiological, orectic) referents (1969, p. 28). As Turner put it, "At one pole cluster a set of referents of a grossly physiological character, relating to *general human experience* of an emotional kind. At the other pole cluster a set of referents to moral norms and principles governing social structure.... Here we have an intimate union of the moral and material" (1969, p. 54; emphasis ours).

It is in the context of the polarization of meaning that Turner argued that these two basic poles become intimately interlinked. They are linked through processes of ritual engagement with cultural symbols that shape individual consciousness according to the dictates set by cultural and social ideals, morals, edicts, roles, and rules. In other words, in his earlier writings it is through a ritually mediated engagement with symbols that Turner grounded the canalization of an individual's subjective, emotional, and physiological experiences according to pre-given social and cultural structures. Moreover, it is also through ritual that the imperceptible world of cultural representations is given coherence in reference to the perceptible world of the senses. As he explains in reference to the Nbembu's (dwelling in West Africa) cultural belief in "shades" (ghosts, ancestors), ritual "connects the known world of sensorily perceptible phenomena with the unknown and invisible realm" (Turner, 1969,

p. 15). In this respect, it can be said that every "symbolic item is related to some empirical item of experience," whether that be "sensorily perceptible objects," feeling states, desires, a sense of purposiveness, or emotions (pp. 42–43). In Turner's early writings (e.g., Turner, 1969), we find that consciousness is most often characterized as having a psychobiological base that is shaped by both culturally patterned and universally structured properties that help give definition to an individual's subjective take on his or her physical, social, and cultural worlds.

Turner's later writings on consciousness (e.g., Turner 1982) were directly inspired by the writings of the German philosopher Wilhelm Dilthey (1833–1911; see Throop, 2002, 2003a). In the context of his dialogue with Dilthey, Turner extended his earlier understanding of consciousness to encompass a trichotomy of cognitive, affective, and volitional dimensions as they are directly lived through by individual actors. It is not until 1982 that we find Turner's first published discussion of conscious experience from the perspective of Dilthey's framework. Turner pointed out that in contrast to Kant's belief that it is only with the conceptual pattering of sensation that the "raw data" of experience are given definite form, Dilthey holds that every distinct unit of experience is given to an individual's awareness with a certain structure that is not merely the result of the categorical impositions of the human mind. Instead, "the data of experience are 'instinct with form,' and thought's work is to draw out 'the structural system' implicit in every distinguishable *Erlebnis* or unit of experience" (1982, p. 13). It is important to point out here that, although focusing upon structures of experience, Turner was also quite familiar with Dilthey's attempt to discuss different moments of experience that are understood to be integral components of the organization of any distinctive structure of experience (see Throop, 2002). After outlining five such moments – the perceptual core, the evocation of past images, the revival of associated feelings, the emergence of meaning and value, and the expression of experience – Turner went on to argue, however, that it is only really in the fifth moment of "expression" that the structured unit of experience can be said to reveal itself (1982, p. 15).

Turner further recognized Dilthey's important distinction between the immediate living through of experience as a sequence of events (*Erleben*) and the retrospective attribution of meaning tied to the structuring of experience as a particular coherent unit or form. In this way, Turner argued that in the context of its expression "experience is both 'living through' and 'thinking back' ... [and it] is also 'willing or wishing forward'" (1982, p. 18). Here, Turner explores the multilayered structuring of "experience in terms of the temporal organization of meaning, value, and ends" (see also Turner, 1985, pp. 214–215; Throop 2003a). According to Turner's reading of Dilthey, "meaning" is essentially a cognitive structure oriented to the past. "Value" is, by contrast, an affective structure tied to the vicissitudes of the present moment, whereas "ends" are volitional structures tied to goal-directed behavior oriented toward an emerging future. Again following Dilthey, he argues that there is little or no cognitive coherence in the "unarticulated quality of value." Instead, it is only with the interconnection of what are otherwise latent "tonal-affinities" that disparate "values" are able to be organized into a coherent structure through the "ligatures" provided by personal and cultural forms of meaning. In contrast to the transient sequentiality that is characteristic of value as it manifests in its immediate immersion in the "conscious present" – "[m]eaning is apprehended by *looking back* over a temporal process" (1982, p. 76; emphasis in original).

In his dialogue with Dilthey, Turner thus highlighted for anthropologists the significance of exploring consciousness in terms of its temporal structure (e.g., retrospection, perception, and anticipation). As is evident from Turner's discussion of value, meaning, and ends, it seems that there may very well be significant variations in the relation between culture and the contents of consciousness, inasmuch as the latter variously articulate with differing temporal orientations in the stream of consciousness (see Throop, 2003a).

Structure and Content III: Contemporary Developments in the Anthropology of Consciousness

Levi-Strauss's structuralism, Geertz's hermeneutics, Bourdieu's practice theory, and Turner's anthropology of experience each set the stage for many of the contemporary approaches to consciousness in the discipline that have arisen during the past 30 years. As we see below, whether it is in terms of a critical reaction to, or an attempt to build upon, the insights of these earlier approaches to consciousness in the discipline, the themes, orientations, and methodological and theoretical tensions found in the past century and a half continue to develop in contemporary anthropology. Meanwhile, new and intriguing approaches to consciousness have developed as well, all within the basic naturalistic framework of ethnological research. In this section, we explore some of the major approaches to consciousness that have emerged in anthropology over the last 30 years.

Transpersonal Anthropology and Altered States of Consciousness

It is perhaps anthropological attempts to document evidence for alterations in states of consciousness cross-culturally that have garnered the most attention from researchers outside the discipline (see Chapter 19). And indeed, it is true that anthropologists have encountered, recorded, and thought about the importance of alternative states of consciousness since the latter part of the 19th century (e.g., see Lang, 1894, 1897, 1898). Moreover, these observations have challenged many of the assumptions about consciousness that have appeared in the context of Western scientific approaches to the topic, including the prevalent "monophasic" bias – the tendency to focus almost exclusively on exploring the contents and structures of consciousness in normal waking.

Such interest continued intermittently throughout the 20th century in a variety of reports of altered states of consciousness. For example, this century saw reports by Lincoln (1935) on dreams and culture, Barnouw (1946) on the paranormal cross-culturally, Aberle (1966) on the use of peyote in the Native American Church, Bourguignon (1973, 1976) on altered states of consciousness cross-culturally, Bharati (1975) on tantric meditation practices, and Furst (1976), Dobkin de Rios (1984), and Dobkin de Rios and Winkelman (1989) on the use of hallucinogens and cultural practices. Moreover, Halifax (1975), Peters (1982), and Peters and Price-Williams (1980) have written on altered states of consciousness related to shamanism, Long (1977) on extrasensory phenomena cross-culturally, Jilik (1982) on altered states of consciousness and healing, and Rouget (1985) on music and trance states.

However, it took developments in psychology to make ethnology more aware that extraordinary experiences were not only important for challenging assumptions about the nature of consciousness in North American and Western Europe but could also be of prime significance for *doing* ethnographic research. Hot on the heels of the rise of transpersonal psychology in the late 1960s and early 1970s (Boucouvalas, 1980; Sutich, 1968), a number of anthropologists began to realize that the experiences associated with some religious texts and ritual practices encountered by ethnographers are of an exceptional nature. They are in fact altered states of consciousness – states not easily accessed by researchers using routine ethnographic field methods (see Campbell & Staniford, 1978; Laughlin, 1989, 1990, 1994a; Laughlin, McManus, & Shearer, 1983; Lee, 1980; Long, 1976; MacDonald, 1981). Moreover, it became clear that such experiences are both very common cross-culturally and fundamental to most of the world's traditional religious systems (Bourguignon, 1973, 1976). At the same time, it also became evi-

dent that few ethnographers had personally experienced and reported on altered states of consciousness related to the peoples they were studying.

Methodological issues were part of the problem – it is very difficult to access altered states of consciousness from "outside" as it were (Braud & Anderson, 1998; Laughlin, 1989). Also, until the latter part of the 20th century, there had been an unwritten tradition in ethnology against using first-person narratives. Only during the last few decades have such reports begun to surface. Among the reports are the following: Grindal (1983) on a profound experience that occurred to him while attending a Sisala funeral in Ghana in 1967; Katz (1982, pp. 6ff) on experiences attendant to trance-dancing among the Bushmen; Laughlin (1994) on altered states of consciousness related to tantric Buddhist practices; Laughlin, McManus, and Webber (1984) on experiences arising while meditating upon complex symbols in Tibetan tantric Buddhism, Lederman (1988, pp. 805–806) on ritually driven altered states of consciousness among Malay shamans, MacDonald et al. (1988) on experiments with the shaman's mirror; Young-Laughlin and Laughlin (1988) and Webber, Stephens, and Laughlin (1983) on the phenomenology and structure of masked performance; Coult (1977) on the ethnological significance of psychedelic experiences; Edith Turner (1996) on perceiving spirit entities; Harner (1973) on hallucinogens and religion; George (1995) on telepathic dreaming; Chagnon (1977, pp. 154ff) on an experiment with hallucinogenics, shamanic dance, and chanting; and Young and Goulet (1994) for a review of such reports.

An excellent example of how an anthropological focus on alternative states of consciousness has contributed to the scientific study of consciousness can be found in the comprehensive treatment of practices of shamanism cross-culturally by Michael Winkelman (2000). In response to a myriad of positions in anthropology and elsewhere that view the states of consciousness evoked by practicing shamans as evidencing various forms of psychopathology – ranging from schizophrenia to epilepsy to dissociation to hysterical neuroses – Winkelman provides an extensive review of the positive interpersonal, neurophysiological, and psychoneuroimmunological effects of shamanic practice, ritual, and the induction of concomitant non-ordinary states of consciousness. Phenomenologically speaking, Winkelman argues that a key difference between shamanic and pathological states of consciousness is found in the control of, and intentional entry into, those states of consciousness that are often associated with shamanic practice (2000, p. 79). Moreover, Winkelman holds that shamans are able to distinguish clearly between experiences had in non-ordinary states of consciousness and those had in everyday waking life; the absence of this ability is generally held to be a key defining characteristic of many forms of psychopathology, including schizophrenia.

All of these insights serve as an important corrective to those scholars who view the intentional alteration of consciousness in the service of shamanic healing to be evidence of psychopathology. Although it is certainly true that we must be careful not to fall prey to an unthinking relativism when exploring the relationship among culture, consciousness, and psychopathology (see Spiro, 2001), it is also true, as Winkelman points out, that we must, in searching for any transcultural criteria for assessing psychopathology, be careful not to fall prey to our own culturally shaped biases.

Following Laughlin, Manus, and D'Aquili (1992), Winkelman suggests that there is in anthropology an all too often unexamined monophasic bias when it comes to investigating states of consciousness that fall outside the boundaries of normal waking states. In Husserlian terms, investigators are limited by their taken-for-granted adherence to their culturally conditioned "natural attitude" (Husserl 1950/1993) – an attitude that tends to privilege what Schutz and Luckmann (1973) have termed the everyday life-world of the "wide-awake and normal adult." Because of this bias, social scientists, psychotherapists, and medical practitioners are often prone to dispense negative evaluations of those states of consciousness that do not conform to what is largely an unquestioned definition of normalcy as calibrated according to the standards of what Winkelman terms a "modern rational bureaucratic consciousness" (2000, p. xi). In highlighting the pervasiveness of this bias in anthropological assessments of shamanic practice, Winkelman thus notably calls our attention to the extent to which scientific assumptions pertaining to consciousness are still often deeply permeated by unexamined cultural assumptions that we must constantly struggle to "bracket" in the context of our ongoing research and theorizing.

Cognitive Anthropology

Cognitive anthropological approaches to consciousness have their roots in the ethnoscientific work of such scholars as Charles Frake, Ward Goodenough, Brent Berlin, and Paul Kay, among others. These approaches arose, much like those of their psychological counterparts, in the context of what is now understood to have been a general backlash against behaviorism in the social sciences occurring during the mid-1960s and early 1970s (see D'Andrade, 1995). Indeed, ethnoscientific approaches in anthropology sought to place consciousness back in the center of anthropological research through exploring how the conceptual categorization of experience in differing cultures could shed light on both the flexibility and limitations inherent in human cognitive capacities.

By the late 1970s and early 1980s, cognitive anthropological approaches to consciousness focused a great deal of attention on the significance of "cultural schemas" – a term that can ultimately be traced back to Bartlett's "schemata" (1932) – in giving definition to the contents of human consciousness; in many ways, this focus contributed significantly to the development of cognitive science as an independent field of study (see D'Andrade, 1995). In this section we discuss three recent, influential approaches to consciousness in cognitive anthropology. Out of all the approaches to consciousness thus far discussed, cognitive anthropology has perhaps been the most innovative in developing methodologies for exploring the impact of culture on consciousness and the impact of consciousness on culture. Indeed, from triad testing to paired comparisons to multidimentional scaling to cultural consensus measures, cognitive anthropology has been at the forefront of the effort to ground anthropological research in systematic methods for data collection and analysis.

Perhaps the single most influential figure in contemporary cognitive anthropology is Roy D'Andrade. D'Adrande (1981) has addressed the relation between culture and consciousness most explicitly through an exploration of a number of differences he notes between symbolically driven computer programs and human cognitive abilities. According to D'Andrade, the most apparent difference is that whereas computer programs acquire information about the world through explicit symbolic encoding of the unambiguous linear ordering of step-by-step instructions, human children in most societies are seldom exposed to explicit instruction and acquire what is often context-specific knowledge and competencies through processes of observation, peripheral participation, modeling, and trial-and-error activity.

In terms of the relation between culture and consciousness, D'Andrade notes that, not only do cultural processes shape the contents and processes of human consciousness but also the innate capacities of human consciousness shape and constrain cultural processes (e.g., see George A. Miller, 1956, for findings with regard to the limits of human memory). D'Andrade attributes the coexistence of the "flexibility" and "sharedness" of cultural forms to the basic ways in which humans acquire knowledge and competencies, which he characterizes as a "curious combination of self-initiated yet other dependent leaning" (D'Andrade, 1981, p. 188). Although D'Andrade is convinced that the computer analogy so prevalent in cognitive science often sheds light upon human mental functioning primarily by acting as a valuable contrast to that functioning, he has also played an important role in generating interest in how computer models based on parallel distributed processing theory may inform our understanding of the relation between culture and human mental processes (D'Andrade 1984, 1987).

Inspired by a number of D'Andrade's insights, two other influential figures in the field, Claudia Strauss and Naomi Quinn (1998), have recently set out to outline a cognitive theory of cultural meaning that focuses squarely upon the relationship between culture and consciousness in the context of a discussion of internalization and the analysis of "intrapersonal culture." Arguing that philosophical and theoretical discussions of cultural meaning have all too often left unexamined the psychological mechanisms underpinning the "internalization" of cultural forms, Strauss and Quinn advocate a theory of signification in which meaning is understood to arise from the mutual interaction of intrapersonal and extrapersonal realms. A central goal of their work is therefore to maintain that cultural forms must be understood in the context of those mental processes that were mostly excised from the anthropological purview with the pervasive and uncritical acceptance of Geertz's Ryleian thesis that cultural processes are found primarily in public symbols (see discussion above). Also like D'Andrade, Strauss and Quinn are interested in exploring how insights from connectionist theory – a theoretical orientation in cognitive science where the encoding of representation is thought to reside in the differential distribution of connection weights in a parallel distributed processing system that is organized according to levels of input and output units (see Quartz & Sejnowski, 1997; Rumelhart, Hinton, & McClelland, 1986; Way 1997) – can shed light upon the psychological and neurophysiological processes that underlie the acquisition, transformation, and transmission of cultural forms. For Strauss and Quinn, an advantage to connectionist models is that they provide a view of encoding cultural schemas that is structurally coherent while still being sensitive to modification through experience. Moreover, these approaches seem to provide a way to account for how schematic knowledge may be encoded, without the concomitant necessity of explicitly stated rules (1998, p. 53; see also the discussion of Bourdieu above). According to Strauss and Quinn, these models are thus able to generate rule-like responses without the need for ever having been exposed to the "rule as such" (1998, p. 75). Because of this feature, they argue that connectionist models do not privilege language-based learning and that "[e]mbodied ideas can be represented as well as (and perhaps even more readily than) highly abstract ones" (1998, p. 53).

Although ultimately endorsing connectionist approaches, Strauss and Quinn also utilize insights from anthropological research to point to some limits of these models. First, they highlight the fact that these models are often overly dependent upon "supervised" learning (e.g., through a back propagation learning algorithm). That is, researchers are needed to guide the training sessions carefully for the proper patterning of weighted distributions to take effect. As Strauss and Quinn make clear, this model does not account for those numerous "real-life" learning situations where there is seldom a teacher around to correct a novice's every mistake. Second, they reveal that, although these systems seem to be quite proficient for dealing with "implicit" knowledge acquisition and "procedural" learning, they do not seem to account for those forms of learning that proceed through "explicit" statements (1988, p. 77). Third, these systems make no attempt to account for the role that emotion and affect play in learning and memory. Finally, Strauss and Quinn argue that connectionism is limited in terms of its tendency to posit too little innate knowledge (1988, p. 79). Their solution is to argue that, although it may be true that we need to postulate a small number of cognitive universals to account for the ability to acquire culturally specific forms, the innate structuring necessary for humans is probably not overly detailed.

Using extensive ethnographic case studies and revisiting Bastian's notion of the psychic unity of humankind (see above), a fur-

ther recent significant contribution to cognitive anthropological approaches to consciousness is found in the work of Bradd Shore (1996). Shore (1996) has built a cognitive theory of culture that links the anthropologist's concern with social action and institutions with the psychologist's concept of mental models. Grounding his discussion in both biogenetic structural theory (see below) and on the "neural Darwinism" of Jean-Pierre Changeux (see Changeux, 1985), Shore demonstrates that no simplistic essentialist, hard-wired brain approach will account for the psychic unity phenomenon (Bastian's idea discussed above that the minds of all people, regardless of their race or culture, operate in the same way). Instead, what is required is a more complex developmental approach of the sort that the biogenetic structuralists, as well as Jean Piaget, Changeux, and others, have taken.

Shore (1996) calls for conceiving of culture as a system of models – "as an extensive and heterogeneous collection of 'models,' models that exist both as public artifacts 'in the world' and as cognitive constructs 'in the mind' of members of the community" (1996, p. 44). Public models and mental models are not the same thing. Public models are analogous to knowledge and take on such myriad forms as dances, houses, paintings, songs, stories, clothing, pottery, and tools. Mental models on the other hand are more like historically patterned, received schemas – the socially transmitted mental structure of knowledge in the heads of people. A cultural model is like an internalized script that is both socially derived and dwells within the head of cultural participants.

The brain, of course, is the organ of mental models – more than that, the brain is a model generator. There is no end to the variety of models that the human brain can produce. According to Shore, the modeling capacity of the brain has two aspects: the personal and the conventional. We can develop our own models, but many of our models are derived from our culture. These socially shared models are generated under the distinct constraints of social interaction (see also Rappaport 1979, 1999, on his notion of "cognized environment"). This is a theme we have encountered earlier in the thinking of Durkheim (see above). Consciousness then is formed from internalized models that are either generated by the person during his or her development or inculcated through the process of enculturation. Both kinds of models are present in any and all moments of consciousness.

Neuroanthropological Approaches to Consciousness

As we have seen, the suggestion that both the variance and the structural commonality among peoples' consciousness and cultures are due in some fashion to an underlying psychophysical basis has been bouncing around in anthropology from its beginnings in the 19th century. And as we noted above, Lévi-Strauss importantly suggested that structural commonalities in expressive culture could be traced to the structure of the human brain. That said, a full-blown neuroanthropology had to await the inspiration of Earl W. Count (1899–1996) in the mid-20th century (1958, 1973). In his book *Being and Becoming Human* (1973), Count argued that each and every species inherits the generalized pattern of adaptation of its "anlage"; that is, its precursor species. Count called the total package of species-typical adaptation patterns that species' "biogram." The heritable architectonics (or structures) of the neuroendocrine system and the brain are very much a part of every species' biogram. Within each species' biogram are the limits of possible organizations of consciousness, which then develop relative to the adaptational circumstances of the individual and the group. Thus, for Count, it was appropriate to speak in terms of the human "brainmind" as inextricably a part of the human biogram and as the one and only organ of human consciousness. Indeed, he argued that only when anthropology reached the point where the brainmind became its central object of study could the discipline be considered a mature science (see also Laughlin, McManus, & d'Aquili, 1990).

Following in the footsteps of Earl Count, the pioneering work of the biogenetic

structuralist group, founded by Charles D. Laughlin, Eugene G. D'Aquili, and John McManus, constructed a culturally informed neuroanthropology of consciousness (D'Aquili, 1982, 1983; D'Aquili & Laughlin, 1975; D'Aquili, Laughlin, & McManus, 1979; D'Aquili & Newberg, 1996; Laughlin, 1991, 1996a; Laughlin & Brady, 1978; Laughlin & D'Aquili, 1974; Laughlin & McManus 1995; Laughlin, McManus, & D'Aquili 1990; Laughlin et al., 1986; Laughlin & Richardson, 1986). This body of literature set out to recognize and explain the centrality of the brain in mediating cultural transmission, social action, and subjective experience. This perspective holds that any and all states, structures, and contents of consciousness are mediated by systems of cells in the nervous system. These systems of cells are termed "models" and are determined in their initial organization by the DNA – they are "neurognositic," and in Count's terms, very much a part of the human biogram. Neural models, being made up of living cells in communication with each other, continue to grow and elaborate, guided in their growth by inherent processes of development, by personal experiences, and by culture (Laughlin, 1991). What it means to "enculturate" (anthropologists' term for the process of instilling culture into the minds of children) a member of society is in fact to influence the organization of the neural systems mediating mental processing and action in any particular instance or relative to any particular object.

Later research in biogenetic structuralism focused particularly upon the problem of how publicly available symbolism has the power to evoke subjective states of consciousness and to channel social understanding and action. The group first considered the universal properties of ritual and how rituals with their embedded techniques, neuroendocrine system "drivers," and symbolism operate to control experience in all cultures (D'Aquili, Laughlin, & McManus, 1979; Laughlin et al., 1986). They defined what they call a culture's "cycle of meaning" by which sociocultural practices operate to integrate the society's worldview (primarily carried around in people's head) and the consciousness of individual group members by expressing that worldview through symbolic texts and ritual activities in such a way that experiences arise that are then typically interpreted in terms of the worldview – producing a kind of feedback loop. For example, ritually enacted aspects of a culture's worldview are able to engender experiences in participants that in turn are interpreted by people as both verifying and enlivening the society's collective representations – engendering an effect that Durkheim (1912/1995) long before termed "collective effervescence" (see above).

This group of theorists had an influence on Victor Turner's later interest in exploring the interconnection of culture, mind, and brain (see Turner, 1983). Other scholars making important contributions to a neuroanthropological approach to consciousness studies include Michael Winkelman (1986, 1994, 2000) on the anthropology of consciousness and the neurophenomenology of shamanism; Stephen Reyna (2002) on the brain, symbolism, and hermeneutics; and Dean Falk (1992) on the evolution of the brain and consciousness. Warren TenHouten (1978–79) has also contributed much to the study on the brain and different modes of thought cross-culturally. Finally, there is recent work exploring biocultural approaches to the emotions (see Hinton, 1999), as well as research in evolutionary psychology (see Barkow, 1989; Barkow, Cosmides, & Tooby, 1992; Pinker, 1997; Sperber, 1996; Sperber & Block, 2002) that holds that the structure of human consciousness is at least partially informed by adaptive modular neural structures that mediated cognition during the long centuries of the Paleolithic (the Old Stone Age).

Cultural Psychology

Cultural psychological approaches to consciousness in anthropology largely emerged as a form of critique of the prevalent application of Piagetian research paradigms in cross-cultural psychology and psychological

anthropology in the late 1960s and early to mid-1970s. In addition to questioning many of the universalist assumptions about the development of human consciousness from a Piagetian paradigm, cultural psychological approaches to consciousness in anthropology and psychology often also draw (both explicitly and implicitly) from early 20th-century Soviet psychology and the writings of Lev Vygotsky and his students.

Influenced by the writings of Lévy-Bruhl (see above), Vygotsky (1930/1978) posited that human consciousness consists of two forms of mental functioning: (1) elementary functions (i.e., unlearned biological functions, such as hunger) and (2) higher mental functions (i.e., language, memory, abstraction). In Vygotsky's estimation, what served to mediate the transition from elementary to higher mental functioning in the context of a child's development are cultural symbols/tools. Not unlike Geertz (see above), Vygotsky understood these symbols/tools to be material manifestations of past generations of human activity and mentation, what some recent theorists have aptly termed "artifacts" (Cole, 1996). For Vygotsky, of all of the artifacts that play a role in enabling the development of higher mental functions in humans, language is the most significant. As a result, the focus of much of Vygotskian-inspired research in cultural psychology is exploring "language and activity-in-context" as the means to understanding the interpenetration of culture and consciousness (see Cole, 1996).

Although the popularizing of Vygotsky's writings in North American can largely be attributed to the influential writings and research of such eminent psychologists as Michael Cole, James Wertsch, Carl Ratner, Jerome Bruner, and others, one of the most influential proponents of a cultural psychological approach to consciousness in anthropology is Richard Shweder (1984). Although not relying as explicitly upon Soviet psychology as did his peers in the discipline of psychology, Shweder has been a champion of a pluralistic contextualism in developing his understanding of the intersection among culture, activity, and consciousness in human societies. Moreover, like his psychological colleagues, he has been staunchly anti-Piagetian in his critique of Kohlberg's theories of moral development from a cross-cultural framework.

Shweder (1984) predicates his version of cultural psychology on an understanding of consciousness as organized according to a trichotomy of mental operations classified according to rational, irrational, and non-rational distinctions. In line with a long history of debates in anthropology over putative differences between modern and primitive mentalities (see Lévy-Bruhl above), Shweder importantly emphasizes that this trichotomy points to the coequal integration of these three forms of consciousness in all cultures, regardless of their degree of "modernization." To this end, Shweder's understanding of consciousness is representative of an important shift in anthropological thinking concerning the structure and function of modern mentalities. According to this perspective, modern mentalities have come to be characterized as equally suffused with irrational and non-rational currents as primitive mentalities were once held to be. Shweder's discussion of the romantic contributions of "semantically induced memory drifts," "paradigms," "cultural frames," and "performatives" illustrates this point. Shweder is thus highly critical of what he characterizes to be Piaget's exaggerated stress upon self-constructed knowledge, personal invention, and predictable progressive development. Shweder maintains that, on the contrary, what cultural psychologists have discovered is the significance of other-dependent learning, social interaction, and the internalization of collective representations in understanding the patterning and functioning of consciousness in any given culture or social group.

Once again we see the tension between structuralist and relativist points of view at play in the anthropology of consciousness. Shweder (1984, 1991, 2003) can be praised for doing what anthropologists have always done best – that is, insisting upon the cultural influence upon learning and

behavior, which is forgotten all too easily by experimental, cognitive, and cross-cultural psychologists. Unfortunately, as is typical of many of the more relativistic approaches to culture and consciousness in anthropology and elsewhere, Shweder tends to overlook the very important distinction between structure (that is, the complexity of organization of information) and content (the information being structured). Moreover, he downplays ethnographic evidence of social institutions designed with the developmental levels of maturation of structure in mind. For instance, there are societies in which the telling of myths and other sacred narratives is done with sensitivity to the maturity of the audience (see Jorgensen, 1980, on the Telefolmin of Papua New Guinea; Barth, 1975, on the Baktaman of New Guinea; Peters, 1982, on the Tamang shamans of Nepal; Reichel-Dolmatoff, 1971, on the Tukano of Amazonia; Griaule, 1965, covering the Dogon of West Africa; and Beyer, 1973, on the instruction of Tibetan lamas).

Psychocultural Anthropology

Another approach to consciousness in anthropology can be broadly termed "psychocultural." Whereas cultural psychologists have focused much of their attention upon activity and social context as a means to understand the organization and functioning of consciousness cross-culturally, psychocultural approaches to consciousness in anthropology (see Briggs 1998; Crapanzano, 1986, 1992; Levy, 1973, 1984; Hollan, 2000, 2001; Obeyesekere, 1981, 1990; Parish, 1994; Spiro, 1987, 1994, 1997) have generally emphasized not only the significance of expanding our understanding of the complexity of the social matrix in defining consciousness but also how the multivariate nature of consciousness influences social interaction and the internalization of cultural meaning (see Throop, 2003b).

At the heart of many of these approaches is an attempt to explore the articulation of personal and cultural processes in the crucible of consciousness while also recognizing that those contents, processes, and structures that scientists have glossed with the term "consciousness" actually consist of multiple modalities that range from explicit conceptual content to non-conceptual feelings and images. In viewing consciousness from the perspective of multiple modalities that may be co-present in any given moment in the stream of consciousness, the scholars approaching the problem of culture and consciousness from a psychocultural perspective have tended to also highlight the significance of discrepancies and conflicts that may arise between differing modes of consciousness, each of which may in turn be affected differently by cultural forms.

Much of this work is explicitly or implicitly Freudian in its approach, inasmuch as it relies upon a view of the mind as structured according to non-conscious, preconscious, and conscious elements. In some of the most recent psychocultural approaches to consciousness, however, theorists have drawn increasingly from insights formulated in relational psychoanalysis (e.g., Mitchell, 1988) and dissociation theory (e.g., Stern, 1997). What all of these approaches share is the idea that culture can differentially influence non-conscious, preconscious, and conscious states and that there may be important divergences among feeling, representation, emotion, and motivation at these differing phases of consciousness. Methodologically, psychocultural approaches to consciousness in many instances also draw from psychoanalytic approaches to clinical interviewing and as a result have often relied upon indepth, open ended, person-centered interviewing strategies (see Levy & Hollan, 1998).

Melford Spiro (e.g., 1987) is one of the most influential figures in this tradition, and his writings on the relations between collective representations and mental representations within the context of a Freudian theory of mind have for decades been considered essential reading for anthropologists interested in the intersection of personal and cultural aspects of consciousness. Spiro's (1997; see also Spiro,1994) most recent formulation of this approach is based on the assumption that one must take into account the interleaving of psychodynamic and cultural processes (e.g., the relation between defense mechanisms and replication of anxiety-provoking cultural ideologies) if one is going to adequately understand both the impact of culture on consciousness and the impact of consciousness on culture. He asserts that it is only in coming to understand the role of "precultural" (e.g., biological and social) contents and structures of consciousness that one can properly understand how proclivities, dispositions, motivations, and susceptibilities emerge for the acquisition and "internalization" of specific kinds of knowledge.

Spiro contends that theories of cultural reproduction that do not address the interrelation between culture and consciousness in the context of psychological preadaptation are at a significant disadvantage in explaining why it is that some cultural propositions are often still internalized by cultural participants. For example, Spiro interprets the "Ideology of the Superior Male" and the "Ideology of the Dangerous Female" in Burma as cultural resources that may be utilized by social actors in the construction of "culturally constituted defense mechanisms." As he notes, although these two ideologies are empirically false and anxiety provoking, they are still readily internalized by Burmese men. According to Spiro, these ideologies are perpetuated in Burma, as well as in other cultures, because they are ultimately beneficial both to the individuals who internalize them and to the culture that constitutes them. Individuals who internalize these belief systems are able to partially fulfill what would otherwise be frustrated unconscious wishes and desires. At the same time, the culture of these individuals facilitates the reproduction of cultural forms by recruiting intrapsychic conflict in the service of cultural propositions and in the process motivates the enactment of socially sanctioned roles.

Robert Levy (1973, 1984) is another important figure in this tradition who has written much about culture's role in differentially patterning the cognitive saliency of various states and processes of consciousness. Although he explores many different aspects of consciousness from rationality to sensation, Levy is most often referenced with regard to his discussion of the cultural patterning of emotion. He has coined the distinction between "hyper- and hypo-cognized" emotions, which serves to draw attention to the role that culture plays in differentially articulating patterns of attention, conceptualization, and sensation in the structuring of emotional experience (see Throop, 2005). Hypercognized emotions are those that are culturally elaborated and thus highly salient, and as a consequence they tend to be centers of recurrent attentional focus for individual culture bearers. In contrast, due to their lack of culturally infused conceptual elaboration, hypocognized emotions tend to resist or defy explicit forms of representation because they tend not to evoke the same culturally attuned attentional focus. Levy formulated these insights through conducting in-depth "person-centered" interviews with informants in Tahiti, where he discovered, for instance, that there seemed to be "no unambiguous terms which represent the concepts of sadness, longing, or loneliness.... [In this light p]eople would name their condition, where I supposed that the context called for 'sadness' or 'depression,' as 'feeling troubled'... as 'not feeling an inner push' as 'feeling heavy' as 'feeling fatigued' and a variety of other terms all referring to a generally troubled or subdued body state" (1973, p. 305).

Building upon the work of Spiro, Levy, and others, Douglas Hollan (2000) has recently argued that any adequate theory of culture must thus be predicated upon an understanding of the relations between cultural processes and "the fluidity and complexity of the psychological states that underlie" them. In line with psychocultural approaches generally in anthropology, Hollan's formulation pivots on the recognition of how both the fluctuating nature of social interaction (self – "not me"-object relations) and the transitional nature of consciousness (conscious-preconscious-unconscious relations) mutually affect those

processes subserving the maintenance, transmission, and creation of cultural meaning. Through developing a complex model of the relationship between the conscious and unconscious dimensions of the mind, which he stresses are seldom organized into discrete or independent realms but instead are held to coexist in ever-shifting and fluid processes of interpenetration, Hollan suggests that researchers interested in understanding the relationship between culture and consciousness must explore how these various intrapsychic, interpsychic, and extrapsycic processes contribute to both the standardization and "personalization of meaning."

Anthropology of the Senses

Influenced by various semiotic and phenomenological traditions, the cultural patterning of olfactory, haptic, and auditory sensations took on a renewed significance during the mid-1970s and early 1980s in the work of Alfred Gell (1977), Valentine Daniel (1983/1991), Steven Feld (1984), and Paul Stoller (1984). Indeed, the wave of interest in non-visual sensation during this period can be tied to more general trends in anthropology concerning the exploration of culture in relation to non-conceptual modes of human existence. Here Bourdieu's writings on the concept of habitus as a culturally inculcated generative structure shaping fields of perception, motivation, judgment, and action (see above); a burgeoning interest in the anthropology of emotion that largely set out to question Cartesian-inspired distinctions between mind-body and thought-feeling (Lutz, 1988; Rosaldo, 1984); critiques of visualist and representationalist biases in modern ethnography (Tyler, 1984); and a movement toward developing theories of practice in the discipline as a whole (Ortner 1984) can all be seen as arising out of the same general *Zeitgeist* of resistance to what a growing number of thinkers perceived to be the overly intellectualist orientations of Lévi-Straussian structuralism and Geertzian textualism (see above).

The early anthropological writings on culture and sensation have played an important role in setting the stage for the great efflorescence of work on sensation that emerged in the discipline during the 1990s. Sensation has clearly emerged as a significant area of theorizing and research in the discipline as a whole and now involves such questions as how sensory modalities are implicated in healing practices (Csordas, 1994; Desjarlais, 1992; Landerman & Roseman, 1996), cultural variations in senses of space and place (Feld & Basso, 1996), the influence of culture on ordering various "ratios of sense"(Classen, 1997; Howes, 1991; Synnott, 1993), and the relation between sensation and moral sensibilities (Geurts, 2002). In addition, there is work exploring the cultural patterning of varying somatic modes of attention (Csordas, 1993; Sobo, 1996; Throop, 2003a); the importance of recognizing differing sensory orders in the context of ethnographic research (Stoller, 1989, 1997); the cultural elaboration of specific sensory modalities, such as audition, olfaction, or taste (Chuengsatiansup, 1999; Rasmussen, 1999); and renewed interest in debates over culture and color perception (Goodwin, 1997; Hardin & Maffi, 1997).

Although a great deal of important work has emerged out of this tradition, there is little doubt that the work of the Concordia Group – consisting of David Howes, Constance Classen, and Anthony Synnott – has provided much of the impetus behind the renewed interest in culture and sensation. In a series of books and articles, these three scholars have argued for the historical rootedness of the senses. Anthropologists are being encouraged to move away from the strictly physicalist assumptions of sensory psychology to a stance that not only explores the effect of cultural assumptions and values on the functioning of any one particular sensory modality but also takes into consideration "inter-sensory relations."

According to Classen (1997), the research of the Concordia Group has challenged three prevalent assumptions in anthropological writing on sensation: (1) that the senses in some way provide a transparent window upon the world and are thus in some way "precultural"(1997, p. 402); (2) that all cultures organize their sensory orders in terms of a structure similar to that of the West with its bias toward visualism; and (3) the deeply ingrained "prejudice against smell, taste, and touch as 'animal senses'" (1997, p. 405) and the tendency to believe that there is little variation within sensory modes cross-culturally. Instead, Classen and her colleagues hold that it is time for anthropologists to recognize that culture not only patterns the relative value assigned to each sensory modality but also that within each modality there are various experiential properties that can serve to fuel cultural elaboration. For instance, the "vision which is deemed rational and analytic in the West...may be associated with irrationality in another society" (1997, p. 404). Or vision may very well be associated primarily with aesthetic values that have little to do with the acquisition of "objective" forms of knowledge about the external world.

Central to the methodology proposed by Howes and Classen (1991) is a phenomenologically grounded effort to penetrate our taken-for-granted sensory attunements toward the world in an attempt to better approximate the sensory orders most valued in a particular culture under study. To discover the various ways that a particular culture sets out to differentially "emphasize or repress" different varieties of sensory experience, Howes and Classen suggest that it is first necessary for the researcher to work to "overcome, to the extent possible, his or her own sensory biases" (1991, p. 260). This effort begins with working to evaluate and discover one's own sensory predispositions. To this end, Howes and Classen suggest that researchers follow an exercise devised by Galton that entails describing a past event in one's life and noting which sensory modalities are most heavily relied upon in recounting the details of that event. The second step in this methodology consists of "training oneself to be sensitive to a multiplicity of sensory expressions" (1991, p. 260). Here the authors recommend following a basic phenomenological principle that is based on "disengaging one's attention from the object itself so as to focus on how each of the sensory properties would impinge on one's consciousness were they not filtered in any way" (1991, p. 260). This disengagement is then complemented with cultivating the ability to be "of two sensoria about things"; that is, to be "able to operate with complete awareness in two perceptual systems or sensory orders simultaneously (the sensory order of one's own culture and that of the culture studied" and constantly comparing notes (1991, p. 260).

Having worked to effectively bracket one's "natural sensory attitude," Howes and Classen then argue that there are several different avenues to explore in attempting to outline the sensory order of any given culture. They advise researchers to begin by investigating the existing words for the different senses, exploring which of the various sensory modalities have the largest vocabulary allotted to them, and determining how the various senses are used in metaphor and other forms of expressive speech. This effort can be complemented by an examination of cultural aesthetics and the realm of material artifacts. Here cultural ideas regarding beauty can be evaluated in terms of the relative contribution of each of the senses. Moreover, an investigator can examine how various cultural artifacts are used to represent or evoke the senses of the creator/user/admirer. For instance, Howes and Classen (1991) assert that a "Tsimshian 'wraparound' representation of Bear corresponds to the experience of sound, which also envelops and surrounds one.... [in other words the] 'ear-minded' Tsimshian would thus seem to transpose visual imagery into auditory imagery in their visual art" (1991, p. 265).

In addition to these two strategies, Howes and Classen point out that the decoration and alteration of the form of the body can further serve as an effective means to explore a culture's sensory order. For example, which of the sense organs are highlighted by decoration? Sensory orders may also be explored through close examination of child-rearing practices where careful attention is paid to which senses are stressed

or utilized by parents when raising their children. This exploration can also be augmented by investigations that look at how the natural and built environment, rituals, mythology, cosmology, and communication media potentiate or dispotentiate the various senses.

Cultural Phenomenological and Neurophenomenological Approaches

As evident in the methodological orientation of sensorial anthropology outlined above, anthropology has in recent years discovered the significance of phenomenology, blending methods derived from various phenomenological approaches into the ethnographic fieldwork "toolkit" (see Csordas 1990, 1993, 1994; Desjarlais, 1997, 2003; Jackson, 1989, 1996; Throop 2002, 2003a, Throop & Murphy, 2002). Methodologically, a phenomenological ethnography requires that the researcher focus on the experiences of individual actors immersed in social interaction (see Jackson, 1996; Chapter 4). The shift is thus toward examining the world of everyday experience and how individuals in their everyday interactions are themselves conscious of their own lifeworlds. In this approach, the stories and experiences of individual social actors in the context of everydayness form the field of investigation for the researcher. This marks, of course, at least a partial return to the fieldwork strategy of Franz Boas (see above).

An excellent example of phenomenological anthropology's contributions to the study of consciousness and culture is found in the influential work of Thomas Csordas (1990, 1993, 1994, 2002). A main thrust of Csordas's writings (1990) is that anthropology as a discipline is in the processes of shifting toward a paradigm of embodiment. He suggests that such a view does not entail that all cultures should be understood to "have the same structures as bodily experience, but that embodied experience is the starting point for analyzing human participation in a cultural world" (1993, p. 135). To this end, a key phenomenological insight (borrowed from Merleau-Ponty, 1962) advanced by Csordas (1990) is that perception does not begin, but, rather ends in objects. That is, perceptual experience is understood to be an active process of constitution whereby otherwise ambiguous stimuli are able to be articulated into personally and culturally meaningful forms. Csordas's cultural phenomenology thus sets out to explore those cultural processes implicated in the constitution of those objects confronting a social actor's consciousness moment by moment.

According to Csordas, embodied experience as a mode of being-in-the-world becomes a complementary perspective to, what has historically been, an all too dominant textualist and representationalist perspective in anthropological theorizing. A major shortcoming of such perspectives, Csordas argues, is that they presume "an unbridgeable gulf between language and experience" that is "predicated on the notion that language can only be about itself" (1994, p. xii). On the contrary, Csordas maintains that cultural phenomenological investigations into the dynamics and structures of consciousness evidence the fact that "language is not only a form of observable behavior but a medium of intersubjectivity, so that it is fair to say that language gives us authentic access to experience" (1994, :xii).

This assertion is based on Csordas' assumption, following Merleau-Ponty's phenomenology (1962) and the practice theory of Bourdieu (see above), that another person's intentions, emotions, thoughts, and desires are manifest preobjectively as an intersubjectively accessible "co-presence" that can be immediately grasped "insofar as we share the same habitus." By relying upon Bourdieu's concept of habitus – which serves to explain how it is that perceptual, affective, motivational, and evaluative orientations can become shared by individuals whose respective consciousnesses have been conditioned in similar social, economic, and cultural environments – Csordas argues that he is able to account for a dispositional resonance between actors that both precedes and informs the structure and use of language.

One of Csordas's (1993) most important contributions to anthropological studies of

consciousness, however, has been to advance the notion of "somatic modes of attention," which he defines as those "culturally elaborated ways of attending to and with one's body in surrounding that include the embodied presence of others" (1993, p. 138). In other words, Csordas wishes to highlight the various ways that culture can pattern individual attention to bodily sensation in relation to both perception and motility. As he explains, to "attend to a bodily sensation is not to attend to the body as an isolated object, but to attend to the body's situation in the world" (1993, p. 138). This approach should not be mistaken for a sensory-based empiricism because Csordas argues that any attempt to compare the sensation of heat, for example, in the context of healing with the experience of heat associated with blushing fails to recognize the extent to which a synthesis exists between interpretive and experiential realms. Examples provided by Csordas drawn from his field work among Catholic Charismatic groups include the interpretation of sensations of "queasiness" as "indicating the activity of evil spirits, and an unexpected sneeze or yawn.... [indicating] that a spirit is passing out of the supplicant through the healer" (1993, p. 141),

Also arguing for an embodied understanding of consciousness, we have incorporated the earlier work of the biogenetic structuralist group (see above) in developing a phenomenology that is grounded in both the neurosciences and cultural anthropology – what we term a "cultural neurophenomenology." Our approach seeks to wed the application of a trained phenomenology that controls for cultural variation in perception and interpretation and is yet still attentive to the personal and cultural influences on everyday experience with information from the neurosciences about how the organ of experience – the brain – is structured and functions.

In previous writings we have suggested that the influence of culture on consciousness is differentially articulated with differing strata of the human nervous system. We have also argued that the phenomenological and neurophysiological structures underlying many apparently diverse cultural institutions – institutions such as ceremonial ritual, cosmological worldviews, myth, and the almost ubiquitous drive among the world's peoples to alter their states of consciousness – may operate to "true-up" the lifeworld of individual members of society in relation to an extra-mental reality within which each person and group must adapt (Laughlin & Throop, 1999, 2001; Throop & Laughlin, 2002). We also incorporate the notion of a "cycle of meaning" (see above) to explore how a culture's myth and ritual purvey a given culture's worldview in such a powerful way that they are able to engender experiences in individuals that in turn verify and enliven the society's collective representations – what Durkheim once termed "collective effervescence."

Perhaps most significant for this review is our attempt to advance a corrective to overly cognitivist and propositionally biased accounts of consciousness and its contents by exploring what we hold to be the multiplex nature of human consciousness. That is, we hold that consciousness is differentially organized according to the conceptual and abstract contents of linguistically mediated thought *and* the imagistic, perceptual, and somatosensory contents of presentational forms of awareness (see also Hunt, 1995; Winkelman, 2000). For instance, in an article investigating the cultural patterning of human emotional experience (Lauglin & Throop, 1999), we suggest that different phenomenologically accessible variants of emotional awareness are grounded in the differing structural and functional strata of the human brain. The significance of these insights for the study of culture and consciousness is tied to the fact that the various neurophysiological structures mediating various conscious modalities may be affected differently by cultural resources and as such may provide researchers with a way to account for both interpsychic variation *and* transcultural similarities in the structuring of subjective experience crossculturally.

Conclusion

Anthropological approaches to consciousness have traditionally been based on the fact that anthropologists, like all human beings on the planet, have been inclined by the very structure of their own consciousness and its intentional nature to focus their attention on objects: thought objects, perceptual objects, sensory objects, physical objects, cultural objects, etc. In the act of focusing on these objects – the contents of consciousness – other processes and structures available for scrutiny within the stream of consciousness are necessarily occluded. Thus anthropologists have played an important role in highlighting the striking variation that is apparent both cross-culturally and interpersonally in terms of the constitution and organization of comparable objects.

Although it is true that some scholars, like Levi-Strauss, have examined how cultural objects (i.e., texts, artifacts, behaviors, symbols) may evidence patterns that resonate across cultures, thus working back from cultural product to the shared structures of human consciousness, the overall tendency in anthropology has been to focus on content in terms of its variation and fluctuation. Indeed, this tendency has served anthropology well inasmuch as it has frequently forced scientists in other disciplines who are interested in exploring invariant aspects of consciousness to take notice of cross-cultural variation. Doing so injects some humility into their otherwise sweeping statements concerning the universality of these structures; a universality that all too often has arisen from the reification of unscrutinized cultural assumptions about the nature of consciousness held by a particular thinker whole cloth onto all of humanity.

That said, anthropology has also demonstrated an equally long history of awareness and concern for the similarity, psychic unity, and shared aspects of consciousness across cultural boundaries. Accordingly, one of the most important points to take away from this review of anthropological approaches to consciousness is that it seems far too simplistic to assume a unidirectional flow of causation from the external organization of socioeconomically determined activity patterns and cultural symbols to the formation of contents and structures of consciousness, just as it is too simplistic to assume that social and cultural forms are merely the externalization of pregiven structures of consciousness. The truth of the matter seems to lie somewhere between these two long-standing polar perspectives concerning the relation between culture and consciousness. Indeed, the truth would appear to lie in attempting to develop perspectives within an anthropological frame that focus equally on exploring content and structure, object and process, or what Edmund Husserl termed *noema* (act) and *noesis* (content; see Ströker, 1993 and Chapter 2).

A second significant insight that readers should take away from this discussion is the fact that anthropologists have long sought to highlight in their research how culture patterns the responses that social scientists receive from their informants. Here the questions that anthropologists have asked concern the cultural frames of reference that are embedded in what scientists perceive to be "culture-free" standardized tests used to gain insight into the structure and content of consciousness. For instance, in the context of cross-cultural research exploring the cultural patterning of cognitive abilities, anthropological research points to the importance of asking whether a refusal to answer a syllogism, which informants may attribute to an "unfamiliarity" with the topic at hand, indicates differences in cognitive functioning or differences in communicative practices. For example, in their important work on language socialization, Ochs and Schieffelin (1984) assert that, although Schieffelin's Kaluli informants often refused to speculate about another individual's thoughts, intentions, and feelings, this observation should not simply be interpreted as an indication that the Kaluli have no theory of mind. Quite the contrary, "Kaluli obviously interpret and assess one another's available

behaviors and internal states, these interpretations are [just] not acceptable as topics of talk" (1984:290).

There are a number of other key insights that have arisen from the anthropological study of consciousness: (1) the abundant evidence in the ethnographic record for the interdependent and dynamic relationship among collective (cultural) knowledge, enculturation, individual subjectivity, and transculturally shared somatic structures in the constitution of consciousness; (2) the suggestion that the drive to alter individual states of consciousness by socially prescribed means is fundamental to both healing, health and producing a worldview that better accords with reality; (3) the contents of consciousness are both structured by the inherent organization of the body, and plastic and adaptively responsive to environmental, personal, and cultural influences; (4) the qualitative research devoted to the study of consciousness as it is manifest in the context of everyday social interaction is crucial to developing a more accurate understanding of the structures and contents of human consciousness cross-culturally; and (5) there still remains in contemporary scientific and philosophical theorizing a number of unexamined assumptions about consciousness that can be traced to particularized cultural orientations to the relation between mind and body.

Considering consciousness from an anthropological point of view has the advantage of grounding consciousness research in the naturalistic everydayness of human experience, a perspective all too easily lost in the laboratory. We are often reminded of the story told by the great comparative psychologist, Emil Menzel (1967), who spent years working with olive baboons in the laboratory, and had pretty much concluded they were a dull and unintelligent species of primate. Then chance took him to Kenya where he took a safari out among olive baboon troops in their natural environment. He suddenly realized that his very erroneous picture of baboon intelligence was based upon experimental questions that had little to do with the natural environment in which they evolved. Ever after Menzel argued very elegantly for the necessity of blending experimental with naturalistic research. Much the same situation confronts consciousness research today, and the main role of anthropology is to broaden our collective perspective by bringing the naturalistic framework back into our scope of inquiry.

References

Aberle, D. (1966). *The peyote religion among the Navajo*. Chicago: Aldine.

Adam, B. (1994). Perceptions of time. In T. Ingold (Ed.), *Companion encyclopedia of anthropology* (pp. 503–526). London: Routledge.

Antze, P., & Lambek, M. (Eds.). (1996). *Tense past: Cultural essays in trauma and memory*. London: Routledge.

Baars, B. J. (1997). *In the theater of consciousness: The workspace of the mind*. New York: Oxford University Press.

Barkow, J. (1989). *Darwin, sex and status: Biological approaches to mind and culture*. Toronto: University of Toronto Press.

Barkow, J., Cosmides, L., & Tooby, J. (Eds). (1992). *The adapted mind: Evolutionary psychology and the generation of culture*. Oxford: Oxford University Press.

Barnouw, V. (1946). Paranormal phenomena and culture. *Journal of the American Society for Psychical Research*, 40, 2–21.

Barrett, H. C. (2004). Descent versus design in Shuar children's reasoning about animals. *Journal of Cognition and Culture*, 4, 25–50.

Barth, F. (1975). *Ritual knowledge among the Baktaman of New Guinea*. New Haven: Yale University Press.

Bartlett, F. C. (1932). *Remembering: A study in experimental and social psychology*. Cambridge: Cambridge University Press.

Bastian, A. (1881). *Vorgeschichte der ethnologie*. Berlin.

Bastian, A. (1887). *Die Welt in ibren spiegelungen unter dem wandel des völkergedankens*. Berlin.

Beyer, S. (1973). *The cult of Tara: Magic and ritual in Tibet*. City, State: Publisher.

Bharati, A. (1975). *The Tantric tradition*. New York: Samuel Weiser.

Boas, F. (1974). On alternating sounds. In G. W. Stocking, Jr. (Ed.), *A Franz Boas reader: The shaping of American anthropology, 1883–1911* (pp. 72–76). Chicago: University of Chicago Press. (Original work published 1889)

Boas, F. (1910/1938). *The mind of primitive man*. New York: The Free Press.

Bock, P. K. (1999). *Rethinking psychological anthropology: Continuity and change in the study of human action*. Prospect Heights, Illinois: Waveland Press, Inc.

Boucouvalas, M. (1980). Transpersonal psychology: A working outline of the field. *Journal of Transpersonal Psychology*, 12(1), 37–46.

Bourdieu, P. (1977). *Outline of a theory of practice*. Cambridge: Cambridge University Press.

Bourdieu, P. (1985). The genesis of the concepts of *habitus* and *field*. *Sociocriticism*, 2(2): 11–24.

Bourdieu, P. (1990). *Logic of practice*. Stanford: Stanford University Press.

Bourdieu, P. (2000). *Pascalian meditations*. Stanford: Stanford University Press.

Bourguignon, E. (1973). *Religion, altered states of consciousness, and social change*. Columbus, OH: Ohio State University Press.

Bourguignon, E. (1976). *Possession*. San Francisco: Chandler and Sharp.

Braud, W., & Anderson, R. (Eds.). (1998). *Transpersonal research methods for the social sciences*. Thousand Oaks, CA: SAGE Publications.

Briggs, J. (1998). *Inuit Morality Play*. New Haven: Yale University Press.

Bruner, J. (1951). Personality dynamics and the process of perceiving. In R. V. Blake, & G. V. Ramsey (Eds.), *Perception: An approach to personality* (pp. 121–147). New York: Ronald Press.

Campbell, R. L., & Staniford, P. S. (1978). Transpersonal anthropology. *Phoenix: The Journal of Transpersonal Anthropology*, 2(1), 28–40.

Chagnon, N. (1977). *Yanomamo: The fierce people*. New York: Holt, Rinehart and Winston.

Changeux, J.-P. (1985). *Neuronal man: The biology of mind*. Oxford: Oxford University Press.

Chuengsatiansup, K. (1999). Sense, symbol, and soma: Illness experience in the soundscape of everyday life. *Culture, Medicine, and Psychiatry*, 23(3), 273–301.

Classen, C. (1997). Foundation for an anthropology of the senses. *International Social Science Journal*, 153, 401–412.

Cole, M. (1996). *Cultural psychology*. Cambridge, MA: Harvard University Press.

Conklin, H. (1969). Lexicographical treatment of folk taxonomies. In S. Tyler (Ed.), *Cognitive anthropology*. New York: Holt, Rinehart and Winston.

Coult, A. (1977). *Psychedelic anthropology: The study of man through the manifestation of the mind*. Philadelphia: Dorrance & Company.

Count, E. W. (1958). The biological basis of human sociality. *American Anthropologist, 60*, 1049–1085.

Count, E. W. (1973). *Being and becoming human*. New York: Van Nostrand Reinhold.

Count, E. W. (1990). Interview with Earl W. Count. *Neuroanthropology Network Newsletter, 3*(1), 5–8.

Crapanzano, V. (1986). *Tuhami: Portrait of a Moroccan*. Chicago: University of Chicago Press.

Crapanzano, V. (1992). *Herme's dilemma and Hamlet's desire; On the epistomology of interpretation*. Cambridge: Harvard University Press.

Csordas, T. J. (1990). Embodiment as a paradigm for anthropology. *Ethos, 18*, 5–47.

Csordas, T. J. (1993). Somatic modes of attention. *Cultural Anthropology, 8*, 135–156.

Csordas, T. J. (1994). *The sacred self: A cultural phenomenology of charismatic healing*. Los Angeles: University of California Press

Csordas, T. J. (2002). *Body/meaning/healing*. New York: Palgrave.

D'Andrade, R. (1981). The cultural part of cognition. *Cognitive Science, 5*, 179–195.

D'Andrade, R. (1984). Cultural meaning systems. In R. Shweder & R. Levine (Eds.), *Culture theory* (pp.88–119). Cambridge: Cambridge University Press,

D'Andrade, R. (1987). A folk model of the mind. In D. Holland & N. Quinn (Eds.), *Cultural models in language and thought* (pp. 112–148). Cambridge: Cambridge University Press.

D'Andrade, R. (1995). *The development of cognitive anthropology*. Cambridge: Cambridge University Press.

Daniel, V. E. (1991). The pulse as an icon in Siddha medicine. In D. Howes (Ed.), *The varieties of sensory experience* (pp. 100–110). Toronto: University of Toronto Press. (Original work published 1983)

D'Aquili, E. G. (1982). Senses of reality in science and religion: A neuroepistemological perspective. *Zygon, 17*(4), 361–384.

D'Aquili, E. G. (1983). The myth-ritual complex: A biogenetic structural analysis. *Zygon, 18*(3), 247–269.

D'Aquili, E. G., & Laughlin, C. D. (1975). The biopsychological determinants of religious ritual behavior. *Zygon, 10*(1), 32–58.

D'Aquili, E. G., Laughlin, C. D., & McManus, J. (1979). *The spectrum of ritual*. New York: Columbia University Press.

D'Aquili, E. G., & Newberg, A. B. (1996). Consciousness and the machine. *Zygon, 31*(2), 235–252.

Desjarlais, R. (1992). *Body and emotion*. Philadelphia: University of Pennsylvania Press.

Desjarlais, R. (1997). *Shelter blues*. Philadelphia: University of Pennsylvania Press.

Desjarlais, R. (2003). *Sensory biographies*. Berkeley: University of California Press.

Dissanayake, E. (1992). *Homo aestheticus: Where art comes from and why*. Seattle: University of Washington Press.

Dobkin de Rios, M. (1984). *Hallucinogens: Cross-cultural perspectives*. Albuquerque: University of New Mexico Press.

Dobkin de Rios, M., & Winkelman, M. (Eds.). (1989). Shamanism and altered states of consciousness. Special issue of the *Journal of Psychoactive Drugs, 21*(1).

Donald, M. (1991). *Origins of the modern mind*. Cambridge, MA: Harvard University Press.

Duranti, A. (1993). Truth and intentionality: An ethnographic perspective. *Cultural Anthropology, 8*, 214–245.

Duranti, A. (2006). The social ontology of intentions. *Discourse Studies, 8*, 31–40.

Durkheim, E., & Mauss, M. (1963). *Primitive classification* (R. Needham, Trans.). Chicago: University of Chicago Press. (Original work published 1903)

Durkheim, E. (1995). *The elementary forms of religious life* (K. Fields, Trans.). London: Allen. (Original work published 1912)

Falk, D..(1992). *Braindance: What new findings reveal about human origins and brain evolution*. New York: Henry Holt.

Feld, S. (1984). Sound structure as social structure. *Ethnomusicology, 28*(3), 383–408.

Feld, S., & Basso, K. H. (Eds.). (1996). *Senses of place*. Santa Fe: School of American Research Press.

Foster, M. L. (1994). Symbolism: The foundation of culture. In T. Ingold (Ed.), *Companion encyclopedia of anthropology* (pp. 366–395). London: Routledge.

Foster, M. L., & Botscharow, L. J. (Eds.). (1990). *The life of symbols.* Boulder, CO: Westview.

Frake, C. O. (1961). The diagnosis of disease among the Subanun of Mindanao. *American Anthropologists, 63*, 113–132.

Furst, P. (1976). *Hallucinogens and culture.* San Francisco: Chandler and Sharp.

Garro, L. (1998). On the rationality of decision making studies: Part 2: Divergent rationalities. *Medical Anthropology Quarterly, 12*(3).

Garro, L. (2000). Remembering what one knows and the construction of the past. *Ethos, 28*(3), 275–319.

Garro, L. (2001). The remembered past in a culturally meaningful life: Remembering as culture, social and cognitive process. In C. Moore & H. Mathews (Eds.), *The psychology of cultural experience* (pp. 105–150). Cambridge: Cambridge University Press.

Geertz, C. (1973). *The interpretation of cultures.* New York: Basic Books.

Geertz, C. (1983). *Local knowledge: Further essays in interpretive anthropology.* New York: Basic Books.

Gell, A. (1977). Magic, perfume, dream. In I. M. Lewis (Ed.), *Symbols and sentiments: Cross-cultural studies in symbolism* (pp. 25–38). London: Academic Press.

Gell, A. (1992). *The anthropology of time: Cultural constructions of temporal maps and images.* Oxford: Berg.

George, M. (1995). Dreams, reality, and the desire and intent of dreamers as experienced by a fieldworker. *Anthropology of Consciousness, 6*(3), 17–33.

Geurts, K. L. (2002). *Culture and the senses: Bodily ways of knowing in an African community.* Berkeley: University of California Press.

Goodenough, W. (1971). *Culture, language, and society.* Reading, MA: Addison-Wesley.

Goodwin, C. (1997). The blackness of black: color categories as situated practices. In L. B. Resnick, et al. (Eds.), *Discourse, tools and reasoning: Essays in situated cognition* (pp. 111–140) Berlin: Springer.

Griaule, M. (1965). *Conversations with Ogotemmeli: an introductin to Dogon religious ideas* (R. Butler, Trans.). London: Oxford University Press.

Grindal, B. T. (1983). Into the heart of Sisala experience: Witnessing death divination. *Journal of Anthropological Research, 39*(1), 60–80.

Gumperz, J. J., & Levinson, S. C. (Eds.). (1996). *Rethinking linguistic relativity.* Cambridge: Cambridge University Press.

Haddon, A. C. (Ed.). (1901). *Reports of the Cambridge expedition to Torres Straits: Vol. II: Physiology and psychology.* Cambridge: Cambridge University Press.

Halifax, J. (1975). *Shamanic voices.* New York: Dutton.

Hallowell, A. I. (1955). *Culture and experience.* Philadelphia: University of Pennsylvania Press.

Hamill, J. F. (1990). *Ethno-logic: The anthropology of human reasoning.* Urbana, IL: University of Illinois Press.

Hardin, C. L., & Maffi, L. (Eds.). (1997). *Color categories in thought and language.* Cambridge: Cambridge University Press.

Harkness, S. (1992). Human development in psychological anthropology. In T. Schwartz, G. M. White, & C. A. Lutz (Eds.), *New directions in psychological anthropology* (pp. 102–124). Cambridge: Cambridge University Press.

Harner, M. (ed.) (1973). Hallucinogens and shamanism. New York: Oxford University Press.

Heelas, P., & Lock, A. (Eds.). (1981). *Indigenous psychologies: The anthropology of the self.* New York: Academic Press.

Henrich, J., Boyd, R., Bowles, S., Camerer, C., Fehr, E., & Gintis, H. (2004). *Foundations of human sociality: Economic experiments and ethnographic evidence from fifteen small-scale societies.* New York: Oxford University Press.

Hinton, A. L. (Ed.). (1999). *Biocultural approaches to the emotions.* Cambridge: Cambridge University Press.

Hollan, D. (2000). Constructivist models of mind, contemporary psychoanalysis, and the development of culture theory. *American Anthropologist, 102*(3), 538–550.

Hollan, D. (2001). Developments in person-centered ethnography. In H. Mathews and C. Moore (Eds.), *The psychology of cultural experience.* New York: Cambridge University Press.

Howes, D. (ed.) (1991). *The varieties of sensory experience*. Toronto: University of Toronto Press.

Howes, D., & Classen, C. (1991). Conclusion: Sounding sensory profiles. In D. Howes (Ed.), *The varieties of sensory experience*. Toronto: University of Toronto Press.

Hunt, E., & Agnoli, F. (1991). The Whorfian hypothesis: A cognitive psychological perspective. *Psychological Review*, 98(3), 377–389.

Hunt, H. T. (1995). *On the nature of consciousness: Cognitive, phenomenological, and transpersonal perspectives*. New Haven, CT: Yale University Press.

Husserl, E. (1962). *Ideas: General introduction to pure phenomenology.* New York: Collier Books. (Original work published 1913)

Husserl, E. (1950/1993). *Cartesian meditations*. Dordrecht: Kluwer Academic Press.

Husserl, E. (1970). *The crisis of European sciences and transcendental phenomenology*. Evanston, IL: Northwestern University Press. (Original work published 1954)

Jackson, M. (1989). *Paths toward a clearing: Radical empiricism and ethnographic inquiry*. Bloomington: Indiana University Press.

Jackson, M. (ed.) (1996). *Things as they are: New directions in phenomenological anthropology*. Bloomington: Indiana University Press.

Jilik, W. G. (1982). *Indian healing*. Surrey, British Columbia, Canada: Hancock House.

Jorgensen, D. (1980). What's in a name? The meaning of meaninglessness in Telefolmin. *Ethos*, 8, 349–66.

Katz, R. (1982). *Boiling energy: Community healing among the Kalahari Kung*. Cambridge, MA: Harvard University Press.

Kay, P., & Kempton, W. (1984). What is the Sapir-Whorf hypothesis? *American Anthropologist*, 86, 65–79.

Koepping, K.-P. (1983). *Adolf Bastian and the psychic unity of mankind: The foundations of anthropology in nineteenth century Germany*. St. Lucia: University of Queensland Press.

Kuklick, H. (1991). *The savage within: The history of British anthropology, 1885–1945*. Cambridge: Cambridge University Press.

Laboratory of Comparative Human Cognition (LCHC). (1983). Culture and cognitive development. In P. Mussen (Ed.), *Handbook of child psychology: History, theory, and methods* (pp. 295–356). New York: Wiley.

Landerman, C., & Roseman, M. (Eds.). (1996). *The performance of healing*. London: Routledge.

Lang, A. (1894). *Cock lane and common sense*. New York: AMS Press.

Lang, A. (1897). *The book of dreams and ghosts*. London. Longmans.

Lang, A. (1898). *The making of religion*. New York: AMS Press.

Laughlin, C. D. (1990). At play in the fields of the lord: The role of metanoia in the development of consciousness. *Play and Culture*, 3(3), 173–192.

Laughlin, C. D. (1991). Pre- and perinatal brain development and enculturation: A biogenetic structural approach. *Human Nature*, 2(3), 171–213.

Laughlin, C. D. (1994a). Transpersonal anthropology, then and now. *Transpersonal Review*, 1(1), 7–10.

Laughlin, C. D. (1994b). Psychic energy and transpersonal experience: A biogenetic structural account of the Tibetan Dumo practice. In D. E. Young & J.-G. Goulet (Eds.), *Being changed by cross-cultural encounters*. Peterborough, Ontario: Broadview Press.

Laughlin, C. D. (1996a). Archetypes, neurognosis and the quantum sea. *Journal of Scientific Exploration*, 10(3), 375–400.

Laughlin, C. D. (1996b). Phenomenological anthropology. In D. Levinson & M. Ember (Eds.), *Encyclopedia of cultural anthropology* (Vol. 3, pp. 924–926). New York: Henry Holt.

Laughlin, C. D. (1989). Transpersonal anthropology: Some methodological issues. *Western Canadian Anthropologist*, 5, 29–60.

Laughlin, C. D., & Brady, I. A. (1978). *Extinction and survival in human populations*. New York: Columbia University Press.

Laughlin, C. D., & D'Aquili, E. G. (1974). *Biogenetic structuralism*. New York: Columbia University Press.

Laughlin, C. D., & McManus, J. (1995). The relevance of the radical empiricism of William James to the anthropology of consciousness. *Anthropology of Consciousness*, 6(3), 34–46.

Laughlin, C. D., McManus, J., & D'Aquili, E. G. (1990). *Brain, symbol and experience: Toward a neurophenomenology of consciousness*. New York: Columbia University Press.

Laughlin, C. D., McManus, J., Rubinstein, R. A., & Shearer, J. (1986). The ritual control of experience. In N. K. Denzin (Ed.), *Studies in symbolic interaction* (Part A). Greenwich, CT: JAI Press.

Laughlin, C. D., McManus, J., & Shearer, J.. (1983). Dreams, trance and visions: What a transpersonal anthropology might look like. *Phoenix: The Journal of Transpersonal Anthropology, 7*(1/2), 141–159.

Laughlin, C. D., McManus, J., & Webber, M. (1984). Neurognosis, individuation, and Tibetan arising yoga practice. *Phoenix: The Journal of Transpersonal Anthropology, 8*(1/2), 91–106.

Laughlin, C. D., & Richardson, S. (1986, June). The future of human consciousness. *Futures*, 401–419.

Laughlin, C. D., & Throop, C. J. (1999). Emotion: A view from biogenetic structuralism. In A. L. Hinton (Ed.), *Biocultural approaches to the emotions* (pp. 329–363). Cambridge: Cambridge University Press.

Laughlin, C. D., & Throop, C. J. (2001). Imagination and reality: On the relations between myth, consciousness, and the quantum sea. *Zygon, 36*(4), 709–736.

Lederman, C. (1988). Wayward winds: Malay archetypes, and theory of personality in the context of shamanism. *Social Science and Medicine, 27*(8), 799–810.

Lee, S. (1980). Association for transpersonal anthropology. *Phoenix: The Journal of Transpersonal Anthropology, 4*(1/2), 2–6.

Lévi-Strauss, C. (1963). *Structural anthropology*. New York: Basic Books. (Original work published 1958)

Lévi-Strauss, C. (1969a). *The elementary structures of kinship*. Boston: Beacon Press. (Original work published 1949)

Lévi-Strauss, C. (1969b). *The raw and the cooked*. Chicago: University of Chicago Press. (Original work published 1964)

Lévi-Strauss, C. (1973). *From honey to ashes*. New York: Harper Row. (Original work published 1966)

Lévi-Strauss, C. (1978). *The origin of table manners*. New York: Harper Row. (Original work published 1968)

Lévi-Strauss, C. (1981). *Naked man*. Chicago: University of Chicago Press. (Original work published 1971)

Levy, R. I. (1973). *Tahitians*. Chicago: University of Chicago Press.

Levy, R. I. (1984). Emotion, knowing and culture. In R. Shweder & R. A. Levine (Eds.), *Culture theory: essays on mind, self, and emotion* (pp. 214–237). Cambridge: Cambridge University Press.

Levy, R., & Hollan, D. (1998). Person-center interviewing and observation. In H. R. Bernard (Ed.), *Handbook of methods in cultural anthropology* (pp. 331–362). New York: Altamira Press.

Lévy-Bruhl, L. (1926). *How natives think*. London: Allen & Unwin

Lévy-Bruhl, L. (1975). *The notebooks on primitive mentality*. New York: Harper & Row.

Lincoln, J. S. (1935). *The dream in primitive culture*. London: Cresset.

Long, J. K. (1976). Shamanism, trance, hallucinogens, and psychical events: Concepts, methods, and techniques for fieldwork among primitives. In A. Bharati (Ed.), *Realm of the extra-human*. The Hague: Mouton.

Long, J. K. (1977). *Extrasensory ecology*. Metuchen, NJ: Scarecrow Press.

Lowie, R. H. (1937). *The history of ethnological theory*. New York: Rhinehart.

Lucy, J. (1985). Whorf's view of the linguistic mediation of thought. In E. Mertz, & R. Parmentier (Eds.), *Semantic mediation*. New York: Academic Press.

Lucy, J. (1992). *Language diversity and thought: A reformulation of the linguistic relativity hypothesis*. Cambridge: Cambridge University Press.

Lutz, C. (1988). *Unnatrual emotions*. Chicago: University of Chicago Press.

Lutz, C., & White, W. (1986). The anthropology of emotion. *Annual Review of Anthropology, 15*, 405–36.

MacDonald, G. F., Cove, J., Laughlin, C. D., & McManus, J. (1988). Mirrors, portals and multiple realities. *Zygon, 23*(4), 39–64.

MacDonald, J. L. (1981). Theoretical continuities in transpersonal anthropology. *Phoenix: The Journal of Transpersonal Anthropology, 5*(1), 31–47.

Mauss, M. (1950). *Les techniques du corps: Sociologie et anthropologie*. Paris: Presses Universitares de France.

McDougall, W. (1901). Cutaneous sensations. In A. C. Haddon (Ed.), *Report of the Cambridge anthropological expedition to the Torres Straits*

(Vol. 2, pp. 189–195). Cambridge: Cambridge University Press.

Menzel, E. W. (1967). Naturalistic and experimental research on primates. *Human Development, 10*, 170–186.

Merleau-Ponty, M. (1962). *Phenomenology of perception*. London: Routledge and Kegan Paul.

Miller, G. A. (1956). The magical number seven, plus or minus two: Some limits on our capacity for processing information. *Psychological Review, 63*, 81–97.

Miller, G. A., Galanter, E., & Pribram, K. H. (1960). *Plans and the structure of behavior*. New York: Holt, Rhinehart & Winston.

Mitchell, S. (1988). *Relational concepts in psychoanalysis*. Cambridge, MA: Harvard University Press.

Morris, B. (1994). *Anthropology of the self: The individual in cultural perspective*. London: Pluto Press.

Munn, N. (1992). The cultural anthropology of time: A critical essay. *Annual Review of Anthropology, 21*, 93–123.

Obeyesekere, G. (1981). *Medusa's hair*. Chicago: University of Chicago Press.

Obeyesekere, G. (1990). *The work of culture*. Chicago: University of Chicago Press.

Ochs, E., & Schieffelin, B. (1984). Language acquisition and socialization: Three developmental stories. In R. Shweder & R. LeVine (Eds.), *Culture theory: Essays in mind, self, and emotion* (pp. 276–320). Cambridge: Cambridge University Press.

O'Nell, C. W. (1976). *Dreams, culture and the individual*. San Francisco: Chandler and Sharp.

Ortner, S. (1984). Theory in anthropology since the sixties. *Comparative Studies in Society and History, 37*(1), 173–193.

Parish, S. (1994). *Moral knowing in a Hindu sacred city: an exploration of mind, emotion, and self.* New York: Columbia University Press.

Peacock, J. L. (1975). *Consciousness & change: Symbolic anthropology in evolutionary perspective*. Oxford: Blackwell.

Peters, L. G. (1982). Trance, initiation, and psychotherapy in Tamang shamanism. *American Ethnologist, 9*(1), 21–46.

Peters, L. G., & Price-Williams, D. (1980). Towards an experiential analysis of shamanism. *American Ethnologist, 7*(3), 397–413.

Pinker, S. (1997). *How the mind works*. New York: WW Norton & Company, Inc.

Pinxton, R., Van Dooren, I., & Harvey, F. (1983). *The anthropology of space*. Philadelphia: University of Pennsylvania Press.

Quartz, S., & Sejnowski, T. J. (1997) The neural basis of cognitive development: A constructivist manifesto. *Behavioral and Brain Sciences, 20*, 537–596

Rappaport, R. A. (1979). *Ecology, meaning and religion*. Richmond: North Atlantic Books

Rappaport, R. A. (1999). *Ritual and religion in the making of humanity*. Cambridge: Cambridge University Press.

Rasmussen, S. (1999). Making better 'scents' in anthropology: Aroma in Tuareg sociocultural systems and the shaping of ethnography. *Anthropological Quarterly, 72*(2), 55–73.

Reichel-Dolmatoff, G. (1971). *Amazonian cosmos: The sexual and religious symbolism of the Turkano Indians*. Chicago: University of Chicago Press.

Reyna, S. P. (2002). *Connections: Brain, mind, and culture in a social anthropology*. New York: Routledge.

Richards, G. (1998). Getting a result: The expeditions's psychological research 1898–1913. In A. Herle & S. Rouse (Eds.), *Cambridge and the Torres Strait: Centenary Essays on the 1898 anthropological expedition* (pp. 136–157). Cambridge: Cambridge University Press.

Rivers, W. H. R. (1901a). Colour vision. In A. C. Haddon (Ed.), *Report of the Cambridge anthropological expedition to the Torres Straits*, Vol 2. Cambridge: Cambridge University Press.

Rivers, W. H. R. (1901b). The colour vision of the natives of Upper Egypt. *Journal of the Royal Anthropological Institute, 31*, 229–247.

Rivers, W. H. R. (1902). The colour vision of the Eskimo. *Proceedings of the Cambridge Philosophical Society, 11*(2), 143–149.

Rivers, W. H. R. (1903). Observations on the vision of the Uralis and the Sholagas. *Bulletin of the Madras Government Museum, 5*, 3–18.

Rivers, W. H. R. (1905). Observations on the senses of the Todas. *British Journal of Psychology, 93*, 10–20.

Rivers, W. H. R., & Head, H. (1908). A human experiment in nerve division. *Brain, 31*, 323–450.

Rouget, G. (1985). *Music and trance: A theory of the relations between music and possession*. Chicago: University of Chicago Press.

Rumelhart, D. E., Hinton, G. E., & McClelland, J. L. (1986). A general framework for parallel distributed processing. In D. E. Rumelhart, J. L. McClelland, & The PDP Research Group (Eds.), *Parallel distributed processing: Explorations in the microstructure of cognition, Vol. 1: Foundations*. Cambridge, MA: MIT Press.

Rumsey, A. (1990). Wording, meaning, and linguistic ideology. *American Anthropologist, 92*, 346–361.

Ryle, G. (1984). *The concept of mind*. London: Hutchinson. (Original work published 1949)

Sahlins, M. (2000). Colors and cultures. In M. Sahlins (Ed.), *Culture in practice: Selected essays* (pp. 139–162). New York: Zone Books.

Sapir, E. (1931). Conceptual categories in primitive languages. *Science, 74*, 578–584.

Sapir, E. (1958). *Culture, language and personality*. Los Angeles: University of California Press. (Original work published 1929)

Scholte, B. (1973). The structural anthropology of Claude Levi-Strauss. In J. J. Honigmann (Ed.), *Handbook of social and cultural anthropology* (pp. 637–716). Chicago: Rand McNally.

Schutz, A., & Luckmann, T. (1973). *The stuctures of the LifeWorld. Vol I*. Evanston: Northwestern University Press.

Segall, M. H., Campbell, D. T., & Herscovits, M. J. (1966). *The influence of culture on visual perception*. Chicago: Bobbs-Merrill.

Shore, B. (1996). *Culture in mind: Cognition, culture, and the problem of meaning*. Oxford: Oxford University Press.

Shweder, R. A. (1984). Anthropology's romantic rebellion against the enlightenment, or there's more to thinking than reason and evidence. In R. A. Shweder & R. A. Levine (Eds.), *Culture history: Essays on mind, self, and emotion* (pp. 27–66). Cambridge: Cambridge University Press.

Shweder, R. A. (1991). *Thinking through cultures*. Cambridge: Harvard University Press.

Shweder, R. A. (2003). *Why do men barbecue?: Recipes for cultural psychology*. Cambridge: Harvard University Press.

Sobo, E. J. (1996). The Jamaican body's role in emotional experience and sense perception: Feelings, hearts, minds and nerves. *Culture, Medicine and Psychiatry, 20*(3), 313–342.

Spencer, H. (1886). *Principles of psychology*, Vol. 5. New York: Appleton.

Spencer, H. (1997). *Gender ideology and psychological reality*. Princeton, NJ: Princeton University Press.

Sperber, D. (1996). *Explaining culture: A naturalistic approach*. Oxford: Blackwell.

Sperber, D., & Block, M. (2002). Kinship and evolved psychological dispositions: The mother's brother controversy reconsidered. *Current Anthropology, 43*(4), 723–748.

Spiro, M. (2001). Cultural determinism, cultural relativism, and the comparative study of psychopathology. *Ethos, 29*, 218–234.

Spiro, M. (1987). *Culture and human nature: Theoretical papers of Melford Spiro*. Chicago: University of Chicago Press.

Spiro, M. (1997). *Gender ideology and psychological reality*. New Haven: Yale University Press.

Spiro, M. (1994). Collective representations and mental representations in religious symbol systems. In B. Kilbourne & L. L. Langness (Eds), *Culture and Human Nature* (pp. 161–184). New Brunswick, NJ: Transactions Publishers. (Original work published 1984)

Stern, D. B. (1997). *Unformulated experience*. Hillsdale, NJ: Analytic Press.

Stoller, P. (1984). Sound in Songhay cultural experience. *American Ethnologist, 11*(3), 559–70.

Stoller, P. (1989). *The taste of ethnographic things: The senses in anthropology*. Philadelphia: University of Pennsylvania Press.

Stoller, P. (1997). *Sensuous scholarship*. Philadelphia: University of Pennsylvania Press.

Strauss, C., & Quinn, N. (1998). *Cognitive theory of cultural meaning*. Cambridge: Cambridge University Press.

Ströker, E. (1993). *Husserl's transcendental phenomenology* (L. Hardy, Trans.). Stanford, CA: Stanford University Press.

Sutich, A. J. (1968). Transpersonal psychology: An emerging force. *Journal of Humanistic Psychology, 8*, 77–79.

Synnott, A. (1993). *The body social: Symbolism, self, and society*. London: Routledge.

Tambiah, S. (1990). *Magic, science, religion and the scope of rationality*. Cambridge: Cambridge University Press.

TenHouten, W. (1978–79). Hemispheric interaction in the brain and the propositional, compositional, and the dialectical modes of thought. *Journal of Altered States of Consciousness, 4*(2), 129–140.

Throop, C. J. (2000). Shifting from a constructivist to an experiential approach to the anthropology of self and emotion. *Journal of Consciousness Studies*, 7(3), 27–52.

Throop, C. J. (2002). Experience, coherence, and culture: The significance of Dilthey's "descriptive psychology" for the anthropology of consciousness. *Anthropology of Consciousness*, 13(1), 2–26.

Throop, C. J. (2003a). Articulating experience. *Anthropological Theory*, 3(2), 219–241.

Throop, C. J. (2003b). On crafting a cultural mind – a comparative assessment of some recent theories of "internalization" in psychological anthropology. *Transcultural Psychiatry*, 40(1), 109–139.

Throop, C. J. (2003c). Minding experience: En exploration of the concept of experience in the French anthropology of Durkheim, Lévy-Bruhl, and Lévi-Strauss. *Journal of the History of the Behavioral Sciences*, 39(4), 365–382.

Throop, C. J. (2005). Hypocognition, a 'sense of the uncanny,' and the anthropology of ambiguity: Reflections on Robert I. Levy's contribution to theories of 'experience' in anthropology. *Ethos*, 33(4), 499–511.

Throop, C. J., & Laughlin, C. D. (2002). Ritual, collective effervescence and the categories: Toward a neo-Durkheimian model of the nature of human consciousness, feeling and understanding. *Journal of Ritual Studies*, 16(1), 40–63.

Throop, C. J., & Murphy, K. M. (2002). Bourdieu and phenomenology: A critical assessment. *Anthropological Theory*, 2(2), 185–207.

Titchener, E. B. (1916). On ethnological tests of sensation and perception, with special reference to tests of color vision and tactile discrimination described in the reports of the Cambridge anthropological expedition to Torres Straits. *Proceedings of the American Philosophical Society*, 55(3), 204–236.

Turner, E. (1996). *The hands feel it: Healing and spirit presence among a northern Alaskan people*. DeKalb, IL: Northern Illinois University Press.

Turner, V. (1969). *The ritual process: Structure and anti-structure*. Chicago: Aldine.

Turner, V. (1982). *From ritual to theatre*. New York: Performing Arts Journal Publications.

Turner, V. (1983). Body, brain, and culture. *Zygon*, 18(3), 221–245.

Turner, V., & Bruner, E. M. (1986) *The anthropology of experience*. Urbana, IL: University of Illinois Press.

Turner, V. (1985). On the edge of the bush. In V. Turner, & E. L. B. Turner (Eds.), *On the edge of the bush*. Tucson: The University of Arizona Press.

Tyler, S. (1984). The vision quest in the West or what the mind's eye sees. *Journal of Anthropological Research*, 40, 23–40.

Tylor, E. B. (1958). *Primitive culture, Vol. 1: The origins of culture*. New York: Harper and Row. (Original work published 1871)

Vygotsky, L. (1978). *Mind in society: The development of higher mental processes*. Cambridge, MA: Harvard University Press. (Original work published 1930)

Walsh, R. N., & Vaughan, F. (1980). *Beyond ego: Transpersonal dimensions in psychology*. Los Angeles: J. P. Tarcher.

Way, E. C. (1997). Connectionism and conceptual structure. *American Behavioral Scientist*, 40(6), 729–753.

Webber, M., Stephens, C. D., & Laughlin, C. D. (1983). Masks: A re-examination, or 'masks? You mean they affect the brain?' In N. R. Crumrine & M. Halpin (Eds.), *The power of symbols* (pp. 204–218). Vancouver, BC: University of British Columbia Press.

White, G., & Kirkpatrick, J. (Eds.). (1986). *Person, self, and experience*. Berkeley: University of California Press.

Whorf, B. L. (1956). *Language, thought, and reality: Selected writings of Benjamin Lee Whorf* (J. B. Carroll, Ed.). Cambridge, MA: MIT Press.

Winkelman, M. (1986). Trance states: A theoretical model and cross-cultural analysis. *Ethos*, 14, 174–203.

Winkelman, M. (1994). Multidisciplinary perspectives on consciousness. *Anthropology of Consciousness*, 5(2), 16–25.

Winkelman, M. (2000). *Shamanism: The neural ecology of consciousness and healing*. Westport, CT: Bergin & Garvey.

Young, A. (1995). *Harmony of illusions: Inventing posttraumatic stress disorder*. Princeton, NJ: Princeton University Press.

Young, D., & Goulet, J.-G. (Eds.). (1994). *Being changed by cross-cultural encounters: The anthropology of extraordinary experience*. Peterborough, Ontario: Broadview Press.

Young-Laughlin, J. & Laughlin, C. D. (1988). How masks work, or masks work how? *Journal of Ritual Studies*, 2(1), 59–86.

H. Psychodynamic Approaches to Consciousness

CHAPTER 24

Motivation, Decision Making, and Consciousness: From Psychodynamics to Subliminal Priming and Emotional Constraint Satisfaction

Drew Westen, Joel Weinberger, and Rebekah Bradley

Abstract

This chapter describes the relevance of clinically derived concepts of conscious and unconscious processes for contemporary theory and research. We first describe models of consciousness that emerged from psychoanalytic clinical observation at the turn of the last century. We argue that, although these models had many flaws, they were prescient in their postulation of unconscious thought, feeling, and motivation; consciousness as a limited-capacity system used for problem solving superimposed on a set of competing, collaborating, and conflicting unconscious processes; expression of memory consciously through explicit recollection or unconsciously in behavior; the influence of unconscious networks of association on consciousness and behavior; and multimodal representations associated with multiple affects. We then describe two areas of psychoanalytically influenced research that bear on contemporary concepts of consciousness: (1) unconscious (subliminal) activation and (2) unconscious affect-regulation processes that affect judgment and decision making. We describe experimental research in both areas, including recent neuroimaging research attempting to identify the neural circuitry involved in motivated reasoning. We conclude by describing how psychodynamic theory and research might inform contemporary accounts of consciousness by disentangling three distinct meanings of *activation* and by refining the *implicit/explicit* and *declarative /non-declarative* distinctions.

Introduction

Although von Helmholtz (1909) used the term "unconscious inference" to describe the way the brain adjusts for distance when assessing the size of objects (and William James, 1890, certainly spilled some ink on the topic of conscious and unconscious mental events; see Weinberger, 2000), for much of its first century, psychology had little interest in the distinction between conscious and unconscious processes. Behaviorism ruled both conscious and unconscious processes out of court for scientific study. The serial processing models of cognition that spurred the cognitive revolution in the 1960s and 1970s rarely addressed the question of consciousness, although they posited a short-term memory system that was essentially its equivalent. Similarly, social psychologists did not distinguish until the 1990s whether the attitudes and stereotypes they were studying were conscious or unconscious, and they tended to make methodological decisions (exclusive reliance on self-reports) that assumed that such processes are conscious or can readily be made conscious by asking.

The situation has radically changed in the last decade. The question of consciousness – and with it, of unconsciousness – has become the Cinderella of contemporary cognitive neuroscience and allied disciplines, as methodological advances and changes in paradigms (both conceptual and experimental) have uncovered the glass slippers that have finally allowed conscious and unconscious (explicit and implicit) processes to dance at the scientific ball. Until the "second cognitive revolution" that ushered in the focus on implicit processes in the 1990s (see Westen, 2000a), however, the primary field of inquiry that focused on the distinction between conscious and unconscious processes and attempted to outline their differential functions was psychology's wicked stepsister, psychoanalysis. For a variety of reasons, the hypotheses about consciousness that emerged from clinical observation of psychopathology over the last hundred years (no different, in principle, from clinical observations of neurological cases that are treated routinely as important sources of hypotheses in contemporary neuroscience) never entered into mainstream theory and research. Indeed, many students of consciousness today take the view that, if anything, the views of consciousness formulated by this wicked stepsister actually set back the study of conscious and unconscious processes by decades (Kihlstrom, 1999, 2000; Kihlstrom, Barnhardt, & Tataryn, 1992).

Our goal in this chapter is to highlight clinically derived conceptions of conscious and unconscious processes that we believe could be profitably integrated into contemporary theory and research. The clinical database has three features that make it particularly useful in hypothesis generation. The first is its basis in the naturalistic study of people's mental lives and behavior longitudinally as they talk about things that matter to them in an ongoing way. The second is the focus on affectively charged, motivationally significant cognition and behavior, which is difficult to approximate in the laboratory. The third is the focus, since the beginning of psychoanalysis, on identifying and tracking implicit associative networks hypothesized to regulate behavior and provide the neural foundation for many forms of psychopathology. Research on implicit processes tends to focus on shared networks – and indeed *presumes* such networks (so that, for example, for most subjects *robin* should facilitate the recognition of *bird*). In contrast, clinical observation focuses on the *unshared* networks that make people different from one another and particularly on the idiosyncratic, affect-laden networks hypothesized to underlie many forms of psychopathology. We would suggest that it was not accidental that clinicians struggling to confer explanatory coherence (Thagard, 1989) on the data of clinical observation needed to assume the existence of unconscious processes a century before data from the laboratory rendered the postulation of such processes indispensable. With different vantage points come different discoveries.

Our aim in this chapter, although partly historical, is not primarily to describe the fossil record of prehistoric (i.e., prescientific) thought on consciousness in psychoanalysis. Rather, our goal is to focus on the theory and research on psychodynamic processes that may contribute to our current understanding of conscious and unconscious processes. We begin by describing the models of consciousness that emerged from psychoanalytic clinical observation at the turn of the last century. We argue that these models were not only prescient in multiple respects but that they also point to phenomena that would be important to integrate with contemporary views of consciousness that have their roots in the laboratory (and hence emerged to answer different questions). We then describe two areas of psychoanalytically influenced research that bear on contemporary concepts of consciousness: (1) unconscious (subliminal) activation and (2) unconscious affect-regulation processes that affect judgment and decision making. We conclude by describing two ways that psychodynamic theory and research might inform contemporary accounts of consciousness, by distinguishing among different meanings of *activation* and between implicit/explicit and declarative/nondeclarative processes.

A History of Psychoanalytic Views of Conscious and Unconscious Processes

From the start, Freud (1900/1953) considered the theory of unconscious processes to be the cornerstone of psychoanalytic theory. He argued that if there is a discontinuity in consciousness – something the person is doing but cannot report or explain – then the relevant mental processes necessary to "fill in the gaps" must be unconscious (see Rapaport, 1944/1967). Early in his career Freud studied aphasia, and he knew then that we cannot be aware of the processes that generate our capacity to speak fluently. He included such processes, along with activated networks that are not currently conscious, among the rubric of mental events that are *descriptively* unconscious, by which he meant simply that they were active but not accessible to introspective awareness. Today we might say that such processes are unconscious by virtue of mental architecture rather than by motivation, a rendering with which Freud would likely have been quite comfortable.

The starting point for Freud's development of a theory of conscious and unconscious processes, however, was the clinical observation of psychopathology. He repeatedly encountered patients who explicitly *wanted* to overcome their symptoms, but could not do so despite their best conscious efforts; for example, obsessive-compulsive patients who would wash their hands repetitively until they bled. What was perhaps most striking about these patients was that they could not offer compelling (conscious) explanations for what they were doing.

Freud thus made a simple deduction. If their behavior was motivated (e.g., not just a tic or physiological event without psychological meaning) but was not consciously intended, there was only one other possibility: It must have been *unconsciously* motivated (see Erdelyi, 1985). He made the corollary assumption that motives may be *kept* from conscious awareness because they would be threatening to acknowledge (e.g., hostility toward significant others, expressed instead as passive-aggressive behavior). He referred to such processes as *dynamically* unconscious and contrasted them with the descriptively unconscious processes described above (e.g., phenomena that emerge in priming studies, in which implicit activation of a network influences reaction time to semantically related words).

Freud proposed his first comprehensive model of the relation between conscious and unconscious process in 1900, but his views changed over the years, and he never completely reconciled what he considered, until the end of his life, works in progress. Developments in psychoanalysis since Freud have also been associated with somewhat different models of consciousness. To cover all (or even most) of these models in any detail would be impossible in a brief chapter (see Weinberger, in press). Our review of the history of psychoanalytic views of unconscious processes is therefore necessarily short and selective. We focus first on Freud's topographic model (conscious, preconscious, unconscious), which was his first and most systematic formulation of the relation between conscious and unconscious processes. We then briefly describe his structural model (id, ego, superego), followed by a brief tour through the conceptualizations of conscious and unconscious processes in the psychoanalytic literature since Freud.

Freud's Topographic Model

Freud's first systematic attempt at a model of the mind (Freud, 1900/1953) was called the topographic model. This model proposed a tripartite division of mental processes into conscious, preconscious, and unconscious systems. These systems were distinguished by the person's capacity to be aware of their mental contents. According to the topographic model, mental processes can be classified by their level of awareness, from fully conscious (conscious system) to capable of becoming conscious (preconscious system) to never in awareness (unconscious system). Like contemporary cognitive neuroscientists, Freud, who was influenced both by his experience as a neurologist and by the Darwinian thinking of his time (the *Origin of Species* was published in the year of Freud's birth), believed that mental processes could be understood as systems and defined by what they did (i.e., by their functions). In his topographic model, these functions were defined by their level of awareness.

THE CONSCIOUS SYSTEM

The conscious system includes what a person is aware of at any particular moment in time. The reader is, for example, conscious of reading this sentence or is perhaps distracted by a smell from the kitchen. The contents of this system are therefore constantly changing and are selected by their perceptual, emotional, or motivational significance. A unique feature of Freud's theory of the selection of mental contents for conscious attention was his suggestion that the emotional significance of representations could either activate *or* inhibit them, with some representations inhibited as a way of managing anxiety (e.g., the representation that a darkening mole could be cancerous). Empirically, this aspect of Freud's theory has stood the test of time (e.g., Ditto, Scepansky, Munro, Apanovitch, & Lockhart, 1998) and could be usefully incorporated into more cognitively inspired models of consciousness, a point to which we return.

THE PRECONSCIOUS SYSTEM

People are necessarily only aware of a very small part of the information potentially available to them at any one moment in time. In modern terms, consciousness (or working

memory) has severe processing constraints imposed by the limited amount of information that can be held in conscious awareness. This means that the vast majority of potentially available information is not in the conscious system. Instead, it is represented elsewhere in the mind (brain), where it can remain potentially accessible for lengthy periods of time. In its latent state, such information is not conscious and is therefore unconscious by definition, although unconscious networks of association can influence conscious thought and behavior. Freud described this latent information as residing in a "preconscious" system or state.

This preconscious system consists of mental contents (memories, experiences, and so on) that a person can usually bring into consciousness when needed but that are not currently conscious. Once preconscious material (e.g., a phone number) is brought into consciousness, it becomes part of the conscious system. Once it is no longer actively conscious, it returns to the preconscious system. Although the preconscious system as we have just described it shares many of the more static features of long-term memory as described in cognitive theories of the 1970s and 1980s, Freud actually proposed a surprisingly contemporary model of representations as distributed processes that vary in their potential for reactivation. In his paper on "The Unconscious," published 90 years ago, he described representations as

> nothing static, but something in the nature of a process . . . start[ing] from a particular point in the cortex and spread[ing] from there over the whole cortex or along certain tracts. When this process is completed, it leaves a modification behind in the cortex that has been affected by it – the possibility of remembering. Our consciousness shows nothing of the sort to justify, from the physical point of view, the name of a 'latent mnemic image.' But whenever the same state of the cortex is provoked again, the psychical aspect comes into being once more as a mnemic image. (Freud, 1915/1957, p. 208)

The topographic model posits a relatively free and easy exchange between the two systems, conscious and preconscious. What is preconscious can usually be brought into consciousness, and what is conscious easily moves to a preconscious state once it is no longer needed. To bring a preconscious content into consciousness, the person has to focus attention on it. The nature of the organization of both the conscious and preconscious systems, according to Freud, is rational and linguistic. That is, their contents can be expressed sensibly and in language. The only difference between the two systems is that of phenomenal awareness, controlled by attention. As a result, Freud sometimes referred to them as a single system, the preconscious/conscious system. (We address below the place of information encoded in sensory modalities other than language in Freud's topographic model.)

THE UNCONSCIOUS SYSTEM

Freud's first two systems, conscious and preconscious, yield a model of the mind that looks a great deal like the serial processing models that dominated cognitive psychology for 30 years. What was perhaps most distinctive about his topographic model, however, was the third system, the unconscious system. Based on his clinical observation as well as his naturalistic observation of the "psychopathology of everyday life" (1901; e.g., slips of the tongue), Freud identified a set of mental processes that operate in ways that differ radically and qualitatively from those of the conscious/preconscious and are, by the standards of those systems, "irrational." The *unconscious* system in the topographic model is a reservoir of desires, needs, and urges. As a scientist steeped in evolutionary theory, as well as an observer of the motives that seemed to get people into trouble in their lives, Freud first posited that these desires are primarily self-preservative (egoistic) and reproductive. Eventually he came to believe that they are primarily sexual and aggressive.[1]

The unconscious system of the topographic model is primarily conative rather than cognitive. It differs, however, from the conscious and preconscious systems in another way: Rather than being organized by logic and language, its thought processes are symbolic, imagistic, and associative. At the risk of reification, one might say that the unconscious system "thinks" in similes, metaphors, and the images of poetry (cf. Schimek, 1975). In the language of contemporary theories of persuasion (Eagly & Chaiken, 1998; Petty & Cacioppo, 1986), it is this system that is involved in "peripheral" routes to persuasion that influence consumers and voters when they are not attending to and rationally weighing the arguments. The beautiful women in the beer commercial "speak" the language of the unconscious, as sirens who promise that Budweiser will bring something more gratifying than a beer gut.

The unconscious system differs from the conscious/preconscious in yet another way: Because it is not bound by rationality, opposing desires can exist side by side without contradiction (Freud, 1933). The mind in this model is often in conflict. Unconscious desires press for satisfaction, without concern for reality, safety, morality, or other motives that may exert equal and opposite pressure for satisfaction. The conscious/preconscious system, in contrast, is connected to reality, morality, and adaptation and hence must weigh the merits of alternative desires, find compromises among them, and keep others in check.

In some cases, desires that are consciously unacceptable slip through the cracks, find alternative outlets, or emerge in disguised form. Freud would likely have looked with a combination of consternation and the delight of recognition at the televangelists of the 1980s, such as Jimmy Swaggart and Jim Baker, who constantly preached about the evils of sex yet (or perhaps consequently) seemed to have sex on their minds much of the time. Apparently, preaching about the evils of sex was not enough to satisfy their sexual desires in the face of highly repressive sexual attitudes, as both men engaged in all kinds of colorful variants of it (e.g., with prostitutes) when the cameras (and their consciences) were turned off.

Freud termed the strategies people use to keep threatening desires at bay or to get their needs met when acknowledging them would be too emotionally threatening *defenses*. (In the topographic model he tended to use the term "repression" more generically to refer to defenses until he and others came to understand better the complex ways people can regulate their emotions; A. Freud, 1936; Vaillant, 1977; Vaillant & McCullough, 1998). Defenses often permit *some* form of satisfaction of unconscious desires without giving them full expression. Frequently this requires substantial compromise. If such a compromise allows for enough satisfaction, all is well. For example, when the first two authors look at themselves in the mirror each morning, they do not typically retch, but neither do they imagine that they are Brad Pitt. (In their most self-congratulatory moments, they might settle for Dustin Hoffman.) When such compromises do not work so well, the person suffers in some way, often through a psychological symptom (e.g., a preoccupation with appearance characteristic of many patients with histrionic personality disorder, body dysmorphic disorder, or anorexia nervosa).

Foresight and Hindsight: Evaluating Freud's First Model of Consciousness

With the benefits of a century of hindsight, theory, and data, we can appreciate both the strengths and weaknesses of the topographic model as a model of the relation between conscious and unconscious processes. As noted above, the model has many features that should be recognizable to contemporary cognitive scientists, such as a serial processing system superimposed on a parallel architecture. Freud's model of associative networks was also remarkably similar to the spreading activation theories that emerged in the 1960s and 1970s (see Blum, 1960; Pribram & Gill, 1976; Westen, 1985). And as argued below, his understanding of the dynamics of unconscious affective and motivational influences on conscious thought and behavior continues to offer insights worth incorporating into theories derived primarily from the laboratory, where the

emotional significance of stimuli is often set to zero.

Nevertheless, the topographic model of consciousness has many limitations, some of which Freud recognized (hence the development of his next model of the mind, the structural model), and others of which he did not. Of particular importance was his tendency to force multiple dichotomies (e.g., conscious/unconscious, rational/irrational, linear/associative, cognitive/emotional, linguistic/imagistic) into a single one, defined by the distinction between the conscious/preconscious and unconscious systems (Westen, 1999b). Here he was clearly wrong. For example, he insisted that emotions and language must be conscious, whereas irrationality must bespeak unconscious processes. Emotional processes can be conscious or unconscious, just as semantic representations can be processed linearly or associatively (as in priming). Interestingly, similar confusions have emerged in the history of thinking about consciousness, as in the widespread confusion of declarative and explicit memory (described below).

Consciousness in Later Psychoanalytic Models

Psychodynamic theorists of all stripes generally adhere to the proposition that much of mental life – including thoughts, feelings, and motives – is unconscious, which means that people can behave in ways or develop symptoms that are inexplicable to them. Likewise, psychodynamic theorists believe that mental processes, including affective and motivational processes, operate in parallel, so that individuals can have conflicting feelings toward the same person or situation that motivate them in opposing ways and often lead to compromise solutions. The psychoanalytic view of these processes is not, however, monolithic. Here we describe three developments in psychoanalytic theory since Freud's original model that bear on the nature of consciousness: the structural model, ego psychology, and object relations theory.

FREUD'S STRUCTURAL MODEL

Whereas Freud's first model categorized mental processes according to the extent to which they were or could become conscious, his second (and final) systematic model of the mind, the structural model (see Freud, 1926, 1933), categorized mental processes by their functions (Jahoda, 1977). With the introduction of the familiar tripartite model of id, ego, and superego in the structural model, Freud's understanding of the dynamics of the mind shifted from conflict between conscious and unconscious to conflict between desires and the dictates of conscience and/or reality. In the structural model, all sides of the conflict could have conscious and unconscious elements.

Perhaps the most central change from the topographic to the structural model can be seen in what had once been the preconscious/conscious system(s), now renamed the "ego" (the "I" in the original German; Bettelheim, 1983). No longer is everything in this system potentially available to awareness. The ego is the part of the mind that must somehow balance the demands of desire, reality, and morality. To do this, it marshals mechanisms of defense as well as creative compromises among competing forces, many of which are unconscious. Thus, unconscious processes are no longer the province of a single mental system (in the topographical model, the unconscious system). All the systems of the mind, now functionally defined, have aspects that are unconscious.[2] Mental processes range from completely unconscious to completely conscious, with conscious and unconscious processes (e.g., conscious coping strategies and unconscious defenses) often serving similar functions.

The structural model placed greater emphasis on morals, values, and ideals (the "superego"; literally, in the original German, "above-me," as in standing in judgment on oneself). Whereas many theorists have assumed that our values are largely conscious or accessible to consciousness (or have not considered the question of level of consciousness of moral values), Freud's clinical experience led him to believe that many aspects of moral experience are unconscious, as when a person with a harsh superego (i.e., unrealistically stringent moral standards or ideals) berates himself or ruminates on things he wishes he had done differently. In Freud's structural model, much of personality reflects the unconscious internalization of such functions as morality, self-restraint, and self-soothing from significant others. We are rarely aware of such internalizations, which tend to operate automatically.

The unconscious system of the topographical model was relatively unchanged in the structural model. It was given the new name, "id" (the "it" in the original German, reflecting the way Freud talked to patients about seemingly "foreign" aspects of themselves, such as symptoms, that felt like "not me"), and was no longer the sole locus of unconscious processes. It continued, however, to be the reservoir for ontogenetically (and phylogenetically) primitive, largely sexual and aggressive, needs, desires, and wishes.

The structural model offered a more accurate view of the relation between conscious and unconscious processes than the topographic model because it recognized that many of the functions ascribed to the ego and superego, particularly those involved in cognition and self-regulation, are unconscious. Nevertheless, few psychoanalysts today rely on the structural model or use the terms id, ego, and superego. This largely reflects a recognition of the dangers of reifying "structures" as real entities or homunculi, rather than treating them, as Freud intended, as constructs denoting functionally related processes (see Klein, 1976; Schafer, 1976).

EGO PSYCHOLOGY

A significant shift in psychoanalytic theory began at about the time of Freud's death with the development of ego psychology. Whereas Freud's primary focus was on motivation and conflict (the province of the topographic unconscious and the structural id), ego psychology focused on the nature and development of the functions Freud ascribed to the ego, such as problem solving, self-regulation, impulse regulation, and affect regulation (see Blanck & Blanck, 1974, 1979). Heinz Hartmann (1939/1958) and his colleagues (e.g., Hartmann, Kris, & Loewenstein, 1946) were, to a significant extent, cognitive psychologists, and they actively read and attempted to integrate into psychoanalytic theory the then-current work of Piaget and Werner. Hartmann (1939/1958) discussed means-end problem solving and the impact of automaticity of thought processes on cognitive development and adaptation in ways that would be familiar to contemporary cognitive psychologists.

Later ego psychologists (Arlow & Brenner, 1964; Brenner, 1982; Gill, 1967) argued that "fantasies" (affect-laden beliefs) form people's templates for understanding and reacting to the world. What they termed fantasy functioned much as schemas later came to do in cognitive and social psychology (cf. Schimek, 1975; Weinberger, in press). The difference was that, unlike most conceptions of schemas, the fantasy templates described by ego psychologists tended to be highly affective and largely unconscious and often included a combination of wishes, fears, and cognitive constructions.[3]

Weiss, Sampson, and their colleagues (1986) developed the notion of unconscious fantasy in a more empirical direction, focusing on "pathogenic beliefs" in psychopathology and psychotherapy. For example, they have studied the phenomenon of survivor guilt (O'Connor, Berry, Weiss, Schweitzer, & Sevier, 2000), first emphasized by psychoanalytic clinicians describing the experience of survivors of concentration camps, who often suffered with the fantasy (i.e., belief/fear/wish) that they should have died instead of their brother, sister, or parent. Of note is that the "fantasy" underlying survivor guilt may include not only a pathogenic *belief* that somehow the survivor could have done something different to save the person who died or that doing penance will somehow undo the unjustice but also a *fear* that the survivor is indeed bad and a

wish that something bad happen to even the score.

The complexity and ambivalence of such a seemingly simple "fantasy" are hallmarks not only of ego psychology but also of the psychoanalytic understanding of meaning more generally. The notion that mental representations of this sort are often complex and ambivalent is another aspect of the psychoanalytic theory of the structure of unconscious networks and their conscious expressions or concomitants that could be profitably integrated with contemporary, more cognitive views of consciousness. Consider, for example, a not infrequently encountered clinical phenomenon, the survivor guilt often seen in children with a mentally retarded sibling, who may as adults unconsciously sabotage their own success as a way of "making up for" having had an intact intellect. Although they are generally aware of some of their guilt, they may be less aware of its patterns of activation and the ramifications on their ongoing thought, feeling, and behavior. From a theoretical point of view, in such cases, networks of association activated by an impending intellectual success may activate an associatively linked network representing self-in-relation-to-retarded sibling. This in turn activates unconscious guilt and efforts to regulate it, for example by failing. We address below some of the empirical data bearing on unconscious emotion and emotion regulation of this sort (see also Westen, 1998b, 1999a).

OBJECT RELATIONS THEORY

Perhaps the most important development in psychoanalysis since Freud is object relations theory (Greenberg & Mitchell, 1983; Guntrip, 1971; Mitchell, 1988; Scharf & Scharf, 1998). The term "object relations" refers to enduring patterns of interpersonal functioning in intimate relationships and the cognitive and affective processes mediating those patterns (Westen, 1991). Object relations theories emerged from the observation of patients with serious interpersonal problems, such as people who rapidly attach to someone they have just met and then feel desperate, betrayed, enraged, or suicidal when the other person does not reciprocate their affection or begins to back off when confronted with what feels like an unrealistic level of emotional investment in a relationship that does not really exist. Whereas classical psychoanalysis focused primarily on sexual and aggressive motives, object relations theories (and related developments, such as relational psychoanalysis; see Aron, 1996) tend to focus on relational motives and on what can happen when these motives go awry. For example, children who are abused by a parent often cling tenaciously to the very person who is abusing them (DiLillo, Long, & Russell, 1994), just as victims of childhood sexual abuse are more likely to find themselves repeatedly in abusive relationships or dangerous situations as adults (Classen, Palesh, & Aggarwal, 2005). From an object relations standpoint, people can have conflicting relational motives and are frequently unaware of both these motives and the interpersonal patterns that they engender (Fonagy, Gergely, Jurist, & Target, 2002; see Westen, 1990b, 1997).

For the present purposes, the major innovation of object relations theory lies in its emphasis on the complex representations of self, others, and relationships hypothesized to mediate interpersonal functioning in close relationships. In the early 1960s, Sandler and Rosenblatt (1962) described the cognitive-affective structure of the "representational world" – that is, of people's representations of the self, others, and relationships. They distinguished between people's conscious representations of self and the complex networks of unconscious self-representations and episodic memories that could influence the "shape" of conscious self-representation at any moment.

Unlike many areas of psychoanalytic theory, object relations theory has amassed a substantial body of empirical research, as researchers have attempted to track down and operationalize the processes that mediate the capacity for intimacy, including the implicit representations, expectations, and ways of construing relationships that guide both normal and pathological interper-

sonal functioning (Ackerman, Hilsenroth, Clemence, Weatherill, & Fowler, 2000; Blatt, Auerbach, & Levy, 1997; Huprich & Greenberg, 2003; Westen, 1991). Perhaps the most widely known object relations theory outside of psychoanalytic circles, and the most generative of research, is attachment theory, which emerged from the work of the psychoanalyst and ethologist John Bowlby (1969, 1973, 1982). A core proposition of attachment theory is that experiences in the close relationships beginning with primary caregivers in infancy and early childhood coalesce into internal representations or "internal working models" of attachment relationships (see Main, Kaplan, & Cassidy, 1985). These working models are cognitive-affective representations that influence the ways people think, feel and behave, particularly in close interpersonal relationships. They form the core of patterns of attachment-related behaviors, often referred to as attachment styles. Two aspects of attachment style of particular significance here are that they operate primarily outside of awareness, similar to the representations postulated by other object relations theorists, and that they are intertwined with unconscious or implicit affect-regulation strategies (defenses) that emerge through interactions (particularly aversive interactions) with attachment figures. These affect-regulation strategies have observable manifestations in the first 12 to 18 months of life and throughout the lifespan (see Mikulincer, Shaver, & Pereg, 2003; Shaver & Mikulincer, 2005).

Kernberg (1975, 2004) has focused on the structure of representations in patients with personality disorders, such as the tendency of patients with borderline personality disorder to have difficulty maintaining balanced representations of significant others. Empirically, patients with borderline pathology are prone to "splitting" their representations into emotionally one-sided, all-good or all-bad views of the self and others, particularly when emotions are strong (Baker, Silk, Westen, Nigg, & Lohr, 1992; Conklin & Westen, 2005; Shedler & Westen, 2004). In the present context, what is particularly relevant about splitting in borderline personality disorder is that in many respects it reflects a deficit in the self-regulation of consciousness, whereby attributes of a person are selected for integration into conscious representations only to the extent that they share the prevailing emotional tone. In some ways, splitting can be understood as an extreme form of mood-dependent memory and cognition, although at times it can also be motivated, as when a person idealizes a troubled spouse or parents and systematically filters out information that might "tarnish" the representation.

Both Kernberg (1975) and Kohut (1966, 1971) focused on the structure of self-representations in narcissistic personality disorder. Of particular relevance to the understanding of consciousness is a characteristic feature of many patients with severe narcissistic disturbances, whose conscious grandiosity often rests on a foundation of unconscious self-devaluation or desperate fear that they are not who they want to think they are (see Russ, Bradley, Shedler, & Westen, 2005; Westen, 1990a). These patients often are at their most (consciously) grandiose when they feel most vulnerable to devaluation, as when they respond with rage, narcissistic tantrums, or grandiose indignation when someone questions their judgment or ability. Clinically, the constant need for mirroring, approbation, and bragging in narcissistic patients often appears to belie a powerful need to bolster unrealistic explicit views of the self (for empirical data, see Baumeister & Vohs, 2001; Rhodewalt & Sorrow, 2003; Shedler & Westen, 2004).

More broadly, the psychoanalytic concept of representations, which has been refined through object relations and relational theorists over the last 50 years, has three features worthy of note. First, representations are multidimensional and multivalent. A person has a large repertoire of implicit representations of the self and significant others that may be mutually inconsistent, encoded in multiple modes, and activated at different times and in different combinations under different circumstances. Representations of significant social others are also always affect-laden and not only ambivalent (i.e., associated with both positive and negative affect) but also multivalent (i.e., associated with a range of different affects). (If the reader has any doubts, try answering the question, "How do you feel about your mother?" We suspect the answer will vary substantially depending on when the question is asked and who is asking it.)

Second, representations of the self and significant others tend to be densely interconnected with wishes, fears, interpersonal patterns (implicit relational procedures; see Westen, 1997), and patterns of affect regulation. As a result, they tend to be slow to change, and efforts to alter maladaptive explicit representations of the self or others may have little enduring impact because they do not address the broader networks in which they are embedded (see Westen, 2000b; Westen, Novotny, & Thompson-Brenner, 2004).

Third, a central point of psychoanalysis since its start, and implicit in most object relations theories, is that it is not incidental whether a representation is conscious or unconscious. Much of the work of contemporary dynamic psychotherapy involves identifying unconscious representations of self, others, and relationships and implicit relational procedures that lead people to experience repetitive, unsatisfying interactions with other people and the negative affect states those interactions typically entail. Some of these unconscious representations and relational procedures are unconscious by virtue of defense (i.e., kept from consciousness because they are threatening), whereas others are likely unconscious simply because they never became the object of introspection.

Psychoanalytically Inspired Research on Unconscious Processes: Subliminal Activation

As with the psychoanalytic theory of unconscious processes, it would be impossible to review psychoanalytic research concerning unconscious processes comprehensively in a chapter. (The interested reader is referred to a series edited by Bornstein & Masling,

1998.) Instead, we describe two lines of research relevant to contemporary theories of consciousness. (To illustrate the psychoanalytic concept of narcissism, we focus on research programs in which we have been centrally involved.)

The first line of research regards subliminal activation. Psychoanalytic theorists and clinicians from Freud through the present have taken as axiomatic that affective processes can influence conscious thought and behavior outside of awareness and that affects themselves can be generated by events that occur outside of awareness (see Weinberger, in press; Westen, 1998c). Research on subliminal activation supports both suppositions.

The New Look

The first systematic effort to examine psychoanalytic views of unconscious processes emerged in the 1950s in what was termed the "New Look" in perception. Dixon (1971, 1981) provides a comprehensive review and critique of this work (see also Weinberger, in press). The basic premise of the New Look was that perception does not just involve a neutral mirroring of environmental stimulation. Instead, perception is influenced by psychological processes, including motivation and emotion. To test this premise, investigators measured detection and recognition thresholds of affectively meaningful and neutral stimulation. This work quickly developed into efforts to investigate psychoanalytic propositions about what should affect perceptual processes. Two constructs directly derived from psychoanalytic theory soon became central to New Look research: defense and repression. Defense was studied in what New Look researchers termed perceptual defense and vigilance; repression was studied in what was termed subception.

Perceptual defense and vigilance were studied by presenting a word or picture tachistoscopically and determining at what speed (measured in milliseconds) it could be accurately identified. Perceptual defense was said to occur if detection of an affectively arousing stimulus required a longer presentation than did detection of a neutral stimulus. Perceptual vigilance was said to occur if an affectively arousing stimulus required a shorter presentation than did a neutral stimulus.

Both defense and vigilance were easy to find. For example, taboo words took longer to identify than did neutral words. This was perceptual defense. Threatening words sometimes took longer to identify (perceptual defense) and sometimes were identified more easily (perceptual vigilance) than were neutral words. These differences seemed to make sense psychoanalytically. For example, hysterics, who are said to avoid threat, showed perceptual defense, whereas paranoids, who see threat everywhere, showed perceptual vigilance. In many respects, this work foreshadowed research conducted decades later using such paradigms as the emotional Stroop task to measure implicit attentional biases (similarly assessed via reaction time) in different psychopathological groups (e.g., spider phobics, depressed patients; Williams, Mathews, & MacLeod, 1996).

Methodological critiques of these studies abounded. Many were justified. For example, some pointed out that taboo words may take longer to identify than neutral words simply because people are reluctant to say them out loud until they are absolutely certain of them so as to avoid embarrassment. No such hesitancy prevented them from saying neutral words out loud. The same could be said of threatening words. Hysterics tend to deny threat and so would not admit to it until absolutely forced to do so. Paranoids see threat everywhere and so will guess a threatening word on minimal evidence. The advent of signal detection theory gave researchers the ability to differentiate between perceptual and psychological threshold setting. However, the literature dealing with these controversies is too large and complex to review in any detail here (see Dixon, 1971, 1981; Weinberger, in press), and the issue was never definitively resolved.

Another argument was theoretical. For perceptual defense to work, the person must first perceive the word or image and then had to not see it (consciously). This process was sometimes called perceiving for the purpose of not perceiving and was seen as a logical impossibility. This argument was based on the major model of perception of the time, a serial processing model wherein a stimulus was first registered, then recognized, and then reacted to. Erdelyi (1974) pointed out that such a model is not necessary because several perceptual processes can occur simultaneously. Today, most researchers recognize that mental processes often occur in parallel (and that affective processing can be quicker than cognitive processing; LeDoux, 1986). It could therefore make sense for someone to react emotionally but show no recognition of a stimulus. These parallel processing and neuroscience models were, unfortunately, not available at the time, and as a result, the critiques of the New Look were perceived as definitive.

Subception did not fare much better than did perceptual defense/vigilance. In subception, a neutral stimulus was associated with electrical shock. It was then presented subliminally, and the person was then asked to say what he or she saw. The person would deny seeing the stimulus while, at the same time, evidencing arousal, in the form of an electrodermal response to it. Such electrodermal responding was held to indicate anxious arousal. Thus it seemed that affective responding (anxiety) occurred in the absence of conscious perception. This, too, was disputed, most elegantly by Eriksen (1959). He pointed out that recognition of a stimulus is an either/or proposition, whereas electrodermal responding is continuous. It is therefore quite easy to imagine a person denying seeing a stimulus when uncertain, but showing some physiological activity indicating perception of the stimulus. Once again, this critique seemed definitive at the time, although today we recognize that cognitive and affective processes may occur in parallel and rely on different (though interdependent) neural circuitry.

As a result of these criticisms, the New Look disappeared from the literature after 1960. Behaviorism was in its heyday, and serial processing models of information processing were dominant in then-emergent

cognitive psychology. Psychoanalytic theory did not have either the empirical base or the intellectual "cachet" in the field to maintain its competing view of a brain characterized by parallel, unconscious processing.

Subliminal Psychodynamic Activation

In the 1960s, Lloyd Silverman began a series of investigations termed subliminal psychodynamic activation, based explicitly on psychoanalytic theories. Reviews of the early work can be found in Silverman, Bronstein, and Mendelsohn (1976); later work in this area was reviewed by Silverman and Weinberger (1985) and Siegel and Weinberger (1998). The basic paradigm for this work involved presenting a stimulus intended to represent a psychoanalytic construct subliminally and seeing if it had the effects predicted by the theory. Much of the research was supportive. The subliminal stimulus was typically presented four times, via a tachistoscope, for 4 ms. Tests for subliminality followed the presentations. Two stimuli were usually compared, one selected for its presumed psychodynamic meaning and the other a control stimulus. Studies employed both within-subject and between-subject designs, and results were similar for both.

Silverman's best-known research focused on the effects of stimulating a wish or representation of being closely connected with the mother of early childhood, on the theory that the infant-mother connection can be one of the most nurturant and non-conflictual periods of life. The phrase MOMMY AND I ARE ONE, presented subliminally, operationalized this representation; the control stimulus was usually PEOPLE ARE WALKING (Siegel & Weinberger, 1998; Silverman, Lachmann, & Milich, 1982; Silverman & Weinberger, 1985).

Initial experiments with schizophrenia patients revealed that what was termed their ego pathology (a variable closely akin to thought disorder) could be temporarily reduced by presenting them with this subliminal message MOMMY AND I ARE

ONE. Subsequent experiments expanded the approach from laboratory demonstrations of transient effects to a more direct test of the general adaptation-enhancing effects of subliminal MOMMY AND I ARE ONE (MIO) stimulation in therapeutic and educational settings. In most of these studies, treatment was more effective when preceded by MIO than by control stimulation. This does not mean that MIO stimulation effected cure; rather, treatment was found to be more efficacious when preceded by MIO than by a control stimulus. Of particular importance, however, a range of semantically similar control stimuli (e.g., MOMMY AND I ARE GOING) did not have the same effects in any of these studies.

Meta-analyses confirmed the effects of these seemingly fantastic findings (see Weinberger, 1992, for a discussion of the counterintuitive nature of these findings and the resultant resistance to them). Hardaway (1990) conducted a meta-analysis of all MIO studies and obtained what Cohen (1977) would call a small to moderate effect size of $d = .41$. Moreover, the effect sizes of studies conducted by or in conjunction with Silverman were identical to the effect sizes conducted in independent laboratories. Weinberger and Hardaway (1990) further demonstrated that published and unpublished studies yielded equivalent effect sizes. They also conducted what Rosenthal (1979) has termed a counter-null analysis aimed at addressing the "file drawer" problem. Such an analysis estimates how many null findings (presumably unreported and stashed in various file drawers) would be required to cancel out the obtained effects and render them non-significant. This analysis revealed that it would require 2,287 studies with null results to abrogate the significant MIO results reported in the literature. Thus, the results are real and reliable.

Weinberger (1992) suggested that MIO results might be mediated by mood effects. That is, MIO stimulation might generate positive mood, which would then mediate positive outcomes in therapeutic and educational venues. Recent research in related areas suggests an alternative and more spe-

cific explanation; namely, that it is the activation of a representation of an important significant other, the mother in this case, that underlies these effects. Baldwin (1994) found that exposing participants to the name of a supportive other led to more positive self-evaluations. Pierce and Lydon (1998) primed proximity-related words and thereby increased participants' reliance on support seeking when faced with stress. Cohen, Towbes, and Flocco (1988) found that priming memories of attachment security caused participants to perceive others in more supportive terms.

The most compelling research in support of the specificity of attachment figures over a general mood-enhancing effect comes from the work of Mikulincer and Shaver. Mikulincer et al. (2000) subliminally primed participants with either a stressful word (failure) or a neutral word (hat). They then asked participants whether a series of word strings were words or not and measured their reaction time in responding (a lexical decision task). The logic behind a lexical decision task of this sort is that words related to the prime become more accessible and therefore should evoke a shorter reaction time. The investigators made a creative (or what Popper would call "risky") prediction based on attachment theory. In attachment theory (Bowlby, 1969), threat leads to a need for security, which activates the attachment system. Mikulincer and colleagues therefore hypothesized that threat words would make attachment-related words more accessible. The hypothesis was supported. The threat prime led to faster reaction times for words related to proximity to attachment figures than for neutral words. More importantly, participants responded more quickly to proximity words than to generally positive or negative words. Thus, the threat prime uniquely affected proximity-related representations, and the effects could not be attributed to the general activation of affect. These findings were replicated when the threat prime was changed to "death" or "illness." Thus, the effects were not unique to any particular threat word, but held for threat in general.

Mikulincer, Gillath, and Shaver (2002) later conducted a study that paralleled the MIO paradigm more closely. In this study, the words used in the lexical decision task (LDT) were not general proximity words, but were instead people's names. The names included current attachment figures, close friends, a current romantic partner, people participants knew of but did not know personally (e.g., famous actors), and people whom participants did not know; other stimuli were non-words. The investigators once again primed participants with either a threat word or a neutral word. Priming facilitated processing only of attachment figures (evidenced in reduced reaction time). The investigators once again replicated the effect using a different threat word and switching from a within-subject to a between-subject design.

It may be that these studies explain the robust effects of what seems like an outlandish stimulus, MOMMY AND I ARE ONE. Mikulincer et al. (2000, 2002) demonstrated the specificity of their effects to attachment figures and proximity seeking. Close relationships did not have the same effects if they were not attachment relationships, just as would be predicted by attachment theory. Because mothers are typically people's most important childhood attachment figures, it may be that MIO effects are attributable to participants' attachment to their mothers. In support of this, Mikulincer and Shaver (personal communication to J. W., February, 2003) noted that the most common attachment figure identified by their participants was their mother.

The studies by Mikulincer and colleagues may also help explain the well- replicated but hard-to-believe findings using MIO studies; namely, that the MIO stimulus led to increases in adaptive behavior in many samples. For example, Mikulincer and Arad (1999) reported that priming memories of attachment security increased cognitive openness in response to belief-discrepant information. Mikulincer and Shaver (2001) found in five studies that priming with stimulation evocative of positive attachment resulted in reduction of out-group bias. The out-groups were homosexuals and Arabs as evaluated by heterosexual Israelis. Because one of the primes employed as a control was evocative of positive affect, the findings could not be attributable to mood variations. Priming positive affect had no more effect than negative or neutral affect. Similarly, Mikulincer et al. (2001) found in multiple studies that activation or priming of attachment led participants to respond to the needs of others more empathically. Once again, a positive affect prime had no effect. These results and others (Mikulincer et al., 2002) suggest that there is something specific about priming attachment relationships that has different effects than priming other positively valenced relationships or, more generally, positive affect.

Together, this body of research work strongly suggests that unconscious activation of representations of attachment leads to multiple positive effects, from threat reduction to treating other people with more understanding. The question of whether mother is somehow special or is just one (albeit the most common) instance of a positive attachment representation remains to be studied.

Subliminal Politics

Three recent studies by Weinberger and Westen (2005) used subliminal priming to examine affective influences on political evaluations and choices. One was based on an ad run during the 2000 presidential election by the Bush campaign; it criticized Al Gore containing what appeared to be the subliminal word RATS (Berke, 2000; Crowley, 2000). Gore supporters suspected foul play. Bush supporters insisted the subliminal appearance was inadvertent. Advertising executives were generally skeptical, likening subliminal effects to belief in astrology and alien abduction (Egan, 2000) or alligators in the sewers of New York City (Shapiro, 2000).

In our experiment, the word RATS was presented subliminally prior to the supraliminal presentation of a photo of an individual ostensibly running for office. Participants were asked to evaluate this individual according to several affect-laden qualities. Participants stimulated with RATS rated the purported candidate more negatively than did participants stimulated with subliminal control stimuli, including STAR (RATS spelled backwards). This experiment suggested that the presentation of the subliminal message RATS by Republicans in the 2000 presidential campaign, whether intended or not, could have affected political evaluations.

A second experiment was designed to test the hypothesis that the Gore campaign shot itself in the foot in the 2000 election by trying to dissociate itself from Bill Clinton. In this study, preceding the same ersatz candidate was a subliminal photo of either the candidate himself or Bill Clinton. Evaluations were less negative after the photo of Clinton than after the photo of the candidate. (In this and the next experiment, only negative evaluations were affected by subliminal stimulation. Positive evaluations were unaffected. Results are therefore described in terms of reduced or increased dislike.)

A third experiment had potentially greater political ramifications. Here the subliminal Clinton photo preceded a photo of former Governor of California Gray Davis. The study was conducted during the recall election that removed Davis from office. The results were complex, but theoretically coherent. Republicans and Democrats were barely affected by the subliminal stimulation, likely reflecting their strong prior attitudes toward Davis. Independents, however, were a different story. Although Independents reported disliking Davis, when Davis was preceded by the subliminal Clinton, their ratings were dramatically less negative. The implication is that subliminal stimulation in politics is unlikely to change attitudes in people whose opinions are strongly held but can have real effects on those whose opinions are not set in concrete. Elections often hinge on the voting decisions made by such individuals, and politicians therefore target them. Apparently such individuals are susceptible to manipulation of unconscious associative processes.

These three experiments had particularly high ecological validity because they were conducted on the Internet. Although people participated at the times of their choosing, and distracting stimuli were not controlled for, significant effects were obtained nonetheless. This suggests that subliminal stimulation can have effects in the real world.

Emotional Constraint Satisfaction in Judgment and Decision Making

A second body of psychodynamically inspired research of relevance to the understanding of conscious and unconscious processes focuses on implicit and explicit emotional influences on judgment and decision making – from the kind of judgments people make in everyday life (e.g., about whether to take one job or another or whether a comment had a hostile "twist") to political, judicial, or boardroom decisions of tremendous significance (e.g., whether Iraq had weapons of mass destruction prior to the U.S. invasion in 2003). Across a number of fields – cognitive science, psychology, economics, political science, and business – the most widely held models of judgment and decision making today are bounded rationality models, or *almost*-rational models. These models suggest that people are *largely* rational but that they rely on (frequently adaptive) shortcuts and have some cognitive quirks (e.g., in making decisions in high- vs. low-risk situations) that can sometimes lead to divergences from rational choice.

These bounded rationality models generally begin with some version of expectancy-value theories, which focus on the explicit (conscious) processes by which people weigh various options and draw conclusions designed to maximize utility. Central to these models is the idea that, when people make decisions, they consider both the *utility* or value to them of different options and the *probability* or estimated likelihood of obtaining the outcomes associated with each option (Edwards, 1977; Edwards & Newman, 1986). A rational judgment, according to such models, requires comparing each potential option on its *expected utility*, calculated by multiplying the utility and expected probability of a given outcome.

Consider the decision-making process that confronted typewriter manufacturers in the 1970s and early 1980s, as the prospect of personal computers (PCs) with word-processing capabilities began to emerge. In weighing the extent to which they should devote capital to the development of then-nonexistent PCs, they had to consider the utility (in terms of potential sales) of devoting resources to this new technology versus the utility of continued development of their current products (which were beginning to have some word-processing capability). Even if the potential utility was astronomical, they also had to assess the probabilities that (a) R&D devoted to computer technology would lead somewhere – which was certainly not a sure thing in the 1970s – and that (b) a market for home computers would ultimately arise that might capture some of the market share then occupied by typewriters. If either utility or probability were judged to be low, executives would have been likely to select the more conservative option of continuing to develop their current product lines. Judging from the relative accessibility today of the names IBM and Smith Corona, we can make some educated guesses about the judgments made in different boardrooms. (Smith Corona eventually went bankrupt.)

With respect to the "almost" or "bounded" part of the almost-rational or bounded rationality models, researchers recognized over 30 years ago that the idealized views of rational decision making in expectancy-value theories left something to be desired as descriptions of how people actually make decisions. Kahneman, Tversky, and others have identified numerous heuristics and cognitive biases that influence judgments (Kahneman & Tversky, 2000; Tetlock & Mellers, 2002; Tversky & Kahneman, 1974). Other theorists have developed bounded

rationality models suggesting that people devote conscious cognitive resources to problems of significance to them, but tend to use cognitive shortcuts in matters of less consequence (Gigerenzer & Goldstein, 1996; Gigerenzer & Selten, 2001; Simon, 1990). Although some researchers (e.g., Mellers, 2000) now posit a greater role of affect in decision making, models of judgment, decision making, and problem solving in cognitive psychology, political science, and economics have always emphasized cognition over affect in accounting for both optimal and suboptimal judgment and decision making (see also Marcus, Newman, & MacKuen, 2000; Simon, 1967, 1984).

Like a number of other emotion theorists (e.g., Panksepp, 2005; Plutchik, 1980; Tomkins, 1962), Westen (1985, 1994) has argued for a much more substantial role of emotion – and emotional regulation – in judgment and decision making. Contemporary views of motivation emphasize approach and avoidance systems motivated by positive and negative affect[4] (Carver, 2001; Davidson, Jackson, & Kalin, 2000; Gray, 1990). Westen (1985) proposes that the "value" component of expectancy-value theories is primarily affective, as people implicitly and explicitly respond with approach and avoidance to various alternatives based on elicited, associated, or anticipated affect (see contemporary research on emotional forecasting; Gilbert, Pinel, Wilson, Blumberg, & Wheatley, 2002). In this view, operant conditioning can be understood as implicit emotion-based decision making, in which humans and other animals gravitate toward or away from actions associatively linked to rewarding or aversive consequences (for relevant data, see Westen, 1985). In explicit judgment and decision making, people similarly approach and avoid alternative conclusions based on their emotional consequences, although these perceived consequences may be much more strongly cognitively mediated.

Of particular relevance to the present discussion is Westen's assertion that precisely the same processes of affect-based approach and avoidance that motivate "rational" decision making also frequently distort the conclusions people reach, the data they consider, and the way they weigh those data. To return to our example of IBM and Smith Corona, imagine the events in the mind of an executive vice president participating in a discussion of whether and how much to devote resources to PC research and development. A traditional decision-making account might describe the events as follows. The vice president collects data on what is known about PC technology, estimates the likelihood that personal computing could actually emerge as a significant "player" in the emerging word-processing market, estimates the level of investment required for his organization to become a significant player in this new technology, estimates the costs of diverting resources from continuing to develop its current product line of word-processing typewriters, calculates the costs and benefits of each alternative multiplied by their probabilities, and makes his presentation to his colleagues.

Now consider the same scenario, adding in, first, some of the explicit (conscious) affective processes hypothesized by the model to occur in decision making. To this executive, the affective value of getting in on the ground floor of the PC industry may be enormous, in two senses. First, to the extent that he is invested in his company (not only emotionally but also financially, e.g., through stock options and retirement income tied to the value of the company's stock), an investment in PC technology, if it pays off, will mean a tremendous windfall. Second, more personally, suppose he is its most vocal champion among the people at the table in the boardroom. If his bet pays off, he is a visionary, and his personal stock will rise astronomically in the organization, perhaps landing him the CEO position he has fantasized about for years. On the other hand, if he is wrong, the costs might also be substantial if it becomes clear that PCs will never take off. These various emotional costs and benefits, which will likely affect both how he feels moment to moment in

the meeting and how he anticipates feeling many years down the road, will determine his decisions both about what he perceives as the best options and how much he speaks up about his opinion.

Now let us factor in the role of implicit affect-regulatory processes in the way he thinks about both the probability and likely consequences – financial, career, and emotional – of various possibilities. Let us suppose, for example, that he is high on the personality dimension of harm avoidance (Ben-Porath, Almagor, Hoffman-Chemi, & Tellegen, 1995; Cloninger, Przybeck, Svrakic, & Wetzel, 1994); that is, he is anxious and highly sensitive to potential dangers and tends to be drawn more to avoid negative outcomes and affect states than to seek pleasure, excitement, and risk. And suppose he is interpersonally relatively astute and can see that the CEO is leaning in a risk-averse direction. As he collects information about the emerging PC industry, he pays particularly close attention to information suggesting that the technology is many years away, likely to be too expensive for the reach of most households for decades, and so forth. At the same time, he questions the motivations of "yaysayers" who seem to him overly enthusiastic while giving particular credence to internal company reports about the likely market for its impressive new word-processing typewriters. The meeting makes him anxious, as his colleagues are expressing strong opinions in opposing directions, and "part of him" responds to the excitement in the room about this new technology and what it could mean for the company's success and his own financial security. He is thus not the first to speak, but he follows up on one of the comments by the CEO with his careful estimates of probabilities – careful estimates that have been substantially biased by the interaction of his personality style with just the kind of situation in which such a style can either by very helpful or very detrimental.

The kinds of biases in reasoning that entered the judgments of the executive in this last account were first described systematically in the psychoanalytic literature on defense (which today we might think of in terms of implicit forms of affect regulation). This literature, like research on implicit forms of affective *activation*, is actually quite well developed empirically as well as theoretically (see Vaillant, 1992; Westen, 1998a; in press). An emerging research literature on motivated reasoning has also begun to put such processes on firm empirical ground (e.g., Ditto, Munro, Apanovitch, Scepansky, & Lockhart, 2003; Ditto et al., 1998; Dunning, 1999; Jost, Glaser, Kruglanski, & Sulloway, 2003; Kunda, 1990). For example, years ago, Mahoney (1977) demonstrated experimentally the effect of motivational biases on manuscript reviewing. He found that scientists identified many more methodological limitations in studies that refuted rather than supported their pre-existing beliefs even though the methods sections were actually identical.

As this last rendering of the vice president's decision-making processes makes clear, people are often called upon not to solve one problem at a time but to solve several affective-motivational problems simultaneously – balancing multiple competing and collaborating emotional "pulls." In this example, the executive had motivations to "get it right" – to process information accurately, given the decisive importance of making a good decision – as well as to manage his anxiety, to protect his investment in his company, to protect his career, to maintain his relationship with the CEO, to respond appropriately to people's realistic excitement about the possibilities of computer technology, and so forth. (For a connectionist account of complex group situations such as this, see Thagard, in press.) The psychological "task" facing our executive was to equilibrate to a number of solutions (about how to weigh the data, how to present what he had learned, and how to manage his relationships in the boardroom) in ways that would be both as faithful as possible to the data *and* emotionally tolerable to him.

In attempting to model complex acts of cognition and emotion regulation of this sort, Westen and colleagues have drawn on the psychoanalytic construct of "compromise formation," which refers to the process whereby the mind generates compromise solutions in the face of multiple, often competing motives (Brenner, 1982; Westen, 1985, 1998b, 1999a; Westen, Blagov, Feit, Arkowitz, & Thagard, 2005). Readers with a background in cognitive science will readily recognize the analogy to equilibration and constraint satisfaction in connectionist networks, whereby the brain equilibrates to a solution that optimizes goodness of fit to the available data. Like connectionist models, models of compromise formation, first proposed by Freud a century ago to account for dream and symptom formation and applied more widely by later psychoanalytic theorists (Brenner, 1982), reject a primarily serial processing view of the mind (in this case, of motives that must come into consciousness one at a time to influence behavior; see Olds, 1994; Westen & Gabbard, 2002). They suggest instead that multiple motives can operative simultaneously and influence thought or action outside of awareness, leading to compromise solutions.

Westen and colleagues have proposed a model of emotion regulation, judgment, and decision making that includes the connectionist focus on constraints imposed by the data as well as a second set of constraints imposed by the *hedonic implications* of different solutions. According to this model, judgments about emotionally meaningful issues (which, in everyday life, include most judgments and decisions) reflect the simultaneous satisfaction of two sets of constraints: cognitive constraints (imposed by data and their logical entailments) and emotional constraints (imposed by emotional associations and anticipated emotions). Just as information provides constraints on the equilibrated solutions that people reach – by spreading activation to networks (and ultimately conclusions) that make sense of the "gestalt" of available data and spreading inhibition to alternatives that make less sense of the totality of the data – feelings and emotion-laden goals provide constraints on the equilibrated solutions people reach by spreading activation to the neural networks or units that lead people toward desired conclusions and inhibiting those that increase the likelihood of undesired ones. Thus, the brain equilibrates to solutions designed not only to maximize goodness of fit to the data but also to maximize positive and minimize negative affect. Where emotional constraints are relatively strong, even in the face of strong cognitive constraints, we would predict that excitation and inhibition of units of relevant networks based on their associations with positive and negative affect will exert a strong influence on judgments, leading to solutions that maximize what Thagard (2000, 2003) has called *emotional coherence*.

We have tested this model in a series of five studies involving three crises over the last 6 years in U.S. politics (the impeachment of Bill Clinton, the disputed presidential election of 2000, and the discovery of torture by the U.S. military at Abu Ghraib prison in Iraq; Westen, Blagov et al., 2005). In all five studies, we collected data from community samples, assessing or manipulating cognitive constraints (the information that would constrain their judgments) and assessing competing emotional constraints, with the goal of predicting judgments that most decision theories would explain in more "cold" cognitive terms. The gist of the findings are, first, that people's political judgments do indeed reflect an interaction of multiple cognitive and emotional constraints; and second, that competing and collaborating emotional pulls dominate judgment and decision making in high-stakes, emotion-laden political situations, generally overriding even relatively strong cognitive constraints.

For example, in three studies conducted at different points of the Clinton-Lewinski crisis, we used cognitive and emotional constraints to predict people's judgments about whether the President likely groped Kathleen Willey in the Oval Office, whether he lied to the grand jury investigating the case, and whether his actions constituted an impeachable offense as defined by the U.S. Constitution. We hypothesized that people's answers (e.g., about the extent to which lying about sex to a grand jury constitutes

"high crimes and misdemeanors" as intended by the framers of the U.S. Constitution) would reflect some combination of cognitive constraints (what participants knew about Clinton and the scandal) and affective constraints (what they felt about the Democratic and Republican parties, Clinton, infidelity, and feminism). We assessed cognitive constraints by asking participants ten factual questions about Clinton's life that would indicate long-standing knowledge about his political and personal history and ten factual questions about the scandal. We assessed emotional constraints by asking multiple questions about participants' feelings toward the Democrats and Republicans, Clinton, infidelity, and feminism, which we predicted would provide overlapping but in many cases competing emotional constraints on judgment.

As predicted, participants' judgments at all three time points reflected a complex balancing act, in which their decisions could be predicted by a combination of their feelings toward the parties, Clinton, infidelity, and feminism (with each set of emotional constraints contributing significantly after holding the others constant) and the constraints imposed by their knowledge. However, the emotional constraints at all three time points swamped cognition. For example, we could predict people's judgments about whether the President's actions crossed the constitutional threshold for impeachment from cognitive and emotional constraints measured 6 to 9 months earlier with remarkable accuracy (88% of the time). However, we could predict the same judgments with 85% accuracy when we included only emotional constraints in the model. People's knowledge about the scandal placed a statistically significant but practically insignificant constraint on people's judgments longitudinally.

We obtained similar findings regarding people's beliefs about the validity of manual versus machine ballot counts in the disputed presidential election of 2000. (Recall that Democrats argued for the importance of a manual recount to assess as accurately as possible the intent of each voter, whereas Republicans argued that such a recount would be less valid than the machine counts that had rendered George W. Bush the victor by a handful of votes in Florida.) We could predict participants' judgments 83.6% of the time from the combination of two sets of cognitive constraints (their knowledge of relevant data and an experimental manipulation) and two sets of emotional constraints (their feelings toward the two candidates and the two parties). Eliminating both sets of cognitive constraints from the model (i.e., including only emotional constraints) decreased our ability to predict – but only to 83.0%. Thagard (2003; Westen, Blagov, et al., 2005) has successfully modeled these processes computationally using his HOTCO 2 (hot cognition) program.

Similar findings emerged in an experimental study in which we manipulated cognitive constraints, providing participants in different experimental conditions with more or less evidence in an alleged case of abuse at Abu Ghraib. The experimental manipulation had a small, marginally significant effect, but this effect was less than one-sixth the magnitude of the effect of feelings toward the parties and was dwarfed as well by the effects of participants' feelings toward the U.S. military and toward human rights as a goal of U.S. policy – none of which, logically, should have affected people's judgments. In all of these studies, data from community samples mirrored decisions made by elected officials and judges, suggesting that the same processes occur in political elites as in the general electorate. The only study thus far in which we have found a more substantial impact of cognitive constraints (although still less powerful than the effects of feelings toward the two parties) is in a study just completed in which we predicted people's beliefs about the state of the national economy from an objective set of economic indicators (e.g., gross domestic product, unemployment), their personal finances, and their feelings toward the political parties (Westen, Kelley, & Abramowitz, 2005). Once again, however, and supporting the model, these various cognitive and emotional constraints

jointly predicted people's judgments in a relatively "cold" cognitive domain (the state of the economy).

We recently completed a study testing this model using functional neuroimaging with a sample of committed Democrats and Republicans during the 3 months prior to the U.S. presidential election of 2004 (Westen, Kilts, Blagov, Harenski, & Hamman, 2006). We presented participants with 18 sets of stimuli, 6 each regarding President Bush, his challenger Senator John Kerry, and neutral male control figures. For each set of stimuli, participants first read a statement from the target (e.g., Bush), followed by a second statement documenting a clear contradiction between the target's words and deeds that would be threatening to a partisan (generally suggesting that the candidate was dishonest or pandering). Next, participants were asked to consider the discrepancy and then to rate the extent to which the target's words and deeds were contradictory. Finally, they were presented with an exculpatory statement that might explain away the apparent contradiction and asked to reconsider and again to rate the extent to which the target's words and deeds were contradictory.

Behavioral data (participants' ratings of the extent to which the first and second statements were contradictory) showed the expected motivated reasoning, with partisans denying obvious contradictions made by their own candidate that they had no difficulty detecting in the opposing candidate. Importantly, in both their behavioral and neural responses, Republicans and Democrats did not differ in the way they responded to apparent contradictions for the neutral control targets, but Democrats responded to Kerry as Republicans responded to Bush (not, as would be predicted by most decision models, similarly weighing similar evidence). While weighing apparent contradictions for their own candidate, partisans showed expected activations throughout the orbital frontal cortex, indicating affective processing and presumably affect-regulatory strategies, as well as lateral orbital and insular cortex activations suggesting the experience of negative affect. They also showed large activations in the anterior and posterior cingulate cortices, suggesting emotion processing, conflict monitoring, and perhaps judgments of forgivability or moral accountability (see, e.g., Farrow et al., 2001). After apparently having found a way to resolve the contradiction, while asked to "consider" (and then rate) the contradiction, partisans showed a large activation in the ventral striatum and nucleus accumbens – indicating reward processing. We suspect this reflects essentially the operant conditioning of a defensive response, associating the participant's "revisionist" account of the data with positive affect or relief.

Conclusion

One can think about the relevance of psychoanalytic views of consciousness to the contemporary understanding of consciousness in one of two ways. The first is historical. Historically, psychoanalysis made some claims, based on clinical data, that not only differed from the dominant perspectives in psychology that emerged over the next 90 years but also turned out to be correct. Most importantly, psychoanalysts argued that much of mental life is unconscious and that this extends to thought, feeling, and motivation (Shevrin & Dickman, 1980; Westen, 1998c). They viewed consciousness as a serial processing system used for problem solving that is superimposed on a mental processing system that operates outside of awareness. They argued that mental events that occur in parallel can compete, collaborate, and conflict in various ways and that nothing guarantees their smooth coordination. They argued that memory can be expressed consciously through explicit recollection or unconsciously in behavior. They argued that much of psychological experience is mediated by networks of association that encode not only our experience but also our feelings and fears and can influence

consciousness and behavior even when they are not readily apparent. They argued that representations are multimodal and usually associated with multiple affects, both positive and negative.

A second way to view psychoanalytic conceptions, however, is in terms of their potential contributions to *contemporary* theory and research on consciousness. We have already noted a number of ways in which psychoanalytic views of consciousness emerging from clinical observation point to important phenomena that need to be addressed by any theory of consciousness, such as differences between implicit and explicit representations that may be active simultaneously, the activation and influence of implicit affective and motivational processes, and the multivalent nature of most networks representing emotionally significant concepts (e.g., attitudes, representations of significant others). Further, psychoanalysis has argued since its inception that meaning is not always manifest in the ways assumed by the widespread use of self-report methods and brief treatments for complex psychological disorders that build in minimal time or techniques for exploration of associative networks. In this view, understanding complex behavior and emotionally significant actions and communications in everyday life (as in the consulting room) requires an ability to frame and test hypotheses about the implicit networks regulating a person's behavior in ways that maximize what Thagard (2002) has called explanatory coherence. Although clinical inference and interpretation of meaning certainly have their pitfalls (e.g., Dawes, Faust, & Meehl, 1989), recent data suggest that clinical inferences can be remarkably reliable and valid in assessing such subtle constructs as narcissism from people's narratives (Westen & Weinberger, 2004, 2005). Indeed, we decode meaning all the time in everyday life, and much of the time observers reach considerable consensus on what they have observed. The same is true when researchers apply coding systems to narratives to quantify both thematic content and structural aspects (e.g., complexity, syntax) that provide insight into implicit meanings (e.g., Main et al., 1985).

We conclude with two final ways that psychoanalytically inspired theory and research may contribute to contemporary theory and research on conscious and unconscious processes: by distinguishing among three types of activation and by distinguishing implicit/explicit from declarative/procedural knowledge.

Three Types of Activation

In our discussion of cognitive and emotional constraint satisfaction, we have essentially argued for the importance of distinguishing two forms of activation, one cognitive and one hedonic (Westen, 1985). Cognitive activation (including both excitation and inhibition) reflects principles of association familiar since Aristotle and refined over the last 40 years by cognitive psychologists. Cognitive excitation occurs as one unit in a network increases the level of activation of another by virtue of some form of sensory, mnemonic, or logical conjunction (i.e., the two units have been activated together before because of some sensory or cognitive relation, such as similarity or temporal association, and hence are more likely to be coactivated in the future). Conversely, cognitive inhibition occurs as one unit in a network (or one network, depending on the extent to which one wants to model more specific processes) inhibits another by virtue of the fact that its presence suggests the absence or low probability of the other.[5]

A second form of activation is hedonic, as affect activates approach or avoidance, either toward stimuli associated with pleasure or pain (behavioral activation and inhibition; see, e.g., Carver, 2001; Corr, 2002; Davidson et al., 2000; Elliot & Thrash, 2002; Gray, 1990) or toward mental processes (e.g., inferences, representations, attributions) associated or expected to be associated with positive or negative feelings. Cognitive theories have focused on the way repeated associations between two units in a network can strengthen their association, leading to heightened activation of unit B

following unit A. What we have suggested is that repeated association of unit A with negative affect can lead to cognitive avoidance (inhibition) of unit A, and repeated association of unit B with positive affect can lead to approach to, or hyperactivation of, unit B. In judgment and decision making, these processes of hedonic activation (excitation and inhibition) can influence the arguments for or against a given position that reach consciousness, the amount of time spent thinking about different arguments or pieces of data, the conscious processes by which people weigh evidence or rationalize their decisions, the amount of activation or inhibition spread to units in a network of association, and so forth (see, e.g., Ditto et al., 2003).

We would note a final distinction vis-à-vis activation, namely between conscious and unconscious activation. Cognitive theorists frequently use the term "activation" without specifying the level of consciousness, on the assumption that if enough activation spreads to a representation it will become conscious. Both psychoanalytic clinical observation and neuroimaging data on the nature of conscious thought processes (usually described in terms of activation of working memory) render this assumption unlikely.

From a neuroimaging standpoint, people process a considerable amount of information using posterior networks without involvement of the dorsolateral prefrontal circuits involved in working memory. From a clinical standpoint, as we have suggested, a person could have a highly active representation that is nonetheless inhibited from conscious awareness because of its emotional significance. For example, as noted earlier, narcissistic patients often appear to be at their most consciously grandiose when their self-esteem is at its most unconsciously precarious. Similarly, people who fancy themselves non-prejudiced may have highly active negative representations of minority group members that motivate subtle forms of devaluation while being consciously aware of nothing but positive feelings toward the target of their implicit prejudice. (This latter example likely explains the oft-heard sentiment among African-Americans that the only thing as aversive as an old-fashioned bigot is a patronizing liberal.) In each of these cases, neural networks appear to have settled simultaneously into *two* solutions, one conscious and one unconscious. (Alternatively, one might consider the combination of the two incongruent representations at different levels of awareness to be a single equilibrated solution.)

What this analysis suggests is that conscious activation is not simply a function of the level of cognitive activation, in which crossing a threshold brings representations into consciousness. Rather, conscious activation is probably a joint function of (1) cognitive activation, (2) affective attention to emotionally significant events, (3) affective inhibition of unpleasant information (which can run counter to attention to emotionally significant events), and (4) affective excitation of pleasurable information. In the case of defended-against information, representations selected for consciousness are not those with the highest level of unconscious cognitive activation.

Implicit/Explicit and Procedural/ Declarative: One Dichotomy or Two?

A second domain in which psychoanalytic theory, research, and data might prove useful is in distinguishing two ways of classifying mental events or forms of memory that are frequently used as synonyms: implicit/explicit and declarative/procedural (or non-declarative). In 1986, Squire introduced the landmark distinction between declarative and procedural knowledge. Declarative knowledge referred to conscious knowledge, typically verbal or semantic, that could be "declared." Procedural knowledge referred to knowledge expressed in behavior that did not require conscious recollection. Squire placed several phenomena under the rubric of procedural knowledge, including priming, skill learning, and conditioning.

Although this distinction was extraordinarily useful in moving the field forward, it was problematic in two respects. First, priming, which Squire defined as a form of procedural knowledge, involves activation of implicit networks, yet the networks on which priming operates are quintessentially declarative. This is particularly apparent in priming procedures involving semantic networks linking words with related meanings. Second, subliminal priming leads to robust effects, suggesting that a "declarative" prime (i.e., a prime with semantic content) can activate implicit networks without itself ever being explicitly processed. Third, from a clinical standpoint, many declarative memories or representations – e.g., warded-off self-representations, beliefs about what happened at Abu Ghraib that a supporter of the U.S. administration would rather not acknowledge – are not consciously declarable because of their affective content.

Squire's distinction, and its subsequent equation in the literature with the implicit/explicit distinction, created a confusion between *type of knowledge* (how-to knowledge, which is procedural, and declarative knowledge, which has content) and *the way that knowledge is expressed* (explicitly, through conscious recollection, or implicitly, through behavior). The declarative/procedural dichotomy refers to the type of knowledge or representational mode (facts versus skills), whereas the explicit/implicit distinction refers to the way this knowledge is retrieved and expressed (with or without conscious awareness).

There is no necessary relation between these two distinctions, which represent orthogonal axes. We know many things unconsciously, and we exercise many choices and instigate and regulate many actions consciously. Declarative knowledge (representations of facts or events) can be either explicit (as when a person remembers a recent event) or implicit (as in semantic priming). Procedural knowledge (representations of internal or external actions) can be either explicit (e.g., conscious decision making, coping skills, or deliberate attempts to remember or forget) or implicit (e.g., skills such as reading facial emotions, responses learned through operant conditioning, defenses against unpleasant feelings). For example, coping strategies are, like

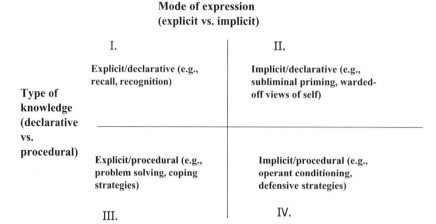

Mode of expression
(explicit vs. implicit)

	I.	II.
Type of knowledge (declarative vs. procedural)	**Explicit/declarative (e.g., recall, recognition)**	**Implicit/declarative (e.g., subliminal priming, warded-off views of self)**
	Explicit/procedural (e.g., problem solving, coping strategies)	**Implicit/procedural (e.g., operant conditioning, defensive strategies)**
	III.	IV.

Figure 24.1. Declarative/procedural and implicit/explicit knowledge.

other habits, procedural, but many of them are quite conscious, as when we remind ourselves that something painful will be over soon. Defenses, in contrast, are implicit procedures whose function is similarly to regulate affect. Thus, a given mental event can be declarative and explicit, declarative and implicit, procedural and explicit, or procedural and implicit. To broaden the distinction to include mental events other than "cold" cognitions, we might distinguish between *type of mental event* (whether the event is an idea, feeling, or motive on the one hand, or a mental or behavioral operation, action, or strategy on the other) and its *mode of expression* (whether the idea, feeling, motive, or action can be consciously recognized or recalled or whether it is expressed in behavior without conscious intention or the necessity of conscious awareness). The type of mental event usually reflects its mode or modes of representation (e.g., words or images vs. action tendencies). Figure 24.1 describes the four quadrants defined by these two axes.

Alongside episodic and generic forms of declarative knowledge, we might also postulate another kind of knowledge that is *quasi-declarative*; namely, memory for feelings and motives. Emotions and motives can be considered quasi-declarative because they have content (a "what"). They can be explicit (conscious emotions, wishes, or fears) or implicit (unconscious and observ-

able only indirectly). Other examples of quasi-declarative knowledge are feelings of knowing and feelings of familiarity. These feelings inform us of something factual and hence have quasi-declarative content (e.g., that we can retrieve this information if we try hard enough or we have seen it before, even though the content is unavailable).

We fear at this point that if we engage in any further distinction-drawing, the clinically sophisticated reader will begin to infer obsessional dynamics on the part of the authors, and hence we stop here. We hope, however, that we have made the point convincingly argued that the clinically informed approaches to consciousness that first emerged from psychoanalytic observation a century ago may be not only of historical interest but may also continue to provide insight into aspects of consciousness in the next century. Just as it would be remarkable if neuroscientists had learned nothing about consciousness from the recent explosion of neuroimaging research, it seems equally unlikely that clinicians learned nothing from a century of listening to people struggle with the things that matter most to them.

Acknowledgments

Preparation of this article was supported in part by NIMH grants MH62377 and MH62378 to the first author.

Notes

1. Interestingly, his first dual-motive model of motivation was closer to contemporary evolution thinking than his late model of sex and aggression as fundamental drives, which perhaps applies best to movies and frat parties. As in his theories of consciousness, Freud's theories of motives always followed his clinical observation, in this case, the observation that these two motives tend to be the ones that get people into the most trouble.

2. Like the conscious/preconscious, the ego also draws upon what Freud termed secondary processes (e.g., rational thought, memory, voluntary behavior) in its efforts to balance the aforementioned demands.

3. Interestingly, this concept of affect-laden representations is much closer to contemporary views of representation, stereotypes, and attitudes in the social psychology literature than were the initial schema theories. Because of the emergence of this concept of fantasy from the clinic, however, the primary focus was on fantasies that are maladaptive and often rooted in painful or conflictual developmental experiences (e.g., the common fantasy of young children that they caused their parents' divorce).

4. We use the terms "affect" and "emotion" throughout interchangeably.

5. Emotional processes can influence this form of activation in ways that do not require different principles. For example, affect orients people to phenomena of adaptive significance, which in turn spreads activation to networks representing those phenomena. In this sense, affect (both positive and negative) may provide one more source of excitatory cognitive (associational) activation.

References

Ackerman, S. J., Hilsenroth, M. J., Clemence, A. J., Weatherill, R., & Fowler, J. C. (2000). The effects of social cognition and object representation on psychotherapy continuation. *Bulletin of the Menninger Clinic*, 64, 386–408.

Arlow, J. A., & Brenner, C. (1964). Psychoanalytic concepts and the structure model. *Journal of the American Psychoanalytic Association*, (Monograph No. 3).

Aron, L. (1996). *A meeting of minds: Mutuality in psychoanalysis* (Vol. 4). New York: Analytic Press.

Baker, L., Silk, K. R., Westen, D., Nigg, J. T., & Lohr, N. E. (1992). Malevolence, splitting, and parental ratings by borderlines. *Journal of Nervous and Mental Disease*, 180, 258–264.

Baldwin, M. W. (1994). Primed relational schemas as a source of self-evaluative reactions. *Journal of Social and Clinical Psychology*, 13, 380–403.

Baumeister, R. F., & Vohs, K. D. (2001). Narcissism as addiction to esteem. *Psychological Inquiry*, 12, 206–210.

Ben-Porath, Y. S., Almagor, M., Hoffman-Chemi, A., & Tellegen, A. (1995). A cross-cultural study of personality with the Multidimensional Personality Questionnaire. *Journal of Cross-Cultural Psychology*, 26, 360–373.

Berke, R. L. (2000, Sept. 12). The 2000 campaign: The ad campaign: Democrats see, and smell, rats in G.O.P. ad. *New York Times*, p. 1.

Bettelheim, B. (1983). *Freud and man's soul*. New York: Knopf.

Blanck, G., & Blanck, R. (1974). *Ego psychology: Theory and practice*. New York: Columbia University Press.

Blanck, G., & Blanck, R. (1979). *Ego psychology II: Theory and practice*. New York: Columbia University Press.

Blatt, S. J., Auerbach, J. S., & Levy, K. N. (1997). Mental representations in personality development, psychopathology, and the therapeutic process. *Review of General Psychology*, 1, 351–374.

Blum, G. S. (1960). Psychoanalytic behavior theory: A conceptual framework for research. In H. P. David & J. C. Brengelmann (Eds.), *Perspectives in personality research* (pp. 107–138). Oxford: Springer.

Bornstein, R. F., & Masling, J. M. (Eds.). (1998). *Empirical perspectives on the psychoanalytic unconscious*. Washington, DC: American Psychological Association.

Bowlby, J. (1969). *Attachment* (Vol. 1). New York: Basic Books.

Bowlby, J. (1973). *Separation* (Vol. 2). London: Hogarth Press.

Bowlby, J. (1982). Attachment and loss: Retrospect and prospect. *American Journal of Orthopsychiatry*, 52, 664–678.

Brenner, C. (1982). The mind in conflict. New York: International Universities Press.

Carver, C. S. (2001). Affect and the functional bases of behavior: On the dimensional structure of affective experience. *Personality and Social Psychology Review, 5*, 345–356.

Classen, C. C., Palesh, O. G., & Aggarwal, R. (2005). Sexual revictimization: A review of the empirical literature. *Trauma, Violence, & Abuse, 6*, 103–129.

Cloninger, C. R., Przybeck, T. R., Svrakic, D. M., & Wetzel, R. D. (1994). *The Temperament and Character Inventory (TCI): A guide to its development and use*. St. Louis: Washington University Center for Psychobiology of Personality.

Cohen, J. (1977). *Statistical power analysis for the behavioral sciences*. Hillsdale, NJ: Erlbaum.

Cohen, L. H., Towbes, L. C., & Flocco, R. (1988). Effects of induced mood on self-reported life events and perceived and received social support. *Journal of Personality and Social Psychology, 55*, 669–674.

Conklin, C. Z., & Westen, D. (2005). Borderline personality disorder in clinical practice. *American Journal of Psychiatry, 162*, 867–875.

Corr, P. J. (2002). J. A. Gray's reinforcement sensitivity theory: Tests of the joint subsystems hypothesis of anxiety and impulsivity. *Personality and Individual Differences, 33*, 511–532.

Crowley, C. (2000, Sept. 12). Bush says "RATS" ad not meant as subliminal message; Gore calls ad "disappointing development." Retrieved from www.CNN.com

Davidson, R. J., Jackson, D. C., & Kalin, N. H. (2000). Emotion, plasticity, context, and regulation: Perspectives from affective neuroscience. *Psychological Bulletin, 126*, 890–909.

Dawes, R. M., Faust, D., & Meehl, P. E. (1989). Clinical versus actuarial judgment. *Science, 243*(4899), 1668–1674.

DiLillo, D. K., Long, P. J., & Russell, L. M. (1994). Childhood coping strategies of intrafamilial and extrafamilial female sexual abuse victims. *Journal of Child Sexual Abuse, 3*, 45–65.

Ditto, P. H., Munro, G. D., Apanovitch, A. M., Scepansky, J. A., & Lockhart, L. K. (2003). Spontaneous skepticism: The interplay of motivation and expectation in responses to favorable and unfavorable medical diagnoses. *Personality & Social Psychology Bulletin, 29*(9), 1120–1132.

Ditto, P. H., Scepansky, J. A., Munro, G. D., Apanovitch, A. M., & Lockhart, L. K. (1998). Motivated sensitivity to preference-inconsistent information. *Journal of Personality & Social Psychology, 75*, 53–69.

Dixon, N. F. (1971). *Subliminal perception: The nature of a controversy*. London: McGraw-Hill.

Dixon, N. F. (1981). *Preconscious processing*. New York: Wiley.

Dunning, D. (1999). A newer look: Motivated social cognition and the schematic representation of social concepts. *Psychological Inquiry, 10*, 1–11.

Eagly, A. H., & Chaiken, S. (1998). Attitude structure and function. In D. T. Gilbert, S. T. Fiske, & G. Lindzey (Eds.), *The handbook of social psychology* (4th ed., pp. 269–322). New York: McGraw-Hill.

Edwards, W. (1977). How to use multiattribute utility measurement for social decisionmaking. *IEEE Transactions on Systems, Man, & Cybernetics, 7*, 326–340.

Edwards, W., & Newman, J. (1986). Multiattribute evaluation. In H. R. Arkes & K. R. Hammond (Eds.), *Judgment and decision making: An interdisciplinary reader* (pp. 13–37). New York: Cambridge University Press.

Egan, J. (2000, Sept. 13). RATS ad: Subliminal conspiracy? Retrieved from www.news.bbc.co.uk.

Elliot, A. J., & Thrash, T. M. (2002). Approach-avoidance motivation in personality: Approach and avoidance temperaments and goals. *Journal of Personality and Social Psychology, 82*, 804–818.

Erdelyi, M. (1974). A new look at the New Look: Perceptual defense and vigilance. *Psychological Review, 81*, 1–25.

Erdelyi, M. H. (1985). *Psychoanalysis: Freud's cognitive psychology*. New York: W. H. Freeman.

Eriksen, C. W. (1959). Discrimination and learning without awareness: A methodological survey and evaluation. *Psychological Review, 67*, 279–300.

Farrow, T. F. D., Zheng, Y., Wilkinson, I. D., Spence, S. A., Deakin, J., Tarrier, N., et al. (2001). Investigating the functional anatomy of empathy and forgiveness. *Neuroreport, 12*, 2433–2438.

Fonagy, P., Gergely, G., Jurist, E. L., & Target, M. (2002). *Affect regulation, mentalization, and the development of the self*. New York: Other Press.

Freud, A. (1936). *The ego and the mechanisms of defense*. New York: International Universities Press.

Freud, S. (1901). *Psychopathology of everyday life*. London: T. Fischer Unwin.

Freud, S. (1953). The interpretation of dreams. In J. Strachey (Ed. & Trans.), *The standard edition of the complete psychological works of Sigmund Freud* (Vol. 4, pp. 1–338). London: Hogarth Press. (Original work published 1900)

Freud, S. (1957). The unconscious. In J. Strachey (Ed. & Trans.), *The standard edition of the complete psychological works of Sigmund Freud* (Vol. 14, pp. 159–215). London: Hogarth Press. (Original work published 1915)

Freud, S. (1926). *The ego and the id*. Honolulu, HI: Hogarth Press.

Freud, S. (1933). *New introductory lectures on psycho-analysis*. New York: W. W. Norton.

Gigerenzer, G., & Goldstein, D. G. (1996). Reasoning the fast and frugal way: Models of bounded rationality. *Psychological Review, 103*, 650–669.

Gigerenzer, G., & Selten, R. (2001). Rethinking rationality. In G. Gigerenzer & R. Selten (Eds.), *Bounded rationality: The adaptive toolbox* (pp. 13–36). Cambridge, MA: MIT Press.

Gilbert, D. T., Pinel, E. C., Wilson, T. D., Blumberg, S. J., & Wheatley, T. P. (2002). Durability bias in affective forecasting. In T. Gilovich, D. Griffin, & D. Kahneman (Eds.), *Heuristics and biases: The psychology of intuitive judgment* (pp. 292–312). New York: Cambridge University Press.

Gill, M. M. (1967). *The collected papers of David Rapaport*. New York: Basic Books.

Gray, J. A. (1990). Brain systems that mediate both emotion and cognition. *Cognition and Emotion, 4*, 269–288.

Greenberg, J. R., & Mitchell, S. (1983). *Object relations in psychoanalytic theory*. Cambridge, MA: Harvard University Press.

Guntrip, H. (1971). *Psychoanalytic theory, therapy, and the self*. New York: Basic Books.

Hardaway, R. A. (1990). Subliminally activated symbiotic fantasies: Facts and artifacts. *Psychological Bulletin, 107*, 177–195.

Hartmann, H. (1958). *Ego psychology and the problem of adaptation*. Oxford: International Universities Press. (Original work published 1939)

Hartmann, H., Kris, E., & Loewenstein, R. M. (1946). Comments on the formation of psychic structure. *Psychoanalytic Study of the Child, 2*, 11–38.

Huprich, S. K., & Greenberg, R. P. (2003). Advances in the assessment of object relations in the 1990s. *Clinical Psychology Review, 23*, 665–698.

Jahoda, M. (1977). *Freud and the dilemmas of psychology*. London: Hogarth Press.

James, W. (1890). *The principles of psychology*. New York: Holt.

Jost, J. T., Glaser, J., Kruglanski, A. W., & Sulloway, F. J. (2003). Political conservatism as motivated social cognition. *Psychological Bulletin, 129*(3), 339–375.

Kahneman, D., & Tversky, A. (Eds.). (2000). *Choices, values, and frames*. New York: Cambridge University Press.

Kernberg, O. (1975). *Borderline conditions and pathological narcissism*. Northvale, NJ: Jason Aronson.

Kernberg, O. F. (2004). Borderline personality disorder and borderline personality organization: Psychopathology and psychotherapy. In J. J. Magnavita (Ed.), *Handbook of personality disorders: Theory and practice* (pp. 92–119). New York: Wiley.

Kihlstrom, J. F. (1999). The psychological unconscious. In L. A. Pervin & O. P. John (Eds.), *Handbook of personality: Theory and research* (2nd ed., pp. 424–442). New York: Guilford Press.

Kihlstrom, J. (2000). Freud's influence on psychology has been that of a dead weight. In R. I. Atkinson, R. C. Atkinson, E. E. Smith, D. J. Bem, & S. Nolen Hieksema (Eds.), *Hilgard's introduction to psychology* (13th ed., pp. 480). New York: Harcourt Brace.

Kihlstrom, J. F., Barnhardt, T. M., & Tataryn, D. J. (1992). The psychological unconscious: Found, lost, and regained. *American Psychologist, 47*, 788–791.

Klein, G. S. (1976). Freud's two theories of sexuality. In L. Breger (Ed.), *Clinical-cognitive psychology* (pp. 136–181). Englewood Cliffs, NJ: Prentice-Hall.

Kohut, H. (1966). Forms and transformations of narcissism. *Journal of the American Psychoanalytic Association, 14*(2), 243–272.

Kohut, H. (1971). *The analysis of the self: A systematic approach to the treatment of narcissistic personality disorders*. New York: International Universities Press.

Kunda, Z. (1990). The case for motivated reasoning. *Psychological Bulletin, 108*, 480–498.

LeDoux, J. E. (1986). Sensory systems and emotion: A model of affective processing. *Integrative Psychiatry*, 4, 237–243.

Mahoney, M. J. (1977). Reflections on the cognitive-learning trend in psychotherapy. *American Psychologist*, 32, 5–13.

Main, M., Kaplan, N., & Cassidy, J. (1985). Security in infancy, childhood, and adulthood: A move to the level of representation. *Monographs of the Society for Research in Child Development*, 50(1–2), 66–104.

Marcus, G. E., Newman, W. R., & MacKuen, M. (2000). *Affective intelligence and political judgment*. Chicago: University of Chicago Press.

Mellers, B. (2000). Choice and the relative pleasure of consequences. *Psychological Bulletin*, 126, 910–924.

Mikulincer, M., & Arad, D. (1999). Attachment working models and cognitive openness in close relationships: A test of chronic and temporary accessibility effects. *Journal of Personality and Social Psychology*, 77, 710–725.

Mikulincer, M., Birnbaum, G., Woddis, D., & Nachmias, O. (2000). Stress and accessibility of proximity-related thoughts: Exploring the normative and intraindividual components of attachment theory. *Journal of Personality and Social Psychology*, 78, 509–523.

Mikulincer, M., Gillath, O., Halevy, V., Avihour, N., Avidan, S., & Eshkoli, N. (2001). Attachment theory and reaction to others' needs: Evidence that activation of the sense of attachment security promotes empathic responses. *Journal of Personality and Social Psychology*, 81, 1205–1224.

Mikulincer, M., Gillath, O., & Shaver, P. R. (2002). Activation of the attachment system in adulthood: Threat-related primes increase the accessibility of mental representations of attachment figures. *Journal of Personality & Social Psychology*, 83, 881–895.

Mikulincer, M., & Shaver, P. R. (2001). Attachment theory and intergroup bias: Evidence that priming the secure base schema attenuates negative reactions to out-groups. *Journal of Personality and Social Psychology*, 81, 97–115.

Mikulincer, M., Shaver, P. R., & Pereg, D. (2003). Attachment theory and affect regulation: The dynamics, development, and cognitive consequences of attachment-related strategies. *Motivation & Emotion*, 27, 77–102.

Mitchell, S. A. (1988). *Relational concepts in psychoanalysis: An integration*. Cambridge, MA: Harvard University Press.

Non-interpretive mechanisms in psychoanalytic therapy: The 'something more' than interpretation. (1998). *International Journal of Psycho-Analysis*, 79, 903–921.

O'Connor, L. E., Berry, J. W., Weiss, J., Schweitzer, D., & Sevier, M. (2000). Survivor guilt, submissive behaviour and evolutionary theory: The down-side of winning in social comparison. *British Journal of Medical Psychology*, 73, 519–530.

Olds, D. D. (1994). Connectionism and psychoanalysis. *Journal of the American Psychoanalytic Association*, 42, 581–611.

Panksepp, J. (2005). Affective consciousness: Core emotional feelings in animals and humans. *Consciousness & Cognition: An International Journal*, 14, 30–80.

Petty, R., & Cacioppo, J. (1986). *Communication and persuasion: Central and peripheral routes to attitude change*. New York: Springer-Verlag.

Pierce, T., & Lydon, J. (1998). Priming relational schemas: Effects of contextually activated and chronically accessible interpersonal expectations on responses to a stressful event. *Journal of Personality and Social Psychology*, 75, 1441–1448.

Plutchik, R. (1980). *Emotions: A psychoevolutionary synthesis*. New York: Harper & Row.

Pribram, K., & Gill, M. (1976). *Freud's project reassessed*. New York: Basic Books.

Rapaport, D. (1967). The scientific methodology of psychoanalysis. In M. Gill (Ed.), *The collected papers of David Rapaport*. New York: Basic Books. (Original work published 1944)

Rhodewalt, F., & Sorrow, D. L. (2003). Interpersonal self-regulation: Lessons from the study of narcissism. In M. R. Leary & J. P. Tangney (Eds.), *Handbook of self and identity* (pp. 519–535). New York: Guilford Press.

Rosenthal, R. (1979). The file drawer problem and tolerance for null results. *Psychological Bulletin*, 86, 638–641.

Russ, E., Bradley, R., Shedler, J., & Westen, D. (2005). *Refining the narcissistic diagnosis: Defining criteria, subtypes, and endophenotypes*. Unpublished manuscript, Emory University, Atlanta, GA.

Sandler, J., & Rosenblatt, B. (1962). The concept of the representational world. *Psychoanalytic Study of the Child*, 17, 128–145.

Schafer, R. (1976). *A new language for psychoanalysis*. New Haven, CT: Yale University Press.

Scharf, J. S., & Scharf, D. (1998). *Object relations individual therapy*. New York: Jason Aronson.

Schimek, J. G. (1975). A critical re-examination of Freud's concept of unconscious mental representation. *International Review of Psycho-Analysis, 2*, 171–187.

Shapiro, W. (2000, Sept. 12). Fear of subliminal advertising is irrational. Retrieved from www.USA.com

Shaver, P. R., & Mikulincer, M. (2005). Attachment theory and research: Resurrection of the psychodynamic approach to personality. *Journal of Research in Personality, 39*, 22–45.

Shedler, J., & Westen, D. (2004). Refining personality disorder diagnoses: Integrating science and practice. *American Journal of Psychiatry, 161*, 1350–1365.

Shevrin, H., & Dickman, S. (1980). The psychological unconscious: A necessary assumption for all psychological theory? *American Psychologist, 35*, 421–434.

Siegel, P., & Weinberger, J. (1998). Capturing the "mommy and I are one" merger fantasy: The oneness motive. In R. F. Bornstein & J. M. Masling (Eds.), *Empirical perspectives on the psychoanalytic unconscious* (pp. 71–97). Washington, DC: American Psychological Association.

Silverman, L. H., Bronstein, A., & Mendelsohn, E. (1976). The further use of the subliminal psychodynamic activation method for the experimental study of the clinical theory of psychoanalysis: On the specificity of the relationship between symptoms and unconscious conflicts. *Psychotherapy: Theory, Research & Practice, 13*, 2–16.

Silverman, L. H., Lachmann, F. M., & Milich, R. (1982). *The search for oneness*. New York: International Universities Press.

Silverman, L. H., & Weinberger, J. (1985). Mommy and I are one: Implications for psychotherapy. *American Psychologist, 40*, 1296–1308.

Simon, H. A. (1967). Motivational and emotional controls of cognition. *Psychological Review, 74*, 29–39.

Simon, H. A. (1984). Commentary. In L. S. Sproull & P. D. Larkey (Eds.), *Advances in information processing in organizations* (pp. 169–171). Greenwich, CT: JAI Press.

Simon, H. A. (1990). Invariants of human behavior. *Annual Review of Psychology, 41*, 1–19.

Tetlock, P., & Mellers, B. (2002). The great rationality debate. *Psychological Science, 13*, 94–99.

Thagard, P. (1989). Explanatory coherence. *Behavioral and Brain Sciences, 12*, 435–467.

Thagard, P. (2000). *Coherence in thought and action*. Cambridge, MA: MIT Press.

Thagard, P. (2002). The passionate scientist: Emotion in scientific cognition. In P. Carruthers, S. Stich, & M. Siegal (Eds.), *The cognitive basis of science* (pp. 235–250). New York: Cambridge University Press.

Thagard, P. (2003). Why wasn't O. J. convicted? Emotional coherence in legal inference. *Cognition and Emotion, 17*, 361–385.

Thagard (in press).

Tomkins, S. S. (1962). *Affect, imagery, consciousness: Vol. I. The positive affects*. Oxford: Springer.

Tversky, A., & Kahneman, D. (1974). Judgment under uncertainty: Heuristics and biases. *Science, 185*, 1124–1131.

Vaillant, G. (1977). *Adaptation to life*. Boston: Little Brown.

Vaillant, G. (Ed.). (1992). *Ego mechanisms of defense: A guide for clinicians and researchers*. Washington, DC: American Psychiatric Association Press.

Vaillant, G. E., & McCullough, L. (1998). The role of ego mechanisms of defense in the diagnosis of personality disorders. In J. W. Barron (Ed.), *Making diagnosis meaningful: Enhancing evaluation and treatment of psychological disorders* (pp. 139–158). Washington, DC: American Psychological Association.

von Helmholtz, H. (1909). *Handbuch der Physiologischen Optik* (3rd ed.). Leipzig: Leopold Voss.

Weinberger, J. (1992). Validating and demystifying subliminal psychodynamic activation. In R. F. Bornstein & T. S. Pittman (Eds.), *Perception without awareness: Cognitive, clinical, and social perspectives* (pp. 170–188). New York: Guilford Press.

Weinberger, J. (2000). William James and the unconscious: Redressing a century-old misunderstanding. *Psychological Science, 6*, 439–445.

Weinberger, J. (in press). *The unconscious*. New York: Guilford Press.

Weinberger, J., & Hardaway, R. (1990). Separating myth from reality in subliminal psychodynamic activation. *Clinical Psychology Review, 10*, 727–756.

Weinberger, J., & Westen, D. (2005). *RATS, we should have used Clinton: Subliminal stimulation and presidential politics*. Unpublished manuscript, Adelphi University.

Weiss, J., & Sampson, H. (1986). *The psychoanalytic process: Theory, clinical observation & empirical research*. New York: Guilford Press.

Westen, D. (1985). *Self and society: Narcissism, collectivism, and the development of morals*. New York: Cambridge University Press.

Westen, D. (1990a). The relations among narcissism, egocentrism, self-concept, and self-esteem: Experimental, clinical and theoretical considerations. *Psychoanalysis & Contemporary Thought*, *13*, 183–239.

Westen, D. (1990b). Towards a revised theory of borderline object relations: Contributions of empirical research. *International Journal of Psycho-analysis*, *71*, 661–693.

Westen, D. (1991). Social cognition and object relations. *Psychological Bulletin*, *109*, 429–455.

Westen, D. (1994). Toward an integrative model of affect regulation: Applications to social-psychological research. *Journal of Personality*, *62*, 641–667.

Westen, D. (1997). Towards a clinically and empirically sound theory of motivation. *International Journal of Psycho-analysis*, *78*, 521–548.

Westen, D. (1998a). Affect regulation and psychopathology: Applications to depression and borderline personality disorder. In W. Flack & J. Laird (Eds.), *Affect and psychopathology*. New York: Oxford University Press.

Westen, D. (1998b). The scientific legacy of Sigmund Freud: Toward a psychodynamically informed psychological science. *Psychological Bulletin*, *124*, 333–371.

Westen, D. (1998c). Unconscious thought, feeling, and motivation: The end of a century-long debate. In R. F. Bornstein & J. M. Masling (Eds.), *Empirical perspectives on the psychoanalytic unconscious* (Vol. 7, pp. 1–43). Washington, DC: American Psychological Association.

Westen, D. (1999a). Psychodynamic theory and technique in relation to research on cognition and emotion: Mutual implications. In T. Dalgleish & M. Power (Eds.), *Handbook of cognition and emotion* (pp. 727–746). New York: Wiley.

Westen, D. (1999b). The scientific status of unconscious processes: Is Freud really dead? *Journal of the American Psychoanalytic Association*, *47*, 1061–1106.

Westen, D. (2000a). Commentary: Implicit and emotional processes in cognitive-behavioral therapy. *Clinical Psychology: Science & Practice*, *7*, 386–390.

Westen, D. (2000b). Integrative psychotherapy: Integrating psychodynamic and cognitive-behavioral theory and technique. In C. R. Snyder & R. Ingram (Eds.), *Handbook of psychological change: Psychotherapy processes and practices for the 21st century* (pp. 217–242). New York: Wiley.

Westen, D., Blagov, P., Feit, A., Arkowitz, J., & Thagard, P. (2005). When reason and passion collide: Cognitive and emotional constraint satisfaction in high-stakes political decision making. Manuscript submitted for publication.

Westen, D., & Gabbard, G. O. (2002). Developments in cognitive neuroscience: I. Conflict, compromise, and connectionism. *Journal of the American Psychoanalytic Association*, *50*, 53–98.

Westen, D., Kelley, M., & Abramowitz, A. (2005). *Is GDP in the eyes of the beholder? Cognitive and emotional constraint satisfaction in voters' perceptions of the economy*. Unpublished manuscript, Emory University, Atlanta, GA.

Westen, D., Kilts, C., Blagov, P., Harenski, K., & Hamman (2006). The neural basis of motivated reasoning: An fMRI study of emotional constraints on political judgment during the U.S. presidential election of 2004. *Journal of Cognitive Neuroscience*, *18*, 1947–1958.

Westen, D., Novotny, C. M., & Thompson-Brenner, H. (2004). The empirical status of empirically supported psychotherapies: Assumptions, findings, and reporting in controlled clinical trials. *Psychological Bulletin*, *130*, 631–663.

Westen, D., & Weinberger, J. (2004). When clinical description becomes statistical prediction. *American Psychologist*, *59*, 595–613.

Westen, D., & Weinberger, J. (2005). In praise of clinical judgment: Meehl's forgotten legacy. *Journal of Clinical Psychology*, *61*, 1257–1276.

Williams, J. M. G., Mathews, A., & MacLeod, C. (1996). The Emotional Stroop Task and psychopathology. *Psychological Bulletin*, *120*, 3–24.

Part II

THE NEUROSCIENCE OF CONSCIOUSNESS

A. Neurophysiological Mechanisms
of Consciousness

CHAPTER 25

Hunting the Ghost: Toward a Neuroscience of Consciousness

Petra Stoerig

Abstract

Consciousness is a term with many meanings. In one sense, we use the term to indicate whether or not an organism is in a conscious *state*. In this sense, consciousness is what is altered, reduced, or even lost when we faint or undergo deep general anaesthesia. In a second sense, it is a trait, an *attribute* of a psychological process; we may think, desire, hear, see, and feel consciously, thereby becoming conscious of thoughts, wishes, voices and music, of colours and textures. Local anaesthesia, by abolishing conscious sensations of touch in the affected limb, thus interferes with the consciousness *of* something. Within trait consciousness, I draw a further distinction between conscious representations and conscious access. Conscious representations are of objects or contents of perceptions, desires, or actions; they are usually phenomenal, like a strawberry that is red, sweet. and heart-shaped and that I see, smell, and desire to eat. To describe the strawberry's looks and taste or to resist its temptation, conscious access to its representation is required (Block, 1995).

This chapter reviews evidence pertaining to the neural basis of state and trait consciousness (Stoerig, 2002). As we (still?) lack an objective marker of conscious representations that is independent of the subjects' overt behaviour, we can assess conscious representations only when our subjects can access and (verbally or non-verbally) express them. The same applies to the conscious state, because it is only observable conscious access that precludes a diagnosis of unconsciousness. If conscious representations as well as state consciousness are attributed on the basis of evidence for conscious access, the neuronal processes that mediate conscious access in its many forms are likely to contaminate what we learn about those that mediate conscious representations and states. A prominent candidate for mediating conscious access is a network of frontoparietal cortical regions that play an important role in attentional and behavioural selection of incoming and stored information. As these regions allocate processing resources and guide behavioural selection, it is not surprising that they are activated both when vegetative state patients recover and when healthy subjects perform demanding perceptual tasks. Although the frontoparietal network has been implicated in the mediation of the conscious state, of conscious representations, and of conscious access, I argue that these different manifestations of consciousness may well depend on different neuronal processes.

Consciousness as a State of an Organism

Is it possible to identify a system of neuronal structures that mediate all conscious states and whose destruction or downregulation abolishes consciousness? It should be a *non-specific* system because we are in a conscious state regardless of whether we listen to a concert, indulge in French cuisine, or suffer from heartburn afterward; we are conscious ('bei Bewusstsein') regardless of what we are conscious *of*. Being in a conscious state is prerequisite to any conscious experience, and alterations in the state cause changes in the experience. The following sections discuss sleep as an example of circadian endogenous state changes; general anaesthesia as an example of chemically induced state changes; and comatose, vegetative, and minimally conscious states as examples of pathology-induced state changes. The purpose is to provide up-to-date information on several aspects of consciousness, as well as their interdependence, and to point out some critical confounds.

Sleep

Sleep is regularly and actively induced by a shift in neuronal activity and neurotransmitter balance in brainstem nuclei. In their seminal work, Morruzzi and Magoun (1949) discovered a network of neurons extending from the medulla oblongata through the midbrain up to the diencephalon that seemed to regulate both the activity of the brain and the spinal cord. We now know that three states are balanced within this network: non-REM sleep, characterized by inhibition of the spinal cord and large parts of the cortex;

wakefulness, characterized by activation of both; and REM sleep (rapid eye movement sleep) during which the cortex becomes regionally activated, but the spinal fibres are actively inhibited. This inhibition is crucial to prevent the motor signals that the cortex generates while we sleep from reaching the muscles. A small lesion in the locus coeruleus interferes with this inhibition, so that a sleeping cat, albeit unresponsive to sensory stimulation, exhibits walking or running movements or even full-fledged fighting behaviour (Jouvet & Delorme, 1965); the intact animal will execute only small twitching movements in REM sleep.

In humans, REM sleep behaviour disorders that are a consequence of dysfunctions of the balance between endogenous activation and inhibition come in different degrees of severity. In severe cases, sleepers can be propelled to perform violent actions that endanger themselves as well as their partners and can be most difficult to stop because external sensory input is inhibited during REM sleep and so fails to wake them. Upon awakening and reconnecting with the environment, the patients may report wild dreams that seem consistent with the behaviour they displayed, indicating dream enactment (Schenck, Bundlie, Ettinger, & Mahowald, 1986). A young man recurrently dreamt he was a big cat let out of his cage by a zookeeper who offered him raw meat that he could not snatch. His behaviour during these periods reflected the dream: He would prowl about the house, open the refrigerator with his mouth, or lift a mattress with his jaws and drag it about (Schenck et al., 1989, p. 195).

These REM sleep behaviour disorders differ from non-REM sleep disorders of which sleep walking is probably the best known; sleep eating and sleep sex are other examples (Schenck & Mahowald, 1994). In all of these disorders, the patients initiate seemingly goal-directed activities; they will for instance get up and walk to the fridge, carry the food they find back to bed, and devour it. Clearly, the behaviours are complex, and sequences may last up to 1 or 2 hours. More tragic results than waking up

Table 25.1. The incidence of dream reports is lower when subjects are woken from non-REM sleep; absolute values depend on which non-REM stage preceded the waking, and what is counted as a dream.

Authors	% Dream Reports From REM	Non-REM
Aserinsky & Kleitmann, 1953	74	22
Dement & Kleitmann, 1957	79.6	7
Foulkes, 1962	87	74
Hobson et al., 1965	87.2	37.2
Kales et al., 1967	83	35
Foulkes and Schmidt, 1983	93	67
Cavallero et al., 1992	89.2	64.5
Bosinelli, 1995	89/93	65/77 (SWS)
Cicogna et al., 2000	93.33	62.62 (SWS)
Nielsen, 2000	81.9+/−.9	43+/−20.8

satiated in a bed messed up with food are evidenced by a series of crimes committed – to the best judgement of the specialists and jury – in this altered state of consciousness (Broughton et al., 1994; Hartmann, 1983). Unlike people awakening from REM sleep behaviours, the non-REM disorder patients usually recall neither a dream nor another aspect of behaviour related to the episodes, indicating that the neurochemistry governing REM and non-REM sleep is likely to differentially affect recall after waking (see Chapter 16 for more information on the neurochemistry of sleep disorders).

The electroencephalographic characteristics of REM sleep – a low-amplitude high-frequency EEG resembling that recorded during waking with eyes open – are suggestive of dream experience. As dynamic, multisensory dreams are reported more often when sleepers are woken from REM rather than non-REM phases, sleep researchers since Kleitman (1963) have tended to equate dream and REM sleep. However, studies that have used more sensitive measures to assess reports of mental activity prior to waking (Foulkes, 1962) have shown that mentation is reported quite commonly after waking from REM as well as non-REM phases (see Table 25.1). Even when woken from the deepest of the non-REM sleep stages, stage 4, which is characterized by a low-frequency, high-amplitude EEG, subjects may report not only some thought-like mentation but

also movie-like dreams (see Bosinelli, 1995, for example). The higher incidence of dream reports from REM sleep is a probability effect, not an absolute difference.

Currently, the EEG is used to classify sleep stages (Rechtschaffen & Kales, 1968), but no physiological marker for the absence or presence of dream mentation has been identified. Therefore functional neuroimaging studies performed on sleeping subjects can provide insights into the regional brain activation patterns that characterize sleep and its different stages, but cannot differentiate between periods with and without mentation. During both REM and non-REM sleep, the prefrontal and parietal cortical regions are deactivated in comparison to the wakeful 'resting state' (Braun et al., 1997; Maquet, 2000; Maquet et al., 1996). 'Resting state' describes a situation in which subjects lie, with their eyes closed, in the scanner and, despite uncontrolled differences in internally ongoing emotional and cognitive activity, are attentive to the environment. The most active regions in the resting state are the (left) dorsolateral and medial prefrontal areas, the inferior parietal cortex, and the posterior cingulate/precuneus (see Maquet, 2000; Shulman et al., 1997, for reviews). In slow-wave sleep (SWS, non-REM stages 3 and 4 with high-amplitude low-frequency EEG), regional cerebral blood flow decreases in these as well as most other parts of the brain including the thalamus and brainstem;

Figure 25.1. The relative contributions of exogenous stimulation (white) and endogenous activity (stippled) to mental life change during the waking period. Here, permeability is considerably higher than during sleep where the contribution of externally induced activity is systematically reduced.

only the perirolandic (sensorimotor) and occipital (visual) cortices were reported to remain unaffected (Kajimura et al., 1999). In REM sleep, despite overall increases in cerebral blood flow and energy demands, relatively low regional cerebral blood flow (rCBF) persists in prefrontal and parietal cortex, whereas relative activations are seen in the brainstem, hypothalamus, and thalamus where the nuclei that regulate sleep stages are housed (Hobson, 1989; Steriade, 2000; Chapter 16) and in the amygdalae and posterior association cortices (Braun et al., 1997; Nofzinger et al., 1997). Interestingly, the posterior cingulate-precuneal region that is significantly deactivated in both SWS and REM sleep (e.g. Braun et al., 1997; Maquet et al., 1996) was selectively activated in a SPECT-study of sleepwalking (Bassetti et al., 2000). The increased activity in this posterior midline area in the face of persistent frontal deactivation suggests that this non-REM sleep, and possibly other sleep behaviour disorders, results from pathological combinations of neurobiological features of sleep and wakefulness (Mahowald & Schenck, 2001).

Activation patterns observed during waking and sleeping indicate that the mental activity during sleep differs from that during waking. The observed deactivation of prefrontal cortex seems to preclude neither the sometimes fantastic creativity expressed in dreams nor the cognitive insights that anecdotally occur during sleep. Only recently has the role that sleep plays for the latter been demonstrated experimentally, when

subjects were found to be significantly more likely to detect hidden rules to a task when they were allowed to sleep before continuing in its execution (Wagner et al., 2004). The activation of limbic structures and sensory association cortices seen during REM sleep may provide the emotional colour and the multisensory phenomenal content of REM sleep dreaming; both higher auditory and visual cortical areas appear quite reliably activated in this sleep stage.

A further and major difference between waking and dreaming experience/mentation lies in its origin. In the waking state, internal (thoughts, imagery, feelings, memories) and external (sensations) components of mental life shift in their relative contributions throughout the day, but always remain penetrable to each other, whereas in the sleeping state, the external contribution is consistently reduced (see Fig. 25.1). Electrophysiological recordings show that sensory stimuli generate only the early components of the waking state evoked potentials (Yamada et al., 1988), and neuroimaging of responses to auditory stimulation (text being read to the sleeper) during non-REM sleep produced less auditory cortical activation than in the waking state. In addition, in the visual cortex a pronounced negative BOLD response was seen not only during text reading (Czisch et al., 2002) but also in response to visual stimulation (8 Hz flickering light), and it corresponded to a decrease in rCBF in the same visual cortical areas (rostromedial occipital cortex) in additional volunteers who underwent $H_2{}^{15}O$ PET during

SWS (Born et al., 2002). One of the possible interpretations of this finding is that external stimulation interferes with endogenous visual cortex activation.

At present we cannot get information about the experiences of sleepers without waking them and thereby changing their state, and therefore we have no means to determine confidently whether a lack of report indicates a lack of experience or a lack of recall. At the same time, reports need not necessarily reflect mentation just before waking; if there were periods of true nothingness, the reports could also reflect the last event that left a reportable trace. Although the amount and movie-like character of dreams may differ during different sleep stages and unconscious periods cannot be ruled out, sleep as such is not an unconscious state, but rather one that alters consciousness by closing the shutters on the largest part of external sensory input.

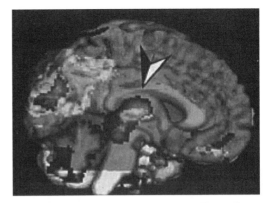

Figure 25.2. The most pronounced effects of propofol (Fiset et al., 1999) are shown together with those induced by halothane and isoflurane inhalation (Alkire et al., 2000). Regional cerebral blood flow was measured in the first and regional cerebral glucose metabolism in the second study. (With kind permission from Michael Alkire.) (See color plates.)

Anaesthesia

General anaesthesia is induced by a variety of very different chemical compounds. This is probably the major reason why, at present, we have no generally accepted theory of general anaesthesia. The major contenders include (1) inhibition of excitatory receptor channels together with potentiation of inhibitory ones that include GABA$_A$ (γ-aminobutyric acid), glycine, nicotinergic acetylcholine, and serotonin (Franks & Lieb, 1994; 1996); (2) interference with NMDA (N-methyl-D-aspartate) receptor function (Anis, Berry, Burton, & Lodge, 1983; Flohr, 1995, Flohr, Glade, & Motzko, 1998); and (3) changes in polymerization of microtubules (Allison & Nunn, 1968; Hameroff, 1998). Although all these hypotheses focus on some specific cell sites, none implies that a particular brain structure (or set of brain structures) is especially involved in the mediation of the conscious state. It is still open to discussion whether this reflects the fact that core structures that really are indispensable for the conscious state can, possibly due to their central placement, be accessed in very different ways, or whether there are no core structures and the conscious state instead depends on a functional property of the network.

Although earlier neuroimaging data that compared general anaesthesia with pre- or post-anaesthetic states showed that the tested pharmaceutical agents produce an overall reduction in brain metabolism (Alkire et al., 1995), more sensitive analysis revealed that in addition to the fronto-parietal resting state network, cerebellar, frontobasal, and thalamo-mesencephalic brain regions are relatively more deactivated (Alkire et al., 2000; Fiset et al., 1999; see Fig. 25.2). Despite some agent-specific differences, the tested anaesthetics – halothane, propofol, and isoflurane – thus produced considerable overlap regarding the most affected brain regions, suggesting the possibility of a central core in the mesencephalic reticular formation and the thalamus (Alkire et al., 2000). Support for a special role of the thalamus and its reciprocal network of connections to the cortex comes from a variety of sources: (1) Functional thalamo-cortical connectivity is altered in anaesthesia (White & Alkire, 2003); (2) the EEG, which at light doses may either increase or decrease its frequency depending on the anaesthetic, changes to slow, large-amplitude patterns at deep levels, indicating thalamocortical synchronization; (3) 3-Hz electrical stimulation applied to thalamic nuclei like the nucleus reticularis thalami during neurosurgery causes behavioural arrest whose appearance resembles the absences observed during certain epileptic seizures; the patient stops responding, looks straight ahead, and cannot remember anything about this 5- to 10-s period after abruptly coming to (Jasper, 1998; Jasper & Droogleever-Fortuyn, 1947); and (4) especially the non-specific thalamic nuclei entertain closely knit connections not only to brainstem nuclei but also to the cortex, the basal ganglia, and the striatum. In view of their central position they are optimally placed to transmit arousal signals as well as exerting both global and local influences on neocortical activity. Originally seen as a dorsal extension of the reticular activating system (Morruzzi & Magoun, 1949), they have been suggested as central players in the mediation of consciousness (e.g. Bogen, 1995; Purpura & Schiff, 1997; Chapter 27). The thalamus, and especially its non-specific nuclei (or neurons, see Jones, 1998), may thus play an important role in maintaining the conscious state.

Although the overall reduction in brain metabolism effected by the majority of compounds suggests a loss of consciousness, all the problems of ascertaining whether such loss occurs in sleep are exacerbated under anaesthesia: Communication in this state is impossible as the subjects do not respond to verbal commands, and post-anaesthetic recall of events is impeded not only by the drugs and their effects on memory but also by the longer recovery period. Regarding sensory information processing, auditory and somatosensory potentials evoked during general anaesthesia in rats (Angel, 1991, 1993) and humans (Madler et al., 1991; Madler & Pöppel, 1987) show that only the earliest deflections (~10 ms) remain unaffected, whereas mid- and long-latency components are much reduced or absent.

Although this effect is reliably induced with such common agents as propofol and isoflurane and indicates severely altered processing of external stimuli, opioids and anaesthetics like ketamine (a dissociative anaesthetic that in small doses is hallucinogenic and in large ones causes general anaesthesia without immobilizing the subjects or producing the appearance of deep sleep) do not flatten the mid- and long-latency components to the same extent; they may in fact even enhance the amplitude both of the auditory mid-latency and the 40-Hz steady-state response (Plourde, Baribeau, & Bonhomme, 1997). Certainly neurons in cortical as well as subcortical structures do not simply stop responding to sensory signals, as is also demonstrated unequivocally by the fact that a vast part of our knowledge on their response properties stems from anaesthetized animals (Hubel & Wiesel, 1968). Recent neuroimaging data on visual processing in anaesthetized monkeys extend these findings, showing activation in numerous cortical and subcortical structures in response to visual stimuli (Leopold, Plettenberg, & Logothetis, 2003; Logothetis, Guggenberger, Peled, & Pauls, 1999). Human subjects stimulated tactually while undergoing stepped propofol (Bonhomme et al., 2001) or isoflurance anaesthesia (Antognini, Buonocore, Disbrow, & Carstens, 1997) showed that activation in somatosensory cortex is decreased at a lower dosage than thalamic activation. Stroboscopic visual flicker stimulation under pentobarbital produced similar decreases of the BOLD signal in visual cortex, culminating in negative responses in subjects who received the highest doses relative to body weight (Martin et al., 2000). Although at increasingly higher concentration these specific stimulus-evoked responses decrease and eventually disappear (Leopold et al., 2003) and the EEG turns isoelectric, they may remain at the dosage used for clinical interventions.

Behavioural evidence, again from both monkeys and humans, provides further evidence for information processing under general anaesthesia. Ketamine-anaesthetized

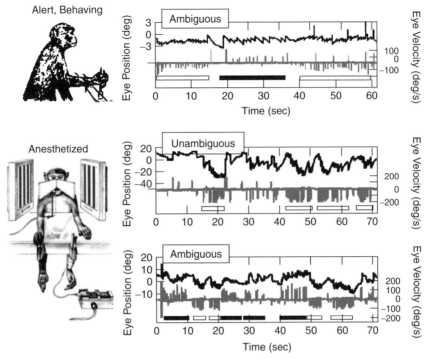

Figure 25.3. (Top) When gratings that move in opposite directions are presented simultaneously, one to each eye, the awake monkey, who is trained to indicate motion direction this way, responds by moving the handle alternately into the one or other direction (white and black bars at bottom). The perceptual switches are also reflected in his optokinetic responses that follow the presently perceived grating, as shown both with respect to eye movement amplitude (left axis) and velocity (right axis). The responses consist of alternating slow phases where the eyes follow the perceived motion, and fast phases in the opposite direction. The changes in the direction of the fast phases are easily seen in the velocity plot (grey). (Bottom) In the ketamine-anaesthetized monkey, optokinetic nystagmus follows the grating in the unambiguous condition. In the rivalry condition, responses again alternate direction.

monkeys can show not only preserved optokinetic nystagmus in response to moving visual patterns but also irregular alternations in its direction when stimuli are presented in binocularly rivalrous conditions (Leopold et al., 2003; see Fig. 25.3). When two patterns moving in opposite direction are presented, one to each eye, the awake subjects' percept switches in a quasi-regular manner between that of the one and that of the other stimulus (Blake & Logothetis, 2002). This perceptual effect is reflected in the eye movements that follow the perceptually dominant direction of stim-ulus motion; as they correspond to manual responses given by monkey and human subjects to indicate the perceived direction of motion, they have been used as indicators of perceptual changes in monkeys (Logothetis & Schall, 1989). The presence of optokinetic responses under unambiguous stimulation indicates that sensorimotor loops continue to function at least under relatively light ketamine anaesthesia. More surprising is the finding that these responses switch direction under ambiguous stimulation, because a behavioural pattern that is regarded as evidence for alternations between conscious percepts in the awake organism (Fig. 25.3) has thus been demonstrated in anaesthetized monkeys.

The second example concerns memory processes. Numerous studies have investigated memory in patients undergoing surgery under general anaesthesia with a wide variety of agents. Stimulation is usually auditory; the most common paradigm involves reading word lists to the patient intraoperatively. Retrieval of this information is tested postoperatively with indirect methods, such as word-stem completion. In this task, stems of used and new words are presented (as in 'mem . . .'), and the subjects are asked to complete these stems with the first word that comes to mind. If overall they use words they have heard during surgery (say 'memory' rather than 'member') significantly more often than an alternative (and equally common) one, this is regarded as evidence for implicit memory. To distinguish this effect more clearly from explicit recall, Jacoby's inclusion-exclusion task has been adapted (Bonnebakker et al., 1996): Here, in addition to word-stem completion with the first word that comes to mind, in different series the patients are explicitly asked NOT to use the word they have heard before. Whereas an implicit memory trace may bias a subject's responses toward repeating what was processed implicitly or explicitly (inclusion), exclusion of this same information requires intentional avoidance of the facilitated word. As this cognitive operation is thought to involve conscious access to the memory, it provides evidence for explicit recall. Remarkably, both inclusion and exclusion procedures as well as two-alternative forced choice (2AFC) have revealed significant memory effects (Bonnebakker et al., 1996), although not every study has yielded this finding. A meta-analysis of 44 studies encompassing 2,517 patients conducted to elucidate the reasons for the divergent results showed that the effect of the stimulation decayed over time. No longer significant 36 hours after surgery, it was highly significant within 12 hours, and still significant but less so when patients were tested between 12 and 36

hours post-surgery (Merikle & Daneman, 1996).

Together, the studies on information processing under general anaesthesia demonstrate not only dose-dependent specific brain activity in response to stimulation but also significant perceptual (in binocular rivalry) and motor organization (OKN) in ketamine-dissociated monkeys (Leopold et al., 2003), and memory formation in human patients under general clinical anaesthesia. Whether this evidence ought to be seen in the context of unconscious cognition (Merikle & Daneman, 1996) or in the context of information being processed in a state of severely altered, dissociated consciousness still needs to be determined. In the former case – cognition in a state of unconsciousness – we would have to believe that (a) perceptual organization continues to a level at which alternative interpretations of ambiguous stimulations are presented and (b) that memory traces laid down in a state of unconsciousness can be accessed when consciousness is recovered. In the latter case – anaesthesia produces a dissociated state of consciousness – both the perceptual organization and the memory formation would occur in a conscious but dissociated subject.

Coma and Vegetative State

Coma is a state of unarousable unresponsiveness resulting from severe pathology. The patient lies with the eyes closed and may appear almost as if in deep sleep (see Table 25.2). However, if this state does not end with recovery or death, within weeks the coma will give way to a vegetative state (VS; Jennett & Plum, 1972) that may continue for months or years (persistent VS). In this state, patients "awake" from their coma and may be able to breathe independently. Importantly, sleep and waking phases alternate in VS (but not in coma), although movies and the popular press often wrongly portray 'comatose' patients who sleep restfully for years. Not only does coma not last that long but also VS patients open and close their eyes, react to strong or painful stimulation with eye opening and

Table 25.2. Overview of best-possible behaviours observed in pathology-induced state changes.

State	Coma	VS	MCS	Locked-in
Reactive eyeopening	No	Yes	Yes	Yes
Cyclic eye opening	No	Yes	Yes	Yes
Verbal utterances	Grunts	Jumble	Intelligible	No
Motor behaviour	Reflex	Reflex	In context	No (eyes only)
Affective behaviour	No	Yes	In context	No
Breathing	Variable	Normal	Normal	Normal
EEG	δ, τ	δ, τ, slow α	α, local γ	Almost normal
Brain metabolism (overall)	50%	~50%	~40%	Small-medium reduction
Pain experience	No	No	Yes	Yes
Self-consciousness	No	No	Yes	Yes

In both VS and MCS patients, stimulation may evoke local brain activation patterns. Note that negative statements on pain experience and self-consciousness are only inferred from the behavioural response patterns.

faster breathing, and may grimace and move their limbs during the waking phases. In addition to pupillary light, cornea, and gagging reflexes, in the waking phases spontaneous movements may be observed; chewing, grunting, swallowing, smiling, teeth gnashing, and brief pursuit eye movements can occur. The state is described as one of 'wakefulness without awareness' (Jennett & Plum, 1972).

The vegetative state has recently been differentiated from the newly introduced category of the minimally conscious state (MCS; Giacino et al., 2002). MCS patients may show islands of relatively preserved brain responses (Boly, Faymonville, & Peigneux, 2004; Schiff et al., 2002), as well as fragments of behaviours interpretable as signs of perception and voluntary movement that preclude the diagnosis of vegetative state (Zeman, 1997). Both the vegetative and the minimally conscious state need to be distinguished from the locked-in syndrome in which the patient is fully conscious but, due to a circumscribed brainstem lesion, is unable to communicate in any way other than by lid closure and vertical eye movements. Overall brain metabolism is less reduced in locked-in patients (Levy et al., 1987; see Table 25.2).

Lesions causing coma, VS, and MCS may be diffuse and metabolic as well as focal.

Among the causes for continued loss of consciousness are extensive fibre degeneration, extensive necrosis of the cerebral cortex or the thalamus, and thalamic-hypothalamic and brainstem lesions that involve the pons and its tegmentum (Plum & Posner, 1982). Support for a special role of the thalamus comes from a recent review of pathology data: Of 35 cases of VS caused by trauma, 80% had thalamic damage; in addition, of 14 non-traumatic VS cases, all had severely damaged thalami (Jennett, 2002). Brain metabolism was relatively most affected in frontal and parietotemporal association cortices of VS patients (Kassubek et al., 2003; Laureys et al., 2002a,b, Laureys, Owen, & Schiff, 2004; see Fig. 25.4); in addition, functional connectivity to the intralaminar nuclei of the thalamus was altered (Laureys et al., 2000a). In contrast, the removal of an entire cerebral hemisphere does not cause coma, indicating that the system that mediates the conscious state is bilateral and that one half of a brain suffices to sustain it. Neither does coma result from bilateral lesions that destroy both occipital, both parietal, both temporal, or both frontal lobes.

Cortical as well as subcortical activation has been observed in response to auditory (Laureys et al., 2000b) and noxious stimulation of VS patients (Kassubek et al., 2003;

Laureys et al., 2002a). The patterns were subnormal and in the case of painful stimuli did not activate the entire pain matrix. In addition, the activated areas' functional connectivity to the higher frontal and parietal cortices seemed impaired in VS patients, but showed recovery when the patients recovered (Boly et al., 2004; Laureys et al., 2002a). Nevertheless, these data do not preclude the possibility that the VS patients still have some conscious experience even if it is not in context.

Conclusion

The body of data on the three states of altered, reduced, dissociated, or lost consciousness demonstrates how difficult it is to provide incontrovertible evidence for even a transient absence of all consciousness. In all instances, we need to 'wake' the person and require a (verbal or non-verbal) report to learn whether anything was experienced before the 'waking'. Even when this is possible – in sleep or anaesthesia, and to some extent after emergence from VS – the effects of the state change on memory make it difficult, if not impossible, to conclude anything from a negative report. Process fractionation, discussed both in the context of sleep behaviour disorders (Mahowald & Schenck, 2001) and anaesthesia (Cariani, 2000; Mashour, 2004) and referring to dissociations within neurobiological patterns that regulate the normal stages of sleep and wakefulness, could be extended to the pathological state changes. Such a dissociation-based concept of state changes in general anaesthesia, the vegetative, and the minimally conscious state could accommodate conscious experiences whether or not they are accessible to the subject after 'waking' and could explain aspects of wakefulness manifest in vegetative state and sleep behaviour disorder patients.

That the thalamus and its thalamo-cortico-thalamic loops that integrate specific and non-specific neurons (Jones, 1998) play a special role in maintaining state consciousness seems likely in the light of both pathology and anaesthesiology.

Consciousness as Attribute or Trait of Psychological Processes

Even when the organism is in a fully conscious and alert state, it is not capable of being conscious of everything dealt with by its brain. Many brain processes are devoted to the regulation of homeostasis, and at least in humans, hormone secretion, digestion, breathing, immune defence, and the like are in principle unconscious. We can learn about them, but have no direct access to them, and only feel the consequences of their functions and dysfunctions. What the organism can be conscious of depends on its sensory, cognitive, and behavioural faculties. Some of the brain processes involved in their mediation are potentially conscious, in that we can consciously perceive, think, feel, wish, and act upon them. However, at any point in time we are in fact only conscious of a small subset of what we can be conscious of. Despite the richness of our moment-to-moment experience, our consciousness is limited in its capacity for simultaneous representation. Broadbent's bottle neck (1974) and Koestler's administration (1968) metaphors both focus on this restriction, illustrating that only a fraction of what goes on in the brain reaches the top representative.

Neuropsychological Approaches to Conscious Representations

How can we learn in which ways brain processes that can cause conscious experiences differ from those that cannot, and how those involved in mediating the presently conscious differ from those that are potentially, but not now, consciously represented? One of the inroads to the first question is the neuropsychological study of patients or animals who have suffered circumscribed brain lesions. If the lesion destroyed the conscious representation of a particular modality or faculty, we can explore whether implicit (non-conscious) processes remain and how the neuronal activity mediating them and the performance they allow differ from their normal conscious counterparts.

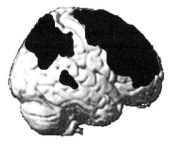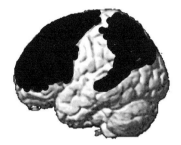

Figure 25.4. The metabolically most impaired brain regions in vegetative state patients were found in prefrontal, premotor, and parietotemporal areas (Fig. 2A from Laureys et al., 2002b, reproduced with kind permission from Steven Laureys).

The best-known examples of this approach are probably the implicit functions that remain in amnesic and in cortically blind patients.

Claparède (1911) was the first to describe telling evidence of implicit memory. His densely amnesic patient refused to shake his hand after he had, on a previous occasion, pricked her with a needle he had hidden between his fingers. When asked about her refusal, she might even explain that sometimes people hide needles in their hands, indicating that the experience had left a trace that could be incorporated into her behaviour as well as her reasoning; however, she could not consciously recall the original painful episode. Results of extensive formal testing rather than anecdotal evidence have been reported on patient HM whose dense anterograde amnesia resulted from bilateral removal of medial temporal cortex. A series of papers impressively demonstrates that HM, despite his superior intelligence, was unable to recall or recognize verbal as well as pictorial material if prevented from constant rehearsal between presentation and recall. Nevertheless, HM showed motor learning and from trial to trial improved his ability to trace a line between the double outlines of a star that, like his pencil, were only visible in a mirror. Despite never recalling having performed these tasks before, HM showed similar improvements in solving the Tower of Hanoi puzzle (Cohen & Corkin, 1981; Milner, Corkin, & Teuber, 1968). Another thoroughly studied case, that of KC who suffered extensive bilateral damage involving

the hippocampal regions, complements previous findings. He too presents with dense anterograde amnesia, but, unlike HM, is incapable of recollecting episodic memories from his life before the accident, although, like HM, he can recall semantic information from that time. In addition to providing evidence for a dissociation between semantic and episodic memory, he implicitly recovered new associations between word pairs and took longer when responding to rearranged or new pairs than to the original intact pairs, although he failed to recollect the items on explicit testing (see Rosenbaum et al., 2004, for a review). More evidence for implicit memory comes from the work of Warrington and Weiskrantz (1968). They introduced the fragmented figure test and found that their amnesic subjects recognized the figures at an earlier, more fragmented stage when having seen the set before. Other forms of implicit memory include various forms of priming, word-stem completion, and conditioning (Rovee-Collier et al., 2001; Schacter, Dobbins, & Schnyer, 2004; Chapter 28).

Amnesic patients thus provide a prime example of implicit access to information that informs behaviour despite being unavailable to conscious recall. The information – the pinprick, the word pairs, the fragmented figures – is phenomenally represented as long as it is present, and the patients' responses to it show that they are perfectly aware of it and able to deal with it in multitudinous ways. The conscious access that manifests itself in their behaviour, however, is lost quickly when the information is no longer present. Implicit memory remains when a form of conscious acess – recall – is lost, and thus differs from the second of the widely known examples of implicit functions that survive the lesion-induced loss of their explicit representation, that of blindsight (Weiskrantz, Warrington, Sanders, & Marshall, 1974), where cortical blindness prevents the conscious phenomenal respresentation of visual information. Cortical blindness results from the destruction or denervation of the primary visual cortex (V1). Patients with absolute field defects consistently claim that they do not see visual stimuli that are confined to the blind field. Nevertheless, they can exhibit non-reflexive visual functions when they are forced to guess whether, where, or what stimulus has been presented and may detect, localize, and discriminate visual stimuli at statistically significant levels (Stoerig, 1999; see Fig. 25.5; Weiskrantz, 1986). Evidence for blindsight has also been reported in hemianopic monkeys (Cowey & Stoerig, 1995) who behaved like the patients; they showed excellent localization performance but nevertheless treated the same stimuli as blanks when given that response option (Stoerig, Zontanou, & Cowey, 2002). Numerous other examples of implicit visual functions include covert processing of colours in cerebral achromatopsia (Heywood, Cowey, & Newcombe, 1991), faces in prosopagnosia (Bruyer et al., 1983), orientation and size in agnosia (Milner & Goodale, 1995), as well as deaf hearing (Mozaz Garde & Cowey, 2000) and unfeeling touch (Paillard, Michel, & Stemach, 1983) following lesions of the auditory or somatosensory cortices, respectively. Probably it is fair to say that most every loss that results from a cortical lesion spares implicit functions that can be revealed with appropriate testing.

Studies of implicit processes and the pathways that mediate them may help us get a better grasp of the neural basis of explicit representations. Blindsight for example seems to involve all the remaining projections from the retina onto subcortical visual nuclei (Pasik & Pasik, 1982) and extrastriate visual cortex (Goebel et al., 2001). The blindness in blindsight can therefore not be attributed to an absence of all cortical involvement, a conclusion supported by evidence for cortical activation in a variety of other neuropsychological syndromes (e.g., Rees et al., 2000). More likely, some functional or quantitative difference accounts for the loss of the conscious representation. Such loss, albeit of a particular visual feature, also characterizes cerebral colour blindness that results from destruction of the colour complex in the fusiform and lingual gyri (see Meadows, 1974; Zeki, 1990, for review) and cerebral motion blindness that results from bilateral destruction of the motion complex (see Zeki, 1991, for review).

Zeki's concept of micro-consciousnesses (Zeki, 2001) is based both on the selective loss of visual qualia from circumscribed lesions of visual cortical areas and on the (re)appearance of residual qualia that Riddoch (1917) first observed in the cortically blind fields of some patients. The concerted activity of the early visual cortical areas is necessary to provide the repertoire of our visual qualia – brightness, depth, colour, and motion – that are the phenomenal fabric of conscious vision (Stoerig, 1996). Although the primary visual cortex plays first violin in this concert, as its destruction abolishes all visual qualia in the vast majority of cases, its precise role is still under debate. Certainly functional blindness also ensues when (V1) is disconnected from the higher visual cortical areas (Bodis-Wollner, Atkin, Raab, & Wolkstein, 1977; Horton & Hoyt, 1991). Whether this finding indicates that vision is only conscious when higher visual, and possibly also non-visual, areas receive retinal input via the retino-geniculo-striate–extrastriate cortical route, or whether the normally massive backprojections from higher to earlier visual areas are required for conscious vision, is still uncertain (Hochstein & Ahissar, 2002; Stoerig & Cowey, 1993; Crick & Koch, 1995; Köhler & Moscovitch, 1997; Lamme, 2001).

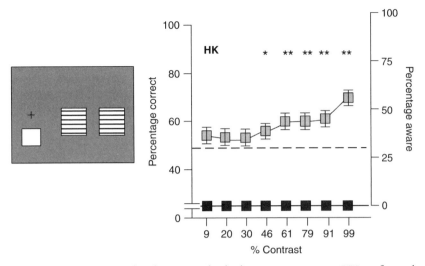

Figure 25.5. In a 2 AFC localization task, the hemianopic patient HK performed significantly above chance with a grating contrast of 46% or higher. When asked to indicate whether or not he was aware of the stimulus, which could appear with equal probability at either of the two target positions when he touched the start light shown beneath the fixation cross in the display (left), he did not report awareness on a single trial, regardless of contrast.

Selective inactivation of feedforward and feedback projections would help disentangle this issue.

Experiments on Normal Observers

How processes that are consciously represented at this moment differ from those that may, but are not, presently so represented has been addressed in normal subjects. The main paradigms manipulate the experimental conditions so that the subjects cannot become aware of parts of the physically presented information; in addition, manipulation of the subjects by means of transcranial magnetic or electrical stimulation is used. Note that unlike the patients who have lost the conscious representation of a sensory modality, the normal subjects consciously perceive information in these manipulations even if they miss whatever target they are seeking. Binocular rivalry, change blindness, inattentional blindness, visual masking, repetition blindness, and the attentional blink are all examples drawn primarily from the visual domain.

Binocular rivalry results from dichoptic stimulation with incompatible images that cannot be fused into a meaningful percept. If one eye sees an upward moving grating while the other sees a downward moving one, rather than perceiving no motion as would happen if the two inputs cancelled each other out, subjects see first upward, then downward, then upward moving gratings in succession. As monkeys also report these changes when trained to indicate upward or downward motion (Logothetis & Schall, 1989), brain processes during rivalrous stimulation have been recorded from both species in the hope that they may help distinguish between processes that are presently conscious and those that are presently not conscious. Results of neural recordings in various areas of the occipito-temporal stream in awake behaving monkeys who constantly indicate which stimulus they presently see have shown that the number of neurons that follow the percept (rather than responding throughout to the always present stimulus direction they prefer) increase substantially from early to late visual cortical areas (see Fig. 25.6). In the motion area MT and in area V4, ~40% of neurons responded to their preferred stimulus only when the monkey indicated seeing it, whereas in inferotemporal (IT) and superior temporal cortex, ~90% of neurons showed this behaviour, indicating that binocular rivalry is largely resolved at this advanced processing stage (Logothetis, 1998).

How do these neurons, which were also found in medial temporal lobe areas of humans (Kreiman et al., 2002), know which stimulus is (or should) just (be) perceived? Do they determine it among themselves, in some kind of oscillating majority vote? If so, do the patterns alternate because fatigue causes the balance to shift to the suppressed population? Or does another brain process determine the perceptual and neuronal switches? Tononi, Srinivasan, Russell, and Edelman (1998) used magnetoencephalography and presented their subjects with dichoptically presented gratings of different colour that flickered at different frequencies to allow attribution of the recorded activity to one or the other grating. In line with previous results (Brown & Norcia, 1997), they found stronger amplitudes correlating with the perceived stimulus. This finding is consistent with more neurons firing in concert, but does not elucidate how the perceptual switches are brought about. Evidence in favour of a switch located outside of the visual areas comes from a neuroimaging study in humans that compared brain activation patterns from rivalrous stimulation with a control condition in which the stimuli were physically alternating so as to produce a rivalrous percept without interocular conflict (Lumer et al., 1998). Such a fake rivalry stimulus is useful for comparison with the real one, because it appears the same to the subject if well done and externally induces the perceptual switches that the subject's brain initiates on its own under conditions of interocular conflict. The results of the comparison of activation patterns evoked by real and fake rivalry indicated that a frontoparietal network was more active in real rivalry. That a frontoparietal network may be involved in initiating the perceptual

switches agrees with observations in patients with damage to the right frontal lobe who may fail to report perceptual alternations of ambiguous figures (Ricci & Blundo, 1990). Leopold and Logothetis (1999) use this finding to back their hypothesis that the (frontoparietal) sensorimotor systems punctuate the visual areas and thereby actively shift the perceptual interpretation by means of attention poised for action.

Frontal regions have also been implicated in change blindness. Here, two complex visual stimuli, such as photographs of real-world scenes or arrangements of symbols, are presented in alternation. The two stimuli are similar overall, but differ in some feature; a person may wear a different pair of trousers, or a mountain may shift position. In between stimulus presentations, a blank screen appears briefly to simulate an eye blink and mask the transient change, rendering change detection difficult enough for subjects to require several cycles of presentation (Rensink, 2000; Simons & Levin, 1997; see Chapter 9). Beck and colleagues (2001) used this phenomenon in a neuroimaging study in which they substituted one image of a face (or a place) for another. They compared activation patterns correlating with stimulus presentations yielding change detection with those in which the change went unreported and found significant differences in frontoparietal (right middle frontal gyrus and bilateral superior parietal lobule) activation. Here, activation was pronounced when the change was detected, whereas the visual areas that are responsive to faces, or places, respectively, appeared not to differentiate between detected and undetected changes.

Results based on a variety of paradigms (e.g., detection of threshold stimuli [Pins and ffytche, 2003]; or detection of a moving target in a field of relative cortical blindness [Sahraie et al., 1997]) support the hypothesis that frontoparietal networks play some role in conscious vision. However, they do not address whether frontoparietal neurons play an important part in the phenomenal rendering of the information and, if they do, which neurons are implicated. Conceivably,

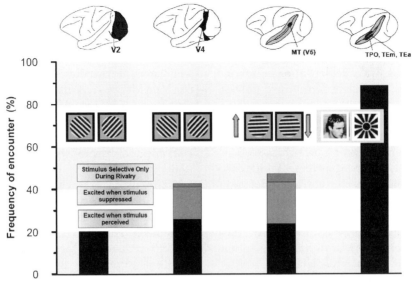

Figure 25.6. In the visual cortical areas of the monkey (top), Logothetis and co-workers recorded neurons' responses to dichoptically presented stimuli tuned to each area's preferences. Orthogonal orientations were used for V1/V2 and V4, gratings moving in opposite directions for MT (V5), and complex images (face and starburst) for the temporal visual areas TPO and TE. The bars show the proportion of neurons that respond to their stimulus when the monkey indicated perceiving it (black) and when it was perceptually suppressed (grey). Like neurons that responded selectively only during rivalry (darker grey), these were encountered only at the intermediate processing stages V4 and MT. Note that the vast majority of neurons in the highest region investigated fired only when their stimulus was also perceived. (With kind permission from Nicos Logothetis).

all or some of these activated neurons are involved in attentional selection, and again all or some of them may be required to provide conscious access to that information. As detection is inferred on the basis of report, and both attention and access are necessary for report, it is premature to ascribe the conscious detection of stimulus or change to the frontoparietal regions.

Some light is shed on this issue by recent studies. An attentional blink paradigm was used in the first such study. In this 'experimental blindness' paradigm, different visual stimuli are presented briefly and in rapid alternation, and two targets are embedded in the series. Although the targets differ in some prominent feature from the distractors – they may be white letters when the distractors are black letters – subjects' detection of the second stimulus is severely impaired provided the second stimulus follows the detected first target after a (distractor-filled) interval of ∼100–300 ms (Chun & Potter, 1995). Marois, Yi, and Chun (2004) found that activity in the parahippocampal place area (PPA) was enhanced when the second of the two target stimuli (a scene) embedded in a rapid series of scrambled versions of the same scenes that served as distractors was consciously perceived; moreover, frontal cortex was activated only when the target was also reported. Whereas the first finding indicates that the PPA, which responds preferentially to images of places and houses, is activated differentially when the appropriate stimulus is consciously perceived, the latter result implicates the frontal activation in report.

This result gains support from a change detection study. Here, subjects had to maintain a sample stimulus in short-term memory in order to decide whether the test stimulus, which appeared 6 s later at the same central position, matched the sample (Pessoa & Ungerleider, 2004). Importantly, the authors used a stimulus/response-contingent analysis of their imaging data, contrasting false alarms (reports of a change that had not occurred) with misses (missing a change that had occurred), as well as hits (correctly reporting a change) with correct rejections (correctly denying a change). In this fashion, they could show that, albeit less strongly, false alarms activated the same frontoparietal network as hits. Missed targets produced less (Marois et al., 2004) or none of this dorsal frontoparietal activation even if subjects indicated high confidence in their responses (Pessoa & Ungerleider, 2004). Instead, focal activation increases were seen in visual areas tuned to the stimuli and in more ventrally situated frontal areas (inferior frontal gyrus: Beck et al., 2001; supplementary eye field: Pessoa & Ungerleider, 2004).

That different brain regions are involved in different aspects of processing, such as phenomenal rendering, report, and attention, is thus more than a conceptual possibility. Moreover, different neuronal populations in the same area also seem to be differentially involved, as indicated by physiological recordings in the frontal eye field (FEF) of monkeys performing a detection task in which a proportion of targets was masked (Thompson & Schall, 2000). Reminiscent of Pessoa and Ungerleider's results, the authors found FEF neurons that responded when the monkeys reported a target, regardless of whether the target had been presented or not. However, visual FEF neurons that do not project to oculomotor structures also showed a selective post-mask activity that was synchronized to target presentation. These neurons may send feedback to extrastriate visual cortex, prompting and questioning them as prefrontal cortex has been suggested to do in several ambiguous and difficult visual tasks. Finally, transcranial magnetic stimulation over the FEF in humans improved the subjects' detec-

tion of backward masked targets when delivered 40 ms before target onset (Grosbras & Paus, 2003). As electrical microstimulation of the FEF in monkeys has been shown to enhance the visually evoked responses in area V4 (Moore & Armstrong, 2003), this finding is in line with a frontal 'prompting' of visual areas as well as a gain effect (i.e., an enhancement of visual responsivity as has been repeatedly demonstrated to result from attention).

In difficult tasks, such as those used for studying processes pertaining to presently invisible or inaccessible information in normal subjects, attention is certainly required. In its different guises (focal, spatial, divided, voluntary, automatic), attention can modulate the activity of sensory neurons (Desimone & Duncan, 1995) even in the absence of stimuli (Kastner et al., 1999), affect the apparent contrast of stimuli that are presented (Carrasco, Ling, & Read, 2004), and enhance spatial resolution and recognition. Depending on guise and context, attention invokes different subcortical and cortical neural networks including dorsal and ventral frontoparietal regions (Corbetta & Shulman, 2002). It may thus account for some aspects of the different stimulus- and response-contingent activation patterns in the change detection and attentional blink results.

Because the effects of attention permeate the entire perceptual process from the phenomenal rendering through recognition and working memory to report of stimuli, its neuronal correlates require careful differentiation from those involved in consciousness. This is both important and difficult. It is difficult because, as just described, attention affects the structures that are involved in perceptual processing. It is important because attention is distinct from consciousness: Like sensory information processing, but unlike consciousness, attention comes in covert as well as explicit forms, being automatically deployed in the first, and intentionally focussed in the second. That voluntary focal attention can be required for above-chance performance in tasks in which the stimuli are not consciously perceived – masking in normally sighted subjects is one example (Naccache, Blandin, & Dehaene, 2002) – further underlines its being different from the conscious representation.

Conclusion

Whether information, which is processed to an extent that makes it behaviourally effective, becomes consciously represented is not determined by attention alone. In the absence of sufficient visual information, as in blindsight or under stringent masking conditions, attention cannot render the representation phenomenal. Both attention and the conscious access to the information that is required for the subjects to be able to communicate that they have a conscious representation of the information invoke frontoparietal cortices. Although their role is thus of great importance in establishing whether a representation is conscious, the process that renders it phenomenal requires the functionality of the systems that provide the information. In the present vision-only examples, it is the destruction or denervation of the visual cortices, rather than that of frontoparietal circuits, that abolishes (aspects of) phenomenal vision or object recognition dependent on what parts are affected. The jury that decides whether these regions are only necessary, as people who argue that it is only by virtue of access that conscious representations are formed contend (see below), or whether they are also sufficient is still out.

Consciousness and Confounds

The neural correlates of conscious sensations and representations depend on many factors. The stimulus itself is one; presentation of a brief beep causes a cascade of brain events that is different from that caused by a briefly presented red blob, and the neuronal response to a red blob depends on stimulus size, position, contrast, and so on. The experimental conditions under which the stimulus is presented – whether it is a singleton, or presented simultaneously with distractors, or in a series of other stimuli – will also influence both the neuronal response it evokes and its detectability. The subjects' task bears on the level of processing that a stimulus achieves; for example, detection of face stimuli among non-face distractors requires a level of processing different from what is required for recognition of individual faces. What the subject senses or experiences depends on the magnitude and probably the kind of neuronal response; the strength of the response, the size of the activated population, and whether its members act in concert are all likely to play a role. What becomes consciously represented may depend on what the subject attends to, and attention invokes extravisual structures that in their turn affect visual neurons. What becomes consciously represented may also depend on the subject's alertness; some events pass unnoticed when one is daydreaming, whereas others, like slipping on a banana skin, reach consciousness if anything does. Whether anything becomes consciously represented depends on the subject being in a conscious state in the first place. Neuronal processes involved in mediating the conscious state, whether via the reticular formation, or through non-specific thalamo-cortico-thalamic loops, or through some other type of process, provide the critical background for any conscious representation. It is therefore not surprising that manipulations of non-specific brain structures alter the stimulus-driven activity of specific neurons (Jasper, 1949) as well as neuronal networks (Munk et al., 1996); Bachmann's approach to the microgenesis of conscious perception takes this non-specific thalamic-enabling effect into account (Bachmann, 2000).

If all of these factors, and the list is not exhaustive, determine what gets to be represented and also to what depth it does so, it is a hard task to define the neural correlate even of a single phenomenal sensation. To make matters worse, observers who want to study conscious processes require a report from the subject that they can confidently use to assert that something was consciously seen, heard, or felt. In view of the possibility of implicitly guided motor behaviour, this (verbal or non-verbal) report cannot be of a kind that could also be elicited when no conscious representation was formed. Giving an unequivocal report requires not only sufficient motor control on the part of the subject but also conscious access to his or her phenomenal percept. In Block's definition (1995), 'access-consciousness' is availability for use in reasoning and rationally guiding speech and action. Conscious access and reportability are the ones most likely to involve additional neuronal processes, which further encumbers the search for the neuronal correlates of trait consciousness, especially if neither access nor reportability is necessary for having the experience in the first place. This point – whether or not access is necessary for the phenomenal representation – is controversial (Block, 1995, 2005; Rosenthal, 1986; Stoerig & Barth, 2001).

Studies tackling the neural substrate of conscious representations indicate that the sensory systems are necessary for the phenomenal rendering of stimuli. However, their activation as such can be insufficient to generate conscious sensation, as demonstrated by the finding that implicit and explicit perceptual processes are mediated by overlapping sensory regions, suggesting that a certain level, type, or pattern of activity is necessary. To what extent non-sensory cortical networks are required for phenomenal perception is still unresolved (see discussion in Köhler & Moscovitch, 1997). My working hypothesis is that the sensory neurons' concerted activity is responsible for providing conscious phenomenal content; reflecting on this content could well be enabled by non-sensory networks that also access the sensory ones during recall and imagery and prompt them continuously – challenging the consistency of their report and requesting different interpretations in the face of ambiguous input. The frontal cortex is indispensable for conscious report because voluntary behaviour is impossible without it, but any interference with reportability is moot regarding the presence or absence of a phenomenal representation.

This argument extends to the interpretation of data from patients in pathological states of consciousness. A marked decrease in frontoparietal network activity is consistent with the patients' inability to give consistent reports about any experiences they may have, but does not preclude that they have any. Functional disconnections between sensory and frontoparietal areas as inferred from neuroimaging of vegetative state patients agree with this cautious interpretation. In fact, the functional neuroanatomy of sleep in its various stages provides experimental support for it, as both REM and non-REM sleep are characterized by a decrease in frontoparietal activation, although extended periods of sleep brim with phenomenal experiences. Although these experiences are not lacking in vividness, they are lacking in immediate and general reportability and other forms of access. If access consciousness depends on phenomenal consciousness, there is no access if the phenomenal representation is lost; but if access is lost while phenomenality remains, only the subject learns about it.

The multiplicity of conjoined factors is likely to contaminate the conclusions we draw from the experimental data. To unconfound them, we need a means to establish whether something is consciously represented, a means that, like a brain potential or some other physiological marker, is independent of a behavioural response. As yet, we do not know whether someone is conscious at all unless he or she displays behaviour we are able to identify as consciously initiated, and we do not know whether something is consciously represented unless he or she informs us about it. Only people who equate access and phenomenal consciousness need not mind what to others appears a barrier large enough to warrant a Nobel prize to reward its dissolution.

Acknowledgements

Thanks to the colleagues who kindly provided figures to illustrate their data – Michael Alkire, David Leopold, Steven Laureys, and Nicos Logothetis – and to

Morris Moscovitch for his helpful comments on the manuscript.

References

Allison. A. C., & Nunn, J. F. (1968). Effects of general anesthetics on microtubules. A possible mechanism of anesthesia. *Lancet*, 2, 1326–1329.

Alkire, M. T., Haier, R. J., Barker, S. J., Shah, N. K., Wu, J. C., & Kao, Y. J. (1995) Cerebral metabolism during propofol anesthesia in humans studied with positron emission tomography. *Anesthesiology*, 82, 393–400.

Alkire, M. T., Haier, R. J., & Fallon, J. H. (2000). Toward a unified theory of narcosis: Brain imaging evidence for a thalamocortical switch as the neurophysiologic basis of anesthetic-induced unconsciousness. *Consciousness and Cognition*, 9, 387–395.

Angel, A. (1991). The G. L. Brown lecture. Adventures in anaesthesia. *Experimental Physiology*, 76, 1–38.

Angel, A. (1993). Central neuronal pathways and the process of anaesthesia. *British Journal of Anaesthesia*, 71, 148–163.

Anis, N. A., Berry, S. C., Burton, N. R., & Lodge, D. (1983). The dissociative anaesthetics, ketamine and phencyclidine, selectively reduce excitation of central mammalian neurons by N-methyl-asparatate. *British Journal of Pharmacology*, 79, 565–575.

Antognini, J. F., Buonocore, M. H., Disbrow, E. A., & Carstens, E. (1997). Isoflurane anesthesia blunts cerebral responses to noxious and innocuous stimuli: A fMRI study. *Life Sciences*, 61, 349–354.

Aserinsky, E., & Kleitman, N. (1953). Regularly occurring periods of eye motility, and concomitant phenomena during sleep. *Science*, 118, 273–274.

Bachmann, T. (2000). *Microgenetic approach to the conscious mind*. Amsterdam: John Benjamins.

Bassetti, C., Vella, S., Donati, F., Wielapp, P., & Weder, B. (2000). SPECT during sleepwalking. *Lancet*, 356, 484–485.

Beck, D. M., Rees, G., Frith, C. D., & Lavie, N. (2001). Neural correlates of change detection and change blindness. *Nature Neuroscience*, 4, 645–650.

Blake, R., & Logothetis, N. K. (2002). Visual competition. *Nature Reviews Neuroscience*, 3, 13–21.

Block, N. (1995). On a confusion about a function of consciousness. *Behavioral and Brain Sciences*, 18, 227–287.

Block, N. (2005). Two neural correlates of consciousness. *Trends in Cognitive Sciences*, 9, 46–52.

Bodis-Wollner, I., Atkin, A., Raab, E., & Wolkstein, M. (1977). Visual association cortex and vision in man: Pattern-evoked occipital potentials in a blind boy. *Science*, 198, 629–631.

Bogen, J. E. (1995). On the neurophysiology of consciousness: I. An overview. *Consciousness and Cognition*, 4, 52–62.

Boly, M., Faymonville, M.-E., Peigneux, P. et al. (2004). Auditory processing in severely brain injured patients: differences between the minimally conscious state and the persistent vegetative state. *Archives of Neurology*, 61, 233–238.

Bonhomme, V., Fiset, P., Meuret, P., Backman, S., Plourde, G., Paus, T., Bushnell, M. C., & Evans, A. C. (2001). Propofol anesthesia and cerebral blood flow changes elicited by vibrotactile stimulation: A positron emission tomography study. *Journal of Neurophysiology*, 85, 1299–1308.

Bonnebakker, A. E., Bonke, B., Klein, J., Wolters, G., Stijnen, T., Passchier, J., & Merikle, P. M. (1996). Information processing during general anesthesia: Evidence for unconscious memory. *Memory and Cognition*, 24, 766–776.

Born, A. P., Law, I., Lund, T. E., Rostrup, E., Hanson, L. G., Wildschiødtz, G., Lou, H. C., & Paulson, O. B. (2002). Cortical deactivation induced by visual stimulation in human slow-wave sleep. *Neuroimage*, 17, 1325–1335.

Bosinelli, M. (1995). Mind and consciousness during sleep. *Behavioral Brain Research*, 69, 195–201.

Braun, A. R., Balkin, T. J., Wesensten, N. J., Carson, R. E., Varga, M., Baldwin, P., Selbie, S., Belenky, G., & Herscovitch, P. (1997). Regional cerebral blood flow throughout the sleep-wake cycle. *Brain*, 120, 1173–1197.

Braun, A. R., Balkin, T. J., Wesensten, N. J., Gwadry, F., Carson, R. E., Varga, M., Baldwin, P., Belenky, G., & Herscovitch, P. (1998). Dissociated pattern of activity in visual cortices and their projections during human rapid eye movement sleep. *Science*, 279, 91–95.

Broadbent, D. E. (1974). Division of function and integration of behavior. In F. O. Schmitt & F. G. Worden (Eds.), *The neurosciences third study program* (pp. 31–42). Cambridge, MA: MIT Press.

Broughton, R. et al. (1994). Homicidal somnambulism: A case report. *Sleep*, *17*, 253–264.

Brown, R. J., & Norcia, A. M. (1997). A method for investigating binocular rivalry in real-time with the steady-state VEP. *Vision Research*, *37*, 2401–2408.

Bruyer, R., Laterre, C., Seron, X., Feyereisen, P., Srypstein, E., Pierrard, E., & Rectern, D. (1983). A case of prosopagnosia with some preserved covert remembrance of familiar faces. *Brain and Cognition*, *2*, 257–284.

Cariani, P. (2000). Anesthesia, neural information processing, and conscious awareness. *Consciousness and Cognition*, *9*, 387–395.

Carrasco, M., Ling, S., & Read, S. (2004). Attention alters appearance. *Nature Neuroscience*, *7*, 208–209.

Cavallero, C., Cicogna, P., Natale, V., Occhionero, M., & Zito, A (1992). Slow wave sleep dreaming. *Sleep*, *15*, 562–566.

Chun, M. M., & Potter, M. C. (1995). A two-stage model for multiple target detection in rapid serial visual presentation. *Journal of Experimental Psychology: Human Perception and Performance*, *21*, 109–127.

Cicogna, P., Natale, V., Occhionero, M., & Bosinelli, M. (2000). Slow wave and REM sleep mentation. *Sleep Research Online*, *3*, 67–72.

Claparède, E. (1911). Recognition et moité. *Archives de Psychologie*, *11*, 79–90.

Cohen, N. J., & Corkin, S. (1981). The amnesic patient H. M.: Learning and retention of a cognitive skill. *Neuroscience Abstracts*, *7*, 235.

Corbetta, M., Shulman G. L. (2002). Control of goal-directed and stimulus-driven attention in the brain. *Nature Reviews Neuroscience*, *3*, 201–215.

Cowey, A., & Stoerig, P. (1995). Blindsight in monkeys. *Nature*, *373*, 247–249.

Crick, F., & Koch, C. (1995). Are we aware of neural activity in primary visual cortex? *Nature*, *375*, 121–123.

Czisch, M., Wetter, T. C., Kaufmann, C., Pollmächer, T., Holsboer, F., & Auer, D. P. (2002). Altered processing of acoustic stimuli during sleep: Reduced auditory activation and visual deactivation detected by a combined fMRI/EEG study. *Neuroimage*, *16*, 251–258.

Dement, W., & Kleitman, N. (1957). Cyclic variations in EEG during sleep and their relation to eye movements, body motility, and dreaming.

Electroencephalography and Clinical Neurophysiology, *9*, 673–690.

Desimone, R., & Duncan, J. (1995). Neural mechanisms of selective attention. *Annual Review of Neuroscience*, *18*, 193–222.

Fiset, P., Paus, T., Daloze, T., Plourde, G., Meuret, P., Bonhomme, V., Haji-Ali, N., Backman, S. B., & Evans, A. C. (1999). Brain mechanisms of propofol-induced loss of consciousness in humans: A positron emission tomography study. *Journal of Neuroscience*, *19*, 5506–5513.

Flohr, H. (1995). An information processing theory of anaesthesia. *Neuropsychologia*, *33*, 1169–1180.

Flohr, H., Glade, U., & Motzko, D., (1998). The role of the NMDA synapse in general anesthesia. *Toxicology Letters*, *100–101*, 23–29.

Foulkes, D., & Schmidt, M. (1983). Temporal sequence and unit composition in dream reports from different stages of sleep. *Sleep*, *6*, 265–80.

Foulkes, W. D. (1962). Dream reports from different stages of sleep. *Journal of Abnormal and Social Psychology*, *65*, 14–25.

Franks, N. P., & Lieb, W. R. (1994). Molecular and cellular mechanisms of general anesthesia. *Nature*, *367*, 607–614.

Franks, N. P., & Lieb, W. R. (1996). An anesthetic-sensitive superfamily of neurotransmitter-gated ion channels. *Journal of Clinical Anesthesia*, *8*, S3–S7.

Giacino, J. T., Ashwal, S., Childs, N., et al. (2002). The minimally conscious state. Definition and diagnostic criteria. *Neurology*, *58*, 349–353.

Goebel, R., Muckli, L., Zanella, F. E., Singer, W., & Stoerig, P. (2001). Sustained extrastriate cortical activation without visual awareness revealed by fMRI studies of hemianopic patients. *Vision Research*, *41*, 1459–1474.

Grosbras, H., & Paus, T. (2003). Transcranial magnetic stimulation of the human frontal eye field facilitates visual awareness. *European Journal of Neuroscience*, *18*, 3121–3126.

Hameroff, S. (1998). Anesthesia, consciousness and hydrophobic pockets – a unitary quantum hypothesis of anesthetic action. *Toxicology Letters*, *100/101*, 31–39.

Hartmann, E. (1983). Two case reports: Night terrors with sleepwalking – a potentially lethal disorder. *Journal of Nervous and Mental Disease*, *171*, 503–505.

Heywood, C. A., Cowey, A., & Newcombe, F. (1991). Chromatic discrimination in a cortically colour blind observer. *European Journal of Neuroscience*, 3, 802–812.

Hobson, J. A. (1989). *Sleep*. New York: Scientific American Library.

Hobson, J. A., Goldfrank, F., & Snyder, F. (1965). Respiration and mental activity during sleep. *Journal of Psychiatric Research*, 3, 79–90.

Hochstein, S., & Ahissar, M. (2002). View from the top: Hierarchies and reverse hierarchies in the visual system. *Neuron*, 36, 791–804.

Horton, J. C., & Hoyt, W. F. (1991). Quadrantic visual field defects. A hallmark of lesions in extrastriate (V2/V3) cortex. *Brain*, 114, 1703–1718.

Hubel, D. H., & Wiesel, T. N. (1968). Receptive fields and functional architecture of monkey striate cortex. *Journal of Physiology (London)*, 195, 215–243.

Jasper, H. H. (1949). Diffuse projection systems: The integrative action of the thalamic reticular system. *Electroencephalography and Clinical Neurophysiology*, 1, 405–420.

Jasper, H. H. (1998). Sensory information and conscious experience. In H. H. Jasper, L. Descarries, V. F. Castellucci, & S. Rossignol (Eds), *Consciousness at the frontiers of neuroscience. Advances in neurology* (Vol. 77, pp. 33–48). Philadelphia, New York: Lippincott-Raven Publishers.

Jasper, H. H., & Droogleever-Fortuyn, J. (1947). Experimental studies of the functional anatomy of petit mal epilepsy. *Proceedings of the association for research in nervous & mental disease*, 26, 272–298.

Jennett, B. (2002). The vegetative state. *Journal of Neurology, Neurosurgery, and Psychiatry*, 73, 355–356.

Jennett, B., & Plum, F. (1972, April 1). Persistent vegetative state after brain damage. *Lancet*, 734–737.

Jouvet, M., & Delorme, F. (1965). Locus coeruleus et sommeil paradoxical. *Societé de Biologie*, 159, 895–899.

Jones, E. G. (1998). A new view of specific and nonspecific thalamocortical connections. In H. H. Jasper, L. Descarries, V. F. Castellucci, & S. Rossignol (Eds), *Consciousness at the frontiers of neuroscience. Advances in neurology* (Vol. 77, pp. 49–71). Philadelphia: Lippincott-Raven Publishers.

Kajimura, N., Uchiyama, M., Takayama, Y., Uchida, S., Uema, T., Kato, M., et al. (1999). Activity of midbrain reticular formation and neocortex during the progression of human non-rapid eye movement sleep. *Journal of Neuroscience*, 19, 10065–10073.

Kales, A., Hoedemaker, F. S., Jacobson, A., Kales, J. D., Paulson, M. J., & Wilson, T. E. (1967). Mentation during sleep: REM and NREM recall reports. *Perceptual and Motor Skills*, 24, 555–60.

Kassubek, J., Juengling, F. D., Els, T., et al. (2003). Activation of residual cortical network during painful stimulation in long-term postanoxic vegetative state: A ^{15}O-H$_2$O PET study. *Journal of Neurological.Science*, 212, 85–91.

Kastner, S., Pinsk, M. A., De Weerd, P., Desimone, R., & Ungerleider, L. G. (1999). Increased activity in human visual cortex during directed attention in the absence of visual stimulation. *Neuron*, 22, 751–761.

Kleitman, N. (1963). *Sleep and wakefulness*. Chicago: University of Chicago Press.

Koestler, A. (1968). *Das Gespenst in der Maschine*. Wien, Zürich, München: Molden:

Köhler, S., & Moscovitch, M. (1997) Unconscious visual processing in neuropsychological syndromes: A survey of the literature and evaluation of models of consciousness. In M. D. Rugg (Ed.), *Cognitive neuroscience* (pp. 305–373). Cambridge, MA: MIT Press.

Kreiman, G., Fried, I., & Koch, C. (2002) Single-neuron correlates of subjective vision in the human temporal lobe. *Proceedings of the National Academy of Science USA*, 99, 8378–8383.

Lamme, V. L. (2001). Blindsight: The role of feedforward and feedback corticocortical connections. *Acta Psychologica (Amsterdam)*, 107, 209–228.

Laureys, S., Faymonville, M.-E., Luxen, A., Lamy, M., Franck, G., & Maquet, P. (2000a). Restoration of thalamocortical connectivity after recovery from persistent vegetative state. *Lancet*, 355, 1790–1791.

Laureys, S., Faymonville M.-E., Degueldre, C., et al. (2000b). Auditory processing in the vegetative state. *Brain*, 123, 1589–1601.

Laureys, S., Faymonville, M.-E., Peigneux, P., et al. (2002a). Cortical processing of noxious somatosensory stimuli in the persistent vegetative state. *Neuroimage*, 17, 732–741.

Laureys, S., Antoine, S., Boly, M., et al. (2002b). Brain function in the vegetative state. *Acta Neurologica (Belgium)*, 102, 177–185.

Laureys, S., Owenm A. M., & Schiff, N. D. (2004). Brain function in coma, vegetative state, and related disorders. *Lancet Neurology*, 3, 537–546.

Leopold, D. A., & Logothetis, N. K. (1999). Multistable phenomena: Changing views in perception. *Trends in Cognitive Sciences*, 3, 254–264.

Leopold, D. A., Plettenberg, H. K., & Logothetis, N. K. (2003). Visual processing in the ketamine-anesthetized monkey. Optokinetic and blood oxygenation-dependent responses. *Experimental Brain Research*, 143, 359–372.

Levy, D. E., Sidtis, J. J., Rottenberg, D. A., Jarden, J. O., et al. (1987). Differences in cerebral blood flow and glucose utilization in vegetative versus locked-in patients. *Annals of Neurology*, 22, 673–682.

Logothetis, N. K. (1998). Single units and conscious vision. *Philosophical Transactions of the Royal Society, London B*, 353, 1801–1818.

Logothetis, N. K., Guggenberger, H., Peled, S., & Pauls, J. (1999). Functional imaging of the monkey brain. *Nature Neuroscience*, 2, 555–562.

Logothetis, N. K., & Schall, J. D. (1989). Neuronal correlates of subjective visual perception. *Science*, 245, 761–763.

Lumer, E. D., Friston, K. J., & Rees, G. (1998) Neural correlates of perceptual rivalry in the human brain. *Science*, 280, 1930–1934.

Madler, C., Keller, I., Schwender, D., & Pöppel, E. (1991). Sensory information processing during general anaesthesia: Effect of isoflurane on auditory evoked neuronal oscillations. *British Journal of Anaesthesiology*, 66, 81–87.

Madler, C., & Pöppel, E. (1987). Auditory evoked potentials indicate the loss of neuronal oscillations during general anaesthesia. *Naturwissenschaften*, 74, 42–43.

Mahowald, M. W., & Schenck, C. H. (2001). Evolving concepts of human state dissociation. *Archives Italienne de Biologie*, 139, 269–300.

Maquet, P. (2000). Functional neuroimaging of normal human sleep by positron emission tomography. *Journal of Sleep Research*, 9, 207–231.

Maquet, P., Péters, J.-M., Aerts, J., Delfiore, G., Degueldre, G., Luxen, A., & Franck, G. (1996). Functional neuroanatomy of human rapid-eye-movement sleep and dreaming. *Nature*, 383, 163–166.

Marois, R., Yi, D.-J., & Chun, M. M. (2004). The neural fate of consciously perceived and missed events in the attentional blink. *Neuron*, 41, 465–472.

Martin, E., Thiel, T., Joeri, P., Loenneker, T., Ekatodramis, E., Huisman, T., Hennig, J., & Marcar, V. L. (2000). Effect of pentobarbital on visual processing in man. *Human Brain Mapping*, 10, 132–139.

Mashour, G. A. (2004). Consciousness unbound. Toward a paradigm of general anesthesia. *Anesthesiology*, 100, 428–433.

Meadows, J. C. (1974). Disturbed perception of colours associated with localized cerebral lesions. *Brain*, 97, 615–632.

Merikle, P. M., & Daneman, M. (1996). Memory for unconsciously perceived events; evidence from anesthetized patients. *Consciousness and Cognition*, 5, 542–561.

Milner, A. D., & Goodale, M. A. (1995). *The visual brain in action*. New York: Oxford University Press.

Milner, B., Corkin, S., & Teuber, H.-L. (1968). Further analysis of the hippocampal amnesic syndrome: 14-year follow-up study of H. M. *Neuropsychologia*, 6, 215–234.

Moore, T., & Armstrong, K. M. (2003). Selective gating of visual signals by microstimulation of frontal cortex. *Nature*, 421, 370–373.

Morruzzi, G., & Magoun, W. (1949). Brain stem reticular formation and activation of the EEG. *Electroencephalography and Clinical Neurophysiology*, 1, 455–473.

Mozaz Garde, M. , & Cowey, A. (2000). 'Deaf hearing': Unacknowledged detection of auditory stimuli in a patient with cerebral deafness. *Cortex*, 36, 71–80.

Munk, M. H. J., Roelfsema, P. R., König, P., Engel, A. K., & Singer, W. (1996). Role of reticular activation in the modulation of intracortical synchronization. *Science*, 272, 271–274.

Nacchache, L., Blandin, E., & Dehaene, S. (2002). Unconscious masked priming depends on temporal attention. *Psychological Science*, 13, 416–424.

Nielsen, T. A. (2000) A review of mentation in REM and NREM sleep: "covert" REM sleep as a possible reconciliation of tow opposing models. *Behavioral and Brain Sciences*, 23, 793–1121.

Nofzinger, E. A., Mintun, N. A., Wiseman, M., Kupfer, D. J., & Moore, R. Y. (1997). Forebrain activation in REM-sleep: An FDG PET study. *Brain Research, 770*, 192–201.

Paillard, J., Michel, F., & Stemach, G. (1983). Localization without content: A tactile analogue of blindsight. *Archives of Neurology, 40*, 548–551.

Pasik, P., & Pasik, T. (1982). Visual function in monkeys after total removal of visual cerebral cortex. *Contributions to Sensory Physiology, 7*, 147–200.

Pessoa, L., & Ungerleider, L. G. (2004). Neural correlates of change detection and change blindness in a working memory task. *Cerebral Cortex, 14*, 511–520.

Pins, D., & ffytche, D. (2003). The neural correlates of conscious vision. *Cerebral Cortex, 13*, 461–474.

Plourde, G., Baribeau, J., & Bonhomme, V. (1997). Ketamine increases the amplitude of the 40-Hz auditory steady-state response in humans. *British Journal of Anaesthesia, 78*, 524–529.

Plum, F., & Posner, J. B. (1982). *The diagnosis of stupor and coma*. Philadephia: F. A. Davis.

Plum, F., Schiff, N., Ribary, U., & Llínas, R. (1998). Coordinated expression in chronically unconscious persons. *Philosophical Transactions of the Royal Society, London B: Biological Science, 353*, 1929–1933.

Pöppel, E. (1997). A hierarchical model of time perception. *Trends in Cognitive Sciences, 1*, 56–61.

Purpura., K. P., & Schiff, N. D. (1997). The thalamic intralaminar nuclei: A role in visual awareness. *The Neuroscientist, 3*, 8–15.

Rechtschaffen, A., & Kales, A. A. (1968). *A manual of standardized terminology, techniques and scoring system for sleep stages of human subjects*. Bethesda, MD: National Institute of Neurological Diseases and Blindness.

Rees, G., Wojciulik, E., Clarke, K., Husain, M., Frith, C., & Driver, J. (2000). Unconscious activation of visual cortex in the damaged right hemisphere of a parietal patient with extinction. *Brain, 123*, 1624–1633.

Rensink, R. A. (2000). Seeing, sensing, scrutinizing. *Vision Research, 40*, 1469–1487.

Ricci, C., & Blundo, C. (1990). Perception of ambiguous figures after focal brain lesions. *Neuropsychologia, 28*, 1163–1173.

Riddoch, G. (1917). Dissociations of visual perception due to occipital injuries, with especial reference to appreciation of movement. *Brain, 40*, 15–57.

Rosenbaum, R. S., Köhler, S., Schacter, D. L., Moscovitch, M., Westmacott, R., Black, S. E., Gao, F., & Tulving, E. (2004). The case of K. C.: Contributions of a memory-impaired person to memory theory. *Neuropsychologia, 43*, 989–1021.

Rosenthal, D. (1986). Two concepts of consciousness. *Philosophical Studies, 94*, 329–359.

Rovee-Collier, C., Hayne, H., & Colombo, M. (2001). *The development of implicit and explicit memory. Advances in consciousness research 24*. Amsterdam: John Benjamins.

Sahraie, A., Weiskrantz, L., Barbur, J. L., Simmons, A., Williams, S., & Brammer, M. J. (1997). Pattern of neuronal activity associated with conscious and unconscious processing of visual signals. *Proceedings of the National Academy of Sciences USA, 94*, 9406–9411.

Schacter, D. L., Dobbins, I. G., & Schnyer, D. M. (2004). Specificity of priming: A cognitive neuroscience perspective. *Nature Reviews Neuroscience, 5*, 853–862.

Schenck, C. H., Bundlie, S. R., Ettinger, M. G., & Mahowald, M. W. (1986). Chronic behavioral disorders of human REM sleep: A new category of parasomnia. *Sleep, 9*, 293–308.

Schenck, C. H., & Mahowald, M. W. (1994). Review of nocturnal sleep-related eating disorders. *International Journal of Eating Disorders, 15*, 343–356.

Schenck, C. H., Milner, D. M., Hurwitz, T. D., Bundlie, S. R., & Mahowald, M. W. (1989). Dissociative disorders presenting as somnambulism: Polysomnographic, video and clinical documentation (8 cases). *Dissociation, 2*, 194–204.

Schiff, N. D., Ribary, U., Moreno, D. R., Beattie, B., et al. (2002). Residual cerebral activity and behavioural fragments can remain in the persistently vegetative brain. *Brain, 125*, 1210–1234.

Shulman, G., Fiez, J., Corbetta, M., Buckner, R. L., Miezin, F. M., Raichle, M. E., & Petersen, S. E. (1997). Common blood flow changes across visual tasks: II. Decreases in cerebral cortex. *Journal of Cognitive Neuroscience, 9*, 648–663.

Simons, D. J., & Levin, D. T. (1997). Change blindness. *Trends in Cognitive Sciences, 1*, 261–267.

Steriade, M. (2000). Corticothalamic resonance, states of vigilance and mentation. *Neuroscience*, *101*, 243–276.

Stoerig, P. (1996). Varieties of vision: From blind processing to conscious recognition. *Trends in Neurosciences*, *19*, 401–406.

Stoerig, P. (1999). Blindsight. In R. Wilson & F. Keil (Eds.), *The MIT encyclopedia of the cognitive sciences* (pp. 88–90). Cambridge, MA: MIT Press.

Stoerig, P. (2002). Neural correlates of consciousness as state and trait. In L. Nadel (Ed.), *Encyclopedia of cognitive neuroscience* (pp. 233–240). London: Macmillan Press.

Stoerig, P., & Barth, E. (2001). Low-level phenomenal vision despite unilateral destruction of primary visual cortex. *Consciousness and Cognition*, *10*, 574–587.

Stoerig, P., & Cowey, A. (1993). Blindsight and perceptual consciousness: neuropsychological aspects of striate cortical function. In B. Gulyas, D. Ottoson, & P. Roland (Eds.), *Functional organisation of the human visual cortex* (pp. 181–193). Oxford, New York: Pergamon Press.

Stoerig, P., & Cowey, A. (1997). Blindsight in man and monkey. *Brain*, *120*, 535–559.

Stoerig, P., Zontanou, A., & Cowey, A. (2002). Aware or unaware? Assessment of cortical blindness in four men and a monkey. *Cerebral Cortex*, *12*, 565–574.

Thompson, K. G., & Schall, J. D. (2000). Antecedents and correlates of visual detection and awareness in macaque prefrontal cortex. *Vision Research*, *40*, 1523–1538.

Tononi, G., Srinivasan, R., Russell, D. P., & Edelman, G. M. (1998). Investigating neural correlates of conscious perception by frequency-tagged neuromagnetic responses. *Proceedings of the National Academy of Science USA*, *95*, 3198–3203.

Wagner, U., Gais, S., Haider, H., Verleger, R., & Born, J. (2004). Sleep inspires insight. *Nature*, *427*, 352–355.

Warrington, E. K., & Weiskrantz, L. (1968). New method of testing long-term retention with special reference to amnesic patients. *Nature*, *217*, 972–972.

Weiskrantz, L. (1986). *Blindsight: A case study and implications*. Oxford: Oxford University Press.

Weiskrantz, L., Warrington, E. K., Sanders, M. D., & Marshall, J. (1974). Visual capacity in the hemianopic field following a restricted cortical ablation. *Brain*, *97*, 709–728.

White, N. S., & Alkire, M. T. (2003). Impaired thalamocortical connectivity in humans during general-anesthetic-induced unconsciousness. *Neuroimage*, *19*, 402–411.

Yamada, T., Kameyama, S., Fuchigami, Y., Nakazumi, Y., Dickins, Q. S., & Kimura, S. (1988). Changes of short latency somatosensory potential in sleep. *Electroencephalography and Clinical Neurophysiology*, *70*, 126–136.

Zeki, S. (1990). A century of cerebral achromatopsia. *Brain*, *113*, 1721–1777.

Zeki, S. (1991). Cerebral akinetopsia. *Brain*, *114*, 811–824.

Zeki, S. (2001). Localization and globilization in conscious vision. *Annual Review of Neuroscience*, *24*, 57–86.

Zeman, A. (1997). Persistent vegetative state. *Lancet*, *350*, 795–798.

CHAPTER 26

Neurodynamical Approaches
to Consciousness

Diego Cosmelli, Jean-Philippe Lachaux, and Evan Thompson

Abstract

One of the outstanding problems in the cognitive sciences is to understand how ongoing conscious experience is related to the workings of the brain and nervous system. Neurodynamics offers a powerful approach to this problem because it provides a coherent framework for investigating change, variability, complex spatiotemporal patterns of activity, and multiscale processes (among others). In this chapter, we advocate a neurodynamical approach to consciousness that integrates mathematical tools of analysis and modeling, sophisticated physiological data recordings, and detailed phenomenological descriptions. We begin by stating the basic intuition: Consciousness is an intrinsically dynamic phenomenon and must therefore be studied within a framework that is capable of rendering its dynamics intelligible. We then discuss some of the formal, analytical features of dynamical systems theory, with particular reference to neurodynamics. We then review several neuroscientific proposals that make use of dynamical systems theory in characterizing the neurophysiological basis of consciousness. We continue by discussing the relation between spatiotemporal patterns of brain activity and consciousness, with particular attention to processes in the gamma frequency band. We then adopt a critical perspective and highlight a number of issues demanding further treatment. Finally, we close the chapter by discussing how phenomenological data can relate to and ultimately constrain neurodynamical descriptions, with the long-term aim being to go beyond a purely correlational strategy of research.

The Intuition

The central idea of this chapter is the notion of dynamics – the dynamics of neural activity, the dynamics of conscious experience, and the relation between them.

Dynamics is a multifarious concept. In a narrow sense, it refers to the change a circumscribed system undergoes in some time-dependent descriptive variable; for example, a neuron's membrane voltage (Abarbanel & Rabinovich, 2001). In a broad sense, dynamics indicates a field of research concerned with non-linear dynamical systems. Such systems range from mathematical models to experimental problems to actual concrete world systems (Van Gelder, 1999). Finally, in a more intimate sense, dynamics refers to the temporal nature of our observations themselves and thus to our conscious experience and how it is deployed in time (Varela, 1999). The interplay of these different senses of dynamics is at the heart of this chapter.

What exactly are the properties of dynamical systems, and why are they of interest in relation to consciousness? The entirety of this chapter is concerned with this question, but to begin addressing it, we wish, in this introductory section, first to give an overview of the basic intuition underlying dynamical approaches to consciousness.

Briefly stated, a complex, non-linear dynamical system can be described, at any time, by a position in a high-dimensional state space (Nicolis & Prigogine, 1989). The n coordinates of such a position are the values of the set of n variables that define the system. This position changes in time and thus defines a trajectory, which will tend to explore a subregion of the total state space. One can then measure the distance between any two points of the trajectory and show that under certain circumstances the trajectory can exhibit spontaneous recurrence: Small portions of the state space will be explored over and over, but never along the exact same path. When perturbed by external events, such a system will change its trajectory in a way that is never quite the same and that depends on its position in the state space at the time of the perturbation.

Given this feature, plus the system's extreme sensitivity to initial conditions, the system's response to perturbations will be unpredictable in practice. It is therefore quite difficult to control such a system and constrain its movement along a predefined trajectory. For example, in the case of chaotic systems, such control involves applying a continuous succession of carefully chosen, delicate inputs, brute force usually being

inefficient (think of what happens when you try to catch a fish out of water; Garfinkel, Spano, Ditto, & Weiss, 1992; Schiff et al., 1994). In general terms, there will be a certain degree of dissociation between the observed behavior of these systems and the patterns of external constraints that can be imposed on them. In other words, these systems exhibit a certain degree of autonomy: When external perturbations cease, the system goes on; when external perturbations become stationary, the system does not. Somehow we intuitively recognize such systems as animated or alive, in contrast to simpler systems that respond in a linear and predictable way to external control (e.g., a stone that flies twice the distance when thrown twice as strong).

Thus, such systems exhibit an intrinsic variability that cannot be attributed to noise, but appears to be constitutive of their functioning. Moreover, in the case of certain types of complex dynamical systems, one can reveal a characteristic spatiotemporal balance of functional segregation and cooperative integration.[1] This balance depends on the actual architecture of the system (its internal connectivity, for example), and is revealed in the transient establishment of distributed couplings among separated subsystems that in themselves present local encapsulated dynamics. Finally, some of these systems display what has been termed 'self-organization'; that is, the emergence of collective coherent behavior starting from random initial conditions. This last feature, although not necessary for a system to be considered dynamical, has proven especially interesting when dealing with biological phenomena (Haken, 1983; Kelso, 1995).

The brain is a major case in point. The nervous system is a complex dynamical structure, in which individual neurons have intrinsic activity patterns and cooperate to produce coherent collective behavior (Llinas, 1988). The explosion of neuroimaging studies in the last 15–20 years, as well as the substantial amount of data produced by electrophysiological techniques since the beginning of the 20th century, has shown that the brain is never silent, but always in a state of ongoing functioning (Wicker, Ruby, Royet, & Fonlupt, 2003). The nervous system has a domain of viability, of allowed functioning, but within this domain it explores a multiplicity of possible states in a recurrent, yet always changing manner (Palus, 1996). Incoming events are not sufficient to determine the system's behavior, for any incoming event will change the system's activity only as a result of how the system, given its current activity, responds to that event (Engel, Fries, & Singer, 2001).

If we now follow the thread of dynamics back to our own conscious experience, we can immediately notice that our consciousness manifests subjectively as a kind of continuously changing or flowing process of awareness, famously called the 'stream of consciousness' by William James (1890/1981). Our experience is made up of recurring perceptions, thoughts, images, and bodily sensations; yet, however similar these events may be over time, there is always something new to each one, something ultimately unpredictable to every forthcoming moment. We can try to plan our day as strictly as we want, but the wanderings of our minds and how we react to the encounters we have in the actual world are things we cannot fully control. There seems to be an endogenous, spontaneous, ongoing flow to experience that is quite refractory to external constraints (Hanna & Thompson, 2003). Indeed, this dissociation can easily be made evident from the first-person perspective. If you sit down and close the windows, turn off the lights, and close your eyes so that external stimulation is greatly reduced *for* you, there is nevertheless still something going on subjectively *in* you, with an apparent temporal dynamics all of its own.[2] Furthermore, at any moment, consciousness appears diverse, complex, and rich with multiple, synchronous, and local contents (images, expectations, sounds, smells, kinesthetic feelings, etc.), yet it seems to hold together as a coherent and globally organized experience.

This intuitive convergence of complex dynamical patterns in experience and in brain activity is highly suggestive. It suggests that the framework of dynamical systems theory could offer a valuable way of bridging the two domains of brain activity and subjective experience. If we wish to study the neurobiological processes related to consciousness, then we must provide a description of these processes that is (somehow) compatible with the dynamics of lived experience. On the other hand, dynamical aspects of experience might serve as a leading clue for uncovering and tracking the neurobiological processes crucial for consciousness.

In the rest of this chapter, we explore this guiding intuition through a discussion of the following topics: formal dynamical systems, neurobiological theories based on dynamical system principles, and the attempt to distinguish dynamical structures within experience that can constrain how we study the neurobiological basis of consciousness.

Neurodynamics

Dynamical Systems

Dynamical cognitive science has been defined as "a confederation of research efforts bound together by the idea that natural cognition is a dynamical phenomenon and best understood in dynamical terms" (Van Gelder, 1999, p. 243). Within this confederation, the job of the neurodynamicist is to model the neural basis of cognition using the tools of dynamical systems theory. Thus, the first thing we need to do is to define more precisely the notion of a dynamical system.

A dynamical system is a collection of interdependent variables that change in time. The state of the system at any time t is defined by the values of all the variables at that time; it can be represented by a position in an abstract 'state space', whose coordinates are the values of all the variables at t. The system's behavior consists of transitions between states and is described geometrically by a trajectory in the state space, which corresponds to the consecutive positions the system occupies as time passes.

At a first level of complexity, in the context of neurodynamics, we can think of the variables as being the membrane potentials of each individual neuron of the nervous system.[3] These membrane potentials are obviously interdependent. Thus, at this level, the state of the nervous system at any time t would be defined by the value of all the membrane potentials at time t.

Although a dynamical system, in the most general terms, is any system that changes in time, dynamical systems theory gives special attention to *non-linear* dynamical systems. The behavior of such systems is governed by non-linear equations; in other words, some of the mathematical functions used to derive the system's present state from its previous states and possible external inputs are non-linear functions (for neurobiological examples, see Abarbanel & Rabinovich, 2001; Faure & Korn, 2001). Non-linearity can endow the system with certain interesting properties. For example, when convection cells in a horizontal water layer are submitted to a thermal gradient above a critical value, the motions of billions of molecules spontaneously organize into long-range correlated macroscopic structures (Chandrasekhar 1961, cited in Le Van Quyen, 2003, p. 69; see also Kelso, 1995). Such properties of non-linear systems led in the 1970s to an increased interest in the mathematics of dynamical system theory (Nicolis & Prigogine, 1977).

Several elements condition the behavior of a dynamical system during a given window of observation. First, the system's behavior is conditioned by the values of a set of so-called *order parameters*. By definition, these parameters determine the exact mathematical equations that govern the system. This set of parameter values is a function of the architecture of the system (e.g., the synaptic weights between neurons), factors external to the system (e.g., outside temperature), and so on. These parameters cannot necessarily be controlled, and their dynamics is slower than that of the system itself.

They can be considered as constant during the given window of observation, but are potentially variable across different observation periods. Their dynamics thus contrasts with that of the external inputs, which can have a dynamics as fast as that of the system. The governing equations of the system are also a function of these inputs, but the temporal evolution of the external inputs cannot be predicted from those equations (otherwise they could be considered as state variables of the system). Finally, all real systems include a noise component, which also counts as a factor in the governing equations and thus affects the trajectory of the system.

Neurodynamics and the Dynamical Approach in Neuroscience

Neurodynamics emerged from the proposal, which can be traced back to Ashby in the 1950s (Ashby, 1952), that the nervous system can be described as a non-linear dynamical system. Although simple in appearance, this proposal deserves some attention: What does the nervous system look like from a dynamical point of view, and why is it non-linear? The majority of the dynamical models of the nervous system describe the temporal evolution of the membrane potentials of neurons (Arbib, 2002). The behavior of any neuron of the system is a function of both its own history of activation and the history of activation of every other neuron, thanks to the intrinsic connectivity of the nervous system. The precise influence of a given neuron on a second one is determined by the weight of the synapse that links them. Thus, the overall synaptic pattern in the nervous system provides the main set of order parameters in such models (see Arbib, 2002).[4] To this desciption, it must be added that the system is not isolated, but under the constant influence of external sensory inputs that shape the behavior of peripheral sensory neurons.

There are many models available for the mathematical functions that link the membrane potentials of individual neurons to the history of the larger system and to the external inputs (Arbib, 2002). At this point, it is sufficient to state that these functions are non-linear and that this is the reason why the nervous system is described as a (spatially extended) non-linear dynamical system (for reviews, see Faure & Korn, 2001; Korn & Faure, 2003).[5]

Chaos in the Brain

As Le Van Quyen (2003, p. 69) notes, there was little echo to Ashby's original proposal to view the nervous system as a non-linear dynamical system, mostly because the appropriate mathematical methods and computational tools to pursue this proposal were lacking at that time. The real boost to neurodynamics came later, in the 1980s and 1990s, with the widespread emergence in the scientific community of interest in the properties of chaotic systems.

Chaotic systems are simply non-linear systems, with their parameters set so that they possess an extreme sensitivity to initial conditions. Such sensitivity means that if one changes the initial position of the system in its state space, however slightly, the subsequent positions on the modified trajectory will diverge exponentially from what they would have been otherwise. Given this sensitive dependence on initial conditions, combined with the impossibility of determining the present state of the system with perfect precision, the future behavior of a chaotic system is unpredictable. The system thus appears to have an inherent source of variability, for it will never react twice in the same way to identical external perturbations, even in the absence of noise.[6]

The possible existence of 'chaos in the brain' sparked much speculation and excitement. There were two related matters of debate: (i) whether the nervous system is actually chaotic (or whether there are subsystems in the brain that are; Faure & Korn, 2001; Korn & Faure, 2003) and (ii) what use the nervous system could make of such chaotic behaviors (Faure & Korn, 2001; Korn & Faure, 2003; Skarda & Freeman, 1987; Tsuda, 2001).

The second question proved to be the easier one. One property of chaotic systems is that their dynamics can organize around the presence of 'strange' attractors. A strange attractor is a pattern of activity that captures nearby states (Arbib, Érdi, & Szentágothai, 1997): It occupies a subregion of the state space, a manifold, and if the trajectory of the system comes into contact with this manifold, the trajectory will stay on it subsequently, in the absence of external perturbations. The precise number and shapes of the attractors are determined by the parameters of the system, such as the intrinsic connectivity of the nervous system. Which particular attractor captures the system is determined by the system's initial position. When the parameters define several strange attractors, then there can be associations between certain initial positions in the state space and certain attractors (Tsuda, 2001). This association is the basis for chaos-based perceptual systems: For example, in a common non-linear model of olfactory processing (as reviewed in Korn & Faure, 2003), each odor is represented by a specific attractor, such that when confronted with slightly different olfactory stimuli, the trajectory of the system will converge onto the same attractor, if the stimuli actually correspond to the same odorant.[7] Thus, in this model, perception is based on several coexisting attractors in a multistable system. An additional and important feature is that external perturbations to the system can make the system jump from one attractor to another; therefore, chaotic systems should not be thought of as 'static' and unreactive to the environment. Moreover, chaotic systems can be controlled; that is, they can be 'forced' to stay within specific portions of the state space via external perturbations. It must immediately be added, however, that the term 'forced' is misleading, for the external perturbations are nothing like brute force; rather, they must be thought of as like a series of subtle touches, carefully chosen to adapt to the system's dynamic properties.

A sobering thought is that it is not clear whether the activity of the nervous system, considered as a whole, is chaotic. One requirement for a system to be chaotic is that its trajectory in the state space be constrained within geometrical structures that have a lower dimension than the space itself (this requirement is needed mainly to distinguish between chaotic and stochastic processes; Wright & Liley, 1996). Unfortunately, the behavior of the nervous system cannot be observed directly in its actual state space, but only via limited sets of measurements that are crude projections of its actual state (like the electroencephalogram or EEG, which retains only the average activity of millions of neurons; Korn & Faure, 2003).[8]

Nevertheless, the debate over the chaotic nature of brain activity proved productive and brought out of the shadows some ideas crucial to neurodynamics. For instance, central to neurodynamical thought is the idea that the variability of neural activity may be an integral part of the nervous system's dynamics. This notion is orthogonal to a number of traditional (and still largely dominant) approaches in neuroscience that attribute this variability to 'meaningless noise'. As a case in point, most brain imaging studies try to get rid of the variability of the neural activity by averaging brain recordings over multiple repetitions of the same process.[9] These averaging procedures most likely give an oversimplified view of brain dynamics. In the near future, neuroscientists will undoubtedly have to go to the trouble of making sense of the neural variability by finding its experiential and behavioral correlates. Fortunately, new approaches along these lines are emerging, such as trying to understand the brain response to sensory stimulation in the context of the brain's active state preceding the stimulation and thus in relation to an active 'baseline' of neural activity that is far from neutral (Lutz, Lachaux, Martinerie, & Varela, 2002; Engel et al., 2001)

This shift in the focus of brain imaging should not be underestimated: The brain's reaction is no longer viewed as a passive 'additive' response to the perturbation, but as an active 'integration' of the perturbation into the overall dynamics (Arieli, Sterkin, Grinvald, & Aertsen, 1996). In other words, the processing of an incoming sensory stimulation is no longer viewed as the simple triggering of a systematic, prespecified, chain of neural operations that would unfold independently of the brain's current activity, as in a computer algorithm. For this reason, the neurodynamical approach is often presented as a sharp alternative to the computer metaphor of the brain (Freeman, 1999a; Kelso, 1995; Van Gelder, 1998).

Self-Organization and the Emergence of Spatiotemporal Patterns

As Crutchfield and Kaneko (1987) note, dynamical system theory has developed largely through the study of low-dimensional systems, with no spatial extension. To be useful for neuroscience, however, dynamical system theory needs to consider the special properties conferred on the nervous system by its spatial extension.

Fortunately, there has been a recent coincidence between, on the theoretical side, the development of a theory of large-scale non-linear systems and, on the experimental side, the advent of multielectrode recordings and imaging techniques to map precisely the electrical activity of entire populations of neurons. This coincidence has led to renewed interest, in the biological community, in large-scale models of neural activity.

The study of large, spatially extended non-linear systems is a field in itself, in which the interest in attractors shifts to the related one of spatiotemporal patterns. (We recommend the reader spend a few minutes looking for pictures of 'cellular automata' with the Google image search engine to see some beautiful examples of spatiotemporal structures.) As a result, the neurodynamical community is now becoming less focused on chaos and more focused on the properties of self-organization in non-linear systems, and particularly the formation of transient spatiotemporal structures in the brain.[10] As noted by Freeman, in the preface to the second (electronic) printing of his seminal book, *Mass Action in the Nervous System* (Freeman, 1975): "The word 'chaos' has lost its value as a prescriptive label and should be dropped in the dustbin of history, but the phenomenon of organized disorder constantly changing with fluctuations across the edge of stability is not to be discarded" (Freeman, 2004).

Spatiotemporal structures are ubiquitous in the brain. Apart from the obvious physical construction of the system, they correspond to the emergence of transient functional couplings between distributed neurons. For a given period of time, the activity of a set of neurons shows an increased level of statistical dependency, as quantified, for example, by mutual information.[11] In pioneering work, Freeman (reviewed in Freeman, 2000a) observed spatiotemporal activity patterns in the olfactory bulb and interpreted them within the framework of dynamical system theory. In an influential theoretical paper with Skarda, he proposed that sensory information was encoded in those patterns (Skarda & Freeman, 1987).

The classic example of spatiotemporal structures in the brain is the Hebbian reverberant cell assembly, which Hebb (1949) hypothesized to be the basis for short-term memory (see Amit, 1994).[12] (This notion is also closely related to Varela's [1995] idea of resonant cell assemblies, described below.) Reverberant cell assemblies are labile sets of neurons that transiently oscillate together at the same frequency, at the level of their membrane potential. They are the best-studied spatiotemporal structures in the brain. Indeed, the cortex has sometimes been modeled as a lattice of coupled oscillators – in other words, as a juxtaposition of reverberant cell assemblies. One advantage of such models is that the behavior of oscillator lattices has been abundantly investigated, mainly using numerical simulations (see Gutkin, Pinto, & Ermentrout, 2003; Kuramoto, 1984; Nunez, 2000; Wright & Liley, 1996).

The formation of spatiotemporal structures in such systems often takes the form of phase-synchronization patterns between the oscillators (Le Van Quyen, 2003).[13] In the brain, phase synchronization of large populations of neural oscillators can produce macroscale oscillations that can be picked up by mesoscale recordings (such as local field potentials) or macroscale recordings (such as an EEG). For this reason, synchronous oscillations have been the easiest form of spatiotemporal structure to measure in the brain and not surprisingly, the first one to be observed (Bressler & Freeman, 1980; Gray, Konig, Engel, & Singer, 1989); see also the discussion of functional connectivity below).

One reason why resonant cell assemblies in particular, and spatiotemporal structures in general, are so appealing to neuroscience is because they provide a flexible and reversible way to bind together distributed neurons that may be primarily involved in very different functional processes. This type of binding has three fundamental features: (i) the ability to integrate distributed neural activities (*integration*); (ii) the ability to promote, and virtually extract, one particular set of neural activities above the rest of the brain activity (*segregation*); and (iii) the capacity to evolve easily through a succession of flexible and adaptive patterns (*metastability*). For example, one resonant assembly could transiently bind together the different populations of neurons involved in analyzing the shape, color, and motion of a visual object, and this temporary assembly would constitute a neural substrate for the transient perception of a visual object. This idea is the starting point of a very active stream of research that we discuss later in this chapter (for an overview, see Roskies, 1999). Some authors have even proposed that every cognitive act corresponds to the formation of such a transient spatiotemporal pattern (Varela, 1995).

In summary, dynamical system theory proposes a precise framework to analyze the spatiotemporal neural phenomena that occur at different levels of organization in the brain, such as the firing of individual neurons and the collective dynamics of synchronous oscillations within large networks. The future challenge is to relate these properties of self-organization to various aspects of mental life. This endeavor is still in its early phases, but the future looks promising.

For example, recent analysis methods making use of the brain's dynamical properties have been proposed as a means to anticipate epileptic seizures (Martinerie et al., 1998). There is now a strong general sense that the properties of metastable, neural spatiotemporal patterns match crucial aspects of conscious experience and that neurodynamics may provide the tools and concepts to understand how the neural activity crucial for consciousness temporally unfolds. This trend is patent in a set of influential neuroscientific models of consciousness that we review in the next section of this chapter.

Examples of Neurodynamical Approaches to Consciousness

Introduction

Although neurodynamics is quite popular in the neurobiology of consciousness, it is still not a widespread practice to formulate theories about the relation between consciousness and the brain in purely dynamical terms. Dynamical concepts are incorporated to varying degrees by different researchers and used alongside concepts from information theory or functionalist models of cognitive processing. In this section, we review some models that make use of dynamical concepts in attempting to explain the phenomenon of consciousness. The list of models we cover is not meant to be exhaustive, but rather a small sample of a large spectrum of dynamical approaches to brain activity and consciousness. Furthermore, we do not intend to scrutinize these models in detail, but instead to highlight some common aspects while providing an overview of their main proposals and hypotheses. The reader is referred to the original sources for more details.

Neurodynamical Models of Consciousness

CONSCIOUSNESS AS ORDER PARAMETER AND DYNAMICAL OPERATOR

Among the different approaches to neural dynamics, the pioneering work of Walter J. Freeman stands out as one of the most elaborate and truly dynamical theories of brain function (Freeman, 1975, 1999a,b, 2000a,b, 2004). His work is based mainly on animal studies, in particular electrophysiological recordings of the olfactory system of awake and behaving rabbits. This approach can be summarized as follows: The point of departure is the neuronal population. A neuronal population is an aggregate of neurons, in which, through positive feedback, a state transition has occurred so that the ensemble presents steady-state, non-zero activity. When negative feedback is established between populations, where one is excitatory and the other inhibitory, oscillatory patterns of activity appear. This change implies a second state transition, where the resulting attractor is a limit cycle that reveals the steady-state oscillation of the mixed (excitatory-inhibitory) population. When three or more mixed populations combine among themselves by further negative and positive feedback, the resulting background activity becomes chaotic. This chaotic activity now distributed among the populations is the carrier of a spatial pattern of amplitude modulation that can be described by the local heights of the recorded waveform.

When an input reaches the mixed population, an increase in the non-linear feedback gain will produce a given amplitude-modulation pattern. The emergence of this pattern is considered to be the first step in perception: *Meaning* is embodied in these amplitude-modulation patterns of neural activity, whose structure is dependent on synaptic changes caused by previous experience. Thus, the whole history of the animal sets the context in which the emerging spatiotemporal pattern is meaningful. Through the divergence and convergence of neural activity onto the entorhinal cortex, the pulse patterns coming from the bulb are smoothed, thereby enhancing the macroscopic amplitude-modulation pattern while attenuating the sensory-driven microscopic activity. Thus, what the cortex 'sees' is a construction made by the bulb, not a mapping of the stimulus.

Hence, in Freeman's view, perception is an essentially active process, closer to hypothesis testing than to passive recovery of incoming information. This active stance is embodied in the process of 'preafference' by which the limbic system (including the entorhinal cortex and the hippocampus in mammals), through corollary discharges to all sensory cortices, maintains an attentive expectancy of what is to come. The stimulus then confirms or disconfirms the hypothesis through state transitions that generate the amplitude-modulation patterns described previously.[14] The multisensory convergence onto the entorhinal cortex becomes the basis for the formation of Gestalts underlying the unitary character of perception.

Finally, through multiple feedback loops, global amplitude-modulation patterns of chaotic activity emerge throughout the entire hemisphere, directing its subsequent activity. These loops comprise feedforward flow from the sensory systems to the entorhinal cortex and the motor systems, and feedback flow from the motor systems to the entorhinal cortex, and from the entorhinal cortex to the sensory systems. Such global brain states "emerge, persist for a small fraction of a second, then disappear and are replaced by other states" (Freeman, 1999b, p. 153).

For Freeman, it is this level of emergent and global cooperative activity that is crucial for consciousness, as these remarks indicate: "Consciousness . . . is a state variable that constrains the chaotic activities of the parts by quenching local fluctuations. It is an order parameter and an operator that comes into play in the action-perception cycle as an action is being concluded, and as the learning phase of perception begins" (Freeman, 1999a, p. 132). Furthermore: "[T]he globally coherent activity . . . may be an objective correlate of awareness. . . . In this view, awareness is basically akin to the intervening state variable in a homeostatic mechanism, which is both a physical quantity, a dynamical operator, and the carrier of influence from the past into the future that supports the relation between a desired set point and an existing state" (Freeman, 1999b, p. 157).

DYNAMIC LARGE-SCALE INTEGRATION AND RADICAL EMBODIMENT

Another proposal that falls squarely within the neurodynamical framework is one formulated initially by Francisco J. Varela (1995) and then developed with his collaborators, especially Evan Thompson (Thompson & Varela, 2001). Varela proposes to address the question of how neural mechanisms bring about "the flow of adapted and unified cognitive moments" (Varela, Lachaux, Rodriguez, & Martinerie, 2001, p. 229). The main working hypothesis is that a specific neuronal assembly underlies the operation of every unitary cognitive act. Here a neuronal assembly is understood as a distributed set of neurons in the brain that are linked through reciprocal and selective interactions, where the relevant variable is no longer single-neuron activity, but rather the dynamic nature of the links that are established between them. Varela and collaborators propose that such dynamical links are mediated by the transient establishment of phase relations (phase synchrony) across multiple frequency bands, especially in the beta (15–30 Hz) and gamma (30–80 Hz) range (Varela et al., 2001). Moreover, the transient nature of such dynamical links (and therefore of the neural assemblies themselves) is central to the idea of large-scale integration, for it brings to the fore the notion that the system, rather than presenting a series of well-defined states (attractors), shows metastable (self-limiting and recurrent) patterns of activity: "In the brain, there is no 'settling down' but an ongoing change marked only by transient coordination among populations, as the attractor itself changes owing to activity-dependent changes and modulations of synaptic connections" (Varela et al., 2001, p. 237). Large-scale integration through phase relations becomes fundamental for understanding brain dynamics as coordinated spatiotemporal patterns and provides a plausible solution to the problem of how to relate the local specificity of activity in specialized cortical regions to the constraints imposed by the connectivity established with other distributed areas. We see in the next two sections below, as well as in the other dynamical approaches described in this section, that this balance of segregation and integration has been considered the hallmark of brain complexity and a plausible prerequisite for consciousness.

Thompson and Varela (2001) then qualify this view by placing it in a 'radical embodiment' framework. They propose that, although the neural processes relevant to consciousness are best mapped at the level of large-scale, transient spatiotemporal patterns, the processes crucial for consciousness are not brain-bound events, but comprise also the body embedded in the environment. By taking into account the notion of *emergent processes* as understood in complex systems theory (order parameters or collective variables and the boundary conditions they impose on local activities), they propose that conscious awareness (as an order parameter or dynamical operator) is efficacious with respect to local neural events (see also Freeman 1999a,b, and above) and that the processes crucial for consciousness so understood span at least three 'cycles of operation' that cut across brain-body-world divisions (Thompson & Varela, 2001, p. 424). The first is the regulatory organismic cycle, in which the maintenance of internal variables within a viable range is achieved "through sensors and effectors to and from the body that link neural activity to the basic homodynamic processes of internal organs." This cycle is supposed to be the basis of the "inescapable affective backdrop of every conscious state," also called 'core consciousness' (Damasio, 1998, 1999) or 'primary-process consciousness' (Panksepp, 1998). The second cycle is sensorimotor coupling between organism and environment, whereby what the organism senses is a function of how it moves and how it moves is a function of what it senses. Here, "transient neural assemblies mediate the coordination of sensory and motor surfaces, and sensorimotor coupling with the environment constrains and modulates this neural dynamics." The third is a cycle of intersubjective interaction involving the recognition of the intentional meaning of actions and (in humans) linguistic communication. This last type of cycle depends on various levels of sensorimotor coupling, mediated in particular by the so-called mirror neuron systems that show similar patterns of activation for both self-generated, goal-directed actions and when one observes someone else performing the same action (Rizzolatti & Craighero, 2004).

As a final aspect of this proposal, Thompson and Varela hypothesize that "consciousness depends crucially on the manner in which brain dynamics are embedded in the somatic and environmental context of the animal's life, and therefore there may be no such thing as a minimal internal neural correlate whose intrinsic properties are sufficient to produce conscious experience" (Thompson & Varela, 2001, p. 425; see also Noë & Thompson, 2004a).

CORTICAL COORDINATION DYNAMICS

Based on extensive work in human motor coordination, J. A. Scott Kelso has developed a detailed dynamical framework for understanding human cognition (Kelso, 1995). His main focus is the appearance of self-organized patterns caused by non-linear interactions between system components, at both the neural and motor levels, as well as their role in human behavior. Kelso views the brain as fundamentally "a pattern forming self-organized system governed by potentially discoverable, non-linear dynamic laws" (Kelso, 1995, p. 257). He proposes that cognitive processes "arise as metastable spatiotemporal patterns of brain activity that themselves are produced by cooperative interactions among neural clusters" (257). He then goes one step further, proposing that "an order parameter isomorphism connects mind and body, will and brain, mental and neural events. Mind itself is a spatiotemporal pattern that molds the metastable dynamic patterns of the brain" (288).

What are the specific neural mechanisms underlying the establishment of such self-organized patterns? Kelso, in collaboration with Steven Bressler, proposes that the answer lies in the notion of 'coordination dynamics' (Bressler & Kelso, 2001). Coordination dynamics is presented as an integrative framework, in which the main issue is "to identify the key variables of coordination (defined as a functional ordering among interacting components) and their dynamics (rules that govern the stability and change of coordination patterns and the non-linear coupling among components that give rise to them)" (Bressler & Kelso, 2001, p. 26). Using this framework, Bressler and Kelso address the question of how interacting, distributed cortical areas allow the emergence of ongoing cognitive functions. On the basis of previous studies of bimanual coordination, they propose more specifically that the relevant collective variable is the relative phase (the continuous phase difference) among the given neural structures, which are themselves considered to be accurately described by non-linear oscillators. They argue that this coordination variable is adequate because (i) it reveals the spatiotemporal ordering between interacting structures, (ii) changes in the relative phase occur more slowly than changes in the local component variables, and (iii) relative phase shows abrupt changes during phase transitions or bifurcations. When the two coordinated local neuronal populations have different intrinsic frequencies, the relative phase shows a metastable regime in the form of 'attractiveness' toward preferred modes of coordination, without settling into any unique one. Accordingly, Bressler and Kelso propose that "a crucial aspect of cognitive function, which can both integrate and segregate the activities of multiple distributed areas, is large-scale relative coordination governed by way of metastable dynamics" (Bressler & Kelso, 2001, p. 30).

THE 'DYNAMIC CORE' HYPOTHESIS

Gerald M. Edelman and Giulio Tononi have developed an account of the neural basis of consciousness that aims to explain two fundamental properties of conscious experience, which they call 'integration' and 'differentiation' (Edelman & Tononi, 2000; Tononi & Edelman, 1998). Integration refers to the unitary character of conscious experience, whereby the multiplicity of aspects, such as color, taste, audition, kinesthetic

sense, etc., come together in a unique coherent experience. Differentiation is the capacity to experience any of a vast number of different possible conscious states. This capacity is intimately tied to what Edelman and Tononi call the informativeness of conscious experience, where each conscious state would be highly informative, given the reduction in uncertainty that is accomplished by the selection of one among a potentially infinite number of possible states.

Edelman and Tononi stress that consciousness is not a thing, but a process, and therefore should be explained in terms of neural processes and interactions and not in terms of specific brain areas or local activities. More specifically, they postulate that to understand consciousness it is necessary to pinpoint neural processes that are themselves integrated, yet highly differentiated. Their answer to this problem is what they call 'the Dynamic Core hypothesis' (Edelman & Tononi, 2000; Tononi & Edelman, 1998). They describe this hypothesis as follows:,

> 1) a group of neurons can contribute directly to conscious experience only if it is part of a distributed functional cluster that achieves high integration in hundreds of milliseconds. 2) To sustain conscious experience, it is essential that this functional cluster be highly differentiated, as indicated by high values of complexity. We call such a cluster of neuronal groups that are strongly interacting among themselves and that have distinct functional borders with the rest of the brain at the time scale of fractions of a second a 'dynamic core,' to emphasize both its integration and its constantly changing composition. A dynamic core is therefore a process, not a thing or a place, and it is defined in terms of neural interactions, rather than in terms of specific neural locations, connectivity or activity (Edelman & Tononi, 2000, p. 144).

In addition, they argue that "the dynamic core is a functional cluster: its participating neuronal groups are much more strongly interactive among themselves than with the rest of the brain. The dynamic core must also have high complexity: its global activity patterns must be selected within less than a second out of a very large repertoire" (Tononi & Edelman, 1998, p. 1849). They hypothesize that the dynamic core achieves integration on the basis of reentrant interactions among distributed neuronal groups, most likely mediated by the thalamocortical system. Specifically, for primary consciousness to arise, interactions are required between sensory cortices in different modalities and value-category and memory systems in frontal, temporal, and parietal areas.[15]

Edelman and Tononi claim that the dynamic core provides a "neural reference space for conscious experience" (Edelman & Tononi, 2000, p. 164). They depict this space as an n-dimensional neural space, where the number of dimensions is given by the number of neuronal groups that are part of the dynamic core at that moment. Such neuronal groups would be segregated into neural domains specialized for various functions, such as form, color, or orientation discrimination, proprioceptive or somatosensory inputs, and so on, and they would be brought together through re-entrant interactions. The local activities of these groups would therefore need to be understood in relation to the unified process constituted by the functional cluster; that is, the entire dynamic core: "The pure sensation of red is a particular neural state identified by a point within the N-dimensional neural space defined by the integrated activity of all the groups of neurons that constitute the dynamic core.... The conscious discrimination corresponding to the quale of seeing red acquires its full meaning only when considered in the appropriate, much larger, neural reference space" (Edelman & Tononi, 2000, p. 167).

Related Models

Several other authors have advanced models in which dynamical system concepts are present, yet appear less explicitly. Nevertheless, these approaches also aim to describe the formation of spatiotemporal patterns of brain activity that are crucial for action, per-ception, and consciousness. Therefore, we believe that it is important to keep these models in mind as part and parcel of the wider research program of neurodynamics.

THE CORTICO-THALAMIC DIALOGUE

Rodolfo Llinas and his collaborators have proposed a model of how consciousness is related to brain activity, in which the notion of emergent collective activity plays a central role (Llinas & Pare, 1991; Llinas & Ribary, 2001; Llinas, Ribary, Contreras, & Pedroarena, 1998). In particular, Llinas postulates that consciousness arises from the ongoing dialogue between the cortex and the thalamus (Llinas & Pare, 1991). He calls attention to the fact that most of the input to the thalamus comes from the cortex, rather than from peripheral sensory systems. On this basis, he proposes that the brain be considered as a 'closed system' that can generate and sustain its own activity thanks to the intrinsic electrical properties of neurons (Llinas, 1988) and the connectivity they establish. The interplay of these two main characteristics underlies the establishment of "global resonant states which we know as cognition" (Llinas & Ribary, 2001, p. 167).

A crucial feature of this proposal is the precise temporal relations established by neurons in the cortico-thalamic loop. This temporal mapping is viewed as a 'functional geometry' and involves oscillatory activity at different spatial scales, ranging from individual neurons to the cortical mantle. In particular, 40-Hz oscillations that traverse the cortex in a highly spatially structured manner are considered as candidates for the production of a "temporal conjunction of rhythmic activity over large ensemble of neurons" (Llinas & Ribary, 2001, p. 168). Such gamma oscillations are believed to be sustained by a thalamo-cortical resonant circuit involving pyramidal neurons in layer IV of the neocortex, relay thalamic neurons, and reticular nucleus neurons. In particular, temporal binding is supposed to be generated by the conjunction of a specific circuit involving specific sensory and motor nuclei projecting to layer IV and the feedback via the reticular nucleus, and a non-specific circuit involving non-specific intralaminar nucei projecting to the most superficial layer of the cortex and collaterals to the reticular and non-specific thalamic nuclei. Thus, the 'specific' system is supposed to supply the *content* that relates to the external world, and the non-specific system is supposed to give rise to the temporal conjunction or the *context* (on the basis of a more interoceptive context concerned with alertness). Together they would generate a single cognitive experience (Llinas & Ribary, 2001, p. 173).

TIMING AND BINDING

Wolf Singer and collaborators have extensively investigated the issue of temporal correlations between cortical neurons and the role this phenomenon could play in solving what has been called 'the binding problem' (Engel & Singer, 2001; Gray et al., 1989; Singer & Gray, 1995). This is the problem of how the signals from the separate neuronal populations concerned with distinct object features (color, shape, motion, etc.) are bound together into a unified perceptual representation. The main idea behind their approach is that there is a "temporary association of neurons into functionally coherent assemblies that as a whole represent a particular content whereby each individual neuron is tuned to one of the elementary features of composite perceptual objects" (Singer, 1998, p. 1831). The specific hypothesis is that neurons become members of such coherent assemblies through the precise synchronization of their discharges; in other words, such synchronization establishes a "code for relatedness" (Singer, 1998, p. 1837).

Recently, Singer and colleagues (Engel & Singer, 2001, Engel et al., 1999) **have** extended this framework to address the issue of phenomenal awareness. Their argument can be summarized as follows: (1) Brains capable of phenomenal awareness should be able to generate metarepresentations of their own cognitive processes. (2) Metarepresentations are realized by an iterative process, in which higher-order cortical areas read low-order (sensory) areas. (3) Combinatorial flexibility of metarepresentations is obtained

via dynamical cell assemblies. (4) Binding of such assemblies is effected by transient synchrony that establishes a code for relatedness among features and facilitates downstream evaluation and impact. (5) Such assemblies need desynchronized EEG[16] (which correlates with phenomenal awareness in the waking state and REM dream state and shows high-frequency beta and gamma oscillatory activity), and are facilitated by attention (Singer, 1998).

Engel, Fries, and Singer (Engel, Fries, & Singer, 2001; Engel & Singer, 2001) also explicitly espouse a 'dynamicist view' of brain function. According to this view, brain processes are not passive, stimulus-driven, and hierarchical, but active, context-dependent, endogenously driven, and distributed. In particular, "spatio-temporal patterns of ongoing activity...translate the functional architecture of the system and its pre-stimulation history into dynamic states of anticipation" (Engel et al., 2001, p. 705). In this dynamicist account of top-down influences, relevant patterns are generated as a result of continuous large-scale interactions, and these patterns can bias the saliency of sensory signals by changes in their temporal correlations. Endogenous, self-generated activity displays distinct spatiotemporal patterns, and these patterns bias the self-organizing process that leads to the temporal coordination of input-triggered responses and their binding into functionally coherent assemblies. This dynamicist approach thus stresses the importance of top-down influence in the form of large-scale dynamics that express contextual influences and stored knowledge in the system and that can modulate local processing and hence the downstream effect of the impinging event (Engel et al., 2001).

THE NEURAL CORRELATES OF CONSCIOUSNESS

Francis Crick and Christof Koch have employed dynamical concepts in a series of proposals regarding the relation between neural activity and conscious perception (Crick & Koch, 1990, 1998, 2003). In their view, the best way for the neuroscience of consciousness to proceed is first to uncover the neural correlates of consciousness (NCCs), in particular the neural contents of visual consciousness. They define a neural correlate of consciousness as a minimal set of neuronal events necessary and sufficient for a given state of phenomenal consciousness (see also Chalmers, 2000). Here we summarize the version of their theory presented in one of their last joint articles on consciousness (Crick & Koch, 2003).

They begin with the notion of an 'unconscious homunculus', which is a system consisting of frontal regions of the brain "looking at the back, mostly sensory region" (Crick & Koch, 2003, p. 120). Crick and Koch propose that we are not conscious of our thoughts, but only of sensory representations of them in imagination. The brain presents multiple unconscious processing modules, mostly feedforward, that act as 'zombie' modes. These modules present stereotyped responses in a sort of 'cortical reflex', whereas conscious modes are necessary only to deal with time-consuming, less stereotyped situations that need planning and decision making. The most important point, however, with regard to the NCC issue, is the existence of dynamic coalitions of neurons in the form of neural assemblies whose sustained activity embodies the contents of consciousness. Explicit representations of particular aspects of the (visual) scene are present in special brain regions ('critical nodes'), and these representations are bound together in the dynamic neural coalitions. Additionally, Crick and Koch suggest that higher levels of cortical processing are first reached by the feedforward sensory sweep and that only through backpropagation of activity from higher to lower levels do the lower levels gain access to this information. They distinguish 'driving' from 'modulating' connections and suggest that the feedforward sweep is mostly driving activity in the frontal regions, whereas the feedback return onto sensory cortices is mainly modulating. In the specific case of conscious perception, they propose that it is not a continuous phenomenon, but rather that it works on the basis of a series of 'snapshots'. Such

snapshots are possibly related to alpha and theta rhythms and are the reflection of a certain threshold that has been overcome (for a certain amount of time) by neural activity, enabling it to become conscious. Conscious coalitions would therefore be continually "forming, growing or disappearing" (Crick & Koch, 2003, p. 122). Crick and Koch propose that attention is fundamental in biasing the competition among coalitions that share critical nodes. Attention produces the effective binding of different attributes of the given conscious content by means of shared "membership in a particular coalition" (Crick & Koch, 2003, p. 123).

Although Crick and Koch recognize that the mechanism to establish such coalitions probably involves synchronous firing between distributed populations, they explicitly state that they no longer believe that 40-Hz oscillatory activity is a sufficient condition for consciousness. Finally, they propose that there is a set of neural processes that, although not part of the NCC, is affected by the NCC, both with respect to its actual firing and with respect to synaptic modifications caused by previous experience. This 'penumbra' (Crick and Koch, 2003, p. 124), could eventually become conscious, if incorporated into the NCC.

CONSCIOUSNESS AS GLOBAL WORKSPACE

Stanislas Dehaene, Jean-Pierre Changeux, and collaborators have explored an alternative model of brain functioning that underlies the accessibility to verbal report of conscious experience (Dehaene, Kerszberg, & Changeux, 1998; Dehaene & Naccache, 2001; Dehaene, Sergent, & Changeux, 2003). The main proposal of their model is the existence of "two main computational spaces within the brain" (Dehaene, Kerszberg, & Changeux, 1998, p. 14529). The first computational space consists of a series of functionally segregated and specialized modules or processors that constitute a parallel distributed network (examples of modular processors would be primary visual cortex (V1) or the mirror neuron system in area F5 of the premotor cortex). The second computational space is not confined to a series of brain areas, but rather is distributed among multiple cortical regions. The main property of this second space is massive reciprocal connectivity on the basis of horizontal projections (long-range cortico-cortical connections). Through descending connections, this 'global workspace' determines the contributions of the modular processors of the first computational space by selecting a specific set while suppressing another. Through this selective mobilization of the specialized processors into the global workspace. a 'brain scale' state can be reached, in which a group of workspace neurons are spontaneously coactivated while the rest are suppressed. As a result, an exclusive 'representation' invades the workspace and

> *may remain active in an autonomous manner and resist changes in peripheral activity. If it is negatively evaluated, or if attention fails, it may however be spontaneously and randomly replaced by another discrete combination of workspace neurons. Functionally, this neural property implements an active 'generator of diversity,' which constantly projects and tests hypotheses (or pre-representations) on the outside world. The dynamics of workspace neuron activity is thus characterized be a constant flow of individual coherent episodes of variable duration (Dehaene, Kerszberg, & Changeux, 1998, p. 14530).*

This postulated workspace has access to the world through 'perceptual circuits'; 'motor programming circuits' enable action guidance'; 'long-term memory circuits' enable access to past experiences; 'evaluation circuits' allow negative-positive judgments; and 'attention circuits' endow the workspace with the capacity to alter its own activity separately from the influence of external inputs. Through connections with motor and language centers, the workspace makes its resident representation available for verbal report by the subject. Thus, Dehaene and Changeux see consciousness as a selective global pattern: "When a piece of information such as the identity of a stimulus accesses a sufficient subset of workspace neurons, their activity becomes self-sustained and can be broadcasted via long-

distance connections to a vast set of defined areas, thus creating a global and exclusive availability for a given stimulus, which is then subjectively experienced as conscious" (Dehaene, Kerszberg, & Changeux, 2003).

SUMMARY

The majority of the approaches reviewed above stress the importance of a certain type of distributed, spatiotemporal pattern of neural activity that 'demarcates' itself from the background activity of the brain. Such patterns are described as ongoing, transient, metastable coordination processes among separate neurons, and they are considered to be crucial for the moment-to-moment emergence and formation of conscious experience. Another related feature crucial to several of the above approaches is that these spatiotemporal patterns reveal the interplay of two apparently fundamental principles of brain organization and function; namely, functional segregation and cooperative interaction or integration. This interplay and the dynamical properties of the brain's spatiotemporal activity patterns are the focus of the following sections.

The Search for Meaningful Spatiotemporal Patterns in the Brain

Introduction

Despite their significant differences, all the above models agree that the constitution of dynamic spatiotemporal patterns of neural activity plays a central role in the emergence of consciousness. This section discusses the practical aspects of the search for such patterns. After a short review of the connectivity of the brain, we discuss the detection of such patterns in real brain data. A short mathematical presentation leads us to the concept of synchrony, which is the preferred candidate to date for such patterns.

Connectivity in the Brain

The organization of the brain's connectivity is what ultimately determines the form of the neural spatiotemporal patterns. For this reason, it is useful to start with a review of some basic facts about this architecture.

The brain is probably one of the most complex biological systems we know (Edelman & Tononi, 2000). Its complexity is certainly due in great part to its histological and morphological structure, and one of the most striking aspects of the brain as a system is the connectivity pattern it exhibits. This pattern is that of a compact but distributed tissue, with local clusters of highly connected neurons that establish long-range interactions. In general, two neurons in the brain are always in interaction either directly or via a certain number of intermediate cells. It is useful to distinguish two levels of connectivity in the brain.

Local connections: Several types of neurons coexist in the neocortex. Within a given portion of neocortex, a complex arrangement of pyramidal, spiny stellate, and smooth stellate cells can be found. This arrangement of collateral axons, dentritic trees, and cell bodies gives rise to clusters of interconnected neurons that extend over a fraction of a millimeter. Neurons tend to organize into radial clusters that share functional characteristics, known as functional columns. These structures are particularly evident in somatic sensory cortex and visual cortex and are believed to play a fundamental role in basic discriminative capacities.

Long-range connections: In addition to the bodies and dentritic trees of the local neurons, axons from deep structures and other cortical regions terminate at different points in the six-layered structure of the neocortex. Likewise, pyramidal neurons in a given region of the neocortex have axons that extend into the white matter and reach both deep structures and other cortical regions. At least four patterns of long-distance connectivity can be distinguished in the brain (Abeles, 1991): (i) between cortical neurons within one hemisphere, (ii) between cortical neurons of different hemispheres, (iii) between cortical neurons and deep nuclei, and (iv) between brainstem modulatory systems and extended areas of the cortex. In general, long-range connectivity obeys a reciprocity rule (Varela, 1995): If A projects to B, then B projects to A. This rule clearly favors the establishment of recursive loops. Nevertheless, some basal ganglia nuclei present a slightly different connectivity structure: Although they receive axons from cortical neurons, they project only through the thalamus into frontal lobe regions (Edelman & Tononi, 2000).

Interestingly, however, no one zone in the brain can be distinguished as the ultimate highest level, at least in terms of the connectivity patterns. Indeed, the massively interconnected nature of the brain suggests that dynamic relations between local and distant activities will *necessarily* be established whatever the observed origin of a given activation is. On the other hand, it is true that clusters of more strongly interconnected regions are evident. Stephan and collaborators recognize at least three main clusters in the primate cortex: (i) visual (occipito-temporal); (ii) somatomotor (mainly pre- and post-central, but extending into parietal regions); and (iii) orbito-temporopolar-insular (Stephan et al., 2000). It is interesting that the overall structural connectivity (Hilgetag & Kaiser, 2004) and functional connectivity (Stephan et al., 2000) show a 'small world' architecture. Networks having such an architecture display remarkable properties, such as reduced average length path (reaching any node from any other node is accomplished in a minimal number of steps), high synchronizability, enhanced signal propagation speed, and stability (one can randomly eliminate links without affecting substantially the network properties; Watts & Strogatz, 1998).

One of the most important conclusions of the study of the brain as a system is that, despite its massive interconnectedness, the brain shows a strong segregation into clusters at both structural and functional levels. The interplay of these two characteristic features of the brain lies at the basis of one of the most interesting issues in contemporary neuroscience – the large-scale integration of brain activity and its role in the unified nature of experience (James, 1890/1981; Varela, 1995; Von der Malsburg, 1981).

The combination of extensive neuropsychological studies since Broca and the explosive use of imaging techniques in the last

15–20 years has highlighted two main principles of brain functioning (Edelman & Tononi, 2000; Friston, 2002a,b, 2005). On the one hand, a functional encapsulation is evident: Distinct regions in the brain contribute differentially to different aspects of adaptive behavior; for instance, bilateral damage to the human homologue of V_5/MT (in the middle temporal area) can lead to a restricted impairment in the capacity to discriminate movement (akinetopsia; Zihl, Von Cramon, & Mai, 1983). On the other hand, for a given cognitive task, it is rarely the case that *only* one isolated region shows significant activation. For example, directing attention to a particular location of the visual field correlates with the concomitant activation of several cortical regions, preferentially right parietal, anterior cingulate, and occipital cortices (Mesulam, 1999).

Indeed, as we saw above, the connectivity pattern of the mammalian brain reveals a complex structure of recursively connected distant areas (Hilgetag & Kaiser, 2004; Stephan et al., 2000). Although the corticocortical connectivity pattern is paradigmatic, the structure of recursive connections is reflected most prominently in the thalamocortical matrix (Edelman & Tononi, 2000; Llinas & Ribary, 2001). For instance, the lateral geniculate nucleus (LGN) of the thalamus receives only around 5–10% of its inputs (not more than 20%) from the retina, whereas the remaining connections come from local inhibitory networks, descending inputs from layer VI of the visual cortex, and ascending inputs from the brainstem (Sherman & Guillery, 2002). Yet the LGN is the major relay in the visual pathway from the retina to the cortex. Such a complex structure of recursive, re-entrant, and interconnected networks that pervade the mammalian brain (Edelman & Tononi, 2000) strongly suggests the existence of constitutive cooperative interactions, and therefore integrative activity, among different regions.

Nevertheless, the presence of anatomical connectivity is not enough to explain effective interactions among separate regions (Friston, 2002a,b). Indeed, in addition to being connected, it is necessary that such regions establish interdependent activation to account adequately for the integration of functionally separate activity (Bressler, 1995). Thus, one task facing the neurodynamicist is to detect such interdependent activation from the brain recordings available today.

Detecting Interdependent Activations from Real Brain Recordings

THE DATA

The activity of the brain can be recorded at several different spatial and temporal scales. The neurodynamicist will be primarily interested in those techniques that are fast enough to follow the formation of spatiotemporal patterns in the time scale of hundreds of milliseconds. Because the construction of such patterns often involves activities at the millisecond time scale (e.g., in the case of fast neural oscillations), the desired temporal resolution is on this order of milliseconds. In practice, this excludes the neuroimaging techniques based on slow metabolic measures, such as functional magnetic resonance imaging (fMRI) or positron emission topography (PET).[17] Millisecond temporal resolution is accessible through direct intracellular and extracellular measurements of individual neurons and recordings of local field potentials (LFPs) or of the electromagnetic fields of large neural populations that produce the electroencephalographic (EEG) and magnetoencephalographic (MEG) signals. LFPs are the summation of the membrane potentials of populations of neurons. The size of the populations depends on the site and precision of the recordings: Local microelectrodes can record small populations, extending over less than a square millimeter of tissue, whereas scalp EEG electrodes or MEG sensors (and optical imaging) record the average activity of several square centimeters of cortex. At an intermediate level, intracranial recordings from human patients can record from a couple of square millimeters of cortex (Lachaux, Rudrauf, & Kahane, 2003). Except in those rare situations justified by therapeutical reasons, human recordings are almost exclusively non-invasive and performed therefore at the centimeter-wide spatial resolution of MEG or EEG.

With this panel of recording techniques, spatiotemporal patterns can in principle be observed at three levels: (i) as interactions between simultaneous recordings of multiple individual neurons, (ii) as interactions between simultaneous recordings of multiple individual LFPs, and (iii) in single LFP recordings. The third level is intermediate between the first two: Because an individual LFP records from a single neural population, the average activity of the LFP is sensitive to the spatiotemporal organization of activity within this population. For example, if all the neurons are coactive periodically, the average activity in the LFP will be a massive oscillation, much stronger than if the neurons are not synchronous.

SOME SIMPLE MATHEMATICAL CONSIDERATIONS

As we have seen, the organization of the brain suggests that interactions among distributed neuronal groups are bound to occur, given their massive interconnectedness. We also mentioned that recordings of neuronal activity can be obtained by a diversity of approaches and at several levels of spatial resolution. With these points in mind, let us return to the central question of this section: How does one detect neural spatiotemporal patterns from real brain data? The definition of the 'dynamic core' by Tononi and Edelman (1998) provides a useful starting point: "The dynamic core is a functional cluster: its participating neuronal groups are much more strongly interactive among themselves than with the rest of the brain." The challenge for the neurodynamicist is therefore to find neurons or groups of neurons with particularly strong (but transient) interactions.

In keeping with the dynamical approach, we can usefully consider this question in geometrical terms. Consider the n simultaneous measures of brain activity that one can record in a typical electrophysiological setting (e.g., 64 measures from 64 EEG channels). At any time t, the n simultaneous measurements define a position in an n-dimensional state space, and the evolution of this position in time defines a trajectory. If the measurements are independent from each other, then the trajectory will progressively completely fill a hypercubic portion of the state space, leaving no hole. In contrast, if there are interactions among the measured neuronal populations, then the trajectory will fit into a restricted portion of the full space and be constrained onto a manifold with a (fractal) dimension less than that of the state space.[18] What this means in informational terms is that, for at least one pair of the measured neural populations, measuring the activity of the first population provides some information about the activity of the second one. The probability distribution of the activity of Population 2 (the probability $p(y)$ that this activity is y), *given that* the activity of Population 1 is x, is different from what it would be if the activity of Population 1 were x'. Consider this metaphor: If we know where John will spend the afternoon, we can predict with some accuracy that his wife Ann will spend the afternoon in the same city, but we cannot predict where Jane, unrelated to John, will be. Certain measures, such as mutual information (David, Cosmelli, & Friston, 2004), quantify exactly this sharpening of the probability distribution.

The transient nature of neural interactions, however, makes general measures based on such geometrical formulations difficult to apply. The main problem is that, to know whether or not the trajectory fills up the whole space, the experimenter needs to observe it during time windows that are typically orders of magnitude longer than the typical lifespan of cell assemblies. This difficulty can be avoided if the researcher assumes a priori what will be the shape of the manifold onto which the trajectory is constrained. Because spatiotemporal patterns can potentially take an infinite number of shapes in the state space, a possible solution is to assume a specific shape and to build a special detector for this shape (surfing on the advances of signal processing). It is easy to see that it takes fewer measurements to test whether the trajectory stays on a circle or whether it follows some general, unknown, geometrical structure.

In the absence of noise, three successive measurements are sufficient to know whether the trajectory stays on a straight line, which would correspond to a linear relationship between the recorded activities. Synchrony between quasi-periodic oscillators – that is, the transient phase-locking of their oscillations – is a good example of such an interaction. But linear relationships can be extended to other trajectories constrained on simple manifolds of dimension 1,[19] such as a circle. This is the case for two oscillators rotating at the same frequency with a constant phase lag.

Synchrony: Perhaps Not the Best Candidate, but at Least the Simplest

The practical reason that synchrony has so far been the best-studied (if not the only) type of transient interaction between neural populations is the ease with which it can be detected. Furthermore, since the development of the EEG, it has been evident that oscillations are ubiquitous in the brain. This fact, combined with the relation between coordinated oscillatory activity and several important cognitive functions (discussed below), has also contributed to the development of approaches that seek to detect the occurrence of synchrony from real neurobiological signals.

In its original neurophysiological formulation, 'synchrony' refers to a positive correlation between the spike timing of a set of neurons. In other words, if we consider two neurons within a synchronous population, the probability of the first neuron to fire a spike is significantly higher at specific delays relative to the spikes of the other neuron.[20] In the simplest case, this delay is zero, which means that the neurons have a high probability of firing simultaneously. In general, this probability, as well as the eventual delay, is quantified by the cross-correlogram between the spike trains of the two neurons (Perkel, Gerstein, & Moore, 1967). One speaks of oscillatory synchrony, or synchronous oscillations, if the neurons tend to fire at periodic latencies. Numerous animal studies conducted over the past 20 years have now established that synchrony is ubiquitous in virtually all sensory and motor modalities. It has often been found to be related to perception, memory, and motor programming (see Roskies, 1999, for a group of excellent reviews that summarize these results).

Synchrony has also been studied in humans as an instance of spatiotemporal patterns of interdependent neural activity, although at a different level from animal studies. Here an important distinction needs to be made between the local recordings of individual neurons, almost always accessible only in animals, and the more global recordings of entire neural populations, accessible in humans through scalp EEG or MEG. EEG and MEG average across large neuronal assemblies, and hence oscillatory synchrony between neurons shows up as changes of power in particular frequency bands. The reason this happens is that groups of synchronously firing neural oscillators can be modeled as oscillators themselves, with the amplitude of the oscillations depending on the number of individual oscillators in the group and on the precision of the synchrony between them. This point entails a further distinction: On the one hand, oscillatory activity as recorded by an individual EEG electrode or MEG sensor implies already a certain amount of local synchronous activity. On the other hand, one can choose to consider synchronization between oscillations produced by distant neuronal populations (separated by several centimeters) to describe distributed spatiotemporal patterns that occur at a more global level. In any case, when dealing with EEG and MEG recording one is always in the presence of noisy data. Hence, any interdependence measure must be understood in a statistical sense throughout a given temporal window (Lachaux et al., 2002; Lachaux, Rodriguez, Martinerie, & Varela, 1999; Le Van Quyen et al., 2001).

Synchrony at the more regional or local level has been demonstrated repeatedly in humans in relation to integrative mechanisms in language, memory, attention, and motor tasks and in virtually all the sensory modalities. For example, the perception of coherent objects in humans is specifically associated with synchronous oscillations in the gamma range (above 30 Hz), the so-called induced gamma response (for a review, see Tallon-Baudry & Bertrand, 1999). This response, although not completely time-locked to the stimulus presentation, typically starts in posterior brain areas (over the occipital cortex) around 200 ms after the stimulus and then returns gradually to the prestimulus level when the stimulus does not require further analysis (Lachaux et al., 2000, 2005; Tallon-Baudry & Bertrand, 1999).

As we mentioned above, oscillations produced by two neural populations can also be synchronous within larger cell assemblies. This synchrony can be detected by a transient phase-locking between the oscillations of the two local fields (Lachaux et al., 1999, 2002; Rodriguez et al., 1999). Such long-range synchrony between distant neural populations has been suggested as a plausible candidate to mediate the integration of activity in functionally specialized and distinct brain regions (Bressler, 1995; Varela et al., 2001). For example, Tallon-Baudry and colleagues have shown in humans that during the maintenance of a complex shape in visual short-term memory, two functionally distinct regions within the ventral visual pathway, the fusiform gyrus and the lateral occipital sulcus, produce synchronous oscillations around 20 Hz (Tallon-Baudry, Bertrand, & Fischer, 2001).

Synchronization is a complex concept that can cover several possibly distinct types of temporal relations, such as coherence, frequency synchronization, phase synchronization, generalized synchronization, as well as others (Brown & Kocarev, 2000; Friston, 1997; Pikovsky et al., 1997). Here we have focused on synchrony as either occurring between stochastic point-processes, such as spike trains, or in terms of phase relations between oscillatory processes (phase-locking synchrony). As mentioned above, we chose this focus mainly because of technical limitations in the estimation of generalized measures of synchronous activation. With this point in mind it is possible to say that synchrony, as presented here, appears as a simple measure of precise temporal relations between neural processes that can enable one to follow the formation of spatiotemporal brain patterns relevant for consciousness. Not surprisingly, this mechanism is referred to in several of the dynamical models reviewed above. In the next section, we review more specifically a set of results concerning the relation between consciousness and the current 'crowd's favorite' among neurodynamicists – synchrony in the gamma range.

The Crowd's Favorite: The Gamma Band

Evidence for a Relation Between Gamma Synchrony and Consciousness

We have mentioned that synchrony among oscillating neural populations is a plausible candidate to mediate functional connectivity and therefore to allow the formation of spatiotemporal structures, such as those reviewed in the previous sections. In this section, we return to this hypothesis in more detail, with a particular focus on gamma band oscillations, which have been repeatedly associated with consciousness in the last 15 years.

The putative role of gamma band oscillations in the formation of conscious experience was proposed by Crick and Koch (Crick & Koch, 1990), shortly after Singer and colleagues (Gray et al., 1989) had completed a series of observations in the cat visual cortex showing that neurons tend to synchronize their spiking activity when stimulated with parts of the same visual object, such as a moving bar (whereas they do not synchronize when stimulated with features that cannot be part of the same object). Those observations matched theoretical predictions by Von der Marlsburg (1981) that synchrony could be used to achieve figure/ground segmentation during perception of the visual scene. Thus, synchrony was assumed to provide a solution to the visual binding problem (the problem, discussed above, of integrating distinct visual features into a unified and coherent perception; see Roskies, 1999).

In their 1990 paper, Crick and Koch pushed this idea further by stating that visual consciousness of the object occurs only when its features are bound together as a result of this type of synchronous activity. This hypothesis was in good agreement with the feature-integration-theory, proposed by Anne Treisman, suggesting that attention is necessary to bind together the features of objects (Treisman & Gelade, 1980).[21] Henceforth, a close relation between gamma synchrony and attention and consciousness has ensued (Fell et al., 2003; Varela, 1995). This association has been very appealing for neurodynamicists addressing the consciousness issue, because it provides ground material for the neural spatiotemporal patterns they associate with consciousness on the appropriate time scale. Indeed, several dynamic models among those reviewed above, specifically those by Singer, Llinas, Varela, and their respective collaborators, consider synchronous activity in high-frequency ranges, most preferentially the gamma range, as crucial for conscious experience.

Fortunately, the association between the gamma band and attention, vigilance, and consciousness is not just based on its theoretical appeal but also on sound experimental evidence. For instance, it is well known that the precise synchronization of neuronal discharges is more prevalent during states characterized by arousal and moreover that gamma oscillations are particularly prominent during epochs of higher vigilance (Herculano-Houzel, Munk, Neuenschwander, & Singer, 1999; Rodriguez, Kallenbach, Singer, & Munk, 2004). In cats, for example, gamma synchrony is stronger after the stimulation of the mesencephalic reticular formation (Munk, Roelfsema, Konig, Engel, & Singer, 1996). Furthermore, EEG/MEG gamma-band activity is present both during REM sleep and awake states, with a much stronger amplitude than during deep sleep (reviewed in Engel et al., 1999).[22]

Several studies have also demonstrated that the presentation of sensory stimuli elicits stronger gamma synchrony when attention is focused on the stimulus than when attention is diverted away. This finding was observed in monkeys for somatosensory stimulations and found again recently for neurons in area V_4 of monkeys presented with small visual gratings (Fries, Reynolds, Rorie, & Desimone, 2001).

There is also evidence for a more direct relation between gamma activity and consciousness. Lachaux and colleagues have recently shown that the perception of faces is associated with strong gamma oscillations in face-specific regions along the ventral visual stream (Lachaux et al., 2005). Epileptic patients with intracranial electrodes that record directly from the fusiform face area (a region along the ventral visual pathway particularly associated with the perception of faces) were presented with high-contrast 'Mooney figures' representing faces. Because the figures were presented briefly, for 200 ms, they were consciously perceived as faces only half of the time. The authors reported that the gamma band response to the images was significantly stronger when the figures were actually consciously perceived as faces than when they were not. This high-resolution study followed a previous one (Rodriguez et al., 1999), using the same protocol in normal subjects with non-invasive scalp EEG recordings; this study showed that gamma oscillations tend to synchronize across widely separated brain areas (typically frontal versus occipital) only when the figures are perceived as faces.

Fries and colleagues (Fries, Roelfsema, Engel, Konig, & Singer, 1997) have shown an even more direct relation between gamma synchrony and consciousness. They showed that, during binocular rivalry in cats, the level of synchrony between visual neurons follows in time the shift of perceptual dominance. Cats were presented with two visual patterns moving simultaneously in different directions: One pattern was presented to the left eye and the other to the right eye. Under such circumstances, the visual percept cannot encompass the two contradictory patterns and instead alternates between them (hence the term 'binocular rivalry'). The results of this study showed that neurons stimulated by the perceived stimulus were strongly synchronized, with strong gamma oscillations, whereas cells stimulated by the suppressed visual pattern showed only weak synchrony. This experiment is highly relevant to the study of visual consciousness, because conscious perception is decoupled from the drive of the sensory inputs (the physical stimulus remains constant while perception does not) and gamma synchrony is used as an indicator of which pattern is being consciously perceived by the cat.

Gamma synchrony has been further associated with consciousness in the context of the attentional blink effect. The attentional blink occurs when a subject must detect two targets in a series of rapidly presented pictures (at a rate of about 10 per second). Typically, the second target is detected (and consciously perceived) less frequently when it comes within 500 ms of the first target, as if the subject had 'blinked'. Fell and colleagues have argued that the blink could be due to the suppression of gamma synchronization shortly after the response to the first target (Fell, Klaver, Elger, & Fernandez, 2002). Once again, gamma synchrony would be necessary for conscious perception.

This proposal is consistent with a recent observation from Lachaux and colleagues, in the face perception paradigm detailed above (Lachaux et al., 2005), that parts of the primary visual cortex shut down, with respect to gamma activity, after the presentation of a Mooney figure: There is a drop of energy in the gamma band, below the baseline level, which lasts a couple of hundreds of milliseconds, and is simultaneous with the induced gamma increase in the fusiform face area. This drop in gamma activity could be the trace of a transient deactivation of the primary visual cortex that could cause the transient attentional blink after a meaningful visual stimulus. The visual cortex would be transiently 'unavailable' while processing particularly meaningful stimuli, as in a reflex protective mode.

Further hints about the role of gamma synchrony come, albeit indirectly, from the experimental contributions of Benjamin Libet (Gomes, 1998; Libet, 2002). In a series of classic experiments in patients mixing direct intracranial electric stimulations and peripheral somatosensory stimulations, Libet revealed a number of interesting properties of somatosensory awareness: (1) An electrical cortical or thalamic stimulus requires a duration of more than 250 ms to be felt, whereas a skin stimulus of 20 ms is sufficient. (2) If a direct cortical (electrical) stimulus occurs within 250 ms after a skin stimulus, it can suppress or enhance the felt perception of the latter stimulus. (3) For a skin stimulus to be felt as synchronous with a non-overlapping cortical stimulus, the skin stimulus must be delayed about 250 ms relative to the latter stimulus. Interestingly, all three properties match quite closely the known temporal dynamics of the cortical gamma response induced by sensory stimuli. This match is particularly intriguing considering the fact that Libet used rhythmic electrical stimulations in the gamma range (typically 60-Hz trains of electric pulses).

If the induced gamma response is involved in the conscious perception of a sensory stimulus, then one would indeed expect that a rhythmic train of electrical stimulations in the gamma range could mimic the effect of the induced gamma response, if it possesses the same temporal properties; that is, if it starts roughly 250 ms after the mimicked stimulus onset and lasts for at least 250 ms. Then it should be felt as synchronous with a corresponding skin stimulus and possibly interfere with perception of that latter stimulus. In brief, Libet's observations can readily be interpreted via the involvement of the sensory-induced gamma response in sensory awareness, at least in the case of somatosensory awareness.

In summary, the previous studies certainly build a strong case for the role of resonant assemblies, oscillating in the gamma range, as neural correlates of sensory awareness. Nevertheless, this assessment is not the end of the story, for a number of arguments make it difficult to equate gamma synchrony and consciousness.

Problems Concerning the Link Between Gamma Synchrony and Consciousness

The first problem to mention is that gamma synchrony can be observed in unconscious anesthetized animals, although it is stronger when animals are awake (see Sewards & Sewards, 2001, for arguments against the role of gamma synchrony in consciousness). Sewards and Sewards further argue that gamma oscillatory activities have been detected in structures that most likely do not participate in the generation of sensory awareness, such as the hippocampal formation: "Obviously hippocampal activities could not contribute to sensory awareness since lesions to that structure do not result in purely sensory deficits of any kind" (Sewards & Sewards, 2001, p. 492). This argument, as well as others, leads them to conclude that "while synchronization and oscillatory patterning may be necessary conditions for activities to participate in generating awareness, they are certainly not sufficient" (Sewards & Sewards, 2001, p. 492).[23]

This point echoes the conclusions from a study by Revonsuo and colleauges (Revonsuo, Wilenius-Emet, Kuusela, & Lehto, 1997). In this study, they recorded the gamma band response of normal subjects during the fusion of random-dot stereograms. They observed that, although 40-Hz synchronized oscillations seemed to participate in the construction of the unified percept, they were not maintained during the continuous viewing (and conscious perception) of the same stimulus once it had been constructed. Lachaux (unpublished findings) repeatedly confirmed this observation with human intracranial recordings: The gamma response induced by durable visual stimuli in the visual system often stops before the end of the stimulus presentation, despite the fact that the subjects still fixate the images and consciously perceive them.[24]

These considerations indicate that other spatiotemporal structures may participate in the emergence and the stabilization of the conscious percept. The presence of such structures is especially the case for short-term memory, which has been proposed as a central component of consciousness (Baars & Franklin, 2003). In visual short-term memory, when an individual has to maintain a conscious representation of a complex visual shape, using mental imagery, for a couple of seconds, synchrony occurs not in the gamma range, but in the lower beta range (between 15 and 20 Hz), between distributed sites of the ventral visual pathway (Tallon-Baudry et al., 2001). Therefore, resonant cell assemblies in the beta range may also subserve continuous visual perception (if only in its imagery aspect).

The above studies emphasize the point that gamma synchrony may be necessary for the emergence of a conscious perception, but perhaps only in this emergence. Once formed, the percept could then continue via other cell mechanisms, in the form of other types of spatiotemporal structures.

Nevertheless, even at the initial level of this emergence, the role of gamma synchrony needs to be clarified. As we have seen, gamma synchrony occurs in anesthetized animals and is therefore not sufficient for consciousness (Sewards & Sewards, 2001). One interesting possibility, in the case of the visual system, is that gamma synchrony could be involved in the formation of visual objects. Visual objects are the preferred targets of visual attention, and yet they present themselves to us only via conscious perception. Furthermore, as argued by the Feature Integration Theory (Treisman & Gelade, 1980), visual objects seem to require visual attention to form. The question thus arises of which comes first: objects or attention. One solution to this problem is that in the absence of attention there are only 'pre-objects'; that is, bundles of features that are object candidates and that are sufficient to attract attention, which would then finish the construction and remain grabbed by them (Wolfe & Bennett, 1997).

Engel and Singer (Engel et al., 1999) propose that gamma synchrony may mediate this mechanism. According to this proposal, proto-objects, based on their physical features and Gestalt properties, assemble in the form of nascent cell assemblies via gamma synchrony. This synchrony corresponds to the kind of 'automatic' synchrony observed in anesthetized animals. This nascent synchrony is reinforced in awake animals, such that there is a formation of the visual object. This process corresponds to the grabbing of attention by the object and is simultaneous with the object's actual formation for perception. In this model, attention and gamma synchrony become two sides of the same coin, as long as one is ready to extend the concept of attention (usually associated with conscious perception) to a general selection mechanism that includes an unconscious preselection mechanism. This preselection mechanism is the one observed in anesthetized animals. Attention, in its classic 'conscious' sense, is thus envisioned as the tip of the selection iceberg.

Can we therefore relate the full formation of resonant gamma assemblies to the emergence of consciousness? The answer would seem to be yes, in a certain sense; namely, that the content that is correlated with the formation of the resonant gamma assembly is accessible to verbal report, working memory, and so on. On this view, gamma synchrony is necessary for any kind of sensory awareness. This view gains support from Engel and Singer's observation that synchrony is related to all of the four presumed component processes of awareness: arousal, segmentation, selection, and working memory (Engel et al., 1999). In the following, however, we examine certain problems with this idea that lead us to qualify it.

Consciousness and Dynamical Structures: Some Qualifications

Introduction

Throughout this chapter we have explored the view that consciousness seems to require the formation of distinct, dynamic spatiotemporal structures in the brain. This view is, after all, one of the main points of agreement among the different neurodynamical proposals we reviewed earlier. In this section, we take a more critical stance regarding this central issue and put forth some qualifications we believe are important to keep in mind.

In several of the neurodynamical theories we have discussed, the notion of a distributed neuronal assembly, understood as some kind of synchronous pattern of activation, is central to explaining the neuronal basis of consciousness. As we saw in the preceding section, the gamma band has been a preferred region of the frequency domain, in which such assemblies have been studied. Whether restricted to this frequency band or spanning multiple frequencies, an emergent and stabilized spatiotemporal pattern is seen as a prerequisite for conscious experience to happen.

This viewpoint, however, raises at least two related questions. On the one hand, if such patterns are necessary for consciousness, and if we can distinguish them as having a certain spatiotemporal unity, what happens between patterns? Are we conscious during such transitions? Or is consciousness a sequence of snapshots, in which the apparently seamless fusion of successive moments into the ongoing flow of experience is achieved by some additional mechanism?

On the other hand, can we define a stable conscious moment within the flow, and are we therefore entitled to suppose that during such a moment, the assembly will 'hold' or 'contain' a certain unity, even though during that moment one can distinguish a change (or changes) in one's experience? Recall that dynamic assemblies are supposed to last for several hundreds of milliseconds, but our sensory experience can change within that duration. Suppose, for example, you are sitting in a train, staring out of the window, and as you look out into the countryside, trees, electricity poles, and other objects swiftly cross your visual field, without your being able to grasp them fully and stably. Yet you know they are trees, electricity poles, and other objects. Does your rapid experience of each of these objects correspond to a distinct assembly? Or is it rather a matter of one global assembly, in which various local assemblies 'ride'? In several neurodynamical proposals, as we have seen, an experience of an object is supposed to depend on the formation of distinct, coherent brain patterns. But a conscious moment can include full-fledged objects as well as less definite visual patterns that, although conscious to a certain extent, cannot be completely described as stable entities.

These two interrelated features – ongoing flow and fleeting experiences – need to be addressed by any neurodynamical approach to consciousness. In the remainder of this section, we discuss both features and propose a simple distinction that may help clarify the issues at hand.

Ongoing Flow and Fleeting Experiences

The issue of the ongoing, fluid nature of conscious experience is certainly not new.[25] William James, in his famous chapter on "The Stream of Thought" (James, 1890/1891, Chapter IX), provides a detailed description of the structure of this flow. He distinguishes at least two fundamental aspects – 'substantive' stable moments, in which one is actually conscious of something, and 'transitive' fleeting moments, in which one passes from one content to another. He describes consciousness as like a bird's life, for it seems to be made up of an alternation of flights and perchings. James remarks that substantive moments can be recognized as such, whereas transitive moments are quite difficult to pinpoint accurately. They present themselves as tendencies and changes between states, and not as distinct contents immediately definable in themselves, save by some retrospective exercise.

How do these phenomenological observations relate to the neurodynamical picture of the brain and its relation to consciousness? As we have seen, most neurodynamical proposals stress that each conscious state depends on a specific neural assembly or emerging dynamic pattern, but the issue of how transitions between states take place

and what they mean in terms of the experiencing subject is addressed less frequently. With regard to this issue, the proposals of Varela and Kelso are the most explicit and developed.[26] These authors stress the *metastable* nature of such patterns, so that successive moments of distributed neural coherence combine in a continuous and ongoing fashion, in contrast to a sequence of clear-cut states.[27] These approaches present attractive alternatives that seem to fit nicely with James's intuitions. They also allow for a different interpretation of what counts as a meaningful dynamic pattern. Rather than seeing these patterns as individual assemblies that arise, maintain themselves for a brief period, and then subside, they can be viewed as one itinerant trajectory, and thus as one pattern (Friston, 1997, 2000; Varela, 1999) in which the rate of change is the only internal definition of the stability of a given moment. In any case, neurodynamical approaches must deal explicitly with this issue of the apparent unity of the flow of consciousness,[28] as opposed to the unity of moment-to-moment experience.

The second question to which we wish to draw attention is related to the stability of actual perceived objects during a conscious moment. As we mentioned above, the notion of an assembly implicitly incorporates a notion of stability during the lifespan of the pattern in question. Our sensory environment, however, can be subject to rapid change in time windows lasting less than several hundred milliseconds, and yet we are, to a certain extent, aware of the change as taking place. This fact would seem to pose a difficulty for any theory that postulates a neural assembly, organized on a slower time scale, as necessary for conscious experience. On the other hand, not every object of the visual scene is perceived as stably as one might naively think. This fact is especially clear in inattentional blindness experiments (Simons, 2000). In such experiments, subjects are asked to focus on a particular task and set of stimuli in a visual scene. If an additional stimulus appears unexpectedly in that scene, the subjects are often unable to report it afterward. What is particularly striking with such 'inattentional blindness' is that it can happen even for very distinctive and salient objects. In one famous example (described in Simons, 2000), subjects watch people passing basketballs. Three people wearing white T-shirts pass a ball to each other, while three other people wearing black T-shirts pass another ball to each other. The subjects have to count the number of passes between the white players, which occur at a fast enough rate to require the full attention of the viewer. After 45 s of the display, a man in a gorilla suit walks across the scene, stops for a moment in between the players, waves his hands in the air, and then exits through the other side 5 s later. It is well documented that a high portion of the viewers fail to report seeing this gorilla.

In models like the one advocated by Singer and collaborators (see above) there is a strong correspondence between a figure/ground distinction (and therefore an object) and the formation of a synchronous assembly. This correspondence would seem to imply that only fully formed assemblies can 'support' some type of perceptual recognition of the object in question. As discussed above, however, both phenomenological observation of one's own experience and experiments such as the unnoticed gorilla suggest that a great deal of experience may be unstable and fleeting. Where would such fleeting experiences of quasi-objects fall in the framework of dynamic neural assemblies? Lamme (2003, 2004) has proposed that such fleeting experiences belong to 'phenomenal consciousness' (i.e., are subjectively experienced, but not necessarily accessible to verbal report), whereas more stable experiences belong also to 'access consciousness' (i.e., are available to verbal report and rational action guidance; see Block, 1997, 2001, for this distinction between phenomenal consciousness and access consciousness).[29] Neurodynamical models need to be able to account for this evanescent aspect of conscious experience in a more explicit way.

More precisely, we propose that the stable/fleeting duality be considered a structural feature of consciousness experience (see also the next section) and dealt with

accordingly. In a certain sense, this duality mirrors the access/phenomenal distinction, but without assuming that there can be fleeting phenomenally conscious experiences that are inaccessible in principle to verbal report. In endorsing the need to make this stable/fleeting distinction, we also stress the need to consider the possibility of the more ephemeral aspects of experience as being accessible to verbal report, if approached with the appropriate first-person and second-person phenomenological methods (Petitmengin, in press; Varela & Shear, 1999).

Given this structural distinction between stable and fleeting aspects of experience, it would be interesting to see how a neurodynamical theory that relates the formation of well-defined spatiotemporal patterns in brain activity to conscious experience would deal with the intrinsic *mobility* of any given perceptual act. For example, the feedforward stream (or sweep, FFS) is defined as the earliest activation of cells in successive areas of the cortical hierarchy. In the visual modality, it starts with the retina, the LGN, V1, and then the extrastriate visual areas and the parietal and temporal cortex. Thorpe and colleagues (Thorpe, Fize, & Marlot, 1996) have shown that the FFS is sufficient to carry out complex visual processing, such as detecting whether a natural scene presented for 20 ms contains an animal. It is tempting to relate the more stable aspect of experience to the formation of spatiotemporal patterns, in the sense of dynamic neural assemblies mediated by recurrent neural interactions, whereas the fleeting, unstable awareness could be embodied through the rapid FFS that *modulates* and continuously affects the formation of such assemblies while not being fully excluded from a certain level of perceptual experience. This proposal is highly speculative, but is intended simply as a way to highlight the necessity of dealing with the stable/fleeting structure that appears to be inherent in each and every conscious moment.

To conclude this section on qualifications to the dynamic approach, we would like briefly to draw the reader's attention to another aspect of consciousness that is significant in light of the preceding discussion and the overall topic of this chapter. This aspect is the subjectivity or subjective character of consciousness. For example, Damasio (1999) has stressed that, in addition to understanding the neurobiological basis for the stream of object-directed conscious experiences, it is also necessary to understand the neurobiological basis for "the sense of self in the act of knowing" (Parvizi & Damasio, 2001; see also Panksepp, 1998, for a convergent argument, and Wicker et al., 2003). The sense of self with which Damasio is concerned is a primitive kind of conscious self-awareness that does not depend on reflection, introspection, or possession of the concept of a self. In phenomenological terms, it corresponds to the fundamental 'ipseity' (I-ness or selfhood, by contrast with otherness or alterity) belonging to subjective experience (see Chapters 4 and 19).

In a related line of argument, Searle (2000) has suggested that a major drawback of current attempts to uncover the neural correlates of consciousness in human beings is that they begin with already conscious subjects. He advocates a 'field of consciousness'[30] viewpoint, in which the perceptual experience of an object arises as a modification of a pre-existing conscious 'ground-state' that is unified, subjective, and qualitative. In this context, the transition between conscious states need not be punctuated by a radical gap in consciousness, but can rather be a modulation of a more basic state of background consciousness, which accounts for the fact that even such transitive moments are felt as belonging to oneself. Here dynamic patterns in the form of transient and distributed coactive assemblies would mainly reflect the nervous system's own homeodynamic activity; that is, its maintenance of a range of internal regularities in the face of its ongoing compensation for the systematic perturbations to which it is exposed from both the sensory environment and the internal bodily milieu (Damasio, 1999; Maturana & Varela, 1980).

Nevertheless, it remains difficult to see how metastable assemblies of coactive neurons could by themselves account for this crucial aspect of the subjectivity of consciousness. This crucial feature is often put to the side as something to deal with once the issue of the neural correlates of perceptual consciousness has been resolved (e.g., Crick & Koch, 2003). Our view, however, is that unless the subjectivity of consciousness is adequately confronted and its biological basis understood, proposals about the neural correlates of perceptual consciousness will provide limited insight into consciousness overall. Thus, the issue of subjectivity is a non-trival matter that any neurodynamical approach must confront sooner or later if it is to become a cogent theory of consciousness. We briefly pick up this thread in the when discussing how to relate phenomenological descriptions to neurodynamical accounts.

The Future: Beyond Correlation?

Introduction

So far we have dealt primarily with the issue of meaningful spatiotemporal patterns in the brain and their relevance to the study of conscious experience. It may have become increasingly evident to the reader, however, that the issue of *how* to relate such patterns to *experience* as a first-person phenomenon has been left untouched. Indeed, one of the major challenges facing the cognitive sciences is precisely how to relate these two domains – the domain of third-person biobehavioral processes and the domain of first-person subjective experience. What is the right way to conceptualize this relation, and what is the best way to approach it methodologically? These questions have not yet received anything near a satisfactory answer from the neuroscientific community. We do not intend to propose an answer to them here. Rather, we wish to highlight some conceptual and practical issues in the quest to understand the relation between these two domains while keeping in mind the dynamical insights we have gained from the previous exposition.

Correlation and Emergence

The first question that comes to mind is the extent to which the entire neurodynamical approach rests on a merely correlational strategy. In coarse terms, one isolates a given target experience, say the perception of a figure; one determines the neural patterns that correlate with the moment the subject sees the figure; and one then concludes that the conscious experience depends on such neural patterns.[31] In the last decade or so this correlational approach, in the form of the search for the neural correlates of consciousness, has undergone important developments and become more sophisticated with regard to its conceptual formulation, methodological commitments, and empirical results (Block, 1996; Crick & Koch, 1990, 1998; Rees, Kreiman, & Koch, 2002). Here the central idea is that, rather than formulating explanatory principles about the relation between neural activity and experience, what has to be done first is to determine those neural processes that can count as a "specific system in the brain whose activity correlates directly with states of consciousness" (according to the Association for the Scientific Study of Consciousness, cited by Chalmers, 2000, pp. 17–18). Once such processes have been found, then one can turn to the issue of how they are causally related to experience itself.[32]

Neurodynamics as a research program is devoted, at least methodologically, to this correlational strategy and in this sense remains closely linked to the NCC program. Of course, this commitment is due to the fact that, in the scientific tradition, establishing a relation between two target events or phenomena is mainly approached by establishing a correlation in their occurrence. Causal relations can then be assessed on the basis of altering one of the target events and observing whether and how the other changes. This 'interventionist' strategy can be employed in the case of brain functioning and consciousness by using microstimulation during surgery or transcranial magentic stimulation (TMS). Nevertheless, by itself this strategy does not guarantee the elucidation of the underlying causal mechanisms.

Several of the proposals reviewed above, however, formulate explicit links between the neural and the experiential in terms of the notion of *emergence* or *emergent phenomena* and thus can be considered as attempts to go beyond a purely correlational description. Although 'emergence' is a complex concept subject to multiple interpretations (see Keslo, 1995; Thompson, 2007; Thompson & Varela, 2001), in simple terms it can be defined as follows: A process is emergent when (i) it belongs to an ensemble or network of elements, (ii) it does not belong to any single element, and (iii) it happens spontaneously given both the way the elements interact locally and the way those interactions are globally constrained and regulated. Thus, an emergent process cannot be understood at the level of local components taken individually, but depends rather on the relations established between them. Furthermore, an emergent process not only depends on the local components but also constrains their degrees of freedom, a two-way process that has been termed 'circular caulality' (Haken, 1983). Especially in Freeman's and Varela's approaches, conscious experience is considered to be an emergent process. The difference between their views is that whereas Freeman (1999a,b) proposes that consciousness is a global brain state, Varela proposes that consciousness may encompass multiple cycles of organismic regulation that are not fully restricted to the brain (Thompson & Varela, 2001). Neverthless, although principles of emergence have been clearly formulated at the level of physical processes and molecular interactions (Nicolis & Prigogine, 1989), in the case of conscious experience, such principles still need to be understood and formulated in a more rigorous way. We believe that the study of complex systems offers a promising approach in this direction (Le Van Quyen, 2003; Thompson, 2007).

Gaining Access to Experience

As mentioned earlier, any neurodynamical approach to consciousness must eventually deal with the issue of how to describe experience itself. In the previous sections of this chapter we have discussed mainly spatiotemporal brain patterns in relation to consciousness, but we now turn to consider the other side of the issue; namely, how to gain access to experience itself and render it accessible to scientific description.

On the more operational side of this question, one can ask how it is possible to set up an experimental paradigm that addresses the issue of gaining access to experience in a way that allows us to study the underlying neuronal processes. Not all that is going on in the brain is necessarily related to what the subject is consciously experiencing. It is known that, during our conscious engagement with the world, a non-negligible part of our adapted behavior depends on non-conscious processes that are carried on without us being aware of their functioning. For example, do you have any feeling whatsoever of the oxygen level in your blood right now? Yet this bodily state of affairs can be crucial to your capacity to be here right now reading this text. Although this example is extreme, carefully crafted experiments reveal that even perceptual information can be used to guide behavior in a non-conscious way. For example, when a subject is presented with a small circle surrounded by larger circles, the small circle appears smaller than if it is presented in isolation. Yet if the subject is asked to reach for it, his fingers adopt a grip size that is consistent with the true size of the circle and not with its illusory dimension (Milner & Goodale, 1995). Another classic example is known as blindsight (Danckert & Goodale, 2000; Weiskrantz, 1990). In this neurological condition, conscious visual experience is impaired due to damage in primary visual cortex, yet subjects can produce quite accurate motor actions, such as introducing an envelope through a horizontal slot or pointing to a target they claim not to see. Thus, the problem arises of how to determine those neural processes that show some kind of direct relation to the actual conscious experience of the subject, in contrast to those that sustain ongoing and non-conscious adaptive behavior in the world.

Several experimental approaches have become paradigmatic in this endeavor. In general, the rationale behind these experiments is to dissociate what is presented to the subject from what the subject sees in order to distinguish the neural patterns that are specific for conscious perception. Among these approaches, three stand out as the most well studied and influential. The first is visual masking (Dehaene & Naccache, 2001; Hollender, 1986), in which short-lived visual stimuli flanked by meaningless masks are not perceived consciously, yet can alter future behavior (an index of non-conscious processing). The second is inattentional blindness and change blindness (O'Regan & Noë, 2001; Simons, 2000), in which diverting the subject's attention can render major changes in the scene unnoticed. The third is binocular rivalry (Blake, 1989; Blake & Logothetis, 2002), in which the presentation to each eye of a different image induces an alternation in conscious perception between the two alternatives, despite the fact that both are always present.

This last experimental paradigm is particularly relevant to the issue of gaining access to experience because it provides an ongoing, slow phenomenon that can be described by the subject. In virtue of its alternating character, the experience lends itself to repetitive scrutiny, in order to better characterize 'what it is like' subjectively to undergo it. Finally, because both stimuli do not change, yet perception changes dramatically, binocular rivalry evidences the endogenous and ongoing character of experience and therefore calls for attending to those neural processes that share this fundamentally dynamical structure.[33]

These considerations suggest that, in addition to using experimental paradigms for dissociating unconscious and conscious processes, we need to be able to capture the dynamics of experience itself. Hence it is necessary for the experimenter to take measurements of each phenomenon – the dynamics of the brain and the dynamics of experience. Measurements should provide public data; that is, information that can be shared with another observer. One recurrent problem with consciousness is that the direct observation of experience is accessible only to the subject, and such observation is not a public measurement in itself. The experience therefore needs to be transcribed into public data in a subsequent step to provide so-called first-person data. What the status of first-person data is and to what extent the subject can play an active role in describing his or her experience are matters of active debate in the science of consciousness (Jack & Roepstorff, 2003; Varela & Shear, 1999). We cannot review these debates here. Rather, in the remainder of this section, we wish to explore two complementary lines of investigation that are relevant to the issue of making experience more scientifically accessible.

A 'Topological Approach' to First-Person Data

In a general sense, one expects measures to be somehow organized in a universe, the measurement universe, that is the set of all the possible 'values' that measure can take. The term 'universe' must be understood in its statistical sense and simply refers to the set of possible values, states, or items that can be valid measurements. For instance, a single word is one particular item among all the possible words. The universe may be discrete (as for words or sentences) or continuous (as for magnetic fields). In any case, a measurement will be the selection of one particular value allowed in a given universe, based on the present state of the observed phenomenon. For a given subjective experience, this may correspond to the selection of one description, among all the possible written descriptions that can be produced (say) in a couple of minutes.[34]

We mentioned that the measurement should be 'organized'. This means that it should be provided with some sort of topology: It should be possible to estimate a distance between two measures. Indeed, it should be possible to say whether measure A is closer to measure B than it is to measure C (see Fell 2004 for a convergent discussion). Without any kind of topology, it would be difficult to compare the dynamics of the two phenomena. For instance, the notion of *sta-*

bility requires distance. Stability means that the phenomenon remains somewhat constant during a certain time interval; it further means that the *distance* between consecutive measures is shorter now than what it was in earlier observation windows. The notion of distance is also central to the concept of *recurrence*: If we find a certain neural pattern that correlates with a conscious experience, we expect this neural pattern to repeat when the same experience repeats. Because neither neural patterns nor experiences repeat in a perfectly reproducible way, we also need a way to know whether a certain neural pattern or experience looks like one that occurred in the past. This requires a quantification of resemblance between two measures; that is, a *distance*.

Note that this first definition is large enough to include many possible measures. In fact, a dance could be considered as a measure or a series of measures if each successive body configuration constitutes by itself a measure. A drawing could also be a measure. But to be actually useful, we insist that the subject and the experimenter should agree on a measure of distance, which enables anybody to evaluate the degree of similarity between two measurements. The Basic Requirement (so called in the following) is that the distance should be consistent with the experience of the subject (as only the subject can tell): If measure A is closer to measure B than to measure C, then the elements of experience that led the subject to select measure A should appear to him as closer to the elements that led him to choose measure B than to the elements associated with measure C.[35] This requirement directly implies, for instance, that recurrences in the subject's experience should translate into recurrences in the measure.

Once provided with measures of (some elements of) the subjective experience and with measures of neural phenomena, it should be possible to establish a relationship between the two phenomena by comparing the dynamics of those measures: Related phenomena should provide sets of measures with compatible dynamics. That is, once again, stability in experience should be associated with stability (or stationarity) in the neural dynamics, whereas moments of change should be correlated with changing (or non-stationary) neural processes.[36]

A 'Structural Invariants' Approach to First-Person Data

As a complement to the fine-grained topological description presented above, it seems possible to adopt what can be termed a 'structural invariant' strategy. Here the main aim is to obtain, through descriptions of the target experience, an account of that which is invariant (or stable) as a feature of the experience, regardless of whether it is one or another subject that undergoes it. The roots of this approach go back to the method adopted in phenomenological philosophy (see Chapter 4). Here, through several repetitions of the same experience in different contexts, one can arrive first at a certain subjective invariant, and then, through contrast with other subjects, intersubjective invariants that are present in the original experience, no matter how many versions of it one tries and no matter how many different subjects engage in it. A traditional example is the structure of the visual field, in which what one sees focally always appears as a relatively detailed center surrounded by an increasingly less detailed region, which, at the limit, fades into an ungraspable indeterminacy. In the particular context of the neurodynamics of consciousness, the relevance of this type of approach can be illustrated by recent work on the experience of binocular rivalry (Cosmelli et al., 2004).

As we briefly described above, binocular rivalry occurs whenever one is presented with dissimilar images, one to each eye. The subjective experience is that of an ongoing alternation between both possible images, with only one of them consciously perceived at a time. If the images are large, then during the transition from one to the other, one can distinguish a mosaic, patchwork pattern composed of both images, but as a rule, if the adequate contrast and luminance con-ditions are met, at any given point of the visual image, only one of the images (or part of it) will be seen (will dominate) in an exclusive way. In general, binocular rivalry is considered a clear-cut alternation between two states, and average measures of the brain state during one or the other dominance period are contrasted. Most commonly, the subject's indication via a button press of the moment when the alternation takes place is used to fix a rigid temporal reference around which the average brain responses are defined.

We recently used this experimental protocol to investigate the underlying neural patterns, but with the specific objective of describing their spatiotemporal evolution throughout extended periods and without presupposing a rigid two-state structure (Cosmelli et al., 2004). To do so, we worked with a group of subjects who were extensively exposed to the experience and produced free, ongoing descriptions of what they were seeing and how they were experiencing it. As conflicting stimuli we used a human face and a moving pattern with an intrinsic frequency (a frequency tag; see Brown & Norcia, 1997; Tononi & Edelman, 1998). This intrinsic frequency was incorporated in order to tag a neural evoked response that could be followed by magnetoencephalography (MEG).

The descriptions produced by the subjects showed some interesting features: In addition to experiencing the well-known alternation between both images, the subjects repeatedly described this alternation as extremely variable in the way it occurred. Although sometimes the alternation from one image to the other started in the center of the field and progressed toward the outer limits, in other occasions it began on one side, from the top or the bottom, or even from the external borders, and then progressively invaded the pre-existing image. Most subjects claimed that it was difficult to give a stable description of how these transitions took place, because at each time they developed in a different way. Nevertheless, all subjects invariantly stated that dominance periods would alternate and recur, no matter what the subjects did or how much they tried to prevent it from happening.

At a first coarse level, these descriptions already provide us with some crucial aspects of the experience of rivalry: This experience is one of an ongoing flow of *recurrent* dominant periods, in which alternations are extremely *variable* in the way they develop. This feature is indeed a hallmark of binocular rivalry that will be experienced by any normal observer and is thus a structural invariant in the sense described above. Although this descriptive feature is not particularly novel, it nevertheless points toward a concrete restriction in the *methods* we need to choose to analyze the underlying neural processes (and consequently what we understand as the neural underpinnings of consciousness). If we wish to reveal neural patterns that are meaningful in the context of this specific experience, then we cannot impose a rigid temporal grid and suppose that there is such a thing as an average transition from one image to the other. This point, however, is rarely acknowledged. We therefore developed a statistical framework that considered significant any neural activity that is recurrent in time, without any restrictions on the temporal pattern of activation. The result was an original description of a network of distributed cortical regions that showed synchronous activation modulated in concert with conscious dominance periods. Moreover, the dynamics of modulation of these brain patterns showed a striking similarity to the bell-type pattern that William James had predicted (more than a century ago) would underlie the occurrence of any given conscious moment (James, 1890/1981).

An important contribution of the structural invariant approach is thus that it can serve as an effective constraint on how we study the dynamic brain patterns. Basic phenomenological observation shows that experience (or the stream of consciousness) is at least (i) dynamic and ongoing; (ii) continuous;[37] (iii) able to be parsed, so one can distinguish in a given subjective experience components or aspects that

are more visual, or more auditory, for instance, and eventually segment it along such dimensions; and (iv) recurrent, in the sense that we recognize objects, feelings, thoughts, memories, etc., as seen or felt before, even though they are never experienced in the same way. These properties, although certainly not exhaustive of our conscious lives, do suggest that methods that allow for processes of compatible dynamics should be preferred if we want to advance in our understanding of the neural underpinnings of consciousness.

In addition to this methodological constraint, however, the structural invariants approach can potentially make a further contribution. As we mentioned above, one of the most prominent structural invariants of consciousness is precisely its subjective character, in the sense of its fundamental prereflective and preconceptual 'ipsiety' (see Zahavi, 2005, for an extended discussion). This backdrop of consciousness pervades the occurrence of specific states of perceptual consciousness. It would appear to call for an explanation not so much in terms of the dynamic behavior of the system (e.g., only in terms of the dynamical properties of the nervous system's patterns of activity), but rather in terms of how a certain *self-referring perspective can emerge from a certain dynamical organization* (Rudrauf et al., 2003; Thompson, 2007). Whether this type of account is beyond the domain of neurodynamics as we have defined it here is an empirical issue. The crucial point is that if, through some enriched neurodynamical plus organismic plus biological approach (e.g., Damasio, 1999; Varela, 1979), one could account for the *conditions of possibility of a minimally subjective system*, then transcending a purely correlational strategy would become a real possibility.

Can We Avoid the Pitfalls of Introspectionism?

One recurrent question, when discussing the use of first-person data, is how to avoid the pitfalls of introspectionism. Introspectionism was an attempt to use introspection as a scientific method to elaborate psychological theories. It was the main scientific approach to mental phenomena at the beginning of psychology, but was later dismissed by the scientific community in favor of behaviorism (reviewed by Vermersch, in Depraz, Varela, & Vermersch, 2003). The main problem with introspection, as used at that time, was that it provided conflicting theories. The root of the problem was in fact methodological: It was never possible to ascertain whether the introspective reports met the Basic Requirement mentioned above, and there were serious doubts about the correspondence between the descriptions of the experiences and the experiences themselves. On the other hand, there was little explicit description of the introspective method by which to proceed to explore and describe experience, and hence the actual testing and refinement of the research method, as opposed to the content of its descriptions, remained underdeveloped (Varela, 1996). Consequently, an important part of the cognitive science community is generally reluctant to use first-person data. Is it therefore possible to build a neurodynamics of consciousness, given that it must rely on first-person data?

Our position is that the whole issue is a technical one: If the measure providing first-person data meets the Basic Requirement described above, then the measure is useful. Alternatively, in the structural invariant approach, if a given invariant is stable across all subjects for a given experimental paradigm, it should be considered valid. In fact, the real question is not whether cognitive scientists should 'trust the subject', but in which conditions they can trust the subject and what they should ask. First-person data, defined as measures of the subjective experience, are continuously being used in psychophysics: When a subject presses a button to indicate that he saw a blue square, and not a red circle, he provides a measure of his immediate perceptual experience in its simplest form. In this extremely simple form, first-person reports are considered as perfectly valid and trustworthy. At the other extreme, first-person data about the precise dynamic of subtle variations of emotions would probably be considered less reliable (this means that they would not meet the Basic Requirement – the same subtle variations would not lead to the *same* first-person data, if repeated).[38] So, in fact, the real question concerning first-person data is, Where shall we draw the line between what is acceptable, perfectly good data, and what is not?[39] A related question of equal importance is whether this line is the same for all individuals and whether it is fixed within a single individual or whether training can move the line (see Chapter 19).[40] We believe that this question should become central in cognitive neuroscience in the near future, especially in view of the advent of new fields, such as the neuroscience of emotions or the neuroscience of consciousness itself. Such emergent fields rely heavily on trustworthy measures of subjective experience.

Conclusion

In summary, the neurodynamics of consciousness is an attempt to relate two dynamical phenomena that take place in a subject – the formation of metastable patterns in the subject's neural activity and the transient emergence of discernible elements or aspects of his or her conscious experience. To establish such a relation, cognitive neuroscientists need to observe systematic similarities between the dynamical properties of these two phenomena. In this sense, the neurodynamical approach works at the level of correlations, albeit refined ones. On the experiential side, this approach requires the subject to provide first-person descriptions that can serve as 'public' measures of experience, with at least two objectives. The first objective is to capture reliably the degree of similarity (or disparity) between different subjective phenomena and produce timings that can be compared to the timing of neural measurements. The second objective is to produce descriptions of the structural invariants of the experience in question, in order to constrain the methods that are chosen to determine which neural activity is to be considered significant. It is not yet clear how much of the complexity of consciousness can be revealed in this way, and this question constitutes an important field of investigation for the future.

Notes

1. We define in more detail the notions of functional segregation and cooperative interaction in the section, "The Search for Meaningful Spatiotemporal Patterns in the Brain." Here we only say that they can be considered analogous to local specialization and collective interaction, respectively.

2. This situation is, of course, only suggestive. A dream state might be a more rigorous case of a true sensory filter (Llinas & Pare, 1991).

3. One might rightly consider other variables, such as the local concentrations of certain neurotransmitters. Quantitative measures of the glial system should probably also be included. In fact, there is no one single way of choosing which variables to include in the system. This choice is largely driven by our current knowledge of the nervous system, which unfortunately remains quite limited. As a starting point, one needs to keep the following three elements in mind when choosing the variables of the system: (1) The time scale: If one candidate variable maintains a constant value during the time of observation of the system, then it does not need to be counted as a variable, but rather can be considered as a parameter (see below). (2) The spatial scale: The nervous system can be modeled at several scales – molecules, neurons, neural populations, etc. The variables should be meaningful at the spatial level of investigation. (3) The interdependence within the system: If the value of one candidate variable is fully determined by the values of the other variables, then it does not need to be included in the system.

4. Alternative definitions of the nervous system as a dynamical system can include the synaptic weights themselves among the variables. At certain time scales, the weights are a function of the evolution of the membrane potentials; for instance, via long-term potentiation (LTP) mechanisms. Models that include a changing connectivity can quickly become unmanageable, however, both mathematically and computationally (but see Ito & Kaneko, 2002).

5. For further details on this subject, we strongly recommend one of the original and most influential sources in neurodynamics by Walter Freeman (Freeman, 1975). See also Bressler & Kelso, 2001.

6. For this reason, it would not necessarily be meaningful to repeat the same perturbation over and over to study the average reaction of a chaotic system, for there is no guarantee that this average reaction would have any meaning. Yet, such averaging procedures are the basis of almost all the imaging studies of the nervous system.

7. Note that the exact reaction of the system – that is, the precise trajectory that the system will follow to converge on the attractor – can be very different from one olfactory stimulation to another, even though the target attractor is the same for all. Therefore, the existence of attractors is compatible with the intrinsic variability of chaotic systems.

8. A recent review notes that "incontrovertible proof that EEG reflects any simple chaotic process is generally lacking. There are grounds for reservation concerning reports of the dimensionality of EEG from direct measurement. Fundamental difficulties lie in the applicability of estimation algorithms to EEG data because of limitation in the size of data sets, noise contamination, and lack of signal stationarity" (Wright & Liley, 1996).

9. In human electrophysiology, for instance, the dominant paradigm is recording the EEG of human subjects while presenting them with series of similar sensory stimulations. The signal studied is the evoked potential: the mean EEG response averaged over all the stimulations. The intertrial variability is considered as noise and disappears in the averaging procedure.

10. As Le Van Quyen (2003, p. 69) notes, "In physics, what is usually referred to as self-organization is the spontaneous formation of well organized structures, patterns, or behaviors, from random initial conditions. Typically, these systems possess a large number of elements or variables interacting in a complex way, and thus have very large state

spaces. However, when started with some initial conditions, they tend to converge to small areas of this space which can be interpreted as a form of emergent eigenbehavior."

11. Mutual information quantifies the ability to predict the behavior of one element in the system from the behavior of one or several other elements (David, Cosmelli, & Friston, 2004). This measure is one of several tools used to quantify statistical dependence within a system. Note that what counts as a spatiotemporal structure will depend on which measure of statistical dependence is used.

12. "It seems that short-term memory may be a reverberation in the closed loops of the cell assembly and between cell assemblies" (Hebb, as cited in Amit, 1994, p. 621).

13. A precise definition of synchronization between chaotic systems can be found in (Pikovsky, Zaks, Rosenblum, Osipov, & Kurths, 1997, p. 680): "The phase synchronization of a chaotic system can be defined as the occurrence of a certain relation between the phases of interacting systems or between the phase of a system and that of an external force, while the amplitudes can remain chaotic and are, in general, uncorrelated (see also Brown & Kocarev, 2000; Rosenblum, Pikovsky, & Kurths, 1996).

14. In Freeman's words, "preafference provides an order parameter that shapes the attractor landscapes, making it easier to capture expected or desired stimuli by enlarging or deepening the basins of their attractors. [. . .] corollary discharges do this by a macroscopic bias that tilts sensory attractor landscapes" (Freeman, 1999a, p. 112).

15. Edelman and Tononi distinguish primary consciousness from higher-order consciousness. The former involves the capacity to construct a mental scene to guide behavior without the semantic, linguistic, and self-reflective capacities unique to the latter.

16. Here we are referring to desynchronized EEG in the classical sleep/wake cycle sense, in which desynchronized gamma and beta frequencies dominate the EEG of the waking state, by contrast with the synchronized slow-wave delta frequency EEG of sleep. This notion of desynchronized and synchronized EEG as a whole should not be confused with the synchronization and desynchronization of particular EEG signals, which is more

accurately termed phase-locking and phase-scattering respectively (see below).

17. Mathematical methods are available to detect correlations between localized metabolic activations as measured by fMRI and PET. The advantage of these methods is that they provide maps of functional connectivity with a high spatial resolution in normal human subjects. These methods, however, measure interactions that occur on the time scale of a couple of seconds at best. This temporal resolution may be sufficient when studying the neural correlates of slow experiential patterns, such as the evolution of certain emotions (Buchel & Friston, 1997).

18. The fractal dimension d of a trajectory can be envisioned as follows: Imagine that each point along the trajectory is in fact a small ball of lead. Then, the total mass of lead contained in a sphere centered on the trajectory will increase as a function of the sphere radius r proportionally to rd. If the trajectory occupies all the space, then d is equal to the dimension of the space. If the trajectory is a straight line or a circle, d equals 1.

19. See the previous note.

20. Note that synchrony can occur between two neurons without an actual direct relation between them, if they are driven by a common driver. This fact reveals one of the limitations of the synchrony measure so far. The three-neuron system that includes the driver, however, can be seen as a larger spatiotemporal pattern revealed by the synchrony measure.

21. This theory was based, among other things, on the observation of false conjunctions in the absence of attention: When presented briefly with a red square and a blue circle outside of the scope of attention, a subject would sometimes report having seen a red circle and a blue square. Such perception is typically an incorrect binding of the color and shape attributes.

22. This has led to the suggestion that gamma-band synchrony is the trace of similar processes in the emergence of dreaming consciousness in REM sleep and waking consciousness (Engel et al., 1999).

23. We do not wish at this point to step into the debate about which brain areas actually participate in the generation of sensory awareness (see Rees, Kreiman, & Koch, 2002).

24. Letter strings presented to the subject for 1 s, for instance, generate an induced gamma response that lasts roughly only for the first 500 ms (Lachaux, unpublished observations).

25. For an extensive presentation of questions concerning the experience of time, we refer the reader to the notable work by Charles Sherover (1991).

26. Varela in particular proposed a neurodynamical account of Husserl's phenomenological account of time consciousness (see Varela, 1999, and for further extensive discussion, Thompson, 2007).

27. Tononi and Edelman (1998) do mention that their dynamic core is constantly changing, but they do not develop this point further.

28. The question of whether this unity is illusory or real remains an unresolved problem (Van-Rullen & Koch, 2003).

29. Lamme's distinction, however, is not completely equivalent to Block's initial proposal (Block, 1996). In its original formulation, phenomenal consciousness is subjective experience, in the sense that there is something it is like for the subject to be in the state. Access consciousness, on the other hand, is an information-theoretical concept that is supposed to account for the availability of conscious information for further rational guidance of behavior, including reportability. The conceptual and empirical validity of this distinction are a matter of lively debate in the science of consciousness (see Block, 1997, 2000; see also the discussion in Thompson, Lutz, & Cosmelli, 2005).

30. The notion that consciousness has a unified field structure goes back to A. Gurwitsch (1964).

31. We see below that this general characterization needs some important qualifications, in particular at the level of determining what counts as a valid conscious experience and how to contrast such a conscious experience with possibly unconscious processing in similar situations.

32. The theoretical validity and empirical plausibility of this approach remain a matter of extensive discussion. Rather than endorse or reject this approach, we wish to highlight it as an influential approach that can serve as a reference for further discussion. The interested reader is referred to several interesting publications (and references therein)

on this controversial and interesting question (Crick & Koch, 2003; Metzinger, 2000; Noë & Thompson, 2004a,b; Pessoa, Thompson, & Noë, 1998).

33. This feature pertains to multistable and ambiguous perception in general (see Leopold & Logothetis, 1999).

34. This way of defining measures of subjective experience should be sufficiently general to include all the measures used in psychophysics: Choosing to press one button among two, or to press one at a particular time, for example, fits into that definition. Psychophysics is indeed partly about first-person data. For example, the experimenter shows a shape to a subject and asks him to press button A if what he sees looks more like a circle, and button B if it looks more like a square. The subject's answer is based on one particular element of his subjective experience (he selects one particular action in the universe of allowed responses, based on the observation of his conscious visual experience). The button press can therefore be seen as a (very crude) description of a conscious content.

35. In other words, what is needed here is first a possible one-to-one *monotonic* correspondence between the phenomena under investigation and the measurements. 'Monotonic' is to be understood in its usual mathematical sense: For three phenomena pa, pb, and pc and their corresponding measurements $m(pa)$, $m(pb)$, and $m(pc)$, it would be desirable that if $D(pa,pb) > D(pa,pc)$ (D being a subjective distance between experiential phenomena), then $d(m(pa), m(pb)) > d(m(pa),m(pc))$ (d being the distance defined by the experimenter and the subject in the universe of measures;for a convergent perspective see also Fell, 2004).

36. This relation implies an additional requirement for the measures of the subjective experience: They should be timed. Indeed, the dynamics of experiential phenomena can only be accessed through *series* of consecutive timed measures (as simple as a series of button presses, for instance, or the time course of the pressure applied on a joystick). Therefore, to establish a strong relation between the dynamics of an experience and the formation of certain patterns of neural activity, one should be able to say that the experience started at time $t = 2s$ and fully developed between $t = 5s$ and $t = 10s$

(this is easy to understand in the case of an emotional reaction to a sound, for example). It does not follow, however, that the *time as experienced* must correspond precisely to the *timing of neural processes*. The former is a matter of the *content* of experience and the latter of the neural *vehicles* that (in ways we do not fully understand) embody or encode those contents. Within certain small temporal windows, a given neural vehicle could encode one *event* as happening *before* another *event*, even though that *neural vehicle* occurs *after* the *neural vehicle* encoding the second event (see Dennett & Kinsbourne, 1992).

37. 'Continuous' here is not meant as the opposite of discrete, but rather is used to mean that consciousness does not jump around with no connection whatsoever from one sort of experience to another.

38. Consider, however, the possibility of working with individuals who can produce and stabilize mental states more reliably (see Chapter 19). The issue of working with 'experts' or trained subjects is important and controversial (Jack & Roepstorff, 2003; Lutz & Thompson, 2003; Varela & Shear, 1999; Chapter 19).

39. Cognitive psychologists sometimes ask subjects very difficult questions, so how can they trust their answers? Why shall we trust the button presses of a subject during a binocular rivalry experiment? The subject is asked to press the button as soon as one pattern dominates completely, but how can one be sure that the subject can actually do this task reliably or that he has this sort of fine capacity to attend to his own visual experience and its dynamics in time?

40. There is a similar problem with the measure of neural events. For instance, with EEG, the noise level is sometimes simply so strong that measures of gamma activity cannot be made: The Basic Requirement is not met.

References

Abarbanel, H. D., & Rabinovich, M. I. (2001). Neurodynamics: Nonlinear dynamics and neurobiology. *Current Opinion in Neurobiology*, 11(4), 423–430.

Abeles, M. (1991). *Corticonics*. New York: Cambridge University Press.

Amit, D. J. (1994). The Hebbian paradigm reintegrated: Local reverberations as internal representations. *Behavioral and Brain Sciences*, 18, 617–626.

Arbib, M. A. (2002). *Handbook of brain theory and neural networks* (2nd ed.). Cambridge, MA: MIT Press.

Arbib, M. A., Érdi, P., & Szentágothai, J. (1997). *Neural organization: Structure, function, and dynamics*. Cambridge, MA: MIT Press.

Arieli, A., Sterkin, A., Grinvald, A., & Aertsen, A..(1996). Dynamics of ongoing activity: Explanation of the large variability in evoked cortical responses. *Science*, 273(5283), 1868–1871.

Ashby, R. (1952). *Design for a brain*. London.: Chapman-Hall.

Baars, B. J., & Franklin, S. (2003). How conscious experience and working memory interact. *Trends in Cognitive Sciences*, 7(4), 166–172.

Blake, R. A. (1989). A neural theory of binocular rivalry. *Psychology Review*, 96, 145–167.

Blake, R., & Logothetis, N. K. (2002). Visual competition. *Nature Reviews Neuroscience*, 3(1), 13–21.

Block, N. (1996). How can we find the neural correlate of consciousness? *Trends in Neurosciences*, 19(11), 456–459.

Block, N. (1997). On a confusion about a function of consciousness. In N. Block, O. Flanagan, & G. Güzeldere (Eds.), *The nature of consciousness: Philosophical debates* (pp. 375–416). Cambridge, MA: MIT Press.

Block, N. (2001). Paradox and cross purposes in recent work on consciousness. *Cognition*, 79, 197–219.

Bressler, S. L. (1995). Large-scale cortical networks and cognition. *Brain Research Review*, 20(3), 288–304.

Bressler, S. L., & Freeman, W. J. (1980). Frequency analysis of olfactory system EEG in cat, rabbit, and rat. *Electroencephalography and Clinical Neurophysiology*, 50(1–2), 19–24.

Bressler, S. L., & Kelso, J. A. (2001). Cortical coordination dynamics and cognition. *Trends in Cognitive Sciences*, 5(1), 26–36.

Brown, R., & Kocarev, L. (2000). A unifying definition of synchronization for dynamical systems. *Chaos*, 10(2), 344–349.

Brown, R. J., & Norcia, A. M. (1997). A method for investigating binocular rivalry in real-time with steady-state VEP. *Vision Research*, 37, 2401–2408.

Buchel, C., & Friston, K. J. (1997). Modulation of connectivity in visual pathways by attention: Cortical interactions evaluated with structural equation modelling and fMRI. *Cerebral Cortex*, 7(8), 768–778.

Chalmers, D. J. (2000). What is a neural correlate of consciousness? In T. Metzinger (Ed.), *Neural correlates of consciousness: Empirical and conceptual questions*. Cambridge, MA: MIT Press.

Chandrasekhar, S. (1961). *Hydrodynamic and hydromagnetic stability*. Oxford: Oxford University Press.

Cosmelli, D., David, O., Lachaux, J. P., Martinerie, J., Garnero, L., Renault, B., et al. (2004). Waves of consciousness: Ongoing cortical patterns during binocular rivalry. *Neuroimage*, 23(1), 128–140.

Crick, F. C., & Koch, C. (1990). Towards a neurobiological theory of consciousness. *Seminars in Neuroscience*, 2, 263–275.

Crick, F. C., & Koch, C. (1998). Consciousness and neuroscience. *Cerebral Cortex*, 8(2), 97–107.

Crick, F. C., & Koch, C. (2003). A framework for consciousness. *Nature Neuroscience*, 6(2), 119–126.

Crutchfield, J. P., & Kaneko, K. (1987). Phenomenology of spatiotemporal chaos. In *Directions in chaos* (pp. 272–353). World Scientific.

Damasio, A. R. (1998). Investigating the biology of consciousness. *Philosophical Transactions of the Royal Society London B: Biological Science*, 353(1377), 1879–1882.

Damasio, A. (1999). *The feeling of what happens: Body and emotion in the making of consciousness*. New York: Harcourt.

Danckert, J., & Goodale, M. A. (2000). A conscious route to unconscious vision. *Current Biology*, 10(2), 64–67.

David, O., Cosmelli, D., & Friston, K. J. (2004). Evaluation of different measures of functional connectivity using a neural mass model. *Neuroimage*, 21(2), 659–673.

Dehaene, S., Kerszberg, M., & Changeux, J. P. (1998). A neuronal model of a global workspace in effortful cognitive tasks. *Proceedings of the National Academy of Sciences USA*, 95(24), 14529–14534.

Dehaene, S., & Naccache, L. (2001). Towards a cognitive neuroscience of consciousness: Basic evidence and a workspace framework. *Cognition*, 79(1–2), 1–37.

Dehaene, S., Sergent, C., & Changeux, J. P. (2003). A neuronal network model linking subjective reports and objective physiological data during conscious perception. *Proceedings of the National Academy of Sciences USA*, 100(14), 8520–8525.

Dennett, D. C., & Kinsbourne, M. (1992). Time and the observer: The where and when of consciousness in the brain. *Behavioral and Brain Sciences*, 15, 183–247.

Depraz, N., Varela, F., & Vermersch, P. (2003). *On becoming aware. A pragmatics of experiencing*. Amsterdam: Benjamins.

Edelman, G. M., & Tononi, G. (2000). *A universe of consciousness: How matter becomes imagination*. New York: Basic Books.

Engel, A. K., Fries, P., Konig, P., Brecht, M., & Singer, W. (1999). Temporal binding, binocular rivalry, and consciousness. *Consciousness and Cognition*, 8(2), 128–151.

Engel, A. K., Fries, P., & Singer, W. (2001). Dynamic predictions: Oscillations and synchrony in top-down processing. *Nature Reviews Neuroscience*, 2(10), 704–716.

Engel, A. K., & Singer, W. (2001). Temporal binding and the neural correlates of sensory awareness. *Trends in Cognitive Sciences*, 5(1), 16–25.

Faure, P., & Korn, H. (2001). Is there chaos in the brain? I. Concepts of nonlinear dynamics and methods of investigation. *Les Comptes rendus de l'Académie des sciences III*, 324(9), 773–793.

Fell, J. (2004). Identifying neural correlates of consciousness: The state space approach. *Consciousness and Cognition*, 13, 709–729.

Fell, J., Fernandez, G., Klaver, P., Elger, C. E., & Fries, P. (2003). Is synchronized neuronal gamma activity relevant for selective attention? *Brain Research: Brain Research Reviews*, 42(3), 265–272.

Fell, J., Klaver, P., Elger, C. E., & Fernandez, G. (2002). Suppression of EEG gamma activity may cause the attentional blink. *Consciousness and Cognition*, 11(1), 114–122.

Freeman, W. J. (1975). *Mass action in the nervous system*. New York: Academic Press.

Freeman, W. J. (1999a). *How brains make up their minds*. London: Weidenfeld and Nicolson.

Freeman, W. J. (1999b). Consciousness, intentionality and causality. *Journal of Consciousness Studies*, 6(11–12), 143–172.

Freeman, W. J. (2000a). *Neurodynamics: An exploration of mesoscopic brain dynamics*. London: Springer-Verlag.

Freeman, W. J. (2000b). Mesoscopic neuro-dynamics: From neuron to brain. *Journal of Physiology Paris*, 94(5–6), 303–322.

Freeman, W. J. (2004). *Mass action in the nervous system* (2nd ed.). Retrieved from http://sulcus.berkeley.edu.

Fries, P., Reynolds, J. H., Rorie, A. E., & Desimone, R. (2001). Modulation of oscillatory neuronal synchronization by selective visual attention. *Science, 291*, 1560–1563.

Fries, P., Roelfsema, P. R., Engel, A. K., Konig, P., & Singer, W. (1997). Synchronization of oscillatory responses in visual cortex correlates with perception in interocular rivalry. *Proceedings of the National Academy of Sciences USA, 94*(23), 12699–12704.

Friston, K. J. (1997). Transients, metastability, and neuronal dynamics. *Neuroimage, 5*(2), 164–171.

Friston, K. J. (2000). The labile brain. I. Neuronal transients and nonlinear coupling. *Philosophical Transactions of the Royal Society London B: Biological Science, 355*(1394), 215–236.

Friston, K. J. (2002a). Beyond phrenology: What can neuroimaging tell us about distributed circuitry? *Annual Review of Neuroscience, 25*, 221–250.

Friston, K. (2002b). Functional integration and inference in the brain. *Progress in Neurobiology, 68*(2), 113–143.

Friston, K. J. (2005). Models of brain function in neuroimaging. *Annual Review of Psychology, 56*, 57–87.

Garfinkel, A., Spano, M. L., Ditto, W. L., & Weiss, J. N. (1992). Controlling cardiac chaos. *Science, 257*, 1230–1235.

Gomes, G. (1998). The timing of conscious experience: A critical review and reinterpretation of Libet's research. *Consciousness and Cognition, 7*(4), 559–595.

Gray, C. M., Konig, P., Engel, A. K., & Singer, W. (1989). Oscillatory responses in cat visual cortex exhibit inter-columnar synchronization which reflects global stimulus properties. *Nature, 338*(6213), 334–337.

Gurwitsch, A. (1964). *The field of consciousness*. Pittsburgh: Duquesne University Press.

Gutkin, B., Pinto, D., & Ermentrout, B. (2003). Mathematical neuroscience: From neurons to circuits to systems. *Journal of Physiology Paris, 97*(2–3), 209–219.

Haken, H. (1983). *Synergetics: An introduction. Nonequilibrium phase transitions and self-organization in physics, chemistry, and biology.* New York: Springer-Verlag.

Hanna, R., & Thompson, E. (2003). The spontaneity of consciousness. *Canadian Journal of Philosophy, 29*, 133–162.

Hebb, D. O. (1949). *The organization of behavior.* New York: Wiley.

Herculano-Houzel, S., Munk, M. H., Neuenschwander, S., & Singer, W. (1999). Precisely synchronized oscillatory firing patterns require electroencephalographic activation. *Journal of Neuroscience, 19*(10), 3992–4010.

Hilgetag, C. C., & Kaiser, M. (2004). Clustered organization of cortical connectivity. *Neuroinformatics, 2*(3), 353–360.

Hollender, D. (1986). Semantic activation without conscious identification in dichotic listening, parafoveal vision, and visual masking: A survey and appraisal. *Behavioral and Brain Sciences, 9*, 1–66.

Ito, J., & Kaneko, K. (2002). Spontaneous structure formation in a network of chaotic units with variable connection strengths. *Physical Review Letters, 88*(2).

Jack, A., & Roepstorff, A. (2003). Trusting the subject (Vol. 1). *Journal of Consciousness Studies, 10*(9–10).

James, W. (1981). *The principles of psychology.* Cambridge, MA: Harvard University Press. (Original work published 1890)

Kelso, J. A. S. (1995). *Dynamic patterns: The self-organization of brain and behavior.* Cambridge, MA: MIT Press.

Korn, H., & Faure, P. (2003). Is there chaos in the brain? II. Experimental evidence and related models. *Comptes rendus biologies, 326*(9), 787–840.

Kuramoto, Y. (1984). Cooperative dynamics of oscillator community: A study based on lattice of rings. *Progress of Theoretical Physics,79* (Suppl.), 223–240.

Lachaux, J.-P., George, N., Tallon-Baudry, C., Martinerie, J., Hugueville, L., Minotti, L., et al. (2005). The many faces of the gamma band response to complex visual stimuli. *Neuroimage, 25*(2), 491–501.

Lachaux, J. P., Lutz, A., Rudrauf, D., Cosmelli, D., Le Van Quyen, M., Martinerie, J., et al. (2002). Estimating the time-course of coherence between single-trial brain signals: An introduction to wavelet coherence. *Neurophysiology Clinics, 32*(3), 157–174.

Lachaux, J. P., Rodriguez, E., Martinerie, J., Adam, C., Hasboun, D., & Varela, F. J. (2000). A quantitative study of gamma-band activity in human intracranial recordings triggered by visual stimuli. *European Journal of Neuroscience*, 12(7), 2608–2622.

Lachaux, J. P., Rodriguez, E., Martinerie, J., & Varela, F. J. (1999). Measuring phase synchrony in brain signals. *Human Brain Mapping*, 8(4), 194–208.

Lachaux, J. P., Rudrauf, D., & Kahane, P. (2003). Intracranial EEG and human brain mapping. *Journal of Physiology Paris*, 97(4–6), 613–628.

Lamme, 2003, 2004

Le Van Quyen, M. (2003). Disentangling the dynamic core: A research program for a neurodynamics at the large-scale. *Biological Research*, 36(1), 67–88.

Le Van Quyen, M., Foucher, J., Lachaux, J.-P., Rodriguez, E., Lutz, A., Martinerie, J., et al. (2001). Comparison of Hilbert transform and wavelet methods for the analysis of neuronal synchrony. *Journal of Neuroscience Methods*, 111(2), 83–98.

Leopold, D. A., & Logothetis, N. K. (1999). Multistable phenomena: Changing views in perception. *Trends in Cognitive Sciences*, 3(7), 254–264.

Libet, B. (2002). The timing of mental events: Libet's experimental findings and their implications. *Consciousness and Cognition*, 11(2), 291–299; discussion 304–233.

Llinas, R. (1988). The intrinsic electrophysiological properties of mammalian neurons: Insights into central nervous system function. *Science*, 242(4886), 1654–1664.

Llinas, R., & Pare, D. (1991). Of dreaming and wakefulness. *Neuroscience*, 44(3), 521–535.

Llinas, R., & Ribary, U. (2001). Consciousness and the brain. The thalamocortical dialogue in health and disease. *Annals of the New York Academy of Sciences*, 929, 166–175.

Llinas, R., Ribary, U., Contreras, D., & Pedroarena, C. (1998). The neuronal basis for consciousness. *Philosophical Transactions of the Royal Society London B: Biological Science*, 353(1377), 1841–1849.

Lutz, A., Lachaux, J. P., Martinerie, J., & Varela, F. J.. (2002). Guiding the study of brain dynamics by using first-person data: Synchrony patterns correlate with ongoing conscious states during a simple visual task. *Proceedings of the Naionatl Academy of Sciences USA*, 99(3), 1586–1591.

Lutz, A., & Thompson, E. (2003). Neurophenomenology: Integrating subjective experience and brain dynamics in the neuroscience of consciousness. *Journal of Consciousness Studies*, 10, 31–52.

Martinerie, J., Adam, C., Le Van Quyen, M., Baulac, M., Clemenceau, S., Renault, B., et al. (1998). Epileptic seizures can be anticipated by non-linear analysis. *National Medicine*, 4(10), 1173–1176.

Maturana, H. R., & Varela, F. J. (1980). *Autopoiesis and cognition: The realization of the living. Boston studies in the philosophy of science*, Vol. 42. Dordrecht: D. Reidel.

Mesulam, M. M. (1999). Spatial attention and neglect: Parietal, frontal and cingulate contributions to the mental representation and attentional targeting of salient extrapersonal events. *Philosophical Transactions of the Royal Society London B: Biological Science*, 354(1387), 1325–1346.

Metzinger, T. (Ed.). (2000). *Neural correlates of consciousness: Empirical and conceptual questions*. Cambridge, MA: MIT Press.

Milner, D., & Goodale, M. (1995). *The visual brain in action*. Oxford: Oxford University Press.

Munk, M. H., Roelfsema, P. R., Konig, P., Engel, A. K., & Singer, W. (1996). Role of reticular activation in the modulation of intracortical synchronization. *Science*, 272(5259), 271–274.

Nicolis, G., & Prigogine, G. (1977). *Self-organization in nonequilibrium systems*. New-York: Wiley.

Nicolis, G., & Prigogine, I. (1989). *Exploring complexity: An introduction*. New York: W. H. Freeman.

Noë, A., & Thompson, E. (2004a). Are there neural correlates of consciousness? *Journal of Consciousness Studies*, 11, 3–28.

Noë, A., & Thompson, E. (2004b). Sorting out the neural basis of consciousness. Authors' reply to commentators. *Journal of Consciousness Studies*, 11, 87–98.

Nunez, P. L. (2000). Toward a quantitative description of large scale neocortical dynamic function and EEG. *Behavioral and Brain Sciences*, 23(3).

O'Regan, K., & Noë, A. (2001). sensorimotor account of vision and visual consciousness.

Behavioral and Brain Sciences, 24(5), 939–973.

Palus, M. (1996). Nonlinearity in normal human EEG: Cycles, temporal asymmetry, nonstationarity and randomness, not chaos. *Biological Cybernetics*, 75, 389–396.

Panksepp, J. (1998). The periconscious substrates of consciousness: Affective states and the evolutionary origins of self. *Journal of Consciousness Studies*, 5, 566–582.

Parvizi, J., Damasio, A. (2001). Consciousness and the brainstem. *Cognition*, 79, 135–159.

Perkel, D. H., Gerstein, G. L., & Moore, G. P. (1967). Neuronal spike trains and stochastic point processes. I. The single spike train. *Biophysical Journal*, 7(4), 391–418.

Pessoa, L., Thompson, E., & Noë, A. (1998). Finding out about filling-in: A guide to perceptual completion for visual science and the philosophy of perception. *Behavioral and Brain Science*, 21(6), 723–748.

Petitmengin, C. (in press). Describing one's subjective experience in the second-person. *Phenomenology and the Cognitive Sciences*.

Pikovsky, A., Zaks, M., Rosenblum, M., Osipov, G., & Kurths, J. (1997). Phase synchronization of chaotic oscillations in terms of periodic orbits. *Chaos*, 7(4), 680–687.

Rees, G., Kreiman, G., & Koch, C. (2002). Neural correlates of consciousness in humans. *Nature Reviews Neuroscience*, 3(4), 261–270.

Revonsuo, A., Wilenius-Emet, M., Kuusela, J., & Lehto, M. (1997). The neural generation of a unified illusion in human vision. *Neuroreport*, 8(18), 3867–3870.

Rizzolatti, G., & Craighero, L. (2004). The mirror-neuron system. *Annual Review of Neuroscience*, 27, 169–192.

Rodriguez, E., George, N., Lachaux, J.- P., Martinerie, J., Renault, B., & Varela, F. J. (1999). Perception's shadow: Long-distance synchronization of human brain activity. *Nature*, 397(6718), 430–433.

Rodriguez, R., Kallenbach, U., Singer, W., & Munk, M. H. (2004). Short- and long-term effects of cholinergic modulation on gamma oscillations and response synchronization in the visual cortex. *Journal of Neuroscience*, 24(46), 10369–10378.

Rosenblum, M., Pikovsky, A., & Kurths, J. (1996). Phase synchronization of chaotic oscillators. *Physical Review Letters*, 76(11), 1804–1807.

Roskies, A. L. (1999). The binding problem [Special issue]. *Neuron*, 24(7–9).

Rudrauf, D., Lutz, A., Cosmelli, D., Lachaux, J.-P., & Le Van Quyen, M. (2003). From autopoiesis to neurophenomenology: Francisco Varela's exploration of the biophysics of being. *Biological Research*, 36, 27–66.

Schiff, S. J., Jerger, K., Duong, D. H., Chang, T., & Spano, M. L. (1994). Controlling chaos in the brain. *Nature*, 8, 615–620.

Searle, J. (2000). Consciousness. *Annual Review of Neuroscience*, 23.

Sewards, T. V., & Sewards, M. A. (2001). On the correlation between synchronized oscillatory activities and consciousness. *Consciousness and Cognition*, 10(4), 485–495.

Sherman, S. M., & Guillery, R. W. (2002). The role of the thalamus in the flow of information to the cortex. *Philosophical Transactions of the Royal Society London B: Biological Science*, 357(1428), 1695–1708.

Sherover, C. (1991). *The human experience of time*. Evanston, IL: Northwestern University Press.

Simons, D. J. (2000). Attentional capture and inattentional blindness. *Trends in Cognitive Science*, 4(4), 147–155.

Singer, W. (1998). Consciousness and the structure of neuronal representations. *Philosophical Transactions of the Royal Society London B: Biological Science*, 353(1377), 1829–1840.

Singer, W., & Gray, C. M. (1995). Visual feature integration and the temporal correlation hypothesis. *Annual Review of Neuroscience*, 18, 555–586.

Skarda, C. A., & Freeman, W. J. (1987). How brains make chaos in order to make sense of the world. *Behavioral and Brain Sciences*, 10(2), 161–195.

Stephan, K. E., Hilgetag, C. C., Burns, G. A., O'Neill, M. A., Young, M. P., & Kotter, R. (2000). Computational analysis of functional connectivity between areas of primate cerebral cortex. *Philosophical Transactions of the Royal Society London B: Biological Science*, 355(1393), 111–126.

Tallon-Baudry, C., & Bertrand, O. (1999). Oscillatory gamma activity in humans and its role in object representation. *Trends in Cognitive Sciences*, 3(4), 151–162.

Tallon-Baudry, C., Bertrand, O., & Fischer, C. (2001). Oscillatory synchrony between human extrastriate areas during visual short-term memory maintenance. *Journal of Neuroscience*, 21(20), RC177.

Thompson, E. (2007). *Mind in life: Biology, phenomenology, and the sciences of mind*. Cambridge, MA: Harvard University Press.

Thompson, E., Lutz, A., & Cosmelli, D. (2005). Neurophenomenology: An introduction for neurophilosophers. In A. Brook & K. Akins (Eds.), *Cognition and the brain: The philosophy and neuroscience movement* (pp. 40–97). New York: Cambridge University Press.

Thompson, E., & Varela, F. J. (2001). Radical embodiment: Neural dynamics and consciousness. *Trends in Cognitive Sciences*, 5(10), 418–425.

Thorpe, S., Fize, D., & Marlot, C. (1996). Speed of processing in the human visual system. *Nature*, 381(6582), 520–522.

Tononi, G., & Edelman, G. M. (1998). Consciousness and complexity. *Science*, 282(5395), 1846–1851.

Treisman, A. M., & Gelade, G. (1980). A feature-integration theory of attention. *Cognitive Psychology*, 12(1), 97–136.

Tsuda, I. (2001). Toward an interpretation of dynamic neural activity in terms of chaotic dynamical systems. *Behavioral and Brain Sciences*, 24(5), 793–810; discussion 810–748.

Van Gelder, T. J. (1998). The dynamical hypothesis in cognitive science. *Behavioral and Brain Sciences*, 21, 1–14.

Van Van Gelder, T. J. (1999). Dynamic approaches to cognition. In R. Wilson & F. Keil (Eds.), *The MIT encyclopedia of cognitive sciences* (pp. 244–246). Cambridge MA: MIT Press.

VanRullen, R., & Koch, C. (2003). Is perception discrete or continuous? *Trends in Cognitive Sciences*, 7(5), 207–213.

Varela, F. (1995). Resonant cell assemblies: A new approach to cognitive functioning and neuronal synchrony. *Biological Research*, 28(81–95).

Varela, F. J. (1996). Neurophenomenology: A methodological remedy for the hard problem.

Journal of Consciousness Studies, 3(4), 330–349.

Varela, F. (1999). The specious present: The neurophenomenology of time consciousness. In J. Petitot, F. J. Varela, B. Pachoud, & J. M. Roy (Eds.), *Naturalizing phenomenology* (pp. 266–314). Stanford: Stanford University Press.

Varela, F., Lachaux, J.-P., Rodriguez, E., & Martinerie, J. (2001). The brainweb: Phase synchronization and large-scale integration. *Nature Reviews Neuroscience*, 2(4), 229–239.

Varela, F. J., & Shear, J. (1999). First-person methodologies: Why, when and how. *Journal of Consciousness Studies*,

Von der Malsburg, C. (1981). *The correlation theory of brain function*. Göttingen: Germany: Max Planck Institute for Biophysical Chemistry.

Watts, D. J., & Strogatz, S. H. (1998). Collective dynamics of 'small-world' networks. *Nature*, 393(6684), 440–442.

Weiskrantz, L. (1990). The Ferrier lecture, 1989. Outlooks for blindsight: Explicit methodologies for implicit processes. *Philosophical Transactions of the Royal Society London B: Biological Science*, 239(1296), 247–278.

Wicker, B., Ruby, P., Royet, J. P., & Fonlupt, P. (2003). A relation between rest and the self in the brain? *Brain Research: Brain Research Review*, 43(2), 224–230.

Wolfe, J. M., & Bennett, S. C. (1997). Preattentive object files: Shapeless bundles of basic features. *Vision Research*, 37(1), 25–43.

Wright, J. J., & Liley, D. T. J. (1996). Dynamics of the brain at global and microscopic scales: Neural networks and the EEG. *Behavioral and Brain Sciences*, 19, 285–320.

Zahavi, D. (2005). *Subjectivity and selfhood: Investigating the first-person perspective*. Cambridge, MA: MIT Press.

Zihl, J., Von Cramon, D., & Mai, N. (1983). Selective disturbance of movement vision after bilateral brain damage. *Brain*, 106(2), 313–340.

B. Neuropsychological Aspects of Consciousness

Disorders and Neuroimaging

CHAPTER 27

The Thalamic Intralaminar Nuclei and the Property of Consciousness

Joseph E. Bogen

Abstract

An anatomico-physiologic approach to consciousness is facilitated by recognizing that the various meanings of the term "consciousness" have in common a crucial core variously called subjectivity, sentience, awareness, conscious itself, consciousness-as-such, consciousness per se, primary consciousness, or simply, by some earlier authors, consciousness. In this chapter it is called C. A sharp distinction is made between the property C and the manifold contents of consciousness, the partial loss of which is typical of circumscribed neocortical lesions. The neuronal mechanism needed for C is here proposed to involve the intralaminar thalamic nuclei. Subsidiary hypotheses are briefly considered concerning volition and episodic memory.

Introduction

The belief that consciousness depends significantly on thalamic function is at least as old as the "automatic apparatus" of Carpenter (1853). Thalamic contributions were a principal emphasis of the landmark Laurentian Symposium entitled "Brain Mechanisms and Consciousness" held a century later (Adrian, Bremer, & Jasper, 1954). However, as argued by Walshe (1965) in his criticism of that emphasis, toward the end of the 19th century the cerebral cortex had become accepted by many neurologists as the "seat of consciousness," as well as of intelligence, ideation, and memory. In the Laurentian Symposium it was Lashley and Bremer who mainly dissented from the thalamic emphasis. Bremer insisted that "it is the dynamic integration of all cerebral processes at a single moment which makes consciousness" (Adrian et al., 1954, p. 497). This so-called global view still appeals to many people although the impressive extent to which "dynamic integration" has since been shown to occur without consciousness (as discussed further below) has somewhat lessened the connection. Lashley reiterated his earlier opinion, possibly the strongest argument against a thalamic "seat" of consciousness. He wrote that "the neurological activity in a psychological event cannot be simpler in structure or in number of elements than the psychological activity which it constitutes.... The complexity of mental processes is too great to be represented by the permutations of a small number of cells" (Lashley, 1952). This argument has perhaps been answered in part by writers who have made a distinction between the property of consciousness and the contents of consciousness, as discussed further on, emphasizing that only an exceedingly small part of the potential contents can be conscious at any moment. Toward the end of the 20th century, brain-oriented books on the subject commonly have supposed that mentation, conscious or not, depends upon thalamocortical interaction while offering varying views as to when or how this activity is endowed with consciousness (Baars, 1988, 1997; Cairns-Smith, 1996; Churchland, 2002: Crick, 1994; Darnasio, 1999; Edelman, 1989, 1992; Koch, 2004; Llinas, 2001; Taylor, 1999).

This chapter is devoted to reviewing some aspects of thalamic structure and function as they may contribute to making small fractions of mentation momentarily conscious, with particular emphasis on those thalamic constituents sometimes called non-specific. Considerable emphasis is given to the effects of certain thalamic lesions. Before presenting a simplified description of thalamic anatomy as a prelude to selected physiologic and pathologic observations, I offer a brief discussion of usages of the word "consciousness" and a few explicit assumptions about neuronal activity patterns.

The Concept of "C" or Elementary Consciousness

Although there is often considerable agreement as to who or what is conscious, the basis on which we make this attribution is not always the same – there seems to be no single universally applicable criterion (Allport, 1988). We often use accurate eye tracking of a moving object as an indicator that someone is conscious, but this can be fallible as well as often inappropriate. I follow Hempel (1966) and Goldman (1993) in the view that insisting on a single criterion for a supposedly unitary property has in science been "long since given up"; a standard example is length, which is measured in different ways depending on the context. And I follow, as described in some detail elsewhere (Bogen, 1995b), those philosophers of science who advise that formal definitions must follow rather than precede understanding of a subject.

Although it seems desirable not to delay a neurobiological approach to consciousness by getting mired down in discussions of definition or of uncertain cases (Crick & Koch, 1990, 2000), it is nonetheless troublesome that the word "consciousness" is used in many differing ways (Galin, 1992; Güzeldere, 1997; Natsoulas, 1983). The variety of usages contributed to the opinion of G. Ryle that "there would seem to be no actual thing or process that our past usages have been getting at" (Güzeldere, 1997, p. 473). Others have taken a less radical approach, recognizing that the many usages have in common (as their intersection or commonality) a crucial, central core for which have been suggested many semi-synonyms. These semi-synonyms include first-person experience (Fessard, 1954), subjectivity (Chalmers, 2002; Flanagan, 1992), awareness (Goldman, 1993; Jennett, 2002), sentience (Searle, 1993, 1998), inner experience (Metzinger, 1995), phenomenal consciousness (Block, 1995), primary consciousness (Edelman, 1992; Revonsuo, 1995), crude consciousness (Cairns, 1952), consciousness-as-such (Baars, 1988, 1993), consciousness per se (Gray, 1995), consciousness itself (Moscovitch, 1995), the crucial core of consciousness (Bogen, 1995a), core consciousness (Damasio, 1999) or simply, consciousness (Grossman, 1980; Moore, 1922). In this chapter I simply refer to consciousness as C.

C Includes One (Minimal) Aspect of the Complex Concept "Self"

The word "self" seems to be used even more variously than the word "consciousness." My

Webster's Collegiate Dictionary has about 350 usages spread over three and a half pages. As a possible example of a relatively narrow usage, Dennett (1991) refers to the "self as the center of narrative gravity." This is a felicitous phrase, but linguistic ability (good or bad) is not essential to the C we share with so many other species. At another extreme, Galin (1992, 2003) proposed that self be defined as "the overall organization that makes a person a unity." A similar concept of self was discussed by P. S. Churchland in a multiauthored discussion entitled "Reflections on Self" in the April 12, 2002 issue of *Science*. This "overall organization" view may not be the most inclusive usage possible, but it is surely a contender, it involving such a multitude of unifying mechanisms, both hormonal and neuronal. We need not attempt a catalogue of all that self might contain in order to point to one aspect that is typically implied when the word "consciousness" is used.

Flanagan (1991, p. 352) quotes William James as saying, "Whatever I may be thinking of, I am always at the same time more or less aware of myself, of my personal existence." Flanagan goes on to observe, "This low level sense of 'me-ness,' of 'something happening here' does seem to underlie all conscious experience. All conscious experiences are, in addition to being experienced, experienced as attached to the subject of these very experiences." As Churchland wrote, "A single thread of "me-ness" runs through the entire fabric of one's existence" (Churchland, 2002, p. 61). There might be arguable exceptions (e.g., certain meditative states) to C having this quite minimal aspect of self, but "me-ness" names what I believe to be an essential characteristic of C.

That a connection with self is an indispensable aspect of any sensible usage of the term "consciousness" has often been maintained. Damasio (1999) suggests repeatedly that consciousness depends upon bringing together what he calls an "object" and the self. Damasio includes as objects not only places and persons but also pains and emotions; he sometimes uses the term "object proxy" (I would refer to the neuronal

activity pattern that represented an object, in his broad sense, as a "pre-percept").

According to Hart and Whitlow (1995), the human sense of self has five facets: None of these, even Hart's "subjective self-awareness," seems terribly close to what Flanagan and Churchland call "me-ness." Hart's other four facets – objective self-awareness, memories of self, representations of self, and theories of self – are even less close to me-ness. That even the "subjective self-awareness" of Hart is not as low level as Flanagan and I have in mind is indicated by maintaining that monkeys do not have even this aspect of self (Hart & Whitlow, 1995). I do believe monkeys know who they are, which infants are theirs, etc. (Bergman et al., 2003) even though they do not understand the function of a mirror à la Gallup's (Gallup, 1995) chimps.

It needs to be emphasized that the me-ness ascribed here to C is neither an aspect of cognition nor does it require cognition; it is, in Thomas Sullivan's term, subconceptual. Taylor (2002) offers a nice summary of authors advocating related concepts of "primitive self" or "minimal self" or "pre-reflective self" or "ipseity." This minimal, subconceptual aspect of self is, of course, a far cry from what some philosophers have in mind. For example, "While a bat, like even the lowly lobster, has a biological self, it has no selfy self to speak of – no Center of Narrative Gravity...no regrets, no complex yearnings, no nostalgic reminiscences, no grand schemes" (Dennett, 1991). According to P. S. Churchland (personal communication, June 30, 2003), Dennett still holds firmly to his 1991 views, including that brains do not have any "hardwiring" for consciousness.

Identification of the neuronal substrates for the richness of a maximally "selfy self" may be a desirable long-term goal; considerably less ambitious is the hope expressed in this chapter of identifying the neuronal requirements for the primitive, low-level sense of me-ness and giving some indication of how this neuronal mechanism is transiently connected to the neuronal representation of a pre-percept, thus embodying what Damasio discussed as the connection of self and "object."

There Is a Lot That C Does Not Include

I have discussed elsewhere (Bogen, 1995a) further philosophical considerations concerning the semantics of C, including Carnap's concept of explication and Naess's notion of precisation. In paraphrase, the concept of Naess says the following: The formulation C is more "precise" than consciousness if there are properties of consciousness that are not properties of C, but there are no properties of C that are not also properties of consciousness. C is a much narrower concept than many people's usage of consciousness. C is intended to include the above described low-level sense of me-ness, accompanying some percept or affect, but C is intended to convey very little else.

Whatever else various usages of consciousness sometimes include (e.g. planning, control, time-binding, monitoring, supervision, language, "higher thoughts," self-image, theory-of mind, sociality), none of these is involved in the concept C, whereas C *does* appear to be involved in most of the more expansive concepts of consciousness.

The view urged here is that we are well served by making a sharp distinction between the property C and the contents, potentially enormous, of consciousness. Most of the authors cited in the previous paragraph using some semi-synonym for C have made this distinction. Other examples include Panksepp's distinction between "the essential foundations of consciousness and the contents of consciousness" (Panksepp, 1998, p. 313) and the view of Grossman (1980) who wrote, "We can also introspectively discriminate between the contents of consciousness... and the quality of being conscious." The earliest example I have found is the distinction made by G. E. Moore. Landesman (1967), quotes Moore (1922) as follows, "The sensation of blue differs from that of green. But it is plain that if both are sensations they also have some

point in common.... I will call this common element 'consciousness'.... We have then in every sensation two distinct terms, (1); consciousness; in respect of which all sensations are alike, and (2) something else [the content], in respect of which one sensation differs from another."

One fact motivating the approach of this chapter is that partial, specific loss of contents is typical of cerebro-cortical lesions that leave C otherwise intact. This chapter concentrates on the search for a process or mechanism providing the property C, without trying to explain everything else that consciousness might include.

Neuronal Activity Patterns

A persistent question about consciousness is, Where does it come from? I take it for granted in this chapter that C depends upon specific brain processes. I assume that every sensation, thought, feeling, memory, and expectation is represented in the brain by a neuronal activity pattern (NAP). This view, although explicitly mechanistic, is not necessarily materialistic or completely deterministic; this is discussed in detail elsewhere (Bogen, 1995b; Bogen et al., 1998) for those who care about the metaphysics. I only assume here that C requires specific neuronal activity that we hope to identify.

This approach suggests the availability to experimentation of various questions: First, what is the change in a NAP that occurs when it is associated with C? This implies that recording from brain cells (electrically or chemically or both) will provide information that distinguishes, in the words of Marcel, "processing without consciousness from processing which is also describable as conscious" (Marcel, 1988, p. 126). Second, is there an identifiable mechanism that produces the change in a NAP? Such a mechanism, which associates NAPs with C, is named in this chapter Mc. A third question is, What determines which NAP will acquire C at any particular time?

Regarding the first question, it is sometimes suggested that the change from NAP to CNAP is simply an increase in activity as measured by neuronal firing rates (Fuster, 2002). As Moutoussis and Zeki (2002) put it, "When certain levels of activation are reached and probably in combination with the activation of other areas as well, there is the generation of a conscious visual percept." On the other hand, recordings from neurons known to respond to a specific stimulus sometimes show a decrease in firing rate when the subject indicates it is aware of that stimulus (Koch, 2004; Logothetis, 2002).

In answer to the second question, it has been suggested that the change in NAPs involves increased synchrony (Singer, 1998). Of particular interest are synchronous discharges in the gamma range (20–70 Hz), most often around 40 Hz. Although originally described in anesthetized animals, the gamma synchrony (at least for vision) is more evident in the alert state, is enhanced by arousal, and is related to the presence and properties of experimental stimuli (Fries et al., 2001; Gray & Viana Di Prisco, 1997; Munk et al., 1996).

As to the third question, what factors determine which NAP will acquire C, the current answers are usually expressed in such psychological terms as "salience" or "attention"; in this chapter, I briefly mention some thalamic contributions to these two important aspects. Mainly, however, I discuss the second question: how to go about finding Mc, a mechanism that can endow a NAP with C.

We Are Looking for Mc, Rather Than C

C is provided by some cerebral mechanism, Mc. It is this mechanism that we hope to identify and ultimately analyze. Trying to point to C may turn out to be like pointing to the wind. We can point to the effects of the wind, and we can usually give a good account of what causes the wind, the causes often being quite distant (in miles) from the effects. We do not actually see the wind itself, only leaves fluttering, or material such as dust or smoke being carried by the wind.

Similarly with C, we commonly detect its presence by its effects. The effects of C, when it is generated by Mc, depend on the specific NAPs involved. Determining which effects might be considered most typical of consciousness is important, but is not the immediate problem, which is to find the mechanisms necessary to achieve any of the various effects.

C Requires a Time-Dependent Process

Most discussants agree that NAPs that are potentially conscious make up a restricted fraction of the NAPs possible in a brain. And of those NAPs that can acquire C at some time or another, a very small fraction are endowed with C at any one moment. There is considerable debate as to how long a "moment" is, probably one to several hundred milliseconds and possibly varying with the NAP involved. The exact time is not essential for most hypotheses about consciousness. Most views currently advocated seem compatible with a metaphor of Pavlov: "If the place of optimal excitability were luminous, then we should see [it] playing over the cerebral surface" (Pavlov, 1928, p. 222). I believe that the "hot spot" can involve the depths, as well as the surface, and to some extent can be multiple. As mentioned in the previous paragraph, "optimal excitability" does not necessarily mean "increased excitability." Evidence is presented that specific, wired-in thalamic structures are needed for Mc; in addition, there needs to be some active process that transiently involves each NAP for the brief time it is endowed with C. This implies an affirmative answer to the question, "Does time help to understand consciousness?" (Engel et al., 1999).

C Is an Emergent Property

A question not always explicitly addressed when looking for some Mc is whether C is an aggregative or an emergent property. The term "emergent" is used variously;

sometimes it simply means "arising from" as a bather emerging from the water. Somewhat idiosyncratic is the definition in Rumbaugh, Beran, and Pate (2003, p. 53): "Emergent behaviors are new patterns of responding with no antecedent in previously learned behavior [and] are applied appropriately to novel situations." A more common meaning among philosophers, not necessarily involving novelty, was adopted by Dudai (2002, p. 218), who noted that in a complex system there may be properties that are "emergent, *i.e.*, appear only at a higher level of organization."

This chapter employs a philosophically technical usage, following Wimsatt (1976, 2000), who contrasts "emergent" with "aggregative." A property possessed by a combination of parts is said to be aggregative if it results from adding up smaller amounts of that property already possessed by the parts; common examples are mass or electrical charge. Sometimes an aggregate reaches what is called "critical mass," as when a forest fire is large enough to create a wind that then fans the flames that created it; this sort of property is sometimes called "emergent." By contrast, according to Wimsatt's usage and in this chapter, an emergent property arises not from an accumulation of smaller amounts possessed by each part, but from *the particular way* in which the parts are put together. A common example of an emergent property is the ability of a wheel to roll – whether it is made of wood, steel, plaster-of-paris, or clay fired in a kiln, it rolls. The property of "rollness" is largely independent of the properties of the parts, although not entirely; one cannot very well make a wheel out of jello or oatmeal.

If, as I urge here, C is an emergent property of some Mc in the Wimsatt sense, there may well be restrictions on the sort of parts that can be assembled for this purpose. At present, many of us believe that neurons are the essential constituents. An open mind on this issue requires remembering that real brains also have an abundance of glial cells and lots of different juices surrounding the neurons. (The wetness of brains is one of the big differences from all known man-made

computers; Bunin & Wightman, 1999; Fuxe & Agnati, 1991; Marder & Bucher, 2001). An extensive review of the possible role of glia is found in Fields and Stevens-Graham (2002).

That C is aggregative has had many advocates; a good example is the suggestion in Greenfield (1998) that the intensity of subjective experience may correlate with the size of a non-specialized neuronal network. In line with the idea of a critical mass of connections is the view of Cairns-Smith (1996) who suggested that consciousness arises by virtue of the extensive white matter making up so much of the cerebrum; this seems to echo R. Sperry's (1980, 1991) discussions of widespread connections leading to an "emergent" consciousness (see also Bogen, 1998). Different, but also suggesting aggregation is the belief of R. Llinás (2001) that each individual neuron has what he called "a modicum of qualia" so that when many are added together there is a substantial amount. (Llinàs also believes that the circuit "architecture" is important.) A similar view was expressed earlier by Lashley who spoke of "consciousness quanta" possessed even by simple reflexes (Lashley, 1954, p. 437).

Claims that an entire brain must be involved are sometimes called "global" theories. Lycan seemed to express such a view when he wrote, "The central nervous system is as central as it gets" (Lycan, 1997, p. 762). More restricted, but non-localized hypotheses include the complexity theory of Tonini and Edelman (1998), which proposes a highly mobile "dynamic core" of activity whose composition "can transcend traditional anatomic boundaries." When the emphasis is on aggregation rather than architecture, theories are often called "global" even when they do not intend that an entire brain is involved. For example, Kinsbourne in his "integrated field theory" maintained that awareness is a property of a sufficiently sizable neural network, "not of any particular locus in the brain" (Kinsbourne & Smith, 1974).

Until we have a more widely agreed-upon understanding of how C is produced, this question remains open. The view in this chapter is that Mc depends upon an anatomically specifiable arrangement of nerve cells, probably including and inducing specific chemical environments.

C Depends upon an Anatomically Localizable Mechanism

Once we agree that C depends upon brain, and we want to decide whether to look for a global or a local mechanism, a relevant question is the following: Are some brain parts more important than others? One can approach a physiologic understanding at levels from the microscopic to the most encompassing. That is, C might be supposed to appear at the subcellular level (e.g., the microtubules as in Hameroff & Penrose, 1996). Another approach is to attribute C to specialized neurons in cortical clusters; this seems implied by the view that processing of information is best described as depending upon a large number of nodes and each of these nodes is capable of generating its own "microconsciousness" (Zeki & Bartels, 1999). The idea that consciousness is generated independently in different places is supported by the finding that color and motion occurring at the same time can sometimes be perceived at different times (Zeki & Bartels, 1999). It is hoped that the reader will find that this phenomenon is also explicable by thalamocortical interaction as described in this chapter.

Special cells or circuits seem implied by the idea that C can accompany the ventral stream but not the dorsal stream. This last suggestion was proposed by Milner and Goodale (1996) and reflects the proposal that visual information flows forward from the primary visual area in two directions: the ventral stream into the temporal lobe, giving rise to knowledge of what an object is, and the dorsal stream into the parietal lobe, giving rise to knowing where it is (Ungerleider & Mishkin, 1982). Milner and Goodale prefer to regard the ventral and dorsal streams as serving perception and action, respectively (Milner & Goodale, 1996, p. 178) and suggest that processing in the dorsal stream is not

normally available to awareness (Milner & Goodale, 1996, p. 200).

A theory emphasizing the role of specialized cells was offered by Jones (1998a). He pointed out that in each thalamus there are cells, staining for the presence of parvalbumin, that project focally to cortex. Others that he calls matrix cells and that stain for calbindin project more diffusely. He suggests that it is the diffusely projecting matrix cells that contribute to "the binding of all aspects of sensory experience into a single framework of consciousness" (Jones, 1998a, p. 69). Jones's proposal is discussed in more detail later in the chapter, after a brief discussion of thalamic anatomy.

Some describe consciousness in terms of much larger frameworks; one of these is the Extended Reticular Thalamocortical Activating System (ERTAS) of Newman and Baars (1993), which can act as a "global workplace" or "theatre of consciousness" (Baars, 1997). Baars (1988) emphasized early on that consciousness of particular data is associated with what might be called a "broadcasting" of those particular data. This aspect of consciousness has now been confirmed by fMRI studies showing that whereas a stimulus can produce cerebral activity without the subject's awareness, when the subject does become aware, then cerebral activity appears in many more locations. This fact about consciousness might suggest that it is the broadcasting of data that makes them conscious. By contrast, the hypothesis advanced in this chapter is that the broadcasting is not the cause of C, but rather is a consequence of data having acquired C. It may be that deciding between these two views will require combining fMRI with some other procedure having finer time resolution.

In contrast to much of the foregoing, I present below evidence for the view that C depends upon centrally located, hard-wired circuits that embody what I have called Mc (Bogen, 1993, 1995a,b, 1997c). That is, Mc is supposed to depend upon a specific arrangement of neurons so organized, so centrally located, and so widely connected to other brain parts that it can transiently endow a

NAP elsewhere in brain with the property C. Kinsbourne (1995) has criticized this concept, facetiously referring to a postulated Mc as "the subjectivity pump"; this term describes precisely what we are trying to find.

NAPs that are potentially conscious undoubtedly number in the billions. However, only a few can have C at any one moment. Probably relevant here is the process of "sparsening" by which complex, distributed material can be rapidly and specifically retrieved using only a fraction of the material to be retrieved (Kanerva, 1988), as concisely explained by Laurent (2002). Because Mc, as conceived here, needs to reflect only a very small set of NAP at any one moment, Mc need not be very large as would be required in a so-called Cartesian theatre; that is, "a place where it all comes together" (Dennett & Kinsbourne, 1992).

Evidence for Localization of Mc

The usual localizationist argument involves two findings. First, a large deficit in some function (f) is produced by a small lesion in the "center" or "node" for that f (this does not imply that the representation of f is wholly contained within some sharp boundary; Bogen, 1976; Bogen & Berker, 2002; Bogen & Bogen, 1976). Second, a large lesion elsewhere results in very little if any disturbance of f. A familiar example is the profound disturbance of speech beginning with "a complete linguistic suppression" (Lecours, Lhermitte, & Bryans, 1983) and often leading to what is called agrammatism, which stems from relatively small lesions in and around Broca's area of the left hemisphere (Henderson, 1990). By contrast, a very large lesion in the right hemisphere or even its complete removal rarely affects the syntactic (grammatic) competence of a right-hander.

With respect to C, quite small bithalamic lesions involving both sets of intralaminar nuclei (ILN) typically impair Mc (detailed below), whereas very large bicortical lesions

typically do not (Benson, 1994: Damasio & Damasio, 1989).

Neocortex Provides Content, But Is Insufficient to Provide the Property C

That C is not produced by cerebral cortex was particularly urged by Penfield and Jasper (1954). Their views derived largely from observations of epilepsy, including that consciousness could be absent during complex behavior (requiring neocortex). Conversely, severe disturbances of function either from cortical removals or cortical hyperactivity (as in focal seizures) need not be accompanied by loss of consciousness.

As early as 1937, Penfield expressed one theme of this chapter: "All parts of the brain may well be involved in normal conscious processes but the indispensable substratum of consciousness lies outside of the cerebral cortex, probably in the diencephalon." (The diencephalon includes both thalamus and hypothalamus). It is an interesting fact that this view has often been ignored by recent theorizers on consciousness, many of whom are fixated almost exclusively on neocortical function. We would do well to keep in mind the point made by Steriade and colleagues that for cortical information processing, "at each step of this information flow, corticothalamic volleys engage synaptically the intrathalamic networks" (Steriade, Jones, & McCormick, 1997, p. 13). These authors go so far as to refer to the thalamus as a "switchboard" for the cerebrum. More recently, Sherman and Guillery (2002) have suggested the likelihood that "the thalamus sits at an indispensable position for the modulation of messages involved in corticocortical processing."

Conscious Content Includes Primitive, Non-Cognitive Components

To Penfield and Jasper's reasons that C is produced outside the cerebral cortex can be added the observation that some important contents of consciousness are quite primitive; that is, they are unneedful of neocortical discrimination, association, or learning. Examples are nausea, fatigue, unelaborated pain (for example, the "electric" jabs of trigeminal neuralgia), thirst, and the like. It may be that Mc evolved to give these percepts greater potency, either to facilitate learning or to provide another layer of control over the stopping of ongoing action. In either case, it would appear that Mc was only subsequently recruited to serve so-called higher functions and more elaborate responses (Seager, 2002). We understand that Mc of humans routinely endows with C patterns of complex cortical activity describable as "representations of representations" or "higher order thoughts" (Rolls, 2000; Rosenthal, 1990). But these are special contents, not the crucial core of consciousness.

Conversely, complex representations can sometimes be effective without consciousness. Earlier experiments that attempted to show that meaningful contents requiring neocortical activity can influence behavior without being conscious have been subject to a variety of methodological criticisms (Hollender, 1986; Perruchet & Vinter, 2002). However, considerable evidence has for most of us established the existence of nonconscious perception and cognition (Bar & Biederman, 1998; Berti & Rizzolatti, 1992; Castiello, Paulignan, & Jeannerod, 1991; Henke et al., 1993; Jeannerod, 1992; Kihlstrom, 1987; Libet, Gleason, Wright, & Pearl, 1983; Milner & Goodale, 1996; Ro & Rafal, 1996; Schacter, McAndrews, & Moscovitch, 1988; Taylor & McCloskey, 1990; Wexler, Warrenburg, Schwartz, & Janer, 1992; Zaidel, Hugdahl, & Johnsen, 1995; Zaidel et al., 1999; see Chapter 9).

An Historical Antecedent: The Centrencephalon

When Penfield and Jasper (1954) argued against cerebral cortex as the source of C, they introduced the concept of a "centren-cephalon." They originally described it as "the neurone systems which are symmetrically connected with both hemispheres and which serve to co-ordinate their functions" (Penfield & Jasper, 1954, p. 27). This original description takes in a great deal of anatomy. including the 200 million fiber corpus callosum. However, in subsequent discussions in that book and in later descriptions (Adrian et al., 1954; Eccles, 1966) they made it clear that they had in mind structures in the diencephalon, and they particularly stressed the role of the ILN. Why was this concept largely abandoned? At least three reasons can be seen:

1. The centrencephalon was supposed to be not only a mechanism for consciousness but also a source of seizures that were "generalized from the start." The concept of centrencephalic seizures has been largely abandoned by epileptologists. However, that Penfield and Jasper combined these two ideas does not require that we do so; arguments for a thalamic role in C can be made quite independently of theories about seizure origin and spread.

2. The centrencephalon was intended to explain the unification of consciousness. However, cerebral commissurotomy (the split-brain, discussed further below) renewed interest in the corpus callosum as an integrating structure and raised doubts about the usefulness of the centrencephalon concept for explaining consciousness (Doty, 1975). On the basis of our current knowledge, the problem of localizing Mc can be approached in terms of a single hemisphere (which we know can have C), postponing to the future the problem of integrating two Mc and the implications of this problem for the unity of consciousness.

3. When Penfield and Jasper emphasized the function of thalamic nuclei, especially the intralaminar nuclei (ILN), objections to their concept arose because of considerable doubt concerning the existence of ILN projections to cortex. This doubt arose because unilateral decortication did not produce rapid degeneration in the ILN as it did in the principal nuclei. However, more

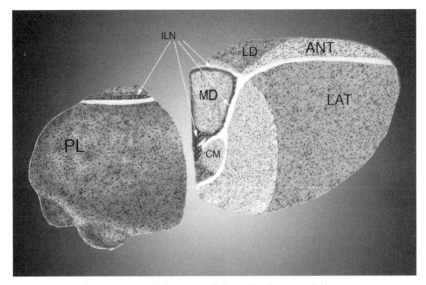

Figure 27.1. This is a stylized drawing of the right, human thalamus as seen from above and behind (the left thalamus is an anatomical mirror image). A thin slice has been taken out about two-thirds of the way back from the anterior (front) end in order to show some of the internal structure. This figure shows what modern anatomists call the "dorsal thalamus" because of its embryonic origin. In reality, the dorsal thalamus is enshrouded by the reticular nucleus (**R**), a thin shell of cells that are of ventral embryonic origin. The **R** is not shown in this figure because it would hide the dorsal thalamus from view. Anatomists of the Renaissance were unaware of both the embryology and the microscopic detail; they applied the term "thalamus" to the entire assembly including **R**, and this is what neurologists usually mean when they use the word thalamus. (The word "thalamus" is Latin for bridal couch; the older anatomists enjoyed a rather randy vocabulary.)

The internal lamina is shown in white. (There are other laminae (layers of fibers) outside of the thalamus, but are not relevant here.) The lamina consists of millions of nerve fibers going to or from nearby neurons. To the right of the lamina are the lateral and ventral parts; they are largely concerned with specific sensory or motor functions and are not discussed further in this chapter. Toward the anterior end the lamina bifurcates, with the lateral branch continuing on toward the cortex. The medial branch dives under the collections of neurons to which most of its fibers are headed.

Each thalamus (the right thalamus is shown here) contains many subparts called nuclei. There are, in each thalamus, about 40 nuclei according to Jones (and about 80 according to Hassler). We do not need to bother with most of these nuclei (they are unrelated to the text), so we do not show the subdivisions of the lateral and anterior parts; and we do not label most of the nuclei, with four exceptions: **MD, PL, LD,** and **CM.**

The medial dorsal nucleus (**MD**) takes up most of the medial thalamus. The **MD** is almost certainly important for emotion because of its large input from the amygdala of the same hemisphere. And **MD** is likely important for thoughts about the future, as its output is to the prefrontal cortex; more specifically the large-celled part of **MD** projects to the orbitofrontal cortex, which is an important part of the so-called emotional brain.

On top of **MD** is the rather thin nucleus called lateral dorsal (**LD**); it is included by Jones (1985) in his discussion of the Anterior nuclei. These have been implicated in both memory and emotion by various authors and may be involved in other processes because they project to the anterior cingulate gyrus, recent tracer techniques have shown that ILN do indeed project to cortex and do so widely.

The centrencephalon concept tried to explain too much. But it contained a germ of truth, which now needs to be nourished in terms of thalamic contributions to the mechanisms that provide us, as well as creatures like us, with consciousness.

Different Kinds of Evidence That Mc Requires the ILN

Evidence for the importance of thalamic nuclei, especially the ILN, is presented here from clinical neurology, neuroanatomy, electrophysiology, and other studies, including experiments with magnetic resonance imaging (MRI). Before getting to these

findings, some introductory anatomy may be helpful.

Simplified Image of a Thalamus

Within each cerebral hemisphere, close to the midline, sits the thalamus of that hemisphere. Each human thalamus is about the size and shape of a pecan in the shell, with a bulbous swelling at the back end called the pulvinar. In other words, each thalamus is an ellipsoid about 4 cm long and about 2 cm wide (see Fig. 27.1).

The neurons in each thalamus are in clusters called nuclei. According to Netter (1953), long a favorite of medical students, each thalamus contains 11 nuclei. According to Hassler (in Schaltenbrand & Wahren, 1977), long favored by neurosurgeons who operate on thalami, there are about 80 different nuclei. According to E. G. Jones

---

Figure 27.1 (cont.)

which itself has been implicated in a wide variety of cognitive, volitional, and emotional processes. Note that, in the human, the **LD** is neither lateral nor dorsal; it acquired its name from its position in more primitive brains, such as rabbit, cat, or the most primitive primates like the bushbaby.

At the posterior end of the dorsal thalamus there is a quite large nucleus, having several subdivisions; it is called the pulvinar (**PL**). (The word "pulvinar" means pillow.) The pulvinar is connected very widely to almost all of the cortex known to respond to external stimuli of whatever nature; it is particularly large in primates where it is thought to help in determining salience of information, and it therefore plays a role in directing attention.

The **ILN** are shown in black, surrounding the **MD**; in reality the nerve cells of the **ILN** are not all in a discrete band, as shown here, because many of them are dispersed within the lamina. The subdivisions of the **ILN** have been given a variety of names, which are unnecessary in this chapter. Because of their arrangement in a shell around the **MD**, they were lumped together by Grünthal (1934) as the "nucleus circularis." This nicely descriptive usage was followed by a half-dozen anatomists subsequently, but is no longer current.

The entromedian nucleus (**CM**), more commonly called centrum medianum in Latin or centre mediane in French, is visible where the slice was taken out. The **CM** is much larger in monkeys than in most mammals and is even bigger in humans. It projects to the motor cortex, which is one of the reasons for thinking that it is probably essential to volition. It has long been customary to consider **CM** to be part of the **ILN** because it is located in the lamina (as shown on the cut surface). Moreover, it has a major output to the striatum, which is a defining characteristic of the **ILN**. At present, in simple terms, we can think of **CM** as the motor part of **ILN** and the rest of **ILN** (the veil surrounding **MD**) as sensory; in other words, roughly speaking, this reflects the difference between the intentional and perceptual aspects of C. [This stylized drawing was done by Michael Stern, using Photoshop, with advice from JEB, referring to the coronal sections in Fig. 6 of Jones (1998a) and the coronal sections of Figs. 1–8 in Munkle et al. (2000).]

(1985, 1998a,b), whose views reflect modern staining techniques, each thalamus has about 40 nuclei. Thalamic nuclei have been delineated and named in conflicting ways, often subject to vociferous argument (Jones & Macchi, 1997; Percheron, 1997). For some, what mattered was whether groups of cells seemed circumscribed by fiber bundles. Also, anatomists gave individual names to groups of cells if they seemed to have the same appearance and were clustered together more closely. Modern terminology also gives major importance to connections, as well as to chemical constituents as shown by various staining techniques. Another source of complexity is that even when anatomists are largely agreed on which thalamic neurons belong together, they use different names. I follow here the usage of Jones (1985, 1998a,b),

For the purposes of this chapter I am not concerned with all the nuclei; most of them contribute to specific sensory or motor functions, like vision or hearing or coordination. In the older literature these are sometimes called "relay nuclei"; more recently the terms "specific nuclei" or "principal nuclei' are preferred. Of greater relevance for this chapter are the intralaminar nuclei (ILN), often called non-specific; it is the case that compared to the specific nuclei, inputs to the ILN are dispersed more widely, and much of their output is distributed more diffusely. One specific nucleus important for present purposes is the medial dorsal nucleus (MD), whose connections from amygdala and with prefrontal cortex give it a special role in emotion. Moreover the location of MD helps in the description of the ILN, as well as suggesting their hypothetical role in the experiencing of emotion.

The medial dorsal nucleus (MD) is an ellipsoid about the size and shape of a single Virginia peanut (out of its shell) located inside the pecan. MD is nestled up against the roof of the thalamus against the medial wall. The ILN are collections of nerve cells draped like a blanket all around the MD, top and bottom, front and back, and all along the side. In rats, cats, and monkeys similar cells also cover the medial surfaces of both right and left MD, and the clusters are merged together so they are given a separate name, the midline nuclei. In humans in whom the midline nuclei are largely absent, the two thalami are for the most part clearly separated. In addition to the "blanket," it is customary to include as one of the ILN the centrum medianum (CM), which resembles a small bean up against the blanket just below the back half of MD. The CM seems to have a different function as judged by the fact that it stains differently from the rest of the ILN. It is notably bigger in primates than in most mammals, and even more so in humans, a fact to which I return.

The Definition of the ILN Has Changed

Modern thalamic terminology was greatly influenced by LeGros Clark (1932). He wrote, "Broadly speaking, the thalamic nuclei may be divided into two groups: principal nuclei and intralaminar nuclei." Further on he wrote, "Among the principal nuclei and outlining them are fiber tracts which form the medullary laminae. These laminae are strewn with cells [which] form the intralaminar nuclei" (LeGros Clark, 1932, p. 418). That is, the ILN originally got their name from their association with the laminae, whether actually inside them or close by outside them. Anatomists have argued about what nuclei should be so characterized; most nowadays accept the view that the ILN are defined mainly by their projection to the striatum (Jones, 1985, 1989, 1998b). The considerable importance of this projection comes up later with respect to volition and procedural memory. First, I consider evidence alluded to earlier that Mc depends on the ILN.

Some Neurologic Evidence: Three Clinical Facts

1. There are two levels in the CNS where very small lesions (less than 1 g) placed bilaterally can abruptly abolish responsiveness: These are either in the brainstem reticular formation (BSRF) or in the thalamic intralaminar nuclei (ILN). These facts are

discussed in more detail, with appropriate references, further on.

Corollary: The effect on consciousness of brain damage depends crucially on its location. One of the most widely used textbooks on human neuropsychology states, "There are no reports that individuals, who have lost a certain restricted portion of the brain have lost their consciousness. The idea that consciousness is a property of a single system or brain area receives no support from clinical studies of people who have suffered brain damage" (Kolb & Wishaw, 2000, p. 484).

People who want to understand consciousness can be led astray by these two sentences. Perhaps the authors had in mind "cortical system or brain area"; if so they were undoubtedly correct.

2. The larger the thalamic lesion, the more widespread the diaschisis (the shock effect that depresses nerve cell function elsewhere; Szelies et al., 1991). Also, the larger the lesion, the more long-lasting the deficit. This follows a basic principle of behavioral neurology (and of neuropsychology); that is, the location of the lesion commonly determines the nature of the behavioral deficit, whereas the size of the lesion is usually the main determinant of the extent of recovery (Kertesz, 1993).

Corollary: The effects on consciousness of appropriately placed focal lesions follow the same rules as the effects produced by focal lesions on other brain functions. The fact that responsiveness returns after small ILN lesions is not evidence against the necessity of ILN for C (Petit, Rousseaux, Clarisse, & Delafosse, 1981; Smythies, 1997) any more than rapid recovery from a small lesion in Broca's area (Dronkers, 2000; Mohr, 1973, 1976; Moutier, 1908) means that this cortical area is irrelevant for aphasia, as once claimed by P. Marie (1906). The ability of brain function to recover significantly (though rarely ever completely) from structural damage is, along with wetness, an important property distinguishing brains from known artifacts.

3. So long as the lesion is unilateral, there will be no loss of consciousness. This is true not only for a small lesion weighing a few grams in one of the two thalami but even for very large damage or removal of an entire hemisphere, in excess of 400 g.

Corollary: The mechanism for consciousness is paired, existing in duplicate. This conclusion is consonant with the bilateralism of the anatomy and is supported experimentally by the results of hemispherectomy and the splitbrain.

The ILN Subserve Mc: The Widespread Connections

Experiments using anatomic tracers have shown that with small lesions in almost every cortical region these regions project to ILN. However, Koch (1995) pointed out that both primary visual cortex (V1) and inferotemporal cortex (IT) in the monkey have not been shown to connect with ILN. There is considerable controversy over V1-ILN connections; if they are indeed absent, this would be consistent with the evidence that processing in V1 is inaccessible to consciousness (Koch, 2004). A systematic search for ILN-IT connections or their absence is needed; if they are not present, our attention will be increasingly focused on the pulvinar because it is widely connected to all of postrolandic cortex and is thought to be essential to the determination of the salience of visual stimuli (Robinson & Cowie, 1997).

Groenewegen and Berendse recently reviewed evidence that ILN has effects more specific than the traditional term "nonspecific" might suggest. They concluded that "the major role of the midline-intralaminar nuclei presumably lies in the regulation of the activity and the ultimate functioning of individual basal-ganglia-thalamocortical circuits" (Groenewegen & Berendse, 1994, p. 56). Moreover, "the midline-intralaminar nuclei are positioned in the forebrain circuits like a spider in its web" (Groenewegen & Berendse, 1994, p. 57).

The emphases placed on the ubiquitous role of thalamus in neocortical function by Steriade et al. (1997) and by Sherman and Guillery (2002) were made with respect to the processing of specific information. A different but related point is that essentially an entire thalamus is engaged in switching between more general states, such as arousal, spindling (as in drowsiness), slow-wave sleep, or seizure activity (Contreras et al., 1997). How large numbers of thalamic cells, located in different nuclei, can be activated collectively for such overall state changes depends upon several mechanisms. Jones (1998a) includes (1) the action on underlying thalamic nuclei of the reticular nucleus whose cells are widely interconnected; (2) interconnections (which are controversial) among the ILN; (3) cortical projections to ILN, which in turn project diffusely to cortex; and (4) the more recent proposal (Jones, 1998b) that the diffusion of activity is effected via the diffusely projecting matrix cells present in all thalamic nuclei, principal as well as ILN. The relative importance of these mechanisms remains unsettled.

Ascending input to ILN can help explain C of primitive percepts. The input to ILN includes a large fraction of the ascending output of the brainstem reticular formation, which not only subserves arousal but also contains information about other bodily states. Other input comes from a phylogenetically old spinothalamic system and trigeminal complex (both conveying temperature and nociceptive information) and from the dentate nuclei in the cerebellum conveying proprioceptive signals. There are also ascending inputs to ILN from deep layers of the periacqueductal gray, substantia nigra, and amygdala with affective information and from the vestibular nuclei with information about body position (Kaufman & Rosenquist, 1985; McGuinness & Krauthamer, 1980; Royce, Bromley, & Gracco, 1991).

The ILN Subserve Mc: Multiple Functional Roles

In addition to observations from clinical cases and the use of anatomical tracers, information on the ILN has come from recording and stimulation. By 1966, Ervin and Mark were stimulating the ILN in pain patients, obtaining diffuse dysphoria and making lesions that (at least for a time) produced "a striking loss of the clinical

pain." When recording, they found neurons responding to visual and auditory as well as somesthetic stimuli. It was emphasized by Jasper (1966) that such responses only appeared when the stimuli were novel and were less evident with repetition, unlike the responses in the sensory (ventrobasal) portion of thalamus that "continue to respond faithfully . . . whether the patient is aware of the stimuli or not" (Jasper, 1966, p. 260). When Albe-Fessard and Besson published their monumental review in 1978, they emphasized the polysensory functions of the ILN although admitting they had "a role to play" in the appreciation of pain. By 1980, McGuinness and Krauthamer had concluded that the ILN acted not only as a thalamic pacemaker and as a relay for cortical arousal but was characterized also by the presence of cells responding to visual, auditory, and somesthetic stimuli. They found further that the suggestion that at least part of the ILN were active in central pain mechanisms and in addition acted as a modulator of both striatal output and input, hence could be considered part of the motor apparatus. Similar conclusions were reached by Schlag and Schlag-Rey (Schlag, 1984) after nearly twenty years of experiments on thalamic function. In addition, they established a major role for ILN in the control of eye movements and visual attention (Orem, 1973).

Purpura and Schiff (Purpura, 1997) concluded that a wide range of data, "suggest that in the state of wakefulness, the ILN neurons promote the formation of an "event-holding" function in the cortex". An abundance of neurological, anatomical and functional evidence was subsequently reviewed in Schiff (1999) who wrote, "cortical and subcortical innervations of the ILN place them in a central position to influence distributed networks underlying arousal, attention, intention, working memory, and sensorimotor integration, including gaze control."

Bilaterality of the Mechanism

A striking example of loss of cerebral tissue is provided by a total hemispherectomy also called "hemicerebrectomy" (including cortex, underlying white matter, and basal ganglia). Of the four patients reported by Austin and Grant (1958), one was stuporous preoperatively. The other three continued speaking and were "acutely aware" of their surroundings throughout the operation, which was done under local anesthesia. Whatever the anatomical basis for producing C, the anatomy exists in duplicate. That only one of the pair suffices for C is clear from total hemispherectomy in humans (Austin & Grant, 1958; Bogen et al., 1998; Peacock, 1996; Smith & Burklund, 1966; Smith & Sugar, 1975). The same conclusion follows from hemicerebrectomy in monkeys and cats (Bogen, 1974; Bogen & Campbell, 1962; Koskoff, Patton, Migler, & Kruper, 1959; Kruper, Patton, & Koskoff, 1971; White et al., 1959). It also follows from temporarily anesthetizing a human hemisphere rather than removing it (Lesser, Dinner, Luders, & Morris, 1986).

Often the term "hemispherectomy" has been applied to operations in humans in which there has been only a hernidecortication (Kossoff et al., 2003). In addition, some operations are "functional hemispherectomies' in which the hemisphere has been disconnected from the rest as fully as possible, but left in situ (Arzimanoglou et al., 2000). In such cases it is always possible that some function is attributable to parts left behind, rather than solely to the residual hemisphere. However, in the cat and monkey experiments described above the sections were precisely in the midline, so no parts of the extirpated hemisphere remained. In the human cases of "total hemispherectomy" cited above, the basal ganglia were removed with all the cortex, as well as all the intervening white matter (Austin & Grant, 1958; Bogen et al., 1998; Smith & Burklund, 1966; Smith & Sugar, 1975). With no targets remaining for their axons, the thalamic cells soon atrophy and are resorbed; half of the supratentorial space is thus left empty, containing only cerebrospinal fluid.

Even before hemispherectomies had been performed, there had been observed naturally occurring cases with resorption of an entire hemisphere; these cases led some of the most prominent neurologists of the late 19th century to speak of a double brain. The rise and subsidence of these views are thoroughly described by Harrington (1987); her book was stimulated by the appearance of new evidence for cerebral duality (the split-brain) as it became well known in the 1970s through the work of Roger Sperry and colleagues.

Because consciousness requires only one hemisphere, many 19th-century neurologists inferred that there can be a doubling of C with two hemispheres. This inference was empirically confirmed in the testing of split-brain cats and monkeys (Sperry, 1961) as well as humans (Sperry, Gazzaniga, & Bogen, 1969). How this duality is negotiated by an assortment of integrating mechanisms in the intact cerebrum is a fascinating and important question (Bogen, 1990, 1993, 1997a; Bogen & Bogen, 1969; Gazzaniga, 1970; Iacoboni & Zaidel, 1996; Kinsbourne & Smith, 1974; Landis & Regard, 1988; Regard, Cook, Wieser, & Landis, 1994; Sperry, 1968; Tramo et al., 1995; Trevarthen, 1974; Zaidel & Iacoboni, 2002). But this problem of interhemispheric integration is not the concern of this chapter. It is pointed out here to emphasize the following conclusion: Because an individual needs only one hemisphere to be conscious, our immediate problem of understanding the physiology of consciousness can be much simplified by restricting our attention to how C is engendered in someone with a single cerebral hemisphere.

It is worth emphasizing at this point that it is a mistake to argue against the possibility of an anatomically specifiable mechanism (an Mc) necessary for consciousness on the ground that no suitable anatomic structure is present in the middle of the head (Dennett & Kinsbourne, 1992; Flanagan, 1991). What is evident on any horizontal or frontal section of the cerebrum is the duality of any and all candidates; they are all present in pairs. The hemispherectomy data have established that either member of a pair is, in general, sufficient for C. If one is looking for a structure located "in the middle" of the hemisphere, one obvious place is the thalamus of that hemisphere. Many people are so accustomed to speak of "the" thalamus or "the" amygdala or "the" limbic system that they easily forget that there are two, one in each hemisphere. We should not let our thinking about the physiology be misdirected by long-standing, convenient figures of speech.

The ILN Subserve Mc: Results of Bithalamic Paramedian Strokes

Support of the proposal that ILN subserve Mc includes the results of thalamic obstructive strokes involving the thalamoperforating (paramedian) arteries (Tatu, Moulin, Bogousslavsky, & Duvernoy, 1998). Simultaneous bimedial thalamic damage can occur because the medial parts of both thalami are occasionally supplied by a single arterial trunk that branches, with one branch to each thalamus. If the trunk is occluded before it branches, both thalami will be affected. When there is simultaneous, partial damage of the two sets of ILN, unresponsiveness typically ensues (see Table 2 of Guberman & Stuss, 1983). Sudden onset of coma can occur even when the lesions are only a few cubic centimeters in volume, as in case 4 of Graff-Radford, Tranel, Van Hoesen, and Brandt (1990). This is in contrast to retention of responsiveness with very large infarctions elsewhere. Even a quite large lesion involving one (and only one) thalamus rarely if ever causes coma (Plum & Posner, 1985).

Correlating thalamic damage with behavioral deficit is more precise with strokes from occlusion of blood supply than from bleeding or from tumors, so that emphasis is given here to cases of occlusion.

Classical autopsy examples of bithalamic occlusion often had extension of the damage downward into subthalamus (Castaigne et al., 1981; Façon, Steriade, & Wertheim, 1958). Many cases carried uncertainties inherent in now outdated imaging techniques. More recently, published cases typically show crisp MRI images of small lesions whose extent is well demonstrated (Tatemichi et al., 1992; van Domburg, ten Donkelaar, & Noterman, 1996; Wiest, Mallek, & Baumgartner, 2000); in these cases it has again been reported that onset of the bilateral damage was accompanied by the abrupt loss of responsiveness.

Emergence from unresponsiveness after incomplete bithalamic lesions depends on the size of the lesion, taking only a few hours if the lesions are tiny, as in case 4 of Graff-Radford et al. (1990). When the lesions are larger, it takes longer for the patient to arouse. With larger lesions, the recovery is commonly accompanied by mental impairments variously described as confusion, dementia, amnesia, and/or hypersomnia. Which of these impairments dominates depends on the precise lesion site and size (Abe, Yokoyama, & Yorifuji, 1993; Bassetti et al., 1996; Bewermeyer et al., 1985; Bogousslavsky & Caplan, 1995; Bogousslavsky et al., 1991; Gentilini, De Renzi, & Crisi, 1987; Graff-Radford et al., 1990; Guberman & Stuss, 1983; Malamut et al., 1992; Markowitsch, Cramon, & Schuri, 1993; Meissner, Sapir, Kokmen, & Stein, 1987; Michel et al., 1982; Mills & Swanson, 1978; Plum & Posner, 1985; Schott et al., 1980; Yasuda et al., 1990).

With quite large bilateral lesions the patients usually remain in coma until they die. However, a patient with extensive ILN lesions may survive for many years, if medically supported, in a persistent vegetative state. That is, such a patient remains unresponsive in spite of relatively intact brainstem and cerebral cortex, as in the case (widely publicized at the time) of Karen Ann Quinlan (Kinney et al., 1994).

Shortness of Breath

Among the most primitive of subjective sensations is the experience of shortness of breath (SOB), sometimes called breathlessness or air hunger. The usual cause of SOB is increased CO_2 in the blood, whether from exertion, inadequate ventilation, lung disease, or direct introduction of CO_2 into the subject's inspired air. Extensive investigations have made it clear that SOB does not depend on feedback from respiratory muscles or the rib cage; it is directly related to "respiratory drive"; that is, the frequency of neuronal firing in the respiratory centers of the medulla (Eldridge & Chen, 1996). The amount of respiratory drive can be measured by recording from medulla, but is measured more conveniently by recording from the phrenic nerve. Because the sensation of SOB does not stem from bodily sensations (SOB occurs even when these sensations are interrupted as in spinal cord injury), its likely source is a corollary discharge traveling upward from the medulla. A search of the midbrain and of thalamus has disclosed neurons whose activity is closely correlated with phrenic nerve activity, as CO_2 levels are manipulated. In the thalamus, the neurons that become active with increased CO_2 appear to be in the ILN (Eldridge & Chen, 1996).

When CO_2 is elevated, the pulse rate and respiratory rate rise along with increased respiratory effort. These compensatory reactions occur automatically. So what advantage is there in also having a subjective experience? The answer is not altogether clear, but likely has to do with encouraging the individual to change whatever else is going on.

Other questions remain, as the experiments of Eldridge and Chen lacked histological controls and have not been replicated to my knowledge. When they are repeated, it would be of interest to know if the ILN neurons correlated with SOB are those already known to be responsive to pain, visual, auditory, and somesthetic stimuli, especially when these stimuli are novel (Jasper, 1966).

Ascending Activation

It is important to distinguish Mc from the ascending activating influences arising from several sources in the brainstem reticular formation (BSRF). First, some background.

It has been known since work conducted by Berger (1930) that transitions from resting to behavioral alertness are reflected in the electroencephalogram (EEG) as transitions from high-voltage low frequencies (HVLF) to lower-voltage higher frequencies (LVHF).

This change has subsequently come to be called arousal of the EEG because of its common coexistence with behavioural arousal. When Bremer (1935, 1936) transected the neuraxis at C_1, the top end of the spinal cord, he found that the isolated brain (encéphale isolé) alternated between HVLF and LVHF and the cat's pupils alternated between small, as in sleep, and dilated as in the aroused animal. In other words, the cat's brain alternated between sleep and wakefulness in spite of being disconnected from its body below the head and in spite of the head being fixed in a frame so the EEG could be recorded. From my own personal experience with the encéphale isolé, I can also add that when the cat is awake, as judged by EEG criteria and pupil size, it follows with its eyes objects or persons moving around the room.

By contrast, Bremer found that after midbrain transection the isolated cerebrum (cerveau isolé) stayed in the HVLF state. That is, without the brainstem the cerebrum was apparently unarousable. Subsequently, Moruzzi and Magoun (1949) found that stimulation within the brainstem reticular formation produced the EEG arousal. As was pointed out above, small (bilateral) lesions in the BSRF can cause immediate unresponsiveness. Together with relevant autopsy studies of coma in humans, this line of research led to the widely accepted notion of an ascending reticular activating system (ARAS; Magoun, 1952; O'Leary & Coben, 1958).

By 1960, it was generally accepted that (1) for consciousness, the cerebrum must remain attached to the upper end of the brainstem and that (2) this fact depended upon ascending activating influences from the BSRF. For several decades, in the 1970s and 1980s, the concept of an ARAS was variously criticized (Brodal, 1969; Jouvet, 1967) and thought by some to be passé. However, newer evidence in the 1980s and 1990s, much of it from Steriade and colleagues, enabled Steriade (1996) to say that the concept of ascending activation from the BSRF "has been rescued from oblivion." Furthermore, it now appears that the BSRF stimulation that arouses the EEG can facilitate synchrony in the gamma range (20–70 spikes/s: Munk et al., 1996). This is important because synchrony in the gamma range has been thought to underlie aspects of cognition, so this finding fits the idea that arousal facilitates thinking. In addition, an imaging study found that procedures that called for focusing attention caused increased activation of both BSRF and the thalamic ILN (Kinomura, Larsson, Gulyas, & Roland, 1996).

The ILN Are Not Simply Relays for Activation

When the concept of ascending activation was first popular, the arrival at cortex of activating influences appeared attributable to an "unspecific thalamocortical system" including the ILN (Jasper, 1954). Since then, it has often been supposed that the function of the ILN is best understood as relaying to cortex the activation originating in the brainstem. This appeared similar to the "relay" function attributed to the specific nuclei. Perhaps the most explicit expression of this is the ERTAS advocated by Newman and Baars (1993). However, considering the ILN to act principally as relays for activation seems incorrect for several reasons.

First, the view that thalamic nuclei act mainly as relays (and are often labeled "relay nuclei" in introductory texts) is no longer tenable (Guillery & Sherman, 2002). In this connection, I note that only 10 to 20% of LGN synapses are from the eyes (LGN is the visual "relay" nucleus of thalamus). This means that information arriving from the eyes is subjected in LGN to modification from a variety of sources. This includes fibers from visual cortex back to LGN that are about ten times as numerous as the fibers carrying information from LGN up to visual cortex (Sherman & Koch, 1986).

Second, the internal organization of the ILN implies selective processing, a conclusion consonant with their diverse inputs from all sensory modalities.

Third, the output of the ILN is not only to cortex, but even more prominently is to the striatum, which suggests a role of ILN in the control of motor output, as discussed further below.

Fourth, activation of cortex occurs independently of ILN as evidenced by rare cases of nearly complete destruction of the ILN but relative sparing of cortex; the resulting vegetative state includes cycling between "sleep" and "wakefulness" (i.e., states with and without cortical arousal; Kinney et al., 1994; Schiff & Plum, 1999).

Thalamic Contribution to Attention

Consideration of the relation of consciousness and attention is made difficult by the various usages of both words. Attention can be synonymous with an orientation of the head and eyes to a brief stimulus, attributable to midbrain function and occurring well before awareness of the stimulus. What we see may or may not correspond to the "spotlight of attention" (He, Cavanagh, & Intriligator, 1997; Jung, 1954). Or attention may refer to an individual's keeping some location "in mind" while fixating vision elsewhere (Treue & Maunsell, 1996) as evidenced, for example, by a faster response to that location than to others. It is not surprising then, that multiple mechanisms have been implicated in attention, including an assortment of cortical regions (Posner & Rothbart, 1992).

Almost completely surrounding each thalamus is a thin layer of cells called the reticular nucleus (which is called R, RE, Ret, Rt, nRt, RTN, or TRN depending on the author). It has long been suggested that R provides part of the physiologic basis for selective attention (Crick, 1984; Guillery, Feig, & Lozsadi, 1998; Jones, 2002; Mitrofanis & Guillery, 1993; Scheibel & Scheibel, 1966; Yingling & Skinner, 1976, 1977). Briefly, a physiologic mechanism for attention is ascribed to R for several reasons: (1) Each R envelops, in a thin layer, most of the thalamic nuclei. The thalamocortical fibers, as well as the fibers returning from cortex to thalamus, when passing through R, give off collaterals as they pass through;

(2) R efferents terminate in the immediately underlying thalamic nuclei; and (3) R efferents are GABAergic (the neurons in R are exclusively inhibitory, using GABA as their transmitter). The likelihood exists, therefore, that thalamocortical communication can be simultaneously inhibited overall with highly selective non-inhibition. Such localized gating could provide a mechanism for selective attention in cognition. How R selectively gates is clearly affected by the fibers from cortex ending in R, which may help explain top-down control of attention. Bottom-up effects on attention may involve several mechanisms, but one probably depends upon the collaterals, ending in R, of thalamic projection to cortex from the sensory nuclei of the thalamus. In addition to the focal gating, R can generally inhibit all the other thalamic nuclei during slow-wave sleep. When the ascending activation from BSRF increases, it has a widespread inhibitory effect throughout R; this suppresses the inhibition exerted by R and momentarily opens up widespread (ungated) communication from thalamus to cortex. As Guillery and Harting (2003) wrote, "Whereas [brainstem and basal forebrain] afferents can be expected to have global actions on thalamocortical transmission, relevant for overall attentive state, the [topographically focal corticothalamic input] will have local actions, modulating transmission through the thalamus to cortex with highly specific local effects."

Appropriate Interaction

There are three main types of thalamic projections: the specific (as for vision, audition), the diffuse (characteristic of the matrix cells according to Jones as mentioned above), and the projection to striatum (essentially all from ILN). The striatal projection is discussed below with respect to volition. The first type, specific projection, conforms more to the concept of the sensory relay of information to cortex. As to the second type, diffuse ILN efferents are widely though sparsely distributed to most

of neocortex; it is this diffuse projection that, I argue here, has to do with C. One can understand how ILN could directly influence ideation, as ideation is a function of cortex. This implies that awareness of content depends upon some as yet unspecified "appropriate interaction" between ILN and the neural representation of that content. The possibility has been raised that what I call appropriate interaction involves synchronization of neuronal activity at 40 Hz: Stimulus-dependent synchronization of cortical cells with ILN cells at 40 Hz could be an example of C plus content (Steriade, Curro Dossi, & Contreras, 1993).

As an example of appropriate interaction between ILN and a specific cortical area, we can consider awareness of the direction of motion of a stimulus. It is now widely understood that motion direction information (MDI) is represented in cortex of the superior temporal sulcus (STS), especially area V5, also called MT (Allman & Kass, 1971; Maunsell & Newsome, 1987; Rodman, Gross, & Albright, 1990; Zeki, 1974, 1993). According to the present hypothesis, for the MDI to have a subjective aspect (i.e., to acquire C) there must occur the appropriate interaction between STS neurons and Mc. Keep in mind that the MDI in STS might well be available for adaptive behavior whether or not it acquires C.

In the neurally intact individual, the appropriate interaction can be on, or off, or in between and is quickly adjustable. However, when V1 (striate cortex) has been ablated, the appropriate interaction for vision typically does not occur. That is, the MDI in STS is not available to verbal output (the individual denies seeing the stimulus). At the same time, the MDI may be available for some other behavior. This is an example of blindsight (Grüsser & Landis, 1991; Ptito, Lepore, Ptito, & Lassonde, 1991; Stoerig & Cowey, 1995, 1997; Weiskrantz, 1986, 1997). When we accept availability to verbal output as the index of C (which we commonly do) it appears that the appropriate interaction between STS and ILN cannot readily occur without an essential influence from striate cortex (V1). An explanation for the fact that

C usually does not accompany the processing of visual information in the absence of V1 is not yet established (Weiskrantz, 1997). However, the excitatory drive of the extrastriate regions by striate cortex may be the essential ingredient; more feeble input from subcortical sources (such as pulvinar) can enable some low-level processing by MT without awareness (Koch, 2004).

When visual processing in the absence of V1 is accompanied by C (Stoerig & Barth, 2001), this may indicate stronger than usual input from pulvinar. Alternatively, Zeki and Bartels (1999) consider visual C without participation of V1 to be evidence for their theory, mentioned above, of multiple microconsciousnesses.

Interruption of Access to C

This chapter's hypothesis suggests that for some content represented by NAPs in cortex to be endowed with C, there must be a connection between the ILN and the region(s) of cortex containing those NAPs. Years ago it was suggested that unawareness of one's bodily derangement (called anosognosia) could be caused by an interruption between thalamus and parietal cortex (Sandifer, 1946). The disconnection of ILN from cortex should result in the unavailability to consciousness of some content; the more extensive the disconnection, the greater the loss of content. An extreme example would be the vegetative state in which there is eye opening to minimal stimuli, cycling between sleeping and waking states, and preservation of many brainstem functions but little if any evidence of mental function (Plum & Posner, 1985). The undetectability of mental function is accompanied by loss of metabolic activity and decreased blood flow in the cerebrum. Although the vegetative state may follow widespread cerebral damage it can also appear either from damage solely to the thalami (Szirmai, Guseo, & Molnar, 1977) or from interruption of thalamocortical connections with little if any damage to the cortex (Jennett, 2002; Kinney et al., 1994; Schiff et al., 2002). A PET study (measuring blood flow) done by Laureys et al. (2000) showed thalamocortical disconnection as the cause of a vegetative state. These authors concluded that "restoration of consciousness seems to be paralleled by the resumption of the functional relation between thalami and associative cortices." The next sections discuss interference with the ILN-cortex connections that are physiologic (functional) rather than anatomic.

Loss of Function from Unbalanced Inhibition

An important principle of neuropsychology is that loss of some ability is not necessarily the result of destruction of a brain part essential to that ability. A fairly common example is the loss of a stroke patient's ability to look toward the side of a cortical lesion; this deficit sometimes subsides in a few hours, but may take much longer. The problem is not primarily in the midbrain circuits controlling eye movement; the problem is that these circuits are receiving from one hemisphere influences that are no longer balanced by those from the damaged hemisphere. There are multiple influences, both inhibitory and facilitatory.

As some of these influences subside, the ability to gaze in either direction returns. Recovery from a brain injury results from a variety of processes; one of these is a rebalancing of the facilitatory and inhibitory influences. When performance has been lost because the competence has lost some facilitation, re-emergence of the performance can result simply from the subsidence of inhibition (Sherrington, 1932). Much the same suggestion was made by von Monakow (1911).

The main point is that a loss of performance is not necessarily the result of damage to the competence for that performance; it may result from unbalanced or excessive inhibition of the competence.

The concept of an appropriate interaction between ILN and a NAP elsewhere implies that C of some representations can be lost not only when the representations are damaged or when anatomical connections are severed. In addition, contents (represented by various NAPs) that are ordinarily available to consciousness can be unavailable because the interaction is inhibited. An example may be found in some cases of parietal hemi-neglect (Bogen, 2003).

The Conviction of Volition

That the basal ganglia (BG) are crucial in controlling motor function is well known. Many of the relevant facts come from studies of Parkinsonism: "Damage to the striatum results in major defects in voluntary movement" (Graybiel, Aosaki, Flaherty, & Kimura, 1994). The BG are particularly involved in self-initiated movement (Taniwaki et al., 2003).

The prominent connections to ILN from globus pallidus suggests a monitoring of motor systems, as do the cortical projections to ILN from sensorimotor and premotor cortex. A role for ILN in the control of motor output can be inferred from the very substantial projections from ILN to striatum (Sadikot, Parent, Smith, & Bolam, 1992; Sidibé & Smith, 1996). We can ask, Is the ILN projection to striatum a pathway for the inhibition (or release from inhibition) of motor plans that have been developing for several hundred milliseconds? Is this the basis for a "volitional" decision?

Closely related to or synonymous with "volitional" are such adjectives as voluntary, discretionary, conative, spontaneous, intentional, deliberate, and the like. We need not consider here how these concepts differ, nor mire down in the centuries-old problem of free will versus either theological or materialistic determinism. We need recognize only the fact that each of us has a conviction of volition that we attach to some of our acts (those for which we feel responsible), but not to some other acts, and that our conviction of volition has a neurophysiological explanation. It helps to consider first acts that are non-volitional. A common example of action for which people do not consider themselves responsible is the pupillary constriction to light. Many activities carry on in the absence not only of voluntary control but

also of any awareness at all. We understand that most bodily adaptations (including postural adjustments, sensorimotor coordination, phoneme generation during speech, as well as most autonomic regulation) not only can proceed independently of C but, more often than not, are also unavailable to C.

The foregoing contrasts with what I call "deliberate" actions. And some activities are only intermittently volitional; probably the commonest example of incessant activity for which we occasionally do take responsibility is breathing. What is the physiological difference among these actions?

Velmans (1991) and Gray (1995) have described a range of processes in which awareness follows rather than precedes the information processing. A famous experiment (Libet, 1993, 2003; Libet et al., 1983) showed that an intent to act develops, as evidenced by development of the readiness potential (RP) several hundred milliseconds before the subject decides to act, as noted by the subject who is watching an indicator sweeping a large clock face marked in milliseconds. This experiment of Libet has been furiously debated for more than 20 years, sometimes regarding the method but mainly with respect to the interpretation. Much of the argumentation has stemmed from suspicions that the experiment has, or has not, some significance for certain metaphysical issues; these debates do not relate to my suggestion here that the experiment tells us something about the conviction of volition. The methodological criticisms have probably been laid to rest by replication of the original findings (Keller & Heckhausen, 1990; Trevena & Miller, 2002). Trevena and Miller (2002) did point out that, although the RP started earlier, what is called the lateralized readiness potential (LRP) appeared at the time indicated by the subjects, probably concordant with activation of motor cortex (their article is part of a thorough discussion in *Consciousness and Cognition* 11(2)). The discussion largely concluded with the statement by Pockett (2002) who was in many respects critical of Libet; however, she wrote, "Thus by no means all of the time difference between the start of the

RP and the consciousness of initiating an action can be accounted for by measurement errors. Clearly there is at least some form of unconscious preparation going on well before a subject consciously initiates a voluntary action" (Pockett, 2002, p. 323).

The foregoing does not mean that intent plays no role in what happens because, although conscious intent appears well after the intent to move has been developing, it appears some 150 ms before the action (pushing of a button). There exists, therefore, time for the subject either to stop the process or allow it to continue. Moreover, motor plans can be voluntarily formulated and stored, the storage probably involving the motor areas in medial frontal cortex (Libet, 1993; Passingham, 1993; Tanji & Shima, 1994). Stored motor plans can be subsequently released by a triggering stimulus that acquires C after the action has been initiated. Indeed, a stored action may be triggered by stimuli that never are "perceived"; that is, never acquire C (Taylor & McCloskey, 1990).

The proposal here is that a motor plan develops over time and that partway through this development or while it is held in readiness but not yet executed, we become aware of it (Libet, 1993). We can readily suppose that appropriate interaction between premotor cortex and ILN occurs early enough (i.e., 150 ms) before action so that the self is associated with the developing motor plan. There would thus be time for ILN to exert an inhibition that would stop the action or to overcome any tonic inhibition and thus allow the action. If the motor plan is permitted to run to completion, self or me-ness would be associated with the action, and the individual would feel responsibility precisely because there had been an opportunity to abort the plan.

Endowing Emotions with C

The present hypothesis, including that a NAP can be converted to CNAP by Mc, implies that the NAPs representing emotions can exist (and cause behavioral signs of emotion) while non-conscious. This is consonant with the common dictionary definition of affect as the conscious aspect of emotion. Attributing Mc to the ILN provides a tangible mechanism for the conscientiation of emotion (i.e., turning a non-conscious emotion into an affect). Before considering the anatomy, it helps to comment briefly on the point that being conscious of emotions may be more fundamental than being conscious of ideas (Damasio, 1999; Panksepp, 1998; Seager, 2002; Watt, 2000).

The C of nausea, thirst, fatigue, and the like is at least as typical of being conscious (having qualia) as having C of time, place, person, meanings, memories, and expectations. In all likelihood C of emotions antedated C of cognition in both phylogeny and ontogeny. An excessive emphasis on C attending cognition by many current students of consciousness may derive, as do so many attitudes, from Descartes who claimed, "I think, therefore I am." A neurobiological understanding of C might come more quickly if we were to aver, I feel, therefore I am (Bogen, 1997b; Prof. T. Sullivan has recently brought to my attention that when Descartes said "thinking," he meant to include feelings as well as thoughts. However, the idea that Descartes meant to exclude emotions seems to be a venerable misunderstanding; see Descartes, 1953, p. 374, where Principle 9 is entitled, "Ce que c'est penser").

Looking for the mechanism endowing emotions with C means finding connections between structures subserving C and structures subserving emotion. The latter are, roughly speaking, the constituents of the limbic system; these include the amygdala, orbital cortex, and, connected to both of these, the medial dorsal nucleus of the thalamus. As pointed out above, the ILN are draped over and around the MD like a blanket. This relationship is particularly well demonstrated by staining for the compound calretinin, which is largely restricted to the ILN (Cicchetti, Lacroix, Beach, & Parent, 1998; Fortin, Asselin, Gould, & Parent, 1998; Munkle, Waldfogel, & Faull, 1999, 2000). So striking is this relation that one is tempted to think of it as the anatomical basis for the statement, "I feel, therefore I am."

Importance of C for Episodic Memory

Understanding the relations between memory and consciousness can help us understand better both of these (Schacter, 1989; Tulving, 1985). One function of C is to facilitate certain kinds of learning. We can consider as examples two forms of learning: trace conditioning (TC) of the blink reflex to a puff of air and the delayed non-match-to-sample (DNMS). The former is relatively simple and has been studied extensively in rabbits as well as humans (Clark & Squire, 1998). The DNMS is more demanding; it has mainly been studied in rats as well as monkeys (Dudai, 2002; Eichenbaum & Cohen, 2001). Both TC and DNMS are dependent on neuronal circuits that include the entorhinal cortex (ento), which is the principal bottleneck for information to and from the hippocampus. C is maintained by structures other than the entorhinal cortex because C persists after removal of entorhinal cortex. If it is correct that both TC and DNMS require consciousness, then they evidently depend not only on ento but also on a connection between ento and other structure(s) important for C. A likely candidate is the "blanket" of ILN. This follows not only because of the evidence presented in this chapter that the ILN are essential to C but also because it is known that damage to the ILN impairs DNMS (Mair, 1994). So far as I am aware, no one has yet examined whether lesions of the ILN would prevent trace conditioning. These facts also suggest that both TC and DNMS could be experimentally impaired by lesions of the tracts connecting the entorhinal cortex with ILN while sparing both termini (Bogen, 2001).

Summary of the Thalamic ILN and the Property C

This chapter includes a series of suggestions:

1. An essential aspect for the understanding of consciousness is its physiologic basis.

2. Our search for that basis will be facilitated by making a sharp distinction between the property of consciousness (here called C) and the contents of consciousness, which vary widely from time to time, from one individual to the next, and from one species to another.

3. The property C depends upon a specific mechanism (here called Mc) that evolved to enable the transient association of self with (a small fraction at any one time) of the thoughts and feelings generated in mammalian (and possibly other) brains.

4. Proper function of Mc requires a state of arousal ordinarily dependent upon activation ascending from the brainstem reticular formation.

5. In mammals the Mc exists in duplicate.

6. Mc crucially includes the intralaminar nuclei of the thalami.

References

Abe, K., Yokoyama, R., Yorifuji, S. (1993). Repetitive speech disorder resulting from infarcts in the paramedian thalami and midbrain. *Journal of Neurology, Neurosurgery, and Psychiatry, 56*, 1024–1026.

Adrian, E. D., Bremer, F., & Jasper, H. H. (Eds.). (1954). *Brain mechanisms and consciousness.* Springfield, IL: C. C. Thomas.

Albe-Fessard, D., & Besson, J. M. (1978). Convergent thalamic and cortical projections, the non-specific system. In A. Iggo (Ed.), *Handbook of sensory physiology: Somatosensory system.* New York: Springer.

Allman, J. M., & Kass, J. H. (1971). A representation of the visual field in the caudal third of the middle temporal gyrus of the owl monkey (*Aotus trivirgatus*). *Brain Research, 31*, 85–105.

Allport, A. (1988). What concept of consciousness? In A. J. Marcel & E. Bisiach (Eds.), *Consciousness in contemporary science.* Oxford: Clarendon Press.

Arzimanoglou, A. A., Andermann, F., Aicardi, J., Sainte-Rose, C., Beaulieu, M. A., Villemure, J. G., Olivier, A., & Rasmussen, T. (2000). Sturge-Weber syndrome: Indications and results of surgery in 20 patients. *Neurology, 55*, 1472–1479.

Austin, G. M., & Grant, F. C. (1958). Physiologic observations following total hemispherectomy in man. *Surgery, 38*, 239–258.

Baars, B. J. (1988). *A cognitive theory of consciousness*. Cambridge: Cambridge University Press.

Baars, B. J. (1993). How does a serial, integrated and very limited stream of consciousness emerge from a nervous system that is mostly unconscious, distributed, parallel and of enormous capacity? In G. Broch & J. F. Marsh (Eds.), *Experimental and theoretical studies of consciousness*. New York: John Wiley and Sons.

Baars, B. J. (1997). *In the theatre of consciousness*. New York: Oxford University Press.

Bar, M., & Biederman, I. (1998). Subliminal visual priming. *Psychological Science, 9*, 464–469.

Bar, M., & Biederman, I. (1999). Localizing the cortical region mediating visual awareness of object identity. *Proceedings of the National Academy of Sciences USA, 96*, 1790–1793.

Bassetti, C., Mathis, J., Gugger, M., Lovblad, K. O., & Hess, C. W. (1996). Hypersomnia following paramedian thalamic stroke: A report of 12 patients. *Annals of Neurology, 39*, 471–480.

Benson, D. F. (1994). *The neurology of thinking*. New York: Oxford University Press.

Berger, H. (1930). Über das Elektrenkephalogram des Menschen, II. *Archives of Psychology and Neurology (Lpz), 40*, 160–169.

Bergman, T. J., Beehner, J. C., Cheney, D. L., & Seyfarth, R. M. (2003). Hierarchical classification by rank and kinship in baboons. *Science, 302*, 1234–1236.

Berti, A., & Rizzolatti, G. (1992). Visual processing without awareness: Evidence from unilateral neglect. *Journal of Cognitive Neuroscience*, 345–351.

Bewermeyer, H., Dreesbach, H. A., Rackl, A., Neveling, M., & Heiss, W. D. (1985) Presentation of bilateral thalamic infarction on CT, MRI and PET. *Neuroradiology, 27*, 414–419.

Block, N. (1995). On a confusion about a function of consciousness. *Behavioral and Brain Sciences, 18*, 227–247.

Bogen, J. E. (1974). Hemispherectomy and the placing reaction in cats. In M. Kinsbourne & W. L. Smith (Eds.), *Hemispheric disconnection and cerebral function*. Springfield, IL: C. C. Thomas.

Bogen, J. E. (1976). Hughlings Jackson's heterogram. In D. Walter, L. Rogers, & J. M. Finzi-Fried (Eds.), *Cerebral dominance*. Los Angeles: UCLA BIS Conference Report.

Bogen, J. E. (1990). Partial hemispheric independence with the neocommissures intact. In C. Trevarthen (Ed.), *Brain circuits and functions of the mind*. Cambridge: Cambridge University Press.

Bogen, J. E. (1993). The callosal syndromes. In K. M. Heilman & E. Valenstein (Eds.), *Clinical neuropsychology* (3rd ed., pp 337–381). New York: Oxford University Press.

Bogen, J. E. (1995a). On the neurophysiology of consciousness: II. Constraining the semantic problem. *Consciousness and Cognition, 4*, 137–158.

Bogen, J. E. (1995b). On the neurophysiology of consciousness: I. An overview. *Consciousness and Cognition, 4*, 52–62.

Bogen, J. E. (1997a). Does cognition in the disconnected right hemisphere require right hemisphere possession of language? *Brain and Language, 57*, 12–21.

Bogen, J. E. (1997b). The crucial central core of consciousness does not require cognition. *Proceedings of the Society for Neuroscience, 23*, 1926.

Bogen, J. E. (1997c). Some neurophysiologic aspects of consciousness. *Seminars in Neurology, 17*, 95–103.

Bogen, J. E. (1998). My developing understanding of Roger Wolcott Sperry's philosophy. *Neuropsychologia, 36*, 1089–1096.

Bogen, J. E. (2001). An experimental disconnection approach to a function of consciousness. *International Journal of Neuroscience, 111*, 135–136.

Bogen, J. E. (2003). Is TPO hemineglect the result of unbalanced inhibition? *International Journal of Neuroscience, 114*(6), 655–670.

Bogen, J. E., & Berker, E. (2002). Face module, face network. *Neurology, 59*, 652–653.

Bogen, J. E., Berker, E., van Lancker, D., Sudia, S., Lipstad, B., Sadun, A., & Weekes, N. (1998). Left hemicerebrectomy: Vision, olfaction and mentation 45 years later. *Proceedings of the Society for Neuroscience, 24*, 173.

Bogen, J. E., & Bogen, G. M. (1969). The other side of the brain. 3. The corpus callosum and creativity. *Bulletin of the Los Angeles Neurology Society, 34*, 191–220.

Bogen, J. E., & Bogen, G. M. (1976). Wernicke's region. Where is it? *Annals of the New York Academy of Sciences, 280*, 834–843.

Bogen, J. E., & Campbell, B. (1962). Recovery of foreleg placing after ipsilateral frontal lobectomy in the hemicerebrectomized cat. *Science*, 135.

Bogousslavsky, J., & Caplan, L. (1995). *Stroke syndromes*. Cambridge: Cambridge University Press.

Bogousslavsky, J., Regli, F., Delaloye, B., Delaloye-Bischof, A., Assal, G., & Uske, A. (1991). Loss of psychic self-activation with bithalamic infarction. Neurobehavioural, CT, MRI and SPECT correlates. *Acta Neurologica Scandinavica*, 83, 309–316.

Bremer, F. (1935). Cerveau isolé et physiologie du sommeil. *Comptes Rendus Societe de la Societe de Biologie*, 118, 1235–1242.

Bremer, F. (1936). Nouvelles recerches sur le mecanisme du sommeil. *Comptes Rendus Societe de la Societe de Biologie*, 122, 460–464.

Brodal, A. (1969). *Neurological anatomy* (2nd ed). London: Oxford University Press.

Bunin, M. A., & Wightman, R. M. (1999). Paracrine neurotransmission in the CNS: Involvement of 5-HT. *Trends in Neuroscience*, 22, 377–382.

Cairns, H. (1952). Disturbances of consciousness with lesions of the brain-stem and diencephalon. *Brain*, 75, 109–146.

Cairns-Smith, A. G. (1996). *Evolving the mind*. Cambridge: Cambridge University Press.

Carpenter, W. B. (1853). *Principles of human physiology*. London: Churchill.

Castaigne, P., Lhermitte, F., Buge, A., Escourolle, R., Hauw, J. J., &Lyon-Caen, O. (1981). Paramedian thalamic and midbrain infarct: Clinical and neuropathological study. *Annals of Neurology*, 10, 127–148.

Castiello, U., Paulignan, Y., & Jeannerod, M. (1991). Temporal dissociation of motor responses and subjective awareness. A study in normal subjects. *Brain*, 114, 2639–2655.

Chalmers, D. J. (2002). The puzzle of conscious experience. *Scientific American*, 12, 90–98.

Churchland, P. S. (2002). *Brain-wise*. Cambridge, MA: MIT Press.

Cicchetti, F., Lacroix, S., Beach, T. G., & Parent, A. (1998). Calretinin gene expression in the human thalamus. *Brain Research: Molecular Brain Research*, 54, 1–12.

Clark, R. E., & Squire, L. R. (1998). Classical conditioning and brain systems: The role of awareness. *Science*, 280, 77–81.

Contreras, D., Destexhe, A., Sejnowski, T. J., & Steriade, M. (1997). Spatiotemporal patterns of spindle oscillations in cortex and thalamus. *Journal of Neuroscience*, 17, 1179–1196.

Crick, F. (1984). Function of the thalamic reticular complex: The search light hypothesis. *Proceedings of the National Academy of Sciences USA*, 81, 4586–4590.

Crick, F. (1994). *The astonishing hypothesis: The scientific search for the soul*. New York: Scribner's.

Crick, F., & Koch, C. (1990). Towards a neurobiological theory of consciousness. *Seminars in the Neurosciences*, 2, 263–275.

Crick, F., & Koch, C. (2000). The problem of consciousness. *Scientific American*, 12, 10–17.

Damasio, A. (1999). *The feeling of what happens: Body and emotion in the making of consciousness*. New York: Harcourt Brace.

Damasio, H., & Damasio, A. R. (1989). *Lesion analysis in neuropsychology*. New York: Oxford University Press.

Dennett, D. C. (1991). *Consciousness explained*. Boston: Little, Brown.

Dennett, D. C., & Kinsbourne, M. (1992). Time and the observer: The where and when of consciousness in the brain. *Behavioral and Brain Sciences*, 15, 183–201.

Descartes, R. (1953) Traite de l'homme. In O *Euvres et letters* (A. Bridoux A, Ed.). Paris: Gallimard.

Doty, R. W., Sr. (1975). Consciousness from neurons. *Acta Neurobiologiae Experimentalis (Warsz)*, 35, 791–804.

Dronkers, N. F. (2000). The gratuitous relationship between Broca's aphasia and Broca's area. *Behavioral and Brain Sciences*, 23, 30–31.

Dudai, Y. (2002). *Memory from A to Z*. Oxford: Oxford University Press.

Eccles, J. C. (1966). Conscious experience and memory. In J. C. Eccles (Ed.), *Brain and conscious experience*. New York: Springer.

Edelman, G. M. (1989). *The remembered present: A biological theory of consciousness*. New York: Basic Books.

Edelman, G. M. (1992). *Bright air, brilliant fire*. New York: Basic Books.

Eichenbaum, H., & Cohen, N. J. (2001). *From conditioning to conscious recollection*. New York: Oxford University Press.

Eldridge, F. L., & Chen, Z. (1996). Respiratory sensation: A neurophysiologic perspective. In L. Adams & A. Guz (Eds.), *Respiratory sensation*. New York: Marcel Dekker.

Engel, A. K., Fries, P., Konig, P., Brecht, M., & Singer, W. (1999). Does time help to understand consciousness? *Consciousness and Cognition*, 8, 260–268.

Ervin, F. R., & Mark, V. H. (1966). Studies of the human thalamus: IV. Evoked responses. *Annals of the New York Academy of Sciences*, 112, 81–92.

Façon, E., Steriade, M., & Wertheim, N. (1958). Hypersomnie prolongée engendrée par des lésions bilatérales du systéme activateur médial lesyndrome thrombotique de la bifurcation du tronc basilaire. *Revue of Neurologique (Paris)*, 98, 117–133.

Fessard, A. E. (1954). Mechanisms of nervous integration and conscious experience. In E. D. Adrian & F. Bremer, Eds.), *Brain mechanisms and consciousness* (pp 200–236). Springfield, IL: C. C. Thomas.

Fields, R. D., & Stevens-Graham, B. (2002). New insights into neuron-glia communication. *Science*, 298, 556–562.

Flanagan, O. (1991). The modularity of consciousness. *Behavioral and Brain Sciences*, 14, 446–447.

Flanagan, O. (1992). *Consciousness reconsidered*. Cambridge: MIT Press.

Fortin, M., Asselin, M. C., Gould, P. V., & Parent, A. (1998). Calretinin-immunoreactive neurons in the human thalamus. *Neuroscience*, 84, 537–548.

Fries, P., Reynolds, J. H., Rorie, A. E., & Desimone, R. (2001). Modulation of oscillatory neuronal synchronization by selective visual attention. *Science*, 291, 1560–1563.

Fuster, J. (2002). *Cortex and mind: Unifying cognition*. New York: Oxford University Press.

Fuxe, K., & Agnati, L. F. (Eds.). (1991). *Volume transmission in the brain: Novel mechanisms for neural transmission*. New York: Raven Press.

Galin, D. (1992). Theoretical reflections on awareness, monitoring, and self in relation to anosognosia. *Consciousness and Cognition*, 1, 152–162.

Galin, D. (2003). The concepts "self," "person" and "I" in Buddhism and in western psychology. In B. A. Wallace (Ed.), *Breaking new ground: Essays on Tibetan Buddhism and modern science* (p. 432). New York: Columbia University Press.

Gallup, G. G. (1995). Mirrors minds, and cetaceans. *Consciousness and Cognition*, 4, 226–228.

Gazzaniga, M. S. (1970). *The bisected brain*. New York: Appleton-Century-Crofts.

Gentilini, M., De Renzi, E. , & Crisi, G. (1987). Bilateral paramedian thalamic artery infarcts: Report of eight cases. *Journal of Neurology, Neurosurgery, and Psychiatry*, 50, 900–909.

Goldman, A. I. (1993). Consciousness, folk psychology and cognitive science. *Consciousness and Cognition*, 2, 364–382.

Graff-Radford, N. R., Tranel, D., Van Hoesen, G. W., & Brandt, J. P. (1990). Diencephalic amnesia. *Brain*, 113, 1–25.

Gray, C. M., & Viana Di Prisco, G. (1997). Stimulus-dependent neuronal oscillations and local synchronization in striate cortex of the alert cat. *Journal of Neuroscience*, 17, 3239–3253.

Gray, J. A. (1995). The contents of consciousness: A neuropsychological conjecture. *Behavioral and Brain Sciences*, 18, 659–722.

Graybiel, A. M., Aosaki, T., Flaherty, A. W., & Kimura, M. (1994). The basal ganglia and adaptive motor control. *Science*, 265, 1826–1831.

Greenfield, S. A. (1998). A rosetta stone for mind and brain? In S. R. Hameroff, A. W. Kaszniak, & A. C. Scott (Eds.), *Toward a science of consciousness: II. The second Tucson discussions and debates* (pp 231–236). Cambridge, MA: MIT Press.

Groenewegen, H. J., & Berendse, H. W. (1994). The specificity of the 'nonspecific' midline and intralaminar thalamic nuclei. *Trends in Neuroscience*, 17, 52–57.

Grossman, R. G. (1980). Are current concepts and methods in neuroscience adequate for studying the neural basis of consciousness and mental activity? In H. M. Pinsker & W. D. Willis, Jr. (Eds.), *Information processing in the nervous system*. New York: Raven Press.

Grünthal, E. (1934). Der Zellbau im Thalamus der Säuger und des Menschen. *Journal of Psychology and Neurology*, 46, 41–112.

Grüsser, O. J., & Landis, T. (1991). *Visual agnosias and other disturbances of visual perception and cognition*. London: Macmillan & Co.

Guberman, A., & Stuss, D. (1983). The syndrome of bilateral paramedian thalamic infarction. *Neurology*, 33, 540–546.

Guillery, R. W., Feig, S. L., & Lozsadi, D. A. (1998). Paying attention to the thalamic reticular nucleus. *Trends in Neuroscience*, 21, 28–32.

Guillery, R. W., & Harting, J. K. (2003). Structure and connections of the thalamic reticular nucleus: Advancing views over half a century. *Journal of Comparative Neurology, 463*, 360–371.

Guillery, R. W., & Sherman, S. M. (2002). Thalamic relay functions and their role in cortico-cortical communication: Generalizations from the visual system. *Neuron, 33*, 163–175.

Güzeldere, G. (1997). The many faces of consciousness: A field guide. In N. Block, O. Flanagan, & G. Güzeldere (Eds.), *The nature of consciousness*. Cambridge, MA: MIT Press.

Hameroff, S. R., & Penrose, R. (1996). Orchestrated reduction of quantum coherence in brain microtubules: A model for consciousness. In S. R. Hameroff, A. W. Kaszniak, & A. C. Scott (Eds.), *Toward a science of consciousness* (pp. 507–540). Cambridge, MA: MIT Press.

Harrington, A. H. (1987). *Medicine, mind, and the doublebrain; a study in 19th century thought*. Princeton: Princeton University Press.

Hart, D., & Whitlow, J. W. (1995). The experience of self in the bottlenose dolphin. *Consciousness and Cognition, 4*, 244–247.

He, S., Cavanagh, P., & Intriligator, J. (1997). Attentional resolution. *Trends in Neuroscience, 1*, 115–121.

Hempel, C. G. (1966). *Philosophy of natural science*. Englewood Cliffs, NJ: Prentice Hall.

Henderson, V. W. (1990). Alalia, aphemia, and aphasia. *Archives of Neurology, 47*, 85–88.

Henke, K., Landis, T., & Markowitsch, H. J. (1993). Subliminal perception of pictures in the right hemisphere. *Consciousness and Cognition, 2*, 225–236.

Hollender, D. (1986). Semantic activation without conscious identification in dichotic listening, parafoveal vision, and visual masking: A survey and appraisal. *Behavioral and Brain Sciences, 9*, 1–66.

Iacoboni, M., & Zaidel, E. (1996). Hemispheric independence in word recognition: Evidence from unilateral and bilateral presentations. *Brain and Language, 53*, 121–140.

Jasper, H. H. (1954). Functional properties of the thalamic reticular system. In J. F. Delofresnaye (Ed.), *Brain mechanisms and consciousness*. Oxford: Blackwell.

Jasper, H. H. (1966). Pathophysiological studies of brain mechanisms in different states of consciousness. In J. C. Eccles (Ed.), *Brain and conscious experience*. Berlin: Springer-Verlag.

Jeannerod, M. (1992). The where in the brain determines the when in the mind. *Behavioral and Brain Sciences, 15*, 212–213.

Jennett, B. (2002). The vegetative state. *Journal of Neurology, Neurosurgery, and Psychiatry, 73*, 355–357.

Jones, E. G. (1985). *The thalamus*. New York: Plenum Press.

Jones, E. G. (1989). Defining the thalamic intralaminar nuclei in primates. In G. Gainotti, M. Bentivoglio, P. Bergonzi, & F. M. Ferro (Eds.), *Neurologia e scienze de base: Scritti in onore di Giorgio Macchi*. Milan: Università Cattolica del Sacro Cuore.

Jones, E. G. (1998a). The thalamus of primates. In F. E. Bloom, A. Björklund, & T. Hökfelt (Eds.), *Handbook of chemical neuroanatomy* (pp. 1–298). Amsterdam: Elsevier.

Jones, E. G. (1998b). A new view of specific and nonspecific thalamocortical connections. In H. H. Jasper, L. Descarries, V. F. Castellucci, & S. Rossignol (Eds.), *Consciousness: At the frontiers of neuroscience*. Philadelphia: Lippincott-Raven.

Jones, E. G. (2002). Thalamic circuitry and thalamocortical synchrony. *Philosophical Transactions of the Royal Society of London. Series B: Biological Sciences (London), 357*, 1659–1673.

Jones, E. G., & Macchi, G. (1997). Terminology of the motor thalamus. *Journal of Neurosurgery, 87*, 981–982.

Jouvet, M. (1967). Neurophysiology of the states of sleep. *Physiological Reviews, 47*, 117–177.

Jung, R. (1954). Correlation of bioelectrical and autonomic phenomena with alterations of consciousness and arousal in man. In E. D. Adrian, R. Bremer, & H. H. Jasper (Eds.), *Brain mechanisms and consciousness*. Springfield, IL: C. C. Thomas.

Kanerva, P. (1988). *Sparse distributed memory*. Cambridge, MA: MIT Press.

Kaufman, E. F., & Rosenquist, A. C. (1985). Afferent connections of the thalamic intralaminar nuclei in the cat. *Brain Research, 335*, 281–296.

Keller, I., & Heckhausen, H. (1990). Readiness potentials preceding spontaneous motor acts: Voluntary vs. involuntary control. *Electroencephalography and Clinical Neurophysiology, 76*, 351–361.

Kertesz, A. (1993). Clinical forms of aphasia. *Acta Neurochirurgica Supplementum (Wien), 56*, 52–58.

Kihlstrom, J. F. (1987). The cognitive unconscious. *Science, 237,* 1445–1452.

Kinney, H. C., Korein, J., Panigrahy, A., Dikkes, P., & Goode, R. (1994). Neuropathological findings in the brain of Karen Ann Quinlan. The role of the thalamus in the persistent vegetative state. *New England Journal of Medicine, 330,* 1469–1475.

Kinomura, S., Larsson, J., Gulyas, B., & Roland, P. E. (1966) Activation by attention of the human reticular formation and thalamic intralaminar nuclei. *Science, 271,* 512–515.

Kinsbourne, M. (1995). The intralaminar thalamic nuclei: Subjectivity pumps or attention action coordinators? *Consciousness and Cognition, 4,* 167–171.

Kinsbourne, M., & Smith, W. L. (1974). *Hemispheric disconnection and cerebral function.* Springfield, IL: C. C. Thomas.

Koch, C. (1995). Visual awareness and the thalamic intralaminar nuclei. *Consciousness and Cognition, 4,* 163–166.

Koch, C. (2004). *The quest for consciousness: A neurobiological approach.* Englewood, CO: Roberts and Company.

Kolb, B., & Wishaw, I. Q. (2000). *Fundamentals of human neuropsychology* (4th ed). New York: W. H. Freeman.

Koskoff, Y. D., Patton, R., Migler, B., & Kruper, D. (1959, Sept-Oct). Hemicerebrectomy in the Rhesus monkey: Surgical technique and preliminary behavioral observations. *Cerebral Palsy.*

Kossoff, E. H., Vining, E. P., Pillas, D. J., Pyzik, P. L., Avellino, A. M., Carson, B. S., & Freeman. J. M. (2003). Hemispherectomy for intractable unihemispheric epilepsy: Etiology vs outcome. *Neurology, 61,* 887–890.

Kruper, D. C., Patton, R. A., & Koskoff, Y. D. (1971). Visual discrimination in hemicerebrectomized monkeys. *Physiology and Behavior, 7,* 173–179.

Landesman, C. (1967). Consciousness. In P. Edwards (Ed.), *Encyclopedia of philosophy* (pp. 191–195). New York: Macmillan.

Landis, T., & Regard, M. (1988). The right hemisphere's access to lexical meaning: A function of its release from left hemisphere control? In C. Chiarello (Ed.), *Right hemisphere contributions to lexical semantics.* New York: Springer.

Lashley, K. S. (1952). The problem of serial order in behavior. In L. A. Jeffress (Ed.), *Cerebral mechanisms in behavior* (pp. 112–136). New York: Wiley.

Lashley, K. S. (1954). Dynamic processes in perception. In E. D. Adrian, F. Bremer, & H. H. Jasper (Eds.), *Brain mechanisms and consciousness.* Springfield, IL: C. C. Thomas.

Laurent, G. (2002). Olfactory network dynamics and the coding of multidimensional signals. *Nature Reviews Neuroscience, 3,* 884–895.

Laureys, S., Faymonville, M. E., Luxenm A., Lamy, M., Franck, G., & Maquet, P. (2000). Restoration of thalamocortical connectivity after recovery from persistent vegetative state. *Lancet, 355,* 1790–1791.

Lecours, A. R., Lhermitte, F., & Bryans, B. (1983). *Aphasiology.* London: Balliere Tindall.

LeGros Clark, W. E. (1932). The structure and connections of the thalamus. *Brain, 55,* 406–470.

Lesser, R. P., Dinner, D. S., Luders, H., & Morris, H. H. (1986). Memory for objects presented soon after intracarotid amobarbïtal sodium injections in patients with medically intractable complex partial seizures. *Neurology, 36,* 889–899.

Libet, B. (1993). *Neurophysiology of consciousness.* Boston: Burkhäuser.

Libet, B. (2003). Timing of conscious experience: Reply to the 2002 commentaries on Libet's findings. *Consciousness and Cognition, 12,* 321–331.

Libet, B., Gleason, C. A., Wright, E. W., & Pearl, D. K. (1983). Time of conscious intention to act in relation to onset of cerebral activities (readiness potential): The unconscious initiation of a freely voluntary act. *Brain, 106,* 623–642.

Llinás, R. R. (2001). *I of the vortex: From neurons to self.* Cambridge, MA: MIT Press.

Logothetis, N. K. (2002). Vision: A window on consciousness. The hidden mind. *Scientific American* [Special issue], 12, 18–25.

Lycan, W. G. (1997). Consciousness as internal monitoring. In N. Block, O. Flanagan, & G. Guzeldere (Eds.), *The nature of consciousness: Philosophical debates.* Cambridge, MA: MIT Press.

Magoun, H. W. (1952). An ascending reticular activating system in the brainstem. *Archives of Neurology and Psychiatry, 57,* 145–154.

Mair, R. G. (1994). On the role of thalamic pathology in diencephalic amnesia. *Reviews in the Neurosciences, 5,* 105–140.

Malamut, B. L., Graff-Radford, N., Chawluk, J., Grossman, R. I., & Gur, R. C. (1992). Memory in a case of bilateral thalamic infarction. *Neurology*, 42, 163–169.

Marcel, A. J. (1988). Phenomenal experience and functionalism. In A. J. Marcel & E. Bisiach (Eds.), *Consciousness in contemporary science* (pp, 121–158). Oxford: Clarendon Press.

Marder, E., & Bucher, D. (2001). Central pattern generators and the control of rhythmic movements. *Current Biology*, 11, R986–996.

Marie, P. (1906). The third left frontal convolution plays no special role in the function of language. *Semaine Medicale*, 26, 241–247.

Markowitsch, H. J., von Cramon, D. Y., & Schuri, U. (1993). Mnestic performance profile of a bilateral diencephalic infarct patient with preserved intelligence and severe amnesic disturbances. *Journal of Clinical and Experimental Neuropsychology*, 15, 627–652.

Maunsell, J. H., & Newsome, W. T. (1987). Visual processing in monkey extrastriate cortex. *Annual Review of Neuroscience*, 10, 363–401.

McGuinness, C. M., & Krauthamer, G. M. (1980). The afferent projections to the centrum medianum of the cat as demonstrated by retrograde transport of horseradish peroxidase. *Brain Research*, 184, 255–269.

Meissner, I., Sapir, S., Kokmen, E., & Stein, S. D. (1987). The paramedian diencephalic syndrome: A dynamic phenomenon. *Stroke*, 18, 380–385.

Metzinger, T. (1995). *The problem of consciousness*. Thorverton, UK: Imprint Academic.

Michel, D., Laurent, B., Foyaher, N., Blanc, A., & Portafaix, M. (1982). Infarctus thalamique paramèdian gauche: tude de la mémoire et du langage. *Revue Neurologique*, 138, 533–550.

Mills, R. P., & Swanson, P. D. (1978). Vertical oculomotor apraxia and memory loss. *Annals of Neurology*, 4, 149–153.

Milner, A. D., & Goodale, M. A. (1996). *The visual brain in action*. Oxford: Oxford University Press.

Mitrofanis, J., & Guillery, R. W. (1993). New views of the thalamicreticular nucleus in the adult and the developing brain. *Trends in Neuroscience*, 16, 240–245.

Mohr, J. P. (1973). Rapid amelioration of motor aphasia. *Archives of Neurology*, 28, 77–82.

Mohr, J. P. (1976). Broca's area and Broca's aphasia. In H. Whitaker & H. A. Whitaker (Eds.), *Studies in neurolinguistics*. New York: Academic Press.

Moore, G. E. (1922). *Philosophical studies*. London: Routledge & Kegan Paul.

Moruzzi, G., & Magoun, H. W. (1949). Brain stem reticular formation and activation of the EEG. *Electroencephalography and Clinical Neurophysiology*, 1, 455–473.

Moscovitch, M. (1995). Models of consciousness and memory. In M. S. Gazzaniga (Ed.), *The cognitive neurosciences*. Cambridge, MA: MIT Press.

Moutier, F. (1908). *L'aphasie de Broca*. Paris: Steinheil.

Moutoussis, K., & Zeki, S. (2002). The relationship between cortical activation and perception investigated with invisible stimuli. *Proceedings of the National Academy of Sciences USA*, 99, 9527–9532.

Munk, M. H., Roelfsema, P. R., Konig, P., Engel, A. K., & Singer, W. (1996). Role of reticular activation in the modulation of intracortical synchronization. *Science*, 272, 271–274.

Munkle, M. C., Waldvogel, H. J., & Faull, R. L. (1999). Calcium-binding protein immunoreactivity delineates the intralaminar nuclei of the thalamus in the human brain. *Neuroscience*, 90, 485–491.

Munkle, M. C., Waldvogel, H. J., & Faull, R. L. (2000). The distribution of calbindin, calretinin and parvalbumin immunoreactivity in the human thalamus. *Journal of Chemical Neuroanatomy*, 19, 155–173.

Natsoulas, T. (1983). Concepts of consciousness. *Journal of Mind and Behavior*, 4, 13–59.

Netter, F. H. (1953). *Nervous system*. Summit, NJ: Ciba.

Newman, J., & Baars, B. J. (1993). A neural attentional model for access to consciousness: A global workspace perspective. *Concepts in Neuroscience*, 4, 255–290.

O'Leary, J. L., & Coben, L. A. (1958). The reticular core. 1957. *Physiological Reviews*, 38, 243–276.

Orem, J., Schlag-Rey, M., & Schlag, J. (1973). Unilateral visual neglect and thalamic intralaminar lesions in the cat. *Experimental Neurology*, 40, 784–797.

Panksepp, J. (1998). *Affective neuroscience*. New York: Oxford University Press.

Passingham, R. (1993). *The frontal lobes and voluntary action*. Oxford: Oxford University Press.

Pavlov, I. P. (1928). *Lectures on conditioned reflexes*. New York: Liveright Publishing.

Peacock, W. J. (1996). Hemispherectomy for intractable seizures in children: A report of 58 cases. *Child's Nervous System, 12*, 376–384.

Penfield, W. (1937). The cerebral cortex and consciousness. In R. H. Wilkins (Ed.), *The Harvey lectures*. New York: Johnson Reprint Corp.

Penfield, W., & Jasper, H. (1954). *Epilepsy and the functional anatomy of the human brain*. Boston: Little & Brown.

Percheron, G. (1997). The motor thalamus. *Journal of Neurosurgery, 87*, 981.

Perruchet, P., & Vinter, A. (2002). The self-organizing consciousness. *Behavioral and Brain Sciences, 25*, 297–330.

Petit, H., Rousseaux, M., Clarisse, J., & Delafosse, A. (1981). Oculocephalomotor disorders and bilateral thalamo-subthalamic infarction. *Revue Neurologique (Paris), 137*, 709–722.

Plum, F., & Posner, J. B. (1985). *The diagnosis of stupor and coma* (3rd ed). Philadelphia: F. A. Davis.

Pockett, S. (2002). Backward referral, flash-lags, and quantum free will: A response to commentaries on articles by Pockett, Klein, Gomes, and Trevena and Miller. *Consciousness and Cognition, 11*, 314–425.

Posner, M. I., & Rothbart, M. K. (1992). Attentional mechanisms and conscious experience. In A. D. Milner & M. D. Rugg (Eds.), *The neuropsychology of consciousness*. San Diego: Academic Press.

Ptito, A., Lepore, F., Ptito, M., & Lassonde, M. (1991). Target detection and movement discrimination in the blind field of hemispherectomized patients. *Brain, 114*, 497–512.

Purpura, K. P., & Schiff, N. D. (1997). The thalamic intralaminar nuclei: A role in visual awareness. *The Neuroscientist, 3*, 8–15.

Regard, M., Cook, N. D., Wieser, H. G., & Landis, T. (1994). The dynamics of cerebral dominance during unilateral limbic seizures. *Brain, 117*, 91–104.

Revonsuo, A. (1995). Conscious and nonconscious control of action. *Behavioral and Brain Sciences, 18*, 265–266.

Ro, T., & Rafal, R. D. (1996). Perception of geometric illusions in hemispatial neglect. *Neuropsychologia, 34*, 973–978.

Robinson, D. L., & Cowie, R. J. (1997). The primate pulvinar: Structural, functional and behavioural components of visual salience. In E. G. Jones, M. Steriade, & D. A. McCormick (Eds.), *The thalamus*. Amstedam: Elsevier.

Rodman, H. R., Gross, C. G., & Albright, T. D. (1990). Afferent basis of visual response properties in area MT of the macaque. II. Effects of superior colliculus removal. *Journal of Neuroscience, 10*, 1154–1164.

Rolls, E. T. (2000). The brain and emotion. *Behavioral and Brain Sciences, 23*, 177–234.

Rosenthal, D. M. (1990). Two concepts of consciousness. In D. M. Rosenthal (Ed.), *The nature of mind*. Oxford: Oxford University Press.

Royce, G. J., Bromley, S., & Gracco, C. (1991). Subcortical projections to the centromedian and parafascicular thalamic nuclei in the cat. *Journal of Comparative Neurology, 306*, 129–155.

Rumbaugh, D. M., Beran, M. J., & Pate, J. L. (2003). Uncertainty monitoring may promote emergents. *Behavioral and Brain Sciences, 26*, 353.

Sadikot, A. F., Parent, A., Smith, Y., & Bolam, J. P. (1992). Efferent connections of the centromedian and parafascicular thalamic nuclei in the squirrel monkey: A light and electron microscopic study of the thalamostriatal projection in relation to striatal heterogeneity. *Journal of Comparative Neurology, 320*, 228–242.

Sandifer, P. H. (1946). Anosognosia and disorders of body scheme. *Brain, 69*, 122.

Schacter, D. L. (1989). On the relation between memory and consciousness: Dissociable interactions and conscious experience. In H.L Roediger & F. I. M. Craik (Eds.), *Varieties of memory and consciousness: Essays in honour of Endel Tulving*. Hillsdale, NJ: Erlbaum.

Schacter, D. L., McAndrews, M. P., Moscovitch, M. (1988). Access to conscousness: Dissociation between implicit and explicit knowledge in neuropsychological syndrome. In L. Weiskrantz (Ed.), *Thought without language*. Oxford: Clarendon Press.

Schaltenbrand, G., & Wahren, W. (1977). *Atlas for stereotaxy of the human brain*, 2nd ed. Stuttgart: Thieme.

Scheibel, M. E., & Scheibel, A. B. (1966). The organization of the nucleus reticularis thalami: A Golgi study. *Brain Research, 1*, 43–62.

Schiff, N. D., & Plum, F. (1999). Web forum: The neurology of impaired consciousness: Global disorders and implied models. http://athena.

english.vt.edu/cgi-bin/netforum/nic/a/34--1.2.1

Schiff, N. D., Ribary, U., Moreno, D. R., Beattie, B., Kronberg, E., Blasberg, R., Gicino, J., McCagg, C., Fins, J. J., Llinas, R., & Plum, F. (2002). Residual cerebral activity and behavioural fragments can remain in the persistently vegetative brain. *Brain, 125*, 1210–1234.

Schlag, J., & Schlag-Rey, M. (1984). Visuomotor functions of central thalamus in monkey. II. Unit activity related to visual events, targeting, and fixation. *Journal of Neurophysiology, 51*, 1175–1195.

Schott, B., Mauguière, F., Laurent, B., Serclerat, O., & Fischer, C. (1980). L'amnésie thalamique. *Revue Neurologique (Paris), 136*, 117–130.

Seager, W. (2002). Emotional introspection. *Consciousness and Cognition, 11*, 666–687.

Searle, J. R. (1993). The problem of consciousness. *Ciba Foundation Symposium, 174*, 61–69; discussion 70–80.

Searle, J. R. (1998). How to study consciousness scientifically. *Philosophical Transactions of the Royal Society of London. Series B: Biological Sciences (London), 353*, 1935–1942.

Sherman, S. M., & Guillery, R. W. (2002). The role of the thalamus in the flow of information to the cortex. *Philosophical Transactions of the Royal Society of London. Series B: Biological Sciences (London), 357*, 1695–1708.

Sherman, S. M., & Koch, C. (1986). The control of retinogeniculate transmission in the mammalian lateral geniculate nucleus. *Experimental Brain Research, 63*, 1–20.

Sherrington, C. S. (1932). *Inhibition as a coordinative factor.* In Amsterdam: Elsevier.

Sidibé, M., & Smith, Y. (1996), Differential synaptic innervation of striatofugal neurones projecting to the internal or external segments of the globus pallidus by thalamic afferents in the squirrel monkey. *Journal of Comparative Neurology, 365*, 445–465.

Singer, W. (1998). Consciousness and the structure of neuronal representations. *Philosophical Transactions of the Royal Society of London. Series B: Biological Sciences (London), 353*, 1829–1840.

Smith, A., & Burklund, C. W. (1966). Dominant hemispherectomy: Preliminary report on neuropsychological sequelae. *Science, 153*, 1280–1282.

Smith, A., & Sugar, O. (1975). Development of above normal language and intelligence 21

years after left hemispherectomy. *Neurology, 25*, 813–818.

Smythies, J. (1997). The functional neuroanatomy of awareness: With a focus on the role of various anatomical systems in the control of intermodal attention. *Consciousness and Cognition, 6*, 455–481.

Sperry, R. W. (1961). Cerebral organization and behavior. *Science, 133*, 749–1757.

Sperry, R. W. (1968). *Mental unity following surgical disconnection of the cerebral hemispheres.* New York: Academic Press.

Sperry, R. W. (1980). Mind-brain interaction: Mentalism, yes; dualism, no. *Neuroscience, 5*, 195–206.

Sperry, R. W. (1991). In defense of mentalism and emergent interaction. *Journal of Mind and Behavior, 12*, 221–245.

Sperry, R. W., Gazzaniga, M. S., & Bogen, J. E. (1969). Interhemispheric relationships: The neocortical commissures; syndromes of hemisphere disconnection. *Handbook of Clinical Neurology, 4*, 273–290.

Steriade, M. (1996). Arousal: Revisiting the reticular activating system. *Science, 272*, 225–226.

Steriade, M., Curró Dossi, R., & Contreras, D. (1993). Electrophysiological properties of intralaminar thalamocortical cells discharging rhythmic (approximately 40 HZ) spike-bursts at approximately 1000 HZ during waking and rapid eye movement sleep. *Neuroscience, 56*, 1–9.

Steriade, M., Jones, E. G., & McCormick, D. A. (1997). *Thalamus I: Organization and function.* New York: Elsevier.

Stoerig, P., & Barth, E. (2001). Low-level phenomenal vision despite unilateral destruction of primary visual cortex. *Consciousness and Cognition, 10*, 574–587.

Stoerig, P., & Cowey, A. (1995). Visual perception and phenomenal consciousness. *Behavioral Brain Research, 71*, 147–156.

Stoerig, P., & Cowey, A. (1997). Blindsight in man and monkey. *Brain, 120*, 535–559.

Szelies, B., Herholz, K., Pawlik, G., Karbe, H., Hebold, I., & Heiss, W. D. (1991). Widespread functional effects of discrete thalamic infarction. *Archives of Neurology, 48*, 178–182.

Szirmai, I., Guseo, A., & Molnar, M. (1977). Bilateral symmetrical softening of the thalamus. *Journal of Neurology, 217*, 57–65.

Taniwaki, T., Okayama, A., Yoshiura, T., Nakamura, Y., Goto, Y., Kira, J., & Tobimatsu, S. J.

(2003). Reappraisal of the motor role of basal ganglia: A functional magnetic resonance image study. *Journal of Neuroscience*, 23, 3432–3438.

Tanji, J., & Shima, K. (1994). Role for supplementary motor area cellsin planning several movements ahead. *Nature*, 371, 413–416.

Tatemichi, T. K., Steinke, W., Duncan, C., Bello, J. A., Odel, J. G., Behrens, M. M., Hilal, S. K., & Mohr, J. P. (1992). Paramedian thalamopeduncular infarction: Clinical syndromes and magnetic resonance imaging. *Annals of Neurology*, 32, 162–171.

Tatu, L., Moulin, T., Bogousslavsky, J., & Duvernoy, H. (1998). Arterial teritories of the human brain. *Neurology*, 50, 1699–1708.

Taylor, J. G. (1999). *The race for consciousness*. Cambridge, MA: MIT Press.

Taylor, J. G. (2002). Paying attention to consciousness. *Trends in Cognitive Science*, 6, 206–210.

Taylor, J. L., & McCloskey, D. I. (1990). Triggering of preprogrammed movements as reactions to masked stimuli. *Journal of Neurophysiology*, 63, 439–446.

Tononi, G., & Edelman, G. M. (1998). Consciousness and complexity. *Science*, 282, 1846–1851.

Tramo, M. J., Baynes, K., Fendrich, R., Mangun, G. R., Phelps, E. A., Reuter-Lorenz, P. A., & Gazzaniga, M. S. (1995). Hemispheric specialization and interhemispheric integration: Insights from experiments with commissurotomy patients. In A. G. Reeves & D. W. Roberts (Eds.), *Epilepsy and the corpus callosum*. New York: Plenum Press.

Treue, S., & Maunsell, J. H. R. (1996). Attentional modulation of visualmotion processing in cortical areas MT and MST. *Nature*, 382, 539–541.

Trevarthen, C. (1974). Functional relations of disconnected hemispheres with the brain stem, and with each other: Monkey and man. In M. Kinsbourne & W. L. Smith (Eds.), *Hemispheric disconnection and cerebral function*. Springfield, IL: C. C. Thomas.

Trevena, J. T., & Miller, J. (2002). Cortical movement preparation before and after a conscious decision to move. *Consciousness and Cognition*, 11, 162–190.

Tulving, E. (1985). Memory and consciousness. *Canadian Psychology*, 26, 1–12.

Ungerleider, L. G., & Mishkin, M. (1982). Two cortical visual systems. In D. J. Ingle, M. A. Goodale, & R. J. W. Mansfield (Eds.), *Analysis of visual behavior* (pp. 549–546). Cambridge, MA: MIT Press.

van Domburg, P. H. M. F., ten Donkelaar, H. J., & Noterman, S. L. H. (1996). Akinetic mutism with bithalamic infarction neurophysiologic correlates. *Journal of Neuroscience*, 139, 58–64.

Velmans, M. (1991). Is human information processing conscious? *Behavioral and Brain Sciences*, 14, 651–726.

von Monakow, C. (Ed.). (1911). *Localization of brain functions*. Springfield, IL: C. C. Thomas.

Walshe, F. M. R. (1965). *Further critical studies in neurology*. London: E & S. Livingstone.

Watt, D. F. (2000). Emotion and consciousness. *Journal of Consciousness Studies*, 7, 72–84.

Weiskrantz, L. (1986). *Blindsight: A case study and implications*. Oxford: Clarendon Press.

Weiskrantz, L. (1997). *Consciousness lost and found*. Oxford: Oxford University Press.

Wexler, B. E., Warrenburg, S., Schwartz, G. E., & Janer, L. D. (1992). EEG and EMG responses to emotion-evoking stimuli processed without conscious awareness. *Neuropsychologia*, 30, 1065–1079.

White, R. J., Schreiner, L. H., Hughes, R. A., MacCarty, C. S., & Grindlay, J. H. (1959). Physiologic consequences of total hemispherectomy in the monkey. *Neurology*, 9, 149–159.

Wiest, G., Mallek, R., & Baumgartner, C. (2000). Selective loss of vergence control secondary to bilateral paramedian thalamic infarction. *Neurology*, 1997–1999.

Wimsatt, W. C. (1976). Reductionism, levels of organization, and the mind-body problem. In G. G. Globus, G. Maxwell, & I. Savodnik (Eds.), *Consciousness and the brain*. New York: Plenum.

Wimsatt, W. C. (2000). Emergence as non-aggregativity and the biases of reductionisms. *Foundations of Science*, 5, 269–297.

Yasuda, Y., Akiguchi, I., Ino, M., Nabatabe, H., & Kameyama, M. (1990). Paramedian thalamic and midbrain infarcts associated with palilalia. *Journal of Neurology, Neurosurgery, and Psychiatry*, 53, 797–799.

Yingling, C. D., & Skinner, J. E. (1976). Selective regulation of thalamic sensory relay nuclei by nucleus reticularis thalami. *Electroencephalography and Clinical Neurophysiology*, 41, 476–482.

Yingling, C. D., & Skinner, J. E. (1977). Gating of thalamic input to cerebralcortex by nucleus reticularis thalami. In J. E. Desmedt (Ed.), *Attention, voluntary contraction and event-related cerebral potentials*. Basel: Krager.

Zaidel, D. W., Hugdahl, K., & Johnsen, B. H. (1995). Physiological responses to verbally inaccessible pictorial information in the left and right hemispheres. *Neuropsychology, 9,* 1–6.

Zaidel, E., Zaidel, D. W., & Bogen, J. E. (1999). The split brain. In G. Adelman & B. Smith (Eds.), *Encyclopedia of neuroscience* (2nd ed.; pp. 1027–1032). Amsterdam: Elsevier.

Zaidel, E., & Iacoboni, M. (Eds.). (2002). *The parallel brain: The cognitive neuroscience of the corpus callosum*. Cambridge, MA: MIT Press.

Zeki, S. (1974). Functional organization of a visual area in the superiortemporal sulcus of the rhesus monkey. *Journal of Physiology, 236,* 549.

Zeki, S. (1993). *A vision of the brain*. Oxford: Blackwell.

Zeki, S., & Bartels, A. (1999). Toward a theory of visual consciousness. *Consciousness and Cognition, 8,* 225–259.

CHAPTER 28

The Cognitive Neuroscience
of Memory and Consciousness

Scott D. Slotnick and Daniel L. Schacter

Abstract

In this chapter, we delineate the neural activity associated with conscious memories characterized by different degrees of 'retrieval content' (i.e., sensory/contextual detail). Based primarily on neuroimaging evidence, we identify the neural regions that are associated most consistently with the following conscious memory processes: retrieval success versus retrieval attempt, remembering versus knowing, and true recognition versus false recognition. A number of patterns emerge from the comparison of memories with high retrieval content (i.e., retrieval success, remembering, and true recognition) and memories with low retrieval content (i.e., retrieval attempt, knowing, and false recognition). Memories with both high and low retrieval content are associated with activity in the prefrontal and parietal cortex, indicating that these regions are generally associated with retrieval. There is also evidence that memories with low retrieval content are associated with activity in the prefrontal cortex to a greater degree than memories with high retrieval content, sug-gesting that low retrieval content memories are associated with greater post-retrieval monitoring (although this activity does not necessarily reflect differential retrieval content per se). Finally, memories with high retrieval content, to a greater degree than memories with low retrieval content, are associated with activity in the parietal cortex and sensory cortex (along with the medial temporal lobe for retrieval success > attempt and remembering > knowing). This increased activity in sensory cortex (and medial temporal lobe) for memories with high retrieval content indicates that conscious memories are constructed by reactivation of encoded item features at retrieval.

Introduction

In 1985, Endel Tulving lamented the lack of interest in the topic of memory and consciousness shown by past and present memory researchers: "One can read article after article on memory, or consult book after book, without encountering the term 'consciousness.' Such a state of affairs must be regarded as rather curious. One might think that memory should have something to do with remembering, and remembering *is* a conscious experience (Tulving, 1985b, p. 11)."

Though Tulving provided an accurate assessment of the field at the time, the year in which he voiced his complaint proved to be a kind of turning point in research on memory and consciousness. Tulving's (1985b) own article focused on the important distinction between *remembering*, which involves specific recollections of past experiences, and *knowing*, which involves a general sense of familiarity without specific recollection, and introduced seminal techniques for experimentally assessing these two forms of memory.

In a different paper published that same year, Tulving (1985a) argued that each of three dissociable memory systems is uniquely associated with a particular type of consciousness. Specifically, he contended that *procedural memory* (learning of motor, perceptual, and cognitive skills) is associated with *anoetic* or "nonknowing" consciousness, which entails simple awareness of external stimuli; *semantic memory* (general factual knowledge) is associated with *noetic* or "knowing" consciousness; and *episodic memory* (recollection of personal experiences) is associated with *autonoetic* or "self-knowing" consciousness.

Finally, in 1985 Graf and Schacter introduced the related distinction between implicit and explicit memory. According to Graf and Schacter (1985), *explicit memory* refers to the conscious recollection of previous experiences, as revealed by standard tests of recall and recognition that require intentional retrieval of previously acquired information. *Implicit memory*, by contrast, refers to non-conscious effects of past experiences on subsequent behavior and performance, such as priming or skill learning, that are revealed by tests that do not require conscious recollection of previous experiences (for precursors, see also Cermak, 1982; Moscovitch, 1984).

During the 20 years that have elapsed since the publication of these papers, a vast amount of research has been published on the distinctions that they introduced. For example, many cognitive studies have used the techniques introduced by Tulving (1985b) to delineate the functional and phenomenological characteristics of remembering and knowing (for reviews and contrasting perspectives, see Dunn, 2004; Gardiner, Ramponi, & Richardson-Klavehn, 2002). Likewise, cognitive studies have also explored numerous aspects of the relation between implicit and explicit forms of memory (for reviews, see Roediger & McDermott, 1993; Schacter, 1987; Schacter & Curran, 2000).

Although purely cognitive studies have played a significant role in advancing our understanding of memory and consciousness, cognitive neuroscience studies – which attempt to elucidate the nature of, and relations between, the brain systems and processes that support various forms of memory – have also been critically important. Indeed, much of the impetus for the distinction between implicit and explicit memory was provided initially by neuropsychological studies of amnesic patients, who exhibit severe impairment of explicit memory for previous experiences as a result of damage to the hippocampus and related structures in the medial temporal lobe (MTL; e.g., Moscovitch, Vriezen, & Goshen-Gottstein, 1993; Nadel & Moscovitch, 1997; Squire, 1992; Squire, Stark, & Clark, 2004). Nonetheless, it has been demonstrated repeatedly that conditions exist in which amnesics can exhibit robust and sometimes normal implicit memory for aspects of prior experiences, as exemplified by such phenomena as preserved priming and skill learning (for recent reviews, see Gooding, Mayes, & van Eijk, 2000; Schacter, Dobbins & Schnyer, 2004). Studies of other neuropsychological syndromes have likewise revealed dissociations between implicit and explicit forms of perception, language, and related cognitive and motor processes (e.g., Goodale & Westwood,

2004; Güzeldere, Flanagan, & Hardcastle, 2000; Köhler & Moscovitch, 1997; Schacter, McAndrews, & Moscovitch, 1988; Warrington & Weiskrantz, 1974; Young, 1994).

Although neuropsychological studies have been crucial to advancing our understanding of the relation between memory and consciousness, during the past decade cognitive neuroscience analyses have focused increasingly on research using functional neuroimaging techniques, such as positron emission tomography (PET) and functional magnetic resonance imaging (fMRI). A vast amount of neuroimaging research has been published, and much of it is well beyond the scope of this chapter. However, we believe that several lines of research concerned with elucidating the neural correlates of explicit memory processes do provide useful insights into the cognitive neuroscience of memory and consciousness (for reviews of neuroimaging studies concerning the neural substrates associated with implicit memory, see Henson, 2003; Schacter & Buckner, 1998; Schacter et al., 2004; Wiggs & Martin, 1998).

Many neuroimaging studies of explicit memory have used a recognition paradigm, where items such as words or objects are studied, and then on a subsequent test, these old items are randomly intermixed with new items, and participants decide whether each item is "old" or "new." Item recognition has been associated most consistently with activity in three neural regions: (1) prefrontal cortex (anterior and dorsolateral), (2) parietal cortex, and (3) the MTL (for reviews, see Buckner & Schacter, 2004; Buckner & Wheeler, 2001; Slotnick, Moo, Segal, & Hart, 2003; Tulving, Kapur, Craik, Moscovitch, & Houle, 1994). The functional role(s) subserved by each of these regions is currently an active area of investigation, as we discuss later in this chapter. At a very general level, prefrontal cortex has been associated with the control of retrieval (e.g., increases in activity that correlate with retrieval demands; Velanova et al., 2003: Wheeler & Buckner, 2003) and in addition has been associated with

post-retrieval monitoring (for a review, see Schacter & Slotnick, 2004). Parietal cortex, particularly in Brodmann Area (BA) 39/40, has recently been associated with the tendency to make "old" responses (Velanova et al., 2003; Wheeler & Buckner, 2003). The MTL, as mentioned previously, is necessary for explicit memory, with the hippocampus proper possibly serving the role of binding together information from disparate cortical regions (Squire, 1992). That is, the hippocampus may serve a central role in combining disparate features to construct a unitary memory (e.g., Moscovitch, 1994; Schacter, Norman, & Koutstaal, 1998a; Squire, 1992).

Providing support for this constructive view of memory, recent neuroimaging evidence indicates that explicit memory evokes activity in the appropriate domain-specific processing regions (i.e., retrieval-related reactivation of processing regions associated with memorial encoding). Specifically, memory for actions activates motor processing regions (Nyberg, Petersson, Nilsson, Sandblom, Åberg, & Ingvar, 2001), memory for sounds activates auditory processing regions (Nyberg, Habib, McIntosh, & Tulving, 2000; Wheeler & Buckner, 2003; Wheeler, Petersen, & Buckner, 2003), memory for odors activates olfactory processing regions (Gottfried, Smith, Rugg, & Dolan, 2004), and memory for visual stimuli (e.g., shapes or objects) activates occipital-temporal regions in the ventral visual processing stream (Moscovitch, Kapur, Köhler, & Houle, 1995; Slotnick et al., 2003; Vaidya, Zhao, Desmond, & Gabrieli, 2002; Wheeler & Buckner, 2003; Wheeler et al., 2000). Such domain-specific sensory reactivation is typically taken as evidence for the conscious re-experiencing of sensory attributes of items from the study episode.

This chapter considers three lines of research that have examined aspects of this memory-related sensory/contextual activity and the associated subjective experience (or phenomenal consciousness; see Block, 1995; also referred to as the 'contents of consciousness' or more simply 'retrieval content'; Wheeler & Buckner, 2003). We believe that each of these lines of research has provided new information regarding the neural underpinnings of conscious experiences of remembering. First, we consider attempts to separate explicit retrieval into separate components that can be grouped broadly into two categories: *retrieval success*, which involves the recovery of information presented during a prior study episode, and *retrieval attempt*, which refers to strategic processes involved in explicit retrieval that operate even when recovery is not successful. Evidence from recent neuroimaging studies points toward different neural substrates subserving these two broad classes of conscious memory processes. Second, we discuss imaging experiments concerned with the distinction between remembering and knowing (Tulving, 1985b) that examine how neural activity correlates with differing degrees or types of conscious experiences. Third, we consider recent work concerned with delineating the neural substrates of true versus false memories, where the role of sensory reactivation in the conscious experience of remembering has been examined in the context of questions concerning the accuracy of explicit retrieval. Although we focus on neuroimaging studies in each of the three lines of research, we also discuss, when relevant, complementary data from neuropsychological studies of brain-damaged patients.

Neural Substrates of Retrieval Success Versus Attempt

When a brain region shows changes in activity during explicit retrieval, the changes are not necessarily associated with the conscious experience of successfully recovering previously studied information. Such changes could instead reflect, entirely or in part, conscious processes involved in the deployment of attention or effort when individuals attempt to retrieve the target material, independent of whether retrieval is successful. Once neuroimaging studies of episodic memory had demonstrated that

explicit retrieval is accompanied by activation in specific brain regions – most prominently, regions within prefrontal cortex, but also within the MTL (e.g., Schacter, Alpert, Savage, Rauch, & Albert, 1996a; Squire et al., 1992; Tulving et al., 1994) – it became important to specify further the nature of the observed activity. Early PET studies adopted two main experimental approaches to this issue: (1) producing high and low levels of successful retrieval by manipulating study conditions and (2) manipulating the number of previously studied items that appear during a particular test. We briefly summarize studies that have used each type of approach.

In a PET study by Schacter et al. (1996a), subjects studied some words four times and judged the number of meanings associated with each item (high-recall condition); they studied other words once and judged the number of t-junctions in each item (low-recall condition). Subjects were then scanned during an explicit retrieval task (stem-cued recall, e.g., tab__ for table), with separate scans for high-recall words and low-recall words. The logic underlying the experiment is that regions that are selectively activated during the high-recall condition, when subjects correctly recall a large proportion of the study list words, are preferentially associated with successful conscious recollection; by contrast, regions that are activated during the low-recall condition, when subjects retrieve only a few study lists words, are preferentially associated with retrieval attempt. Analysis of PET data revealed blood flow increases in the hippocampal formation during the high-recall but not the low-recall condition, and a significant difference between the two conditions, thereby suggesting that hippocampal activation is associated with some aspect of the successful conscious recall of a previously studied word, rather than retrieval attempt (see also, Nyberg, McIntosh, Houle, Nilsson, & Tulving, 1996; Rugg, Fletcher, Frith, Frackowiak, & Dolan, 1997). Schacter et al. (1996a) also found that anterior/dorsolateral areas within prefrontal cortex were preferentially activated in the low-recall condition, thus raising the possibility that blood flow increases in anterior prefrontal cortex during stem-cued recall are associated with retrieval orientation effects (cf., Nyberg et al., 1995). Such findings accord well with theoretical proposals that have linked the MTL/hippocampal region with the automatic recovery of stored information and regions within prefrontal cortex with strategic aspects of retrieval (e.g., Moscovitch, 1994).

In a related PET study by Rugg et al. (1997), subjects studied word lists and either generated sentences for each word (deep encoding) or made judgments about the letters in each word (shallow encoding). Following each type of encoding task, they were given either an old-new recognition test (intentional retrieval) or an animate/inanimate decision task (unintentional retrieval). Deep encoding produced more accurate memory on the intentional retrieval task. Performance was at ceiling levels on the unintentional task, but subjects reported spontaneously noticing that test words came from the study list more often after deep than shallow encoding, perhaps providing a rough index of unintentional conscious recollection. There was greater activation in left MTL areas after deep encoding than after shallow encoding during both intentional and unintentional retrieval. Thus, these data suggest that hippocampal activity during retrieval is observed with high levels of conscious recollection, regardless of whether subjects voluntarily try to remember the study list items. By contrast, there was greater right prefrontal activation during intentional retrieval than during unintentional retrieval after both deep and shallow encoding.

Several PET studies have attempted to separate retrieval success and retrieval attempt by manipulating the proportion of old items presented to subjects during a particular scan. The reasoning here is that presenting large numbers of old items during a particular scan will produce more successful retrieval than presenting only a few old items. In general, these studies focused on issues concerning the characterization of

retrieval-related activation observed in right anterior prefrontal cortex. However, results from these studies were inconclusive, with some evidence linking right prefrontal activation with retrieval attempt (e.g., Kapur, Craik, Jones, Brown, Houle, & Tulving, 1995) and others reporting evidence for retrieval success effects (e.g., Rugg, Fletcher, Frith, Frackowiak, & Dolan, 1996; for an attempt to reconcile some of these conflicting early results, see Wagner, Desmond, Glover, & Gabrieli, 1998).

The development of event-related fMRI in the late 1990s provided a more direct means of examining brain activations associated with retrieval success and retrieval attempt. The PET studies reviewed above used blocked designs in which items from different conditions were presented in separate blocks, and data concerning brain activity were collapsed across subjects' behavioral responses. Taking advantage of the superior temporal resolution of fMRI compared with PET, event-related fMRI allows intermixing of items from different conditions and, more importantly, permits analysis of brain activity conditional on subjects' responses (Dale & Buckner, 1997). Thus, for example, in a recognition memory task, "old" and "new" responses can be analyzed separately for old and new items. Thus, retrieval success should be maximal when subjects make "old" responses to old items (hits) and minimized when subjects make "new" responses to new items (correct rejections).

A number of studies have used event-related fMRI to examine retrieval success versus retrieval attempt with an old-new recognition test for previously studied items intermixed with new, non-studied items. The critical comparison involves a contrast of brain activity during hits and correct rejections. A number of early studies using these procedures failed to reveal clear evidence of brain activation differences during hit versus correct rejection trials (e.g., Buckner, Koutstaal, Schacter, Dale, Rotte, & Rosen, 1998; Schacter, Buckner, Koutstaal, Dale, & Rosen, 1997a). However, as discussed by Konishi, Wheeler, Donaldson, and Buckner (2000), these failures to observe evidence for retrieval success effects likely reflected technical limitations of early event-related fMRI procedures, such as low statistical power resulting from the use of long intertial intervals and a correspondingly low number of items per experimental condition. Consistent with this possibility, studies using more powerful event-related methods revealed evidence for greater activation during hits than during correct rejections in a number of cortical regions, most consistently in prefrontal and parietal cortices (e.g., Konishi et al., 2000; McDermott, Jones, Petersen, Lageman, & Rodeiger, 2000; Nolde, Johnson, & D'Esposito, 1998) but also in the MTL (as is discussed below).

The results of the foregoing studies are consistent with the conclusion that regions within prefrontal and parietal cortices are specifically related to successful conscious recollection of some aspects of a previous experience. However, this conclusion depends critically on the assumption that comparing hits with correct rejections isolates successful retrieval. Although the assumption appears straightforward enough, the comparison between hits and correct rejections necessarily confounds subjects' responses ("old" or "new") and item type (old and new). It is conceivable, therefore, that hit greater than correct rejection-related brain activations do not exclusively reflect differences in conscious experience related to subjects' responses (e.g., calling an item "old" versus calling it "new"), but instead reflect differences in responses to old versus new items, irrespective of subjects' experiences. For example, differential responses to old and new items might reflect the occurrence of priming or related processes that can occur independently of conscious memory (Schacter & Buckner, 1998; Schacter et al., 2004; Wiggs & Martin, 1998).

Dobbins, Rice, Wagner, and Schacter (2003) approached this issue within the context of the theoretical distinction between *recollection* (i.e., memory for the contextual details of a prior encounter) and *familiarity* (i.e., recognition without recollection of contextual details). Both recollection and familiarity can, in principle, operate on a par-

ticular memory test (for a contrasting view, see Slotnick & Dodson, 2005). Moreover, each of the two processes are potentially separable into the two components on which we have focused in this section of the chapter, retrieval success and retrieval attempt (Dobbins et al. used the closely related phrase, *retrieval orientation* to refer to the extent to which subjects recruit each process during particular retrieval tasks). With respect to the issues raised in the preceding paragraph, Dobbins et al. (2003) noted that, when presented with new items, subjects could rely entirely on familiarity-based processes, rejecting new items when they are not familiar, and might not even attempt to engage in recollection-based retrieval. Thus, it is conceivable that previous findings of prefrontal and parietal activations associated with hits greater than correct rejections might reflect *attempted* recollective retrieval, rather than successful conscious recollection.

To address this issue, Dobbins et al. (2003) used a different type of experimental design in which all items had been presented previously, and task demands were varied to require differential reliance on recollection and familiarity. Prior to scanning, subjects were presented visually with a long list of nouns, and then they alternated between two semantic encoding tasks (pleasant/unpleasant and concrete/abstract judgments). Subjects were then scanned during two different two-alternative forced-choice tests: a source memory test and a recency memory test. During source memory, subjects selected the member of the pair previously associated with a particular encoding task; that is, they had to recollect some type of detail associated with the particular encoding judgment performed earlier. In contrast, the recency judgment required subjects to select the most recently encountered item of the pair, regardless of how it had been encoded. The source memory test is assumed to rely on recollection, whereas recency decisions can rely on a familiarity signal. Furthermore, successful and unsuccessful trials within each retrieval task were contrasted to determine whether retrieval success effects occurred in

Table 28.1. Neural regions associated most consistently with conscious memory processes

Region	Prefrontal Cortex	Parietal Cortex	MTL	Sensory Cortex
Retrieval Success & Attempt	X	X		
Retrieval Success > Attempt			X	
Retrieval Attempt > Success	X			
Remembering & Knowing	X	X		
Remembering > Knowing		X	X	X
Knowing > Remembering	X			
True & False Recognition	X	X	X	
True > False Recognition		X		X
False > True Recognition	X			

Note: Regions of common (&) and differential (>) activity were identified via review of the neuroimaging literature.

overlapping or dissimilar brain regions compared to those associated with each retrieval orientation.

Results revealed left lateral prefrontal and parietal activations that distinguished attempted source recollection from judgments of relative recency; these retrieval attempt or orientation effects were largely independent of retrieval success. Importantly, these activations occurred largely in the same left prefrontal and parietal regions that had been previously identified with retrieval success. Because these regions were not associated with successful retrieval in the Dobbins et al. (2003) design, which controlled for old-new item differences present in previous studies, it is plausible that the prefrontal and parietal activations in earlier studies reflect attempted, rather than successful, conscious recollection (for further relevant analyses, see Dobbins, Foley, Schacter, & Wagner, 2002). In contrast, Dobbins et al. (2003) found that MTL structures (hippocampus and parahippocampal gyrus) were differentially more active during successful recollection, showing similarly reduced responses during failed source recollection and judgments of recency. These findings complement previous data linking MTL regions with successful conscious recollection (e.g., Maril, Simons, Schwartz, Mitchell, & Schacter, 2003; Rugg et al., 1997; Schacter et al., 1996a; but see, Buckner et al., 1998; Rugg, Henson, & Robb, 2003), as well as other results from related paradigms considered later in the chapter.

Kahn, Davachi, and Wagner (2004) have provided converging evidence on the foregoing conclusions using an old-new recognition test for previously presented words and new words in which subjects also made a source memory judgment (whether they had read a word at study or imagined a scene related to the word). They concluded that left prefrontal/parietal regions are related to attempted recollection of source information, but not to successful recollection of that information; by contrast, MTL activation (in the parahippocampal region) was related to successful source recollection. Importantly, Kahn et al. (2004) also provided evidence indicating that left frontal/parietal activity is related to familiarity-based retrieval success. Thus, the general distinction between retrieval success and retrieval attempt (or orientation) may be too coarse to prove useful theoretically. Instead, it may be necessary to specify a particular form of retrieval to make sense of neuroimaging data concerning the neural correlates of successful and attempted retrieval (e.g., recollection versus familiarity, or remembering versus knowing, which are considered in detail below).

The results summarized in this section indicate that neuroimaging studies are beginning to dissociate components of conscious retrieval that are related to activity in particular brain regions. In particular, three patterns of results can be observed (Table 28.1). First, both retrieval success and retrieval attempt were associated with activity in the prefrontal cortex and parietal cortex. Second, retrieval success to a greater degree than retrieval attempt was associated with activity in the MTL. Third, there is some evidence that retrieval attempt may be associated with greater prefrontal cortex activity than with retrieval success. As research in this area progresses, increasingly finer distinctions will be made regarding the neural substrates associated with particular aspects of conscious memorial experience. Of note, the fact that retrieval success – which can be assumed to reflect greater retrieval content than retrieval attempt – is preferentially associated with the MTL suggests this region plays a role during conscious remembering.

Neural Activity Associated with Remembering and Knowing

We reviewed research in the preceding section that attempts to dissociate recollection and familiarity by manipulating task demands. However, as noted earlier, recollection and familiarity can be assessed directly by asking participants about their subjective experiences during a memory task; that is, to classify "old" responses based on the associated memorial experience of remembering or knowing. Remember responses indicate recollection of specific contextual detail associated with a previous experience, whereas know responses refer to a sense of familiarity without contextual detail (Tulving, 1985b). Comparing the neural activity associated with remember and know responses is thus expected to provide additional insight into the substrates of specific types of conscious experiences considered under the general rubric of explicit memory.

In an event-related fMRI study of remembering and knowing (Henson, Rugg, Shallice, Josephs, & Dolan, 1999), subjects first studied a list of words. For each item on a subsequent recognition test, participants responded "remember" or "know" to items they judged to be "old" and otherwise responded "new." Both correct remem-

ber responses and correct know responses, relative to new-correct rejections, were associated with activity in prefrontal cortex (dorsolateral and medial) and medial parietal cortex (precuneus). Relative to new-correct rejections, remember judgments (but not know judgments) were also associated with additional activity in parietal cortex (superior parietal lobule and inferior parietal lobule) and the MTL (parahippocampal gyrus). The direct contrast between remember and know responses complemented these results by showing activity in the parietal cortex (superior parietal lobule and inferior parietal lobule). Although the MTL activation did not survive this direct contrast, it should be noted that only remember responses (versus new-correct rejections) evoked activity in the MTL, providing some indication that this region is preferentially associated with remembering. The reverse contrast between know and remember was associated with activity in the prefrontal cortex (dorsolateral and medial), albeit to a less extensive degree than that associated with remember or know responses (versus new-correct rejections), and medial parietal cortex (precuneus).

A subsequent event-related fMRI recognition memory study, also using words as study and test materials, replicated and extended the previous pattern of results by focusing on differential neural activity associated with remember and know responses (Eldrige, Knowlton, Furmanski, Bookheimer, & Engel, 2000). The contrast between remember and know responses was associated with activity in the prefrontal cortex (dorsolateral), the parietal cortex (inferior parietal lobule), the MTL (both hippocampus and parahippocampal gyrus), and the fusiform gyrus. This fusiform gyrus activity (coupled with the MTL activity) likely reflects a greater degree of sensory reactivation associated with remember as compared to know responses. The know greater than remember contrast was associated with a distinct region in the (anterior) prefrontal cortex.

In an event-related fMRI remember-know paradigm conducted by Wheeler and

Buckner (2004; adapted from a paradigm originally designed to investigate memory-related domain specific sensory reactivation; see Wheeler & Buckner, 2003; Wheeler et al., 2000), words were paired with either sounds or pictures at study. On the subsequent recognition test, old words (those previously paired with pictures, the only type of old items considered in the analysis) and new words were presented. Participants responded "remember," "know," or "new." Correct remember and know responses were associated with the same degree of activity in one subregion of the parietal cortex, whereas another subregion was associated with greater activity for remember than know responses (both regions were in the inferior parietal lobule). The contrast of remember versus know was also associated with activity in the prefrontal cortex (medial), the MTL (hippocampus), and the fusiform cortex. Because subjects were remembering previously studied pictures, the fusiform cortex activity in this study likely reflects memory-related sensory reactivation. Know versus remember responses were associated with activity in the (dorsolateral) prefrontal cortex.

Across the studies reviewed, a number of patterns emerge (Table 28.1). First, remembering and knowing, as compared to new-correct rejections, were associated with activity in prefrontal cortex and parietal cortex. Second, remembering evoked greater activity than knowing most consistently in parietal cortex, the MTL, and sensory cortex. Third, knowing evoked greater activity than remembering in the prefrontal cortex. These findings are largely consistent with evidence from remember-know ERP studies, which have shown greater remember than know activity at parietal scalp electrodes (approximately 400–800 ms from stimulus onset) in addition to similar remember and know activity (both greater than new) at frontal scalp electrodes (approximately 1000–1600 ms from stimulus onset; Curran, 2004; Duarte, Ranganath, Winward, Hayward, & Knight, 2004; Düzel, Yonelinas, Mangun, Heinze, & Tulving, 1997; Smith, 1993; Trott, Friedman, Ritter,

Fabiani, & Snodgrass, 1999; see also Wilding & Rugg, 1996).

Neuropsychological evidence converges to some extent with the neuroimaging (and ERP) findings. In a study by Knowlton and Squire (1995), amnesic patients with MTL damage studied a list of unrelated words and then made "remember," "know," or "new" judgments on a subsequent recognition test. Amnesic patients showed a large decrement in remember responses as compared to control participants and a more modest but still significant decline in know responses (at a 10-minute delay between study and test). Subsequent studies showed a similar pattern of results, where amnesic patients showed a severe impairment in remembering along with more modest trends for impairments in knowing (Schacter, Verfaellie, & Anes, 1997b; Schacter, Verfaellie, & Pradere, 1996c; Yonelinas, Kroll, Dobbins, Lazzara, & Knight, 1998) and unilateral temporal lobectomy patients have been shown to only be impaired in remembering (Moscovitch & McAndrews, 2002).

Although these group studies include patients with damage to a variety of MTL structures, more recent studies have attempted to distinguish between patients with damage restricted to the hippocampal formation and those with more extensive MTL damage. Yonelinas et al. (2002) found deficits in both remembering and knowing in patients with damage to both the hippocampus and surrounding parahippocampal gyrus. By contrast, they found impairments of remembering – but not knowing – in patients who developed memory deficits as a result of hypoxia, which is known to produce damage restricted to the hippocampal formation in patients whose deficits are restricted to memory (see Yonelinas et al., 2002). Note, however, that anatomical information was not provided concerning the precise lesion sites of the hypoxic patients included in the Yonelinas et al. (2002) study, so the anatomical implications of these findings are uncertain. Manns, Hopkins, Reed, Kitchener, and Squire (2003) reported significant and comparable deficits of remembering and knowing in amnesics with restricted hippocampal damage, compared with controls. By contrast, a recent case study of patient B.E., who has selective bilateral hippocampal damage, suggests that damage to the hippocampal region alone can result in a specific deficit in remembering with relative sparing of knowing (Holdstock, Mayes, Gong, Roberts, & Kapur, 2005; see also Holdstock et al., 2002).

In summary, although all neuropsychological studies of amnesic patients with MTL or restricted hippocampal damage reveal severe deficits of remembering, the evidence is mixed concerning the role of the MTL generally, and of hippocampus specifically, in knowing. Given current controversies in the interpretation of remember/know data (cf., Dunn, 2004; Gardiner et al., 2002; Rotello, Macmillan, & Reeder, 2004; Wixted & Stretch, 2004), it is perhaps not entirely surprising that clarification of the relative status of remembering and knowing in amnesic patients will require further study. Nonetheless, these neuropsychological studies complement imaging data by providing evidence that the MTL is critically involved in remembering, which reflects a rich form of conscious recollective experience (see discussion in Moscovitch, 1995, 2000).

Sensory Reactivation in True and False Memory

In the type of recognition memory paradigms we have considered thus far, analyses of cognitive and brain activity typically focus on accurate responses: "old" responses to studied items (old-hits) or "new" responses to non-studied items (new correct rejections). False alarms to new items in such paradigms are usually too few to allow meaningful analysis. However, cognitive psychologists have developed a number of paradigms that yield much larger numbers of false alarms, thus allowing comparison of the cognitive and neural properties of true memories and false memories (for a recent review, see Schacter & Slotnick, 2004). For example,

Roediger and McDermott (1995), extending earlier work by Deese (1959), reported a paradigm that produces extremely high levels of false memories (now commonly referred to as the DRM paradigm). In the DRM paradigm, participants are presented with lists of associated words (e.g., *fly*, *bug*, *insect*, *web*, and other related words) that are related to a non-studied lure item (e.g., *spider*). Roediger and McDermott's (1995) study showed that subjects falsely recognized a high proportion of these related lure items and often claimed to specifically "remember" (versus "know") that the lure items appeared on the study list. A similar paradigm has been used to study false memory for visual shapes, in which subjects study physically related shapes and later produce high levels of false alarms to perceptually similar shapes that had not been previously seen (Koutstaal, Schacter, Verfaellie, Brenner, & Jackson, 1999). From the perspective of the present chapter, the development of such paradigms allows us to examine the similarities and differences in the neural correlates of conscious experiences associated with accurate and inaccurate memories.

In the first neuroimaging study to compare true and false memory (Schacter, Reiman, Curran, Yun, Bandy, McDermott, & Roediger, 1996b), participants heard DRM-associated lists followed by a recognition test (consisting of studied/old words, lures/non-studied related words, and non-studied unrelated/new words). Each item type at test (old, related, and new), in addition to a baseline passive fixation condition, was presented in a separate PET scanning block. Both true and false recognition, compared to baseline fixation, were associated with activity that included anterior/dorsolateral prefrontal cortex (BA 10/46), precuneus (medial parietal cortex), and parahippocampal gyrus (within the MTL). The direct contrast between true and false recognition was associated with activity in a left temporal parietal cortex, a region linked to auditory processing. This latter finding can be taken as evidence for greater sensory reactivation (i.e., auditory cortex activation during memory for previously spoken words) during true memory as compared to false memory.

A similar experiment was conducted using event-related fMRI (Schacter et al. 1997a), where event types during the recognition test were intermixed, and it showed that both true and false recognition (compared to baseline fixation) were associated with similar patterns of activity including the prefrontal cortex, parietal cortex, and the MTL. However, unlike the previous study, the true greater than false recognition contrast did not reveal activity in any region. At the same time, an ERP experiment suggested that true greater than false recognition-related activity could be attributed to differences in blocked versus event-related designs (Johnson, Nolde, Mather, Kounios, Schacter, & Curran, 1997). Although this latter finding suggests common neural substrates underlying true and false recognition, subsequent fMRI studies have shown more convincing evidence of true/false differences in brain activity and have begun to elucidate the nature of that activity.

In an event-related fMRI study conducted by Cabeza, Rao, Wagner, Mayer, and Schacter (2001), a male or female (on videotape, a relatively rich contextual environment) spoke words from DRM lists of semantic associates or similar categorized lists (e.g., *onion*, *cucumber*, and *pea* are exemplars of the category 'vegetable'). Participants were instructed to remember each word and whether it was spoken by the male or female. At test, old words, related words (non-presented associates and categories), or new words were presented, and participants made an old-new recognition decision. True recognition and false recognition, as compared to new items, were associated with activity in the dorsolateral prefrontal cortex, parietal cortex (medial and inferior parietal lobule), and the MTL, specifically the hippocampus. The contrast of false recognition versus true recognition was associated with greater activity in ventromedial prefrontal cortex. True recognition versus false recognition was associated

with greater activity in the parietal cortex (inferior parietal lobule) and another region of the MTL, the parahippocampal gyrus. This parahippocampal gyrus activity (which has also been reported in a true/false recognition paradigm by Okado and Stark, 2003) may reflect greater true than false recognition-related contextual reactivation (possibly reflecting memory for the videotaped speakers), because this region has been associated with processing visual context (Bar & Aminoff, 2003; Epstein & Kanwisher, 1998).

Slotnick and Schacter (2004) used event-related fMRI to investigate the neural substrates of true and false recognition for abstract visual shapes. During the study phase, participants viewed sets of exemplar shapes that were similar to a non-presented prototype shape (analogous to DRM word lists). At test, old shapes, related shapes (e.g., non-studied but similar shapes), or new shapes were presented, and participants made an old-new recognition judgment. True recognition and false recognition, as compared to new-correct rejections (i.e., responding "new" to unrelated new items), were associated with activity in the anterior/dorsolateral and medial prefrontal cortex, parietal cortex (superior parietal lobule, inferior parietal lobule, and precuneus), the MTL (hippocampus), and ventral occipital-temporal visual processing regions (BA 17/18/19/37). Although the true greater than false recognition contrast and the reverse contrast were each associated with activity in different regions of the dorsolateral prefrontal cortex and parietal cortex (including precuneus and inferior parietal lobule), only the true greater than false recognition contrast was associated with activity in visual processing regions, specifically in BA 17 and BA 18. These latter regions may reflect greater visual sensory reactivation associated with true recognition as compared to false recognition. The results of ERP studies investigating the neural basis of true and false visual spatial memory are consistent with these findings (Fabiani, Stadler, & Wessels, 2000; Gratton, Corballis, & Jain, 1997).

Thus, across a number of studies, cortical activity that is likely associated with sensory/contextual processing is greater for true than false recognition. Such differential activity might be taken as reflecting conscious recollection of sensory/contextual details that are remembered during true but not false recognition, an idea that has received some support from behavioral studies (e.g., Mather, Henkel, & Johnson, 1997; Norman & Schacter, 1997). Slotnick and Schacter (2004) attempted to identify visual processing regions that reflect conscious memory by contrasting old-hits (responding "old" to old items) and old-misses (responding "new" to old items; see also, Wheeler & Buckner, 2003, 2004). If activity within such regions reflects conscious memory, then brain activity should be greater for old-hits than for old-misses. Conversely, regions that reflect non-conscious memory should respond equivalently during old-hits and old-misses, but in both cases to a greater degree than during new correct rejections (Rugg, Mark, Walla, Schloerscheidt, Birch, & Allan, 1998). Slotnick and Schacter found that conscious memory, as identified by the old-hits greater than old-misses contrast, was associated with activity in later visual processing regions (BA 19/37), whereas non-conscious memory – identified by contrasting both old-hits and old-misses each with new-correct rejections – was associated with activity in earlier visual processing regions (BA 17/18). The same functional-anatomic dichotomy was also observed in a follow-up experiment. Both the true greater than false recognition activity and the old-hits and old-misses greater than new-correct rejections results provide convergent evidence that activity in BA17/18 reflects nonconscious memory, at least in the paradigm used by Slotnick and Schacter.

We have proposed that this early visual area activity may reflect the influence of priming, which as noted earlier is a non-conscious form of memory (Slotnick & Schacter, 2004). One possible problem with this idea is that neuroimaging studies have often shown that priming is associated with decreases in activity following repetition of familiar items, such as words and pictures of common objects (for reviews, see Henson, 2003; Schacter & Buckner, 1998; Schacter et al., 2004; Wiggs & Martin, 1998). However, it has also been found that repetition of novel (or masked) faces, objects, or shapes elicits increases in regional brain activity (e.g., Henson, Shallice, & Dolan, 2000; James, Humphrey, Gati, Menon, & Goodale, 2000; Schacter, Reiman, Uecker, Polster, Yun, & Cooper, 1995; Uecker, Reiman, Schacter, Polster, Cooper, Yun, & Chen, 1997). Because novel abstract shapes served as materials in the Slotnick and Schacter study, the priming hypothesis remains viable. Note also that Slotnick and Schacter used the identical shapes at study and test, thus allowing for repetition priming to occur (see also, Slotnick et al., 2003), whereas other visual memory studies that failed to observe memory-related activity in early visual regions (but found memory-related activity in late visual regions BA 19/37) did not use the identical stimuli at study and test, thus reducing the possibility of repetition priming (Vaidya et al., 2002; Wheeler & Buckner, 2003; Wheeler et al., 2000).

The overall pattern of results thus suggests that memory-related activity in BA 17/18 may be non-conscious. This observation has ramifications for interpreting activity associated with performance on explicit memory tests. Typically, activation associated with explicit memory tests such as old-new recognition is attributed to conscious processing; however, the present analysis indicates this is not always the case. Rather, additional analyses (such as the old-hits versus old-misses contrast) appear necessary to investigate and characterize the nature of activity associated with explicit memory.

The idea that activity in early visual regions that distinguishes between true and false recognition reflects non-conscious memory processes may also help explain why false recognition occurs at high levels, even though brain activity can distinguish between true and false memories. If the activity in early visual regions that distinguished between true and false memories had been consciously accessible, participants should have used this activity to avoid making false alarms to the related shapes. The fact that there was nonetheless a high rate of false recognition makes sense if the activity within these regions reflects a non-conscious form of memory.

Across the true and false recognition studies reviewed, a number of patterns can be observed (Table 28.1). First, consistent with regions previously associated with explicit retrieval, true and false recognition (versus new-correct rejections) were both associated with activity in prefrontal cortex, parietal cortex, and the MTL (most consistently within the hippocampus). Second, true greater than false recognition was associated with activity in the parietal cortex and sensory/contextual processing regions. Third, false greater than true recognition was associated with activity in the prefrontal cortex (distinct from the commonly active regions).

Neuropsychological studies have provided convergent evidence, particularly regarding the role of the MTL in both true and false recognition. In a study by Schacter et al. (1996c), amnesic patients (with MTL damage) took part in a recognition memory paradigm that used associative word lists. As expected, these patients showed lower levels of true recognition (and higher levels of false alarms to new words) as compared to control participants; in addition, the patients had lower levels of false recognition (i.e., a reduced rate of false alarms to semantically related words; see also, Melo, Winocur, & Moscovitch, 1999; Schacter, Verfaellie, Anes, & Racine, 1998b). Similarly, reduced levels of both true and false recognition in amnesic patients have also been shown in recognition memory paradigms that have employed conceptually related words (e.g., "twister," "funnel") and perceptually related words (e.g., "hate," "mate"; Schacter et al., 1997b), or abstract visual patterns (Koutstaal et al., 1999; similar to those used by Slotnick & Schacter, 2004). Furthermore, Alzheimer's disease patients (with neuropathology that includes, but is not limited to, the MTL regions) also have lower levels of false recog-

nition as compared to control participants (Balota, Watson, Duchek, & Ferraro, 1999; Budson, Daffner, Desikan, & Schacter, 2000; Budson, Desikan, Daffner, & Schacter, 2001; Budson, Sullivan, Daffner, & Schacter, 2003). These neuropsychological studies indicate that the MTL is critically involved in both true and false recognition.

Concluding Comments

In this chapter we have reviewed cognitive neuroscience evidence concerning three distinctions that illuminate different aspects of the relation between memory and consciousness: retrieval success versus attempt, remembering versus knowing, and true versus false recognition. Retrieval success involves memory of a previously experienced item or event, whereas retrieval attempt refers to the effort associated with remembering (without success). As such, successful retrieval (based on the associated memorial experience/details) can be said to reflect high retrieval content. whereas retrieval attempt can be said to reflect low retrieval content. By definition, remember-know studies are used to study distinctions between contextual differences in explicit memory: Remember responses are associated with greater sensory/contextual detail (i.e., high retrieval content), whereas know responses are not associated with sensory/contextual detail (i.e., low retrieval content). True recognition has been associated with access to greater sensory/contextual detail as compared to false recognition (Mather et al., 1997; Norman & Schacter, 1997; Schooler, Gerhard, & Loftus, 1986). Accordingly, retrieval content can be considered greater during true as compared to false memory (although not to such a degree as to preclude the occurrence of false memories). Thus, although both true and false recognition are forms of explicit memory, where common neural substrates likely reflect mechanisms of general retrieval, regions differentially associated with true and false recognition can be assumed to reflect high and low retrieval content, respectively.

As reflected in our summaries at the conclusion of each section of the chapter, the patterns of results for retrieval success and attempt, for remembering and knowing, and for true and false recognition show striking parallels (Table 28.1). The patterns of results for retrieval success and attempt differed from the patterns for remembering and knowing only in that remembering greater than knowing (and not retrieval success greater than attempt) was associated with activity in parietal and sensory cortex (which may simply reflect general differences in the use of stimulus materials; e.g., pictures versus words). The patterns of results for true versus false recognition were largely identical to the patterns of results for remembering versus knowing, except that true and false recognition were both associated with MTL activity, whereas some data indicate remembering but not knowing were associated with MTL activity (as noted earlier, however, the neuropsychological evidence for this conclusion is uncertain, with some data indicating a link between knowing and MTL structures). That the MTL is associated with false recognition may provide some explanation why participants respond "old" despite the fact there may be less contextual detail associated with these items.

We now consider the common neural activity associated with high retrieval content (i.e., retrieval success, remembering, and true recognition) and low retrieval content (i.e., retrieval attempt, knowing, and false recognition). Memories with both high and low retrieval content were associated with activity in the prefrontal cortex and parietal cortex, which indicates these regions are generally associated with explicit retrieval. There was also some evidence that memories with low retrieval content, to a greater degree than those with high retrieval content, may be associated with increased prefrontal cortex activity; however, this activity has been attributed to greater low retrieval content-related post-retrieval monitoring (Schacter & Slotnick, 2004). That is, although there may be more effortful conscious processing with

low retrieval content items (which can be considered access-consciousness; see Block, 1995), and is perhaps attributable to greater task difficulty, this is typically not the central focus in discussions of consciousness and memory. Rather, high retrieval content and low retrieval content refer to the sensory/contextual experience associated with retrieval of episodic memories. Relevant to this point, high retrieval content memories, to a greater degree than low retrieval content memories, were associated with activity in the parietal cortex (most consistently the inferior parietal lobule) and sensory processing regions (at least for remembering and true recognition, with a null result for retrieval success). The parietal activity may reflect a greater degree of attention during retrieval of memories with high retrieval content as compared to those with low retrieval content (Corbetta & Shulman, 2002; Hopfinger, Buonocore, & Mangun, 2000). Critically, however, the greater degree of sensory activity associated with memories with high versus low retrieval content provides evidence that memories are constructed by reactivation of features that comprised a previous item or event (Squire, 1992; Schacter et al., 1998a).

The present chapter shows that a cognitive neuroscience approach can illuminate the relation between memory and consciousness, highlighting how explicit memories with different degrees of retrieval content can be linked to distinct neural substrates. Although we would be remiss not to point out that this area of research is in its infancy, we also believe that the field has advanced significantly since the publication of Tulving's (1985b) lament concerning the lack of interest in memory and consciousness. We suspect that advances during the next 20 years will be even more impressive than those of the past two decades.

Acknowledgments

Preparation of this chapter was supported by grants NIA AG08441 and NIMH MH060951.

References

Balota, D. A., Watson, J. M., Duchek, J. M., & Ferraro, F. R. (1999). Cross-modal semantic and homograph priming in healthy young, healthy old, and Alzheimer's disease individuals. *Journal of International Neuropsychological Society*, 5, 626–640.

Bar, M., & Aminoff, E. (2003). Cortical analysis of visual context. *Neuron*, 38, 347–358.

Block, N. (1995). On a confusion about a function of consciousness. *Behavioral and Brain Sciences*, 18, 227–287.

Buckner, R. L., Koutstaal, W., Schacter, D. L., Dale, A. M., Rotte, M., & Rosen, B. R. (1998). Functional-anatomic study of episodic retrieval: Selective averaging of event-related fMRI trials to test the retrieval success hypothesis. *NeuroImage*, 7, 163–175.

Buckner, R. L., & Schacter, D. L. (2004). Neural correlates of memory's successes and sins. In M. S. Gazzaniga (Ed.), *The cognitive neurosciences* (3rd ed., pp. 739–752). Cambridge, MA: MIT Press.

Buckner, R. L., & Wheeler, M. E. (2001). The cognitive neuroscience of remembering. *Nature Reviews Neuroscience*, 2, 624–634.

Budson, A. E., Daffner, K. R., Desikan, R., & Schacter, D. L. (2000). When false recognition is unopposed by true recognition: Gist-based memory distortion in Alzheimer's disease. *Neuropsychology*, 14, 277–287.

Budson, A. E., Desikan, R., Daffner, K. R., & Schacter, D. L. (2001). Perceptual false recognition in Alzheimer's disease. *Neuropsychology*, 15, 230–243.

Budson, A. E., Sullivan, A. L., Daffner, K. R., & Schacter, D. L. (2003). Semantic versus phonological false recognition in aging and Alzheimer's disease. *Brain and Cognition*, 51, 251–261.

Cabeza, R., Rao, S. M., Wagner, A. D., Mayer, A. R., & Schacter, D. L. (2001). Can medial temporal lobe regions distinguish true from false? An event-related functional MRI study of veridical and illusory recognition memory. *Proceedings of the National Academy of Sciences USA*, 98, 4805–4810.

Cermak, L. S. (1982). *Human memory and amnesia*. Hillsdale, NJ: Erlbaum.

Corbetta, M., & Shulman, G. L. (2002). Control of goal-directed and stimulus-driven attention in the brain. *Nature Reviews Neuroscience*, 3, 201–215.

Curran, T. (2004). Effects of attention and confidence on the hypothesized ERP correlates of recollection and familiarity. *Neuropsychologia*, 42, 1088–1106.

Dale, A. M., & Buckner, R. L. (1997). Selective averaging of rapidly presented individual trials using fMRI. *Human Brain Mapping*, 5, 329–340.

Deese, J. (1959). On the prediction of occurrence of particular verbal intrusions in immediate recall. *Journal of Experimental Psychology*, 58, 17–22.

Dobbins, I. G., Foley, H., Schacter, D. L., & Wagner, A. D. (2002). Executive control during episodic retrieval: Multiple prenfrontal processes subserve source memory. *Neuron*, 35, 989–996.

Dobbins, I. G., Rice, H. J., Wagner, A. D., & Schacter, D. L. (2003). Memory orientation and success: Separable neurocognitive components underlying episodic recognition. *Neuropsychologia*, 41, 318–333.

Dobbins, I. G., Schnyer, D. M., Verfaellie, M., & Schacter, D. L. (2004). Cortical activity reductions during repetition priming can result from rapid response learning. *Nature*, 428, 316–319.

Duarte, A., Ranganath, C., Winward, L., Hayward, D., & Knight, R. T. (2004). Dissociable neural correlates for familiarity and recollection during the encoding and retrieval of pictures. *Cognitive Brain Research*, 18, 255–272.

Dunn, J. C. (2004). Remember-know: A matter of confidence. *Psychological Review*, 111, 524–542.

Düzel, E., Yonelinas, A. P., Mangun, G. R., Heinze, H., & Tulving, E. (1997). Event-related brain potential correlates of two states of conscious awareness in memory. *Proceedings of the National Academy of Sciences USA*, 94, 5973–5978.

Eldridge, L. L., Knowlton, B. J., Furmanski, C. S., Bookheimer, S. Y., & Engel, S. A. (2000). Remembering episodes: A selective role for the hippocampus during retrieval. *Nature Reviews Neuroscience*, 3, 1149–1152.

Epstein, R., & Kanwisher, N. (1998). A cortical representation of the local visual environment. *Nature*, 392, 598–601.

Fabiani, M., Stadler, M. A., & Wessels, P. M. (2000). True but not false memories produce a sensory signature in human lateralized brain potentials. *Journal of Cognitive Neuroscience, 12*, 941–949.

Gardiner, J. M., Ramponi, C., & Richardson-Klavehn, A. (2002). Recognition memory and decision processes: A meta-analysis of remember, know, and guess responses. *Memory, 10*, 83–98.

Goodale, M. A., & Westwood, D. A. (2004). An evolving view of duplex vision: Separate but interacting cortical pathways for perception and action. *Current Opinion in Neurobiology, 14*, 203–211.

Gooding, P. A., Mayes, A. R., & van Eijk, R. (2000). A meta-analysis of indirect memory tests for novel material in organic amnesics. *Neuropsychologia, 38*, 666–676.

Gottfried, J. A., Smith, A. P. R., Rugg, M. D., & Dolan, R. J. (2004). Remembrance of odors past: Human olfactory cortex in cross-modal recognition memory. *Neuron, 42*, 687–695.

Graf, P., & Schacter, D. L. (1985). Implicit and explicit memory for new associations in normal subjects and amnesic patients. *Journal of Experimental Psychology: Learning, Memory, and Cognition, 11*, 501–518.

Gratton, G., Corballis, P. M., & Jain, S. (1997). Hemispheric organization of visual memories. *Journal of Cognitive Neuroscience, 9*, 92–104.

Guzeldere, G., Flanagan, O., & Hardcastle, V. G. (2000). The nature and function of consciousness: Lessons from blindsight. In M. S. Gazzaniga (Ed.), *The cognitive neurosciences* (2nd ed., pp. 1277–1284). Cambridge, MA: MIT Press.

Henson, R. N. (2003). Neuroimaging studies of priming. *Progress in Neurobiology, 70*, 53–81.

Henson, R. N. A., Rugg, M. D., Shallice, T., Josephs, O., & Dolan, R. J. (1999). Recollection and familiarity in recognition memory: An event-related functional magnetic resonance imaging study. *Journal of Neuroscience, 19*, 3962–3972.

Henson, R., Shallice, T., & Dolan, R. (2000). Neuroimaging evidence for dissociable forms of repetition priming. *Science, 287*, 1269–1272.

Holdstock, J. S., Mayes, A. R., Gong, Q. Y., Roberts, N., & Kapur, N. (2005). Item recognition is less impaired than recall and associative recognition in a patient with selective hippocampal damage. *Hippocampus, 15*, 203–215.

Holdstock, J. S., Mayes, A. R., Roberts, N., Cezayirli, E., Isaac, C. L., O'Reilly, R. C., & Norman, K. A. (2002). Under what conditions is recognition spared relative to recall after selective hippocampal damage in humans? *Hippocampus, 12*, 341–351.

Hopfinger, J. B., Buonocore, M. H., & Mangun, G. R. (2000). The neural mechanisms of top-down attentional control. *Nature Neuroscience, 3*, 284–291.

James, T. W., Humphrey, G. K., Gati, J. S., Menon, R. S., & Goodale, M. A. (2000). The effects of visual object priming on brain activation before and after recognition. *Current Biology, 10*, 1017–1024.

Johnson, M. K., Nolde, S. F., Mather, M., Kounios, J., Schacter, D. L., & Curran, T. (1997). The similarity of brain activity associated with true and false recognition memory depends on test format. *Psychological Science, 8*, 250–257.

Kahn, I., Davachi, L., & Wagner, A. D. (2004). Functional-neuroanatomic correlates of recollection: Implications for models of recognition memory. *Journal of Neuroscience, 24*, 4172–4180.

Kapur, S., Craik, F. I., Jones, C., Brown, G. M., Houle, S., & Tulving, E. (1995). Functional role of the prefrontal cortex in retrieval of memories: A PET study. *NeuroReport, 6*, 1880–1884.

Knowlton, B. J., & Squire, L. R. (1995). Remembering and knowing: Two different expressions of declarative memory. *Journal of Experimental Psychology: Learning, Memory, & Cognition, 21*, 699–710.

Köhler, S., & Moscovitch, M. (1997). Unconscious visual processing in neuropsychological syndromes: A survey of the literature and evaluation of models of consciousness. In M. D. Rugg (Ed.), *Cognitive neuroscience* (pp. 305–373). Cambridge, MA: MIT Press.

Konishi, S., Wheeler, M. E., Donaldson, D. I., & Buckner, R. L. (2000). Neural correlates of episodic retrieval success. *NeuroImage, 12*, 276–286.

Koutstaal, W., Schacter, D. L., Verfaellie, M., Brenner, C., & Jackson, E. M. (1999). Perceptually based false recognition of novel objects in amnesia: Effects of category size and similarity to category prototypes. *Cognitive Neuropsychology, 16*, 317–341.

Manns, J. R., Hopkins, R. O., Reed, J. M., Kitchener, E. G., & Squire, L. R. (2003). Recognition memory and the human hippocampus. *Neuron, 37*, 171–180.

Maril, A., Simons, J. S., Mitchell, J. P., Schwartz, B. L., & Schacter, D. L. (2003). Feeling-of-knowing in episodic memory: An event-related fMRI study. *NeuroImage, 18*, 827–836.

Mather, M., Henkel, L. A., & Johnson, M. K. (1997). Evaluating characteristics of false memories: Remember/know judgments and memory characteristics questionnaire compared. *Memory & Cognition, 25*, 826–837.

McDermott, K. B., Jones, T. C., Petersen, S. E., Lageman, S. K., & Roediger, H. L. III. (2000). Retrieval success is accompanied by enhanced activation in anterior prefrontal cortex during recognition memory: An event-related fMRI study. *Journal of Cognitive Neuroscience, 12*, 965–976.

Melo, B., Winocur, G., & Moscovitch, M. (1999). False recall and false recognition: An examination of the effects of selective and combined lesions to the medial temporal lobe/diencephalon and frontal lobe structures. *Cognitive Neuropsychology, 16*, 343–359.

Moscovitch, M. (1984). The sufficient conditions for demonstrating preserved amnesia: A task analysis. In L. R. Squire & N. Butters (Eds.), *Neuropsychology of memory* (pp. 104–114). New York: Guilford Press.

Moscovitch, M. (1994). Memory and working with memory: Evaluation of a component process model and comparisons with other models. In D. L. Schacter & E. Tulving (Eds.) *Memory systems 1994* (pp. 269–331). Cambridge, MA: MIT Press.

Moscovitch, M. (1995). Recovered consciousness: A hypothesis concerning modularity and episodic memory. *Journal of Clinical and Experimental Neuropsychology, 17*, 276–290.

Moscovitch, M. (2000). Theories of memory and consciousness. In E. Tulving & F. I. M. Craik (Eds.), *Oxford handbook of memory* (pp. 609–625). London: Oxford University Press.

Moscovitch, M., Kapur, S., Köhler, S., & Houle, S. (1995). Distinct neural correlates of visual long-term memory for spatial location and object identity: A positron emission tomography study in humans. *Proceedings of the National Academy of Sciences USA, 92*, 3721–3725.

Moscovitch, M., & McAndrews, M. P. (2002). Material-specific deficits in "remembering" in patients with unilateral temporal lobe epilepsy and excisions. *Neuropsychologia, 40*, 1335–1342.

Moscovitch, M., Vriezen, E., & Goshen-Gottstein, Y. (1993). Implicit tests of memory in patients with focal lesions or degenerative brain disorders. In F. Boller & J. Grafman (Eds.), *Handbook of neuropsychology* (Vol. 8, pp. 133–173). Amsterdam: Elsevier.

Nadel, L., & Moscovitch, M. (1997). Memory consolidation, retrograde amnesia and the hippocampal complex. *Current Opinion in Neurobiology, 7*, 217–227.

Nolde, S. F., Johnson, M. K., & D'Esposito, M. (1998). Left prefrontal activation during episodic remembering: An event-related fMRI study. *NeuroReport, 9*, 3509–3514.

Norman, K. A., & Schacter, D. L. (1997). False recognition in younger and older adults: Exploring the characteristics of illusory memories. *Memory & Cognition, 25*, 838–848.

Nyberg, L., Habib, R., McIntosh, A. R., & Tulving, E. (2000). Reactivation of encoding-related brain activity during memory retrieval. *Proceedings of the National Academy of Sciences USA, 97*, 11120–11124.

Nyberg, L., McIntosh, A. R., Houle, S., Nilsson, L. G., & Tulving, E. (1996). Activation of medial temporal structures during episodic memory retrieval. *Nature, 380*, 715–717.

Nyberg, L., Petersson, K. M., Nilsson, L., Sandblom, J., Åberg, C., & Ingvar, M. (2001). Reactivation of motor brain areas during explicit memory for actions. *NeuroImage, 14*, 521–528.

Nyberg, L., Tulving, E., Habib, R., Nilsson, L. G., Kapur, S., Houle, S., Cabeza, R., & McIntosh, A. R. (1995). Functional brain maps of retrieval mode and recovery of episodic information. *NeuroReport, 7*, 249–252.

Okado, Y., & Stark, C. (2003). Neural processing associated with true and false memory retrieval. *Cognitive, Affective, & Behavioral Neuroscience, 3*, 323–334.

Roediger, H. L. III, & McDermott, K. B. (1993). Implicit memory in normal human subjects. In H. Spinnler & F. Boller (Eds.), *Handbook of neuropsychology* (Vol. 8, pp. 63–131). Amsterdam: Elsevier.

Roediger, H. L.III, & McDermott, K. B. (1995). Creating false memories: Remembering words not presented in lists. *Journal of Experimental Psychology: Learning, Memory, and Cognition, 21*, 803–814.

Rotello, C. M., Macmillan N. A., & Reeder, J. A. (2004). Sum-difference theory of remembering and knowing: A two-dimensional signal-detection model. *Psychological Review*, 111, 588–616.

Rugg, M. D., Fletcher, P. C., Frith, C. D., Frackowiak, R. S., & Dolan, R. J. (1996). Differential activation of the prefrontal cortex in successful and unsuccessful memory retrieval. *Brain*, 119, 2073–2083.

Rugg, M. D., Fletcher, P. C., Frith, C. D., Frackowiak, R. S., & Dolan, R. J. (1997). Brain regions supporting intentional and incidental memory: A PET study. *NeuroReport*, 24, 1283–1287.

Rugg, M. D., Henson, R. N. A., & Robb, W. G. K. (2003). Neural correlates of retrieval processing in the prefrontal cortex during recognition and exclusion tasks. *Neuropsychologia*, 41, 40–52.

Rugg, M. D., Mark, R. E., Walla, P., Schloerscheidt, A. M., Birch, C. S., & Allan, K. (1998). Dissociation of the neural correlates of implicit and explicit memory. *Nature*, 392, 595–598.

Schacter, D. L. (1987). Implicit memory: History and current status. *Journal of Experimental Psychology: Learning, Memory, and Cognition*, 13, 501–518.

Schacter, D. L., Alpert, N. M., Savage, C. R., Rauch, S. L., & Albert, M. S. (1996a). Conscious recollection and the human hippocampal formation: Evidence from positron emission tomography. *Proceedings of the National Academy of Sciences USA*, 93, 321–325.

Schacter, D. L., & Buckner, R. L. (1998). Priming and the brain. *Neuron*, 20, 185–195.

Schacter, D. L., Buckner, R. L., Koutstaal, W., Dale, A. M., & Rosen, B. R. (1997a). Late onset of anterior prefrontal activity during true and false recognition: An event-related fMRI study. *NeuroImage*, 6, 259–269.

Schacter, D. L., & Curran, T. (2000). Memory without remembering and remembering without memory: Implicit and false memories. In M. S. Gazzaniga (Ed.), *The cognitive neurosciences* (2nd ed., pp. 829–840). Cambridge, MA: MIT Press.

Schacter, D. L., Dobbins, I. G., & Schnyer, D. M. (2004). Specificity of priming: A cognitive neuroscience perspective. *Nature Reviews Neuroscience*, 5, 853–862.

Schacter, D. L., McAndrews, M. P., & Moscovitch, M. (1988). Access to consciousness: Dissociations between implicit and explicit knowledge. In L. Weiskrantz (Ed.), *Thought without language* (pp. 242–278). New York: Oxford University Press.

Schacter, D. L., Norman, K. A., & Koutstaal, W. (1998a). The cognitive neuroscience of constructive memory. *Annual Review of Psychology*, 49, 289–318.

Schacter, D. L., Reiman, E., Curran, T., Yun, L. S., Bandy, D., McDermott, K. B., & Roediger, H. L. III. (1996b). Neuroanatomical correlates of veridical and illusory recognition memory: Evidence from positron emission tomography. *Neuron*, 17, 267–274.

Schacter, D. L., Reiman, E., Uecker, A., Polster, M. R., Yun, L. S., & Cooper, L. A. (1995). Brain regions associated with retrieval of structurally coherent visual information. *Nature*, 376, 587–590.

Schacter, D. L., & Slotnick, S. D. (2004). The cognitive neuroscience of memory distortion. *Neuron*, 44, 149–160.

Schacter, D. L., Verfaellie, M., & Anes, M. D. (1997b). Illusory memories in amnesic patients: Conceptual and perceptual false recognition. *Neuropsychology*, 11, 331–342.

Schacter, D. L., Verfaellie, M., Anes, M. D., & Racine, C. (1998b). When true recognition suppresses false recognition: Evidence from amnesic patients. *Journal of Cognitive Neuroscience*, 10, 668–679.

Schacter, D. L., Verfaellie, M., & Pradere, D. (1996c). The neuropsychology of memory illusions: False recall and recognition in amnesic patients. *Journal of Memory and Language*, 35, 319–334.

Schooler, J. W., Gerhard, D., & Loftus, E. F. (1986). Qualities of the unreal. *Journal of Experimental Psychology: Learning, Memory, and Cognition*, 12, 171–181.

Slotnick, S. D., & Dodson, C. S. (2005). Support for a continuous (single-process) model of recognition memory and source memory. *Memory & Cognition*, 33, 151–170.

Slotnick, S. D., Moo, L. R., Segal, J. B., & Hart, J. Jr. (2003). Distinct prefrontal cortex activity associated with item memory and source memory for visual shapes. *Cognitive Brain Research*, 17, 75–82.

Slotnick, S. D., & Schacter, D. L. (2004). A sensory signature that distinguishes true from false memories. *Nature Neuroscience*, 7, 664–672.

Smith, M. E. (1993). Neurophysiological manifestations of recollective experience during recognition memory judgments. *Journal of Cognitive Neuroscience, 5*, 1–13.

Squire, L. R. (1992). Memory and the hippocampus: A synthesis from findings with rats, monkeys, and humans. *Psychological Review, 99*, 195–231.

Squire, L. R., Ojemann, J. G., Miezin, F. M., Petersen, S. E., Videen, T. O., & Raichle, M. E. (1992). Activation of the hippocampus in normal humans: A functional anatomical study of memory. *Proceedings of the National Academy of Sciences USA, 89*, 1837–1841.

Squire, L. R., Stark, C. E. L., & Clark, R. E. (2004). The medial temporal lobe. *Annual Review of Neuroscience, 27*, 279–306.

Trott, C. T., Friedman, D., Ritter, W., Fabiani, M., & Snodgrass, J. G. (1999). Episodic priming and memory for temporal source: Event-related potentials reveal age-related differences in prefrontal functioning. *Psychology and Aging, 14*, 390–413.

Tulving, E. (1985a). How many memory systems are there? *American Psychologist, 40*, 385–398.

Tulving, E. (1985b). Memory and consciousness. *Canadian Psychology, 26*, 1–12.

Tulving, E., Kapur, S., Craik, F. I. M., Moscovitch, M., & Houle, S. (1994). Hemispheric encoding/retrieval asymmetry in episodic memory: Positron emission tomography findings. *Proceedings of the National Academy of Sciences USA, 91*, 2016–2020.

Uecker, A., Reiman, E. M., Schacter, D. L., Polster, M. R., Cooper, L. A., Yun, L. S., & Chen, K. (1997). Neuroanatomical correlates of implicit and explicit memory for structurally possible and impossible visual objects. *Learning & Memory, 4*, 337–355.

Vaidya, C. J., Zhao, M., Desmond, J. E., & Gabrieli, J. D. E. (2002). Evidence for cortical encoding specificity in episodic memory: Memory-induced re-activation of picture processing areas. *Neuropsychologia, 40*, 2136–2143.

Velanova, K., Jacoby, L. L., Wheeler, M. E., McAvoy, M. P., Petersen, S. E., & Buckner, R. L. (2003). Functional-anatomic correlates of sustained and transient processing components engaged during controlled retrieval. *Journal of Neuroscience, 23*, 8460–8470.

Wagner, A. D., Desmond, J. E., Glover, G. H., & Gabrieli, J. D. E. (1998). Prefrontal cortex and recognition memory: Functional-MRI evidence for context-dependent retrieval processes. *Brain, 121*, 1985–2002.

Warrington, E. K., & Weiskrantz, L. (1974). The effect of prior learning on subsequent retention in amnesic patients. *Neuropsychologia, 12*, 419–428.

Wheeler, M. E., & Buckner, R. L. (2003). Functional dissociation among components of remembering: Control, perceived oldness, and content. *Journal of Neuroscience, 23*, 3869–3880.

Wheeler, M. E., & Buckner, R. L. (2004). Functional-anatomic correlates of remembering and knowing. *NeuroImage, 21*, 1337–1349.

Wheeler, M. E., Petersen, S. E., & Buckner, R. L. (2000). Memory's echo: Vivid remembering reactivates sensory-specific cortex. *Proceedings of the National Academy of Sciences USA, 97*, 11125–11129.

Wiggs, C. L., & Martin, A. (1998). Properties and mechanisms of perceptual priming. *Current Opinion in Neurobiology, 8*, 227–233.

Wilding, E. L., & Rugg, M. D. (1996). An event-related potential study of recognition memory with and without retrieval of source. *Brain, 119*, 889–905.

Wixted, J. T., & Stretch, V. (2004). In defense of the signal detection interpretation of remember/know judgments. *Psychonomic Bulletin & Review, 11*, 616–641.

Yonelinas, A. P., Kroll, N. E. A., Dobbins, I., Lazzara, M., & Knight, R. T. (1998). Recollection and familiarity deficits in amnesia: Convergence of remember-know, process dissociation, and receiver operating characteristic data. *Neuropsychology 12*, 323–339.

Yonelinas, A. P., Kroll, N. E., Quamme, J. R., Lazzara, M. M., Sauve, M. J., Widarman, K. F., & Knight, R. T. (2002). Effects of extensive temporal lobe damage or mild hypoxia on recollection and familiarity. *Nature Neuroscience, 5*, 1236–1241.

Young, A. W. (1994). Conscious and nonconsious recognition of familiar faces. In C. Umiltà & M. Moscovitch (Eds.), *Attention and performance 15: Conscious and nonconscious information processing* (pp. 153–178). Cambridge, MA: MIT Press.

C. Affective Neuroscience of Consciousness

CHAPTER 29

The Affective Neuroscience of Consciousness: Higher-Order Syntactic Thoughts, Dual Routes to Emotion and Action, and Consciousness

Edmund T. Rolls

Abstract

In this chapter, a theory of the nature of emotion and the functions of emotions are described. A Higher-Order Syntactic Thought theory of consciousness is then developed. It is argued that the adaptive value of higher-order thoughts is to solve the credit assignment problem that arises if a multistep syntactic plan needs to be corrected. It is then suggested that it feels like something to be an organism that can think about its own linguistic and semantically based thoughts. It is suggested that qualia and raw sensory and emotional feels arise secondary to having evolved such a higher-order thought system and that sensory and emotional processing feels like something because it would be unparsimonious for it to enter the planning, higher-order thought system and *not* feel like something.

Emotions as States

Emotions can usefully be defined as states elicited by rewards and punishers that have particular functions (Rolls, 1999a, 2005a). A reward is anything for which an animal (which includes humans) will work. A punisher is anything that an animal will escape from or avoid. An example of an emotion might thus be happiness produced by being given a reward, such as a pleasant touch, praise, or winning a large sum of money. Another example of an emotion might be fear produced by the sound of a rapidly approaching bus or the sight of an angry expression on someone's face. We will work to avoid such stimuli, which are punishing. Another example would be frustration, anger, or sadness produced by the omission of an expected reward. such as a prize, or the termination of a reward, such as the death of a loved one. Another example would be relief, produced by the omission or termination of a punishing stimulus, such as the removal of a painful stimulus, or sailing out of danger. These examples indicate how emotions can be produced by the delivery, omission, or termination of rewarding or punishing stimuli and go some way to indicate how different emotions could be produced and classified in terms of the rewards and punishments received, omitted, or terminated. A diagram summarizing some of the emotions associated with the delivery of reward or punishment or a stimulus associated with them, or with the omission of a reward or punishment, is shown in Figure 29.1.

Before accepting this approach, we should consider whether there are any exceptions to the proposed rule. Are any emotions caused by stimuli, events, or remembered events that are not rewarding or punishing? Do any rewarding or punishing stimuli not cause emotions? We consider these questions in more detail below. The point is that if there are no major exceptions, or if any exceptions can be clearly encapsulated, then we may have a good working definition at least of what causes emotions. Moreover, it is worth pointing out that many approaches to or theories of emotion (see Strongman, 1996) have in common that part of the process involves "appraisal" (e.g., Frijda, 1986; Lazarus, 1991; Oatley & Jenkins, 1996). In all these theories the concept of appraisal presumably involves assessing whether something is rewarding or punishing. The description in terms of reward or punishment adopted here seems more tightly and operationally specified. I next consider a slightly more formal definition than rewards or punishments, in which the concept of reinforcers is introduced, and show how there has been a considerable history in the development of ideas along this line.

The proposal that emotions can be usefully seen as states produced by instrumental reinforcing stimuli (Rolls, 2005a) follows earlier work by Millenson (1967), Weiskrantz (1968), Gray (1975, 1987), and Rolls (1986a, b, 1990, 1999a, 2000a). (Instrumental reinforcers are stimuli that, if their occurrence, termination, or omission is made contingent upon the making of a response, alter the probability of the future emission of that response.) Some stimuli are unlearned reinforcers (e.g., the taste of food if the animal is hungry, or pain), whereas others may become reinforcing by learning, because of their association with such primary reinforcers, thereby becom-ing "secondary reinforcers". This type of learning may thus be called "stimulus-reinforcement association" and occurs via a process like classical conditioning. If a reinforcer increases the probability of emission of a response on which it is contingent, it is said to be a "positive reinforcer" or "reward"; if it decreases the probability of such a response it is a "negative reinforcer" or "punisher". For example, fear is an emotional state that might be produced by a sound (the conditioned stimulus) that has previously been associated with an electrical shock (the primary reinforcer).

The converse reinforcement contingencies produce the opposite effects on behavior. The omission or termination of a positive reinforcer ("extinction" and "time out", respectively, sometimes described as "punishing") decreases the probability of responses. Responses followed by the omission or termination of a negative reinforcer increase in probability, this pair of negative reinforcement operations being termed "active avoidance" and "escape" respectively (see further Gray, 1975; Mackintosh, 1983).

This foundation has been developed (see Rolls, 1986a, b, 1990, 1999a, 2000a, 2005a,) to show how a very wide range of emotions can be accounted for by the operation of six factors:

1. The *reinforcement contingency* (e.g., whether reward or punishment is given or withheld; see Fig. 29.1).
2. The *intensity* of the reinforcer (see Fig. 29.1).
3. Any environmental stimulus might have a *number of different reinforcement associations*. (For example, a stimulus might be associated both with the presentation of a reward and of a punisher, allowing such states as conflict and guilt to arise.)
4. Emotions elicited by stimuli associated with *different primary reinforcers* will be different.
5. Emotions elicited by *different secondary reinforcing stimuli* will be different from each other (even if the primary reinforcer is similar).

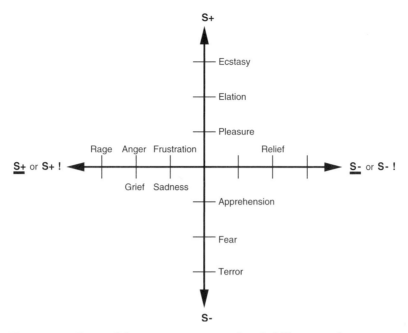

Figure 29.1. Some of the emotions associated with different reinforcement contingencies are indicated. Intensity increases away from the centre of the diagram, on a continuous scale. The classification scheme created by the different reinforcement contingencies consists of (1) the presentation of a positive reinforcer (S+), (2) the presentation of a negative reinforcer (S –), (3) the omission of a positive reinforcer (S̲+̲) or the termination of a positive reinforcer (S+!), and (4) the omission of a negative reinforcer (S̲ –̲) or the termination of a negative reinforcer (S–!).

6. The emotion elicited can depend on whether an *active or passive behavioral response* is possible. (For example, if an active behavioral response can occur to the omission of a positive reinforcer, then anger might be produced, but if only passive behavior is possible, then sadness, depression, or grief might occur.)

It is also worth noting that emotions can be produced just as much by the recall of reinforcing events as by external reinforcing stimuli and that cognitive processing (whether conscious or not) is important in many emotions, for very complex cognitive processing may be required to determine whether or not environmental events are reinforcing. Indeed, emotions normally consist of (1) cognitive processing that analyses the stimulus and then determines its reinforcing valence and then (2) an elicited mood change if the valence is positive or

negative. In that an emotion is produced by a stimulus, philosophers say that emotions have an object in the world and that emotional states are intentional, in that they are about something. We note that a mood or affective state may occur in the absence of an external stimulus, as in some types of depression, but that normally the mood or affective state is produced by an external stimulus, with the whole process of stimulus representation, evaluation in terms of reward or punishment, and the resulting mood or affect being referred to as emotion.

It is worth raising the issue that philosophers usually categorize fear as an emotion, but not pain. The distinction they make may be that primary (unlearned) reinforcers do not produce emotions, whereas secondary reinforcers (stimuli associated by stimulus-reinforcement learning with primary reinforcers) do. They describe the pain as a sensation. But neutral stimuli (such as a table) can produce sensations when touched. It accordingly seems to be much more useful to categorise stimuli according to whether they are reinforcing (in which case they produce emotions) or are not reinforcing (in which case they do not produce emotions). Clearly there is a difference between primary reinforcers and learned reinforcers; but this is most precisely caught by noting that this is the difference, and that it is whether a stimulus is reinforcing that determines whether it is related to emotion.

The Functions of Emotion

The functions of emotion also provide insight into the nature of emotion. These functions, described more fully elsewhere (Rolls 1990, 1999a, 2000a, 2005a), can be summarized as follows:

1. The *elicitation of autonomic responses* (e.g., a change in heart rate) and *endocrine responses* (e.g., the release of adrenaline). These prepare the body for action.
2. *Flexibility of behavioral responses to reinforcing stimuli*. Emotional (and motivational) states allow a simple interface between sensory inputs and action systems. The essence of this idea is that goals for behavior are specified by reward and punishment evaluation. When an environmental stimulus has been decoded as a primary reward or punishment or (after previous stimulus-reinforcer association learning) as a secondary rewarding or punishing stimulus, then it becomes a goal for action. The animal can then perform any action (instrumental response) to obtain the reward or to avoid the punisher. Thus there is flexibility of action, and this is in contrast with stimulus-response, or habit, learning in which a particular response to a particular stimulus is learned. It also contrasts with the elicitation of species-typical behavioral responses by sign-releasing stimuli (such as pecking at a spot on the beak of the parent herring gull in order to be fed; see Tinbergen, 1951), where there is inflexi-

bility of the stimulus and the response, and which can be seen as a very limited type of brain solution to the elicitation of behavior. The emotional route to action is flexible not only because any action can be performed to obtain the reward or avoid the punishment but also because the animal can learn in as little as one trial that a reward or punishment is associated with a particular stimulus, in what is termed "stimulus-reinforcer association learning".

To summarize and formalize, two processes are involved in the actions being described. The first is stimulus-reinforcer association learning, and the second is instrumental learning of an operant response made to approach and obtain the reward or to avoid or escape from the punisher. Emotion is an integral part of this, for it is the state elicited in the first stage by stimuli that are decoded as rewards or punishers, and this state has the property that it is motivating. The motivation is to obtain the reward or avoid the punisher, and animals must be built to obtain certain rewards and avoid certain punishers. Indeed, primary or unlearned rewards and punishers are specified by genes that effectively specify the goals for action. This is the solution that natural selection has found for how genes can influence behavior to promote their fitness (as measured by reproductive success) and for how the brain could interface sensory systems to action systems.

Selecting among available rewards with their associated costs, and avoiding punishers with their associated costs, is a process that can take place both implicitly (unconsciously) and explicitly using a language system to enable long-term plans to be made (Rolls, 1999a, 2005a). These many different brain systems, some involving implicit evaluation of rewards, and others explicit, verbal, conscious, evaluation of rewards and planned long-term goals, must all enter into the selector of behavior (see Fig. 29.2). This selector is poorly understood, but it might include a process of competition between

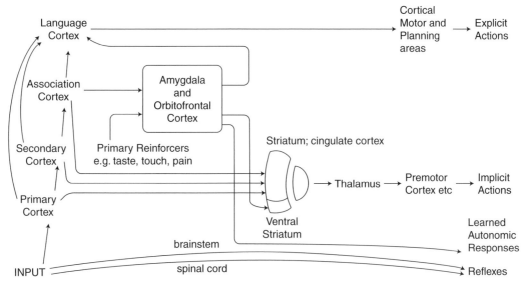

Figure 29.2. Dual routes to the initiation of action in response to rewarding and punishing stimuli. The inputs from different sensory systems to brain structures, such as the orbitofrontal cortex and amygdala, allow these brain structures to evaluate the reward- or punishment-related value of incoming stimuli or of remembered stimuli. The different sensory inputs enable evaluations within the orbitofrontal cortex and amygdala based mainly on the primary (unlearned) reinforcement value for taste, touch, and olfactory stimuli and on the secondary (learned) reinforcement value for visual and auditory stimuli. In the case of vision, the 'association cortex' that outputs representations of objects to the amygdala and orbitofrontal cortex is the inferior temporal visual cortex. One route for the outputs from these evaluative brain structures is via projections directly to such structures as the basal ganglia (including the striatum and ventral striatum) to enable implicit, direct behavioural responses based on the reward- or punishment-related evaluation of the stimuli to be made. The second route is via the language systems of the brain, which allow explicit (verbalizable) decisions involving multistep syntactic planning to be implemented.

all the competing calls on output and might involve the basal ganglia in the brain (see Fig. 29.2 and Rolls, 2005a).

3. Emotion is *motivating*, as just described. For example, fear learned by stimulus-reinforcement association provides the motivation for actions performed to avoid noxious stimuli.

4. *Communication*. Monkeys, for example, may communicate their emotional state to others by making an open-mouth threat to indicate the extent to which they are willing to compete for resources, and this may influence the behavior of other animals. This aspect of emotion was emphasized by Darwin and has been studied more recently by Ekman (1982, 1993). He reviews evidence that humans can categorize facial expressions into the categories happy, sad, fearful, angry, surprised, and disgusted and that this categorization may operate similarly in different cultures. He also describes how the facial muscles produce different expressions. Further investigations of the degree of cross-cultural universality of facial expression, its development in infancy, and its role in social behavior are described by Izard (1991) and Fridlund (1994). As shown elsewhere (Rolls, 2000c, d, 2005a, Rolls and Deco, 2002), there are neural systems in the amygdala and overlying temporal cortical visual areas that are specialized for the face-related aspects of this processing.

5. *Social bonding*. Examples of this function are the emotions associated with the attachment of the parents to their young

and the attachment of the young to their parents.

6. The current mood state can affect the *cognitive evaluation of events or memories* (see Oatley & Jenkins, 1996). This may facilitate continuity in the interpretation of the reinforcing value of events in the environment. A hypothesis that backprojections from parts of the brain involved in emotion such as the orbitofrontal cortex and amygdala implement this evaluation of events or memories is described in *Emotion Explained* (Rolls, 2005a).

7. Emotion may facilitate the *storage of memories*. One way this occurs is that episodic memory (i.e., one's memory of particular episodes) is facilitated by emotional states. This may be advantageous in that storing many details of the prevailing situation when a strong reinforcer is delivered may be useful in generating appropriate behavior in situations with some similarities in the future. This function may be implemented by the relatively nonspecific projecting systems to the cerebral cortex and hippocampus, including the cholinergic pathways in the basal forebrain and medial septum and the ascending noradrenergic pathways (see Rolls, 2005a; Rolls & Treves, 1998). A second way in which emotion may affect the storage of memories is that the current emotional state may be stored with episodic memories, providing a mechanism for the current emotional state to affect which memories are recalled. A third way that emotion may affect the storage of memories is by guiding the cerebral cortex in the representations of the world that are set up. For example, in the visual system it may be useful for perceptual representations or analyzers to be built that are different from each other if they are associated with different reinforcers, and for these to be less likely to be built if they have no association with reinforcement. Ways in which backprojections from parts of the brain important in emotion (such as the amygdala) to parts of the cerebral cor-

tex could perform this function are discussed by Rolls and Treves (1998).

8. Another function of emotion is that, by enduring for minutes or longer after a reinforcing stimulus has occurred, it may help produce *persistent and continuing motivation and direction of behavior* to help achieve a goal or goals.

9. Emotion may trigger the *recall of memories* stored in neocortical representations. Amygdala backprojections to the cortex could perform this function for emotion in a way analogous to how the hippocampus implements the retrieval in the neocortex of recent (episodic) memories (Rolls & Treves 1998; Rolls & Stringer, 2001).

Reward, Punishment, and Emotion in Brain Design: An Evolutionary Approach

The theory of the functions of emotion is further developed in Chapter 3 of *Emotion Explained* (Rolls, 2005a), and some of the points made there help elaborate greatly on the above section. Rolls (1999a) and (2005a) considers the fundamental question of why we and other animals are built to use rewards and punishments to guide or determine our behavior. Why are we built to have emotions, as well as motivational states? Is there any reasonable alternative around which evolution could have built complex animals? In this section I outline several types of brain design, with differing degrees of complexity, and suggest that evolution can operate to influence action with only some of these types of design.

Taxes

A simple design principle is to incorporate mechanisms for *taxes* into the design of organisms. At their simplest, taxes consist of orientation toward stimuli in the environment; for example, the bending of a plant toward light, which results in maximum light collection by its photosynthetic surfaces. When just turning rather than locomotion is possible, such responses are called tropisms. When locomotion is possible, as in animals, taxes include movements toward sources of nutrient and movements away from hazards, such as very high temperatures. The design principle here is that animals have through a process of natural selection built receptors for certain dimensions of the wide range of stimuli in the environment and have linked these receptors to mechanisms for particular responses in such a way that the stimuli are approached or avoided.

Reward and Punishment

As soon as we have an approach toward stimuli at one end of a dimension (e.g., a source of nutrient) and away from stimuli at the other end of the dimension (in this case lack of nutrient), we can start to wonder when it is appropriate to introduce the terms "rewards" and "punishers" for the stimuli at the different ends of the dimension. By convention, if the response consists of a fixed reaction to obtain the stimulus (e.g., locomotion up a chemical gradient), we shall call this a taxis, not a reward. On the other hand, if an arbitrary operant response can be performed by the animal in order to approach the stimulus, then we call this rewarded behavior, and the stimulus the animal works to obtain is a reward. (The operant response can be thought of as any arbitrary action the animal will perform to obtain the stimulus.) This criterion of an arbitrary operant response is often tested by bidirectionality. For example, if a rat can be trained either to raise or lower its tail to obtain a piece of food, then we can be sure that there is no fixed relation between the stimulus (e.g., the sight of food) and the response, as there is in a taxis.

The role of natural selection in this process is to guide animals to build sensory systems that will respond to dimensions of stimuli in the natural environment along which actions can lead to a better ability to pass genes on to the next generation; that is, to increased fitness. The animals must

be built by such natural selection to make responses that will enable them to obtain more rewards; that is, to work to obtain stimuli that will increase their fitness. Correspondingly, animals must be built to make responses that will enable them to escape from, or learn to avoid, stimuli that will reduce their fitness. There are likely to be many dimensions of environmental stimuli along which actions can alter fitness. Each of these dimensions may be a separate reward-punishment dimension. An example of one of these dimensions might be food reward. It increases fitness to be able to sense nutrient need, to have sensors that respond to the taste of food, and to perform behavioral responses to obtain such reward stimuli when in that need or motivational state. Similarly, another dimension is water reward, in which the taste of water becomes rewarding when there is body fluid depletion (see Chapter 6 of *Emotion Explained*).

With many reward/punishment dimensions for which actions may be performed (see Table 2.1 of *Emotion Explained* for a non-exhaustive list!), a selection mechanism for actions performed is needed. In this sense, rewards and punishers provide a *common currency* for inputs to response selection mechanisms. Evolution must set the magnitudes of each of the different reward systems so that each will be chosen for action in such a way as to maximize overall fitness. Food reward must be chosen as the aim for action if a nutrient is depleted, but water reward as a target for action must be selected if current water depletion poses a greater threat to fitness than the current food depletion. This indicates that each reward must be carefully calibrated by evolution to have the right value in the common currency for the competitive selection process. Other types of behavior, such as sexual behavior, must be selected sometimes, but probably less frequently, to maximise fitness (as measured by gene transmission into the next generation). Many processes contribute to increasing the chances that a wide set of different environmental rewards will be chosen over a period of time, including not only need-related satiety mechanisms that decrease the rewards within a dimension but also sensory-specific satiety mechanisms, which facilitate switching to another reward stimulus (sometimes within and sometimes outside the same main dimension) and attraction to novel stimuli. Finding novel stimuli rewarding is one way that organisms are encouraged to explore the multidimensional space in which their genes are operating.

The above mechanisms can be contrasted with typical engineering design. In the latter, the engineer defines the requisite function and then produces special-purpose design features that enable the task to be performed. In the case of the animal, there is a multidimensional space within which many optimisations to increase fitness must be performed. The solution is to evolve reward/punishment systems tuned to each dimension in the environment that can increase fitness if the animal performs the appropriate actions. Natural selection guides evolution to find these dimensions. In contrast, in the engineering design of a robot arm, the robot does not need to tune itself to find the goal to be performed. The contrast is between design by evolution, which is 'blind' to the purpose of the animal, and design by a designer who specifies the job to be performed (cf. Dawkins, 1986). Another contrast is that for the animal the space will be high-dimensional, so that the most appropriate reward for current behavior (taking into account the costs of obtaining each reward) needs to be selected, whereas for the robot arm, the function to perform at any one time is specified by the designer. Another contrast is that the behavior (the operant response) most appropriate to obtain the reward must be selected by the animal, whereas the movement to be made by the robot arm is specified by the design engineer.

The implication of this comparison is that operation by animals of reward and punishment systems tuned to dimensions of the environment that increase fitness provides a mode of operation that can work in organisms that evolve by natural selection. It is clearly a natural outcome of Darwinian evolution to operate using reward and punishment systems tuned to fitness-related dimensions of the environment, if arbitrary responses are to be made by the animals, rather than just preprogrammed movements such as tropisms and taxes. Is there any alternative to such a reward/punishment-based system in this evolution by natural selection situation? It is not clear that there is, if the genes are to control behavior. The argument is that genes can specify actions that will increase their fitness if they specify the goals for action. It would be very difficult for them in general to specify in advance the particular responses to be made to each of a myriad of different stimuli. This may be why we are built to work for rewards, avoid punishers, and to have emotions and needs (motivational states). This view of brain design in terms of reward and punishment systems built by genes that gain their adaptive value by being tuned to a goal for action offers, I believe, a deep insight into how natural selection has shaped many brain systems, and is a fascinating outcome of Darwinian thought.

To What Extent Is Consciousness Involved in the Different Types of Processing Initiated by Emotional States?

It might be possible to build a computer that would perform the functions of emotions described above and in more detail by Rolls (1999a, 2000a, 2005a), and yet we might not want to ascribe emotional *feelings* to the computer. We might even build the computer with some of the main processing stages present in the brain and implemented using neural networks that simulate the operation of the real neural networks in the brain (see Rolls & Deco, 2002; Rolls & Treves, 1998), yet we might not still wish to ascribe emotional feelings to this computer. This point often arises in discussions with undergraduates, who may say that they follow the types of point made above about emotion, yet believe that almost the most important aspect of emotions, the feelings, have not been accounted for nor their neural basis described. In a sense, the functions of reward and punishment in emotional behaviour are described by the above types of process and their underlying brain mechanisms in such structures as the amygdala and orbitofrontal cortex as described by Rolls (1999a, 2000b, c, 2002), but what about the subjective aspects of emotion, what about the pleasure? A similar point arises when we consider the parts of the taste, olfactory, and visual systems in which the reward value of the taste, smell, and sight of food is represented. One such brain region is the orbitofrontal cortex (Rolls, 1997, 1999a, 2000b, 2002, 2005a). Although the neuronal representation in the orbitofrontal cortex is clearly related to the reward value of food, is this where the pleasantness (the subjective hedonic aspect) of the taste, smell, and sight of food is represented? Again, we could (in principle at least) build a computer with neural networks to simulate each of the processing stages for the taste, smell, and sight of food that are described by Rolls (2005a, and more formally in terms of neural networks by Rolls & Deco, 2002; Rolls & Treves, 1998), and yet would probably not wish to ascribe feelings of pleasantness to the system we have simulated on the computer.

What is it about neural processing that makes it feel like something when some types of information processing are taking place? It is clearly not a general property of processing in neural networks, for there is much processing – for example that concerned with the control of our blood pressure and heart rate – of which we are not aware. Is it then that awareness arises when a certain type of information processing is being performed? If so, what type of information processing? And how do emotional feelings and sensory events come to feel like anything? These feels are called qualia. These are great mysteries that have puzzled philosophers for centuries. They are at the heart of the problem of consciousness, for why it should feel like something at all is the great mystery. Other aspects of consciousness, such as the fact that often when

we "pay attention" to events in the world, we can process those events in some better way – that is process or access as opposed to phenomenal aspects of consciousness – may be easier to analyse (Allport, 1988; Block, 1995; Chalmers, 1996). The puzzle of qualia – that is of the phenomenal aspect of consciousness – seems to be rather different from normal investigations in science, in that there is no agreement on criteria by which to assess whether we have made progress. So, although the aim of this chapter is to address the issue of consciousness, especially of qualia, in relation to emotional feelings and actions, what is written cannot be regarded as being establishable by the normal methods of scientific enquiry. Accordingly, I emphasize that the view on consciousness that I describe is only preliminary, and theories of consciousness are likely to develop considerably. Partly for these reasons, this theory of consciousness, at least, should not be taken to have practical implications.

A Theory of Consciousness

A starting point is that many actions can be performed relatively automatically, without apparent conscious intervention. An example sometimes given is driving a car. Such actions could involve control of behaviour by brain systems that are old in evolutionary terms, such as the basal ganglia. It is of interest that the basal ganglia (and cerebellum) do not have backprojection systems to most of the parts of the cerebral cortex from which they receive inputs (see e.g., Rolls, 1994; Rolls & Johnstone, 1992; Rolls & Treves, 1998). In contrast, parts of the brain, such as the hippocampus and amygdala, which are involved in such functions as episodic memory and emotion, respectively, about which we can make (verbal) declarations (hence declarative memory, Squire, 1992) do have major backprojection systems to the high parts of the cerebral cortex from which they receive forward projections (Rolls, 1996a, 2000e; Rolls & Deco, 2002; Rolls & Treves, 1998; Treves & Rolls, 1994). It may be that evolutionarily newer parts of the brain, such as the language areas and parts of the prefrontal cortex, are involved in an alternative type of control of behaviour, in which actions can be planned with the use of a (language) system that allows relatively arbitrary (syntactic) manipulation of semantic entities (symbols).

The general view that there are many routes to behavioural output is supported by the evidence that there are many input systems to the basal ganglia (from almost all areas of the cerebral cortex) and that neuronal activity in each part of the striatum reflects the activity in the overlying cortical area (Rolls, 1994, 2005a; Rolls & Johnstone, 1992; Rolls & Treves, 1998). The evidence is consistent with the possibility that different cortical areas, each specialised for a different type of computation, have their outputs directed to the basal ganglia, which then select the strongest input and map it into action (via outputs directed for example to the premotor cortex; Rolls & Johnstone, 1992; Rolls & Treves, 1998). Within this scheme, the language areas would offer one of many routes to action, but one that is particularly suited to planning actions because of the syntactic manipulation of semantic entities that may make long-term planning possible. A schematic diagram of this suggestion is provided in Fig. 29.2. Consistent with the hypothesis of multiple routes to action, only some of which utilise language, is the evidence that split-brain patients may not be aware of actions being performed by the "non-dominant" hemisphere (Gazzaniga, 1988, 1995; Gazzaniga & LeDoux, 1978). Also consistent with multiple routes to action, including non-verbal routes, is the finding that patients with focal brain damage – for example to the prefrontal cortex – may perform actions, yet comment verbally that they should not be performing those actions (e.g., Hornak et al., 2003, 2004; Rolls, 1999b; Rolls, Hornak, Wade, & McGrath, 1994). The actions that appear to be performed implicitly, with surprise expressed later by the explicit system, include making behavioral responses to a no-longer rewarded visual stimulus in a visual

discrimination reversal (Hornak et al., 2004; Rolls et al., 1994). In these types of patients, confabulation may occur, in that a verbal account of why the action was performed may be given, which may not be related at all to the environmental event that actually triggered the action (Gazzaniga, 1988, 1995; Gazzaniga & LeDoux, 1978; Rolls et al., 1994).

It is possible that sometimes in normal humans when actions are initiated as a result of processing in a specialized brain region, such as those involved in some types of rewarded behaviour, the language system may subsequently elaborate a coherent account of why that action was performed (i.e., confabulate). This would be consistent with a general view of brain evolution in which, as areas of the cortex evolve, they are laid on top of existing circuitry connecting inputs to outputs, and in which each level in this hierarchy of separate input-output pathways may control behaviour according to the specialised function it can perform (see schematic in Fig. 29.2). (It is of interest that mathematicians may get a hunch that something is correct, yet not be able to verbalise why. They may then resort to formal, more serial, and language-like theorems to prove the case, and these seem to require conscious processing. This is a further indication of a close association between linguistic processing and consciousness. The linguistic processing need not, as in reading, involve an inner articulatory loop.)

We may next examine some of the advantages and behavioural functions that language, present as the most recently added layer to the above system, would confer. One major advantage would be the ability to plan actions through many potential stages and to evaluate the consequences of those actions without having to perform the actions. For these functions, the ability to form propositional statements and to perform syntactic operations on the semantic representations of states in the world would be important. Also important in this system would be the ability to have second-order thoughts about the type of thought that I have just described (e.g., I think that he thinks that . . .), as this would allow much better modelling and prediction of others' behaviour, and therefore of planning, particularly planning when it involves others[1]. This capability for higher-order thoughts would also enable reflection on past events, which would also be useful in planning. In contrast, non-linguistic behaviour would be driven by learned reinforcement associations, learned rules, etc., but not by flexible planning for many steps ahead that involves a model of the world including others' behaviour. (For an earlier view that is close to this part of the argument see Humphrey, 1980.) (The examples of behaviour from non-humans that may reflect planning may reflect much more limited and inflexible planning. For example, the dance of the honeybee to signal to other bees the location of food may be said to reflect planning, but the symbol manipulation is not arbitrary. There are likely to be interesting examples of non-human primate behaviour, perhaps in the great apes, that reflect the evolution of an arbitrary symbol-manipulation system that could be useful for flexible planning (cf. Cheney & Seyfarth, 1990.) It is important to state that the language ability referred to here is not necessarily human verbal language (though this would be an example). What it is suggested is important to planning is the syntactic manipulation of symbols, and it is this syntactic manipulation of symbols that is the sense in which language is defined and used here.

It is next suggested that this arbitrary symbol manipulation using important aspects of language processing and used for planning but not in initiating all types of behaviour is close to what consciousness is about. In particular, consciousness may *be* the state that arises in a system that can think about (or reflect on) its own (or other peoples') thoughts; that is, in a system capable of second- or higher-order thoughts (Carruthers, 2000; Dennett, 1991; Gennaro, 2004; Rolls, 2004b, 2005a; Rosenthal, 1986, 1990, 1993, 2004, 2005). On this account, a mental state is non-introspectively (i.e., non-reflectively) conscious if one has a roughly simultaneous thought that one is in that mental state. Following from this, introspec-

tive consciousness (or reflexive consciousness or self-consciousness) is the attentive, deliberately focused consciousness of one's mental states. It is noted that not all of the higher-order thoughts need themselves be conscious (many mental states are not). However, according to the analysis, having a higher-order thought about a lower-order thought is necessary for the lower-order thought to be conscious. A slightly weaker position than Rosenthal's (and mine) on this is that a conscious state corresponds to a first-order thought that has the *capacity* to cause a second-order thought or judgement about it (Carruthers, 1996). Another position that is close in some respects to that of Carruthers and the present position is that of Chalmers (1996) that awareness is something that has *direct availability for behavioral control*, which amounts effectively for him in humans to saying that consciousness is what we can report (verbally) about. This analysis is consistent with the points made above that the brain systems that are required for consciousness and language are similar. In particular, a system that can have second- or higher-order thoughts about its own operation, including its planning and linguistic operation, must itself be a language processor in that it must be able to bind correctly to the symbols and syntax in the first-order system. According to this explanation, the feeling of anything is the state that is present when linguistic processing that involves second- or higher-order thoughts is being performed.

It might be objected that this captures some of the process aspects of consciousness, what it is good for in an information-processing system, but does not capture the phenomenal aspect of consciousness. (Chalmers, following points made in his 1996 book, might make this point.) I agree that there is an element of "mystery" that is invoked at this step of the argument, when I say that it feels like something for a machine with higher-order thoughts to be thinking about its own first- or lower-order thoughts. But the return point (discussed further below) is the following: *If a human with second-order thoughts is thinking about its own first-order thoughts, surely it is very difficult for us to conceive that this would NOT feel like something?* (Perhaps the higher-order thoughts in thinking about the first-order thoughts would need to have some sense of continuity or self, so that the first-order thoughts would be related to the same system that had thought of something else a few minutes ago. But even this continuity aspect may not be a requirement for consciousness. Humans with anterograde amnesia cannot remember what they felt a few minutes ago, yet their current state does feel like something.)

It is suggested that part of the evolutionary adaptive significance of this type of higher-order thought is that it enables correction of errors made in first-order linguistic or in non-linguistic processing. Indeed, the ability to reflect on previous events is extremely important for learning from them, including setting up new long-term semantic structures. It was shown above that the hippocampus may be a system for such "declarative" recall of recent memories. Its close relation to "conscious" processing in humans (Squire, 1992, has classified it as a declarative memory system) may be simply that it enables the recall of recent memories, which can then be reflected upon in conscious, higher-order processing (Rolls, 1996a). Another part of the adaptive value of a higher-order thought system may be that, by thinking about its own thoughts in a given situation, it may be able to better understand the thoughts of another individual in a similar situation and therefore predict that individual's behaviour better (cf. Barlow, 1997; Humphrey, 1980, 1986).

As a point of clarification, I note that according to this theory, a language-processing system is not *sufficient* for consciousness. What defines a conscious system according to this analysis is the ability to have higher-order thoughts, and a first-order language processor (that might be perfectly competent at language) would not be conscious in that it could not think about its own or others' thoughts. One can perfectly well conceive of a system that obeyed the rules of language (which is the aim of much connectionist modelling) and implemented a first-order linguistic system that would not be conscious. [Possible examples of language processing that might be performed non-consciously include computer programs implementing aspects of language or ritualized human conversations (e.g., about the weather). These might require syntax and correctly grounded semantics and yet be performed non-consciously. A more complex example, illustrating that syntax could be used, might be, "If A does X, then B will probably do Y, and then C would be able to do Z." A first-order language system could process this statement. Moreover, the first-order language system could apply the rule usefully in the world, provided that the symbols in the language system (A, B, X, Y etc.) are grounded (have meaning) in the world.]

In line with the argument on the adaptive value of higher-order thoughts and thus consciousness given above, that they are useful for correcting lower-order thoughts, I now suggest that correction using higher-order thoughts of lower-order thoughts would have adaptive value primarily if the lower-order thoughts are sufficiently complex to benefit from correction in this way. The nature of the complexity is specific: It should involve syntactic manipulation of symbols, probably with several steps in the chain, and the chain of steps should be a one-off (or in American, "one-time", meaning used once) set of steps, as in a sentence or in a particular plan used just once, rather than a set of well-learned rules. The first- or lower-order thoughts might involve a linked chain of "if" . . . "then" statements that would be involved in planning, an example of which has been given above. It is partly because complex lower-order thoughts, such as these that involve syntax and language, would benefit from correction by higher-order thoughts that I suggest that there is a close link between this reflective consciousness and language. The hypothesis is that by thinking about lower-order thoughts, the higher-order thoughts can discover what may be weak links in the chain of reasoning at the lower-order level and, having detected the weak link, might alter the plan to see if doing so gives better success. In our example above, if it transpired that C could not do Z, how might the plan have failed? Instead of having to go through endless random changes to the plan to see if by trial and error some combination does happen to produce results, what I am suggesting is that by thinking about the previous plan, one might, for example using knowledge of the situation and the probabilities that operate in it, guess that the step where the plan failed was that B did not in fact do Y. So by thinking about the plan (the first- or lower-order thought), one might correct the original plan in such a way that the weak link in that chain, that "B will probably do Y", is circumvented.

To draw a parallel with neural networks, there is a *"credit assignment"* problem in such multistep syntactic plans: If the whole plan fails, how does the system assign credit or blame to particular steps of the plan? (In multilayer neural networks, the credit assignment problem is that if errors are being specified at the output layer, the problem arises about how to propagate back the error to earlier, hidden layers of the network to assign credit or blame to individual synaptic connection; see Rolls & Deco, 2002; Rumelhart, Hinton, & Williams, 1986). The suggestion is that this is the function of higher-order thoughts and is why systems with higher-order thoughts evolved. The suggestion I then make is that if a system were doing this type of processing (thinking about its own thoughts), it would then be very plausible that it should feel like something to be doing this. I even suggest to the reader that it is not plausible to suggest that it would not feel like anything to a system if it were doing this.

Two other points in the argument should be emphasized for clarity. One is that the system that is having syntactic thoughts about its own syntactic thoughts (higher-order syntactic thoughts or HOSTs) would have to have its symbols grounded in the real world for it to feel like something to be having higher-order thoughts. The intention of this clarification is to exclude systems, such as a computer running a program when there is in addition some sort of control or even overseeing program checking the operation of the first program. We would want to say that in such a situation it would feel like something to be running the higher-level control program only if the first-order program was symbolically performing operations on the world and receiving input about the results of those operations, and if the higher-order system understood what the first-order system was trying to do in the world. The issue of symbol grounding is considered further by Rolls (2005a, Chapter 10; 2000a). The symbols (or symbolic representations) are symbols in the sense that they can take part in syntactic processing. The symbolic representations are grounded in the world in that they refer to events in the world. The symbolic representations must have a great deal of information about what is referred to in the world, including the quality and intensity of sensory events, emotional states, etc. The need for this is that the reasoning in the symbolic system must be about stimuli, events, and states, and remembered stimuli, events, and states; for the reasoning to be correct, all the information that can affect the reasoning must be represented in the symbolic system, including for example just how light or strong the touch was, etc.

Indeed, it is pointed out in *Emotion Explained* that it is no accident that the shape of the multidimensional phenomenal (sensory etc.) space maps so clearly onto the space defined by neuronal activity in sensory systems, for if this were not the case, reasoning about the state of affairs in the world would not map onto the world and would not be useful. Good examples of this close correspondence are found in the taste system, in which subjective space maps simply onto the multidimensional space represented by neuronal firing in primate cortical taste areas. In particular, if a three-dimensional space reflecting the distances between the representations of different tastes provided by macaque neurons in the cortical taste areas is constructed, then the distances between the subjective ratings by humans of different tastes is very similar (Plata-Salaman, Smith-Swintowsky,

& Scott, 1996; Smith-Swintowsky, Plata-Salaman, & Scott, 1991; Yaxley, Rolls, & Sienkiewicz, 1990; Kadohisa, Rolls, & Verhagen, 2005). Similarly, the changes in human subjective ratings of the pleasantness of the taste, smell, and sight of food parallel very closely the responses of neurons in the macaque orbitofrontal cortex (see *Emotion Explained*, Chapter 5). The representations in the first-order linguistic processor that the HOSTs process include beliefs (for example "Food is available", or at least representations of this), and the HOST system would then have available to it the concept of a thought (so that it could represent "I believe [or there is a belief] that food is available").

However, as summarised by Rolls (2000a, 2005a), representations of sensory processes and emotional states must be processed by the first-order linguistic system, and HOSTs may be about these representations of sensory processes and emotional states capable of taking part in the syntactic operations of the first-order linguistic processor. Such sensory and emotional information may reach the first-order linguistic system from many parts of the brain, including those parts, such as the orbitofrontal cortex and amygdala, that are implicated in emotional states (see *Emotion Expalined*, Fig. 10.3 and p. 408). When the sensory information is about the identity of the taste, the inputs to the first-order linguistic system must come from the primary taste cortex, in that the identity of taste, independent of its pleasantness (in that the representation is independent of hunger), must come from the primary taste cortex. In contrast, when the information that reaches the first-order linguistic system is about the pleasantness of taste, it must come from the secondary taste cortex, in that there the representation of taste depends on hunger.

The second clarification is that the plan would have to be a unique string of steps, in much the same way as a sentence can be a unique and one-off (or one-time) string of words. The point here is that it is helpful to be able to think about particular one-off plans and to correct them; this type of operation is very different from the slow learning of fixed rules by trial and error or the application of fixed rules by a supervisory part of a computer program.

This analysis does not yet give an account for sensory qualia ("raw sensory feels"; for example, why "red" feels red), for emotional qualia (e.g., why a rewarding touch produces an emotional feeling of pleasure), or for motivational qualia (e.g., why food deprivation makes us *feel* hungry). The view I suggest on such qualia is as follows. Information processing in and from our sensory systems (e.g., the sight of the colour red) may be relevant to planning actions using language and the conscious processing thereby implied. Given that these inputs must be represented in the system that plans, we may ask whether it is more likely that we would be conscious of them or that we would not. I suggest that it would be a very special-purpose system that would allow such sensory inputs, and emotional and motivational states, to be part of (linguistically based) planning and yet remain unconscious. It seems to be much more parsimonious to hold that we would be conscious of such sensory, emotional, and motivational qualia because they would be being used (or are available to be used) in this type of (linguistically based) higher-order thought processing, and this is what I propose.

The explanation for emotional and motivational subjective feelings or qualia that this discussion has led toward is thus that they should be felt as conscious because they enter into a specialised linguistic symbol-manipulation system that is part of a higher-order thought system that is capable of reflecting on and correcting its lower-order thoughts involved, for example, in the flexible planning of actions. It would require a very special machine to enable this higher-order linguistically based thought processing, which is conscious by its nature, to occur without the sensory, emotional, and motivational states (which must be taken into account by the higher-order thought system) becoming felt qualia. The qualia are thus accounted for by the evolution of the linguistic system that can reflect on and correct its own lower-order processes and thus has adaptive value.

This account implies that it may be especially those animals with a higher-order belief and thought system and with linguistic symbol manipulation that have qualia. It may be that much non-human animal behaviour, provided that it does not require flexible linguistic planning and correction by reflection, could take place according to reinforcement guidance (using e.g., stimulus-reinforcement association learning in the amygdala and orbitofrontal cortex; Rolls, 1990, 1996b, 1999a, 2000b, c, 2002, 2004a, 2005a), and rule following (implemented, for example, using habit or stimulus-response learning in the basal ganglia, Rolls, 1994; Rolls & Johnstone, 1992). Such behaviours might appear very similar to human behaviour performed in similar circumstances, but would not imply qualia. It would be primarily by virtue of a system for reflecting on flexible, linguistic, planning behaviour that humans (and animals close to humans, with demonstrable syntactic manipulation of symbols and the ability to think about these linguistic processes) would be different from other animals and would have evolved qualia.

For processing in a part of our brain to be able to reach consciousness, appropriate pathways must be present. Certain constraints arise here. For example, in the sensory pathways, the nature of the representation may change as it passes through a hierarchy of processing levels, and to be conscious of the information in the form in which it is represented in early processing stages, the early processing stages must have access to the part of the brain necessary for consciousness. An example is provided by processing in the taste system. In the primate primary taste cortex, neurons respond to taste independently of hunger, yet in the secondary taste cortex, food-related taste neurons (e.g., responding to sweet taste) only respond to food if hunger is present and gradually stop responding to that taste during feeding to satiety (see Rolls, 1997, 2005a; Rolls & Scott, 2003). Now the quality of the tastant (sweet, salt etc.) and its intensity

are not affected by hunger, but the pleasantness of its taste is decreased to zero (neutral) or even becomes unpleasant after we have eaten it to satiety. The implication of this is that for quality and intensity information about taste, we must be conscious of what is represented in the primary taste cortex (or perhaps in another area connected to it that bypasses the secondary taste cortex), and not of what is represented in the secondary taste cortex. In contrast, for the pleasantness of a taste, consciousness of this could not reflect what is represented in the primary taste cortex, but instead what is represented in the secondary taste cortex (or in an area beyond it). The same argument arises for reward in general, and therefore for emotion, which in primates is not represented early on in processing in the sensory pathways (nor in or before the inferior temporal cortex for vision), but in the areas to which these object analysis systems project, such as the orbitofrontal cortex, where the reward value of visual stimuli is reflected in the responses of neurons to visual stimuli (see Rolls, 1990, 1995a, b, 2005a). It is also of interest that reward signals (e.g., the taste of food when we are hungry) are associated with subjective feelings of pleasure (see Rolls, 1990, 1995a,b, 1997, 2005a). I suggest that this correspondence arises because pleasure is the subjective state that represents in the conscious system a signal that is positively reinforcing (rewarding) and that inconsistent behaviour would result if the representations did not correspond to a signal for positive reinforcement in both the conscious and the nonconscious processing systems.

Do these arguments mean that the conscious sensation of, for example, taste quality (i.e., identity and intensity) is represented or occurs in the primary taste cortex, and of the pleasantness of taste in the secondary taste cortex, and that activity in these areas is sufficient for conscious sensations (qualia) to occur? I do not suggest this at all. Instead the arguments I have put forward above suggest that we are only conscious of representations when we have higher-order thoughts about them. The implication then is that pathways must connect from each of the brain areas in which information is represented about which we can be conscious, to the system that has the higher-order thoughts, which as I have argued above, requires language. Thus, in the example given, there must be connections to the language areas from the primary taste cortex, which need not be direct, but which must bypass the secondary taste cortex, in which the information is represented differently (see Rolls, 1995a, 2005a). There must also be pathways from the secondary taste cortex, not necessarily direct, to the language areas so that we can have higher-order thoughts about the pleasantness of the representation in the secondary taste cortex. There would also need to be pathways from the hippocampus, implicated in the recall of declarative memories, back to the language areas of the cerebral cortex (at least via the cortical areas that receive backprojections from the amygdala, orbitofrontal cortex, and hippocampus, see Fig. 29.2), which would in turn need connections to the language areas).

One question that has been discussed is whether there is a causal role for consciousness (e.g., Armstrong & Malcolm, 1984). The position to which the above arguments lead is that indeed conscious processing does have a causal role in the elicitation of behaviour, but only under the set of circumstances when higher-order thoughts play a role in correcting or influencing lower-order thoughts and that it is a property of the higher-order thought system that it feels like something when it is operating. As we have seen, some behavioural responses can be elicited when there is not this type of reflective control of lower-order processing nor indeed any contribution of language (see further Rolls, 2003, for relations between implicit and explicit processing). There are many brain processing routes to output regions, and only one of these involves conscious, verbally represented processing that can later be recalled (see Fig. 29.2).

It is of interest to comment on how the evolution of a system for flexible planning might affect emotions. Consider grief, which may occur when a reward is terminated and no immediate action is possible (see Rolls, 1990, 1995b, 2005a). Grief may be adaptive by leading to a cessation of the formerly rewarded behaviour and thus facilitating the possible identification of other positive reinforcers in the environment. In humans, grief may be particularly potent because it becomes represented in a system that can plan ahead and can understand the enduring implications of the loss. (Thinking about or verbally discussing emotional states may also in these circumstances help, because doing so can lead toward the identification of new or alternative reinforcers and the realization that for example negative consequences may not be as bad as feared.)

This account of consciousness also leads to a suggestion about the processing that underlies the feeling of free will. Free will would in this scheme involve the use of language to check many moves ahead on a number of possible series of actions and their outcomes, and then with this information to make a choice from the likely outcomes of different possible series of actions. (If in contrast choices were made only on the basis of the reinforcement value of immediately available stimuli, without the arbitrary syntactic symbol manipulation made possible by language, then the choice strategy would be much more limited, and we might not want to use the term "free will", as all the consequences of those actions would not have been computed.) It is suggested that when this type of reflective, conscious information processing is occurring and leading to action, the system performing this processing and producing the action would have to believe that it could cause the action, for otherwise inconsistencies would arise, and the system might no longer try to initiate action. This belief held by the system may partly underlie the feeling of free will. At other times, when other brain modules are initiating actions (in the implicit systems), the conscious processor (the explicit system) may confabulate and believe that it caused the action or at least give an account (possibly wrong) of why the action was initiated. The fact that the conscious processor may have the belief even in these circumstances that it initiated the action may be a property of it being inconsistent for a system that can take overall control using conscious verbal processing to believe that it was overridden by another system. This may be the reason why confabulation occurs.

In the operation of such a free will system, the uncertainties introduced by the limited information possible about the likely outcomes of series of actions, and the inability to use optimal algorithms when combining conditional probabilities, would be much more important factors than whether the brain operates deterministically or not. (The operation of brain machinery must be relatively deterministic, for it has evolved to provide reliable outputs for given inputs.)

Before leaving these thoughts, it may be worth commenting on the feeling of continuing self-identity that is characteristic of humans. Why might this arise? One suggestion is that if one is an organism that can think about its own long-term multistep plans, then for those plans to be executed consistently and thus adaptively, the goals of the plans would need to remain stable, as would memories of how far one had proceeded along the execution path of each plan. If one felt each time one came to execute, perhaps on another day, the next step of a plan, that the goals were different; or if one did not remember which steps had already been taken in a multi step plan, the plan would never be usefully executed. So, given that it does feel like something to be doing this type of planning using higher-order thoughts, it would have to feel as if one were the same agent, acting toward the same goals, from day to day. Thus it is suggested that the feeling of continuing self-identity falls out of a situation in which there is an actor with consistent long-term goals and long-term recall. If it feels like anything to be the actor, according to the suggestions of the higher-order thought theory, then it should feel like the same thing from occasion to occasion to be the actor, and no special further construct is needed to account for self-identity. Humans without such a feeling of being the same person from day to day might be expected to have for exam-

ple inconsistent goals from day to day or a poor recall memory. It may be noted that the ability to recall previous steps in a plan and bring them into the conscious, higher-order thought system is an important prerequisite for long-term planning that involves checking each step in a multistep process.

These are my initial thoughts on why we have consciousness and are conscious of sensory, emotional, and motivational qualia, as well as qualia associated with first-order linguistic thoughts. However, as stated above, one does not feel that there are straightforward criteria in this philosophical field of enquiry for knowing whether the suggested theory is correct. Therefore, it is likely that theories of consciousness will continue to undergo rapid development, and current theories should not be taken to have practical implications.

Dual Routes to Action

According to the present formulation, there are two types of route to action performed in relation to reward or punishment in humans (see also Rolls, 2003, 2005a). Examples of such actions include emotional and motivational behaviour.

The first route is via the brain systems that have been present in non-human primates, such as monkeys, and to some extent in other mammals for millions of years. These systems include the amygdala and, particularly well developed in primates, the orbitofrontal cortex. These systems control behaviour in relation to previous associations of stimuli with reinforcement. The computation that controls the action thus involves assessment of the reinforcement-related value of a stimulus. This assessment may be based on a number of different factors. One is the previous reinforcement history, which involves stimulus-reinforcement association learning using the amygdala and its rapid updating especially in primates using the orbitofrontal cortex. This stimulus-reinforcement association learning may involve quite specific information about a stimulus; for example, of the energy associated with each type of food, by the process of conditioned appetite and satiety (Booth, 1985). A second is the current motivational state; for example, whether hunger is present, whether other needs are satisfied, etc.

A third factor that affects the computed reward value of the stimulus is whether that reward has been received recently. If it has been received recently but in small quantity, this may increase the reward value of the stimulus. This is known as incentive motivation or the "salted peanut" phenomenon. The adaptive value of such a process is that this positive feedback of reward value in the early stages of working for a particular reward tends to lock the organism onto behaviour being performed for that reward. This means that animals that are for example almost equally hungry and thirsty will show hysteresis in their choice of action, rather than continually switching from eating to drinking and back with each mouthful of water or food. This introduction of hysteresis into the reward evaluation system makes action selection a much more efficient process in a natural environment, for constantly switching between different types of behaviour would be very costly if all the different rewards were not available in the same place at the same time. (For example, walking a half-mile between a site where water was available and a site where food was available after every mouthful would be very inefficient.) The amygdala is one structure that may be involved in this increase in the reward value of stimuli early on in a series of presentations, in that lesions of the amygdala (in rats) abolish the expression of this reward-incrementing process, which is normally evident in the increasing rate of working for a food reward early on in a meal (Rolls & Rolls, 1982).

A fourth factor is the computed absolute value of the reward or punishment expected or being obtained from a stimulus; for example, the sweetness of the stimulus (set by evolution so that sweet stimuli will tend to be rewarding because they are generally associated with energy sources) or the pleasantness of touch (set by evolution to be pleasant according to the extent to which it brings animals of the opposite sex together,

and depending on the investment in time that the partner is willing to put into making the touch pleasurable, a sign that indicates the commitment and value for the partner of the relationship). After the reward value of the stimulus has been assessed in these ways, behaviour is then initiated based on approach toward or withdrawal from the stimulus. A critical aspect of the behaviour produced by this type of system is that it is aimed directly toward obtaining a sensed or expected reward, by virtue of connections to brain systems, such as the basal ganglia, which are concerned with the initiation of actions (see Fig. 29.2). The expectation may of course involve behaviour to obtain stimuli associated with reward, which might even be present in a chain.

Now part of the way in which the behaviour is controlled with this first route is according to the reward value of the outcome. At the same time, the animal may only work for the reward if the cost is not too high. Indeed, in the field of behavioural ecology, animals are often thought of as performing optimally on some cost-benefit curve (see e.g., Krebs & Kacelnik, 1991). This does not at all mean that the animal thinks about the rewards and performs a cost-benefit analysis using a lot of thoughts about the costs, other rewards available, and their costs, etc. Instead, it should be taken to mean that in evolution, the system has evolved so that the way in which the reward varies with the different energy densities or amounts of food and the delay before it is received can be used as part of the input to a mechanism that has also been built to track the costs of obtaining the food (e.g., energy loss in obtaining it, risk of predation, etc.), and to then select, given many such types of reward and the associated cost, the current behaviour that provides the most "net reward". Part of the value of having the computation expressed in this reward-minus-cost form is that there is then a suitable "currency", or net reward value, to enable the animal to select the behaviour with currently the most net reward gain (or minimal aversive outcome).

The second route in humans involves a computation with many "if...then" statements used to implement a plan to obtain a reward. In this case, the reward may actually be *deferred* as part of the plan, which might involve working first to obtain one reward and only then to work for a second more highly valued reward, if this was thought to be overall an optimal strategy in terms of resource usage (e.g., time). In this case, syntax is required, because the many symbols (e.g., names of people) that are part of the plan must be linked or bound correctly. Such linking might be of the form: "If A does this, then B is likely to do this, and this will cause C to do this...". The requirement of syntax for this type of planning implies that an output to language systems in the brain is required for this type of planning (see Fig. 29.2). Thus, the explicit language system in humans may allow working for deferred rewards by enabling use of a one-off, individual plan appropriate for each situation. Another building block for such planning operations in the brain may be the type of short-term memory in which the prefrontal cortex is involved. For example in non-human primates, this short-term memory may be of where in space a response has just been made. A development of this type of short-term response memory system in humans to enable multiple short-term memories to be held in place correctly, preferably with the temporal order of the different items in the short-term memory coded correctly, may be another building block for the multiple-step "if...then" type of computation required to form a multiple step plan. Such short-term memories are implemented in the (dorsolateral and inferior convexity) prefrontal cortex of non-human primates and humans (see Goldman-Rakic, 1996; Petrides, 1996), and may be part of the reason why prefrontal cortex damage impairs planning (see Shallice & Burgess, 1996).

Of these two routes (see Fig. 29.2), it is the second that I have suggested above is related to consciousness. The hypothesis is that consciousness is the state that arises by virtue of having the ability to think about one's own thoughts, which has the adaptive value of enabling one to correct long multistep syntactic plans. This latter system is thus the one in which explicit, declarative processing occurs. Processing in this system is frequently associated with reason and rationality, in that many of the consequences of possible actions can be taken into account. The actual computation of how rewarding a particular stimulus or situation is or will be probably still depends on activity in the orbitofrontal cortex and amygdala, as the reward value of stimuli is computed and represented in these regions and verbalised expressions of the reward (or punishment) value of stimuli are dampened by damage to these systems. (For example, damage to the orbitofrontal cortex renders painful input still identifiable as pain, but without the strong affective, "unpleasant", reaction to it.) This language system that enables long-term planning may be contrasted with the first system in which behaviour is directed at obtaining the stimulus (including the remembered stimulus) that is currently most rewarding, as computed by brain structures that include the orbitofrontal cortex and amygdala. There are outputs from this system, perhaps those directed at the basal ganglia, which do not pass through the language system, and behaviour produced in this way is described as implicit, and verbal declarations cannot be made directly about the reasons for the choice made. When verbal declarations are made about decisions made in this first system, those verbal declarations may be confabulations, reasonable explanations, or fabrications of reasons why the choice was made. These reasonable explanations would be generated to be consistent with the sense of continuity and self that is a characteristic of reasoning in the language system.

The question then arises of how decisions are made in animals such as humans that have both the implicit, direct reward-based and the explicit, rational, planning systems (see Fig. 29.2). One particular situation in which the first, implicit, system may be especially important is when rapid reactions to stimuli with reward or punishment value must be made, for then the direct connections from structures such as the orbitofrontal cortex to the basal ganglia may allow rapid actions (e.g., Rolls et al., 1994). The implicit system may be used to guide action when there may be too many factors to be taken into account easily by the explicit, rational, planning, system. In contrast, when the implicit system continually makes errors, it would then be beneficial for the organism to switch from automatic, direct action based on obtaining what the orbitofrontal cortex system decodes as being the most positively reinforcing choice currently available, to the explicit conscious control system that can evaluate with its long-term planning algorithms what action should be performed next. Indeed, it would be adaptive for the explicit system to regularly be assessing performance by the more automatic system and to switch itself in to control behaviour quite frequently, as otherwise the adaptive value of having the explicit system would be less than optimal. Another factor that may influence the balance between control by the implicit and explicit systems is the presence of pharmacological agents such as alcohol, which may alter the balance toward control by the implicit system, may allow the implicit system to influence more the explanations made by the explicit system, and may within the explicit system alter the relative value it places on caution and restraint versus commitment to a risky action or plan.

There may also be a flow of influence from the explicit, verbal system to the implicit system, in that the explicit system may decide on a plan of action or strategy and exert an influence on the implicit system that will alter the reinforcement evaluations made by and the signals produced by the implicit system. An example of this might be that if a pregnant woman feels that she would like to escape a cruel mate, but is aware that she may not survive in the jungle, then it would be adaptive if the explicit system could suppress some aspects of her implicit behaviour toward her mate, so that she does not give signals that she is displeased with her situation. (In the literature on self-deception, it has been suggested that unconscious desires may not be made explicit in consciousness (or may actually be repressed), so as not to compromise the explicit system in what it produces; see e.g.,

Alexander, 1975, 1979; Trivers, 1976, 1985; and the review by Nesse & Lloyd, 1992). Another example might be that the explicit system might because of its long-term plans influence the implicit system to increase its response to, for example, a positive reinforcer. One way in which the explicit system might influence the implicit system is by setting up the conditions in which, for example when a given stimulus (e.g., person) is present, positive reinforcers are given to facilitate stimulus-reinforcement association learning by the implicit system of the person receiving the positive reinforcers. Conversely, the implicit system may influence the explicit system, for example by highlighting certain stimuli in the environment that are currently associated with reward, to guide the attention of the explicit system to such stimuli.

However, it may be expected that there is often a conflict between these systems, in that the first, implicit system is able to guide behaviour particularly to obtain the greatest immediate reinforcement, whereas the explicit system can potentially enable immediate rewards to be deferred and longer-term, multistep, plans to be formed. This type of conflict will occur in animals with a syntactic planning ability; that is, in humans and any other animals that have the ability to process a series of "if ... then" stages of planning. This is a property of the human language system, and the extent to which it is a property of non-human primates is not yet fully clear. In any case, such conflict may be an important aspect of the operation of at least the human mind, because it is so essential for humans to correctly decide, at every moment, whether to invest in a relationship or a group that may offer long-term benefits or whether to directly pursue immediate benefits (Nesse & Lloyd, 1992).

As Nesse and Lloyd (1992) describe, analysts have come to a somewhat similar position, for they hold that intrapsychic conflicts usually seem to have two sides, with impulses on one side and inhibitions on the other. Analysts describe the source of the impulses as the *id*, and the modules that inhibit the expression of impulses, because of external and internal constraints, the *ego* and *superego*, respectively (Leak & Christopher, 1982; Trivers, 1985; see also Nesse & Lloyd, 1992, p. 613). The superego can be thought of as the conscience, whereas the ego is the locus of executive functions that balance satisfaction of impulses with anticipated internal and external costs. The present position differs because it is based on the identification of dual routes to action implemented by different systems in the brain, each with its own selective advantage.

Some investigations in non-human primates on deception have been interpreted as showing that animals can plan to deceive others (see e.g., Griffin, 1992); that is, to utilize "Machiavellian intelligence". For example, a baboon may "deliberately" mislead another animal in order to obtain a resource, such as food (e.g., by screaming to summon assistance in order to have a competing animal chased from a food patch) or sex (e.g., a female baboon who moved very gradually into a position from which the dominant male could not see her grooming a subadult baboon; see Dawkins, 1993). The attraction of the Machiavellian argument is that the behaviour for which it accounts seems to imply that there is a concept of another animal's mind and that one animal is trying occasionally to mislead another, which implies some planning. However, such observations tend by their nature to be field-based and may have an anecdotal character, in that the previous experience of the animals in this type of behaviour, and the reinforcements obtained, are not known (Dawkins, 1993). It is possible for example that some behavioural responses that appear to be Machiavellian may have been the result of previous instrumental learning in which reinforcement was obtained for particular types of response or of observational learning, with again learning from the outcome observed. However, in any case, most examples of Machiavellian intelligence in non-human primates do not involve multiple stages of "if . . . then" planning requiring syntax to keep the symbols apart (but may involve learning of the type "if the dominant male sees me grooming a subadult male,

I will be punished"; see Dawkins, 1993). Nevertheless, the possible advantage of such Machiavellian *planning* could be one of the adaptive guiding factors in evolution that provided advantage to a multistep, syntactic system that enables long-term planning, the best example of such a system being human language.

However, another, not necessarily exclusive, advantage for the evolution of a linguistic multistep planning system could well be not Machiavellian planning, but planning for social cooperation and advantage. Perhaps in general an "if . . . then" multistep syntactic planning ability is useful primarily in evolution in social situations of the type: "if X does this, then Y does that; then I would/should do that, and the outcome would be . . .". It is not yet at all clear whether such planning is required in order to explain the social behaviour of social animals, such as hunting dogs or socialising monkeys (Dawkins, 1993). However, in humans there is evidence that members of "primitive" hunting tribes spend hours recounting tales of recent events (perhaps who did what, when, who then did what, etc.), perhaps to help learn from experience about good strategies, which is necessary for example when physically weak men take on large animals (see Pinker & Bloom, 1992). Thus, social cooperation may be as powerful a driving force in the evolution of syntactical planning systems as Machiavellian intelligence. What is common to both is that they involve social situations. However, such a syntactic planning system would have advantages not only in social systems, for such planning may be useful in obtaining resources purely in a physical (non-social) world. An example might be planning how to cross terrain given current environmental constraints in order to reach a particular place.

The thrust of this argument thus is that much complex animal, including human, behaviour can take place using the implicit, non-conscious route to action. We should be very careful not to postulate intentional states (i.e., states with intentions, beliefs, and desires) unless the evidence for them is strong, and it seems to me that a flexible, one-off linguistic processing system that can handle propositions is needed for intentional states. What the explicit, linguistic system does allow is exactly this flexible, one-off, multistep planning-ahead type of computation, which allows us to defer immediate rewards based on such a plan.

This discussion of dual routes to action has been with respect to the behaviour produced. There is of course, in addition, a third output of brain regions, such as the orbitofrontal cortex and amygdala involved in emotion, which is directed to producing autonomic and endocrine responses. Although it has been argued by Rolls (2005a, Chapter 2) that the autonomic system is not normally in a circuit through which behavioural responses are produced (i.e., against the James-Lange and related somatic theories), there may be some influence from effects produced through the endocrine system (and possibly the autonomic system, through which some endocrine responses are controlled) on behaviour, or on the dual systems just discussed that control behaviour. For example, during female orgasm the hormone oxytocin may be released, and this may influence the implicit system to help develop positive reinforcement associations and thus attachment.

Discussion

Some ways in which the current theory may be different from other related theories follow. The current theory holds that it is higher-order *syntactic* thoughts (HOSTs) that are closely associated with consciousness, and this may differ from Rosenthal's higher-order thoughts (HOTs) theory (Rosenthal, 1986, 1990, 1993, 2005) in the emphasis on language. Language in the current theory is defined by syntactic manipulation of symbols and does not necessarily imply verbal language. The type of language required in the theory described here is sometimes termed "mentalese" by philosophers (Fodor, 1994). The reason that strong emphasis is placed on language is that it is as a result of having a multistep flexible

"on the fly" reasoning procedure that errors that cannot be corrected easily by reward or punishment received at the end of the reasoning, need 'thoughts about thoughts'– that is, some type of supervisory and monitoring process – to detect where errors in the reasoning have occurred. This suggestion on the adaptive value in evolution of such a higher-order linguistic thought process for multistep planning ahead, and correcting such plans, may also be different from earlier work. Put another way, this point is that *credit assignment* when reward or punishment is received is straightforward in a one-layer network (in which the reinforcement can be used directly to correct nodes in error or responses). However, credit assignment is very difficult in a multistep linguistic process executed once "on the fly". Very complex mappings in a multilayer network can be learned if hundreds of learning trials are provided. But once these complex mappings are learned, their success or failure in a new situation on a given trial cannot be evaluated and corrected by the network. Indeed, the complex mappings achieved by such networks (e.g., backpropagation nets) mean that after training they operate according to fixed rules and are often quite impenetrable and inflexible. In contrast, to correct a multistep, single occasion, linguistically based plan or procedure, recall of the steps just made in the reasoning or planning and perhaps of related episodic material needs to occur, so that the link in the chain that is most likely to be in error can be identified. This may be part of the reason why there is a close relation between declarative memory systems, which can explicitly recall memories, and consciousness.

Some computer programs may have supervisory processes. Should these count as higher-order linguistic thought processes? My current response to this question is that they should not, to the extent that they operate with fixed rules to correct the operation of a system that does not itself involve linguistic thoughts about symbols grounded semantically in the external world. If on the other hand it were possible to implement on a computer such a higher-order linguistic thought supervisory correction process to correct first-order one-off linguistic thoughts with symbols grounded in the real world, then this process would prima facie be conscious. If it were possible in a thought experiment to reproduce the neural connectivity and operation of a human brain on a computer, then prima facie it would also have the attributes of consciousness. It might continue to have those attributes for as long as power was applied to the system.

Another possible difference from earlier theories is that raw sensory feels are suggested to arise as a consequence of having a system that can think about its own thoughts. Raw sensory feels, and subjective states associated with emotional and motivational states, may not necessarily arise first in evolution.

A property often attributed to consciousness is that it is *unitary*. The current theory would account for this property by the limited syntactic capability of neuronal networks in the brain, which render it difficult to implement more than a few syntactic bindings of symbols simultaneously (see McLeod, Plunkett, & Rolls, 1998 and Rolls & Treves, 1998). This limitation makes it difficult to run several "streams of consciousness" simultaneously. In addition, given that a linguistic system can control behavioural output, several parallel streams might produce maladaptive behaviour (apparent as, for example, indecision), and might be selected against. The close relation between and the limited capacity of both the stream of consciousness and auditory-verbal short term memory may be that both implement the capacity for syntax in neural networks. Whether syntax in real neuronal networks is implemented by temporal binding (see von der Malsburg, 1990) is still very much an unresolved issue (Rolls & Deco, 2002; Rolls & Treves, 1998; Rolls, 2007a). [For example, the code about which visual stimulus has been shown can be read off from the end of the visual system without taking the temporal aspects of the neuronal firing into account; much of the information about which stimulus is shown is available in short periods of

30–50 ms, and cortical neurons need fire for only this long during the identification of objects (Rolls, 2003; Rolls & Deco, 2002; Rolls & Tovee, 1994; Rolls, Tovee, & Panzeri, 1999; Rolls & Treves, 1998; Rolls, Tovee, Purcell, Stewart, & Azzopardi, 1999; Tovee & Rolls, 1995; Tovee, Rolls, Treves, & Bellis, 1993): These are rather short time windows for the expression of multiple separate populations of synchronized neurons). In addition, oscillations, at least, are not an obvious property of neuronal firing in the primate temporal cortical visual areas involved in the representation of faces and objects (Tovee & Rolls, 1992; see further Rolls & Treves, 1998).] However, the hypothesis that syntactic binding is necessary for consciousness is one of the postulates of the theory I am describing (for the system I describe must be capable of correcting its own syntactic thoughts), and the fact that the binding must be implemented in neuronal networks may well place limitations on consciousness, which lead to some of its properties, such as its unitary nature. The postulate of Crick and Koch (1990) that oscillations and synchronization are necessary bases of consciousness could thus be related to the present theory if it turns out that oscillations or neuronal synchronization is the way the brain implements syntactic binding. However, the fact that oscillations and neuronal synchronization are especially evident in anaesthetized cats does not impress as strong evidence that oscillations and synchronization are critical features of consciousness, for most people would hold that anaesthetized cats are *not* conscious. The fact that oscillations and synchronization are much more difficult to demonstrate in the temporal cortical visual areas of awake behaving monkeys (Aggelopoulos, Franco, & Rolls, 2005) might just mean that during evolution to primates the cortex has become better able to avoid parasitic oscillations, as a result of developing better feedforward and feedback inhibitory circuits (see Rolls & Deco, 2002 and Rolls & Treves, 1998).

The current theory holds that consciousness arises by virtue of a system that can think linguistically about its own linguistic thoughts. The advantages for a system of being able to do this have been described, and this has been suggested as the reason why consciousness evolved. The evidence that consciousness arises by virtue of having a system that can perform higher-order linguistic processing is however, and I think may remain, circumstantial. (Why must it feel like something when we are performing a certain type of information processing? The evidence described here suggests that it does feel like something when we are performing a certain type of information processing, but does not produce a strong reason for why it has to feel like something. It just does, when we are using this linguistic processing system capable of higher-order thoughts.) The evidence, summarized above, includes the points that we think of ourselves as conscious when for example we recall earlier events, compare them with current events, and plan many steps ahead. Evidence also comes from neurological cases, from for example split-brain patients who may confabulate conscious stories about what is happening in their other, non-language hemisphere; and from frontal lobe patients who can tell one consciously what they should be doing, but nevertheless may be doing the opposite. (The force of this type of case is that much of our behaviour may normally be produced by routes about which we cannot verbalize and are not conscious about.)

This raises the issue of the causal role of consciousness. Does consciousness cause our behaviour?[2] The view that I currently hold is that the information processing that is related to consciousness (activity in a linguistic system capable of higher-order thoughts and used for planning and correcting the operation of lower-order linguistic systems) can play a causal role in producing our behaviour (see Fig. 29.2). It is, I postulate, a *property* of processing in this system (capable of higher-order thoughts) that it feels like something to be performing that type of processing. It is in this sense that I suggest that consciousness can act causally to influence our behaviour: Consciousness is the prop-

erty that occurs when a linguistic system is thinking about its lower-order thoughts. The hypothesis that it does feel like something when this processing is taking place is at least to some extent testable: Humans performing this type of higher-order linguistic processing, for example recalling episodic memories and comparing them with current circumstances, who denied being conscious, would prima facie constitute evidence against the theory. Most humans would find it very implausible, though, to posit that they could be thinking about their own thoughts, and reflecting on their own thoughts, without being conscious. This type of processing does appear to be for most humans to be necessarily conscious.

Finally, I provide a short specification of what might have to be implemented in a neural network to implement conscious processing. First, a linguistic system, not necessarily verbal, but implementing syntax between symbols implemented in the environment would be needed (i.e., a mentalese language system). Then a higher-order thought system also implementing syntax, able to think about the representations in the first-order language system, and able to correct the reasoning in the first-order linguistic system in a flexible manner would be needed. So my view is that consciousness can be implemented in neural networks, (and that this is a topic worth discussing), but that the neural networks would have to implement the type of higher-order linguistic processing described in this chapter.

Conclusions and Comparisons

It is suggested that it feels like something to be an organism or machine that can think about its own (linguistic and semantically based) thoughts. It is suggested that qualia, raw sensory, and emotional feels arise secondary to having evolved such a higher-order thought system and that sensory and emotional processing feels like something because it would be unparsimonious for it to enter the planning, higher-order thought system and *not* feel like something. The adaptive value of having sensory and emotional feelings, or qualia, is thus suggested to be that such inputs are important to the long-term planning, explicit processing system. Raw sensory feels and subjective states associated with emotional and motivational states may not necessarily arise first in evolution. Some issues that arise in relation to this theory are discussed by Rolls (2000a, 2004b, 2005a); reasons why the ventral visual system is more closely related to explicit than implicit processing are considered by Rolls (2003) and by Rolls and Deco (2002); and reasons why explicit, conscious processing may have a higher threshold in sensory processing than implicit processing are considered by Rolls (2003, 2005b).

The theory is different from some other theories of consciousness (Carruthers, 2000; Gennaro, 2004; Rosenthal, 1990, 1993, 2004, 2005) in that it provides an account of the evolutionary, adaptive value of a higher-order thought system in helping solve a credit assignment problem that arises in a multistep syntactic plan, links this type of processing to consciousness, and therefore emphasises a role for syntactic processing in consciousness. The type of syntactic processing need not be at the natural language level (which implies a universal grammar), but could be at the level of mentalese (Rolls, 1999a, 2004b, 2005a; cf Fodor, 1994).

The theory described here is also different from other theories of affect, which in some cases consider the issue of consciousness. James (1884) and Lange (1885/1922) held that emotional feelings arise when feedback from the periphery (about for example heart rate) reach the brain, but had no theory of why some stimuli and not others produced the peripheral changes, and thus of why some but not other events produce emotion. Moreover, the evidence that feedback from peripheral autonomic and proprioceptive systems is essential for emotions is very weak; for example, blocking peripheral feedback does not eliminate emotions, and producing peripheral (e.g., autonomic) changes does not elicit emotion (Reisenzein, 1983; Rolls, 1999a, 2005a; Schachter & Singer, 1962).

Damasio's theory of emotion (1994, 2003) is similar to the James-Lange theory (and is therefore subject to some of the same objections), but holds that the peripheral feedback is used in decision making rather than in consciousness. He does not formally define emotions, but holds that body maps and representations are the basis of emotions. When considering consciousness, he assumes that all consciousness is self-consciousness (Damasio, 2003, p. 184) and that the foundational images in the stream of the mind are images of some kind of body event, whether the event happens in the depth of the body or in some specialized sensory device near its periphery (Damasio, 2003, p. 197). His theory does not appear to be a fully testable theory, in that he suspects that "the ultimate quality of feelings, a part of why feelings feel the way they feel, is conferred by the neural medium" (Damasio 2003, p. 131). Thus, presumably if processes he discusses (Damasio, 1994, 2003) were implemented in a computer, then the computer would not have all the same properties with respect to consciousness as the real brain. In this sense he appears to be arguing for a non-functionalist position and for something crucial about consciousness being related to the particular biological machinery from which the system is made. It is in this respect that the theory seems somewhat intangible.

LeDoux's (1996) approach to emotion is largely (to quote him) one of automaticity, with emphasis on brain mechanisms involved in the rapid, subcortical mechanisms involved in fear. LeDoux, in line with Johnson-Laird (1988) and Baars (1988), emphasises the role of working memory in consciousness, where he views working memory as a limited-capacity serial processor that creates and manipulates symbolic representations (p. 280). He thus holds that much emotional processing is unconscious and that when it becomes conscious it is because emotional information is entered into a working memory system. However, LeDoux (1996) concedes that consciousness, especially its phenomenal or subjective nature, is not completely explained by the computational processes that underlie working memory (p. 281; see Rolls, 2007b).

Panksepp's (1998) approach to emotion has its origins in neuroethological investigations of brainstem systems that when activated lead to behaviours like fixed action patterns, including escape, flight, and fear behaviour. His views about consciousness include the postulate that feelings may emerge when endogenous sensory and emotional systems within the brain that receive direct inputs from the outside world, as well as the neurodynamics of the SELF (a Simple Ego-type Life Form), begin to reverberate with each other's changing neuronal firing rhythms (Panksepp, 1998, p. 309).

Notes

1. Second order thoughts are thoughts about thoughts. Higher order thoughts refer to second order, third order etc. thoughts about thoughts...

2. This raises the issue of the causal relation between mental events and neurophysiological events, part of the mind-body problem. My view is that the relation between mental events and neurophysiological events is similar (apart from the problem of consciousness) to the relation between the program running in a computer and the hardware on the computer. In a sense, the program causes the logic gates to move to the next state. This move causes the program to move to its next state. Effectively, we are looking at different levels of what is overall the operation of a *system*, and causality can usefully be understood as operating both within levels (causing one step of the program to move to the next), as well as between levels (e.g., software to hardware and vice versa). This is the solution I propose to this aspect of the mind-body (or mind-brain) problem.

References

Aggelopoulos, N. C., Franco, L., & Rolls, E. T. (2005). Object perception in natural scenes: Encoding by inferior temporal cortex simultaneously recorded neurons. *Journal of Neurophysiology*, 93, 1342–1357,

Alexander, R. D. (1975). The search for a general theory of behavior. *Behavioral Sciences*, 20, 77–100.

Alexander, R. D. (1979). *Darwinism and human affairs*. Seattle: University of Washington Press.

Allport, A. (1988). What concept of consciousness? In A. J. Marcel & E. Bisiach (Eds.), *Consciousness in contemporary science* (pp. 159–182). Oxford: Oxford University Press.

Armstrong, D. M., & Malcolm, N. (1984). *Consciousness and causality*. Oxford: Blackwell.

Baars, B. J. (1988). *A cognitive theory of consciousness*. New York: Cambridge University Press.

Barlow, H. B. (1997). Single neurons, communal goals, and consciousness. In M. Ito, Y. Miyashita, & E. T. Rolls (Eds.), *Cognition, computation, and consciousness* (pp. 121–136). Oxford: Oxford University Press.

Block, N. (1995). On a confusion about a function of consciousness. *Behavioral and Brain Sciences*, 18, 227–247.

Booth, D. A. (1985). Food-conditioned eating preferences and aversions with interoceptive elements: Learned appetites and satieties. *Annals of the New York Academy of Sciences*, 443, 22–37.

Carruthers, P. (1996). *Language, thought and consciousness*. Cambridge: Cambridge University Press.

Carruthers, P. (2000). *Phenomenal consciousness*. Cambridge: Cambridge University Press.

Chalmers, D. J. (1996). *The conscious mind*. Oxford: Oxford University Press.

Cheney, D. L., & Seyfarth, R. M. (1990). *How monkeys see the world*. Chicago: University of Chicago Press.

Crick, F. H. C., & Koch, C. (1990). Towards a neurobiological theory of consciousness. *Seminars in the Neurosciences*, 2, 263–275.

Damasio, A. R. (1994). *Decartes' error*. New York: Putnam.

Damasio, A. R. (2003). *Looking for Spinoza*. London: Heinemann.

Dawkins, M. S. (1993). *Through our eyes only? The search for animal consciousness*. Oxford: Freeman.

Dawkins, R. (1986). *The blind watchmaker*. Harlow: Longman.

Dennett, D. C. (1991). *Consciousness explained*. London: Penguin.

Ekman, P. (1982). *Emotion in the human face* (2nd ed.). Cambridge: Cambridge University Press.

Ekman, P. (1993). Facial expression and emotion. *American Psychologist*, 48, 384–392.

Fodor, J. A. (1994). *The elm and the expert: Mentalese and its semantics.* Cambridge, MA: MIT Press.

Fridlund, A. J. (1994). *Human facial expression: An evolutionary view.* San Diego: Academic Press.

Frijda, N. H. (1986). *The emotions.* Cambridge: Cambridge University Press.

Gazzaniga, M. S. (1988). Brain modularity: Towards a philosophy of conscious experience. In A. J. Marcel & E. Bisiach (Eds.), *Consciousness in contemporary science* (pp. 218–238). Oxford: Oxford University Press.

Gazzaniga, M. S. (1995). Consciousness and the cerebral hemispheres. In M. S. Gazzaniga (Ed.), *The cognitive neurosciences* (pp. 1392–1400). Cambridge, MA: MIT Press.

Gazzaniga, M. S., & LeDoux, J. (1978). *The integrated mind.* New York: Plenum.

Gennaro, R. J. (Ed.) (2004). *Higher order theories of consciousness.* Amsterdam: Benjamins.

Goldman-Rakic, P. S. (1996). The prefrontal landscape: Implications of functional architecture for understanding human mentation and the central executive. *Philosophical Transactions of the Royal Society B*, 351, 1445–1453.

Gray, J. A. (1975). *Elements of a two-process theory of learning.* London: Academic Press.

Gray, J. A. (1987). *The psychology of fear and stress* (2nd ed.). Cambridge: Cambridge University Press.

Griffin, D. R. (1992). *Animal minds.* Chicago: University of Chicago Press.

Hornak, J., Bramham, J., Rolls, E. T., Morris, R. G., O'Doherty, J., Bullock, P. R., et al. (2003). Changes in emotion after circumscribed surgical lesions of the orbitofrontal and cingulate cortices. *Brain*, 126, 1691–1712.

Hornak, J., O'Doherty, J., Bramham, J., Rolls, E. T., Morris, R. G., Bullock, P. R., et al. (2004). Reward-related reversal learning after surgical excisions in orbitofrontal and dorsolateral prefrontal cortex in humans. *Journal of Cognitive Neuroscience*, 16, 463–478.

Humphrey, N. K. (1980). Nature's psychologists. In B. D. Josephson & V. S. Ramachandran (Eds.), *Consciousness and the physical world* (pp. 57–80). Oxford: Pergamon.

Humphrey, N. K. (1986). *The inner eye.* London: Faber.

Izard, C. E. (1991). *The psychology of emotions.* New York: Plenum.

James, W. (1884). What is an emotion? *Mind*, 9, 188–205.

Johnson-Laird, P. N. (1988). *The computer and the mind: An introduction to cognitive science.* Cambridge, MA: Harvard University Press.

Kadohisa, M., Rolls, E. T., & Verhagen, J. V. (2005). Neuronal representations of stimuli in the mouth: the primate insular taste cortex, orbitofrontal cortex, and amygdala. *Chemical Senses*, 30, 401–419.

Krebs, J. R., & Kacelnik, A. (1991). Decision making. In J. R. Krebs & N. B. Davies (Eds.), *Behavioural ecology* (3rd ed., pp. 105–136). Oxford: Blackwell.

Lange, C. (1922). The emotions. In E. Dunlap (Ed.), *The emotions.* Baltimore: Williams & Wilkins. (Original work published 1885)

Lazarus, R. S. (1991). *Emotion and adaptation.* New York: Oxford University Press.

Leak, G. K., & Christopher, S. B. (1982). Freudian psychoanalysis and sociobiology: A synthesis. *American Psychologist*, 37, 313–322.

LeDoux, J. (1996). *The emotional brain.* New York: Simon and Shuster.

Mackintosh, N. J. (1983). *Conditioning and associative learning.* Oxford: Oxford University Press.

McLeod, P., Plunkett, K., & Rolls, E. T. (1998). *Introduction to connectionist modelling of cognitive processes.* Oxford: Oxford University Press.

Millenson, J. R. (1967). *Principles of behavioral analysis.* New York: MacMillan.

Nesse, R. M., & Lloyd, A. T. (1992). The evolution of psychodynamic mechanisms. In J. H Barkow, L. Cosmides, & J. Tooby (Eds.), *The adapted mind* (pp. 601–624). New York: Oxford University Press.

Oatley, K., & Jenkins, J. M. (1996). *Understanding emotions.* Oxford: Blackwell.

Panksepp, J. (1998). *Affective neuroscience: The foundations of human and animal emotions.* New York: Oxford University Press.

Petrides, M. (1996). Specialized systems for the processing of mnemonic information within the primate frontal cortex. *Philosophical Transactions of the Royal Society B*, 351, 1455–1462.

Pinker, S., & Bloom, P. (1992). Natural language and natural selection. In J. H. Barkow, L. Cosmides, & J. Tooby (Eds.), *The adapted mind* (pp. 451–493). New York: Oxford University Press.

Plata-Salaman, C. R., Smith-Swintosky, V. L., & Scott, T. R. (1996). Gustatory neural coding in the monkey cortex: Mixtures. *Journal of Neurophysiology, 75*, 2369–2379.

Reisenzein, R. (1983). The Schachter theory of emotion: Two decades later. *Psychology Bulletin, 94*, 239–264.

Rolls, B. J., & Rolls, E. T. (1982). *Thirst.* Cambridge: Cambridge University Press.

Rolls, E. T. (1986a). Neural systems involved in emotion in primates. In R. Plutchik & H. Kellerman (Eds.), *Emotion: Theory, research, and experience: Vol. 3. Biological foundations of emotion* (pp. 125–143). New York: Academic Press.

Rolls, E. T. (1986b). A theory of emotion, and its application to understanding the neural basis of emotion. In Y. Oomura (Ed.), *Emotions. neural and chemical control* (pp. 325–344). Tokyo: Japan Scientific Societies Press.

Rolls, E. T. (1990). A theory of emotion, and its application to understanding the neural basis of emotion. *Cognition and Emotion, 4*, 161–190.

Rolls, E. T. (1994). Neurophysiology and cognitive functions of the striatum. *Revue Neurologique, 150*, 648–660.

Rolls, E. T. (1995a). Central taste anatomy and neurophysiology. In R. L. Doty (Ed.), *Handbook of olfaction and gustation* (pp. 549–573). New York: Dekker.

Rolls, E. T. (1995b). A theory of emotion and consciousness, and its application to understanding the neural basis of emotion. In M. S. Gazzaniga (Ed.), *The cognitive neurosciences* (pp. 1091–1106). Cambridge, MA: MIT Press.

Rolls, E. T. (1996a). A theory of hippocampal function in memory. *Hippocampus, 6*, 601–620.

Rolls, E. T. (1996b). The orbitofrontal cortex. *Philosophical Transactions of the Royal Society B, 351*, 1433–1444.

Rolls, E. T. (1997). Taste and olfactory processing in the brain. *Critical Reviews in Neurobiology, 11*, 263–287.

Rolls, E. T. (1999a). *The brain and emotion.* Oxford: Oxford University Press.

Rolls, E. T. (1999b). The functions of the orbitofrontal cortex. *Neurocase, 5*, 301–312.

Rolls, E. T. (2000a). Précis of *The Brain and Emotion. Behavioral and Brain Sciences, 23*, 177–233.

Rolls, E. T. (2000b). The orbitofrontal cortex and reward. *Cerebral Cortex, 10*, 284–294.

Rolls, E. T. (2000c). Neurophysiology and functions of the primate amygdala, and the neural basis of emotion. In J. P. Aggleton (Ed.), *The amygdala: A functional analysis* (2nd ed., pp. 447–478). Oxford: Oxford University Press.

Rolls, E. T. (2000d). Functions of the primate temporal lobe cortical visual areas in invariant visual object and face recognition. *Neuron, 27*, 205–218.

Rolls, E. T. (2000e). Hippocampo-cortical and cortico-cortical backprojections. *Hippocampus, 10*, 380–388.

Rolls, E. T. (2002). The functions of the orbitofrontal cortex. In D. T. Stuss & R. T. Knight (Eds.) *Principles of frontal lobe function* (pp. 354–375). New York: Oxford University Press.

Rolls, E. T. (2003). Consciousness absent and present: A neurophysiological exploration. *Progress in Brain Research, 144*, 95–106.

Rolls, E. T. (2004a). The functions of the orbitofrontal cortex. *Brain and Cognition, 55*, 11–29.

Rolls, E. T. (2004b). A higher order syntactic thought (HOST) theory of consciousness. In R. J. Gennaro (Ed.), *Higher order theories of consciousness* (pp. 137–172). Amsterdam: John Benjamins.

Rolls, E. T. (2005a). *Emotion explained.* Oxford: Oxford University Press.

Rolls, E. T. (2005b). Consciousness absent and present: A neurophysiological exploration of masking. In H. Ogmen & B. G. Breitmeyer (Eds.), *The first half second: The microgenesis and temporal dynamics of unconscious and conscious visual processes* (pp 89–108). Cambridge, MA: MIT Press.

Rolls, E. T. (2007a). *Memory, attention, and decision-making.* Oxford: Oxford University press.

Rolls, E. T. (2007b). Emotion, higher-order syntactic thoughts, and consciousness. In M. Davies & L. Weiskrantz (Eds.), *Frontiers of consciousness.* Oxford: Oxford University Press.

Rolls, E. T., & Deco, G. (2002). *Computational neuroscience of vision.* Oxford: Oxford University Press.

Rolls, E. T., Hornak, J., Wade, D., & McGrath, J. (1994). Emotion-related learning in patients with social and emotional changes associated with frontal lobe damage. *Journal of Neurology, Neurosurgery and Psychiatry, 57*, 1518–1524.

Rolls, E. T., & Johnstone, S. (1992). Neurophysiological analysis of striatal function. In G. Vallar,

S. F. Cappa, & C. Wallesch (Eds.), *Neuropsychological disorders associated with subcortical lesions* (pp. 61–97). Oxford: Oxford University Press.

Rolls, E. T., & Scott, T. R. (2003). Central taste anatomy and neurophysiology. In R. L. Doty (Ed.), *Handbook of olfaction and gustation* (2nd ed., pp. 679–705). New York: Dekker.

Rolls, E. T., & Stringer, S. M. (2001). A model of the interaction between mood and memory. *Network: Computation in Neural Systems, 12,* 89–109.

Rolls, E. T., & Tovee, M. J. (1994). Processing speed in the cerebral cortex and the neurophysiology of visual masking. *Proceedings of the Royal Society of London B, 257,* 9–15.

Rolls, E. T., Tovee, M. J., & Panzeri, S. (1999). The neurophysiology of backward visual masking: Information analysis. *Journal of Cognitive Neuroscience, 11,* 335–346.

Rolls, E. T., Tovee, M. J., Purcell, D. G., Stewart, A. L., & Azzopardi, P. (1994). The responses of neurons in the temporal cortex of primates, and face identification and detection. *Experimental Brain Research, 101,* 474–484.

Rolls, E. T., & Treves, A. (1998). *Neural networks and brain function.* Oxford: Oxford University Press.

Rosenthal, D. M. (1990). *A theory of consciousness.* ZIF Report No. 40. Bielefeld: Germany: Zentrum fur Interdisziplinaire Forschung.

Rosenthal, D. M. (1986). Two concepts of consciousness. *Philosophical Studies, 49,* 329–359.

Rosenthal, D. M. (1993). Thinking that one thinks. In M. Davies & G. W. Humphreys (Eds.), *Consciousness* (pp. 197–223). Oxford: Blackwell.

Rosenthal, D. M. (2004). Varieties of higher order theory. In R. J. Gennaro (Ed.), *Higher order theories of consciousness* (pp. 17–44). Amsterdam: John Benjamins.

Rosenthal, D. M. (2005) *Consciousness and mind.* Oxford: Oxford University Press.

Rumelhart, D. E., Hinton, G. E., & Williams, R. J. (1986). Learning internal representations by error backpropagation. In D. E. Rumelhart & J. L. McClelland, et al. (Eds.), *Parallel distributed processing: Explorations in the microstructure of cognition,* Vol 1. Cambridge, MA: MIT Press.

Schacter, S., & Singer, J. E. (1962). Cognitive, social and physiological determinants of emotional state. *Psychological Review, 69,* 379–99

Shallice, T., & Burgess, P. (1996). The domain of supervisory processes and temporal organization of behaviour. *Philosophical Transactions of the Royal Society of London B, 351,* 1405–1411.

Smith-Swintosky, V. L., Plata-Salaman, C. R., & Scott, T. R. (1991). Gustatory neural coding in the monkey cortex: Stimulus quality. *Journal of Neurophysiology, 66,* 1156–1165.

Squire, L. R. (1992). Memory and the hippocampus: A synthesis from findings with rats, monkeys and humans. *Psychological Review, 99,* 195–231.

Strongman, K. T. (1996). *The psychology of emotion* (4th ed.). Chichester: Wiley.

Tinbergen, N. (1951). *The study of instinct.* Oxford: Clarendon Press.

Tovee, M. J., & Rolls, E. T. (1992). Oscillatory activity is not evident in the primate temporal visual cortex with static stimuli. *Neuroreport, 3,* 369–372.

Tovee, M. J., & Rolls, E. T. (1995). Information encoding in short firing rate epochs by single neurons in the primate temporal visual cortex. *Visual Cognition, 2,* 35–58.

Tovee, M. J., Rolls, E. T., Treves, A., & Bellis, R. P. (1993). Information encoding and the responses of single neurons in the primate temporal visual cortex. *Journal of Neurophysiology, 70,* 640–654.

Treves, A., & Rolls, E. T. (1994). A computational analysis of the role of the hippocampus in memory. *Hippocampus, 4,* 374–391.

Trivers, R. L. (1976). Foreword. In R. Dawkins (Ed.), *The selfish gene.* Oxford: Oxford University Press.

Trivers, R. L. (1985). *Social evolution.* California: Benjamin/Cummings.

von der Malsburg, C. (1990). A neural architecture for the representation of scenes. In J. L. McGaugh, N. M. Weinberger, & G. Lynch (Eds.), *Brain organization and memory: Cells, systems and circuits* (pp. 356–372). New York: Oxford University Press.

Weiskrantz, L. (1968). Emotion. In L. Weiskrantz (Ed.), *Analysis of behavioural change* (pp. 50–90). London: Harper and Row.

Yaxley, S., Rolls, E. T., & Sienkiewicz, Z. J. (1990). Gustatory responses of single neurons in the insula of the macaque monkey. *Journal of Neurophysiology, 63,* 689–700.

D. Social Neuroscience of Consciousness

CHAPTER 30

Consciousness: Situated and Social

Ralph Adolphs

Abstract

Conscious experience is usually presumed to depend in a direct way only on events in the brain. For instance, thought experiments in which events in the brain are held constant, but events outside the brain are changed, are assumed to leave the nature of the conscious experience also unchanged. Here I argue to the contrary that conscious experience depends in a direct way on a wider set of events, including events outside the brain and in the past. Nonetheless, not all events matter equally. For events outside the brain, social relations appear especially important. A complex social environment has shaped much of the architecture of the brain and can be partially internalized by the brain via simulation. This view suggests that understanding conscious experience requires understanding the phylogenetic, ontogenetic, and current social relations in which an individual brain is embedded.

Introduction: The Problem of Conscious Experience

No other topic has stirred so much debate as has the question of conscious experience. Approaches have ranged from denying that we are conscious at all to claiming that we already know how we are conscious. One reason for the diversity of approaches is that different thinkers take up fairly different questions, a situation resulting at least in part because there is no single problem of consciousness, but rather quite a heterogeneous collection of problems. To simplify the discussion in this chapter, I will discuss consciousness in the restricted sense of conscious sensory experience, such as the experiences of seeing a certain color, hearing a certain sound, smelling a rose, and the various other examples usually cited by those who want to make a convincing case for so-called qualia. Furthermore, I restrict the aspect of conscious experience under scrutiny to what has been the focus in some recent philosophical discussions. Many readers are familiar with the views of the philosopher Thomas Nagel, who has defended the view that our difficulty in providing a scientific explanation of conscious experience arises from an essential feature of conscious experience: its subjectivity (Nagel, 1974, 1993). Of course, there are other reasons why explaining conscious experience is not easy, but subjectivity looms as the paramount obstacle, because we cannot at present even conceive of how this feature could be made commensurate with our scientific, objective understanding of the world.

By subjectivity, Nagel means that feature of conscious experience that generates a point of view on the world by the owner of the experience. In Nagel's words, there is "something it is like to be" an organism undergoing a conscious experience. This ontological notion of subjectivity needs to be distinguished from epistemic subjectivity (the way the word is used colloquially) – that is, the meaning that something is a matter of opinion. Ontological subjectivity, the meaning of the term that concerns us here, is a particular mode of existence of a phenomenon (existence as seen "from the inside"). It is important also to acknowledge that an experience is rendered phenomenal in virtue of a collection of properties, the instantiation of more than one of which is necessary for actually having a conscious experience. Thus, phenomenality consists of quite a few different properties or features, and it is possible to distinguish conceptually among these (cf. Metzinger, 2003). For our purposes it is important to note that subjectivity, in the sense in which Nagel is using the term and in which I intend to use it here, is separate from ownership or from self-consciousness. It may well be that subjectivity itself, upon further analysis, fragments into a collection of disparate properties.

For present purposes it suffices to use our pretheoretical concept that there is something it is like for a conscious organism in the act of becoming aware of a sensory object, such as opening one's eyes and seeing a red sunset; something it is like from the organism's own point of view at the time that the sunset is seen by the organism. Although it is important to distinguish this meaning of subjectivity from its more common everyday usage, it is also critical not to attach to it properties that would prevent any possibility of an epistemologically objective account of the phenomenon and that would bar reductive explanation. It is easy to jump from the realization that conscious experience is subjective in Nagel's sense to the conclusion that therefore it is not material. The "hard problem" of consciousness arises because what it is like to have a conscious experience seems so clearly contingent on all possible objective accounts of the physical or functional machinery on which the conscious experience supervenes. Let us consider one such apparent example.

David Chalmers has championed thought experiments about the conceivability of "zombies." These are conceivably possible (logically possible, rather than nomologically possible) creatures identical to a human in all physical and functional respects, minus the conscious experience (Chalmers, 1997). All objective accounts of consciousness we have at present, all accounts that describe consciousness from "the outside" as it were, fail to provide an understanding of how consciousness fits into the rest of the world as a natural feature of its constituents. They fail to do so precisely because in every case we can imagine a system meeting all the criteria of the objective theory, yet not be conscious. The converse is also conceivable: that the conscious experience remains the same while its physical substrate is very different (or even non-existent, as in the conceivability of disembodied spirits).

It is instructive to compare what we might want to say about conscious experience to what we would say about how mental states refer to events in the world. One much-defended answer about propositional attitudes, such as beliefs, is to say that they indeed are *not* specified or identified by pointing to events occurring in the brain, but rather by pointing to events outside of the brain (in fact, outside of the person and the current physical events). The philosopher

Hilary Putnam (1979) has defended this view on the basis of his famous "twin earth" examples, and a similar thought experiment has been provided by the late Donald Davidson with the invention of "swampman"; let us consider the latter (Davidson, 1987).

Swampman is a molecular duplicate of Davidson that was created by a spontaneous assembly of the requisite atoms when lightning struck a swamp. If physical determinism is true, Swampman does and says exactly the things that Davidson would do and say; their behavior is indistinguishable. But Davidson tells us that his swamp duplicate could nonetheless not have any of the beliefs that he, the real Davidson, has, because the swamp being does not share any of Davidson's history that is necessary for having such beliefs. That is, although Swampman would, like Davidson, say that it believes it was born on such and such a date, is married to such and such a person, etc., all of these beliefs could not refer to the said events, because they depend on the correct historical embeddedness, which Swampman lacks and Davidson has. So, Swampman's physical constituency would cause him to utter the words, "I remember playing in the sand when I was a little boy," a statement he believes to be true and one that would be true if Davidson uttered it (let us suppose). But in Swampman's case it could not possibly refer to the stated event: Swampman didn't play in the sand as a little boy; instead, he was spontaneously created only a few minutes ago in the swamp (and it would certainly sound bizarre to suppose that Swampman's utterance somehow refers to Davidson's early life). The same goes for all the other things that Swampman might honestly say about his history preceding his actual existence. The way in which mental events refer to states of affairs in the world depends not just on how we are constituted, on what goes on in our brains and bodies; it matters also how we are in fact situated with respect to the environment and our history of interaction within it.

The opposite conclusion can now be reached in the case of David Chalmers turning himself into a zombie, the first example I mentioned above. If Chalmers by some unexplained and mysterious accident were to suddenly lose all ability to have conscious experiences, but nonetheless remained physically identical, his behavior would, we suppose, remain unchanged and so would his beliefs. (We could further suppose that this would be so even if his physical constituency changed but his functional architecture remained invariant, but for present purposes this is irrelevant.) What he tells us and believes that was true before is still true in the absence of the conscious experience. He would, like Swampman, be physically indistinguishable from his earlier incarnation, and he would say all the things the prior, conscious person would say. But, unlike Swampman, he would still be right about the beliefs he avows (perhaps with one exception: he might still, and now incorrectly, believe that he is conscious).

These examples seem to show that the representational properties of brain events can come apart despite invariance in their physical composition. Moreover, they can come apart in directions opposite to the way in which conscious experience might come apart: Swampman arguably still has conscious experiences indistinguishable from those Davidson would have, despite the vacuous representations of his past; the zombie on the other hand has (by stipulation) no conscious experiences although he still has the same representational powers.

It is not hard (I think) to see how these examples work in the case of intentional states like beliefs, because it is not hard to acknowledge that beliefs might not be intrinsic states. Beliefs, like desires, wants, and other such attitudes, are, as the name "attitude" already tells us, relational states: They depend on the historical relations between the believer and events in the world. But what about conscious experiences? Are they, like beliefs, relational states specified in part by the historical context?

The argument sounds implausible for conscious experiences. Quite the opposite: We seem to be able to imagine that Swampman has conscious experiences indistinguishable from Davidson's and that zombie

Chalmers has none although he believes he does. The reason we give these answers is that our concept of conscious experience ties it to intrinsic properties of the person (and specifically the brain, at least in modern day), rather than to relational properties as in the case of beliefs. This ability of ours to imagine the above scenarios, of course, in no way shows that they are actually possible. What it shows is that we can imagine them, that they are conceivable, and that therefore our current concept of conscious experience fails to be explained by our current concepts of the objective criteria that determine it. And this is where the problem lies: If conscious experiences were like beliefs, we could explain them in virtue of the relations between organisms and their interactions with the environment. Given that we are unwilling to take this step with conscious experiences, that we insist on an intrinsic account, we run into problems. On the one hand, we want to insist that conscious experience depends only on its proximal neural substrate, only on events in the brain, and hence both Swampman and brains in vats have conscious experiences identical to those of normal humans. On the other hand, the possibility of zombies seems to show that conscious experience is contingent on all physical events occurring inside the person who has the experience, and hence the two cannot be identified with one another. We are faced with a dilemma: Consciousness seems completely unaccounted for by any of the intrinsic physical facts about a person despite our firm belief that it must arise from or be identical with such physical facts. What to do? One might postulate by fiat conscious experience as a brute addition to our objective understanding of the world. But this, of course, does not count as an explanation – it does not make transparent why conscious experience should accompany certain events that can also be described physically or functionally.

I have dwelled on these difficulties for two reasons: I think that (1) an externalist view of mental content may provide clues toward a similar treatment also of conscious experience and (2) their difficulty (and their persuasiveness) are a good warning signal. These difficulties tell us that we need to put on hold many of the preconceptions that we may have about explanations of conscious experience. The problem cannot be solved simply by thinking about it, because the concepts we would currently employ in its analysis are misguided.

What kinds of concepts would we need? To make the relationship between objective physical events and the subjectivity of conscious experience transparent, Nagel tells us in a more recent paper that we would need to see how conscious experience is a necessary accompaniment of the objective events, rather than a contingent one (Nagel, 2001). We would need to be able to understand not just that, but why, certain physical events or information-processing events also have a subjective nature to them. This would mean that the identification of conscious experience with such physical or functional events would be a necessary truth, but one that we could only appreciate a posteriori. That is, once we would have the conceptual apparatus to see how conscious experience is realized physically or functionally, we would see the relationship to be necessary, not contingent. But we do not see this now, and it cannot be seen using the concepts we have currently available – hence it is not an a priori truth, but only one we could see to be true if we change the way in which are able to think about the problem.

Does the Mind Supervene on the Brain Alone?

Situated Cognition

The preceding section served to sharpen the kind of difficulty with which we are dealing. The problem stems in large part from what we can currently conceive or not. In this chapter, I work my way toward proposing an account of conscious experience that, a priori, may seem rather counter-intuitive, perhaps even inconceivable. The task, therefore, is to make it seem, a posteriori, conceivable that what I write might be right. By way of introducing the proposal, let us review what has been written recently, not specifically regarding conscious experience, but regarding the mind and cognition in general.

Picking up some of the strands we discussed in the preceding section, a major issue is whether we should think of mental events as intrinsic to the brain or as relations between brains and their environment. Recent proposals have argued that we should think of them as relational. These proposals have been motivated by a variety of findings that demonstrate that, at least at the level of information processing, much of such information processing doesn't happen inside the skulls of people alone, but draws on information that is distributed throughout the environment with which the person interacts. Let's consider some examples.

You are able, presumably, to calculate the square of a five-digit number. The way in which you do so (presumably) draws (for example) on pencil and paper: You manipulate objects in your environment to take up some of the computational load (specifically, working memory load, in this example) with which your brain in isolation is unable to deal. So calculating the square of a five-digit number involves physical events outside of your brain and indeed outside of your body. Yet it is your brain that is guiding these external computations. Your brain is able to structure events occurring in the body and environment in such a way as to use them in information processing. The cognitive scientist Andy Clark has championed a comprehensive account of how the relational interactions between a brain, a body, and the external environment are all necessary for cognition (Clark, 1997). And one can go further: Not only are all these relational interactions necessary for cognition but they are also necessary for conscious experience. You as a subject of conscious experience are not identical with your brain, but rather arise from the relational interactions of that brain with its environment (Clark, 1995).

Similar comments apply to cases where we do not actively manipulate the external environment, such as when you are able to glean lots of information about a complex visual scene. For instance, you can identify targets in it, count objects, and report on innumerable other features in an image. But you can't do it by first inspecting the visual scene and then simply closing your eyes and reading off all the information from an internal representation of the scene. The information is not in your brain; it is in the environment to be obtained by investigation (in this example, by moving your eyes and your visual attention to particular locations in the image about which you want to obtain information). A popular demonstration of this fact comes from the phenomenon of "change blindness." People often fail to notice rather large changes in a visual scene, despite the fact that they are looking right at those changes and nothing is preventing them from noticing the changes (Rensink, O'Regan, & Clark, 1997).

If we reflect carefully on our conscious visual experience, we can realize that it arises rather directly from how we probe the external world, rather than from what is happening in our brains alone. The visual world appears very rich and full of information – but much of that information is not in our head; it is available for inspection in the world. The sense we have of a rich visual experience is not as of an image in our mind that offers this richness, but rather as of the world out there that provides it if we choose to look here and there (Noe, 2004; O'Regan & Noe, 2001). And this is all as it should be; if we didn't rely on the external world as a rich source of information, our brains would be overwhelmed. The idea then is that we don't have detailed, rich, internal representations of the features of the world, but rather that our representations consist (at least in good part) of prescriptions of how to obtain such information by exploring our environment.

This is not to say that we don't represent anything in our brains. It is just to say that what we represent is not the sole source of information of which we can become aware and that the format of the representation is often sensorimotor in nature, rather than just sensory. The motor aspect emphasizes the idea that we are situated (Suchman, 1987), embedded in our environments: Our relationship with the environment is bidirectional – it affects us and we affect it, and the way in which we affect it in turn influences the way in which it affects us. So, clever manipulation of the way in which we change our bodies and the environment will permit us to use physical events outside our brains to do information processing for us.

There is still a weak version of this view, according to which the environment influences the mind only insofar as it influences the brain. That is, events external to us can certainly contribute to cognition, but they do so only through the proximal substrate of cognition, namely the brain. However, there is also a stronger version of the view, according to which the entire, coupled system of brain and environment is the proximal substrate of cognition. The "active externalism" proposed by Clark and Chalmers (1998), suggests this second view. If this is right, then it would appear that cognition does not supervene solely on neural events, but depends on events in our bodies, sense organs, and the environment with which they interact as well.

Extended Conscious Experience?

You have probably guessed where this discussion is going. If cognitive abilities depend on resources external to our brains, might conscious experiences have a similar dependency? Might our minds literally extend outside of our brains and bodies, not just with respect to their information-processing capacities, but with respect to conscious experience?

Of course, the above discussion already indicates that this is so in a certain sense, but perhaps only an indirect sense. Situated cognition, the view espoused in some of the writings quoted earlier (Clark 1997; O'Regan & Noe, 2001), has a long history of acknowledging that sensation requires action onto the environment and that sensation and action are not temporally and functionally separate phenomena, but concurrent aspects of how an organism interacts with its world. The philosopher John Dewey

provided some of the first examples of this idea:

> Upon analysis, we find that we begin not with a sensory stimulus, but with a sensori-motor coördination, the optical-ocular, and that in a certain sense it is the movement which is primary, and the sensation which is secondary, the movement of body, head and eye muscles determining the quality of what is experienced. In other words, the real beginning is with the act of seeing; it is looking, and not a sensation of light. The sensory quale gives the value of the act, just as the movement furnishes its mechanism and control, but both sensation and movement lie inside, not outside the act (Dewey, 1896).

The idea that the mind is embodied and situated in the world has been developed in considerable detail recently (Varela, Thompson, & Rosch, 1991) and has been combined with findings in cognitive neuroscience. In particular, the idea is that complex dynamical patterns of brain activity arise from the way in which the brain and body interact with the external environment and that it is such dynamical brain patterns that generate conscious experience (Thompson & Varela, 2001).

One can agree with all these points as providing a useful analysis of how the contents of our conscious experience depend on relational facts about brains, bodies, and the rest of the world, and yet one can still adhere to the belief that it is in fact only the events happening in the brain that directly determine conscious experience. That is, one can agree that interaction with the world shapes the inputs the brain receives, but that if we were to strip away the world and keep the events in the brain unchanged, we would keep the conscious experience unchanged. That, after all, is the idea that conscious experience supervenes solely on the brain, even though what happens in the brain will of course be influenced by events outside it (under normal circumstances).

We have noted that at least some are willing to view beliefs as literally and directly supervenient on external and historical events, as we saw in the case of

Swampman earlier. And as reviewed above, many are willing to view cognition and information processing that contribute to our conscious experience as similarly externalized. But it sounds very odd indeed to suppose that conscious experience itself should depend on events external to the brain, although some proposals have indeed been made along exactly those lines (e.g., Rowlands, 2003).

What I propose is to bite the bullet and literally consider conscious experience as supervening on events occurring outside the brain. That is, brains in vats and perhaps Swampman also could not in fact be conscious in the way that we imagine them to be. They lack some of the necessary environmental and historical relations. Note that this is a radical claim – we are not claiming merely that such relations can affect conscious experience via their effects on events in the brain, but that they are constitutive of conscious experience. Of course, the idea seems nonsensical at first, a priori. It seems an impossibility because we are wedded to the view that the subjectivity of conscious experience is an intrinsic property of the brain. But we saw earlier that this view faces serious problems.

Under the new proposal, conscious awareness is best thought of as arising not from events in the brain, but rather from the act of becoming conscious of an external event or object in the environment through our brain's and body's interaction with it. If we thus attach phenomenal properties to the act of apprehending that of which we become consciously aware, we can see that conscious awareness is situated in the same way in which cognition in general was proposed to be situated in our earlier discussion. Like situated cognition, the subjectivity of conscious awareness depends not only on the subject's brain but also on the relation that the subject has to the object of conscious awareness in the environment and indeed to his or her history of interaction with objects in the environment.

Several perspectives follow naturally from this idea. In retrospect, thinking of subjectivity as an intrinsic property of events

in the brain now seems misguided, because their very subjectivity presupposes a distinction between subject and object; that is, a relation. What it is like to have a conscious experience of a red sunset depends not only on the subject undergoing the experience but also on the red sunset toward which the subject's point of view can be directed. In this respect, the subjectivity of conscious experience is no different from the directedness of intentional states like beliefs or from the situatedness of the mind's information processing. None of these supervenes solely on events intrinsic to the brain, but literally arises from the brain's relational interaction with its environment. The extended system as a whole – brain, body, and environment and their interactions (now as well as historically) – is what makes the subject consciously aware of objects and events. The subvenience base of conscious experience has thus been radically broadened: Even if everything in the brain is held constant, a change in the web of relations that are linked to the brain would change the conscious experience. Despite his claims to the contrary, Swampman would not have the conscious experiences that he avows, for the same reason that he does not have the beliefs he avows.

Social Cognition

The Social Brain Hypothesis

We have covered a lot of ground so far, mostly philosophical, and of necessity I've sketched only the roughest kind of picture. The question that a scientist might now like to ask is, How are we to think of this environment with which a subject interacts and that is doing so much work according to the arguments above? At a minimum, some partitions of the environment must be more important to conscious experience than others. If there is an explosion on alpha centauri, it cannot be that my conscious experience suddenly undergoes a large change. Presumably, some set of the relations between the brain and the rest of the world matter more than others to conscious experience. An initial visual metaphor would be that subjectivity is centered in the head, as it were, but leaks out into the body and past the bounds of the body, becoming fainter the more distally that events are located. Of course, it is not spatial location as such that matters here, but the strength of the relational interaction within the web of relations that involves the brain: Breaking some of these relations introduces a large perturbation into the entire relational network, whereas breaking others has a negligible effect.

One aspect of the external environment is of course just the non-biological environment of mountains and tables and chairs that surrounds us. Another critical aspect of the external environment, however, is the social environment: the other people, the other minds, with whom we interact. The social environment has several features that distinguish it: It is more complex than the non-social environment, it is reciprocally interactive with us, and it includes other minds and other subjects of conscious awareness. How important is this distinction?

According to some views, very important. One influential line of thinking has proposed that the cognitive abilities that make us distinctively human in fact arose precisely from the need to function in a socially complex environment, with other minds and the reciprocal interactions they provide us. As a source of competition for resources like shared food and mates, the social environment would arguably have driven the evolution of our abilities to predict other people's behavior and to guide our behavior accordingly. Given that everyone would have been driven in the same fashion, something like a "mental arms race" might thus have provided the impetus for the evolution of many of our cognitive abilities, abilities that collectively allow us to outsmart others. I next briefly review this issue in somewhat more detail.

It is clear that primates are exceedingly adept at negotiating the social environment. This ability is most striking in the most social primate, *Homo sapiens*, suggesting the hypothesis that our exceptional cognitive skills may be traced to evolution in an environment in which there was a premium on social skills. In support of this idea, there is a correlation between mean group size among various primate species and their neocortex volume (Dunbar, 1998); to be exact, it is the ratio of their neocortex volume to their total brain volume, but the details are not important here. Such a correlation has been found also for several other mammals that all feature a complex social structure (e.g., bats, carnivores, and toothed whales): The larger the social groups, the larger the brains. Although brain size has been argued to correlate with a number of other factors, including dietary foraging strategy, tool use, and longevity (Allman, 1999), it may be that large brain size is at least a partial consequence of the fact that primates have a complex ecological niche with respect to social structure (including its effect on food and mate availability). This hypothesis, variously dubbed the Machiavellian Intelligence Hypothesis (Whiten & Byrne, 1997) or the Social Brain Hypothesis (Dunbar, 1998), argues that the complexity of primate social structure, together with certain of its unique features, such as cooperativity and deception, led to an advantage for larger brains.

Primates are clearly highly skilled at predicting other individuals' behavior, but there is presently vigorous debate regarding how to interpret such an ability. Research into how we represent other minds began with a question about whether or not chimpanzees might possess a theory of mind (Premack & Woodruff, 1978), a question that is still the subject of debate (Povinelli & Vonk, 2003; Tomasello, Call, & Hare, 2003). In humans, the question was posed concretely in terms of the ability to attribute beliefs, specifically false beliefs, to other individuals, an ability that begins to emerge around age 4 or possibly earlier (Wimmer & Perner, 1983). The abilities that constitute a theory of mind have been fractionated into several distinct components, such as the ability to attribute desires, to recognize objects of shared attention, and to monitor others' direction of gaze (Baron-Cohen, 1995). All these different components appear at distinct developmental stages in humans, and there is evidence that some of them may be disproportionately impaired in subjects with autism, a disorder that exhibits marked difficulties in social behavior.

There is thus considerable support (although by no means unequivocal support) for the idea that social interactions gave rise to the kinds of complex cognitive abilities seen in humans. If the human mind, with respect to cognition, arose out of the need to function in a complex social environment, might the same be true of human consciousness? Returning to our metaphor of the mind as literally leaking out beyond the bounds of our skull to encompass the web of relations in which our brains participate, social relations may be some of the strongest links in this web.

I have argued that relational facts about a brain's interactions with its environment are just as important to conscious experience as they have been claimed to be important for propositional attitudes like beliefs and for cognitive abilities in general. There is now the further argument that a very important, and perhaps the most important, component of those relations concern relations between an individual and others of its kind. At least at the gross level of evolution of the brain, the nature of social relations appears to have been a driving force in that evolution. The critically social nature of the environment in which our brains are embedded also has not escaped the notice of neuroscientists, and there is now a burgeoning literature on how socially relevant stimuli are processed by the brain. This literature is briefly reviewed next.

Social Cognitive Neuroscience

Social cognitive neuroscience, the study of the neurological underpinnings of social cognition, has recently exploded as a field. Data are pouring in from cross-disciplinary studies using techniques that range from fMRI, lesion, and behavioral studies in humans to cellular and molecular studies in rats and flies (Adolphs, 2003; Cacioppo et al., 2001). Many recent neuroscience studies

have started at the input end, as it were: by showing subjects (often under passive viewing conditions) pictures of social relevance and associating differences in the social content of stimuli with differences in the neural structures engaged in their processing. This work has found covariances between stimulus dimensions and brain structures, primarily from functional imaging studies.

Investigations have focused on the visual modality in primates. Social visual signals include information about the face, such as its expression and direction of gaze, as well as about body posture and movement. There is a wealth of signals available in the face, reviewed further below, that illustrates the tight reciprocal link between action and perception. We look at someone's face to pick up salient information, but doing so may well result in the other person also noticing that he is being scrutinized and changing his face in response.

Human viewers are surprisingly adept also at making reliable judgments about social information contained in rather impoverished stimuli, such as very faint changes in facial expression or only a few seconds of videos of full-body interpersonal interactions. For instance, very brief and sparse depictions of biological motion depicting people can already trigger a rich social interpretation (Ambady & Rosenthal, 1992). Not only are we exceedingly sensitive to the social signal itself but we also are sensitive to the details of the context in which it occurs. A good example of this is direction of eye gaze – direct gaze is a potent social signal, but it can mean different things, such as threat or flirtation, depending on who it is that is doing the gazing. Moreover, there are clear differences in the brain when social signals are embedded in different contexts (Pelphrey, Singerman, Allison, & McCarthy, 2003), and the influence of such social context on brain function appears to be impaired in people with autism.

Regions of non-primary sensory cortices already appear to be relatively specialized to process certain socially relevant attributes of stimuli. The evidence is best in regard to faces, for which higher-order visual cortices can be regarded as an assembly of modules that process distinct attributes, as borne out by a variety of lesion studies, scalp and intracranial recordings, and a rapidly growing list of functional imaging studies. The data point to the fusiform gyrus in processing the structural, static properties of faces that are reliable indicators of personal identity, and to regions more anterior and dorsal in the temporal lobe (such as the superior temporal gyrus and sulcus) in processing information about the changeable configurations of faces, such as facial expressions, eye movements, and mouth movements (Haxby, Hoffman, & Gobbini, 2000). Activation along the superior temporal sulcus and gyrus has been found when subjects view stimuli depicting biological motion, such as eye gaze shifts and mouth movements. The fusiform gyrus, the superior temporal gyrus, and other as yet less well-specified regions of occipitotemporal cortex could thus be thought of as an interconnected system of regions that together construct a spatially distributed perceptual representation of different aspects of faces (Haxby et al., 2001). There is good evidence that activation in all of these regions can be modulated by attention (Vuilleumier, Armony, Driver, & Dolan, 2001) and by the context in which the visual social signal appears. All of these findings certainly indicate that the brain is exquisitely tuned to respond to socially relevant signals with which it can interact.

A growing body of work has used visual stimuli that signal biological motion. Social psychologists first demonstrated our propensity to make social inferences from visual motion of abstract shapes in the 1940s (Heider & Simmel, 1944), and recent studies suggest that specific movement cues generate attributions of animacy, intentionality, and agency (Scholl & Tremoulet, 2000). Visual motion stimuli elicit attributions of intentionality and animacy in infants, and robustly elicit intentional, emotional, and personality attributions in adults, even when only static depictions of their trajectories are shown. Point-light displays offer more specific information about the movements made by a human body (Johansson, 1973)

and generate exceptionally robust shape-from-motion cues that permit recognition of identity, gender, emotions, and personality traits. In line with the role of superior temporal cortices in processing dynamic aspects of faces, this region is also activated by viewing biological motion in whole bodies or their point-light displays (Grossman & Blake, 2002) and by more abstract movements of geometric shapes, likely reflecting its role in processing biological motion information on the basis of which we make social attributions. In these examples, relatively subtle or impoverished trigger stimuli in the environment are sufficient to result in a large neural modulation. In this case it is the brain that is providing most of the information generated, rather than the stimulus – but of course the brain does so on the basis of its history of interaction within a social environment.

Several brain regions are activated not only as a function of properties inherent to the stimuli but also as a function of the psychological judgments we make about them. In a sense, the influence of such judgments reflects a progressive decoupling from responses dictated by the stimulus itself to information that is generated by the brain via associations and inferences. The amygdala is one structure that is anatomically positioned to participate in such post-perceptual processing, as it receives highly processed visual information (from anterior temporal cortices) and stores codes for subsequent processing of such perceptual information in other brain regions. In this way, it can influence memory, attention, decision making, and other cognitive functions on the basis of the social significance of the stimuli being processed.

The bulk of research on the human amygdala has used emotional facial expressions as stimuli and has pointed most consistently to processing of fear and related emotions (Adolphs, Tranel, Damasio, & Damasio, 1994; Calder et al., 1996), although recent evidence suggests that its role is probably considerably broader than that. Functional imaging studies demonstrate processing at multiple stages: rapid, automatic evaluation and tagging of stimuli for further processing, feedback modulation of attentional processing in visual cortices, and modes of processing subject to self-regulation and volitional guidance. The first and last of these in fact illustrate complementary roles for the amygdala, probably operating at complementary time scales. On the one hand, some amygdala activation is seen early, regardless of conscious perception of the stimulus and regardless of attention allocation in some tasks. On the other hand, effortful self-regulation of the emotions induced by stimuli, reappraisal of the emotional significance of the stimuli, and difficult attentional tasks all modulate amygdala activation. These findings urge caution in the rigid assignment of cognitive processes to neural structures, because it is likely that a given structure participates in multiple processes, depending on the point in time at which its activity is sampled and on the details of the task and context in which the subject is engaged. It is plausible that the amygdala participates both in the initial, rapid evaluation of the emotional significance of stimuli and in their later assessment within a given context and goals.

Beyond its role in the recognition of basic emotions, the amygdala is involved in more complex social judgments. It shows differential habituation of activation to faces of people of another race, and amygdala activation has been found to correlate with racial stereotypes of which the viewer may be unaware (Phelps et al., 2000). However, the amygdala's role in processing information about race is still unclear: Other brain regions, in extrastriate visual cortex, are also activated differentially as a function of race, and lesions of the amygdala do not appear to impair race judgments.

All of this demonstrates that the neural events that generate knowledge, behavior, and awareness of the social world unfold over multiple iterations of processing, iterations that include multiple interactions with the environment. There is a recent particularly clear example of such action-perception coupling in regard to the amygdala. It turns out that the amygdala not only processes visual information by interacting with other visual regions of the brain but that it does so also by directing gaze to specific features of stimuli. Damage to the amygdala results in an inability to recognize certain emotions from facial expressions, but it appears to do so, at least in good part, via an impairment in exploring the social environment with one's eyes. In one case, a patient with bilateral damage to the amygdala failed to look normally at other people's faces and consequently failed to pick up and use visual information normally in judging the emotion that was shown on the face (Adolphs et al., 2005). This example brings us back to our discussion of situated cognition and examples like change blindness: The visual world we experience is not entirely in our heads. Rather, our brains possess strategies for actively and efficiently probing the external environment in order to seek out relevant visual information – for instance, by deciding where to direct our gaze in the first place.

Abilities that have been dubbed "theory of mind" enable the attribution of mental states to other people (Siegal & Varley, 2002). Particularly studied have been attributions of beliefs, specifically false beliefs, to other individuals. As we discussed earlier in this section, such abilities emerge around age 4, may be unique to humans, and may be assembled out of a collection of more basic skills by which we assign animacy, actions, goals, and intentions to stimuli, an issue that has seen intense recent investigation using visual motion stimuli (Blakemore & Decety, 2001). In addition to the reliable activation of superior temporal gyrus already mentioned earlier, a number of functional imaging studies have demonstrated activation of cortex in the medial frontal lobe, as well as the inferior parietal lobule, when people view visual motion or eye gaze stimuli that signal such directed mental states.

Many of the same stimuli that engage the superior temporal gyrus and that lead viewers to attribute actions, intentions, and goals also activate regions of neocortex involved in representing actions. These regions include premotor-related cortices as well as somatosensory-related cortices, the efferent and afferent sides of actions. A series of recent studies have investigated the role of right somatosensory-associated cortices and left premotor cortex in making emotional and personality attributions also from point-light displays and movements of geometric shapes; damage in both regions impairs the ability to make such attributions.

There is a rapidly growing literature supporting the idea that we understand other people's behavior in part by simulation (Rizzolatti, Fogassi, & Gallese, 2001). Observing another's actions results in desynchronization in motor cortex as measured with magnetoencephalography (Hari et al., 1998); imitating another's actions via observation activates premotor cortex in functional imaging studies (Iacoboni et al., 1999), and such activation is somatotopic with respect to the body part that is observed to perform the action, even in the absence of any overt action on the part of the subject (Buccino et al., 2001). In fact, in both humans (Hutchison, Davis, Lozano, Tasker, & Dostrovsky, 1999) and monkeys (Gallese & Goldman, 1999), so-called mirror neurons have been discovered that respond both when the subject is doing something specific and when he or she observes another person doing the same thing. Damage restricted to somatosensory cortex impairs the ability to recognize complex blends of emotions in facial expressions (Adolphs, Damasio, Tranel, Cooper, & Damasio, 2000), and there is an association between impaired somatic sensation of one's own body and impaired ability to judge other people's emotions (Adolphs et al., 2000). Functional imaging studies also support a role for right somatosensory-related cortices in representing the actions we observe others to perform, as distinct from those we perform ourselves (Ruby & Decety, 2001).

All of the above review might seem to suggest that, after all, richer minds arise from larger and more complex brains; richer conscious experience depends on richer brains; and perhaps we should jettison everything I argued for in the first half of this chapter and return to the idea that conscious experience arises entirely out of the complex internal dynamics of the brain processes that were just outlined. Well, there is certainly some consequence of the more elaborated social information processing that primate brains afford. But, following the metaphor outlined earlier, the consequence of more elaborate neural processing is that it brings certain relevant relations closer to the nexus of the web in which they are embedded.

Let us return briefly to the example of calculating the square of a five-digit number. With some training, one could do so in the absence of pencil and paper. Perhaps one strategy of doing so might even be to concentrate very hard to create a detailed visual image as if one were doing it with pencil and paper. What has been achieved by this is to bring what used to require relations with events in the external environment into a simulation of those relations within the brain. But that in no way shows that the cognitive ability to square a five-digit number now depends only on the brain. It depends on events happening in the brain, as well as on historical relations between the brain and the environment. Without that history of interaction, there would have been nothing to internalize. This issue, of how the brain might come to internalize relevant aspects of its relational interaction with body and environment, requires some further treatment.

Simulation

Like all cognition, social knowledge goes beyond the mere information present in the evidence on which it is based; it is inferential and creative in nature. But do the mechanisms that subserve it literally extend outside the brain, as I've been suggesting? One starting point is to view brains as containing emulators that are in the business of constructing models of the world, including the social world. The mechanisms required by the theory-of-mind abilities reviewed above can be considered to use emulators of sorts. The simulation theory of mind, for instance, might consist in an "articulated" emulator: a model that mimics aspects of what it is modeling to achieve its predictive power (Grush, 2003).

The notion of an articulated emulator has substantial support from findings in cognitive neuroscience. As reviewed above, there is considerable empirical evidence that humans obtain knowledge about other people's emotional states, for example, at least in part, via some kind of articulated emulation. Premotor cortices are engaged when we observe others behaving emotionally, as are somatosensory cortices and insula. These components would correspond to the initial goal command for emotional behaviors and to representation of the feedback signal from such behavior, respectively, raising the question of what happens between the two to connect them: Where is the emulator itself?

One possibility is that we engage some of the same machinery during emulation as during actual emotions: the body outside the brain. There is good evidence for this idea as well: Observing other people express emotions results in some mirroring of the physiological emotional state in the viewer. In this case it seems that the emulator is the same as the system in normal operation, although it may engage only a subset of a hierarchically structured system. The possibility of using the body itself as the emulator when we model another person's emotion would be not only economical but also suggests an interesting way in which actual, analog physical processes – state changes in various parameters of the body that normally comprise an emotional response – can be used in information processing. The body might be thought of as a "somatic scratchpad" that we can probe with efferent signals in order to reconstruct knowledge about the details of an emotional state. Given the complexity of interaction among multiple somatic parameters, in action as well as emotion, it may not be feasible to emulate this entirely neurally.

Typically, of course, our emulation should be less than the real thing. Thus, emotion emulation involves faint somatic changes that are a subset of having the emotion oneself and that involve active inhibition of expression of some of the components. Much the same happens when we dream: As in waking emulation, we construct models that include responses in our bodies, and although there are indeed somatic responses during dreaming, these responses are actively inhibited from full expression. It would seem odd to have evolved such efferent processing and inhibition if the body itself did not play an important role in building the models that help us predict the world.

We can now imagine extending the modeling outside the bounds of the body. To obtain social information, we may query not only our own bodies but also those of other people. Clearly, this is the case in a general sense: We probe other people's reactions to initial and often subtle behaviors on our own part and use their response as feedback in constructing a more accurate model of the social world.

Conclusions

The picture that emerges from the above discussion is more subtle and complex than the one we previously had in mind. The relations between brain, body, and external environment are still the base out of which the mind is generated, but the brain has some control over the relative importance of these relations insofar as it can internalize some of them and externalize others. Thus, depending on the particular cognitive and behavioral requirements, relations can be modeled internally to provide greater processing speed or can be externalized where very large or detailed computations are required that go beyond what the brain in isolation could compute. But nowhere is there an independence of brain from environment – the only way in which the environment can, by certain brains under certain circumstances, be partially modeled is through a history of interaction with that environment in the first place. The mind, including conscious experience, arises from a web of relations that involve the brain, but the brain remains the hub in this web, in the sense that neural events contribute substantially to mental events and the brain has a role in orchestrating the relational web as its organizing center.

Needless to say, and despite the length of the chapter here, I've only begun to sketch, in the barest outline, how precisely the fact that we are embedded in a web of social interactions would inform our understanding of consciousness. My aim has been to focus the philosophical problem on one particular view of the problem of consciousness, to suggest reasons for doubting that we can understand consciousness through intrinsic properties of the brain, and to argue that we need to look instead at relational properties – between the brain and the social environment (i.e., between multiple brains). My review of social neuroscience has, of course, not directly addressed the deeper issue at hand. But I hope it has provided a brief overview of what we do know about the neural underpinnings of social behavior and social cognition and, in so doing, emphasized the fact that, as in the case of situated cognition more generally, our representation of the social world depends both on events in our brains and events external to us. We perceive other people's behavior, they in turn perceive ours, and mutual interaction permits one to construct a model of the other. Moreover, I hope that even this very brief sketch of an overview of social neuroscience suggested that our brains are indeed highly adapted for a socially interactive environment. The evolutionary evidence I mentioned supports the idea that much of what has driven the evolution of the brain was the nature of the complex social environment in which brains were situated. The neurobiological evidence reinforced the idea that the brain is replete with mechanisms for processing socially relevant information, is exceedingly sensitive to such information and its context, and has evolved clever tools for actively probing the social environment.

At this stage, my feeling is that we have enough ammunition available to begin formulating experiments that would test some of the ideas put forth in this chapter. There is good evidence, as reviewed above, that social information processing draws more on some structures than on others. What happens when those structures are lesioned? What happens if they are artificially stimulated? If we find that changes in conscious aware-ness are often correlated with changes in social cognition, this would be preliminary evidence in support of the idea that consciousness is related to our social nature. There is already some evidence for such a correlation from experiments in patients who have damage to the frontal lobes: Not only is their social behavior severely compromised but also the nature of their conscious experience may well be altered. It is likely, for instance, that their ability to experience certain emotions, perhaps especially social ones, is severely diminished and, at the same time, their social relations with others are severely disturbed (Anderson et al., 1999; Damasio, 1994).

More direct evidence for the idea that consciousness literally depends on relational social events would require other kinds of data. One could imagine developmental studies in which the social environment is systematically manipulated that might investigate the issue. One could also imagine comparative studies between different species that are more or less social. Of course, all of these would run up against another, separate practical difficulty, one that I have not mentioned here: how to decide on convincing observable criteria for conscious awareness in the first place.

References

Adolphs, R. (2003). Cognitive neuroscience of human social behavior. *Nature Reviews Neuroscience, 4*, 165–178.

Adolphs, R., Damasio, H., Tranel, D., Cooper, G., & Damasio, A. R. (2000). A role for somatosensory cortices in the visual recognition of emotion as revealed by 3-D lesion mapping. *Journal of Neuroscience, 20*, 2683–2690.

Adolphs, R., Gosselin, F., Buchanan, T. W., Tranel, D., Schyns, P., & Damasio, A. R. (2005). A mechanism for impaired fear recognition following amygdala damage. *Nature, 433*, 68–72.

Adolphs, R., Tranel, D., Damasio, H., & Damasio, A. (1994). Impaired recognition of emotion in facial expressions following bilateral damage to the human amygdala. *Nature, 372*, 669–672.

Allman, J. M. (1999). *Evolving brains.* New York: Scientific American Library.

Ambady, N., & Rosenthal, R. (1992). Thin slices of expressive behavior as predictors of interpersonal consequences: A meta-analysis. *Psychological Bulletin, 111*, 256–274.

Anderson, S. W., Bechara, A., Damasio, H., Tranel, D., & Damasio A. R. (1999). Impairment of social and moral behavior related to early damage in human prefrontal cortex. *Nature Neuroscience, 2*, 1032–1037.

Baron-Cohen, S. (1995). *Mindblindness: An essay on autism and theory of mind.* Cambridge, MA: MIT Press.

Blakemore, S.-J., & Decety, J. (2001). From the perception of action to the understanding of intention. *Nature Reviews Neuroscience, 2*, 561–568.

Buccino, G., Binkofski, F., Fink, G. R., Fadiga, L., Fogassi, L., Gallese, V. V., et al. (2001). Action observation activates premotor and parietal areas in a somatotopic manner: An fMRI study. *European Journal of Neuroscience, 13*, 400–404.

Cacioppo, J. T., Berntson, G. G., Adolphs, R., Carter, C. S., Davidson, R. J., McClintock, M. K., et al. (Eds.). (2001). *Foundations in social neuroscience.* Cambridge, MA: MIT Press.

Calder, A. J., Young, A. W., Rowland, D., Perrett, D. I., Hodges, J. R., & Etcoff, N. L. (1996). Facial emotion recognition after bilateral amygdala damage: Differentially severe impairment of fear. *Cognitive Neuropsychology, 13*, 699–745.

Chalmers, D. J. (1997). *The conscious mind.* Oxford: Oxford University Press.

Clark, A. (1997). *Being there: Putting brain, body and world together again.* Cambridge, MA: MIT Press.

Clark, A. (1995). I am John's brain. *Journal of Consciousness Studies, 2*, 144–148.

Clark, A., & Chalmers, D. J. (1998). The extended mind. *Analysis, 58*, 10–23.

Damasio, A. R. (1994). *Descartes' error: Emotion, reason, and the human brain.* New York: Putnam.

Davidson, D. (1987). Knowing one's own mind. In D. Davidson (Ed.), *Subjective, intersubjective, objective: Philosophical essays of Donald Davidson* (pp. 15–38). New York: Oxford University Press.

Dewey, J. (1896). The reflex arc concept in psychology. *Psychological Review, 3*, 357–370.

Dunbar, R. (1998). The social brain hypothesis. *Evolutionary Anthropology, 6*, 178–190.

Gallese, V., & Goldman, A. (1999). Mirror neurons and the simulation theory of mind-reading. *Trends in Cognitive Sciences, 2*, 493–500.

Grossman, E., & Blake, R. (2002). Brain areas active during visual perception of biological stimuli. *Neuron, 35*, 1167–1175.

Grush, R. (2003). The emulation theory of representation: Motor control, imagery and perception. *Behavioral and Brain Sciences, 27*, 377–442.

Hari, R., Forss, N., Avikainen, S., Kirveskari, E., Salenius, S., & Rizzolatti, G. (1998). Activation of human primary motor cortex during action observation: A neuromagnetic study. *Proceedings of the National Academy of Sciences, 95*, 15061–15065.

Haxby, J. V., Gobbini, M. I., Furey, M. L., Ishai, A., Schouten, J. L., & Pietrini, P. (2001). Distributed and overlapping representation of faces and objects in ventral temporal cortex. *Science, 293*, 2425–2429.

Haxby, J. V., Hoffman, E. A., & Gobbini, M. I. (2000). The distributed human neural system for face perception. *Trends in Cognitive Sciences, 4*, 223–233.

Heider, F., & Simmel, M. (1944). An experimental study of apparent behavior. *American Journal of Psychology, 57*, 243–259.

Hutchison, W. D., Davis, K. D., Lozano, A. M., Tasker, R. R., & Dostrovsky, J. O. (1999). Pain-related neurons in the human cingulate cortex. *Nature Neuroscience, 2*, 403–405.

Iacoboni, M., Woods, R. P., Brass, M., Bekkering, H., Mazziotta, J. C., & Rizzolatti, G. (1999). Cortical mechanisms of human imitation. *Science, 286*, 2526–2528.

Johansson, G. (1973). Visual perception of biological motion and a model of its analysis. *Perception and Psychophysics, 14*, 202–211.

Metzinger, T (2003). *Being no one: The self model of subjectivity.* Cambridge, MA: The MIT Press.

Nagel, T. (1974). What is it like to be a bat? *Philosophical Review, 83*, 435–450.

Nagel, T. (1993). What is the mind-body problem? In *Experimental and theoretical studies of consciousness* (Vol. 174, Ciba Foundation Symposium, pp. 1–13). New York: John Wiley.

Nagel, T. (2001). The psychophysical nexus. In P. Boghossian & C. Peacocke (Eds.), *New essays on the a priori* (pp. 433–471). New York: Oxford University Press.

Noe, A. (2002). Is the visual world a grand illusion? *Journal of Consciousness Studies, 9*, 1–12.

Noe, A. (2004). *Action in perception*. Cambridge, MA: MIT Press.

O'Regan, J. K., & Noe, A. (2001). A sensorimotor account of vision and visual consciousness. *Behavioral and Brain Sciences, 24*, 939–1031.

Pelphrey, K. A., Singerman, J. D., Allison, T., & McCarthy, G. (2003). Brain activation evoked by the perception of gaze shifts: The influence of timing and context. *Neuropsychologia, 41*, 156–170.

Phelps, E. A., O'Connor, K. J., Cunningham, W. A., Funayama, E. S., Gatenby, J. C., Gore, J. C., et al. (2000). Performance on indirect measures of race evaluation predicts amygdala activation. *Journal of Cognitive Neuroscience, 12*, 729–738.

Povinelli, D. J., & Vonk, J. (2003). Chimpanzee minds: Suspiciously human? *Trends in Cognitive Sciences, 7*, 157–160.

Premack, D., & Woodruff, G. (1978). Does the chimpanzee have a theory of mind? *Behavioral and Brain Sciences, 1*, 515–526.

Putnam, H. (1979). The meaning of 'meaning'. In *Mind, language and reality: Philosophical papers* (Vol. 2, pp. 215–272). Cambridge: Cambridge University Press

Rensink, R. A., O'Regan, J. K., & Clark, J. J. (1997). To see or not to see: The need for attention to perceive changes in scenes. *Psychological Science, 8*, 368–373.

Rizzolatti, G., Fogassi, L., & Gallese, V. (2001). Neurophysiological mechanisms underlying the understanding and imitation of action. *Nature Reviews Neuroscience, 2*, 661–670.

Rowlands, M. (2003). *Externalism: Putting mind and world back together again*. Chesham: Acumen.

Ruby, P., & Decety, J. (2001). Effect of subjective perspective taking during simulation of action: A PET investigation of agency. *Nature Neuroscience, 4*, 546–550.

Scholl, B. J., & Tremoulet, P. D. (2000). Perceptual causality and animacy. *Trends in Cognitive Sciences, 4*, 299–308.

Siegal, M., & Varley, R. (2002). Neural systems involved in 'theory of mind'. *Nature Reviews Neuroscience, 3*, 463–471.

Suchman, L. (1987). *Plans and situated actions*. Cambridge: Cambridge University Press.

Thompson, E., & Varela, F. J. (2001). Radical embodiment: neural dynamics and consciousness. *Trends in Cognitive Sciences, 5*, 418–425.

Tomasello, M., Call, J., & Hare, B. (2003). Chimpanzees understand psychological states – the question is which ones and to what extent. *Trends in Cognitive Sciences, 7*, 153–156.

Varela, J. F., Thompson, E., & Rosch, E. (1991). *The embodied mind: Cognitive science and human experience*. Cambridge, MA: MIT Press.

Vuilleumier, P., Armony, J. L., Driver, J., & Dolan, R. J. (2001). Effects of attention and emotion on face processing in the human brain. An event-related fMRI study. *Neuron, 30*, 829.

Whiten, A., & Byrne, R. W. (Eds.). (1997). *Machiavellian intelligence II: Extensions and evaluations*. Cambridge: Cambridge University Press.

Wimmer, H., & Perner, J. (1983). Beliefs about beliefs: Representation and constraining function of wrong beliefs in young children's understanding of deception. *Cognition, 13*, 103–128.

Part III

QUANTUM APPROACHES TO CONSCIOUSNESS

CHAPTER 31

Quantum Approaches to Consciousness

Henry Stapp

Abstract

The concepts of classical physics and the implied doctrine of the causal closure of the physical description fail to accommodate observed behaviors of macroscopic systems when those behaviors depend sensitively upon the properties of atomic-sized particles. To adequately describe such behaviors physicists were forced to replace, in the mathematics, the numbers that describe the intrinsic properties of a system by actions that correspond to the probing actions performed upon that system by an observing system. According to orthodox quantum theory these probing actions are "freely" chosen by human agents, where "freely" means that these choices are not fixed by the known laws of physics or laws of any yet-known kind. But these choices influence the course of physical events. Von Neumann's orthodox formulation of quantum mechanics makes this influence of our conscious choices into influences, described by specified causal laws, of a person's conscious choices on the state of his or her brain. Classical physics is an approximation to quantum mechanics that eliminates this effect. That makes the physical efficacy of our conscious choices a strictly quantum effect. The Penrose, Bohm, and Eccles-Beck quantum approaches to the mind-brain system are discussed, along with the orthodox von Neumann approach.

Introduction

Quantum approaches to consciousness are sometimes said to be motivated simply by the idea that quantum theory is a mystery and consciousness is a mystery, so perhaps the two are related. That opinion betrays a profound misunderstanding of the nature of quantum mechanics, which consists fundamentally of a pragmatic scientific solution to the problem of the connection between mind and matter.

The key philosophical and scientific achievement of the founders of quantum theory was to forge a rationally coherent and practically useful linkage between the two kinds of descriptions that jointly comprise the foundation of science. Descriptions of the first kind are accounts of psychologically experienced empirical findings, expressed in a language that allows us to communicate to our colleagues what we have done and what we have learned. Descriptions of the second kind are specifications of physical properties, which are expressed by assigning mathematical properties to space-time points, and formulating laws that determine how these properties evolve over the course of time. Bohr, Heisenberg, Pauli, and the other inventors of quantum theory discovered a useful way to connect these two kinds of descriptions by causal laws; their seminal discovery was extended by John von Neumann from the domain of atomic science to the realm of neuroscience and in particular to the problem of understanding and describing the causal connections between the minds and the brains of human beings.

The magnitude of the difference between the quantum and classical conceptions of the connection between mind and brain can scarcely be exaggerated. All approaches to this problem based on the precepts of classical physics founder first on the problem of the lack of any need within classical mechanics for consciousness to exist at all, and second on a conceptual gap that blocks any rational understanding of how the experiential realities that form our streams of consciousness could ever be produced by, or naturally come to be associated with, the motions of the things that classical physics claims the physical world to be made of. The first problem is that, according to precepts of classical physics, the causal properties that it explicitly mentions suffice, by themselves, with no acknowledgment of the existence of consciousness, to completely specify all physical properties of the universe, including the activities of our bodies and brains. According to the conceptual structure of classical physics, everything physical would go on just the same if nothing existed but the physical properties explicitly mentioned in the theory. The second problem is that within that conceptual framework of classical physics neither planets nor electrons,

nor any of the other entities, nor combinations of the entities that populate the world *make choices on the basis of ideas*. The world described by the concepts of classical physics has been systematically stripped of, and is consequently bereft of, the concept of choices based on consciously experienced ideas. Thus, the stubborn fact that idea-like realities do exist enforces an awkward departure of science from a purely naturalistic stance. Non-physical features, such as conscious thoughts, ideas, and feelings, must be added, for no apparent naturalistic, physical, or rational reason, to the features that enter into the putative laws of nature. There is thus a conceptual mismatch between the world described by the basic laws of classical physics and the world we inhabit and do science in.

These difficulties have been much discussed by many philosophers, who have proposed many different approaches. But in view of the known failure of classical physics to be able to describe the *macroscopic properties* of systems whose behaviors can depend sensitively on the behaviors of their atomic constituents, and the further fact that orthodox contemporary physical theory brings conscious choices by human agents into physical theory in an essential way, the question must be asked whether these philosophical efforts accord with 20th-century science or are, instead, clever ways of trying to justifying the use of approximately valid but fundamentally incorrect 19th-century physics in a domain where that approximation is inadequate.

Both of the above-mentioned difficulties are resolved in a rationally coherent and practically useful way by quantum mechanics. On the one hand, a key basic precept of the quantum approach, as it is both practiced and taught, is that choices made by human beings play a key and irreducible role in the dynamics. On the other hand, the great disparity within classical physics between the experiential and physical aspects of nature is resolved in the quantum approach by altering the assumptions about the nature of the physical universe. The physical world, as it appears in the theory, is transformed from a structure based on *substance* or *matter* to one based on *events*, each of which has both experiential aspects and physical aspects: Each such event injects information, or "knowledge," into an information-bearing mathematically described physical state. An important feature of this radical revamping of the conceptual foundations is that it leaves unchanged, at the practical level, most of classical physics. Apart from making room for, *and a strict need for*, efficacious conscious choices, the radical changes introduced at the foundational level by quantum mechanics preserve at the pragmatic level almost all of classical physics.

In the remainder of this introductory section I sketch out the transition from the classical physics conception of reality to von Neumann's application of the principles of quantum physics to our conscious brains. In succeeding sections I describe the most prominent of the many efforts now being made by physicists to apply von Neumann's theory to recent developments in neuroscience.

The quantum conception of the connection between the psychologically and physically described components of scientific practice was achieved by abandoning the classical picture of the physical world that had ruled science since the time of Newton, Galileo, and Descartes. The building blocks of science were shifted from descriptions of the behaviors of tiny bits of mindless matter to accounts of *the actions that we take to acquire knowledge* and of the *knowledge that we thereby acquire*. Science was thereby transformed from its 17th-century form, which effectively excluded our conscious thoughts from any causal role in the mechanical workings of Nature, to its 20th-century form, which focuses on our active engagement with Nature and on what we can learn by taking appropriate actions.

Twentieth-century developments have thus highlighted the fact that *science is a human activity* that involves us not as passive witnesses of a mechanically controlled universe, but as agents who can freely choose to perform causally efficacious actions. The basic laws of nature, as they are now understood, not only fail to determine how we will act, but, moreover, inject our *choices about how to act* directly into the dynamical equations.

This altered role of conscious agents is poetically expressed by Bohr's famous dictum:

> *In the great drama of existence we ourselves are both actors and spectators. (Bohr, 1958, p. 81; 1963, p. 15)*

It is expressed more concretely in statements such as the following:

> *The freedom of experimentation, presupposed in classical physics, is of course retained and corresponds to the free choice of experimental arrangement for which the mathematical structure of the quantum mechanical formalism offers the appropriate latitude. (Bohr, 1958, p. 73)*

The most important innovation of quantum theory, from a philosophical perspective, is the fact that it is formulated in terms of an *interaction* between the physically described world and conscious agents who are, *within the causal structure defined by the known physical laws, free to choose* which aspect of nature they will probe. This crack, or gap, in the mechanistic world view leads to profound changes in our conception of nature and the place of human beings within it.

Another key innovation pertains to the *nature* of the *stuff* of the physically/mathematically described universe. The switch is succinctly summarized in Heisenberg's famous assertion:

> *The conception of the objective reality of the elementary particles has thus evaporated not into the cloud of some obscure new reality concept, but into the transparent clarity of a mathematics that represents no longer the behavior of the particle but rather our knowledge of this behavior. (Heisenberg, 1958a)*

What the quantum mathematics describes is not the locations of tiny bits of matter. What is described by the mathematics is a causal structure embedded in space-time that carries or contains information or knowledge, but no material substance. This structure is, on certain occasions, abruptly altered by *discrete events* that inject new information into it. But this carrier structure is not purely passive. It has an active quality. It acts as a bearer of "objective tendencies" or "potentia" or "propensities" for new events to occur (Heisenberg, 1958b, p. 53).

To appreciate this new conception of the connection between the psychologically described empirical part and the mathematically described physical part of the new scientific description of physical phenomena, one needs to contrast it with what came before.

The Classical-Physics Approach

Classical physics arose from the theoretical effort of Isaac Newton to account for the findings of Johannes Kepler and Galileo Galilei. Kepler discovered that the planets move in orbits that depend on the location of other physical objects – such as the sun – but not on the manner or the timings of our observations: Minute-by-minute viewings have no more influence on a planetary orbit than daily, monthly, or annual observations. The nature and timings of our observational acts have no effect at all on the orbital motions described by Kepler. Galileo observed that certain falling terrestrial objects have similar properties. Newton then discovered that he could explain *simultaneously* the celestial findings of Kepler and the terrestrial findings of Galileo by postulating, in effect, that all objects in our solar system are composed of tiny planet-like particles whose motions are controlled by *laws* that refer to the relative locations of the various particles and that make no reference to any conscious acts of experiencing. These acts are taken to be simply passive witnessings of macroscopic properties of large conglomerations (such as tables and chairs and measuring devices) of the tiny individually invisible particles.

Newton's laws involve instantaneous action at a distance: Each particle has an instantaneous effect on the motion of every other particle, no matter how distant. New-

ton considered this non-local feature of his theory to be unsatisfactory, but proposed no alternative. Eventually, Albert Einstein, building on ideas of James Clerk Maxwell, constructed a *local* classical theory in which all dynamical effects are generated by contact interactions between mathematically described properties localized at space-time points and in which no effect is transmitted faster than the speed of light.

All classical physics models of Nature are *deterministic*: The state of any isolated system at any time is completely fixed by the state of that system at any earlier time. The Einstein-Maxwell theory is deterministic in this sense; it is also "local" in the just-mentioned sense that all interactions are via contact interactions between neighboring localized mathematically describable properties, and no influence propagates faster than the speed of light.

By the end of the 19th century certain difficulties with the general principles of classical physical theory had been uncovered. One such difficulty was with "black-body radiation." If one analyzes the electromagnetic radiation emitted from a tiny hole in a big hollow heated sphere, then it is found that the manner in which the emitted energy is distributed over the various frequencies depends on the temperature of the sphere, but not upon the chemical or physical character of the interior surface of the sphere: The spectral distribution depends neither on whether the interior surface is smooth or rough nor on whether it is metallic or ceramic. This universality is predicted by classical theory, but the specific form of the predicted distribution differs greatly from what is empirically observed.

In 1900 Max Planck discovered a universal law of black-body radiation that matches the empirical facts. This new law is incompatible with the basic principles of classical physical theory and involves a new constant of Nature, which was identified and measured by Planck and is called "Planck's Constant." By now a huge number of empirical effects have been found that depend upon this constant and that conflict with the predictions of classical physical theory.

During the 20th century a theory was devised that accounts for all of the successful predictions of classical physical theory and also for all of the departures of the predictions of classical theory from the empirical facts. This theory is called quantum theory. No confirmed violation of its principles has ever been found.

The Quantum Approach

The core idea of the quantum approach is the seminal discovery by Werner Heisenberg that the classical model of a physical system can be considered to be an *approximation* to a quantum version of that model. This quantum version is constructed by replacing each numerical quantity of the classical model by an *action*: by an entity that acts on other such entities and for which the order in which the actions are performed matters. The effect of this replacement is to convert each point-like particle of the classical conceptualization – such as an electron – to a smeared-out cloudlike structure that evolves, almost always, in accordance with a quantum mechanical law of motion called the Schroedinger equation. This law, like its classical analog, is local and deterministic: The evolution in time is controlled by contact interactions between localized parts, and the physical state of any isolated system at any time is completely determined from its physical state at any earlier time by these contact interactions. The cloudlike structure that represents an individual "particle," such as an electron or proton, tends, under the control of the Schroedinger equation, to spread out over an ever-growing region of space, whereas according to the ideas of classical physics an electron always stays localized in a very tiny region.

The local deterministic quantum law of motion is, in certain ways, incredibly accurate: It correctly fixes *to one part in a hundred million* the values of some measurable properties that classical physics cannot predict. However, it does not correlate directly to human experience. For example, if the state of the universe were to have developed from the big bang solely under the control of the local deterministic Schroedinger equation, then the location of the *center* of the moon would be represented in the theory by a structure spread out over a large part of the sky, in direct contradiction to normal human experience.

This smeared-out character of the position of (the center-point of) a macroscopic object is a consequence of the famous Heisenberg Uncertainty Principle, combined with the fact that tiny uncertainties at the microscopic level usually get magnified over the course of time, *by the Schroedinger equation acting alone*, to large uncertainties in macroscopic properties, such as location.

Thus a mathematical equation – the Schroedinger equation – that is a direct mathematical generalization of the laws of motion of classical physical theory and that yields many predictions of incomparable accuracy – strongly conflicts with many facts of everyday experience (e.g., with the fact that the apparent location of the center of the moon is well defined to within, say 10 degrees, as observed from a location on the surface of the earth). Contradictions of this kind must be eliminated by a satisfactory formulation of quantum theory.

To put the accurate predictions of the quantum mathematics into the framework of a rationally coherent and practically useful physical theory, the whole concept of what physical science is was transformed from its 19th-century form – as a theory of the properties of a mechanical model of Nature in which we ourselves are mechanical parts – to a theory of the connection between the physically and psychologically described aspects of actual scientific *practice*. In actual practice we are agents that probe nature in ways of our own choosing in order to acquire knowledge that we can use. I now describe in more detail how this pragmatic conception of science works in quantum theory.

"The Observer" and "The Observed System" in Copenhagen Quantum Theory

The original formulation of quantum theory is called the Copenhagen Interpretation because it was created by the physicists that Niels Bohr had gathered around him in Copenhagen. A central precept of this approach is that, in any particular application of quantum theory, Nature is to be considered divided into two parts: "the observer" and "the observed system." The observer consists of the stream of consciousness of a human agent, together with the brain and body of that person, and also the measuring devices that he or she uses to probe the observed system.

Each observer describes himself and his knowledge in a language that allows him to communicate to colleagues two kinds of information: *how he has acted* in order to prepare himself – his mind, his body, and his devices – to receive recognizable and reportable data and *what he has learned* from the data he thereby acquires. This description is in terms of the conscious experiences of the agent himself. It is a description of his intentional probing actions and of the experiential feedbacks that he subsequently receives.

In actual scientific practice the experimenters are free to choose which experiments they perform: The empirical procedures are determined by the protocols and aims of the experimenters. This element of freedom is emphasized by Bohr in statements such as the following:

> To my mind there is no other alternative than to admit in this field of experience, we are dealing with individual phenomena and that our possibilities of handling the measuring instruments allow us to make a choice between the different complementary types of phenomena that we want to study. (Bohr, 1958, p. 51)

This freedom to choose is achieved in the Copenhagen formulation of quantum theory by placing the empirically/psychologically described observer outside the observed system that is being probed and then subjecting only the observed system to the rigorously enforced mathematical laws.

The observed system is, according to both classical theory and quantum theory, describable in terms of mathematical properties assigned to points in space-time. How-ever, the detailed forms of the laws that govern the evolution in time of this mathematical structure, and of the rules that specify the connection of this mathematical structure to the empirical facts, are very different in the two theories.

I am endeavoring here to avoid mathematical technicalities. But the essential conceptual difference between the two approaches rests squarely on a certain technical difference. This difference can be illustrated by a simple two-dimensional picture.

The Paradigmatic Example

Consider an experiment in which an experimenter puts a Geiger counter at some location with the intention of finding out whether or not this device will "fire" during some specified time interval. The experiment is designed to give one of two possible answers: 'Yes', the counter will fire during the specified interval, or 'No', the counter will not fire during this specified interval. This is the paradigmatic quantum measurement process.

This experiment has *two* alternative mutually exclusive possible responses, 'Yes' or 'No.' *Consequently*, the key mathematical connections can be pictured in a *two*-dimensional space, such as the top of your desk.

Consider two distinct points on the top of your desk called *zero* and *p*. The displacement that would move a point placed on *zero* to the point *p* is called a *vector*. Let it be called V. Suppose V has unit length in some units, say meters. Consider any two other displacements V_1 and V_2 on the desk top that start from zero, have unit length, and are perpendicular to each other. The displacement V can be formed in a unique way by making a (positive or negative) displacement along V_1 followed by a (positive or negative) displacement along V_2. Let the lengths of these two displacements be called X_1 and X_2, respectively. The theorem of Pythagoras says that X_1 squared plus X_2 squared is one (unity).

Quantum theory is based on the idea that the various experiencable outcomes have "images" in a vector space. The vector V_1

mentioned above is the image, or representation, in the vector space of the possible outcome 'Yes,' whereas V_2 represents 'No.' I do not try to describe here how this mapping of possible experiencable outcomes into corresponding vectors is achieved. But the basic presumption in quantum theory is that such a mapping exists.

The vector V represents the state of the to-be-observed system, which has been prepared at some earlier time and has been evolving in accordance with the Schroedinger equation. The vector V_1 represents the state that this observed system would be known to be in if the observed outcome of the measurement were 'Yes.' The vector V_2 represents the state that the observed system would be known to be in if the observed result of the measurement were 'No.' Of course, the directions of the two perpendicular vectors V_1 and V_2 depend upon the exact details of the experiment: on exactly where the experimenters have placed the Geiger counter and on other details controlled by the experimenters.

The outcome of the probing measurement will be either V_1 (Yes) or V_2 (No). The predicted probability for the outcome to be 'Yes' is X_1 squared, and the predicted probability for the outcome to be 'No' is X_2 squared. These two probabilities sum to unity, by virtue of the theorem of Pythagoras. The sudden jump of the state from V to either V_1 or V_2 is called a "quantum jump." The *general* theory is expressed in terms of a many-dimensional generalization of your desktop. This generalization is called a Hilbert space, and every observable state of a physical system is a represented by a "vector" in such a space.

The crucial, though trivial, logical point can now be stated: The two alternative possible outcomes, 'Yes' or 'No' of the chosen-by-the-experimenter experiment, are associated with a pair of perpendicular unit-length vectors called "basis vectors." The *orientation* (i.e., directions) of the set of basis vectors, V_1 and V_2, enters into the dynamics as a *free variable* controlled by the experimental conditions, which are specified in practice by choices made by experimenters.

The orientation of the set of basis vectors is thus, from a mathematical standpoint, a variable that can be, and is, specified *independently* of the state V of the system being probed.

This entry into the dynamics of choices made by the experimenters is not at all surprising. If the experimenters are considered to stand outside, and apart from, the system being observed, as specified by the Copenhagen approach, then it is completely reasonable and natural that the choices made by the experimenters (about how to probe the observed system) should be treated as variables that are independent of the variables that specify the physical state of the system they are probing.

Bohr (1958, p. 100) argued that quantum theory should not be applied to living systems. He also argued that the classical concepts were inadequate for that purpose. So the strict Copenhagen approach is simply to renounce the applicability of *contemporary* physical theories, both classical and quantum, to neurobiology.

Von Neumann's Formulation

The great mathematician and logician John von Neumann (1955/1932) rigorized and extended quantum theory to the point of being able to corporate the devices, the body, and the brain of the observers into the physically described part of the theory, leaving, in the psychologically described part, only the stream of conscious experiences of the agents. The part of the physically described system being directly acted upon by a psychologically described "observer" is, according to von Neumann's formulation, *the brain of that observer* (von Neumann, 1955, p. 421). The quantum jump of the state of the brain of an observer to the 'Yes' basis state (vector) then becomes the representation, *in the state of that brain*, of the conscious acquisition of the knowledge associated with that answer 'Yes.' Thus the physical features of the brain state actualized by the quantum jump to the state V_1 associated with the answer 'Yes' constitute the *neural correlate* of that person's conscious experience of the feedback

'Yes.' This fixes the essential quantum link between consciousness and neuroscience.

This is the key point! Quantum physics is built around "events" that have both physical and phenomenal aspects. The events are physical because they are represented in the physical/mathematical description by a quantum jump to one or another of the basis state vectors defined by the agent/observer's choice of what question to ask. If the resulting event is such that the 'Yes' feedback experience occurs, then this event "collapses" the prior physical state to a new physical state compatible with that phenomenal experience. Mind and matter thereby become dynamically linked in a way that is causally tied to the agent's free choice of how he or she will act. Thus, a causal dynamical connection is established between (1) a person's conscious choices of how to act, (2) that person's consciously experienced increments in knowledge, and (3) the physical actualizations of the neural correlates of the experienced increments in knowledge.

This conceptualization of the structure of basic physical theory is radically different from what it was in classical physics. Classical physics was based on a guess that worked very well for two centuries; namely, the notion that the concepts that provided an "understanding" of our observations of planets and falling apples would continue to work all the way down to the elementary particle level. That conjecture worked well until science became able to explore what was happening at the elementary particle or atomic level. Then it was found that that simple "planetary" idea could not be right. Hence scientists turned to a more sophisticated approach that was based *less* on simplistic ontological presuppositions and *more* on the empirical realities of actual scientific practice.

This new conceptual structure is not some wild philosophical speculation. It rationally yields – when combined with the statistical rule associated with the theorem of Pythagoras described above – all the pragmatic results of quantum theory, which include, as special cases, all the valid predictions of classical physics!

Von Neumann shifted the boundary between the observer and the observed system, in a series of steps, until the bodies and brains of all observers, and everything else that classical physics would describe as "physical," were included as part of the observed system, and he showed that this form of the theory is essentially equivalent, in practice, to the Copenhagen interpretation. But it evades an unnatural feature imposed by Bohr: It bypasses the ad hoc separation of the dynamically unified physical world into two differently described parts. Von Neumann's final placement of the boundary allows the psychological description to be – as is natural – the description of a stream of conscious experiences that are the experiential sides of a sequence of events whose physical sides actualize the neural correlates of those experiences.

It is important that von Neumann's systematic enlargement of the physical system to include eventually the bodies and brains of the observers *does not disrupt the basic mathematical structure of the theory*. In particular, it does not alter *the critical need to specify the orientation of the set of basis vectors* (e.g., V_1 and V_2) to make the theory work. *The specification of the basis states continues to be undetermined by anything in contemporary physical theory, even when the physical description is extended to include the entire physical world, including the bodies and brains of all human observers.*

This leap by von Neumann from the realm of atomic physics to the realm of neuroscience was way ahead of its time. Neuroscience was then in a relatively primitive state compared to what it is today. It had a long way to go before mainstream interest turned to the question of the connection between brains and conscious experiences. But 70 years of brain science has brought the empirical side up to the level where the details of the mind-brain connections are being actively probed, and intricate results are being obtained that can be compared to the predictions of the psychophysical theory prepared long ago by John von Neumann.

It is evident that a scientific approach to brain dynamics must *in principle* use quantum theory in order to deal properly with brain processes that depend heavily on chemical and ionic processes. For example, the release of neurotransmitter from a nerve terminal is controlled by the motions of calcium ions, and these ions are small enough so that the deterministic laws of classical physics necessarily fail. *Quantum theory must in principle be used to describe the ion dynamics.* But once one goes over to a quantum-mechanical description of the ionic components of the brain, one must follow through and treat also the conglomeration of these cloudlike entities and the other similar components of the brain by the quantum rules in order to recover the connection of that mathematical structure to our conscious experiences!

According to this quantum description, the state of the brain is itself an expanding cloudlike structure in a high-dimensional space. Just as the various points in the cloud that describes a single particle represent different classically conceived possibilities for that single particle (where it is and how it is moving), so do the various points in the cloud that describe the brain represent different classically conceived possible states of that brain. This cloudlike structure can, and generally will, encompass, with appreciable weights, many conflicting classical possibilities.

The job of the brain is to accept clues from the environment and then to construct a "Template for Action" (an "executive" pattern of neurological activity) that, if it endures, will issue the sequence of neural signals that will cause some specific (and, it is hoped, appropriate) action to unfold. In the cloudlike structure that represents a brain, many alternative conflicting Templates for Action can arise. The generation, within the quantum state of the brain, of important components representing conflicting classical possibilities should occur particularly when the low-level (essentially mechanical) processes cannot come to agreement on the best course of action. In this circumstance, the quantum mechanical rules allow choices to be made that produce quantum jumps that, on the psychological side, inject new

experiences, associated with a newly chosen course of action, into the stream of consciousness of the human agent and that, on the physical side, actualize brain states that contain the neural correlates of those experiences. This is the basic dynamical process that underlies the quantum approach to consciousness.

Summary

The essential difference at the basic conceptual level between the quantum and classical approaches to consciousness is that the classical principles make no mention of consciousness. The causal structure is in principle completely "bottom up." Everything is, in principle, fully determined by what goes on at the microscopic atomic level, and any dependence of microscopic properties upon macroscopic properties, or on consciousness, is, in the end, a round-about consequence of laws expressible exclusively in terms of properties of atomic particles and of the physical fields that they produce. But in quantum theory the local-deterministic (i.e., bottom-up) physical process is *in principle causally incomplete*. It fixes, by itself, neither our actions nor our experiences, nor even any statistical prediction about how we will act or what we will experience. The bottom-up process *alone* is unable to make statistical predictions, because the statistical predictions depend upon the choice of a set of basis vectors, and the bottom-up local-deterministic quantum process does not fix this choice.

This reorganization of the dynamical structure leads to an altered perspective on the entire scientific enterprise. The psychologically described empirical side of scientific practice is elevated from its formerly subservient status – as something that should be *deduced* from, or constructed from, the already dynamically complete physical side – to the new status of coequal dynamical partner. Science becomes the endeavor to describe the *two-way interplay* between the psychologically and physically described aspects of nature, rather than an attempt to deduce the existence and properties of our streams of conscious experiences from a presumed-to-be-dynamically complete local mechanical model.

Within the von Neumann framework our conscious choices fix the orientations of the basis vectors. These choices can strongly influence our actions. Thus these influences need not be illusions. The theory provides, as we see in the section on the von Neumann/Stapp approach, a specific mechanism that allows our conscious "free" choices to significantly influence our physical actions.

Pragmatic Neuroscience

Von Neumann, in his 1932 book, followed the Copenhagen tack of focusing on scientific practice, rather than ontological issues. Indeed, it can be argued that science is intrinsically pragmatic, rather than ontological. The true nature of things, other than our experiences themselves, can never be provably ascertained by the methods of science. Thus von Neumann's formulation of quantum theory provides the foundations of a *pragmatic* neuro-psycho-dynamics that is built on contemporary physical theory, rather than an inadequate classical physics. All quantum approaches to consciousness build upon this foundation laid by von Neumann, but various physicists have proposed different ways of developing that core structure. We now turn to the descriptions of a number of these proposals.

The Penrose-Hameroff Approach

Perhaps the most ambitious attempt to create a quantum theory of consciousness is the one of Roger Penrose and Stuart Hameroff. Their proposal has three parts: the Gödel Part, the Gravity Part, and the Microtubule Part.

The Gödel Part, which is due to Penrose, is an effort to use the famous Gödel Incompleteness Theorem to prove that human beings have intellectual powers that they could not have if they functioned in accordance with the principles of classical physical theory. Proving this would reaffirm a

conclusion of the von Neumann formulation of quantum theory; namely, that a conscious human being can behave in ways that a classical mechanical model cannot. Penrose's argument, if valid, would yield this same conclusion, but within a framework that relies not on quantum concepts, which are generally unknown to cognitive scientists, but rather on Gödel-type arguments, which are familiar to some of them.

The general idea of Penrose's argument is to note that, because of the mathematically deterministic character of the laws of classical physics, the output at any specified finite time of any computer behaving in accordance with the classical laws should in principle be deducible, to arbitrarily good accuracy, from a finite-step procedure based on a finite set of mutually consistent rules that encompass the laws of arithmetic. But then a human being who can be adequately modeled as a classical computer should be able to know, at any finite time, the truth *only* of those statements that can be deduced from a finite-step computation based on the finite set of rules that govern that computer. Yet, Gödel-theorem-type arguments allow real mathematicians to know, given *any* finite set of consistent logical rules that encompass the laws of arithmetic, the truth of mathematical statements that cannot be deduced by any finite-step proof based on those rules. This seems to imply that a real mathematician can know things that no classical physics model of himself could ever know; namely, the truth of statements that his classical computer simulation could not establish in a finite time.

Filling in the details of this argument is not an easy task. Penrose spends the better part of five chapters in *The Emperor's New Mind* (Penrose, 1986) and some 200 pages in *Shadows of the Mind* (Penrose, 1994) explaining and defending this thesis. However, the Harvard philosopher Hilary Putnam challenged Penrose's conclusion in a debate appearing in the *New York Times Review of Books* (Putnam, 1994), and numerous logicians have since weighed in, all, to my knowledge, challenging the validity of Penrose's argument. Thus, the Gödel Part of the Penrose-Hameroff approach cannot now be regarded as having been established successfully.

The Gravity Part of the Penrose-Hameroff approach addresses a key question pertaining to quantum dynamics: Exactly *when* do the sudden quantum jumps occur? In von Neumann's theory these jumps should presumably occur when the neural correlates of conscious thoughts become sufficiently well formed. But von Neumann gives no precise rule for when this happens.

The lack of specificity on this issue of precisely *"when"* is a serious liability of the von Neumann theory, insofar as it is construed as a description of the ontological mind-matter reality itself. That difficulty is the basic reason why both the original Copenhagen formulation and von Neumann's extension of it eschew traditional ontological commitments. They hew rather to the pragmatic position that the job of science is to establish useful practical connections between empirical findings and theoretical concepts, rather than advancing shaky speculations about the ultimate nature of reality. The pragmatic position is that theoretical ideas that optimally provide reliable practical connections between human experiences constitute, themselves, our best *scientific* understanding of "reality." Added ontological superstructures are viewed as not true science, because additions that go beyond optimal theoretical descriptions of connections between human experiences cannot be tested empirically.

Penrose wants to provide an ontology that has "real quantum jumps." Hence he must face the question: When do these jumps occur? He seeks to solve this problem by linking it to a problem that arises when one attempts to combine quantum theory with Einstein's theory of gravity.

Einstein's theory of gravity, namely General Relativity, is based on the idea that space-time is not a rigid flat structure, as had previously been thought, but is rather a *deformable medium*, and that the way it is deformed is connected to the way that matter is distributed within it. This idea was developed within the framework of classical physical theory, and most applications of it are made within a classical physics idealization. But serious problems arise when the quantum character of matter is considered. For, according to orthodox quantum theory, a particle, such as an electron or an ion, has no well-defined location: Its location is specified by a smeared-out "probability cloud." But if the locations of the material particles are not well defined then, according to General Relativity, neither is the form of the space-time structure in which the particle structures are embedded.

Penrose conjectures that Nature abhors uncertainty in the structure of space-time and that when too much ambiguity arises in the space-time structure a quantum jump to some less ambiguous structure will occur. This "principle" allows him to tie quantum jumps to the amount of uncertainty in the structure of space-time.

There is no compelling reason why Nature should be any more perturbed by an uncertainty in the structure of space-time than by an uncertainty in the distribution of matter. However, by adopting the principle that Nature finds intolerable an *excessive ambiguity in the structure of space-time* Penrose is able to propose a specific rule about when the quantum jumps occur.

Penrose's rule depends on the fact that Planck's constant gives a connection between energy and time: This constant divided by any quantity of energy gives a corresponding interval of time. Thus if an energy associated with a possible quantum jump can be defined, then a time interval associated with that potential jump becomes specified.

To identify the pertinent energy, consider a simple case in which, say, a small object is represented quantum mechanically by a small cloud that divides into two similar parts, one moving off to the right and the other moving off to the left. Both parts of the cloud are simultaneously present, and each part produces *a different distortion* of the underlying space-time structure, because matter is distributed differently in the two cases. One can compute the amount of energy that it would take to pull apart, against their gravitational attraction, two copies of the object, if each copy is located at the position specified by one of the two clouds. If one divides Planck's constant by this "gravitational energy," then a time interval associated with this distortion of space-time into these two disparate structures becomes defined. Penrose proposes that this time interval is the duration of time for which Nature will *endure* this bifurcation of its space-time structure into the two incompatible parts before jumping to one or the other of these two forms.

This conjectured rule is based on two very general features of Nature: Planck's universal constant of action and the Newton-Einstein universal law of gravitation. This universality makes the rule attractive, but no reason is given why Nature must comply with this rule.

Does this rule have any empirical support?

An affirmative answer can be provided by linking Penrose's rule to Hameroff's belief that consciousness is closely linked to the *microtubular substructure of the neuron* (Hameroff & Penrose, 1996).

It was once thought that the interiors of neurons were basically structureless fluids. That conclusion arose from direct microscopic examinations. But it turns out that in those early studies the internal substructure was wiped out by the fixing agent. It is now known that neurons are filled with an intricate structure of *microtubules*.

Each microtubule is a cylindrical structure that can extend over many millimeters. The surface of the cylinder is formed by a spiral chain of tubulin molecules, with each circuit formed by 13 of these molecules. The tubulin molecule has a molecular weight of about 110,000, and it exists in two slightly different configurational forms. Each tubulin molecule has a single special electron that can be in one of two relatively stable locations. The molecule's configurational state depends on which of these two locations this special electron is occupying.

Hameroff is an anesthesiologist, and he noted that there is close correspondence between, on the one hand, the measured effects of various anesthetics upon consciousness and, on the other hand, the capac-

ity of these anesthetics to diminish the ability of the special electron to move from one stable location to the other. This suggests a possible close connection between consciousness and the configurational activity of microtubules.

This putative linkage allows an empirical test of Penrose's rule to be made.

Suppose, in keeping with the case considered by Penrose, you are in a situation where one of two possible experiences will probably occur. For example, you might be staring at a Necker Cube, or walking in a dark woods when a shadowy form jumps out and you must choose "fight" or "flight," or perhaps you are checking your ability to freely choose to raise or not raise your arm. Thus one of two alternative possible experiences is likely to occur. Various experiments suggest that it takes about a half-second for an experience to arise. Given this time interval, Penrose's formula specifies a certain corresponding energy. Then Hameroff can compute, on the basis of available information concerning the two configurational states of the tubulin molecule, how many tubulin-molecule configurational shifts are needed to give this energy.

The answer is about 1% of the estimated number of tubulin molecules in the human brain. This result seems reasonable. Its reasonableness is deemed significant because the computed fraction could have come out to be perhaps billions of times smaller than or billions of times greater than 100%. The fact that the computed value is "in the ballpark" supports the idea that consciousness may indeed be connected *via gravity* to tubulin configurational activity.

Given this rather radical idea – it was previously thought that gravity was not essential to consciousness (orbiting astronauts can think) and that the microtubules were merely a construction scaffolding for the building and maintenance of the physical structure of the neurons – many other exotic possibilities arise. The two configurational forms of the tubulin molecule mean that it can hold a "bit" of information, so maybe the microtubular structure forms the substrate of a complex *computer* located within each neuron, thus greatly expanding the computational power of the brain. And maybe each such computer is in fact a "quantum computer." And maybe these quantum computers are all linked together to form one giant brain-wide quantum computer. And maybe these hollow microtubes form wave guides for quantum waves.

These exotic possibilities are exciting and heady. They go far beyond what conservative physicists are ready to accept and far beyond what the 1% number derived from Penrose's rule actually supports. What is supported is merely a connection between consciousness and microtubular activity, *without the presence* of the further stringent *coherence conditions* required for the functioning of a quantum computer.

Coherence means preservation of the "phase" relationships that allow waves that have traveled via different paths to come back together so that, for example, crest meets crest and trough meets trough to build an enhanced effect. Quantum computation requires an effective isolation of the quantum informational waves from the surrounding environment, because any interaction between these waves and the environment tends to destroy coherence and the required isolation is difficult to maintain in a warm, wet, noisy brain.

The simplest system that exhibits a behavior that depends strongly on quantum interference effects, and for which the maintenance of *coherence* is essential, is the famous double-slit experiment. When photons of a single wave length are allowed to pass, one at a time, through a pair of closely spaced narrow slits, and each photon is later detected by some small detection device that is embedded in a large array of such devices, one finds that *if the photonic system is not allowed to perceptibly influence any environmental degree of freedom* on its way to the detection device, then the pattern of detected events depends on an *interference* between the parts of the beam passing through the two different slits. This pattern is very different from what it is if the photon is allowed to perceptibly disturb the surrounding environment. Disturbing the environment produces a "decoherence" effect (i.e., a weakening or disappearance of the interference effects).

If a system interacts with its environment, it is difficult to prevent a "perceptible influence" of the system on the environment. If even *a single one* of the thousands of particles in the environment is displaced by a discernible amount, then the coherence is lost, and the quantum interference effect will disappear.

Because the medium in which the putative quantum information waves are moving involves different conformational states of huge tubulin molecules of molecular weight ~110,000, it would seemingly be exceedingly hard to ensure that the passage of these waves will not disturb even one particle of the environment by a discernible amount.

Max Tegmark wrote an influential paper in *Physical Review E* (Tegmark, 2000) that mathematically buttressed the intuition of most physicists that the macroscopic coherence required by Penrose-Hameroff – namely that the microtubular conformal states can form the substrate of a quantum computer that extends over a large part of the brain – could not be realized in a living human brain. Tegmark concluded that the coherence required for macroscopic quantum computation would be lost in a ten-trillionth of a second and hence should play no role in consciousness. This paper was widely heralded. However, Hagan, Hameroff, and Tuszynski (2002) wrote a rejoinder in a later issue of the same journal. They argued that some of Tegmark's assumptions departed significantly from those of the Penrose-Hameroff model. The associated corrections lengthened the coherence time by 8 or 9 orders of magnitude, thus bringing the situation into a regime where the non-equilibrium conditions in a living brain might become important: Energetic biological processes might conceivably intervene in a way that would make up the still-needed factor of ten thousand. However, the details of how this might happen were not supplied. Hence the issue is, I believe, still up in the air, with no detailed explanation available to show how the needed macroscopic quantum coherence could be maintained in a living human brain.

It must be stressed, however, that these exotic "quantum computer" effects are not necessary for the emergence of strong quantum effects within the general framework supplied by the combination of Penrose's rule pertaining to gravity and Hameroff's claim concerning the importance of microtubules. According to von Neumann's general formulation, the state of the brain – or of the microtubular part of the brain – is adequately represented by what physicists call the "reduced density matrix" of that subsystem. This representation depends only on the variables of that subsystem itself (i.e., the brain, or microtubular array), but nevertheless takes adequate account of the interactions of that system with the environment. It keeps track of the quantum coherence or lack thereof. Penrose's rule can be stated directly in terms of the reduced density matrix, which displays, ever more clearly as the interaction with the environment grows, the two alternative states of the brain – or of the microtubular array – that Nature must choose between. This reduced-density-matrix representation shows that the powerful decoherence effect produced by strong interactions with the environment actually *aids* the implementation of Penrose's rule, which is designed to specify *when* the quantum jump occurs (and perhaps to which states the jump occurs). The capacity of the brain to be or not to be *a quantum computer* is a very different question, involving enormously more stringent conditions. It thus is important, for logical clarity, to separate these two issues of the requirements for *quantum computation* and for *quantum jumps*, even though they happen to be interlocked in the particular scenario described by Penrose and Hameroff.

The Bohm Approach

The Copenhagen and von Neumann formulations of quantum theory are nondeterministic. Both specify that human choices enter into the dynamics, but neither specifies the causal origins of these choices.

The question thus arises: What determines these choices?

One possibility is that these choices arise in some yet-to-be-specified way from what we conceive to be the *idealike aspect of reality*. That option was pursued by Penrose, with his suggestion that our thoughts are linked to Plato's world of ideal forms. Another – seemingly different – possibility is that a *physical description* exists that is more detailed than the smeared-out cloudlike structures of the orthodox formulations and that this *more detailed physical description* determines all features left undetermined in the orthodox formulations.

This second approach was developed by David Bohm (1952: Bohn & Hiley, 1993). His formulation of quantum theory postulates, in effect, the existence of the old-fashioned world of classical physical theory. This classical-type world is supposed to exist *in addition to the cloudlike wave function of orthodox quantum theory* and is supposed to evolve in a way completely determined by what precedes it in time. Bohm specifies new laws of motion that are able to reinstate determinism in a way compatible with the predictions of quantum theory, but at the expense of a very explicit abandonment of locality: Bohm's theory entails very strong, and very long-range, instantaneous action-at-a-distance.

One serious failing of Bohm's approach is that it was originally formulated in a non-relativistic context, and it has not yet – after a half-century and great effort – been extended to cover deterministically the most important domain in physics; namely, the realm of quantum electrodynamics. This is the theory that covers the atoms that make up our bodies and brains, along with the tables, chairs, automobiles, and computers that populate our daily lives. This deficiency means that Bohm's theory is, at present, primarily a philosophically interesting curiosity, not a viable deterministic physical theory.

Also, Bohm's theory, at least in its original form, is not really germane to the issue of consciousness. For Bohm's theory *successfully achieved its aim*, which was precisely to get rid of consciousness (i.e., to eliminate consciousness from the basic dynamical equations, just as classical physics had done).

Bohm recognized, later on, that some understanding of consciousness was needed, but he was led instead to the notion of an infinite tower of mechanical levels, each controlling the one below, with consciousness somehow tied to the mystery of the infinite limit (Bohm, 1986, 1990). This infinite-tower idea tends to diminish the great achievement of the original theory, which was to reinstate physical determinism in a simple way.

Perhaps the most important use of Bohm's model is to provide an understanding of the consequences of assuming, as some philosophers do, that we live in a world in which everything is deterministically fixed by purely physical processes and our conscious choices are epiphenomenal.

Bohm's model is an example of such a theory, which moreover agrees with the predictions of quantum theory, at least in the non-relativistic regime. It is thus instructive to examine Bohm's model and see how, within that deterministic framework in which consciousness plays no fundamental causal role, consciousness nevertheless enters, *at the level of scientific practice*, in just the way specified by the orthodox formulations.

As explained in the introductory section, actual scientific practice involves setting up experimental conditions that promote consciously conceived objectives. In von Neumann's theory these consciously chosen actions influence the subsequent course of events in the observed system, which, according to von Neumann's version of quantum theory, is primarily the brain of the human participant. A key point is that these choices, made by the experimenter about how he or she will act, are treated in von Neumann's theory, and also by Copenhagen quantum theory, as *input data*, to be fixed by the experimenter: No matter what these choices actually are, or where they come from, or what they actually do, these conscious choices are *treated* in orthodox quantum theory as free,

controllable, and knowable input boundary conditions.

In Bohm's theory these choices are not *actually* free: Freedom is an illusion. The apparently free choice is, at a deeper dynamical level, completely determined by *physical* conditions, just as it was in classical physics. However, the putative existence of this deeper dynamical underpinning does not upset scientific practice. It does not displace, within science, the orthodox quantum dynamics. The analysis by Heisenberg shows that, even within the context of a deterministic Bohmian mechanics, the human observers can never determine, or *know*, to which of the conceivable logically possible classical Bohmian worlds their experiences belong. The Heisenberg Uncertainty Principle is a limitation upon human knowledge that is not evaded by Bohm's deterministic dynamics. The most that "experiencers" can ever *know* about the Bohmian classical world of which they are a putative part is represented by a quantum mechanical cloudlike wave function.

This limitation *in human knowledge* is acknowledged by Bohm. Indeed, Bohm's theory leaves actual scientific practice the same as it is in the Copenhagen approach. This *equivalence at the practical level* of Bohm's model to the Copenhagen formulation means that the unavoidable gap *in human knowledge* mandated by the uncertainty principle forces a return, at the level of scientific practice, to Copenhagen quantum theory. The theoretically specified, *but in principle unknowable and uncontrollable information about the supposedly deterministic microscopic realities* are replaced in actual practice by *knowable and controllable realities*; namely, our human conscious choices about which actions we will take and their consciously experienced feedbacks. But this means that the structure added by Bohm lies beyond the scope of science, in the sense that it adds nothing testable. It is pure speculation.

An important feature of quantum theory, as it is understood by physicists, is the never rebutted argument of the founders that any added superstructure of the general kind proposed by Bohm can never add anything testable, and hence lies outside science. Quantum physicists tend to be skeptical of any claim that ascribes reality to properties that are unknowable *in principle* and give nothing testable. They identify science with actual scientific practice, not untestable philosophical speculations. This attitude may be as beneficial in neuroscience as it is in atomic physics.

The von Neumann/Stapp Approach

John von Neumann converted Copenhagen quantum theory, in a series of steps, into a form in which the entire physical universe, including the brain of each agent, is represented in one basic quantum state, which is called the state of the universe. The state of any subsystem, such as a brain, is formed by averaging (tracing) this basic state over all variables *other* than those that describe the state of that subsystem. The dynamics consists of *three* processes.

Process 1 is the choice on the part of the experimenter about how to act. This choice is sometimes called the Heisenberg Choice because Heisenberg strongly emphasized its crucial role in quantum dynamics. At the pragmatic level it is a "free choice" because it is controlled *in practice* by the conscious intentions of the experimenter/participant, and neither the Copenhagen nor von Neumann formulations provide any description of the *causal origins* of this choice, apart from the thoughts, ideas, and feelings of the agent. Each intentional action involves an effort to produce a conceived experiential feedback, which, if it occurs, will be an experiential confirmation of the success of that effort.

Process 2 is the quantum analog of the equations of motion of classical physics. As in classical physics, these equations of motion are local: All interactions are between immediate neighbors. They are also deterministic. They are obtained from the classical equations by a certain *quantization* procedure and are reduced to the classical equations by taking the *classical approximation* of setting to zero the value of Planck's constant everywhere it appears. Evolution via the quantum Process 2 normally has the effect of *expanding* the microscopic uncertainties beyond what is demanded by the Heisenberg Uncertainty Principle: The cloud of microscopic possibilities *spreads out*. This growth in the microscopic regime, if unchecked by any other process, spreads into the macroscopic domain and causes even the *centers* of large objects to tend to become diffused over large regions. The disparity between this Process-2-generated theoretical indefiniteness of the locations of the centers of large objects and the consciously experienced definiteness of the positions of visible objects is resolved by Process 3.

Process 3 is sometimes called the Dirac Choice. Dirac called it a "choice on the part of Nature." It can be regarded as Nature's answer to the question posed by Process 1. This posed question might be, Will the detecting device be found to be in the state that signifies "Yes, a detection has occurred"? Or, "Will the Geiger counter be observed to 'fire' in accordance with the experiential conditions that define a 'Yes' response?" Each Process 3 reply must be preceded by a Process 1 question. This is because Process 2 generates a *continuous infinity* of possible questions that cannot all be answered consistently within the mathematical framework provided by quantum theory. Process 1 specifies a set of distinct allowed possible answers such that the Pythagoras Rule for probabilities yields the conclusion that the probabilities for the allowed possible answers sum to unity.

Process 1 brings the conscious choices made by the observer/participant directly into the dynamics. On the other hand, there is a tendency for the effect of the Process 1 choices (of the questions) on the state of observed system to be washed out, in the long run, by the averaging over the two possible answers, 'Yes' and 'No.' However, it has been stressed by Stapp (1999) that if willful effort can control the *rate* at which a sequence of similar Process 1 events occur then the course of brain events could be strongly affected by mental effort. The timing of the Process 1 events is, within the orthodox Copenhagen/von Neumann quantum theoretical framework, governed by the choice made by the experimenter/agent, and this choice is not specified by any known law of physics. But a rapid sequence of pairs of questions and answers (Process 1/ Process 3 events) can, by virtue of the quantum laws themselves, hold a particular pattern of neurological activity in place, against the physical forces that would, both in the absence of such pairs, and also in classical physics, tend quickly to disrupt it. If this pattern of neurological activity were to be a Template for Action (i.e., an executive pattern of neurological activity that tends to produce a specific action) then the prolongation of the activation of this executive pattern of brain activity can tend to cause the intended bodily action to occur, in accordance with William James's "ideo-motor" theory of action (James, 1890, p. 522). (According to that theory, it is the holding in place of the idea of an action that tends to make that action happen.)

This fact that a sufficiently rapid sequence of consciously selected probing events can hold the associated pattern of physical activity in place longer than what would be specified either by the classical laws of motion or its quantum analog, Process 2, is *an automatic consequence of the quantum laws of motion*. It has been extensively studied by quantum physicists, both empirically (Itano, Heinzen, Bollinger, & Wineland, 1990) and theoretically (Misra & Sudarshan, 1977), under the title "Quantum Zeno Effect."

This quantum process can provide a physics-based account of the causal efficacy of conscious willful effort. This account corresponds closely to the ideas of William James, as is made evident by the following quotations:

> *Thus we find that we reach the heart of our inquiry into volition when we ask by what process is it that the thought of any given action comes to prevail stably in the mind. (James, 1890, p. 564)*

and later

> *The essential achievement of the will, in short, when it is most 'voluntary,' is to attend to a difficult object and hold it fast before the mind. . . . Effort of attention is thus the essential phenomenon of will.*

Still later, James says,

> *Everywhere, then, the function of effort is the same: to keep affirming and adopting the thought which, if left to itself, would slip away.*

The conclusion here is that the apparent capacity of our conscious efforts/choices to influence our physical actions, which seems so puzzling and necessarily illusory within classical physics, has a straightforward explanation within quantum theory. This causal connection follows directly from the orthodox quantum laws of motion. Moreover, the details of how the process works is in close accord with William James's account of how willful effort brings about intended actions. Unlike the situation in classical physics, these willful choices themselves are not controlled by the known laws of physics. There is, therefore, no warrant in contemporary physical theory for the assumption that our human choices are strict consequences of local mechanical processes akin to, or analogous to, those appearing in the classical physics approximation. The classical approximation completely wipes out the uncertainties within which the free choices are allowed to act. This approximation contracts the spreading cloudlike structures of quantum theory into narrow pencil-like beams, thus eliminating the freedom provided by quantum theory that Bohr strongly emphasized. In contrast to the Process 3 choices on the part of Nature, which are subject to statistical laws, and hence are forced to be "random," the Process 1 choices on the part of agents are not subject to any known law, statistical or otherwise, and hence need not be ruled by pure chance. This is important, because it is often claimed by the ill-informed that all of the indeterminateness introduced by quantum theory is controlled by statistical laws, and is hence random. But the crucial Process 1 choices on the part of the agents are not subject to any known *statistical or deterministic* conditions.

In quantum theory the connection between mental effort and physical action can be explained as a *causal consequence of the laws of quantum physics*, combined with an assumption that an agent's conscious effort to produce some experientially characterized effect increases the rapidity of a set of Process 1 probing actions that focus attention on the intended experience. The experiential side of each such Process 1 action/event is specified by an intended (projected) experiential state. The physical side collapses the prior physical state of the brain to a sum of two parts. The first part is the part of the prior state in which the neural correlate (Template for Action) of the conscious intention is definitely present. The second part is the part of the prior state in which the neural correlate of the conscious intention is definitely not present. In quantum theory there are generally parts of the prior state that are not compatible with either of those possibilities. Those parts are eliminated by Process 1, which is thus associated with *asking* a question. Process 3 gives Nature's immediate answer: It collapses the state to the 'Yes' part or to the 'No' part. These pairs of abrupt events can be regarded as the "posing by agents" and the "answering by Nature" of specific experientially formulated questions with 'Yes' or 'No' answers. *These events with their associated experiential and physical sides are the basic building blocks of quantum mechanics.* Between such event-pairs the state evolves via the local mechanical Process 2 that is analogous to the local deterministic law of motion in classical physics.

This tripartite quantum dynamics involving Choice, Causation, and Chance (Processes 1, 2, & 3, respectively) and the implementation of Will (Volition) via the conscious control of the rapidity of Process 1 events provides the mathematical and logical foundation of a *pragmatic* quantum approach to neuropsychology. How well does this pragmatic quantum approach work in actual practice?

Pashler's Analysis

A great deal of experimental work in the field of the psychology of attention is summarized in Harold Pashler's recent book of that title (Pashler, 1998).

Pashler organizes his discussion by separating perceptual processing from post-perceptual processing. The former covers processing that, first of all, identifies such basic properties of stimuli as location, color, loudness, and pitch, and, secondly, identifies stimuli in terms of categories of meaning. The post-perceptual process covers the tasks of producing motor and cognitive actions beyond mere categorical identification. Pashler emphasizes (p. 33) that "the empirical findings of attention studies specifically argue for a distinction between perceptual limitations and more central limitations involved in thought and the planning of action." The existence of these two different processes, with different characteristics, is a principal theme of Pashler's book (pp. 33, 263, 293, 317, 404). He argues that the former processes are carried out in parallel, but that the latter processes, which seem to require effortful choosing, operate in series and have a capacity that, although limited, can often be enlarged by willful effort.

Pashler's conclusion is based on the analysis of a huge array of recent experiments. But the central finding is succinctly illustrated in a finding dating from the 19th century; namely, that mental exertion reduces the amount of physical force that a person can apply. He notes, "This puzzling phenomena remains unexplained" (p. 387). However, if we take the sequence of Process 1 events associated with an agent to have a limited "capacity" in terms of events per second, then this effect is a natural consequence of quantum theory. Creating a physical force by muscle contraction requires a *conscious effort* that prolongs the existence of the neural template for action, in opposition to the Process-2-generated tendency of the brain to evolve toward a more relaxed state. This prolongation is produced by the Quantum Zeno Effect, and its effect is roughly proportional to the number of bits per second of central processing capacity that is devoted to the task. So if part of this processing capacity is directed to another task, then the applied force will diminish.

This example is just one simple case, but it illustrates the general principle. The identification of Pashler's limited central se-rial "capacity" with the rate of occurrence of Process 1 events, assumed to be increasable by willful effort, up to a limit, appears to explain the general features of all of the many diverse empirical results cited by Pash-ler in support of his thesis (Schwartz, Stapp, & Beauregard, 2003; Stapp, 2001).

The apparent success of this quantum psychophysical theory in accounting for Pashler's data does not mean that classical physics could not be supplemented in some ad hoc way that would enable it to match that performance. However, the von Neu-mann theory allows the data to be explained directly in terms of *the already existing explic-itly described tripartite process that constitutes the core of contemporary basic physical the-ory*, whereas an explanation based on clas-sical physics is predicated on the untenable idea that the classical concepts of causation can be extrapolated from the motions of planets and falling apples to the motions of ions inside nerve terminals. It rests on a the-ory that is not only demonstrably false but that also claims to be dynamically and log-ically complete without entailing the exis-tence of a part of reality that we know does exist, namely human consciousness. In con-trast, von Neumann's equations specify def-inite dynamical connections between con-sciousness and brain activity, and they do so in a theoretical framework that auto-matically entails all of the valid predictions of classical physics. So what is the ratio-nale, in neuropsychology, for rejecting the fundamental equations and ideas of con-temporary physics, which can mathemat-ically account for the "directly observed" causal efficacy of consciousness and also explain all of the valid classical features of phenomena, in favor of an extrapola-tion of "planetary" concepts into a micro-scopic regime where they are known to fail?

The Libet Experiment

Perhaps the best way to understand the essence of the quantum approach to con-sciousness is to see how it applies to the famous Libet experiments pertaining to will-ful action (Libet, 2003; see Chapter 12).

The empirical fact established by the Libet data is that when an action is 'willed' – such as 'willing' a finger to rise – a readiness potential (RP) appears *before* the conscious experience of willing appears. The most straightforward conclusion is that the causal efficacy of free will is an illusion. The motion of the finger seems clearly to be caused by neural activity that began well before the conscious act of willing occurs. Thus, consciousness is seemingly a *conse-quence* of neural activity, not a *cause* of it.

The quantum mechanical analysis of this experiment leads to a more subtle conclusion.

In the Libet experiment the original com-mitment by the subject to, say, "raise my finger within the next minute" will condi-tion his brain to tend to produce *a sequence* of potential RPs distributed over the next minute. That is, the cloud of quantum pos-sibilities will begin to generate a sequence of possible RPs, each one beginning at a dif-ferent time. Each such RP will be associ-ated with the 'Yes' answer to the question, "Shall I choose (make an effort) to raise my finger now?" If the answer is 'No' then the 'template for the action of making an effort to raise the finger at that moment' will not be actualized, and the brain state associated with the answer 'No' will then evolve until the possibility of actualizing the template and RP corresponding to a later moment of choice arrives. When the brain activity asso-ciated with any *one* of these RPs reaches a certain triggering condition the Process 1 action associated with that particular RP will occur. Because the original commitment is spread over a minute the probability, for any individual RP in this sequence, for Nature's answer to be 'Yes' will be small. Hence most of the possible RPs up to the one correspond-ing to some particular moment will *not be actualized*: They will be eliminated by the 'No' answer on the part of Nature. But for one of these Process 1 events the associated Process 3 will deliver the answer 'Yes,' and the associated experience E will occur. Up to this point the conscious will has entered only via the original commitment to raise the finger at some time within the next minute.

But to be efficacious the later experience E must contain an element of effort, which will cause the Process 1 associated with this experience (or a very similar one) to occur quickly again, and then again and again, thereby activating the Quantum Zeno Effect. This will cause the finger-raising template for action to be held in place, and the effect of this will be the issuing of the neural messages to the muscles that will cause the finger to rise. Without this willful effort, which occurs in conjunction with the answer 'Yes', the sustained activation of the template for action will not occur and the finger will not rise. The willful effort causes the rapid repetition of the Process 1 action to occur. This holds the template in place, which causes the finger to rise. Thus the rising of the finger is caused, in the quantum formulation, by the willful effort, in concordance with the idea expressed by James (1892, p. 227):

> I have spoken as if our attention were wholly determined by neural conditions. I believe that the array of things we can attend to is so determined. No object can catch our attention except by the neural machinery. But the amount of the attention which an object receives after it has caught our attention is another question. It often takes effort to keep mind upon it. We feel that we can make more or less of the effort as we choose. If this feeling be not deceptive, if our effort be a spiritual force, and an indeterminate one, then of course it contributes coequally with the cerebral conditions to the result. Though it introduces no new idea, it will deepen and prolong the stay in consciousness of innumerable ideas which else would fade more quickly away.

Applications in Neuropsychology

This theory has been applied to neuropsychology (Oschner, Bunge, Gross, & Gabrieli, 2002; Schwartz, Stapp, & Beauregard, 2003). In these studies human subjects are first instructed how to alter their mental reactions to emotionally charged visual stimuli by adopting certain mental strategies. For example, the subjects are trained how to reduce their emotional reaction to a violent or sexual visual scene by cognitively re-evaluating the content; for example, by interpreting or contextualizing it in a different way. Their reactions to such stimuli are then studied using fMRI under differing choices of mental set. The brain scans reveal profoundly different patterns of response to the stimuli according to whether the subject does or does not apply the cognitive re-evaluation. Without cognitive re-evaluation the brain reaction is focused in the limbic system, whereas when cognitive re-evaluation is employed the focus shifts to prefrontal regions. This demonstrates the powerful effect of cognitive choices upon brain functioning.

This effect is not surprising. Within the pragmatic framework this effect appears as a causal connection between a psychologically described input variable, namely a knowable and controllable free conscious choice, and an ensuing brain behavior. Quantum theory contains a mechanism that can explain this empirically observed apparent causal effect of the conscious choice upon the ensuing brain activity, but can provide no explanation of any causal effect of brain process upon our conscious choices. The contending classical approach asserts that the causal connections are wholly in the opposite direction. It claims that both the conscious choice and the subsequent brain behavior are both consequences of prior physical processes.

Superficially, it might seem that there is no way to decide between these contending theories, and hence that a scientist is free here to choose between classical physics and quantum physics. It might be argued that the dispute is all words, with no empirical or theoretical content. However, the claim that the sufficient *cause* of the subject's subsequent brain state does not include the controllable variable that *empirically* controls it is prima facie unreasonable. It would become reasonable only if supported by strong theoretical arguments or empirical evidence. But there is no strong theoretical support. The only theoretical support for this prima facie implausible claim comes from a physical theory, classical physics, whose domain of applicability fails in principle to cover the phenomena in question. The more accurate physical theory that *should* cover these phenomena provides no support at all for an epiphenomenal explanation of this data.

This argument does not *prove* that a classical-type causal explanation that leaves consciousness out is rationally untenable. However, if one were to search for evidence to support the classical idea then most scientists would probably agree that one must, at this point in time, expect the data to be at least *compatible* with the predictions of quantum theory. But then the example provided by Bohm's model becomes instructive. That model is deterministic at the purely physical level, without reference to consciousness. To be sure, it involves, in a direct way, instantaneous long-range action at a distance, and it has not been made compatible with the special theory of relativity. But the model does give an idea of how consciousness *might* in principle be rendered impotent in a model compatible with the *predictions* of quantum theory. However, as discussed in the section on Bohm's model, the Heisenberg uncertainty principle excludes the possibility of knowing anything about, or testing for the presence of, the proposed causal substructure. This circumstance argues for the adoption in neuroscience of the attitude adopted in atomic physics: Avoid the introduction of speculative concepts that are unknowable and untestable in principle, and instead treat conscious choices in the way that they actually enter scientific practice; namely, as empirically knowable and controllable input parameters.

The basic elements of von Neumann's theory are the experiences of conscious agents and the neural correlates of those experiences, the NCCs. The fundamental building blocks of quantum theory are "information/action events." On the psychological level, each Process 1 event focuses attention and effort on an intended experiential/informational feedback. On the physical level this event reduces (collapses) the state of the brain to a sum of two terms, one of which is the neural correlate of the intended experience and the other of which is the neural correlate of the negation of that possibility. Contemporary physical theory gives no statistical or deterministic conditions on the choice of the intended action. But Nature's feedback is required to conform to the Pythagoras statistical rule described above.

How is the necessary connection between the experiential and physical regimes established? The answer is by trial-and-error empirical testing of the correspondence between "the feeling of the conscious effort" and "the feeling of the experiential feedback." Every healthy alert infant is incessantly engaged in mapping out the correspondences between efforts and feedbacks, and he or she builds up over the course of time a repertoire of correspondences between the feel of the effort and the feel of the feedback. This is possible because different effortful choices have, according to the quantum equations, different physical consequences, which produce different experiential consequences. This whole process of learning depends crucially upon the causal efficacy of chosen willful efforts: If efforts have no actual consequences then how can learning occur and the fruits of learning be obtained by appropriate effort?

The focus here has been on the theoretical foundations of pragmatic neuroscience. However, von Neumann's formulation makes the theory more amenable to ontological interpretation.

The essential difference between quantum theory and classical physics, both ontologically construed, is that the classical state of the universe represents a purported *material* reality, whereas the von Neumann quantum state of the universe represents a purported *informational* reality. This latter reality has certain matter-like features. It can be expressed in terms of micro-local entities (local quantum fields) that evolve by direct interactions with their neighbors, *except* when certain abrupt "reductions" or "collapses" occur. These sudden changes are sometimes called quantum jumps. In orthodox pragmatic quantum theory what the state represents is the collective knowledge of all agents. Hence it abruptly changes whenever the knowledge of any agent changes. This behavior is concordant with the term "our knowledge" used by the founders of quantum theory. Thus the quantum state has a *form* that manifests *certain* of the mechanical properties of matter, but a *content* that is basically idea-like: It represents an objective kind of knowledge that changes when someone acquires knowledge.

This radical revamping of physics was not something lightly entered into by the founders of quantum theory or docilely accepted by their colleagues. A blithe disregard, in the study of the mind-brain connection, of this profound and profoundly relevant revision by scientists of the idea of the interplay between the experiential and physical aspects of nature is not easy to justify.

If one shifts over to an explicitly ontological interpretation, the question arises, What systems besides human beings are *agents*? There is currently a lack of replicable empirical data that bear on this question, and I shall therefore not enter into philosophical speculation.

It needs to be emphasized that everything said about the von Neumann theory is completely compatible with there being very strong interactions between the brain and its environment. The state S(t) of the brain is what is known as the statistical operator (reduced density matrix) corresponding to the brain. It is formed by averaging (tracing) over all non-brain degrees of freedom, and it automatically incorporates all of the decoherence effects arising from interactions with the environment. The key point is that strong environmental decoherence does not block the Quantum Zeno Effect.

There is an approach to quantum theory that tries to ignore von Neumann's Process 1 (and Process 3 as well). This approach is called the "many-minds" or "many-worlds" approach. No demonstration has been given that such a radical break with orthodox quantum theory is mathematically possible. Hence I do not include it among the possible quantum approaches to consciousness described here.

Von Neumann's theory provides a general physics-based psycho-physical framework for studying the neuroscience of consciousness. We now turn to some efforts to tie this structure to the detailed structure of the brain.

The Eccles-Beck Approach

Sir John Eccles suggested in 1990, in the Proceedings of the Royal Society (Eccles, 1990), that quantum theory plays a key role in the workings of the conscious brain. Based in part on his discussions with Henry Margenau, Eccles noted that the statistical element in quantum theory allows an escape from the rigid determinism of classical physics that has plagued philosophy since the time of Isaac Newton. In his later book, *How the Self Controls Its Brain*, Eccles (1994) notes, "There is of course an entrenched materialist orthodoxy, both philosophic and scientific, that rises to defend its dogmas with a self-righteousness scarcely equaled in the ancient days of religious dogmatism." He says at the outset,"Following Popper (1968) I can say: I wish to confess, however, at the very beginning, that I am a realist: I suggest somewhat like a naïve realist that there is a physical world and a world of states of consciousness, and that these two interact."

Eccles gives "two most weighty reasons" for rejecting the classical-physics-based concept of materialism (Eccles 1994, p, 9). First, classical physics does not entail the existence or emergence of the defining characteristic of consciousness, namely "feelings," and hence entails no theory of consciousness. Second, because the nature of the mapping between brain states and states of consciousness never enters into the behavior of an organism, there is no evolutionary reason for consciousness to be closely connected to behavior, which it clearly is.

Eccles' approach to the mind-brain problem has three main points. The first is that consciousness is composed of elemental mental units called psychons and that each psychon is associated with the activation of a corresponding macroscopic physical structure in the cerebral cortex that Eccles calls a *dendron*. It is anatomically defined and is connected to the rest of the brain via a large number of synapses.

The second point is the claim that quantum theory enters brain dynamics in connection with exocytosis, which is the release of the contents of a "vesicle" – filled with neurotransmitter – from a nerve terminal into a synaptic cleft.

The third point is a model developed by the physicist Friedrich Beck that describes the quantum mechanical details of the process of exocytosis.

The first claim, that psychological processes have elemental units associated with dendrons, places Eccles' theory somewhat apart from the currently widespread belief that the neural correlates of our conscious experiences are spead out over larger regions of the brain, which may be related more by phase synchronization in time than by very restictive localization in space.

More germane to our topic is the second component of Eccles' proposal; namely, that quantum effects are important in brain dynamics in connection with cerebral exocytosis. This conclusion is plausible and indeed inescapable. Exocytosis is instigated by an action potential pulse that triggers an influx of calcium ions through ion channels into a nerve terminal. These calcium ions migrate from the ion channel exits to sites on or near the vesicles, where they trigger the release of the contents of the vesicle into the synaptic cleft. The diameter of the ion channel through which the calcium ion enters the nerve terminal is very small, less than a nanometer, and this creates, in accordance with the Heisenberg uncertainty principle, a correspondingly large uncertainly in the direction of the motion of the ion. That means that the quantum wave packet that describes the location of the ion spreads out, during its travel from ion channel to trigger site, to a size much larger than the trigger site (Stapp, 1993/2004). That means that the issue of whether or not the calcium ion (in combination with other calcium ions) produces an exocytosis is a quantum question basically similar to the question of whether or not a quantum particle passes through one or the other slit of a double-slit experiment. According to quantum theory the answer

is both. Until the brain process reaches the level of organization corresponding to the occurrence of a Process 1 action, one must in principle retain *all* of the possibilities generated by the Schroedinger equation, Process 2. In particular, one must retain both the possibility that the ion activates the trigger, and exocytosis occurs, and also the possibility that the ion misses the trigger site, and exocytosis does not occur.

For cortical nerve terminals the observed fraction of action potential pulses that result in exocytosis is considerably less than 100%. This can be modeled classically (Fogelson & Zucker, 1985). But the large Heisenberg uncertainty in the locations of the triggering calcium ions entails that the classical uncertainties will carry over to similar quantum uncertainties, and the two possibilities at each synapse, exocytosis and no exocytosis, will, prior to the occurrence of the Process 3 action, *both be present* in the quantum state S(t). If N such synaptic events occur in the brain during some interval of time in which no Process 3 events occur, then the state S(t) of the brain will evolve during that interval into a form that contains (at least) 2^N contributions, one for each of the alternative possible combinations of the exocytosis and no exocytosis options at each of the N synapse events.

There is a lot of parallel processing and redundancy in brain dynamics, and many of these possible contributions may correspond to exactly the same possible experience E. But in real-life situations where there could be several different reasonable actions, one cannot expect that every one of the 2^N alternative possible brain states will be a neural correlate of *exactly* the same possible E. If the agent is conscious then the von Neumann Processes 1 and 3 must enter to determine which of the various alternative possible experiences E actually occurs.

The analysis just given assumes, in accordance with the model of Fogelson and Zucker, that the condition that triggers exocytosis is the presence of a specified number of calcium ions on a trigger site. Beck and Eccles (2003) consider another possibility. They say that the "low exocytosis probability per excitatory impulse . . . means that there is an activation barrier against opening an ion channel in the PVG (presynaptic vesicular grid)."

They propose that "an incoming nerve pulse excites some electronic configuration to a metastable level, separated energetically by a potential barrier $V(q)$ from the state that leads to the unidirectional process of exocytosis." In this scenario the state in which the exocytosis does occur can be considered to be connected by a *quantum tunneling process* to the state where it does not occur.

Beck's tunneling mechanism would achieve the same result as the mechanism, described above, which is based simply on the spreading of the wave packets of the calcium ions due to Heisenberg's uncertainty principle. Both mechanisms lead to the result that the brain state $S(t)$ will contain 2^N states, defined by the independent exocytosis or no exocytosis option at each of the N synapses. Hence the Eccles-Beck model does not lead to any essential difference, as regards this key point, from the model that emphasizes the spreading of the calcium ions inside the nerve terminal. (Of course, it should not be thought that these explicitly considered effects are the *only* places where quantum effects enter into brain dynamics. These explicitly treated processes are just special cases where enough empirical evidence is available to make a calculation and where the alternative possibilities should feed into the generation of non-identical brain states.)

The Eccles-Beck proposal does, however, differ significantly from the von Neumann/ Stapp proposal in regard to its third point. The von Neumann/Stapp theory attributes the efficacy of will to the assumed power of mental effort to increase the rate of Process 1 actions, whereas the Eccles-Beck proposal attributes the efficacy of will to the assumed power of mental effort to modify *the probabilities associated with the Process 3 action*, the collapse of the quantum state.

The von Neumann/Stapp proposal stays rigorously within the framework of relativistic quantum field theory and hence produces no causal anomalies, such as the possibility of sending messages backward in time. The Eccles-Beck proposal, by violating the basic quantum probability rules, would in principle allow such anomalies to occur.

It is often emphasized, *correctly*, in connection with quantum approaches to brain dynamics, that "the environment" will be affected differently by interactions with the brain states in which an exocytosis has or has not occurred, and that this difference will destroy, almost immediately, all (practically achievable) interference effects between these macroscopically distinct states.

This *environmental decoherence effect* is automatically included in the formulas used here, which refer explicitly to the brain state $S(t)$, which is the brain-state statistical operator obtained by averaging (tracing) over all non-brain variables.

It is then sometimes concluded, *incorrectly*, that one can immediately replace the brain state $S(t)$ by just *one* of these 2^N components. That conclusion might follow if one were to ignore Process 1, which is part of the brain process that defines which of our alternative possible thoughts occurs next. Because Process 1 is part of the process that determines which thought occurs next, it should depend upon the state $S(t)$ of the brain *before* the thought occurs, not on the part of that state that will eventually be actualized. Hence all of the 2^N components of $S(t)$ should be retained prior to the Process 3 collapse, whether they interfere or not:

The model of the brain used above, with its 2^N well defined distinct components is, of course, highly idealized. A more realistic model would exhibit the general smearing out of all properties that follows from the quantum smearing out of the positions and velocities of all the particles. Thus the state $S(t)$ prior to the collapse cannot be expected ever to be rigorously divided, solely by Process 2 action, including interaction with the environment, into strictly orthogonal non-interfering components corresponding to distinct experiences. It is Process 1 that makes this crucial separation, not Process 2. The recognition of the need to bring in a separate process to define the question is the critical element of the Copenhagen approach, and it was formalized by von Neumann as Process 1. Any attempt to leave out Process 1 faces daunting challenges.

The Jibu-Yasue Approach

The preceding sections are conservative and incomplete. They are conservative because they (1) build on the orthodox philosophy of quantum theory, which recognizes that science, like every human endeavor, arises from the fact that human beings choose their actions and experience the feedbacks; and they (2) exploit the quantum laws that relate these choices to those feedback.

The preceeding sections are incomplete because they say very little about the actual brain mechanisms.

In regard to this second point there is a related question of how memories are stored. Karl Pribram (1966, 1991) has suggested that consciousness operates on principles similar to that of a hologram, in which tiny variations of a myriad of physical variables, dispersed over a large region, combine to modulate a carrier wave. These physical variables might be the strengths of the synaptic junctions. Pribram identifies the dendritic network (a dense set of neural fibers) as the likely substrate of such a brain process.

This holographic model would appear to be implementable within quantum electrodynamics, which is the physical theory that would normally be expected to control brain dynamics. However, Umezawa and co-workers (Riccardi & Umezawa, 1967; Stuart, Takahashi, & Umezawa, 1978, 1979) have suggested that an exotic physical process is involved; namely, a process similar to what appears in the theory of superconductivity. That theory is characterized by the existence of a continuum of states of the same (lowest) energy, and Umezawa has suggested that long-term memory is associated with breaking the symmetry of these ground states, instead of, for example, enduring changes in the physical structures of nerve cells.

Jibu and Yasue (1995) have attempted to weave these ideas of Pribram and Umezawa into a unified quantum theory of brain dynamics (QBD). Their theory takes the substrate associated with Umezawa's ideas to be the water that pervades the brain. Excitations of certain states of the water system are called corticons, and they interact with photons in the electromagnetic fields of, for example, the dendritic network. They say:

> With the help of quantum field theory, we have found that the creation and annihilation dynamics of corticons and photons in the QBD system in the sub-microscopic world of the brain to be the entity we call consciousness or mind.

However, they have not made clear why "the creation and annihilation dynamics of corticon and photons" should possess the defining characteristics of conscious processes; namely, the fact that they are "feelings." Conscious experiences have a quality of "feelingness" about them that is not contained in, or entailed by, the physical concepts of corticons and photons, or of the dynamics of these entities that they claim "to be the entity we call consciousness or mind." Thus their work does not address the basic question of how rationally to get the concepts that characterize the experiential aspects of reality out of the concepts of the physical theory. That question is the one that was answered by the work of von Neumann, and that has been the primary focus of this chapter.

Glossary

Quantum Jumps. The mystery of quantum theory is concentrated wholly in the peculiarities of the quantum jumps, which seem to have both subjective experiential aspects associated with "increases in knowledge" and also objective physical aspects associated with changes in the expectations or potentialities for future quantum jumps. In the chapter "The Copenhagen Interpretation" in his book *Physics and Philosophy*, Heisenberg (1958b, p. 54) says, "When the old adage '*natura non facit saltus*' (nature makes no jumps), is used as a basis for criticism of quantum theory, we can reply that certainly our knowledge can change suddenly and that this fact justifies the use of the term 'quantum jump.'" This explanation stresses the subjective/experiential knowledge-increasing aspect of the quantum jumps and is very much in line with the words of Bohr. But Heisenberg then begins a further discourse with the words, "If we want to know what happens in an atomic event" and then speaks of "the transition from 'possible' to 'actual' that takes place as soon as the interaction of the object with the measuring device, and hence with the rest of the world, comes into play." He says that this transition is "is not connected to the registration of the result in the mind of the observer," but that "the discontinuous change in *the probability function*, however, takes place with the act of registration, because it is the discontinuous change of our knowledge in the instant of registration that has its image in the discontinuous change in the probability function." In this account there are two different kinds of jumps, one purely physical and occurring at the device, and one purely psychological/experiential and occurring in the mind of the observer. The idea is that the probability function is a mathematical construct that lives in the minds of human scientists and represents "our knowledge" and that it consequently "jumps" when our knowledge increases. There are also physical jumps that occur at the devices.

But what happens in a person's *brain* when an abrupt increase in knowledge occurs? A brain is similar in many ways to a measuring device: There is energy available to magnify quickly the effects of some small triggering event. And how does one explain the fantastic accuracy of quantum calculations if the quantum mathematics that exists in our minds is not closely related to what is really happening? The von Neumann formulation answers these questions by shifting the boundary between the observed system and the observer so that the physically described state includes the brain of the observer, and the two kinds of "jumps" described by Heisenberg become two aspects of a single kind of quantum jump that occurs at the mind-brain interface. Von Neumann's Process 1 is the physical aspect of the choice on the part of the human agent. Its psychologically described aspect is experienced and described as a focusing of attention and effort on some intention, and the physically described aspect consists of the associated choice of the basis vectors and of the timings of the action. Then there is a feedback quantum jump whose psychologically described aspect is experienced and described as an increment in knowledge and whose physical aspect is a "quantum jump" to a new physical state that is compatible with that increment in knowledge. Thus the two aspects of the conceptual foundation of science, the objective/mathematical and the subjective/experiential, are linked together, *within the theory*, in the conceptual structure of the quantum jump.

Planck's Constant. This number, discovered by Max Planck in 1900, is a number that characterizes quantum phenomena. It specifies a definite connection between energy and frequency. The energy carried by a quantum entity, such as an electron or photon (a quantum of "light"), divided by Planck's constant, defines a "frequency" (the number of oscillations per second) that is associated with this entity. Thus Planck's constant links together a discrete "lump" or "quantum" of energy with an oscillatory motion of specified frequency. This constant thus forms the basis for linking a property normally associated with a "particle" – namely, a discrete amount of energy – with a property that is associated in quantum theory with a wave motion. In classically describable phenomena the products of energy and frequency of the individual quantum entities that combine to produce the macroscopic phenomena are so small on the scale of observable parameters as to be individually undetectable, even though the macroscopically measurable properties of materials depend strongly upon the quantum properties of their constituent elements.

Quantum Zeno Effect. The equations of motion of a quantum system differ in many ways from the classical equations.

One such way is this: The motion of a planet, as described by Kepler's empirical laws and by Newton's theoretical ones, are such that the motion does not depend on how often we look at it. But the evolution in time of an observed quantum system depends on Process 1, which is specified in the theory by observational choices made by the experimenter/observer/agent. In the case of a planet the effect of our observations is negligible. But experiments on atoms (Itano, Heinzen, Bollinger, & Wineland, 1990) show that the behavior of atoms can be strongly affected by the rapidity at which Process 1 events are occurring. If these events occur sufficiently rapidly then the normal behavior of the atom, such as a transition from an excited state to a state of lower energy, is slowed down. This was predicted by quantum theory, and the empirical results are in good agreement with theoretical predictions. This slowing effect is called the Quantum Zeno Effect (Misra & Sudarshan, 1977). If the observed system is the brain of an agent then, as a consequence of evolutionary and educational processing, this brain could be expected to become very sensitive to variations in the character of the Process 1 events. This is because Templates for Action could be held in place longer than normal by "free" choices made by agents, and this could strongly influence behavior. Such an effect would elevate the choices made by human agents from their status in classical physics as mechanically determined epiphenomenal side effects to causes that, *in principle*, are not fully traceable within contemporary physical theory to purely physical processes, and hence are properly treatable as empirical inputs.

Template for Action. This is an "executive" patterns of neurological activity that if held in place for an extended period will issue the sequence of neural signals that will initiate and monitor a particular physical (or perhaps mental) action.

Gödel's Incompleteness Theorem. "Any finite set of rules that encompass the rules of arithmetic is either inconsistent or incomplete: it entails either statements that can be proved to be both true and false, or statements that cannot be proved to be either true or false."

Heisenberg's Uncertainty Principle. This principle asserts the mathematical fact that within the logical framework provided by quantum theory the position and momentum (velocity times mass) of a quantum entity cannot be simultaneously defined to arbitrary accuracy. The product of the uncertainties in these two quantities is given by Planck's constant. This principle renders the classical concept of the deterministic motions of the planets in the solar system inapplicable to the motions of the ions in a human brain.

References

Beck, F., & Eccles, J. (2003). Quantum processes in the brain: A scientific basis of consciousness. In N. Osaka (Ed.), *Neural basis of consciousness* (pp. 141–166). Amsterdam: Benjamins.

Bohm, D. (1952). A suggested interpretation of quantum theory in terms of hidden variables. *Physical Review, 85*, 166–179.

Bohm, D. J. (1986). A new theory of the relationship of mind to matter. *Journal of the American Society for Psychical Research, 80*, 113–135.

Bohm, D. J. (1990). A new theory of the relationship of mind to matter. *Philosophical Psychology, 3*, 271–286.

Bohm, D., & Hiley, D. J. (1993). *The undivided universe*. London: Routledge.

Bohr, N. (1958). *Atomic physics and human knowledge*. New York: Wiley.

Bohr, N. (1963). *Essays 1958/1962 on atomic physics and human knowledge*. New York: Wiley.

Eccles, J. C. (1990). A unitary hypothesis of mind-brain interaction in the cerebral cortex. *Proceedings of the Royal Society of London, 240*, 433–451.

Eccles, J. C. (1994). *How the self controls its brain*. Berlin: Springer.

Fogelson, A., & Zucker, R., (1985). Presynaptic calcium diffusion from various arrays of single channels. *Biophysical Journal, 48*, 1003–1017.

Hagen, S., Hameroff, S., & Tuszynski, J. (2002). Quantum computation in brain microtubules: Decoherence and biological feasibility. *Physical Review, E65*, 061901–1 – 061901–11.

Hameroff, S., & Penrose, R. (1996). Orchestrated reduction of quantum coherence in brain microtubules: A model for consciousness. *Journal of Consciousness Studies, 3*, 36–53.

Heisenberg, W. (1958a). The representation of Nature in contemporary physics. *Daedalus, 87*, 95–108.

Heisenberg, W. (1958b). *Physics and philosophy*. New York: Harper,

Itano, A., Heinzen, D., Bollinger, J., & Wineland, D. (1990). Quantum Zeno effect. *Physical Review, A41*, 2295–2300.

James, W. (1890). *The principles of psychology, Vol. II*. New York: Dover.

James, W. (1892). *Psychology: The briefer course*. In *William James: Writings 1879–1899*. New York: Library of America.

Jibu, M., & Yasue, K. (1995). *Quantum brain dynamics and consciousness*. Amsterdam: Benjamins.

Libet, B. (1985). Unconscious cerebral initiative and the role of conscious will in voluntary action. *Behavioral and Brain Sciences, 8*, 529–566.

Libet, B. (2003). Cerebral physiology of conscious experience: Experimental studies. In N. Osaka (Ed.), *Neural basis of consciousness*. Amsterdam: Benjamins.

Misra, B., & Sudarshan, E. C. G. (1977). The Zeno's paradox in quantum theory. *Journal of Mathematical Physics, 18*, 756–763.

Ochsner, K. N., Bunge, S. J., Gross, J. J., & Gabrieli, J. D. (2002). Rethinking feelings: An fMRI study of the cognitive regulation of emotion. *Journal of Cognitive Neuroscience, 14*, 1215–1229.

Pashler, H. (1998). *The psychology of attention*. Cambridge, MA: MIT Press.

Penrose, R. (1986). *The emperor's new mind*. New York: Oxford University Press.

Penrose, R. (1994). *Shadows of the mind*. New York: Oxford University Press.

Pribram, K. H. (1966). Some dimensions of remembering: Steps towards a neurophysiological theory of memory. In J. Gaito (Ed.), *Macromolecules and behavior* (pp. 165–187). New York: Academic Press.

Pribram, K. H. (1991). *Brain and perception*. Hillsdale, NJ: Erlbaum.

Putnam, H. (1994, November 20). Review of Roger Penrose, *Shadows of the Mind. New York Times Book Review*, p. 7. Retrieved from www.ams.org/journals/bull/pre-1996data/199507/199507015.tex.html.

Riccardi, L. M., & Umezawa, H. (1967). Brain and physics of many-body problems. *Kybernetik, 4*, 44–48.

Schwartz, J., Stapp, H., & Beauregard, M. (2003). The volitional influence of the mind on the brain, with special reference to emotional self regulation. In M. Beauregard (Ed.), *Consciousness, emotional self-regulation and the brain*. Amsterdam: Benjamins.

Stapp, H. (1999). Attention, intention, and will in quantum physics. *Journal of Consciousness Studies, 6*, 143–164.

Stapp, H. (2001). Quantum theory and the role of mind in Nature. *Foundations of Physics, 31*, 1465–1499.

Stapp, H. (1993/2004). *Mind, matter, and quantum mechanics*. Heidelberg, Berlin, New York: Springer. Sections 5.7 and 6.4.

Stuart, C. I. J. M., Takahashi, Y., & Umezawa, H. (1978). On the stability and nonlocal properties of memory. *Journal of Theoretical Biology, 71*, 605–618.

Stuart, C. I. J. M., Takahashi, Y., & Umezawa, H. (1979). Mixed-system brain dynamics: Neural memory as a macroscopic ordered state. *Foundations of Physics, 9*, 301–327.

Tegmark, M. (2000). Importance of quantum decoherence in brain process. *Physical Review, E61*, 4194–4206.

von Neumann, J. (1955). *Mathematical foundations of quantum mechanics* (R. T. Rever, Trans.). Princeton: Princeton University Press. (Original work published 1932.)

Author Index

Subject Index